Financial Management and Analysis

Analysis

Second Edition

THE FRANK J. FABOZZI SERIES

Financial Management and Analysis

Analysis

Second Edition

FRANK J. FABOZZI

PAMELA P. PETERSON

WILEY

John Wiley & Sons, Inc.

FJF
To my wife and children, Francesco, Patricia, and Karly

PPP
To my children, Ken and Erica

For general information on our other products and services, or technical support, please contact our Customer Care Department within the United States at 800-762-2974, outside the United States at 317-572-3993, or fax 317-572-4002.

Wiley also publishes its books in a variety of electronic formats. Some content that appears in print may not be available in electronic books.

For more information about Wiley, visit our web site at www.wiley.com.

ISBN: 0-471-23484-2

Printed in the United States of America

10 9 8 7 6 5 4 3 2 1

Contents

Preface

Financial Management and Analysis is an introduction to the concepts, tools, and applications of finance. The purpose of this textbook is to communicate the fundamentals of financial management and financial analysis. This textbook is written in a way that will enable students who are just beginning their study of finance to understand financial decision-making and its role in the decision-making process of the entire firm.

Throughout the textbook, you'll see how we view finance. We see financial decision-making as an integral part of the firm's decision-making, not as a separate function. Financial decision-making involves coordination among personnel specializing in accounting, marketing, and production aspects of the firm.

The principles and tools of finance are applicable to all forms and sizes of business enterprises, not only to large corporations. Just as there are special problems and opportunities for small family-owned businesses (such as where to obtain financing), there are special problems and opportunities for large corporations (such as agency problems that arise when management of the firm is separated from the firm's owners). But the fundamentals of financial management are the same regardless of the size or form of the business. For example, a dollar today is worth more than a dollar one year from today, whether you are making decisions for a sole proprietorship or a large corporation.

We view the principles and tools of finance as applicable to firms around the globe, not just to U.S. business enterprises. While customs and laws may differ among nations, the principles, theories, and tools of financial management do not. For example, in evaluating whether to buy a particular piece of equipment, you must evaluate what happens to the firm's future cash flows (How much will they be? When will they occur? How uncertain are they?), whether the firm is located in the United States, Great Britain, or elsewhere.

In addition, we believe that a strong foundation in finance principles and the related mathematical tools are necessary for you to understand how investing and financing decisions are made. But building that foundation need not be strenuous. One way that we try to help you build that foundation is to present the principles and theories of finance using intuition, instead of with proofs and theorems. For example, we walk you through the intuition of capital structure theory with numerical and real world examples, not equations and proofs. Another way we try to assist you is to approach the tools of finance using careful, step-by-step examples and numerous graphs.

ORGANIZATION

Financial Management and Analysis is presented in seven parts. The first two parts (Parts One and Two) cover the basics, including the objective of financial management, valuation principles, and the relation between risk and return. Financial decision-making is covered in Parts Three, Four, and Five where we present long-term investment management (commonly referred to as capital budgeting), the management of long-term sources of funds, and working capital management. Part Six covers financial statement analysis which includes financial ratio analysis, earnings analysis, and cash flow analysis. The last part (Part Seven) covers several specialized topics: international financial management, borrowing via structured financial transactions (i.e., asset securitization), project financing, equipment leasing, and financial planning and strategy.

DISTINGUISHING FEATURES OF THE TEXTBOOK

Logical structure. The text begins with the basic principles and tools, followed by long-term investment and financing decisions. The first two parts lay out the basics; Part Three then focuses on the "left side" of the balance sheet (the assets) and the Part Four is the "right side" of the balance sheet (the liabilities and equity). Working capital decisions, which are made to support the day-to-day operations of the firm, are discussed in Part Five. Part Six provides the tools for analyzing a firm's financial statements. In the last chapter of the book, you are brought back full-circle to the objective of financial management: the maximization of owners' wealth.

Graphical illustrations. Graphs and illustrations have been carefully and deliberately developed to depict and provide visual reinforcement of mathematical concepts. For example, we show the growth of a bank balance through compound interest several ways: mathematically, in a time-line, and with a bar graph.

Applications. As much as possible, we develop concepts and mathematics using examples of actual practice. For example, we first present financial analysis using a simplified set of financial statements for a fictitious company. After you've learned the basics using the fictitious company, we demonstrate financial analysis tools using data from Wal-Mart Stores, Inc. Actual examples help you better grasp and retain major concepts and tools. We integrate over 100 actual company examples throughout the text, so you're not apt to miss them. Considering both the examples throughout the text and the research questions and problems, you are exposed to hundreds of actual companies.

Extensive coverage of financial statement analysis. While most textbooks provide some coverage of financial statement analysis, we have provided you with much more detail in Part Six of the textbook. Chapter 6 and the three chapters in Part Six allow an instructor to focus on financial statement analysis.

Extensive coverage of alternative debt instruments. Because of the innovations in the debt market, alternative forms debt instruments can be issued by a corporation. In Chapter 15, you are introduced to these instruments. We then devote one chapter to the most popular alternative to corporate bond issuance, the creation and issuance of asset-backed securities.

Coverage of leasing and project financing. We provide in-depth coverage of leasing in Chapter 27, demystifying the claims about the advantages and disadvantages of leasing you too often read about in some textbooks and professional articles. Project financing has grown in importance for not only corporations but for countries seeking to develop infrastructure facilities. Chapter 28 provides the basic principles for understanding project financing.

Early introduction to derivative instruments. Derivative instruments (futures, swaps, and options) play an important role in finance. You are introduced to these instruments in Chapter 4. While derivative instruments are viewed as complex instruments, you are provided with an introduction that makes clear their basic investment characteristics. By the early introduction of derivative instruments, you will be able to appreciate the difficulties of evaluating securities that have embedded options (Chapter 9), how there are real options embedded in capital budgeting decisions (Chapter14), and how derivative instruments can be used to reduce or to hedge the cost of borrowing (Chapter 15).

Stand-alone nature of the chapters. Each chapter is written so that chapters may easily be rearranged to fit different course structures. Concepts, terminology, and notation are presented in each chapter so that no chapter is dependent upon another. This means that instructors can tailor the use of this book to fit their particular time frame for the course and their students' preparation (for example, if students enter the course with sufficient background in accounting and taxation, Chapters 5 and 6 can be skipped).

We believe that our approach to the subject matter of financial management and analysis will help you understand the key issues and provide the foundation for developing a skill set necessary to deal with real world financial problems.

Frank J. Fabozzi
Pamela P. Peterson

About the Authors

Frank J. Fabozzi, Ph.D., CFA, CPA is the Frederick Frank Adjunct Professor of Finance in the School of Management at Yale University. Prior to joining the Yale faculty, he was a Visiting Professor of Finance in the Sloan School at MIT. Professor Fabozzi is a Fellow of the International Center for Finance at Yale University and the editor of the *Journal of Portfolio Management*. He earned a doctorate in economics from the City University of New York in 1972. In 1994 he received an honorary doctorate of Humane Letters from Nova Southeastern University and in 2002 was inducted into the Fixed Income Analysts Society's Hall of Fame. He is the honorary advisor to the Chinese Asset Securitization website.

Pamela Parrish Peterson, Ph.D., CFA is a Professor of finance at Florida State University where she teaches undergraduate courses in corporate finance and doctoral courses in valuation theory. She received her Ph.D. from the University of North Carolina and has taught at FSU since receiving her degree in 1981. Professor Peterson is a co-author with Don Chance of *Real Options* (AIMR Research Foundation, 2002), is a co-author with Frank J. Fabozzi of *Capital Budgeting* (John Wiley & Sons, 2002) and *Analysis of Financial Statements* (published by Frank J. Fabozzi Associates, 1999), co-author with David R. Peterson of the AIMR monograph *Company Performance and Measures of Value Added* (1996), and author of *Financial Management and Analysis* (published by McGraw-Hill, 1994). Professor Peterson has published articles in journals including the *Journal of Finance*, the *Journal of Financial Economics*, the *Journal of Banking and Finance*, *Financial Management*, and the *Financial Analysts Journal*.

Foundations

CHAPTER 1

Introduction to Financial Management and Analysis

Finance is the application of economic principles and concepts to business decision-making and problem solving. The field of finance can be considered to comprise three broad categories: financial management, investments, and financial institutions:

- *Financial management.* Sometimes called *corporate finance* or *business finance*, this area of finance is concerned primarily with financial decision-making within a business entity. Financial management decisions include maintaining cash balances, extending credit, acquiring other firms, borrowing from banks, and issuing stocks and bonds.
- *Investments.* This area of finance focuses on the behavior of financial markets and the pricing of securities. An investment manager's tasks, for example, may include valuing common stocks, selecting securities for a pension fund, or measuring a portfolio's performance.
- *Financial institutions.* This area of finance deals with banks and other firms that specialize in bringing the suppliers of funds together with the users of funds. For example, a manager of a bank may make decisions regarding granting loans, managing cash balances, setting interest rates on loans, and dealing with government regulations.

No matter the particular category of finance, business situations that call for the application of the theories and tools of finance generally involve either investing (using funds) or financing (raising funds).

Managers who work in any of these three areas rely on the same basic knowledge of finance. In this book, we introduce you to this common body of knowledge and show how it is used in financial decision-making. Though the emphasis of this book is financial management, the basic principles and tools also apply to the areas of investments and financial institutions. In this introductory chapter, we'll consider the types of decisions financial managers make, the role of financial analysis, the forms of business ownership, and the objective of managers' decisions. Finally, we will describe the relationship between owners and managers.

FINANCIAL MANAGEMENT

Financial management encompasses many different types of decisions. We can classify these decisions into three groups: investment decisions, financing decisions, and decisions that involve both investing and financing. Investment decisions are concerned with the use of funds— the buying, holding, or selling of all types of assets: Should we buy a new die stamping machine? Should we introduce a new product line? Sell the old production facility? Buy an existing company? Build a warehouse? Keep our cash in the bank?

Financing decisions are concerned with the acquisition of funds to be used for investing and financing day-to-day operations. Should managers use the money raised through the firms' revenues? Should they seek money from outside of the business? A company's operations and investment can be financed from outside the business by incurring debts, such as though bank loans and the sale of bonds, or by selling ownership interests. Because each method of financing obligates the business in different ways, financing decisions are very important.

Many business decisions simultaneously involve both investing and financing. For example, a company may wish to acquire another firm— an investment decision. However, the success of the acquisition may depend on how it is financed: by borrowing cash to meet the purchase price, by selling additional shares of stock, or by exchanging existing shares of stock. If managers decide to borrow money, the borrowed funds must be repaid within a specified period of time. Creditors (those lending the money) generally do not share in the control of profits of the borrowing firm. If, on the other hand, managers decide to raise funds by selling ownership interests, these funds never have to be paid back. However, such a sale dilutes the control of (and profits accruing to) the current owners.

Whether a financial decision involves investing, financing, or both, it also will be concerned with two specific factors: expected return and risk. And throughout your study of finance, you will be concerned with these factors. *Expected return* is the difference between potential benefits and potential costs. *Risk* is the degree of uncertainty associated with these expected returns.

Financial Analysis

Financial analysis is a tool of financial management. It consists of the evaluation of the financial condition and operating performance of a business firm, an industry, or even the economy, and the forecasting of its future condition and performance. It is, in other words, a means for examining risk and expected return. Data for financial analysis may come from other areas within the firm, such as marketing and production departments, from the firm's own accounting data, or from financial information vendors such as Bloomberg Financial Markets, Moody's Investors Service, Standard & Poor's Corporation, Fitch Ratings, and Value Line, as well as from government publications, such as the *Federal Reserve Bulletin*. Financial publications such as *Business Week*, *Forbes*, *Fortune*, and the *Wall Street Journal* also publish financial data (concerning individual firms) and economic data (concerning industries, markets, and economies), much of which is now also available on the Internet.

Within the firm, financial analysis may be used not only to evaluate the performance of the firm, but also its divisions or departments and its product lines. Analyses may be performed both periodically and as needed, not only to ensure informed investing and financing decisions, but also as an aid in implementing personnel policies and rewards systems.

Outside the firm, financial analysis may be used to determine the creditworthiness of a new customer, to evaluate the ability of a supplier to hold to the conditions of a long-term contract, and to evaluate the market performance of competitors.

Firms and investors that do not have the expertise, the time, or the resources to perform financial analysis on their own may purchase analyses from companies that specialize in providing this service. Such companies can provide reports ranging from detailed written analyses to simple creditworthiness ratings for businesses. As an example, Dun & Bradstreet, a financial services firm, evaluates the creditworthiness of many firms, from small local businesses to major corporations. As another example, three companies—Moody's Investors Service, Standard & Poor's, and Fitch—evaluate the credit quality of debt obligations issued by corporations and express these views in the form of a rating that is published in the reports available from these three organizations.

FORMS OF BUSINESS ENTERPRISE

Financial management is not restricted to large corporations: It is necessary in all forms and sizes of businesses. The three major forms of business organization are the sole proprietorship, the partnership, and the corporation. These three forms differ in a number of factors, of which those most important to financial decision-making are:

- The way the firm is taxed.
- The degree of control owners may exert on decisions.
- The liability of the owners.
- The ease of transferring ownership interests.
- The ability to raise additional funds.
- The longevity of the business.

Sole Proprietorships

The simplest and most common form of business enterprise is the *sole proprietorship*, a business owned and controlled by one person—the proprietor. Because there are very few legal requirements to establish and run a sole proprietorship, this form of business is chosen by many individuals who are starting up a particular business enterprise. The sole proprietor carries on a business for his or her own benefit, without participation of other persons except employees. The proprietor receives all income from the business and alone decides whether to reinvest the profits in the business or use them for personal expenses.

A proprietor is liable for all the debts of the business; in fact, it is the proprietor who incurs the debts of the business. If there are insufficient business assets to pay a business debt, the proprietor must pay the debt out of his or her personal assets. If more funds are needed to operate or expand the business than are generated by business operations, the owner either contributes his or her personal assets to the business or borrows. For most sole proprietorships, banks are the primary source of borrowed funds. However, there are limits to how much banks will lend a sole proprietorship, most of which are relatively small.

For tax purposes, the sole proprietor reports income from the business on his or her personal income tax return. Business income is treated as the proprietor's personal income.

The assets of a sole proprietorship may also be sold to some other firm, at which time the sole proprietorship ceases to exist. Or the life of a sole proprietorship ends with the life of the proprietor, although the assets of the business may pass to the proprietor's heirs.

Partnerships

A *partnership* is an agreement between two or more persons to operate a business. A partnership is similar to a sole proprietorship except instead of one proprietor, there is more than one. The fact that there is more than one proprietor introduces some issues: Who has a say in the day-to-day operations of the business? Who is liable (that is, financially responsible) for the debts of the business? How is the income distributed among the owners? How is the income taxed? Some of these issues are resolved with the partnership agreement; others are resolved by laws. The partnership agreement describes how profits and losses are to be shared among the partners, and it details their responsibilities in the management of the business.

Most partnerships are *general partnerships*, consisting only of general partners who participate fully in the management of the business, share in its profits and losses, and are responsible for its liabilities. Each general partner is personally and individually liable for the debts of the business, even if those debts were contracted by other partners.

A *limited partnership* consists of at least one general partner and one *limited partner*. Limited partners invest in the business but do not participate in its management. A limited partner's share in the profits and losses of the business is limited by the partnership agreement. In addition, a limited partner is not liable for the debts incurred by the business beyond his or her initial investment.

A partnership is not taxed as a separate entity. Instead, each partner reports his or her share of the business profit or loss on his or her personal income tax return. Each partner's share is taxed as if it were from a sole proprietorship.

The life of a partnership may be limited by the partnership agreement. For example, the partners may agree that the partnership is to exist only for a specified number of years or only for the duration of a specific business transaction. The partnership must be terminated when any one of the partners dies, no matter what is specified in the partnership agreement. Partnership interests cannot be passed to heirs; at the death of any partner, the partnership is dissolved and perhaps renegotiated.

One of the drawbacks of partnerships is that a partner's interest in the business cannot be sold without the consent of the other partners. So a partner who needs to sell his or her interest because of, say, personal financial needs may not be able to do so.[1]

Another drawback is the partnership's limited access to new funds. Short of selling part of their own ownership interest, the partners can

---

[1] Still another problem involves ending a partnership and settling up, mainly because it is difficult to determine the value of the partnership and of each partner's share.

raise money only by borrowing from banks—and here too there is a limit to what a bank will lend a (usually small) partnership.

In certain businesses—including accounting, law, architecture, and physician's services—firms are commonly organized as partnerships. The use of this business form may be attributed primarily to state laws, regulations of the industry, and certifying organizations meant to keep practitioners in those fields from limiting their liability.[2]

Corporations

A *corporation* is a legal entity created under state laws through the process of incorporation. The corporation is an organization capable of entering into contracts and carrying out business under its own name, separate from it owners. To become a corporation, state laws generally require that a firm must do the following: (1) file articles of incorporation, (2) adopt a set of bylaws, and (3) form a board of directors.

The *articles of incorporation* specify the legal name of the corporation, its place of business, and the nature of its business. This certificate gives "life" to a corporation in the sense that it represents a contract between the corporation and its owners. This contract authorizes the corporation to issue units of ownership, called *shares*, and specifies the rights of the owners, the *shareholders*.

The bylaws are the rules of governance for the corporation. The bylaws define the rights and obligations of officers, members of the board of directors, and shareholders. In most large corporations, it is not possible for each owner to participate in monitoring the management of the business. For example, at the end of 2001, Emerson Electric Co. had approximately 33,700 shareholders. It would not be practical for each of these owners to watch over Emerson's management directly. Therefore, the owners of a corporation elect a board of directors to represent them in the major business decisions and to monitor the activities of the corporation's management. The board of directors, in turn, appoints and oversees the officers of the corporation. Directors who are also employees of the corporation are called *insider directors*; those who have no other position within the corporation are *outside directors* or *independent directors*. In the case of Emerson Electric Co., for example, there were 18 directors in 2002, six inside directors and 13 outside directors. Generally it is believed that the greater the proportion of outside directors, the greater the board's independence from the management of the company. The proportion of

---

[2] Many states have allowed some types of business, such as accounting firms, that were previously restricted to the partnership form to become limited liability companies (a form of business discussed later in this chapter).

outside directors on corporate boards varies significantly. For example, in 2002 only 44% of Kraft Foods' board are outsiders, whereas 89% of Texas Instrument's board is comprised of outside directors.

The state recognizes the existence of the corporation in the corporate charter. Corporate laws in many states follow a uniform set of laws referred to as the *Model Business Corporations Act*.[3] Once created, the corporation can enter into contracts, adopt a legal name, sue or be sued, and continue in existence forever. Though owners may die, the corporation continues to live. The liability of owners is limited to the amounts they have invested in the corporation through the shares of ownership they purchased.

Unlike the sole proprietorship and partnership, the corporation is a taxable entity. It files its own income tax return and pays taxes on its income. That income is determined according to special provisions of the federal and state tax codes and is subject to corporate tax rates different from personal income tax rates.

If the board of directors decides to distribute cash to the owners, that money is paid out of income left over after the corporate income tax has been paid. The amount of that cash payment, or dividend, must also be included in the taxable income of the owners (the shareholders). Therefore, a portion of the corporation's income (the portion paid out to owners) is subject to double taxation: once as corporate income and once as the individual owner's income.

The dividend declared by the directors of a corporation is distributed to owners in proportion to the numbers of shares of ownership they hold. If Owner A has twice as many shares as Owner B, he or she will receive twice as much money.

The ownership of a corporation, also referred to as *stock* or *equity*, is represented as shares of stock. A corporation that has just a few owners who exert complete control over the decisions of the corporation is referred to as a *close corporation* or a *closely-held corporation*. A corporation whose ownership shares are sold outside of a closed group of owners is referred to as a *public corporation* or a *publicly-held corporation*. Mars Inc., producer of M&M candies and other confectionery products, is a closely-held corporation; Hershey Foods, also a producer of candy products among other things, is a publicly-held corporation.

The shares of public corporations are freely traded in securities markets, such as the New York Stock Exchange. Hence, the ownership of a publicly-held corporation is more easily transferred than the ownership of a proprietorship, a partnership, or a closely-held corporation.

---

[3] A Model act is a statute created and proposed by the National Conference of Commissioners of Uniform State Laws. A Model act is available for adoption—with or without modification—by state legislatures.

Companies whose stock is traded in public markets are required to file an initial registration statement with the *Securities and Exchange Commission* (SEC), a federal agency created to oversee the enforcement of U. S. securities laws. The statement provides financial statements, articles of incorporation, and descriptive information regarding the nature of the business, the debt and stock of the corporation, the officers and directors, any individuals who own more than 10% of the stock, among other items.

Other Forms of Business

In addition to the proprietorship, partnership, and corporate forms of business, an enterprise may be conducted using other forms of business, such as the master limited partnership, the professional corporation, the limited liability company, and the joint venture.

A *master limited partnership* is a partnership with limited partner ownership interests that are traded on an organized exchange. For example, more than two dozen master limited partnerships are listed on the New York Stock Exchange, including the Boston Celtics, Cedar Fair, and Red Lion Inns partnerships. Ownership interests, which represent a specified ownership percentage, are traded in much the same way as the shares of stock of a corporation. One difference, however, is that a corporation can raise new capital by issuing new ownership interests, whereas a master limited partnership cannot. It is not possible to sell more than a 100% interest in the partnership, yet it is possible to sell additional shares of stock in a corporation. Another difference is that the income of a master limited partnership is taxed only once, as partners' individual income.

Another variant of the corporate form of business is the professional corporation. A *professional corporation* is an organization that is formed under state law and treated as a corporation for federal tax law purposes, yet that has unlimited liability for its owners—the owners are personally liable for the debts of the corporation. Businesses that are likely to form such corporations are those that provide services and require state licensing, such as physicians', architects', and attorneys' practices, since it is generally felt that it is in the public interest to hold such professionals responsible for the liabilities of the business.

More recently, companies are using a hybrid form of business, the *limited liability company* (LLC), which combines the best features of a partnership and a corporation. In 1988 the Internal revenue Service ruled that the LLC be treated as a partnership for tax purposes, while its owners are not liable for its debts. Since this ruling, every state has passed legislation permitting limited liability companies.

Though state laws vary slightly, in general, the owners of the LLC have limited liability. The IRS considers the LLC to be taxed as a partnership if the company has no more than two of the following characteristics: (1) limited liability, (2) centralized management, (3) free transferability of ownership interests, and (4) continuity of life. If the company has more than two of these, it will be treated as a corporation for tax purposes, subjecting the income to taxation at both the company level and the owners'.

A *joint venture*, which may be structured as either a partnership or as a corporation, is a business undertaken by a group of persons or entities (such as a partnership or corporation) for a specific business activity and, therefore, does not constitute a continuing relationship among the parties. For tax and other legal purposes, a joint venture partnership is treated as a partnership and a joint venture corporation is treated as a corporation.

U.S. corporations have entered into joint ventures with foreign corporations, enhancing participation and competition in the global marketplace. For example, the Coca-Cola Company entered a joint venture with FEMSA, Mexico's largest beverage company, in 1993, expanding its opportunities within Mexico. Joint ventures are an easy way of entering a foreign market and of gaining an advantage in a domestic market. For example, Burger King, the second largest fast food chain in America, entered the Japanese market through a joint venture with Japan Tobacco Inc., which is two-thirds owned by Japan's Ministry of Finance, to form Burger King Japan. This joint venture gives Burger King (owned by the British firm, Grand Metropolitan PLC) a fighting chance in competing against McDonald's almost 2,000 outlets in Japan.

Joint ventures are becoming increasingly popular as a way of doing business. Participants—whether individuals, partnerships, or corporations—get together to exploit a specific business opportunity. Afterward, the venture can be dissolved. Recent alliances among communication and entertainment firms have sparked thought about what the future form of doing business will be. Some believe that what lies ahead is a virtual enterprise—a temporary alliance without all the bureaucracy of the typical corporation—that can move quickly and decisively to take advantage of profitable business opportunities.

Prevalence

The advantages and disadvantages of the three major forms of business from the point of view of financial decision-making are summarized in Exhibit 1.1. Firms tend to evolve from proprietorship to partnership to corporation as they grow and as their needs for financing increase. Sole proprietorship is the choice for starting a business, whereas the corporation is the choice to accommodate growth. The great majority of business firms in the United States are sole proprietorships, but most business income is generated by corporations.

The Objective of Financial Management

So far we have seen that financial managers are primarily concerned with investment decisions and financing decisions within business organizations. The great majority of these decisions are made within the corporate business structure, which better accommodates growth and is responsible for 89% of U.S. business income. Hence, most of our discussion in the remainder of this book focuses on financial decision-making in corporations, but many of the issues apply generally to all forms of business.

EXHIBIT 1.1   Characteristics of the Three Basic Forms of Business

---

Sole Proprietorship

Advantages

1. The proprietor is the sole business decision-maker.
2. The proprietor receives all income from business.
3. Income from the business is taxed once, at the individual taxpayer level.

Disadvantages

1. The proprietor is liable for all debts of the business (unlimited liability).
2. The proprietorship has a limited life.
3. There is limited access to additional funds.

General Partnership

Advantages

1. Partners receive income according to terms in partnership agreement.
2. Income from business is taxed once as the partners' personal income.
3. Decision-making rests with the general partners only.

Disadvantages

1. Each partner is liable for all the debts of the partnership.
2. The partnership's life is determined by agreement or the life of the partners.
3. There is limited access to additional funds.

Corporation

Advantages

1. The firm has perpetual life.
2. Owners are not liable for the debts of the firm; the most that owners can lose is their initial investment.
3. The firm can raise funds by selling additional ownership interest.
4. Income is distributed in proportion to ownership interest.

Disadvantages

1. Income paid to owners is subjected to double taxation.
2. Ownership and management are separated in larger organizations.

One such issue concerns the objective of financial decision-making. What goal (or goals) do managers have in mind when they choose between financial alternatives—say, between distributing current income among shareholders and investing it to increase future income? There is actually one financial objective: the maximization of the economic well-being, or wealth, of the owners. Whenever a decision is to be made, management should choose the alternative that most increases the wealth of the owners of the business.

The Measure of Owner's Economic Well-Being

The price of a share of stock at any time, or its *market value*, represents the price that buyers in a free market are willing to pay for it. The *market value of shareholders' equity* is the value of all owners' interest in the corporation. It is calculated as the product of the market value of one share of stock and the number of shares of stock outstanding:

Market value of shareholders' equity
= Market value of a share of stock × Number of shares of stock outstanding

The number of shares of stock outstanding is the total number of shares that are owned by shareholders. For example, at the end of June 2002 there were 2,040 million Walt Disney Company shares outstanding. The price of Disney stock at the end of June 2002 was $18.90 per share. Therefore, the market value of Disney's equity at the end of June 2002 was over $38.5 billion.

Investors buy shares of stock in anticipation of future dividends and increases in the market value of the stock. How much are they willing to pay today for this future—and hence uncertain—stream of dividends? They are willing to pay exactly what they believe it is worth today, an amount that is called the *present value*, an important financial concept explained in Chapter 7. The present value of a share of stock reflects the following factors:

- The uncertainty associated with receiving future payments.
- The timing of these future payments.
- Compensation for tying up funds in this investment.

The market price of a share is a measure of owners' economic well-being. Does this mean that if the share price goes up, management is doing a good job? Not necessarily. Share prices often can be influenced by factors beyond the control of management. These factors include expectations regarding the economy, returns available on alternative investments (such as bonds), and even how investors view the firm and the idea of investing.

These factors influence the price of shares through their effects on expectations regarding future cash flows and investors' evaluation of those cash flows. Nonetheless, managers can still maximize the value of owners' equity, given current economic conditions and expectations. They do so by carefully considering the expected benefits, risk, and timing of the returns on proposed investments.

Economic Profit versus Accounting Profit: Share Price versus Earnings Per Share

When you studied economics, you saw that the objective of the firm is to maximize profit. In finance, however, the objective is to maximize owners' wealth. Is this a contradiction? No. We have simply used different terminology to express the same goal. The difference arises from the distinction between accounting profit and economic profit.

Economic profit is the difference between revenues and costs, where costs include both the actual business costs (the explicit costs) and the implicit costs. The implicit costs are the payments that are necessary to secure the needed resources, the *cost of capital*. With any business enterprise, someone supplies funds, or capital, that the business then invests. The supplier of these funds may be the business owner, an entrepreneur, or banks, bondholders, and shareholders. The cost of capital depends on both the time value of money—what could have been earned on a risk-free investment—and the uncertainty associated with the investment. The greater the uncertainty associated with an investment, the greater the cost of capital.

Consider the case of the typical corporation. Shareholders invest in the shares of a corporation with the expectation that they will receive future dividends. But shareholders could have invested their funds in any other investment, as well. So what keeps them interested in keeping their money in the particular corporation? Getting a return on their investment that is better than they could get elsewhere, considering the amount of uncertainty of receiving the future dividends. If the corporation cannot generate economic profits, the shareholders will move their funds elsewhere.

Accounting profit, however, is the difference between revenues and costs, recorded according to accounting principles, where costs are primarily the actual costs of doing business. The implicit costs—opportunity cost and normal profit—which reflect the uncertainty and timing of future cash flows, are not taken into consideration in accounting profit. Moreover accounting procedures, and hence the computation of accounting profit, can vary from firm to firm. For both these reasons, accounting profit is not a reasonable gauge of shareholders' return on their investment, and the maximization of accounting profit is not equivalent to the maximization of shareholder wealth.[4]

Many U. S. corporations, including Coca–Cola, Briggs & Stratton, and Boise Cascade, are embracing a relatively new method of evaluating and rewarding management performance that is based on the idea of compensating management for economic profit, rather than for accounting profit. The most prominent of recently developed techniques to evaluate a firm's performance are economic value–added and market value-added.[5]

Economic value-added (*EVA*®) is another name for the firm's economic profit. Key elements of estimating economic profit are:

1. calculating the firm's operating profit from financial statement data, making adjustments to accounting profit to better reflect a firm's operating results for a period,
2. calculating the cost of capital, and
3. comparing operating profit with the cost of capital.

The difference between the operating profit and the cost of capital is the estimate of the firm's economic profit, or economic value–added.

A related measure, *market value added* (*MVA*), focuses on the market value of capital, as compared to the cost of capital. The key elements of market value added are:

1. calculating the market value of capital,
2. calculating the amount of capital invested (i.e., debt and equity), and
3. comparing the market value of capital with the capital invested.

The difference between the market value of capital and the amount of capital invested is the market value added. In theory, the market value added is the present value of all expected future economic profits.

The application of economic profit is relatively new in the measurement of performance, yet the concept of economic profit is not new. What this recent emphasis on economic profit has accomplished is to focus attention away from accounting profit and toward clearing the cost of capital hurdle.

---

[4] When economic profit is zero, as an example, investors are getting a return that just compensates them for bearing the risk of the investment. When accounting profit is zero, investors would be much better off investing elsewhere and just as well off by keeping their money under their mattresses.

[5] One of the first to advocate using economic profit in compensating management is G. Bennett Stewart III, *The Quest for Value* (New York: HarperCollins Publishers, Inc., 1991).

Share Prices and Efficient Markets

We have seen that the price of a share of stock today is the present value of the dividends and share price the investor expects to receive in the future. What if these expectations change?

Suppose you buy a share of stock of IBM. The price you are willing to pay is the present value of future cash flows you expect from dividends paid on one share of IBM stock and from the eventual sale of that share. This price reflects the amount, the timing, and the uncertainty of these future cash flows. Now what happens if some news—good or bad—is announced that changes the expected IBM dividends? If the market in which these shares are traded is efficient, the price will fall very quickly to reflect that news.

In an efficient market, the price of assets—in this case shares of stock—reflects all publicly available information. As information is received by investors, share prices change rapidly to reflect the new information. How rapidly? In U.S. stock markets, which are efficient markets, information affecting a firm is reflected in share prices of its stock within minutes.

What are the implications for financing decisions? In efficient markets, the current price of a firm's shares reflects all publicly available information. Hence, there is no good time or bad time to issue a security. When a firm issues stock, it will receive what that stock is worth—no more and no less. Also, the price of the shares will change as information about the firm's activities is revealed. If the firm announces a new product, investors will use whatever information they have to figure out how this new product will change the firm's future cash flows and, hence, the value of the firm—and the share price—will change accordingly. Moreover, in time, the price will be such that investors' economic profit approaches zero.

Financial Management and the Maximization of Owners' Wealth

Financial managers are charged with the responsibility of making decisions that maximize owners' wealth. For a corporation, that responsibility translates into maximizing the value of shareholders' equity. If the market for stocks is efficient, the value of a share of stock in a corporation should reflect investors' expectations regarding the future prospects of the corporation. The value of a stock will change as investors' expectations about the future change. For financial managers' decisions to add value, the present value of the benefits resulting from decisions must outweigh the associated costs, where costs include the costs of capital.

If there is a separation of the ownership and management of a firm—that is, the owners are not also the managers of the firm—there are additional issues to confront. What if a decision is in the best interests of the firm, but not in the best interest of the manager? How can owners insure that managers are watching out for the owners' interests? How can owners motivate managers to make decisions that are best for the owners? We will address these issues, and more, in the next section.

THE AGENCY RELATIONSHIP

If you are the sole owner of a business, then you make the decisions that affect your own well-being. But what if you are a financial manager of a business and you are not the sole owner? In this case, you are making decisions for owners other than yourself; you, the financial manager, are an agent. An *agent* is a person who acts for—and exerts powers of—another person or group of persons. The person (or group of persons) the agent represents is referred to as the *principal*. The relationship between the agent and his or her principal is an *agency relationship*. There is an agency relationship between the managers and the shareholders of corporations.

Problems with the Agency Relationship

In an agency relationship, the agent is charged with the responsibility of acting for the principal. Is it possible the agent may not act in the best interest of the principal, but instead act in his or her own self-interest? Yes—because the agent has his or her own objective of maximizing personal wealth.

In a large corporation, for example, the managers may enjoy many fringe benefits, such as golf club memberships, access to private jets, and company cars. These benefits (also called perquisites, or "perks") may be useful in conducting business and may help attract or retain management personnel, but there is room for abuse. What if the managers start spending more time at the golf course than at their desks? What if they use the company jets for personal travel? What if they buy company cars for their teenagers to drive? The abuse of perquisites imposes costs on the firm—and ultimately on the owners of the firm. There is also a possibility that managers who feel secure in their positions may not bother to expend their best efforts toward the business. This is referred to as shirking, and it too imposes a cost to the firm.

Finally, there is the possibility that managers will act in their own self-interest, rather than in the interest of the shareholders when those interests clash. For example, management may fight the acquisition of their firm by some other firm even if the acquisition would benefit shareholders. Why? In most takeovers, the management personnel of the acquired firm generally lose their jobs. Envision that some company is making an offer to acquire the firm that you manage. Are you happy that the acquiring firm is offering the shareholders of your firm more for their stock than its current market value? If you are looking out for their best interests, you should be. Are you happy about the likely prospect of losing your job? Most likely not.

Many managers faced this dilemma in the merger mania of the 1980s. So what did they do? Among the many tactics,

- Some fought acquisition of their firms—which they labeled *hostile takeovers*—by proposing changes in the corporate charter or even lobbying for changes in state laws to discourage takeovers.
- Some adopted lucrative executive compensation packages—called *golden parachutes*—that were to go into effect if they lost their jobs.

Such defensiveness by corporate managers in the case of takeovers, whether it is warranted or not, emphasizes the potential for conflict between the interests of the owners and the interests of management.

Costs of the Agency Relationship

There are costs involved with any effort to minimize the potential for conflict between the principal's interest and the agent's interest. Such costs are called *agency costs*, and they are of three types: monitoring costs, bonding costs, and residual loss.

Monitoring costs are costs incurred by the principal to monitor or limit the actions of the agent. In a corporation, shareholders may require managers to periodically report on their activities via audited accounting statements, which are sent to shareholders. The accountants' fees and the management time lost in preparing such statements are monitoring costs. Another example is the implicit cost incurred when shareholders limit the decision-making power of managers. By doing so, the owners may miss profitable investment opportunities; the foregone profit is a monitoring cost.

The board of directors of corporation has a *fiduciary duty* to shareholders; that is the legal responsibility to make decisions (or to see that decisions are made) that are in the best interests of shareholders. Part of that responsibility is to ensure that managerial decisions are also in the best interests of the shareholders. Therefore, at least part of the cost of having directors is a monitoring cost.

Bonding costs are incurred by agents to assure principals that they will act in the principal's best interest. The name comes from the agent's promise or bond to take certain actions. A manager may enter into a contract that requires him or her to stay on with the firm even though another company acquires it; an implicit cost is then incurred by the manager, who foregoes other employment opportunities.

Even when monitoring and bonding devices are used, there may be some divergence between the interests of principals and those of agents. The resulting cost, called the *residual loss*, is the implicit cost that results because the principal's and the agent's interests cannot be perfectly aligned even when monitoring and bonding costs are incurred.

Motivating Managers: Executive Compensation

One way to encourage management to act in shareholders' best interests, and so minimize agency problems and costs, is through executive compensation—how top management is paid. There are several different ways to compensate executives, including:

Salary. The direct payment of cash of a fixed amount per period.

Bonus. A cash reward based on some performance measure, say earnings of a division or the company.

Stock appreciation right. A cash payment based on the amount by which the value of a specified number of shares has increased over a specified period of time (supposedly due to the efforts of management).

Performance shares. Shares of stock given the employees, in an amount based on some measure of operating performance, such as earnings per share.

Stock option. The right to buy a specified number of shares of stock in the company at a stated price—referred to as an *exercise price* at some time in the future. The exercise price may be above, at, or below the current market price of the stock.

Restricted stock grant. The grant of shares of stock to the employee at low or no cost, conditional on the shares not being sold for a specified time.

The salary portion of the compensation—the minimum cash payment an executive receives—must be enough to attract talented executives. But a bonus should be based on some measure of performance that is in the best interests of shareholders—not just on the past year's accounting earnings. For example, a bonus could be based on gains in market share. Recently, several companies have adopted programs that base compensation, at least in part, on value added by managers as measured by economic profits.

The basic idea behind stock options and restricted stock grants is to make managers owners, since the incentive to consume excessive perks and to shirk are reduced if managers are also owners. As owners, managers not only share the costs of perks and shirks, but they also benefit financially when their decisions maximize the wealth of owners. Hence, the key to motivation through stock is not really the *value* of the stock, but rather *ownership* of the stock. For this reason, stock appreciation rights and performance shares, which do not involve an investment on the part of recipients, are not effective motivators.

Stock options do work to motivate performance if they require owning the shares over a long time period; are exercisable at a price *above* the current market price of the shares, thus encouraging managers to get the share price up, and require managers to tie up their own wealth in the shares.

Currently, there is a great deal of concern in some corporations because executive compensation is not linked to performance. In recent years, many U.S. companies have downsized, restructured, and laid off many employees and allowed the wages of employees who survive the cuts to stagnate. At the same time, corporations have increased the pay of top executives through both salary and lucrative stock options. If these changes lead to better value for shareholders, shouldn't the top executives be rewarded?

There are two issues here. First, such a situation results in anger and disenchantment among both surviving employees and former employees. Second, the downsizing, restructuring, and lay-offs may not result in immediate (or even, eventual) increased profitability. Consider AT&T in 1995: In a year in which the company restructured, barely made a profit, eliminated 40,000 jobs, and its stock had lackluster returns, the chief executive officer (CEO) received salary and bonuses of $5.2 million and options valued at $11 million. If the restructuring pays off in the long-run, the CEO's pay may be justified, but meanwhile, there may be some unhappy AT&T shareholders: The average annual return on AT&T stock over the period 1996–2001 was –23.19%.[6]

Another problem is that compensation packages for top management are designed by the board of directors, which often includes top management. Moreover, reports disclosing these compensation packages to shareholders (the proxy statements) are often confusing. Both problems can be avoided by adequate and understandable disclosure of executive compensation to shareholders, and with compensation packages determined by board members who are not executives of the firm.

---

[6] Joann S. Lublin, "AT&T Board Faces Protest Over CEO Pay," *Wall Street Journal* (April 16, 1996), pp. A3, A6.

Owners have one more tool with which to motivate management—the threat of firing. As long as owners can fire managers, managers will be encouraged to act in the owners' interest. However, if the owners are divided or apathetic—as they often are in large corporations—or if they fail to monitor management's performance and the reaction of directors to that performance, the threat may not be credible. The removal of a few poor managers can, however, make this threat palpable.

Shareholder Wealth Maximization and Accounting "Irregularities"

Recently, there have been a number of scandals and allegations regarding the financial information that is being reported to shareholders and the market. Financial results reported in the income statements and balance sheets of some companies indicated much better performance than the true performance or much better financial condition than actual. Examples include Xerox, which was forced to restate earnings for several years because it had inflated pre-tax profits by $1.4 billion, Enron, which is accused of inflating earnings and hiding substantial debt, and Worldcom, which failed to properly account for $3.8 billion of expenses. Along with these financial reporting issues, the independence of the auditors and the role of financial analysts have been brought to the forefront.[7]

It is unclear at this time the extent to which these scandals and problems were the result of simply bad decisions or due to corruption. The eagerness of managers to present favorable results to shareholders and the market appears to be a factor in several instances. And personal enrichment at the expense of shareholders seems to explain some cases. Whatever the motivation, chief executive officers (CEOs), chief financial officers (CFOs), and board members are being held directly accountable for financial disclosures. For example, in 2002, the Securities and Exchange Commission ordered sworn statements attesting to the accuracy of financial statements. The first deadline for such statements resulted in several companies restating financial results.

The accounting scandals are creating an awareness of the importance of corporate governance, the importance of the independence of the public accounting auditing function, the role of financial analysts, and the responsibilities of CEOs and CFOs.

---

[7] For example, the public accounting firm of Arthur Andersen was found guilty of obstruction of justice in 2002 for their role in the shredding of documents relating to Enron. As an example of the problems associated with financial analysts, the securities firm of Merrill Lynch paid a $100 million fine for their role in hyping stocks to help win investment-banking business.

Shareholder Wealth Maximization and Social Responsibility

When financial managers assess a potential investment in a new product, they examine the risks and the potential benefits and costs. If the risk-adjusted benefits do not outweigh the costs, they will not invest. Similarly, managers assess current investments for the same purpose; if benefits do not continue to outweigh costs, they will not continue to invest in the product but will shift their investment elsewhere. This is consistent with the goal of shareholder wealth maximization and with the allocative efficiency of the market economy.

Discontinuing investment in an unprofitable business may mean closing down plants, laying off workers, and, perhaps destroying an entire town that depends on the business for income. So decisions to invest or disinvest may affect great numbers of people.

All but the smallest business firms are linked in some way to groups of persons who are dependent to a degree on the business. These groups may include suppliers, customers, the community itself, and nearby businesses, as well as employees and shareholders. The various groups of persons that depend on a firm are referred to as its *stakeholders*; they all have some *stake* in the outcome of the firm. For example, if the Boeing Company lays off workers or increases production, the effects are felt by Seattle and the surrounding communities.

Can a firm maximize the wealth of shareholders and stakeholders at the same time? Probably. If a firm invests in the production of goods and services that meet the demand of consumers in such a way that benefits exceed costs, the firm will be allocating the resources of the community efficiently, employing assets in their most productive use. If later the firm must disinvest—perhaps close a plant—it has a responsibility to assist employees and other stakeholders who are affected. Failure to do so could tarnish its reputation, erode its ability to attract new stakeholder groups to new investments, and ultimately act to the detriment of shareholders.

The effects of a firm's actions on others are referred to as *externalities*. Pollution is an externality that keeps increasing in importance. Suppose the manufacture of a product creates air pollution. If the polluting firm acts to reduce this pollution, it incurs a cost that either increases the price of its product or decreases profit and the market value of its stock. If competitors do not likewise incur costs to reduce their pollution, the firm is at a disadvantage and may be driven out of business through competitive pressure.

The firm may try to use its efforts at pollution control to enhance its reputation in the hope that this will lead to a sales increase large enough to make up for the cost of reducing pollution. This is called a *market solution*: The market places a value on the pollution control and rewards the firm (or an industry) for it. If society really believes that pollution is bad and that pollution control is good, the interests of owners and society can be aligned.

It is more likely, however, that pollution control costs will be viewed as reducing owners' wealth. Then firms must be forced to reduce pollution through laws or government regulations. But such laws and regulations also come with a cost—the cost of enforcement. Again, if the benefits of mandatory pollution control outweigh the cost of government action, society is better off. In such a case, if the government requires all firms to reduce pollution, then pollution control costs simply become one of the conditions under which owner wealth-maximizing decisions are to be made.

SUMMARY

- Finance comprises three areas: financial management, investments, and financial institutions. These three areas are linked together through a common body of knowledge that includes the theories and tools of finance.
- The decision-making of financial managers can be broken down into two broad classes: investment decisions and financing decisions. Investment decisions are those decisions that involve the use of the firm's funds. Financing decisions are those decisions that involve the acquisition of the firm's funds.
- Financial managers assess the potential risks and rewards associated with investment and financing decisions through the application of financial analysis.
- The information necessary for financial decisions and analysis includes the accounting information that describes the company and its industry as well as economic information relating to the company, the industry, and the economy in general.
- A business enterprise may be formed as a sole proprietorship, a partnership, corporation, or a hybrid of one or more of these forms. The hybrid forms include the master limited partnership, the professional corporation, the limited liability company, and the joint venture. The choice of the form of business is influenced by concerns about the life of the enterprise, the liability of its owners, the taxation of income, and access to funds. In turn, the form of business influences financial decision-making through its effect on taxes, governance, and the liability of owners.

■ Corporations are entities created by law that limit the liability of owners and subject income to an additional layer of taxation. The corporation's owners—the shareholders—are represented by the board of directors, which oversees the management of the firm.

■ The objective of financial decision-making in a business is the maximization of the wealth of owners. For a corporation, this is equivalent to the maximization of the market value of the stock.

■ If markets for securities are price efficient, share prices will reflect all available information. When information is revealed to investors, it is rapidly figured into share prices.

■ Since managers' self-interest may not be consistent with owners' best interests, owners must devise ways to align mangers' and owners' interests. One means of doing this is through executive compensation. By designing managers' compensation packages to encourage long-term investment in the stock of a corporation, the interests of managers and shareholders can be aligned.

■ Recent scandals have created an awareness of the responsibility of CEOs, CFOs, and board members to shareholders and the market.

■ Shareholder wealth maximization is consistent with the best interests of stakeholders and society if market forces reward firms for taking actions that are in society's interest or if the government steps in to force actions that are in society's interest.

QUESTIONS

1. Which of following actions are the result of a financing decision? Which of the following actions are the result of an investment decision?
   a. A firm introduces a new product.
   b. A firm issues new bonds.
   c. A corporation issues new shares of stock.
   d. A firm expands its existing manufacturing facilities.
   e. A firm leases a new building to be used in its manufacturing.

2. Suppose you are the financial manager of a large national food processing firm. In your travels, you run across a small regional food processor that you believe will provide your firm with annual returns of over 30%. Returns on your firm's typical investments are around 20%. Should you propose that your firm acquire this regional food processor? What factors need to be considered in this decision?

3. McDonald's Corporation, licensor and operator of a chain of fast-food restaurants, was founded in 1953 as a partnership and within

six months was incorporated. Why would this operator of fast-food restaurants incorporate so soon after being established? What factors influence the decision to incorporate?

4. Briefly describe each of the following forms of business: (a) master limited partnership, (b) professional corporation, (c) joint venture.

5. Corporations contribute the greatest share of business income in the United States, yet there are fewer corporations than sole proprietorships. Explain why these facts seem reasonable, considering the evolution of a firm.

6. If the share price of a corporation's stock declines, does this mean that the management of the company is not maximizing shareholder wealth? If the share price of a corporation's stock increases, does this mean that the management of the company is maximizing shareholder wealth? Explain.

7. Why is the maximizing of shareholder wealth not necessarily equivalent to the maximizing of earnings per share?

8. Through 1997, the Burlington Coat Factory Warehouse Corporation had not paid any dividends. Why were investors willing to pay over $10 for a share of Burlington stock in 1997?

9. The Rising Corporation has had 20 consecutive quarters of increasing earnings per share, but its share price has remained at about the same price over this same time period. Is this consistent? Explain.

10. Which forms of business have limited liability for all owners? Which forms of business have unlimited liability for all owners?

11. Why may a firm's share price increase when the firm announces lower earnings?

12. The Clockwork Corporation would like to issue $2 million in new shares of stock. The President of Clockwork believes that if the company waits two weeks, they could get a better price for their shares. The Chair of the board of directors disputes this. She says that because markets are price efficient, there is no "timing" possible on the stock issue and Clockwork should issue the shares when they need the funds, and not worry about "timing." Who is right?

13. What is an agency cost? Give three examples of agency costs.

14. The Sununu Corporation is having a bit of a problem: The executives are using the corporation's jets for personal reasons, such as traveling on vacation and visiting doctors in other cities. The board of directors wants management to cut down on this type of activity.

   a. In terms of the different types of agency costs, how would we classify the misuse of corporate jets?

   b. What measures can the board take to reduce or eliminate the misuse of the corporate jets?

15. Suppose that you start your own small retail business. As business increases, you expand the hours and hire someone to manage the business during the evening hours.
    a. Describe the agency relationship involved in your business.
    b. What possible problems can arise in this relationship?
    c. How could you reduce the costs associated with this agency relationship?
16. List four kinds of compensation for a firm's management. Identify the arrangements that would be most effective in aligning the interests of shareholders and management.
17. Can shareholder wealth maximization be consistent with a firm's social responsibility? Explain. Consider International Business Machines (IBM), whose headquarters are located in Armonk, New York, but whose manufacturing and sales operations span the globe. Who are IBM's stakeholders? If IBM trims is work force, what obligations does it have to its stakeholders?
18. On Tuesday, February 16, 2000, the L Corp. announced that its fourth quarter 1999 earnings per share rose to 67 cents, up from 55 cents for the fourth quarter of 1991. On the same day, M Corp. announced fourth quarter earnings of 63 cents per share, compared to the previous year's fourth quarter earnings of 66 cents. On February 16, 2000, L Corp.'s share price fell from \$27.375 to \$25.375 and M Corp.'s share price fell from \$40.125 to \$37.375. Why would the share prices of both companies fall when these earnings figures are announced?
19. Why would a firm choose to be a closely-held corporation instead of a publicly-held corporation? Why would a firm choose to be a publicly-held corporation instead of a closely-held corporation?
20. Compare performance shares with a restricted stock grant as a means of motivating management to act in shareholders' best interests. Which do you believe is more effective? Explain your reasoning.
21. Mary, Martin, and Michael invested \$20,000, \$30,000, and \$50,000, respectively, in a business enterprise. After operating the business unsuccessfully for five years, they decided to terminate it. At the time they ceased business operations, the assets of the business were worth only \$40,000 and the debts of the business were \$10,000.
    a. If this business were formed as a partnership, with the sharing of profits and losses based on the proportion of each partner's original investment, what would be the financial consequences of the dissolution of the business to Mary, Martin, and Michael?
    b. If this business were formed as a corporation, with the proportion of ownership based on the proportion of each shareholder's original investment, what would be the financial consequences of the dissolution of the business to Mary, Martin, and Michael?

CHAPTER 2

Securities and Markets

The objective of any financial decision, whether it is a financing or investment decision, should be to maximize owners' wealth. For a corporation this translates into maximizing the market value of the ownership interest—the value of the stock. So a financial manager's decisions must be made with an eye on the value of the firm's stock and the markets in which the stock is traded.

If a firm needs funds, should it issue stock or borrow? If it issues new stock, will present investors lose? If it borrows, what interest rate will its lenders—the investors in its bonds—require? How soon could the loan be paid off? How soon should it be paid off?

If a firm has funds to invest, should financial managers invest it until it is needed? In what kind of financial instrument? What characteristics must the investment vehicle have? What types of risk must they take on with their investment?

Financial managers must understand the wide range of securities available and the markets in which they are bought and sold. This chapter provides an overview of both. Its purpose is twofold. First, we acquaint you with the terms and definitions we use in this book. Then, we give you an idea how markets for securities function so that you will know how security prices are determined.

SECURITIES

A *security* is a document that gives the owner a claim on future cash flows. A security may represent an ownership claim on an asset (such as a share of stock) or a claim on the repayment of borrowed funds, with interest (such as a bond). The document may be a piece of paper (such as a stock certificate or a bond) or an entry in a register (which may, in turn, be a computer record). A *securities market* is an arrangement for buying and selling securities. It may be a physical location or simply a computer or telephone network.

Securities are classified into three groups: money market securities, capital market securities, and derivative securities—based on their maturity and the source of their value. The word "maturity" is often used loosely to refer to the length of time before repayment of a debt. Other terms using the word "maturity" are more specific. The *maturity date* of a security is the pre-set date on which the amount borrowed (called the *face value*, the *par value*, the *principal*, or the *maturity value*) is repaid. The security is said to mature on its maturity date. The *original maturity* is the time between the date a security is issued and its maturity date.

Money Market Securities

Money market securities are short-term indebtedness. By "short term" we usually imply an original maturity of one year or less. The most common money market securities are Treasury bills, commercial paper, negotiable certificates of deposit, and bankers acceptances.

Treasury bills (*T-bills*) are short-term securities issued by the U.S. government; they have original maturities of either four weeks, three months, or six months. Unlike other money market securities, T-bills carry no stated interest rate. Instead, they are sold on a *discounted basis*: Investors obtain a return on their investment by buying these securities for less than their face value and then receiving the face value at maturity. T-Bills are sold in $10,000 denominations; that is, the T-Bill has a face value of $10,000.

Commercial paper is a promissory note—a written promise to pay—issued by a large, creditworthy corporation. These securities have original maturities ranging from one day to 270 days and usually trade in units of $100,000. Most commercial paper is backed by bank lines of credit, which means that a bank is standing by ready to pay the obligation if the issuer is unable to. Commercial paper may be either interest-bearing or sold on a discounted basis.

Certificates of deposit (CDs) are written promises by a bank to pay a depositor. Nowadays they have original maturities from six months to three years. *Negotiable certificates of deposit* are CDs issued by large commercial banks that can be bought and sold among investors. Negotiable CDs typically have original maturities between one month and one year and are sold in denominations of $100,000 or more. Negotiable certificates of deposit are sold to investors at their face value and carry a fixed interest rate. On the maturity date, the investor is repaid the amount borrowed, plus interest.

Eurodollar certificates of deposit are CDs issued by foreign branches of U.S. banks, and *Yankee certificates of deposit* are CDs issued by foreign banks located in the United States. Both Eurodollar CDs and Yankee CDs are denominated in U.S. dollars. In other words, interest payments and the repayment of principal are both in U.S. dollars.

Bankers' acceptances are short-term loans, usually to importers and exporters, made by banks to finance specific transactions. An acceptance is created when a draft (a promise to pay) is written by a bank's customer and the bank "accepts" it, promising to pay. The bank's acceptance of the draft is a promise to pay the face amount of the draft to whomever presents it for payment. The bank's customer then uses the draft to finance a transaction, giving this draft to her supplier in exchange for goods. Since acceptances arise from specific transactions, they are available in a wide variety of principal amounts. Typically, bankers' acceptances have maturities of less than 180 days. Bankers' acceptances are sold at a discount from their face value, and the face value is paid at maturity. Since acceptances are backed by both the issuing bank *and* the purchaser of goods, the likelihood of default is very small.

Money market securities are backed solely by the issuer's ability to pay. With money market securities, there is no *collateral*; that is, no item of value (such as real estate) is designated by the issuer to ensure repayment. The investor relies primarily on the reputation and repayment history of the issuer in expecting that he or she will be repaid.

CAPITAL MARKET SECURITIES

Capital market securities are long-term securities issued by corporations and governments. Here "long-term securities" refers to securities with original maturities greater than 1 year and perpetual securities (those with no maturity). There are two types of capital market securities: those that represent shares of ownership interest, also called *equity*, issued by corporations, and those that represent indebtedness, issued by corporations and by the U.S. and state and local governments.

Equity

The equity of a corporation is referred to as "stock"; ownership of stock is represented by shares. Investors who own stock are referred to as *shareholders*. Every corporation has common stock, and some corporations have another type of stock, preferred stock, as well.

Common stock is the most basic ownership interest in a corpora-tion. Common shareholders are the residual owners of the firm. If the business is liquidated, the common shareholders can claim the business' assets, but only those assets that remain after all other claimants have been satisfied.

Since common stock represents ownership of the corporation, and since the corporation has a perpetual life, common stock is a perpetual security; it has no maturity. Common shareholders may receive cash payments—dividends—from the corporation. They may also receive a return on their investment in the form of increased value of their stock as the corporation prospers and grows.

Preferred stock also represents ownership interest in a corporation and, like common stock, is a perpetual security. However, preferred stock differs from common stock in several important ways. First, pre-ferred shareholders are usually promised a fixed annual dividend, whereas common shareholders receive what the board of directors decides to distribute. And although the corporation is not legally bound to pay the preferred stock's dividend, preferred shareholders must be paid their dividends before any common dividends are paid. Second, preferred shareholders are not residual owners; their claim on a liqui-dated corporation takes precedence over that of common shareholders. And finally, preferred shareholders generally do not have a say in cor-porate matters, whereas common stockholders have the right to vote for members of the board of directors and on major issues.

Indebtedness

A capital market debt obligation is a financial instrument whereby the bor-rower promises to repay the face amount of the obligation by the maturity date and, in most cases, to make periodic interest payments to the holder of the debt obligation, referred to as the *lender*. These debt obligations can be broken into two categories: bank loans and debt securities.

While at one time, bank loans were not considered capital market instruments, in recent years a market for the buying and selling of these debt obligations has developed. One form of bank loan that is bought and sold in the market is a *syndicated bank loan*. This is a loan in which a group (or syndicate) of banks provides funds to the borrower. The need for a group of banks arises because the amount sought by a borrower may be too large for any one bank to be exposed to the credit risk of that borrower.

Debt securities include (1) bonds, (2) notes, (3) medium-term notes, and (4) asset-backed securities. The distinction between a bond and a note has to do with the number of years until the obligation matures when the security is originally issued. Historically, a note is a debt security with a maturity at issuance of 10 years or less; a bond is a debt security with a maturity greater than10 years.[1] The distinction between a note and a medium-term note has nothing to do with the maturity but rather the way the security is issued and we will explain this in Chapter 15. Throughout most of this book we will simply refer to a bond, a note, or a medium-term note as simply a bond. We will refer to the investors in any debt obligation as either the *debtholder, bondholder,* or *note holder.*

A debt security may provide a promise to pay the investor periodic interest (referred to as a *coupon*); a debt security that does not include a promise to pay interest is referred to as a *zero-coupon debt.* In the case of debt that pays interest, interest is generally paid at regular intervals (say, semi-annually) and may be a fixed or floating (or variable) rate. The interest rate for a floating rate security is usually tied to the interest rate on a market interest rate, the price of a commodity, or the return on some financial instrument.

Bonds, notes, and medium-term notes are issued by corporations, the U.S. government, U.S. government agencies, and municipal governments. Corporate debt securities backed by specific assets as collateral are referred to as *secured notes* or *secured bonds.* If they are not backed by specific assets, they are referred to as *debentures.* If a debt obligation is secured and the borrower is unable to make interest or principal payments when promised, in theory the creditors may be able to force the sale of the collateral for the purpose of collecting what is due them. Collateral therefore reduces the security's riskiness and the level of return, or *yield,* the issuer (the borrower) must pay. As we will see in later chapters in this book, riskiness is an important determinant of the return on as investment. The claims of debtholders take precedence over those of shareholders, but debtholders are unlikely to be paid the full face value for their securities if a corporation must be liquidated.

U.S. government notes and bonds are interest-bearing securities backed by the "full faith and credit" of the United States; there is little uncertainty regarding whether the interest and principal will be paid as promised. The bonds and notes of U.S. government agencies, such as the Tennessee Valley Authority, are also backed by the government. The securities of government sponsored enterprises, such as the United

---

[1] This distinction between notes and bonds is not precisely true, but is consistent with common usage of the terms "note" and "bond." In fact, notes and bonds are distinguished by whether or not there is an indenture agreement, a legal contract specifying the terms of the borrowing and any restrictions, and identifying a trustee to watch out for the debtholders' interests. A bond has an indenture agreement, whereas a note does not. For our purposes in this chapter, we will use the terms notes and bonds in their common usage, distinguished on the term to maturity.

States Postal Service and the Federal Home Loan Bank are not explicitly backed by the government, yet there is little uncertainty whether the interest and principal on these securities will be paid as promised.

Bonds issued by state and local governments are called municipal bonds. They are either *general obligation bonds*, which are backed by the general taxing power of the issuing government, or *revenue bonds*, which are bonds issued to finance a specific project and are repaid with the revenues from that project.

Interest on federal government bonds is taxed as income by the federal government, but in most cases not by the states. The interest on municipal bonds is generally taxed as income by the states, but not by the federal government. The exclusion of interest on municipal bonds from federal income tax makes these bonds attractive to investors. It also allows local governments to pay lower-than-average interest on their bonds.

The major financing instrument for corporations that developed in the 1990s was the *asset-backed security*. This is a debt security that is backed by loans or receivables. For example, Ford Credit, a subsidiary of Ford Motor Company, has issued securities backed by a pool of automobile loans. The process of issuing securities backed by a pool of loans or receivables is referred to as *securitization*. We'll see the advantages of a corporation issuing an asset-backed security relative to a corporate bond in Chapter 26.

Derivative Instruments

A *derivative instrument* is any contract that gets its value directly from another security, a market interest rate, the price of a commodity, or a financial index. Derivative instruments include: (1) options, (2) futures/forwards, (3) swaps, and (4) caps and floors. In Chapter 4 we will discuss these derivative instruments.

What is important to understand is that derivative instruments can be used to control the wide range of risk faced by corporations and investors. This is one reason why derivatives are often referred to as *risk control instruments*. We must postpone a detailed discussion of the risk reducing role of derivative instruments at this juncture since we have not discussed the various risks faced by corporations and investors. This key role played by derivative instruments in global financial markets was stated in a 1994 report published by the U.S. General Accounting Office:

> Derivatives serve an important function of the global financial marketplace, providing end-users with opportunities to better manage financial risks associated with their business transactions. The rapid growth and increasing

complexity of derivatives reflect both the increased demand from end-users for better ways to manage their financial risks and the innovative capacity of the financial services industry to respond to market demands.[2]

Unfortunately, derivative markets are too often viewed by the general public—and sometimes regulators and legislative bodies—as vehicles for pure speculation (that is, legalized gambling). Without derivative instruments and the markets in which they trade, the financial systems throughout the world would not be as integrated as they are today and it would be difficult for corporations and investors to protect themselves against unwanted risks.

SECURITIES MARKETS

The primary function of a securities market—whether or not it has a physical location—is to bring together buyers and sellers of securities. Securities markets can be classified by whether they are involved in original sales or resales of securities, and by whether or not they involve a physical trading location.

Primary and Secondary Markets

When a security is first issued, it is sold in the primary market. This is the market in which new issues are sold and new capital is raised. So it is the market whose sales directly benefit the issuer of the securities.

There are three ways to raise capital in the primary market. The first is the direct sale, in which the investor purchases, say, stock directly from the issuer. Many venture capital firms invest in small, growing businesses in this way. Also, many corporations sell securities directly to large investors, such as pension funds. By doing so, the issuer can tailor the features of the security (such as maturity) to suit the desires of the investor. This type of selling is referred to as *private placement.*

A second method is through *financial institutions,* which are firms that obtain money from investors in return for the institution's securities and then invest that money. For example, a bank issues bank accounts in return for depositors' money and then loans that money to a firm. Besides banks, firm such as mutual funds and pension funds operate as financial institutions.

---

[2] U.S. General Accounting Office (GAO), *Financial Derivatives: Actions Needed to Protect the Financial System,* May 1994, p. 6.

EXHIBIT 2.1 The Three Methods of Raising Capital in the Primary Markets

Directly to investors

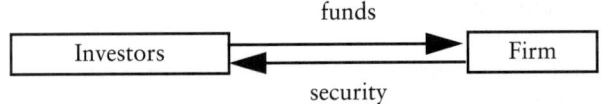

Through a financial institution

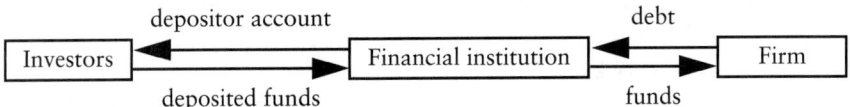

Through an investment banker

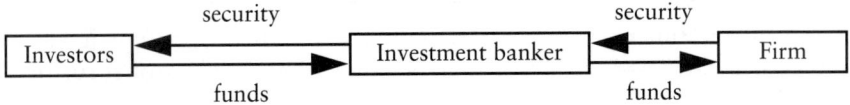

The third method for primary market transactions operates through investment bankers, who buy the securities issued by corporations and then sell those securities to investors for a higher price. This process of buying shares from the issuer and reselling them to investors is called *underwriting*. For example, Kraft Foods' 2001 offering of newly issued common shares was underwritten by a syndicate of 15 underwriters, including Credit Suisse First Boston, Salomon Smith Barney, Deutsche Banc Alexander Brown, and J. P. Morgan. The offering raised $8.7 billion, with Kraft Foods receiving over $8.4 billion:

	Per share	Total proceeds
Initial public offering price	$31.0000	$8,680,000,000
Underwriting discount	$0.8471	$237,181,000
Proceeds, before expenses, to Kraft	$30.1529	$8,442,819,000

The three methods of raising capital in the primary market are illustrated in Exhibit 2.1. We discuss the underwriting of securities and the role of investment bankers in the next chapter.

A *secondary market* is one in which securities are resold among investors. No new capital is raised and the issuer of the security does not benefit directly from the sale. Trading takes place among investors. Investors who buy and sell securities on the secondary markets may obtain the services of *stock brokers*, individuals who buy or sell securities for their clients.

We can use the market for college textbooks to illustrate the difference between primary and secondary markets. Suppose one of your instructors decides to use this book, *Financial Management and Analysis*, as the class text. The instructor notifies the school bookstore, which buys copies of the text from the publisher, John Wiley & Sons, and then puts them up for sale at a somewhat higher price than was paid. You then buy your new copy of this book from the bookstore. The market for new books, in which you, the publisher, and the bookstore have operated as buyer, seller, and intermediary, respectively, is a ***primary market***. The bookstore has acted as a sort of textbook "investment banker," but most of the money invested in the book has gone to the issuer (the publisher). The bookstore received a profit for performing as an intermediary, a facilitator of the transaction between you and the publisher. The publisher would have been hard put to sell to each member of the class individually.

At the end of the term you may wish to sell your used copy of *Financial Management and Analysis*. You can sell it directly to a friend who is about to take the course, or you can sell it back to the bookstore for resale to another student. Both these transactions take place in the secondary textbook market, because the publisher (the issuer) is not a party to them.

If a firm can raise new funds only through the primary market, why should financial managers be concerned about the secondary market on which the firm's securities trade? Because investors may not be interested in buying securities that are not liquid—that they could not sell at a fair price at any time. And the secondary markets provide the liquidity. For example, suppose IBM wants to issue new common shares to pay for its expansion program; investors would not be willing to buy such shares if they could not expect to sell them on the secondary market should the need arise. IBM counts on the existence of a healthy secondary market to entice investors to buy its new stock issue.

Exchanges and Over-the-Counter Markets

There are two types of secondary securities markets: exchanges and over-the-counter markets. *Exchanges* are actual places where buyers and sellers (or their representatives) meet to trade securities. Examples are the New York Stock Exchange and the Tokyo Stock Exchange. *Over-the-counter* (OTC) *markets* are arrangements in which investors or their representatives trade securities without sharing a physical location. For the most part, computer and telephone networks are used for this purpose. These networks are owned and managed by the market's members. An example is the Nasdaq system, which is operated by the National Association of Securities Dealers (NASD).

Exchanges may be privately owned, as are those in the United States and the United Kingdom. Privately owned exchanges are managed by their owners, or members (typically brokerage firms), who may pay hundreds of thousands of dollars for the privilege of owning a seat (a membership) on the exchange. Private exchanges are self-regulated; that is, they determine the rules and regulations that must be followed by their members, by traders, and by companies whose securities are *listed*, or accepted for trading, on the exchange.

Exchanges may be owned and operated by banks or banking organizations, as are many European exchanges—those in Luxembourg and Germany, for example. If the exchanges are owned by the banking institutions, these institutions then control both the primary and secondary markets for securities. Both bank-owned and privately owned exchanges are, of course, subject to regulation by the countries in which they are located.

Finally, there are state-controlled exchanges, such as those in France, Belgium, and several Latin American countries. These are generally the most restrictive exchanges and are characterized by stringent listing standards, especially for foreign companies.

There are two types of pricing systems for securities: the pure auction and the dealer market. In the *pure auction process*, investors wanting to buy or sell shares of stock submit their bids through their brokers, who relay these bids to a centralized location, where bids are matched and the transaction is executed. The party that does the matching is referred to as the *specialist*. For each stock in the market, there is only one matchmaker, one specialist. In a *dealer market*, individual dealers buy and sell shares of stock, trading with individuals and other dealers. We refer to these dealers as market makers since they "make" a market in the stock, providing liquidity to the market. In a dealer market, there may be many dealers for a given stock. Though a market can use either or some combination of the two systems, exchanges tend to use the auction process and over-the-counter markets use a dealer market.

Markets in the United States

Governments provide no guarantees regarding securities. However, through legislation and regulation of markets, transactions, and transactors, the U.S. government has attempted to guard against fraudulent practices and manipulative behavior on the part of market participants. The federal organization charged with the regulation of U.S. financial markets is the Securities and Exchange Commission (SEC). The SEC is a federal agency that administers federal securities laws and was established by the Securities and Exchange Act of 1934. The SEC consists of five members, each appointed by the President of the United States for a term of five years. The SEC carries out the following activities:

- Issues rules that clarify securities laws or trading procedure issues.
- Requires disclosure of specific information.
- Makes public statements on current issues.
- Oversees self-regulation of the securities industry by the stock exchanges and professional groups such as the National Association of Securities Dealers.

Major federal legislation is listed in Exhibit 2.2; in addition, the states have all passed laws that reinforce or extend federal legislation.

EXHIBIT 2.2   Federal Regulation of Securities Markets in the United States

Law	Description
Securities Act of 1933	Regulates new offerings of securities to the public. It requires the filing of a registration statement containing specific information about the issuing corporation and prohibits fraudulent and deceptive practices related to security offers.
Securities and Exchange Act of 1934	Establishes the Securities and Exchange Commission (SEC) to enforce securities regulations and extends regulation to the secondary markets.
Investment Company Act of 1940	Gives the SEC regulatory authority over publicly-held companies that are in the business of investing and trading in securities.
Investment Advisers Act of 1940	Requires registration of investment advisors and regulates their activities.
Federal Securities Act of 1964	Extends the regulatory authority of the SEC to include the over-the-counter securities markets.
Securities Investor Protection Act of 1970	Creates the Securities Investor Protection Corporation, which is charged with the liquidation of securities firms that are in financial trouble and which insures investors' accounts with brokerage firms.
Insider Trading Sanctions Act of 1984	Provides for treble damages to be assessed against violators of securities laws.
Insider Trading and Securities Fraud Enforcement Act of 1988	Provides preventative measures against insider trading and establishes enforcement procedures and penalties for the violation of securities laws.

Money Markets

Money market securities are not traded in a physical location; rather these securities are traded over-the-counter through banks and dealers that are networked together by telephone and computer lines. These intermediaries bring together buyers and sellers from around the world. In the United States, most trading is centered around large banks (called *money center banks*) located in the major financial centers of the country. Many banks and dealers specialize in specific instruments, such as commercial paper or bankers' acceptances.

Equity Markets

In the United States, there are two national stock exchanges: (1) the New York Stock Exchange (NYSE), commonly called the "Big Board," and (2) the American Stock Exchange (AMEX or ASE), also called the "Curb." National stock exchanges trade stocks of not only U.S. corporations but also non-U.S. corporations. In addition to the national exchanges, there are regional stock exchanges in Boston, Chicago (called the Midwest Exchange), Cincinnati, San Francisco (called the Pacific Coast Exchange), and Philadelphia. Regional exchanges primarily trade stocks from corporations based within their region.

The major OTC market in the United States is Nasdaq (the National Association of Securities Dealers Automated Quotation System), which is owned and operated by the NASD (the National Association of Securities Dealers). The NASD is a securities industry self-regulatory organization (SRO) that operates subject to the oversight of the SEC. Nasdaq is a national market. During 1998, Nasdaq and AMEX merged to form the Nasdaq–AMEX Market Group, Inc., each maintaining their respective markets and forming a large market that takes advantage of both the floor-based market structure and the OTC market structure.

The NYSE is the largest exchange in the United States, with approximately 2,800 companies' shares listed and dominates other markets in terms of the value and volume of shares traded. The AMEX is the second largest national stock exchange in the United States, with more than 750 issues listed for trading. Nasdaq has a greater number of listed stocks (4,200) but with much less market capitalization than the NYSE.

According to the Securities Act of 1934 (see Exhibit 2.2), there are two categories of traded stocks. The first is exchange traded stocks, which are also called *listed stocks*. The second is OTC stocks, which are also non-exchange traded stocks and are, thereby, by inference, non-listed. However, as we will describe later in this chapter, certain Nasdaq stocks have listing requirements (the Nasdaq National Market and the

Nasdaq Small Capitalization Market). Thus, a more useful and practical categorization of these categories is as follows:

■ Exchange listed stocks (national and regional exchanges).
■ Nasdaq listed OTC stocks.
■ Non-Nasdaq OTC stocks.

Stock Exchanges

Stock exchanges are formal organizations, approved and regulated by the Securities and Exchange Commission (SEC). They are made up of members who use the exchange facilities and systems to exchange or trade listed stocks. These exchanges are physical locations where members assemble to trade. Stocks that are traded on an exchange are said to be listed stocks. That is, these stocks are individually approved for trading on the exchange by the exchange. To be listed, a company must apply and satisfy requirements established by the exchange for minimum capitalization, shareholder equity, average closing share price, and other criteria. Even after being listed, exchanges may delist a company's stock if it no longer meets the exchange requirements.

To have the right to trade securities or make markets on an exchange floor, firms or individuals must become a member of the exchange, which is accomplished by buying a seat on the exchange. The number of seats is fixed by the exchange and the cost of a seat is determined by supply and demand of those who want to sell or buy seats. In early 2001, there were 1,366 seats on the NYSE.

Two kinds of stocks are listed on the five regional stock exchanges: (1) stocks of companies that either could not qualify for listing on one of the major national exchanges or could qualify for listing but chose not to list; and (2) stocks that are also listed on one of the major national exchanges. The latter are called *dually listed stocks*. The motivation of a company for dual listing is that a local brokerage firm that purchases a membership on a regional exchange can trade their listed stocks without having to purchase a considerably more expensive membership on the national stock exchange where the stock is also listed. Alternatively, a local brokerage firm could use the services of a member of a major national stock exchange to execute an order, but in this case it would have to give up part of its commission.

The regional stock exchanges compete with the NYSE for the execution of smaller trades. Major national brokerage firms have in recent years routed such orders to regional exchanges because of the lower fee they charge for executing orders or better prices, as we will discuss later.

OTC Market

The OTC market is called the market for unlisted stocks. As explained previously, technically while there are listing requirements for exchanges, there are also listing requirements for the Nasdaq National and Small Capitalization OTC markets. Nevertheless, exchange traded stocks are called listed, and stocks traded on the OTC markets are called unlisted. There are three parts to the OTC market: two under the aegis of NASD (the Nasdaq markets) and a third market for truly unlisted stocks, the non-Nasdaq OTC markets.

The Nasdaq stock market is the flagship market of the NASD. Nasdaq is essentially a telecommunication network that links thousands of geographically dispersed, market-making participants. Nasdaq is an electronic quotation system that provides price quotations to market participants on Nasdaq listed stocks. Although there is no central trading floor, Nasdaq has become an electronic "virtual trading floor." Some 535 dealers, known as market-makers, representing some of the world's largest securities firms, provide competing bids to buy and offers to sell Nasdaq stocks to investors.

The Nasdaq stock market has two broad tiers of securities: (1) the Nasdaq National Market and the Small Capitalization Market. Newspapers contain separate sections for these two tiers of stocks (sections labeled the "Nasdaq National Market" and the "Nasdaq Small Capitalization Market"). The Nasdaq National Market is the dominant OTC market in the United States.

Whereas the Nasdaq stock markets are the major parts of the U.S. OTC markets, the vast majority of the OTC issues (about 8,000) do not trade on either of the two Nasdaq systems. There are two types of markets for these stocks. The securities traded on these markets are not listed; that is, they have no listing requirements. The first of these two non-Nasdaq OTC markets is the OTC Bulletin Board (OTCBB), sometimes called simply the Bulletin Board. It includes stocks not traded on NYSE, AMEX, or Nasdaq. The second non-Nasdaq OTC market is the *Pink Sheets* that are published weekly. In addition, an electronic version of the Pink Sheets is updated daily and disseminated over market data vendor terminals. Pink Sheet securities are often pejoratively called *penny stocks*.

Alternative Trading Systems

It is not necessary for two parties to a transaction to use an intermediary. That is, the services of a broker or a dealer are not required to execute a trade. The direct trading of stocks may take place between two customers without the use of a broker. A number of proprietary alternative trading systems (ATSs) are operated by the NASD members or member affiliates. These ATSs are for-profit "broker's brokers" that match investor orders and report trading activity to the marketplace via Nasdaq or the third market. In a sense, ATSs are similar to exchanges because they are designed to allow two participants to meet directly on the system and are maintained by a third party who also serves a limited regulatory function by imposing requirements on each subscriber.

Broadly, there are two types of ATSs: electronic communications networks and crossing networks. *Electronic communications networks* (ECNs) are privately owned broker-dealers that operate as market participants within the Nasdaq system. They display quotes that reflect actual orders and provide institutions and Nasdaq market-makers with an anonymous way to enter orders. Instinet was the first ECN. *Crossing networks* are systems developed to allow institutional investors to cross trade—that is, match buyers and sellers directly—typically via computer. These networks are batch processes that aggregate orders for execution at prespecified times.

Stock Market Indicators

Stock market indicators have come to perform a variety of functions, from serving as benchmarks for evaluating the performance of professional investors to answering the question "How did the market do today?" Thus, stock market indicators (indexes or averages) have become a part of everyday life.

The most commonly quoted stock market indicator is the Dow Jones Industrial Average (DJIA). Other stock market indicators cited in the financial press are the Standard & Poor's 500 Composite (S&P 500), the New York Stock Exchange Composite Index (NYSE Composite), the Nasdaq Composite Index, and the Value Line Composite Average (VLCA). Other stock market indicators include the Wilshire stock indexes and the Russell stock indexes, which are followed primarily by institutional money managers.

In general, market indexes rise and fall in fairly similar patterns. Although the correlation is high, the indexes do not move in exactly the same ways at all times. The differences in movement reflect the different ways in which the indexes are constructed. Three factors enter into that construction: the universe of stocks represented by the sample underlying the index, the relative weights assigned to the stocks included in the index, and the method of averaging across all the stocks.

Some indexes represent only stocks listed on an exchange. Examples are DJIA and the NYSE Composite, which represent only stocks listed on the Big Board. By contrast, the Nasdaq Composite Index includes only stocks traded over the counter. A favorite of professionals is the S&P 500 because it contains both NYSE-listed and OTC-traded shares.

Each index relies on a sample of stocks from its universe, and that sample may be small or quite large. The DJIA uses only 30 of the largest corporations, while the NYSE Composite includes every one of the NYSE listed shares. The Nasdaq Composite Index also includes all shares in its universe, while the S&P 500 has a sample that contains only 500 of the more than 8,000 shares in the universe it represents.

The stocks included in a stock market indicator must be combined in certain proportions, and each stock must be given a weight. The three main approaches to weighting are these: (1) weighting by the market capitalization of the stock's company, which is the value of the number of shares times price per share; (2) weighting by the price of the stock; and (3) equal weighting for each stock, regardless of its price or its firm's market value. With the exception of the Dow Jones averages (such as the DJIA) and the VLCA, all of the most widely used indices are market-value weighted. The DJIA is a price-weighted average, and the VLCA is an equally weighted index.

Stock market indicators can be classified into three groups: (1) those produced by stock exchanges based on all stocks traded on the exchanges; (2) those produced by organizations that subjectively select the stocks to be included in indices; and (3) those where stock selection is based on an objective measure, such as the market capitalization of the company. The first group includes the New York Stock Exchange Composite Index, which reflects the market value of all stocks traded on the exchange. Although it is not an exchange, the Nasdaq Composite Index falls into this category because the index represents all stocks tracked by the Nasdaq system.

The three most popular stock market indicators in the second group are the Dow Jones Industrial Average, the Standard & Poor's 500, and the Value Line Composite Average. The DJIA is constructed from 30 of the largest blue-chip industrial companies. The companies included in the average are those selected by Dow Jones & Company, publisher of the *Wall Street Journal*. The S&P 500 represents stocks chosen from the two major national stock exchanges and the over-the-counter market. The stocks in the index at any given time are determined by a committee of Standard & Poor's Corporation, which may occasionally add or delete individual stocks or the stocks of entire industry groups. The aim of the committee is to capture present overall stock market conditions as reflected in a very broad range of economic indicators. The VLCA, produced by Value Line, Inc., covers a broad range of widely held and actively traded NYSE, AMEX, and OTC issues selected by Value Line.

In the third group, we have the Wilshire indexes produced by Wilshire Associates (Santa Monica, California) and Russell indexes produced by the Frank Russell Company (Tacoma, Washington), a consultant to pension funds and other institutional investors. The criterion for inclusion in each of these indexes is solely a firm's market capitalization. The most comprehensive index is the Wilshire 5000, which currently includes more than 6,500 stocks, up from 5,000 at its inception. The Wilshire 4500 includes all stocks in the Wilshire 5000 except for those in the S&P 500. Thus, the shares in the Wilshire 4500 have a smaller capitalization than those in the Wilshire 5000. The Russell 3000 encompasses the 3,000 largest companies in terms of their market capitalization. The Russell 1000 is limited to the largest 1,000 of those, and the Russell 2000 has the remaining smaller firms.

Does it matter in which market a corporation's securities are traded? Yes and no. It is desirable to have your securities traded in a market where there is sufficient activity so that an investor who wants to buy or sell the security can do so readily. Therefore, the marketability that the market provides to the security is important. The more easily a security can be bought and sold, the less its *marketability risk*, which is the risk than an owner will not be able to sell the security when he or she wants to sell it. Investors are willing to take a lower return when the marketability risk is lower, allowing the corporation to raise additional funds at a lower cost. Therefore, firms want to list their stocks in a market that provides marketability for the stock.

Bond Markets

Almost all bond trading takes place in OTC markets, with the remainder (around 1%) occurring mainly on the New York Stock Exchange Fixed Income Market and the American Stock Exchange. The bond trading that does take place on exchanges consists primarily of small orders, whereas bond trading in the OTC market is for larger—sometimes huge—blocks of bonds, purchased by institutional investors.

Within the OTC market, large banks and large trading firms "make a market" in bonds; that is, they connect buyers with sellers. They negotiate directly with large bond investors such as pension funds, insurance companies, and corporations, and are connected through a computerized network.

As with the stock market, there are bond market indexes that are followed by investors. The wide range of bond market indexes available can be classified as broad-based bond market indexes and specialized bond market indexes. The three broad-based bond market indexes most commonly used by institutional investors are the Lehman Brothers U.S. Aggregate Index, the Salomon Smith Barney (SSB) Broad Investment-Grade Bond Index (BIG), and the Merrill Lynch Domestic Market Index. There are more than 5,500 issues in each index. The specialized bond market indexes focus on one sector of the bond market or a subsector of the bond market. Indexes on sectors of the market are published by the three firms that produce the broad-based bond market indexes. Non-brokerage firms have created specialized indexes for sectors.

Options and Futures Markets

The first formal options market was the *Chicago Board Options Exchange* (CBOE), begun in 1973. Soon after, several exchanges introduced options contracts to their "product lines." Now options are traded on such exchanges as the CBOE, the Chicago Board of Trade (CBOT), the Pacific Stock Exchange, the Philadelphia Stock Exchange, and the American Stock Exchange. As an indicator of the growing interest in options, we note that the dollar value of options traded annually on the CBOE now exceeds the value of the stocks traded annually on the AMEX. Options are traded on both exchanges and in the over-the-counter market, with most of the recent growth in the over-the-counter market.

Futures contracts are traded on (among others) the CBOT, the Chicago Mercantile Exchange, the Mid-America Commodity Exchange, and the New York Futures Exchange. Some futures markets specialize in certain contracts, either by preference or by state law. For example, the International Petroleum exchange specializes in petroleum products such as crude oil and gas oil. However, most commodities exchanges deal with a variety of futures contracts.

Like the equity markets, options and futures markets are subject to state and federal regulations (to different degrees), as well as to self-regulation by the markets themselves.[3]

Efficient Markets

Investors do not like risk and they must be compensated for taking on risk—the larger the risk, the more the compensation. But can investors earn a return on securities beyond that necessary to compensate them for the risk? In other words, can investors earn an *abnormal profit* on the secondary markets? Can they beat the market? The answer is "maybe."

An *efficient market* is a market in which asset prices rapidly reflect all available information, and the securities markets in the United States are typically thought of as being highly efficient. This means that all available information is already impounded in a security's price, so investors should expect to earn a return necessary to compensate them for their opportunity cost, anticipated inflation, and risk. That would seem to preclude abnormal profits. But according to at least one theory, there are several levels of efficiency: weak form efficient, semi-strong form efficient, and strong form efficient.[4]

---

[3] For example, the *Commodity Futures Trading Commission* (CFTC) is a regulatory body established by Congress to approve new types of futures contracts and to establish trading rules for futures exchanges.

[4] Eugene F. Fama, "Efficient Capital Markets: A Review of Theory and Empirical Work," *Journal of Finance*, Volume 25, Number 2 (May 1970), pp. 383–417.

In the *weak form of market efficiency*, current securities prices reflect all past prices and price movements. In other words, all worthwhile information about previous prices of the stock has been used to determine today's price; the investor cannot use that same information to predict tomorrow's price and still earn abnormal profits.[5]

Empirical evidence shows that the securities markets are at least weak-form efficient. In other words, you cannot beat the market by using information on past securities prices.

In the *semi-strong form of market efficiency*, the current market prices of securities reflect all publicly-available information. So if you trade on the basis of publicly-available information, you cannot earn abnormal profits. This does not mean that prices change instantaneously to reflect new information, but rather that information is impounded *rapidly* into the prices of securities.

Empirical evidence supports the idea that U.S. securities markets are semi-strong form efficient. This, in turn, implies that careful analysis of securities and issuing firms cannot produce abnormal profits.[6]

In the *strong form of market efficiency*, stock prices reflect all public and private information. In other words, the market (which includes all investors) knows everything about all securities, including information that has not been released to the public.

The strong form implies that you cannot make abnormal profits from trading on inside information, where inside information is information that is not yet public.[7] This form of market efficiency is not supported by the evidence. In fact, we know from recent events that the opposite is true; gains are available from inside information.

As pointed out above, U.S. securities markets are essentially semi-strong efficient. This means that investors can, for the most part, expect securities to be fairly priced. So when a firm issues new securities, it should expect investors to pay a price for those shares that reflects their value. This also means that if new information about the firm is revealed

---

[5] This doesn't mean that trying it once may not prove fruitful. What it does mean is that, over the long run, you cannot earn abnormal profits from reading charts of past prices and predicting future prices from these charts. Do investors actually try this? Well, there are financial services in business today that perform analysis of stock prices (called technical analysis), so someone out there is doing it.

[6] Does this mean that financial analysis is worthless? No. We still need financial analysis to help us sort out risk and expected return so that we can properly manage our investments.

[7] There is no exact definition of "inside information" in law. Laws pertaining to insider trading remain a gray area, subject to clarification mainly through judicial interpretation.

to the public (for example, concerning a new product), the price of the stock should change to reflect that new information.

But a semi-strong efficient market also means that an investor can make abnormal profits through trading using information not known to the public. Such trading tends to distort the prices of affected securities and thus to harm at least some investors. For that reason, and because investigators found evidence of such trading during the corporate merger mania of the 1980s, existing anti-insider trading legislation has recently been strengthened and reinforced. Strengthening such legislation tends to ensure the fairness of securities prices.

In essence, it is illegal for any person with an agency relationship to a firm to benefit financially through non-public information obtained as a result of that relationship. This does *not* mean that executives of a corporation cannot buy and sell shares of the firm. Trading by insiders (members of the board of directors and the employees of the firm) is legal *if* it is not motivated by the use of non-public information. What it does mean is that insiders cannot use inside information to make their personal investment decisions; doing so would be ***illegal insider trading***. As another example, an investment banker who is negotiating the merger of two corporations cannot legally purchase the stock of those corporations knowing that the market prices will rise when news of the merger is made public.

SUMMARY

- A security is an instrument that represents ownership in an asset or debt obligation. Securities are classified as either money market securities, capital market securities, or derivative securities.
- Money market securities are marketable securities with original maturities of less than a year and include U.S. T-bills, commercial paper, certificates of deposit, and bankers acceptances. Capital market securities have maturities beyond one year and include common stocks, corporate bonds, and government bonds.
- Derivative instruments are contracts that derive their value from some security or asset, interest rate, exchange rate, or financial index. Derivative instruments include options, futures/forwards, swaps, and caps/floors.
- A securities market is any arrangement in which securities can be bought and sold and can be a formalized market, such as a stock exchange, or an informal market, such as banks acting as dealers in the over-the-counter market for bonds. Securities are bought and sold in primary markets, which provide the issuer with new capital, or in sec-

ondary markets, which involves trading among investors and no new capital for the issuer.

■ Stocks, bonds, options, and futures are traded in securities markets. These financial markets may be specialized for one type of security, or may trade in more than one type of security. For example, bonds, futures, and options are all traded on markets organized under the New York Stock Exchange.

■ More and more, securities are being bought and sold in countries other than their country of origin. The actual security may not trade outside its domestic market, yet there are means of trading securities that represent ownership of a foreign security, such as ADRs and unit trusts.

■ Market indicators provide us with a gauge of the securities markets, giving us an idea of the general movements of securities prices.

■ An efficient market is one in which information is quickly reflected in the prices of securities. We can further classify efficient markets according to the kind of information that is reflected: In weak form markets all past price information is contained in securities prices; in semi-strong form markets all publicly available information is reflected in securities prices; and in semi-strong form markets, all public and private information is reflected in securities prices. Evidence supports the idea that U.S. securities markets are semi-strong efficient markets. Trading on inside information, which disrupts market operations and efficiency, is illegal in the United States.

QUESTIONS

1. Ahsin, Inc., is a publicly traded company, but it does not intend to raise any new capital in the next few years. Why should Ahsin's financial managers concern themselves with securities markets?
2. What is the primary distinction between a money market security and a capital market security? From an investor perspective, which security would tend to be riskier? Why?
3. How risky is buying the commercial paper of a corporation relative to, say, buying its common stock? What factors affect the riskiness of a corporation's commercial paper? What factors affect the riskiness of a corporation's common stock?
4. How does collateral affect a security's riskiness? How does collateral affect the return required by investors?
5. Suppose individual income tax rates increase. Ignoring any other changes that may be made in the tax law, how should this affect the demand for municipal bonds?

6. Consider a convertible security that gives the owner the right to exchange it for another security within a specified period of time. Is this right to exchange a call or a put option? Explain.

7. What are derivative instruments and why are they used?

8. Describe the maturity and cash flow characteristics of common stock, preferred stock, and corporate debt securities. Rank these securities in terms of the uncertainty of their future cash flow.

9. What are the main differences between common and preferred stock? From the perspective of an investor, which security is riskier? Why?

10. Suppose International Business Machines (IBM) needs to raise new capital. List and briefly describe the three methods of raising capital.

11. Blockbuster Entertainment initially listed their stock on the Nasdaq system in 1983 and then changed its listing to the NYSE in 1989. Why would they initially list on the Nasdaq system? Why would they want to change their listing to the NYSE?

12. Determine whether each statement is consistent with the semi-strong form of market efficiency.
    a. *Statement X:* A local brokerage firm claims that following their strategy of investing in securities whose company name begins with the letter M, investors can earn a return that more than makes up for the risk associated with these securities.
    b. *Statement Y:* Company Big invested in stocks during 1992 and earned a return of 10%. Company Little earned 15% during the same year.
    c. *Statement Z:* Larry's investment strategy requires him to buy stocks of those companies that announced earnings higher than last year's. He claims that he can earn returns that are more than necessary to compensate him for the securities' risks.

13. What is insider trading? What is illegal insider trading?

14. Suppose an executive exercises her stock options just prior to the year, buying the shares and then selling them immediately, in order to avoid an anticipated increase in tax rates with the new administration. Is this illegal insider trading?

15. Suppose a member of the board of directors is involved in negotiating a merger of the firm with another firm. But suppose the negotiations are not complete and will not be for several months. If the board member buys stock of the other company while the negotiations are going on (but not completed), is this illegal insider trading?

16. Suppose you are manager of a corporation and you feel that it will do better in the future than most analysts believe. Can you buy stock of this firm? Is this illegal insider trading?

CHAPTER 3

Financial Institutions and the Cost of Money

Businesses make their investment and financing decisions in a dynamic financial environment. Financial managers must understand the economy, the role of government in the economy, and the markets in which financial institutions operate. We have already taken a look at the financial markets in Chapter 2. Now we focus on other aspects of the financial environment. In particular, we examine the role of the following:

- the U.S. Federal Reserve System in determining the money supply
- the key role of financial intermediaries in the financial market with a focus on two of them—commercial banks and investment banks
- interest rates, the factors that influence them, and the cost of borrowing.

THE FEDERAL RESERVE SYSTEM

The United States has a central monetary authority known as the Federal Reserve System. The *Federal Reserve System* (often referred to as the "Fed") acts as the U.S. central bank, much like the Bank of England and the Bank of France are central banks in their respective countries. The role of a central bank is to carry out monetary policy that serves the best interests of the country's economic well-being. *Monetary policy* is the set of tools that a central bank can use to control the availability of loanable funds. These tools can be used to achieve goals for the nation's economy. Along with the U.S. Treasury, the Fed determines policies that affect employment and prices.

49

EXHIBIT 3.1 The Federal Reserve System

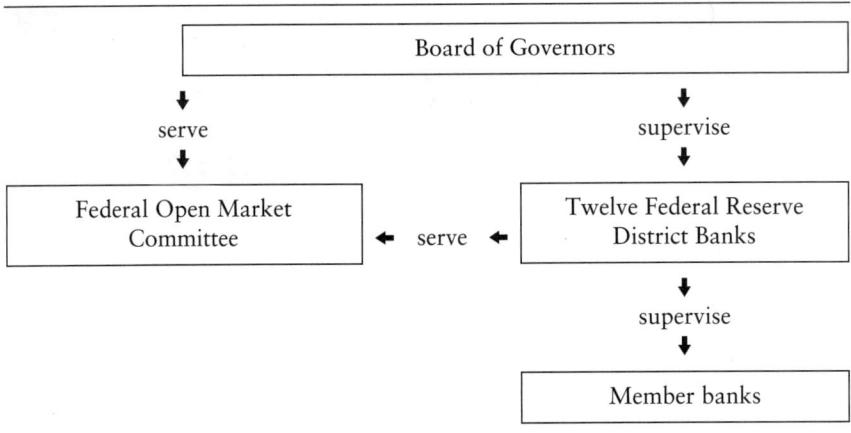

The Federal Reserve System is comprised of 12 district banks, with the Federal Reserve Board of Governors overseeing the activities of the district banks. The members of the Board are appointed by the President of the United States and confirmed by the U.S. Senate, and each serves a term of 14 years, with terms staggered through time. The president also appoints the chairman of the board from among the members on the board. The chairman serves in this capacity for a term of four years. What's the role of the Board? The Board creates rules and regulations that govern all depository institutions, as shown in Exhibit 3.1.

The Federal Reserve District Banks are not-for-profit institutions. Their responsibilities include (1) handling the vast majority of check-clearing in the United States, (2) issuing money, and (3) acting as the bankers' bank, accepting deposits from other financial institutions

The Federal Reserve System consists of the Federal Reserve Banks and member commercial banks. All nationally chartered banks must join the system, but state-chartered banks may also join. A nationally chartered bank is a bank that receives its charter of incorporation (its right to do business) from the federal government, granted by the Comptroller of the Currency; a state-chartered bank receives its charter from the state. The *Comptroller of the Currency* is a division of the U.S. Treasury and was established in 1863. The role of the Comptroller is to monitor periodically banks' financial condition and compliance with regulations; states have similar agencies that monitor state-chartered banks. Because national banks represent the largest banking institutions in the United States, more than two-thirds of all bank assets are held by national banks.

The *Federal Open Market Committee* (FOMC) is a policy making group within the Federal Reserve System. The committee is comprised of the seven members of the Federal Reserve Board, plus presidents or vice-presidents of five Reserve banks. The FOMC is charged with making decisions regarding the Federal Reserve's open market operations, which consist of buying and selling of U.S. government securities. The open market operations of the Fed affect the cost and availability of credit in the economy.

The Fed and the Money Supply

Financial managers and investors are interested in the supply and demand for money because it is the interaction of supply and demand that ultimately affects the interest rates paid to borrow funds and the amount of interest earned on investing funds. The demand for money is determined by the availability of investment opportunities. The supply of money is determined, in large part, by the actions of a nation's central bank.

The decisions of the Fed affect the money supply of the United States. The *money supply* consists of cash and cash-like items. In fact, there are different definitions of the money supply, depending on the cash-like items you include. For example, the most basic definition of money supply, *M1*, consists of:

- cash (currency and bills) in circulation,
- demand deposits (non-interest earning deposits at banking institutions that can be withdrawn on demand),
- other deposits that can be readily withdrawn using checks, and
- travelers' checks.

A broader definition of money supply is *M2*, which consists of everything in M1, plus

- savings deposits,
- small denomination time deposits,
- money market mutual funds, and
- money market deposit accounts.

A still broader definition of money supply is *M3*, which consists of everything in M2, plus:

- large denomination time deposits,
- term repurchase agreements issued by commercial banks and thrift institutions, term Eurodollars held by U.S. residents, and
- institution-owned balances in money market funds.

A *savings deposit* is an amount held in an account with a financial institution for the purpose of accumulating money. A *time deposit* is a type of savings account at a financial institution. A *certificate of deposit* (CD) is an example of a time deposit. The term "time" is used to describe the account because originally these accounts required that the saver notify the institution in advance (e.g., 90 days) of making a withdrawal. Though this practice of advance notification is no longer around, the term "time deposit" remains. *Money market mutual funds* are funds invested in an account that invests in short-term securities. *Money market deposit accounts* are funds deposited at financial institutions such as a bank or a thrift, that can be readily withdrawn. *Eurodollars* are deposits of U.S. dollars in foreign banks or in foreign branches of U.S. banks.

The money supply, whether defined as M1, M2, or M3, is managed by the government, and is one of the many tools that the government has to affect the economy. The role of non-M2 elements of the money supply has gained in importance in the money supply over this period, due primarily to the increasing popularity of money market funds.

The Fed affects the country's money supply and, ultimately, its economy through three devices. One device is a change in the *reserve requirement*, the fraction of deposits that a bank accepts that must be held either on deposit with the district Federal Reserve Bank or in cash in the bank's own vault. The money not held in reserve can be used to make loans and purchase securities. Changing the reserve requirement affects monetary expansion; the lower the reserve requirement, the more funds that can be put into the economy through loans and investments and, hence, the greater the supply of money in the economy. Raising the required ratio reduces the effects of money expansion, and hence the money supply.

Another device is the use of open market operations. The FOMC affects the money supply through its decisions regarding *open market operations*, which are purchases and sales of government securities by the Fed. Buying securities injects money into the economy; selling securities reduces the amount of money available.

Still another device is the change in the *discount rate*, the interest rate charged by the Fed for loans to banks for reserves. These loans are secured—that is, backed—by U.S. government securities or other, suitable collateral. These loans are made by the district Federal Reserve Banks through a source referred to as the *discount window*. Banks can borrow from the discount window to shore up their reserves for short periods of time (generally less than fifteen days). Increasing the discount rate discourages borrowing by banks, which in turn discourages banks from lending funds. Lowering the discount rate has the opposite effect—encouraging bank lending.

These three devices are used by the Fed to control the money supply. Since these devices have an effect on interest rates and the availability of loanable funds, many businesses watch the actions of the Fed with great interest.

The Future of Money: Electronic Cash

Nowadays, what we think of as "money" is quickly changing: electronic cash has entered the picture. *Electronic cash*, sometimes referred to as *e-cash*, *cybercash*, or *digicash*, is money that is created electronically and that exists outside the world of banks, checks, coin, and currency overseen by the Federal Reserve, and is created electronically. Though still in its infancy, electronic cash exists in the computer world of the Internet and on plastic cards. Who creates this money? Just about anyone. Electronic cash is replacing traditional cash, credit cards, and checks as a medium of exchange. It is more convenient than other forms of money and can result in lower costs of transacting business.

While seen as a universal medium of exchange that can span countries' borders, the existence of electronic cash raises some important issues:

- Who should be able to issue electronic cash?
- Who will regulate the issuers?
- How will transactions be monitored for compliance with tax laws?
- How secure are these transactions? (That is, can someone else wind up using your electronic cash?)
- How will consumers be protected from fraudulent issuers and users?
- How will regulators deal with money laundering and counterfeiting?

Currently, the Federal Reserve and banks are the money creators through the fractional reserve system. The emergence of electronic cash opens up money creation to almost anyone. The Fed may therefore lose its ability to control the economy by manipulating the reserve requirement, open market operations, and the discount rate. Though there are few players in electronic cash creation today on the Internet, several joint ventures between major corporations such as Microsoft, Xerox, and AT&T will bring electronic cash to consumers in the near future.

FINANCIAL INSTITUTIONS

Business entities include nonfinancial and financial enterprises. Nonfinancial enterprises manufacture products (e.g., cars, steel, computers) and/or provide nonfinancial services (e.g., transportation, utilities, computer programming). Financial enterprises, more popularly referred to as *financial institutions*, provide services related to one or more of the following:

1. Transforming financial assets acquired through the market and constituting them into a different, and more widely preferable, type of asset—which becomes their liability. This is the function performed by *financial intermediaries*, the most important type of financial institution.
2. Exchanging of financial assets on behalf of customers.
3. Exchanging of financial assets for their own accounts.
4. Assisting in the creation of financial assets for their customers, and then selling those financial assets to other market participants.
5. Providing investment advice to other market participants.
6. Managing the portfolios of other market participants.

Financial intermediaries include *depository institutions* (commercial banks, savings and loan associations, savings banks, and credit unions), which acquire the bulk of their funds by offering their liabilities to the public mostly in the form of deposits; insurance companies (life and property and casualty companies); pension funds; and finance companies.

The second and third services in the list above are the *broker and dealer functions*. The fourth service is referred to as *underwriting*. As we explain later, typically a financial intermediary that provides an underwriting service also provides a brokerage and/or dealer service. Some nonfinancial enterprises have subsidiaries that provide financial services. For example, many large manufacturing firms have subsidiaries that provide financing for their parent company's customer. These financial institutions are called *captive finance companies*. Examples include General Motors Acceptance Corporation (a subsidiary of General Motors) and General Electric Credit Corporation (a subsidiary of General Electric).

Role of Financial Intermediaries

As we have seen, financial intermediaries obtain funds by issuing financial claims against themselves to market participants, and then investing those funds. The investments made by financial intermediaries—their assets—can be in loans and/or securities. These investments are referred to as *direct investments*. Market participants who hold the financial claims issued by financial intermediaries are said to have made *indirect investments*.

Two examples will illustrate this. Most readers of this book are familiar with what a commercial bank does. Commercial banks accept deposits and may use the proceeds to lend funds to consumers and businesses. The deposits represent a liability of the commercial bank and a financial asset owned by the depositor. The loan represents a liability of the borrowing entity and a financial asset of the commercial bank. The commercial bank has made a direct investment in the borrowing entity; the depositor effectively has made an indirect investment in that borrowing entity.

As a second example, consider an investment company or mutual fund, a financial intermediary we focus on later, which pools the funds of market participants and uses those funds to buy a portfolio of securities such as stocks and bonds. Investors providing funds to the investment company receive an equity claim that entitles the investor to a pro rata share of the outcome of the portfolio. The equity claim is issued by the investment company. The portfolio of financial assets acquired by the investment company represents a direct investment that it has made. By owning an equity claim against the investment company, those who invest in the investment company have made an indirect investment.

We have stressed that financial intermediaries play the basic role of transforming financial assets that are less desirable for a large part of the public into other financial assets—their own liabilities—which are more widely preferred by the public. This transformation involves at least one of four economic functions: (1) providing maturity intermediation; (2) reducing risk via diversification; (3) reducing the costs of contracting and information processing; and (4) providing a payments mechanism. Each function is described below.

Maturity Intermediation

In our example of the commercial bank, two things should be noted. First, the maturity of at least a portion of the deposits accepted is typically short term. For example, certain types of deposits are payable upon demand. Others have a specific maturity date, but most are less than two years. Second, the maturity of the loans made by a commercial bank may be considerably longer than two years. In the absence of a commercial bank, the borrower would have to borrow for a shorter term, or find an entity that is willing to invest for the length of the loan sought, and/or investors who make deposits in the bank would have to commit funds for a longer length of time than they want. The commercial bank, by issuing its own financial claims, in essence transforms a longer-term asset into a shorter-term one by giving the borrower a loan for the length of time sought and the investor/depositor a financial asset for the desired investment horizon. This function of a financial intermediary is called *maturity intermediation*.

Maturity intermediation has two implications for financial markets. First, it provides investors with more choices concerning maturity for their investments; borrowers have more choices for the length of their debt obligations. Second, because investors are naturally reluctant to commit funds for a long period of time, they will require that long-term borrowers pay a higher interest rate than short-term borrowers. A financial intermediary is willing to make longer-term loans, and at a lower cost to the borrower than an individual investor would, by counting on successive deposits providing the funds until maturity (although at some risk—see below). Thus, the second implication is that the cost of longer-term borrowing is likely to be reduced.

Reducing Risk via Diversification

Consider the example of the investor who places funds in an investment company. Suppose that the investment company invests the funds received in the stock of a large number of companies. By doing so, the investment company has diversified and reduced its risk. Investors who have a small sum to invest would find it difficult to achieve the same degree of diversification because they do not have sufficient funds to buy shares of a large number of companies. Yet by investing in the investment company for the same sum of money, investors can accomplish this diversification, thereby reducing risk.

This economic function of financial intermediaries—transforming more risky assets into less risky ones—is called *diversification*. Although individual investors can do it on their own, they may not be able to do it as cost-effectively as a financial intermediary, depending on the amount of funds they have to invest. Attaining cost-effective diversification in order to reduce risk by purchasing the financial assets of a financial intermediary is an important economic benefit for financial markets.

Reducing the Costs of Contracting and Information Processing

Investors purchasing financial assets should take the time to develop skills necessary to understand how to evaluate an investment. Once those skills are developed, investors should apply them to the analysis of specific financial assets that are candidates for purchase (or subsequent sale). Investors who want to make a loan to a consumer or business will need to write the loan contract (or hire an attorney to do so).

Although there are some people who enjoy devoting leisure time to this task, most prefer to use that time for just that—leisure. Most of us find that leisure time is in short supply, so to sacrifice it, we have to be compensated. The form of compensation could be a higher return that we obtain from an investment.

In addition to the opportunity cost of the time to process the information about the financial asset and its issuer, there is the cost of acquiring that information. All these costs are called *information processing costs*. The costs of writing loan contracts are referred to as *contracting costs*. There is also another dimension to contracting costs, the cost of enforcing the terms of the loan agreement.

With this in mind, consider our two examples of financial intermediaries—the commercial bank and the investment company. People who work for these intermediaries include investment professionals who are trained to analyze financial assets and manage them. In the case of loan agreements, either standardized contracts can be prepared, or legal counsel can be part of the professional staff that writes contracts involving more complex transactions. The investment professionals can monitor compliance with the terms of the loan agreement and take any necessary action to protect the interests of the financial intermediary. The employment of such professionals is cost-effective for financial intermediaries because investing funds is their normal business.

In other words, there are economies of scale in contracting and processing information about financial assets because of the amount of funds managed by financial intermediaries. The lower costs accrue to the benefit of the investor who purchases a financial claim of the financial intermediary and to the issuers of financial assets, who benefit from a lower borrowing cost.

Providing a Payments Mechanism

Although the previous three economic functions may not have been immediately obvious, this last function should be. Most transactions made today are not done with cash. Instead, payments are made using checks, credit cards, debit cards, and electronic transfers of funds. These methods for making payments, called *payment mechanisms*, are provided by certain financial intermediaries.

The ability to make payments without the use of cash is critical for the functioning of a financial market. In short, depository institutions transform assets that cannot be used to make payments into other assets that offer that property.

Below we review each of the financial institutions and their role as intermediaries. The majority of our discussion will focus on the role of commercial banks (a form of depository institution) and investment banks. You will see why these entities are of particular interest to us because of the role that they play in either providing funds directly to entities needing to raise funds, assisting entities in raising funds, and/or facilitating the trading of securities. You will also see that while we made a distinction between commercial banks and investment bank, today a financial institution can provide all of the services provided by both of them.

Deposit Institutions

Traditionally, the United States has had several types of deposit institutions: commercial banks, savings and loan associations (referred to as thrift institutions or simply "thrifts"), mutual savings banks, and credit unions. In addition to accepting deposits, these institutions make loans and provide other financial services. These types of institutions are distinguished by their type of ownership (investor or depositor owned) and the type of loans (business or personal).

Commercial banks are corporations that are owned by investors. These banks lend primarily to businesses. Commercial banks may be independent corporations or may be subsidiaries of bank holding companies. *Bank holding companies* are organizations that own one or more other companies in addition to a bank. A common use of a bank holding company is as a device to circumvent regulations regarding bank branching or merging with banks across state lines. The Federal Reserve Board permits bank holding companies to own subsidiaries that are in lines of business related to banking.

Savings and loan associations are owned by their depositors and specialize in making home mortgage loans. The mission of savings and loan associations is to serve the thrift (that is, savings) and home ownership needs of consumers. Federally chartered savings and loans are overseen by the Office of Thrift Supervision (formerly the Federal Home Loan Bank Board, which was created in 1933). *Mutual savings banks* are also owned by their depositors and focus primarily on loans to the local community. *Credit unions* are non-profit associations that are owned by the members, the depositors, and their primary focus is making personal loans to their members. Exhibit 3.2 is a summary of the features of several of the deposit institutions.

EXHIBIT 3.2   Summary of Types of Financial Institutions

Type	Ownership	Primary Mission
Commercial bank	Corporations; owned by investors	Lend to businesses
Savings and loan (S&L)	Either corporations or owned by depositors	Offer savings accounts for individuals and make loans for home ownership
Mutual savings bank	Owned by depositors	Lend to the local community
Credit union	Non-profit; owned by depositors	Lend and provide other financial services to members

Commercial banks traditionally have the widest range of services, including checking accounts, savings accounts, credit cards, business loans, and personal loans. The *Depository Institutions Deregulation and Monetary Control Act of 1980* (DIDMC) reduced some of the distinctions between commercial banks and other institutions by eliminating restrictions on the type of loans, the interest rates on accounts, and the types of investments these other institutions could make. The effect of this act was to allow savings and loans, mutual savings banks, and credit unions to do business much like commercial banks. Adding to these new freedoms, the *Garn-St. Germain Depository Act of 1982* permitted both commercial banks and thrifts to provide money market accounts, enabling these institutions to compete with non-bank companies, such as brokerage firms, that offered money market accounts to individuals.

Deposits of commercial banks and savings institutions are insured by the *Federal Deposit Insurance Corporation* (FDIC), which is an agency created in 1934. Deposits with FDIC-insured institutions are insured up to $100,000 for each depositor and $100,000 for each depositor's retirement account. The role of the FDIC is to monitor these institutions' earnings and capital. Deposit insurance is intended to make the financial system more stable, preventing bank runs or panics—sudden and massive withdrawals of funds by customers.

Commercial Bank Services

Commercial banks play an important role in the country's money supply. Our purpose in this chapter is not to discuss this role; this topic is typically covered in a course on money and banking or financial markets. Rather, we will discuss the services commercial banks provide to entities seeking to raise funds. These services can be broadly classified as follows: (1) individual banking; (2) institutional banking; and (3) global banking. Of course, different banks are more active in certain of these activities than others.

Individual banking encompasses consumer lending, residential mortgage lending, consumer installment loans, credit card financing, automobile and boat financing, brokerage services, student loans, and individual-oriented financial investment services such as personal trust and investment services. Interest income and fee income are generated from mortgage lending and credit card financing.

Loans to nonfinancial corporations, financial corporations (such as life insurance companies), and government entities (state and local governments in the United States and foreign governments) fall into the category of *institutional banking*. Also included in this category are commercial real estate financing and other activities that will be discussed elsewhere in this book, leasing and factoring.

It is in the area of global banking that banks began to compete head-to-head with investment banking (or securities) firms. *Global banking* covers a broad range of activities involving corporate financing and capital market and foreign-exchange products and services.

Corporate financing involves two components. First is the procuring of funds for a bank's customers. This can go beyond traditional bank loans to involve the underwriting of securities. As we shall explain later, legislation in the form of the Glass-Steagall Act at one time limited bank activities in this area. In assisting customers in obtaining funds, banks also provide bankers acceptances, letters of credit, and other types of guarantees for their customers. That is, if a customer has borrowed funds backed by a letter of credit or other guarantee, its lenders can look to the customer's bank to fulfill the obligation. The second area of corporate financing involves advice on such matters as strategies for obtaining funds, corporate restructuring, divestitures, and acquisitions.

Capital market and foreign exchange products and services involve transactions where the bank may act as a dealer or broker in a service. Some banks, for example, are dealers in U.S. government or other securities. Customers who wish to transact in these securities can do so through the government desk of the bank. Similarly, some banks maintain a foreign-exchange operation, where foreign currency is bought and sold. Bank customers in need of foreign exchange can use the services of the bank.

Regulation of Commercial Bank Activities

Because of the special role that commercial banks play in the financial system, banks are regulated and supervised by several federal and state government entities. At the federal level, supervision is undertaken by the Federal Reserve Board, the Office of the Comptroller of the Currency, and the Federal Deposit Insurance Corporation. While much of the legislation defining these activities dates back to the late 1930s, the nature of financial markets and commercial banking has changed since the 1970s.

The most sweeping legislation in bank regulation in recent years has produced changes in the permissible activities for banks and bank holding companies. The key legislation is the Financial Services Modernization (FSM) Act of 1999, more commonly referred to as the Gramm-Leach-Bliley (GLB) Act, which has changed the shape of the financial services sector by lowering the firewalls that existed between different financial service businesses. To appreciate the major impact of this legislation, we must first review the regulations on permissible bank activities prior to the passage of this legislation.

Early legislation governing bank activities developed because transactions between commercial banks and their securities affiliates that were permitted led to abuses. Against this background, Congress passed the Banking Act of 1933, which, among other provisions, contained four sections that are popularly referred to as the *Glass-Steagall Act*. Specifically, banks could neither (1) underwrite securities and stock, nor (2) act as dealers in the secondary market for securities and stock (although there were some exceptions).

The Gramm-Leach-Bliley Act of 1999 created a new financial holding company authorized to engage in underwriting and selling securities. Consequently, the underwriting activities described later and the secondary securities market that were primarily the domain of financial entities referred to as investment banking firms were now opened to banks. As a result, subsequent to the act there have been several mergers of large bank holding companies and investment banking firms.

Investment Banking

The primary market involves the distribution to investors of newly issued securities by corporations and other entities seeking to raise funds. The entity issuing a security is referred to as the *issuer*. The participants in the marketplace that work with issuers to distribute newly issued securities are called *investment bankers*. The activity of investment banking is undertaken by basically two types of firms: securities houses and commercial banks.

Traditional Process for Underwriting New Issues

The traditional process in the United States for issuing new securities involves investment bankers performing one or more of the following three functions:

1. advising the issuer on the terms and the timing of the offering,
2. buying the securities from the issuer, and
3. distributing the issue to the public.[1]

In the sale of new securities, investment bankers need not undertake the second function—buying the securities from the issuer. An investment banker may merely act as an advisor and/or distributor of the new security. The function of buying the securities from the issuer is what we

---

[1] When an investment banking firm commits its own funds on a long-term basis by either taking an equity interest or creditor position in companies, this activity is referred to as *merchant banking*.

referred to earlier as "underwriting." When an investment banking firm buys the securities from the issuer and accepts the risk of selling the securities to investors at a lower price, it is referred to as an "underwriter." When the investment banking firm agrees to buy the securities from the issuer at a set price, the underwriting arrangement is referred to as a *firm commitment*. In contrast, in a *best efforts arrangement*, the investment banking firm agrees only to use its expertise to sell the securities—it does not buy the entire issue from the issuer.

The fee earned from underwriting a security is the difference between the price paid to the issuer and the price at which the investment bank reoffers the security to the public. This difference is called the *gross spread*, or the *underwriter discount*. There are numerous factors that affect the size of the gross spread.

The typical underwritten transaction involves so much risk of capital loss that a single investment banking firm undertaking it alone would be exposed to the danger of losing a significant portion of its capital. To share this risk, an investment banking firm forms a syndicate of firms to underwrite the issue. The gross spread is then divided among the lead underwriter(s) and the other firms in the underwriting syndicate. The lead underwriter manages the deal (or "runs the books" for the deal). In many cases, there may be more than one lead underwriter.

A successful underwriting of a security requires that the underwriter have a strong sales force. The sales force provides feedback on advance interest in the security, and the traders (also called market makers) provide input in pricing the security as well. It would be a mistake to think that once the securities are all sold the investment banking firm's ties with the deal are ended. In the case of bonds, those who bought the securities will look to the investment banking firm to make a market in the issue.

Regulation of the Primary Market

Underwriting activities are regulated by the Securities and Exchange Commission (SEC). The Securities Act of 1933 governs the issuance of securities. The act requires that a registration statement be filed with the SEC by the issuer of a security. The type of information contained in the registration statement is the nature of the business of the issuer, key provisions or features of the security, the nature of the investment risks associated with the security, and the background of management. Financial statements must be included in the registration statement, and they must be certified by an independent public accountant.

The registration is actually divided into two parts. Part I is the *prospectus*. It is this part that is typically distributed to the public as an offering of the securities. Part II contains supplemental information, which is not distributed to the public as part of the offering but is available from the SEC upon request. The act provides for penalties in the form of fines and/or imprisonment if the information provided is inaccurate or material information is omitted. One of the most important duties of an underwriter is to perform due diligence.

The filing of a registration statement with the SEC does not mean that the security can be offered to the public. The registration statement must be reviewed and approved by the SEC's Division of Corporate Finance before a public offering can be made. If the staff is satisfied, the SEC will issue an order declaring that the registration statement is "effective," and the underwriter can solicit sales. The approval of the SEC, however, does not mean that the securities have investment merit or are properly priced or that the information is accurate. It merely means that the appropriate information appears to have been disclosed.

The time interval between the initial filing of the registration statement and the time the registration statement becomes effective is referred to as the waiting period: (also called the "cooling-off period"). During the waiting period, the SEC does allow the underwriters to distribute a preliminary prospectus. Because the prospectus has not become effective, its cover page states this in red ink and, as a result, the preliminary prospectus is commonly called a *red herring*. During the waiting period, the underwriter cannot sell the security, nor may it accept written offers from investors to buy the security.

In 1982 the SEC approved Rule 415, which permits certain issuers to file a single registration document indicating that they intend to sell a certain amount of a certain class of securities at one or more times within the next two years.[2] Rule 415 is popularly referred to as the shelf registration rule because the securities can be viewed as sitting on a "shelf," and can be taken off that shelf and sold to the public without obtaining additional SEC approval. In essence, the filing of a single registration document allows the issuer to come to market quickly because the sale of the security has been preapproved by the SEC. Prior to establishment of Rule 415, there was a lengthy period required before a security could be sold to the public. As a result, in a fast-moving market, issuers could not come to market quickly with an offering to take advantage of what they perceived to be attractive financing opportunities. For example, if a corporation felt that interest rates were low and wanted to issue a bond, it had to file a registration statement and could

---

[2] The issuer qualifes for Rule 415 registration if the securities are investment-grade securities and/or are the securities of companies that have historically filed registration statements and whose securities comply with minimum flotation requirements.

not issue the bond until the registration statement became effective. The corporation was then taking the chance that during the waiting period interest rates would rise, making the bond offering more costly.

Variations in the Underwriting Process

Not all deals are underwritten using the traditional syndicate process we have described. Variations in the United States and foreign markets include the bought deal for the underwriting of bonds, the auction process for both stocks and bonds, and a rights offering for underwriting common stock.

The mechanics of a *bought deal* are as follows. The lead manager or a group of managers offers a potential issuer of debt securities a firm bid to purchase a specified amount of the securities. The issuer is given a day or so (maybe even only a few hours) to accept or reject the bid. If the bid is accepted, the underwriting firm has bought the deal. It can, in turn, sell the securities to other investment banking firms for distribution to their clients and/or distribute the securities to its clients.

Another variation for underwriting securities is the *auction process*. In this method, the issuer announces the terms of the issue, and interested parties submit bids for the entire issue. The auction form is mandated for certain securities of regulated public utilities and many municipal debt obligations. It is more commonly referred to as a *competitive bidding underwriting*. For example, suppose that a public utility wishes to issue $300 million of bonds. Various underwriters will form syndicates and bid on the issue. The syndicate that bids the lowest cost to the issuer wins the entire $300 million bond issue and then reoffers it to the public.

A *preemptive rights offering* is a method for issuing new common stock directly to existing shareholders. A preemptive right grants existing shareholders the right to buy some proportion of the new shares issued at a price below market value. The price at which the new shares can be purchased is called the *subscription price*. A rights offering ensures that current shareholders may maintain their proportionate equity interest in the corporation. For the shares sold via a preemptive rights offering, the underwriting services of an investment banker are not needed. However, the issuing corporation may use the services of an investment banker for the distribution of common stock that is not subscribed to. A *standby underwriting arrangement* will be used in such instances. This arrangement calls for the underwriter to buy the unsubscribed shares. The issuing corporation pays a standby fee to the investment banking firm. In the United States, the practice of issuing common stock via a preemptive rights offering is uncommon. In other countries it is much more common; in some countries, it is the only means by which a new offering of common stock may be sold.

Private Placement of Securities

In addition to underwriting securities for distribution to the public, securities may be placed with a limited number of financial institutions. *Private placement*, as this process is known, differs from the public offering of securities that we have described so far. Life insurance companies are the major investors in private placements.

Public and private offerings of securities differ in terms of the regulatory requirements that the issuer must satisfy. The Securities Act of 1933 and the Securities Exchange Act of 1934 require that all securities offered to the general public must be registered with the SEC, unless there is a specific exemption. One exemption from registration under the 1933 act is for "transactions by an issuer not involving any public offering." Regulation D, adopted by the SEC in 1982, sets forth the guidelines that determine if an issue is qualified for exemption from registration. The guidelines require that, in general, the securities cannot be offered through any form of general advertising or general solicitation that would prevail for public offerings. Most importantly, the guidelines restrict the sale of securities to "sophisticated" investors. Such "accredited" investors are defined as those who (1) have the capability to evaluate (or who can afford to employ an advisor to evaluate) the risk and return characteristics of the securities, and (2) have the resources to bear the economic risks.

The exemption of an offering does not mean that the issuer need not disclose information to potential investors. In fact, the issuer must still furnish the same information deemed material by the SEC. The issuer supplies this information in a private placement memorandum, as opposed to a prospectus for a public offering. The distinction between the private placement memorandum and the prospectus is that the former does not include information deemed "nonmaterial" by the SEC, if such information is required in a prospectus. Moreover, unlike a prospectus, the private placement memorandum is not subject to SEC review.

Investment banking firms assist in the private placement of securities in several ways. They work with the issuer and potential investors on the design and pricing of the security. Often it has been in the private placement market that investment bankers first design new security structures. The investment bankers may be involved with lining up the investors as well as designing the issue. Or, if the issuer has already identified the investors, the investment banker may serve only in an advisory capacity. An investment banker can also participate in the transaction on a best efforts underwriting arrangement.

In the United States, one restriction imposed on buyers of privately placed securities is that they may not be resold for two years after acquisition. Thus, there is no liquidity in the market for that time period. Buyers of privately placed securities must be compensated for the lack of liquidity, which raises the cost to the issuer of the securities. In April 1990, however, SEC Rule 144A became effective. This rule eliminates the two-year holding period by permitting large financial institutions to trade securities acquired in a private placement among themselves without having to register these securities with the SEC. Private placements are now classified as *Rule 144A offerings* or *non-Rule 144A offerings*. The latter are more commonly referred to as traditional private placements. Rule 144A offerings are underwritten by investment bankers.

Other Financial Institutions

There are a number of non-deposit financial institutions that hold financial assets. In this section, we briefly describe the role of trust companies, investment companies, pension funds, and insurers.

Trust Companies

A *trust company* is corporation formed to act as a trustee according to the terms of a contract (referred to as a trust agreement). A *trustee* is a person or a business that has the responsibility of overseeing the management of funds, making sure that they are managed in a way that is in the best interests of the beneficiaries (the persons for whose benefit the trust is established). Though many banks have their own trust departments to serve this function, independent trust companies exist to accept and manage funds according to a trust agreement.

Investment Companies

Investment companies sell shares to individuals and use these funds to invest in a pool of assets. These assets may be stocks, bonds, or some other investment. Investment companies that buy and sell shares in the pool at any time the customer wishes are referred to as *open-end investment companies*, which are also referred to as *mutual funds*. Investment companies that sell only a specific number of shares in the pool are referred to as *closed-end investment companies*. Pools invested in short-term assets are referred to as *money market funds*. Pools invested in real estate investments are referred to as *real estate investment trusts*.

Pension Funds

Workers set aside a portion of their income in *pension funds* to protect against a loss of income in retirement years. The pension fund then invests the money in stocks, bonds, or other assets, building up the value of the funds to provide for the workers' future retirement.

Life Insurance Companies

Individuals and companies purchase insurance policies that protect policy-holders and their families or employers against the risks of premature death or disability. The life insurance company invests and manages the funds, building up these funds for the eventual payout of insurance policy benefits.

Property-Casualty Insurers

Individuals and businesses purchase insurance policies that protect them against risks of loss from weather, crime, personal negligence, or some other type of event. Like the life insurers, property-casualty insurers invest and manage these funds to accommodate future payments to insured individuals and businesses.

THE COST OF MONEY

Money is not a free good. Those who need money are willing to pay for it and those who lend money expect to be compensated. The *interest rate* is the cost of money. If you put $1,000 in an account in a savings and loan that pays interest of 5% per year, you will earn $50 interest in one year. The savings and loan is paying you $50 for the use of your $1,000. Similarly, if you buy a $1,000 face value bond with a coupon rate of 5%, you earn $50 interest each year. The issuer is paying $50 interest each year for the use of your $1,000.

Interest Rates and Yields

Because bonds are traded in the secondary market, the price of the bond may change as the supply and demand for funds changes. The interest paid on your bond does not change (you get $50 per year), but the bond's price does. Suppose instead you buy the $1,000 face value bond for $900. The bond still pays $50 interest per year, but you only paid $900 for it. Therefore, you are earning more than the 5% interest rate ($50/$900 = 5.56%). The 5.56% is the *yield* on the bond, and 5% is the *interest rate* on the bond.

Most bonds are issued at their face or par value, so when they are issued the yield is often equal to the coupon rate. And if you buy a bond when it is issued and hold it until it matures, you will earn the bond's interest rate (i.e., pay $1,000 and get $50 per year). As time marches on, a bond's value change and its yield (that is, what investors can earn if they buy the bond at the time) will often deviate from its interest rate. If you hold the bond to maturity, you don't care about its changing value. But if you buy the bond sometime after it is issued or sell the bond before it matures, you do care about its changing value.

We often use the terms "interest rate" and "yield" interchangeably because they tell us how much we get for the amount we invest. When we are talking about what investors are getting in terms of a return, we generally talk about the "yield"—the return investors get if they buy a security at its current price. And, to make returns comparable across securities with different maturities, we quote these yields in terms of a common time frame—a year. This allows us to compare the yield on, say, a 3-month Treasury Bill with a 1-year Treasury Bill.

Determinants of Interest Rates

Interest rates are determined by the supply and demand for money. The supply of money depends in large part on the actions of the Fed, as we discussed previously. Therefore, let's focus on the demand for money.

The demand for money arises from two sources: transactions demand and asset demand. The *transactions demand* arises from individuals' and businesses' need to use money as a medium of exchange in transactions. The more goods and services exchanges take place in the economy, the greater the transactions demand. The *asset demand* is individuals' and businesses' need to use money as a store of value—they keep some of their wealth in the form of money (instead of in, say, stocks or bonds), which is risk-free and liquid.

Firms raise funds to invest in capital projects, which are investments that have long-term future cash flow consequences. If a firm has many possible ways to invest—to build a new plant, to start an advertising campaign—it will rank these projects based on profitability and invest in those whose profit exceeds the cost of the funds. Meanwhile, other firms are doing the same thing. As a result, firms compete for funds for their investment projects. Firms with the most profitable investment opportunities get the necessary funds, and firms with the least profitable investment opportunities do not. In other words, money is distributed to the capital projects that are most profitable.

Since money earns little or nothing, how much wealth individuals or firms are willing to keep in the form of money depends not only on how they feel about liquidity and risk, but also on what they could earn on the funds if they invested them elsewhere (say, in bonds). Therefore, the demand for money is affected by interest rates: the higher the interest rate, the lower the demand for money.

The Structure of Interest Rates

There is not one interest rate in any economy. Rather, there is a structure of interest rates. The interest rate that a borrower will have to pay depends on a myriad of factors. We discuss these factors next.

The Base Interest Rate

The securities issued by the U.S. Department of the Treasury, popularly referred to as Treasury securities or simply Treasuries, are backed by the full faith and credit of the U.S. government. Consequently, market participants throughout the world view them as having no credit risk. As a result, historically the interest rates on Treasury securities have served as the benchmark interest rates throughout the U.S. economy as well as in international capital markets.

The U.S. Treasury is the largest single issuer of debt in the world and the large size of any single issue has contributed to making the Treasury market the most active and, hence, the most liquid market in the world. However, in recent years, the U.S. Department of the Treasury has reduced its issuance of Treasury securities, particularly long-term securities, as well as buying back long-term Treasury securities in the market. This has decreased the supply of these securities and, as a result, there are market participants who feel that the yields on Treasury securities are no longer a suitable benchmark for interest rates throughout the world. As a result, as of this writing, there is a search for other possible benchmarks.

The Risk Premium

Market participants talk of interest rates on non-Treasury securities as "trading at a spread" to a particular on-the-run Treasury security (or a spread to any particular benchmark interest rate selected). For example, if the yield on a 10-year non-Treasury security is 7% and the yield on a 10-year Treasury security is 6%, the spread is 100 basis points. This spread reflects the additional risks the investor faces by acquiring a security that is not issued by the U.S. government and, therefore, can be called a risk premium. Thus, we can express the interest rate offered on a non-Treasury security as:

$$\text{Interest rate} = \text{Base interest rate} + \text{Spread}$$

or equivalently,

$$\text{Interest rate} = \text{Base interest rate} + \text{Risk premium}$$

We have discussed the factors that affect the base interest rate. One of the factors is the expected rate of inflation. That is, the base interest rate can be expressed as:

$$\text{Base interest rate} = \text{Real rate of interest} + \text{Expected rate of inflation}$$

Turning to the spread, the factors that affect it are (1) the issuer's perceived creditworthiness; (2) the term or maturity of the instrument; (3) provisions that grant either the issuer or the investor the option to do something; (4) the taxability of the interest received by investors; and (5) the expected liquidity of the issue.

It is important to note that yield spreads must be interpreted relative to the benchmark interest rate used. This is particularly important to keep in mind for the second and last factors that affect the spread when the benchmark interest rate is other than the yield on U.S. Treasury securities.

Perceived Creditworthiness of Issuer   Credit risk refers to the risk that the issuer of a debt obligation may be unable to make timely payment of interest and/or the principal amount when it is due. Most market participants rely primarily on commercial rating companies to assess the default risk of an issuer. These companies perform credit analyses and express their conclusions by a system of ratings. The three commercial rating companies in the United States are (1) Moody's Investors Service, (2) Standard & Poor's Corporation, and (3) Fitch Ratings.

In all systems the term *high grade* means low credit risk, or conversely, high probability of future payments. The highest-grade bonds are designated by Moody's by the symbol Aaa, and by S&P and Fitch by the symbol AAA. The next highest grade is denoted by the symbol Aa (Moody's) or AA (S&P and Fitch); for the third grade all rating systems use A. The next three grades are Baa or BBB, Ba or BB, and B, respectively. There are also C grades. Moody's uses 1, 2, or 3 to provide a narrower credit quality breakdown within each class, and S&P and Fitch use plus and minus signs for the same purpose.

Bonds rated triple A (AAA or Aaa) are said to be *prime*; double A (AA or Aa) are of *high quality*; single A issues are called *upper medium grade*, and triple B are *medium grade*. Lower-rated bonds are said to have speculative elements or be distinctly speculative. Bond issues that are assigned a rating in the top four categories are referred to as *investment-grade bonds*. Issues that carry a rating below the top four categories are referred to as *noninvestment-grade bonds*, or more popularly as high-yield bonds or junk bonds. Thus, the bond market can be divided into two sectors: the investment-grade and noninvestment-grade markets. The spread between Treasury securities and non-Treasury securities that are identical in all respects except for quality is referred to as a *quality spread* or *credit spread*.

Term to Maturity   The price of a financial asset will fluctuate over its life as yields in the market change. It can be demonstrated that the price volatility of a bond is dependent on its maturity. More specifically, with all other factors being constant, the longer the maturity of a bond, the greater the price volatility resulting from a change in market yields. The spread between any two maturity sectors of the market is called a *maturity spread* or *yield curve spread*. The relationship between the yields on comparable securities but different maturities is called the *term structure of interest rates*. The term-to-maturity topic is of such importance that we discuss in more detail later in this chapter.

Inclusion of Options   It is not uncommon for a bond issue to include a provision that gives either the bondholder and/or the issuer an option to take some action against the other party. An option that is included in a bond issue is referred to as an *embedded option*. The most common type of option in a bond issue is a *call provision*. This provision grants the issuer the right to retire the debt, fully or partially, before the scheduled maturity date. The inclusion of a call feature benefits issuers by allowing them to replace an old bond issue with a lower interest cost issue should interest rates in the market decline. Effectively, a call provision allows the issuer to alter the maturity of a bond. A call provision is detrimental to the bondholder because the bondholder will be uncertain about maturity and might have to reinvest the proceeds received at a lower interest rate if the bond is called and the bondholder wants to keep his or her funds in issues of similar risk of default.

An issue also may include a provision that allows the bondholder to change the maturity of a bond. An issue with a *put provision* grants the bondholder the right to sell the issue back to the issuer at par value on designated dates. Here, the advantage to the investor is that, if interest rates rise after the issue date and result in a price that is less than the par value, the investor can force the issuer to redeem the bond at par value.

A *convertible bond* is an issue giving the bondholder the right to exchange the bond for a specified number of shares of common stock. This feature allows the bondholder to take advantage of favorable movements in the price of the issuer's common stock.

The presence of these embedded options has an effect on the spread of an issue relative to a Treasury security and the spread relative to otherwise comparable issues that do not have an embedded option. In general, market participants require a larger spread over a comparable Treasury security for an issue with an embedded option that is favorable to the issuer (e.g., a call option) than for an issue without such an option. In contrast, market participants require a smaller spread over a comparable Treasury security for an issue with an embedded option that is favorable to the investor (for example, put option and conversion option). In fact, for a bond with an option that is favorable to an investor, the interest rate on an issue may be less than that on a comparable Treasury security!

Taxability of Interest   Unless exempted under the federal income tax code, interest income is taxable at the federal level. In addition to federal income taxes, there may be state and local taxes on interest income. The federal tax code specifically exempts the interest income from qualified municipal bond issues from taxation at the federal level. Municipal bonds are securities issued by state and local governments and by their creations, such as "authorities" and special districts. The large majority of outstanding municipal bonds are tax-exempt securities. Because of the tax-exempt feature of municipal bonds, the yield on municipal bonds is less than that on Treasuries with the same maturity.

Expected Liquidity of an Issue   Bonds trade with different degrees of liquidity. The greater the expected liquidity with which an issue trades, the lower the yield that investors require. As noted earlier, Treasury securities are the most liquid securities in the world. The lower yield offered on Treasury securities relative to non-Treasury securities reflects, to a significant extent, the difference in liquidity.

Term Structure of Interest Rates

One of the factors that we stated affects the risk premium is the maturity of a debt obligation. The relationship between the yield on a bond and its maturity is the *term structure of interest rates*. The graphic that depicts the relationship between the yield on bonds of the same credit quality but different maturities is known as the *yield curve*. Market participants have tended to construct yield curves from observations of prices and yields in the Treasury market. Two reasons account for this tendency. First, Treasury securities are free of default risk, and differences in creditworthiness do not affect yield estimates. Second, as the largest and most active bond market, the Treasury market offers the fewest problems of illiquidity or infrequent trading. Exhibit 3.3 shows the shape of three hypothetical Treasury yield curves that have been observed from time to time in the United States. However, as noted earlier, new benchmarks are being considered by market participants because of the dwindling supply of U.S. Treasury securities. Nevertheless, the principles set forth here apply to any other benchmark selected.

From a practical viewpoint, the Treasury yield curve functions mainly as a benchmark for setting yields in many other sectors of the debt market—bank loans, mortgages, corporate debt, and international bonds. However, a Treasury yield curve based on observed yields on the Treasury market is an unsatisfactory measure of the relation between required yield and maturity. The key reason is that securities with the same maturity may actually provide different yields. Hence, it is necessary to develop more accurate and reliable estimates of the Treasury yield curve. Specifically, the key is to estimate the theoretical interest rate that the U.S. Treasury would have to pay assuming that the security it issued is a zero-coupon security. We will not explain how this is done. At this point, all that is necessary to know is that there are procedures for estimating the theoreitical interest rate or yield that the U.S. Treasury would have to pay for bonds with different maturities. These interest rates are called *Treasury spot rates*.

Valuable information for market participants can be obtained from the Treasury spot rates. These rates are called *forward rates*. First, we will see how these rates are obtained and then we will discuss theories about what determines forward rates. Finally, we will see how issuers can use the forward rates in making financing decisions.

Foward Rates To see how a forward rate can be computed, consider the following two Treasury spot rates. Suppose that the spot rate for a zero-coupon Treasury security maturing in one year is 4% and a zero-coupon Treasury security maturing in two years is 5%. Let's look at this situation from the perspective of an investor who wants to invest funds for two years. The investors choices are as follows:

EXHIBIT 3.3 Three Observed Shapes for the Yield Curve

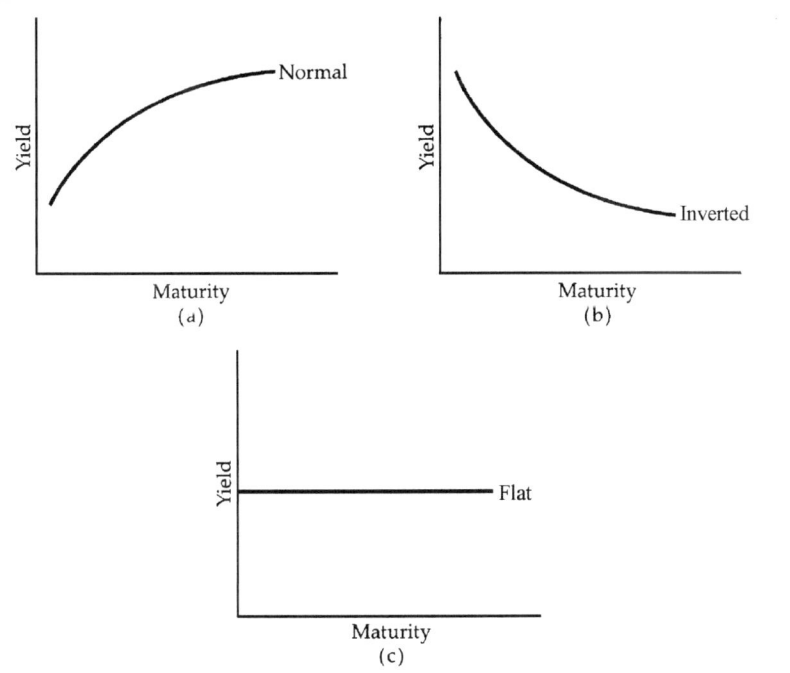

Alternative 1: Investor buys a two-year zero-coupon Treasury security

Alternative 2: Investor buys a one-year zero-coupon Treasury security and when it matures in one year the investor buys another one-year instrument.

With Alternative 1, the investor will earn the two-year spot rate and that rate is known with certainty. In contrast, with Alternative 2, the investor will earn the one-year spot rate, but the one-year spot one year from now is unknown. Therefore, for Alternative 2, the rate that will be earned over one year is not known with certainty.

Suppose that this investor expected that one year from now the one-year spot rate will be higher than it is today. The investor might then feel Alternative 2 would be the better investment. However, this is not necessarily true. To understand why and to appreciate the need to understand why it is necessary to know what a forward rate is, let's continue with our illustration.

The investor will be indifferent to the two alternatives if they produce the same total dollars over the two-year investment horizon. Given the two-year spot rate, there is some spot rate on a one-year zero-coupon Treasury security one year from now that will make the investor indifferent between the two alternatives. We will denote that rate by f.

The value of f can be readily determined given the two-year spot rate and the one-year spot rate. If an investor placed $100 in the two-year zero-coupon Treasury security (Alternative 1) earning 5%, the total dollars that will be generated at the end of two years is:[3]

$$\text{Total dollars at the end of two years for Alternative 1} = \$100(1.05)^2$$
$$= \$110.25$$

The proceeds from investing in the one-year Treasury security at 4% will generate the following total dollars at the end of one year:

$$\text{Total dollars at the end of two years for Alternative 2} = \$100(1.04)$$
$$= \$104$$

If one year from now this amount is reinvested in a zero-coupon Treasury security maturing in one year, which we denoted f, then the total dollars at the end of two years would be:

$$\text{Total dollars at the end of two years for Alternative 2} = \$104(1 + f)$$

---

[3] We will discuss this compounding of returns in Chapter 7.

The investor will be indifferent between the two alternatives if the total dollars are the same. Setting the two equations for the total dollars at end of two years for the two alternatives equal we get:

$$\$110.25 = \$104(1 + f)$$

Solving the preceding equation for f, we get

$$f = \frac{\$110.25}{\$104} - 1 = 0.06 = 6\%$$

Here is how we use this rate of 6%. If the one-year spot rate one year from now is less than 6%, then the total dollars at the end of two years would be higher by investing in the two-year zero-coupon Treasury security (Alternative 1). If the one-year spot rate one year from now is greater than 6%, then the total dollars at the end of two years would be higher by investing in a one-year zero-coupon Treasury security and reinvesting the proceeds one year from now at the one-year spot rate at that time (Alternative 2). Of course, if the one-year spot rate one year now is 6%, the two alternatives give the same total dollars at the end of two years.

Now that we have the forward rate f in which we are interested and we know how that rate can be used, let's return to the question we posed at the outset. Suppose that the investor expects that one year from now, the one-year spot rate will be 5.5%. That is, the investor expects that the one-year spot rate one year from now will be higher than its current level. Should the investor select Alternative 2 because the one-year spot rate one year from now is expected to be higher? The answer is no. As we explained in the previous paragraph, if the spot rate is less than 6%, then Alternative 1 is the better alternative. Since this investor expects a rate of 5.5%, then he or she should select Alternative 1 despite the fact that he or she expects the one-year spot rate to be higher than it is today.

This is a somewhat surprising result for some investors. But the reason for this is that the market prices its expectations of future interest rates into the rates offered on investments with different maturities. This is why knowing the forward rates is critical. Some market participants believe that the forward rate is the market's consensus of future interest rates.

Similarly, borrowers need to understand what a forward rate is. For example, suppose a borrower must choose between a two-year loan and a series of two one-year loans. If the forward rate is less than the borrower's expectations of one-year rates one year from now, then the borrower will be better off with a two-year loan. If, instead, the borrower's expectations are that the one-year rate one year from now will be less than the forward rate, the borrower will be better off by choosing a series of two one-year loans.

In practice, a corporate treasurer needs to know both forward rates and what future spreads will be. Recall that a corporation pays the Treasury rate (i.e., the benchmark) plus a spread.

Forward Rates as a Hedgeable Rate   A natural question about forward rates is how well they do at predicting future interest rates. Studies have demonstrated that forward rates do not do a good job in predicting future interest rates.[4] Then, why the big deal about understanding forward rates? The reason, as we demonstrated in our illustration of how to select between two alternative investments, is that the forward rates indicate how an investor's and borrower's expectations must differ from the market consensus in order to make the correct decision.

In our illustration, the one-year forward rate may not be realized. That is irrelevant. The fact is that the one-year forward rate indicated to the investor that if expectations about the one-year rate one month from now are less than 6%, the investor would be better off with Alternative 1.

For this reason, as well as others explained later, some market participants prefer not to talk about forward rates as being market consensus rates. Instead, they refer to forward rates as being *hedgeable rates*. For example, by investing in the two-year Treasury security, the investor was able to hedge the one-year rate one year from now. Similarly, a corporation issuing a two-year security is hedging the one-year rate one year from now. (Note, however, that it is only the benchmark interest rate that is being hedged. The spread that the corporation or the issuer will pay can change.)

Determinants of the Shape of the Term Structure   If we plot the term structure—the yield to maturity, or the spot rate, at successive maturities against maturity—what is it likely to look like? Exhibit 3.3 shows three shapes that have appeared with some frequency over time. Panel A shows an upward-sloping yield curve; that is, yield rises steadily as maturity increases. This shape is commonly referred to as a normal or positive yield curve. Panel B shows a downward-sloping or inverted yield curve, where yields decline as maturity increases. Finally, panel C shows a flat yield curve.

Two major theories have evolved to account for these observed shapes of the yield curve: the expectations theory and the market segmentation theory.

---

[4] See Eugene F. Fama, "Forward Rates as Predictors of Future Spot Rates," *Journal of Financial Economics* (1976), pp. 361–377.

There are several forms of the expectations theory—the pure expectations theory, the liquidity theory, and the preferred habitat theory. All share a hypothesis about the behavior of short-term forward rates and also assume that the forward rates in current long-term debt contracts are closely related to the market's expectations about future short-term rates. These three theories differ, however, on whether or not other factors also affect forward rates, and how. The pure expectations theory postulates that no systematic factors other than expected future short-term rates affect forward rates; the liquidity theory and the preferred habitat theory assert that there are other factors. Accordingly, the last two forms of the expectations theory are sometimes referred to as *biased expectations theories.*

According to the pure expectations theory, the forward rates exclusively represent the expected future rates. Thus, the entire term structure at a given time reflects the market's current expectations of the family of future short-term rates. Under this view, a rising term structure, as in Panel A of Exhibit 3.3, must indicate that the market expects short-term rates to rise throughout the relevant future. Similarly, a flat term structure reflects an expectation that future short-term rates will be mostly constant, while a falling term structure must reflect an expectation that future short rates will decline steadily.

Unfortunately, the pure expectations theory suffers from one shortcoming, which, qualitatively, is quite serious. It neglects the risks inherent in investing in bonds and like instruments. If forward rates were perfect predictors of future interest rates, then the future prices of bonds would be known with certainty. The return over any investment period would be certain and independent of the maturity of the instrument initially acquired and of the time at which the investor needed to liquidate the instrument. However, with uncertainty about future interest rates and hence about future prices of bonds, these instruments become risky investments in the sense that the return over some investment horizon is unknown.

Similarly, from a borrower or issuer's perspective, the cost of borrowing for any required period of financing would be certain and independent of the maturity of the instrument initially sold if the rate at which the borrower must refinance debt in the future is known. But with uncertainty about future interest rates, the cost of borrowing is uncertain if the borrower must refinance at some time over the periods in which the funds are initially needed.

There are two biased expectations theories that recognize the shortcomings in the pure expectations theory—the liquidity theory and the preferred habitat theory. According to the liquidity theory, the forward rates will not be an unbiased estimate of the market's expectations of future interest rates because they embody a liquidity premium. This liquidity premium reflects the risks of holding a bond for a longer time period. Thus, an upward-sloping yield curve may reflect expectations that future interest rates either (1) will rise, or (2) will be flat or even fall, but with a liquidity premium increasing fast enough with maturity so as to produce an upward-sloping yield curve.

The preferred habitat theory also adopts the view that the term structure reflects the expectation of the future path of interest rates as well as a risk premium. However, the habitat theory rejects the assertion that the risk premium must rise uniformly with maturity. Proponents of the habitat theory say that the latter conclusion could be accepted if all investors intend to liquidate their investment at the first possible date, while all borrowers are eager to borrow long, but that this is an assumption that can be rejected for a number of reasons. The argument is that different financial institutions have different investment horizons and have a preference for the maturities in which they invest. The preference is based on the maturity of their liabilities. To induce a financial institution out of that maturity sector, a premium must be paid. Thus, the forward rates include a liquidity premium and compensation for investors to move out of their preferred maturity sector. Consequently, forward rates do not reflect the market's consensus of future interest rates.

There is one more theory about the terms structure of interest rates. The *market segmentation theory* also recognizes that investors have preferred habitats dictated by saving and investment flows. This theory also proposes that the major reason for the shape of the yield curve lies in asset/liability management constraints (either regulatory or self-imposed) and/or creditors (borrowers) restricting their lending (financing) to specific maturity sectors. However, the market segmentation theory differs from the preferred habitat theory in that it assumes that neither investors nor borrowers are willing to shift from one maturity sector to another to take advantage of opportunities arising from differences between expectations and forward rates. Thus, for the segmentation theory, the shape of the yield curve is determined by supply of and demand for securities within each maturity sector.

Understanding Issuer Costs

We now understand that a corporation or other entity wishing to issue debt must pay the benchmark interest rate plus a risk premium. The risk premium is the spread and is affected by the various factors we discussed. In fact, when a potential issuer inquires of its investment bankers about the interest rate it would have to pay if it issued securities, the investment banker typically does *not* talk about the rate. The issuer talks about the "spread" at which the securities can be sold.

Consequently, when an issuer must decide on whether or not to issue a security, say a 15-year bond, the treasurer or chief financial officer will assess the benchmark interest rate and the spread. The forward rates along with forecasts by economists can be used to evaluate whether or not to issue a security now if rates are expected to rise or postpone issuance (and borrow short term) if rates are expected to fall. The expected change in the spread also affects the decision. The benchmark interest rate may be expected to fall but the spread increase such that the interest rate that the issuer would pay would be higher in the future. All of these elements go into the financing decision.

In Chapter 15 we will see how issuers can hedge the interest rate at which they have to pay. We will see that they can hedge the benchmark interest rate and/or hedge the spread.

Finally, the yield or cost of borrowing for an issuer of securities will depend on the benchmark interest rate plus a spread to reflect the risk premium that the market will demand. In addition, the issuance will have to pay various fees to issue a security. These fees include the payment to the SEC to register the securities, attorney fees, and fees to investment bankers. The latter fees are the underwriting spread—the difference between the price at which the securities are offered to the public by the investment banking firm and the price that the investment banking firm pays to the issuer to purchase the security—the gross spread. When an issuer evaluates its cost, it must recognize these issuance costs. In Chapter 11, we will see how the cost of funds is calculated for an issuer taking into account issuance costs. This measure is referred to as the "all in cost of funds."

SUMMARY

- The Federal Reserve System (the "Fed") is a network of banks that acts as the central banker for the United States.
- The money supply consists of cash and cash-like items. There are different definitions of what constitutes the money supply, depending on which cash-like items are included.
- The Fed affects the money supply by changing the reserve requirements, open market operations, and changing in the discount rate. Changes in the money supply affect interest rates and the availability of funds.
- Financial institutions provide various types of financial services. Financial intermediaries are a special group of financial institutions that obtain funds by issuing claims to market participants and use these funds to purchase financial assets. Intermediaries transform funds they

acquire into assets that are more attractive to the public by (1) providing maturity intermediation; (2) providing risk reduction via diversification at lower cost; (3) reducing the cost of contracting and information processing; or (4) providing a payments mechanism.

■ Depository institutions (commercial banks, savings and loan associations, savings banks, and credit unions) accept various types of deposits. With the funds raised through deposits and other funding sources, they make loans to various entities and invest in securities.

■ Investment bankers advise the issuer of a security on the terms of the offering, distributing the security to the public, and making a market for the security. Variations of the traditional underwriting of securities include the bought deal, distribution via an auction process, and private placements.

■ Interest rates are determined by the base rate (rate on a Treasury security) plus a risk premium. The factors that affect the risk premium are (1) the perceived creditworthiness of the issuer, (2) term to maturity, (3) inclusion of options, (4) taxability of interest, and (5) expected liquidity of an issue.

■ The term structure of interest rates shows the relationship between the yield on a bond and its maturity; the yield curve is the graph of the relationship between the yield on bonds of the same credit quality but different maturities.

■ Valuable information for issuers and investors is provided in forward rates.

■ Two major theories are offered to explain the observed shapes of the yield curve: the expectations theory (which includes the pure expectations theory, the liquidity theory, and the preferred habitat theory) and the market segmentation theory.

QUESTIONS

1. a. What is money?
   b. What is meant by M1? M2? M3?
2. What role does the Federal Reserve Bank play in determining the supply of money?
3. What is the Board of Governors and what types of decisions does this board make?
4. If the Federal Reserve uses the discount rate to encourage banks to lend funds, is this rate raised or lowered? Explain.
5. Distinguish between the transactions demand and the asset demand for money.

6. Describe the relation between the real rate of interest and the nominal rate of interest.

7. Suppose the nominal interest rate is 8% for a one-year security. If the expected real rate of interest next year is 5%, what is the inflation premium? What is the implied inflation rate?

8. Explain how a financial intermediary reduces the cost of contracting and information processing.

9. a. What are the three ways in which an investment banking firm may be involved in the issuance of a new security?
   b. What is meant by the underwriting function?

10. What is the difference between a firm commitment underwriting arrangement and a best efforts arrangement?

11. What is meant by a bought deal?

12. a. What is a preemptive right?
    b. What is a preemptive rights offering?

13. What is meant by the "base interest rate"?

14. a. Typically, how do market participants gauge the credit risk associated with a bond issue?
    b. What is the relationship between credit risk and the risk premium?

15. How does the taxability of interest affect the yield offered on a bond?

16. Suppose that the 1-year spot rate is 4.1% and the 2-year spot rate is 4.6%. What is the 1-year forward rate one year from now?

17. a. Comment on the following statement: "Forward rates are good predictors of future interest rates."
    b. Why can forward rates be viewed as hedgeable rates?

18. Consider the following yields to maturity:

Years to Maturity	Yield to Maturity
1	3.0%
2	3.5%
3	3.9%
4	4.4%
5	4.8%
6	5.2%

a. Graph the yield to maturity against the time to maturity.
b. Is this yield curve consistent with any of the yield curve theories? Explain.

19. A corporate treasurer is considering borrowing funds for 10 years. How can the corporate treasurer use forward rates in determining whether or not to borrow today or postpone borrowing?

20. Why are "biased" expectation theories of the term structure of interest rates biased?
21. Comment on the following: "There is no theory of the term structure of interest rates that would explain a yield curve in which interest rates increase with maturity for the first two years, decline with maturity until year 5, and then increase with maturity after year 5."

CHAPTER 4

Introduction to Derivatives

Firms are exposed to several risks in the ordinary course of operations and when borrowing funds. For some risks, management can obtain protection from an insurance company. For example, management can insure a plant against destruction by fire by obtaining a fire insurance policy from a property and casualty insurance company. There are capital market products available to management to protect against certain risks that are not insurable by an insurance company. Such risks include risks associated with a rise in the price of commodity purchased as an input, a decline in a commodity price of a product the firm sells, a rise in the cost of borrowing funds, and an adverse exchange rate movement. The instruments that can be used to provide such protection are called *derivative instruments*, so named because they derive their value from whatever the contract is based on. These instruments include futures contracts, forward contracts, option contracts, swap agreements, and cap and floor agreements.

There has been public concern about the use of derivative instruments by firms. This concern arises from major losses resulting from positions in derivative instruments.[1] However, an investigation of the reason for major losses would show that the losses were not due to derivatives per se, but the improper use of them by management that was either ignorant about the risks associated with using derivative instruments or management that sought to use them in a speculative manner rather than a means for managing risk. Another term for speculative purposes is trading purposes.

In this chapter we will discuss the basic features of each type of derivative instrument.

---

[1] Well-publicized losses in the 1990s include Procter & Gamble's losses related to foreign exchange derivatives, Gibson Greetings losses related to interest rates swaps, and Pier 1 Imports losses due to the trading of bond futures and options.

FUTURES CONTRACTS AND FORWARD CONTRACTS

A *futures contract* is an agreement that requires a party to the agreement either to buy or sell something at a designated future date at a predetermined price. The something that the two parties agree will be bought and sold is referred to as the **underlying for the contract** or simply the **underlying**. The basic economic function of futures markets is to provide an opportunity for market participants to hedge against the risk of adverse price movements.

Futures contracts are products created by exchanges. Futures contracts involving traditional agricultural commodities (such as grain and livestock), imported foodstuffs (such as coffee, cocoa, and sugar), or industrial commodities are traded. Collectively, such futures contracts are known as **commodity futures**. Futures contracts based on a financial instrument or a financial index are known as **financial futures**. Financial futures can be classified as (1) stock index futures, (2) interest rate futures, and (3) currency futures.

Mechanics of Futures Trading

A futures contract is an agreement between a buyer (seller) and an established exchange or its clearinghouse in which the buyer (seller) agrees to take (make) delivery of the underlying at a specified price at the end of a designated period of time. The price at which the parties agree to transact in the future is called the **futures price**. The designated date at which the parties must transact is called the **settlement date** or **delivery date**.

To illustrate, suppose there is a futures contract traded on an exchange where the underlying is Asset X, and the settlement date is three months from now. Assume further that Brent buys this futures contract, and Susan sells this futures contract, and the price at which they agree to transact in the future is $60. Then $60 is the futures price. At the settlement date, Susan will deliver Asset X to Brent; Brent will give Susan $60, the futures price. This transaction is illustrated in Exhibit 4.1.

EXHIBIT 4.1   Illustration of a Futures Contract for the Delivery of Asset X in Three Months at a Futures Price of $60

Today ———————— *Three months* ————————— Settlement date

Susan agrees to sell Asset X to Brent in the future.
Susan sells a future contract to Brent.
Agreed upon futures price is $60.

Susan delivers Asset X to Brent.
Brent pays Susan $60.

Liquidating a Position

Most futures contracts have settlement dates in the months of March, June, September, or December. This means that at a predetermined time in the contract settlement month the contract stops trading, and a price is determined by the exchange for settlement of the contract. A party to a futures contract has two choices on liquidation of the position. First, the position can be liquidated prior to the settlement date. For this purpose, the party must take an offsetting position in the same contract. For the buyer of a futures contract, this means selling the same number of identical futures contracts; for the seller of a futures contract, this means buying the same number of identical futures contracts.

The alternative is to wait until the settlement date. At that time the party purchasing a futures contract accepts delivery of the underlying (financial instrument, currency, or commodity) at the agreed-upon price; the party that sells a futures contract liquidates the position by delivering the underlying at the agreed-upon price. For some futures contracts, settlement is made in cash only. Such contracts are referred to as *cash-settlement contracts*.

The Role of the Clearinghouse

Associated with every futures exchange is a *clearinghouse*, which performs several functions. One of these functions is guaranteeing that the two parties to the transaction will perform. To see the importance of this function, consider potential problems in the futures transaction described earlier from the perspective of the two parties—Brent, the buyer and Susan, the seller. Each must be concerned with the other's ability to fulfill the obligation at the settlement date. Suppose that at the settlement date the price of Asset X in the cash market is $40. Susan can buy Asset X for $40 and deliver it to Brent who, in turn, must pay her $60 (the futures price agreed upon when the two parties entered into the agreement). If Brent does not have the capacity to pay $60 or refuses to pay, however, Susan has lost the opportunity to realize a profit of $20. Suppose, instead, that the price of Asset X in the cash market is $90 at the settlement date. In this case, Brent is ready and willing to accept delivery of Asset X and pay the agreed-upon price of $60. If Susan does not have the ability or refuses to deliver Asset X, Brent has lost the opportunity to realize a profit of $30.

The clearinghouse exists to meet this problem. When a party takes a position in the futures market, the clearinghouse takes the opposite position and agrees to satisfy the terms set forth in the contract. Because of the clearinghouse, the parties to a futures contract need not worry about the financial strength and integrity of the other party that has taken the opposite side of the contract (called the *counterparty*). After initial execution of an order, the relationship between the two parties ends. The clearinghouse interposes itself as the buyer for every sale and the seller for every purchase. Thus either party is free to liquidate a position without involving the counterparty in the original futures contract, and without worry that the counterparty may default. This is the reason why we define a futures contract as an agreement between a party and a clearinghouse associated with an exchange.

Besides its guarantee function, the clearinghouse makes it simple for parties to a futures contract to unwind their positions prior to the settlement date. Suppose that Brent wants to get out of his futures position. He will not have to seek out Susan and work out an agreement with her to terminate the original agreement. Instead, Brent can unwind his position by selling an identical futures contract. As far as the clearinghouse is concerned, its records will show that Brent has bought and sold an identical futures contract. At the settlement date, Susan will not deliver Asset X to Brent but will be instructed by the clearinghouse to deliver to someone who bought and still has an open futures position. In the same way, if Susan wants to unwind her position prior to the settlement date, she can buy an identical futures contract.

Margin Requirements

When a position is first taken in a futures contract, the investor must deposit a minimum dollar amount per contract as specified by the exchange. This amount is called the *initial margin* and is required as deposit for the contract. The initial margin may be in the form of an interest-bearing security. As the price of the futures contract fluctuates, the value of the investor's equity in the position changes. At the end of each trading day, the exchange determines the settlement price for the futures contract. This price is used to determine the investor's position, so that any gain or loss from the position is reflected in the investor's equity account. In financial markets, the process of recording the market value of a position is referred to as *marking a position to market* or simply *marking to market.*

Maintenance margin is the minimum level (specified by the exchange) by which an investor's equity position may fall as a result of an unfavorable price movement before the investor is required to deposit additional margin. The additional margin deposited is called *variation margin*, and it is an amount necessary to bring the equity in the account back to its initial margin level. Unlike initial margin, variation margin must be in cash, not interest-bearing instruments. Any excess margin in the account may be withdrawn by the investor. If a party to a futures contract who is required to deposit variation margin fails to do so within 24 hours, the futures position is closed out.[2]

Futures versus Forward Contracts

A *forward contract,* just like a futures contract, is an agreement for the future delivery of the underlying at a specified price at the end of a designated period of time. Futures contracts are standardized agreements as to the delivery date (or month) and quality of the deliverable, and are traded on organized exchanges. A forward contract differs in that it is usually nonstandardized (that is, the terms of each contract are negotiated individually between buyer and seller), there is no clearinghouse, and secondary markets are often nonexistent or extremely thin. Unlike a futures contract, which is an exchange-traded product, a forward contract is an over-the-counter instrument.

Although both futures and forward contracts set forth terms of delivery, futures contracts are not intended to be settled by delivery. In fact, generally less than 2% of outstanding contracts are settled by delivery. Forward contracts, in contrast, are intended for delivery.

Futures contracts are marked to market at the end of each trading day. Consequently, futures contracts are subject to interim cash flows as additional margin may be required in the case of adverse price movements, or as cash is withdrawn in the case of favorable price movements. A forward contract may or may not be marked to market, depending on the wishes of the two parties. For a forward contract that is not marked to market, there are no interim cash flow effects because no additional margin is required.

Finally, the parties in a forward contract are exposed to credit risk because either party may default on the obligation. The risk that the counterparty may default is referred to as *counterparty risk.* Counterparty risk is minimal in the case of futures contracts because the clearinghouse associated with the exchange guarantees the other side of the transaction.

Other than these differences, most of what we say about futures contracts applies equally to forward contracts.

---

[2] Although there are initial and maintenance margin requirements for buying securities on margin, the concept of margin differs for securities and futures. When securities are acquired on margin, the difference between the price of the security and the initial margin is borrowed from the broker. The security purchased serves as collateral for the loan, and the investor pays interest. For futures contracts, the initial margin, in effect, serves as "good faith" money, an indication that the investor will satisfy the obligation of the contract. Normally no money is borrowed by the investor.

Risk and Return Characteristics of Futures Contracts

When an investor takes a position in the market by buying a futures contract, the investor is said to be in a *long position* or to be *long futures*. If, instead, the investor's opening position is the sale of a futures contract, the investor is said to be in a *short position* or *short futures*.

The buyer of a futures contract will realize a profit if the futures price increases; the seller of a futures contract will realize a profit if the futures price decreases. For example, suppose one month after Brent and Susan take their positions in the futures contract, the futures price of Asset X increases to $80. Brent, the buyer of the futures contract, could then sell the futures contract and realize a profit of $20 ($80 minus the futures price of $60). Effectively, at the settlement date he has agreed to buy Asset X for $60 but can sell Asset X for $80. Susan, the seller of the futures contract, will realize a loss of $20.

If the futures price falls to $45 and Susan buys the contract, she realizes a profit of $15 because she agreed to sell Asset X for $60 and now can buy it for $45. Brent would realize a loss of $15. Thus, if the futures price decreases, the buyer of the futures contract realizes a loss while the seller of a futures contract realizes a profit.

How Futures are Used to Manage Risk

We will use an example to illustrate how futures contracts can be used to manage risk. Consider a producer of crude oil and a company that uses crude oil in the operations of its business. The concern of the crude oil producer is that the price of crude oil will decline, thereby forcing it to sell crude oil at a lower price. The concern of the user of crude oil is that the price of crude oil will increase, resulting in a rise in its production costs.

Consider first the producer of crude oil. Suppose management expects that the crude oil will be available in two months and that management can sell a crude oil futures contract to deliver crude oil two months from now for $19 per barrel. The number of barrels that is expected to be sold will determine how many barrels of crude oil the firm will seek to deliver. By selling futures, management has locked in a price of $19 per barrel two months from now. Consequently, even if the price of crude oil two months from now is, say, $17 per barrel, management will receive $19 per barrel. If, instead, the price of crude oil two months from now is $20 per barrel, management has given up the opportunity to benefit from a higher price since it has agreed to accept $19 per barrel.

Now let's look at the user of crude oil. By buying a crude oil futures contract that settles in two months, management can assure that the price at which it must purchase crude oil will be no higher than $19 per barrel. So, if crude oil increases to $20 per barrel, management only needs to pay $19 per barrel. In contrast, if the price of crude oil two months from now decreases to $17 per barrel, management gave up the opportunity to benefit from a lower cost for crude oil.

In the same way that these two firms are able to use a futures contract to lock in the future price of crude oil, a firm can use futures contracts to lock in a foreign exchange rate or an interest rate.

OPTIONS

An option is a contract in which the *writer of the option* grants the *buyer of the option* the right, but not the obligation, to purchase from or sell to the writer an asset at a specified price within a specified period of time (or at a specified date). The writer, also referred to as the *seller*, grants this right to the buyer in exchange for a certain sum of money, which is called the *option price* or *option premium*. The price at which the asset may be bought or sold is called the *exercise price* or *strike price*. The date after which an option is void is called the *expiration date*. As with a futures contract, the asset that the buyer has the right to buy and the seller is obligated to sell is referred to as the underlying.

When an option grants the buyer the right to purchase the underlying from the writer (seller), it is referred to as a *call option*, or *call*. When the option buyer has the right to sell the underlying to the writer, the option is called a *put option*, or *put*.

An option is also categorized according to when the option buyer may exercise the option. There are options that may be exercised at any time up to and including the expiration date. Such an option is referred to as an *American option*. There are options that may be exercised only at the expiration date. An option with this feature is called a *European option*. An option that can be exercised before the expiration date but only on specified dates is called a *Bermuda option*.

To illustrate the characteristics of an option contract, suppose that Patricia buys a call option for $2 (the option price) with the following terms:

1. The underlying is one unit of Asset X.
2. The exercise price is $60.
3. The expiration date is three months from now, and the option can be exercised any time up to and including the expiration date (that is, it is an American option).

At any time up to and including the expiration date, Patricia can decide to buy from the writer of this option one unit of Asset X, for which she will pay a price of $60. If it is not beneficial for Patricia to exercise the option, she will not. Whether Patricia exercises the option or not, the $2 she paid for the option will be kept by the option writer. If Patricia buys a put option rather than a call option, then she would be able to sell Asset X to the option writer for a price of $60.

The maximum amount that an option buyer can lose is the option price. The maximum profit that the option writer can realize is the option price. The option buyer has substantial upside return potential, while the option writer has substantial downside risk. The risk/reward relationship for option positions will be discussed later.

There are no margin requirements for the buyer of an option once the option price has been paid in full. Because the option price is the maximum amount that the investor can lose, no matter how adverse the price movement of the underlying, there is no need for margin. Because the writer of an option has agreed to accept all of the risk (and none of the reward) of the position in the underlying, the writer is generally required to put up the option price received as margin. In addition, as price changes occur that adversely affect the writer's position, the writer is required to deposit additional margin (with some exceptions) as the position is marked to market.

Exchange-Traded versus Over-the-Counter Options

Options, like other financial instruments, may be traded either on an organized exchange or in the over-the-counter (OTC) market. The advantages of an exchange-traded option are as follows. First, the exercise price and expiration date of the contract are standardized. Second, as in the case of futures contracts, the direct link between buyer and seller is severed after the order is executed because of the interchangeability of exchange-traded options. The clearinghouse associated with the exchange where the option trades performs the same function in the options market that it does in the futures market. Finally, the transactions costs are lower for exchange-traded options than for OTC options.

The higher cost of an OTC option reflects the cost of customizing the option for the many situations where a corporation seeking to use an option to manage risk needs to have a tailor-made option because the standardized exchange-traded option does not satisfy its objectives. Some commercial and investment and banking firms act as principals as well as brokers in the OTC options market. OTC options are sometimes referred to as *dealer options*. While an OTC option is less liquid than an exchange-traded option, this is typically not of concern to the user of such an option. Most corporations who use OTC options do so as part of a financing strategy or price protection against unfavorable changes in prices of its inputs or exchange rates.

Differences between Options and Futures Contracts

Notice that, unlike in a futures contract, one party to an option contract is not obligated to transact—specifically, the option buyer has the right but not the obligation to transact. The option writer does have the obligation to perform. In the case of a futures contract, both buyer and seller are obligated to perform. Of course, a futures buyer does not pay the seller to accept the obligation, while an option buyer pays the seller an option price.

Consequently, the risk/reward characteristics of the two contracts are also different. In the case of a futures contract, the buyer of the contract realizes a dollar-for-dollar gain when the price of the futures contract increases and suffers a dollar-for-dollar loss when the price of the futures contract drops. The opposite occurs for the seller of a futures contract. Because of this relationship, futures are referred to as having a "linear payoff."

Options do not provide this symmetric risk/reward relationship. The most that the buyer of an option can lose is the option price. While the buyer of an option retains all the potential benefits, the gain is always reduced by the amount of the option price. The maximum profit that the writer may realize is the option price; this is offset against substantial downside risk. Because of this characteristic, options are referred to as having a "nonlinear payoff."

The difference in the type of payoff between futures and options is extremely important because market participants can use futures to protect against symmetric risk and options to protect against asymmetric risk.

Risk and Return Characteristics of Options

Here we illustrate the risk and return characteristics of the four basic option positions—buying a call option, selling a call option, buying a put option, and selling a put option. The illustrations assume that each option position is held to the expiration date and not exercised early. Also, to simplify the illustrations, we ignore transactions costs.[3]

---

[3] In addition, the illustrations do not address the cost of financing the purchase of the option price or the opportunity cost of investing the option price. Specifically, the buyer of an option must pay the seller the option price at the time the option is purchased. Thus, the buyer must finance the purchase price of the option or, assuming the purchase price does not have to be borrowed, the buyer loses the income that can be earned by investing the amount of the option price until the option is sold or exercised. In contrast, assuming that the seller does not have to use the option price as margin for the short position or can use an interest-earning asset as security, the seller has the opportunity to earn income from the proceeds of the option sale.

Buying Call Options

The purchase of a call option creates a position referred to as a *long call position*. To illustrate this position, assume that there is a call option on Asset X that expires in one month and has an exercise price of $60. The option price is $2. What is the profit or loss for the investor who purchases this call option and holds it to the expiration date?

The profit and loss from the strategy will depend on the price of Asset X at the expiration date. A number of outcomes are possible.

1. If the price of Asset X at the expiration date is less than $60 (the option price), then the investor will not exercise the option. It would be foolish to pay the option writer $60 when Asset X can be purchased in the market at a lower price. In this case, the option buyer loses the entire option price of $2. Notice, however, that this is the maximum loss that the option buyer will realize regardless of how low Asset X's price declines.

2. If Asset X's price is equal to $60 at the expiration date, there is again no economic value in exercising the option. As in the case where the price is less than $60, the buyer of the call option will lose the entire option price, $2.

3. If Asset X's price is more than $60 but less than $62 at the expiration date, the option buyer will exercise the option. By exercising, the option buyer can purchase Asset X for $60 (the exercise price) and sell it in the market for the higher price. Suppose, for example, that Asset X's price is $61 at the expiration date. The buyer of the call option will realize a $1 gain by exercising the option. Of course, the cost of purchasing the call option was $2, so $1 is lost on this position. By failing to exercise the option, the investor loses $2 instead of only $1.

4. If Asset X's price at the expiration date is equal to $62, the investor will exercise the option. In this case, the investor breaks even, realizing a gain of $2 that offsets the cost of the option, $2.

5. If Asset X's price at the expiration date is more than $62, the investor will exercise the option and realize a profit. For example, if the price is $70, exercising the option will generate a profit on Asset X of $10. Reducing this gain by the cost of the option ($2), the investor will realize a net profit from this position of $8.

Exhibit 4.2 shows in graph form the profit and loss for the buyer of the hypothetical call option. While the break-even point and the loss will depend on the option price and the exercise price, the profile shown in Exhibit 4.2 will hold for all buyers of call options. The shape indicates that the maximum loss is the option price and that there is substantial upside potential.

EXHIBIT 4.2   Profits and Losses on the Exercise of a Call Option to Buy the Stock at $60. The investor Pays $2 for this Call Option.

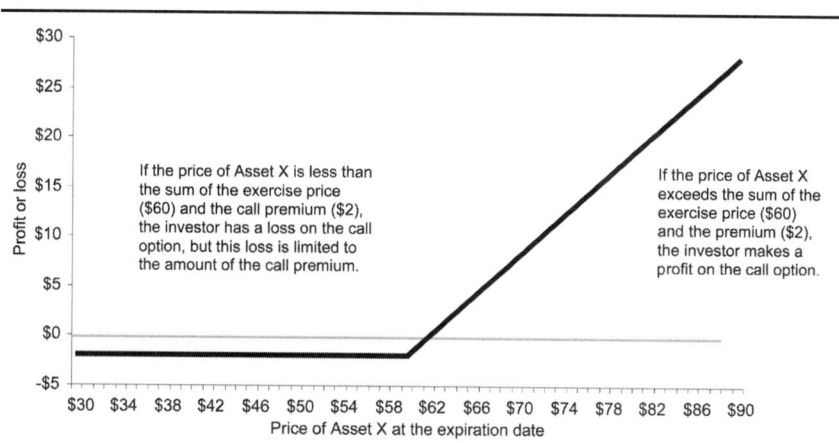

Writing (Selling) Call Options

The writer of a call option is said to be in a *short call position*. To illustrate the option seller's (writer's) position, we use the same call option we used to illustrate buying a call option. The profit and loss profile of the short call position (that is, the position of the call option writer) is the mirror image of the profit and loss profile of the long call position (the position of the call option buyer). That is, the profit of the short call position for any given price for Asset X at the expiration date is the same as the loss of the long call position. Consequently, the maximum profit that the short call position can produce is the option price. The maximum loss is not limited because it is the highest price reached by Asset X on or before the expiration date, less the option price; this price can be indefinitely high. Exhibit 4.3 shows the profit/loss profile for a short call position.

Buying Put Options

The buying of a put option creates a financial position referred to as a *long put position*. To illustrate this position, we assume a hypothetical put option on one unit of Asset X with one month to maturity and an exercise price of $100. Assume the put option is selling for $3 and the price of Asset X at the expiration date is $60. The profit or loss for this position at the expiration date depends on the market price of Asset X. The possible outcomes are:

EXHIBIT 4.3 Profits and Losses on the Writing of a Call Option that Allows the Call Option Buyer to Buy the Stock at $60. The Call Writer Receives $2 for this Option.

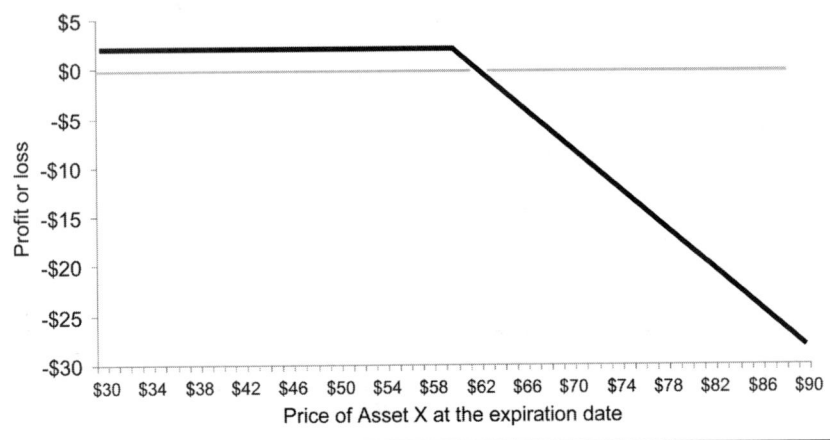

1. If Asset X's price is greater than $60, the buyer of the put option will not exercise it because exercising would mean selling Asset X to the writer for a price that is less than the market price. A loss of $3 (the option price) will result in this case from buying the put option. Once again, the option price represents the maximum loss to which the buyer of the put option is exposed.
2. If the price of Asset X at expiration is equal to $60, the put will not be exercised, leaving the put buyer with a loss equal to the option price of $3.
3. Any price for Asset X that is less than $60 but greater than $57 will result in a loss; exercising the put option, however, limits the loss to less than the option price of $1. For example, suppose that the price is $59 at the expiration date. By exercising the option, the option buyer will realize a loss of $2. This is because the buyer of the put option can sell Asset X, purchased in the market for $59, to the writer for $60, realizing a gain of $1. Deducting the $3 cost of the option results in a loss of $2.
4. At a $57 price for Asset X at the expiration date, the put buyer will break even. The investor will realize a gain of $3 by selling Asset X to the writer of the option for $60, offsetting the cost of the option ($3).
5. If Asset X's price is below $57 at the expiration date, the long put position (the put buyer) will realize a profit. For example, suppose the price falls at expiration to $46. The long put position will produce a profit of $11: a gain of $14 for exercising the put option less the $3 option price.

EXHIBIT 4.4   Profits and Losses on the Exercise of a Put Option to Sell the Stock at $60. The Investor Pays $2 for this Put Option.

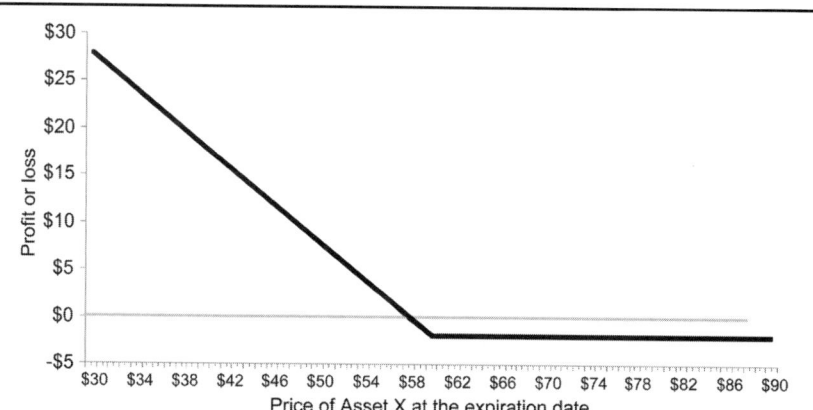

The profit and loss profile for the long put position is shown in graphical form in Exhibit 4.4. As with all long option positions, the loss is limited to the option price. The profit potential, however, is substantial: The theoretical maximum profit is generated if Asset X's price falls to zero. Contrast this profit potential with that of the buyer of a call option. The theoretical maximum profit for a call buyer cannot be determined beforehand because it depends on the highest price that can be reached by Asset X before or at the option expiration date.

Writing (Selling) Put Options

Writing a put option creates a position referred to as a *short put position*. The profit and loss profile for a short put option is the mirror image of the long put option. The maximum profit from this position is the option price. The theoretical maximum loss can be substantial should the price of the underlying fall; at the extreme, if the price were to fall all the way to zero, the loss would be as large as the exercise price less the option price. Exhibit 4.5 graphically depicts this profit and loss profile.

To summarize, buying calls or selling puts allows the investor to gain if the price of the underlying rises. Selling calls and buying puts allows the investor to gain if the price of the underlying falls.

Basic Components of the Option Price

The option price is a reflection of the option's *intrinsic value* and any additional amount over its intrinsic value. The premium over intrinsic value is often referred to as the *time premium*.

EXHIBIT 4.5   Profits and Losses on the Writing of a Put Option that Allows the Put Option Buyer to Sell the Stock at $60. The Put Writer Receives $2 for this Option.

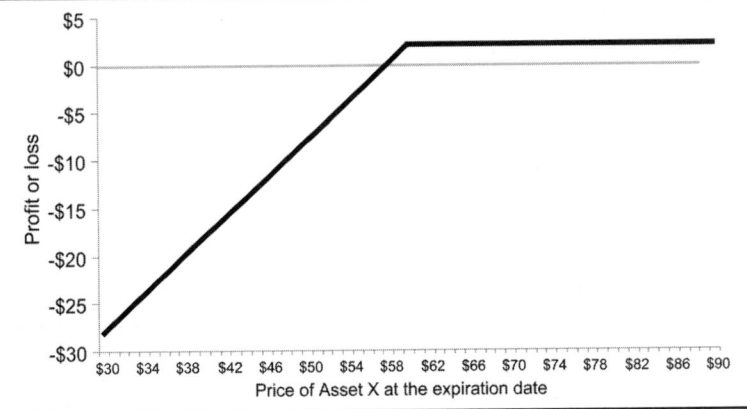

Intrinsic Value of an Option

The *intrinsic value* of an option is the economic value of the option if it is exercised immediately, except that if there is no positive economic value that will result from exercising it immediately, then the intrinsic value is zero.

The intrinsic value of a call option is the difference between the current price of the underlying and the exercise price if positive; it is otherwise zero. For example, if the exercise price for a call option is $60 and the current asset price is $67, the intrinsic value is $7. That is, an option buyer exercising the option and simultaneously selling the underlying asset would realize $67 from the sale of the underlying, which would be covered by acquiring the underlying from the option writer for $60, thereby netting a $7 gain.

When an option has intrinsic value, it is said to be "in the money." When the exercise price of a call option exceeds the current price of the underlying, the call option is said to be "out of the money"—it has no intrinsic value. An option for which the exercise price is equal to the current price of the underlying is said to be "at the money." Both at-the-money and out-of-the-money options have an intrinsic value of zero because it is not profitable to exercise the option. Our call option with an exercise price of $60 would be: (1) in the money when the current price of the underlying is greater than $60, (2) out of the money when the current price of the underlying is less than $60, and (3) at the money when the current underlying price is equal to $60.

For a put option, the intrinsic value is equal to the amount by which the current price of the underlying is below the exercise price. For example, if the exercise price of a put option is $60 and the current price of the underlying is $52, the intrinsic value is $8. That is, the buyer of the put option who exercises the put option and simultaneously sells the underlying will net $8 by exercising. The asset will be sold to the writer for $60 and purchased in the market for $52. For our put option with an exercise price of $60, the option would be: (1) in the money when the price of the underlying is less than $60, (2) out of the money when the current price of the underlying exceeds the exercise price, (3) at the money when the exercise price is equal to the underlying's price.

Time Premium of an Option

The time premium of an option is the amount by which the option price exceeds its intrinsic value. The option buyer hopes that, at some time prior to expiration, changes in the market price of the underlying will increase the value of the rights conveyed by the option. For this prospect, the option buyer is willing to pay a premium above the intrinsic value. For example, if the price of a call option with an exercise price of $60 is $9 when the current price of the underlying is $65, the time premium of this option is $4 ($9 minus its intrinsic value of $5). Had the current price of the underlying been $50 instead of $65, then the time premium of this option would be the entire $9 because the option has no intrinsic value.

There are two ways in which an option buyer may realize the value of a position taken in the option. First is to exercise the option. The second is by selling the call option for $9. Selling the call is preferable because the exercise of an option will realize a gain of only $5—it will cause the immediate loss of any time premium. There are circumstances under which an option may be exercised prior to the expiration date; they depend on whether the total proceeds at the expiration date would be greater by holding the option or exercising and reinvesting any cash proceeds received until the expiration date.

How Options are Used for Managing Risk

We can use our illustration of the producer of crude oil and the user of crude oil to explain how buying options can be used. Suppose that there are options on crude oil. Management of the producer of crude oil wants to set a minimum price it will have to pay for crude oil two months from now. It does so by buying a put option on crude oil. The exercise price for the put option is the price that management can sell crude oil. Suppose the exercise price for a put option on crude oil that expires in two months is $19. Then if two months from now crude oil falls below $19, say to $17, then management will exercise the put option and sell the crude oil to the writer of the put option for $19. What is the effective minimum price that management will be selling crude oil? It is not the exercise price of $19. Rather, that price must be reduced by the cost of the put option (i.e., option price).

To appreciate the difference between a futures contract and an option, consider the scenario wherein two months from now the price of crude oil is $20 per barrel. In that case, management will not exercise the put option. Instead, it can sell the crude oil for $20 per barrel in the market to benefit from the higher price. The effective price it sold the crude oil for is $20 less the option price. So, with a put option management has set a minimum price for how much it will sell crude oil two months from now (exercise price less the option price) but has maintained the opportunity to benefit from a price that is higher than the exercise price. In contrast, with a futures contract on crude oil that has a futures price of $19 per barrel, management has fixed a price and cannot benefit from a higher price for crude oil two months from now.

Now let's consider the user of crude oil. Management wants to set a maximum price for crude oil two months from now. It can do so by buying a call option. For example, suppose that the exercise price for a call option that expires in two months is $19 per barrel. Then if the price of crude oil two months from now is higher than $19 per barrel, management will exercise the call option and buy crude oil for $19 per barrel. The effective maximum price it will buy crude oil for is the exercise price plus the price of the call option.

Again, let's see the difference between buying a call option and buying a futures contract. If the price of crude oil two months from now is $17 per barrel (a price that is less than the exercise price), management will not exercise the call option and, instead, buy crude oil in the market for $17. The effective purchase price is equal to $17 plus the option price. In contrast, with a futures contract to buy crude oil, management has locked in a futures price of $19 per barrel and has given up the opportunity to buy crude oil at a lower price.

SWAPS

A *swap* is an agreement whereby two parties (called counterparties) agree to exchange periodic payments. The dollar amount of the payments exchanged is based on some predetermined dollar principal, which is called the **notional principal amount** or simply **notional amount**. The dollar amount each counterparty pays to the other is the agreed-upon periodic rate times the notional amount. The only dollars that are exchanged between the parties are the agreed-upon payments, not the notional amount.

A swap is an over-the-counter contract. Hence, the counterparties to a swap are exposed to counterparty risk.

The three types of swaps typically used by non-finance corporations are interest rate swaps, currency swaps, and commodity swaps. We illustrate these types of swaps below.

Interest Rate Swap

In an *interest rate swap*, the counterparties swap payments in the same currency based on an interest rate. For example, one of the counterparties can pay a fixed interest rate and the other party a floating interest rate. The floating interest rate is commonly referred to as the *reference rate*.

For example, suppose the counterparties to a swap agreement are Farm Equip Corporation (a manufacturing firm) and PNC Bank. The notional amount of this swap is $100 million and the term of the swap is five years. Every year for the next five years, Farm Equip Corporation. agrees to pay PNC Bank 9% per year, while PNC Bank agrees to pay Farm Equip Corporation the one-year London interbank offered rate (LIBOR). LIBOR is the reference rate. This means that every year, Farm Equip Corporation will pay $9 million (9% times $100 million) to PNC Bank. The amount PNC Bank will pay Farm Equip Corporation depends on LIBOR. For example, one-year LIBOR is 6%, PNC Bank will pay Farm Equip Corporation $6 million (6% times $100 million).

It is too early in this book to appreciate the motivation for the treasurer of Farm Equipment Corporation to use an interest rate swap. The motivation will be seen when we discuss financing techniques.

Currency Swaps

In a *currency swap*, two parties agree to swap payments based on different currencies. To illustrate a currency swap, suppose two counterparties are the High Quality Electronics Corporation (a U.S. manufacturing firm) and Citibank. The notional amount is $100 million and its Swiss franc (SF) equivalent at the time the contract was entered into is SF 127 million. The swap term is eight years. Every year for the next eight years the U.S. manufacturing firm agrees to pay Citibank Swiss francs equal to 5% of the Swiss franc notional amount, or SF 6.35 million. In turn, Citibank agrees to pay High Quality Electronics 7% of the U.S. notional principal amount of $100 million, or $7 million.

Again, the motivation for the management of High Quality Electronics Corporation for using a currency swap is difficult to appreciate because we have not covered how a firm finances itself. Currency swaps are used by corporations to raise funds outside of their home currency and then swap the payments into their home currency. This allows a corporation to eliminate currency risk (i.e., unfavorable exchange rate or currency movements) when borrowing outside of its domestic currency.

Commodity Swaps

In a commodity swap, the exchange of payments by the counterparties is based on the value of a particular physical commodity. Physical commodities include precious metals, base metals, energy stores (such as natural gas or crude oil), and food (including pork bellies, wheat, and cattle). Most commodity swaps involve oil.

For example, suppose that the two counterparties to this swap agreement are Comfort Airlines Company, a commercial airline, and Prebon Energy (an energy broker). The notional amount of the contract is 1 million barrels of crude oil each year and the contract is for three years. The swap price is $19 per barrel. Each year for the next three years, Comfort Airlines Company agrees to buy 1 million barrels of crude oil for $19 per barrel. So, each year Comfort Airlines Company pays $19 million to Prebon Energy ($19 per barrel times 1 million barrels) and receives 1 million barrels of crude oil.

The motivation for Comfort Airlines of using the commodity swap is that it allows the company to lock-in a price for 1 million barrels of crude oil at $19 per barrel regardless of how high crude oil's price increases over the next three years.

Interpretation of a Swap

If we look carefully at a swap, we can see that it is not a new derivative instrument. Rather, it can be decomposed into a package of derivative instruments that we have already discussed. To see this, consider our first illustrative swap.

Every year for the next five years Farm Equip Corporation agrees to pay PNC Bank 9%, PNC Bank agrees to pay Farm Equip Corporation the reference rate, one-year LIBOR. Since the notional amount is $100 million, Farm Equip Corporation Manufacturing agrees to pay $9 million. Alternatively, we can rephrase this agreement as follows: Every year for the next five years, PNC Bank agrees to deliver something (one-year LIBOR) and to accept payment of $9 million. Looked at in this way, the counterparties are entering into multiple forward contracts: One party is agreeing to deliver something at some time in the future, and the other party is agreeing to accept delivery. The reason we say that there are multiple forward contracts is that the agreement calls for making the exchange each year for the next five years.

While a swap may be nothing more than a package of forward contracts, it is not a redundant contract for several reasons. First, in many markets where there are forward and futures contracts, the longest maturity does not extend out as far as that of a typical swap. Second, a swap is a more transactionally efficient instrument. By this we mean that in one transaction an entity can effectively establish a payoff equivalent to a package of forward contracts. The forward contracts would each have to be negotiated separately. Third, the liquidity of certain types of swaps has grown since the inception of swaps in 1981; some swaps now are more liquid than many forward contracts, particularly long-dated (i.e., long-term) forward contracts.

CAP AND FLOOR AGREEMENTS

There are agreements available in the financial market whereby one party, for a fee (premium), agrees to compensate the other if a designated reference is different from a predetermined level. The party that will receive payment if the designated reference differs from a predetermined level and pays a premium to enter into the agreement is called the buyer. The party that agrees to make the payment if the designated reference differs from a predetermined level is called the seller.

When the seller agrees to pay the buyer if the designated reference exceeds a predetermined level, the agreement is referred to as a *cap*. The agreement is referred to as a *floor* when the seller agrees to pay the buyer if a designated reference falls below a predetermined level.

In a typical cap or floor, the designated reference is either an interest rate or commodity price. The predetermined level is called the *exercise value*. As with a swap, a cap and a floor have a notional amount. Only the buyer of a cap or a floor is exposed to counterparty risk.

In general, the payment made by the seller of the cap to the buyer on a specific date is determined by the relationship between the designated reference and the exercise value. If the former is greater than the latter, then the seller pays the buyer an amount delivered as follows:

Notional amount × [Actual value of designated reference – Exercise value]

If the designated reference is less than or equal to the exercise value, then the seller pays the buyer nothing.

For a floor, the payment made by the seller to the buyer on a specific date is determined as follows. If the designated reference is less than the exercise value, then the seller pays the buyer an amount delivered as follows:

Notional amount × [Exercise value – Actual value of designated reference]

If the designated reference is greater than or equal to the exercise value, then the seller pays the buyer nothing.

The following example illustrates how a cap works. Suppose that the FPK Bookbinders Company enters into a five-year cap agreement with Fleet Bank with a notional amount of $50 million. The terms of the cap specify that if one-year LIBOR exceeds 8% on December 31 each year for the next five years, Fleet Bank (the seller of the cap) will pay FPK Bookbinders Company the difference between 8% (the exercise value) and LIBOR (the designated reference). The fee or premium FPK Bookbinders Company agrees to pay Fleet Bank each year is $200,000.

The payment made by Fleet Bank to FPK Bookbinders Company on December 31 for the next five years based on LIBOR on that date will be as follows. If one-year LIBOR is greater than 8%, then Fleet Bank pays $50 million × [Actual value of LIBOR – 8%]. If LIBOR is less than or equal to 8%, then Fleet Bank pays nothing.

So, for example, if LIBOR on December 31 of the first year of the cap is 10%, Fleet Bank pays FPK Bookbinders Company $1 million as shown below:

$$\$50 \text{ million} \times [10\% - 8\%] = \$1 \text{ million}$$

Interpretation of a Cap and Floor

In a cap or floor, the buyer pays a fee which represents the maximum amount that the buyer can lose and the maximum amount that the seller of the agreement can gain. The only party that is required to perform is the seller. The buyer of a cap benefits if the designated reference rises above the exercise value because the seller must compensate the buyer. The exercise value can be a reference interest rate or an exchange rate, for example. The buyer of a floor benefits if the designated reference falls below the exercise value because the seller must compensate the buyer.

In essence the payoff of these contracts is the same as that of an option. A call option buyer pays a fee and benefits if the value of the option's underlying (or equivalently, designated reference) is higher than the exercise price at the expiration date. A cap has a similar payoff. A put option buyer pays a fee and benefits if the value of the option's underlying (or equivalently, designated reference) is less than the exercise price at the expiration date. A floor has a similar payoff. An option seller is only entitled to the option price. The seller of a cap or floor is only entitled to the fee.

Motivation for a Cap or Floor

We can easily see the use of a cap or a floor. In a cap that involves an interest rate, a corporation seeking funds can use a swap to set a maximum interest rate for its borrowing cost. In a cap that involves the price of a commodity, the cap sets a maximum price for the commodity and is therefore used by a manufacturer to eliminate the price risk associated with buying that commodity. In a floor that involves a commodity, a manufacturer can use such a contract to protect against a decline in a product it sells.

SUMMARY

- The traditional purpose of derivative instruments is to provide an important opportunity to manage against the risk of adverse future price, exchange rate, or interest rate movements.
- Futures contracts are creations of exchanges, which require initial margin from parties. Each day positions are marked to market. Additional (variation) margin is required if the equity in the position falls below the maintenance margin. The clearinghouse guarantees that the parties to the futures contract will satisfy their obligations.
- A forward contract differs in several important ways from a futures contract. In contrast to a futures contract, the parties to a forward contract are exposed to the risk that the other party to the contract will fail to perform. The positions of the parties are not necessarily marked to market, so there are no interim cash flows associated with a forward contract. Finally, unwinding a position in a forward contract may be difficult.
- A buyer (seller) of a futures contract realizes a profit if the futures price increases (decreases). The buyer (seller) of a futures contract realizes a loss if the futures price decreases (increases).
- An option grants the buyer of the option the right either to buy from (in the case of a call option) or to sell to (in the case of a put option) the seller (writer) of the option the underlying at a stated price called the exercise (strike) price by a stated date called the expiration date.
- The price that the option buyer pays to the writer of the option is called the option price or option premium.
- An American option allows the option buyer to exercise the option at any time up to and including the expiration date; a European option may be exercised only at the expiration date.
- The buyer of an option cannot realize a loss greater than the option price, and has all the upside potential. By contrast, the maximum gain

that the writer (seller) of an option can realize is the option price; the writer is exposed to all the downside risk.

■ The option price consists of two components: the intrinsic value and the time premium. The intrinsic value is the economic value of the option if it is exercised immediately (except that if there is no positive economic value that will result from exercising immediately, then the intrinsic value is zero). The time premium is the amount by which the option price exceeds the intrinsic value.

■ In a swap, the counterparties agree to exchange periodic payments. The dollar amount of the payments exchanged is based on the notional principal amount.

■ Swaps typically used by non-finance companies are interest rate swaps, currency swaps, and commodity swaps.

■ A swap has the risk/return profile of a package of forward contracts.

■ A cap is an agreement whereby the seller agrees to pay the buyer when a designated reference exceeds a predetermined level (the exercise value). A floor is an agreement whereby the seller agrees to pay the buyer when a designated reference is less than a predetermined level (the exercise value). The designated reference could be a specific interest rate or a commodity price.

■ A cap is equivalent to a package of call options; a floor is equivalent to a package of put options.

QUESTIONS

1. The following appears in the 2000 10-K of International Business Machines:

   "The company employs a number of strategies to manage these risks, including the use of derivative financial instruments. Derivatives involve the risk of non-performance by the counterparty."

   Explain what is meant in the last sentence of this quotation.

2. A manufacturer of furniture is concerned that the price of lumber will increase over the next three months. Explain how the manufacturer can protect against a rise in the price of lumber using lumber futures contracts.

3. The treasurer of a corporation wants to use futures contracts to protect against a decline in the price of one of the products it sells. Explain why the treasurer must be prepared to put up cash when using a futures contract.

4. The chief financial officer of the corporation you work for recently told you that he had a strong preference to use forward contracts rather than futures contracts to hedge: "You can get contracts tailor-made to suit your needs." Comment on the CFO's statement. What other factors influence the decision to use futures or forward contracts?

5. In discussing hedging instruments, you overhead the following statement: "Unlike a futures contract, a forward contract is not marked to market."
   a. Explain what is meant by "marked to market."
   b. Explain whether you agree or disagree with the above statement.

6. What is the difference between a put option and a call option?

7. What is the difference between an American option and a European option?

8. Why does an option writer need to post margin?

9. Identify two important ways in which an exchange-traded option differs from an over-the-counter option.

10. "There's no real difference between options and futures. Both are hedging tools, and both are derivative products. It's just that with options you have to pay an option price, while futures require no upfront payment except for a 'good faith' margin. I can't understand why anyone would use options." Do you agree with this statement?

11. a. What option strategy (position) can a treasurer take to protect against a rise in the cost of one of its inputs in the production process assuming that there is an option available?
    b. What option strategy (position) can a treasurer take to protect against a decline in the selling price of one of its products assuming that there is an option available?

12. How does the price of an option and the exercise price affect the minimum price that the underlying can be sold for or the maximum price that the underlying can be purchased for?

13. Suppose an investor bought both a call option and a put option on an asset. Both options have an exercise price of $50 and both options have an option premium of $5.
    a. Draw the profit-loss diagram for each option considered individually.
    b. Draw the profit-loss diagram for the strategy that involves buying both options.
    c. What is an investor with this combination of options hoping will happen to the price of the underlying asset?

14. a. Suppose that the price of the underlying is $40 and that the option price is $5. If the exercise price for a put option is $50, what is the intrinsic value and the time premium for this option?

b. Suppose that the price of the underlying is $40 and that the option price is $5. If the exercise price for a call option is $50, what is the intrinsic value and the time premium for this option?

15. Burlingame Bank and the ABC Manufacturing Corp. enter into the following 7-year swap with a notional amount of $75 million and the following terms: Every year for the next seven years, Burlingame Bank agrees to pay ABC Manufacturing 7% per year and receive from ABC Manufacturing LIBOR.

    a. What type of swap is this?

    b. In the first year payments are to be exchanged, suppose that LIBOR is 4%. What is the amount of the payment that the two parties must make to each other?

16. Explain why a swap is similar to a package of forward contracts.

17. Why would a corporate treasurer want to use a commodity swap to manage the price risk of a product it purchases?

18. What is the relationship between a cap and an option?

CHAPTER 5

Taxation

In assessing a company's current and future cash flows, the financial analyst requires information concerning a company's tax obligations. Unfortunately, the company's tax return is not publicly available, requiring the analyst to understand the basics of corporate taxation and to work with information disclosed in the financial statements.

The tax laws are changed almost constantly and are likely being changed as you read this chapter. Hence, no purpose would be served by covering all the details of present tax laws; they might be outdated as soon as you learn them. Instead, we discuss some of the principles behind the tax laws and in doing so provide an opportunity for you to learn some terminology, do some basic taxation calculations, and see how taxes affect a company's cash flows. We use the rates in the 2001 tax laws for demonstration purposes.

Following are the main kinds of taxes:

- *Income taxes* are taxes specifically levied on the basis of income.
- *Employment taxes* are also based on income, but specifically on wage and salary income. In the United States, employment taxes are paid by the employee and the employer, and they are designated specifically for social insurance programs (i.e., retirement and unemployment).
- *Excise taxes* are taxes on certain commodities, such as alcoholic beverages, tobacco products, telephone service, and gasoline. Excise taxes provide an easy way of raising revenue, and they can be imposed to discourage the use of specific products, such as tobacco.
- *Import and export taxes* (or tariffs) are taxes based on trade with other countries and are imposed to achieve specific economic goals in world trade.

In this chapter, we focus on income taxes and, specifically, U.S. federal corporate income taxes. However, any of the other types of taxes may have a strong influence on the cash flows of industries or firms. For example, excise taxes and import and export taxes will influence the demand for a firm's products and therefore the firm's cash flows.

THE U.S. TAX LAW

In the United States, the federal tax law is the product of all three branches of federal government. Congress passes the tax legislation that comprises the *Internal Revenue Code* (IRC). The *Internal Revenue Service* (IRS), a part of the Treasury Department, interprets these laws, adds the details, and implements them. The IRS does this by providing and processing tax forms, collecting tax payments, explaining the law in its regulations, and even providing decisions regarding the law (called rulings) in some situations. The courts are also called on to interpret the law through specific court cases, and there is now a well-developed case law related to the IRC. Together the Internal Revenue Code, IRS regulations, IRS rulings, and the case law make up federal tax law.

In forecasting future cash flows, the financial analyst needs to be aware that tax rates change frequently. The financial analyst cannot simply assume that the tax rate in existence today will be the same in five or ten years. Moreover, in comparing the after-tax performance of a firm over time, changes in tax rates must be considered.

U.S. FEDERAL TAX RATES

Exhibit 5.1 shows the 2001 U.S. federal income tax rate schedules for corporations. We can look at the schedule for a corporation to see how the income tax is computed. Each line of the schedule represents a layer of taxable income, sometimes called a "tax bracket"; the lower limit of each bracket is called its base. So the first line, for example, represents the taxable income layer with base $0 and maximum taxable income of $50,000.

Each line of the schedule also tells us the dollar amount of the tax on the base and the rate at which income above the base is taxed in that bracket. Suppose a corporation has taxable income of $12 million. Using the tax rate schedule, we see that the tax is 15% on the first $50,000, 25% on the next $25,000, 34% on the next $25,000, 39% on the next $235,000, 34% on the next $9,665,000, and 35% on the last $2,000,000, or:

EXHIBIT 5.1   Federal Income Tax Rate Schedule for Corporations, 2001

If taxable income is:

over ...	but not over ...	tax is ...	of the amount over ...
$0	$50,000	15%	$0
50,000	75,000	$7,500 + 25%	50,000
75,000	100,000	13,750 + 34%	75,000
100,000	335,000	22,250 + 39%	100,000
335,000	10,000,000	113,900 + 34%	335,000
10,000,000	15,000,000	3,400,000 + 35%	10,000,000
15,000,000	18,333,333	5,150,000 + 38%	15,000,000
18,333,333	—	35%	0

$$\text{Tax on } \$12,000,000 = \$3,400,000 + 0.35(\$12,000,000 - 10,000,000)$$
$$= \$3,400,000 + 700,000 = \$4,100,000$$

The *marginal tax rate* is the rate at which the next dollar of income would be taxes. It is the rate that defines the tax bracket. For a corporation with income falling between $50,000 and $75,000, the marginal tax rate in 2001 is 25%; for a corporation with income between $10 million and $15 million, the marginal tax rate is 35%.

The *average tax rate* is the ratio of the tax paid on the taxable income. So, for example, the corporation with $12 million in taxable income paid an average tax rate of:

$$\text{Average tax rate on } \$12,000,000 = \frac{\$4,100,000}{\$12,000,000} = 0.3417 \text{ or } 34.17\%$$

Note that this average tax rate is lower than the marginal tax rate, 35%. This is true for all progressive taxes, such as the U.S. federal income tax. A *progressive tax* is one that levies a higher average tax rate on higher incomes.

The marginal and average tax rates for a range of 2001 taxable corporate incomes are graphed in Exhibit 5.2. It is apparent from this diagram that as corporate incomes increase, the average rate approaches the marginal rate of tax. It is also apparent that the corporate income tax is progressive. Note, however, that the corporate tax rate schedule in 2001 has a "bubble" of 39% in the $100,000 to $335,000 bracket, where the rate is lower in the next higher tax bracket. These bubbles appear occasionally in the tax rate schedules mainly to increase revenues, and many times they disappear from the schedules after a year or two. They usually do not change the progressive nature of the tax.

It is important to realize that taxable income is taxed at the appropriate *marginal* rate for each bracket, and not at the average rate. Therefore, when a company's investment or financing decision is likely to affect taxable income—and hence cash flow—it will do so through the *marginal* income tax rate.

Corporate Taxable Income

There are many areas in which companies are permitted to use different methods of accounting for financial statements and tax purposes. These differences may arise from mandated methods of accounting for tax purposes (e.g., depreciation) or from the deductibility of certain expenses for the determination of income for one but not the other (e.g., goodwill). The result of these differences is a timing difference between reported tax expense and actual tax expense. If the reported tax expense exceeds the actual tax expense, the difference is a deferred tax liability and if the reported tax expense is less than the actual tax expense, the difference is a deferred tax asset. The deferred tax asset or liability therefore reflects a temporary difference between expense and revenue recognition for an accounting period.

EXHIBIT 5.2 Marginal and Average Tax Rates from the 2001 Corporate Tax Rate Schedule

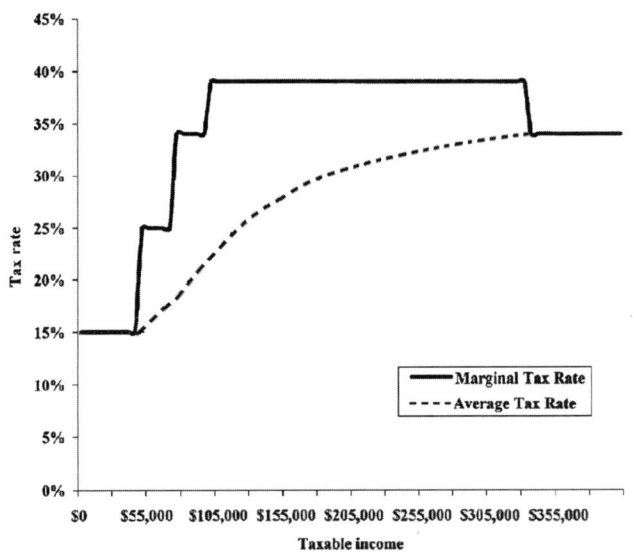

There are many potential sources of differences between income per accounting statements and taxable income and, as we will see in Chapter 6, these differences can be useful in analyzing a company's financial situation. Examples of temporary sources of differences between accounting income and taxable income include the methods of recognition method for accruals and reserves, depreciation deductions, and tax loss carry-overs. The sources of the deferred tax liability or asset are summarized in the company's income tax note to the financial statements.

Recognizing that some temporary differences persist over time, Statement of Financial Accounting Standard No. 109 requires that deferred taxes be adjusted for the expected permanent difference in tax liability per financial statements and tax books; this adjustment is referred to as a *valuation allowance*. The result of including the valuation allowance is a deferred tax liability or asset that better reflects temporary differences between accounting and tax books.

In addition to these temporary differences, there are permanent differences between financial and tax income. For example, dividends received from other corporations are included fully in the financial income, but are permitted to be deducted in whole or part for tax purposes, which result in a permanent difference between taxable income and accounting income. Permanent differences such as this do not affect the deferred tax accounts.

The basic calculation of a corporation's taxable income is shown in Exhibit 5.3. To better understand how different features of the tax law affect a firm's taxes and, hence, its cash flows, we take a closer look at the dividends-received deduction, depreciation for tax purposes, and capital gains taxation.

The Dividends-Received Deduction

We have seen that corporate income distributed to shareholders (in the form of dividends) is taxed twice—first as corporate income and then as shareholders' income—and then if the shareholder is another corporation, that income could be taxed a third time. To minimize the chance of triple (or even quadruple) taxation of the same income, the tax laws permit a *dividends-received deduction*: A corporate recipient of dividends may deduct a portion of its dividend income from its taxable income.

With respect to dividend income received by corporations, the 1997 tax law, for example, specifies deductions of either 100%, 80%, or 70%, as follows:

■ Deduction of 100% of dividends received may be deducted if the corporation is (1) a small business investment company operated under the Small Business Investment Act or (2) a member of an affiliated group of corporations, as in the case of a parent corporation and its wholly owned subsidiaries.

- Deduction of 80% if the dividends are received from a 20% or more owned corporation.
- Deduction of 70% if none of the conditions above applies.

Fox example, suppose the Inc. Corporation has operating income of $2 million. Further suppose that it received $1 million in dividends and $500,000 in interest, and it paid $800,000 dividends and $600,000 interest. If the dividends received deduction is 70%, Inc's taxable income is:

Operating income	$2,000,000
Plus: Included dividend income (30% of $1,000,000)	300,000
Plus: Interest income	500,000
Less: Interest expense	(600,000)
Taxable income	$2,200,000

EXHIBIT 5.3 Corporate Taxable Income

Gross receipts
− Cost of goods sold
Gross profit
+ Dividend income
+ Interest income
+ Gross rents
+ Gross royalties
+ Capital gain income
+ Other income
Total income
− Salaries and wages
− Repairs and maintenance
− Bad debt expense
− Rents
− Taxes and licenses
− Interest
− Charitable contributions
− Depreciation
− Depletion
− Advertising
− Pension, profit-sharing plans
− Employee benefit programs
− Other deductions
Total deductions

Taxable income

The remaining $700,000 in dividends received are not taxed—these dividends are excluded from income. The $800,000 dividends paid do not affect taxable income.

The dividends-received deduction either eliminates the tax on dividend income or reduces the effective tax rate considerably. Suppose a corporation has a marginal tax rate of 34% and the dividends it receives qualify for the 80% deduction. Then the effective tax rate on that dividend income is 20% of 34%, or 6.8%.

The dividends-received deduction increases the after-tax return of a corporation *investing* in another corporation's stock. Since corporate investors get a tax break on dividend income, they require a lower return on these securities, thus lowering the cost of capital for the corporation that *issues* these securities. The recent trend in tax law is to reduce the dividends-received deduction, increasing the multiple taxation effect and increasing the cost of capital to issuers of these securities.

While a corporation's dividend income receives special treatment, its interest income does not: Interest received by a corporation is taxed like any other income. Dividends and interest *paid* by a corporation receive different treatment as well: Interest paid by a corporation is fully deductible when computing taxable income, whereas dividends paid are not deductible. The taxation of dividend and interest received and paid enters into financial decision-making since it affects the cost of capital.

Depreciation for Tax Purposes

For accounting purposes, a firm can select a method of depreciation based on a number of factors, including the expected rate of physical depreciation of its asset and the effect on reported income. For federal income tax purposes, however, businesses are limited by law with regard to both the depreciation method and the period of time over which an asset can be depreciated.

The current depreciation tax laws are the result of an ongoing trend to create more uniformity in depreciation methods among business taxpayers while at the same time simplifying the calculations and allowing accelerated depreciation and shorter asset lives.

Currently, the two methods of depreciation available to business taxpayers are an accelerated method and straight-line. The accelerated method, referred to as the *modified accelerated cost recovery system* (MACRS), has four features:

1. The depreciation rate used each year is either 150% or 200% of the straight-line rate (referred to as 150 declining balance (DB) and 200 DB, respectively), depending on the type of property, applied against the undepreciated cost of the asset. Since the rate is applied against a

declining amount, this method is a declining balance method, but not the same declining balance method as that used for financial statement reporting purposes.

2. The salvage value of the asset is ignored; so the depreciable cost is the original cost and the asset's value is depreciated to zero.

3. The *half-year convention* is used on most property, that is, a half-year of depreciation is taken in the year the asset is acquired, no matter whether it is owned for one day or 365 days.

4. The depreciation method is switched to the straight-line method when straight-line depreciation produces a higher depreciation expense than the accelerated method.

Because the MACRS is an accelerated method, it yields greater depreciation expenses in earlier years and thus reduces taxable income and taxes relative to straight-line depreciation. However, the law allows some firms to use straight-line depreciation if they don't have the income necessary to take advantage of the faster depreciation of the MACRS. The use of MACRS for tax purposes and straight-line for financial reporting purposes, which is often the case for U.S. corporations, results in a difference in income for tax and financial accounting. This difference gives rise to deferred tax liabilities because actual taxes (calculated using MACRS depreciation) are less than reported taxes (calculated using straight-line depreciation) when MACRS results in a greater amount of depreciation, as in the earlier years of an asset's life.[1]

Congress (and the IRS) have taken much of the work out of calculating depreciation expenses for tax purposes.[2] Exhibit 5.4 outlines the depreciable life for each class of assets and the depreciation rates used for assets of each classified life. First, as panel *a* shows, depreciable lives are assigned to the various classes of assets that might be used by businesses. Second, tables are provided showing the depreciation rates to be applied to the asset's cost for each year in the life of each class of asset (panel *b* of Exhibit 5.4.)

Notice in panel *b* that each asset type is depreciated over its life plus one year: There are four years of depreciation for a 3-year asset, six years of depreciation for a 5-year asset, and so on. This is because of the half-year convention: Only half a year's depreciation is used up at the start, leaving half a year's depreciation to be taken after the asset's "life" is over for tax purposes.

---

[1] In Exhibit 5.4, for example, we see that most of the deferred tax liabilities arise from the depreciation of property, plant, and equipment.

[2] There are occasional changes to this system. For example, for a limited period of time (2001 through 2005), businesses are entitled to an additional 30% depreciation in the asset's first year for qualifying assets (Job Creation and Worker Assistance Act of 2002).

EXHIBIT 5.4 Modified Accelerated Cost Recovery System (MACRS)
Panel a. Classified Lives

3-year:	Tractor units, racehorses over two years old, special tools
5-year:	Cars, light and heavy trucks, computer and peripheral equipment, semi-conductor manufacturing equipment
7-year:	Office furniture and fixtures, railroad property
10-year:	Means of water transportation, fruit trees, nut trees
15-year:	Municipal wastewater plants, depreciable land improvements, pipelines, service station buildings
20-year:	Farm buildings, municipal sewers
27.5-year:	Residential rental property
31.5-year:	Non-residential real property, such as elevators and escalators
50-year:	Railroad grading and tunnel bores

Panel b. Depreciation Rates for 3-Year, 5-Year, 7-Year, 10-Year, 15-Year, and 20-Year Classified Assets

	Depreciation Rate (%)					
Year	3-Year	5-Year	7-Year	10-Year	15-Year	20-Year
1	33.33	20.00	14.29	10.00	5.00	3.750
2	44.45	32.00	24.49	18.00	9.50	7.219
3	14.81	19.20	17.49	14.40	8.55	6.677
4	7.41	11.52	12.49	11.52	7.70	6.177
5		11.521	8.93	9.22	6.93	5.713
6		5.76	8.92	7.37	6.23	5.285
7			8.93	6.55	5.90	4.888
8			4.46	6.55	5.90	4.522
9				6.56	5.91	4.462
10				6.55	5.90	4.461
11				3.28	5.91	4.462
12					5.90	4.461
13					5.91	4.462
14					5.90	4.461
15					5.91	4.462
16					2.95	4.461
17						4.462
18						4.461
19						4.462
20						4.461
21						2.231

These rates reflect depreciation calculated using the 200% (for 3-year, 5-year, 7-year, and 10-year property) or 150% (for 15-year and 20-year property) declining-balance method, with a switch to straight-line, using the half-year convention.

EXHIBIT 5.5   MACRS Depreciation of a $50,000 Truck, Using MACRS Rates

Year	Depreciation Rate	Depreciation Expense = Rate Times $50,000
2001	20.00%	$10,000
2002	32.00	16,000
2003	19.20	9,600
2004	11.52	5,760
2005	11.52	5,760
2006	5.76	2,880
Total	100%	$50,000

Let's see how depreciation expense is calculated using the information in Exhibit 5.5. Suppose a firm buys a truck for $50,000. According to panel *a* of the table, the truck has a 5-year class life. According to panel *b*, the first year's depreciation rate is 20%, the next year's is 32%, and so on. The results of applying these rates to the cost of the truck over six years are shown in Exhibit 5.5. The total cost is recouped over the six years, with most of the depreciation expense taken in the earlier years.

From the perspective of a financial analyst, understanding current and expected depreciation rates is important because depreciation, while not itself a cash flow, affects a corporation's taxes and hence its cash flows. If the corporation has a depreciation expense of $100 million and a 35% marginal tax rate, the benefit from the depreciation deduction for tax purposes is to reduce taxable income by $100 million and hence reduce taxes by 35% times $100 million, or $35 million. This reduction in taxes of $35 million is referred to as the *depreciation tax-shield*. Over the life of an asset, the total dollar amount of depreciation is the same regardless of the rate of depreciation. However, changes in depreciation rates affect the *timing* of the depreciation tax-shield and hence their value today.

Capital Gains

We tend to use the term "capital gain" loosely to mean an increase in the value of an asset. however, in tax law a *capital gain* is specifically a realized gain that results when an asset is sold for more than was paid for it. Because tax rates are progressive, taxing capital gains in one lump in one year at higher rates seems unfair, so Congress has traditionally granted special treatment—via lower effective tax rates—to capital gains.

Special treatment for capital gains has come in either of two ways: (1) an exclusion of a portion of the gain or (2) a cap on the tax rate applied to capital gains. A cap is a "ceiling" on the tax rate applied to capital gains and is lower than the tax rate applied to other income. In 2001, for example, the tax rate cap on capital gains was 35% for corporations.

Suppose that in 2001 the Taxit Corporation has ordinary taxable income (that is, taxable income not including capital gains) of $50,000 and a capital gain of $10,000. Taxit's tax bracket is 25%, which is below 2001's corporate capital gains rate of 35%. So Taxit's tax on its $60,000 of income is:

Tax on $60,000 = $7,500 + 0.25($60,000 – $50,000) = $10,000

Suppose instead that Taxit has ordinary income of $200,000 and a capital gain of $10,000. Taxit's tax is:

$$
\begin{array}{ccc}
\text{Tax} & = & \underbrace{\$22,250 + 0.39\,(\$200,000 - 100,000)}_{\text{tax on ordinary income}} + \underbrace{0.35\,(\$10,000)}_{\text{tax on capital gain income}} \\
& = & \$61,250 \qquad\qquad\qquad\qquad + \qquad 3,500 \\
& = & \$64,750
\end{array}
$$

The other way of giving special treatment to capital gains for tax purposes is the exclusion. A capital gains exclusion excludes a portion, say 60%, of the capital gain from taxation and taxes the remainder at the ordinary tax rate. Consider Taxit Corporation's income. If 60% of its capital gain is excluded, only 60% of the $10,000, or $6,000 is included in taxable income.

After a while, Congress caught on that for a depreciable asset, a part of the gain was really the result of "over-depreciating" it (for tax purposes) during its life; that is, depreciation expenses taken over the life of the asset (which reduced taxable income and taxes) do not represent the actual amount the asset depreciated in value. So, Congress inserted provisions in the tax laws that require breaking the gain into two parts:

1. The *recapture of depreciation,* the difference between (a) the lower of the original cost or the sales price and (b) the under-depreciated portion of the asset's cost for tax purposes.
2. The capital gain, which is the sales price less the original cost.

The recapture portion of the gain is taxed at ordinary rates, and the capital gain portion is given special treatment (so effectively, it is taxed at less than ordinary rates).

Suppose Reclaim Inc. bought a depreciable asset ten years ago for $100,000, and its book value (cost less accumulated depreciation) for tax purposes is now $30,000. This means that the firm has taken $70,000 of depreciation expense over the ten years and has reduced its taxable income by that amount. If it now sells this asset for $125,000, it has a capital gain of $25,000:

Sales price	$125,000
Cost	100,000
Capital gain	$25,000

But Reclaim has also recaptured its entire depreciation expense by selling the asset. The tax code requires that recaptured depreciation be added to ordinary income and, thus, taxed at the ordinary income tax rate. Reclaim would have to pay ordinary income tax on the recaptured $70,000 of depreciation and capital gains tax on $25,000.

Original cost	$100,000
Less book value	30,000
Recapture (taxed as ordinary income)	$70,000

If only part of the asset's depreciation is recaptured when it is sold, only the recaptured part is taxed, and there would be no capital gain. The recaptured portion is the difference between sales price and book value. For example, if Reclaim sold the asset for $75,000, instead of $125,000, it would have:

Sales price	$75,000
Less book value	30,000
Recapture (taxed as ordinary income)	$45,000

As you can see, taxes, depreciation, and capital gains are all mutually related. Furthermore, they all become considerations in investment decisions, which almost always deal in some way with the purchase and sale of assets, and in cash flow, which is directly affected by tax law.

TAX CREDITS

From time to time Congress allows business credits against calculated income tax. One such credit that has popped up now and then in the tax law is the *investment tax credit* (ITC). The ITC may or may not exist at the time you read this chapter.

A tax credit is a direct reduction of the computed income tax. Suppose, for example, that the tax code allows an ITC of 10%. If a company invests $100 million, say, in new machinery, it is entitled to a direct reduction in taxes based on the cost of the machinery: 10% of $100 million, or $10 million.

The ITC is not the only tax credit that Congress has offered businesses. At one time or another there have been energy tax credits, targeted job credits, alcohol fuel credits, disabled access credits, and more.

Tax Credit versus Tax Deduction

Deductions and credits both reduce taxes payable. A *deduction* reduces taxable income and thus indirectly reduces the taxes paid. A tax *credit* is subtracted from the taxes paid, and thus directly reduces taxes.

For example, suppose a corporation has $100 million in taxable income, without considering a potential deduction or credit, and for simplicity assume a flat tax rate of 40%. Let's look at the effect on the firm's taxes of a $10 million deduction compared to a $10 million tax credit:

	No Deduction, No Credit	Deduction, No Credit	Credit, No Deduction
Taxable income without deduction	$100	$100	$100
Deduction	0	10	0
Taxable income	$100	$90	$100
Tax rate	0.40	0.40	0.40
Tax before credit	$40	$36	$40
Credit	0	0	10
Tax	$40	$36	$30

The benefit from the deduction is $4, whereas the benefit from the credit is $10.

NET OPERATING LOSS CARRYBACKS AND CARRYOVERS

A *net operating loss* is an excess of business deductions over business gross income in a tax year. The Internal Revenue Code allows businesses to carry back a net operating loss to preceding years and to carry forward the loss to future years to reduce the taxes payable for those years. The current tax law, for example, permits net operating losses of corporations to be carried back three years from the year of the loss and carried over (forward through time) 15 years.

Here's how carrybacks and carryovers work. Suppose that in the year 2000, a corporation has a $100 million net operating loss. To simplify the calculations, let's also assume that the corporate tax rate is a flat 40% of income. Suppose further that the corporation paid taxes on income as follows in the three years prior to 2000:

Year	Taxable Income	Taxes Paid
1997	$10,000,000	$4,000,000
1998	50,000.000	20,000,000
1999	50,000,000	20,000,000

To use the 2000 loss, the corporation begins by carrying it back to the earliest year (1997 in this example), applying it to reduce that year's taxable income, and then recomputing the tax. Any loss that is left over is carried to the next year, and so on. The 2000 tax law allows a 3-year carryback, so the computation would look like this:

Year	Taxable Income	Amount of Loss Applied	Refigured Taxable Income	Refigured Taxes	Refund
1997	$10,000,000	$10,000,000	$0	$0	$4,000,000
1998	50,000,000	50,000,000	0	0	20,000,000
1999	50,000,000	40,000,000	10,000,000	4,000,000	16,000,000
		$100,000,000			$40,000,000

The corporation would then apply for a $40 million refund of 1997-to-1999 taxes on the basis of its 2000 loss.

What if the corporation's loss was larger than the sum of the previous three years' taxable incomes? Then the corporation could carryover any unused portion of the loss to future tax years, applying it to taxable income in the tax returns for those years. As an example, assume the corporation's loss was $200 million, instead of $100 million. The corporation would be able to apply $110 million of that to taxable income and then could carryover the remaining loss of $90 million. The corporation would apply as much as possible to its 2001 taxable income, carryover any remainder to 2002, and so on, until either the loss was exhausted or the time limit prescribed in the IRC—currently 15 years—was reached.

STATE AND LOCAL TAXES

In addition to the federal income tax, individuals and corporations may also be assessed state and local income taxes. State and local tax structures are, for the most part, dependent upon the federal tax system. With some exceptions and an occasional adjustment to taxable income, state and local taxes are levied as a percentage of the federal income.

EXHIBIT 5.6   KPMG International's Corporate Tax Rate Survey, January 2002

Country	Corporate Tax Rate January 1, 2001 (%)	Corporate Tax Rate January 1, 2002 (%)
Argentina	35	35
Australia	34	30
Brazil	34	34
Canada	42.1	38.6
Czech Republic	31	31
France	35.33	35.33
Germany	38.36	38.36
Italy	40.25	40.25
Japan	42	42
Switzerland	24.7	24.5
United Kingdom	30	30
United States	40	40

Source: http://www.tax.kpmg.net

State and local taxes can be significant, with rates ranging from 1% to 12%, depending on the locality in which the corporation conducts its business. For example, in fiscal year 2001, the Walt Disney Company paid federal taxes—with a top rate of 35%—and state taxes—with an effective rate of 7.5%—together an effective marginal tax rate of 42.5%.[3]

TAXATION OUTSIDE OF THE UNITED STATES

The basic corporate income tax imposed by central governments is a fixed percentage or an increasing percentage of the statutorily determined corporate income. Countries typically tax resident corporations on worldwide income regardless of whether the income is repatriated. Nonresident corporations, that is, corporations whose corporate seat and place of management are outside the country, are typically subject only to corporate taxes derived from within the country.

The rate varies significantly from country to country. The range of corporate tax rates is shown in Exhibit 5.6. These tax rates, which are

[3] *The Walt Disney Company 2001 Annual Report,* p. 69. Because state taxes are deductible for federal income tax purposes, the state tax rate reflects this benefit and, hence, is lower than the statutory state corporate tax rate.

from KPMG International's *Corporate Tax Rate Survey* for January 2002, are estimates of the corporate tax burden, considering both national and local tax rates. Several countries impose no tax or minimal tax rates. These countries are referred to as *tax havens*.

The basic tax rates shown in Exhibit 5.6 may be misleading for several reasons. These reasons are given in Chapter 26.

Consequently, when an analyst computes the average tax rate for a U.S. firm with significant operations overseas, this rate can vary greatly by the allocation of its activities throughout the world.

SUMMARY

- Tax rates change often and the financial analyst needs to consider the changing tax environment in making evaluation of a firm's future cash flows.
- The dividend income that a corporation receives from another corporation is effectively taxed at a lower rate than other income because of the dividends received deduction. Interest income of a corporation does not receive special treatment.
- Dividends paid by a corporation are not deductible in arriving at taxable income. Interest paid by a corporation is deductible for tax purposes.
- Depreciation for tax purposes is prescribed by the tax code. The method of depreciation for tax purposes may differ from the method used for financial statement accounting purposes.
- Special tax provisions for capital gains effectively reduce the tax paid on these gains. However, tax provisions regarding how much of a gain on a sale of an asset is given special treatment requires breaking out the gain into two components: recaptured depreciation (depreciation taken in the past but not really reflective of the asset's decline in value) and capital gain (the appreciation in the asset's value).
- Net operating loss carryovers effectively smooth out the taxes of a business in those cases where taxable income varies significantly from year to year.
- Tax rates vary by country and a comparison of basic tax rates among countries is complicated.

QUESTIONS

1. Distinguish between an average tax rate and a marginal tax rate. Under what circumstance are the two the same?

2. Using the tax rate schedule provided in Exhibit 5.1, what is the amount of tax, the marginal tax rate, and the average tax rate for a corporation with the following taxable income: a. $35,000 b. $120,000 c. $300,000 d. $1,000,000 e. $2,000,000

3. What is the role of the dividends-received deduction?

4. The PARENT Corporation received $3 million in dividends from the SUB Corporation. PARENT'S income is taxed at a flat rate of 40%. How much tax must PARENT Corporation pay on these dividends if the relationship between the two companies for purposes of the dividends-received deduction is:
   a. SUB and PARENT have no affiliation.
   b. SUB is 10%-owned by PARENT.
   c. SUB is wholly owned by PARENT.

5. DIV Corporation received $5 million in dividends and had $10 million in other taxable income. DIV's income is taxed at a flat rate of 30%.
   a. What is DIV's tax bill if there is no dividends-received deduction?
   b. What is DIV's tax bill if a 60% dividends-received deduction is allowed?
   c. What is DIV's tax bill if a 70% dividends-received deduction is allowed?
   d. What is DIV's tax bill if a 80% dividends-received deduction is allowed?

6. The NOL Company had a loss of $1 million for 2001. The firm had income and paid taxes in the four prior years of:

Year	Taxable Income	Taxes Paid (30% of Taxable Income)
1997	$2,000,000	$600,000
1998	500,000	150,000
1999	300,000	90,000
2000	100,000	30,000

Suppose the tax law allows losses to be carried back three years and forward 15 years.
   a. How much of a refund of prior taxes can NOL receive?
   b. How much of the loss, if any, can be carried forward to future years?

7. The Loser Corporation had a loss of $200,000 in 2000. The firm had income and paid taxes in the three prior years of:

Year	Taxable Income	Taxes Paid (40% of Taxable Income)
1997	$100,000	$40,000
1998	200,000	80,000
1999	100,000	40,000

Suppose the tax law allows losses to be carried back three years and forward 15 years.

a. How much of a refund of prior taxes can Loser receive?

b. How much of the loss, if any, can be carried forward to future years?

8. The Mayberry Company purchased equipment for $100,000. Assume that this equipment qualifies as a five-year asset under the MACRS.

a. What is the depreciation expense for tax purposes for each year the equipment is depreciated?

b. If Mayberry's marginal tax rate is 40%, what is the depreciation tax shield for each year?

9. The USA Company purchased equipment for $1 million. Assume this equipment qualifies as a seven-year asset under the MACRS. What is the depreciation expense for tax purposes for each year the equipment is depreciated?

10. In 2000, NI Corporation had sales of $1 million, cost of goods sold of $600,000, and depreciation of $100,000. The corporation received $200,000 in dividends, paid $100,000 in dividends, and bought equipment for $300,000. Its tax rate was 30%, and the dividends-received deduction was 80%.

a. What was the taxable income of NI Corporation?

b. How much must NI pay in taxes?

11. In 1999, TI Corporation had sales of $2 million, cost of goods sold of $1 million, and depreciation of $500,000. The firm received $300,000 in dividends and $100,000 in interest income, and paid $150,000 in dividends and $200,000 in interest. It bought equipment for $300,000. The firm's tax rate was 30%, and the dividends-received deduction was 70%.

a. What was the taxable income of TI Corporation?

b. How much must TI pay in taxes?

CHAPTER 6

Financial Statements

Financial statements are summaries of the operating, financing, and investment activities of a business. Financial statements should provide information useful to both investors and creditors in making credit, investment, and other business decisions. And this usefulness means that investors and creditors can use these statements to predict, compare, and evaluate the amount, timing, and uncertainty of potential cash flows. In other words, financial statements provide the information needed to assess a company's future earnings and therefore the cash flows expected to result from those earnings. In this chapter, we discuss the four basic financial statements: the balance sheet, the income statement, the statement of cash flows, and the statement of shareholders' equity. The analysis of financial statements is provided in Part Six of this book.

ACCOUNTING PRINCIPLES AND ASSUMPTIONS

The accounting data in financial statements are prepared by the firm's management according to a set of standards, referred to as *generally accepted accounting principles* (GAAP).

The financial statements of a company whose stock is publicly traded must, by law, be audited at least annually by independent public accountants (i.e., accountants who are not employees of the firm). In such an audit, the accountants examine the financial statements and the data from which these statements are prepared and attest—through the published auditor's opinion—that these statements have been prepared according to GAAP. The auditor's opinion focuses on whether the statements conform to GAAP and that there is adequate disclosure of any material change in accounting principles.

The financial statements are created using several assumptions that affect how we use and interpret the financial data:

- *Transactions are recorded at historical cost.* Therefore, the values shown in the statements are not market or replacement values, but rather reflect the original cost (adjusted for depreciation, in the case of depreciable assets).
- *The appropriate unit of measurement is the dollar.* While this seems logical, the effects of inflation, combined with the practice of recording values at historical cost, may cause problems in using and interpreting these values.
- *The statements are recorded for predefined periods of time.* Generally, statements are produced to cover a chosen fiscal year or quarter, with the income statement and the statement of cash flows spanning a period's time and the balance sheet and statement of shareholders' equity as of the end of the specified period. But because the end of the fiscal year is generally chosen to coincide with the low point of activity in the firm's operating cycle, the annual balance sheet and statement of shareholders' equity may not be representative of values for the year.
- *Statements are prepared using accrual accounting and the matching principle.* Most businesses use accrual accounting, where income and revenues are matched in timing such that income is recorded in the period in which it is earned and expenses are reported in the period in which they are incurred to generate revenues. The result of the use of accrual accounting is that reported income does not necessarily coincide with cash flows. Because the financial analyst is concerned ultimately with cash flows, he or she often must understand how reported income relates to a company's cash flows.
- *It is assumed that the business will continue as a going concern.* The assumption that the business enterprise will continue indefinitely justifies the appropriateness of using historical costs instead of current market values because these assets are expected to be used up over time instead of sold.
- *Full disclosure requires providing information beyond the financial statements.* The requirement that there be full disclosure means that, in addition to the accounting numbers for such accounting items as revenues, expenses, and assets, narrative and additional numerical disclosures are provided in notes accompanying the financial statements. An analysis of financial statements is therefore not complete without this additional information.
- *Statements are prepared assuming conservatism.* In cases in which more than one interpretation of an event is possible, statements are prepared using the most conservative interpretation.

EXHIBIT 6.1 Fictitious Corporation Balance Sheets for Years Ending December 31, in Thousands

	2003	2002
ASSETS		
Cash	$400	$200
Marketable securities	200	0
Accounts receivable	600	800
Inventories	1,800	1,000
Total current assets	$3,000	$2,000
Gross plant and equipment	$11,000	$10,000
Accumulated depreciation	(4,000)	(3,000)
Net plant and equipment	7,000	7,000
Intangible assets	1,000	1,000
Total assets	$11,000	$10,000
LIABILITIES AND SHAREHOLDERS' EQUITY		
Accounts payable	$500	$400
Other current liabilities	500	200
Long-term debt	4,000	5,000
Total liabilities	$5,000	$5,600
Common stock, $1 par value;		
Authorized 2,000,000 shares		
Issued 1,500,000 and 1,200,000 shares	1,500	1,200
Additional paid-in capital	1,500	800
Retained earnings	3,000	2,400
Total shareholders' equity	6,000	4,400
Total liabilities and shareholders' equity	$11,000	$10,000

The financial statements and the auditors' findings are published in the firm's annual and quarterly reports sent to shareholders and the 10K and 10Q filings with the Securities and Exchange Commission (SEC). Also included in the reports, among other items, is a discussion by management, providing an overview of company events. The annual reports are much more detailed and disclose more financial information than the quarterly reports.

THE BALANCE SHEET

The *balance sheet* is a summary of the assets, liabilities, and equity of a business at a particular point in time—usually the end of the firm's fiscal year (see Exhibit 6.1). The balance sheet is also known as the *statement of financial condition* or the *statement of financial position*. The values shown for the different accounts on the balance sheet are not purported to reflect current market values; rather, they reflect historical costs.

Assets are the resources of the business enterprise, such as plant and equipment, that are used to generate future benefits. If a company owns plant and equipment that will be used to produce goods for sale in the future, the company can expect these assets (the plant and equipment) to generate cash inflows in the future.

Liabilities are obligations of the business. They represent commitments to creditors in the form of future cash outflows. When a firm borrows, say, by issuing a long-term bond, it becomes obligated to pay interest and principal on this bond as promised.

Equity, also called *shareholders' equity* or *stockholders' equity*, reflects ownership. The equity of a firm represents the part of its value that is not owed to creditors and therefore is left over for the owners. In the most basic accounting terms, equity is the difference between what the firm owns—its assets—and what it owes its creditors—its liabilities.

The balance sheets for Fictitious Corporation, shown in Exhibit 6.1, provide an example. At the end of the 1999 accounting year, the firm has $11 million in assets, financed by $5 million in liabilities and $6 million in equity.

ASSETS

There are two major categories of assets: current assets and noncurrent assets, where noncurrent assets include plant assets, intangibles, and investments. Assets that do not fit neatly into these categories may be recorded as either *other assets, deferred charges,* or *other noncurrent assets.*

Current Assets

Current assets (also referred to as *circulating capital* and *working assets*) are assets that could reasonably be converted into cash within one operating cycle or one year, whichever takes longer. An operating cycle begins when the firm invests cash in the raw materials used to produce its goods or services and ends with the collection of cash for the sale of those same goods or services. For example, if Fictitious manufactures and sells candy products, its operating cycle begins when it purchases the raw materials for the products (e.g., sugar) and ends when it receives cash for selling the candy to retailers. Because the operating

cycle of most businesses is less than one year, we tend to think of current assets as those assets that can be converted into cash in one year.

Current assets consist of cash, marketable securities, accounts receivable, and inventories. *Cash* comprises both currency—bills and coins—and assets that are immediately transformable into cash, such as deposits in bank accounts. *Marketable securities* are securities that can be readily sold when cash is needed. Every company needs to have a certain amount of cash to fulfill immediate needs, and any cash in excess of immediate needs is usually invested temporarily in marketable securities. Investments in marketable securities are simply viewed as a short-term place to store funds; marketable securities do not include those investments in other companies' stock that are intended to be long term. Some financial reports combine cash and marketable securities into one account referred to as *cash and cash equivalents* or *cash and marketable securities*.

Accounts receivable are amounts due from customers who have purchased the firm's goods or services but haven't yet paid for them. To encourage sales, many firms allow their customers to "buy now and pay later," perhaps at the end of the month or within 30 days of the sale. Accounts receivable therefore represents money that the firm expects to collect soon. Because not all accounts are ultimately collected, the gross amount of accounts receivable is adjusted by an estimate of the uncollectible accounts, the *allowance for doubtful accounts*, resulting in a *net accounts receivable* figure.

Inventories represent the total value of the firm's raw materials, work-in-process, and finished (but as yet unsold) goods. A manufacturer of toy trucks would likely have plastic and steel on hand as raw materials, work-in-process consisting of truck parts and partly completed trucks, and finished goods consisting of trucks packaged and ready for shipping. There are three basic methods of accounting for inventory, including:

- FIFO (first in, first out), which assumes that the first items purchased are the first items sold,
- LIFO (last in, first out), which assumes that the last items purchased are the first items sold, and
- Average cost, which assumes that the cost of items sold is the average of the cost of all items purchased.

The choice of inventory accounting method is significant because it affects values recorded on both the balance sheet and the income statement, as well as tax payments and cash flows.

EXHIBIT 6.2   Current Assets for Wal-Mart Stores, Procter & Gamble, and Walt Disney Company (2001)

Current Asset	Wal-Mart Stores		Procter & Gamble		Walt Disney Company	
	in Millions	% of Total	in Millions	% of Total	in Millions	% of Total
Cash and cash equivalents	$2,161	7.6%	$2,306	21.2%	$618	8.8%
Accounts receivable	2,000	7.1	3,328	30.5	3,965	56.4
Inventory	22,614	80.1	3,384	31.1	671	9.5
Other	1,471	5.2	1,871	17.2	1,775	25.3
Total	$28,246	100.0%	$10,889	100.0%	$7,029	100.0%

Source: The 2001 10-K reports for the respective companies.

Another current asset account that a company may have is prepaid expenses. *Prepaid expenses* are amounts that have been paid but not as yet consumed. A common example is the case of a company paying insurance premiums for an extended period of time (say, a year), but for which only a portion (say, three months) is applicable to the insurance coverage for the current fiscal year; the remaining insurance that is prepaid as of the end of the year is considered an asset. Prepaid expenses may be reported as part of *other current liabilities*.

Companies' investment in current assets depends, in large part, on the industry in which they operate. Consider the breakdown of current assets by asset type for three companies for 2001 reported in Exhibit 6.2. Retailers, such as Wal-Mart, have a relatively large investment in inventory, whereas manufacturing firms, such as consumer product manufacturer Procter & Gamble, have substantial investments in both accounts receivable and inventory. Companies that generate a large portion of their operating revenues from patents, copyrights, and other such intangibles (e.g., film libraries) tend to have a relatively larger investment in accounts receivable, as we can see with the Walt Disney Company.

Noncurrent Assets

Noncurrent assets are assets that are not current assets; that is, it is not expected that noncurrent assets can be converted into cash within an operating cycle. Noncurrent assets include physical assets, such as plant and equipment, and nonphysical assets, such as intangibles.

Plant assets are the physical assets, such as the equipment, machinery, and buildings, that are used in the operation of the business. We describe a firm's current investment in plant assets by using three values: gross plant assets, accumulated depreciation, and net plant assets. *Gross plant and equipment*, or gross plant assets, is the sum of the original costs of all equipment, buildings, and machinery the firm uses to produce its goods and services. *Depreciation*, as you will see in the next chapter, is a charge that accounts for the using up of an asset over the length of an accounting period; it is a means for allocating the asset's cost over its useful life. *Accumulated depreciation* is the sum of all the depreciation charges taken so far for all the company's assets. *Net plant and equipment*, or *net plant assets*, is the difference between gross plant assets and accumulated depreciation. The net plant and equipment amount is hence the value of the assets—historical cost less any depreciation—according to the accounting books and is therefore often referred to as the *book value* of the assets.

Intangible assets are the current value of nonphysical assets that represent long-term investments of the company. Such intangible assets include patents, copyrights, and goodwill. The cost of some intangible assets is amortized ("spread out") over the life of the asset. *Amortization* is akin to depreciation: The asset's cost is allocated over the life of the asset; the reported value is the original cost of the asset, less whatever has been amortized. The number of years over which an intangible asset is amortized depends on the particular asset and its perceived useful life. For example, a *patent* is the exclusive right to produce and sell a particular, uniquely defined good and has a legal life of 17 years, though the useful life of a patent—the period in which it adds value to the company—may be much less than 17 years. Therefore the company may choose to amortize a patent's cost over a period less than 17 years. As another example, a *copyright* is the exclusive right to publish and sell a literary, artistic, or musical composition, and is granted for 50 years beyond the author's life, though its useful life in terms of generating income for the company may be much less than 50 years. More challenging is determining the appropriate amortization period for goodwill. *Goodwill* was created when one company buys another company at a price that exceeds the acquired company's fair market value of its assets.

A company may have additional noncurrent assets, depending on their particular circumstances. A company may have a noncurrent asset referred to as *investments*, which are assets that are purchased with the intention of holding them for a long term, but which do not generate revenue or are not used to manufacture a product. Examples of investments include equity securities of another company and real estate that is held for speculative purposes. Other noncurrent assets include *long-term prepaid expenses*, arising from prepayment for which a benefit is received over an extended period of time, and *deferred tax assets*, arising from timing differences between reported income and tax income, whereby reported income exceeds taxable income.

Long-term investment in securities of other companies may be recorded at cost or market value, depending on the type of investment; investments held to maturity are recorded at cost, whereas investments held as trading securities or available for sale are recorded at market value. Whether the unrealized gains or losses affect earnings on the income statement depend on whether the securities are deemed trading securities or available for sale.[1]

LIABILITIES

Liabilities, a firm's obligations to its creditors, are made up of current liabilities, long-term liabilities, and deferred taxes.

Current Liabilities

Current liabilities are obligations that must be paid within one operating cycle or one year, whichever is longer. Current liabilities include:

- *Accounts payable*, which are obligations to pay suppliers. They arise from goods and services that have been purchased but not yet paid.
- *Accrued expenses*, which are obligations such as wages and salaries payable to the employees of the business, rent, and insurance.
- *Current portion of long-term debt* or the *current portion of capital leases*. Any portion of long-term indebtedness—obligations extending beyond one year—due within the year.
- Short-term loans from a bank or notes payable within a year.

The reliance on short-term liabilities and the type of current liabilities depends, in part, on the industry in which the firm operates. Consider the breakdown of current liabilities for three firms for 2001 reported in Exhibit 6.3. These three companies differ quite a bit in their use of the different types of current liabilities, with Wal-Mart more reliant on accounts payable (i.e., trade credit) and Disney using accounts payable the least.

---

[1] If the securities are considered trading securities, the unrealized gains or losses (that is, the changes in market value each period) affect earnings; if the securities are available-for-sale, unrealized gains or losses bypass the income statement and only affect shareholders' equity on the balance sheet.

EXHIBIT 6.3   Current Liabilities for Wal-Mart Stores, Procter & Gamble, and the Walt Disney Company

Current Liability	Wal-Mart Stores		Procter & Gamble		Walt Disney Company	
	in Millions	% of Total	in Millions	% of Total	in Millions	% of Total
Accounts payable	$24,134	88.5%	$7,613	77.3%	$4,603	74.0%
Short-term and current long-term debt	3,148	11.5	2,233	22.7	829	13.3
Other current liabilities	0	0.0	0	0.0	787	12.7
Total	$27,282	100.0%	$9,846	100.0%	$6,219	100.0%

Source: The 2001 10-K reports for the respective companies.

Long-Term Liabilities

Long-term liabilities are obligations that must be paid over a period beyond one year. They include notes, bonds, capital lease obligations, and pension obligations. Notes and bonds both represent loans on which the borrower promises to pay interest periodically and to repay the principal amount of the loan.

A *lease* obligates the lessee—the one leasing and using the leased asset—to pay specified rental payments for a period of time. Whether the lease obligation is recorded as a liability or is expensed as lease payments made depends on whether the lease is a capital lease or an operating lease. The rules for classifying a lease as a capital lease or an operating lease and the accounting treatment of each are explained in Chapter 27.

A company's pension and post-retirement benefit obligations may give rise to long-term liabilities. The pension benefits are commitments by the company to pay specific retirement benefits, whereas post-retirement benefits include any other retirement benefit besides pensions, such as health care. Basically, if the fair value of the pension plan's assets exceeds the *projected benefit obligation* (the estimated present value of projected pension costs), the difference is recorded as a long-term asset. If, on the other hand, the plan's assets are less than the projected benefit obligation, the difference is recorded as a long-term liability. In a similar manner, the company may have an asset or a liability corresponding to post-retirement benefits.

Deferred Taxes

Along with long-term liabilities, the analyst may encounter another account, deferred taxes. *Deferred taxes* are taxes that will have to be paid to the federal and state governments based on accounting income, but are not due yet. Deferred taxes arise when different methods of accounting are used for financial statements and for tax purposes. These differences are temporary and are the result of different timing of revenue or expense recognition for financial statement reporting and tax purposes. The deferred tax liability arises when the actual tax liability is less than the tax liability shown for financial reporting purposes (meaning that the firm will be paying the difference in the future), whereas the deferred tax asset, mentioned earlier, arises when the actual tax liability is greater than the tax liability shown for reporting purposes.

EQUITY

Equity is the owner's interest in the company. For a corporation, ownership is represented by common stock and preferred stock. Shareholders' equity is also referred to as the *book value of equity,* since this is the value of equity according to the records in the accounting books.

The value of the ownership interest of preferred stock is represented in financial statements as its *par value,* which is also the dollar value on which dividends are figured. For example, if you own a share of preferred stock that has a $100 par value and a 9% dividend rate, you receive $9 in dividends each year. Further, your ownership share of the company is $100. Preferred shareholders' equity is the product of the number of preferred shares outstanding and the par value of the stock; it is shown that way on the balance sheet.

The remainder of the equity belongs to the common shareholders. It consists of three parts: *common stock outstanding* (listed at par or at stated value), additional paid-in capital, and retained earnings. The par value of common stock is an arbitrary figure; it has no relation to market value or to dividends paid on common stock. Some stock has no par value, but may have an arbitrary value, or *stated value,* per share. Nonetheless, the total par value or stated value of all outstanding common shares is usually entitled "capital stock" or "common stock." Then, to inject reality into the equity part of the balance sheet, an entry called *additional paid-in capital* is added; this is the amount received by the corporation for its common stock in excess of the par or stated value. If a firm sold 10,000 shares of $1 par value common stock at $40 a share, its equity accounts would show:

Common stock, $1 par value	$10,000
Additional paid-in capital	$390,000

In Exhibit 6.1, Fictitious' common stock represents the stock's par value and the amount paid in excess of par value is recorded as additional paid-in capital. Some corporations eliminate this arbitrary division of accounts and instead report the entire amount paid for the common stock as *capital stock* or *common stock*.

If some of the stock is bought back by the firm, the amount it pays for its own stock is recorded as *treasury stock*. Because these shares are not owned by shareholders, common shareholders' equity is reduced by the cost of the treasury stock.

There are actually four different labels that can be applied to the number of shares of a corporation on a balance sheet:

- The number of shares *authorized* by the shareholders.
- The number of shares *issued* and sold by the corporation, which can be less than the number of shares authorized.
- The number of shares currently *outstanding*, which can be less than the number of shares issued if the corporation has bought back (repurchased) some of its issued stock.
- The number of shares of *treasury stock*, which is stock that the company has repurchased.

The outstanding stock is reported in the stock accounts, and adjustments must be made for any treasury stock. In the case of Fictitious Corporation, shown in Exhibit 6.1, in 2003 there were 2 million authorized shares, 1.5 million issued shares, and (since there was no treasury stock) 1.5 million shares outstanding.

As another example, consider the numbers of shares for the Walt Disney Company. For the fiscal year ended September 30, 2001, Disney had 3.6 billion shares authorized, 2.1 billion shares issued, and 2.019 billion shares outstanding.

The number of shares actually issued by Disney is well below the number of shares the company is authorized to issue; as of the end of 2001, Disney could issue 3.6 − 2.1 = 1.5 billion common shares without shareholder approval.

The bulk of the equity interest in a company is in its retained earnings. *Retained earnings* is the accumulated net income of the company, less any dividends that have not been paid, over the life of the corporation. Retained earnings are *not* strictly cash and any correspondence to cash is coincidental. Any cash generated by the firm that has not been paid out in dividends has been reinvested in the firm's assets—to finance accounts receivable, inventories, equipment, and so forth.

The book value of equity—the sum total of retained earnings, common stock, and (if applicable) preferred stock—represents the equity interest of the corporation's owners, stated in terms of historical costs. However, historical costs often bear little resemblance to the value of equity stated in terms of market values. Consider the case of several companies at the end of their fiscal 2001 year:

Company	Book Value of Equity in Millions	Market Value of Equity (in Millions)
Amazon	$(1,440)	$4,038
Coca-Cola	11,366	117,224
General Electric	54,824	397,830
Microsoft	47,289	385,659
Sprint	11,714	17,847
Wal-Mart Stores	35,102	267,091

Source: Book values of equity are drawn from the company's 2001 annual report. Market value, as of the end of the company's fiscal year-end, is from Yahoo! Finance, biz.yahoo.com.

In most cases, the market value of equity exceeds the company's book value by a wide margin, as typified by Coca-Cola, General Electric, and Wal-Mart. Yet there are cases in which the book value of equity is negative (as illustrated by Amazon), which bears no relation to the company's market value of equity. And in other, relatively uncommon cases such as Sprint, the market value of equity is close to the company's book value.

THE INCOME STATEMENT

An *income statement* is a summary of the revenues and expenses of a business over a period of time, usually either one month, three months, or one year. This statement is also referred to as the *profit and loss statement*. It shows the results of the firm's operating and financing decisions during that time. Income statements for Fictitious Corporation are presented in Exhibit 6.4.

The operating decisions of the company—those that apply to production and marketing—generate *sales* or *revenues* and incur the *cost of goods sold* (also referred to as the *cost of sales* or the *cost of products sold*). The difference between sales and cost of goods sold is *gross profit*. Operating decisions also result in administrative and general expenses, such as advertising fees and office salaries. Deducting these expenses from gross profit leaves *operating profit*, which is also referred to as *earnings before interest and taxes* (EBIT), *operating income*, or *operating earnings*. Operating decisions take the firm from sales to EBIT on the income statement. Exhibit 6.4 shows that Fictitious Corporation generated sales of $10 million in 2003, which produced an operating profit of $2 million.

The results of financing decisions are reflected in the remainder of the income statement. When interest expenses and taxes, which are both influenced by financing decisions, are subtracted from EBIT, the result is net income. Net income is, in a sense, the amount available to owners of the firm. If the firm has preferred stock, the preferred stock dividends are deducted from net income to arrive at *earnings available to common shareholders*. If the firm does not have preferred stock (as is the case with Fictitious and most nonfictitious corporations), net income is equivalent to earnings available for common shareholders. The board of directors may then distribute all or part of this as common stock dividends, retaining the remainder to help finance the firm. As shown in Exhibit 6.4, Fictitious Corporation had a net income for 2003 of $1.2 million. Of this, $600,000 was paid to common shareholders. The remaining $600,000 went into retained earnings.

EXHIBIT 6.4 Fictitious Corporation Income Statements for Years Ending December 31 (in Thousands)

	2003	2002
Sales	$10,000	$9,000
Cost of goods sold	(6,500)	(6,000)
Gross profit	$3,500	$3,000
Lease expense	(1,000)	(1,000)
Administrative expense	(500)	(500)
Earnings before interest and taxes (EBIT)	$2,000	$2,000
Interest	(400)	(500)
Earnings before taxes	$1,600	$1,500
Taxes	(400)	(500)
Net income	$1,200	$1,000
Preferred dividends	(100)	(100)
Earnings available to common shareholders	$1,100	$900
Common dividends	(500)	(400)
Retained earnings	$600	$500

The entry "retained earnings" in the balance sheet is the record of accumulated earnings, less any dividends paid since the inception of the corporation. The entry "retained earnings" in the income statement is the amount of earnings retained (that is, not paid out) during that period. As you can see, Fictitious retained $600,000 of its 2003 earnings (Exhibit 6.4), increasing its retained earnings from $2.4 million in 2002 to $3 million in 2003 (Exhibit 6.1).

Companies must report comprehensive income prominently within their financial statements. *Comprehensive income* is a net income amount that includes all revenues, expenses, gains, and losses items and is based on the idea that all results of the firm—whether operating or nonoperating—should be reflected in the earnings of the company. This is referred to as the *all-inclusive income concept.* The all-inclusive income concept requires that these items be recognized in the financial statements as part of comprehensive income.

It is important to note that net income does not represent the actual cash flow from operations and financing. Rather, it is a summary of operating performance measured over a given time period, using specific accounting procedures. Depending on these accounting procedures, net income may or may not correspond to cash flow.

THE STATEMENT OF CASH FLOWS

The *statement of cash flows* is a summary over a period of time of a firm's cash flows from operating, investment, and financing activities. The statement of cash flows for Fictitious is shown in Exhibit 6.5.

The firm's statement of cash flows lists separately its operating cash flows, investing cash flows, and financing cash flows. By analyzing these individual flows, current and potential owners and creditors can examine such aspects of the business as:

■ The source of financing for business operations, whether through internally generated funds or external sources of funds.
■ The ability of the company to meet debt obligations (interest and principal payments).
■ The ability of the company to finance expansion through operating cash flow.
■ The ability of the company to pay dividends to shareholders.
■ The flexibility the business has in financing its operations.

A firm that generates cash flows only by selling off its assets (obtaining cash flows from investments) or by issuing more securities (obtaining cash flows from financing) cannot keep that up for very long. For future prosperity the firm must be able to generate cash flows from its operations.

Cash Flows from Operating Activities

The cash flow from operating activities is the most complex of the three. Ideally, we could obtain it directly, by summing all cash receipts (inflows) and disbursements (outflows) for the periods covered by the statement. However, in spite of its usefulness, this sum is, in practice, burdensome to prepare. Instead, the cash flow from operations is generally obtained indirectly. Using the indirect method, we begin with net income as reported on the income statement and adjust it for each change in current assets and current liabilities and each noncash operating item; what remains is the cash flow from (used for) operations, as shown in Exhibit 6.5.

EXHIBIT 6.5   Fictitious Company Statement of Cash Flows, Years Ended December 31, in Thousands

	2003	2002
Cash flow from (used for) operating activities		
Net income	$1,200	$1,000
Add or deduct adjustments to cash basis:		
Change in accounts receivables	$200	$(200)
Change in accounts payable	100	400
Change in marketable securities	(200)	200
Change in inventories	(800)	(600)
Change in other current liabilities	300	0
Depreciation	1,000	1,000
	600	800
Cash flow from operations	$1,800	$1,800
Cash flow from (used for) investing activities		
Purchase of plant and equipment	$(1,000)	$0
Cash flow from (used for) investing activities	$(1,000)	$0
Cash flow from (used for) financing activities		
Sale of common stock	$1,000	$0
Repayment of long-term debt	(1,000)	(1,500)
Payment of preferred dividends	(100)	(100)
Payment of common dividends	(500)	(400)
Cash flow from (used for) financing activities	(600)	(1,900)
Increase (decrease) in cash flow	$200	$(100)
Cash at the beginning of the year	200	300
Cash at the end of the year	$400	$200

EXHIBIT 6.6 Adjustment of Net Income for Changes in Working Capital Accounts to Arrive at Cash Flow from Operations

Change in Working Capital Account	Adjustment to Net Income
An increase in a current asset account	Deduct the change
A decrease in a current asset account	Add the change
An increase in a current liability account	Add the change
A decrease in a current liability account	Deduct the change

The basic adjustments to net income for changes in current assets and current liabilities are summarized in Exhibit 6.6. Income is adjusted for noncash revenues and expenses, such as depreciation, by adding them because they have been deducted in the computation for net income but do not require cash to be paid out.

We adjust net income for changes in current assets and liabilities because those changes represent the difference between accrual accounting and cash accounting. For example, an increase in the inventories account is the result of an investment of cash to generate sales in the near future. Exhibit 6.1 shows that Fictitious Corporation invested $800,000 in inventories during 2003 ($1 million in 2002 versus $1.8 million in 2003). Since that investment was an operating cash flow, we must *subtract* it from net income. As another example, Exhibit 6.1 shows that accounts receivable decreased by $200,000. That decrease in a current asset represents a flow of cash to the firm—the return of cash invested in accounts receivable. So the $200,000 must be *added* to net income to obtain cash flow. These adjustments are shown in the "Cash flow from operating activities" section of Exhibit 6.5, along with the other adjustments required to obtain Fictitious Corporation's operating activities.

Cash Flows from Investing and Financing Activities

The computation of the cash flows from investing and financing activities is straightforward. The *cash flow from (used for) investing activities* includes cash flow due to investments in plant assets, the disposal of plant assets, acquisitions of other companies, and divestitures of subsidiaries. For Fictitious Corporation, the $1 million invested in plant and equipment shows up as a net outflow on the statement of cash flows.

The *cash flow from (used for) financing activities* includes cash flows due to the sale or repurchase of common or preferred stock, the issuing or retirement of long-term debt securities, and the payment of common and preferred dividends.

The flows attributed to these activities are shown in Exhibit 6.5 for Fictitious Corporation. By design, the statement of cash flows is a reconciliation of the cash flows from the firm's three cash sources: operations, investing, and financing. It takes us from net income to the change in the cash account over the accounting period. For example, for Fictitious Corporation the net change in the cash balance during 1999 is an increase of $200,000 as shown in the first line of Exhibit 6.1. Exhibit 6.5 shows us that this increase is the result of net cash flows during 1999 of $1.8 million from operations, *less* $1 million from investing activities, *less* $600,000 from financing activities.

Consider another example. Suppose the Pretend Corporation has the following financial results:

- Net income of $40,000
- Increase in current assets of $5,000
- Increase in current liabilities of $2,000
- Sale of $10,000 of plant and equipment
- Purchase $20,000 of plant of equipment
- Depreciation of $12,000
- Repurchase $20,000 of common stock
- Dividends on common stock of $2,000

What is the Pretend's cash flow? The first step is to adjust net income for the changes in the working capital accounts: a downward adjustment of $5,000 for the increase in current assets and an upward adjustment of $2,000 for the increase in current liabilities. Adding depreciation, the cash flow from operating activities is $49,000. The cash flows from investing activities consists of the flow for Pretend's sale and purchase of plant and equipment. The cash flow from financing activities involves Pretend's repurchase of common stock and its payment of common dividends. The statement of cash flows for Pretend Corporation is shown in Exhibit 6.7.

The financial analyst can use the statement of cash flows to learn more about a company's financial health. Consider the cash flows shown in Exhibit 6.8 for different companies in 2001. Wal-Mart Stores, Dell, Disney, and Intel have cash flows that are typical of healthy, growing companies: funds are generated internally (that is, through operating activity) and funds are applied to investing activities. Motorola is generating funds from both operations and investments (that is, selling off assets). Wal-Mart Stores and Walt Disney are generating sufficient funds to fund their investment activity and reduce their dependence on externally-raised funds (as indicated by the cash flow used for financing activities). Dell and Disney are able to generate sufficient cash flows through operating activities to reduce dependence on external financing.

EXHIBIT 6.7 Pretend Corporation Statement of Cash Flows

Cash flow from operations	
Net income	$40,000
Increase in current assets	(5,000)
Increase in current liabilities	2,000
Depreciation	12,000
Cash flow from operations	$49,000
Cash flow from investing activities	
Sale of plant and equipment	$10,000
Purchase of plant and equipment	(20,000)
Cash flow used for investing activities	$(10,000)
Cash flow from financing activities	
Repurchase of common stock	$(20,000)
Dividends on common stock	(2,000)
Cash flow used for financing activities	$(22,000)
Increase in cash flow	$17,000

EXHIBIT 6.8 Cash Flows from (Used for) Operating, Investment, and Financing Activities (In millions)

Company	Cash Flows from (for) Operating Activities	Cash Flows from (for) Investment Activities	Cash Flows from (for) Financing Activities	Increase (Decrease) in Cash and Cash Equivalents
Dell Computer	$4,195	$(757)	$(2,305)	$1,101
Disney	3,048	(2,015)	(1,257)	(224)
Motorola	2,124	2,477	(1,802)	2,781
Intel	8,654	(195)	(3,465)	4,994
Wal-Mart Stores	10,260	(7,146)	113	107

Source: Statement of cash flows from the 2001 10-K reports for the respective companies.

EXHIBIT 6.9   Fictitious Corporation Statement of Shareholders' Equity

	Shares	Common Stock	Retained Earnings	Total
Balance at December 31, 2001	1,200	$2,000	$1,900	$3,900
Common stock sold (repurchased)	—	—	—	—
Net income		—	900	900
Cash dividend declared		—	(400)	(400)
Balance at December 31, 2002	1,200	$2,000	$2,400	$4,400
Common stock sold (repurchased)	300	1,000	—	1,000
Net income		—	1,100	1,100
Cash dividend declared		—	(500)	(500)
Balance at December 31, 2003	1,500	$3,000	$3,000	$6,000

THE STATEMENT OF SHAREHOLDERS' EQUITY

Additional information about equity can be found in the *statement of shareholders' equity*, which is a breakdown of the amounts and changes in equity accounts. This statement serves as a connecting link between the balance sheet and the income statement, providing the analyst with more detail on changes in the individual equity accounts.

Whereas the balance sheet provides information on the number of shares outstanding at the specific point in time, the statement of shareholders' equity provides more detail on any changes, including shares issued to satisfy the exercise of stock options and repurchased shares. This statement can be expanded to accommodate treasury stock, if appropriate. The statement of shareholders' equity for Fictitious is shown in Exhibit 6.9.

The statement of shareholders' equity can provide a useful brief history of not only the effects of options, but also of items that may bypass the income statement.

NOTES TO FINANCIAL STATEMENTS

The financial statements of a corporation contain information beyond that presented in the balance sheet, the income statement, the statement of cash flows, and the statement of shareholders' equity. This additional information is presented in the notes to these financial statements. The first note summarizes the company's accounting policies including the methods of inventory accounting, methods of depreciation, and foreign currency translation. Depending on the circumstances of the company and the nature of its business, there may be additional notes providing, for example, supplemental balance sheet data, information on mergers or acquisitions, lease arrangements, or information on joint ventures.

SUMMARY

- The annual report of a company provides financial data, in the form of financial statements and notes, management discussion, and the auditor's opinion.
- The financial statements (the balance sheet, income statement, statement of cash flows, and statement of shareholders' equity), along with the accompanying notes, provide information necessary to assess the operating performance and the financial condition of the firm. Using this information, in conjunction with an understanding of accounting, analysts can see where a business has been, which may tell us something about where it is going.
- The balance sheet provides information about the value of accounts at a point in time, generally at the end of the fiscal year or the end of the fiscal quarter.
- The income statement provides information about the operating performance of a company over a period of time (typically a fiscal year or fiscal quarter).
- The statement of cash flows provides data on the cash flows of the company over time and the sources of these cash flows.
- The statement of shareholders' equity details the changes in the equity accounts over a period of time.
- The notes to financial statements provide more detail on many accounts.

QUESTIONS

1. What is meant by generally accepted accounting principles?
2. What is meant by accrual accounting and the matching principle?
3. Describe the type of information provided in each of the three financial statements:
   a. The balance sheet.
   b. The income statement.
   c. The statement of cash flows.

4. Comment on the following two statements:
   a. "Asset values reported in the balance sheet are shown at market value."
   b. "The cash of a company is equal to its retained earnings."
5. Distinguish between accounts receivable and accounts payable.
6. Define each of the following: (a) current assets, (b) intangible assets, (c) deferred taxes, (d) retained earnings, and (e) earnings before interest and taxes.
7. Distinguish between accounts receivable and accounts payable.
8. Complete the following balance sheet:

Cash	$100	Accounts payable	$200
Inventory	_____	Notes payable	300
Gross plant and equipment	1,800	Long-term debt	_____
Accumulated depreciation	_____	Common equity	1,000
Net plant and equipment	1,500		
Total assets	$2,000	Total liabilities and equity	_____

9. Calculate the amount of retained earnings from the following information:

   ■ Common stock dividends are 40% of earnings available to common shareholders.
   ■ Earnings before taxes are $3,000.
   ■ Preferred stock dividends are $200.
   ■ Taxes are 30% of earnings.

5. 10. Construct the statement of cash flows given the following information:

   ■ $10,000 in new long-term debt is issued.
   ■ $30,000 of common stock is repurchased.
   ■ Common stock dividends are $15,000.
   ■ Current assets are increased by $20,000.
   ■ Current liabilities are decreased by $40,000.
   ■ Depreciation is $10,000.
   ■ Net income is $100,000.
   ■ Plant and equipment purchased during the period are $30,000.

CHAPTER 7

Mathematics of Finance

The notion that money has a time value is one of the most basic concepts in investment analysis. Making decisions today regarding future cash flows requires understanding that the value of money does not remain the same throughout time.

A dollar today is worth less than a dollar some time in the future for two reasons.

Reason No. 1: Cash flows occurring at different points in time have different values relative to any one point in time.

One dollar one year from now is not as valuable as one dollar today. After all, you can invest a dollar today and earn interest so that the value it grows to next year is greater than the one dollar today. This means we have to take into account the *time value of money* to quantify the relation between cash flows at different points in time.

Reason No. 2: Cash flows are uncertain.

Expected cash flows may not materialize. Uncertainty stems from the nature of forecasts of the timing and/or the amount of cash flows. We do not know for certain when, whether, or how much cash flows will be in the future. This uncertainty regarding future cash flows must somehow be taken into account in assessing the value of an investment.

Translating a current value into its equivalent future value is referred to as *compounding*. Translating a future cash flow or value into its equivalent value in a prior period is referred to as *discounting*. This chapter outlines the basic mathematical techniques used in compounding and discounting.

Suppose someone wants to borrow $100 today and promises to pay back the amount borrowed in one month. Would the repayment of only the $100 be fair? Probably not. There are two things to consider. First,

147

if the lender didn't lend the $100, what could he or she have done with it? Second, is there a chance that the borrower may not pay back the loan? So, when considering lending money, we must consider the opportunity cost (i.e., what could have been earned or enjoyed), as well as the uncertainty associated with getting the money back as promised.

Let's say that someone is willing to lend the money, but that they require repayment of the $100 plus some compensation for the opportunity cost *and* any uncertainty the loan will be repaid as promised. The amount of the loan, the $100, is the *principal*. The compensation required for allowing someone else to use the $100 is the *interest*.

Looking at this same situation from the perspective of time and value, the amount that you are willing to lend today is the loan's *present value*. The amount that you require to be paid at the end of the loan period is the loan's *future value*. Therefore, the future period's value is comprised of two parts:

$$\text{Future Value} = \text{Present value} + \text{Interest}$$

The interest is compensation for the use of funds for a specific period. It consists of (1) compensation for the length of time the money is borrowed and (2) compensation for the risk that the amount borrowed will not be repaid exactly as set forth in the loan agreement.

DETERMINING THE FUTURE VALUE

Suppose you deposit $1,000 into a savings account at the Surety Savings Bank and you are promised 10% interest per period. At the end of one period you would have $1,100. This $1,100 consists of the return of your principal amount of the investment (the $1,000) and the interest or return on your investment (the $100). Let's label these values:

- $1,000 is the value today, the present value, PV
- $1,100 is the value at the end of one period, the future value, FV
- 10% is the rate interest is earned in one period, the interest rate, i

To get to the future value from the present value:

$$FV = \underset{\uparrow}{PV} + \underset{\uparrow}{(PV \times i)}$$
$$\quad\quad \text{principal} \quad \text{interest}$$

This is equivalent to:

$$FV = PV(1 + i)$$

In terms of our example,

$$FV = \$1,000 + (\$1,000 \times 0.10) = \$1,000(1 + 0.10) = \$1,100$$

If the $100 interest is withdrawn at the end of the period, the principal is left to earn interest at the 10% rate. Whenever you do this, you earn *simple interest*. It is simple because it repeats itself in exactly the same way from one period to the next as long as you take out the interest at the end of each period and the principal remains the same. If, on the other hand, both the principal and the interest are left on deposit at the Surety Savings Bank, the balance earns interest on the previously paid interest, referred to as *compound interest*. Earning interest on interest is called compounding because the balance at any time is a combination of the principal, interest on principal, and *interest on accumulated interest* (or simply, *interest on interest*).

If you compound interest for one more period in our example, the original $1,000 grows to $1,210.00:

$$
\begin{aligned}
FV &= \text{principal} &&+ \text{first period interest} &&+ \text{second period interest} \\
&= \$1,000.00 &&+ (\$1,000.00 \times 0.10) &&+ (\$1,100.00 \times 0.10) \\
&= \$1,210.00
\end{aligned}
$$

The present value of the investment is $1,000, the interest earned over two years is $210, and the future value of the investment after two years is $1,210.

The relation between the present value and the future value after two periods, breaking out the second period interest into interest on the principal and interest on interest, is:

$$
FV = \underset{\substack{\uparrow \\ \text{principal}}}{PV} + \underset{\substack{\uparrow \\ \text{first period's} \\ \text{interest on} \\ \text{the principal}}}{(PV \times i)} + \underset{\substack{\uparrow \\ \text{second period's} \\ \text{interest on} \\ \text{the principal}}}{(PV \times i)} \quad \underset{\substack{\uparrow \\ \text{second period's} \\ \text{interest on the first} \\ \text{period's interest}}}{(PV \times i \times i)}
$$

or, collecting the PV's from each term and applying a bit of elementary algebra,

$$FV = PV(1 + 2i + i^2) = PV (1 + i)^2$$

The balance in the account two years from now, $1,210, is comprised of three parts:

1. the principal, $1,000,
2. interest on principal, $100 in the first period plus $100 in the second period
3. interest on interest, 10% of the first period's interest, or $10

To determine the future value with compound interest for *more* than two periods, we follow along the same lines:

$$FV = PV(1 + i)^N \tag{7-1}$$

The value of N is the number of *compounding periods*, where a compounding period is the unit of time after which interest is paid at the rate i. A period may be any length of time: a minute, a day, a month, or a year. The important thing is to make sure the same compounding period is reflected throughout the problem being analyzed. The term "$(1 + i)^N$" is referred to as the *compound factor*. It is the rate of exchange between present dollars and dollars N compounding periods into the future. Equation (7-1) is the *basic valuation equation*—the foundation of financial mathematics. It relates a value at one point in time to a value at another point in time, considering the compounding of interest.

The relation between present and future values for a principal of $1,000 and interest of 10% per period through 10 compounding periods is shown graphically in Exhibit 7.1. For example, the value of $1,000, earning interest at 10% per period, is $2,593.70 ten periods into the future:

$$FV = \$1,000 \,(1 + 0.10)^{10} = \$1,000 \,(2.5937) = \$2,593.70$$

As you can see in this exhibit, the $2,593.70 balance in the account at the end of 10 periods is comprised of three parts:

1. the principal, $1,000
2. interest on the principal of $1,000, which is $100 per period for 10 periods or $1,000
3. interest on interest totaling $593.70

We can express the change in the value of the savings balance (i.e., the difference between the ending value and the beginning value) as a growth rate. A *growth rate* is the rate at which a value appreciates (a positive growth) or depreciates (a negative growth) over time. Our $1,000 grew at a rate of 10% per year over the 10-year period to $2,593.70. The average annual growth rate of our investment of $1,000 is 10%—the value of the savings account balance increased 10% per year.

EXHIBIT 7.1   The Value of $1,000 Invested 10 Years in an Account that Pays 10% Compounded Interest per Year

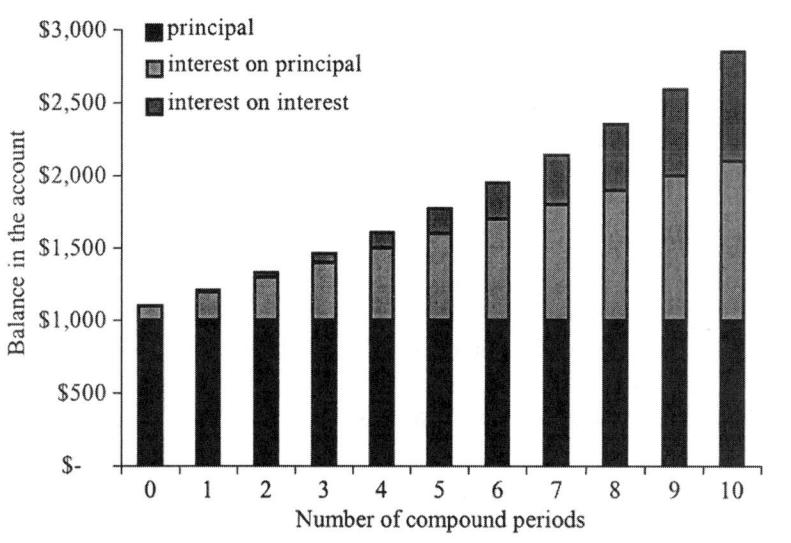

We could also express the appreciation in our savings balance in terms of a return. A *return* is the income on an investment, generally stated as a change in the value of the investment over each period divided by the amount of the investment at the beginning of the period. We could also say that our investment of $1,000 provides an average annual return of 10% per year. The average annual return is *not* calculated by taking the change in value over the entire 10-year period ($2,593.70 − $1,000) and dividing it by $1,000. This would produce an *arithmetic average return* of 159.37% over the 10-year period, or 15.937% per year. But the arithmetic average ignores the process of compounding. The correct way of calculating the average annual return is to use a *geometric average return*:

$$i = \sqrt[N]{\frac{FV}{PV}} - 1 \tag{7-2}$$

which is a rearrangement of equation (7-1). Using the values from the example,

$$i = \sqrt[10]{\frac{\$2,593.70}{\$1,000.00}} - 1 = \left(\frac{\$2,593.70}{\$1,000.00}\right)^{1/10} - 1 = 1.10 - 1 = 10\%$$

Therefore, the annual return on the investment—sometimes referred to as the *compound average annual return* or the *true return*—is 10% per year.

Here is another example for calculating a future value. A common investment product of a life insurance company is a guaranteed investment contract (GIC). With this investment, an insurance company guarantees a specified interest rate for a period of years. Suppose that the life insurance company agrees to pay 6% annually for a 5-year GIC and the amount invested by the policyholder is $10 million. The amount of the liability (that is, the amount this life insurance company has agreed to pay the GIC policyholder) is the future value of $10 million when invested at 6% interest for five years. In terms of equation (7-1), $PV = \$10,000,000$, $i = 6\%$, and $N = 5$, so that the future value is:

$$FV = \$10,000,000 \, (1 + 0.06)^5 = \$13,382,256.$$

Compounding More than One Time Per Year

An investment may pay interest more than one time per year. For example, interest may be paid semiannually, quarterly, monthly, weekly, or daily, even though the stated rate is quoted on an annual basis. If the interest is stated as, say, 10% per year, compounded semiannually, the nominal rate—often referred to as the *annual percentage rate* or APR—is 10%. The basic valuation equation handles situations in which there is compounding more frequently than once a year if we translate the nominal rate into a rate *per compounding period*. Therefore, an APR of 10% with compounding semiannually is 5% per period—where a period is six months—and the number of periods in one year is 2.

Consider a deposit of $50,000 in an account for five years that pays 8% interest, compounded quarterly. The interest rate per period, i, is $8\%/4 = 2\%$ and the number of compounding periods is $5 \times 4 = 20$. Therefore the balance in the account at the end of five years is:

$$FV = \$50,000(1 + 0.02)^{20} = \$50,000(1.4859474) = \$74,297.37$$

As shown in Exhibit 7.2, through 50 years with both annual and quarterly compounding, the investment's value increases at a faster rate with the increased frequency of compounding.

The last example illustrates the need to correctly identify the "period" because this dictates the interest rate per period and the number of compounding periods. Because interest rates are often quoted in terms of an APR, we need to be able to translate the APR into an interest rate per period and to adjust the number of periods. To see how this works, let's use an example of a deposit of $1,000 in an account that pays interest at a rate of 12% per year, with interest compounded for different compounding frequencies. How much is in the account after, say, five years depends on the compounding frequency:

Compounding Frequency	Period	Rate per Compounding Period, i	Number of Periods in 5 Years, N	FV at the End of Five Years
Annual	one year	12%	5	$1,762.34
Semiannual	six months	6%	10	1,790.85
Quarterly	three months	3%	20	1,806.11
Monthly	one month	1%	60	1,816.70

As you can see, both the rate per period, i, and the number of compounding periods, N, are adjusted and depend on the frequency of compounding. Interest can be compounded for any frequency, such as daily or hourly.

Let's work through another example for compounding with compounding more than once a year. Suppose we invest $200,000 in an investment that pays 4% interest per year, compounded quarterly. What will be the future value of this investment at the end of 10 years?

EXHIBIT 7.2 Value of $50,000 Invested in the Account that Pays 8% Interest Per Year: Quarterly versus Annual Compounding

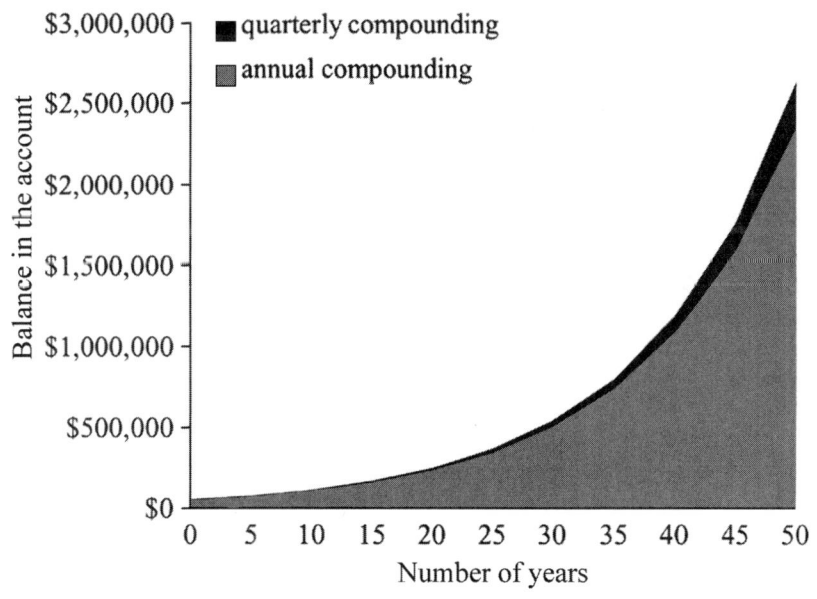

The given information is $i = 4\%/4 = 1\%$ and $N = 10 \times 4 = 40$ quarters. Therefore,

$$FV = \$200,000(1 + 0.01)^{40} = \$297,772.75$$

Continuous Compounding

The extreme frequency of compounding is *continuous compounding*—interest is compounded instantaneously. The factor for compounding continuously for one year is e^{APR}, where e is 2.71828..., the base of the natural logarithm. And the factor for compounding continuously for two years is $e^{APR}e^{APR}$ or e^{2APR}. The future value of an amount that is compounded continuously for N years is:

$$FV = PVe^{N(APR)} \tag{7-3}$$

where APR is the annual percentage rate and $e^{N(APR)}$ is the compound factor.

If \$1,000 is deposited in an account for five years with interest of 12% per year, compounded continuously,

$$FV = \$1,000e^{5(0.12)} = \$1,000(e^{0.60}) = \$1,000(1.82212) = \$1,822.12$$

Comparing this future value with that if interest is compounded annually at 12% per year for 5 years, \$1,762.34, we see that the effects of this extreme frequency of compounding.

Multiple Rates

In our discussion thus far, we have assumed that the investment will earn the same periodic interest rate, i. We can extend the calculation of a future value to allow for different interest rates or growth rates for different periods. Suppose an investment of \$10,000 pays 9% during the first year and 10% during the second year. At the end of the first period, the value of the investment is \$10,000(1 + 0.09), or \$10,900. During the second period, this \$10,900 earns interest at 10%. Therefore the future value of this \$10,000 at the end of the second period is:

$$FV = \$10,000(1 + 0.09)(1 + 0.10) = \$11,990$$

We can write this more generally as:

$$FV = PV(1 + i_1)(1 + i_2)(1 + i_3) \ldots (1 + i_N) \tag{7-4}$$

where i_N is the interest rate for period N.

Consider a $50,000 investment in a one-year bank certificate of deposit (CD) today and rolled over annually for the next two years into one-year CDs. The future value of the $50,000 investment will depend on the one-year CD rate each time the funds are rolled over. Assuming that the one-year CD rate today is 5% and that it is expected that the one-year CD rate one year from now will be 6%, and the one-year CD rate two years from now will be 6.5%, then we know:

$$FV = \$50,000(1 + 0.05)(1 + 0.06)(1 + 0.065) = \$59,267.25$$

Continuing this example, what is the average annual interest rate over this period? We know that the future value is $59,267.25, the present value is $50,000, and $N = 3$:

$$i = \sqrt[3]{\frac{\$59,267.25}{\$50,000.00}} - 1 = \sqrt[3]{1.185345} = 5.8315\%$$

which is also:

$$i = \sqrt[3]{(1 + 0.05)(1 + 0.06)(1 + 0.065)} - 1 = 5.8315\%$$

DETERMINING THE PRESENT VALUE

Now that we understand how to compute future values, let's work the process in reverse. Suppose that for borrowing a specific amount of money today, the Yenom Company promises to pay lenders $5,000 two years from today. How much should the lenders be willing to lend Yenom in exchange for this promise? This dilemma is different than figuring out a future value. Here we are given the future value and have to figure out the present value. But we can use the same basic idea from the future value problems to solve present value problems.

If you can earn 10% on other investments that have the same amount of uncertainty as the $5,000 Yenom promises to pay, then:

- the future value, $FV = \$5,000$
- the number of compounding periods, $N = 2$
- the interest rate, $i = 10\%$

We also know the basic relation between the present and future values:

$$FV = PV(1 + i)^N$$

Substituting the known values into this equation:

$$\$5{,}000 = PV(1 + 0.10)^2$$

To determine how much you are willing to lend now, PV, to get \$5,000 one year from now, FV, requires solving this equation for the unknown present value:

$$PV = \frac{\$5{,}000}{(1 + 0.10)^2} = \$5{,}000\left(\frac{1}{1 + 0.10}\right)^2 = \$5{,}000(0.82645) = \$4{,}132.25$$

Therefore, you would be willing to lend \$4,132.25 to receive \$5,000 one year from today if your opportunity cost is 10%. We can check our work by reworking the problem from the reverse perspective. Suppose you invested \$4,132.25 for two years and it earned 10% per year. What is the value of this investment at the end of the year?

We know: $PV = \$4{,}132.25$, $N = 10\%$ or 0.10, and $i = 2$.

Therefore the future value is:

$$FV = PV(1 + i)^N = \$4{,}132.25 \, (1 + 0.10)^2 = \$5{,}000.00$$

Compounding translates a value in one point in time into a value at some future point in time. The opposite process translates future values into present values: Discounting translates a value back in time. From the basic valuation equation:

$$FV = PV \, (1 + i)^N$$

we divide both sides by $(1 + i)^N$ and exchange sides to get the present value,

$$PV = \frac{FV}{(1 + i)^N} \tag{7-5}$$

$$\text{or } PV = FV\left(\frac{1}{1 + i}\right)^N \quad \text{or } PV = FV\left[\frac{1}{(1 + i)^N}\right]$$

The term in brackets [ ] is referred to as the *discount factor* since it is used to translate a future value to its equivalent present value. The present value of \$5,000 for discount periods ranging from 0 to 10 is shown in Exhibit 7.3.

EXHIBIT 7.3 Present Value of $5,000 Discounted at 10%

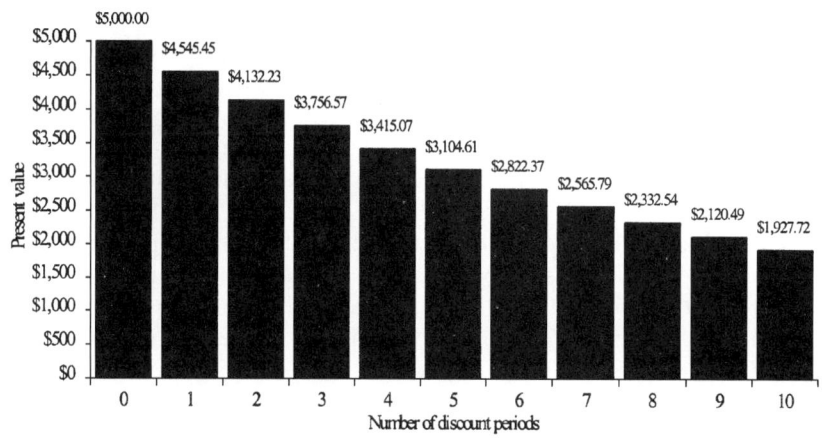

If the frequency of compounding is greater than once a year, we make adjustments to the rate per period and the number of periods as we did in compounding. For example, if the future value five years from today is $100,000 and the interest is 6% per year, compounded semiannually, $i = 6\%/2 = 3\%$ and $N = 5 \times 2 = 10$, and the present value is:

$$PV = \$100,000(1 + 0.03)^{10} = \$100,000(1.34392) = \$134,392$$

Here is an example of calculating a present value. Suppose that the goal is to have $75,000 in an account by the end of four years. And suppose that interest on this account is paid at a rate of 5% per year, compounded semiannually. How much must be deposited in the account today to reach this goal? We are given $FV = \$75,000$, $i = 5\%/2 = 2.5\%$ per six months, and $N = 4 \times 2 = 8$ six-month periods. The amount of the required deposit is therefore:

$$PV = \frac{\$75,000}{(1 + 0.025)^8} = \$61,555.99$$

Compound and Discount Factor Tables

There are different ways to translate values forward and backward in time. The basic way is through equations (7-1) and (7-5), using whichever values of PV, FV, N, or i given, and solving for the present or future value required by the problem.

Another way is to use tables of discount factors and compound factors. A table of compound factors for periods ranging from 1 to 20 and for rates of interest from 1% to 15% is provided in Exhibit 7.4. Similarly, a table of discount factors for the same range of periods and interest rates is provided in Exhibit 7.5. The compound factor to use for a problem is determined by choosing the table value corresponding to the row for the number of periods and the column for the interest rate per period given in the problem. A discount factor is determined in a like manner.

To see how to use a table of factors, let's find the compound factors for several combinations of periods and interest rates. The compound factor for 10 periods and an interest rate of 5% per period is 1.6289. The compound factor for five periods and an interest rate of 10% per period is 1.6105. The compound factor for three periods and an interest rate of 6% per period is 1.1910.

The table of compound factors can also be used for situations where you need to determine the number of periods or the interest rate. For example, suppose that you are asked to find out how long it takes to double your money if the interest rate per period is 8%. Doubling your money would mean that the future value is twice the present value. Using the equation:

$$FV = PV \, (1 + i)^N$$

and inserting the known values:

$$2.0000 = 1.0000(1 + 0.08)^N \text{ or } 2.0000 = (1 + 0.08)^N$$

the compound factor is 2.0000.

The compound factor for 8% per period over some unknown number of periods is 2.0000. Looking at the top panel, going down the 8% interest rate column, we see that the factor closest to 2.0000 is nine periods (compound factor = 1.9990). Therefore, it takes nine periods to double your money if interest is compounded at 8% per period.

Consider another example. If you want to invest $1,000 for six periods, at what interest rate must the account pay compounded interest in order for you to have $1,500 after six periods? We know

$$FV = PV(1+i)^N$$
$$\$1,500 = \$1,000(1+i)^6$$
$$1.5000 = (1+i)^6$$

EXHIBIT 7.4 Table of Compound Factors

Number of Periods	Compounding Rate											
	1%	2%	3%	4%	5%	6%	7%	8%	9%	10%	11%	12%
1	1.0100	1.0200	1.0300	1.0400	1.0500	1.0600	1.0700	1.0800	1.0900	1.1000	1.1100	1.1200
2	1.0201	1.0404	1.0609	1.0816	1.1025	1.1236	1.1449	1.1664	1.1881	1.2100	1.2321	1.2544
3	1.0303	1.0612	1.0927	1.1249	1.1576	1.1910	1.2250	1.2597	1.2950	1.3310	1.3676	1.4049
4	1.0406	1.0824	1.1255	1.1699	1.2155	1.2625	1.3108	1.3605	1.4116	1.4641	1.5181	1.5735
5	1.0510	1.1041	1.1593	1.2167	1.2763	1.3382	1.4026	1.4693	1.5386	1.6105	1.6851	1.7623
6	1.0615	1.1262	1.1941	1.2653	1.3401	1.4185	1.5007	1.5869	1.6771	1.7716	1.8704	1.9738
7	1.0721	1.1487	1.2299	1.3159	1.4071	1.5036	1.6058	1.7138	1.8280	1.9487	2.0762	2.2107
8	1.0829	1.1717	1.2668	1.3686	1.4775	1.5938	1.7182	1.8509	1.9926	2.1436	2.3045	2.4760
9	1.0937	1.1951	1.3048	1.4233	1.5513	1.6895	1.8385	1.9990	2.1719	2.3579	2.5580	2.7731
10	1.1046	1.2190	1.3439	1.4802	1.6289	1.7908	1.9672	2.1589	2.3674	2.5937	2.8394	3.1058
11	1.1157	1.2434	1.3842	1.5395	1.7103	1.8983	2.1049	2.3316	2.5804	2.8531	3.1518	3.4785
12	1.1268	1.2682	1.4258	1.6010	1.7959	2.0122	2.2522	2.5182	2.8127	3.1384	3.4985	3.8960
13	1.1381	1.2936	1.4685	1.6651	1.8856	2.1329	2.4098	2.7196	3.0658	3.4523	3.8833	4.3635
14	1.1495	1.3195	1.5126	1.7317	1.9799	2.2609	2.5785	2.9372	3.3417	3.7975	4.3104	4.8871
15	1.1610	1.3459	1.5580	1.8009	2.0789	2.3966	2.7590	3.1722	3.6425	4.1772	4.7846	5.4736
16	1.1726	1.3728	1.6047	1.8730	2.1829	2.5404	2.9522	3.4259	3.9703	4.5950	5.3109	6.1304
17	1.1843	1.4002	1.6528	1.9479	2.2920	2.6928	3.1588	3.7000	4.3276	5.0545	5.8951	6.8660
18	1.1961	1.4282	1.7024	2.0258	2.4066	2.8543	3.3799	3.9960	4.7171	5.5599	6.5436	7.6900
19	1.2081	1.4568	1.7535	2.1068	2.5270	3.0256	3.6165	4.3157	5.1417	6.1159	7.2633	8.6128
20	1.2202	1.4859	1.8061	2.1911	2.6533	3.2071	3.8697	4.6610	5.6044	6.7275	8.0623	9.6463
21	1.2324	1.5157	1.8603	2.2788	2.7860	3.3996	4.1406	5.0338	6.1088	7.4002	8.9492	10.8038
22	1.2447	1.5460	1.9161	2.3699	2.9253	3.6035	4.4304	5.4365	6.6586	8.1403	9.9336	12.1003
23	1.2572	1.5769	1.9736	2.4647	3.0715	3.8197	4.7405	5.8715	7.2579	8.9543	11.0263	13.5523
24	1.2697	1.6084	2.0328	2.5633	3.2251	4.0489	5.0724	6.3412	7.9111	9.8497	12.2392	15.1786
25	1.2824	1.6406	2.0938	2.6658	3.3864	4.2919	5.4274	6.8485	8.6231	10.8347	13.5855	17.0001
26	1.2953	1.6734	2.1566	2.7725	3.5557	4.5494	5.8074	7.3964	9.3992	11.9182	15.0799	19.0401
27	1.3082	1.7069	2.2213	2.8834	3.7335	4.8223	6.2139	7.9881	10.2451	13.1100	16.7386	21.3249
28	1.3213	1.7410	2.2879	2.9987	3.9201	5.1117	6.6488	8.6271	11.1671	14.4210	18.5799	23.8839
29	1.3345	1.7758	2.3566	3.1187	4.1161	5.4184	7.1143	9.3173	12.1722	15.8631	20.6237	26.7499
30	1.3478	1.8114	2.4273	3.2434	4.3219	5.7435	7.6123	10.0627	13.2677	17.4494	22.8923	29.9599

EXHIBIT 7.5   Table of Discount Factors

Number of Periods	Discount Rate											
	1%	2%	3%	4%	5%	6%	7%	8%	9%	10%	11%	12%
1	0.9901	0.9804	0.9709	0.9615	0.9524	0.9434	0.9346	0.9259	0.9174	0.9091	0.9009	0.8929
2	0.9803	0.9612	0.9426	0.9246	0.9070	0.8900	0.8734	0.8573	0.8417	0.8264	0.8116	0.7972
3	0.9706	0.9423	0.9151	0.8890	0.8638	0.8396	0.8163	0.7938	0.7722	0.7513	0.7312	0.7118
4	0.9610	0.9238	0.8885	0.8548	0.8227	0.7921	0.7629	0.7350	0.7084	0.6830	0.6587	0.6355
5	0.9515	0.9057	0.8626	0.8219	0.7835	0.7473	0.7130	0.6806	0.6499	0.6209	0.5935	0.5674
6	0.9420	0.8880	0.8375	0.7903	0.7462	0.7050	0.6663	0.6302	0.5963	0.5645	0.5346	0.5066
7	0.9327	0.8706	0.8131	0.7599	0.7107	0.6651	0.6227	0.5835	0.5470	0.5132	0.4817	0.4523
8	0.9235	0.8535	0.7894	0.7307	0.6768	0.6274	0.5820	0.5403	0.5019	0.4665	0.4339	0.4039
9	0.9143	0.8368	0.7664	0.7026	0.6446	0.5919	0.5439	0.5002	0.4604	0.4241	0.3909	0.3606
10	0.9053	0.8203	0.7441	0.6756	0.6139	0.5584	0.5083	0.4632	0.4224	0.3855	0.3522	0.3220
11	0.8963	0.8043	0.7224	0.6496	0.5847	0.5268	0.4751	0.4289	0.3875	0.3505	0.3173	0.2875
12	0.8874	0.7885	0.7014	0.6246	0.5568	0.4970	0.4440	0.3971	0.3555	0.3186	0.2858	0.2567
13	0.8787	0.7730	0.6810	0.6006	0.5303	0.4688	0.4150	0.3677	0.3262	0.2897	0.2575	0.2292
14	0.8700	0.7579	0.6611	0.5775	0.5051	0.4423	0.3878	0.3405	0.2992	0.2633	0.2320	0.2046
15	0.8613	0.7430	0.6419	0.5553	0.4810	0.4173	0.3624	0.3152	0.2745	0.2394	0.2090	0.1827
16	0.8528	0.7284	0.6232	0.5339	0.4581	0.3936	0.3387	0.2919	0.2519	0.2176	0.1883	0.1631
17	0.8444	0.7142	0.6050	0.5134	0.4363	0.3714	0.3166	0.2703	0.2311	0.1978	0.1696	0.1456
18	0.8360	0.7002	0.5874	0.4936	0.4155	0.3503	0.2959	0.2502	0.2120	0.1799	0.1528	0.1300
19	0.8277	0.6864	0.5703	0.4746	0.3957	0.3305	0.2765	0.2317	0.1945	0.1635	0.1377	0.1161
20	0.8195	0.6730	0.5537	0.4564	0.3769	0.3118	0.2584	0.2145	0.1784	0.1486	0.1240	0.1037
21	0.8114	0.6598	0.5375	0.4388	0.3589	0.2942	0.2415	0.1987	0.1637	0.1351	0.1117	0.0926
22	0.8034	0.6468	0.5219	0.4220	0.3418	0.2775	0.2257	0.1839	0.1502	0.1228	0.1007	0.0826
23	0.7954	0.6342	0.5067	0.4057	0.3256	0.2618	0.2109	0.1703	0.1378	0.1117	0.0907	0.0738
24	0.7876	0.6217	0.4919	0.3901	0.3101	0.2470	0.1971	0.1577	0.1264	0.1015	0.0817	0.0659
25	0.7798	0.6095	0.4776	0.3751	0.2953	0.2330	0.1842	0.1460	0.1160	0.0923	0.0736	0.0588
26	0.7720	0.5976	0.4637	0.3607	0.2812	0.2198	0.1722	0.1352	0.1064	0.0839	0.0663	0.0525
27	0.7644	0.5859	0.4502	0.3468	0.2678	0.2074	0.1609	0.1252	0.0976	0.0763	0.0597	0.0469
28	0.7568	0.5744	0.4371	0.3335	0.2551	0.1956	0.1504	0.1159	0.0895	0.0693	0.0538	0.0419
29	0.7493	0.5631	0.4243	0.3207	0.2429	0.1846	0.1406	0.1073	0.0822	0.0630	0.0485	0.0374
30	0.7419	0.5521	0.4120	0.3083	0.2314	0.1741	0.1314	0.0994	0.0754	0.0573	0.0437	0.0334

Therefore, the compound factor is 1.5. Using Exhibit 7.4, we see going across the row corresponding to six periods that the compound factor is 1.5000 at (approximately) a 7% interest rate. Therefore, if you save $1,000 in an account that provides 7% per period compounded interest for 6 periods, you will have a balance of approximately $1,500 after six periods.

To see how to use Exhibit 7.5, let's find the discount factors for several combinations of periods and interest rates. The discount factor for ten periods and an interest rate of 5% per period is 0.6139. The discount factor for five periods and an interest rate of 10% per period is 0.6209. The discount factor for three periods and an interest rate of 6% per period is 0.8396. Just as we did for the compound factors, these discount factors can be used to solve for N, given a value of the discount factor and an interest rate, or to solve for the interest rate, given the value for the discount factor and the number of discounting periods.

If we look at equations (7-1) and (7-5) and think about them for a moment, it becomes apparent that inverting the values in one table produces the values in the other. For example, using the corresponding factors for $N = 10$ and $r = 5\%$, we see this inverse relation:

$$\text{Compound factor} = 1/\text{Discount factor}$$
$$1.6289 = 1/0.6139$$

Likewise,

$$\text{Discount factor} = 1/\text{Compound factor}$$
$$0.6139 = 1/1.6289$$

The compound and discount factors are inversely related to one another for any pair of N and i values.

Using a Financial Calculator

The financial math of discounting and compounding can also be performed using a financial calculator. The basic idea is to input the known values and let the calculator solve for the one unknown value—the financial math is programmed into the calculator. To use a financial calculator effectively, you need to understand how to input the known values. For example, in most financial calculators the present value is input as a negative value. Consider using the financial calculator to solve the following problem: You invest $5,000 today in an account that pays 8% interest. What is the balance in the account at the end of five years?

The known values are the following: $PV = \$5,000$, $i = 8\%$, and $N = 5$. The one unknown is the future value. Using several popular financial cal-

culators, we can readily solve this problem to arrive at the answer of
$7,346.64:

Hewlett-Packard 10B	Hewlett-Packard 12C	Hewlett-Packard 17B	Texas Instruments BA-II Plus
5000 ± PV	5000 CHS PV	FIN TVM	5000 ± PV
8 I/YR	8 i	5000 ± PV	8 I
5 N	5 n	8 I%YR	5 N
FV	FV	5 N	FV
		FV	

DETERMINING THE UNKNOWN INTEREST RATE

As we saw earlier in our discussion of growth rates, we can rearrange
the basic equation to solve for i:

$$i = \sqrt[N]{\frac{FV}{PV}} - 1 = \left(\frac{FV}{PV}\right)^{1/N} - 1$$

As an example, suppose that the value of an investment today is
$100 and the expected value of the investment in five years is expected
to be $150. What is the annual rate of appreciation in value of this
investment over the five-year period?

$$i = \sqrt[5]{\frac{\$150}{\$100}} - 1$$
$$= \sqrt[5]{1.5} - 1 = 0.0845 \text{ or } 8.45\% \text{ per year}$$

As we saw earlier, we can approximate the interest rate using
Exhibit 7.4 or Exhibit 7.5. From the formulas for the present value and
future value, you can see that the compounding factor is the ratio of the
future value to the present value, whereas the discounting factor is the
ratio of the present value to the future value. That is,

$$\text{Compounding factor} = (1 + i)^N = \frac{FV}{PV}$$

and

$$\text{Discounting factor} = \left(\frac{1}{1+i}\right)^N = \frac{PV}{FV}$$

In this example,

$$\frac{FV}{PV} = 1.500 \quad \text{and} \quad \frac{PV}{FV} = 0.6667$$

In Exhibit 7.4, the factor closest to 1.5 in the row corresponding to five periods is in the column for a 9% interest rate. In Exhibit 7.5, the factor closest to 0.6667 in the row corresponding to five periods is in the 9% interest rate column. Therefore, investing $100 today will produce $150 five years from now if the investment appreciates approximately 9% per year, as before.

There are many applications in which managers need to determine the rate of change in values over a period of time. If values are increasing over time, we refer to the rate of change as the growth rate. To make comparisons easier, we usually specify the growth rate as a rate per year.

For example, if we wish to determine the rate of growth in these values, we solve for the unknown interest rate. Consider the growth rate of dividends for Bell Atlantic. Bell Atlantic paid dividends of $1.18 per share in 1990 and $1.55 in 1998. We have dividends for two different points in time: 1990 and 1998. Using equation (7-3), with 1990 dividends as the present value, 1998 dividends as the future value, and $N = 8$:

Growth rate in Bell Atlantic's dividends 1990–1998

$$= \sqrt[8]{\frac{\$1.55}{\$1.18}} - 1 = 3.468\%$$

Therefore, Bell Atlantic's dividends grew at a rate of almost 3.5% per year over this eight-year period.

DETERMINING THE NUMBER OF COMPOUNDING PERIODS

Given the present and future values, calculating the number of periods when we know the interest rate is a bit more complex than calculating the interest rate when we know the number of periods. Nevertheless, we can develop an equation for determining the number of periods, beginning with the valuation formula given by equation (7-1) and rearranging to solve for N,

$$N = \frac{\ln FV - \ln PV}{\ln(1 + i)} \qquad (7\text{-}6)$$

where ln indicates the natural logarithm, which is the log of the base e.[1]

Suppose that the present value of an investment is \$100 and you wish to determine how long it will take for the investment to double in value if the investment earns 6% per year, compounded annually:

$$N = \frac{\ln 200 - \ln 100}{\ln 1.06} = \frac{5.2983 - 4.6052}{0.0583}$$
$$= 11.8885 \text{ or approximately 12 years}$$

You'll notice that we round off to the next whole period. To see why, consider this last example. After 11.8885 years, we have doubled our money if interest were paid 88.85% the way through the twelfth year. But, we stated earlier that interest is paid *at the end of each period*—not part of the way through. At the end of the eleventh year, our investment is worth \$189.93, and at the end of the twelfth year, our investment is worth \$201.22. So, our investment's value doubles by the twelfth period—with a little extra, \$1.22.

The factors presented in Exhibits 7.4 and 7.5 can be used to approximate the number of periods. The approach is similar to the way we approximated the interest rate. The compounding factor in this example is 2.0000 and the discounting factor is 0.5000 (that is, $FV/PV = 2.0000$ and $PV/FV = 0.5000$). Using Exhibit 7.4, following down the column corresponding to the interest rate of 6%, the compound factor closest to 2.0000 is for 12 periods. Likewise, using Exhibit 7.5, following down the column corresponding to the interest rate of 6%, the discount factor closest to 0.5000 is for 12 periods.

THE TIME VALUE OF A SERIES OF CASH FLOWS

Managers regularly need to determine the present or future value of a *series* of cash flows rather than simply a single cash flow. The principles of determining the future value or present value of a series of cash flows are the same as for a single cash flow, yet the math becomes a bit more cumbersome.

Suppose that the following deposits are made in a Thrifty Savings and Loan account paying 5% interest, compounded annually:

---

[1] e is approximately equal to 2.718. The natural logarithm function can be found on most calculators, usually indicated by "ln".

Time when Deposit is Made	Amount of Deposit
Today	$1,000
At the end of the first year	2,000
At the end of the second year	1,500

What is the balance in the savings account at the end of the second year if no withdrawals are made and interest is paid annually?

Let's simplify any problem like this by referring to today as the end of period 0, and identifying the end of the first and each successive period as 1, 2, 3, and so on. Represent each end-of-period cash flow as "CF" with a subscript specifying the period to which it corresponds. Thus, CF_0 is a cash flow today, CF_{10} is a cash flow at the end of period 10, and CF_{25} is a cash flow at the end of period 25, and so on.

Representing the information in our example using cash flow and period notation:

Period	Cash Flow	End of Period Cash Flow
0	CF_0	$1,000
1	CF_1	$2,000
2	CF_2	$1,500

The future value of the series of cash flows at the end of the second period is calculated as follows:

Period	End of Period Cash Flow	Number of Periods Interest is Earned	Compounding Factor	Future Value
0	$1,000	2	1.1025	$1,102.50
1	2,000	1	1.0500	2,100.00
2	1,500	0	1.0000	1,500.00
				$4,702.50

The last cash flow, $1,500, was deposited at the very end of the second period—the point of time at which we wish to know the future value of the series. Therefore, this deposit earns no interest. In more formal terms, its future value is precisely equal to its present value.

Today, the end of period 0, the balance in the account is $1,000 since the first deposit is made but no interest has been earned. At the end of period 1, the balance in the account is $3,050, made up of three parts:

1. the first deposit, $1,000
2. $50 interest on the first deposit
3. the second deposit, $2,000

The balance in the account at the end of period 2 is $4,702.50, made up of five parts:

1. the first deposit, $1,000
2. the second deposit, $2,000
3. the third deposit, $1,500
4. $102.50 interest on the first deposit, $50 earned at the end of the first period, $52.50 more earned at the end of the second period
5. $100 interest earned on the second deposit at the end of the second period

These cash flows can also be represented in a time line. A *time line* is used to help graphically depict and sort out each cash flow in a series. The time line for this example is shown in Exhibit 7.6. From this example, you can see that the future value of the entire series is the sum of each of the compounded cash flows comprising the series. In much the same way, we can determine the future value of a series comprising any number of cash flows. And if we need to, we can determine the future value of a number of cash flows before the end of the series.

For example, suppose you are planning to deposit $1,000 today and at the end of each year for the next ten years in a savings account paying 5% interest annually. If you want to know the future value of this series after four years, you compound each cash flow for the number of years it takes to reach four years. That is, you compound the first cash flow over four years, the second cash flow over three years, the third over two years, the fourth over one year, and the fifth you don't compound at all because you will have just deposited it in the bank at the end of the fourth year.

EXHIBIT 7.6 Time Line for the Future Value of a Series of Uneven Cash Flows Deposited to Earn 5% Compounded Interest Per Period

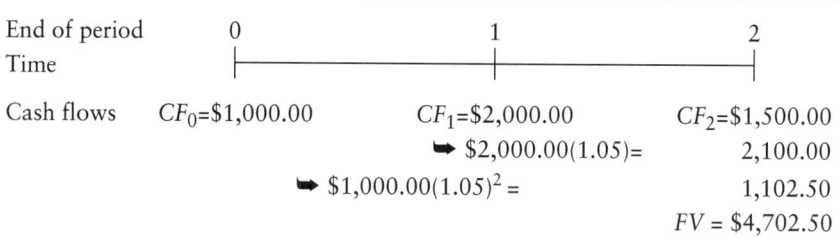

To determine the present value of a series of future cash flows, each cash flow is discounted back to the present, where the beginning of the first period, today, is designated as 0. As an example, consider the Thrifty Savings & Loan problem from a different angle. Instead of calculating what the deposits and the interest on these deposits will be worth in the future, let's calculate the present value of the deposits. The present value is what these future deposits are worth today.

In the series of cash flows of $1,000 today, $2,000 at the end of period 1, and $1,500 at the end of period 2, each are discounted to the present, 0, as follows:

Period	End of Period Cash Flow	Number of Periods of Discounting	Discount Factor	Present Value
0	$1,000	0	1.00000	$1,000.00
1	$2,000	1	0.95238	1,904.76
2	$1,500	2	0.90703	1,360.54
				$FV = \$4,265.30$

The present value of the series is the sum of the present value of these three cash flows, $4,265.30. For example, the $1,500 cash flow at the end of period 2 is worth $1,428.57 at the end of the first period and is worth $1,360.54 today.

The present value of a series of cash flows can be represented in notation form as:

$$PV = CF_0\left(\frac{1}{1+i}\right)^0 + CF_1\left(\frac{1}{1+i}\right)^1 + CF_2\left(\frac{1}{1+i}\right)^2 + \ldots + CF_N\left(\frac{1}{1+i}\right)^N$$

For example, if there are cash flows today and at the end of periods 1 and 2, today's cash flow is not discounted, the first period cash flow is discounted one period, and the second period cash flow is discounted two periods.

We can represent the present value of a series using summation notation as shown below:

$$PV = \sum_{t=0}^{N} CF_t\left(\frac{1}{1+i}\right)^t \qquad (7\text{-}7)$$

This equation tells us that the present value of a series of cash flows is the sum of the products of each cash flow and its corresponding discount factor.

We can also use the cash flow program in a financial calculator to solve for the present value of an uneven series of cash flows:

Hewlett-Packard 10B	Hewlett-Packard 12C	Hewlett-Packard 17B	Texas Instruments BA-II Plus
1000 CFj	1000 CF$_0$	FIN CFLO	CF
2000 CFj	2000 CFj	1000 INPUT	1000 ENTER
1500 CFj	1500 CFj	1 INPUT	↑ 1 ENTER
5 I/YR	5 i	2000 INPUT	↑ 2000 ENTER
■ NPV	f NPV	1 INPUT	↑ 1 ENTER
		1500 INPUT	↑ 1500 ENTER
		1 INPUT	↑ 1 ENTER
		CALC	CPT NPV 5 I/Y ↑ CPT
		5 I%	
		NPV	

Shortcuts: Annuities

There are valuation problems that require us to evaluate a series of level cash flows—each cash flow is the same amount as the others—received at regular intervals. Let's suppose you expect to deposit $2,000 at the end of each of the *next* four years (2000, 2001, 2002, and 2003) in an account earning 8% compounded interest. How much will you have available at the end of 2003, the fourth year?

As we just did for the future value of a series of uneven cash flows, we can calculate the future value (as of the end of 2003) of each $2,000 deposit, compounding interest at 8%:

$$FV = \$2,000(1 + 0.08)^3 + \$2,000(1 + 0.08)^2 + \$2,000(1 + 0.08)^1$$
$$+ \$2,000(1 + 0.08)^0$$
$$= \$2,519.40 + \$2,332.80 + \$2,160.00 + \$2,000 = \$9,012.20$$

Exhibit 7.7 shows the contribution of each deposit and the accumulated interest at the end of each period.

- At the end of 1998, there is $2,000.00 in the account since you have just made your first deposit.
- At the end of 1999, there is $4,160.00 in the account: two deposits of $2,000 each, plus $160 interest (8% of $2,000).
- At the end of 2000, there is $6,492.80 in the account: three deposits of $2,000.00 each, plus accumulated interest of $492.80 [$160.00 + (0.08 × $4,000) + (0.08 × $160)].

EXHIBIT 7.7   Balance in an Account in which Deposits of $2,000 Each are Made Each Year. The Balance in the Account Earns 8%.

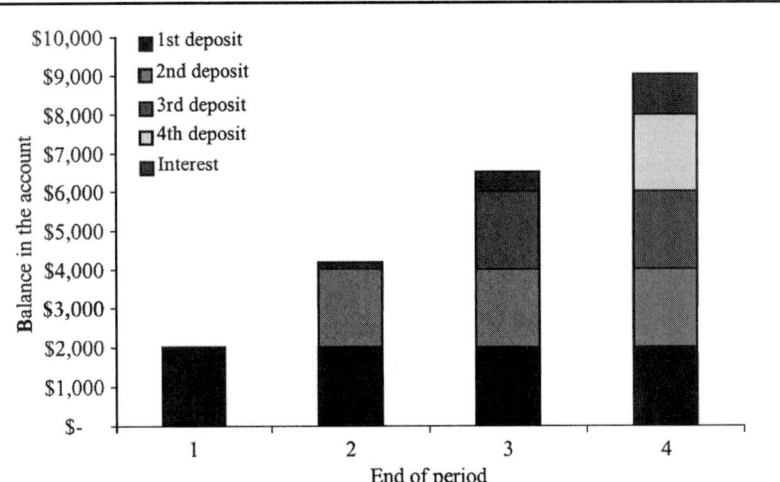

- At the end of the fourth year, you would have $9,012.20 available: four deposits of $2,000 each, plus $1,012.20 accumulated interest [$160.00 + $492.80 + (0.08 × $6,000) + (0.08 × ($160.00 + 492.80))].

Notice that in our calculations, each deposit of $2,000 is multiplied by a factor that corresponds to an interest rate of 8% and the number of periods that the deposit has been in the savings account. Since the deposit of $2,000 is common to each multiplication, we can simplify the math a bit by multiplying the $2,000 by the sum of the factors to get the same answer:

$$FV = \$2,000(1.2597) + \$2,000(1.1664) + \$2,000(1.0800)$$
$$\text{ⅼ } \$2,000(1.0000) = \$9,012.20$$

A series of cash flows of equal amount, occurring at even intervals is referred to as an annuity. Determining the value of an annuity, whether compounding or discounting, is simpler than valuing uneven cash flows. If each CF_t is equal (that is, all the cash flows are the same value) and the first one occurs at the end of the first period $(t = 1)$, we can express the future value of the series as:

$$FV = \sum_{t=1}^{N} CF_t(1+i)^{N-t}$$

N is last and t indicates the time period corresponding to a particular cash flow, starting at 1 for an ordinary annuity. Since CF_t is shorthand for: $CF_1, CF_2, CF_3, \ldots, CF_N$, and we know that $CF_1 = CF_2 = CF_3 = \ldots CF_N$, let's make things simple by using CF to indicate the same value for the periodic cash flows. Rearranging the future value equation we get:

$$FV = CF \sum_{t=1}^{N} (1+i)^{N-t} \qquad (7\text{-}8)$$

This equation tells us that the future value of a level series of cash flows, occurring at regular intervals beginning one period from today (notice that t starts at 1), is equal to the amount of cash flow multiplied by the sum of the compound factors.

In a like manner, the equation for the present value of a series of level cash flows beginning after one period simplifies to:

$$PV = \sum_{t=1}^{N} CF_t \left(\frac{1}{1+i}\right)^t = CF \sum_{t=1}^{N} \left(\frac{1}{1+i}\right)^t$$

or

$$PV = CF \sum_{t=1}^{N} \frac{1}{(1+i)^t} \qquad (7\text{-}9)$$

This equation tells us that the present value of an annuity is equal to the amount of one cash flow multiplied by the sum of the discount factors.

Equations (7-8) and (7-9) are the valuation—future and present value—formulas for an *ordinary annuity*. An ordinary annuity is a special form of annuity, where the first cash flow occurs *at the end of the first period*.

To calculate the future value of an annuity we multiply the amount of the annuity (that is, the amount of one periodic cash flow) by the sum of the compound factors. The sum of these compounding factors for a given interest rate, i, and number of periods, N, is referred to as the *future value annuity factor*. Likewise, to calculate the present value of an annuity we multiply one cash flow of the annuity by the sum of the discount factors. The sum of the discounting factors for a given i and N is referred to as the *present value annuity factor*.

Suppose you wish to determine the future value of a series of deposits of $1,000, deposited each year in the No Fault Vault Bank for five years, with the first deposit made at the end of the first year. If the NFV

Bank pays 5% interest on the balance in the account at the end of each year and no withdrawals are made, what is the balance in the account at the end of the five years?

Each $1,000 is deposited at a different time, so it contributes a different amount to the future value. For example, the first deposit accumulates interest for four periods, contributing $1,215.50 to the future value (at the end of period 5), whereas the last deposit contributes only $1,000 to the future value since it is deposited at exactly the point in time when we are determining the future value, hence there is no interest on this deposit.

The future value of an annuity is the sum of the future value of each deposit:

Period	Amount of Deposit	Number of Periods Interest is Earned	Compounding Factor	Future Value
1	$1,000	4	1.2155	$1,215.50
2	1,000	3	1.1576	1,157.60
3	1,000	2	1.1025	1,102.50
4	1,000	1	1.0500	1,050.00
5	1,000	0	1.0000	1,000.00
Total			5.5256	$5,525.60

The future value of the series of $1,000 deposits, with interest compounded at 5%, is $5,525.60. Since we know the value of one of the level period flows is $1,000, and the future value of the annuity is $5,525.60, and looking at the sum of the individual compounding factors, 5.5256, we can see that there is an easier way to calculate the future value of an annuity. If the sum of the individual compounding factors for a specific interest rate and a specific number of periods were available, all we would have to do is multiply that sum by the value of one cash flow to get the future value of the entire annuity.

In this example, the shortcut is multiplying the amount of the annuity, $1,000, by the sum of the compounding factors, 5.5256:

$$FV = \$1,000 \times 5.5256 = \$5,525.60$$

For large numbers of periods, summing the individual factors can be a bit clumsy—with possibilities of errors along the way. An alternative formula for the sum of the compound factors—that is, the future value annuity factor—is:

$$\text{Future value annuity factor} = \frac{(1+i)^N - 1}{i} \qquad (7\text{-}10)$$

In the last example, $N = 5$ and $i = 5\%$:

$$\text{Future value annuity factor} = \frac{(1 + 0.05)^5 - 1}{0.05} = \frac{1.2763 - 1.000}{0.05} = 5.5256$$

Let's use the long method to find the present value of the series of five deposits of \$1,000 each, with the first deposit at the end of the first period. Then we'll do it using the shortcut method. The calculations are similar to the future value of an ordinary annuity, except we are taking each deposit back in time, instead of forward:

Period	Amount of Deposit	Discounting Periods	Discounting Factor	Present Value
1	\$1,000	1	0.9524	\$952.40
2	1,000	2	0.9070	907.00
3	1,000	3	0.8638	863.80
4	1,000	4	0.8227	822.70
5	1,000	5	0.7835	783.50
Total			4.3294	\$4,329.40

The present value of this series of five deposits is \$4,329.40.

This same value is obtained by multiplying the annuity amount of \$1,000 by the sum of the discounting factors, 4.3294:

$$PV = \$1,000 \times 4.3294 = \$4,329.40$$

Another, more convenient way of solving for the present value of an annuity is to rewrite the factor as:

$$\text{Present value annuity factor} = \frac{1 - \dfrac{1}{(1 + i)^N}}{i} \tag{7-11}$$

If there are many discount periods, this formula is a bit easier to calculate. In our last example,

$$\text{Present value annuity factor} = \frac{\left[1 - \dfrac{1}{(1 + 0.05)^5}\right]}{0.05} = \frac{1 - 0.7835}{0.05} = 4.3295$$

which is different from the sum of the factors, 4.3294, due to rounding.

We can turn this present value of an annuity problem around to look at it from another angle. Suppose you borrow $4,329.40 at an interest rate of 5% per period and are required to pay back this loan in five installments ($N = 5$): one payment per period for five periods, starting one period from now. The payments are determined by equating the present value with the product of the cash flow and the sum of the discount factors:

$$PV = CF(\text{sum of discount factors})$$
$$= CF \sum_{t=1}^{5} \frac{1}{(1 + 0.05)^t}$$
$$= CF(0.9524 + 0.9070 + 0.8638 + 0.8227 + 0.7835)$$
$$= CF(4.3294)$$

substituting the known present value,

$$\$4,329.40 = CF(4.3294)$$

and rearranging to solve for the payment:

$$CF = \$4,329.40/4.3290 = \$1,000.00$$

We can convince ourselves that five installments of $1,000 each can pay off the loan of $4,329.40 by carefully stepping through the calculation of interest and the reduction of the principal:

Beginning of Periods Loan Balance	Payment	Interest (Principal × 5%)	Reduction in Loan Balance (Payment – Interest)	End of Period Loan Balance
$4,329.40	$1,000.00	$216.47	$783.53	$3,545.87
3,545.87	1,000.00	177.29	822.71	2,723.16
2,723.16	1,000.00	136.16	863.84	1,859.32
1,859.32	1,000.00	92.97	907.03	952.29
952.29	1,000.00	47.61	952.29*	0

* The small difference between calculated reduction ($952.38) and reported reduction is due to rounding differences.

For example, the first payment of $1,000 is used to: (1) pay interest on the loan at 5% ($4,329.40 × 0.05 = $216.47) and (2) pay down the principal or loan balance ($1,000.00 – 216.47 = $783.53 paid off). Each successive payment pays off a greater amount of the loan—as the principal amount of the loan is reduced, less of each payment goes to paying off interest and more goes to reducing the loan principal. This analysis of the repayment of a loan is referred to as loan amortization. *Loan amortization* is the repayment of a loan with equal payments, over a specified period of time. As we can see from the example of borrowing $4,329.40, each payment can be broken down into its interest and principal components.

Shortcuts: Tables and Calculators

Annuity factor tables simplify the task of valuing annuities. Exhibit 7.8 is a table of future value of annuity factors for interest rates and periods from 1% to 20% and from 1 to 20 payments, respectively. Exhibit 7.9 is the corresponding table for present value of annuity factors. For example, the future value annuity factor from Exhibit 7.8 for five periodic payments and an interest rate of 10% is 6.1051 and the present value annuity factor from Exhibit 7.9 for five periodic payments and an interest rate of 10% is 3.7908; the factor for 10 periodic payments and an interest rate of 5% is 7.7217.

Like the tables of compound and discount factors, we can use the annuity factor tables to solve for N (given i and the appropriate factor) or for i (given N and the appropriate factor). Suppose that we deposit $1,000 at the end of each year in an account that pays 6% compounded annual interest. How many years must we make deposits in the account to have a balance of $7,000? We can work this using the future value annuity factor in Exhibit 7.8. We know that the future value is $7,000, the interest rate is 6%, and the periodic payments are $1,000. We substitute this information into the formula for the future value of an annuity and solve for the future value annuity factor:

$$FV = CF\left[\sum_{t=1}^{N} (1+i)^{N-t}\right]$$

where the term in brackets is the future value annuity factor. That is,

$$\text{Future value annuity factor} = \sum_{t=1}^{N} (1+i)^{N-t}$$

Substituting the known future value and the known value of CF:

$$\$7,000 = \$1,000 \text{ (future value annuity factor)}$$

we know that the future value annuity factor is 7.0000.

EXHIBIT 7.8 Table of Factors for the Future Value of a $1 Annuity

Number of Cash Flows	Compounding Rate											
	1%	2%	3%	4%	5%	6%	7%	8%	9%	10%	11%	12%
1	1.0000	1.0000	1.0000	1.0000	1.0000	1.0000	1.0000	1.0000	1.0000	1.0000	1.0000	1.0000
2	2.0100	2.0200	2.0300	2.0400	2.0500	2.0600	2.0700	2.0800	2.0900	2.1000	2.1100	2.1200
3	3.0301	3.0604	3.0909	3.1216	3.1525	3.1836	3.2149	3.2464	3.2781	3.3100	3.3421	3.3744
4	4.0604	4.1216	4.1836	4.2465	4.3101	4.3746	4.4399	4.5061	4.5731	4.6410	4.7097	4.7793
5	5.1010	5.2040	5.3091	5.4163	5.5256	5.6371	5.7507	5.8666	5.9847	6.1051	6.2278	6.3528
6	6.1520	6.3081	6.4684	6.6330	6.8019	6.9753	7.1533	7.3359	7.5233	7.7156	7.9129	8.1152
7	7.2135	7.4343	7.6625	7.8983	8.1420	8.3938	8.6540	8.9228	9.2004	9.4872	9.7833	10.0890
8	8.2857	8.5830	8.8923	9.2142	9.5491	9.8975	10.2598	10.6366	11.0285	11.4359	11.8594	12.2997
9	9.3685	9.7546	10.1591	10.5828	11.0266	11.4913	11.9780	12.4876	13.0210	13.5795	14.1640	14.7757
10	10.4622	10.9497	11.4639	12.0061	12.5779	13.1808	13.8164	14.4866	15.1929	15.9374	16.7220	17.5487
11	11.5668	12.1687	12.8078	13.4864	14.2068	14.9716	15.7836	16.6455	17.5603	18.5312	19.5614	20.6546
12	12.6825	13.4121	14.1920	15.0258	15.9171	16.8699	17.8885	18.9771	20.1407	21.3843	22.7132	24.1331
13	13.8093	14.6803	15.6178	16.6268	17.7130	18.8821	20.1406	21.4953	22.9534	24.5227	26.2116	28.0291
14	14.9474	15.9739	17.0863	18.2919	19.5986	21.0151	22.5505	24.2149	26.0192	27.9750	30.0949	32.3926
15	16.0969	17.2934	18.5989	20.0236	21.5786	23.2760	25.1290	27.1521	29.3609	31.7725	34.4054	37.2797
16	17.2579	18.6393	20.1569	21.8245	23.6575	25.6725	27.8881	30.3243	33.0034	35.9497	39.1899	42.7533
17	18.4304	20.0121	21.7616	23.6975	25.8404	28.2129	30.8402	33.7502	36.9737	40.5447	44.5008	48.8837
18	19.6147	21.4123	23.4144	25.6454	28.1324	30.9057	33.9990	37.4502	41.3013	45.5992	50.3959	55.7497
19	20.8109	22.8406	25.1169	27.6712	30.5390	33.7600	37.3790	41.4463	46.0185	51.1591	56.9395	63.4397
20	22.0190	24.2974	26.8704	29.7781	33.0660	36.7856	40.9955	45.7620	51.1601	57.2750	64.2028	72.0524
21	23.2392	25.7833	28.6765	31.9692	35.7193	39.9927	44.8652	50.4229	56.7645	64.0025	72.2651	81.6987
22	24.4716	27.2990	30.5368	34.2480	38.5052	43.3923	49.0057	55.4568	62.8733	71.4027	81.2143	92.5026
23	25.7163	28.8450	32.4529	36.6179	41.4305	46.9958	53.4361	60.8933	69.5319	79.5430	91.1479	104.6029
24	26.9735	30.4219	34.4265	39.0826	44.5020	50.8156	58.1767	66.7648	76.7898	88.4973	102.1742	118.1552
25	28.2432	32.0303	36.4593	41.6459	47.7271	54.8645	63.2490	73.1059	84.7009	98.3471	114.4133	133.3339
26	29.5256	33.6709	38.5530	44.3117	51.1135	59.1564	68.6765	79.9544	93.3240	109.1818	127.9988	150.3339
27	30.8209	35.3443	40.7096	47.0842	54.6691	63.7058	74.4838	87.3508	102.7231	121.0999	143.0786	169.3740
28	32.1291	37.0512	42.9309	49.9676	58.4026	68.5281	80.6977	95.3388	112.9682	134.2099	159.8173	190.6989
29	33.4504	38.7922	45.2189	52.9663	62.3227	73.6398	87.3465	103.9659	124.1354	148.6309	178.3972	214.5828
30	34.7849	40.5681	47.5754	56.0849	66.4388	79.0582	94.4608	113.2832	136.3075	164.4940	199.0209	241.3327

EXHIBIT 7.9 Table of Factors for the Present Value of a $1 Annuity

Number of Cash Flows	Discount Rate											
	1%	2%	3%	4%	5%	6%	7%	8%	9%	10%	11%	12%
1	0.9901	0.9804	0.9709	0.9615	0.9524	0.9434	0.9346	0.9259	0.9174	0.9091	0.9009	0.8929
2	1.9704	1.9416	1.9135	1.8861	1.8594	1.8334	1.8080	1.7833	1.7591	1.7355	1.7125	1.6901
3	2.9410	2.8839	2.8286	2.7751	2.7232	2.6730	2.6243	2.5771	2.5313	2.4869	2.4437	2.4018
4	3.9020	3.8077	3.7171	3.6299	3.5460	3.4651	3.3872	3.3121	3.2397	3.1699	3.1024	3.0373
5	4.8534	4.7135	4.5797	4.4518	4.3295	4.2124	4.1002	3.9927	3.8897	3.7908	3.6959	3.6048
6	5.7955	5.6014	5.4172	5.2421	5.0757	4.9173	4.7665	4.6229	4.4859	4.3553	4.2305	4.1114
7	6.7282	6.4720	6.2303	6.0021	5.7864	5.5824	5.3893	5.2064	5.0330	4.8684	4.7122	4.5638
8	7.6517	7.3255	7.0197	6.7327	6.4632	6.2098	5.9713	5.7466	5.5348	5.3349	5.1461	4.9676
9	8.5660	8.1622	7.7861	7.4353	7.1078	6.8017	6.5152	6.2469	5.9952	5.7590	5.5370	5.3282
10	9.4713	8.9826	8.5302	8.1109	7.7217	7.3601	7.0236	6.7101	6.4177	6.1446	5.8892	5.6502
11	10.3676	9.7868	9.2526	8.7605	8.3064	7.8869	7.4987	7.1390	6.8052	6.4951	6.2065	5.9377
12	11.2551	10.5753	9.9540	9.3851	8.8633	8.3838	7.9427	7.5361	7.1607	6.8137	6.4924	6.1944
13	12.1337	11.3484	10.6350	9.9856	9.3936	8.8527	8.3577	7.9038	7.4869	7.1034	6.7499	6.4235
14	13.0037	12.1062	11.2961	10.5631	9.8986	9.2950	8.7455	8.2442	7.7862	7.3667	6.9819	6.6282
15	13.8651	12.8493	11.9379	11.1184	10.3797	9.7122	9.1079	8.5595	8.0607	7.6061	7.1909	6.8109
16	14.7179	13.5777	12.5611	11.6523	10.8378	10.1059	9.4466	8.8514	8.3126	7.8237	7.3792	6.9740
17	15.5623	14.2919	13.1661	12.1657	11.2741	10.4773	9.7632	9.1216	8.5436	8.0216	7.5488	7.1196
18	16.3983	14.9920	13.7535	12.6593	11.6896	10.8276	10.0591	9.3719	8.7556	8.2014	7.7016	7.2497
19	17.2260	15.6785	14.3238	13.1339	12.0853	11.1581	10.3356	9.6036	8.9501	8.3649	7.8393	7.3658
20	18.0456	16.3514	14.8775	13.5903	12.4622	11.4699	10.5940	9.8181	9.1285	8.5136	7.9633	7.4694
21	18.8570	17.0112	15.4150	14.0292	12.8212	11.7641	10.8355	10.0168	9.2922	8.6487	8.0751	7.5620
22	19.6604	17.6580	15.9369	14.4511	13.1630	12.0416	11.0612	10.2007	9.4424	8.7715	8.1757	7.6446
23	20.4558	18.2922	16.4436	14.8568	13.4886	12.3034	11.2722	10.3711	9.5802	8.8832	8.2664	7.7184
24	21.2434	18.9139	16.9355	15.2470	13.7986	12.5504	11.4693	10.5288	9.7066	8.9847	8.3481	7.7843
25	22.0232	19.5235	17.4131	15.6221	14.0939	12.7834	11.6536	10.6748	9.8226	9.0770	8.4217	7.8431
26	22.7952	20.1210	17.8768	15.9828	14.3752	13.0032	11.8258	10.8100	9.9290	9.1609	8.4881	7.8957
27	23.5596	20.7069	18.3270	16.3296	14.6430	13.2105	11.9867	10.9352	10.0266	9.2372	8.5478	7.9426
28	24.3164	21.2813	18.7641	16.6631	14.8981	13.4062	12.1371	11.0511	10.1161	9.3066	8.6016	7.9844
29	25.0658	21.8444	19.1885	16.9837	15.1411	13.5907	12.2777	11.1584	10.1983	9.3696	8.6501	8.0218
30	25.8077	22.3965	19.6004	17.2920	15.3725	13.7648	12.4090	11.2578	10.2737	9.4269	8.6938	8.0552

Examining the future value annuity table for the 6% interest rate, we don't find a factor of 7.0000, but we do see one very close, 6.9753, which corresponds to $N = 6$ payments. In this example, six payments of $1,000 each year produces $7,000 at the end of the sixth year.

We can also use financial calculators to do the work. The present value of the series of five $1,000 cash flows, using a 5% interest rate, is:

Hewlett-Packard 10B	Hewlett-Packard 12C	Hewlett-Packard 17B	Texas Instruments BA-II Plus
1000 PMT	1000 PMT	FIN TVM	1000 PMT
5 I/YR	5 i	5000 PMT	5 I
5 N	5 n	5 I%YR	5 N
PV	PV	5 N	PV
		PV	

The future value of an annuity is calculated in a like manner.

VALUING CASH FLOWS WITH DIFFERENT TIME PATTERNS

Valuing a Perpetual Stream of Cash Flows

There are some circumstances where cash flows are expected to continue forever. For example, a corporation may promise to pay dividends on preferred stock forever, or, a company may issue a bond that pays interest every six months, forever. How do you value these cash flow streams? Recall that when we calculated the present value of an annuity, we took the amount of one cash flow and multiplied it by the sum of the discount factors that corresponded to the interest rate and number of payments. But what if the number of payments extends forever—into infinity?

A series of cash flows that occur at regular intervals, forever, is a *perpetuity*. Valuing a perpetual cash flow stream is just like valuing an ordinary annuity. It looks like this:

$$PV = CF_1\left(\frac{1}{1+i}\right)^1 + CF_2\left(\frac{1}{1+i}\right)^2 + CF_3\left(\frac{1}{1+i}\right)^3 + \ldots + CF_\infty\left(\frac{1}{1+i}\right)^\infty$$

Simplifying, recognizing that the cash flows CF_t are the same in each period, and using summation notation,

$$PV = CF \sum_{t=1}^{\infty} \left(\frac{1}{1+i} \right)^t$$

As the number of discounting periods approaches infinity, the summation approaches $1/i$. To see why, consider the present value annuity factor for an interest rate of 10%, as the number of payments goes from 1 to 200:

Number of Discounting Periods, N	Present Value Annuity Factor
1	0.9091
10	6.1446
40	9.7791
100	9.9993
200	9.9999

For greater numbers of payments, the factor approaches 10, or $1/0.10$. Therefore, the present value of a perpetual annuity is very close to:

$$PV = \frac{CF}{i} \qquad (7\text{-}12)$$

Suppose you are considering an investment that promises to pay $100 each period forever, and the interest rate you can earn on alternative investments of similar risk is 5% per period. What are you willing to pay today for this investment?

$$PV = \frac{\$100}{0.05} = \$2,000$$

Therefore, you would be willing to pay $2,000 today for this investment to receive, in return, the promise of $100 each period forever.

Let's look at the value of a perpetuity another way. Suppose that you are given the opportunity to purchase an investment for $5,000 that promises to pay $50 at the end of every period forever. What is the periodic interest per period—the return—associated with this investment?

We know that the present value is $PV = \$5,000$ and the periodic, perpetual payment is $CF = \$50$. Inserting these values into the formula for the present value of a perpetuity:

$$\$5,000 = \frac{\$50}{i}$$

Solving for i,

$$i = \frac{\$50}{\$5,000} = 0.01 \text{ or } 1\% \text{ per period}$$

Therefore, an investment of $5,000 that generates $50 per period provides 1% compounded interest per period.

Valuing an Annuity Due

The ordinary annuity cash flow analysis assumes that cash flows occur at the end of each period. However, there is another fairly common cash flow pattern in which level cash flows occur at regular intervals, but the first cash flow occurs immediately. This pattern of cash flows is called an *annuity due*. For example, if you win the Florida Lottery Lotto grand prize, you will receive your winnings in 20 installments (after taxes, of course). The 20 installments are paid out annually, beginning immediately. The lottery winnings are therefore an annuity due.

Like the cash flows we have considered thus far, the future value of an annuity due can be determined by calculating the future value of each cash flow and summing them. And, the present value of an annuity due is determined in the same way as a present value of any stream of cash flows.

Let's consider first an example of the future value of an annuity due, comparing the values of an ordinary annuity and an annuity due, each comprising three cash flows of $500, compounded at the interest rate of 4% per period. The calculation of the future value of both the ordinary annuity and the annuity due at the end of three periods is:

$$\textit{Ordinary annuity} \qquad\qquad \textit{Annuity due}$$

$$FV = \$500 \sum_{t=1}^{3} (1 + 0.04)^{3-t} \qquad FV_{\text{due}} = \$500 \sum_{t=1}^{3} (1 + 0.04)^{3-t+1}$$

The future value of each of the $500 payments in the annuity due calculation is compounded for *one more period* than for the ordinary annuity. For example, the first deposit of $500 earns interest for two periods in the ordinary annuity situation [$500 $(1 + 0.04)^2$], whereas the first $500 in the annuity due case earns interest for three periods [$500 $(1 + 0.04)^3$].

In general terms,

$$FV_{\text{due}} = CF \sum_{t=1}^{N} (1 + i)^{N-t+1} \qquad\qquad (7\text{-}13)$$

which is equal to the future value of an ordinary annuity multiplied by a factor of $1 + i$:

$FV_{due} = CF$[Future value annuity factor (ordinary) for N and i]$(1 + i)$

The present value of the annuity due is calculated in a similar manner, adjusting the ordinary annuity formula for the different number of discount periods:

$$PV_{due} = CF \sum_{t=1}^{N} \frac{1}{(1+i)^{t-1}} \qquad (7\text{-}14)$$

Since the cash flows in the annuity due situation are each discounted one less period than the corresponding cash flows in the ordinary annuity, the present value of the annuity due is greater than the present value of the ordinary annuity for an equivalent amount and number of cash flows. Like the future value an annuity due, we can specify the present value in terms of the ordinary annuity factor:

$PV_{due} = CF$[Present value annuity factor (ordinary) for N and i]$(1 + i)$

Financial calculators make your calculations easier by automatically adjusting the present or future value annuity factor if you specify the "begin" or "due" mode. For example, if you are using the HP12C calculator and want to calculate the future value of $500 to be received at the beginning of each of three periods, you first put the calculator in the annuity due mode [[g][BEG]], then specify the cash flow (the $500), the number of payments (3), and the interest rate (4%).

Valuing a Deferred Annuity

A *deferred annuity* has a stream of cash flows of equal amounts at regular periods starting at some time *after* the end of the first period. When we calculated the present value of an annuity, we brought a series of cash flows back to the beginning of the first period—or, equivalently the end of the period 0. With a deferred annuity, we determine the present value of the ordinary annuity and then discount this present value to an earlier period.

To illustrate the calculation of the present value of an annuity due, suppose you deposit $20,000 per year in an account for 10 years, starting today, for a total of 10 deposits. What will be the balance in the account at the end of 10 years if the balance in the account earns 5% per year? The future value of this annuity due is:

$$FV_{\text{due, 10}} = \$20,000 \sum_{t=1}^{10} (1 + 0.05)^{10-t+1}$$

$$= \$20,000 \binom{\text{Future value annuity factor (ordinary)}}{\text{for 10 periods and 5\%}}(1 + 0.05)$$

$$= \$20,000(12.5779)(1 + 0.05) = \$264,135.74$$

Suppose you want to deposit an amount today in an account such that you can withdraw \$5,000 per year for four years, with the first withdrawal occurring five years from today. We can solve this problem in two steps:

Step 1: Solve for the present value of the withdrawals.
Step 2: Discount this present value to the present.

The first step requires determining the present value of a four-cash flow ordinary annuity of \$5,000. This calculation provides the present value as of the end of the fourth year (one period prior to the first withdrawal):

$$PV_4 = \$5,000 \sum_{t=1}^{4} \frac{1}{(1 + 0.04)^t}$$

$$= \$5,000(\text{present value annuity factor } N = 4, \ i = 4\%)$$

$$= \$18,149.48$$

This means that there must be a balance in the account of \$18,149.48 at the end of the fourth period to satisfy the withdrawals of \$5,000 per year for four years.

The second step requires discounting the \$18,149.48—the savings goal—to the present, providing the deposit today that produces the goal:

$$PV_0 = \frac{\$18,149.48}{(1 + 0.04)^4} = \$15,514.25$$

The balance in the account throughout the entire eight-year period is shown in Exhibit 7.10, with the balance indicated both before and after the \$5,000 withdrawals.

Let's look at a more complex deferred annuity. Consider making a series of deposits, beginning today, to provide for a steady cash flow beginning at some future time period. If interest is earned at a rate of 4% compounded per year, what amount must be deposited in a savings account each year for four years, starting today, so that $1,000 may be withdrawn each year for five years, beginning five years from today? As with any deferred annuity, we need to perform this calculation in steps:

Step 1: Calculate the present value of the $1,000 per year five-year ordinary annuity as of the end of the fourth year:

The present value of the annuity deferred to the end of the fourth period is

$$PV_4 = \$1,000 \sum_{t=1}^{5} \frac{1}{(1+0.04)^t} = \$1,000(4.4518) = \$4,451.80$$

Therefore, there must be $4,451.80 in the account at the end of the fourth year to permit five $1,000 withdrawals at the end of each of the years 5, 6, 7, 8, and 9.

Step 2: Calculate the cash flow needed to arrive at the future value of that annuity due comprising four annual deposits earning 4% compounded interest, starting today.

EXHIBIT 7.10   Balance in the Account that Requires a Deposit Today (Year 0) that Permits Withdrawals of $5,000 Each Starting at the End of Year 5

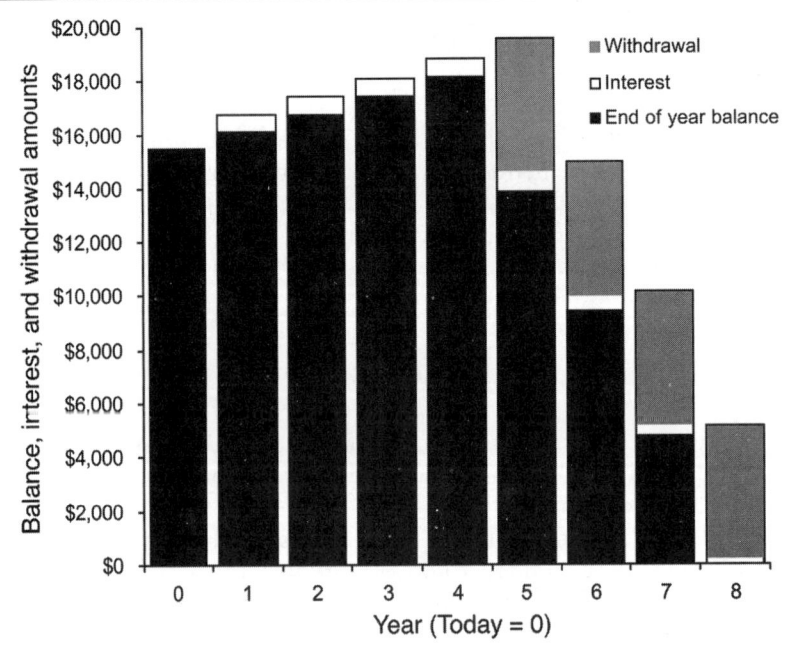

The present value of the annuity at the end of the fourth year, \$4,451.80, is the future value of the annuity due of four payments of an unknown amount. Using the formula for the future value of an annuity due,

$$\$4,451.80 = CF \sum_{t=1}^{4} (1 + 0.04)^{4-t+1} = CF(4.2465)(1.04)$$

and rearranging,

$$CF = \$4,451.80/4.4164 = \$1,008.02$$

Therefore, by depositing \$1,008.02 today and the same amount on the same date each of the next three years, we will have a balance in the account of \$4,451.80 at the end of the fourth period. With this period 4 balance, we will be able to withdraw \$1,000 at the end of the following five periods.

THE CALCULATION OF INTEREST RATES

A common problem in finance is comparing alternative financing or investment opportunities when the interest rates are specified in a way that makes it difficult to compare terms. The Truth in Savings Act requires institutions to provide the annual percentage yield for savings accounts. As a result of this law, consumers can compare the yields on different savings arrangements. But this law does not apply beyond savings accounts. One investment may pay 10% interest compounded semiannually, whereas another investment may pay 9% interest compounded daily. One financing arrangement may require interest compounding quarterly, whereas another may require interest compounding monthly. To compare investments or financing with different frequencies of compounding, we must first translate the stated interest rates into a common basis. There are two ways to convert interest rates stated over different time intervals so that they have a common basis: the annual percentage rate and the effective annual interest rate.

One obvious way to represent rates stated in various time intervals on a common basis is to express them in the same unit of time—so we annualize them. The annualized rate is the product of the stated rate of interest per compound period and the number of compounding periods in a year. Let i be the rate of interest per period and n be the number of compounding periods in a year. The annualized rate, also referred to as the *nominal interest rate* or the *annual percentage rate* (APR) is:

$$APR = i \times n$$

Consider the following example. Suppose the Lucky Break Loan Company has simple loan terms: Repay the amount borrowed, plus 50%, in six months. Suppose you borrow $10,000 from Lucky. After six months, you must pay back the $10,000 plus $5,000. The annual percentage rate on financing with Lucky is the interest rate per period (50% for six months) multiplied by the number of compound periods in a year (two six-month periods in a year). For the Lucky Break financing arrangement:

$$APR = 0.50 \times 2 = 1.00 \text{ or } 100\% \text{ per year}$$

But what if you cannot pay Lucky back after six months? Lucky will let you off this time, but you must pay back the following at the end of the next six months:

- the $10,000 borrowed,
- the $5,000 interest from the first six months, and
- the 50% of interest on both the unpaid $10,000 and the unpaid $5,000 interest ($15,000 (0.50) = $7,500).

So, at the end of the year, knowing what is good for you, you pay off Lucky:

Amount of the original loan	$10,000
Interest from first six months	5,000
Interest on second six months	7,500
Total payment at end of the year	$22,500

Using the Lucky Break method of financing, you have to pay $12,500 interest to borrow $10,000 for one year's time. Because you have to pay $12,500 interest to borrow $10,000 over one year's time, you pay not 100% interest, but rather 125% interest per year ($12,500/ $10,000 = 1.25 = 125%). What's going on here? It looks like the APR in the Lucky Break example ignores the compounding (interest on interest) that takes place after the first six months. And that's the way it is with all APRs. The APR ignores the effect of compounding. Therefore, this rate understates the true annual rate of interest if interest is compounded at any time prior to the end of the year. Nevertheless, APR is an acceptable method of disclosing interest on many lending arrangements, since it is easy to understand and simple to compute. However, because it ignores compounding, it is not the best way to convert interest rates to a common basis.

Effective versus Annualized Rates of Interest

Another way of converting stated interest rates to a common basis is the effective rate of interest. The effective annual rate (EAR) is the true economic return for a given time period—it takes into account the compounding of interest—and is also referred to as the effective rate of interest.

Using our Lucky Break example, we see that we must pay $12,500 interest on the loan of $10,000 for one year. Effectively, we are paying 125% annual interest. Thus, 125% is the effective annual rate of interest. In this example, we can easily work through the calculation of interest and interest on interest. But for situations where interest is compounded more frequently, we need a direct way to calculate the effective annual rate. We can calculate it by resorting once again to our basic valuation equation:

$$FV = PV (1 + i)^n$$

Next, we consider that a return is the change in the value of an investment over a period and an annual return is the change in value over a year. Using our basic valuation equation, the relative change in value is the difference between the future value and the present value, divided by the present value:

$$EAR = \frac{FV - PV}{PV} = \frac{PV(1 + i)^n}{PV}$$

Canceling PV from both the numerator and the denominator,

$$EAR = (1 + i)^n - 1 \qquad (7\text{-}15)$$

Let's look how the EAR is affected by the compounding. Suppose that the Safe Savings and Loan promises to pay 6% interest on accounts, compounded annually. Since interest is paid once, at the end of the year, the effective annual return, EAR, is 6%. If the 6% interest is paid on a semiannual basis—3% every six months—the effective annual return is larger than 6% since interest is earned on the 3% interest earned at the end of the first six months. In this case, to calculate the EAR, the interest rate per compounding period—six months—is 0.03 (that is, 0.06/2) and the number of compounding periods in an annual period is 2:

$$EAR = (1 + 0.03)^2 - 1 = 1.0609 - 1 = 0.0609 \text{ or } 6.09\%$$

Extending this example to the case of quarterly compounding with a nominal interest rate of 6%, we first calculate the interest rate per period, i, and the number of compounding periods in a year, n:

i = 0.06/4 = 0.015 per quarter
n = 4 quarters in a year

The EAR is:

$$EAR = (1 + 0.015)^4 - 1 = 1.0614 - 1 = 0.0614 \text{ or } 6.14\%$$

As we saw earlier in this chapter, the extreme frequency of compounding is continuous compounding. Continuous compounding is when interest is compounded at the smallest possible increment of time. In continuous compounding, the rate per period becomes extremely small:

$$i = \frac{APR}{\infty}$$

And the number of compounding periods in a year, n, is infinite. The EAR is therefore:

$$EAR = e^{APR} - 1 \qquad (7\text{-}16)$$

where e is the natural logarithmic base.

For the stated 6% annual interest rate compounded continuously, the EAR is:

$$EAR = e^{0.06} - 1 = 1.0618 - 1 = 0.0618 \text{ or } 6.18\%$$

The relation between the frequency of compounding for a given stated rate and the effective annual rate of interest for this example indicates that the greater the frequency of compounding, the greater the EAR.

Frequency of Compounding	Calculation	Effective Annual Rate
Annual	$(1 + 0.060)^1 - 1$	6.00%
Semiannual	$(1 + 0.030)^2 - 1$	6.09%
Quarterly	$(1 + 0.015)^4 - 1$	6.14%
Continuous	$e^{0.06} - 1$	6.18%

Figuring out the effective annual rate is useful when comparing interest rates for different investments. It doesn't make sense to compare the APRs for different investments having a different frequency of compounding within a year. But since many investments have returns stated in terms of APRs, we need to understand how to work with them.

To illustrate how to calculate effective annual rates, consider the rates offered by two banks, Bank A and Bank B. Bank A offers 9.2% compounded semiannually and Bank B other offers 9% compounded daily. We can compare these rates using the EARs. Which bank offers the highest interest rate? The effective annual rate for Bank A is $(1 + 0.046)^2 - 1 = 9.4\%$. The effective annual rate for Bank B is $(1 + 0.000247)^{365} - 1 = 9.42\%$. Therefore, Bank B offers the higher interest rate.

SUMMARY

- We can translate a present value into a value in the future through compounding. We can translate a future value into an equivalent value today through discounting. Financial mathematics consists of the mathematical tools we use to perform compounding and discounting.
- The basic valuation equation, $FV = PV\,(1 + i)^N$, is used to translate present values into future values and to translate future values into present values. This basic relationship includes interest compounding— that is, interest earnings on interest already earned.
- Using the basic valuation equation, we can translate any number of cash flows into a present or future value. When faced with a series of cash flows, we must value each cash flow individually, and then sum these individual values to arrive at the present value of the future value of the series. Our work can be cut a bit shorter if these cash flows are equal and occur at periodic intervals of time, referred to as an annuity.
- Tables containing present value factors, future value factors, present value annuity factors, and future value annuity factors can be used to reduce the computations involved in financial math.
- We can use financial mathematics to value many different patterns of cash flows, including perpetuities, annuity due, and deferred annuities. Applying the tools to these different patterns of cash flows requires us to take care in specifying the timing of the various cash flows.
- If the interest on alternative investments is stated in different terms, we can put these interest rates on a common basis so that we can determine the best alternative.
- Typically we specify an interest rate on an annual basis, using either the annual percentage rate or the effective annual rate. The latter method is preferred since it takes into consideration the compounding of interest within a year.
- Effective rates on loans are calculated like annual percentage yields on savings accounts, by calculating the periodic rate and translating it into an effective annual rate.

QUESTIONS

1. If you are offered two investments, one that pays 5% simple interest per year and one that pays 5% compound interest per year, which would you choose? Why?

2. Suppose you make a deposit today in a bank account that pays compounded interest annually. After one year, the balance in the account has grown.
   a. What has caused it to grow?
   b. After two years, the balance in the account has grown even more. What has caused the balance to increase during the second year?

3. The Florida lottery pays out winnings, after taxes, on the basis of 20 equal annual installments, providing the first installment at the time that the winning ticket is turned in.
   a. What type of cash flow pattern is the distribution of lottery winnings?
   b. How would you value such winnings?

4. Rent is typically paid at the first of each month. What pattern of cash flows, an ordinary annuity or an annuity due, does a rental agreement follow?

5. a. Under what conditions does the effective annual rate of interest (EAR) differ from the annual percentage rate (APR)?
   b. As the frequency of compounding increases within the annual period, what happens to the relation between the EAR and the APR?

6. Using the appropriate table, find the compound factor for each of the following combinations of interest rate per period and number of compounding periods:

Number of Periods	Interest Rate per Period	Compound Factor
2	2%	_____
4	3%	_____
3	4%	_____
6	8%	_____
8	6%	_____

7. Using the appropriate table, find the discount factor for each of the following combinations of interest rate per period and number of discounting periods:

Number of Periods	Interest Rate Per Period	Discount Factor
2	2%	_____
4	3%	_____
3	4%	_____
6	8%	_____
8	6%	_____

8. Using the appropriate table, find the future value annuity factor for each of the following combinations of interest rate per period and number of payments:

Number of Payments	Interest Rate Per Period	Future Value Annuity Factor
2	2%	_____
4	3%	_____
3	4%	_____
6	8%	_____
8	6%	_____

9. Using the appropriate table, find the present value annuity factor for each of the following combinations of interest rate per period and number of payments:

Number of Payments	Interest Rate Per Period	Present Value Annuity Factor
2	2%	_____
4	3%	_____
3	4%	_____
6	8%	_____
8	6%	_____

10. Using an 8% compounded interest rate per period, calculate the future value of a $100 investment:
    a. one period into the future.
    b. two periods into the future.
    c. three periods into the future.
    d. four periods into the future.
    e. five periods into the future.
    f. 40 periods into the future.

11. Suppose you deposit $1,000 into a savings account that earns interest at the rate of 4%, compounded annually. What would be the balance in the account:
    a. after two years?
    b. after four years?
    c. after six years?
    d. after 20 years?

12. If you deposit $10,000 in an account that pays 6% compounded interest per period, assuming no withdrawals:
    a. What will be the balance in the account after two periods?
    b. After the two periods, how much interest has been paid on the principal amount?
    c. After the two periods, how much interest has been paid on interest?

13. Using an 8% compounded interest rate, calculate the present value of $100 to be received:
    a. one period into the future.
    b. two periods into the future.
    c. three periods into the future.
    d. four periods into the future.
    e. five periods into the future.
    f. 40 periods into the future.
14. Ted wants to borrow from Fred. Ted is confident that he will have $1,000 available to pay off Fred in two years. How much will Fred be willing to lend to Ted in return for $1,000 two years from now if he uses a compounded interest rate per year of:
    a. 5%? b. 10%? c. 15%?
15. How much would you have to deposit into a savings account that earns 2% interest compounded quarterly, to have a balance of $2,000 at the end of four years, if you make no withdrawals?
16. What is the present value of $5,000 to be received five years from now, if the nominal annual interest rate (APR) is 12% and interest is compounded: a. annually? b. semiannually? c. quarterly? d. monthly?
17. Calculate the future value at the end of the second period of this series of end-of-period cash flows, using an interest rate of 10% compounded per period:

Period	End of Period Cash Flow
0	$100
1	200
2	400

18. An investor is considering the purchase of an investment at the end of Year 0 that will yield the following cash flows:

Year	End of Year Cash Flow
Year 1	$2,000
Year 2	$3,000
Year 3	$4,000
Year 4	$5,000

   If the appropriate discount rate for this investment is 10%, what will this investor be willing to pay for this investment?
19. Calculate the present value (that is, the value at the end of period 0) of the following series of end of period cash flows:

Period	End of Period Cash Flow
0	$100
1	200
2	400

20. Suppose that an investment promises to provide the following cash flows:

Year	End of Year Cash Flow
Year 1	$0
Year 2	$1,000
Year 3	$0
Year 4	−$1,000

If interest is compounded annually at 5%, what is the value of the investment at the end of: a. Year 1? b. Year 0?

21. Calculate the future value at the end of the third period an ordinary annuity consisting of three cash flows of $2,000 each. Use a 5% rate of interest per period.

22. What is the present value of $10 to be received each period, forever, if the interest rate is 6%?

23. If an investor is willing to pay $40 today to receive $2 every year forever, what is this investor's opportunity cost used to value this investment?

24. Calculate the present value of an annuity due consisting of three cash flows of $1,000 each, each one year apart. Use a 6% compounded interest rate per year.

25. Calculate the future value at the end of the third period of an annuity due consisting of three cash flows of $1,000 each, each one year apart. Use a 6% compounded interest rate per year.

26. Suppose that you have won the Florida Lotto worth $18 million. Further suppose that the State of Florida will pay you the winnings in 20 annual installments, starting immediately, of $900,000 each. If your opportunity cost is 10%, what is the value today of these 20 installments?

27. Calculate the required deposit to be made today so that a series of ten withdrawals of $1,000 each can be made beginning five years from today. Assume an interest rate of 5% per period on end of period balances.

28. How much would you need to deposit today so that you can withdraw $4,000 per year for ten years, starting three years from today?

29. Suppose you wish to invest $2,000 today so that you have $4,000 six years from now. What must the compounded annual interest rate be in order to achieve your goal?

30. The Bert and Ernie Bathtub Company is planning to finance a new truck with a loan of $20,000. This loan requires the company to pay five end-of-year-installments of $5,276 each. What is the effective annual interest rate that the company is paying for its new truck financing?

31. If interest is earned at the rate of 5%, compounded annually, how long will it take an investment of $10,000 to grow to:
    a. $15,000? b. $20,000? c. $30,000?

32. If interest is earned at the rate of 5%, compounded annually, how long would it take an investment to:
    a. double in value? b. triple in value?

33. Suppose you invest $2,500 today. How long would it take to grow to $5,000 if interest is compounded at the rate of 4% per quarter?

34. If interest is paid at a rate of 5% per quarter, what is the:
    a. annual percentage rate? b. effective annual rate?

35. L. Shark is willing to lend you $10,000 for three months. At the end of six months, L. Shark requires you to repay the $10,000, plus 50%.
    a. What is the length of the compounding period?
    b. What is the rate of interest per compounding period?
    c. What is the annual percentage rate associated with L. Shark's lending activities?
    d. What is the effective annual rate of interest associated with L. Shark's lending activities?

36. The Consistent Savings and Loan is designing a new account that pays interest quarterly. It wishes to pay, effectively, 16% per year on this account. Consistent desires to advertise the annual percentage rate on this new account, instead of the effective rate, since its competitors state their interest on an annualized basis. What is the APR that corresponds to an effective rate of 16% for this new account?

37. Which of the following financing arrangements offers the lowest cost of credit on an effective annual basis?
    a. Simple interest loan of 15% per year.
    b. Trade credit, on terms 1/10, net 40, paying on the net day.
    c. Pawn shop credit, on terms 25%, payable after 50 days.
    d. A bank loan with a nominal interest of 14%, with interest compounded monthly.

38. Ken invested $6,000 in an a savings account that pays interest at the rate of 1% per quarter. At the end of five years, Ken withdraws only the interest. How much does he withdraw?

39. The ABC Company wished to invest a sum of money today in an investment that grows at the rate of 12% per year, so that it may withdraw $1,000 at the end of every year for the next ten years. How much must be invested?

The Fundamentals of Valuation

CHAPTER 8

Principles of Asset Valuation and Investment Returns

There are a number of factors that affect a stock's price and its value to investors. The financial manager regularly has to figure out whether a particular investment is good or bad. A good investment will enhance shareholder wealth. A bad one won't. To decide whether an investment is good or bad, the manager must determine whether the benefits from the investment—often expected in future periods—will outweigh its costs.

To make the best investment decisions, the financial manager must also consider the way the investment is financed. If the firm takes on more debt, is this harmful to shareholders? If the firm issues more shares of equity, how does this affect the value of equity? Furthermore, recognizing that the value of equity is the difference between the value of the firm's assets and its debt obligations, we must be aware of how debt securities are valued as well.

Valuation compares the benefits of a future investment decision with its cost. Another way of evaluating an investment is to answer the question: Given its cost and its expected future benefits, what return will a particular investment provide? In this chapter we focus on the principles of valuation and how to calculate the return on investments. In the next chapter we focus on the valuation of stocks and bonds.

PRINCIPLES OF ASSET VALUATION

Suppose you are offered the following investment opportunity by a company: Lend the company $90 today, and you will be paid $100 one year from today by the company. Whether or not this is a good investment depends on:

- what you could have done with your $90 instead of investing it with the company, and
- how certain you are that the company will pay the $100 in one year.

If your other opportunities with the same amount of uncertainty provide a return of 10%, is this loan a good investment? There are two ways to evaluate this.

First, you can figure out what you could have wound up with after one year, investing your $90 at 10%:

$$\text{Value at the end of one year} = \$90 + 10\% \text{ of } \$90$$
$$= \$90(1 + 0.10) = \$99$$

Since the $100 promised is more than $99, you are better off with the investment offered by the company.

Another way of looking at this is to figure out what the $100 promised in the future is worth today. To calculate its present value, we must discount the $100 at some rate. The rate we'll use is the opportunity cost of funds, which in this case is 10%:

$$\text{Value today of } \$100 \text{ in one year} = \frac{\$100}{(1 + 0.10)^1} = \$90.91$$

This means that you consider $90.91 today to be worth the same as $100 in one year. In other words, if you invested $90.91 today in an investment that yields 10%, you end up with $100 in one year. Since today's value of the receipt of $100 in the future is $90.91 and it only costs $90 to get into this deal, the investment is attractive: it costs *less* than what you have determined it is worth.

Since there are two ways to look at this—through its future value or through its present value—which way should you go? While both approaches get you to the same decision, the approach in terms of the present value of the investment is usually easier.

Let's look at another example. Suppose you have an opportunity to buy an asset expected to give you $500 in one year and $600 in two years. If your other investment opportunities with the same amount of risk give you a return of 5% a year, how much are you willing to pay today to get these two future receipts?

We can figure this out by discounting the $500 in year 1 at 5% and $600 in year 2 at 5%:

$$\text{Present value of an investment} = \frac{\$500}{(1+0.05)^1} + \frac{\$600}{(1+0.05)^2}$$

$$= \$476.19 + \$544.22 = \$1{,}020.41$$

This investment is worth $1,020.41 today, so you will be willing to pay $1,020.41 *or less* for this investment:

- if you pay more than $1,020.41, you get a return of less than 5%;
- if you pay less than $1,020.41 you get a return of more than 5%; and,
- if you pay $1,020.41 you get a return of 5%.

Suppose you are evaluating an investment that promises $10 every year forever. The value of this investment is the present value of the stream of $10 to be received each year to infinity where each $10 is discounted at the appropriate number of years at some annual rate i:

Present value of an investment

$$= \frac{\$10}{(1+i)^1} + \frac{\$10}{(1+i)^2} + \frac{\$10}{(1+i)^3} + \ldots + \frac{\$10}{(1+i)^\infty}$$

which we can write in shorthand notation using summation notation as:

$$\text{Present value of an investment} = \sum_{t=1}^{\infty} \frac{\$10}{(1+i)^t} = \$10 \sum_{t=1}^{\infty} \frac{1}{(1+i)^t}$$

Or, since the last term is equal to $1/i$, we can rewrite the present value of this perpetual stream as:

$$\text{Present value of investment} = \$10\,(1/i) = \$10/i$$

If the discount rate to translate this future stream into a present value is 10%, the value of the investment is $100:

$$\text{Present value of investment} = \$10\,(1/0.10) = \$10/0.10 = \$100$$

The 10% is the discount rate, also referred to as the *capitalization rate*, for the future cash flows comprising this stream. Let's look at this investment from another angle: If you consider the investment to be worth $100 today, you are capitalizing—translating future flows into a present value—the future cash flows at 10% per year.

As you see from these examples, the value of an investment depends on:

1. the amount and timing of the future cash flows, and
2. the discount rate used to translate these future cash flows into a value today.

This discount rate represents how much an investor is willing to pay today for the right to receive a future cash flow. Or, to put it another way, the discount rate is the rate of return the investor requires on an investment, given the price he or she is willing to pay for its expected future cash flow.

We can generalize this relationship a bit more. Let CF_t represent the cash flow from the investment in period t, so that CF_1 is the cash flow at the end of period 1, CF_2 is the cash flow at the end of period 2, and so on, until the last cash flow at the end of period N, CF_N. If the investment produces cash flows for N periods and the discount rate is i, the value of the investment—the present value—is:

Present value of an investment

$$= \frac{CF_1}{(1+i)^1} + \frac{CF_2}{(1+i)^2} + \frac{CF_3}{(1+i)^3} + \ldots + \frac{CF_N}{(1+i)^N}$$

which we can write more compactly as:

$$\text{Present value of an investment} = \sum_{t=1}^{N} \frac{CF_t}{(1+i)^t}$$

In the special case where the cash flows are all equal, we can simplify this by letting CF represent each cash flow and use CF in place of CF_1, CF_2, and so on. The valuation relation becomes:

$$\text{Present value of an investment} = \sum_{t=1}^{N} \frac{CF}{(1+i)^t} = CF \sum_{t=1}^{N} \frac{1}{(1+i)^t}$$

which we can write in terms of the annuity factor,

Present value of an investment $=$ CF(Present value annuity factor)

If the cash flow stream is level and is promised each period forever, N is infinite. As the number of future periods approaches infinity, the present value annuity factor approaches $1/i$. Therefore, the present value of a perpetual stream of cash flows is equal to:

$$\text{Present value of an investment with a perpetual cash flow} = \frac{CF}{i}$$

Whether we are talking about a single future cash flow, a series of level cash flows, a series of cash flows having different amounts, or a perpetual series of cash flows, to determine its present value we need to know:

- the amount and timing of the future cash flows, and
- the discount rate that reflects the uncertainty of these cash flows.

The Role of the Marketplace in the Valuation of Assets

If you are faced with a decision whether to make a particular investment, you figure out what it is worth to you—its value—and compare it with what it will cost you. If the investment costs less than you think it is worth, you will buy it; if it costs more than you think it is worth, you will not buy it.

Now suppose several people are considering buying the same, one-of-a-kind asset. Each potential investor evaluates whether the asset is priced at more or less than what he or she thinks it is worth by making this comparison and either buying or selling the asset based on whether they think it is over- or underpriced, the buyers and sellers determine its price.

Let's see how this works. Three investors, A, B, and C, have an opportunity to buy an asset expected to generate $100 each period forever. This is a perpetuity whose value is the ratio of the $100 to the discount rate. If each investor thinks that this asset represents an investment that has a different amount of risk, they each will use a different discount rate to value it. If investors are *risk averse*—they do not like risk—they will value an asset using a higher discount rate the more uncertain they are about the future cash flows.

Suppose:

Investor	uses the discount rate ...	and values the asset as...
A	8.0%	$1,250
B	10.0%	$1,000
C	12.5%	$800

And suppose the asset is owned by Investor C who has been looking at alternative investment opportunities with similar risk that offer a return of 12.5% and as a result figures that the asset is worth only $800. Both Investors A and B would be interested in buying it from C for more than $800 and C would be willing to sell it for more than $800. Since both A and B want this asset, they would bid for it.

So what is the market price of the asset? If its price is $1,000, Investor B would be indifferent between this asset and his other investments of similar risk. At $1,000, Investor A would still think it is underpriced and want to buy it. So the price is bid up to reflect the highest value investors are willing to pay: $1,250. If Investor A buys the asset for $1,250, he gets a return of 8%, which is what he thinks is appropriate given his assessment of the asset's risk.

What makes this process work is the desire of investors to exploit profitable opportunities: C to sell it for more than she thinks it is worth and A and B to buy it for less than they think it is worth. If we assume that investors are interested in maximizing their wealth, those investors thinking an asset is overpriced will want to sell it and those thinking it is underpriced will want to buy it.

Buyers and sellers will continue to buy and sell until they have exhausted what they believe are all the profitable opportunities. When that happens, the assets are neither over- or underpriced. This point where buying and selling is in balance is referred to as a ***market equilibrium***. The price of an asset is determined by the investor with the highest valuation of the asset. If the price of an asset is above or below its market equilibrium price, investors will buy and sell it until its price is the market equilibrium price.

As long as an asset can be traded without any restrictions in a market, buying and selling will determine its price. However, if there is a barrier to trading—such as a limit on the quantity that can be sold—this trading is inhibited and the asset's price will not reflect the valuation of the highest valuer.

In addition, if there are costs to trading—such as a fee each time a trade is made—investors will figure the costs into their bidding. For example, if there is a $100 fee to buy the asset, the most Investor A would be willing to pay is $1,150 and the most Investor B would be willing to pay is $900, considering there is a $100 fee to buy it.

RETURNS ON INVESTMENTS

As we have seen, whether investors are willing to make an investment, and the price they are willing to pay, depends on the return they expect. A *return*, the benefit an investor receives from an investment, can be in the form of:

- a change the in the value of the asset—it's appreciation or depreciation,
- a cash flow from the investment, such as a dividend or an interest payment, or
- both a cash flow and a change in value.

The return on an investment is also referred to as the *yield*. We saw the role of the yield in the value of an asset. Now let's see how to calculate returns on different investments.

Return on Investments with No Intermediate Cash Flows

Let's start by looking at an investment that involves no cash flows other than its purchase and then its sale. Suppose you bought a comic book in 1991 for the cover price of $1.00. In 2001, this comic book, in mint condition, was worth $3.00. If you sold at this time, your return on your investment would have been:

Return on investment = (Sales price − cost)/cost = ($3.00 − $1)/$1 = 200%

Before any commission by the comic book dealer, you have made a return of 200% over the ten years.

Because different investments have different lives, or are valued at different points in their lives, we will need to put their yields on some common basis to compare them. The most common way of reporting a return or yield is on an annual basis, expressed as the average annual return per year. We can translate the six-year return on our comic book investment into a return per year given the following:

Future value (sale price) = FV = $3.00
Present value (cost)   = PV = $1.00
Number of periods   = N = 10 years

We can represent the return over the six years on a per year basis. Let i be the annual return on the investment. Using the basic valuation equation, where FV is the future value, PV is the present value, N is the number of compounding periods, and r is the interest rate per period:

$$FV = PV (1 + i)^N$$

$$\$3.00 = \$1.00 (1 + i)^{10}$$

solving for i,

$$(1 + i)^{10} = \$3/\$1$$

Taking the tenth root of both sides:

$$1 + i = \sqrt[10]{\$3/\$1} = \sqrt[10]{3} = 3^{0.10} = 1.1161$$

and therefore i is equal to $1.1161 - 1 = 0.1161$.

The annual return is 11.61%. Holding onto the comic book for ten years provided an average return of 11.61% per year. Another name for this return is the ***internal rate of return*** (IRR).

The average annual return on an investment is the geometric average, not the arithmetic average. What's the difference? Compounding. Suppose today you invest $100 that will earn 5% per year for two years. After two years your investment is worth $100 (1 + 0.05)^2 = $110.25. You have earned $10.25 or 10.25% over two years. But what have you earned per year? Five percent, which happens, not coincidentally, to be the geometric average return:

$$\text{Geometric average annual return} = \sqrt[2]{\frac{FV}{PV}} - 1$$

$$= \sqrt[2]{\frac{\$110.25}{\$100.00}} - 1 = \sqrt[2]{1.1025} - 1$$

$$= 1.05 - 1 = 5\%$$

The arithmetic average annual return is:

$$\text{Arithmetic average annual return} = \frac{\$10.25/\$100.00}{2} = 5.13\%$$

But the arithmetic average ignores any compounding! It says that we earn 5.13% of $100 in the first year, 5.13% in the second year, and do not earn interest on interest during the second period.

If we want to compare investments that have different time horizons and different frequencies of compounding, we need to place returns on a common basis. Since the geometric average gives us a return that considers compounding, this is the average we can compare meaningfully. So, when we refer to the average annual return or average annual yield, we are talking about the average that considers compounding: the geometric average.

Return on Investments with Even Cash Flows

For the comic book, we calculated a return that was derived solely from the appreciation in value. Now let's look at an example where the return is derived solely from a stream of cash inflows.

Suppose you buy an investment for $10,000 that promises to pay $4,000 per year for three years, beginning one year from the date you buy it. The return on this investment is the discount rate that equates its cost, $10,000, with the benefits it produces—the three cash inflows of $4,000 each—considering the time value of money. This is a present value problem. We use CF_t to indicate the cash flow at the end of period t:

Present value (cost of investment)　　　　　 = PV　= $10,000
Cash flow at the end of the first year　　　 = CF_1 = $4,000
Cash flow at the end of the second year　 = CF_2 = $4,000
Cash flow at the end of the third year　　 = CF_3 = $4,000

The return is the value of i that solves:

$$PV = \frac{CF_1}{(1+i)^1} + \frac{CF_2}{(1+i)^2} + \frac{CF_3}{(1+i)^3}$$

Inserting the known values,

$$\$10{,}000 = \frac{\$4{,}000}{(1+i)^1} + \frac{\$4{,}000}{(1+i)^2} + \frac{\$4{,}000}{(1+i)^3}$$

Because the cash flows are level, we can represent this equation in summation form:

$$\$10,000 = \sum_{t=1}^{3} \frac{\$4,000}{(1+i)^t} = \$4,000 \sum_{t=1}^{3} \frac{1}{(1+i)^t}$$

Recognizing that

$$\sum_{t=1}^{3} \frac{1}{(1+i)^t}$$

is the present value annuity factor for three periods and some unknown i, the equation becomes:

$\$10,000 = \$4,000$(Present value annuity factor for $N = 3$ and $i = ?$)

We can calculate i either by:

1. trial and error,
2. using present value of annuity factors from a table of factors, or
3. using a financial calculator.

Using a financial calculator,

Hewlett-Packard 10B	Hewlett-Packard 12C	Hewlett-Packard 17B	Texas Instruments BA-II Plus
10000 ± PV	10000 CHS PV	FIN TVM	10000 ± PV
4000 PMT	4000 PMT	10000 ± PV	4000 PMT
3 N	3 n	4000 PMT	3 N
I/YR	i	3 N	I
		I%YR	

The value of i that solves this equation is $i = 0.09701$ or 9.701% per period. So, we say that this investment yields 9.701% per year.

Return on Investments with Uneven Cash Flows

If we are calculating a return on an investment from a change in the value of an investment, we can use the basic valuation equation to determine the return on the investment. If we are calculating a return on an investment that produces even cash flows throughout its life, we can use the annuity shortcut to figure out its return. But it is more difficult to calculate the return when the cash flows are neither the same amount each period nor a single lump sum. If an investment produces cash flows in different amounts, there are only two ways to solve for i:

1. trial and error, or
2. using a financial calculator.

Suppose you are offered an investment costing $10,000 that promises cash flows of $1,000 after one year, $2,000 after two years, and returns the original $10,000 at the end of the second year. The return on this investment is the rate i that solves:

$$\$10,000 = \frac{\$1,000}{(1+i)^1} + \frac{\$2,000}{(1+i)^2} + \frac{\$10,000}{(1+i)^2}$$

Combining the cash flows that occur at the end of the second year,

$$\$10,000 = \frac{\$1,000}{(1+i)^1} + \frac{\$12,000}{(1+i)^2}$$

The discount rate that solves this problem is 14.66% per year, the annual return on this investment.

Hewlett-Packard 10B	Hewlett-Packard 12C	Hewlett-Packard 17B	Texas Instruments BA-II Plus
10000 ± CFj	10000 CHS CF$_0$	FIN CFLO	CF
1000 CFj	1000 CFj	FLOW(0)=? 10000 ±	CF 10000 ± ENTER
12000 CFj	12000 CFj	INPUT	↑ 1 ENTER
☐ IRR	f IRR	FLOW(1)=? 1000	↑ 1000 ENTER
		INPUT	↑ 1 ENTER
		#TIMES(1)=1	↑ 12000 ENTER
		INPUT	↑ 1 ENTER
		FLOW(2)=? 12000	CPT IRR
		INPUT	
		#TIMES(1)=1	
		INPUT	
		EXIT CALC IRR%	

The Reinvestment Assumption

The discount rate that equates an investment's initial cost with value of the future cash flows it produces is the internal rate of return. The internal rate of return is aptly named since we are assuming that the cash inflows are reinvested at the same return as the rest of the investment—its internal return.

How does this reinvestment work? Let's look again at the preceding problem. Suppose that instead of reinvesting the $1,000 you received after the first year, you place it under your mattress, where it earns nothing. The total value of the cash flows at the end of the second year is:

Year	Cash Flow	Value at the End of the Second Year
1	$1,000	$1,000
2	12,000	12,000
Total		$13,000

This reinvestment strategy provides you $13,000 at the end of the second year. The *effective annual return* on your investment—what you earn considering compounding—is calculated from the basic valuation equation:

$$FV = PV\,(1 + i)^N$$

Substituting the known values of FV, PV, and N,

$$\$13,000 = \$10,000\,(1 + i)^2$$

$$(1 + i)^2 = \frac{\$13,000}{\$10,000} = 1.3000$$

therefore,

$$i = \sqrt{1.3000} - 1 = 0.1402 \text{ or } 14.02\% \text{ per year}$$

By stuffing your first year's end-of-period cash flow into a mattress, where it earns no interest during the second year, your return is 14.02%.

If, instead of the mattress, you invested the $1,000 for the one year at 10%, what would be the return on your total investment?

Year	Cash Flow	Value at the End of the Second Year	
1	$1,000	$1,100	← $1,000 invested one period at 10%
2	$12,000	12,000	
Total		$13,100	

In this case, the return on your investment is:

$$i = \sqrt{\frac{\$13,100}{\$10,000}} - 1 = 14.46\% \text{ per year}$$

which is larger than mattress stuffing because the $1,000 earns $100 of interest during the second period.

But suppose you reinvest this $1,000 at a return = 14.66%?

Year	Cash Flow	Value at the End of the Second Year	
1	$1,000	$1,147	← $1,000 invested one period at 14.66%
2	$12,000	12,000	
Total		$13,147	

$$i = \sqrt{\frac{\$13,147}{\$10,000}} - 1 = 0.1466 \text{ or } 14.66\%$$

In this case, the return on your investment is 14.66%, the IRR!

When we solve for the internal rate of return, whether by trial and error, annuity tables, or the financial calculator, we are assuming that the cash flows are reinvested at the same rate as the rate of the investment that generated those cash flows. This is true whether we are calculating yields on stocks, bonds, comic books, or any other investment.

If we assume the cash flows are reinvested at a different return, the return on the investment is referred to as the **modified internal rate of return** (MIRR). For example, assuming reinvestment of the cash inflows at 10% provides us with a modified internal rate of return of 14.46%, which is less than the internal rate of return, 14.66%.

SUMMARY

■ The value of any asset today depends on its expected future cash flows. These future cash flows may be a level, perpetual stream (as in the case of a preferred stock), a growing stream of cash flows (as in the case of many common stocks), or a series of uneven cash flows (as in the case of a bond).
■ No matter the pattern of future cash flows, the basic valuation of these flows is the same: Each future cash flow is discounted to the present at

an interest rate that reflects both the time value of money and the uncertainty of the cash flow.

■ Prices of assets are determined in a market. A market is in equilibrium if there is a balance between buying and selling.

■ The price of an asset in the market is the most someone is willing to pay for it; in other words, prices are determined by the highest valuation of the asset.

■ If there are transactions costs, these costs will affect the price of an asset in the market.

■ The annual return on an investment is calculated as the geometric mean return. The geometric mean considers the compounding of returns. The geometric mean return also considers that any intermediate cash flows from the investment are reinvested at the average return.

■ There is an inverse relation between the value of an asset and the discount rate applied to future cash flows: The higher this discount rate, the lower today's value, and the lower the discount rate, the higher today's value.

■ The valuation of an asset requires discounting the expected future cash flows at some rate—the yield required by investors. Turning the problem around, we can figure out, for a given asset value, the yield on the asset. It's the same math as we performed with valuation, but instead of solving for the present value of future cash flows, we are solving for the discount rate—the yield.

■ When we calculate the yield on a security, we are interested in translating that yield into some common basis—a year—so we can compare alternative investments.

QUESTIONS

1. What is the relation between the discount rate applied to future cash flows from an investment and the value of the investment today?
2. a. What is meant by the required rate of return?
   b. What is the relation between the required rate of return and the discount rate used to value future cash flows?
3. Consider the following three investments:

Investment 1:
Invest $10,000 today and get $15,000 three years from now.
Investment 2:
Invest $10,000 today and get $5,000 at the end of each of the next three years.

Investment 3:
Invest $10,000 today and get $2,500 at the end of every six months for three years.

If the cash flows from these investments have the same degree of uncertainty, which investment should you choose? Why?

4. Suppose an you have an opportunity to invest $1,000 today an get $1,200 one year from today. If your required rate of return on investments of similar risk is 10%, should you make this investment? Why?

5. Suppose you have the opportunity to invest in a project that provides you with $4,000 every year forever. If you require an 8% return on investments with similar risk, what is the most you would be willing to pay for this project?

6. Calculate the average annual return for the following investments that have no intermediate cash flows:

	Beginning Price	Ending Price	Number of Years
(a)	$1,000	$1,500	2
(b)	$10,000	$9,000	10
(c)	$978	$1,000	3

7. Island Corporation invested $1,000,000 in a new product on January 1, 2000. This product generated cash flows of $800,000 the first year, $400,000 the second year, and $200,000 the third year. At the end of the third year, Island abandoned the new product and disposed of the production equipment for $400,000 at the end of the third year. If these are the only cash flows from this new product, what was Island's return on their investment in this product?

8. Suppose you invest $10,000 in an investment that provides a return of 10% in the first year, 15% in the second and third years, and 12% in the fourth year. The investment has no cash flows, but rather the value of the investment grows each year.
   a. What is your investment worth at the end of the fourth year?
   b. What is the average annual return on this investment?

9. The Abel Company invested $100,000 in an investment that produced cash flows of $35,000 at the end of the first year, $45,000 at the end of the second year, and $50,000 at the end of the third year. If these are the only cash flows from this investment, what is Abel's annual return on its investment?

10. The Baker Company is considering an investment of $1 million. The investment is expected to produce the following cash flows:

Year	Cash Flow
Year 1	$400,000
Year 2	$300,000
Year 3	$300,000
Year 4	$400,000

a. What is the annual return on Baker Company's investment if it invests $1 million?

b. What is the most the Baker Company would invest so that the return on its investment is at least 10%?

CHAPTER 9

Valuation of Securities and Options

In Chapter 8, we explained and illustrated the principles of asset valuation and how to calculate the return on an investment. In this chapter we look at how to value three types of securities: common stock, preferred stock, and debt. We also discuss the key factors affecting the value of an option.

CASH FLOW CHARACTERISTICS

These securities have different types of cash flows and the uncertainty of each is different. We briefly describe the characteristics of the cash flows for these securities. By necessity, our discussion does not cover the finer points associated with the investment characteristics of these securities. These points will be covered in later chapters when we describe common stock (in Chapter 16), preferred stock (in Chapter 17), and various types of debt obligations (in Chapter 15).

If you invest in common stock, you buy shares that represent an ownership interest in a corporation. Shares of common stock are a perpetual security—there is no maturity. Owners of common stock have the right to receive a certain portion of any dividends—but dividends are *not* a sure thing. Typically we see some pattern in the dividends companies pay—dividends are either constant or grow at a somewhat constant rate.

There are three major differences between the dividends of preferred and common shares. First, the dividends on preferred stock usually are specified at a fixed contractual amount. This can be based on a fixed dividend rate or a variable dividend rate. The key point is that with the

211

exception of certain types of preferred stock which are rarely issued, the amount that the investor can receive cannot exceed a contractually specified amount. Second, preferred shareholders' dividends must be paid before any dividends are paid on common stock. Third, if the preferred stock has a *cumulative feature*, dividends not paid in one period accumulate and are carried over to the next period. Therefore, the dividends on preferred stock are more certain than those on common shares.

Notes and bonds are debt securities obligating the borrower to pay interest at regular intervals and to repay the principal amount borrowed, referred to as the *face value*. The repayment of the principal can be at maturity or there can be scheduled principal repayments over the life of the debt obligation. Some notes and bonds can be paid off before the scheduled principal repayment date. The prepayment can be to retire the entire obligation at once by calling an issue before maturity or one or more scheduled payments before the maturity date. Debt securities are senior to equity securities. This means that the corporate borrower must satisfy its obligations to creditors before making payments to owners. Therefore, cash flows from debt securities are viewed as more certain than cash flows from either preferred stock or common stock. The features of preferred stock, common stock, and corporate debt are summarized in Exhibit 9.1.

EXHIBIT 9.1   Summary of Features of Securities

Security	Cash Flow	Certainty of Cash Flow	Maturity
Common stock	Dividend, no fixed rate or amount.	No obligation to pay, but paid at the discretion of the board of directors.	None
Preferred stock	Dividend; can be either a fixed rate or a contractually determined variable rate.	No obligation to pay but preferential to common stock if dividends are paid.	None
Debt	Includes interest and principal repayment. Many variations. Interest can be a fixed or a contractually determined variable rate. Principal repayment can be at maturity or repaid over the life of the debt. The principal repayment provision may allow the firm to prepay.	Legal obligation and given preference over common and preferred stocks. Possibility of early call or prepayments create uncertainty about the cash flow pattern.	Fixed

Valuation of Common Stock

When you buy a share of common stock, it is reasonable to assume that the price you pay reflects what you expect to receive from it in the form of a return on your investment. What you receive are cash dividends in the future. How can we relate that return to the value of a share of common stock? The value of a share of stock should be equal to the present value of all the future cash flows you expect to receive from that share:

Price of a share of common stock
$$= \frac{\text{Dividends in first period}}{(1 + \text{Discount rate})^1} + \frac{\text{Dividends in second period}}{(1 + \text{Discount rate})^2} + \ldots$$

Because common stock never matures, today's value is the present value of an infinite stream of cash flows. And also, common stock dividends are not fixed, as in the case of preferred stock. Not knowing the amount of the dividends—or even if there will be future dividends—makes it difficult to determine the value of common stock.

So what are we to do? Well, we can attempt to determine the valuation of common stock by looking at its current dividend and making assumptions about any future dividends it may pay. We will describe the dividend valuation model and then focus on two related issues: determining the required rate of return and dealing with different assumptions regarding dividend growth.

Dividend Valuation Model

If dividends are constant forever, the value of a share of stock is the present value of the dividends per share per period, in perpetuity. Let D represent the constant dividend per share of common stock expected next period and each period thereafter, forever, P_0 represent the price of a share of stock today, and r_e the required rate of return on common stock. The *required rate of return* (RRR) is the return shareholders demand to compensate them for the time value of money tied up in their investment and the uncertainty of the future cash flows from these investments.

The current price of a share of common stock, P_0, is:

$$P_0 = \frac{D}{(1 + r_e)^1} + \frac{D}{(1 + r_e)^2} + \ldots + \frac{D}{(1 + r_e)^x}$$

which we can write using summation notation,

$$P_0 = \sum_{t=1}^{\infty} \frac{D}{(1+r_e)^t}$$

The summation of a constant amount discounted from perpetuity simplifies to:

$$P_0 = D/r_e$$

As an example, if the current dividend is $2 per share and the required rate of return is 10%, the value of a share of stock is:

$$P_0 = \$2/0.10 = \$20$$

Therefore, if you pay $20 per share and dividends remain constant at $2 per share, you will earn a 10% return per year on your investment every year. But dividends on common stock often change through time.

If dividends grow at a constant rate, the value of a share of stock is the present value of a *growing* cash flow. Let D_0 indicate this period's (i.e., end of period 0) dividend. If dividends grow at a constant rate, g, forever, the present value of the common stock is the present value of all future dividends:

$$P_0 = \frac{D_0(1+g)^1}{(1+r_e)^1} + \frac{D_0(1+g)^2}{(1+r_e)^2} + \dots + \frac{D_0(1+g)^{\infty}}{(1+r_e)^{\infty}}$$

Pulling today's dividend D_0, from each term,

$$P_0 = D_0 \left[\frac{(1+g)^1}{(1+r_e)^1} + \frac{(1+g)^2}{(1+r_e)^2} + \dots + \frac{(1+g)^{\infty}}{(1+r_e)^{\infty}} \right]$$

Using summation notation:

$$P_0 = D_0 \sum_{t=1}^{\infty} \frac{(1+g)^t}{(1+r_e)^t}$$

which simplifies to:

$$P_0 = D_0 \frac{(1+g)}{(r_e - g)}$$

If we represent the next period's dividend, D_1, in terms of this period's dividend, D_0, compounded one period at the rate g (that is, $D_1 = D_0(1+g)$) and substitute for D_0:

$$P_0 = \frac{D_1}{r_e - g}$$

This equation is referred to as the ***Dividend Valuation Model*** (DVM).[1]

As an example, consider a firm expected to pay a constant dividend of $2 per share, forever. If this dividend is capitalized at 10%, the value of a share is $20. If, on the other hand, the current dividend is $2 but these dividends are expected to grow at a rate of 6% per year, forever, the value of a share of stock is $53:

$$P_0 = \frac{\$2(1 + 0.06)}{0.10 - 0.06} = \frac{\$2.12}{0.04} = \$53$$

Does this make sense compared to the constant *amount* case where dividends are unchanged at $2 per year? Yes: If dividends are expected to grow in the future, the stock is worth more than if the dividends are expected to remain the same.

If today's value of a share is $53, what are we saying about the value of the stock next year? If we move everything up one year, D_1 is no longer $2.12, but the current dividend of $2 grows at 6% to $2(1 + 0.06)^2 = \$2.2472$. Therefore, we expect the price of the stock at the end of one year, P_1, to be $5:

$$P_1 = \frac{\$2(1 + 0.06)^2}{0.10 - 0.06} = \frac{\$2.2472}{0.04} = \$56.18$$

---

[1] The Dividend Valuation Model is attributed to Myron Gordon, who popularized the constant growth model. A more formal presentation of this model can be found in published works by Gordon entitled "Dividends, Earnings and Stock Prices," (*Review of Economics and Statistics*, May 1959, pp. 99–105) and *The Investment Financing and Valuation of the Corporation* (Homewood, IL: R. D. Irwin, 1962). However, the foundation of common stock valuation is laid out—for both constant and growing dividends—by John Burr Williams in *The Theory of Investment Value* (Amsterdam: North-Holland Publishing Company, 1938), Chapters V, VI, and VII.

EXHIBIT 9.2   The Price of a Share of Stock with a Current Dividend of $2, a 6% Growth in Dividends, and a 10% Required Rate of Return

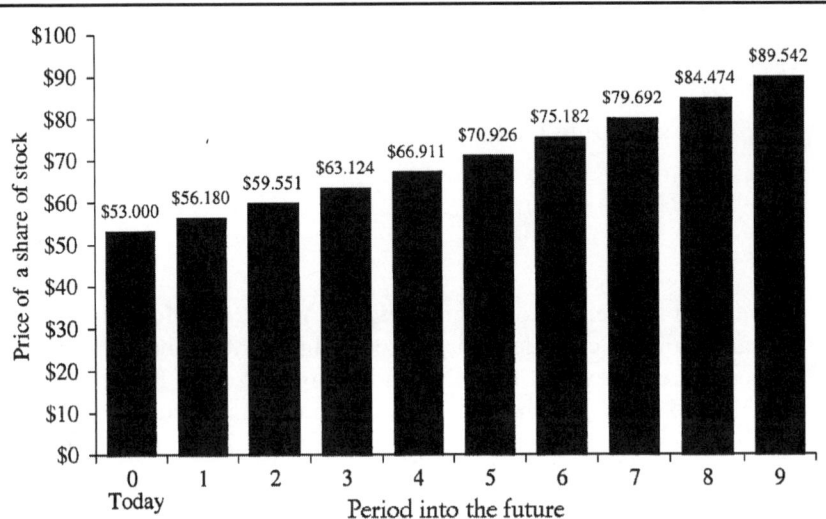

At the end of two years, the price will be $59.55. Since we expect dividends to grow each year, we also are expecting the price of the stock to grow through time as well. In fact, the price is expected to grow at the same rate as the dividends: 6% per period.

The relation between the growth rate of dividends, g, and the price of the stock expected in the future is illustrated in Exhibit 9.2. For a given required rate of return and dividend—in this case $r_e = 10\%$ and $D_0 = \$2$—we see that the price of a share of stock is expected to grow each period at the rate g.

What if the dividends are expected to decline each year? That is, what if g is negative? We can still use the Dividend Valuation Model, but each dividend in the future is expected to be *less* than the one before it. For example, suppose a stock has a current dividend of $2 per share and the required rate of return is 10%. If dividends are expected to *decline* 6% each year, what is the value of a share of stock today? We know that $D_0 = \$2$, $r_e = 10\%$, and $g = -6\%$. Therefore,

$$P_0 = \frac{\$2(1 - 0.06)}{0.10 + 0.06} = \frac{\$1.88}{0.16} = \$11.75$$

Two periods from now, the expected price is even lower:

$$P_1 = \frac{\$2(1-0.06)^2}{0.10+0.06} = \frac{\$1.7672}{0.16} = \$11.045$$

Let's look at another situation, one in which growth is expected to *change* but at different growth rates as time goes on. Consider a share of common stock whose dividend is currently $3.00 per share and is expected to grow at a rate of 8% per year for five years and afterward at a rate of 4% per year after five years. To tackle this problem, let's break it into two manageable parts: the first five years and after five years, or:

P_0 = Present value of dividends in the first five years
       + Present value of dividends received after the first five years to infinity

Assuming a required rate of return of 10%,

$$P_0 = \frac{D_1}{(1+0.10)^1} + \frac{D_2}{(1+0.10)^2} + \frac{D_3}{(1+0.10)^3} + \frac{D_4}{(1+0.10)^4} + \frac{D_5}{(1+0.10)^5}$$

$\uparrow$

Dividends growing at a rate of 8% per year

$$+ \frac{D_6}{(1+0.10)^6} + \frac{D_7}{(1+0.10)^7} + \dots + \frac{D_\infty}{(1+0.10)^\infty}$$

$\uparrow$

Dividends growing at a rate of 4% per year

The present value of the dividends in the first five years is:

Present value of dividends received during the first five years
$$= \frac{\$3.24}{1.1000} + \frac{\$3.4992}{1.2100} + \frac{\$3.7791}{1.3310} + \frac{\$4.0815}{1.4641} + \frac{\$4.4080}{1.6105}$$
$$= \$2.9455 + \$2.8919 + \$2.8393 + \$2.7877 + \$2.7370 = \$14.2014$$

The present value of dividends received after the fifth year—evaluated five years from today—is the expected price of the stock in five years, P_5:

$$P_5 = \frac{D_5(1+0.04)}{0.10-0.04} = \frac{\$4.5843}{0.06} = \$76.4053$$

The price expected at the end of five years is $76.4053, which we translate into a value today by discounting it five years at 10%:

Present value of dividends to be received after the first five years

$$= \frac{\$76.4053}{(1+0.10)^5} = \frac{\$76.4053}{1.6105} = \$47.4420$$

Putting together the two pieces,

$$P_0 = \$14.2014 + \$47.4420 = \$61.6434$$

The value of a share of this stock is $61.6434.

We can represent the Dividend Valuation Model in terms of a share's price to earnings ratio (P/E ratio). Let's start with the Dividend Valuation Model with constant growth in dividends:

$$P_0 = \frac{D_1}{r_e - g}$$

If we divide both sides of this equation by earnings per share, we can represent the dividend valuation model in terms of the price-earnings (P/E) ratio:

$$\frac{P_0}{EPS_1} = \frac{\dfrac{D_1}{EPS_1}}{r_e - g}$$

$$P/E = \frac{\text{Dividend payout ratio}}{r_e - g}$$

This tells us the P/E ratio is influenced by the dividend payout ratio, the required rate of return on equity, and the expected growth rate of dividends.

The Dividend Valuation Model makes some sense regarding the relation between the value of a share of stock, the growth in dividends, and the discount rate:

■ The greater the current dividend, the greater the value of a share of stock.

- The greater the expected growth in dividends, the greater the value of a share of stock.
- The more uncertainty regarding future dividends, the greater the discount rate and the lower the value of a share of stock.

However, the DVM has some drawbacks. How do you deal with dividends that do not grow at a constant rate? As you can see in the last example, this model does not accommodate nonconstant growth easily. What if the firm does not pay dividends now? In that case, D_0 would be zero and the expected price would be zero. But the price of a share of stock cannot be zero. Therefore, the DVM may be appropriate to use to value the stock of companies with stable dividend policies, but it is not applicable for all firms.

Despite its drawbacks, the DVM captures the valuation for many companies' securities. We can use the DVM to take a closer look at investors' required rate of return and the expected rate of growth in future dividends. Moreover, the DVM has been modified to allow for different types of dividend patterns.[2]

Required Rate of Return

The DVM is based on the idea that future cash flows—dividends in the case of common stock—are discounted to the present at some rate that reflects the share owners' opportunity cost. This opportunity cost is what they could have earned on alternative investments with similar risk. This minimum return is the required rate of return—it's the discount rate compensating the share owners for the time value of money and risk:

> Required rate of return
> = Time value of money + Compensation for bearing risk

To calculate the required rate of return, we start with the DVM with a constant growth rate, and solve for r_e:

$$r_e = (D_1/P_0) + g$$

we see that the required rate of return is made up of the *dividend yield*, D_1/P_0, plus the rate we expect share price to grow, the *capital yield*, g:

$$r_e = \text{Dividend yield} + \text{Capital yield}$$

---

[2] For a discussion of these models, see William J. Hurley and Frank J. Fabozzi, "Dividend Discount Models," Chapter 9 in *Handbook of Portfolio Management* (New Hope, PA: Frank J. Fabozzi Associates, 1998).

In other words, if we know next period's dividend, the current price, and the expected growth rate, we can determine the required rate of return. For example, suppose a share of stock is currently selling for $40 per share. If next period's dividend is expected to be $2 and dividends are expected to grow at a rate of 4% per year, the required rate of return is:

$$r_e = (\$2/\$40) + 4\% = 5\% + 4\% = 9\%$$

In other words, a share of stock is valued so that it yields 9%.

Growth Rate of Future Dividends

If we assume that a constant proportion of earnings are paid in dividends—a constant dividend payout—we can tie the growth rate of dividends to the return on equity. Let's start with the DVM with constant growth. If we divide both sides by earnings per share for the next period, EPS_1, we get:

$$\frac{P_0}{EPS_1} = \frac{\dfrac{D_1}{EPS_1}}{r_e - g}$$

Inverting both sides,

$$\frac{EPS_1}{P_0} = \frac{r_e - g}{\dfrac{D_1}{EPS_1}}$$

Recognizing that the return on equity, r_e, is equal to EPS_1/P_0 and simplifying to solve for the growth rate,

$$g = r_e\left(1 - \frac{D_1}{EPS_1}\right)$$

or,

Expected growth rate of dividends
= Return on equity(1 − Dividend payout ratio)

From this we see that:

- the greater the return on equity, the greater the expected growth rate of dividends; and
- the greater the dividend payout, the lower the growth rate of dividends.

Does this make sense? Yes. The more the firm can earn, the greater the expected future growth in dividends. Also, the more the firm pays out in dividends, the less it has to reinvest into the firm for the future and the lower the expected growth rate of dividends in the future.

Returns on Common Stock

As we saw in the preceding section, the value of a stock is the present value of future cash flows, discounted at the required rate of return. If we know the future cash flows and the required rate of return, we can determine today's value. Suppose that instead of determining today's value, we wish to determine the return on a stock. For example, we may want to determine whether a particular stock provides a return over the next five years that is appropriate for its risk. In this case, we know the value of the stock today, we estimate its value in five years, and estimate any intermediate cash flows (e.g., dividends). The missing piece is the return.

We can calculate the return on an investment in common stocks just as we did the internal rate of return in the preceding example. The return on stock is comprised of two components: (1) the appreciation (or depreciation) in the market price of the stock—the capital yield—and (2) the return in the form of dividends—the dividend yield:

$$\text{Return on stock} = \text{Capital yield} + \text{Dividend yield}$$

Let's first ignore dividends. The return on common stock over a period of time where there are no dividends is the change in the stock's price divided by the beginning share price:

$$\text{Return on stock} = \frac{(\text{End-of-period price} - \text{Beginning-of-period price})}{\text{Beginning-of-period price}}$$

Suppose that at the beginning of 2000, Hype.com stock was $10 per share, and at the end of 2001 Hype.com stock was $15 a share. The return on Hype.com during 2000–2001 was:

$$\text{Return on Hype.com stock} = \frac{\$15 - \$10}{\$10} = 50\%$$

Hype.com stock appreciated $5.00 per share, providing a return of 50% for the two years. To make the return comparable to returns on other investments, we usually restate the return as a return per year. The return on Hype.com per year is calculated using the time value of money relationship:

$$PV = \$10 \quad FV = \$15 \quad N = 2$$

Solving for r, the return is 22.47% per year.

Let's work through another illustration. Suppose you bought one share of Berkshire Hathaway stock at the end of 1986 for $2,430. And suppose you sold this share of stock at the end of 1998 for $70,000. Over the twelve years, you earned over 2,700%! But in order to compare this return with other stocks' returns, we need to place it on a common basis, a year. Given the following, we can translate the twelve-year return on Berkshire Hathaway stock into a return per year:

Future value (sales price) = FV = $70,000
Present value (cost) = PV = $2,430
Number of periods = N = 12 years

We can represent the return over the nine years on a per-year basis. Let r be the annual return on the investment. Using the basic valuation equation, $FV = PV (1 + r_e)^N$, we substitute the known elements into the basic valuation equation,

$$\$70,000 = \$2,430 (1 + r_e)^{12}$$

Next, we rearrange in terms of r_e:

$$r_e = \sqrt[23]{\frac{\$70,000}{\$2,430}} - 1 = 32.32\%$$

The return on your investment (not considering any commissions paid) is 32.32% per year.

If a stock pays dividends, we need to consider them as cash inflows, as well as the change in the share's price, in determining the return. The simplest way to calculate the return is to assume that dividends are received at the end of the period:

Return on a stock
$$= \frac{\text{End-of-period price} - \text{Beginning-of-period price} + \text{Dividends at end of period}}{\text{Beginning-of-period price}}$$

Or, if we let:

P_0 = beginning-of-period price
P_1 = end-of-period price
D_1 = dividends received at the end of period

we can write:

$$\text{Return on a stock} = \frac{P_1 - P_0 + D_1}{P_0}$$

We can break this return into one part representing the return due to the change in price and another part representing the return due to dividends:

$$\text{Return on a stock} = \underbrace{\frac{P_1 - P_0}{P_0}}_{\uparrow} + \underbrace{\frac{D_1}{P_0}}_{\uparrow}$$

$$\text{capital yield} \qquad \text{dividend yield}$$

The first part is the capital yield and the second part is the dividend yield. If a company doesn't pay dividends, the dividend yield is zero and the return on the stock is its capital yield.

When using this equation, be careful to specify the timing of the prices at the beginning and the end of the period and the timing of the dividends. Because we're dealing with the time value of money, we have to be very careful to be exact about the timing of all cash flows.

To simplify our analysis, let's ignore our stockbroker's commission, though we will discuss these costs later in this chapter. Suppose we bought 100 shares of Internet.com common stock at the end of 1997 at 35¼. We have invested 100 × $35.25 = $3,525 in Internet.com stock. During 1997, Internet.com paid $0.43 per share in dividends, so we earned $43.00 in dividends. If we sold the Internet.com shares at the end of 1997 for 43 ($43.00 per share, or $4,300.00 for all 100 shares), what was the return on our investment? It depends on when the dividends were received. If we assume that the dividends were received at the end of 1997, our return was:

$$\text{Return on Internet.com for 1997} = \frac{\$4,300.00 - \$3,525.00 + \$43.00}{\$3,525.00}$$

$$= \frac{\$818.00}{\$3,525.00} = 0.2321 \text{ or } \$23.21\%$$

We can break this return into its capital yield and dividend yield components:

$$\text{Return on Internet.com for 1997} = \frac{\$4,300.00 - \$3,525.00}{\$3,525.00} + \frac{\$43.00}{\$3,525.00}$$

	Capital yield	+Dividend yield
=	0.2199	+ 0.0122
=	21.99%	+ 1.22%
=	23.21%	

Most of the return on Internet.com stock was from the capital yield—the appreciation in the stock's price.

Now suppose instead that Internet.com is not sold at the end of 1997, but rather sold at the end of 1999 at $50 per share. This is a more complicated problem to solve because we not only have to consider each cash flow—the purchase price, any dividends paid during the 1997–1999, and the sale price—and the time value of money.

$$P_0 = \frac{D_{1997}}{(1+r_e)^1} + \frac{D_{1998}}{(1+r_e)^2} + \frac{D_{1999}}{(1+r_e)^3} + \frac{P_{1999}}{(1+r_e)^3}$$

If dividends in 1998 and 1999 are the same as those in 1997,

$$\$3,525 = \frac{\$43}{(1+r_e)^1} + \frac{\$43}{(1+r_e)^2} + \frac{\$43}{(1+r_e)^3} + \frac{\$5,000}{(1+r_e)^3}$$

or

$$\$3,525 = \frac{\$43}{(1+r_e)^1} + \frac{\$43}{(1+r_e)^2} + \frac{\$5,043}{(1+r_e)^3}$$

Where do we begin? We can solve this using a financial calculator or trial and error. Using trial and error, we want to find the return that equates the present value of the investment—the $3,525—with the present value of the future cash flows. For example, if we try an r_e of 10%, the present value of the future cash flows is $3,863.51. Since this value is not equal to $3,525, 10% is not the rate we seek.

To reduce the present value, we must use a larger value of r_e. If we try 15%, the present value is $3,385.76 and therefore 15% is not the value we seek. So we know that the return is between 10% and 15%. Using a financial calculator we would find that the answer is 13.45%.

You can see that we can compute returns on investments whether or not we have sold them. In the cases where we do not sell the asset represented in the investment, we compute the capital yield (gain or loss) based on the market value of the asset at the point of time we are evaluating the investment. It becomes important to consider whether or not we actually realize the capital yield only when we are dealing with taxes. We must pay taxes on the capital gain only when we realize it. As long we don't sell the asset, we are not taxed on its capital appreciation.

VALUATION OF PREFERRED STOCK

The value of preferred stock is the present value of all future dividends. If a share of preferred stock has a 5% dividend (based on a $100 par value), paid at the end of each year, today's price is the present value of the stream of $5's forever, discounted at the rate r_p:

Present value of preferred stock

$$= \frac{\$5}{(1+r_p)^1} + \frac{\$5}{(1+r_p)^2} + \frac{\$5}{(1+r_p)^3} + \ldots + \frac{\$5}{(1+r_p)^\infty} = \frac{\$5}{r_p}$$

If the discount rate is 10%, the present value of the preferred stock is $50. That is, investors are willing to pay $50 today for the promised stream of $5 per year since they consider 10% to be sufficient compensation for both the time value of money and the risk associated with the perpetual stream of $5s.

Let's rephrase this relation, letting P_p indicate today's price, D_p indicate the perpetual dividend per share per period, and r_p indicate the discount rate, (i.e., the required rate of return on the preferred stock). Then:

$$P_p = D_p/r_p$$

We can make some generalizations about the value of preferred stock:

■ The greater the dividend rate, the greater the value of a share of preferred stock.
■ The greater the required rate of return—the discount rate—the lower value of a share of preferred stock.

Here is another example of valuing a share of preferred stock. Consider a share of preferred stock with a par value of $100 and a dividend rate of 12%. If the required rate of return is 15%, the value of the preferred stock is less than $100:

$$P_p = \$12/0.15 = \$80$$

If the required rate of return declines to 10%, the price would rise to $120.

Let's look at a feature of preferred stock that may affect its value: the call feature. If preferred stock has a **call feature**, the issuer has the right to call it—buy it back—at a specified price per share, referred to as the **call price**.

Suppose the dividend rate on preferred stock is $6 per share and the preferred stock is callable after three years at par value, $100. If the preferred stock has a required rate of return of 5%, the value of a share of preferred stock without the call is:

$$P_p = \$6/0.05 = \$120$$

Considering the call feature and assuming the issue is called in three years, we need to alter our valuation equation so that we find the present value of the first three dividends and the present value of the call price:

$$P_p = \underbrace{\frac{\$6.00}{(1+0.05)^1} + \frac{\$6.00}{(1+0.05)^2} + \frac{\$6.00}{(1+0.05)^3}}_{\$5.71 + \$5.44 + \$5.18} + \underbrace{\frac{\$100.00}{(1+0.05)^3}}_{+\ \$86.38}$$

$$= \$102.71$$

If the preferred shares did not have a call feature, they would be worth more—the call feature reduces the value of the shares. What is the likelihood that the firm will call in the preferred shares? If the required rate of return is 5%—that is, investors demand a 5% return—and the stock pays $6 on the par of $100, or 6%, the firm can call in the 6% preferred shares and issue 5% shares. Since calling in the preferred shares makes sense—the firm can lower its costs of raising capital—it is very likely the firm will call in the preferred shares when they can.

VALUATION OF LONG-TERM DEBT SECURITIES

Long-term debt securities, such as notes and bonds, are promises by the borrower to repay the principal amount. Notes and bonds typically require the borrower to pay interest periodically, typically semiannually in the United States, and are generally stated as a percentage of the face value of the bond or note. We refer to the interest payments as coupon payments or *coupons* and the percentage rate as the **coupon rate**. If these coupons are a constant amount, paid at regular intervals, we refer to the security paying them as having a **straight coupon**. A debt security that does not have a promise to pay interest periodically but only at the maturity date is referred to as a *zero-coupon* note or bond.

The value of a debt security today is the present value of the promised future cash flows—the interest and the maturity value. Therefore, the present value of a debt is the sum of the present value of the interest payments and the present value of the maturity value:

> Value of debt security = Present value of future interest payments
> + Present value of maturity value

To figure out the value of a debt security, we have to discount the future cash flows—the interest and maturity value—at some rate that reflects both the time value of money and the uncertainty of receiving these future cash flows. We refer to this discount rate as the *yield*. The more uncertain the future cash flows, the greater the yield. It follows that the greater the yield, the lower the present value of the future cash flows—hence, the lower the value of the debt security.

In the case of a straight coupon security, the present value of the interest payments is the present value of an annuity. In the case of a zero-coupon security, the present value of the interest payments is zero, so the present value of the debt is the present value of the maturity value.

We can rewrite the formula for the present value of a debt security using some new notation and some familiar notation. Since there are two different cash flows—interest and maturity value—let C represent the coupon payment promised each period and M represent the maturity value. Also, let N indicate the number of periods until maturity, t indicate a specific period, and r_d indicate the yield. The present value of a debt security, V, is:

$$V = \underbrace{\sum_{t=1}^{N} \frac{C}{(1+r_d)^t}}_{\substack{\text{Present value of future} \\ \text{interest payments}}} + \underbrace{\frac{M}{(1+r_d)^t}}_{\substack{\text{Present value of} \\ \text{maturity value}}}$$

To see how the valuation of future cash flows from debt securities works, let's look at the valuation of a straight coupon bond and a zero-coupon bond.

Straight Coupon Bond

Suppose you are considering investing in a straight coupon bond that:

- Promises interest of $100, paid at the end of each year.
- Promises to pay the principal amount of $1,000 at the end of 12 years.
- Investors require an annual yield of 5%.

What is this bond worth today? We are given the following:

Interest, C = $100 every year
Number of periods, N = 12 years
Maturity value, M = $1,000
Yield, r_d = 5% per year

$$V = \sum_{t=1}^{12} \frac{\$100}{(1+0.05)^t} + \frac{\$1,000}{(1+0.05)^t} = \$886.32 + \$556.84 = \$1,443.16$$

Using a financial calculator,

Hewlett-Packard 10B	Hewlett-Packard 12C	Hewlett-Packard 17B	Texas Instruments BA-II Plus
100 PMT	100 PMT	100 PMT	100 PMT
12 N	12 n	12 N	12 N
1000 FV	1000 FV	1000 FV	1000 FV
5 I/YR	5 i	5 I%YR	5 I/Y
PV	PV	PV	CPT PV

This bond has a present value greater than its maturity value, so we say that the bond is selling at a **premium** from its maturity value. Does this make sense? Yes: The bond pays interest of 10% of its face value every year. But what investors require on their investment—the capitalization rate considering the time value of money and the uncertainty of the future cash flows—is 5%. So what happens? The bond paying 10% is attractive—*so* attractive that its price is bid upward to a price that gives investors the going rate, 5%. In other words, an investor who buys the bond for $1,443.16 will get a 5% return on it if it is held until maturity. We say that at $1,443.16, the bond is priced to yield 5% per year.

Suppose, instead, the interest on the bond is $50 every year—a 5% coupon rate—instead of $100 every year. Then,

Interest, C = $50 every year
Number of periods, N = 12 years
Maturity value, M = $1,000
Yield, r_d = 5% per year

$$V = \sum_{t=1}^{12} \frac{\$50}{(1+0.05)^t} + \frac{\$1,000}{(1+0.05)^t} = \$443.16 + \$556.84 = \$1,000.00$$

The bond's present value is equal to its maturity value and we say that the bond is selling "at par." Investors will pay the maturity value for a bond that pays the going rate for bonds of similar risk. In other words, if an investor buys the 5% coupon bond for $1,000.00, the investor will earn a 5% annual return on the investment if the bond is held until maturity.[3]

Suppose, instead, the interest on the bond is $20 every year—a 2% coupon rate. Then,

Interest, C = $20 every year
Number of periods, N = 12 years
Maturity value, M = $1,000
Yield, r_d = 5% per year

$$V = \sum_{t=1}^{12} \frac{\$20}{(1+0.05)^t} + \frac{\$1,000}{(1+0.05)^t} = \$177.26 + \$556.84 = \$734.10$$

The bond sells below its maturity value and is said to be trading at a *discount* from its maturity value. Why? Because investors are not going to pay the maturity value for a bond that pays less than the going rate for bonds of similar risk. If an investor can buy other bonds that yield 5%, why pay the maturity value—$1,000 in this case—for a bond that pays only 2%? They wouldn't. Instead, the price of this bond would fall to a price that provides an investor a yield of 5%. In other words, if an investor buys the 2% coupon bond for $734.10, the investor will earn a 5% annual return on the investment if the bond is held until maturity.

---

[3] This statement will be qualified later when we discuss assumptions inherent in a yield-to-maturity calculation.

So when we look at the value of a bond, we see that its present value is dependent on the relation between the coupon rate and the yield. We can see this relation in our example:

If a bond has a yield of 5% and a coupon rate of ...	it will sell for ...	so we say it is selling at ...
10%	$1,443.16	a premium
5%	$1,000.00	par
2%	$734.10	a discount

As another example for valuing a straight coupon bond, suppose we have a $1,000 face value bond with a 10% coupon rate, that pays interest at the end of each year and matures in five years. If the required yield is 5%, the value of the bond is:

$$V = \sum_{t=1}^{5} \frac{\$100}{(1+0.05)^t} + \frac{\$1,000}{(1+0.05)^5} = \$432.95 + \$783.53 = \$1,216.48$$

If the yield is 10%, the same as the coupon rate, the bond sells at maturity value:

$$V = \sum_{t=1}^{5} \frac{\$100}{(1+0.10)^t} + \frac{\$1,000}{(1+0.10)^5} = \$379.08 + \$620.92 = \$1,000.00$$

If the yield is 15%, the bond's value is less than its maturity value:

$$V = \sum_{t=1}^{5} \frac{\$100}{(1+0.15)^t} + \frac{\$1,000}{(1+0.15)^5} = \$335.21 + \$497.18 = \$832.39$$

When we hold the coupon rate constant and vary the required yield, we see that:

If a bond has a coupon rate of 10% and a yield of ...	it will sell for ...	so we say it is selling at ...
5%	$1,216.48	a premium
10%	$1,000.00	par
15%	$832.39	a discount

We see a relation developing between the coupon rate, the yield, and the value of a debt security:

- If the coupon rate is more than the yield, the security is worth more than its maturity value—it sells at a premium.
- If the coupon rate is less than the yield, the security is less than its maturity value—it sells at a discount.
- If the coupon rate is equal to the yield, the security is valued at its maturity value.

We can extend the valuation of debt to securities that pay interest every six months. But before we do this, we must grapple with a bit of semantics. In Wall Street parlance, the term *yield-to-maturity* is used to describe an annualized yield on a security if the security is held to maturity. For example, if a bond has a return of 5% over a six-month period, the annualized yield-to-maturity for a year is 2 times 5% or 10%.

$$\text{Yield-to-maturity} = r_d \times 2$$

If a debt security promises interest every six months, there are a couple of things to watch out for in calculating the security's value. First, the r_d we use to discount cash flows is the *six-month yield*, not an annual yield. Second, the number of periods is the number of *six-month periods* until maturity, not the number of years to maturity.

Suppose we are interested in valuing a bond with a maturity value of $1,000 that matures in five years and promises a coupon of 4% per year, with interest paid semiannually. This 4% coupon rate tells us that 2%, or $20, is paid every six months. What is the bond's value if the yield-to-maturity is 6%? From the bond's description we know that:

Interest, C	= $20 every six months
Number of periods, N	= 5 × 2 = 10 six-month periods
Maturity value, M	= $1,000
Yield, r_d	= 6%/2 = 3% for six-month period

The value of the bond is:

$$V = \sum_{t=1}^{10} \frac{\$20}{(1+0.03)^t} + \frac{\$1,000}{(1+0.03)^{10}} = \$170.60 + \$744.09 = \$914.70$$

If the yield-to-maturity is 8%, then:

Interest, C = \$20 every six months
Number of periods, N = $5 \times 2 = 10$ six-month periods
Maturity value, M = \$1,000
Yield, r_d = $8\%/2 = 4\%$ for six-month period

and the value of the bond is:

$$V = \sum_{t=1}^{10} \frac{\$20}{(1+0.04)^t} + \frac{\$1,000}{(1+0.04)^{10}} = \$162.22 + \$675.56 = \$837.78$$

We can see the relation between the yield-to-maturity and the value of the 4% coupon bond in Exhibit 9.3. The greater the required yield, the lower the present value of the bond. This makes sense since a higher yield-to-maturity required by the market means that the future cash flows are discounted at higher rates.

EXHIBIT 9.3   Value of a 4% Coupon Bond with Five Years to Maturity and Semiannual Interest

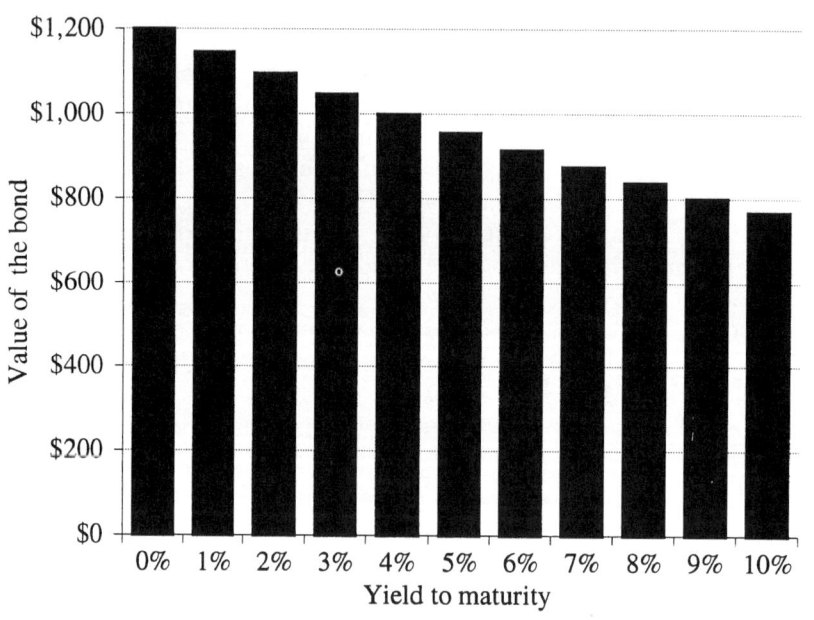

Bond-Equivalent Yield

Notice in dealing with straight-coupon bonds that pay interest semiannually, we moved from the six-month yield-to-maturity to the annual yield-to-maturity by simply doubling the six-month yield-to-maturity. The shortcoming of this approach follows from our discussion of the time value of money in Chapter 7. What the investor is interested in is the effective annual yield computed as follows for bonds that pay interest semiannually:

$$\text{Effective annual yield} = (1 + r_d)^2 - 1$$

For now, it is important to understand that the *convention* in the bond market for annualizing a six-month yield is to double it. The yield computed following this convention is called the *bond-equivalent yield*. Or equivalently, a yield computed by doubling a semiannual yield is said to be computed on a *bond-equivalent basis.*

This convention for annualizing yields must be kept in mind. We'll see why next when we show how to compute the yield on a zero-coupon bond. In addition, there are bonds that are issued in other countries that pay interest annually rather than semiannually. Consequently, the yield on either the bond that pays interest semiannually or the bond that pays interest annually must be adjusted to compare yields. While we have looked at this from the perspective of an investor, from an issuer's perspective this difference in the frequency of payments must be recognized when comparing bonds that may be issued in the U.S. bond market as well as countries such as Japan which pay interest semiannually, and bond markets in many European countries which pay interest annually.

In fact, in Chapter 26 we will discuss a funding source for corporations called asset-backed securities. Such securities typically pay interest monthly. A yield to maturity for such securities can be computed. (Actually, the yield computed for such securities is called a "cash flow yield.") However, the yield-to-maturity calculated is a monthly yield. How is that monthly yield annualized? The convention is to compute the effective six-month yield (we discuss the effective yield later in this chapter) and then to double that yield.

If this makes little sense to you—doubling a six-month yield—it should. All that is important is that you recognize that there is a convention used in the bond market for annualizing a yield and that an investor who is deciding among different bond alternatives or a manager considering issuing bonds in different countries should take this into consideration.

Zero-Coupon Bond

The value of a zero-coupon bond is easier to figure out than the value of a coupon bond. Let's see why. Suppose we are considering investing in a zero-coupon bond that matures in five years and has a maturity value of $1,000. If this bond does not pay interest every period no one will buy it at its maturity value. Instead, investors pay some amount *less* than the maturity value, with its return based on the difference between its maturity value and what they pay for it—assuming they hold it to maturity.

The yield to maturity on bonds with semiannual coupons is determined by taking the six-month yield and multiplying it by two—following the bond-equivalent basis convention. Though this yield is not the effective or true yield on the bond because we have not considered compounding within the year. Now what happens when we are dealing with yields on bonds that have no coupon? Convention still has us dealing with a yield-to-maturity calculated by taking the six-month yield and multiplying it by two.

If a zero-coupon bonds is priced to yield 10% its price is the present value of $1,000, discounted five years at 10%. We are given:

Maturity value, M = $1,000
Number of periods, N = 5 years × 2 = 10 six-month periods
Yield, r_d = 10%/2 = 5% per year

The value of the debt security is:

$$V = \frac{\$1,000}{(1 + 0.05)^{10}} = \$613.91$$

If, instead, these bonds are priced to yield 5%,

Maturity value, M = $1,000
Number of periods, N = 5 years × 2 = 10
Yield, r_d = 5%/2 = 2.5% per year

and the value of a bond is:

$$V = \frac{\$1,000}{(1 + 0.025)^{10}} = \$781.20$$

Returns on Bonds

If you invest in a bond, you realize a return from the interest it pays (if it is a coupon bond) and from either the sale, the maturity, or call of the bond. We calculate the return on a bond in the same way we calculate the return for a stock, except in the case of stock the cash flow is dividend income, rather than interest income.

There is another dimension to consider with bonds that we needn't consider with common stocks: Bonds have a finite life since they either mature or are called. Therefore, we are interested in:

- the realized return, which is the return over a specific period of time,
- the yield if the bond is held to maturity, which is the return assuming the bond is held to maturity, and
- the yield to call, which is the return on the bond assuming the bond is called.

Realized Return

A bond's return comprises the return from the appreciation or depreciation in the value of the bond over the period—the capital yield—and the return from the interest received during the period—the *coupon yield.*

$$Return = Capital\ yield + Coupon\ yield$$

Let's look at an investment in 100 Olympic Power bonds that mature in the year 2007 with a coupon rate of 8⅞ and a par value of 1000. At the beginning of 1997, these bonds were selling at 96½ (that is, 96.5% of face value, or $965.00 per bond); at the end of 1997, they were selling for 97½. The coupon rate of 8⅞% means that they pay 8.875% on the par value of $1,000, or $88.75 for the year. If interest were paid at the end of the year, the return on 100 bonds for 1997 is:

$$Return\ on\ Olympic\ Power\ 8⅞\ bonds\ maturing\ in\ 2007$$
$$= \frac{\$97,500 - \$96,500 + \$8,875}{\$96,500} = \frac{\$9,875}{\$96,500} = 10.2332\%$$

Breaking down this return into its capital yield and coupon yield:

$$\begin{array}{c} Return\ on\ Olympic \\ Power\ 8⅞\ bonds \\ maturing\ in\ 2007 \end{array} = \frac{\$97,500 - \$96,500}{\$96,500} + \frac{\$8,875}{\$96,500} = 10.2332\%$$

$$\underbrace{\qquad\qquad}_{\substack{\uparrow \\ Capital\ yield \\ \downarrow}} \quad \underbrace{\qquad\qquad}_{\substack{\uparrow \\ Coupon\ yield \\ \downarrow}}$$

$$= \quad 1.0363\% \quad + \quad 9.1969\%$$

Because the interest is paid semiannually (each bond pays $44.375 on June 30th and December 31st), what return could you have earned if you bought 100 of these bonds on January 1, 1997 and held them through December 31, 1997? The semiannual interest payments make our computations a bit more complicated. But we can make our job easier if we lay out the cash flows in an orderly fashion:

	Beginning of January 1997	End of June 1997	End of December 1997
Bond value	$96,500.00		$97,500.00
Interest		$4,437.50	4,437.50
Total	$96,500.00	$4,437.50	$101,937.50

The yield on these bonds is such that an investment of $96,500.00 will produce cash flows of $4,437.50 after six months and $101,947.50 after 12 months. Stated in the form of a present value equation, with r_d representing the six-month yield,

$$\$96,500.00 = \frac{\$4,437.50}{(1 + r_d)^1} + \frac{\$101,947.50}{(1 + r_d)^2}$$

Where do we start to solve for r_d? We can begin at either of two places.

For one, we know these bonds are selling at a discount from their par value of $1,000. This tells us the yield is greater than the coupon rate because investors are not willing to pay the maturity value, $1,000, to get interest of 8.875% per year. Therefore, the market rate must be something greater than 8.875%. So, we know the effective annual yield must be greater than 8.875%, which means that the six-month yield must be greater than 8.875%/2 = 4.4375%.

What we know, then, is that the semiannual yield is above 4.992% Using a financial calculator, r_d is 5.1087%. If the yield over six months is 5.1087%, the effective annual yield for a year is 5.1087% compounded for two six-month periods:

Effective annual yield = $(1 + 0.051087)^2 - 1 = 10.48\%$

Now let's look at an example of the return on a zero-coupon bond. Suppose on January 1, 2001, you bought 10 Dot.com zero-coupon bonds maturing on December 31, 2011 for 47¾ or $477.50 per bond. On December 31, 2000, these bonds sold for 50¼, or $502.50 per bond. What is your effective annual return on these bonds during 2000?

$$\text{Return on Dot.com bonds during 2000}$$
$$= \frac{\$5,020 - \$4,775}{\$4,775} = \frac{\$245}{\$4,775} = 5.13\%$$

Yield-to-Maturity

The annual return on a bond is a measure of the yield or benefit (realized or unrealized) over a year. But for some bonds, we may be interested in knowing what yield we would earn over the longer term, such as holding them until maturity. Yield-to-maturity is the annual yield on an investment assuming the investor *holds the bond until maturity*. It considers all an investment's expected cash flows—in the case of a bond, the interest and principal. When we look at yield-to-maturity, we once again see a relation between a bond's yield and its value today.

Zero-Coupon Bonds

Looking again at the Dot.com bonds, let's figure out the return if they were held to maturity. If you hold these bonds to maturity, you will receive the $1,000 par value on each of your bonds, or $10,000.[4] To make the calculations simpler, let's assume they mature on December 31st of 2011. If you buy the bonds and hold them to maturity, you would hold them for 12 years.

The return on these bonds over the 12-year period is:

$$\text{Return on Dot.com bonds 2000–2001}$$
$$= \frac{\$10,000 - \$4,775}{\$4,775} = \frac{\$5,225}{\$4,775} = 109.42\%$$

Looks impressive! But this return is over 12 years. Let's see what this return is on an annual basis so that we can compare it with the annual return of other investments. And to make the yield comparable with that on a coupon bond, let's calculate the yield-to-maturity on a bond equivalent basis.

For this example:

PV = \$4,775.00
FV = \$10,000.00
N = 12 years $\times$ 2 = 24 six-month periods

---

[4] Of course we are assuming that the issuer of the bond, in this case Dot.com, will be able to pay the principal at maturity.

Using the basic valuation equation and inserting the known values for FV, PV, and N, and solving for the annual return:

$$FV = PV(1 + r_d)^N$$
$$\$10,000 = \$4,775.00(1 + r_d)^{24}$$
$$(1 + r_d)^{24} = \$10,000/\$4,775.00 = 2.0942$$
$$1 + r_d = \sqrt[24]{2.0942} = 1.0312788$$
$$r_d = 1.0312788 - 1 = 3.12788\%$$

The yield to maturity is therefore 3.12788% × 2 = 6.25577%. Buying these bonds at the beginning of 1990 and holding them to maturity provides an average annual return of 6.26%—the yield-to-maturity. Using a financial calculator,

Hewlett-Packard 10B	Hewlett-Packard 12C	Hewlett-Packard 17B	Texas Instruments BA-II Plus
24 N	24 n	24 N	24 N
10000 FV	10000 FV	10000 FV	10000 FV
4775 ± PV	4775 ± PV	4775 ± PV	4775 ± PV
I/YR	i	I%YR	CPT I/Y
× 2 =	2×	× 2 =	× 2 =

Coupon Bonds

The present value of a bond is its current market price, which is the discounted value of all future cash flows of the bond—the interest and principal. The yield to maturity on a coupon bond is the discount rate, put on an annual basis, that equates the present value of the interest and principal payments to the present value of the bond. So, in the case of a bond that pays interest semiannually, we first solve for the six-month yield, and then translate it to its equivalent annual yield-to-maturity.

Now let's look at a the yield-to-maturity on a coupon bond. Going back to the Olympic Power 8⅞% coupon bonds maturing in 2007 and with interest paid semiannually, what is the yield to maturity on these bonds if you bought them on January 1, 1997 for $96,500.00? Or, put another way, what annual yield equates the investment of $96,500.000 with the present value of the 22 interest cash flows and maturity value?

In this example, we know the following:

$$V = \$1,000 \times 96.5\% \times 100 = \$96,500.00$$
$$C = (0.08875/2) \times \$1,000 \times 100 \text{ bonds} = \$4,437.50$$

$$M = \$1,000 \times 100 \text{ bonds} \qquad = \$100,000.00$$
$$N = 11 \text{ years} \times 2 \qquad = 22 \text{ six-month periods}$$

and t identifies the six-month period we're evaluating. Therefore,

$$\$96,500 = \sum_{t=1}^{22} \frac{\$4,437.50}{(1+r_d)^t} + \frac{\$100,000.00}{(1+r_d)^{22}}$$

Where do we start looking for a solution to r_d? Before we revert to our financial calculators, let's think about the value of r_d. If the bonds yielded 8⅞%, they would be selling close to par ($100,000 for our 100 bonds). This would be equivalent to a six-month value of $r_d = 4.4375\%$ for six months.

But these bonds are priced *below* par. That is, investors are not willing to pay the maturity value for these bonds because they can get a better return on similar bonds elsewhere. As a result, the price of the bonds is driven downward until these bonds provide a return or yield-to-maturity equal to that of bonds with similar risk.

Given this reasoning, the yield on these bonds must be greater than the coupon rate, so the six-month yield must be greater than 4.4375%. Using the trial and error approach, we would start with 5% as the six-month yield and look at the relation between the present value of the cash inflows (interest and principal) discounted at 5% and the price of the bonds (the $96,500.00):

Present value of bonds using a 5% discount rate

$$= \sum_{t=1}^{22} \frac{\$4,437.50}{(1+0.05)^t} + \frac{\$100,000.00}{(1+0.05)^{22}} = \$92,595.81$$

or,

Present value of bonds using a 5% discount rate $\neq$ Present value of bonds

$$\$92,595.81 \neq \$96,500.00$$

In fact, using 5%, we have discounted too much, since the present value of the bonds using 5% is less than the present value of the bonds. Therefore, we know that r_d should be less than 5%. We now have an idea of where the yield lies: between 4.4375% and 5%. Using a financial calculator, we find the value of $r_d = 4.70\%$, a six-month yield:

Hewlett-Packard 10B	Hewlett-Packard 12C	Hewlett-Packard 17B	Texas Instruments BA-II Plus
4437.5 PMT	4437.5 PMT	4437.5 PMT	4437.5 PMT
22 N	22 n	22 N	22 N
100000 FV	100000 FV	100000 FV	100000 FV
96500 ± PV	96500 CHS PV	96500 ± PV	96500 ± PV
I/YR	i	I%YR	CPT I/Y

Translating the six-month yield into an annual yield, we find that these bonds are valued such that the yield-to-maturity is 9.4%:

$$\text{Yield to maturity} = 4.7\% \times 2 = 9.4\%$$

Another way of saying this is that the bonds are priced to yield 9.4% per year.

Why is the yield to maturity different from the annual yield of 10.48% that we calculated earlier? The annual yield was calculated using the beginning and end-of-year values of the bonds ($96,500.00 and $97,500.00), as well as the two interest payments. But the yield-to-maturity assumes that we buy the bonds for $96,500 and *hold them until 2007*, getting 22 interest payments and the $100,000 principal. So, we know that if we buy and hold these bonds for one year, we would have gotten a 10.48% annual return on our investment. But if we held onto these bonds, we would have gotten a 9.4% annual return. Remember: When we bought the bonds at the beginning of 1997, we didn't know if the price of the bonds was going to go up, down, or stay the same since we didn't know what was going to happen to interest rates during the year. But when we buy the bonds at the beginning of 1997 we do know what we will get at maturity—assuming the bond issuer is able to pay the principal at that time.

The bond's price changes from January 1, 1997 to December 31, 1997 for two reasons:

■ As time progresses, the value of a bond tends toward its maturity value (we'll show why and how next).
■ The value of the bonds change as yields change.

We now take a brief look at both of these considerations.

The Value of Bonds as They Approach Maturity

Let's focus on maturity, holding the yield constant at the January 1, 1997 yield. What is value of the bond if the yield-to-maturity is 9.4% per year and there are now 20 interest payments left, instead of 22? This is the same as asking: What is the value of the bonds as of December 1997—two six-month periods later—if the yield-to-maturity does not change?

Present value of bonds on December 31, 1997

$$= \sum_{t=1}^{20} \frac{\$4,437.50}{(1+0.047)^t} + \frac{\$100,000.00}{(1+0.047)^{22}} = \$96,643.83$$

Moving ahead one more year, to December of 1992:

Present value of bonds on December 31, 1998

$$= \sum_{t=1}^{18} \frac{\$4,437.50}{(1+0.047)^t} + \frac{\$100,000.00}{(1+0.047)^{22}} = \$96,858.27$$

In Exhibit 9.4, we continue this calculation for each year to maturity. We see that the value of the bond increases until it approaches the maturity value. The interest payments contribute less to the bond's present value as time goes on since there are fewer interest payments through time, yet the maturity value contributes more as the bond approaches maturity—and hence more valuable—as we get closer to maturity. The change in the value of the bond as it approaches maturity is referred to as the *time path* of the bond.

EXHIBIT 9.4   Value of Olympic Power 8⅞% Bonds, Interest Paid Semiannually, Maturing December 31, 2000 as Maturity Approaches

Date	Number of Periods Remaining to Maturity	Present Value of Interest Payments	Present Value of Maturity Value	Present Value of Bonds
December 31, 1997	20	$56,735.24	$39,908.59	$96,643.83
December 31, 1998	18	53,110.12	43,748.15	96,858.27
December 31, 1999	16	49,136.23	47,957.12	97,093.35
December 31, 2000	14	44,780.01	52,571.03	97,351.04
December 31, 2001	12	40,004.69	57,628.83	97,633.53
December 31, 2002	10	34,769.94	63,173.24	97,943.19
December 31, 2003	8	29,031.56	69,251.08	98,282.64
December 31, 2004	6	22,741.10	75,913.66	98,654.75
December 31, 2005	4	15,845.43	83,217.23	99,062.66
December 31, 2006	2	8,286.34	91,223.48	99,506.82
December 31, 2007	0	0	100,000.00	100,000.00

The Value of Bonds as Yields Change

If the yield-to-maturity had remained constant at 9.4% per year, what would these bonds be worth at the end of 1997? According to Exhibit 9.4, $96,643.83. What is their value at the end of 1997 in our previous example? $97,500. Why isn't the actual value of the bonds equal to the value predicted according to the time path of the bond? Because yields have changed. At the beginning of 1997, the bonds were priced to yield 9.4% per year to maturity. At the end of 1997, however, the value of the bonds is greater than what we would expect, given simply the passage of time.

The yield to maturity as of December 31, 1997, given a value of $97,500, is calculated by solving for the six-month yield that equates the new market value to the present value of the interest and maturity value:

Present value of bonds on December 31, 1997

$$= \sum_{t=1}^{20} \frac{\$4,437.50}{(1+r_d)^t} + \frac{\$100,000.00}{(1+r_d)^{20}} = \$97,500$$

which gives us:

$$r_d = 4.632\% \text{ semiannually,}$$

or a 4.632% × 2 = 9.264% yield-to-maturity.

If yields did not change during the year and the bonds were valued to yield 9.4% per year to maturity, the value of the bonds would have crept up to $96,643.83 by the end of 1997. But instead, the value of the bonds increased from $96,500 to $97,500. Since the cash flows have not changed, the only thing that could cause the value of the bonds to deviate from $96,643.83 is the discount rate—the yield.

As we saw from the calculations, the yield-to-maturity decreased from 9.4% to 9.264% per year. As the yield decreased, the value of the bond increased.

Let's look once again at the value of a bond:

$$V = \sum_{t=1}^{N} \frac{C}{(1+r_d)^t} + \frac{M}{(1+r_d)^t}$$

If we hold C, T, and M constant, we see that an increase in r_d—the six-month yield—decreases the present value of the bond. Likewise, a decrease in r_d increases the present value of the bond. The value of bonds is therefore sensitive to the yield.

EXHIBIT 9.5   Value of Olympic Power Bonds for Different Yields-to-Maturity

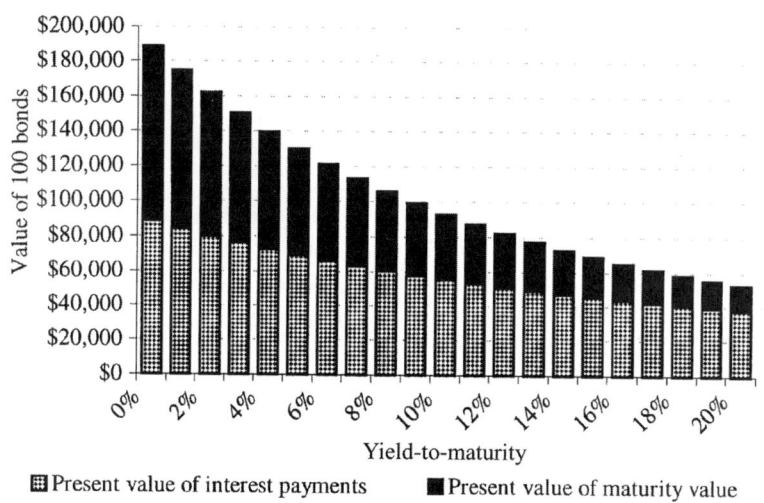

How sensitive is the value to different yields? Let's look at an example using the Olympic Power bonds as of the end of 1997. We saw that if the bonds are valued at $97,500, this is equivalent to saying their yield to maturity is 9.264% per year. We also saw that if the bonds are valued at $96,643.83, their yield-to-maturity is 9.4% per year.

We can see the different values of the bonds as of December 1997 for different yields in Exhibit 9.5. If the bonds are priced to yield 2%, they would be worth $162,032. If the bonds are price to yield 20%, they would be worth $52,643.

Callable Bonds

Some bonds have a feature, referred to as a *call feature*, that allows the bond issuer to buy back the bonds from the investor at a specified price—the call price—during a specified period prior the bond's maturity date. A bond with this feature is referred to as a *callable bond*. If a bond is callable, investors are concerned with not just its yield-to-maturity, but also its return if the bond is called away. *Yield-to-call* is a concept similar to the yield-to-maturity. It is the yield to the date when the bond is expected to be called, instead of a yield to a bond's maturity. The yield-to-call is calculated like the yield-to-maturity, except:

■ instead of the number of periods to the maturity date, N is the number of periods to some date when the bonds are expected to be called, and

■ the call price of the bond is used as the maturity value, M.

The *call price* is specified in the bond indenture. When the bond may be called is also specified in the indenture, but it is usually a range of dates, so the precise date the firm will actually call the bond is not specified. Therefore, some assumption has to be made regarding when the bond will be called away.

Let's look at a callable bond to see how this works. Illinois Bell Telephone 8¼ debentures due in 2016 are callable in any year before maturity until the year 2011. But the call price depends on the year called. For example, if Illinois Bell calls in the bonds in 1991, the company must pay 104.95, or $1,049.50 per bond; if called in 2011, it's 100.24 or $1,002.40 per bond.

On January 1, 1991, the price was 88, or $880 per bond. This bond pays $82.50 interest each year, or $41.25 every six months. As of January 1, 1991, there were 52 interest payments remaining to maturity. Therefore, the yield to maturity as of January 1, 1991 will be the annual yield equivalent to the six-month rate that solves:

$$\$880 = \sum_{t=1}^{52} \frac{\$41.25}{(1+r_d)^t} + \frac{\$1,000}{(1+r_d)^{52}}$$

We know that since this is a discount bond (the value is less than its par value), the yield-to-maturity is greater than the 8¼% coupon rate. Using a financial calculator, the six-month rate is 0.0475 or 4.75%. The yield-to-maturity is therefore 4.75% × 2 = 9.5%.

The yield-to-call is calculated is a similar manner. For example, if the bonds are called at the end of 1991, Illinois Bell must pay $1,049.50 per bond at the call date and prior to the call has paid two interest payments since January 1, 1991: June and December of 1991.

Using this information (M = $1,049.50 and N = 2), the yield-to-call is calculated by determining the six-month yield and translating it into an annual yield:

$$\$880 = \sum_{t=1}^{2} \frac{\$41.25}{(1+r_d)^t} + \frac{\$1,049.50}{(1+r_d)^2}$$

The six-month rate is 13.7% and the yield-to-call is 27.4% per year.

Though the yield-to-call is usually calculated using the first available call date, we can calculate the yield-to-call for any possible call date. For bonds called at the end of the year 2000, the yield-to-call is the annual yield equivalent to the six-month yield solving using the call price for 2000 of 102.83:

$$\$880 = \sum_{t=1}^{20} \frac{\$41.25}{(1+r_d)^t} + \frac{\$1,028.30}{(1+r_d)^{20}}$$

The six-month yield is 5.19% and the yield-to-call is 10.38% per year.

VALUATION OF OPTIONS

In Chapter 4, we discussed options and how the price of an option can be decomposed into intrinsic value and time premium. The factors that affect the time value of an option are:

1. the value of the underlying asset;
2. the exercise price;
3. the time value of money;
4. the expected volatility in the value of the underlying asset; and
5. the time to maturity.

To see how these factors influence the value of an option, let's look at a simple option—a stock option. A *stock option* is the right to buy or sell a particular common stock at a specified price within a specified period. These options are not created by the company that issued the underlying stock; rather, they are created by the exchange on which the option is to be traded.

To illustrate the influence of these factors an option's value, consider the following stock option:

> *The right to buy a share of ABC stock at $40 a share before December 15th.*

Since this is a right to buy an asset, we refer to this as a *call option.* This option gives the investor the right to buy a share of ABC stock at $40 per share—the *exercise price,* also called the *strike price*—before December 15th—the *expiration date.*

If ABC stock is currently trading for $35 a share, this option is referred to as *out-of-the-money*; that is, the current stock price is less that the exercise price of $40. Is this option worthless? The answer is no. The option to buy ABC stock at $40 a share is valuable (that is, the option is worth more than $0) since there is *some* chance that the price of ABC stock will rise above $40 a share prior to December 15th.[5]

If ABC stock is currently trading for $40 a share, this option is referred to as *at-the-money*; that is, the current stock price is equal to the strike price. Again, the option would be worth something since ABC stock may rise above the exercise price prior to December 15th.

If the ABC stock is currently trading for $45 a share, this option is referred to as *in-the-money*; that is, the current stock price is greater than the strike price. The option will be worth more than $5. Why? Because an investor today can buy the stock at $40 (exercising the option) and then sell it for $45 in the market, making a $5 profit. Therefore, the option is at least worth $5. Again, since the stock price has a chance of rising further prior to December 15th, the option will be worth more than $5.

From this analysis, we can see that the greater the price of the underlying asset (the stock, in this case), the greater the value of the call option. That is, there is a direct relation between the price of the underlying asset and the value of the call option.

The option value is also affected by the exercise price. For a given price of ABC stock, the lower the exercise price, the greater the value of the option. For example, assume that the price of ABC stock is $45. The option with an exercise price of $40 will have a value greater than $5. Compare this with an option on ABC with an exercise price of $35. In this latter case, the ABC option will trade for some value greater than $10. Therefore, there is an inverse relation between the exercise price and the value of the call option.

The value of the option is also affected by the time value of money. The call option is the right to buy an asset sometime in the future. Since the option represents buying in the future, the greater the opportunity cost of funds, the greater the value of the option. By delaying the purchase of the asset, you can invest your funds in other assets—the greater the return available, the greater is the value of deferring the purchase of the asset. In other words, the greater the opportunity cost, the more valuable it is to have the option, which allows you to purchase the asset in the future (instead of today).

The value of the option is also influenced by the volatility of the value of the underlying asset. If ABC stock is currently trading for $35 a

---

[5] Of course, the price of the stock may fall below $40. If the price of the stock is below $40, the option owner will not choose to exercise the option (that is, the option owner will not purchase the stock). Since a call option is an option to buy and not an option to sell the stock, the option's value depends on the probability that the stock's price will be *above* the strike price prior to expiration.

share, the value of the option to buy ABC stock at $40 a share is influenced by the probability that ABC stock will rise above $40 prior to the expiration date. What affects this probability? The more volatile the value of the underlying asset is expected to be, the more likely that it may increase in value prior to the expiration date. Therefore, there is a direct relation between the expected volatility of the underlying asset's value and the value of the call option.

The time remaining to expiration also affects the value of the option. For example, if today is October 15th, and the ABC stock is trading for $35 a share, there would be two months prior to the option's expiration. If, instead, today is November 15th and the ABC stock is trading for $35 a share, there is one month prior to expiration. In which case is it more likely that the option will become in-the-money before expiration? October 15th, because there is more time for the stock price to move upward. Therefore, there is a direct relation between the time to maturity of an option and the option's value.

If we alter our example to make the option a *put option* in ABC stock—that is, an option to *sell* ABC stock—we would have a different set of relations between these factors and the value of the option. Consider a put option on ABC stock:

The right to sell a share of ABC stock at $40 a share before December 15th.

The put becomes more valuable in the following circumstances:

- the lower the value of the asset, since the investor in the put option gains when the exercise price is more than the asset's actual value,
- the higher the exercise price, since this means the investor can sell the asset for a higher price,
- the lower the time value of money, since the investor is delaying selling the asset and getting the proceeds from that sale,
- the more the expected volatility of the underlying asset's value, since there is no profit if the price of the underlying asset does not move, and
- the longer the time to maturity, since there is more time for the underlying asset's price to move below the exercise price.

The factors that affect the value of call and put options and their relation to the value of an option are summarized in Exhibit 9.6. Incorporating these factors mathematically into the valuation of an option or option-like security is quite complex. That's part of your advanced studies in finance.

EXHIBIT 9.6   Relation between Call and Put Option Features and the
Value of an Option

Feature	Relation to a Call Option Value	Relation to a Put Option Value
Value of the underlying asset	*Direct relation* The greater the value of the underlying asset, the greater the value of the option.	*Inverse relation* The greater the value of the underlying asset, the lower the value of the option.
Exercise price	*Inverse relation* The lower the exercise price, the greater the value of the option.	*Direct relation* The greater the exercise price, the greater the value of the option.
Time value of money	*Direct relation* The greater the time value of money, the greater the value of the option.	*Inverse relation* The greater the time value of money, the lower the value of the option.
Volatility of the underlying asset's value	*Direct relation* The greater the volatility of the value of the underlying asset, the greater the value of the option.	*Direct relation* The greater the volatility of the value of the underlying asset, the greater the value of the option.
Time to maturity	*Direct relation* The greater the time remaining to maturity, the greater the value of the option.	*Direct relation* The greater the time remaining to maturity, the greater the value of the option.

In addition to options on stocks, as we discussed in our ABC example, there are other types of option securities.

■ A *warrant* is the right to buy a specified stock at a specified price in a specified time period, generally attached to a corporate bond as a "sweetener" to make the bond more attractive. A warrant is therefore a call option.

■ A *detachable warrant* is a warrant that can be sold separately from the bond and traded as a security.

■ A *right* is a call option given to shareholders to buy additional stock in the issuing corporation (usually at a discount from the current market price) for a limited period of time. Rights can be sold by shareholders or exercised. If they are sold to another investor, they are traded as securities.

In addition to these option securities, there are also securities with option-like features. A *convertible bond* is a bond that can be converted into common stock at the option of the investor. This bond is therefore a combination of a straight bond (a bond without such a conversion feature) and an option to convert the bond to shares of stock. Another example is the putable bond. A *putable bond* is a bond that gives the investor the right to put or sell the bonds back to the issuer at a specified price, under certain specified conditions.

There are many option-like features that may affect the value of the security. These features include callability and convertibility. A bond with a call feature gives the bond issuer the right to buy back the bond from the investor for a specified price during a specified period. This feature provides the issuer with flexibility—for example, if interest rates decline, the issuer can call, or buy back, the bonds and then sell new bonds with a lower interest rate. Since the issuer is likely to call the bond when interest rates have declined below the bond's coupon rate, the investor must reinvest the proceeds received when the bond is called at a lower interest rate. Consequently, a call feature increases the risk to the investor because the investor is exposed to the risk that the proceeds received will have to be reinvested at a lower rate. As a result of this risk, investors demand a higher yield to invest in a bond that has a call feature relative to an otherwise comparable bond that does not have this feature. Looked at from the issuer's perspective, the issuer must pay a higher cost (in the form of a higher coupon rate) by issuing a bond with a call feature than one without a call feature.

A bond with a convertible feature gives the investor the right to exchange the bond for common stock of the issuer at a specified rate of exchange. This feature gives the investor flexibility. For example, if the common stock's price increases sufficiently, the investor could exchange the bond for common stock. A convertible feature therefore increases the potential return on the bond since it could be turned into stock when it is attractive to do so.

We already know the value of a debt security is affected by its return (in the form of interest and principal payments) and the uncertainty associated with these interest and principal payments. Now we know features such as callability and convertibility also affect the value of debt securities.

In addition to the options found in securities, the financial manager faces investment decisions that have options. In deciding whether or not to invest in a new product, the financial manager has the option to postpone or defer investment. This is a call option—the option to invest in the product at some future point in time.

Another example is the abandonment option. In evaluating an investment that was made in the past, the financial manager has the option to abandon the investment—stop production and sell off the assets. The option to abandon is a put option, since it is an option to *sell* the investment.

Looking at options in a broader perspective, we see that the owners of a firm have the option to not pay the creditors, halting operations, selling off assets, and distributing the proceeds. This is a put option held by the owners since they control whether or not to pay off creditors or to default.

Whether we are talking about securities that are options, securities with option-like features, or financial decisions that contain options, the same five factors listed in Exhibit 9.6 apply in valuing them. Though the precise calculation of the value of options is beyond the scope of this text, you should be able to recognize the factors affecting the value of an option and how they could influence the financial decisions you will have to make.

SUMMARY

- The value of any asset depends on the expected cash flows and the uncertainty associated with those cash flows.
- The value of a share of stock is the present value of all future dividends on the stock. These dividends may be fairly predictable and constant, as in the case of a preferred stock, or fairly unpredictable in amount and timing, as in the case of some common stock.
- The value of a debt security is the present value of the promised interest and principal payments, discounted at a rate that reflects the uncertainty associated with these cash flows.
- The Dividend Valuation Model (also known as the Gordon Model) is a formula that can be used to value a share of stock if the dividend is either constant or grows at a constant rate. The model states that the value of a share of stock is equal to the ratio of next period's dividend to the difference between the required rate of return and the growth rate of dividends.
- If dividends on a stock are expected to grow at one rate for a finite number of years and to grow at another rate after that time, the Dividend Valuation Model can be modified to accommodate these two growth rates.
- Using the Dividend Valuation Model, we can see that the required rate of return on a stock is a function of the stock's dividend yield and its capital yield. Using the same model, we also can see that the growth rate is a function of the dividend payout such that the lower the payout, the greater the growth of future dividends.

- Calculating returns on an asset uses the same tools we used to value the asset, but this time we solve for the return instead of the present value.
- The return on an asset over a specified time interval involves determining the return based on the given present value, future value, any intermediate cash flows (such as interest or dividends), and the number of periods.
- The return on a bond if it is held to maturity is referred to as the yield-to-maturity. The yield-to-maturity is the annualized return assuming that any interest earned is reinvested at the yield-to-maturity and that the bond is held until maturity. For the case of bonds of U.S. corporations or governmental entities, interest is paid semiannually; therefore, the calculation of the yield-to-maturity requires first calculating the six-month yield then multiplying this yield by two.
- To be consistent with conventions, the value and returns of zero-coupon bonds are calculated using an annualized six-month yield.
- The value of a bond may change when either the bond's yield-to-maturity changes or time passes. As a bond approaches maturity, the value of the bond converges upon the maturity value.
- If a bond is callable, an additional yield is also calculated: the yield-to-call. This is the annualized yield on the bond assuming the bond is called at a specified time and at the specified call price.
- The value of an option—whether an actual security, a security with option-like features, or embedded in an investment or financing decision—is influenced by the exercise price, the time remaining to the expiration of the option, the value of the underlying asset, the expected volatility of the value of the underlying asset, and the time value of money.

QUESTIONS

1. What are the major differences between the dividends expected to be paid to preferred stockholders and common stockholders?
2. a. Why do investors view the cash flows from debt securities of a corporation as more certain than the common stock of the corporation?
   b. What is the uncertainty regarding the cash flows for a bond that is callable?
3. Using the dividend valuation model with dividends growing at a constant rate, what is the relation between dividend growth, share price growth, and earnings growth?
4. Which of the following situations does not work with the dividend valuation model? a. no growth in dividends. b. growth in dividends

that is greater than the required rate of return. c. negative growth in dividends. d. no current dividends.

5. What is the relation between the price-earnings ratio and the growth rate of dividends?

6. If the dividend rate on preferred stock is reset every year to the going market yield on preferred stocks of similar risk, at what price would a share of preferred stock trade?

7. a. What is the relation between the expected growth rate of common stock dividends and the dividend payout?

   b. What is the rationale behind this relation?

8. The Goofy Gadget Company currently pays a dividend of $2.50 per common share. If dividends are expected to grow at a rate of 5% per year and the required rate of return on Goofy common stock is 8%, what is the value of a share of Goofy stock?

9. The Common Company has paid the following dividends during the past four years of:

Year	Dividend per Share
1997	$2.00
1998	$2.10
1999	$2.30
2000	$2.52

   If dividends are expected to grow at the same rate as the past four years and the required rate of return on Common common is 10%, what is the expected price of a share of Common common at the end of 2000?

10. The Grow-all Company has 1,000,000 shares of common stock outstanding. The company paid dividends of $6,000,000 on common stock this year. Dividends are expected to grow at a rate of 4% per year and the required rate of return on common stock is 7%. Using the dividend valuation model, what is the value of a share of Grow-all common stock?

11. The Change-all Company currently pays $2.00 of dividends on each share of common stock. The required rate of return on Change-all stock is 10%.

    a. If the expected dividend growth rate is 5% each year, forever, what is the value of a share of Change-all common stock?

    b. If the expected dividend growth rate is 2% each year, forever, what is the value of a share of Change-all common stock?

    c. If the dividend growth is expected to be 5% for the next five years and 2% thereafter, what is the value of a share of Change-all common stock?

12. The AlterG Corporation currently pays $3.00 of dividends per share of common stock. The required rate of return on AlterG stock is 5%.
   a. If the expected dividend growth rate is 2% per year, forever, what is the value of a share of AlterG common stock?
   b. If the expected dividend growth rate is 4% per year, forever, what is the value of a share of AlterG common stock?
   c. If the dividend growth rate is expected to be 4% per year of the next four years and 2% thereafter, what is the value of a share of AlterG common stock?

13. Ross purchased 100 shares of stock for $30 a share on January 1, 1996. On December 31, 2001, he sold these shares for $25 per share. What was the yield on his investment?

14. The Babson Software Company common stock currently pays dividends of $2.00 per share. Babson's stock earnings are expected to grow at a rate of 10% for the next three years and then grow at a rate of 5% thereafter. Investors demand a return of 12% on Babson's stock. Using the dividend valuation model, what is the value of Babson common stock?

15. Burlington Northern Santa Fe, Inc., paid the following dividends per share (DPS) on its common stock:

Year	DPS	Year	DPS	Year	DPS
1984	$1.10	1988	$2.20	1992	$1.20
1985	$1.45	1989	$1.20	1993	$1.20
1986	$1.55	1990	$1.20	1994	$1.20
1987	$2.05	1991	$1.20	1995	$1.20

Source: Value Line Investment Survey, Edition 2 (March 22, 1996) p. 285.
Calculate the average annual growth rate in dividends from:
   a. 1984 through 1987
   b. 1984 through 1991
   c. 1984 through 1995

16. The Perpetual Corporation issued shares of preferred at a price of $90 per share. If the dividend is fixed at $9 per share, what is the yield on the preferred shares?

17. Suppose the Everlasting Company has shares of preferred stock outstanding that pay $5 per share and are priced to yield 10%. If the yield on this stock were to change to 8%, what would be the expected effect on the shares' price?

18. For each of the following pairs of coupon rates and yields, assuming interest is paid at the end of each year, determine whether the bond will sell for more than, at, or less than its par value:

Bond	Coupon Rate	Yield-to-Maturity
A	5%	7%
B	2%	3%
C	6%	6%
D	3%	6%
E	8%	4%

19. Consider two bonds, Bond X and Bond Y, each with a maturity value of $1,000 and maturing in five years. Bond X has a coupon rate of 5% and Bond Y has a no coupon. If Bond X and Bond Y are considered to be of equal risk, which bond will have a higher value today?

20. If you determine that the yield-to-maturity on a bond with annual coupons is 10%, what rate of return are we assuming that these coupons earn when they are reinvested?

21. Consider a bond with a face value of $1,000, a coupon rate of 8% (paid annually), and a maturity in three years. What is the value of the bond if it is priced to yield 6%?

22. The IM Company issued a bond with a maturity value of $1,000, a coupon rate of 5% (paid annually), and it reaches maturity in five years. What is the value of the IM bond today if the yield-to-maturity is 4%?

23. Suppose three years ago you bought an ABC Company bond that pays 6% per year (paid semiannually) and it has three years to maturity at its par value of $1,000.
    a. If you sell the bond when it is priced to yield 8%, what is your gain or loss on this investment?
    b. If you sell the bond when it is priced to yield 4%, what is your gain or loss on this investment?
    c. If you sell the bond when it is priced to yield 10%, what is your gain or loss on this investment?

24. Arthur purchased a zero-coupon bond on January 1, 1990 for $500. On December 31, 2001, Arthur sold this bond for $750. What was the yield on this investment?

25. Consider a bond that has a current value of $1,081.11, a face value of $1,000.00, a coupon rate of 10% (paid semiannually) and five years remaining to maturity.
    a. What is the bond's yield-to-maturity today?
    b. If the bond's yield does not change, what is its value one year from today?
    c. If the bond's yield does not change, what is its value two years from today?

26. What is the value today of a zero-coupon bond with a maturity value of $1,000 and five years remaining to maturity if it is priced to yield: a. 5%? b. 8%? c. 10%? d. 12%? e. 14%?

27. The R. T. Ely Corporation issued bonds at par on January 1, 1995, with a face value of $1,000, an original maturity of five years and a coupon rate of 5% (paid annually). What is the price of one Ely bond on January 1, 1998 if Ely bonds are priced to yield 6%?

28. On January 1, 1981, the Huntington Railroad Company issued $100 million of 9⅝ bonds due 2020. Interest is paid semiannually in January and June of each year. These bonds are callable according to the following schedule:

1990–2000 at 103.0
2001–2005 at 102.0
2006–2010 at 101.0
2011–2015 at 100.5
2016–2020 at 100.0

These bonds are also convertible into shares of stock, with each $1,000 face value bond convertible into 15 shares of Huntington common stock. Huntington common stock paid a dividend of $2 per share in 1997. Its dividends are expected to grow at a rate of 10% per year for the years 1998–2002 and then slow to a rate of 5% per year thereafter. The current required rate of return on Huntington common stock is 14%.

The current yield (i.e., annual interest/market price) on the Huntington bonds is 7.5%. Interest rate forecasts for the next six years are as follows:

1998	8.00%	2001	8.75%
1999	8.50%	2002	9.00%
2000	8.50%	2003	9.00%

All indications are that yields will remain at 9% through 2020.

a. Calculate the yield-to-call for the Huntington bonds for each year from today, the end of 1997, to maturity. Plot the yield-to-call against time.

b. Forecast the stock price of Huntington common stock for each year from 1998 through 2020. Plot the predicted stock price against time.

c. Based on the yield and dividend growth forecasts, at what point in the future would it be profitable to convert the Huntington bonds into stock? Explain the basis of your decision. What other factors enter into this decision?

29. Suppose you are offered an option on an asset. This option gives you the right to buy the asset for $1,000 any time before December 31st of this year. Currently, this asset is worth $800.
    a. Is this a call option or a put option?
    b. What determines the value of this option?
    c. Currently, is this option "at-the-money," in-the-money," or "out-of-the money"?
    d. Since the exercise price is more than the asset's value today, does this mean the option is worthless? Explain.
30. a. Why is a warrant an option?
    b. Why is a right an option?
31. Explain why each of the following bonds can be viewed as a bond with an embedded option?
    a. a callable bond
    b. a putable bond
    c. a convertible bond.
32. For which type of option (put or call) does the price of the option vary inversely with the:
    a. exercise price?
    b. value of the underlying asset?
33. If the expected volatility of the underlying asset's value increases, what would happen to the price of
    a. a call option?
    b. a put option?
34. If interest rates in the market decline below the coupon rate on a callable bond that is currently callable, why would an investor say that the embedded call option is "in the money"?

CHAPTER 10

Risk and Expected Return

By now it should be clear that to make any investment or financing decision you must make your best determination of the costs involved and the benefits, or return, that will result from it. What may not yet be as clear is that there is always risk that returns may not turn out to be what you though they would be. What we're getting at, of course, is risk. Specifying a return by itself doesn't mean very much unless you also specify its risk.

After we have explained the concept of risk, we will look at how to quantify the risk of an expected return and how to incorporate risk in financial decision-making. By becoming familiar with modern portfolio theory and the role of risk in valuing assets, you will understand how a financial manager can manage risk and its relation to expected return.

RISK

Whenever you make a financing or investment decision, there is some uncertainty about the outcome. *Uncertainty* means not knowing exactly what will happen in the future. There is uncertainty in most everything we do as financial managers, because no one knows precisely what changes will occur in such things as tax laws, consumer demand, the economy, or interest rates.

Though the terms "risk" and "uncertainty" are often used to mean the same thing, there is a distinction between them. Uncertainty is not knowing what's going to happen. *Risk* is how we characterize *how much* uncertainty exists: The greater the uncertainty, the greater the risk. Risk is the degree of uncertainty.

In financing and investment decisions there are many types of risk we must consider. These include:

- Cash flow risk
    - Business risk
        - Sales risk
        - Operating risk
    - Financial risk
    - Default risk
- Reinvestment risk
    - Prepayment risk
    - Call risk
- Interest rate risk
- Purchasing power risk
- Currency risk
- Portfolio risk
    - Diversifiable risk
    - Nondiversifiable risk

Let's take a look at each of these types of risk.

Cash Flow Risk

Cash flow risk is the risk that the cash flows of an investment will not materialize as expected. For any investment, the risk that cash flows may not be as expected—in timing, amount, or both—is related to the investment's business risk.

Business Risk

Business risk is the risk associated with operating cash flows. Operating cash flows are not certain because neither are the revenues nor the expenditures comprising the cash flows.

> *Revenues:* depending on economic conditions and the actions of competitors, prices or quantity of sales (or both) may be different from what is expected. This is *sales risk*.
>
> *Expenditures:* operating costs are comprised of fixed costs and variable costs. The greater the fixed component of operating costs, the less easily a company can adjust its operating costs to changes in sales.

The mixture of fixed and variable costs depends largely on the type of business. For example, fixed operating costs make up a large portion of an airline's operating costs: No matter how many passengers are flying, the airline still needs to pay gate fees, pay a pilot, and buy fuel. The variable costs for an airline—the costs that change depending on the number of passengers—amount to a little bit of fuel and the cost of the meal.

Even within the same line of business, companies can vary their fixed and variable costs. For example, an airline could develop a system that allows it to vary the number of cabin stewards and baggage handlers according to passenger traffic, varying more of its operating costs as demand changes.

We refer to the risk that comes about from the mix of fixed and variable costs as *operating risk*. The greater the fixed operating costs relative to variable operating costs, the greater the operating risk.

Let's take a look at how operating risk affects cash flow risk. Remember back in economics when you learned about elasticity? That's a measure of the sensitivity of changes in one item to changes in another. We can look at how sensitive a firm's operating cash flows are to changes in demand, as measured by unit sales. We'll calculate the operating cash flow elasticity, which we call the *degree of operating leverage (DOL)*.

The degree of operating leverage is the ratio of the percentage change in operating cash flows to the percentage change in units sold. Let's simplify things and assume that we sell all that we produce in the same period. Then,

$$\text{DOL} = \frac{\text{Percentage change in operating cash flows}}{\text{Percentage change in units sold}}$$

Suppose the price per unit is $30, the variable cost per unit is $20, and the total fixed costs are $5,000. If we go from selling 1,000 units to selling 1,500 units, an increase of 50% of the units sold, operating cash flows change from:

	1,000 Units Sold	1,500 Units Sold
Sales	$30,000	$45,000
Less variable costs	20,000	30,000
Less fixed costs	5,000	5,000
Operating cash flow	$5,000	$10,000

Operating cash flows doubled when units sold increased by 50%. What if the number of units decreases by 25%, from 1,000 to 750?

	1,000 Units Sold	750 Units Sold
Sales	$30,000	$22,500
Less variable costs	20,000	15,000
Less fixed costs	5,000	5,000
Operating cash flow	$5,000	$2,500

Operating cash flows decline by 50%. For any 1% change in units sold, the operating cash flow changes by 2%, in the same direction. So if units sold increased by 10%, operating cash flows would increase by 20%; if units sold decreased by 10%, operating cash flows would decrease by 20%.

We can represent the degree of operating leverage in terms of the basic elements of the price per unit, variable cost per unit, number of units sold, and fixed operating costs. Operating cash flows are:

Operating cash flow = (Price per unit)(Number of units sold)
    – (Variable cost per unit)(Number of units sold)
    – (Fixed operating costs)

How much do operating cash flows change when the number of units sold changes? It changes by the difference between the price per unit and the variable cost per unit—called the **contribution margin**—times the change in units sold. The percentage change in operating cash flows for a given change in units sold is:

$$\text{DOL} = \frac{\begin{pmatrix}\text{Number}\\\text{of units}\\\text{sold}\end{pmatrix}\begin{pmatrix}\text{Price}\\\text{per} - \text{cost}\\\text{unit}\quad\text{per unit}\end{pmatrix}}{\begin{pmatrix}\text{Number}\\\text{of units}\\\text{sold}\end{pmatrix}\begin{pmatrix}\text{Price}\\\text{per} - \text{cost}\\\text{unit}\quad\text{per unit}\end{pmatrix} - \begin{pmatrix}\text{Fixed}\\\text{operating}\\\text{costs}\end{pmatrix}} \tag{10-1}$$

Applying the formula for DOL using the data in the example, we can figure out the sensitivity to change in units sold from 1,000 units:

$$\text{DOL for 1,000 units} = \frac{1,000(\$30 - \$20)}{1,000(\$30 - \$20) - \$5,000} = 2$$

A DOL of 2.0 means that a 1% change in units sold results in a 1% × 2.0 = 2% change in operating cash flow.

Why do we specify that the DOL is at a particular quantity sold (in this case 1,000 units)? Because the DOL will be different at different numbers of units sold. For example, at 10,000 units,

$$\text{DOL for 10,000 units} = \frac{10,000(\$30 - \$20)}{10,000(\$30 - \$20) - \$5,000} = 1.05$$

Let's look at situation in which the firm has shifted some of the operating costs away from fixed costs and into variable costs. Suppose the firm has a unit sales price of $30, a variable cost of $24 a unit, and $1,000 in fixed costs. A change in units sold from 1,000 to 1,500—a 50% change—changes operating cash flows from $5,000 to $8,000, or 60%:

	1,000 Units Sold	1,500 Units Sold
Sales	$30,000	$45,000
Less variable costs	24,000	36,000
Less fixed costs	1,000	1,000
Operating cash flow	$5,000	$8,000

Then:

$$\text{DOL at 1,000 units} = \frac{1,000(\$30 - \$24)}{1,000(\$30 - \$24) - \$1,000} = 1.2$$

and

Percentage change inoperating cash flows
= DOL(Percentage change in units sold)
= 1.2(50%) = 60%

What we see in our calculations here is what we saw a bit earlier in our reasoning of fixed and variable costs: The greater use of fixed, relative to variable operating costs, the more sensitive operating cash flows are to changes in units sold and, therefore, more operating risk.

At 1,000 units produced and sold, we see that the DOL is 2.0; at 10,000 units, the DOL is 1.2. The degree of operating leverage is sensitive to the number of units produced and sold.

We can gain additional insight into the firm's profitability and its uncertainty by looking at the relation between profitability and the number of units produced and sold. What number of units must be produced and sold to just break even (that is, to just cover the fixed operating costs)? The answer to this question is found by rearranging the operating cash flow equation:

$$\$0 = (\text{Price per unit})(\text{Number of units sold})$$
$$- (\text{Variable cost per unit})(\text{Number of units sold})$$
$$- (\text{Fixed operating costs})$$

The break-even number of units, Q_{BE}, is:

$$Q_{BE} = \frac{(\text{Fixed operating costs})}{(\text{Price per unit} - \text{Variable cost per unit})} \qquad (10\text{-}2)$$

Consider the example in which fixed operating costs are \$5,000, price per unit is \$30, and variable cost per unit is \$20. The break-even quantity is:

$$Q_{BE} = \frac{\$5,000}{(\$30 - \$20)} = 500 \text{ units}$$

If the firm produces and sells 500 units, there are no operating profits and the DOL is undefined.

Both sales risk and operating risk influence a firm's operating cash flow risk. And both sales risk and operating risk are determined in large part by the type of business the firm is in. But management has more opportunity to manage and control operating risk than they do sales risk.

Suppose a firm is deciding on which equipment to buy to produce a particular product. The sales risk is the same no matter what equipment is chosen to produce the product. But the available equipment may differ in terms of fixed and variable operating costs of producing the product. Financial managers need to consider the operating risk associated with their investment decisions.

Financial Risk

When we refer to the cash flow risk of a security, we expand our concept of cash flow risk. Since a security represents a claim on the income and assets of a business, the risk of the security is not just the risk of the cash flows of the business, but also the risk related to how these cash flows are distributed among the claimants—the creditors and owners of the business. Therefore, cash flow risk of a security includes both its business risk *and* its financial risk.

Financial risk is the risk associated with how a company finances its operations. If a company finances with debt, it is a legally obligated to pay the amounts comprising its debts when due. By taking on fixed obligations, such as debt and long-term leases, the company increases its financial risk. If a company finances its business with equity, either generated from operations (retained earnings) or from issuing new equity, it does not incur fixed obligations.

The more fixed-cost obligations (i.e., debt) incurred by the firm, the greater its financial risk. We can quantify this risk somewhat in the same way we did for operating risk, looking at the sensitivity of the cash flows available to owners when operating cash flows change. This sensitivity, which we refer to as the *degree of financial leverage (DFL)*, is:

$$DFL = \frac{\text{Percentage change in cash flows to owners}}{\text{Percentage change in operating cash flows}}$$

The cash flows to owners are equal to operating cash flows, less interest and taxes. If operating cash flows change, how do cash flows to owners change? Suppose operating cash flows change from $5,000 to $6,000 and suppose the interest payments are $1,000 and, for simplicity and wishful thinking, the tax rate is 0%:

	Operating Cash Flow of $5,000	Operating Cash Flow of $6,000
Operating cash flow	$5,000	$6,000
Less interest	1,000	1,000
Cash flows to owners	$4,000	$5,000

A change in operating cash flow from $5,000 to $6,000—a 20% increase—increased cash flows to owners by $1,000—a 25% increase.

What if, instead, our fixed financial costs are $3,000? A 20% change in operating cash flows results in a 50% change in the cash flows available to owners:

	Operating Cash Flow of $5,000	Operating Cash Flow of $6,000
Operating cash flow	$5,000	$6,000
Interest	3,000	3,000
Cash flows to owners	$2,000	$3,000

Using more debt financing increases the sensitivity of owners' cash flows.

We can write the sensitivity of owners' cash flows to a change in operating cash flows as:

$$
\text{DFL} = \frac{\left(\begin{array}{c}\text{Number}\\ \text{of units}\\ \text{sold}\end{array}\right)\left(\begin{array}{cc}\text{Price} & \text{Variable}\\ \text{per} & -\text{cost}\\ \text{unit} & \text{per unit}\end{array}\right) - \left(\begin{array}{c}\text{Fixed}\\ \text{operating}\\ \text{costs}\end{array}\right)}{\left(\begin{array}{c}\text{Number}\\ \text{of units}\\ \text{sold}\end{array}\right)\left(\begin{array}{cc}\text{Price} & \text{Variable}\\ \text{per} & -\text{cost}\\ \text{unit} & \text{per unit}\end{array}\right) - \left(\begin{array}{c}\text{Fixed}\\ \text{operating}\\ \text{costs}\end{array}\right) - \left(\begin{array}{c}\text{Fixed}\\ \text{financing}\\ \text{costs}\end{array}\right)} \tag{10-3}
$$

If

Number of units sold = 1,000
Price per unit   = \$30
Variable cost per unit = \$20
Fixed operating costs = \$5,000
Fixed financing costs = \$1,000

$$
\text{DFL for 1,000 units} = \frac{1,000(\$30 - \$20) - \$5,000}{1,000(\$30 - \$20) - \$5,000 - \$1,000} = 1.25
$$

Again, we need to qualify our degree of leverage by the level of production since DFL is different at different levels operating cash flows.

The firm must produce and sell a sufficient number of units to make a profit for owners. How many units are necessary? The answer is similar to what we did for the break-even in terms of operating profits, but this time we have to also cover the fixed financial costs (that is, interest). The break-even number of units considering both operating and financial costs, indicated as Q_{BE}^{*}, is:

$$
Q_{BE}^{*} = \frac{(\text{Fixed operating costs}) + (\text{Fixed financing costs})}{(\text{Price per unit} - \text{Variable cost per unit})} \tag{10-4}
$$

In other words, the firm must produce and sell more than Q_{BE}^{*} units to make a profit. In our example, the break-even number of units, with total fixed costs of \$6,000, is:

$$
Q_{BE}^{*} = \frac{\$6,000}{(\$30 - \$20)} = 600 \text{ units}
$$

If the firm sells 600 units, profits to owners will be zero. If the firm sells less than the 600 units, the firm has a loss and if the firm sells more than the 600 units, the firm has a profit.[1]

---

[1] If the firm produces and sells exactly 600 units, the DFL is undefined.

The greater the use of financing sources that require fixed obligations, such as interest, the greater the sensitivity of cash flows to owners to changes in operating cash flows.

Operating and Financial Risk

The degree of operating leverage gives us an idea of the sensitivity of operating cash flows to changes in sales. And the degree of financial leverage gives us an idea of the sensitivity of owners' cash flows to changes in operating cash flows. But often we are concerned about the *combined* effect of both operating leverage and financial leverage. Owners are concerned about the combined effect because both contribute to the risk associated with their future cash flows. And financial managers, making decisions to maximize owners' wealth, need to be concerned with how investment decisions (which affect the operating cost structure) and financing decisions (which affect the capital structure) affect owners' risk.

Let's look back on the example using fixed operating costs of $5,000 and fixed financial costs of $1,000. The sensitivity of owners' cash flow to a given change in units sold is affected by both operating and financial leverage.

Consider increasing the units sold up 50%. If there was no interest (and therefore no financial leverage), the owners' cash flow would equal operating cash flow. Then a 50% increase in units sold would result in a 100% increase in cash flows to owners. Now consider decreasing units sold by 50%. This would result in a 100% decrease in cash flows to owners.

But if there is financial leverage, this leverage exaggerates the effect of operating leverage. Consider again the case where there is $1,000 of interest:

	1,000 Units Sold	1,500 Units Sold	500 Units Sold
Sales	$30,000	$45,000	$15,000
Less variable costs	20,000	30,000	10,000
Less fixed costs	5,000	5,000	5,000
Operating cash flow	$5,000	$10,000	$0
Less interest	1,000	1,000	1,000
Cash flows to owners	$4,000	$9,000	-$1,000

If the number of units sold increases by 50%, from 1,000 to 1,500 units,

■ Operating cash flows increase by 100%.

■ Cash flows to owners increase by 125%.

If units sold decrease by 50%, from 1,000 to 500 units,

■ Operating cash flows decrease by 100%.
■ Cash flows to owners decrease by 125%.

Combining a firm's degree of operating leverage with its degree of financial leverage results in the *degree of total leverage (DTL)*, a measure of the sensitivity of the cash flows to owners to changes in unit sales:

$$DTL = \frac{\text{Percentage change in cash flows to owners}}{\text{Percentage change in units sold}}$$

which is the same as:

$$DFL = \frac{\left(\begin{array}{c}\text{Number}\\\text{of units}\\\text{sold}\end{array}\right)\left(\begin{array}{cc}\text{Price} & \text{Variable}\\\text{per} & -\text{cost}\\\text{unit} & \text{per unit}\end{array}\right)}{\left(\begin{array}{c}\text{Number}\\\text{of units}\\\text{sold}\end{array}\right)\left(\begin{array}{cc}\text{Price} & \text{Variable}\\\text{per} & -\text{cost}\\\text{unit} & \text{per unit}\end{array}\right) - \left(\begin{array}{c}\text{Fixed}\\\text{operating}\\\text{costs}\end{array}\right) - \left(\begin{array}{c}\text{Fixed}\\\text{financing}\\\text{costs}\end{array}\right)} \qquad (10\text{-}5)$$

and which simplifies to:

$$DTL = DOL \times DFL$$

Suppose:

Number of unit sold   = 1,000
Price per unit   = \$30
Variable cost per unit = \$20
Fixed operating cost = \$5,000
Fixed financing cost = \$1,000

Then,

$$DTL \text{ for } 1,000 \text{ units} = \frac{1,000(\$30 - \$20)}{1,000(\$30 - \$20) - \$5,000 - \$1,000}$$
$$= \frac{\$10,000}{\$4,000} = 2.5$$

which we could also have gotten from multiplying the DOL, 2, by the DFL, 1.25. This means that a 1% increase in units sold will result in a 2.5% increase in cash flows to owners; a 50% increase in units sold results in a 125% increase in cash flows to owners; a 5% decline in units sold results in a 12.5% decline in cash flows to owners; and so on.

In the case of operating leverage, the fixed operating costs act as a fulcrum: The greater the proportion of operating costs that are fixed, the more sensitive are operating cash flows to changes in sales. In the case of financial leverage, the fixed financial costs, such as interest, act as a fulcrum: The greater the proportion of financing with fixed cost sources, such as debt, the more sensitive cash flows available to owners are to changes in operating cash flows. Combining the effects of both types of leverage, we see that fixed operating and financial costs together act as a fulcrum that increases the sensitivity of cash flows available to owners to changes in the umber of units sold.

Default Risk

When you invest in a bond, you expect interest to be paid (usually semi-annually) and the principal to be paid at the maturity date. However, the more burdened a firm is with debt—required interest and principal payments—the more likely it is that payments promised to bondholders will not be made and that there will be nothing left for the owners. We refer to the cash flow risk of a debt security as *default risk* or *credit risk*.

Technically, default risk on a debt security depends on the specific obligations comprising the debt. Default may result from:

- Failure to make an interest payment when promised (or within a specified period).
- Failure to make the principal payment as promised.
- Failure to make sinking fund payments (that is, amounts set aside to pay off the obligation), if these payments are required.
- Failure to meet any other condition of the loan.
- Bankruptcy.

Why do financial managers need to worry about default risk? Because they invest their firm's funds in the debt securities of other firms; because they are concerned about how investors perceive the risk of their own debt securities; and because the greater the perceived default risk of a firm's securities, the greater the firm's cost of financing.

Default risk is affected by both business risk—which includes sales risk and operating risk—and financial risk. We need to consider the effects operating and financing decisions have on the default risk of the securities a firm issues, since the risk accepted through the financing decisions affects the firm's cost of financing.

Reinvestment Rate Risk

Another type of risk is the uncertainty associated with reinvesting cash flows, not surprisingly called *reinvestment rate risk.*

Suppose you buy a U.S. Treasury Bond that matures in five years. There is no default risk, since the U.S. government could simply print more money to pay the interest and principal. Does this mean there is no risk when you own a Treasury bond? No. You need to do something with the interest payments as you receive them and the principal amount when it matures. You could stuff them under your mattress, reinvest in another Treasury bond, or invest them otherwise. If yields have been falling, however, you cannot reinvest the interest payments from the bond and get the same return you are getting on the bond. When your Treasury bond matures, you face reinvestment risk.

If we look at an investment that produces cash flows before maturity or sale, such as a stock (with dividends) or a bond (with interest), we face a more complicated reinvestment problem. In this case we're concerned with the reinvestment of the final proceeds (at maturity or sale), but also with the reinvestment of the intermediate dividend or interest cash flows (between purchase and maturity or sale).

Let's look at the case of a five-year bond issued by Company Y, that pays 10% interest (at the end of each year, to keep things simple), and has a par value of $1,000. This bond is a *coupon bond*; that is, interest is paid at the coupon rate of 10% per year, or $100 per bond. If you buy the bond when it is issued at the beginning of Year 1 and hold it to maturity, you will have the following cash flows:

Company Y Bond

Date	Cash Flow
January 1, Year 1	–$1,000.00 ← Purchase of bond
December 31, Year 1	100.00
December 31, Year 2	100.00
December 31, Year 3	100.00
December 31, Year 4	100.00
December 31, Year 5	1,100.00 ← Proceeds of maturity and last interest payment

You face five reinvestment decisions along the life of this bond: the four intermediate flows at the end of each year, and the last and largest cash flow that consists of the last interest payment and the par value.

Suppose we wish to compare the investment in the Company Y bond with another five-year bond, issued by Company Z, that has a different cash flow stream, but a yield that is nearly the same. Company Z's bond is a zero-coupon bond; that is, it has no interest payments, so the only cash flow to the investor is the face value at maturity:

Company Z bond

Date	Cash Flow		
January 1, Year 1	−$1,000.00	←	Purchase of bond
December 31, Year 5	+$1,610.51	←	Proceeds at maturity

Both bonds have the same annual yield-to-maturity of 10%. If the yield is the same for both bonds, does this mean that they have the same reinvestment rate risk? No. Just from looking at the cash flows from these bonds we see there are intermediate cash flows to reinvest from Company Y's bond, but not from Company Z's bond.

Let's see just how sensitive the yield on the investment is to changes in the assumptions on the reinvestment of intermediate cash flows. Suppose we can reinvest the interest payments at 5%, not 10%. We calculate the yield on the bonds assuming reinvestment at 5%—a *modified internal rate of return*—by calculating the future value of the reinvested cash flows and determining the discount rate that equates the original investment of $1,000 to this future value:

	Company Y Bond		Company Z Bond	
Date	Cash Flow	Values as of December 31, Year 5	Cash Flow	Values as of December 31, Year 5
December 31, Year 1	$100.00	$121.55		
December 31, Year 2	100.00	115.76		
December 31, Year 3	100.00	110.25		
December 31, Year 4	100.00	105.00		
December 31, Year 5	1,100.00	1,100.00	$1,610.50	$1,610.51
Future value, with cash flows reinvested at 5%		$1,552.56		$1,610.51

Using the value of the cash flow as of December 31, Year 5 as the future value and the $1,000 investment as the present value, the modified internal rates of return are 9.2% for Company Y's bond and 10% for Company Z's bond. You'll notice that the modified internal rate of return for Company Z's bond is the same as its yield-to-maturity—because there are no intermediate cash flows.

If we compare two bonds with the same yield-to-maturity and the same coupon rate, the bond with the *longer* maturity has *more* reinvestment risk. That's because it has more cash flows to reinvest throughout its life.

If we compare two bonds with the same yield-to-maturity and the same time to maturity, the bond with the *greater* coupon rate has *more* reinvestment rate risk. That's because it has more of its value coming sooner in the form of cash flows.

Two types of risk closely related to reinvestment risk of debt securities are prepayment risk and call risk. **Prepayment risk** is associated with certain asset-backed securities. These securities, which are discussed in Chapter 26, are created by pooling loans and using the pool as collateral for the securities. Examples of asset-backed securities issued by corporations are those backed by residential mortgage loans, automobile loans, and equipment leases. The loans have a schedule for the repayment of principal. Typically the borrower has the right to prepay a loan without a penalty at any time prior to the scheduled principal prepayment date. A payment made in excess of the schedule principal repayment is referred to as a **prepayment.** A borrower may benefit from exercising the option to prepay if interest rates decline below the loan's interest rate. A prepayment that occurs when interest rates decline below the loan's interest rate is a disadvantage to the investor in an asset-backed security because it forces the investor to reinvest the proceeds received at a lower interest rate. This risk is referred to as prepayment risk.

Call risk is the risk that a callable security will be called by the issuer. If you invest in a callable security, there is a possibility that the issuer may call it in (buy it back). While you may receive a call premium (a specified amount above the par value), you have to reinvest the funds you receive.

There is reinvestment risk for assets other than stocks and bonds, as well. if you are investing in a new product—investing in assets to manufacture and distribute it—you expect to generate cash flows in future periods. You face a reinvestment problem with these cash flows: What can you earn by investing these cash flows? What are your future investment opportunities?

If we assume that investors do not like risk—a safe assumption—then they will want to be compensated if they take on more reinvestment rate risk. The greater the reinvestment rate risk, the greater the expected return demanded by investors.

Reinvestment rate risk is relevant to investment decisions no matter the asset and you must consider this risk in assessing the attractiveness of investments. The greater the cash flows during the life of an investment, the greater the reinvestment rate risk of the investment. And if an investment has a greater reinvestment rate risk, this must be factored into decisions.

Interest Rate Risk

Interest rate risk is the sensitivity of the change in an asset's value to changes in market interest rates. And, you should remember that market interest rates determine the rate we must use to discount a future value to a present value. The value of any investment depends on the rate used to discount its cash flows to the present. If the discount rate changes, the investment's value changes.

Suppose you invest in a project that you expect to have in operation for ten years. Two years into the project, you find that returns on alternative investments have increased. Does this affect the value of this two-year-old project? Sure. You now have a higher opportunity cost—the return on your best investment opportunity. Therefore the value of the two-year-old project is now less, and you need to determine whether to continue or terminate it. Reassessment is necessary, also, if the opportunity cost declines as well. If the return on your next best investment opportunity declines, the existing project will look even better.

Interest rate risk also is present in debt securities. If you buy a bond and intend to hold it until its maturity, you don't need to worry about its value changing as interest rates change: your return is the bond's yield-to-maturity. But if you do not intend to hold the bond to maturity, you need to worry about how changes in interest rates affect the value of your investment. As interest rates go up, the value of your bond goes down. As interest rates go down, the value of your bond goes up. This may seem wrong to you. But it's not, it's correct. Here's why.

Let's compare the change in the value of the Company Y bond to the change in the value of the Company Z bond as the market interest rate changes. (We presented these bonds in the previous section.) Suppose that it is now January 1, Year 2. If yields remain at 10%, the value of the bonds are:

Value of Company Y bond

$$= \frac{\$100.00}{(1+0.10)^1} + \frac{\$100.00}{(1+0.10)^2} + \frac{\$100.00}{(1+0.10)^3} + \frac{\$1,100.00}{(1+0.10)^4} = \$1,000.00$$

and

$$\text{Value of Company Z bond} = \frac{\$1,610.51}{(1+0.10)^4} = \$1,100.00$$

If market interest rates change causing the bonds to yield 12%, the value of the Company Y and Company Z bonds are less:

Value of Company Y bond
$$= \frac{\$100.00}{(1+0.12)^1} + \frac{\$100.00}{(1+0.12)^2} + \frac{\$100.00}{(1+0.12)^3} + \frac{\$1,100.00}{(1+0.12)^4}$$
$$= \$939.25$$

and

$$\text{Value of Company Z bond} = \frac{\$1,610.51}{(1+0.12)^4} = \$1,023.51$$

If market interest rates change causing the bonds to yield 8%, the value of the Company Y and Company Z bonds is more than $1,000:

Value of Company Y bond
$$= \frac{\$100.00}{(1+0.08)^1} + \frac{\$100.00}{(1+0.08)^2} + \frac{\$100.00}{(1+0.08)^3} + \frac{\$1,100.00}{(1+0.08)^4}$$
$$= \$1,066.24$$

and

$$\text{Value of Company Z bond} = \frac{\$1,610.51}{(1+0.08)^4} = \$1,183.77$$

But how sensitive are the values of the bond to changes in market interest rates? If the bonds' yield changed on January 1, Year 2 from 10% to 12%, the value of Company Y bond would drop from $1,000.00 to $938.25—a drop of $61.75, or 6.18% of the bond's value. The drop would be greater for Company Z's bond—a drop of $76.50 or 6.95% of its value. Looking at changes in the value of the bonds for different yield changes, we see that the Company Z bond's value is more sensitive to changes in yields than is Company Y's.

The values of the two bonds for different yields as of January 1, Year 2 are shown in Exhibit 10.1. As you can see, the Company Z bond's value is more sensitive to the yield changes than is Company Y's bond.

■ For a given maturity, the *greater the coupon rate*, the *less sensitive* the bond's value to a change in the yield. Why? The greater the coupon rate, the more of the bond's present value is derived from cash flows that are affected less by discounting.

EXHIBIT 10.1   The Value of Company Y and Company Z bonds on January 1, Year 2, for Different Yields

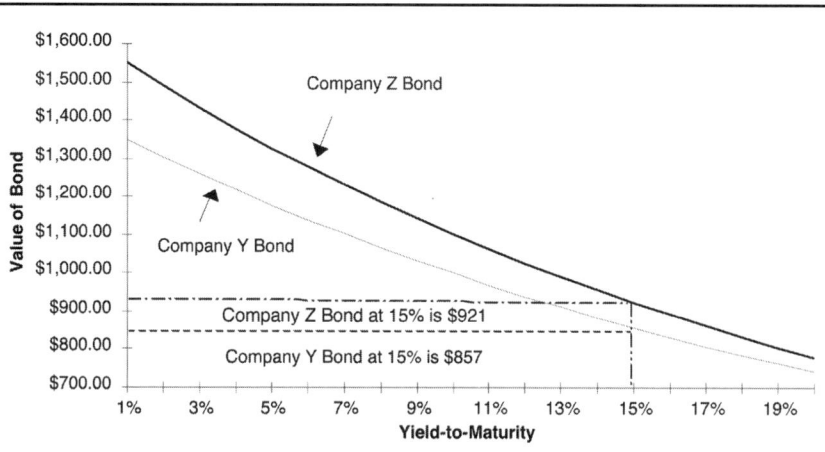

As another example, compare two bonds that have the same time remaining to maturity, five years, the same face value, $1,000, and both are priced to yield 10%. If Bond HC has a 10% coupon and Bond LC has a 5% coupon, a change in the yield has a greater effect on the value of Bond LC than on Bond HC. When yields change from 10% to 12%,

Bond HC's value changes from $1,000 to $928, down 7.20%
Bond LC's value changes from $810 to $748, down 7.65%

We can make an additional generalization about the sensitivity of a bond's value to changes in yields.

■ For a given coupon rate, the *longer the maturity* of the bond, the *more sensitive* the bond's value to changes in market interest rates.

Compare the change in the value of two bonds that have the same coupon rate, 10% and the same face value, $1,000, with interest paid annually. If Bond SM has five years remaining to maturity and Bond LM has ten years remaining to maturity, a change in the yield on the bonds from 10% to 12% results in a greater change in Bond LM's value. When interest changes from 10% to 12%,

Bond SM's value changes from $1,000 to $928, down 7.2%
Bond LM's value changes from $1,000 to $887, down 11.3%

Purchasing Power Risk

Purchasing power risk is the risk that the price level may increase unexpectedly. If a firm locks in a price on your supply of raw materials through a long-term contract and the price level increases, it benefits from the change in the price level and your supplier loses—the firm pays the supplier in cheaper currency. If a firm borrows funds by issuing a long-term bond with a fixed coupon rate and the price level increases, the firm benefits from an increase in the price level and its creditor is harmed since interest and the principal are repaid in a cheaper currency.

Consider the 11.0% and 9.1% inflation rates for the years Year 1 and Year 2, respectively. If you borrowed $1,000 at the beginning of Year 1 and paid it back two years later, you are paying back $1,000 in end-of-Year 2 dollars. But how much is a Year 2 dollar worth relative to beginning-of-Year 1 dollars? We can use the compounding relation to work this out. We know that the future value is $1,000. We also know that the rate of inflation over the two-year period is determined from compounding the two inflation rates:

$$
\begin{aligned}
r &= (1 + \text{Inflation rate for Year 1})(1 + \text{Inflation rate for Year 2}) - 1 \\
&= (1 + 0.110)(1 + 0.091) - 1 \\
&= 0.2110 \text{ or } 21.10\% \text{ over the two years}
\end{aligned}
$$

We can solve the basic valuation relation for today's value, PV, considering r to be a *two-year rate* (that is, a period is defined as the two-year stretch from the beginning of Year 1 through the end of Year 2):

$$
\begin{aligned}
FV &= PV(1 + r) \\
\$1,000 &= PV(1 + 0.2110)
\end{aligned}
$$

and rearranging to solve for PV,

$$
PV = \frac{\$1,000}{(1 + 0.2110)} = \$825.76
$$

Therefore, the $1,000 you paid back at the end of Year 2 was really only worth $825.80 at the beginning of Year 1. As a borrower, you have benefitted from inflation and your lender has lost.

Purchasing power risk is the risk that future cash flows may be worth less or more in the future because of inflation or deflation, respectively, *and* that the return on the investment will not compensate for the unanticipated inflation. If there is risk that the purchasing power of a currency will change, investors—who do not like risk—will demand a higher return.

Financial managers need to assess purchasing power risk in terms of both their investment decisions—making sure to figure in the risk from a change in purchasing power of cash flows—and their financing decisions—understanding how purchasing power risk affects the costs of financing.

Currency Risk

In assessing the attractiveness of an investment, we estimated future cash flows from the investment to see whether their value today—the benefits—out-weigh the cost of the investment. If we are considering making an investment that generates cash flows in another currency (some other nation's currency), there is some risk that the value of that currency will change relative to the value of our domestic currency. We refer to the risk of the change in the value of the currency as *currency risk*. It is discussed further in Chapter 25.

Currency risk is the risk that the *relative values* of the domestic and foreign currencies will change in the future, changing the value of the future cash flows. As financial managers, we need to consider currency risk in our investment decisions that involve other currencies and make sure that the returns on these investments are sufficient compensation for the risk of changing values of currencies.

RETURN AND RISK

We refer to both future benefits and future costs as expected returns. *Expected returns* are a measure of the tendency of returns on an investment. This doesn't mean that these are the only returns possible, just our best measure of what we expect.

Expected Return

Suppose you are evaluating the investment in a new product. You do not know and cannot know precisely what the future cash flows will be. But from past experience, you can at least get an idea of possible flows and the likelihood—the probability—they will occur. After consulting with colleagues in marketing and production management, you determine that there are two possible cash flow outcomes, success or failure, and the probability of each outcome. Next, consulting with colleagues in production and marketing for sales prices, sales volume, and production costs, we develop the following possible cash flows in the first year:

Scenario	Cash Flow	Probability of Cash Flow
Product success	$4,000,000	40%
Product flop	−2,000,000	60%

But what is the expected cash flow in the first year? The expected cash flow is the average of the possible cash flows, weighted by their probabilities of occurring:

$$\text{Expected cash flow} = 0.40(\$4,000,000) + 0.60(-\$2,000,000)$$
$$= \$400,000$$

The expected cash flow is $400,000.

The expected value is a guess about the future outcome. It is not necessarily the *most likely* outcome. The most likely outcome is the one with the highest probability. In the case of our example, the most likely outcome is −$2,000,000.

A general formula for any expected value is:

$$\text{Expected value} = E(x) = p_1 x_1 + p_2 x_2 + p_3 x_3 + \dots + p_n x_n + \dots + p_N x_N$$

where

$E(x)$ = the expected value
n = possible outcome
N = number of possible outcomes
p_n = probability of the nth outcome
x_n = value of the nth outcome

We can abbreviate this formula by using summation notation:

$$\text{Expected value} = E(x) = \sum_{n=1}^{N} p_n x_n \qquad (10\text{-}6)$$

The calculation of the expected value requires that all possible outcomes be included. Therefore, the probabilities (the p_i's) must sum to 1.00 or 100%—if not, you have left out a possible outcome.

Applying the general formula to our example,

N = 2 (there are two possible outcomes)
p_1 = 0.40
p_2 = 0.60

$$x_1 = \$4,000,000$$
$$x_2 = -\$2,000,000$$

$$E(\text{cash flow}) = \sum_{n=1}^{2} p_n x_n$$
$$= p_1 x_1 + p_2 x_2$$
$$= (0.40(\$4,000,000) + 0.60(-\$2,000,000) = \$400,000)$$

Considering the possible outcomes and their likelihoods, we expect a $400,000 cash flow.

Standard Deviation of the Possible Outcomes

The expected return gives us an idea of the tendency of the future outcomes—what we expect to happen, considering all the possibilities. But the expected return is a single value and does not tell us anything about the diversity of the possible outcomes. Are the possible outcomes close to the expected value? Are the possible outcomes much different than the expected value? Just how much uncertainty *is* there about the future?

Since we are concerned about the degree of uncertainty (risk), as well as the expected return, we need some way of quantifying the risk associated with decisions.

Suppose we are considering two products, Product A and Product B, with estimated returns under different scenarios and their associated probabilities:

Scenario	Probability of Outcome	Possible Return on Investment
Product A		
Success	25%	24%
Moderate success	50	10
Failure	25	−4
Product B		
Success	10%	40%
Moderate success	30	30
Failure	60	−5

We refer to a product's set of the possible outcomes and their respective probabilities as the ***probability distribution*** for those outcomes.

We can calculate the expected cash flow for each product as follows:

Scenario	p_n	x_n	$p_n x_n$
Product A			
Success	0.25	0.24	0.0600
Moderate success	0.50	0.10	0.0500
Failure	0.25	−0.04	−0.0100
Expected return			0.1000 or 10%
Product B			
Success	0.10	0.40	0.0400
Moderate success	0.30	0.30	0.0900
Failure	0.60	−0.05	−0.0300
Expected return			0.1000 or 10%

Both Product A and Product B have the same expected return. Let's now see if there is any difference in the possible outcomes for the two products.

The possible returns for Product A range from −4% to 24%, where the possible returns for Product B range from −5% to 40%. The *range* is the span of possible outcomes. For Product A the span is 28%; for Product B the it is 45%. A wider span indicates more risk, so Product B has more risk than Product A.

If we represent graphically the possible cash flow outcomes for Products A and B, with their corresponding probabilities, as in Exhibit 10.2, we see there is more dispersion of possible outcomes with Product B—they are more spread out—than those of Product A.

But the range by itself doesn't tell us much about the possible cash flows at these extremes nor within the extremes. Nor does the range tell us anything about the probabilities at or within the extremes.

A measure of risk that does tell us something about how much to expect and the probability that it will happen is the standard deviation. The *standard deviation* is a measure of dispersion that considers the values and probabilities for each possible outcome. The larger the standard deviation, the greater the dispersion of possible outcomes from the expected value. The standard deviation considers the distance (deviation) of each possible outcome from the expected value and the probability associated with that distance:

Standard deviation of possible outcomes

$$= \sigma(x) = \sqrt{\sum_{n=1}^{N} p_n [x_n - E(x)]^2} \tag{10-7}$$

EXHIBIT 10.2   Probability Distribution for Product A

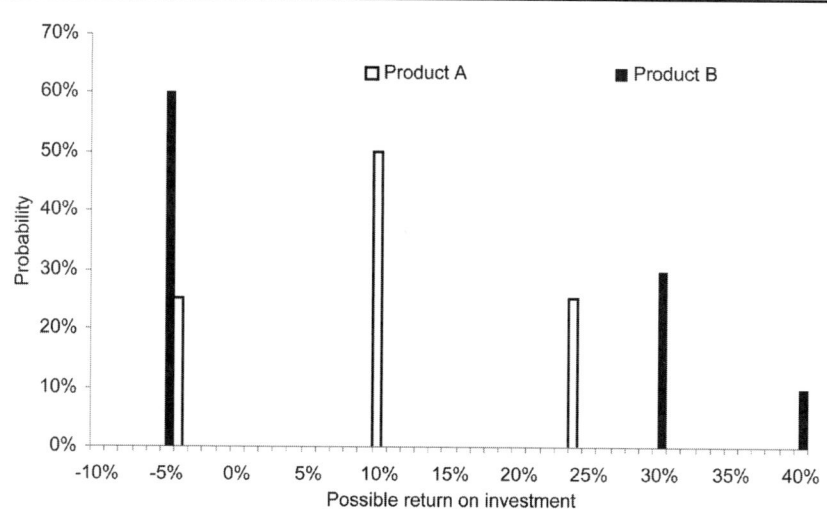

THE VARIANCE AND THE STANDARD DEVIATION

The variance and the standard deviation are both measures of dispersion. In fact, they are related: The standard deviation is the square root of the variance. So why do we go beyond the calculation of the variance to get the standard deviation? For two reasons.

First, the variance is in terms of squared units of measure (say, squared dollars or squared returns), whereas the standard deviation is in terms of the original unit of measure. It gets tough trying to interpret squared dollars or squared returns.

Second, if the probability distribution is approximately normally distributed (that is, bell-shaped, with certain other characteristics), we can use the standard deviation to compactly describe the probability distribution; not so with the variance. There are uses for the variance in statistical analysis, but for purposes of describing and comparing probability distributions, we focus on the expected value and the standard deviation.

The calculation of the standard deviation can be made manageable with a worksheet such as Exhibit 10.3, used to calculate the standard deviations of possible outcomes for Products A and B.

EXHIBIT 10.3 Calculation of the Standard Deviation of Possible Outcomes for Product A and Product B

Product A

Outcome	p	x	px	$x - E(x)$	$(x - E(x))^2$	$p(x - E(x))^2$
1	0.25	0.24	0.0600	0.1400	0.0196	0.0049
2	0.50	0.10	0.0500	0.0000	0.0000	0.0000
3	0.25	-0.04	-0.0100	-0.1400	0.0196	0.0049
			0.1000			$\sigma^2 = 0.0098$
						$\sigma = 0.0990 = 9.90\%$

Product B

Outcome	p	x	px	$x - E(x)$	$(x - E(x))^2$	$p(x - E(x))^2$
1	0.10	0.40	0.0400	0.3000	0.0900	0.0090
2	0.30	0.30	0.0900	0.2000	0.0400	0.0120
3	0.60	-0.05	-0.0300	-0.1500	0.0225	0.0135
			0.1000			$\sigma^2 = 0.0345$
						$\sigma = 0.1857 = 18.57\%$

Summarizing, we have calculated the following:

	Expected Return	Standard Deviation of Possible Outcomes
Product A	10%	9.90%
Product B	10%	18.57%

While both products have the same expected value, they differ in the distribution of possible outcomes. When we calculate the standard deviation around the expected value, we see that Product B has a larger standard deviation. The larger standard deviation for Product B tells us that Product B has more risk than Product A since its possible outcomes are more distant more from its expected value.

Return and the Tolerance for Bearing Risk

Which product investment do you prefer, A or B? Most people would choose A since it provides the same expected return with less risk. Most people do not like risk—they are **risk averse**. Does this mean a risk averse person will not take on risk? No—they will take on risk if they feel they are compensated for it.

A *risk neutral* person is indifferent toward risk. Risk neutral persons do not need compensation for bearing risk. A *risk preference* person likes risk—someone even willing to pay to take on risk. Are there such people? Yes. Consider people who play the state lotteries, where the expected value is always negative: The expected value of the winnings is less than the cost of the lottery ticket.

When we consider financing and investment decisions, we assume that most people are risk averse. Managers, as agents for the owners, make decisions that consider risk "bad" and that if risk must be borne, they make sure there is sufficient compensation for bearing it. As agents for the owners, managers cannot have the "fun" of taking on risk for the pleasure of doing so.

Risk aversion is the link between return and risk. To evaluate a return you must consider its risk: Is there sufficient compensation (in the form of an expected return) for the investment's risk?

EXPECTED RETURN, RISK, AND DIVERSIFICATION

As managers, we rarely are consider investing in only one project at time. Small businesses and large corporations alike can be viewed as collections of different investments, made at different points in time. We refer to a collection of investments as a *portfolio.*

While we usually think of a portfolio as a collection of securities (stocks and bonds), we can think of a business in much the same way— a portfolio of assets such as buildings, inventories, trademarks, patents, and so forth. As managers, we are concerned about the overall risk of the business's portfolio of assets.

Suppose you invested in two assets, Thing One and Thing Two, having 20% and 8% returns over the next year.

Suppose you invest equal amounts, say $10,000, in each asset for one year. At the end of the year you expect to have $10,000(1 + 0.20) = $12,000 from Thing One and $10,000(1 + 0.08) = $10,800 from Thing Two, or a total value of $22,800 from our original $20,000 investment. The return on our portfolio is therefore:

$$\text{Return} = \frac{\$22,800 - \$20,000}{\$20,000} = 14\%$$

If instead, we invested $5,000 in Thing One and $15,000 in Thing Two, the value of our investment at the end of the year would be:

$$\text{Value of investment} = \$5,000(1 + 0.20) + \$15,000(1 + 0.08)$$
$$= \$6,000 + \$16,200 = \$22,200$$

and the return on our portfolio would be:

$$\text{Return} = \frac{\$5,000(1 + 0.20) + \$15,000(1 + 0.08) - \$20,000}{\$20,000} = 11\%$$

which we can also write as:

$$\text{Return} = \frac{\$5,000}{\$20,000}(0.20) + \frac{\$15,000}{\$20,000}(0.08) = 11\%$$

As you can see more immediately by the second calculation, the return on our portfolio is the weighted average of the returns on the assets in the portfolio, where the weights are the proportion invested in each asset.

We can generalize the formula for a portfolio return, r_p, as the weighted average of the returns of *all* assets in the portfolio, letting:

i = a particular asset in the portfolio
w_i = proportion invested in asset i
r_i = return on asset i
S = number of assets in the portfolio

Thus, $r_p = w_1 r_1 + w_2 r_2 + \ldots + w_S r_S$.

We can write more compactly as:

$$r_p = \sum_{i=1}^{S} w_i r_i \tag{10-8}$$

Diversification and Risk

In any portfolio, one investment may do well while another does poorly. The projects' cash flows may be "out of sync" with one another. Let's see how this might happen.

Suppose you own Asset P that produces the returns over time shown in Exhibit 10.4(a). These returns vary up and down within a wide range. Suppose you also invested in Asset Q whose returns over time are shown in Exhibit 10.4(b). These returns also vary over time within a wide band. But since the returns on Asset P and Asset Q are out of sync, each tends to provide returns when the other doesn't. The result is that your portfolio's returns vary within a narrower range as shown in Exhibit 10.4(c).

EXHIBIT 10.4   Returns on Asset P, Asset Q, and a Portfolio over Time
Panel A: Returns on Asset P over Time

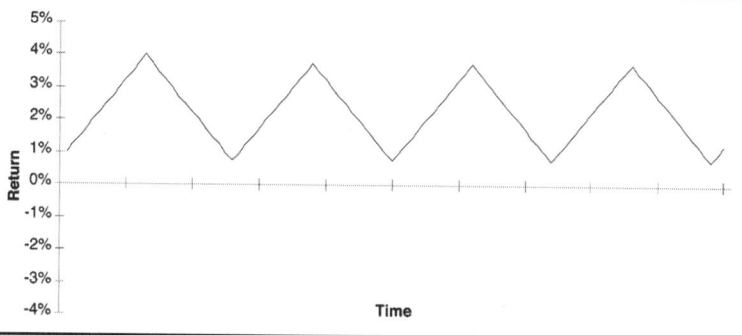

Panel B: Returns on Asset Q over Time

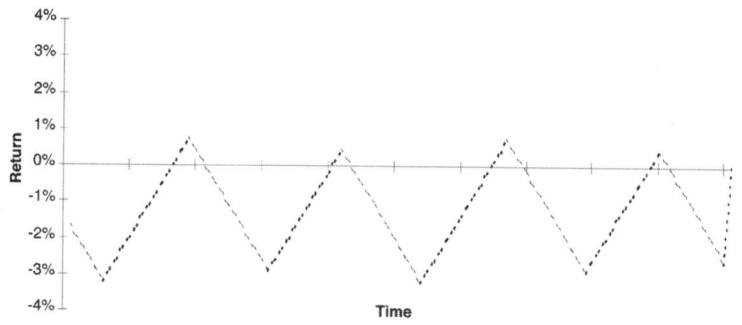

Panel C: Returns on a Portfolio Comprised of Asset P and Asset Q over Time

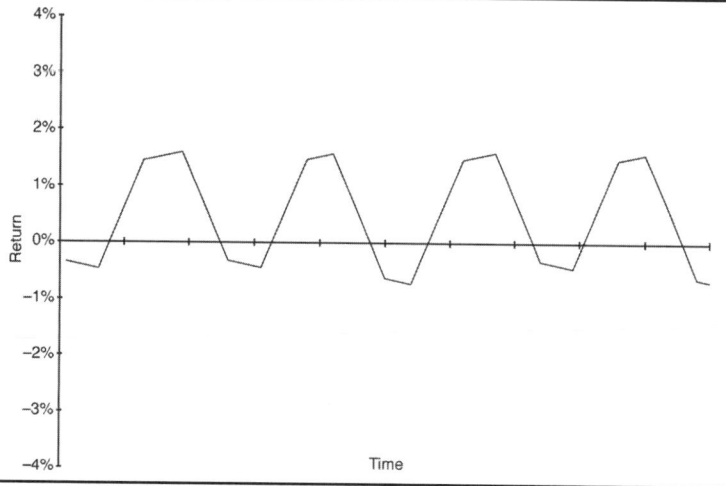

Let's look at the idea of "out-of-syncness" in terms of expected returns, since this is what we face when we make financial decisions. Consider Investment C and Investment D and their probability distributions:

Scenario	Probability of Scenario	Return on Investment C	Return on Investment D
Boom	30%	20%	–10%
Normal	50	0	0
Recession	20	–20	45

We see that when Investment C does well, in the boom scenario, Investment D does poorly. Also, when Investment C does poorly, as in the recession scenario, Investment D does well. In other words, these investments are out of sync with one another.

Now let's look at how their "out-of-syncness" affects the risk of the portfolio of C and D. Suppose we invest an equal amount in C and D. The calculation of the expected return and standard deviation for Investment C, Investment D, and the portfolio consisting of C and D is shown in Exhibit 10.5. The expected return on Investment C is 2% and the expected return on Investment D is 6%. The return on a portfolio comprised of equal investments of C and D is expected to be 4%. The standard deviation of Investment C's return is 14% and of Investment D's return is 19.97%, but the *portfolio's* standard deviation, calculated using the weighted average of the returns on Investment C and D in each scenario, is 4.77%. This is *less* than the standard deviations of each of the individual investments because the returns of the two investments do not move in the same direction at the same time, but rather tend to move in opposite directions.

The portfolio comprised of Investments C and D has less risk than the individual investments because each moves in different directions with respect to the other. A statistical measure of how two variables—in this case, the returns on two different investments—move together is the *covariance*. Covariance is a statistical measure of how one variable changes in relation to changes in another variable. Covariance in this example is calculated in four steps:

Step 1: For each scenario and investment, subtract the investment's expected value from its possible outcome.

Step 2: For each scenario, multiply the deviations for the two investments.

Step 3: Weight this product by the scenario's probability.

Step 4: Sum these weighted products to arrive at the covariance.

EXHIBIT 10.5 Calculation of the Standard Deviations for Investment C, Investment D, and the Portfolio Comprised of Investment C and Investment D

Investment C

Scenario	Probability p_n	Return x_n	Probability Times Return $p_n x_n$	Deviation from Expected Value $x_n - E(x)$	Squared Deviation from Expected Value $(x_n - E(x))^2$	Weighted Squared Deviations $p_n(x_n - E(x))^2$
Boom	30%	20%	0.0600	0.1800	0.0324	0.00972
Normal	50	0	0.0000	-0.0200	0.0004	0.00020
Recession	20	-20	-0.0400	-0.2200	0.0484	0.00968
	100%		$E(x) = 0.0200$			$\sigma^2(x) = 0.01960$
						$\sigma(x) = 0.1400$ or 14%

Investment D

Scenario	Probability p_n	Return x_n	Probability Times Return $p_n x_n$	Deviation from Expected Value $x_n - E(x)$	Squared Deviation from Expected Value $(x_n - E(x))^2$	Weighted Squared Deviations $p_n(x_n - E(x))^2$
Boom	30%	-10%	-0.0300	-0.1600	0.0256	0.00768
Normal	50	0	0.0000	-0.0600	0.0036	0.00018
Recession	20	45	0.0900	0.3900	0.1521	0.03042
	100%		$E(x) = 0.0600$			$\sigma^2(x) = 0.03990$
						$\sigma(x) = 0.1997$ or 19.97%

285

EXHIBIT 10.5 (Continued)

Portfolio of Investment C and Investment D

Scenario	Probability p_n	Return x_n	Probability Times Return $p_n x_n$	Deviation from Expected Value $x_n - E(x)$	Squared Deviation from Expected Value $(x_n - E(x))^2$	Weighted Squared Deviations $p_n(x_n - E(x))^2$
Boom	30%	5.0%	0.0150	0.0100	0.0001	0.00003
Normal	50	0.0	0.0000	-0.0400	0.0016	0.00080
Recession	20	12.5	0.0250	0.0850	0.0072	0.00145
	100%		$E(x) = 0.0400$			$\sigma^2(x) = 0.002275$
						$\sigma(x) = 0.477$ or 4.77%

Notes:

p_n = probability of outcome n occurring

x_n = outcome n

$E(x)$ = expected value

$\sigma(x)$ = standard deviation

$\sigma^2(x)$ = variance

Scenario	Probability	Step 1: Deviation of Return on Investment from its Expected Return		Step 2: Multiply Deviations Together	Step 3: Weight the Product by the Probability
		Investment C	Investment D		
Boom	0.30	0.1800	−0.1600	−0.0288	−0.00864
Normal	0.50	−0.0200	−0.0600	0.0012	0.00060
Recession	0.20	−0.2200	0.3900	−0.0858	−0.01716
				Step 4: Covariance =	−0.02520

As you can see in these calculations, in a boom economic environment, when Investment C is above its expected return (deviation is positive), Investment D is below its expected return (deviation is negative). In a recession, Investment C's return is below its expected value and Investment D's return is above its expected value. The tendency is for the returns on these portfolios to co-vary in *opposite* directions—producing a *negative* covariance of −0.0252.

Let's see the effect of this negative covariance on the risk of the portfolio. The portfolio's variance depends on:

- The weight of each asset in the portfolio.
- The standard deviation of each asset in the portfolio.
- The covariance of the assets' returns.

Let $cov_{1,2}$ represent the covariance of two assets' returns. We can write the portfolio variance as:

$$\text{Portfolio variance} = w_1^2\sigma_1^2 + w_2^2\sigma_2^2 + 2cov_{1,2}w_1w_2 \qquad (10\text{-}9)$$

The portfolio standard deviation is:

$$\text{Portfolio standard deviation} = \sqrt{\text{Portfolio variance}} \qquad (10\text{-}10)$$

We can apply this general formula to our example, with Investment C's characteristics indicated with a 1 and Investment D's with a 2,

w_1 = 0.50 or 50%
w_2 = 0.50 or 50%
σ_1 = 0.1400 or 14.00%
σ_2 = 0.1997 or 19.97%
$cov_{1,2}$ = -0.0252

Then:

Portfolio variance
$$= 0.50^2(0.1400^2) + 0.50^2(0.1997^2) + 2(-0.0252)(0.50)(0.50)$$
$$= 0.002275$$

and:

Portfolio standard deviation $= \sqrt{0.002275} = 0.0477$ or 4.77%

which, not coincidentally, is what we got when we calculated the standard deviation directly from the portfolio returns under the three scenarios.[2]

As we saw above, the standard deviation of the portfolio is lower than the standard deviations of each of the investments because the returns on Investments C and D are negatively related: When one is doing well the other may be doing poorly, and vice-versa. That is, the covariance is negative. The investment in assets whose returns are out of step with one another is the whole idea behind diversification. *Diversification* is the combination of assets whose returns do not vary with one another in the same direction at the same time.

If the returns on investments move together, we say that they are *correlated* with one another. *Correlation* is the tendency for two or more sets of data—in our case returns—to vary together. The returns on two investments are:

- *Positively correlated* if one tends to vary in the same direction at the same time as the other.
- *Negatively correlated* if one tends to vary in the opposite direction with respect to the other.
- *Uncorrelated* if there is no relation between the changes in one with changes in the other.

Statistically, we can measure correlation with a *correlation coefficient*. The correlation coefficient reflects how the returns of two securities vary together and is measured by the covariance of the two securities' returns, divided by the product of their standard deviations:

$$\text{Correlation coefficient} = \frac{\text{Covariance of two assets' returns}}{\left(\begin{array}{c}\text{Standard deviation of}\\ \text{returns on first asset}\end{array}\right)\left(\begin{array}{c}\text{Standard deviation of}\\ \text{returns on second asset}\end{array}\right)} \quad (10\text{-}11)$$

---

[2] If we can calculate the standard deviation directly from the portfolio's returns, why calculate it using the individual assets' standard deviations and the covariance? We did it to illustrate the role of the assets' covariance in the portfolio's risk.

By construction, the correlation coefficient is bounded between –1 and +1.[3] We can interpret the correlation coefficient as follows:

■ **A correlation coefficient of +1** indicates a perfect, positive correlation between the two assets' returns.
■ **A correlation coefficient of –1** indicates a perfect, negative correlation between the two assets' returns.
■ **A correlation coefficient of 0** indicates no correlation between the two assets' returns.
■ **A correlation coefficients falling between 0 and +1** indicates positive, but not perfect positive correlation between the two assets' returns.
■ **A correlation coefficient falling between –1 and 0** indicates negative, but not perfect negative correlation between the two assets' returns.

In the case of Investments C and D, the covariance of their returns is:

$$
\begin{aligned}
&\text{Correlation of returns on Investments C and D} \\
&= \frac{\text{Covariance of returns Investments C and D}}{\left(\begin{array}{c}\text{Standard deviation of}\\ \text{returns on Investment C}\end{array}\right)\left(\begin{array}{c}\text{Standard deviation of}\\ \text{returns on Investment D}\end{array}\right)} \\
&= \frac{-0.0252}{(0.1400)(0.1997)} = -0.9014
\end{aligned}
$$

Therefore, the returns on Investment C and Investment D are negatively correlated with one another.

By investing in assets with less than perfectly correlated cash flows, you can get rid of—diversify away—some risk. The less correlated the cash flows, the more risk you can diversify away—to a point.

Let's think about what this means for a company. Consider Proctor & Gamble whose products include Tide detergent, Prell shampoo, Pampers diapers, Jif peanut butter, and Old Spice cologne. Are the cash flows from these products positively correlated? To a degree, yes. The cash flows from these products depend on consumer spending for consumption goods. But are they *perfectly* correlated? No. For example, diaper sales depend on the diaper wearing population, whereas cologne products depend on the male cologne-wearing population. The cash flows of these different products also depend on the actions of competitors—the degree of competition may be different for the diaper market than for the peanut butter market. Further,

---

[3] Dividing the covariance by the product of the standard deviations insures (mathematically) that this statistic is bounded by –1 and +1, allowing a cleaner interpretation of the relation between assets' returns.

the cash flows of the products are affected by different input pricing—the costs of the raw inputs to make these products. If there is a bad year for the peanut crop, the price of peanuts may increase substantially, reducing cash flows from Jif—but this increase in peanut prices is not likely to affect the costs of, say, producing laundry detergent.

Portfolio Size and Risk

What we have seen for a portfolio with two assets can be extended to include any number of assets. The calculations become very complicated, because we have to consider the covariance between *every possible pair of assets*! But the basic idea is the same. The risk of a portfolio declines as it includes more assets whose returns are not perfectly correlated with the returns of the assets already in the portfolio.

The idea of diversification is based on beliefs about what will happen in the future: expected returns, standard deviation of all possible returns, and expected covariance between returns. How valid are our beliefs about anything in the future? We can get an idea by looking at the past. So we look at historical returns on assets—returns over time—to get an idea of how some asset's returns increase while at the same time others do not or decline.

Let's look at the effects of diversification with common stocks. As we add common stocks to a portfolio, the standard deviation of returns on the portfolio declines—to a point. We can see this in Exhibit 10.6, where the portfolio standard deviation is plotted against the number of different stocks in the portfolio. After around twenty different stocks, the portfolio's standard deviation is about as low as it is going to get.

Why does the risk seem to reach some point and not decline any farther? Because common stocks' returns, in general, are positively correlated with one another. There just aren't enough negatively correlated stocks' returns to reduce portfolio risk beyond a certain point.

We refer to the risk that goes away as we add assets as *diversifiable risk*. We refer to the risk that *cannot* be reduced by adding more assets as *nondiversifiable risk*. Diversifiable and nondiversifiable components of a portfolio's risk are shown in Exhibit 10.6.

The idea that we can reduce the risk of a portfolio by introducing assets whose returns are not highly correlated with one another is the basis of *modern portfolio theory (MPT)*. MPT tells us that by combining assets whose returns are not correlated with one another, we can determine combinations of assets that provide the least risk for each possible expected portfolio return.

Though the mathematics involved in determining the optimal combinations of assets are beyond this text, the basic idea is provided in

Exhibit 10.7. In panel (a), the expected return and standard deviation for all possible portfolios is shown. Each point in the graph represents a *possible* portfolio that can be put together comprising different assets and different weights. The points in this graph represent every possible portfolio. As you can see in this diagram:

- Some portfolios have a higher expected return than other portfolios with the same level of risk.
- Some portfolios have a lower standard deviation than other portfolios with the same expected return.

Because investors like high returns and low risk, some portfolios are preferable to others. Portfolio that deliver the highest return for the level of risk make up what is called the *efficient frontier.* If investors are rational, they will go for the portfolios that fall on this efficient frontier. All the possible portfolios, as well as the efficient frontier, are diagrammed in Exhibit 10.7, panel (b).

So what is the relevance of MPT to financial managers? MPT tells us that:

- We can manage risk by judicious combinations of assets in our portfolios.
- There are some combinations of assets that are preferred over others.

In the next section, we will see what MPT can teach us about valuation.

EXHIBIT 10.6   The Average Standard Deviation of a Portfolio for Different Portfolio Sizes

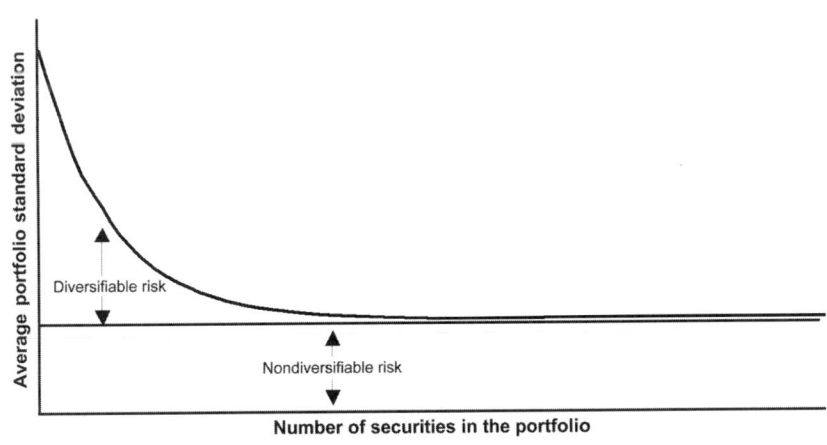

EXHIBIT 10.7   Possible Portfolios and the Efficient Frontier
Panel A: The Expected Return and Risk for Different Portfolios

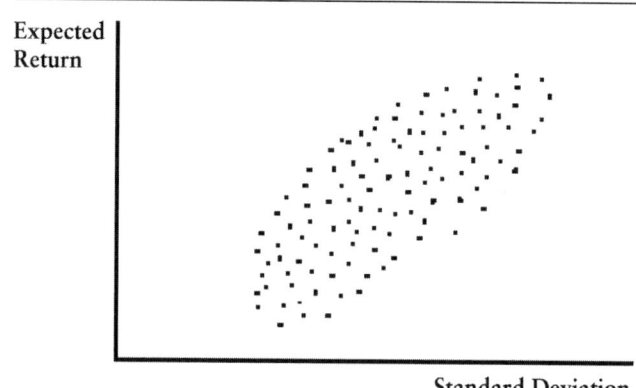

Panel B: The Efficient Frontier

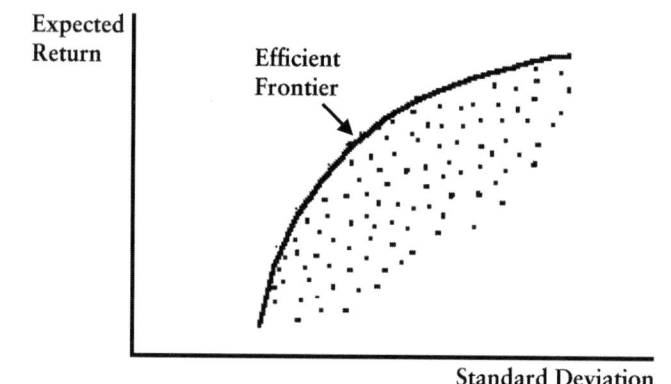

MODERN PORTFOLIO THEORY AND ASSET PRICING

The relation between portfolio returns and portfolio risk was recognized by two Nobel Laureates in Economics, Harry Markowitz and William Sharpe. Harry Markowitz tuned us into the idea that investors hold portfolios of assets and therefore their concern is focused upon the portfolio return and the portfolio risk, not on the return and risk of individual assets.[4]

---

[4] Harry M. Markowitz, "Portfolio Selection," *Journal of Finance* (March 1952) pp. 77–91.

The *relevant risk* to an investor is the portfolio's risk, not the risk of an individual asset. If an investor considers buying an additional asset or selling an asset from the portfolio, what must be considered is how this change will affect the *risk* of the portfolio. This concept applies whether we are talking about an investor who holds 30 different stocks or a business that has invested in 30 different projects. The important thing in valuing an asset is its contribution to the portfolio's return and risk.

The Capital Asset Pricing Model

William Sharpe took the idea that portfolio return and risk are the only elements to consider and developed a model that deals with how assets are priced.[5] This model is referred to as the *capital asset pricing model (CAPM)*.

We just saw in Exhibit 10.7 that there is a set of portfolios that make up the efficient frontier—the best combinations of expected return and standard deviation. All the assets in each portfolio, even on the frontier, have some risk. Now let's see what happens when we add an asset with no risk—referred to as the risk-free asset. Suppose we have a portfolio along the efficient frontier that has a return of 4% and a standard deviation of 3%. Suppose we introduce into this portfolio the risk-free asset, which has an expected return of 2% and, by definition, a standard deviation of zero. If the risk-free asset's expected return is certain, there is *no* covariance between the risky portfolio's returns and the returns of the risk-free asset.

A portfolio comprised of 50% of the risky portfolio and 50% of the risk-free asset has an expected return of $(0.50)4\% + (0.50)2\% = 3\%$ and a portfolio standard deviation calculated as follows:

$$\text{Portfolio standard deviation}$$
$$= \sqrt{0.50^2(0.03) + 0.50^2(0.00) + 2(0.00)0.50(0.50)}$$
$$= \sqrt{0.0075} = 0.0866$$

If we look at all possible combinations of portfolios along the efficient frontier and the risk-free asset, we see that the best portfolios are no longer those along the entire length of the efficient frontier; rather, the best portfolios are now the combinations of the risk-free asset and one—and only one—portfolio of risky assets on the frontier. The portfolios comprised of the risk-free asset and this one risky portfolio are shown in Exhibit 10.8. These portfolios differ from one another by the proportion invested in the risk-free asset; as less is invested in the risk-free asset, both the portfolio's expected return and standard deviation increase.

---

[5] William F. Sharpe, "A Simplified Model of Portfolio Analysis," *Management Science* (January 1963), pp. 277–293.

EXHIBIT 10.8   The Expected Return and Risk for All Possible Portfolios of Assets, Including a Risk-Free Asset

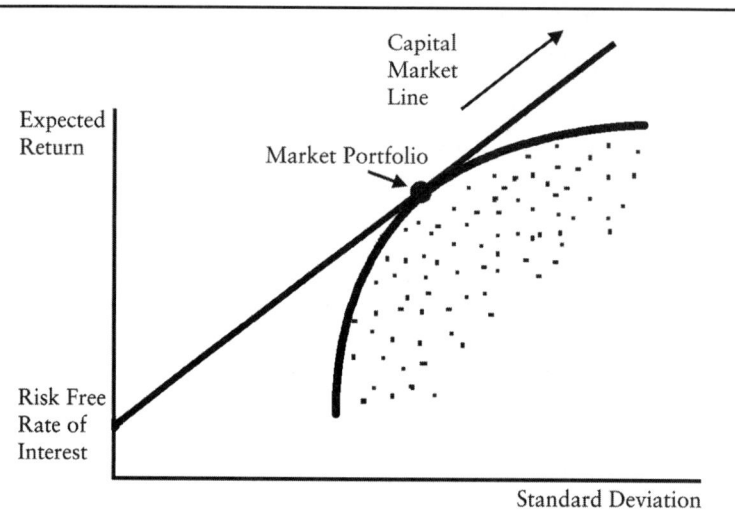

Sharpe demonstrates that this one and only one portfolio of risky assets is the *market portfolio*—a portfolio that consists of all assets, with the weights of these assets being the ratio of their market value to the total market value of all assets.

If investors are all risk averse—they only take on risk if there is adequate compensation—and if they are free to invest in the risky assets as well as the risk-free asset, the best deals lie along the line that is tangent to the efficient frontier. This line is referred to as the *capital market line* (*CML*). If the portfolios along the capital market line are the best deals and are available to all investors, it follows that the returns of these risky assets will be priced to compensate investors for the risk they bear *relative to that of the market portfolio.* Since the portfolios along the capital market line are the best deals, they are as diversified as they can get—no other combination of risky assets or risk-free asset provides a better expected return for the level of risk or provides a lower risk for the level of expected return.

The CML specifies the returns an investor can expect for a given level of risk. The CAPM uses this relationship between expected return and risk to describe how assets are priced.

The CAPM specifies that the return on any asset is a function of the return on a risk-free asset plus a risk premium. The return on the risk-free asset is compensation for the time value of money. The *risk premium* is the compensation for bearing risk. Putting these components of return together, the CAPM says:

> Expected return on an asset
> = Expected return on a risk-free asset + Risk premium

The market portfolio therefore represents the most well-diversified portfolio—the portfolio that consists of all the assets in a market. The only risk in a portfolio comprising all assets is nondiversifiable risk. As far as diversification goes, the market portfolio is the best you can do, because you have included everything in it.

Thus, if we assume that investors hold well-diversified portfolios (approximating the market portfolio), the only risk they have is non-diversifiable risk. If assets are priced to compensate for the risk of assets *and* if the only risk in your portfolio is nondiversifiable risk, then it follows that compensation for risk applies to only nondiversifiable risk. Let's refer to this nondiversifiable risk as *market risk*.

Because the market portfolio is made up of all assets, each asset possesses some degree of market risk. Since market risk is systematic across assets, it is often referred to as *systematic risk*, and diversifiable risk is referred to as *unsystematic risk*. Further, the risk that is not associated with the market as a whole is often referred to as *company-specific risk* when referring to stocks, since it is risk that is specific to the company's own situation—such as the risk of lawsuits and labor strikes—and is not part of the risk that pervades all securities.

The measure of an asset's return sensitivity to the market's return, its market risk, is referred to as that asset's *beta, ß*.

The expected return on an individual asset is the sum of the expected return on the risk-free asset and the premium for bearing market risk. Let r_i represent the expected return on asset i, r_f represent the expected return on the risk-free asset, r_m represent the expected return on the market, and β_i represent the degree of market risk for asset i. Then:

$$r_i = r_f + (r_m - r_f)\beta_i \qquad (10\text{-}12)$$

The term $(r_m - r_f)$, is the *market risk premium*—if you owned all the assets in the market portfolio, you would expect to be compensated $(r_m - r_f)$ for bearing the risk of these assets. β is measure of market risk, which serves to fine-tune the risk premium for the individual asset. For example, if the market risk premium were 2% and the β for an individual asset were 1.5, you would expect to receive a risk premium of 3% since you are taking on 50% more risk than the market.

For each asset there is a beta. If we represent the expected return on each asset and its beta as a point on a graph and connect all the points, the result is the *security market line (SML)*, as shown in Exhibit 10.9.[6] As you can see in the figure:

1. The greater the β, the greater the expected return.
2. If there were no market risk (beta = 0.0) on an asset, its expected return would be the expected return on the risk-free asset.
3. If the asset's risk is similar to the risk of the market as a whole (beta = 1.0), that asset's expected return is the return on the market portfolio.

For an individual asset, beta is a measure of sensitivity of its returns to changes in return on the market portfolio. If beta is *one*, we expect that for a given change of 1% in the market portfolio return, the asset's return is expected to change by 1%. If beta is *less than one*, then for a 1% change in the expected market return, the asset's return is expected to change by less than 1%. If the beta is *greater than one*, then for a 1% change in the expected market return, the asset's return is expected to change by more than 1%.

We typically estimate the beta for a common stock by looking at the historical relation between its return and the return on the market as a whole. The betas of some U.S. companies' common stocks are listed in Exhibit 10.10.

EXHIBIT 10.9   Security Market Line that Describes the Relation Between Expected Asset Returns and Beta

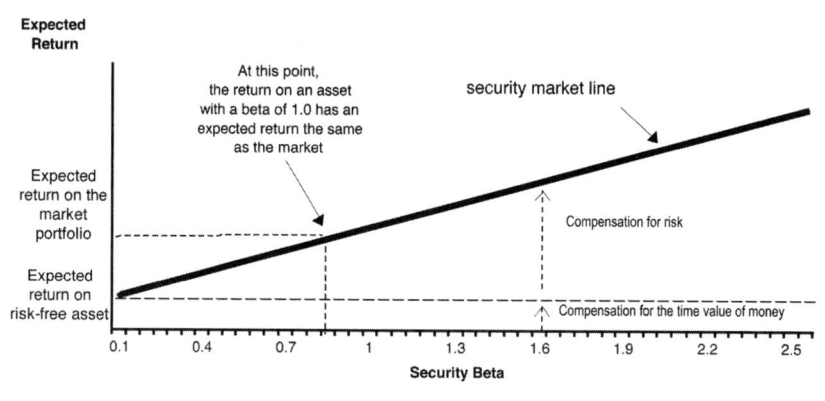

---

[6] You'll notice that in the discussion of the asset pricing models we refer to the risk and expected return for *assets*, which can be any asset, not exclusively stocks. The Security Market Line describes a relation between expected return and market risk that is applicable to any asset, even though the name implies securities.

EXHIBIT 10.10   Security Betas of U.S. Companies' Common Stock

Company	Industry	Security Beta
Amazon.com	Retailer (Internet)	1.85
Bank of America	Financial services	1.30
Baxter International, Inc.	Pharmaceuticals	0.80
Carnival Corporation	Recreation	1.50
Coca-Cola	Beverages	0.80
Cooper Tire and Rubber	Tire and rubber	0.95
Dole Foods	Food processing	0.75
FedEx Corporation	Air transport	0.80
Hershey Foods	Food processing	0.60
Home Depot	Retail (building supply)	1.40
Limited brands	Retail (clothing)	1.20
Mattel Inc.	Recreation	0.75
N.Y. Times	Newspaper	1.00
Papa John's International	Restaurant	0.75
Toys R Us	Retail (special lines)	1.15
Unisys	Computer and office equipment	1.25

Source: Value Line Investment Survey, September 20, 2002

The betas of some firms' stocks are close to 1.0, indicating that the returns on these stocks tend to move along with the market. There are several with betas less than 1.0, indicating that the return on this security does not move along with the market: If the market were to go up 10%, we would expect the return to go down only about 8% for FedEx, for example. Then there are some stocks whose beta is much higher than 1.0. For example, Amazon.com has a beta of 1.85. This means that if the market is expected to go up 1%, we expect Amazon's return to go up 1.85%; if the market is expected to go down 1%, we expect Amazon's return to go down 1.85%.

If we know part of the risk of a particular asset is common to all assets, and we have a large enough representation of all in the assets in our portfolio, then we don't need to be concerned with the diversifiable risk. We are concerned about the market risk of each asset in the portfolio and how it contributes to the market risk of the entire portfolio.

We can get a good idea of the portfolio's market risk by using a beta that represents the composition of the assets in the portfolio. To determine the portfolio's beta, we need to know the weighted average of the betas of the assets that make up the portfolio, where each weight is the proportion invested in each asset. Let β_p indicate the beta of the portfolio, w_i indicate the proportion invested in each the asset i, and β_i indicate the beta for asset i. If there are S assets in the portfolio, then:

$$\beta_p = w_1\beta_1 + w_2\beta_2 + w_3\beta_3 + \ldots + w_S\beta_S \qquad (10\text{-}13)$$

or more compactly,

$$\beta_p = \sum_{i=1}^{S} w_i\beta_i \qquad (10\text{-}14)$$

Suppose we have three securities in our portfolio, with the amount invested in each and their security beta as follows:

Security	Security Beta	Amount Invested
AAA	1.00	$10,000
BBB	1.50	$20,000
CCC	0.75	$20,000

The portfolio's beta is:

$$\beta_p = \frac{\$10,000}{\$50,000}1.00 + \frac{\$20,000}{\$50,000}1.50 + \frac{\$20,000}{\$50,000}0.75 = 1.10$$

If the expected risk-free rate of interest is 4% and the expected return on the market is 7%, the $\beta_p = 1.1$ means:

> Expected return on portfolio of AAA, BBB, and CCC
> $= 4\% + 1.10(7\% - 4\%) = 7.3\%$

Limitations of the CAPM

As we have seen, the CAPM allows us to focus on the risk that is important in asset pricing—market risk. However, there are some drawbacks to applying the CAPM.

1. A beta is an estimate. For stocks, the beta is typically estimated using historical returns. But the estimate for beta depends on the method and period in which is it is measured. For assets other than stocks, beta estimation is more difficult.
2. The CAPM includes some unrealistic assumptions. For example, it assumes that all investors can borrow and lend at the same rate.

3. The CAPM is really not testable. The market portfolio is theoretical and not really observable, so we cannot test the relation between the expected return on an asset and the expected return of the market to see if the relation specified in the CAPM holds.
4. In studies of the CAPM applied to common stocks, the CAPM does not explain the differences in returns for securities that differ over time, differ on the basis of dividend yield, and differ on the basis of the market value of equity (the so called "size effect").

Though it lacks realism and is difficult to apply, the CAPM makes some sense regarding the role of diversification and the type of risk we need to consider in investment decisions.

The Arbitrage Pricing Model

An alternative to CAPM in relating risk and return is the arbitrage pricing model, which was developed by Stephen Ross. The *arbitrage pricing model (APM)* is an asset pricing model that is based on the idea that identical assets in different markets should be priced identically.[7]

While the CAPM is based on a market portfolio of assets, the APM doesn't mention a market portfolio at all. Instead, the APM states that an asset's returns should compensate the investor for the risk of the asset where the risk is due to a number of economic influences or company factors. Therefore, the expected return on the asset i, r_i, is:

$$r_i = r_f + \delta_1 \text{First factor} + \delta_2 \text{Second factor} + \delta_3 \text{Third factor} + \dots \quad (10\text{-}15)$$

where each of the δ's reflect the asset's return sensitivity to the corresponding economic factor. The APM looks much like the CAPM, but the CAPM has one factor—the market portfolio. There are many factors in the APM.

What if an asset's price is out of line with what is expected? That's where arbitrage comes in. Any time an asset's price is out of line with how market participants feel it should be priced—based on the basic economic influences—investors will enter the market and buy or sell the asset until its price is in line with what they think it should be.

The APM provides theoretical support for an asset pricing model where there is more than one risk factor. Consequently, models of this type are referred to as *multifactor risk models*. There are three types of

---

[7] Stephen A. Ross, "The Arbitrage Theory of Capital Asset Pricing," *Journal of Economic Theory*, December 1976.

multifactor risk models: statistical factor models, macroeconomic factor models, and fundamental factor models.[8]

In a *statistical factor model* a statistical technique called factor analysis is used to derive risk factors that best explain observed asset returns. Let's suppose that there are six "factors" identified by the model that are statistically found to best explain common stock returns. These "factors" are statistical artifacts. The objective in a statistical factor model then becomes to determine the economic meaning of each of these statistically derived factors. Because of the problem of interpretation, it is difficult to use the factors from a statistical factor model. Instead, practitioners prefer the two other models described below, which allow them to prespecify meaningful factors, and thus produce a more intuitive model.

In a *macroeconomic factor model*, observable macroeconomic variables are used to try to explain observed asset returns. An example of a proprietary macroeconomic factor model is the Burmeister, Ibbotson, Roll, and Ross model.[9] In this model, there are five macroeconomic factors that have been found that do a good job of explaining common stock returns. They are unanticipated changes in the following macroeconomic variables: investor confidence (confidence risk); interest rates (time horizon risk); inflation (inflation risk); real business activity (business cycle risk); and market index (market timing risk).

The most common model used by practitioners is the *fundamental factor model*. It uses company and industry attributes and market data to determine the factors that best explain observed asset returns.[10] The most often used fundamental factor model for explaining common stock returns is the one developed by the firm of Barra. In the Barra model the risk factors, referred to as risk indexes, are indexes of stock price volatility, stock price momentum, market capitalization (size) of the firm, earnings growth, earnings yield, book-to-value ratio, earnings variability, exposure to foreign currencies, dividend yield, and leverage. In addition, the Barra model indicates that the industry that a firm is in is another factor that explains the return on common stock. In the Barra model there are 55 industry groups.

---

[8] Gregory Connor, "The Three Types of Factor Models: A Comparison of Their Explanatory Power," *Financial Analysts Journal* (May–June 1995), pp. 42–57.

[9] Edwin Burmeister, Roger Ibbotson, Richard Roll, and Stephen A. Ross, "Using Macroeconomic Factors to Control Portfolio Risk," unpublished paper. The information used in this chapter regarding the BIRR model is obtained from various pages of the BIRR website (*www.birr.com*).

[10] For a further discussion of fundamental factor models, see Frank J. Fabozzi, Frank J. Jones, and Raman Vardharaj, "Multi-Factor Equity Risk Models," Chapter 13 in Frank J. Fabozzi and Harry M. Markowitz, *The Theory and Practice of Investment Management* (New York: John Wiley & Sons, 2002).

Financial Decision Making and Asset Pricing

Portfolio theory and asset pricing models lay the groundwork for financial decisions. While portfolio theory and asset pricing theory are complex and rely on many assumptions, they do get us thinking about what is important:

- Return and risk must both be considered.
- Because investors must be compensated for risk, a greater return is expected for bearing greater risk.
- Investors hold portfolios of assets, therefore the relevant risk in the valuation of assets is the portfolio's risk.

If a corporation is considering investing in a new product, there are two levels of thinking to work through in evaluating its risk and returns:

- If a firm takes on the product, it is adding it to its portfolio of assets and needs to consider the effect of this product on the firm's overall risk.
- Because a firm is owned by the investors, who themselves may own portfolios of assets, the relevant risk to consider is how the change in the firm's risk affects the owners' portfolio risk.

Therefore, when we evaluate the new product's future cash flows, the discount rate that we apply to value these future cash flows must reflect how that product affects the owners' portfolio risk.

SUMMARY

- Financial decision makers must consider both expected return and risk from investments.
- To evaluate an investment, the financial manager needs to consider the different types of risk, including cash flow risk, reinvestment rate risk, interest rate risk, purchasing power risk, and currency risk.
- Cash flow risk comprises sales risk, operating risk, and financial risk. Sales risk is the degree of uncertainty regarding the number of units of a good or service the firm will be able to sell and the price of these units. Operating risk is the uncertainty arising from the mix of variable and fixed operating costs. Financial risk is the uncertainty arising from the firm's financing decisions.
- Interest rate risk is the uncertainty associated with the change in the value of an asset that is caused by changes in the discount rate used to

translate future values into present ones. With a bond, for example, interest rate risk is the sensitivity of the bond's price to change in the yield on the bond.

■ Purchasing power risk is the uncertainty associated with the change in the value of the currency. The greater the unanticipated inflation, the greater the purchasing power risk.

■ Currency risk is the uncertainty arising from the change in exchange rates between different currencies. If future cash flows are denominated in a currency other than the domestic currency, the value of those cash flows is dependent, in part, on the exchange rate between the domestic and the foreign currency.

■ When a firm invests in assets whose cash flows are not perfectly correlated with the firm's other assets, the firm's risk may be reduced. This is diversification.

■ The risk that cannot be diversified away, the asset's market risk, is what investors demand compensation for in the form of higher expected returns.

■ The Capital Asset Pricing Model and the Arbitrage Pricing Model are descriptions of the relation between risk and expected return. The CAPM specifies the expected return on an asset in terms of the expected return on a risk-free asset plus a premium for market risk.

■ The Arbitrage Pricing Model specifies the expected return on an asset in terms of the expected return on the risk-free asset plus premiums for several risk factors. These models are called multifactor risk models.

QUESTIONS

1. The Global Company is considering investing in a project in another country. This project will generate cash flows—in the other country's currency—each year for ten years, at which time the project will be terminated. What types of risk does Global need to consider in its investment decision?

2. Consider the two firms Tweedle Dee and Tweedle Dum. Both firms operate in the same industry, but Tweedle Dum has a greater portion of fixed operating costs relative to variable costs than does Tweedle Dee. Which firm has greater operating risk? Which firm has a higher degree of operating leverage?

3. Abel, an astute investor, buys bonds and always holds them to maturity. He claims that because he holds these bonds to maturity, there is no risk. Is he correct? Explain.

4. If you invest in corporate bonds, what types of risk do you assume?

5. Consider the following investments and their expected returns and standard deviations of expected returns:

Investment	Expected Return	Standard Deviation
1	10%	10%
2	11%	10%
3	9%	9%
4	11%	9%

If you a risk averse investor, which investment would he or she prefer from each of the following pairs?
a. 1 and 2
b. 2 and 4
c. 3 and 4
d. 1 and 4

6. The covariance of returns on Asset A and Asset B are negative. What does this tell us about the correlation coefficient for their returns? If we form a portfolio comprised of Asset A and Asset B, what is the relation between the portfolio's risk and that of Asset A and Asset B considered separately?

7. Consider the following common stocks and their return characteristics:

Stock	Expected Return	Standard Deviation	Security Beta
1	10%	5%	1.00
2	8%	5%	1.20
3	10%	6%	0.80

Which stock would a risk averse investor prefer between:
a. 1 and 2?
b. 1 and 3?
c. 2 and 3?

8. a. What are the major features of the capital asset pricing model and the arbitrage pricing model that distinguish them from one another?
b. What are the three types of arbitrage pricing models?

9. The Gearing Company has provided you with the following information regarding their operating and financing costs:

Price per unit = $50
Variable cost per unit = $30
Fixed operating cost = $100,000
Fixed financing cost = $50,000

    a. Calculate its degree of operating leverage at 10,000 units sold.

    b. Calculate its degree of financial leverage at 10,000 units sold.

    c. Calculate its degree of total leverage at 10,000 units sold.

    d. If there is a 1% increase in units sold, what do you expect to be the change in operating cash flows?

    e. If there is a 3% decrease in units sold, what do you expect to be the change in cash flows to owners?

10. Suppose that the contribution margin is $55 per unit. If fixed costs (operating and financing combined) are $10 million, what is the break-even number of units produced and sold?

11. The Jonhaux Company produces a product that has a contribution per unit of $40. Fixed operating costs are $140,000. The Jonhaux Company currently has $10 million of bonds outstanding with a coupon rate of 5%.

    a. What is the current break-even number of units for Jonhaux considering all fixed costs?

    b. The board of Jonhaux is considering a proposal to issue $1 million additional bonds, with a a coupon rate of 6%. How would this proposed financing affect the break-even point?

    c. If 20,000 units are produced and sold, what is the degree of operating leverage, the degree of financial leverage, and the degree of total leverage under the current and proposed financial structures?

12. Consider two bonds, MM and NN:

    ■ Bond MM has face value of $1,000, matures in five years, and pays 6% interest semiannually.

    ■ Bond NN has a face value of $1,000, matures in five years, and pays 2% interest semiannually.

    a. If the yield-to-maturity on these bonds changes from 4% to 6%, which bond's value changes the most?

    b. Which bond has the greatest interest rate risk? Why?

    c. Which bond has the greatest reinvestment rate risk? Why?

13. Suppose you want to earn a rate of 8% after inflation. If you expect inflation to be 4% during the next year, what nominal rate of return would you require on your investment?

14. Your firm is considering investing in a new product. Marketing research has determined that the sales of the new product depend, in large part, on the whether or not competitors jump in to mimic the product. Their assessment of sales, and the likelihood of mimicking is as follows:

Competitor's Reaction	Probability	Sales
Mimic	80%	$1,000,000
Do not mimic	20%	$10,000,000

a. What are the expected sales from this new product?

b. What is the standard deviation of possible sales of this new product?

15. Suppose you are offered two investments with the following expected cash flows:

Economic Scenario	Probability of Economic Scenario	Possible Outcome for Investment 1	Possible Outcome for Investment 2
Boom	20%	$1,000	$1,200
Normal	50%	750	750
Bust	30%	250	117

a. Calculate the expected value of each investment.

b. Calculate the standard deviation for each investment's possible outcomes.

c. Which investment is riskier? Explain.

16. Consider two bonds, HI and LI. The HI bond has a 10% coupon rate and the LI bond has a 5% coupon rate. Both bonds pay interest annually and are priced to yield 10%. Suppose the following interest scenarios are possible at the point in time when both bonds have five years remaining to maturity:

Possible Interest Rate	Probability of Interest Rate
5%	10%
10	50
15	40

a. Calculate the expected value for each bond.

b. Calculate the standard deviation of possible values for each bond.

c. Which bond is riskier? Why?

17. Consider a portfolio comprised of Security A and Security B, with an equal investment in each. Security A's returns have an expected return of 3% and a standard deviation of 4%. Security B's returns have an expected return of 5% and standard deviation of 6%. Complete the following table:

Correlation Coefficient of Returns on Securities A and B	Portfolio Return	Covariance between Returns on Securities A and B	Portfolio Variance	Portfolio Standard Deviation
1.00	_____	_____	_____	_____
0.50	_____	_____	_____	_____
0.00	_____	_____	_____	_____
−0.50	_____	_____	_____	_____
−1.00	_____	_____	_____	_____

18. Consider a portfolio comprised of Asset P and Asset Q. The expected return on Asset P is 10% and the standard deviation is 6%. The expected return on Asset Q is 12% and the standard deviation is 8%. The correlation between the returns on these two assets is 0.500. Complete the following table.

Proportion of Portfolio Invested in Asset P	Proportion of Portfolio Invested in Asset Q	Portfolio Return	Covariance Between Returns on Assets P and Q	Portfolio Variance	Portfolio Standard Deviation
100%	0%	_____	_____	_____	_____
0%	100%	_____	_____	_____	_____
50%	50%	_____	_____	_____	_____
25%	75%	_____	_____	_____	_____
75%	25%	_____	_____	_____	_____

19. If the expected return on a risk-free asset is 5% and the market premium is 4%, what is the expected security return if the security's beta is: a. 0.00? b. 0.50? c. 1.00? d. 1.25? e. 2.00?

20. Suppose the expected risk-free rate is 5% and the expected return on the market is 12%. Further suppose that you have a portfolio comprised of the four securities, with equal investments in each:

Security	Security Beta
AA	1.00
BB	1.25
CC	1.50
DD	1.00

a. What is the expected return for each security in your portfolio?
b. What is the portfolio's beta?
c. What is the expected return on your portfolio?

CHAPTER 11

The Cost of Capital

In Chapters 8 through 10, we discussed and practiced techniques for valuing assets and weighing risk and return. These are all topics we will apply in Part Three of this book, when we turn to the methods and techniques used in making decisions about actual projects: capital budgeting. In this chapter, we focus on a crucial element in both valuation and capital budgeting: the cost of capital.

The *cost of capital* is the return that must be provided for the use of an investor's funds. If the funds are borrowed, the cost is related to the interest that must be paid on the loan. If the funds are equity, the cost is the return that investors expect, both from the stock's price appreciation and dividends. From the investor's point of view, the cost of capital is the same as the required rate of return, which we discussed in Chapter 10.

The required rate of return on an investment and its value are intertwined. If you buy a bond, you expect to receive interest and the repayment of the principal in the future. The price you pay reflects your required rate of return. What determines your required rate? Your opportunity cost—the return you could have received on an investment with similar risk. Suppose that after you buy this bond, market interest rates increase. Your own required rate of return also rises. When your required rate of return increases, the value of your bond's future interest and principal fall since the discount rate—the rate you use to translate future cash flows into today's value—increases. The discount rate increases because its is a reflection of market interest rates.

The cost of capital and the required rate of return are *marginal* concepts. That is, the cost of capital is the cost associated with raising one more dollar of capital, whereas the required rate of return is the return expected on one more dollar invested. For example, suppose I have already borrowed $10,000, promising to pay 5% interest per year. And suppose that if I need to borrow any more, I would have to pay 6% per year of the amount I borrow above $10,000. Six percent is the *marginal* cost. The cost of what we have already borrowed is history, sort of. How much we have already borrowed and what we committed ourselves to pay will influence what we will have to pay to borrow further. That's because the more you are already paying for your borrowings, the greater the rate lenders will require to lend you more. That's why when we analyze the cost of a new investment, we should be thinking about the *marginal* costs of capital.

To make investment decisions of any kind, we need to know the cost of capital. In economics, you learned that a firm should produce goods to the point where the firm's marginal benefit from producing them equals the marginal cost to produce them. At that level of production, profit is maximized.

It's the same in investment and financing decisions: Invest in a project until the marginal cost of funds to invest is equal to the marginal benefit the project provides. The benefit from an investment is its return, which we refer to as its ***internal rate of return*** (from the investor's perspective) or the ***marginal efficiency of capital*** (from the firm's perspective). This means that managers keep on raising funds to invest in projects until the marginal cost of these funds is equal to the marginal benefit (which decreases as we take on more and more projects). Therefore, you need to know the marginal cost of funds before you can determine how much to invest in projects in your attempt to maximize shareholder wealth.

When we refer to the cost of capital for a firm, we are usually referring to the cost of financing its assets. In other words, we mean the cost of capital for all the firm's projects taken together and, hence, the cost of capital for the average project risk of the firm.

When we refer to the cost of capital of a project, we are referring to the cost of capital that reflects the risk of that project. So why determine the cost of capital for the firm as a whole? For two reasons.

First, the cost of capital for the firm is often used as a starting point (a benchmark) for determining the cost of capital for a specific project. The firm's cost of capital is adjusted upward or downward depending on whether the project's risk is more than or less than the firm's typical project.

Second, many of a firm's projects have risk similar to the risk of the firm as a whole. So the cost of capital of the firm is a reasonable approximation for the cost of capital of one of its projects that are under consideration for investment.

A firm's cost of capital is the cost of its long-term sources of funds: debt, preferred stock, and common stock. And the cost of each source reflects the risk of the assets the firm invests in. A firm that invests in assets having little risk will be able to bear lower costs of capital than a firm that invests in assets having a high risk. For example, a discount retail store has much less risk than an oil drilling firm. Moreover, the cost of each source of funds reflects the hierarchy of the risk associated with its seniority over the other sources. For a given firm, the cost of funds raised through debt is less than the cost of funds from preferred stock which, in turn, is less than the cost of funds from common stock. Why? Because creditors have seniority over preferred shareholders, who have seniority over common shareholders. If there are difficulties in meeting obligations, the creditors receive their promised interest and principal before the preferred shareholders who, in turn, receive their promised dividends before the common shareholders.

For a given firm, debt is less risky than preferred stock, which is less risky than common stock. Therefore, preferred shareholders require a greater return than the creditors and common shareholders require a greater return than preferred shareholders.

Figuring out the cost of capital requires us to first determine the cost of each source of capital we expect the firm to use, along with the relative amounts of each source of capital we expect the firm to raise. Then we can determine the marginal cost of raising additional capital.

We can do this in three steps:

Step 1: Determine the proportions of each source to be raised as capital.
Step 2: Determine the marginal cost of each source.
Step 3: Calculate the weighted average cost of capital.

In this chapter, we look at each step. We first discuss how to determine the proportion of each source of capital to be used in our calculations. Then we calculate the cost of each source. The proportions of each source must be determined before calculating the cost of each source since the proportions may affect the costs of the sources of capital.

We then put together the cost and proportions of each source to calculate the firm's marginal cost of capital. We also demonstrate the calculations of the marginal cost of capital for an actual company, showing just how much judgment and how many assumptions go into calculating the cost of capital. That is, we show that it's an estimate. We will use this information in Part Three when we evaluate capital projects.

DETERMINING THE PROPORTION OF EACH CAPITAL COMPONENT

The cost of capital for a firm is the cost of raising an additional dollar of capital. Suppose that a firm raises capital in the following proportions: debt 40%, preferred stock 10%, and common stock 50%. This means an additional dollar of capital will comprise 40 of debt, 10 of preferred stock, and 50 of common stock. We need to take into account the different costs of these different sources of capital.

Our goal as financial managers is to estimate *the optimum proportions* for our firm to issue new capital—not just in the next period, but well beyond. If we assume that the firm maintains the same *capital structure*—the mix of debt, preferred stock, and common stock—throughout time, our task is simple. We just figure out the proportions of capital the firm has at present. If we look at the firm's balance sheet, we can calculate the book value of its debt, its preferred stock, and its common stock. With these three book values, we can calculate the proportion of debt, preferred stock, and common stock that the firm has presently. We could even look at these proportions over time to get a better idea of the typical mix of debt, preferred stock, and common stock.

But will book values tell us what we want to know? Probably not. What we are trying to determine is the mix of capital that the firm considers appropriate. Financial managers recognize that the book values of capital are historical measures and look instead at the *market* values of capital. Therefore, we must obtain the market value of debt, preferred stock, and common stock.

If the securities represented in a firm's capital are publicly traded— that is, listed on exchanges or traded in the over-the-counter market— we can obtain market values. If some capital is privately placed, such as an entire debt issue that was bought by an insurance company or not actively traded, our job is tougher but not impossible. For example, if we know the interest, maturity value, and maturity of a bond that is not traded and the yield on similar risk bonds, we can get a rough estimate of the market value of that bond even though it is not traded.

Once we determine the market value of debt, preferred stock, and common stock, we calculate the sum of the market values of each, and then figure out what proportion of this sum each source of capital represents.

But the mix of debt, preferred stock, and common stock that a firm has now may not be the mix it intends to use in the future. So while we may use the present mix as an approximation of the future, we really are interested in the firm's analysis and resulting decision regarding its *future* mix. In Part Four, when we turn to the subject of capital structure, we will see how the capital structure decision may affect a firm's cost of capital.

DETERMINING THE COSTS OF EACH CAPITAL COMPONENT

The *cost of debt* is the cost associated with raising one more dollar by issuing debt. Suppose you borrow one dollar and promise to repay it in one year, plus pay 10 cents to compensate the lender for the use of her money.

The Cost of Debt

Because Congress allows you to deduct from your taxable income the interest you paid, how much does this dollar of debt *really* cost you? It depends on your ***marginal tax rate***—the tax rate on your next dollar of taxable income. Why the marginal tax rate? Because we are interested in seeing how the interest deduction changes your tax bill in order to see how we will compare your taxes with and without the interest deduction.

Suppose that before considering interest expense you have $2 of taxable income subject to a tax rate of 40%:

$$\text{Taxes} = \$2.00 \times 0.40 = \$0.80$$

Suppose your interest expense reduces your taxable income by 10, reducing your taxes from 80 cents to 76 cents:

$$\text{Taxes} = \$1.90 \times 0.40 = \$0.76$$

By deducting the 10-cent interest expense, you have reduced your tax bill by 4 cents. You pay out the 10 cents and get a benefit of 4 cents. In effect, the cost of your debt is not 10 cents, but 6 cents—4 cents is the government's subsidy of your debt financing!

We can generalize this benefit from the tax deductibility of interest. Let r_d represent the cost of debt per year before considering the tax deductibility of interest, r_d^* represent the cost of debt after considering the tax deductibility of interest, and τ be the marginal tax rate. The effective cost of debt for a year is:

$$r_d^* = r_d(1 - \tau) \tag{11-1}$$

Suppose that you borrow $100,000 and must repay the amount borrowed plus $10,000. Also suppose that your tax rate is 40%:

$$r_d = \frac{\$10,000}{\$100,000} = 10\%$$

the effective cost of debt is:

$$r_d^* = 0.10(1 - 0.40) = 0.06 \text{ or } 6\% \text{ per year}$$

Creditors *require* a return of 10% per year on the funds they lend us. But it only *costs* us 6% per year.

In our example, the required rate of return is easy to figure out: We borrow $100,000, repay $110,000, so your lender's required rate of return is 10% per year. But your cost of debt capital is 6% per year, less than the required rate of return, thanks to Congress. Most debt financing is not as straightforward, requiring us to figure out the yield on the debt—the lender's required rate of return—given information about interest payments and maturity value.

Let's look at an example of the firm's cost of a straight coupon bond. Suppose a firm issues new bonds that have a face value of $1,000, mature in 20 years, and pay interest at a rate of 10% semiannually. If these bonds are issued at face value, the required rate of return of this new debt capital, r_d, is the yield-to-maturity, YTM, of the bonds. The *yield-to-maturity* for these bonds is the discount rate that causes the present value of the future cash flows—the interest and maturity value—to equal today's price of the bonds:

Present value of a coupon bond
= Present value of interest payments + Present value of maturity value

Let C indicate the interest payment, t the period, T the number of periods left until maturity, M the maturity value, and r the six-month yield.

Then putting together the present values of the interest payments and the maturity value:

$$\text{Present value of a coupon bond} = \sum_{t=1}^{T} \frac{C}{(1+r_d)^t} + \frac{M}{(1+r_d)^T} \qquad (11\text{-}2)$$

or, stated differently,

$$\text{Present value of a coupon bond} = \underbrace{C \sum_{t=1}^{T} \frac{1}{(1+r)^t}}_{\substack{\uparrow \\ \text{Present value} \\ \text{annuity factor}}} + \underbrace{M \frac{1}{(1+r)^T}}_{\substack{\uparrow \\ \text{Discount} \\ \text{factor}}}$$

Investors are willing to pay today a price for the bond that reflects the present value of its future cash flows, so today's price is the bond's present value. Let's apply this valuation to the bond in our example, solving first for the six-month yield, r, and then translating this six-month yield into an annual yield-to-maturity, r_d:

$$\text{Present value of bond} = \$1,000$$

$$\text{Interest, } C = \$1,000 \times \frac{10\%}{2} = \$50 \text{ every six months}$$

$$\text{Number of periods, } T = 20 \times 2 = 40 \text{ six-month periods}$$

$$\text{Maturity value, } M = \$1,000$$

We solve for r, the six-month yield:

$$\$1,000 = \sum_{t=1}^{40} \frac{\$50}{(1+r)^t} + \frac{\$1,000}{(1+r)^{40}}$$

$$r = 5\% \text{ per six-month period}$$

This six-month yield is equivalent to an annual yield, r_d:

$$r_d = 0.05 \times 2 = 0.10 \text{ or } 10\%$$

We can solve for r_d in two ways:

■ Trial and error—try different values for r_d until the right-hand side of the equation (the discounted value of interest and principal) is equal to the left-hand side (the value of the bond), or
■ Using calculator or spreadsheet programs.

As we saw in Chapter 9, the yield obtained from doubling the six-month yield is called the *bond-equivalent yield.*

Suppose the firm is able to issue the 10% bonds at a price of $900 per bond and interest is not deductible from the firm's income. The cost of debt would be greater than 10% because we are paying 10% based on the face value of $1,000, but we only get the use of $900. Using the equation for the present value of the bond, we first identify what we know:

$$\text{Present value of bond} = \$900$$

$$\text{Interest, } C = \$1,000 \times \frac{10\%}{2} = \$50 \text{ every six months}$$

Number of periods, $T = 20 \times 2 = 40$ six-month periods

Maturity value, $M = \$1,000$

Again, solve for r

$$\$900 = \sum_{t=1}^{40} \frac{\$50}{(1+r)^t} + \frac{\$1,000}{(1+r)^{40}}$$

$r = 5.6342\%$ per period

which we convert into an annual yield:

$$r_d = 0.056342 \times 2 = 0.112685 \text{ or } 11.2685\%$$

In this case, the return expected on the bond (the lender's [the investor's] required rate of return) and the cost of funds for the firm (the cost of debt) are 11.2685% since there is no other cost associated with raising funds from debt. Any costs associated with the issuance of debt—borrowing—are incorporated directly into the calculation of the cost of debt to the issuer since the present value of the bond is the proceeds of the bond issuer—the price of the bond less costs of issuance.

Now let's consider the costs of issuance, called the *flotation costs*, which are the payments to lawyers, accountants, and investment bankers who assist the firm in issuing debt securities (as well as preferred stock and common stock). There are also SEC registration fees. If these bonds are sold at $900 per bond, investors will require the rate of return of 11.2685%, as we just determined.

But if the firm only gets $890 per bond (the flotation costs are $10 per bond), this means the cost to the firm is *more* than 11.2685% per year:

$$\$890 = \sum_{t=1}^{40} \frac{\$50}{(1+r)^t} + \frac{\$1,000}{(1+r)^{40}}$$

$r = 5.7040\%$ per period

which we convert into an annual yield:

$$r_d = 0.057040 \times 2 = 0.11408 \text{ or } 11.408\%$$

Flotation costs of $10 per bond increase the cost of the bond to the firm from 11.2685% to 11.408%. This rate is referred to as the *all-in-cost of debt*. But investors pay $900 a bond, which reflects their *required rate of return* of 11.2685%.

Next we consider the tax deductibility of interest. If a dollar of interest is paid, is the interest cost to the firm one dollar? No, because interest on debt *is* deductible for tax purposes. Since interest expense reduces income, a dollar of interest reduces taxable income by one dollar. If the firm issues the 10% bonds at par, with interest paid annually and no flotation costs, and has a 40% marginal tax rate, the after-tax cost of debt is 6% per year:

$$r_d^* = 0.10(1 - 0.40) = 0.06 \text{ or } 6\% \text{ per year}$$

If the firm issues the 10% bonds at 90 (this is the way prices are quoted in the bond market), meaning 90% of the bond's face value, or $900 per bond with a $1,000 par value, with no flotation costs, the before-tax cost of debt is 11.2685% and the after-tax cost of debt is:

$$r_d^* = 0.112685(1 - 0.40) = 0.06761 \text{ or } 6.761\% \text{ per year}$$

But to be more complete we must include flotation costs, therefore using the all-in-cost of debt. If the firm issues the 10% bonds at 90, receiving only $890 per bond after flotation costs, the after-tax cost of debt, r_d^*, is:

$$r_d^* = 0.11408(1 - 0.40) = 0.6845 \text{ or } 6.845\% \text{ per year}$$

Therefore, the tax deductibility of interest reduces the cost of debt to the borrower.

The greater the marginal tax rate, the greater this benefit from deductibility and hence the lower the cost of debt. For example, the cost of the 10% bonds for different marginal tax rates, with annual interest and no flotation costs, is shown in Exhibit 11.1.

EXHIBIT 11.1 Cost of Debt at Varying Tax Rates

Marginal Tax Rate	After-Tax Cost of Debt (r_d^*)
20%	8%
40%	6%
60%	4%
80%	2%

Not all bonds are straight coupon bonds. Suppose you issue a zero-coupon bond. Though no interest is paid in cash each year, there is *implicit* interest, which you are allowed to deduct each period for tax purposes.

Suppose you issue a zero-coupon bond at the beginning of 1999 that matures in five years and has a face value of $1,000. If this bond does not pay interest—not explicitly at least—no one will buy it at its face value. Instead, investors will pay some amount *less* than the face value, and their reported return will be based on the difference between what they pay for the bond and (assuming they hold it to maturity) the face value. If the bonds are issued at 60% of the $1,000 face value or $600, what is the yield-to-maturity? We compare the present value of the bond, which is $600, with the maturity value, which is $1,000. We can start with the basic valuation relation:

$$FV = PV(1 + r)^t$$

where

FV = future value
PV = present value
r = interest per period
T = number of periods

Modifying this to fit our needs:

$$\text{Maturity value} = \text{Present value}(1 + r_d)^T$$

First, let's identify the known values:

Maturity value, M = $1,000
Present value, PV = $600
Number of periods, T = 5

We then insert these known values into this equation and solving for the one unknown, r_d:

$$\$1,000 = \$600(1 + r_d)^5$$

$$\frac{\$1,000}{\$600} = (1 + r_d)^5$$

$$1.6667 = (1 + r_d)^5$$

$$r_d = \sqrt[5]{1.6667} - 1 = 0.1076 \text{ or } 10.76\% \text{ per year}$$

EXHIBIT 11.2   Implicit Interest on a Zero-Coupon Bond

Year	End-of-Period Accrued Value	Previous-Period Accrued Value	Implicit Interest
1	$664.56	$600.00	$64.56
2	736.07	664.56	71.51
3	815.27	736.07	79.20
4	902.99	815.27	87.72
5	1,000.00	902.99	97.01

The implicit interest over the life of the bond is the difference between the face value and the issue price, $600. The implicit interest for a *given year* is the growth in the value of the bond during the year that is expected *at the time the bond is issued*.[1] For example, the implicit interest for the first year is the difference between the $600 issue price and $600 grown one year—accrued—at 10.76% per year:

$$\text{Implicit interest in first year} = \underset{\substack{\uparrow \\ \text{Value of the bond} \\ \text{at the end of the} \\ \text{first year}}}{\$600(1 + 0.1076)} - \underset{\substack{\uparrow \\ \text{Issue} \\ \text{price}}}{\$600} = \$64.56$$

We can see the growth in the implicit interest (due to compounding) for each year, comparing the end of period accrued value of the bond with the previous period's accrued value, as shown in Exhibit 11.2.

Each period, we deduct the implicit interest on our tax return to arrive at taxable income.

There is a cost of raising this capital, just as there was with a coupon bond. For example, in year 5, the accrued interest is $64.56, which is 10.76% of the beginning of the year value of $600.00. The issuer deducts $64.56 interest from its income for tax purposes. If the marginal tax rate is 40%, the effective cost per bond is:

$$r_d^* = 0.1076(1 - 0.40) = 0.646 \text{ or } 6.46\% \text{ per year}$$

As you can see from our calculations with a straight coupon bond and a zero-coupon bond, the starting point is the investor's required

---

[1] The implicit interest does not depend on what happens to the actual price of the bond, rather it depends only on the price of the bond at issuance and its time path, assuming the bond is held to maturity.

rate of return. Once we have that rate, we adjust it for flotation costs and the issuer's tax-benefit from interest deductibility.

The Cost of Preferred Stock

The *cost of preferred stock* is the cost associated with raising one more dollar of capital by issuing shares of preferred stock. As explained in Chapter 17, preferred stock may or may not have a maturity. Preferred stock without a maturity date is called *perpetual preferred stock*. Consider perpetual preferred stock with a fixed dividend rate, where the dividend is expressed as a percentage of the par value of a share.[2]

The value of this type of preferred stock is the present value of all future dividends to be received by the investor. If a share of preferred stock has a 5% dividend (based on a $100 par value) paid at the end of each year, the value of the stock today is the present value of the stream of $5's forever:

$$\text{Present value of preferred stock} = \frac{\$5}{(1+r)^1} + \frac{\$5}{(1+r)^2} + \dots + \frac{\$5}{(1+r)^\infty}$$

$$= \sum_{t=1}^{\infty} \frac{\$5}{(1+r)^t}$$

This series of constant amounts divided by a denominator that is growing at a constant rate collapses to:

$$\text{Present value of preferred stock} = \frac{\$5}{r}$$

If the discount rate is 10% per year:

$$\text{Present value of preferred stock} = \frac{\$5}{0.10} = \$50$$

That is, investors are willing to pay $50 today for the promised stream of $5 per year since they consider 10% per year to be sufficient compen-

---

[2] The determination of the cost of preferred equity becomes much more complex for dividend rates that are not fixed or nearly constant. If the dividend rate is adjusted frequently, the preferred shares will trade around their par value and the required rate of return (and hence the cost of capital) will fluctuate as market rates on preferred shares fluctuate.

sation for the time value of money and the risk associated with the perpetual stream of $5 annual dividends.

Let's rephrase this relationship, letting P_p indicate today's price, which is the present value of the preferred stock, D_p indicate the perpetual dividend per share per period, and r_p indicate the discount rate, which is the cost of preferred stock capital. Then:

$$P_p = \frac{D_p}{r_p}$$

We can turn this equation around to solve for r_p, given P_p and D_p:

$$r_p = \frac{D_p}{P_p} \qquad (11\text{-}3)$$

Consider a share of perpetual preferred stock with a price of $100 and a dividend rate of 12% per year:

$$D_p = \$100 \times 12\% = \$12 \text{ per share}$$

$$P_p = \$100$$

We want to solve for the discount rate that equates the discounted value of future dividends with today's price. This discount rate is the cost of preferred stock, r_p, which is also the required rate of return on perpetual preferred stock:

$$r_p = \frac{\$12}{\$100} = 0.12 \text{ or } 12\%$$

But an issuer must pay flotation costs. In this case, the proceeds of the issue would not be $100 per share, but less. If the flotation costs are 2% of the price of the stock when it is issued (thus, $2 per share), the issuer's proceeds from the sale of a share of preferred stock would be $98, instead of $100. Therefore, the issuer's all-in-cost of preferred stock is *more* than 12% because of the flotation costs. We know:

$$D_p = \$100 \times 12\% = \$12 \text{ per share}$$

$$P_p = \$98$$

and wish to solve for the issuer's cost of preferred stock, r_p:

$$r_p = \frac{\$12}{\$98} = 0.1225 \text{ or } 12.25\% \text{ per year}$$

But the investor's required rate of return on the preferred stock is 12% per year, since they are willing to pay $100 to get a future perpetual stream of $12 per year.

We can rewrite the equation for the cost of perpetual preferred stock to include flotation costs. Let f represent the percentage of the share's price that is paid in flotation costs. Then,

$$r_p = \frac{D_p}{P_p(1-f)} \qquad (11\text{-}4)$$

Substituting the figures in our example,

$$r_p = \frac{\$12}{\$100(1-0.02)} = \frac{\$12}{\$98} = 0.1225 \text{ or } 12.25\% \text{ per year}$$

Because dividends paid on preferred stock are not deductible as an expense for the issuer's tax purposes, the cost of preferred stock is not adjusted for taxes—dividends paid on this stock are paid out of *after-tax* dollars. Therefore, the difference between the investor's required rate of return and the issuer's cost of preferred stock is due only to flotation costs.

The Cost of Common Stock

The *cost of common stock* is the cost of raising one more dollar of common equity capital, either internally (from earnings retained in the firm)[3] or externally (by issuing new shares of common stock). There are costs associated with both internally and externally generated capital.

How can internally generated capital—retained earnings—have a cost? As a firm generates internal funds, some portion is used to pay off creditors and preferred shareholders. The remainder are funds owned by the common shareholders. The firm may either retain these funds (investing in assets) or pay them out to the shareholders in the form of cash dividends.

---

[3] The balance sheet account retained earnings is a record of the accumulation of earnings generated from the firm, less any dividends paid to owners. This accumulation starts when the firm first incorporates, so it is the sum of *all* past earnings less *all* past dividends.

Shareholders will require their firm to use retained earnings to generate a return that is at least as large as the return they could have generated for themselves if they had received as dividends the amount of funds represented in the retained earnings.

Retained funds are *not* a free source of capital. The cost of internal equity funds is the opportunity cost of funds of the firm's shareholders. This opportunity cost is what shareholders could earn on these funds for the same level of risk.

The only difference between the cost of internally and externally generated funds is the cost of issuing new common stock. The cost of internally generated funds is the opportunity cost of those funds—what shareholders could have earned on these funds. But the cost of externally generated funds (that is, funds from selling new shares of stock) includes both the sum of the opportunity cost and cost of issuing the new stock.

The cost of issuing common stock is difficult to estimate because of the nature of the cash flow streams to common shareholders. Common shareholders receive their return (on their investment in the stock) in the form of dividends and the change in the price of the shares they own. The dividend stream is not fixed, as in the case of fixed-rate preferred stock. How often and how much is paid as dividends is at the discretion of the board of directors. Therefore, this stream is unknown so it is difficult to determine its value.

The change in the price of shares is also difficult to estimate; the price of the stock at any future point in time is influenced by investors' expectations of cash flows further into the future beyond that point.

Nevertheless, two methods are commonly used to estimate the cost of common stock: the dividend valuation model and the capital asset pricing model. Each method relies on different assumptions regarding the cost of equity; each produces different estimates of the cost of common equity.

Cost of Common Stock Using the Dividend Valuation Model

In Chapter 9, we reviewed the *dividend valuation method* (DVM) for valuing common stock. The DVM states that the price of a share of stock is the present value of all its future cash dividends, where the future dividends are discounted at the required rate of return on equity, r.

If these dividends are constant forever (similar to the dividends of perpetual preferred stock, as we just covered), the cost of common stock is derived from the value of a perpetuity. Let D represent the constant dividend per share of common stock that is expected next period and each period after that forever; P_0, the current price of a share of stock; and r_e, the cost of common stock. The current price of a share of common stock is:

$$P_0 = \frac{D}{r_e}$$

We can solve for r_e:

$$r_e = \frac{D}{P_0}$$

However, common stock dividends do not usually remain constant. It's typical for dividends to grow at a constant rate. Let D_0 indicate this period's dividend. If dividends grow at a constant rate, g, forever, the present value of the common stock is the present value of all *future* dividends:

$$P_0 = \frac{D_0(1+g)^1}{(1+r_e)^1} + \frac{D_0(1+g)^2}{(1+r_e)^2} + \ldots + \frac{D_0(1+g)^\infty}{(1+r_e)^\infty}$$

Pulling today's dividend D_0 from each term,

$$P_0 = D_0 \left[\frac{(1+g)^1}{(1+r_e)^1} + \frac{(1+g)^2}{(1+r_e)^2} + \ldots + \frac{(1+g)^\infty}{(1+r_e)^\infty} \right]$$

Expressing this in summation notation:

$$P_0 = D_0 \sum_{t=1}^{\infty} \frac{(1+g)^t}{(1+r_e)^t}$$

The summation term is approximately equal to $(1+g)/(r_e - g)$, so we can rewrite the price of the common stock as:

$$P_0 = D_0 \frac{(1+g)}{(r_e - g)}$$

If we refer to the next period's dividend, D_1, as this period's dividend, D_0, compounded one period at the rate g,

$$D_1 = D_0(1+g)$$

then:

$$P_0 = \frac{D_1}{(r_e - g)}$$

Rearranging this equation to solve instead for r_e,

$$r_e = \frac{D_1}{P_0} + g \qquad (11\text{-}5)$$

we see that the cost of common stock is the sum of next period's *dividend yield*, D_1/P_0, plus the growth rate of dividends:

Cost of common stock = Dividend yield + Growth rate of dividends

Consider a firm expected to pay a constant dividend of $2 per share per year, forever. If the firm issues stock at $20 a share, the firm's cost of common stock is:

$$r_e = \frac{\$2}{\$20} = 0.10 \text{ or } 10\% \text{ per year}$$

But, if dividends are expected to be $2 in the next period and grow at a rate of 3% per year, and the required rate of return is 10% per year, the expected price per share (with $D_1 = \$2$ and $g = 3\%$) is:

$$P_0 = \frac{\$2}{0.10 - 0.03} = \$28.57$$

which is more than $8 above the price if there is no expected growth in dividends.

The DVM reflects two ideas that make some sense about the relation between the cost of equity and the dividend payments:

■ The greater the current dividend yield, the greater the cost of equity.
■ The greater the growth in dividends, the greater the cost of equity.

However, the DVM has some drawbacks:

■ How do you deal with dividends that do not grow at a constant rate? This model does not accommodate nonconstant growth easily.

■ What if the firm does not pay dividends now? In that case, D_1 would be zero and the expected price would be zero. But a zero price for stock does not make any sense! And if dividends are expected in the future, but there are no current dividends, what do you do?

■ What if the growth rate of dividends is greater than the required rate of return? This implies a negative stock price, which isn't possible.

■ What if the stock price is not readily available, say in the case of a privately-held firm? This would require an estimate of the share price.

Therefore, the DVM may be appropriate to use to determine the cost of equity for companies with stable dividend policies, but it may not applicable for all firms.

Cost of Common Stock Using the Capital Asset Pricing Model

The investor's required rate of return is compensation for both the time value of money and risk. To figure out how much compensation there should be for risk, we first have to understand *what* risk we are talking about.

As we saw in Chapter 10, the *capital asset pricing model* (CAPM) assumes an investor holds a *diversified portfolio*—a collection of investments whose returns do not move in the same direction nor at the same time nor by the same amount. The result is that the only risk left in the portfolio as a whole is the risk related to movements in the market as a whole—*market risk*.

If we assume all shareholders' hold diversified portfolios, the risk that is relevant in valuing a particular investment is the market risk of that investment. The greater the market risk, the greater the compensation—meaning a higher yield—for bearing this risk. And the greater the yield, the lower the present value of the asset because expected future cash flows are discounted at a higher rate that reflects the higher risk.

The cost of common stock is the sum of the investor's compensation for the time value of money and the investor's compensation for the market risk of the stock:

Cost of common stock = Compensation for the time value of money
+ Compensation for market risk

Let's represent the compensation for the time value of money as the expected risk-free rate of interest, r_f. The *risk-free rate of interest* is the rate that is earned on an asset that has no risk. If a particular common stock has market risk that is *the same* as the risk of the market as a whole, then the compensation for that stock's market risk is the **market risk premium**. The market's risk premium is the difference between the expected return on the market, r_m, and the expected risk-free rate, r_f:

$$\text{Market risk premium} = r_m - r_f$$

If the expected risk-free rate is 3% and the expected return on the market is 11%, the market risk premium is 8%.

But if a particular common stock has market risk that is *different* from the risk of the market as a whole, we need to adjust that stock's market risk premium to reflect its different risk. Suppose the market risk premium is 8%. If a stock's market risk is twice the whole market's risk, the stock's premium for its market risk is 2 × 8%, or 16%. If a stock's market risk is half the risk of the market as a whole, the stock's premium for market risk is 0.5 × 8%, or 4%. What we are doing here is fine tuning the compensation investors will need to accept that stock's market risk. We fine tune by starting with our benchmark of the risk of the market as a whole and adjust it to reflect the market's premium for the stock's relative market risk to come up with the stock's premium.

Let β represent the adjustment factor. Then the compensation for market risk is:

$$\text{Compensation for market risk} = \beta(r_m - r_f)$$

Because we know the compensation for the time value of money, r_f, and now we know the compensation for market risk, we see that the cost of common stock, r_e, is:

$$r_e = r_f + \beta(r_m - r_f) \tag{11-6}$$

- The term $(r_m - r_f)$ represents the risk premium required by investors for bearing the risk of owning the market portfolio.
- The multiplier, β, fine tunes this market risk premium to compensate for the market portfolio associated with the individual firm. β, commonly referred to as **beta**, is a measure of the sensitivity of the returns on a particular security (or group of securities) to changes in the returns on the market—a measure of market risk.

A common stock having a β greater than 1.0 has more risk than the average security in the market. A common stock having a β less than 1.0 has less risk than the average security in the market.

Suppose a firm's stock has a β of 2.0. This means its market risk is twice the risk of the average security in the market. If the expected risk-free rate of interest is 6% and the expected return on the market is 10%, the cost of common stock, r_e, is:

$$r_e = 0.06 + 2.0(0.10 - 0.06) = 0.14 \text{ or } 14\%$$

In this example, the market risk premium is $(10\% - 6\%) = 4\%$. A market risk premium of 4% means that if you own a portfolio with the same risk as the market as a whole (that is, with a beta of 1.0), you would expect to receive a 10% return comprising: 6% to compensate you for the price of time and 4% to compensate you for the price of market risk. If you invest in a security with a β of 2.0, you would expect a return of 14% comprising: 6% to compensate you for the price of time and 2.0 times $4\% = 8\%$ to compensate you for the price of that security's particular risk.

The CAPM is based on two ideas that make sense: Investors are risk averse and they hold diversified portfolios. But the CAPM is not without its drawbacks. First, the estimates rely heavily on historical values—returns on the stock and returns on the market. These historical values may not be representative of the future, which is what we are trying to gauge. Also, the sensitivity of a firm's stock returns may change over time; for example, when the firm changes its capital structure. Second, if the firm's stock is not publicly-traded, there are no data sources even for historical values.

PUTTING IT ALL TOGETHER: THE COST OF CAPITAL

The cost of capital is the average of the cost of each source, weighted by its proportion of the total capital it represents. Hence, it is also referred to as the *weighted average cost of capital (WACC)* or the *weighted cost of capital (WCC)*. The weighted average cost of capital is a *weighted average* of the different costs of capital. But each of these costs is a *marginal* cost—the cost of raising additional capital using that source. So the WACC is a *marginal* cost—what it costs to raise additional capital—*averaged* across the different sources of capital.

Let w_d, w_p, and w_e represent the proportion of debt, preferred stock, and common stock in the capital structure, respectively, and r_d, r_p, and r_e equal the after-tax cost of debt, the cost of preferred stock, and the cost of common stock, respectively. The weighted average cost of capital is:

$$\text{WACC} = w_d r_d^* + w_p r_p + w_e r_e \tag{11-7}$$

Consider the following weights and marginal costs of the different sources of capital shown in Exhibit 11.3.

The WACC is:

WACC = (0.40)(0.06) + (0.10)(0.12) + (0.50)(0.14) = 0.106 or 10.6%

The Marginal Cost of Capital Schedule

As you raise more and more money, the cost of each additional dollar of new capital may increase. The reasons are the flotation costs and the demand for the security representing the capital to be raised.

For example, the cost of internal funds from retained earnings will differ from the cost of funds from issuing common stock due to flotation costs. If a firm expects to generate $1,000,000 entirely from what's available in internal funds—retained earnings—there are no flotation costs. But if the firm needs $1,000,001, that $1 above $1,000,000 will have to be raised *externally*, requiring flotation costs.

Let's consider a simple example using the dividend valuation method for the cost of common stock. Suppose a firm pays a dividend of $5 per share this year and dividends are expected to grow at a rate of 5% per year, forever. The current price of the stock is $50. The cost of this internal source of funds is:

$$r_e = \frac{\$5(1 + 0.05)}{\$50} + 0.05$$

$$= 0.1550 \text{ or } 15.5\% \text{ per year}$$

If the firm is expected to generate $2,000,000 in retained earnings in the next period, it will cost 15.5% per year to use this amount as capital.

If the firm needs *more than* $2,000,000, each additional dollar of equity capital will cost more than 15.5% because it will be raised from the other two sources and both have flotation costs.

EXHIBIT 11.3   Costs of Capital

Source	Weight	Cost of Capital
Debt	40%	$r = 6\%$
Preferred stock	10%	$r_p = 12\%$
Common stock	50%	$r_e = 14\%$

Suppose in addition to the retained earnings the firm expects to be able to issue new shares at $50 per share, but receives only $48 per share—the investment bankers get the $2 difference. The cost of this external equity is:

$$r_e = \frac{\$5(1 + 0.05)}{\$48} + 0.05$$

$$= 0.1594 \text{ or } 15.94\% \text{ per year}$$

The first $2,000,000 costs 15.5% per year and anything over that costs 15.94% per year. So, the marginal cost of common stock capital is 15.5% per year to raise from $1 to $2,000,000 from equity, and is 15.94% per year to raise each dollar above $2,000,000 from common stock.

Flotation costs also play a role in creating layers of cost for debt. For example, a firm may expect to be able to privately place a debt issue of $1,000,000 with an insurance company. If more than $1,000,000 of new debt capital is needed, the firm would have to sell another debt issue publicly, incurring higher issuance costs. The first $1,000,000 of debt capital would be at one cost, and any additional debt capital is at a higher cost.

Additional capital may be more costly since the firm must offer higher yields to entice investors to purchase ever larger issues of securities.

Considering the effects of flotation costs and the additional yield necessary to entice investors, we most likely face a schedule of marginal costs of debt capital and a schedule of marginal costs of equity capital. Hence, we need to determine at what level of raising funds the marginal cost of capital for the firm changes.

Capital structure is the mix of long-term sources of funds. Suppose a firm has a target capital structure of 40% debt and 60% common stock and will raise new funds in these proportions. In consultation with its investment bankers, the firm has determined the cost of raising new capital from debt and equity, for different levels of financing. These costs are shown in Exhibit 11.4. For example, if the firm issues $1,500,000 of new debt, the first $1,000,000 costs 5% per year and the next $500,000 costs 6% per year.

Suppose the firm raises capital in the proportions of 40% debt and 60% equity and raises $2,000,000 of new capital comprising $800,000 debt and $1,200,000 common stock. Looking at the schedules, we see the cost of debt is 5% up to the first $1,000,000 of debt. However, the cost of equity changes once we have raised $1,000,000: The first $1,000,000 of equity costs 9% and the additional $200,000 costs 10%. The cost of capital of the first $2,000,000 of new capital is:

$$= \frac{\$800,000}{\$2,000,000}0.05 + \frac{\$1,000,000}{\$2,000,000}0.09 + \frac{\$200,000}{\$2,000,000}0.10$$

$$\uparrow \qquad\qquad \uparrow \qquad\qquad \uparrow$$

Debt　　　　Equity at 9%　　　Equity at 10%

$$= \quad 0.020 \quad + \quad 0.045 \quad + \quad 0.010$$
$$= 0.075 \text{ or } 7.5\% \text{ per year}$$

The average cost of raising a dollar of capital for the first \$2,000,000 of capital is 7.5%. The marginal cost of capital for the first \$1,800,000 is

Marginal cost of capital for first \$1,800,000

$$= \frac{\$720,000}{\$1,800,000}0.05 + \frac{\$1,080,000}{\$1,800,000}0.09$$

$$= 7.4\% \text{ per year}$$

EXHIBIT 11.4　Marginal Costs of Debt and Common Stock

Debt

Amount of New Debt	Marginal Cost of Debt per Year
Up to \$1,000,000	5%
\$1,000,001 to \$2,000,000	6
\$2,000,001 to \$3,000,000	7
\$3,000,001 to \$4,000,000	8
\$4,000,001 to \$5,000,000	9

Equity

Amount of New Equity	Marginal Cost of Common Stock per Year
Up to \$1,000,000	9%
\$1,000,001 to \$3,000,000	10
\$3,000,001 to \$5,000,000	11
\$5,000,001 to \$8,000,000	12

and the marginal cost of capital for the next $200,000 is:

$$= \frac{\$80,000}{\$200,000}0.05 + \frac{\$120,000}{\$200,000}0.10$$
$$= 8\% \text{ per year}$$

If we raise one more dollar of capital beyond the $2,000,000, but not more than $1,000,000 in total debt nor more than $3,000,000 in total equity, then it costs 5% for the additional debt and 10% for the additional equity:

$$\begin{array}{l} \text{Weighted average cost of capital beyond} \\ \$2,000,000 \text{ but less than } \$4,000,000 \end{array} = 0.40(0.05) + 0.60(0.10)$$
$$= 0.08 \text{ or } 8\% \text{ per year}$$

The marginal cost of capital is 8% at $2,000,001 of new capital.

The marginal cost of capital at $4,000,000 of capital ($1,600,000 debt and $2,400,000 equity) is 8.4%. The cost of debt is 6% and the cost of equity is 10%:

$$\text{Weighted average cost of capital} = 0.40(0.06) + 0.60(0.10)$$
$$= 0.084 \text{ or } 8.4\% \text{ per year}$$

Each time the marginal cost of *either* the equity or the debt changes, the marginal cost of capital changes. These changes are referred to as ***break-points***. We can see break-points in Exhibit 11.5, which represents graphically how the marginal cost of capital ratchets upward as the total dollars raised increases. The set of marginal costs of capital for different levels of capital raised makes up the ***marginal cost of capital schedule***.

We can figure out where these break-points occur by looking at:

- The marginal cost of debt schedule.
- The marginal cost of stock schedule.
- The capital structure proportions.

Let's first look at the marginal cost of debt schedule. The marginal cost of capital breaks when the marginal cost of debt changes from 5% to 6%—once we have used up the first $1,000,000 of debt capital. Because our total capital structure consists of 40% debt:

$$0.40(\text{Total capital raised}) = \$1,000,000$$

EXHIBIT 11.5   Marginal Costs of Capital for Different Levels of Capital

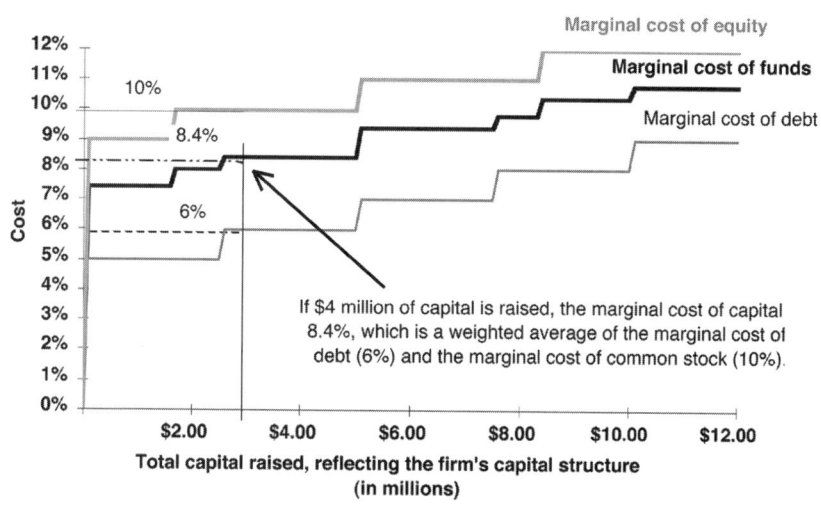

Using a bit of algebra,

$$\text{Total capital raised} = \frac{\$1,000,000}{0.40} = \$2,500,000$$

Once we have raised $2,500,000 of capital, we have hit the $1,000,000 break in the marginal cost of debt capital schedule.

We can repeat this for each break in the marginal cost of debt schedule and each break in the marginal cost of equity capital schedule. The results of computing the breaks in the marginal cost of capital schedule are shown in Exhibit 11.6. By comparing the breaks in this table with the graph in Exhibit 11.5, you see a correspondence between these break-points in the graph and the shifts in the marginal cost of capital schedule. For example, if $5 million new capital is raised, the marginal cost of debt is 7% and the marginal cost of equity is 10%, resulting in a marginal cost of capital of 8.4%. If one more dollar of capital is raised (that is, $5,000,001 in total) the marginal cost of debt remains at 7%, the marginal cost of equity jumps from 10% to 11%, and the marginal cost of capital becomes 9.4%. The $5 million represents a break-point because the marginal cost of capital changes after that amount of new capital is raised.

EXHIBIT 11.6 Marginal Cost of Capital Schedule

Amount of Capital Raised	Amount of Debt Raised	Amount of Common Stock Raised	Marginal Cost of Debt	Marginal Cost of Common Stock	Marginal Cost of Capital
$0 to $1,000,000	$400,000	$600,000	5%	9%	7.4%
1,000,000 to 2,000,000	800,000	1,200,000	5	10	8.0
2,000,001 to 3,000,000	1,200,000	1,800,000	6	10	8.4
3,000,001 to 4,000,000	1,600,000	2,400,000	6	10	8.4
4,000,001 to 5,000,000	2,000,000	3,000,000	7	10	8.4
5,000,001 to 6,000,000	2,400,000	3,600,000	7	11	9.4
6,000,001 to 7,000,000	2,800,000	4,200,000	7	11	9.4
7,000,001 to 8,000,000	3,200,000	4,800,000	8	11	9.8
8,000,001 to 9,000,000	3,600,000	5,400,000	8	12	10.4
9,00,000 to 10,000,000	4,000,000	6,000,000	8	12	10.4
10,000,001 to 11,000,000	4,400,000	6,600,000	9	12	10.8
11,000,001 to 12,000,000	4,800,000	7,200,000	9	12	10.8

We an generalize the calculation of the break-point in the marginal cost of capital schedule as:

Break-point in marginal cost of capital

$$= \frac{\text{Break-point in marginal cost of capital from source}}{\text{Proportion of capital from source}} \qquad (11\text{-}8)$$

In general, as the marginal cost of any component of capital changes, so does the marginal cost of capital.

Marginal Cost of Capital and Shareholder Wealth Maximization

Let's see what maximizing shareholder wealth means in terms of making investment and financing decisions.

To maximize shareholder wealth we must invest in a project until the marginal cost of capital is equal to its marginal benefit. What is the benefit from an investment? It is the internal rate of return—also known as the marginal efficiency of capital. If we begin by investing in the best projects (those with highest returns), and then proceed by investing in the next best projects, and so on, the marginal benefit from investing in more and more projects declines.

Also, as we keep on raising funds and investing them, the marginal cost of funds increases. To maximize shareholders' wealth, we should invest in projects to the point where the increasing marginal cost of funds is equal to the marginal benefit from our investment.

We can see this concept illustrated in Exhibit 11.7. Here we plot the marginal cost of capital and marginal efficiency of investment against the capital expenditure. The *optimal capital budget* is the capital expenditure where the marginal cost of capital intersects the marginal efficiency of capital. In this graph, the optimal capital budget is $2,750,000. This is the amount of capital investment where the marginal cost equals the marginal benefit which equals 8.85%. This means that the firm should take on an investment as long as its return exceeds or is equal to the marginal cost of capital to make the investment.

Practical Problems with the Marginal Cost of Capital

Determining the cost of capital appears straightforward: Find the cost of each source of capital and weight it by the proportion it will represent in the firm's new capital. But it is *not* so simple. There are many problems in determining the cost of capital for an individual firm. Consider, for example:

EXHIBIT 11.7 Determining the Optimal Capital Budget with the Marginal Cost of Capital and the Marginal Efficiency of Investment

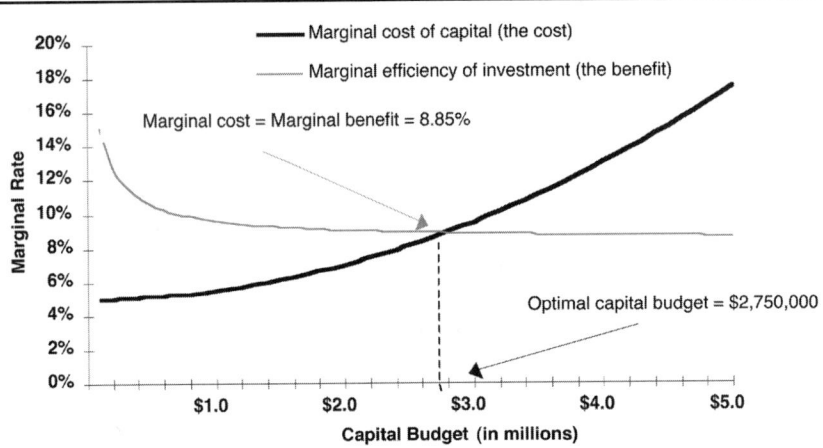

- How do you know what it will cost to raise an additional dollar of new debt? You may seek the advice of an investment banker. You may look at recent offerings of debt with risk similar to yours. But until you issue your debt, you will not know for sure.
- Determining the cost of preferred stock looks easy. But how do you know, for a given dividend rate, what the price of the preferred stock will be? Again, you can seek advice or look at similar risk issues outstanding in the market. But until you issue your preferred stock, you will not know for sure.
- Determining the cost of common stock is still more perplexing. There are problems associated with both the DVM and the CAPM.
- In the case of the DVM: What if dividends are not constant? What if there are no current dividends? And the expected growth rate of dividends is merely an estimate of the future.
- In the case of the CAPM, what is the expected risk-free rate of interest into the future? What is the expected return on the market into the future? What is the expected sensitivity of a particular's asset's returns to that of the market's return? To answer many of these questions, we may derive estimates from looking at historical data. But this can be hazardous.

Estimating the cost of capital requires a good deal of judgment. It requires an understanding of the current risk and return associated with the firm and its securities, as well as of the firm's and securities' risk and return in the future.

If you are able to derive estimates of the costs of each of the sources of capital, you then need to determine the proportions in which the firm will raise capital. If your firm is content with its current capital structure and you expect to raise capital according to the proportions already in place, your job is simpler. In this case, the proportions can be determined by estimating the market value of existing capital and calculating the weights.

On the other hand, if your firm raises capital in proportions *other* than its current capital structure, there is a problem of estimating how this change in capital structure affects the costs of the components. Consider a firm that has a current capital structure, in market value terms, of 50% debt and 50% common stock. What happens to the market value of each component if the firm undergoes a large expansion and raises new funds solely from debt? This increase in debt may *increase* the cost of debt and the cost of common stock. This will occur if this additional debt is viewed as significantly increasing the financial risk of the firm—the chance that the firm may encounter financial problems— thereby increasing the cost of capital. But this increase in the use of debt may also *decrease* the cost of capital. This could result because the firm will be using more of the lower cost capital—debt.

Whether the cost of financial risk outweighs the benefit from the tax deductibility of interest is not clear—and cannot be reasonably forecasted.

INTEGRATIVE EXAMPLE: ESTIMATING THE COST OF CAPITAL FOR DUPONT

Although a precise determination of the cost of capital is not possible, we can develop estimates that are useful in decision-making. Let's estimate the cost of capital for E. I. Du Pont De NeMours & Company, a large U.S. chemical company whose products range from oil to pharmaceuticals. Let's estimate DuPont's cost of capital for 2002, using all published financial data through 2001.

Step 1: Determine the Proportions of Each Component of Capital

If new capital is raised in the same proportions as existing capital, the weights applied to the costs of capital would be the market value proportions of capital—the firm's use of each source of capital, based on its market value. For example, if the market value of debt is $100 and the market value of common stock is $400, the market value proportion of debt is 20% and the market value proportion of common stock is 80%. Because many firms maintain a relatively stable capital structure, that makes it easier to determine the proportions of each capital.

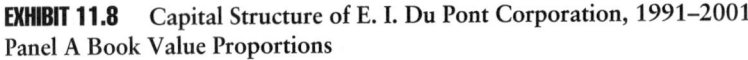

EXHIBIT 11.8   Capital Structure of E. I. Du Pont Corporation, 1991–2001
Panel A Book Value Proportions

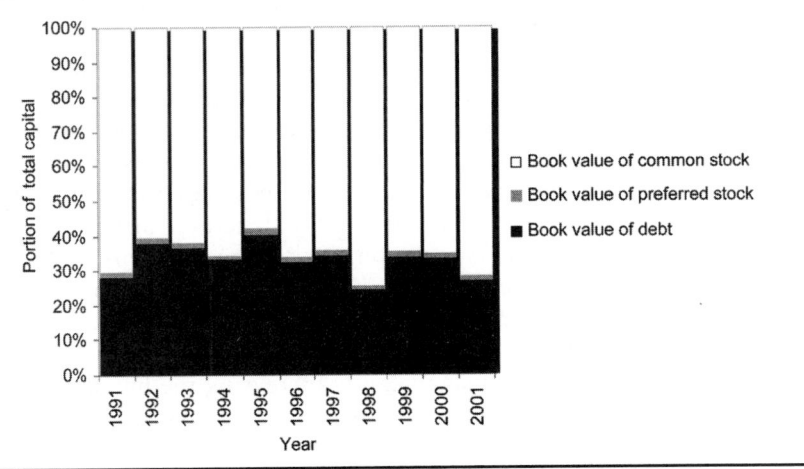

Panel B Market Value Proportions

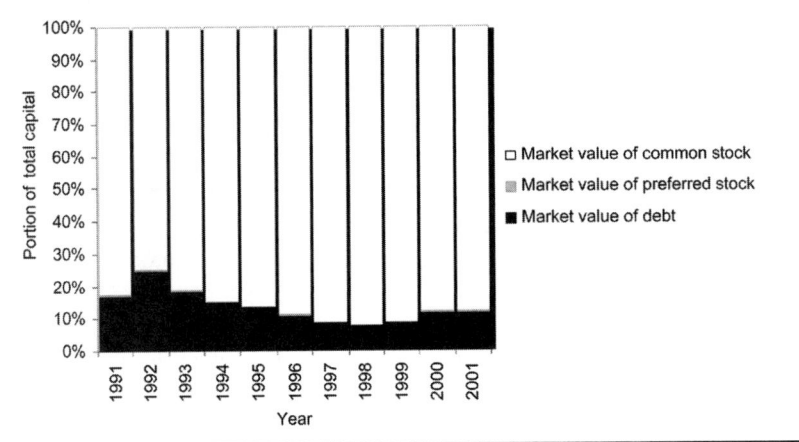

One practical problem is determining the market value of the components of capital. The market values of publicly-traded common stock are readily available. But not all debt is publicly traded—some may be privately placed. If the firm has securities that are not publicly traded, their market values may not be available.

Du Pont has raised capital from three sources: long-term debt, preferred stock, and common stock. The debt and equity proportions, based on book values and market values, are also shown in Exhibit 11.8.

The market value of the preferred and common stock was calculated from information provided in Yahoo! Finance. The information on the market value of debt was obtained from footnotes to the annual financial statements.

Using the market-value proportions, we see that, on average, Du Pont's capital structure consists of 13.4% debt, 0.3% preferred stock, and 86.3% common equity. If we look at book values over the same period, we get a slightly different idea of the proportions: 32.9% debt, 1.30% preferred stock, and 65.8% common stock. If we assume Du Pont will issue new securities in proportion to its capital structure based on recent years' market values, we expect the firm to raise capital according to the market value proportions of 13.4%, 0.3%, and 86.3%.

Comparing the book and market values, we see that the book value of common stock understates its market value. For example, at the end of 2001 the book value of equity is $14,215 million and the market value is $42,595 million. One reason for this discrepancy is that retained earnings (which typically represent a large portion of common stock) are the accumulation of earnings less any dividends paid since the beginning of the corporation's existence. These accumulated earnings are a sum of earnings for the *entire* corporate life of the firm, so in Du Pont's case, earnings in 1995 are added to earnings from, say, 1950, which are added to earnings from 1935, and so on back to 1915.

Aside from this problem, the sum of earnings reinvested in the firm do not reflect what the firm does with them when they are reinvested, whereas the market value of equity reflects this earnings growth potential.

The book value of debt understates the true value of Du Pont debt by several hundred million dollars. Most of the Du Pont debt is selling at a premium from face value—implying that the coupon rates of outstanding debt are above the current market rates. This is because interest rates are currently at lower rates than when the debt was issued.

The use of book values results in an understatement of the use of common stock—the highest cost source—and a slight understatement of the use of debt—the lowest cost source. And since the firm's decision-makers are most likely to look at market values in assessing the firm's current and future capital structure, it seems reasonable to focus more on the market value proportions.

Step 2: Determine the Costs of Each Source of Capital

We must estimate the cost of each of DuPont's sources of capital. To simplify our chore, let's ignore flotation costs.

The Cost of Debt

There are several ways we could estimate the cost of raising an additional dollar of new debt. We could look at:

1. Yields on recent debt offerings with similar risk.
2. Yields on recent debt offerings made by Du Pont.
3. Yields on outstanding debt of Du Pont.

Du Pont debt is rated as high quality by both Moody's and Standard & Poor's: Aa3 in Moody's system, AA in Standard & Poor's system. This means that the debt is considered high quality in terms of default risk. That is, there is little risk Du Pont will be unable to pay the promised interest and principal on its current debt issues.

Using the three ways to estimate Du Pont's cost of new debt, we obtain the following results:

1. Recent debt offerings with similar risk: For firms with Aa-rated debt that was issued late in 2001, the yield was 7.1%.
2. Recent Du Pont offerings: Du Pont did not issue debt securities in 2001. The latest issue was in mid-2000, and hence is not representative of rates at the end of 2001.
3. Outstanding Du Pont debt: At the end of 2001, the yields on Du Pont's current debt issues were slightly lower than the coupon rates, as evidenced by the market values being $250 million greater than the book values at the end of 2001. The coupon rates on current debt range from 6.5% to 8.5%.

Compiling these estimates we can see that there is quite a discrepancy between the rates, with estimates between 6.85% and 8.57% per year:

Approach	Yield
Yield on recently issued debt of similar risk	7.1%
Yield on currently outstanding debt	6.5% to 8.5%

Which do we use? Which one will be enough to get investors to put their money into new Du Pont debt? Most of Du Pont debt now consists of debentures without any sinking fund and with maturities of at least ten years. This persuades us to choose a cost on the upper end of the possible estimates. Because the debt yielding around 7% per year is more typical of the debt Du Pont issues, let's estimate the yield on new debt to be 7%.

Though the required rate of return on new Du Pont debt is estimated to be 7%, the *cost* of debt to Du Pont is less since the interest on debt is tax deductible. Considering the tax rates on corporations for 1995, with the top marginal rate of 35%, the estimated cost of debt, r_d^*, is:

$$r_d^* = 0.07(1 - 0.35) = 0.0455 \text{ or } 4.55\% \text{ per year}$$

The Cost of Preferred Stock

The cost of preferred stock can be estimated in a manner similar to that of debt. But since firms do not issue preferred stock with the same frequency as debt, it is likely that there is no recent preferred stock issue by the same company. We can, however, look at current yields on existing issues.

At the end of 2001, Du Pont had two preferred stock issues outstanding, one with a $3.50 dividend and the other with a $4.50 dividend. We can calculate the yield on the preferred stock using the current market value of the preferred stock and the dividend. From Standard & Poor's *Daily Stock Price Record*, we see that the $3.50 dividend stock's price at the end of 2001 is $59.50. Therefore the required rate of return on this preferred stock, with $P_p = \$59.50$ and $D_p = \$3.50$, is:

$$r_p = \frac{\$3.50}{\$59.50} = 0.0585 \text{ or } 5.85\% \text{ per year}$$

Looking at the same source, we see that the price of the stock that pays $4.50 per share is $74.00 at the end of 1995. Therefore the required rate of return on this preferred stock is:

$$r_p = \frac{\$4.50}{\$74.00} = 0.0608 \text{ or } 6.08\% \text{ per year}$$

We arrive at two estimates of the cost of preferred stock:

Approach	Yield
Current yield on $3.50 dividend preferred stock	5.85%
Current yield on $4.50 dividend preferred stock	6.08%

Let's use an estimate mid-way between the two current yields: 6% per year.

The Cost of Common Stock

We can estimate the cost of equity using either the DVM or an asset pricing model. An asset pricing model specifies the risk factors that are believed to determine the expected return investors seek from buying a security. We discussed one such model, the capital asset pricing model

(CAPM) in Chapter 10. CAPM specifies that there is only one risk factor, the overall market (i.e., market risk) that determines the expected return. Other asset pricing models that are discussed in textbooks on investment management allow for multiple risk factors. These models are called multifactor risk models. Below we will see how to estimate the cost of equity using the DVM and the CAPM. Multifactor risk models are used in the same way as the CAPM to determine the cost of equity.

Using the Dividend Valuation Model   One of the key ingredients in the DVM is the growth rate of dividends. Ideally, we would like to have an estimate of the growth rate of future dividends in perpetuity. But this information is not available.

As an alternative, we look at the dividend history of Du Pont and see if the pattern of dividend payments indicates a trend. The yearly dividends per share paid over the period 1960 through 2001 are shown in Exhibit 11.9. They do not follow a constant pattern in the earlier years. But if we focus on the past few years, we get a pattern that resembles a constant dividend growth.

Du Pont paid dividends on common stock over the past four years as follows:

Year	Dividends per Share
1998	$1.37
1999	1.38
200	1.40
2001	1.40

EXHIBIT 11.9   Dividends on E. I. du Pont Corporation Common Stock, 1960–2001

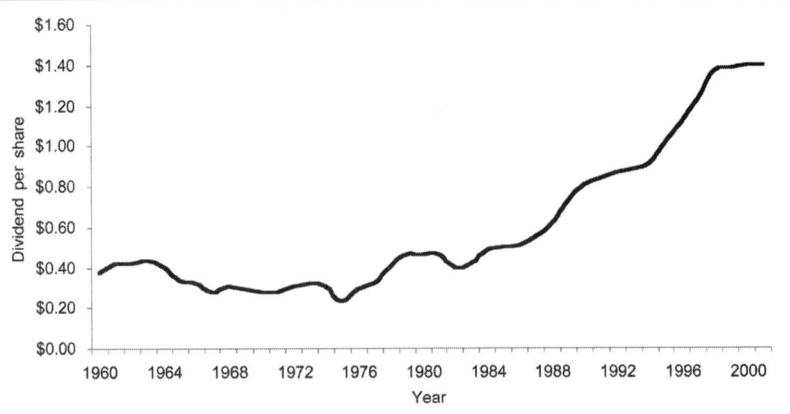

We can calculate the growth rate of dividends by applying the basic valuation equation,

$$FV = PV(1 + r)^t$$

Let the present value be the dividends for 1998, $1.37, and the future value of dividends be the dividends three years later, $1.40. The growth rate, g, is the rate the dividends change each year, which is r in the basic valuation equation. Dividends have grown from $1.37 to $1.40 over three years. Therefore,

$$\$1.40 = \$1.37(1 + g)^3$$

And we solve this equation for the growth rate in dividends, g,

$$(1 + g)^3 = \frac{\$1.40}{\$1.37}$$

$$g = \sqrt[3]{\frac{\$1.40}{\$1.37}} - 1 = 0.0072 \text{ or } 0.72\% \text{ per year}$$

Since the most recent dividend, D_0, is $1.40 per share, the estimate of next period's dividend, D_1, is:

$$D_1 = \$1.40(1 + 0.0072) = \$1.41$$

The price of the stock at the end of 2001 is $42.51 per share. Substituting the known values of D_1 and P into the equation:

$$r_e = \frac{\$1.41}{\$42.51} + 0.0072$$

$$= 0.03317 + 0.0072$$

$$= 0.04037 \text{ or } 4.037\% \text{ per year}$$

Using the Capital Asset Pricing Model   To estimate the cost of equity using the CAPM we first need to estimate:

- r_f, the expected risk free rate of interest
- r_m, the expected return on the market
- β, the stock's return's sensitivity to changes in the market's return

We first need an estimate of the risk-free rate that is expected in the long term. Though there are no risk-free perpetual securities, we can use the yield on a long-term government bond. Using the yield on 30-year U.S. Treasury bonds as of the end of 2001, we estimate the risk-free rate of interest to be 5% per year.[4]

We also need an estimate of the expected market return in the future. The best we can do is determine a typical recent return on the market. If we assume that the market is represented well by an index, say Standard & Poor's 500 Stock Index, we could look at the typical return on the index and use this as our best estimate of the future market return. We can estimate the return on the market by looking at the most recent year's return, or an average market return over a broader time period. The average annual return on the S&P 500 for 30 years (1972–2001) and and 10 years (1992–2001) is:

Period	Average Annual Return
1972–2001	9.133%
1992–2001	12.949%

We will use 11.0% as our best guess of the return on the market.

Because the sensitivity of the returns on the common stock to returns on the market is specific to the individual stock, we need information on the returns on Du Pont stock. We can see this relation between the returns on Du Pont's common stock and the returns on the market by looking at Exhibit 11.10. In this graph, each point represents a month's return on Du Pont common stock and a month's return on the S&P 500 Index, representing the entire market. For example, during the month of February 1998, the return on Du Pont common stock was 8.8% and the return on the S&P 500 was 7%.

We can describe the relation between the returns on the stock and returns of the market by looking at their relation over time We do this using regression analysis, which measures the sensitivity of one variable (in our example, the returns on Du Pont stock) to changes in another (the returns on the S&P 500).

The regression of the monthly returns on Du Pont common stock against the monthly returns on the market, represented by the S&P 500, for the sixty months from January 1996 through December 2001 produces a measure of the average relation between Du Pont stock's returns and the returns of the market. This average is represented graphically as the regression line (see Exhibit 11.10). The slope of this line—0.54—indicates the

---

[4] We found this rate in the *Federal Reserve Bulletin*.

sensitivity—on average over the sixty months—of the returns on Du Pont stock to changes in the returns on the market and is our estimate for market risk, beta (β).[5]

We could also obtain an estimate of β from financial services, such as the *Value Line Investment Survey*. Because there are many different ways to estimate β—using different periods of time or a different market index—there may be slight differences between estimates from different financial services. The β for Du Pont taken from *Value Line* is 0.95, but the beta from Yahoo! Finance is 0.7 which is close to our estimate. For purposes of this example, we will use 0.7.

Is an historical beta a good estimate of the future beta? For some stocks yes, for others no. It depends on whether the market risk of the firm is expected to change in the future.

We have gathered the following:[6]

r_f = 5% per year, which is 0.41667% per month
r_m = 11% per year, which is 0.91667% per month
β = 0.70

EXHIBIT 11.10   Returns on E. I. Du Pont Corporation Common Stock versus Returns on the S&P 500 Index, Monthly, 1996–2001

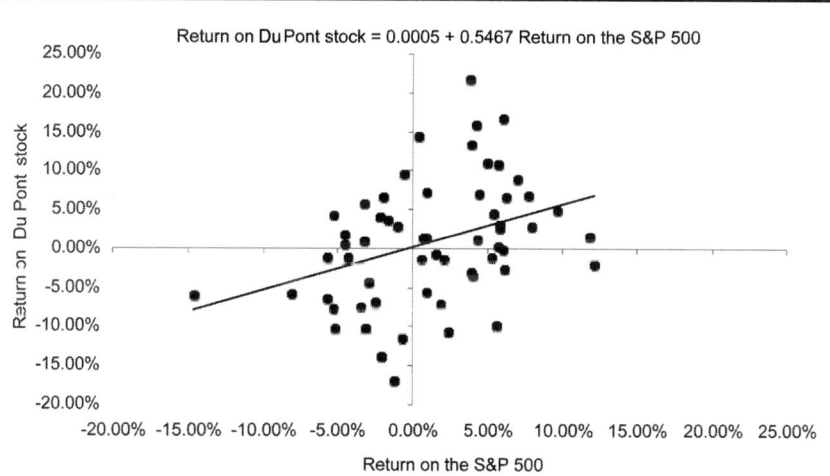

---

[5] The calculations necessary to estimate a regression line can be performed using a spreadsheet program, such as Microsoft's EXCEL, or using a calculator regression program.

[6] We use returns on a monthly basis when calculating the cost of equity because we are applying a beta estimate that is based on monthly returns.

Putting these pieces together, we find that the cost of common stock is:

$$r_e = 0.00417 + 0.70(0.00917 - 0.00417) = 0.00767 \text{ per month}$$

which, on an annual basis translates to:

$$r_e = 0.00767 \times 12 = 9.20\%$$

What does this mean? It means that we expect the market as a whole to generate a return of 11% per year in the future, which is 6% above the expected risk-free rate. Our estimate suggests that investors require a return of 9.2% per year on Du Pont stock, since Du Pont stock is less risky than the market as a whole.

Reconciling the Two Estimates   The different models produced different estimates for the cost of common stock:

CAPM: $r_e = 9.2\%$ per year   DVM: $r_e = 4.04\%$ per year.

This is expected since we are approaching the estimate from different paths. The CAPM evaluates the cost assuming investors hold diversified portfolios and are only concerned about market risk. The DVM evaluates the cost assuming a particular pattern of dividends in the future. Moreover, the different approaches of these two models require us to make certain estimates along the way.

So which approach is better? The one that provides the best estimate for the cost of common stock. Which does that? It's the model that fits our firm's situation better than the other. To determine the better fit in the case of Du Pont, we could ask ourselves:

- Do dividends grow at approximately a constant rate?
- Do changes in the market return tend to explain movements in the common stock's returns?

Du Pont's dividends do not appear to grow at a constant rate, at least when we look at them over a broad period, as shown in Exhibit 11.9. But Du Pont's common stock returns do tend to be explained by movements in the market's return. We can see this in Exhibit 11.10, where the points that represent Du Pont stock return in relation to the market's return tend to be clustered around the regression line, telling us that the market return does explain some portion of the returns on Du Pont's stock.

The answers to these questions—the growth in dividends and the fit of the regression line—tell us to rely more heavily on the CAPM model in estimating the cost of equity for Du Pont rather than on the DVM model. Therefore, we will use the cost of equity from our CAPM analysis to estimate our marginal cost of capital.

Step 3: Put It All Together

Using the market value weights of capital, we estimate the marginal cost of capital for Du Pont as:

Source of Capital	Weight	Marginal Cost	Weight times Cost
Debt	13.4%	4.55%	0.00610
Preferred stock	0.3	6.00	0.00018
Common stock	86.3	9.20	0.07940
Weighted average cost of capital			0.08568 or 8.568% per year

We estimate the cost of capital for Du Pont to be 8.568% per year. In other words, if Du Pont raises additional capital, we estimate that the cost of this additional capital will be 8.568% per year.

Final Considerations

The calculations we made to determine the cost of capital can mislead us into thinking that the result we obtain is precise. Rather, what we get is a ball-park estimate. Our estimate is accompanied by a number of limitations:

- **We get different estimates of the marginal cost of capital using different costs of components.** For example, we get a cost of capital of 4.115% instead of 8.568% if we use the DVM instead of the CAPM. Each model relies on different assumptions.
- **We get different estimates of the marginal cost of capital using different weights.** For example if we used book weights instead of market weights, the cost of capital is 8.6%, instead of 10.02%.[7] Also, if we look at the change in the capital structure over time, we see that Du

---

[7] Using book value weights,

Source of Capital	Weight	Marginal Cost	Weight times Cost
Debt	32.9%	4.55%	0.01497
Preferred stock	1.3	6.00	0.00078
Common stock	65.8	9.20	0.06054
Weighted average cost of capital			0.07629

Pont is using more debt in recent years, so we may wish to use a greater proportion for debt.

■ *Flotation costs must be considered.* We have ignored flotation costs, but these could be substantial, especially if we are raising a large proportion of common equity capital.

■ *Changes in costs for different levels of capital need to be considered.* There may be quite a difference in the cost of capital if Du Pont raised, say $2 billion versus $20 billion in new capital.

The cost of capital of 8.568% is an estimate. With all the assumptions and judgment that go into this figure, we at least have a starting point—an estimate of the cost of capital. Knowing more about Du Pont's target capital structure, future dividend plans, and flotation costs would help us refine our estimate, providing a more useful figure for decision-making.

SUMMARY

■ The cost of capital is the marginal cost of raising additional funds. This cost is important in our investment decision-making because we ultimately want to compare the cost of funds with the benefits from investing these funds.

■ The cost of capital is determined in three steps: (1) determine what proportions of each source of capital we intend to use; (2) calculate the cost of each source of capital; and (3) put the cost and the proportions together to determine the weighted average cost of capital.

■ The required rate of return on debt is the yield demanded by investors to compensate them for the time value of money and the risk they bear in lending their money. The cost of debt to the firm differs from this required rate of return due to: (1) flotation costs, and (2) the tax benefit from the deductibility of interest expense. The cost after flotation costs is called the all-in-cost of debt.

■ The required rate of return on preferred stock is the yield demanded by investors and differs from the firm's cost of preferred stock because of the costs of issuing additional shares (the flotation costs).

■ The required rate of return on common stock is more difficult to estimate than the cost of debt or preferred stock because of the nature of the return on stock: Dividends are not guaranteed nor fixed in amount, and part of the return is from the change in the value of the stock.

■ The dividend valuation method and the capital asset pricing model are two methods commonly used to estimate the required rate of return on common stock. The DVM deals with the expected dividend yield and is based on an assumption that dividends grow at some constant rate into the future. The CAPM assumes that investors hold diversified portfolios, so they require compensation for the time value of money and the market risk they bear by owning the stock.

■ The proportion of each source of capital that we use in calculating the cost of capital is based on what proportions we expect when the firm raises new capital. If the firm already has a capital structure—a mix of debt and equity it feels is appropriate—then that same proportion of each source of capital, in market value terms, is a good estimate of the proportions of new capital.

■ The cost of capital is the cost of raising new capital. The weighted average cost of capital is the cost of all new capital for a given level of financing. The cost of capital is a *marginal* cost—the cost of an additional dollar of new capital at a given level of financing.

■ In determining the optimal amount to spend on investments, the relevant cost is the marginal cost, since we are interested in investing until the marginal cost of the funds is equal to the marginal benefit from our investment. The point where marginal cost equals marginal benefit results in the optimal capital budget.

■ The actual estimation of the cost of capital for a firm requires a bit of educated guesswork, and lots of reasonable assumptions. Using readily available financial data, we can, at least, arrive at a good enough estimate of the cost of capital.

QUESTIONS

1. Why does the cost of debt differ from the required rate of return on debt for the same firm?
2. a. How does a change in the corporate tax rates affect the cost of debt?
   b. In particular, how would an increase in the corporate tax rate affect the cost of debt?
3. What is the difference between the required rate of return on common stock and the cost of common stock?
4. a. Why is it that there is a cost to the firm for internally generated capital?
   b. Why does the cost of externally generated equity capital differ from the cost of internally generated equity capital?
5. Why is it that, for a given firm, the required rate of return on equity is greater than the required rate of return on debt?
6. Why are market value proportions preferred to book value proportions in the calculation of the weighted average cost of capital?

7. List at least three problems that are encountered in calculating the cost of capital for an actual firm.

8. a. List at least two drawbacks associated with the Dividend Valuation Model in the calculation of the cost of common stock.

   b. List at least two drawbacks associated with the Capital Asset Pricing Model in the calculation of the cost of common stock.

9. If both the Dividend Valuation Model and the Capital Asset Pricing Model produce estimates of the cost of common stock, how is it possible to end up with two different numerical estimates?

10. a. What are flotation costs?

    b. Explain how flotation costs affect the cost of capital.

11. The Athens Airline Company has consulted with its investment bankers and determined that they could issue new debt with a yield of 8%. If Athens' marginal tax rate is 40%, what is the after-tax cost of debt to Athens?

12. The Oshkosh Travel Company is considering issuing additional debt. They wish to use the yield on their existing debt as a guide to the cost of new debt. They currently have a 5% coupon bond, paying interest semiannually, that matures in ten years and has a current market price of 80, or $800 per $1,000 face value bond. If Oshkosh's marginal tax rate is 30%, what is their expected cost of new debt?

13. The Richardson Oil Company is considering issuing additional debt. They wish to use the yield on their existing debt as a guide to the cost of new debt. They currently have a zero-coupon bond outstanding that has five years to maturity and a current market price of 74⅞, or $747.50 per $1,000 par value.

    a. If Richardson's marginal tax rate is 20%, what is the cost of debt?

    b. If Richardson's marginal tax rate is 30%, what is the cost of debt?

14. The Oxford Company is evaluating its financing strategy. They estimate that they can sell an issue of $50 par value preferred stock that has a dividend rate of 6% (with dividends paid at the end of each year).

    a. What is the cost of preferred stock if the they sell the issue at par value with no flotation costs?

    b. What is the all-in-cost of preferred stock if they sell the issue at par value with flotation costs of $3 per share?

    c. What is the all-in-cost of preferred stock if they sell the issue at par value with flotation costs of 1% of par value?

    d. What is the cost of preferred stock if they sell the issue at $52 per share and incur no flotation costs?

    e. What is the all-in-cost of preferred stock if they sell the issue at $52 per share and incur flotation costs of $1 per share?

15. The Bloomington Flower Corporation is evaluating its cost of fixed-rate perpetual preferred stock. Bloomington's management believes that it can issue new preferred stock at yields close that of its outstanding preferred stock issues. There are three outstanding preferred stock issues, which we will identify as A, B, and C. The following information has been gathered on these issues:

Issue	Dividend per Share	Current Market Price per Share
A	$3.00	$35¼
B	$2.50	$29½
C	$4.50	$52⅞

Assume, for simplicity, that dividends are paid at the end of each year.
a. What is the current yield on each of these preferred stock issues?
b. What would you recommend as the expected yield on preferred stock?

16. The Clemson Cat Supply Company is considering issuing new stock and is requesting your assistance in evaluating the cost of common stock. The current dividend per share is $2.00 and the current price of the stock is $40 per share. The management of Clemson expects dividends to grow at a rate of 10% per year for the foreseeable future. Using the Dividend Valuation Model, what is the cost of common stock to Clemson?

17. The Charlotte Honey Company is considering issuing new stock and is evaluating its cost of equity capital. Charlotte expects a risk-free rate of interest of 5% and a return on the market of 12%.
a. If Charlotte's common stock has a beta of 1.0, what is the expected cost of common stock using the Capital Asset Pricing Model?
b. If Charlotte's common stock has a beta of 2.0, what is the expected cost of common stock using the Capital Asset Pricing Model?
c. If Charlotte's common stock has a beta of 3.0, what is the expected cost of common stock using the Capital Asset Pricing Model?

18. Yellowjacket Honey, Inc. is evaluating its cost of capital under alternative financing arrangements. In consultation with investment bankers, Yellowjacket, Inc., expects to be able to issue new debt at par with a coupon rate of 10% and to issue new preferred stock with a $4.00 per share dividend at $25 a share. The common stock of Yellowjacket is currently selling for $20.00 a share. Yellowjacket expects

to pay a dividend of $2.50 per share next year. Market analysts foresee a growth in dividends in Invest stock at a rate of 5% per year. Invest does not expect its cost of debt, preferred stock or common stock, to be different under the two possible financing arrangements. Yellowjacket's marginal tax rate is 40%.

The two arrangements are:

	Percentage of New Capital Raised		
Financing Arrangement	Debt	Preferred Stock	Common Stock
1	20%	30%	50%
2	50%	30%	20%

What is the cost of capital to Yellowjacket Honey, Inc., under each financing arrangement?

19. The Walla Walla Washing Company has a capital structure comprised of 40% debt and 60% equity. If the required rate of return on debt is 10% and the cost of common stock is 16%, what is the cost of capital to Walla Walla if there are no flotation costs and:
    a. the marginal tax rate on corporate income is 40%?
    b. the marginal tax rate on corporate income is 60%?

20. The Stillwater Corporation is evaluating its marginal cost of capital schedule. They presently do not use debt or preferred stock in their capital structure and do not plan to do so in the foreseeable future. Stillwater paid $3.00 in dividends per share on its common stock this year. They expect the dividend to grow at a constant rate of 5% per year into the future. The current price of Stillwater common stock is $30 per share. If they issue new stock, they expect to incur a flotation cost of $1 per share. They expect to generate retained earnings of $1,000,000 during the next period.
    a. If they raise $1,000,000, what is the weighted average cost of capital?
    b. If they raise $2,000,000, what is the weighted average cost of capital?
    c. At what level of new financing does the cost of equity change?

21. The UM Company is evaluating its marginal cost of capital. In consultation with their investment bankers, they have determined that the cost of raising new debt and equity is as follows:

Amount of New Debt Capital	Cost
$1 to $1,000,000	5%
$1,000,001 to $2,000,000	7%

$2,000,000 and above	9%

Amount of New Equity Capital	Cost
$1 to $3,000,000	10%
$3,000,001 to $6,000,000	12%
$6,000,001 and above	14%

Any new capital that UM raises will be in the proportions of 40% debt and 60% equity.

a. What is the marginal cost of capital if UM raises $1,000,000 new capital? How much of this new capital is debt? How much of this new capital is equity?

b. Calculate the marginal cost of capital schedule, determining the level and cost at each break-point in the schedule.

22. The Donaldson Corporation is a food processor, producing canned vegetables that are sold to food service companies. The sales and costs of goods sold of the Donaldson Corporation are seasonal, reflecting the seasonality of the primary product line, processed vegetables. Donaldson's capital structure consists of 40% debt and 60% equity. There are 50,100 common shares outstanding as of the end of the most recent fiscal year. The common stock is traded on a national securities market, with a current price (that is, at the end of 2003) of $35 per share.

23. Dividends per share, DPS, over the past ten years, 1994–2003 are as follows:

Year	DPS	Year	DPS
1994	$1.20	1999	$1.36
1995	1.20	2000	1.43
1996	1.25	2001	1.50
1997	1.25	2002	1.59
1998	1.30	2003	1.68

24. Earnings are expected to grow at a rate of 6% for the next three to five years. The returns on Donaldson common stock and those of the market for each of the past 24 months are:

Month	Return on Donaldson Stock	Return on the Market	Month	Return on Donaldson Stock	Return on the Market
1/02	+1.0%	+1.5%	1/03	+1.2%	+2.0%
2/02	+0.5	+0.75	2/03	+0.5	+0.8
3/02	−0.5	−0.70	3/03	−0.5	−0.7
4/02	+0.5	+0.7	4/03	+0.5	+0.7
5/02	−0.3	−0.3	5/03	−0.2	−0.3
6/02	+0.2	+0.1	6/03	+0.1	+0.1
7/02	+0.1	+0.1	7/03	+0.1	+0.1
8/02	−0.1	−0.5	8/03	−0.1	−0.4
9/02	0.0	+0.1	9/03	0.0	+0.1
10/02	−0.1	−0.2	10/03	−0.1	−0.1
11/02	+0.2	+0.1	11/03	+0.2	+0.1
12/02	−0.1	−0.1	12/03	−0.1	0.0

Donaldson's management is interested in calculating the firm's cost of capital. A key ingredient in this cost is the cost of equity.

a. Estimate the cost of equity capital for the Donaldson Corporation using the dividend valuation model. List all assumptions.

b. Estimate the cost of equity capital for the Donaldson Corporation using the capital asset pricing model. List all assumptions.

c. Which model is most appropriate in estimating Donaldson's cost of equity? Support your choice.

Three

Long-Term Investment Decisions

CHAPTER **12**

Capital Budgeting: Cash Flows

The value of a particular asset isn't always easy to determine. However, managers are continually faced with decisions about which assets to invest in. In this chapter, we will look at the different types of investment decisions the financial manager faces. We will also discuss ways to estimate the benefits and costs associated with these decisions.

The financial manager's objective is to maximize owners' wealth. To accomplish this, the manager must evaluate investment opportunities and determine which ones will add value to the firm. For example, consider three firms, Firms A, B and C, each having identical assets and investment opportunities, but that:

- Firm A's management does not take advantage of its investment opportunities and simply pays all of its earnings to its owners;
- Firm B's management only makes those investments necessary to replace deteriorating plant and equipment, paying out any leftover earnings to its owners; and
- Firm C's management invests in all those opportunities that provide a return better than what the owners could have earned if they had invested the funds themselves.

In the case of Firm A, the owners' investment in the firm will not be as profitable as it would be if the firm had taken advantage of better investment opportunities. By failing to invest even to replace deteriorating plant and equipment, Firm A will eventually shrink until it has no more assets. Firm B's management is not taking advantage of all profitable investments. This means that there are forgone opportunities, and owners' wealth is not maximized. But Firm C's management is making all profitable investments and is thus maximizing owners' wealth. Firm

C will continue to grow as long as there are profitable investment opportunities and its management takes advantage of them.

In this chapter, we will describe the process of making investment decisions. We will look at estimating how much a firm's cash flows will change in the future as a result of an investment decision. The main topic of this chapter, estimating cash flow, is an imprecise art at best. Therefore, after we describe in detail a method for estimating cash flows, including two integrative examples, we will explain some ways in which managers sometimes deviate from the ideal method in actual practice.

In the next chapter, Chapter 13, we will analyze the change in the firm's cash flows using techniques that lead the financial manager to a decision regarding whether to invest in a project. In Chapter 14, we see how uncertainty affects the cost of capital and, hence, the investment decision.

THE INVESTMENT PROBLEM

Firms continually invest funds in assets and these assets produce income and cash flows that the firm can then either reinvest in more assets or pay to the owners. These assets represent the firm's capital. *Capital* is the firm's total assets. It includes all tangible and intangible assets. These assets include physical assets (such as land, buildings, equipment, and machinery), as well as assets that represent property rights (such as accounts receivable, securities, patents, copyrights). When we refer to *capital investment*, we are referring to the firm's investment in its assets.

The term "capital" also has come to mean the funds used to finance the firm's assets. In this sense, capital consists of notes, bonds, stock, and short-term financing. We use the term "capital structure" to refer to the mix of these different sources of capital used to finance a firm's assets.

The firm's capital investment decision may be comprised of a number of distinct decisions, each referred to as a project. A *capital project* is a set of assets that are contingent on one another and are considered together. For example, suppose a firm is considering the production of a new product. This capital project would require the firm to acquire land, build facilities, and purchase production equipment. And this project may also require the firm to increase its investment in its *working capital*—inventory, cash, or accounts receivable. Working capital is the collection of assets needed for day-to-day operations that support a firm's long-term investments.

The investment decisions of the firm are decisions concerning a firm's capital investment. When we refer to a particular decision that financial managers must make, we are referring to a decision pertaining to a capital project.

Investment Decisions and Owners' Wealth Maximization

Managers must evaluate a number of factors in making investment decisions. Not only does the financial manager need to estimate how much the firm's future cash flows will change if it invests in a project, but the manager also must evaluate the uncertainty associated with these future cash flows.

We already know that the value of the firm today is the present value of all its future cash flows. But we need to understand better where these future cash flows come from. They come from:

■ assets that are already in place, which are the assets accumulated as a result of all past investment decisions, and
■ future investment opportunities.

The value of the firm is therefore,

Value of firm = Present value of all future cash flows
= Present value of cash flows from all assets in place
+ Present value of cash flows from future investment opportunities

Future cash flows are discounted at a rate that represents investors' assessments of the uncertainty that these cash flows will flow in the amounts and the timeframe expected. To evaluate the value of the firm, we need to evaluate the risk of these future cash flows.

Cash flow risk comes from two basic sources:

■ *Sales risk*, which is the degree of uncertainty related to the number of units that will be sold and the price of the good or service; and
■ *Operating risk*, which is the degree of uncertainty concerning operating cash flows that arises from the particular mix of fixed and variable operating costs.

Sales risk is related to the economy and the market in which the firm's goods and services are sold. Operating risk, for the most part, is determined by the product or service that the firm provides and is related to the sensitivity of operating cash flows to changes in sales. We refer to the combination of these two risks as *business risk*.

A project's business risk is reflected in the discount rate, which is the rate of return required to compensate the suppliers of capital (bondholders and owners) for the amount of risk they bear. From the perspective of investors, the discount rate is the *required rate of return* (RRR). From the firm's perspective, the discount rate is the *cost of capital*— what it costs the firm to raise a dollar of new capital.

For example, suppose a firm invests in a new project. How does the investment affect the firm's value? If the project generates cash flows that *just* compensate the suppliers of capital for the risk they bear on this project (that is, it earns the cost of capital), the value of the firm does not change. If the project generates cash flows *greater* than needed to compensate them for the risk they take on, it earns more than the cost of capital, increasing the value of the firm. If the project generates cash flows *less* than needed, it earns less than the cost of capital, decreasing the value of the firm.

How do we know whether the cash flows are more than or less than needed to compensate for the risk that they will indeed need? If we discount all the cash flows at the cost of capital, we can assess how this project affects the present value of the firm. If the expected change in the value of the firm from an investment is:

- positive, the project returns more than the cost of capital;
- negative, the project returns less than the cost of capital;
- zero, the project returns the cost of capital.

Capital budgeting is the process of identifying and selecting investments in long-lived assets, or assets expected to produce benefits over more than one year. In Chapter 13, we discuss how to evaluate cash flows in deciding whether or not to invest. We cover how to determine cash flow risk and factor this risk into capital budgeting decisions in Chapter 14.

CAPITAL BUDGETING

Because a firm must continually evaluate possible investments, capital budgeting is an ongoing process. However, before a firm begins thinking about capital budgeting, it must first determine its *corporate strategy*— its broad set of objectives for future investment. For example, the Quantum Corporation's goal is to "... be the leading mass storage company in the world....In order for Quantum to achieve our goals, we must build and maintain leadership positions in all of our businesses—in profitability, as well as in market share."[1]

Consider the corporate strategy of Mattel, Inc., manufacturer of toys such as Barbie and Disney toys. Mattel's strategy is to become a full-line toy company and grow through expansion into the international toy market. In the early 1990s, Mattel entered into the activity toy, games, and plush toy markets, and, through acquisitions in Mexico, France, and

---

[1] *Quantum Corporation 1996 Annual Report*, pp. 4–5.

Japan, increased its presence in the international toy market.[2] By 2001, Mattel generated over 30% of its revenues from its non-U.S. sales.[3]

How does a firm achieve its corporate strategy? By making investments in long-lived assets that will maximize owners' wealth. Selecting these projects is what capital budgeting is all about.

Stages in the Capital Budgeting Process

There are five stages in the capital budgeting process.

Stage 1: *Investment screening and selection*
Projects consistent with the corporate strategy are identified by production, marketing, and research and development management of the firm. Once identified, projects are evaluated and screened by estimating how they affect the future cash flows of the firm and, hence, the value of the firm.

Stage 2: *Capital budget proposal*
A capital budget is proposed for the projects surviving the screening and selection process. The budget lists the recommended projects and the dollar amount of investment needed for each. This proposal may start as an estimate of expected revenues and costs, but as the project analysis is refined, data from marketing, purchasing, engineering, accounting, and finance functions are put together.

Stage 3: *Budgeting approval and authorization*
Projects included in the capital budget are authorized, allowing further fact gathering and analysis, and approved, allowing expenditures for the projects. In some firms, the projects are authorized and approved at the same time. In others, a project must first be authorized, requiring more research before it can be formally approved. Formal authorization and approval procedures are typically used on larger expenditures; smaller expenditures are at the discretion of management.

Stage 4: *Project tracking*
After a project is approved, work on it begins. The manager reports periodically on its expenditures, as well as on any revenues associated with it. This is referred to as **project tracking**, the communication link between the decision makers and the operating management of the firm. For example: tracking can identify cost overruns and uncover the need for more marketing research.

---

[2] *Mattel, Inc., 1991 Annual Report*, pp. 4–5, 15.
[3] *Mattel, Inc., 2001 Annual Report*, p.11.

Stage 5: *Post-completion audit*

Following a period of time, perhaps two or three years after approval, projects are reviewed to see whether they should be continued. This re-evaluation is referred to as a *post-completion audit*. Thorough post-completion audits are typically performed on selected projects, usually the largest projects in a given year's budget for the firm or for each division. Post-completion audits show the firm's management how well the cash flows realized correspond with the cash flows forecasted several years earlier.

Classifying Investment Projects

In this section, we discuss different ways managers classify capital investment projects. One way of classifying projects is by project life, whether short-term or long-term. We do this because in the case of long-term projects, the time value of money plays an important role in long-term projects. Another way of classifying projects is by their risk. The riskier the project's future cash flows, the greater the role of the cost of capital in decision-making. Still another way of classifying projects is by their dependence on other projects. The relationship between a project's cash flows and the cash flows of some other project of the firm must be incorporated explicitly into the analysis since we want to analyze how a project affects the total cash flows of the firm.

Classification According to Their Economic Life

An investment generally provides benefits over a limited period of time, referred to as its economic life. The *economic life* or *useful life* of an asset is determined by:

■ physical deterioration;
■ obsolescence; or
■ the degree of competition in the market for a product.

The economic life is an estimate of the length of time that the asset will provide benefits to the firm. After its useful life, the revenues generated by the asset tend to decline rapidly and its expenses tend to increase.

Typically, an investment requires an immediate expenditure and provides benefits in the form of cash flows received in the future. If benefits are received only within the current period—within one year of making the investment—we refer to the investment as a *short-term investment*. If these benefits are received beyond the current period, we refer to the investment as a *long-term investment* and refer to the expenditure as a *capital expenditure*. An investment project may comprise one or more capital expenditures. For example, a new product may require investment in production equipment, a building, and transportation equipment.

Short-term investment decisions involve, primarily, investments in current assets: cash, marketable securities, accounts receivable, and inventory. The objective of investing in short-term assets is the same as long-term assets: maximizing owners' wealth. Nevertheless, we consider them separately for two practical reasons:

1. Decisions about long-term assets are based on projections of cash flows far into the future and require us to consider the time value of money.
2. Long-term assets do not figure into the daily operating needs of the firm.

Decisions regarding short-term investments, or current assets, are concerned with day-to-day operations. And a firm needs some level of current assets to act as a cushion in case of unusually poor operating periods when cash flows from operations are less than expected.

Classification According to Their Risk

Suppose you are faced with two investments, A and B, each promising a $100 cash inflow ten years from today. If A is riskier than B, what are they worth to you today? If you do not like risk, you would consider A less valuable than B because the chance of getting the $100 in ten years is less for A than for B. Therefore, valuing a project requires considering the risk associated with its future cash flows.

The investment's risk of return can be classified according to the nature of the project represented by the investment:

- *Replacement projects:* investments in the replacement of existing equipment or facilities.
- *Expansion projects:* investments in projects that broaden existing product lines and existing markets.
- *New products and markets:* projects that involve introducing a new product or entering into a new market.
- *Mandated projects:* projects required by government laws or agency rules.

Replacement projects include the maintenance of existing assets to continue the current level of operating activity. Projects that reduce costs, such as replacing old equipment or improving the efficiency, are also considered replacement projects. To evaluate replacement projects we need to compare the value of the firm with the replacement asset to the value of the firm without that same replacement asset. What we're really doing in this comparison is looking at *opportunity costs*: what cash flows would have been if the firm had stayed with the old asset.

There's little risk in the cash flows from replacement projects. The firm is simply replacing equipment or buildings already operating and producing cash flows. And the firm typically has experience in managing similar new equipment.

Expansion projects, which are intended to enlarge a firm's established product or market, also involve little risk. However, investment projects that involve introducing new products or entering into new markets are riskier because the firm has little or no management experience in the new product or market.

A firm is forced or coerced into its mandated projects. These are government-mandated projects typically found in "heavy" industries, such as utilities, transportation, and chemicals, all industries requiring a large portion of their assets in production activities. Government agencies, such as the Occupational Health and Safety Agency (OSHA) or the Environmental Protection Agency (EPA), may impose requirements that firms install specific equipment or alter their activities (such as how they dispose of waste).

We can further classify mandated projects into two types: contingent and retroactive. Suppose, as a steel manufacturer, we are required by law to include pollution control devices on all smoke stacks. If we are considering a new plant, this mandated equipment is really part of our new plant investment decision—the investment in pollution control equipment is contingent on our building the new plant.

On the other hand, if we are required by law to place pollution control devices on existing smoke stacks, the law is retroactive. We do not have a choice. We must invest in the equipment whether it increases the value of the firm or not. In this case we either select from among possible equipment that satisfies the mandate, or we weigh the decision whether to halt production in the offending plant.

Classification According to Their Dependence on Other Projects

In addition to considering the future cash flows generated by a project, a firm must consider how it affects the assets already in place—the results of previous project decisions—as well as other projects that may be undertaken. Projects can be classified as follows according to the degree of dependence with other projects: independent projects, mutually exclusive projects, contingent projects, and complementary projects.

An ***independent project*** is one whose cash flows are not related to the cash flows of any other project. Accepting or rejecting an independent project does not affect the acceptance or rejection of other projects. Projects are ***mutually exclusive*** if the acceptance of one precludes the acceptance of other projects. For example, suppose a manufacturer is considering whether to replace its production facilities with more modern equipment. The firm may solicit bids among the different manufacturers of this equipment. The decision consists of comparing two choices, either keeping its existing production facilities or replacing the facilities with the modern equipment of one manufacturer. Because the firm cannot use more than one production facility, it must evaluate each bid and choose the most attractive one. The alternative production facilities are mutually exclusive projects: the firm can accept only one bid.

Contingent projects are dependent on the acceptance of another project. Suppose a greeting card company develops a new character, Pippy, and is considering starting a line of Pippy cards. If Pippy catches on, the firm will consider producing a line of Pippy T-shirts—but *only* if the Pippy character becomes popular. The T-shirt project is a contingent project.

Another form of dependence is found in ***complementary projects***, where the investment in one enhances the cash flows of one or more other projects. Consider a manufacturer of personal computer equipment and software. If it develops new software that enhances the abilities of a computer mouse, the introduction of this new software may enhance its mouse sales as well.

CASH FLOW FROM INVESTMENTS

A firm invests only to increase the value of their ownership interest. A firm will have cash flows in the future from its past investment decisions. When it invests in new assets, it expects the future cash flows to be *greater than without this new investment.*

Incremental Cash Flows

The difference between the cash flows of the firm *with* the investment project and the cash flows of the firm *without* the investment project—both over the same period of time—is referred to as the project's ***incremental cash flows.***

To evaluate an investment, we'll have to look at how it will change the future cash flows of the firm, and, hence, the value of the firm.

The change in a firm's value as a result of a new investment is the difference between its benefits and its costs:

Project's change in the value of the firm = Project's benefits − Project's costs

A more useful way of evaluating the change in the value is the breakdown of the project's cash flows into two components:

1. The present value of the cash flows from the project's operating activities (revenues minus operating expenses), referred to as the project's *operating cash flows* (OCF); and
2. The present value of the *investment cash flows*, which are the expenditures needed to acquire the project's assets and any cash flows from disposing the project's assets.

or,

Change in the value of the firm
= Present value of the change in operating cash flows provided by the project
+ Present value of investment cash flows

The present value of a project's operating cash flows is typically positive (indicating predominantly cash inflows) and the present value of the investment cash flows is typically negative (indicating predominantly cash outflows).

Investment Cash Flows

When we consider the cash flows of an investment we must also consider all the cash flows associated with acquiring and disposing of assets in the investment. Let's first become familiar with cash flows related to acquiring assets; then we'll look at cash flows related to disposing of assets.

Asset Acquisition

In acquiring any asset, there are three types of cash flows to consider:

1. Cost of the asset,
2. Set-up expenditures, including shipping and installation; and
3. Any tax credit.

The tax credit may be an investment tax credit or a special credit—such as a credit for a pollution control device—depending on the prevailing tax law.

Cash flow associated with acquiring an asset is:

Cash flow from acquiring assets = Cost + Set-up expenditures − Tax credit

Suppose the firm buys equipment that costs $100,000 and it costs $10,000 to install it. If the firm is eligible for a 10% tax credit on this equipment (that is, 10% of the total cost of buying and installing the equipment) the change in the firm's cash flow from acquiring the asset of $99,000 is as follows:

Cash flow from acquiring assets
= $100,000 + $10,000 − 0.10($100,000 + $10,000)
= $100,000 + $10,000 − $11,000 = $99,000

The cash outflow is $99,000 when this asset is acquired: $110,000 *out* to buy and install the equipment and $11,000 *in* from the reduction in taxes.

What about expenditures made in the past for assets or research that would be used in the project we're evaluating? Suppose the firm spent $1,000,000 over the past three years developing a new type of toothpaste. Should the firm consider this $1,000,000 spent on research and development when deciding whether to produce this new project we are considering? No: These expenses have already been made and do not affect how the new product changes the future cash flows of the firm. We refer to this $1,000,000 as a **sunk cost** and do not consider it in the analysis of our new project. Whether or not the firm goes ahead with this new product, this $1,000,000 has been spent. A sunk cost is any cost that has already been incurred that does not affect future cash flows of the firm.

Let's consider another example. Suppose the firm owns a building that is currently empty. Let's say the firm suddenly has an opportunity to use it for the production of a new product. Is the cost of the building relevant to the new product decision? The cost of the building itself is a sunk cost since it was an expenditure made as part of some *previous* investment decision. The cost of the building does not affect the decision to go ahead with the new product.

We have assumed that the building is empty and there is no opportunity to sell the building. In this case, the building's cost is truly a sunk cost. But if the company intended to sell the building, instead of leaving it empty, the foregone sales price of the building is an opportunity cost associated with the new product.

Suppose the firm was using the building in some way producing cash (say, renting it) and the new project is going to take over the entire building. The cash flows given up represent opportunity costs that must be included in the analysis of the new project. However, these forgone cash flows are not asset acquisition cash flows. Because they represent operating cash flows that could have occurred but will not because of the new project, they must be considered part of the project's future operating cash flows.

Further, if we incur costs in renovating the building to manufacture the new product, the renovation costs are relevant and should be included in our asset acquisition cash flows.

Asset Disposition

At the end of the useful life of an asset, the firm may be able to sell it or may have to pay someone to haul it away. If the firm is making a decision that involves replacing an existing asset, the cash flow from disposing of the old asset must be figured in since it is a cash flow relevant to the acquisition of the new asset.

If the firm disposes of an asset, whether at the end of its useful life or when it is replaced, two types of cash flows must be considered:

1. what you receive or pay in disposing of the asset; and
2. any tax consequences resulting from the disposal.

> Cash flow from disposing assets
> = Proceeds or payment from disposing assets
> − Taxes from disposing assets

The proceeds are what you expect to sell the asset for if you can get someone to buy it. If the firm must pay for the disposal of the asset, this cost is a cash outflow.

Consider the investment in a gas station. The current owner wants to sell the station to another gas station proprietor. But if a buyer cannot be found and the station abandoned, the current owner may be required to remove the underground gasoline storage tanks to prevent environmental damage. Thus, a cost is incurred at the end of the asset's life.

The tax consequences are a bit more complicated. Taxes depend on: (1) the expected sales price, (2) the book value of the asset for tax purposes at the time of disposition, and (3) the tax rate at the time of disposal.

If a firm sells the asset for more than its book value but less than its original cost, the difference between the sales price and the book value for tax purposes (called the *tax basis*) is a gain, taxable at ordinary tax rates. If a firm sells the asset for more than its original cost, then the gain is broken into two parts:

1. *Capital gain*: the difference between the sales price and the original cost; and
2. *Recapture of depreciation*: the difference between the original cost and the tax basis.

The *capital gain* is the benefit from the appreciation in the value of the asset and may be taxed at special rates, depending on the tax law at the time of sale. The *recapture of depreciation* represents the amount by which the firm has *over*depreciated the asset during its life. This means that more depreciation has been deducted from income (reducing taxes) than necessary to reflect the usage of the asset. The recapture portion is taxed at the ordinary tax rates, since the excess depreciation taken all these years has reduced taxable income.

If a firm sells an asset for less than its book value, the result is a *capital loss*. In this case, the asset's value has decreased by more than the amount taken for depreciation for tax purposes. A capital loss is given special tax treatment:

- If there are capital gains in the same tax year as the capital loss, they are combined, so that the capital loss reduces the taxes paid on capital gains, and
- If there are no capital gains to offset against the capital loss, the capital loss is used to reduce ordinary taxable income.

The benefit from a loss on the sale of an asset is the amount by which taxes are reduced. The reduction in taxable income is referred to as a *tax shield*, since the loss *shields* some income from taxation. If the firm has a loss of $1,000 on the sale of an asset and has a tax rate of 40%, this means that its taxable income is $1,000 less and its taxes are $400 less than they would have been without the sale of the asset.

Suppose you are evaluating an asset that costs $10,000 that you expect to sell in five years. Suppose further that the tax basis of the asset for tax purposes will be $3,000 after five years and that the firm's tax rate is 40%. What are the expected cash flows from disposing this asset?

If the firm expects to sell the asset for $8,000 in five years, $10,000 − $3,000 = $7,000 of the asset's cost will be depreciated; yet the asset lost only $10,000 − $8,000 = $2,000 in value. Therefore, the firm has overdepreciated the asset by $5,000. Because this overdepreciation represents deductions to be taken on the firm's tax returns over the five years that don't reflect the actual depreciation in value (the asset doesn't lose $7,000 in value, only $2,000), this $5,000 is taxed at ordinary tax rates. If the firm's tax rate is 40%, the tax will be 40% × $5,000 = $2,000.

The cash flow from disposition is the sum of the direct cash flow (someone pays us for the asset or the firm pays someone to dispose of it) and the tax consequences. In this example, the cash flow is the $8,000 we expect someone to pay the firm for the asset, less the $2,000 in taxes we expect the firm to pay, or $6,000 cash inflow.

Suppose instead that the firm expects to sell this asset in five years for $12,000. Again, the asset is overdepreciated by $7,000. In fact, the asset is not expected to depreciate, but rather *appreciate* over the five years. The $7,000 in depreciation is recaptured after five years and taxed at ordinary rates: 40% of $7,000, or $2,800. The $2,000 capital gain is the appreciation in the value of the asset and may be taxed at special rates. If the tax rate on capital gain income is 30%, you expect the firm to pay 30% of $2,000, or $600 in taxes on this gain. Selling the asset in five years for $12,000 therefore results in an expected cash inflow of $12,000 – $2,800 – $600 = $8,600.

Suppose the firm expects to sell the asset in five years for $1,000. If the firm can reduce its ordinary taxable income by the amount of the capital loss, $3,000 – $1,000 = $2,000, its tax bill will be 40% of $2,000, or $800 because of this loss. We refer to this reduction in the taxes as a tax shield, since the loss "shields" $2,000 of income from taxes. Combining the $800 tax reduction with the cash flow from selling the asset, the $1,000, gives the firm a cash inflow of $1,800.[4]

The calculation of the cash flow from disposition for the alternative sales prices of $8,000, $12,000, and $1,000 are shown in Exhibit 12.1.

EXHIBIT 12.1   Expected Cash Flows from the Disposition of an Asset

The firm pays $10,000 for an asset and expects to dispose of it in five years, when the asset has a book value of $3,000. The firm's ordinary tax rate is 40% and the tax rate on capital gains is 30%.

Original cost > Expected sales price > Tax Basis

Tax on disposition:

Sales price	$8,000
Tax basis	3,000
Gain	$5,000
Ordinary tax rate	0.40
Tax on recapture	$2,000

Cash flows:

Proceeds from disposition	$8,000
Less tax on gain	2,000
Cash flow on disposition	$6,000

---

[4] On the other hand, if the firm expects other capital gains five years from now, the amount of the tax shield would be less since this loss would be used to first offset any capital gains taxed at 30%. In this case, the expected tax shield is only 30% of $2,000, or $600 because we must first use the capital loss to reduce any capital gains.

EXHIBIT 12.1 (Continued)

Expected sales price > Original cost > Tax basis

Tax on disposition:

Sales price	$12,000
Original cost	10,000
Capital gain	$2,000
Capital gains tax rate	0.30
Tax on capital gain	$600

Original cost	$10,000
Tax basis	3,000
Gain (recapture)	$7,000
Ordinary tax rate	0.40
Tax on recapture	$2,800

Cash flows:

Proceeds from disposition	$12,000
Less tax on capital gain	600
Less tax on recapture	2,800
Cash flow on disposition	$8,600

Tax basis > Expected sales price

Tax shield on disposition:

Book value	$3,000
Tax basis	1,000
Loss	$2,000
Ordinary tax rate	0.40
Tax shield on loss	$800

Cash flows:

Proceeds from disposition	$1,000
Plus tax shield on loss	800
Cash flow on disposition	$1,800

Let's also not forget about disposing of any existing assets. Suppose the firm bought equipment ten years ago and at that time expected to be able to sell it 15 years later for $10,000. If the firm decides *today* to replace this equipment, it must consider what it is giving up by *not* disposing of an asset *as planned*. If the firm does not replace the equipment today, it would continue to depreciate it for five more years and then sell it for $10,000; if the firm replaces the equipment today, it would not have five more years' depreciation on the replaced equipment and it would not have $10,000 in five years (but perhaps some other amount today). This $10,000 in five years, less any taxes, is a foregone cash flow that we must figure into the investment cash flows. Also, the depreciation the firm would have had on the replaced asset must be considered in analyzing the replacement asset's operating cash flows.

Operating Cash Flows

As we saw in the previous section, in the simplest form of investment there is a cash outflow when the asset is acquired and there may be either a cash inflow or an outflow at the end of its economic life. In most cases these are not the only cash flows—the investment may result in changes in revenues, expenditures, taxes, and working capital. These are *operating cash flows* since they result directly from the operating activities—the day-to-day activities of the firm.

What we are after here are *estimates* of operating cash flows. We cannot know for certain what these cash flows will be in the future, but we must attempt to estimate them. What is the basis for these estimates? We base them on marketing research, engineering analyses, operations research, analysis of our competitors—and our managerial experience.

Change in Revenues

Suppose you are a financial analyst for a food processor considering a new investment in a line of frozen dinner products. If you introduce a new ready-to-eat dinner product, your marketing research will indicate how much you should expect to sell. But where do these new product sales come from? Some may come from consumers who do not already buy ready-to-eat products. But some sales may come from consumers who choose to buy other types of ready-to-eat products. It would be nice if these consumers are giving up buying your competitors' ready-to-eat dinners. Yet some of them may be giving up buying your company's other ready-to-eat dinner products. So, when you introduce a new product, you are really interested in how it changes the sales of the entire firm (that is, the incremental sales), rather than the sales of the new product alone.

We also need to consider any foregone revenues—opportunity costs—related to an investment. Suppose a firm owns a building currently being rented to another firm. If we are considering terminating that rental agreement so we can use the building for a new project, we need to consider the foregone rent—what we would have earned from the building. Therefore, the revenues from the new project are really only the additional revenues—the revenues from the new project minus the revenue we could have earned from renting the building.

So, when a firm undertakes a new project, the financial managers want to know how it changes the firm's total revenues, not merely the new product's revenues.

Change in Expenses

When a firm takes on a new project, the costs associated with it will change the firm's expenses. If the investment changes the sales of an existing product, the decision maker must estimate the change in unit sales. Based on that estimate, the estimate of the additional costs of producing the additional number of units is derived by consulting with production management. In addition, an estimate of how the product's inventory may change when production and sales of the product change is also needed.

If the investment involves changes in the costs of production, we compare the costs without this investment with the costs with this investment. For example, if the investment is the replacement of an assembly line machine with a more efficient machine, we need to estimate the change in the firm's overall production costs such as electricity, labor, materials, and management costs.

A new investment may change not only production costs but also operating costs, such as rental payments and administration costs. Changes in operating costs as a result of a new investment must be considered as part of the changes in the firm's expenses.

Increasing cash expenses are cash outflows, and decreasing cash expenses are cash inflows.

Change in Taxes

Taxes figure into the operating cash flows in two ways. First, if revenues and expenses change, taxable income and therefore, taxes change. That means we need to estimate the change in taxable income resulting from the changes in revenues and expenses resulting from a new project to determine the effect of taxes on the firm.

Second, the deduction for depreciation reduces taxes. Depreciation itself is not a cash flow, but depreciation reduces the taxes that must be paid, shielding income from taxation. The tax shield from depreciation is like a cash inflow.

Suppose a firm is considering a new product that is expected to generate additional sales of $200,000 and increase expenses by $150,000. If the firm's tax rate is 40%, considering only the change in sales and expenses, taxes go up by $50,000 × 40% or $20,000. This means that the firm is expected to pay $20,000 more in taxes because of the increase in revenues and expenses.

Let's change this around and consider that the product will generate $200,000 in revenues and $250,000 in expenses. Considering only the change in revenues and expenses, if the tax rate is 40%, taxes go *down* by $50,000 × 40%, or $20,000.[5] This means that we reduce our taxes by $20,000, which is like having a cash inflow of $20,000 from taxes.

Now, consider depreciation. When a firm buys an asset that produces income, the tax laws allow it to depreciate the asset, reducing taxable income by a specified percentage of the asset's cost each year. By reducing taxable income, the firm is reducing its taxes. The reduction in taxes is like a cash inflow since it reduces the firm's cash outflow to the government.

Suppose a firm has taxable income of $50,000 before depreciation and a flat tax rate of 40%. If the firm is allowed to deduct depreciation of $10,000, how has this changed the taxes it pays?

	Without Depreciation	With Depreciation
Taxable income	$50,000	$40,000
Tax rate	0.40	0.40
Taxes	$20,000	$16,000

Depreciation *reduces* the firm's tax-related *cash outflow* by $20,000 − $16,000 = $4,000 or, equivalently, by $10,000 × 40% = $4,000. A reduction is an outflow (taxes in this case) is an inflow. We refer to the effect depreciation has on taxes as the *depreciation tax shield*.

Depreciation itself is not a cash flow. But in determining cash flows, we are concerned with the effect depreciation has on our taxes—and we all know that taxes are a cash outflow. Because depreciation reduces taxable income, depreciation reduces the tax outflow, which amounts to a cash inflow. For tax purposes, firms are permitted to use accelerated depreciation (specifically the rates specified under the Modified Accelerated Cost Recovery System [MACRS]) or straight-line. An accelerated method is preferred in most situations since it results in larger deductions

---

[5] This loss creates an immediate cash inflow *if* (1) the firm has other income in the same tax year to apply the $50,000 loss against, or (2) the firm has income in prior tax years so it can carry back this loss and apply for a refund of prior year's taxes. Otherwise, this loss is carried forward to reduce future tax years' income. In this case, this loss is worth less because the benefit from the loss (the reduction in taxable income) is realized in the future, not today.

sooner in the asset's life than using straight-line depreciation. Therefore, accelerated depreciation, if available, is preferable to straight-line due to the time value of money.

Under the present tax code, assets are depreciated to a zero book value. Salvage value—what we expect the asset to be worth at the end of its life—is not considered in calculating depreciation. So is salvage value totally irrelevant to the analysis? No. Salvage value is our best guess today of what the asset will be worth at the end of its useful life some time in the future. Salvage value is our estimate of how much we can get when we dispose of the asset. Just remember you can ignore it to figure depreciation for tax purposes.

Let's look at another depreciation example, this time considering the effects that replacing an asset has on the depreciation tax shield cash flow. Suppose you are replacing a machine that you bought five years ago for $75,000. You were depreciating this old machine using straight-line depreciation over ten years, or $7,500 depreciation per year. If you replace it with a new machine that costs $50,000 and is depreciated over five years, or $10,000 each year, how does the change in depreciation affect the cash flows if the firm's tax rate is 30%?

We can calculate the effect two ways:

1. We can compare the depreciation and related tax shield from the old and the new machines. The depreciation tax shield on the old machine is 30% of $7,500, or $2,250. The depreciation tax shield on the new machine is 30% of $10,000, or $3,000. Therefore, the change in the cash flow from depreciation is $3,000 – $2,250 = $750.
2. We can calculate the change in depreciation and calculate the tax shield related to the change in depreciation. The change in depreciation is $10,000 – 7,500 = $2,500. The change in the depreciation tax shield is 30% of $2,500, or $750.

Let's look at another example. Suppose a firm invests $50,000 in an asset. And suppose the firm has a choice of depreciating the asset using either:

- An accelerated method over four years, with the rates of 33.33%, 44.45%, 14.81%, and 7.41%, respectively, where these depreciation rates are a percentage of the original cost of the asset; or
- The straight-line method over four years.

If the firm's tax rate is 40% and the cost of capital is 10%, what is the present value of the difference in the cash flows from the depreciation tax shield each year? It is $796 as shown below:

Year	Depreciation Using the Accelerated Method	Depreciation Using the Straight-Line Method	Difference in Depreciation	Difference in Depreciation Tax Shield	Present Value of Difference
First	$16,665	$12,500	$4,165	$1,666	$1,515
Second	22,225	12,500	9,725	3,890	3,215
Third	7,405	12,500	−5,095	−2,038	−1,531
Fourth	3,705	12,500	−8,795	−3,518	−2,403
	$50,000	$50,000	$0	$0	$796

Using both the accelerated and straight-line methods, the entire asset's cost is depreciated over the four years. But the accelerated method provides greater tax shields in the first and second years than the straight-line method. Since larger depreciation tax shields are generated under the accelerated method in the earlier years, the present value of the tax shields using the accelerated method is more valuable than the present value of the tax shields using the straight-line method. How much more? $796.

Change in Working Capital

Working capital consists of short-term assets, also referred to as current assets, that support the day-to-day operating activity of the business. *Net working capital* is the difference between current assets and current liabilities. Net working capital is what would be left over if the firm had to pay off its current obligations using its current assets.

The adjustment we make for changes in net working capital is attributable to two sources:

1. A change in current asset accounts for transactions or precautionary needs; and
2. The use of the accrual method of accounting.

An investment may increase the firm's level of operations, resulting in an increase in the net working capital needed. If the investment is to produce a new product, the firm may have to invest more in inventory (raw materials, work-in-process, and finished goods). If increasing sales means extending more credit, then the firm's accounts receivable will increase. If the investment requires maintaining a higher cash balance to handle the increased level of transactions, the firm will need more cash. If the investment makes the firm's production facilities more efficient, it may be able to reduce the level of inventory.

Because of an increase in the level of transactions, the firm may want to keep more cash and inventory on hand. As the level of operations increase, the effect of any fluctuations in demand for goods and services may increase, requiring the firm to keep additional cash and inventory "just in case." The firm may also increase working capital as a precaution because if there is greater variability of cash and inventory, a greater safety cushion will be needed. On the other hand, if a project enables the firm to be more efficient or lowers costs, it may lower its investment in cash, marketable securities, or inventory, releasing funds for investment elsewhere.

We also use the change in working capital to adjust accounting income (revenues less expenses) to a cash basis because cash flow is ultimately what we are valuing, not accounting numbers. But since we generally have only the accounting numbers to work from, we use this information, making adjustments to arrive at cash.

To see how this works, let's look at the cash flow from sales. Not every dollar of sales is collected in the year of sale: Some customers may pay later. This means that the annual sales figure does not represent the cash inflow from sales, because some of these sales are collected in the next period. This also means that at the end of the year, there will be some accounts receivable from customers who have not paid yet.

For example, suppose you expect sales in the first year to increase by $20,000 per month and customers typically take 30 days to pay. The change in cash flow from sales in the first year is not $20,000 × 12 = $240,000, but rather $20,000 × 11 = $220,000 because one month's worth of sales has not been collected in cash by the end of the year. You adjust for the difference between what is sold and what is collected in cash by keeping track of the change in working capital, which in this case is the increase in accounts receivable, as shown below:

Change in revenues	$240,000
Less: increase in accounts receivable	20,000
Change in cash inflow from sales	$220,000

On the other side of the balance sheet, if the firm increases its purchases of raw materials and incurs higher production costs, such as labor, the firm may increase its level of short-term liabilities, such as accounts payable and salary and wages payable. Suppose expenses for materials and supplies are forecasted at $10,000 per month for the first year and it takes the firm 30 days to pay. Expenses for the first year are $10,000 × 12 = $120,000, yet cash outflow for these expenses is only $10,000 × 11 = $110,000. Accounts payable increases by $10,000, representing one month's of expenses. The increase in net working capital (increase in accounts payable ⇒ increases current liabilities ⇒ decreases net working capital) reduces the cost of goods sold to give us the cash outflow from expenses:

Cost of goods sold	$120,000
Less: increase in accounts payable	10,000
Change in cash flow for expenses	$110,000

A new project may have one of three effects on working capital: an increase, a decrease, or no change. Furthermore, working capital may change at the beginning of the project or at any point during the life of the project. For example, as a new product is introduced, sales may be terrific in the first few years, requiring an increase in cash, accounts receivable, and inventory to support these increased sales. But all of this requires an increase in working capital—a cash outflow.

But later sales may fall off as competitors enter the market. As sales and production fall off, the need for the increased cash, accounts receivable, and inventory also falls off. As cash, accounts receivable, and inventory are reduced, there is a cash inflow in the form of the reduction in the funds that become available for other uses within the firm.

A change in net working capital can be thought of as part of the initial investment—the amount necessary to get the project going. Or it can be considered generally as part of operating activity—the day-to-day business of the firm. So where do we classify the cash flow associated with net working capital? With the asset acquisition and disposition represented in the new project, or with the operating cash flows?

If a project requires a change in the firm's net working capital accounts that persists for the duration of the project—say, an increase in inventory levels starting at the time of the investment—we tend to classify the change as part of the acquisition costs at the beginning of the project and as part of disposition proceeds at the end of project. If, on the other hand, the change in net working capital is due to the fact that accrual accounting does not coincide with cash flows, we tend to classify the change as part of the operating cash flows.

In many applications, however, we can arbitrarily classify the change in working capital as either investment cash flows or operating cash flows. And the classification doesn't really matter since it's the bottom line—the change in net cash flows—that matter. How we classify the change in working capital doesn't affect a project's attractiveness. For purposes of illustrating the calculation of cash flows, we will assume that changes in working capital occur only at the beginning and the end of the project's life. Therefore, changes in working capital will be classified along with acquisition and disposition cash flows in the examples in this chapter.

EXHIBIT 12.2 An Example of the Calculation of the Change in Operating Cash Flow

	Change in sales	$200,000
	Less: change in expenses	150,000
	Less: change in depreciation	10,000
Change in Taxable Income	Change in taxable income	$40,000
↓		
Adjust for the change in taxes	Less taxes	16,000
	Change in income after taxes	$24,000
↓		
Add back noncash expenses such as depreciation	Add: depreciation	10,000
↓		
Change in Operating Cash Flow	Change in operating cash flow	$34,000

Putting It All Together

Here's what we need to put together to calculate the change in the firm's operating cash flows related to a new investment we are considering:

- Changes in revenues and expenses;
- Cash flow from changes in taxes from changes in revenues and expenses;
- Cash flow from changes in cash flows from depreciation tax shields; and
- Changes in net working capital.

There are many ways of compiling the component cash flow changes to arrive at the change in operating cash flow. We will start by first calculating taxable income, making adjustments for changes in taxes, noncash expenses, and net working capital to arrive at operating cash flow.

Suppose you are evaluating a project that is expected to increase sales by $200,000 and expenses by $150,000. The project's assets will have a $10,000 depreciation expense for tax purposes. If the tax rate is 40%, what is the operating cash flow from this project? As you can see in Exhibit 12.2, the change in operating cash flow is $34,000.

When we can mathematically represent how to calculate the change in operating cash flows for a project, let's use the symbol "Δ" to indicate "change in":

ΔOCF = change in operating cash flow
ΔR = change in revenues

ΔE = change in expenses
ΔD = change in depreciation
τ = tax rate

The change in the operating cash flow is:

$$\Delta OCF = (\Delta R - \Delta E - \Delta D)(1 - \tau) + \Delta D \qquad (12\text{-}1)$$

     ↑   ↑   ↑

Change in firm's   Change in   Change in
operating cash flows   after-tax income   depreciation

We can also write this as:

$$\Delta OCF = (\Delta R - \Delta E)(1 - \tau) + \Delta D\tau \qquad (12\text{-}2)$$

     ↑   ↑   ↑

Change in   Change in after-tax   Change in
firm's operating   income without   depreciation
cash flow   considering depreciation   tax shield

Applying equation (12-1) to the previous example,

$$
\begin{aligned}
\Delta OCF &= (\Delta R - \Delta E - \Delta D)(1 - \tau) &&+ \Delta D \\
&= (\$200{,}000 - 150{,}000 - 10{,}000)(1 - 0.40) &&+ \$10{,}000 \\
&= \$24{,}000
\end{aligned}
$$

or, using the rearrangement as in equation (12-2),

$$
\begin{aligned}
\Delta OCF &= (\Delta R - \Delta E)(1 - \tau) &&+ \Delta D\tau \\
&= (\$200{,}000 - \$150{,}000)(1 - 0.40) &&+ \$10{,}000(0.40) \\
&= \$24{,}000
\end{aligned}
$$

Let's look at one more example for the calculation of operating cash flows. Suppose you are evaluating modern equipment which you expect will reduce expenses by $100,000 during the first year. The old machine cost $200,000 and was depreciated using straight-line over ten years, with five years remaining. The new machine cost $300,000 and will be depreciated using straight-line over ten years. If the firm's tax rate is 30%, what is the expected operating cash flow in the first year?

Let's identify the components:

$\Delta R = \$0$ ⇔ The new machine does not affect revenues
$\Delta E = -\$100{,}000$ ⇔ The new machine reduces expenses which will
                                   reduce taxes and increase cash flows

ΔD = +\$10,000   ⇐   The new machine increases the depreciation expense from \$20,000 to \$30,000

τ = 30%

The operating cash flow from the first year is therefore:

$$
\begin{aligned}
\Delta\text{OCF} &= (\Delta R - \Delta E - \Delta D)\,(1 - \tau) &&+ \Delta D \\
&= (\$100,000 - 10,000)\,(1 - 0.30) &&+ \$10,000 \\
&= \$63,000 &&+ \$10,000 = \$73,000
\end{aligned}
$$

Net Cash Flows

As we have seen, an investment's cash flows consist of two types of cash flows: (1) cash flows related to acquiring and disposing the assets represented in the investment and (2) cash flows related to operations. To evaluate any investment project, we must consider both cash flows.

The sum of the cash flows from asset acquisition and disposition and from operations is referred to as *net cash flows* (NCF). The net cash flows are therefore the incremental cash flows related to an investment. The net cash flow is calculated for each period of the project's life. In each period, we add the cash flow from asset acquisition and disposition and the cash flow from operations. For a given period,

Net cash flow
= (Investment cash flow + Change in operating cash flow (ΔOCF))

The analysis of the cash flows of investment projects can become quite complex. But by working through any problem systematically, line-by-line, you will be able to sort out the information and focus on those items that determine cash flows.

Simplifications

To actually analyze a project's cash flows, we need to make several simplifications:

- We assume that cash will flow into or out of the firm at certain points in time, typically at the end of the year, although we realize that cash actually flows into and out of the firm at irregular intervals.
- We assume that the assets are purchased and put to work immediately.
- By combining inflows and outflows in each period, we are assuming that all inflows and outflows in a given period have the same risk.

Because there are so many flows to consider, we focus on flows within a period (say a year), assuming they all occur at the end of the period. We assume this to reduce the number of things we have to keep track of. Whether or not this assumption matters depends on: (1) the difference between the actual time of cash flow and when we assume it flows at the end of the period (that is, a flow on January 2 is 364 days from December 31, but a flow on December 30 is only one day from December 31), and (2) the opportunity cost of funds. Also, assuming that cash flows occur at specific points in time simplifies the financial mathematics we use in valuing these cash flows.

Keeping track of the different cash flows of an investment project can be taxing. Developing a checklist of things to consider can help you wade through the analysis of a project's cash flows. Exhibit 12.3 provides a checklist for the new investment and the replacement investment decisions. When you begin your analysis of an investment decision, take a look at the appropriate checklist to make sure you've covered everything.

In the next two sections, we use two hypothetical examples to illustrate the net cash flow calculations. We then end the chapter by considering the problems of cash flow estimation in the real world.

INTEGRATIVE EXAMPLE 1: THE EXPANSION OF THE WILLIAMS 5 & 10

The Williams 5 & 10 Company is a discount retail chain, selling a variety of goods at low prices. Business has been very good lately and the Williams 5 & 10 Company is considering opening one more retail outlet in a neighboring town at the end of 2003. Management figures that it would be about five years before a large national chain of discount stores moves into that town to compete with its store. So it is looking at this expansion as a five-year prospect. After five years, it would most likely retreat from this town.

The Problem

Williams' managers have researched the expansion and determined that the building needed could be built for $400,000 and it would cost $100,000 to buy the equipment. Under MACRS, the building would be classified as 31.5-year property and depreciated using the straight-line method, with no salvage value. This means that $1/31.5$ of the $400,000 is depreciated each year. Also under MACRS, the equipment would be classified as five-year property. Management expects to be able to sell the building for $350,000 and the equipment for $50,000 after five years.

EXHIBIT 12.3   Capital Budgeting Checklists

Capital Budgeting Checklist Nonreplacement Decision

Investment Cash Flows:
- Asset cost
- Shipping and installation costs
- Asset disposition
- Tax effect of asset disposition

Operating Cash Flows:
- Change in firm's revenues
- Change in firm's expenses
- Tax on change in firm's revenues and expenses
- Depreciation on asset
- Tax shield from depreciation
- Change in working capital to adjust accounting income to cash flows

Capital Budgeting Checklist Replacement Decision

Investment Cash Flows:
- New asset cost
- Shipping and installation costs on new asset
- Old asset disposition
- Tax effect of old asset disposition
- New asset disposition
- Tax effect of new asset disposition
- Change in working capital (transactions or precautionary needs)

Operating Cash Flows:
- Change in firm's revenues
- Change in firm's expenses
- Tax on change in firm's revenues and expenses
- Change in depreciation (new versus old)
- Tax shield from change in depreciation
- Change in working capital to adjust accrual accounting to cash flows

The Williams 5 & 10 extends no credit on its sales and pays for all its purchases immediately. The projections for sales and expenses for the new store for the next five years are:

Year	Sales	Expenses
2004	$200,000	$100,000
2005	300,000	100,000
2006	300,000	100,000
2007	300,000	100,000
2008	50,000	20,000

The new store requires $50,000 of additional inventory. Because all sales are in cash, there is no expected increase in accounts receivable. The tax rate is a flat 30% and there are no tax credits associated with this expansion. Also, capital gains are taxed at the ordinary tax rate.

The Analysis
To determine the relevant cash flows to evaluate this expansion, let's look at this problem bit-by-bit.

> *The Williams 5 & 10 Company is a discount retail chain, selling a variety of goods at low prices. Business has been very good lately and the Williams 5 & 10 Company is considering opening one more retail outlet in a neighboring town at the end of 2003.*

This is an expansion of the business into a new market. Williams has other similar outlets, so this is most likely a low risk type of investment.

> *Management figures that it would be about five years before a large national chain of discount stores moves into that town to compete with its store. So it is looking at this expansion as a five-year prospect. After five years it would most likely retreat from this town.*

The economic life of this project is five years. Management expects to expand into this market for only five years, leaving when a competitor enters.

> *Williams' managers have researched the expansion and determined that the building needed could be built for $400,000 and it would cost $100,000 to buy the cash registers, shelves, and other equipment necessary to start up this outlet.*

The initial outlay for the building and equipment is $500,000. There are no set-up charges, so we can assume that all other initial investment costs are included in these figures.

> *Under MACRS, the building would be classified as 31.5-year property and depreciated using the straight-line method with no salvage value. This means that $1/31.5$ of the $400,000 is depreciated each year. Also under MACRS, the equipment would be classified as five-year property.*

The depreciation expense for each year is:

Year	Depreciation on the Building	Depreciation on the Equipment	Total Depreciation Expense
1	$12,698	$20,000	$32,698
2	12,698	32,000	44,698
3	12,698	19,200	31,898
4	12,698	11,520	24,218
5	12,698	11,520	24,218
Total	$63,490	$94,240	

The tax basis of the building and equipment at the end of the fifth year are:

$$\text{Tax basis of building} = \$400,000 - 63,490 = \$336,510$$

and

$$\text{Tax basis of equipment} = \$100,000 - 94,240 = \$5,760$$

The Williams 5 & 10 expects to sell the building for $350,000 and the equipment for $50,000 after five years.

The sale of the building is a cash inflow of $350,000 at the end of the fifth year. The building is expected to be sold for more than its book value, creating a taxable gain of $350,000 − $336,510 = $13,490. The tax on this gain is $4,047.

The sale of the equipment is a cash inflow of $50,000. The gain on the sale of the equipment is $50,000 − $5,760 = $44,240. The tax on this gain is 30% of $44,240, or $13,272.

Williams extends no credit on its sales and pays for all its purchases immediately. The projections for sales and expenses for the new store for the next five years are:

Year	Sales	Expenses
2004	$200,000	$100,000
2005	300,000	100,000
2006	300,000	100,000
2007	300,000	100,000
2008	50,000	20,000

The change in revenues, ΔR, and the change in cash expenses, ΔE, correspond to the sales and costs figures.

> *The new store would require $50,000 of additional inventory. All sales are in cash, so there is no expected increase in accounts receivable.*

The increase in inventory is an investment of cash when the store is opened, a $50,000 cash outflow. That's the amount Williams has to invest to maintain inventory while the store is in operation. When the store is closed in five years, there is no need to keep this increased level of inventory. If we assume that the inventory at the end of the fifth year can be sold for $50,000, that amount will be a cash inflow at that time. Because this is a change in working capital for the duration of the project, we include this cash flow as part of the asset acquisition (initially) and then its disposition (at the end of the fifth year). We will classify the change in inventory as part of the investment cash flows.

> *The tax rate is a flat 30% and there are no tax credits associated with this expansion. Also, capital gains are taxed at the ordinary tax rate of 30%.*

Once we know the tax rate we can calculate the cash flows related to acquiring and disposing of assets and the cash flow from operations.

We can calculate the cash flows fron operations using equation (12-1):[6]

Year	Change in Revenues ΔR	Change in Expenses ΔE	Change in Depreciation ΔD	Change in Income After Taxes $(\Delta R - \Delta E - \Delta D)(1-\tau)$	Change in Operating Cash Flow $(\Delta R - \Delta E - \Delta D)(1-\tau) + \Delta D$
2004	$200,000	$100,000	$32,698	$47,111	$79,809
2005	300,000	100,000	44,698	108,711	153,409
2006	300,000	100,000	31,898	117,671	149,569
2007	300,000	100,000	24,218	123,047	147,265
2008	50,000	20,000	24,218	4,047	28,265

Or, we can calculate the incremental operating cash flows from the new store using equation (12-2):

---

[6] Remember that the changes in working capital have been classified along with acquisition and disposition cash flows.

Year	Change in Revenues ΔR	Change in Expenses ΔE	Change in Revenues and Expenses After Taxes $(\Delta R - \Delta E)(1-\tau)$	Change in Depreciation Tax Shield $\Delta D\tau$	Change in Operating Cash Flow $(\Delta R - \Delta E)(1-\tau) + \Delta D\tau$
2004	$200,000	$100,000	$70,000	$9,809	$79,809
2005	300,000	100,000	140,000	13,409	153,409
2006	300,000	100,000	140,000	9,569	149,569
2007	300,000	100,000	140,000	7,265	147,265
2008	50,000	20,000	21,000	7,265	28,265

The pieces of this cash flow puzzle are put together in Exhibit 12.4, which identifies the cash inflows and outflows for each year, with acquisition and disposition cash flows at the top and operating cash flows below. Investing $550,000 initially is expected to result in cash inflows during the following five years. Our next task, which we take up in the next chapter, is to see whether investing in this project as represented by the cash flows in this time line will increase owners' wealth.

INTEGRATIVE EXAMPLE 2: THE REPLACEMENT OF FACILITIES AT THE HIRSHLEIFER COMPANY

The management of the Hirshleifer Company is evaluating the replacement of its existing manufacturing equipment with a new equipment. The old equipment cost $200,000 five years ago, currently has a tax basis of $100,000, has been depreciated on the straight-line basis over a ten-year life with no salvage value. If Hirshleifer keeps the old equipment, it is expected to last another five years, at which time the ten-year-old equipment is expected to be sold for $10,000. The old equipment could be sold today for $120,000.

The Problem
The new equipment costs $300,000 and is expected to have a useful life of five years. The new equipment will be depreciated for tax purposes using MACRS and a five-year classified life. At the end of its useful life, management expects to sell the new equipment for $100,000. Meanwhile, the new equipment is expected to reduce production costs by $60,000 each year. In addition, since it is more efficient, Hirshleifer can reduce its raw material and work-in-process inventories. Hirshleifer expects to reduce its inventory by $10,000 as soon as the new equipment is placed in service.

EXHIBIT 12.4 Estimated Incremental Cash Flows from the Williams 5 & 10 Expansion

			End of Year			
	Initial	2004	2005	2006	2007	2008
Investment cash flows						
Purchase and sale of building	−$400,000					+$350,000
Tax on sale of building						−4,047
Purchase and sale of equipment	−100,000					+50,000
Tax on sale of equipment						−13,272
Change in working capital	−50,000					+50,000
Investment cash flows	−$550,000					+$432,681
Change in operating cash flows						
Change in revenues, ΔR		+$200,000	+$300,000	+$300,000	+$300,000	+$50,000
Less: change in expenses, ΔE		−100,000	−100,000	−100,000	−100,000	−20,000
Less: change in depreciation, ΔD		−32,698	−44,698	−31,898	−24,218	−24,218
Change in taxable income		+$67,302	+$155,302	+$168,102	+$175,782	+$5,782
Less: taxes, $\tau(\Delta R - \Delta E - \Delta D)$		−20,191	−46,591	−50,531	−52,735	−1,735
Change in income after tax, $(1-\tau)(\Delta R - \Delta E - \Delta D)$		+$47,111	+$108,711	+$117,671	+$123,047	+$4,047
Add: depreciation, ΔD		+32,698	+44,698	+31,898	+24,218	+24,218
Change in operating cash flows, ΔOCF		+$79,809	+$153,409	+$149,569	+$147,265	+$28,265
Net cash flows	−$550,000	+$79,809	+$153,409	+$149,569	+$147,265	+$460,946

386

The income of Hirshleifer is taxed at a rate of 35%. There are no tax credits available for this equipment. What cash flows would result for each of the five years from this replacement?

The Analysis

This is a replacement project. We need to decide whether to continue with the present equipment or replace it. To do this, we look at the change in cash flows if we replace the equipment—relative to the cash flows of keeping the existing equipment. Instead of analyzing the problem line-by-line as we did for the Williams 5&10, we first look at the cash flows related to acquiring and disposing assets and then look at the operating cash flows.

Investment Cash Flows

The new equipment requires an immediate cash outlay of $300,000. It will be depreciated using the specified rates, where 20.00% + 32.00% + 19.20% + 11.52% + 11.52% = 94.24% of its cost is depreciated by the end of the fifth year. That leaves a tax basis of 5.76% of $300,000, or $17,280. The expected sale price of the new equipment at the end of the fifth year is greater than the equipment's book value, so there is a gain on the sale of the equipment of $100,000 − $17,280 = $82,720.

Because the sales price is less than the original cost, this gain is taxed as a recapture of depreciation at ordinary tax rates. The sale of the new equipment in the fifth year creates a gain of $82,720. The cash outflow for taxes on this gain is 0.35 × $82,720 = $28,952.

The $200,000 cost of the old equipment is a sunk cost and is not directly relevant to our analysis. However, we need to consider the tax basis of the old equipment in computing a gain or loss on its sale. We also need to consider the cost of the old equipment to assess whether any gain on its sale would be a capital gain or a recapture of depreciation.

By selling the old equipment for $120,000, the firm will incur a gain of the selling price less the tax basis, or $120,000 − $100,000 = $20,000. This is a recapture of depreciation—taxed at 35%—since the sales price is less than the original cost, the $200,000.

Disposing of the old equipment has two tax-related cash flows: the tax on the sale of the old equipment when the new equipment is purchased, an outflow of 0.35 × $20,000 = $7,000; and the tax we would have had to pay on the sale of the old equipment in the fifth year, an inflow of 0.35 × $10,000 = $3,500.

If the firm replaces the old equipment today, it foregoes the sale of the equipment in five years for $10,000. We need to consider both the foregone cash flow from this sale, as well as any forgone taxes or tax benefit on this sale.

And let's not forget about the change in net working capital. The reduction in inventory is a cash inflow since inventory can be reduced. If we assume it is reduced immediately, there is a $10,000 cash inflow initially. Assuming that inventory returns to its previous level at the end of the new equipment's life, there will be a $10,000 cash outflow at the end of the fifth year.

Let's summarize the investment cash flows:

Initially:

Purchase of new equipment	−$300,000
Sale of old equipment	+120,000
Tax on sale of old equipment	−7,000
Decrease in inventory	+10,000
Total investment cash flow	−$177,000

Fifth year:

Sale of new equipment	+$100,000
Tax on sale of new equipment	−28,952
Foregone sale of old equipment	−10,000
Foregone tax on sale of old equipment	+3,500
Increase in inventory	−10,000
Total investment cash flow	+$54,548

Operating Cash Flows

If the old equipment is kept, depreciation would continue to be $200,000/10 years = $20,000 per year for each of the next five years. If it is replaced, there would no longer be this depreciation expense.

The new equipment will be depreciated over five years. Comparing the depreciation expense with the old and the new equipment, we determine the change in the taxes from the change in the depreciation tax shield:

Year	Rate of Depreciation on New Equipment	Depreciation Expense of New Equipment	Depreciation Expense of Old Equipment	Change in Depreciation Expense
1	20.00%	$60,000	$20,000	$40,000
2	32.00%	96,000	20,000	76,000
3	19.20%	57,600	20,000	37,600
4	11.52%	34,560	20,000	14,560
5	11.52%	34,560	20,000	14,560
		$282,720	$100,000	

The reduction in costs is a cash inflow—less cash is paid out with the new than with the old equipment. But there is also additional taxable income—the new machine will reduce expenses by \$60,000 each year, so that increases taxable income by \$60,000 each year, increasing taxes each year.

Using equation (12-1),

Year	Change in Revenues ΔR	Change in Expenses ΔE	Change in Depreciation ΔD	Change in Income After Taxes $(\Delta R - \Delta E - \Delta D)$ $(1-\tau)$	Change in Operating Cash Flow $(\Delta R - \Delta E - \Delta D)(1-\tau)$ $+\Delta D$
First	\$0	-\$60,000	\$40,000	\$13,000	\$53,000
Second	0	-60,000	76,000	-10,400	65,600
Third	0	-60,000	37,600	14,560	52,160
Fourth	0	-60,000	14,560	29,536	44,096
Fifth	0	-60,000	14,560	29,536	44,096

Or, using equation (12-2),

Year	Change in Revenues ΔR	Change in Expenses ΔE	Change in Revenues and Expenses After Taxes $(\Delta R - \Delta E)(1-\tau)$	Change in Depreciation Tax Shield $\Delta D\tau$	Change in Operating Cash Flow $(\Delta R - \Delta E)(1-\tau)$ $+\Delta D$
First	\$0	-\$60,000	\$39,000	\$14,000	\$53,000
Second	0	-60,000	39,000	26,600	65,600
Third	0	-60,000	39,000	13,160	52,160
Fourth	0	-60,000	39,000	5,096	44,096
Fifth	0	-60,000	39,000	5,096	44,096

The project's cash flows are shown in Exhibit 12.5. Investing \$177,000 initially is expected to generate cash inflows shown in the time line in the next five years. Our task, which we will take up in the next chapter, is to evaluate these cash flows to see whether taking on this project will increase owners' wealth.

CASH FLOW ESTIMATION IN PRACTICE

Now that we have described how firms ideally estimate cash flows, we turn to the question of how managers actually make these important decisions. Surveys of U.S. corporations provide the following important information:[7]

---

[7] Randolph A. Pohlman, Emmanuel S. Santiago, and F. Lynn Markel, "Cash Flow Estimation Practices of Large Firms," *Financial Management* (Summer 1988), pp. 71–79.

EXHIBIT 12.5 Estimated Incremental Cash Flows from the Replacement of Facilities at the Hirshleifer Company

			End of Year			
	Initial	Year 1	Year 2	Year 3	Year 4	Year 5
Investment cash flows						
Purchase and sale of new equipment	−$300,000					+$100,000
Tax on sale of new equipment						−28,952
Sale of old equipment	+120,000					−10,000
Tax on sale of old equipment	−7,000					+3,500
Change in working capital	+10,000					−10,000
Investment cash flows	−$177,000					+$54,548
Change in operating cash flows						
Change in revenues, ΔR		$0	$0	$0	$0	$0
Less: change in expenses, ΔE		+60,000	+60,000	+60,000	+60,000	+60,000
Less: change in depreciation, ΔD		40,000	76,000	37,600	14,560	14,560
Change in taxable income		−$20,000	−$16,000	+$22,400	+$45,440	+$45,440
Less: taxes, $\tau(\Delta R - \Delta E - \Delta D)$		+7,000	+5,600	−7,840	−15,904	−15,904
Change in income after tax, $(1-\tau)(\Delta R - \Delta E - \Delta D)$		−$13,000	−$10,400	+$14,560	+$29,536	+$29,536
Add: depreciation, ΔD		+40,000	+76,000	+37,600	+14,560	+14,560
Change in operating cash flows, ΔOCF		+$53,000	+$65,600	−$52,160	+$44,096	+$44,096
Net cash flows	−$177,000	+$53,000	+$65,600	+$52,160	+$44,096	+$98,644

■ The person estimating cash flows is an accountant, an analyst, Treasurer, Controller, Vice President of Finance, or a person reporting directly to the Treasurer or Vice President of Finance.
■ Most firms have standard procedures for estimating cash flows.
■ Most firms rely mainly on the subjective judgment of management.
■ Most firms consider working capital requirements in their analysis of cash flows.
■ Sales and operating expense forecasts are a key ingredient in estimating cash flows.

Estimating cash flows for capital projects is perhaps the most difficult part of the investment screening and selection process. With regard to the process of capital budgeting, most firms use some type of post-completion auditing, yet few firms have well developed, sophisticated systems for evaluating ongoing projects.[8]

We know that it is necessary to consider cash flows related to acquiring the assets, to disposing of the assets, and to operations. In our analysis, we must not forget to consider working capital and the cash flows related to taxes. But all the while, we are working with estimates—forecasts of the future. Thus, when managers estimate cash flows, they rely on their best guess as to:

■ The cost of the assets.
■ The benefits or costs of disposing the assets at the end of the project.
■ Sales in each future period.
■ Expenses in each future period.
■ Tax rates in each future period.
■ Working capital needs in each future period.

Implicit in cash flow forecasts are judgments pertaining to:

■ Competitors' reactions to the investment.
■ Changes in the tax code.
■ The costs of materials and labor.
■ The time it takes to get the project underway.

Looking at how cash flows are estimated, we see that corporations analyze all the key elements—sales, expenses, taxes, working capital—yet apply judgment in arriving at the estimates of these elements. Thus, cash flow estimation does not lend itself well to the application of mechanical

---

[8] Kimberly J. Smith, "Postauditing Capital Investments," *Financial Practice and Education* (Spring/Summer 1994), pp. 129–137.

formulae. Though managers can apply formulas that help them put the key elements together, they must always remember that cash flow estimates are determined, in large part, through marketing analyses, engineering studies, and, most important, managerial experience.

SUMMARY

- The capital budgeting process requires identifying, screening, and selecting investment projects. These projects provide benefits in the future by increasing the firm's cash flows in future years.
- Estimating future cash flows requires estimating cash flows of the firm with and without the investment: How do the cash flows of the firm change if the investment is made? These changes in cash flows are the incremental cash flows that we consider in our analysis of an investment.
- Estimating incremental cash flows requires forecasting future sales, expenses, and taxes, as well as the effect on net working capital.
- Cash flows from acquiring and disposing of assets must consider: (1) the direct cash flows from purchases and sales of assets, (2) the tax consequences of sales, and (3) any foregone cash flows from the sale of assets.
- Changes in net working capital arise in an investment project from two sources: (1) increased need for cash, accounts receivable, or inventory to meet a larger scale of operations; or (2) to adjust accounting estimates that are on the accrual basis to a cash basis.
- Putting these estimates together with the estimated cash flows from acquiring and disposing of the assets of the investment project, we calculate the net cash flows for each future period. We then evaluate whether this investment is consistent with owners' wealth maximization, applying evaluation techniques developed in Chapter 13.

QUESTIONS

1. Suppose a toy manufacturer is faced with the following collection of investment projects:
   a. Opening a retail outlet.
   b. Introducing a new line of dolls.
   c. Introducing a new action figure in an existing line of action figures.
   d. Adding another packaging line to the production process.
   e. Adding pollution control equipment to avoid environmental fines.

f. Computerizing the doll molding equipment.

g. Introducing a child's version of an existing adult board game.

Classify each project into one of the four categories: expansion, replacement, new product or market, or mandated.

2. A shoe manufacturer is considering introducing a new line of boots. When evaluating the incremental revenues from this new line, what should be considered?

3. If you sell an asset for more than its tax basis, but less than its original cost, we refer to this gain as a recapture of depreciation and it is taxed at ordinary income tax rates. Why?

4. How does a capital loss on the disposition of an asset generate a cash inflow?

5. If a project's projected revenues and expenses are on a cash basis, is there any need to adjust for a change in working capital? Explain.

6. If a firm replaces its production line with equipment with lower depreciation expenses, will the tax cash flow from depreciation be an inflow or an outflow? Explain.

7. Classify each of the following changes as increasing or decreasing the operating cash flow:

a. An increase in raw materials inventory.

b. An increase in salaries and wages payable.

c. An increase in accounts receivable.

d. A decrease in raw materials inventory.

e. A decrease in accounts receivable.

f. A decrease in accounts payable.

g. A decrease in finished goods inventory.

h. A decrease in accounts receivable.

8. Depreciation does not involve a cash flow, yet we consider cash flows from the depreciation tax shield. What is the depreciation tax shield and how does it produce a cash flow?

9. Suppose you buy an asset for $1,000,000. If it costs $100,000 for shipping and installation, how much is your investment outlay?

10. The Schwab Steel Company is considering two different wire soldering machines. Machine 1 has an initial cost of $100,000, costs $20,000 to set up, and is expected to be sold for $20,000 after 10 years. Machine 2 has an initial cost of $80,000, costs $30,000 to set up, and is expected to be sold for $10,000 after ten years. Both machines would be depreciated over ten years using straight-line depreciation. Schwab has a tax rate of 35%.

a. What are the cash flows related to the acquisition of each machine?

b. What are the cash flows related to the disposition of each machine?

11. The Tinbergen Company is considering a new polishing machine. The existing polishing machine cost $100,000 five years ago and is

being depreciated using straight-line over a ten-year life. Tinbergen's management estimates that they can sell the old machine for $60,000. The new machine costs $150,000 and would be depreciated over five years using MACRS. At the end of the fifth year, Tinbergen's management expects to be able to sell the new polishing machine for $75,000. The marginal tax rate is 40%.

a. What are the cash flows related to the acquisition of the new machine?

b. What are the cash flows related to the disposition of the old machine?

c. What are the cash flows related to the disposition of the new machine?

12. Mama's Goulash Company is considering purchasing a dishwasher. The dishwasher costs $50,000 and would be depreciated over three years using MACRS. After three years, Mama's plans to sell the dishwasher for $10,000. The marginal tax rate is 40%.

a. What are the cash flows related to the acquisition of the dishwasher?

b. What are the cash flows related to the disposition of the dishwasher?

13. If an investment is expected to increase revenues by $100,000 per year for five years, with no effect on expenses or working capital, what is the operating cash flow per year if depreciation is $20,000 each year and the tax rate is: a. 20%? b. 30%? c. 40%? d. 50%?

14. Calculate the change in operating cash flow for each year using the following information:

■ The machine costs $1,000,000, and is depreciated using straight-line over five years.

■ The machine will increase sales by $150,000 per year for five years.

■ The tax rate is 40%.

■ Working capital needs increase by $10,000 when the machine is placed in service and are reduced at the end of the life of the machine.

■ There is no salvage value at the end of the five years.

15. Calculate the change in operating cash flow for each year using the following information:

■ The equipment costs $200,000 and is depreciated using MACRS over five years.

■ The equipment will reduce operating expenses by $25,000 per year for five years.

■ The tax rate is 30%.

- Working capital needs increase by $10,000 when the machine is placed in service and are reduced at the end of the life of the machine.
- There is no salvage value at the end of five years.

16. The Smith Company is a beauty products company that is considering a new hair growth product. This new product would encourage hair growth for persons with thinning hair. The new product is expected to generate sales of $500,000 per year and would cost $300,000 to produce each year. It is expected that the patent on the new product would prevent competition from entering the market for at least seven years.

    The Smith Company spent $1,000,000 developing the new product over the past four years. The equipment to produce the new product would cost $1,500,000 and would be depreciated for tax purposes as a five-year MACRS asset. Smith's management estimates that the equipment could be sold after seven years for $400,000. The marginal tax rate for Smith is 40%.
    a. What are the initial cash flows related to the new product?
    b. What are the cash flows related to the disposition of the equipment after seven years?
    c. What are the operating cash flows for each year?
    d. What are the net cash flows for each year?

17. The Nobel Dynamite Company is considering a new packing machine. The existing packing machine cost $500,000 five years ago and is being depreciated using straight-line over a ten-year life. Nobel's management estimates that the old machine can be sold for $100,000. The new machine costs $600,000 and would be depreciated over five years using straight-line. There is no salvage value for the new machine. The new machine is more efficient and would reduce packing expenses (damaged goods) by $120,000 per year for the next five years. The marginal tax rate is 30%.
    a. What are the cash flows related to the acquisition of the new machine?
    b. What are the cash flows related to the disposition of the old machine?
    c. What are the cash flows related to the disposition of the new machine?
    d. What are the operating cash flows for each year?
    e. What are the net cash flows for each year?

18. Consider a project that is expected to reduce expenses each year for the next five years by $1 million. After considering taxes, what is the contribution to operating cash flows solely from the change in expenses from this project if the tax rate is 30%?

19. Suppose that you are evaluating an asset that costs $400,000 and that is depreciated for tax purposes using MACRS rates for a five-year asset. Assume a marginal tax rate of 30%.
    a. What is the amount of the depreciation expense in the second year?
    b. What is the amount of the depreciation tax shield in the second year?
    c. If you plan to dispose of the asset at the end of the third year, what is the asset's tax basis at the time of sale?
    d. If you can sell the asset for $50,000 at the end of the fifth year, do you have a gain or a loss? What are the tax consequences of this sale? What are the cash flow consequences?
    e. If you can sell the asset for $100,000 at the end of the fifth year, do you have a gain or a loss? What are the tax consequences of this sale? What are the cash flow consequences?

20. The president of Cook Airlines has asked you to evaluate the proposed acquisition of a new jet. The jet's price is $40 million, and it is classified in the ten-year MACRS class. The purchase of the jet would require an increase in net working capital of $200,000. The jet would increase the firm's before-tax revenues by $20 million per year, but would also increase operating costs by $5 million per year. The jet is expected to be used for three years and then sold for $25 million. The firm's marginal tax rate is 40%.
    a. What is the amount of the investment outlay required at the beginning of the project?
    b. What is the amount of the operating cash flow each year?
    c. What is the amount of the nonoperating cash flow in the third year?
    d. What is the amount of the net cash flow for each year?

21. The financial manager of the Villard Electric Company, Fred Taylor, has presented his estimates of cash flows resulting from the possible investment in a new computer system, the Webnet. Mr. Taylor's estimates of net cash flows immediately and over the following four years are as follows:

Item	Initial	First Year	Second Year	Third Year	Fourth Year
Purchase of computer system	−$200,000				
Sale of computer system					$40,000
Tax on sale of computer system					12,442
Acquisition and disposition cash flows	−$200,000	$0	$0	$0	$52,442
Change in expenses		$50,000	$50,000	$50,000	$50,000
Change in depreciation		40,000	64,000	38,400	23,040
Change in taxable income		$10,000	−$14,000	$11,600	$26,960
Less: change in tax		3,600	−5,040	4,176	9,706
Change in income after tax		$6,400	−$8,960	$7,424	$17,254
Change in depreciation		40,000	64,000	38,400	23,040
Change in operating cash flows		$46,400	$55,040	$45,824	$40,294
Change in net cash flows	−$200,000	$46,400	$55,040	$45,824	$92,736

Mr. Taylor has based his estimates on the following assumptions:

■ The cost of the system (including installation) is $200,000.
■ The system will be depreciated as a 5-year asset under the MACRS, but it will be sold at the end of the fourth year for $50,000.
■ Villard's expenses will decline by $50,000 in each of the four years.
■ The company's tax rate will be 36%.
■ Working capital will not be affected.

When he made his presentation to Villard's board of directors, Mr. Taylor was asked to perform additional analyses to consider the following uncertainties:

■ The cost of the system may be as much as 20% higher or as low as 20% lower.
■ The change in expenses may be 30% higher or 20% lower than anticipated.
■ The tax rate may be lowered to 30%.

a. Reestimate the project's cash flows to consider each of the possible variations in the assumptions, altering only one assumption each time. Using a spreadsheet program will help with the calculations.
b. Discuss the impact that each of the changes in assumptions has on the project's cash flows.

CHAPTER 13

Capital Budgeting Techniques

The value of a firm today is the present value of all its future cash flows. These future cash flows come from assets that are already in place and from future investment opportunities. These future cash flows are discounted at a rate that represents investors' assessments of the uncertainty that they will flow in the amounts and when expected:

Value of firm = Present value of all future cash flows
= Present value of cash flows from all assets in place
+ Present value of cash flows from future investment opportunities

The objective of the financial manager is to maximize the value of the firm and, therefore, owners' wealth. As we saw in the previous chapter, the financial manager makes decisions regarding long-lived assets in the process referred to as *capital budgeting*. The capital budgeting decisions for a project require analysis of:

■ Its future cash flows,
■ The degree of uncertainty associated with these future cash flows, and
■ The value of these future cash flows considering their uncertainty.

We looked at how to estimate cash flows in Chapter 12 where we were concerned with a project's incremental cash flows. These comprise changes in operating cash flows (change in revenues, expenses, and taxes), and changes in investment cash flows (the firm's incremental cash flows from the acquisition and disposition of the project's assets).

In the next chapter, we introduce the second required element of capital budgeting: *risk*. In the study of valuation principles, we saw that the more uncertain a future cash flow, the less it is worth today. The degree of uncertainty, or risk, is reflected in a project's cost of capital.

399

The *cost of capital* is what the firm must pay for the funds needed to finance an investment. The cost of capital may be an explicit cost (for example, the interest paid on debt) or an implicit cost (for example, the expected price appreciation of shares of the firm's common stock).

In this chapter, we focus on the third element of capital budgeting: valuing the future cash flows. Given estimates of incremental cash flows for a project and given a cost of capital that reflects the project's risk, we look at alternative techniques that are used to select projects.

For now, we will incorporate risk into our calculations in either of two ways: (1) we can discount future cash flows using a higher discount rate, the greater the cash flow's risk, or (2) we can require a higher annual return on a project, the greater the risk of its cash flows. We will look at specific ways of estimating risk and incorporating risk in the discount rate in Chapter 14.

EVALUATION TECHNIQUES

Exhibit 13.1 shows four pairs of projects for evaluation. Look at the incremental cash flows for Investments A and B shown in the table. Can you tell by looking at the cash flows for Investment A whether or not it enhances wealth? Or, can you tell by just looking at Investments A and B which one is better? Perhaps with some projects you may think you can pick out which one is better simply by gut feeling or eyeballing the cash flows. But why do it that way when there are precise methods to evaluate investments by their cash flows?

To evaluate investment projects and select the one that maximizes wealth, we must determine the cash flows from each investment and then assess the uncertainty of all the cash flows. In this section, we look at six techniques that are commonly used to evaluate investments in long-term assets:

1. Payback period
2. Discounted payback period
3. Net present value
4. Profitability index
5. Internal rate of return
6. Modified internal rate of return

We are interested in how well each technique discriminates among the different projects, steering us toward the projects that maximize owners' wealth.

An evaluation technique should consider all the following elements of a capital project:

- All the future incremental cash flows from the project;
- The time value of money; and
- The uncertainty associated with future cash flows.

Projects selected using a technique that satisfies all three criteria will, under most general conditions, maximize owners' wealth. Such a technique should include objective rules to determine which project or projects to select.

In addition to judging whether each technique satisfies these criteria, we will also look at which ones can be used in special situations, such as when a dollar limit is placed on the capital budget. We will demonstrate each technique and determine in what way and how well it evaluates each of the projects described in Exhibit 13.1.

EXHIBIT 13.1   Projects Evaluated

Investments A and B
Each requires an investment of $1,000,000 at the end of the year 2000 and has a cost of capital of 10% per year.

End of Year Cash Flow		
Year	Investment A	Investment B
2001	$400,000	$100,000
2002	400,000	100,000
2003	400,000	100,000
2004	400,000	1,000,000
2005	400,000	1,000,000

Investments E and F
Each requires $1,000,000 at the end of the year 2000 and has a cost of capital of 5% per year.

End of Year Cash Flows		
Year	Investment E	Investment F
2001	$300,000	$0
2002	300,000	0
2003	300,000	0
2004	300,000	1,200,000
2005	300,000	200,000

Investments C and D
Each requires $1,000,000 at the end of the year 2000 and has a cost of capital of 10% per year.

End of Year Cash Flows		
Year	Investment C	Investment D
2001	$300,000	$300,000
2002	300,000	300,000
2003	300,000	300,000
2004	300,000	300,000
2005	300,000	10,000,000

Investments G and H
Each requires $1,000,000 at the end of the year 2000. Investment G has a cost of capital of 5% per year; Investment H's cost of capital is 10% per year.

End of Year Cash Flows		
Year	Investment G	Investment H
2001	$250,000	$250,000
2002	250,000	250,000
2003	250,000	250,000
2004	250,000	250,000
2005	250,000	250,000

Payback Period

The *payback period* for a project is the length of time it takes to get your money back. It is the period from the initial cash outflow to the time when the project's cash inflows add up to the initial cash outflow. The payback period is also referred to as the *payoff period* or the *capital recovery period*. If you invest $10,000 today and are promised $5,000 one year from today and $5,000 two years from today, the payback period is two years—it takes two years to get your $10,000 investment back.

Suppose you are considering Investments A and B in Exhibit 13.1, each requiring an investment of $1,000,000 today (we're considering today to be the last day of the year 2000) and promising cash flows at the end of each of the following five years. How long does it take to get your $1,000,000 investment back? The payback period for Investment A is three years:

End of Year	Expected Cash Flow	Accumulated Cash Flow	
2001	$400,000	$400,000	
2002	400,000	800,000	
2003	400,000	1,200,000	⇦ $1,000,000 investment is paid back
2004	400,000	1,600,000	
2005	400,000	2,000,000	

By the end of 2002, the full $1 million is not paid back, but by 2003, the accumulated cash flow exceeds $1 million. Therefore, the payback period for Investment A is three years. Using a similar approach of comparing the investment outlay with the accumulated cash flow, the payback period for Investment B is four years—it is not until the end of 2004 that the $1,000,000 original investment (and more) is paid back.

We have assumed that the cash flows are received at the end of the year, so we always arrive at a payback period in terms of a whole number of years. If we assume that the cash flows are received, say, uniformly, such as monthly or weekly, throughout the year, we arrive at a payback period in terms of years and *fractions* of years. For example, assuming we receive cash flows uniformly throughout the year, the payback period for Investment A is 2 years and 6 months, and the payback period for Investment B is 3.7 years or 3 years and 8.5 months. Our assumption of end-of-period cash flows may be unrealistic, but it is convenient to demonstrate how to use the various evaluation techniques. We will continue to use this end-of-period assumption throughout this chapter.

Payback Period Decision Rule

Is Investment A or B more attractive? A shorter payback period is thought to be better than a longer payback period. Yet there is no clear-cut rule for how short is better. Investment A provides a quicker payback than B. But that doesn't mean it provides the better value for the firm. All we know is that A "pays for itself" quicker than B. We do not know in this particular case whether quicker is better.

In addition to having no well-defined decision criteria, payback period analysis favors investments with "front-loaded" cash flows: An investment looks better in terms of the payback period the sooner its cash flows are received no matter what its later cash flows look like!

Payback period analysis is a type of "break-even" measure. It tends to provide a measure of the economic life of the investment in terms of its payback period. The more likely the life exceeds the payback period, the more attractive the investment. The economic life beyond the pay-back period is referred to as the *post-payback duration*. If post-payback duration is zero, the investment is worthless, *no matter how short the payback*. This is because the sum of the future cash flows is no greater than the initial investment outlay. And since these future cash flows are really worth less today than in the future, a zero post-payback duration means that the present value of the future cash flows is *less* than the project's initial investment.

Payback should only be used as a coarse initial screen of investment projects. But it can be a useful indicator of some things. Because a dollar of cash flow in the early years is worth more than a dollar of cash flow in later years, the payback period method provides a simple yet crude measure of the value of the investment.

The payback period also offers some indication of risk. In industries where equipment becomes obsolete rapidly or where there are very competitive conditions, investments with earlier paybacks are more valuable. That's because cash flows farther into the future are more uncertain and therefore have lower present value. In the personal computer industry, for example, the fierce competition and rapidly changing technology require investment in projects that have a payback of less than one year as there is no expectation of project benefits beyond one year.

Further, the payback period gives us a rough measure of the liquidity of the investment—how soon we get cash flows from our investment. However, because the payback method doesn't tell us the particular payback period that maximizes wealth, we cannot use it as the primary screening device for investments in long-lived assets.

Payback Period as an Evaluation Technique

Let's look at the payback period technique in terms of the three criteria listed earlier.

Criterion 1: Does Payback Consider All Cash Flows?   Look at Investments C and D in Exhibit 13.1 and let's assume that their cash flows have similar risk, require an initial outlay of $1,000,000, and have cash flows at the end of each year. Both investments have a payback period of four years. If we used only the payback period to evaluate them, it's likely we would conclude that both investments are identical. Yet, Investment D is more valuable because of the cash flow of $10,000,000 in 2005. The payback method *ignores* the $10,000,000! We know C and D cannot be equal. Certainly Investment D's $10 million in the year 2005 is more valuable in 2000 than Investment C's $300,000.

Criterion 2: Does Payback Consider the Timing of Cash Flows?   Look at Investments E and F. They have similar risk, require an investment of $1,000,000, and have the expected end-of-year cash flows described in Exhibit 13.1. The payback period of both investments is four years. But the cash flows of Investment F are received later in the 4-year period than those of Investment E. We know that there is a time value to money—receiving money sooner is better than later—which is not considered in a payback evaluation. The payback period method ignores the timing of cash flows.

Criterion 3: Does Payback Consider the Riskiness of Cash Flows?   Look at Investments G and H. Each requires an investment of $1,000,000 and both have identical cash inflows. If we assume that the cash flows of Investment G are less risky than the cash flows of Investment H, can the payback period help us to decide which is preferred?

The payback period of both investments is four years. The payback period is *identical* for these two investments, even though the cash flows of Investment H are riskier and therefore less valuable today than those of Investment G. But we know that the more uncertain the future cash flow, the less valuable it is today. The payback period ignores the risk associated with the cash flows.

Is Payback Consistent with Owners' Wealth Maximization?   There is no connection between an investment's payback period and its profitability. The payback period evaluation ignores the time value of money, the uncertainty of future cash flows, and the contribution of a project to the value of the firm. Therefore, the payback period method is not going to indicate projects that maximize owners' wealth.

Discounted Payback Period

The *discounted payback period* is the time needed to pay back the original investment in terms of *discounted* future cash flows. Each cash flow is discounted back to the beginning of the investment at a rate that reflects both the time value of money and the uncertainty of the future cash flows. This rate is the cost of capital—the return required by the suppliers of capital (creditors and owners) to compensate them for the time value of money and the risk associated with the investment. The more uncertain the future cash flows, the greater the cost of capital.

From the perspective of the investor, the cost of capital is the *required rate of return* (RRR), the return that suppliers of capital demand on their investment (adjusted for tax deductibility of interest). Because the cost of capital and the RRR are basically the same concept but from different perspectives, we sometimes use the terms interchangeably in our study of capital budgeting.

Returning to Investments A and B, suppose that each has a cost of capital of 10%. The first step in determining the discounted payback period is to discount each year's cash flow to the beginning of the investment (the end of the year 2000) at the cost of capital:

	Investment A		Investment B	
Year	End of Year Cash Flow	Value at the End of 2000	End of Year Cash Flow	Value at the End of 2000
2001	$400,000	$363,636	$100,000	$90,909
2002	400,000	330,579	100,000	82,644
2003	400,000	300,526	100,000	75,131
2004	400,000	273,205	1,000,000	683,013
2005	400,000	248,369	1,000,000	620,921

How long does it take for each investment's discounted cash flows to pay back its $1,000,000 investment? The discounted payback period for A is four years:

	Investment A		
End of Year	Value at the End of 2000	Accumulated Discounted Cash Flows	
2001	$363,640	$363,640	
2002	330,580	694,220	
2003	300,530	994,750	
2004	273,205	1,267,955	⇐ $1,000,000 investment paid back
2005	248,369	1,516,324	

The discounted payback period for B is five years:

End of Year	Investment B Value at the End of 2000	Accumulated Discounted Cash Flows	
2001	$90,910	$90,910	
2002	86,240	177,150	
2003	75,130	252,280	
2004	683,010	935,290	
2005	620,921	1,556,211	⇐ $1,000,000 investment paid back

This example shows that it takes one more year to pay back each investment with discounted cash flows than with nondiscounted cash flows.

Discounted Payback Decision Rule

It appears that the shorter the payback period, the better, whether using discounted or nondiscounted cash flows. But how short is better? We don't know. All we know is that an investment "breaks-even" in terms of discounted cash flows at the discounted payback period—the point in time when the accumulated discounted cash flows equal the amount of the investment. Using the length of the payback as a basis for selecting investments, A is preferred over B. But we've ignored some valuable cash flows for both investments.

Discounted Payback as an Evaluation Technique

Here is how discounted payback measures up against the three criteria.

Criterion 1: Does Discounted Payback Consider All Cash Flows?   Look again at Investments C and D. The main difference between them is that D has a very large cash flow in 2005, relative to C. Discounting each cash flow at the 10% cost of capital,

Year	Investment C End of Year Cash Flow	Value at the End of 2000	Investment D End of Year Cash Flow	Value at the End of 2000
2001	$300,000	$272,727	$300,000	$272,727
2002	300,000	247,934	300,000	247,934
2003	300,000	225,394	300,000	225,394
2004	300,000	204,904	300,000	204,904
2005	300,000	186,276	10,000,000	6,209,213

The discounted payback period for C is four years:

End of Year	Investment C Value at the End of 2000	Accumulated Discounted Cash Flows	
2001	$272,727	$272,727	
2002	247,934	520,661	
2003	225,394	746,055	
2004	204,904	950,959	
2005	186,276	1,137,235	⇐ $1,000,000 investment paid back

The discounted payback period for D is also four years, with each year-end cash flow from 2001 through 2004 contributing the same as those of Investment C. However, D's cash flow in 2005 contributes over $6 million more in terms of the present value of the project's cash flows:

End of Year	Investment D Value at the End of 2000	Accumulated Discounted Cash Flows	
2001	$272,727	$272,727	
2002	247,934	520,661	
2003	225,394	746,055	
2004	204,904	950,959	
2005	6,209,213	7,160,172	⇐ $1,000,000 investment paid back

The discounted payback period method ignores the remaining discounted cash flows: $950,959 + $186,276 – $1,000,000 = $137,235 from Investment C in year 2005 and $950,959 + $6,209,213 – $1,000,000 = $6,160,172 from Investment D in year 2005.

Criterion 2: Does Discounted Payback Consider the Timing of Cash Flows?

Look at Investments E and F. Using a cost of capital of 5% for both E and F, the discounted cash flows for each period are:

	Investment E		Investment F	
Year	End of Year Cash Flow	Value at the End of 2000	End of Year Cash Flow	Value at the End of 2000
2001	$300,000	$285,714	$0	$0
2002	300,000	272,109	0	0
2003	300,000	259,151	0	0
2004	300,000	246,811	1,200,000	987,243
2005	300,000	235,058	300,000	235,058

The discounted payback period for E is four years:

	Investment E	
End of Year	Value at the End of 2000	Accumulated Discounted Cash Flows
2001	$285,714	$285,714
2002	272,109	557,823
2003	259,151	816,974
2004	246,811	1,063,785	⇐ $1,000,000 investment paid back
2005	235,058	1,298,843

The discounted payback period for F is five years:

	Investment F	
End of Year	Value at the End of 2000	Accumulated Discounted Cash Flows
2001	$0	$0
2002	0	0
2003	0	0
2004	$987,243	$987,243
2005	235,058	1,222,301	⇐ $1,000,000 investment paid back

The discounted payback period is able to distinguish investments with different timing of cash flows. E's cash flows are expected sooner than those of F. E's discounted payback period is shorter than F's—four years versus five years.

Criterion 3: Does Discounted Payback Consider the Riskiness of Cash Flows?

Look at Investments G and H. Suppose the cost of capital for G is 5% and the cost of capital for H is 10%. We are assuming that H's cash flows are more uncertain than G's. The discounted cash flows for the two investments, using the appropriate discount rate, are:

	Investment G		Investment H	
Year	End of Year Cash Flow	Value at the End of 2000	End of Year Cash Flow	Value at the End of 2000
2001	$250,000	$238,095	$250,000	$227,273
2002	250,000	226,757	250,000	206,612
2003	250,000	215,959	250,000	187,829
2004	250,000	205,676	250,000	170,753
2005	250,000	195,882	250,000	155,230

The discounted payback period for G is five years:

	Investment G	
End of Year	Value at the End of 2000	Accumulated Discounted Cash Flows
2001	$238,095	$238,095
2002	226,757	464,852
2003	215,959	680,811
2004	205,676	886,487
2005	195,882	1,082,369 ⇐ $1,000,000 investment paid back

According to the discounted payback period method, H does not pay back its original $1,000,000 investment not in terms of discounted cash flows:

	Investment H	
End of Year	Value at the End of 2000	Accumulated Discounted Cash Flows
2001	$227,273	$227,273
2002	206,612	433,885
2003	187,829	621,714
2004	170,753	792,467
2005	155,230	947,697 ⇐ Less than $1,000,000 paid back

Because risk is reflected through the discount rate, risk is explicitly incorporated into the discounted payback period analysis. The discounted payback period method is able to distinguish between Investment G and the riskier Investment H.

Is Discounted Payback Consistent with Owners' Wealth Maximization?

Discounted payback cannot provide us any information about how profitable an investment is—because it ignores everything after the "break-even" point! The discounted payback period can be used as an initial screening device—eliminating any projects that don't pay back over the expected term of the investment. But since it ignores some of the cash flows that contribute to the present value of investment (those above and beyond what is necessary for the investment's payback), the discounted payback period technique is not consistent with owners' wealth maximization.

Net Present Value

If offered an investment that costs $5,000 today and promises to pay you $7,000 two years from today and if your opportunity cost for projects of similar risk is 10%, would you make this investment? You need to compare your $5,000 investment with the $7,000 cash flow you expect in two years. Because you feel that a discount rate of 10% reflects the degree of uncertainty associated with the $7,000 expected in two years, today it is worth:

Present value of $7,000 to be received in two years

$$= \frac{\$7,000}{(1 + 0.10)^2} = \$5,785.12$$

By investing $5,000 today, you are getting in return a promise of a cash flow in the future that is worth $5,785.12 today. You increase your wealth by $785.12 when you make this investment.

Another way of stating this is that the present value of the $7,000 cash inflow is $5,785.12, which is more than the $5,000, today's cash outflow to make the investment. When we subtract the $5,000 from the present value of the cash inflow from the investment, the difference is the increase or decrease in our wealth referred to as the net present value.

The *net present value* (NPV) is the present value of *all* expected cash flows.

Net Present Value = Present value of all expected cash flows or, in terms of the incremental operating and investment cash flows,

Net present value = Present value of the change in operating cash flows
+ Present value of the investment cash flows

The term "net" is used because we want to determine the difference between the change in the operating cash flows and the investment cash flows. Often the change in operating cash flows are inflows and the investment cash flows are outflows. Therefore we tend to refer to the net present value as the difference between the present value of the cash inflows and the present value of the cash outflows.

We can represent the net present value using summation notation, where t indicates any particular period, CF_t represents the cash flow at the end of period t, r represents the cost of capital, and N the number of periods comprising the economic life of the investment:

$$NPV = \sum_{t=0}^{N} \frac{CF_t}{(1+r)^t} \qquad (13\text{-}1)$$

Cash inflows are positive values of CF_t and cash outflows are negative values of CF_t. For any given period t, we collect all the cash flows (positive and negative) and net them together. To make things a bit easier to track, let's just refer to cash flows as inflows or outflows, and not specifically identify them as operating or investment cash flows.

Let's take another look at Investments A and B. Using a 10% cost of capital, the present values of inflows are:

| | Investment A | | Investment B | |
Year	End of Year Cash Flow	Value at the End of 2000	End of Year Cash Flow	Value at the End of 2000
2001	$400,000	$363,636	$100,000	$90,909
2002	400,000	330,579	100,000	82,645
2003	400,000	300,526	100,000	75,131
2004	400,000	273,205	1,000,000	683,013
2005	400,000	248,369	1,000,000	620,921
Present value of the cash inflows		$1,516,315		$1,552,620

The present value of the cash outflows is the outlay of $1,000,000. The net present value of A is $516,315:

$$\text{NPV of A} = \$1,516,315 - \$1,000,000 = \$516,315$$

and the Net Present Value of B is $552,620:

$$\text{NPV of B} = \$1,552,620 - \$1,000,000 = \$552,620$$

These NPVs tell us if we invest in A, we expect to increase the value of the firm by $516,315. If we invest in B, we expect to increase the value of the firm by $552,620.

Net Present Value Decision Rule

A positive net present value means that the investment increases the value of the firm—the return is more that sufficient to compensate for the required return of the investment. A negative net present value means that the investment decreases the value of the firm—the return is less than the cost of capital. A zero net present value means that the return just equals the return required by owners to compensate them for the degree of uncertainty of the investment's future cash flows and the time value of money. Therefore,

If...	this means that...	and you...
NPV > 0	the investment is expected to increase shareholder wealth	should accept the project.
NPV < 0	the investment is expected to decrease shareholder wealth	should reject the project.
NPV = 0	the investment is expected not to change shareholder wealth	should be indifferent between accepting or rejecting the project.

Investment A increases the value of the firm by $516,315 and B increases it by $552,620. If these are independent investments, both should be taken on because both increase the value of the firm. If A and B are *mutually exclusive*, such that the only choice is either A *or* B, then B is preferred since it has the greater NPV.

Net Present Value as an Evaluation Technique

Now let's compare the net present value technique in terms of the three criteria.

Criterion 1: Does Net Present Value Consider All Cash Flows? Look at Investments C and D, which are similar except for the cash flows in 2005. The net present value of each investment, using a 10% cost of capital, is:

$$\text{NPV of C} = \$1,137,236 - \$1,000,000 = \$137,236$$

$$\text{NPV of D} = \$7,160,172 - \$1,000,000 = \$6,160,172$$

Because C and D each have positive net present values, each is expected to increase the value of the firm. And because D has the higher NPV, it provides the greater increase in value. If we had to choose between them, D is much better because it is expected to increase owners' wealth by over $6 million.

The net present value technique considers all future incremental cash flows. D's NPV with a large cash flow in year 2005 is much greater than C's NPV.

Criterion 2: Does Net Present Value Consider the Timing of

Cash Flows? Let's look again at projects E and F whose total cash flow is the same but their yearly cash flows differ. The net present values are:

$$\text{NPV of E} = \$1,298,843 - \$1,000,000 = \$298,843$$

$$\text{NPV of F} = \$1,222,301 - \$1,000,000 = \$222,301$$

Both E and F are expected to increase owners' wealth. But E, whose cash flows are received sooner, has a greater NPV. Therefore, NPV does consider the timing of the cash flows.

Criterion 3: Does Net Present Value Consider the Riskiness of

Cash Flows? For this we'll look again at Investments G and H. They have identical cash flows, although H's inflows are riskier than G's. For G, the net present value is positive and for H it is negative:

$$\text{NPV of G} = \$1,082,369 - \$1,000,000 = \$82,369$$

$$\text{NPV of H} = \$947,697 - \$1,000,000 = -\$52,303$$

G is acceptable since it is expected to *increase* owners' wealth. H is not acceptable since it is expected to *decrease* owners' wealth. The net present value method is able to distinguish among investments whose cash flows have different risk.

Is Net Present Value Consistent with Owners'

Wealth Maximization? Because the net present value is a measure of how much owners' wealth is expected to increase with an investment, NPV can help us identify projects that maximize owners' wealth.

EXHIBIT 13.2   Investment Profile of Investment A

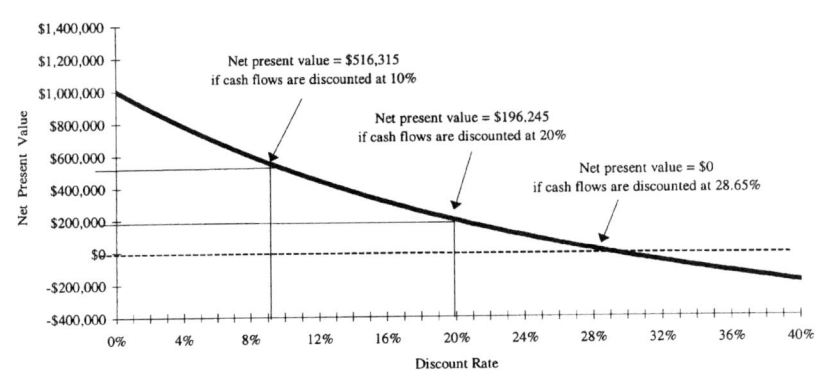

The Investment Profile

The net present value technique also allows you to determine the effect of changes in cost of capital on a project's profitability. A project's *investment profile*, also referred to as the *net present value profile*, shows how NPV changes as the discount rate changes. The investment profile is a graphical depiction of the relation between the net present value of a project and the discount rate. It shows the net present value of a project for a range of discount rates.

The net present value profile for Investment A is shown in Exhibit 13.2 for discount rates from 0% to 40%. To help you get the idea behind this graph, we've identified the NPVs of this project for discount rates of 10% and 20%. The graph shows that the NPV is positive for discount rates from 0% to 28.65%, and negative for discount rates higher than 28.65%. Therefore, Investment A increases owners' wealth if the cost of capital on this project is less than 28.65% and decreases owners' wealth if the cost of capital on this project is greater than 28.65%.

Let's impose A's NPV profile on the NPV profile of Investment B, as shown in Exhibit 13.3. If A and B are mutually exclusive projects, this graph shows that the project we invest in depends on the discount rate. For higher discount rates, B's NPV falls faster than A's. This is because most of B's present value is attributed to the large cash flows four and five years into the future. The present value of the more distant cash flows is more sensitive to changes in the discount rate than is the present value of cash flows nearer the present.

If the discount rate is less than 12.07%, B increases wealth more than A. If the discount rate is more than 12.07% but less than 28.65%, A increases wealth more than B. If the discount rate is greater than 28.65%,

EXHIBIT 13.3 Investment Profile of Investments A and B

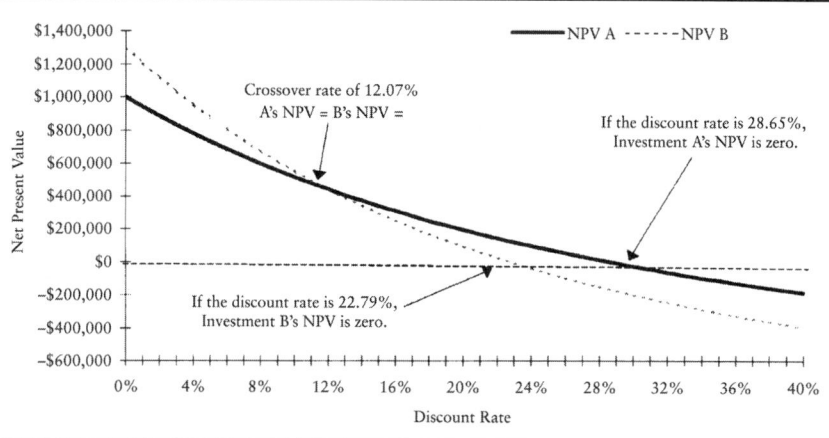

we should invest in neither project, since both would decrease wealth. The 12.07% is the *crossover discount rate* which produces identical NPV's for the two projects. If the discount rate is 12.07%, the net present value of both investments is $439,414.[1]

---

[1] We can solve for the crossover rate directly. For Investments A and B, the crossover rate is the rate i that equates the net present value of Investment A with the net present value of Investment B:

$$\underbrace{-\$1,000,000 + \sum_{t}^{5} \frac{\$400,000}{(1+r)^t}}_{NPV_A} = \underbrace{-\$1,000,000 + \frac{\$100,000}{(1+r)^1} + \frac{\$100,000}{(1+r)^2} + \frac{\$100,000}{(1+r)^3} + \frac{\$1,000,000}{(1+r)^4} + \frac{\$1,000,000}{(1+r)^5}}_{NPV_B}$$

Combining like terms—those with the same denominators,

$$\frac{\$400,000-\$100,000}{(1+r)^1} + \frac{\$400,000-\$100,000}{(1+r)^2} + \frac{\$400,000-\$100,000}{(1+r)^3}$$
$$+ \frac{\$400,000-\$1,000,000}{(1+r)^4} + \frac{\$400,000-\$1,000,000}{(1+r)^5} = 0$$

Simplifying,

$$\frac{\$300,000}{(1+r)^1} + \frac{\$300,000}{(1+r)^2} + \frac{\$300,000}{(1+r)^3} + \frac{-\$600,000}{(1+r)^4} + \frac{-\$600,000}{(1+r)^5} + 0$$

This last equation is in the form of a yield problem: The crossover rate is the rate of return of the *differences* in cash flows of the investments. The i that solves this equation is 12.07%, the crossover rate.

NPV and Further Considerations

The net present value technique considers:

1. All expected future cash flows;
2. The time value of money; and
3. The risk of the future cash flows.

Evaluating projects using NPV will lead us to select the ones that maximize owners' wealth. But there are a couple of things we need to take into consideration using net present value.

First, NPV calculations result in a dollar amount, say $500 or $23,413, which is the incremental value to owners' wealth. However, investors and managers tend to think in terms of percentage returns: Does this project return 10%? 15%?

Second, to calculate NPV we need to know a cost of capital. This is not so easy. The concept behind the cost of capital is simple. It is compensation to the suppliers of capital for (1) the time value of money and (2) the risk they accept that the cash flows they expect to receive may not materialize as projected. Getting an estimate of how much compensation is needed is not so simple. That's because to estimate a cost of capital we have to make a judgment on the risk of a project and how much return is needed to compensate for that risk—an issue we address in another chapter.

Profitability Index

The *profitability index* (PI) is the ratio of the present value of change in operating cash inflows to the present value of investment cash outflows:

$$PI = \frac{\text{Present value of the change in operating cash inflows}}{\text{Present value of the investment cash outflows}} \quad (13\text{-}2)$$

Instead of the *difference* between the two present values, as in equation (13-1), PI is the *ratio* of the two present values. Hence, PI is a variation of NPV. By construction, if the NPV is zero, PI is one.

Suppose the present value of the change in cash inflows is $200,000 and the present value of the change in cash outflows is $200,000. The NPV (the difference between these present values) is zero and the PI (the ratio of these present values) is 1.0.

Looking at Investments A and B, the PI for A is:

$$PI \text{ of } A = \frac{\$1,516,315}{\$1,000,000} = 1.5163$$

and the PI for B is:

$$PI \text{ of } B = \frac{\$1,552,620}{\$1,000,000} = 1.5526$$

The PI of 1.5163 means that for each \$1 invested in A, we get approximately \$1.52 in value; the PI of 1.5526 means that for each \$1 invested in B, we get approximately \$1.55 in value.

The PI is often referred to as the *benefit-cost ratio*, since it is the ratio of the benefit from an investment (the present value of cash inflows) to its cost (the present value of cash outflows).

Profitability Index Decision Rule

The profitability index tells us how much value we get for each dollar invested. If the PI is greater than one, we get more than \$1 for each \$1 invested—if the PI is less than one, we get less than \$1 for each \$1 invested. Therefore, a project that increases owners' wealth has a PI greater than one.

If ...	this means that ...	and you ...
PI > 1	the investment returns more than \$1 in present value for every \$1 invested	should accept the project.
PI < 1	the investment returns less than \$1 in present value for every \$1 invested	should reject the project.
PI = 1	the investment returns \$1 in present value for every \$1 invested	should be indifferent between accepting or rejecting the project.

Profitability Index as an Evaluation Technique

How does the profitability index technique stack up against the three criteria? Here's how.

Criterion 1: Does the Profitability Index Consider All Cash Flows?　For Investment C,

$$PI \text{ of } C = \frac{\$1,137,236}{\$1,000,000} = 1.1372$$

which indicates that the present value of the change in operating cash flows exceeds the present value investment cash flows. For Investment D,

$$PI \text{ of } D = \frac{\$7,160,172}{\$1,000,000} = 7.1602$$

which is much larger than the PI of C, indicating that D produces more value per dollar invested than C.

The PI includes all cash flows.

Criterion 2: Does the Profitability Index Consider the Timing of Cash Flows?

From the data representing Investments E and F, which differ on the timing of the future cash flows:

$$\text{PI of E} = \frac{\$1,298,843}{\$1,000,000} = 1.0824 \text{ and PI of F} = \frac{\$1,222,301}{\$1,000,000} = 1.2223$$

The PI of Investment E, whose cash flows occur sooner is higher than the PI of F. Hence, the PI considers the time value of money.

Criterion 3: Does the Profitability Index Consider the Riskiness of Cash Flows?

Back again to Investments G and H, which have different risk.

$$\text{PI of G} = \frac{\$1,082,369}{\$1,000,000} = 1.0824 \text{ and PI of H} = \frac{\$947,697}{\$1,000,000} = 0.9477$$

The less risky project, G, has a higher PI and is therefore preferred to H, the riskier project.

The PI is able to distinguish between Investment G and the riskier investment, H. The PI of G is greater than the PI of H, even though the expected future cash flows of G and H are the same. The PI does consider the riskiness of the investment's cash flows.

Is the Profitability Index Consistent with Owners' Wealth Maximization?

Rejecting or accepting investments having PI's greater than 1.0 is consistent with rejecting or accepting investments whose NPV is greater than $0. However, in ranking projects, PI might result in one order while NPV might order the same projects differently. This can happen when trying to rank projects that require different amounts to be invested.

Consider the following:

Investment	Present Value of Cash Inflows	Present Value of Cash Outflows	PI	NPV
J	$110,000	$100,000	1.10	$10,000
K	315,000	300,000	1.05	15,000

Investment K has a larger net present value, so it is expected to increase the value of owners' wealth by more than J. But the profitability index values are different: J has a higher PI than K. According to the PI, J is preferred even though it contributes less to the value of the firm. The source of this conflict is the different amounts of investments—scale differences. Because of the way the PI is calculated (as a ratio, instead of a difference), projects that produce the same present value may have different PIs.

Consider two mutually exclusive projects, P and Q:

Project	Present Value of Inflows	Present Value of Outflows	PI	NPV
P	$110,000	$100,000	1.10	$10,000
Q	20,000	10,000	2.00	$10,000

If we rank according to the profitability index, Project Q is preferred, although they both contribute the same value, $10,000, to the firm.

Consider two mutually exclusive projects, P and R:

Project	Present Value of Inflows	Present Value of Outflows	PI	NPV
P	$110,000	$100,000	1.10	$10,000
R	11,000	10,000	1.10	1,000

According to the profitability index, P and R are the same, yet P contributes more value to the firm, $10,000 versus $1,000.

Consider two mutually exclusive projects, P and S:

Project	Present Value of Inflows	Present Value of Outflows	PI	NPV
P	$110,000	$100,000	1.10	$10,000
S	120,000	110,000	1.09	10,000

Ranking on the basis of the profitability index, P is preferred to S, even though they contribute the same value to the firm, $10,000.

Seen enough? If the projects are mutually exclusive and have different scales, selecting a project on the basis of the profitability index may not provide the best decision in terms of owners' wealth. As long as we don't have to choose among projects, so that we can take on all profitable projects, using PI produces the same decision as NPV. If the projects are *mutually exclusive* and they are *different scales*, PI cannot be used.

If there is a limit on how much we can spend on capital projects, PI is useful. Limiting the capital budget is referred to as *capital rationing*. Capital rationing limits the amount that can be spent on capital investments during a particular period of time—that is, a limit on the capital budget. These constraints may arise out some policy of the board of directors, or may arise externally, say from creditor agreements that limit capital spending. If a firm has limited management personnel, the board of directors may not want to take on more projects than they feel they can effectively manage.

Consider the following three projects:

Project	Investment	NPV	PI
X	$10,000	$6,000	1.6
Y	$10,000	$5,000	1.5
Z	$20,000	$8,000	1.4

If there is a limit of $20,000 on what we can spend, which project or group of projects are best in terms of maximizing owners' wealth? If we base our choice on NPV, choosing the projects with the highest NPV, we would choose Z, whose NPV is $8,000. If we base our choice on PI, we would choose Projects X and Y—those with the highest PI—providing a NPV of $6,000 + 5,000 = $11,000.

Our goal in selecting projects when the capital budget is limited is to select those projects that provide the highest *total NPV*, given our constrained budget. We could use NPV to select projects, but we cannot *rank* projects on the basis of NPV and always get the greatest value for our investment. As an alternative, we could calculate the total NPV for all possible combinations of investments, or use a management science technique, such as linear programming, to find the optimal set of projects. If we have many projects to choose from, we can also rank projects on the basis of their PIs and choose those projects with the highest PIs that fit into our capital budget.

Selecting projects based on PI when capital is limited provides us with the maximum total NPV for our total capital budget. The overriding goal of the firm is to maximize owners' wealth. But if you limit capital spending, the firm may have to forego projects that are expected to increase owners' wealth and therefore owners' wealth is not maximized.

Internal Rate of Return

Suppose you are offered an investment opportunity that requires you to put up $50,000 and has expected cash inflows of $28,809.52 after one year and $28,809.52 after two years. We can evaluate this opportunity using the following time line:

Today	One year from today	Two years from today
-$50,000.00	$28,809.52	$28,809.52

The return on this investment is the discount rate that causes the present values of the $28,809.52 cash inflows to equal the present value of the $50,000 cash outflow:

$$\$50,000.00 = \frac{\$28,809.52}{(1+r)^1} + \frac{\$28,809.52}{(1+r)^2}$$

Solving for the return r:

$$\$50,000.00 = \$28,809.52\left[\frac{1}{(1+r)^1} + \frac{1}{(1+r)^2}\right]$$

$$\frac{\$50,000.00}{\$28,809.52} = \left[\frac{1}{(1+r)^1} + \frac{1}{(1+r)^2}\right]$$

$$1.7355 = \left(\begin{array}{c}\text{present value annuity factor}\\ N = 2, r = ?\end{array}\right)$$

The right side is the present value annuity factor, so we can use the tables to determine i, where N is the number of cash flows. Using the present value annuity table or a calculator annuity function, $r = 10\%$. The yield on this investment is therefore 10% per year.

Let's look at this problem from a different angle so we can see the relation between the net present value and the internal rate of return. Calculate the net present value of this investment at 10% per year:

$$\text{NPV} = -\$50,000.00 + \frac{\$28,809.52}{(1+0.10)^1} + \frac{\$28,809.52}{(1+0.10)^2} = \$0$$

Therefore, the net present value of the investment is zero when cash flows are discounted at the yield.

An investment's *internal rate of return* (IRR) is the discount rate that makes the present value of all expected future cash flows equal to zero; or, in other words, the IRR is the discount rate that causes NPV to equal $0.

We can represent the IRR as the rate that solves:

$$\$0 = \sum_{t=1}^{N} \frac{CF_t}{(1+IRR)^t} \qquad (13\text{-}3)$$

Let's return to Investments A and B. The IRR for Investment A is the discount rate that solves:

$$\$0 = -\$1,000,000 + \frac{\$400,000}{(1+IRR)^1} + \frac{\$400,000}{(1+IRR)^2}$$
$$+ \frac{\$400,000}{(1+IRR)^3} + \frac{\$400,000}{(1+IRR)^4} + \frac{\$400,000}{(1+IRR)^5}$$

Recognizing that the cash inflows are the same each period and rearranging,

$$\frac{\$1,000,000}{\$400,000} = 2.5$$

Using the present value annuity factor table, we see that the discount rate that solves this equation is approximately 30% per year. Using a calculator or a computer, we get the more precise answer of 28.65% per year.

Let's calculate the IRR for B so that we can see how we can use IRR to value investments. The IRR for Investment B is the discount rate that solves:

$$\$0 = -\$1,000,000 + \frac{\$100,000}{(1+IRR)^1} + \frac{\$100,000}{(1+IRR)^2} + \frac{\$100,000}{(1+IRR)^3}$$
$$+ \frac{\$100,000}{(1+IRR)^4} + \frac{\$100,000}{(1+IRR)^5}$$

The cash inflows are not the same amount each period, so we cannot use the shortcut of solving for the present value annuity factor, as we did for Investment A. We can solve for the IRR of Investment B by: (1) trial and error, (2) calculator, or (3) computer.

Trial and error requires a starting point. To make the trial and error a bit easier, let's rearrange the equation, putting the present value of the cash outflows on the left-hand side:

$$\$1,000,000 = \frac{\$100,000}{(1+IRR)^1} + \frac{\$100,000}{(1+IRR)^2} + \frac{\$100,000}{(1+IRR)^3}$$
$$+ \frac{\$100,000}{(1+IRR)^4} + \frac{\$100,000}{(1+IRR)^5}$$

If we try IRR = 10% per year, the right-hand side is greater than the left-hand side:

$$\$1,000,000 \neq \$1,552,620$$

This tells us that we have not discounted enough. Increasing the discount rate to 20% per year,

$$\$1,000,000 \neq \$1,094,779$$

We *still* haven't discounted the cash flows enough. Increasing the discount rate still further, to 25% per year,

$$\$1,000,000 \neq \$932,480$$

We discounted *too* much—we drove the right-hand side below $1,000,000. But at least now we know the IRR is between 20% and 25%. Using a calculator or computer, the precise value of IRR is 22.79% per year.[2]

Looking back at Exhibit 13.3, the investment profiles of Investments A and B, you'll notice that each profile crosses the horizontal axis (where NPV = $0) at the discount rate that corresponds to the investment's internal rate of return. This is no coincidence: By definition, the IRR is the discount rate that causes the project's NPV to equal zero.

Internal Rate of Return Decision Rule

The internal rate of return is a yield—what we earn, on average, per year. How do we use it to decide which investment, if any, to choose? Let's revisit Investments A and B and the IRRs we just calculated for each. If, for similar risk investments, owners earn 10% per year, then both A and B are attractive. They both yield *more* than the rate owners require for the level of risk of these two investments:

---

[2] Your calculator does not arrive at the solution directly. Your calculator's program uses trial and error also—and keeps you waiting as it tries different discount rates.

Investment	IRR	Cost of Capital
A	28.65% per year	10% per year
B	22.79%	10%

The decision rule for the internal rate of return is to invest in a project if it provides a return greater than the cost of capital. The cost of capital, in the context of the IRR, is a hurdle rate—the minimum acceptable rate of return.

If ...	this means that ...	and you ...
IRR > cost of capital	the investment is expected to return more than required	should accept the project.
IRR < cost of capital	the investment is expected to return less than required	should reject the project.
IRR = cost of capital	the investment is expected to return what is required	should be indifferent between accepting or rejecting the project.

The IRR and Mutually Exclusive Projects   What if we were forced to choose *between* projects A and B because they are mutually exclusive? A has a higher IRR than B—so at first glance we might want to accept A. But wait! What about the NPV of A and B? What does the NPV tell us to do?

Investment	IRR	NPV
A	28.65%	$516,315
B	22.79%	$552,620

If we use the higher IRR, it tells us to go with A. If we use the higher NPV, we go with B. Which is correct? If 10% is the cost of capital we used to determine both NPVs and we choose A, we will be foregoing value in the amount of $552,620 − $516,315 = $36,305. Therefore, we should choose B, the one with the higher NPV.

In this example, if for both A and B the cost of capital were different, say 25%, we would calculate different NPVs and come to a different conclusion. In this case:

Investment	IRR	NPV
A	28.65%	$75,712
B	22.79%	−$67,520

Investment A still has a positive NPV, since its IRR > 25%, but B has a negative NPV, since its IRR < 25%.

When evaluating mutually exclusive projects, the one with the highest IRR may not be the one with the best NPV. The IRR may give a different decision than NPV when evaluating mutually exclusive projects because of the reinvestment assumption:

- NPV assumes cash flows are reinvested at the cost of capital.
- IRR assumes cash flows are reinvested at the internal rate of return.

This reinvestment assumption may lead to different decisions in choosing among mutually exclusive projects when any of the following factors apply:

- The timing of the cash flows is different among the projects,
- There are scale differences (that is, very different cash flow amounts), or
- The projects have different useful lives.

Let's see the effect of the timing of cash flows in choosing between two projects: Investment A's cash flows are received sooner than B's. Part of the return on each investment comes from the reinvestment of its cash inflows. And in the case of A, there is more return from the reinvestment of cash inflows. The question is "What do you do with the cash inflows when you get them?" We generally assume that if you receive cash inflows, you'll reinvest those cash flows in other assets.

Now we turn to the reinvestment rate assumption in choosing between these projects. Suppose we can reasonably expect to earn only the cost of capital on our investments. Then, for projects with an IRR above the cost of capital, we would be overstating the return on the investment using the IRR. Consider Investment A once again. If the best you can do is reinvest each of the $400,000 cash flows at 10%, these cash flows are worth $2,442,040:

Future value of Investment A's cash flows each invested at 10%

$$= \$400,000 \binom{\text{future value annuity factor}}{N = 5 \text{ and } r = 10\%}$$

$$= \$400,000(6.1051) = \$2,442,040$$

Investing $1,000,000 at the end of 2000 produces a value of $2,442,040 at the end of 2005 (cash flows plus the earnings on these cash flows at 10%). This means that if the best you can do is reinvest cash flows at 10%, then you earn not the IRR of 28.65%, but rather 19.55%:

$$FV = PV(1 + r)^n$$
$$\$2,442,040 = \$1,000,000(1 + r)^5$$
$$r = 19.55\%$$

If we evaluate projects on the basis of their IRR, we may select one that does not maximize value.

Remember that the NPV calculation assumes reinvestment at the cost of capital. If the reinvestment rate is assumed to be the project's cost of capital, we would evaluate projects on the basis of the NPV and select the one that maximizes owners' wealth.

The IRR and Capital Rationing   What if there is capital rationing? Suppose Investments A and B are independent projects. *Independent projects* means that the acceptance of one does not prevent the acceptance of the other. And suppose the capital budget is limited to $1,000,000. We are therefore forced to choose between A or B. If we select the one with the highest IRR, we choose A. But A is expected to increase wealth *less* than B. Ranking investments on the basis of their IRRs may not maximize wealth.

We can see this dilemma in Exhibit 13.3. The discount rate at which A's NPV is $0.00—A's IRR—28.65%, where A's profile crosses the horizontal axis. Likewise, B's IRR is 22.79%. The discount rate at which A's and B's profiles cross is the crossover rate, 12.07%. For discount rates less than 12.07%, B has the higher NPV. For discount rates greater than 12.07%, A has the higher NPV. If you choose A because it has a higher IRR, and if A's cost of capital is more than 12.07%, you have not chosen the project that produces the greatest value.

Suppose you evaluate four independent projects characterized by the following data:

Project	Investment Outlay	NPV	IRR
L	$2,000,000	$150,000	23%
M	3,000,000	250,000	22
N	5,000,000	500,000	21
O	10,000,000	1,000,000	20

If there is no capital rationing, you would spend $20 million since all four have positive NPVs. And we would expect owners' wealth to increase by $1,900,000, the sum of the NPVs.

But suppose the capital budget is limited to $10 million. If you select projects on the basis of their IRRs, you would choose projects L, M, and

N. But is this optimal in the sense of maximizing owners' wealth? Let's look at the value added from different investment strategies:

	Investment Selection	Amount of Investment	Total NPV
Selection based on highest IRRs	L, M, and N	$10,000,000	$900,000
Selection based on highest NPVs	O	10,000,000	1,000,000

We can increase the owners' wealth more with Project O than with the combined investment in Projects L, M, and N. Therefore, when there is capital rationing, selecting investments on the basis of IRR rankings is not consistent with maximizing wealth.

The source of the problem in the case of capital rationing is that the IRR is a percentage, not a dollar amount. Because of this, we cannot determine how to distribute the capital budget to maximize wealth because the investment or group of investments producing the highest yield does not mean they are the ones that produce the greatest wealth.

Internal Rate of Return as an Evaluation Technique

Here is how the internal rate of return technique stacks up against the three criteria.

Criterion 1: Does IRR Consider All Cash Flows? Looking at Investments C and D, the difference between them is D's cash flow in the last year. The internal rate of return for C is 15.24% per year and for D the IRR is 73.46% per year. The IRR considers all cash flows and, as a result, D's IRR is much larger than C's due to the cash flow in the last period.

Criterion 2: Does IRR Consider the Timing of Cash Flows? To see if the IRR can distinguish investments whose cash flows have different time values of money, let's look at Investments E and F. The IRR of E is 15.24% per year.

Notice that Investments C and E have identical cash flows, but C's cost of capital is 10% per year and E's cost of capital is 5% per year. Do the different costs of capital affect the calculation of net present value? Yes, since cash flows for C and E are discounted at different rates. Does this affect the calculation of the internal rate of return? No, since we are solving for the discount rate—we do not use the cost of capital. The cost of capital comes into play in making a decision, comparing IRR with the cost of capital.

The IRR of F is 10.15%. Investment E, whose cash flows are received sooner, has a higher IRR than F. The IRR does consider the timing of cash flows.

Criterion 3: Does IRR Consider the Riskiness of Cash Flows?   To examine whether the IRR considers the riskiness of cash flows, let's compare Investments G and H. The IRR for G is 7.93%. The cash flows of H are the same as those of G, so its IRR is the same, 7.93% per year.

The IRR of G exceeds the cost of capital, 5% per year, so we would accept G. The IRR of H is less than its cost of capital, 10% per year, so we would reject H. So how does the IRR method consider risk? The calculation of IRR doesn't consider risk, but when we compare a project's IRR with its cost of capital—that is, applying the decision rule—we do consider the risk of the cash flows.

Is IRR Consistent with Owners' Wealth Maximization?   Evaluating projects with IRR indicates the ones that maximize wealth so long as: (1) the projects are independent, and (2) they are not limited by capital rationing. For mutually exclusive projects or capital rationing, the IRR may—but not always—lead to projects that do not maximize wealth.

Multiple Internal Rates of Return

The typical project usually involves only one large negative cash flow initially, followed by a series of future positive flows. But that's not always the case. Suppose you are involved in a project that uses environmentally sensitive chemicals. It may cost you a great deal to dispose of them, which will cause a negative cash flow at the end of the project.

Suppose we are considering a project that has cash flows as follows:

Period	End of Period Cash Flow
0	−$100
1	+$474
2	−$400

What is the internal rate of return on this project? Solving for the internal rate of return:

$$\$0 = -\$100 + \frac{\$474}{(1 + IRR)^1} + \frac{-\$400}{(1 + IRR)^2}$$

One possible solution is IRR = 10%. Yet *another* possible solution is IRR = 2.65 or 265%. Therefore, there are two possible solutions, IRR = 10% per year and IRR = 265% per year.

We can see this graphically in Exhibit 13.4, where the NPV of these cash flows are shown for discount rates from 0% to 300%. Remember that the IRR is the discount rate that causes the NPV to be zero. In terms of this graph, this means that the IRR is the discount rate where the NPV is $0, the point at which the present value changes sign—from positive to negative or from negative to positive. In the case of this project, the present value changes from negative to positive at 10% and from positive to negative at 265%.

Multiple solutions to the yield on a series of cash flows occurs whenever there is more than one change from positive to negative or from negative to positive in the sequence of cash flows. For example, the cash flows in the previous example above followed a pattern of negative positive negative. There are two sign changes: from minus to plus and from plus to minus. There are also two possible solutions for IRR, one for each sign change.

If you end up with multiple solutions, what do you do? Can you use any of these? None of these? If there are multiple solutions, there is no unique internal rate of return. And if there is no unique solution, the solutions we get are worthless as far as making a decision based on IRR. This is a strike against the IRR as an evaluation technique.

Modified Internal Rate of Return

The *modified internal rate of return* technique is similar to the IRR, but using a more realistic reinvestment assumption. As we saw in the previous section, there are situations in which it's not appropriate to use the IRR.

EXHIBIT 13.4 Investment Profile of a Project with an Initial Cash Outlay of $100, a First Period Cash Inflow of $474, and a Second Period Cash Outflow of $400, Resulting in Multiple Internal Rates of Return

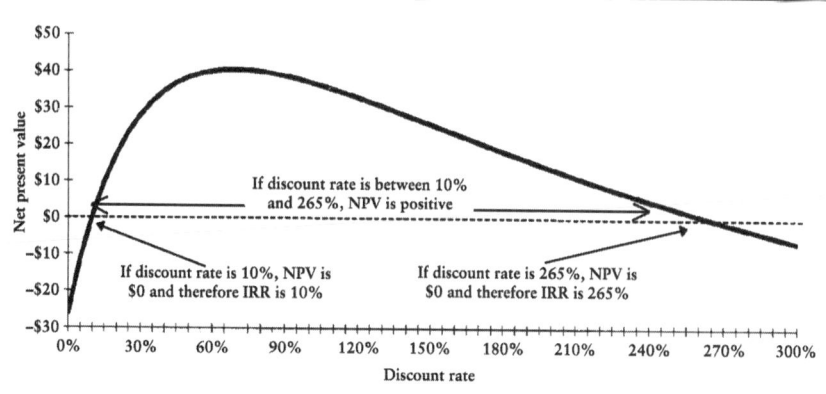

Let's look again at A's IRR of 28.65% per year. This means that when the first $400,000 comes into the firm, it is reinvested at 28.65% per year for four more periods, when the second $400,000 comes into the firm, it is reinvested at 28.65% per year for three more periods, and so on. If you reinvested all of A's cash inflows at the IRR of 28.65%—that is, you had other investments with the same 28.65% yield—you would have by the end of the project:

End of Year	Cash Inflow		Value at the End of the Project
2001	$400,000	$400,000 (1 + 0.2865)^4 =	$1,095,719
2002	400,000	$400,000 (1 + 0.2865)^3 =	$851,705
2003	400,000	$400,000 (1 + 0.2865)^2 =	$662,033
2004	400,000	$400,000 (1 + 0.2865)^1 =	$514,600
2005	400,000	$400,000 (1 + 0.2865)^0 =	$400,000
			$3,524,057

Investing $1,000,000 in A contributes $3,524,057 to the future value of the firm in the fifth year, providing a return on the investment of 28.65% per year. Let FV = $3,524,057, PV = $1,000,000, and $n = 5$. Using the basic valuation equation,

$$FV = PV(1 + i)^n$$

and substituting the known values for FV, PV, and n, and solving for r, the IRR,

$$\$3,524,057 = \$1,000,000(1 + i)^5$$
$$i = 28.65\% \text{ per year}$$

Therefore, by using financial math to solve for the annual return, i, we have assumed that the cash inflows are reinvested at the IRR.

Assuming that cash inflows are reinvested at the IRR is strike two against IRR as an evaluation technique if it is an unrealistic rate. One way to get around this problem is to modify the reinvestment rate built into the mathematics.

Suppose you have an investment with the following expected cash flows:

Year	End of Year Cash Flow
0	−$10,000
1	+$3,000
2	+$3,000
3	+$6,000

The IRR of this project is 8.55% per year. This IRR assumes you can reinvest each of the inflows at 8.55% per year. To see this, consider what you would have at the end of the third year if you reinvested each cash flow at 8.55%:

Year	End of Year Cash Flow	Future Value at End of Third Year, Using 8.55%
1	+$3,000	$3,000 (1 + 0.0855)^2 = $3,534.93
2	+$3,000	$3,000 (1 + 0.0855)^1 = $3,256.50
3	+$6,000	$6,000 (1 + 0.0855)^0 = $6,000.00
FV_3		$12,791.43

Investing $10,000 today produces a value of $12,791.43 at the end of the third year. The return on this investment is calculated using the present value of the investment (the $10,000), the future value of the investment (the $12,791.43) and the number of periods (3 in this case):

$$\text{Return on investment} = \sqrt[3]{\frac{\$12,791.43}{\$10,000.00}} - 1 = 8.55\%$$

Let's see what happens when we change the reinvestment assumption. If you invest in this project and each time you receive a cash inflow you stuff it under your mattress, you accumulate $12,000 by the end of the third year: $3,000 + 3,000 + 6,000 = $12,000. What return do you earn on your investment of $10,000? You invest $10,000 and end up with $12,000 after three years. The $12,000 is the future value of the investment, which is also referred to as the investment's *terminal value*.

We solve for the return on the investment by inserting the known values (PV = $10,000, FV = $12,000, n = 3) into the basic valuation equation and solving for the discount rate, r:

$$\$12,000 = \$10,000(1 + r)^3$$
$$(1 + r)^3 = \$12,000 / \$10,000$$
$$(1 + r) = \sqrt[3]{1.2} = 1.0627$$
$$r = 0.0627 \text{ or } 6.27\% \text{ per year}$$

EXHIBIT 13.5   Modified Internal Rate of Return

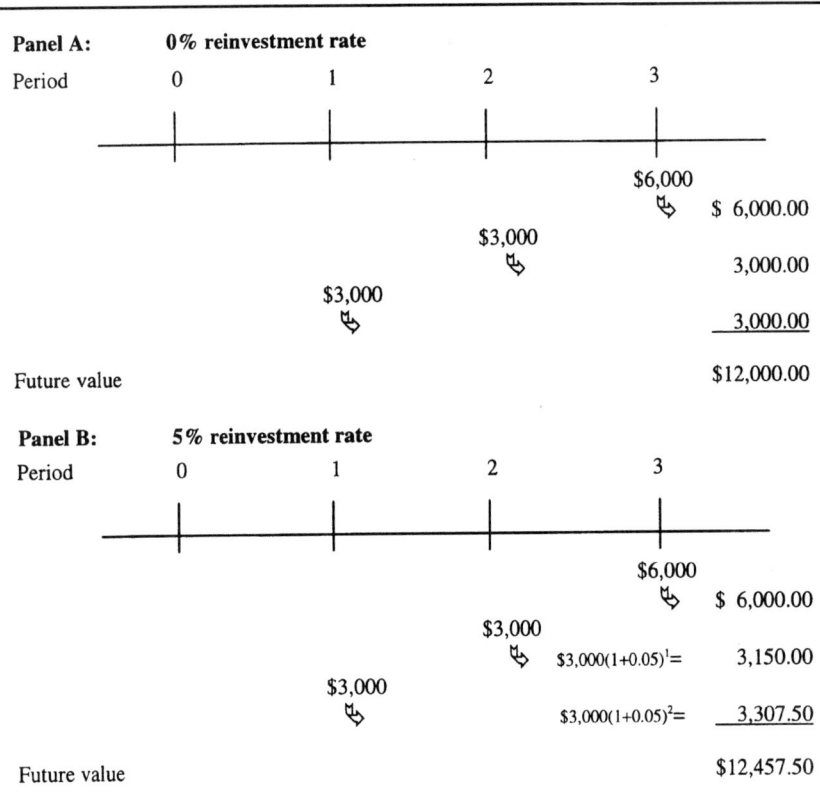

The return from this investment, with no reinvestment of cash flows, is 6.27%. We refer to this return as a *modified internal rate of return* (MIRR) because we have *modified* the reinvestment assumption. In this case, we modified the reinvestment rate from the IRR of 8.55% to 0%.

But what if, instead, you could invest the cash inflows in an investment that provides an annual return of 5%? Each cash flow earns 5% annually compounded interest until the end of the third period. We can represent this problem in a time line, shown in Exhibit 13.5. The future value of the cash inflows, with reinvestment at 5% annually, is:

$$FV = \$3,000(1 + 0.05)^2 + \$3,000(1 + 0.05)^1 + \$6,000$$
$$= \$3,307.50 + \$3,150.00 + \$6,000 = \$12,457.50$$

The MIRR is the return on the investment of $10,000 that produces $12,457.50 in three years:

$$\$12,457.50 = \$10,000(1 + MIRR)^5$$
$$MIRR = 0.0760 \text{ or } 7.60\% \text{ per year}$$

A way to think about the modified return is to consider breaking down the return into its two components:

1. the return you get if there is no reinvestment (our mattress stuffing), and
2. the return from reinvestment of the cash inflows.

We can also represent MIRR in terms of a formula that combines terms we are already familiar with. Consider the two steps in the calculation of MIRR:

Step 1: Calculate the present value of all cash outflows, using the reinvestment rate as the discount rate.

Step 2: Calculate the future value of all cash inflows reinvested at some rate.

Step 3: Solve for rate—the MIRR—that causes future value of cash inflows to equal present value of outflows:

In this last example,

Reinvestment Rate	Modified Internal Rate of Return (MIRR)
0.00%	6.27%
5.00%	7.60%
8.55%	8.55%

If instead of reinvesting each cash flow at 0%, we reinvest at 5% per year, then the reinvestment adds 7.60% − 6.27% = 1.33% to the investment's return. But wait—we reinvested at 5%. Why doesn't reinvestment add 5%? Because you only earn on reinvestment of intermediate cash flows—the first $3,000 for two periods at 5% and the second $3,000 for one period at 5%—not all cash flows.

Let's calculate the MIRR for Investments A and B, assuming reinvestment at the 10% cost of capital.

Step 1: Calculate the present value of the cash outflows. In both A's and B's case, this is $1,000,000.

Step 2: Calculate the future value by figuring the future value of each cash flow as of the end of 2005:[3]

	Investment A		Investment B	
Year	End of Year Cash Flows	End of Year 2005 Value of Cash Flow	End of Year Cash Flow	End of Year 2005 Value of Cash Flow
2001	$400,000	$585,640	$100,000	$146,410
2002	400,000	532,400	100,000	133,100
2003	400,000	484,000	100,000	121,000
2004	400,000	440,000	1,000,000	1,100,000
2005	400,000	400,000	1,000,000	1,000,000
Future value		$2,442,040		$2,500,510

Step 3: For A, solve for the rate that equates $2,442,040 in five years with $1,000,000 today:

$$\$2,442,040 = \$1,000,000(1 + MIRR)^5$$
$$MIRR = 0.1955 \text{ or } 19.55\% \text{ per year}$$

Following the same steps, the MIRR for Investment B is 20.12% per year.

Modified Internal Rate of Return Decision Rule

The modified internal rate of return is a return on the investment, assuming a particular return on the reinvestment of cash flows. As long as the MIRR is greater than the cost of capital—that is, MIRR > cost of capital—the project should be accepted. If the MIRR is less than the cost of capital, the project does not provide a return commensurate with the amount of risk of the project.

If ...	this means that ...	and you ...
MIRR > cost of capital	the investment is expected to return more than required	should accept the project.
MIRR < cost of capital	the investment is expected to return less than required	should reject the project.
MIRR = cost of capital	the investment is expected to return what is required	should be indifferent between accepting or rejecting the project.

---

[3] We have taken each cash flow and determined its value at the end of the year 2005. We could cut down our work by recognizing that these cash inflows are even amounts—simplifying the first step to the calculation of the future value of an ordinary annuity.

Consider Investments A and B and their MIRRs with reinvestment at the cost of capital:

Investment	MIRR	IRR	NPV
A	19.55%	28.65%	$516,315
B	20.12%	22.79%	$552,619

Assume for now that these are mutually exclusive investments. We saw the danger trying to rank projects on their IRRs if the projects are mutually exclusive. But what if we ranked projects according to MIRR? In this example, there seems to be a correspondence between MIRR and NPV. In the case of Investments A and B, MIRR and NPV provide identical rankings.

Modified Internal Rate of Return as an Evaluation Technique

Now we'll go through our usual drill of assessing this technique according to the three criteria.

Criterion 1: Does MIRR Consider All Cash Flows? Assume the cash inflows from Investments C and D are reinvested at the cost of capital of 10% per year. We find that the modified internal rate of return for C is 12.87% per year and for D is 63.07% per year.[4] D's larger cash flow in year 2005 is reflected in the larger MIRR. MIRR does consider all cash flows.

Criterion 2: Does MIRR Consider the Timing of Cash Flows? To see whether the MIRR can distinguish investments whose cash flows occur at different points in time, calculate the MIRR for Investments E and F. Using the terminal values for E and F of $1,831,530 and $1,620,000, respectively, we solve for the rate that equates the terminal value in five years with each investment's $1,000,000 outlay. The MIRR of E is 12.87% per year and the MIRR of F is 10.13% per year. E's cash flows are expected sooner than F's. This is reflected in the higher MIRR. Both E and F are acceptable investments because they provide a return above the cost of capital. If we had to choose between E and F, we would choose E because it has a higher MIRR. MIRR does consider the timing of cash flows.

Criterion 3: Does MIRR Consider the Riskiness of Cash Flows? Let's look at the MIRR for Investments G and H, which have identical expected cash flows, although H's inflows are riskier. Assuming that cash flows are reinvested at the 5% per year cost of capital for G and 10% per year for H, the

---

[4] The terminal values for C and D are $1,831,530 and $11,531,530, respectively.

future values are \$1,381,408 and \$1,526,275, respectively. The MIRR for G is 6.68%, calculated using the investment of \$1,000,000 as the present value and the terminal value of \$1,381,408. Using the same procedure, the MIRR for H is 8.82% per year. Comparing the MIRRs with the costs of capital,

Investment	MIRR	Cost of Capital	Decision
G	6.68%	5%	Accept
H	8.82%	10%	Reject

If we reinvest cash flows at the cost of capital and if the costs of capital are different, we get different terminal values and hence different MIRRs for G and H. If we then compare each project's MIRR with the project's cost of capital, we can determine the projects that would increase owners' wealth.

MIRR distinguishes between the investments, but choosing the investment with the highest MIRR may not give the value maximizing decision. In the case of G and H, H has a higher MIRR. But, when each project's MIRR is compared to the cost of capital, we see that Investment H should not be accepted. This points out the danger of using MIRR when capital is rationed or when choosing among mutually exclusive projects: Ranking and selecting projects on the basis of their MIRR may lead to a decision that does not maximize owners' wealth. If projects are not independent or if capital is rationed, we are faced with some of the same problems we encountered with the IRR in those situations: MIRR may not produce the decision that maximizes owners' wealth.

Is MIRR Consistent with Owners' Wealth Maximization? MIRR can be used to evaluate whether to invest in independent projects and identify the ones that maximize owners' wealth. However, decisions made using MIRR are not consistent with maximizing wealth when selecting among mutually exclusive projects or when there is capital rationing.

COMPARING TECHNIQUES

The results of our calculations using the six techniques we have discussed are summarized in Exhibit 13.6. If each of the eight projects are independent and are not limited by capital rationing, all projects except Investment H are expected to increase owners' wealth.

EXHIBIT 13.6 Summary of the Evaluation of the Investment Projects

Investment	Required Rate of Return	Payback Period	Discounted Payback Period	Net Present Value	Profitability Index	Internal Rate of Return	Modified Internal Rate of Return
A	10%	3 years	4 years	$516,315	1.5163	28.65%	19.55%
B	10%	4 years	5 years	552,620	1.5526	22.79%	20.12%
C	10%	4 years	4 years	137,236	1.1372	15.24%	12.87%
D	10%	4 years	4 years	6,160,172	7.1602	73.46%	63.07%
E	5%	4 years	4 years	298,843	1.2988	15.24%	12.87%
F	5%	4 years	5 years	222,301	1.2223	10.15%	10.13%
G	5%	4 years	5 years	82,369	1.0823	7.93%	6.68%
H	10%	4 years	not paid back	-52,303	0.9477	7.93%	8.82%

Suppose each project is independent, yet we have a capital budget limit of $5 million on the total amount we can invest. Since each of the eight projects requires $1 million, we can only invest in five of them. Which five projects do we invest in? In order of NPV, we choose: D, B, A, E, and F. We would expect the value of owners' wealth to increase by $6,160,172 + 552,620 + 516,315 + 298,843 + 222,301 = $7,750,251.

Now suppose that each pair of projects is a set of mutually exclusive projects. Which project of each mutually exclusive pair is preferred? Investments B, D, E, and G are preferred, choosing the projects with the higher NPV of each pair.

If you are considering mutually exclusive projects, the NPV method leads us to invest in projects that maximize wealth. If your capital budget is limited, the NPV and PI methods lead us to the set of projects that maximize wealth.

Scale Differences

Scale differences—differences in the amount of the cash flows—between projects can lead to conflicting investment decisions among the discounted cash flow techniques. Consider two projects, Project Big and Project Little, that each have a cost of capital of 5% per year with the following cash flows:

End of Period	Project Big	Project Little
0	−$1,000,000	−$1.00
1	+400,000	+0.40
2	+400,000	+0.40
3	+400,000	+0.50

Applying the discounted cash flow techniques to each project,

Discounted Cash Flow Technique	Project Big	Project Little
NPV	$89,299	$0.1757
PI	1.0893	1.1757
IRR	9.7010%	13.7789%
MIRR	8.0368%	10.8203%

Mutually Exclusive Projects

If Big and Little are mutually exclusive projects, which project should a firm prefer? If the firm goes strictly by the PI, IRR, or MIRR criteria, it would choose Project Little. But is this the better project? Project Big provides more value—$89,299 versus 18¢. The techniques that ignore the scale of the investment—PI, IRR, and MIRR—may lead to an incorrect decision.

Capital Rationing

If the firm is subject to capital rationing—say a limit of $1 million—and Big and Little are independent projects, which project should the firm choose? The firm can only choose one—spend $1 or $1,000,000, but not $1,000,001. If you go strictly by the PI, IRR, or MIRR criteria, the firm would choose Project Little. But is this the better project? Again, the techniques that ignore the scale of the investment—PI, IRR, and MIRR—lead to an incorrect decision.

Choosing the Appropriate Technique

The advantages and disadvantages of each of the techniques for evaluating investments are summarized in Exhibit 13.7. We see in this chart that the discounted cash flow techniques are preferred to the non-discounted cash flow techniques. The discounted cash flow techniques—NPV, PI, IRR, MIRR—are preferable because they consider (1) all cash flows, (2) the time value of money, and (3) the risk of future cash flows. The discounted cash flow techniques are also useful because we can apply objective decision criteria—criteria we can actually use that tells us when a project increases wealth and when it does not.

We also see in Exhibit 13.7 that not all of the discounted cash flow techniques are right for every situation. There are questions we need to ask when evaluating an investment and the answers will determine which technique is the one to use for that investment:

- Are the projects mutually exclusive or independent?
- Are the projects subject to capital rationing?
- Are the projects of the same risk?
- Are the projects of the same scale of investment?

If projects are independent and not subject to capital rationing, we can evaluate them and determine the ones that maximize wealth based on any of the discounted cash flow techniques. If the projects are mutually exclusive, have the same investment outlay, and have the same risk, we must use only the NPV or the MIRR techniques to determine the projects that maximize wealth. If projects are mutually exclusive and are of different risks or are of different scales, NPV is preferred over MIRR. If the capital budget is limited, we can use either the NPV or the PI. We must be careful, however, not to select projects on the basis of their NPV (that is, ranking on NPV and selecting the highest NPV projects), but rather how we can maximize the NPV of the total capital budget.

EXHIBIT 13.7   Summary of Characteristics of the Evaluation Techniques

PAYBACK PERIOD

Advantages
1. Simple to compute.
2. Provides some information on he risk of the investment.
3. Provides a crude measure of liquidity.

Disadvantages
1. No concrete decision criteria to tell us whether an investment increases the firm's value.
2. Ignores cash flows beyond the payback period.
3. Ignores the time value of money.
4. Ignores the riskiness of future cash flows.

DISCOUNTED PAYBACK PERIOD

Advantages
1. Considers the time value of money.
2. Considers the riskiness of the cash flows involved in the payback.

Disadvantages
1. No concrete decision criteria that tells us whether the investment increases the firm's value.
2. Calls for a cost of capital.
3. Ignores cash flows beyond the payback period.

NET PRESENT VALUE

Advantages
1. Decision criteria that tells us whether the investment will increase the firm's value.
2. Considers all cash flows.
3. Considers the time value of money.
4. Considers the riskiness of future cash flows.

Disadvantages
1. Requires a cost of capital for calculation.
2. Expressed in terms of dollars, not as a percentage.

PROFITABILITY INDEX

Advantages
1. Decision criteria that tells us whether an investment increases the firm's value.
2. Considers all cash flows.
3. Considers the time value of money.
4. Considers the riskiness of future cash flows.
5. Useful in ranking and selecting projects when capital is rationed.

Disadvantages
1. Requires a cost of capital for calculation.
2. May not give correct decision when comparing mutually exclusive projects.

EXHIBIT 13.7   (Continued)

INTERNAL RATE OF RETURN

Advantages
1. Decision criteria that tells us whether an investment increases the firm's value.
2. Considers the time value of money.
3. Considers all cash flows.
4. Considers riskiness of future cash flows.

Disadvantages
1. Requires a cost of capital for decision.
2. May not give value maximizing decision when comparing mutually exclusive projects.
3. May not give value maximizing decision when choosing projects with capital rationing.

MODIFIED INTERNAL RATE OF RETURN

Advantages
1. Decision criteria that tells us whether the investment increases the firm's value.
2. Considers the time value of money.
3. Considers all cash flows.
4. Considers riskiness of future cash flows.

Disadvantages
1. May not give value maximizing decision when comparing mutually exclusive projects with different scales or different risk.
2. May not give value maximizing decision when choosing projects with capital rationing.

CAPITAL BUDGETING TECHNIQUES IN PRACTICE

Among the evaluation techniques in this chapter, the one we can be sure about is the net present value method. NPV will steer us toward the project that maximizes wealth in the most general circumstances. But what evaluation technique do financial decision makers really use?

We learn about what goes on in practice by anecdotal evidence and through surveys. These indicate that:

■ There is an increased use of more sophisticated capital budgeting techniques.

■ Most financial managers use more than one technique to evaluate the same projects, with a discounted cash flow technique (NPV, IRR, PI) used as a primary method and payback period used as a secondary method.

■ The most commonly used is the internal rate of return method, though the net present value method is gaining acceptance.

■ There is evidence that firms use hurdle rates (that is, costs of capital) that are higher than most cost of capital techniques would suggest.

The IRR is popular most likely because it is a measure of yield and therefore easy to understand. Moreover, since NPV is expressed in dollars—the expected increment in the value of the firm—and financial managers are accustomed to dealing with yields, they may be more comfortable dealing with the IRR than the NPV.

The popularity of the IRR method is troublesome since it may lead to decisions about projects that are not in the best interest of owners. However, the NPV method is becoming more widely accepted and, in time, may replace the IRR as the more popular method.

Is the use of the payback period troublesome? Not necessarily. The payback period is generally used as a screening device, eliminating those projects that cannot break even. Further, the payback period can be viewed as a measure of a yield. If the future cash flows are the same amount each period and if these future cash flows can be assumed to be received each period forever—essentially, a perpetuity—then the reciprocal of the payback period is a rough guide to a yield on the investment. Suppose you invest $100 today and expect $20 each period, forever. The payback period is five years. The inverse, 1/5 = 20% per year, is the yield on the investment.

Now let's turn this relation around and create a payback period rule. Suppose we want a 10% per year return on our investment. This means that the payback period should be less than or equal to 10 years. So while the payback period may seem to be a rough guide, there is some rationale behind it.

Use of the simpler techniques, such as payback period, does not mean that a firm has unsophisticated capital budgeting. Remember that evaluating the cash flows is only one aspect of the process:

- Cash flows must first be estimated.
- Cash flows are evaluated using NPV, PI, IRR, MIRR, or a payback method.
- Project risk must be assessed to determine the cost of capital.

SUMMARY

- Techniques to evaluate the expected cash flows from investment projects include the payback period, the discounted payback period, the net present value, the profitability index, the internal rate of return, and the modified internal rate of return.
- Not all of these six techniques consider all cash flows, the timing of the cash flows, and the risk of the cash flows, nor are they all consistent with owners' wealth maximization.

- The payback period and the discount payback period are measures of how long it takes the future cash flows to pay back the initial investment. The payback period looks only at the amount of the future cash flows, whereas the discounted payback period looks at the present value of the future cash flows. Both methods give us some information on the attractiveness of an investment, though these methods provide little guidance in the decision of whether a project will enhance owners' wealth.
- The net present value is the dollar amount that the value of the firm is increased if the investment is made. It is the difference between the present value of the future operating cash flows and the present value of the investment cash flows.
- The sensitivity of a project's worth can be represented as an investment profile, which is a graphical portrayal of a project's NPV for different discount rates.
- The profitability index is the ratio of the present value of the future operating cash inflows to the present value of the investment cash flows. Similar to the net present value, the profitability index tells us whether the investment would increase owners' wealth. Because the profitability index does not give us a dollar measure of the increase in value, we cannot use it to choose among mutually exclusive projects. But the profitability index does help us rank projects when there is capital rationing.
- The internal rate of return is the yield on the investment. It is the discount rate that causes the net present value to be equal to zero. IRR is hazardous to use when selecting among mutually exclusive projects or when there is a limit on capital spending.
- The modified internal rate of return is a yield on the investment, assuming that cash inflows are reinvested at some rate other than the internal rate of return. This method overcomes the problems associated with unrealistic reinvestment rate assumptions inherent with the internal rate of return method. However, MIRR is hazardous to use when selecting among mutually exclusive projects or when there is a limit on capital spending.
- Each technique we look at offers some advantages and disadvantages. The discounted flow techniques—NPV, PI, IRR, and MIRR—are superior to the nondiscounted cash flow techniques—the payback period and the discounted payback period.
- To evaluate mutually exclusive projects or projects subject to capital rationing, we have to be careful about the technique we use. The net present value method is consistent with owners' wealth maximization whether we have mutually exclusive projects or capital rationing.

■ Looking at capital budgeting in practice, we see that firms do use the discounted cash flow techniques, with IRR being the most widely used. Over time, however, we see a growing use of the net present value technique.

QUESTIONS

1. What criteria must be satisfied for an investment evaluation technique to be ideal?
2. Distinguish between the payback period and the discounted payback period.
3. Can the payback period method of evaluating projects identify the ones that will maximize wealth? Explain.
4. Can the discounted payback period method of evaluating projects identify the ones that will maximize wealth? Explain.
5. Consider two projects, AA and BB, that have identical, positive net present values, but Project BB is riskier than AA. If these projects are mutually exclusive, what is your investment decision?
6. Can the net present value method of evaluating projects identify the ones that will maximize wealth? Explain.
7. The decision rules for the net present value and the profitability index methods are related. Explain the relationship between these two sets of decision rules.
8. What is the source of the conflict between net present value and the profitability index decision rules in evaluating mutually exclusive projects?
9. Suppose you calculate a project's net present value to be $3,000. What does this mean?
10. Suppose you calculate a project's profitability index to be 1.4. What does this mean?
11. The internal rate of return is often referred to as the yield on an investment. Explain the analogy between the internal rate of return on an investment and the yield-to-maturity on a bond.
12. The net present value method and the internal rate of return method may produce different decisions when selecting among mutually exclusive projects. What is the source of this conflict?
13. The net present value method and the internal rate of return method may produce different decisions when selecting projects under capital rationing. What is the source of this conflict?
14. The modified internal rate of return is designed to overcome a deficiency in the internal rate of return method. Specifically, what problem is the MIRR designed to overcome?

15. Based upon our analysis of the alternative techniques to evaluate projects, which method or methods are preferable in terms of maximizing owners' wealth?

16. You are evaluating an investment project, Project ZZ, with the following cash flows:

Period	Cash Flow
0	−$100,000
1	35,027
2	35,027
3	35,027
4	35,027

Calculate the following:
a. Payback period
b. Discounted payback period, assuming a 10% cost of capital
c. Discounted payback period, assuming a 16% cost of capital
d. Net present value, assuming a 10% cost of capital
e. Net present value, assuming a 16% cost of capital
f. Profitability index, assuming a 10% cost of capital
g. Profitability index, assuming a 16% cost of capital
h. Internal rate of return
i. Modified internal rate of return, assuming reinvestment at 0%
j. Modified internal rate of return, assuming reinvestment at 10%

17. You are evaluating an investment project, Project YY, with the following cash flows:

Period	Cash Flow
0	−$100,000
1	43,798
2	43,798
3	43,798

Calculate the following:
a. Payback period
b. Discounted payback period, assuming a 10% cost of capital
c. Discounted payback period, assuming a 14% cost of capital
d. Net present value, assuming a 10% cost of capital
e. Net present value, assuming a 14% cost of capital
f. Profitability index, assuming a 10% cost of capital
g. Profitability index, assuming a 14% cost of capital
h. Internal rate of return

   i. Modified internal rate of return, assuming reinvestment at 10%
   j. Modified internal rate of return, assuming reinvestment at 14%
18. You are evaluating an investment project, Project XX, with the following cash flows:

Period	Cash Flow
0	-$200,000
1	65,000
2	65,000
3	65,000
4	65,000
5	65,000

Calculate the following:
a. Payback period
b. Discounted payback period, assuming a 10% cost of capital
c. Discounted payback period, assuming a 15% cost of capital
d. Net present value, assuming a 10% cost of capital
e. Net present value, assuming a 15% cost of capital
f. Profitability index, assuming a 10% cost of capital
g. Profitability index, assuming a 15% cost of capital
h. Internal rate of return
i. Modified internal rate of return, assuming reinvestment at 10%
j. Modified internal rate of return, assuming reinvestment at 15%
19. Suppose you are evaluating two mutually exclusive projects, Thing 1 and Thing 2, with the following cash flows:

	End of Year Cash Flows	
Year	Thing 1	Thing 2
2000	-$10,000	-$10,000
2001	3,293	0
2002	3,293	0
2003	3,293	0
2004	3,293	14,641

a. If the cost of capital on both projects is 5%, which project, if any, would you choose? Why?
b. If the cost of capital on both projects is 8%, which project, if any, would you choose? Why?
c. If the cost of capital on both projects is 11%, which project, if any, would you choose? Why?

d. If the cost of capital on both projects is 14%, which project, if any, would you choose? Why?

e. At what discount rate would you be indifferent between choosing Thing 1 and Thing 2?

f. On the same graph, draw the investment profiles of Thing 1 and Thing 2. Indicate the following items:

- crossover discount rate
- NPV of Thing 1 if the cost of capital is 5%
- NPV of Thing 2 if cost of capital is 5%
- IRR of Thing 1
- IRR of Thing 2

20. Consider the results from analyzing the following five projects:

Project	Outlay	NPV
AA	$300,000	$10,000
BB	400,000	20,000
CC	200,000	10,000
DD	100,000	10,000
EE	200,000	−15,000

Suppose there is a limit on the capital budget of $600,000. Which projects should we invest in, given our capital budget?

21. Consider these three independent projects:

Period	FF	GG	HH
0	−$100,000	−$200,000	−$300,000
1	30,000	40,000	40,000
2	30,000	40,000	40,000
3	30,000	40,000	40,000
4	40,000	120,000	240,000
Cost of capital	5%	6%	7%

a. If there is no limit on the capital budget, which projects would you choose? Why?

b. If there is a limit on the capital budget of $300,000, which projects would you choose? Why?

22. The Mighty Mouse Computer company is considering whether or not to install a packaging robot. The robot costs $500,000, including shipping and installation. The robot can be depreciated using MACRS as a five-year asset. (MACRS depreciation rates for a five-year asset: 20%, 32%, 19.2%, 11.52%, 11.52%, and 5.76%.) The

robot is expected to last for five years, at which time management expects to sell it for parts for $100,000. The robot is expected to replace five employees in the shipping department, saving the company $150,000 each year. Mighty's tax rate is 30%.

a. What are the net cash flows for each year of the robot's five-year life?

b. What is the net present value of the robot investment if the cost of capital is 10%?

c. What is the net present value of the robot investment if the cost of capital is 5%?

d. What is the profitability index of this investment if the cost of capital is 5%?

e. What is the payback period of the robot investment?

f. What is the discounted payback period of the robot investment if the cost of capital is 5%?

g. What is the internal rate of return of the robot investment?

h. What is the modified internal rate of return of the robot investment if the cash flows are reinvested at 5%?

i. If the cost of capital is 5%, should Mighty Mouse invest in this robot?

23. The Sopchoppy Motorcycle Company is considering an investment of $600,000 in a new motorcycle. They expect to increase sales in each of the next three years by $400,000, while increasing expenses by $200,000 each year. They expect that they can carve out a niche in the marketplace for this new motorcycle for three years, after which they intend to cease production on this motorcycle and sell the manufacturing equipment for $200,000. Assume the equipment is depreciated at the rate of $200,000 each year. Sopchoppy's tax rate is 40%.

a. What are the net cash flows for each year of the motorcycle's three-year life?

b. What is the net present value of the investment if the cost of capital is 10%?

c. What is the net present value of the motorcycle investment if the cost of capital is 5%?

d. What is the profitability index of this investment if the cost of capital is 5%?

e. What is the payback period of the investment?

f. What is the discounted payback period of the investment if the cost of capital is 5%?

g. What is the internal rate of return of the investment?

h. What is the modified internal rate of return of the motorcycle investment if the cash flows are reinvested at 5%?

i. If the cost of capital is 10%, should Sopchoppy invest in this motorcycle?

24. The Leontif Company is evaluating the purchase of a new computer for its marketing department, replacing its existing computer. The current computer is fully depreciated and has little or no resale value. The new computer would cost $40,000 and would be depreciated for tax purposes as a five-year asset using MACRS. The new computer would not enhance revenues, but would reduce expenses due to increased operating efficiency. It is expected that the computer would be used for four years, at which time it would have a resale value of $1,000.

25. The Leontif Company's income is taxed at 37%. Leontif requires projects with similar risk to provide a return of 10%. What would the amount of expense reduction have to be in order for this computer to be considered attractive to Leontif? Assume that any expense reduction is the same for each year of operating this new computer.

26. The B. Bowden Company is evaluating the purchase of a stadium, the B. B. Dome. The stadium would cost Bowden $1 million and would be depreciated for tax purposes using straight-line over 20 years (that is, $50,000 per year). It is expected that the stadium will increase B. Bowden revenues by $400,000 per year, but would also increase expenses by $200,000 per year. B. Bowden would be expected to increase its working capital by $20,000 to accommodate the increased investment in ticket accounts receivable. B. Bowden Company intends to sell the stadium to the city after ten years for $600,000. The marginal tax rate for B. Bowden is 40%. For purposes of identifying the timing of cash flows, consider the purchase to be made at the end of 2000, the first year of operations the year 2001, and the last year of operations the year 2010.

    a. Calculate the net cash flows for each year, 2000 through 2010.

    b. If the cost of capital for this project is 10%, should B. Bowden invest in the new stadium?

    c. Over what range of cost of capital would this project be attractive? Over what range of cost of capital would this project be unattractive?

27. National Foods is considering producing a new candy, Nasty-As-Can-Be. National has spent two years and $450,000 developing this product. National has also test marketed Nasty, spending $100,000 to conduct consumer surveys and tests of the product in 25 states.

    Based on previous candy products and the results in the test marketing, management believes consumers will buy 4 million packages each year for ten years at 50 cents per package. Equipment to produce Nasty will cost National $1,000,000 and $300,000 of additional net working capital will be required to support Nasty sales. National expects production costs to average 60% of Nasty's net revenues, with overhead and sales expenses totaling $525,000 per year. The equipment has a life of ten years, after which time it will have no salvage value. Working capital is assumed to be fully recovered at the end of ten years. Depreciation is straight-line (no salvage) and National's tax rate is 45%. The required rate of return for projects of similar risk is 8%.

a. Should National Foods produce this new candy? What is the basis of your recommendation?

b. Would your recommendation change if production costs average 65% of net revenues instead of 60%? How sensitive is your recommendation to production costs?

c. Would your recommendation change if the equipment were depreciated according to MACRS as a ten-year asset instead of using straight-line?

d. Suppose that competitors are expected to introduce similar candy products to compete with Nasty, such that dollar sales will drop by 5% each year following the first year. Should National Foods produce this new candy considering this possible drop in sales? Explain.

CHAPTER 14

Capital Budgeting and Risk

All new projects involve risk. Capital budgeting decisions require that managers analyze the following factors for each project they consider:

- Future cash flows,
- The degree of uncertainty of these future cash flows, and
- The value of these future cash flows considering their uncertainty.

We described how to estimate future cash flows in Chapter 12 where we saw that a project's incremental cash flows comprise two types: (1) operating cash flows (the change in the revenues, expenses, and taxes) and (2) investment cash flows (the acquisition and disposition of the project's assets).

In Chapter 13, we focused on evaluating future cash flows. *Given* estimates of incremental cash flows for a project and *given* a discount rate that reflects the uncertainty that the project will produce those flows as expected, we looked at alternative techniques that are used to select projects to invest in.

In deciding whether a project increases shareholder wealth, managers must weigh its benefits and its costs. The costs are:

1. The cash flow necessary to make the investment (the investment outlay) and
2. The opportunity costs of using the cash tied up in this investment.

The benefits are the future cash flows generated by the investment. But the future is uncertain, therefore future cash flows are uncertain. So, for an evaluation of any investment to be meaningful, we must evaluate the risk that its cash flows will differ from what is expected, in terms of the amount and the timing of the cash flows. **Risk** is the *degree of uncertainty.*

451

Managers incorporate risk into their calculations in one of two ways: (1) by discounting future cash flows using a higher discount rate, the greater the cash flow's risk, or (2) by requiring a higher annual return on a project, the greater the cash flow's risk. In this chapter, we look at the sources of cash flow uncertainty and how to incorporate risk in the capital budgeting decision.

We begin by describing what we mean by risk in the context of long-lived projects. We then propose several commonly used statistical measures of risk, taking what we learned about risk in Chapter 10, expanding on it, and applying it to capital projects. Then we look at the relation between risk and return, specifically for capital projects, and we conclude by showing how risk can be incorporated in the capital budgeting decision.

RISK AND CASH FLOWS

When managers estimate what it costs to invest in a given project and what its benefits will be in the future, they are coping with uncertainty. The uncertainty arises from different sources, depending on the type of investment being considered, as well as the circumstances and the industry in which it is operating. Uncertainty may result from:

- *Economic conditions.* Will consumers be spending or saving? Will the economy be in a recession? Will the government stimulate spending? Will there be inflation?
- *Market conditions.* Is the market competitive? How long does it take competitors to enter into the market? Are there any barriers, such as patents or trademarks, that will keep competitors away? Is there sufficient supply of raw materials and labor? How much will raw materials and labor cost in the future?
- *Taxes.* What will tax rates be? Will Congress alter the tax system?
- *Interest rates.* What will be the cost of raising capital in future years?
- *International conditions.* Will the exchange rate between different countries' currencies change? Are the governments of the countries in which the firm does business stable?

These sources of uncertainty influence future cash flows. To choose projects that will maximize owners' wealth, we need to assess the uncertainty associated with a project's cash flows. In evaluating a capital project, we are concerned with measuring its risk.

The Required Rate of Return

Financial managers worry about risk because the suppliers of capital—the creditors and owners—demand compensation for taking on risk. They can either provide their funds to your firm to make investments or they could invest their funds elsewhere. Therefore, there is an opportunity cost to consider: what the suppliers of capital could earn elsewhere for the same level of risk. We refer to the return required by the suppliers of capital as the *cost of capital*, which comprises the compensation to suppliers of capital for their opportunity cost of not having the funds available (the time value of money) and compensation for risk.

$$\text{Cost of capital} = \text{Compensation for the time value of money}$$
$$+ \text{Compensation for risk}$$

Using the net present value criterion, if the present value of the future cash flows is greater than the present value of the cost of the project, the project is expected to increase the value of the firm, and therefore is acceptable. And under certain circumstances, using the internal rate of return criterion, if the project's return exceeds the project's cost of capital, the project increases owners' wealth. From the perspective of the firm, this required rate of return is what it costs to raise capital, so we also refer to this rate as the cost of capital.

We refer to the compensation for risk as a *risk premium*—the additional return necessary to compensate investors for the risk they bear. How much compensation for risk is enough? 2%? 4%? 10%?

How do we assess the risk of a project? We begin by recognizing that the assets of a firm are the result of its prior investment decisions. Therefore, a firm is really a collection or portfolio of projects. So when the firm adds another project to its portfolio, should we be concerned only about the risk of that additional project? Or should we be concerned about the risk of the entire portfolio when the new project is included in it? To answer this question, let's look at the different dimensions of risk of a project.

Stand-Alone versus Market Risk

If we have some idea of the uncertainty associated with a project's future cash flows—its possible outcomes—and the probabilities associated with these outcomes, we will have a measure of the risk of the project. But this is the project's risk in isolation from the firm's other projects, also referred to as the project's *total risk*, or *stand-alone risk*.

Because most firms have many assets, the stand-alone risk of a project under consideration may not be the relevant risk for analyzing the project. A firm is a portfolio of assets, and the returns of these different assets are not perfectly positively correlated with one another. We are therefore not concerned about the stand-alone risk of a project, but rather *how the addition of the project to the firm's portfolio of assets changes the risk of the firm's portfolio.*

Now let's take it a step further. Shareholders own shares of many firms and these shareholders are investors who *themselves* may hold diversified portfolios. These investors are concerned about how the firm's investments affect the risk of their own personal portfolios. When owners demand compensation for risk, they are requiring compensation for market risk, the risk they can't get rid of by diversifying. Recognizing this, a firm considering taking on a new project should be concerned with how it changes its market risk. Therefore, if the firm's owners hold diversified investments, it is the project's *market* risk that is relevant to the firm's decision making.

If the Microsoft Corporation introduces a new operating system, the relevant risk to consider in evaluating this new product is not its stand-alone risk, but rather it market risk. Microsoft has many computer software products and services—they have a portfolio of investments. And while its investments are all related somewhat to computers, the products' fortunes do not rise and fall perfectly in sync with one another—in other words, some of the risk is diversified away. Additionally, investors who hold Microsoft common stock in their portfolios also own stock of other corporations (and perhaps own some bonds, real estate, or cash). What risk is relevant for Microsoft to consider in its decision regarding the new product? It is the market risk of the product since some risk is diversified away at the company level and some risk is diversified away at the investors' level.

Even though we generally believe that it's the project's market risk that is important to analyze, stand-alone risk should not be ignored. If we are making decisions for a small, closely-held firm whose owners do not hold well-diversified portfolios, the stand-alone risk gives us a good idea of the project's risk. And many small businesses fit into this category.

And even if we are making investment decisions for large corporations that have many products and whose owners are well-diversified, the analysis of stand-alone risk is useful. Stand-alone risk is often closely related to market risk: In many cases, projects with higher stand-alone risk may also have higher market risk. And a project's stand-alone risk is easier to measure than its market risk. We can get an idea of a project's stand-alone risk by evaluating the project's future cash flows using statistical measures, sensitivity analysis, and simulation analysis. We now consider these evaluation techniques.

MEASUREMENT OF PROJECT RISK

The financial decision-maker needs to measure risk to incorporate it into the capital budgeting decision. We next look at several methods of evaluating risk, focusing first on stand-alone risk and then on market risk.

Measuring a Project's Stand-Alone Risk

We will first look at a project's stand alone risk.

Statistical Measures of Cash Flow Risk

We will look at three statistical measures used to evaluate the risk associated with a project's possible outcomes: the range, the standard deviation, and the coefficient of variation. Let's demonstrate each using new products as examples. Based on experience with our firm's current product lines and the market research for new Product A, we can estimate that it may generate one of three different cash flows in its first year, depending on economic conditions:

Economic Condition	Cash Flow	Probability
Boom	$10,000	20% or 0.20
Normal	5,000	50% or 0.50
Recession	−1,000	30% or 0.30

Looking at this table we can see there is more than one possible outcome. There are three possible outcomes, each representing a possible cash flow, and its probability of occurring. Product A's three possible cash flows are represented graphically in Exhibit 14.1. Looking at this graph, we see that there is some chance of getting a −$1,000 cash flow and some chance of getting a +$10,000 cash flow, though the most likely possibility (the one with the greatest probability) is a +$5,000 cash flow.

But to get an idea of Product A's risk, we need to know a bit more. The more spread out the possible outcomes, the greater the degree of uncertainty (the risk) of what is expected in the future. We refer to the degree to which future outcomes are "spread out" as *dispersion*. In general, the greater the dispersion, the greater the risk.

There are several measures we could use to describe the dispersion of future outcomes. We will focus on the range, the standard deviation, and the coefficient of variation.

The Range The *range* is a statistical measure representing how far apart are the two extreme outcomes of the probability distribution. The range is calculated as the difference between the best and the worst possible outcomes:

Range = Best possible outcome − Worst possible outcome

For Product A, the range of possible outcomes is $10,000 − (−$1,000) = $11,000. The larger the range, the farther apart are the two extreme possible outcomes and therefore, the greater the risk.

The Standard Deviation   Though easy to calculate, the range doesn't tell us anything about the likelihood of the possible cash flows at or between the extremes. In financial decision-making, we are interested in not just the extreme outcomes, but all the possible outcomes.

One way to characterize the dispersion of all possible future outcomes is to look at how the outcomes differ from one another. This would require looking at the differences among all possible outcomes and trying to summarize these differences in a usable measure.

An alternative to this is to look at how each possible future outcome differs from a single value, comparing each possible outcome with this one value. A common approach is to use a measure of central location of a probability distribution, the *expected value.*

Let's use N to designate the number of possible future outcomes, x_n to indicate the nth possible outcome, p_n to indicate the probability of the nth outcome occurring, and $E(x)$ to indicate the expected outcome. The expected cash flow is the weighted average of the cash flows, where the weights are the probabilities:

$$E(x) = x_1 p_1 + x_2 p_2 + x_3 p_3 + ... + x_n p_n + ... + x_N p_N$$

EXHIBIT 14.1   Probability Distribution for Product A's Cash Flow

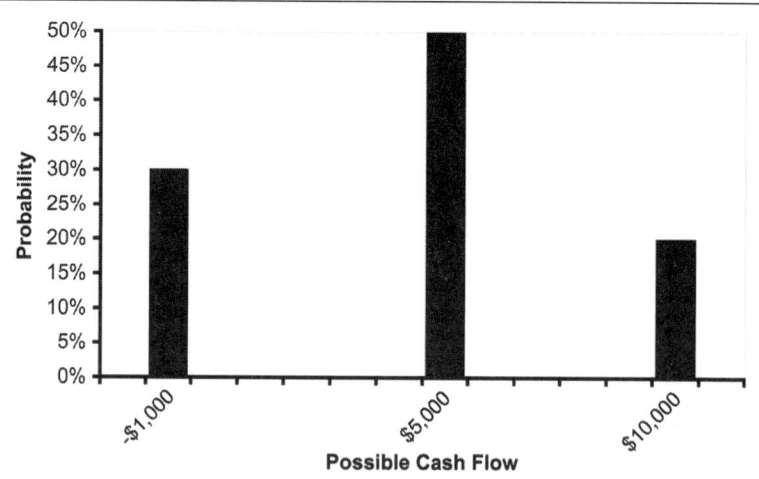

EXHIBIT 14.2 Calculation of the Standard Deviation of the Possible Cash Flows of Product A

Economic Conditions	Cash Flow	Probability	$x_n p_n$	$x_n - E(x)$	$(x_n - E(x))^2$	$p_n(x_n - E(x))^2$
Boom	$10,000	0.20	$2,000	$5,800	33,640,000	6,728,000
Normal	5,000	0.50	2,500	800	640,000	320,000
Recession	−1,000	0.30	−300	−5,200	27,040,000	9,112,000
		$E(x) =$	$4,200		$\sigma^2(x) =$	15,160,000

Standard deviation = $\sigma(x) = \sqrt{15,160,000} = \$3,894$

or, using summation notation,

$$E(x) = \sum_{n=1}^{N} p_n x_n$$

The *standard deviation* is a measure of how each possible outcome deviates—that is, differs—from the expected value. The standard deviation provides information about the dispersion of possible outcomes because it provides information on the distance each outcome is from the expected value and the likelihood the outcome will occur. The standard deviation is:

$$\sigma(x) = \sqrt{\sum_{n=1}^{N} p_n [x_n - E(x)]^2}$$

The calculation of the standard deviation is shown in Exhibit 14.2. As you can see, it is necessary to calculate the expected value before calculating the standard deviation. The standard deviation of Product A's future cash flows is $3,894.

The standard deviation is a statistical measure of dispersion of the possible outcomes about the expected outcome. The larger the standard deviation, the greater the dispersion and, hence, the greater the risk.

Let's look at another example. Suppose the possible cash flows and their corresponding probabilities in the first year for Product B are:

Cash Flow	Probability
$10,000	5%
9,000	10
8,000	20
7,000	30
6,000	20
5,000	10
4,000	5

Expected value and standard deviation calculated similar to that of Product A is shown in Exhibit 14.2. We can describe the probability distribution with several measures:

■ The expected value is $7,000.
■ The most likely outcome—the one that has the highest probability of occurring—is $7,000.
■ The range of possible outcomes is $10,000 – 4,000 = $6,000.
■ The standard deviation of the possible outcomes is $1,449.

Let's compare the risk associated with Product B's cash flows with the risk of still another project, Product C, which has the following possible cash flows:

Cash Flow	Probability
$10,000	2%
9,000	8
8,000	20
7,000	40
6,000	20
5,000	8
4,000	2

Describing the possible outcomes for Product C (which you can determine on your own applying what we did for Products A and B),

■ The expected value is $7,000.
■ The most likely outcome is $7,000.
■ The range of possible outcomes is $6,000.
■ The standard deviation of the possible outcome is $1,183.

EXHIBIT 14.3   Probability Distributions of Product B and Product C

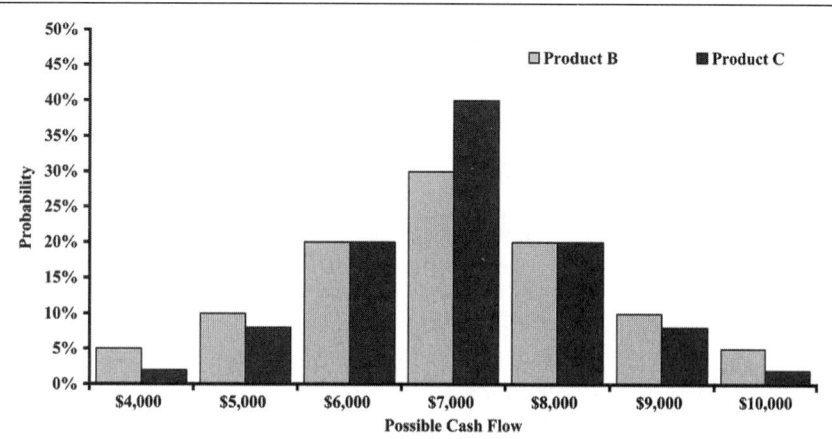

Both B and C have the same most likely outcome, the same expected value, and the same range of possible outcomes. But the standard deviation of the cash flows for C is less than it is for B. This confirms what we see when comparing the probability distributions of Product C, as shown in Exhibit 14.3—the distribution of possible outcomes of Product C are less disperse than that of Product B.

The Coefficient of Variation   The standard deviation provides a useful measure of dispersion. It is a measure of how widely dispersed the possible outcomes are from the expected value. However, we cannot compare standard deviations of different projects' cash flows if they have different expected values. To see this, consider the possible cash flows from Product D:

Cash Flow	Probability
$100,000	5%
90,000	10
80,000	20
70,000	30
60,000	20
50,000	10
40,000	5

We can describe the probability distribution of Product D's possible cash flows:

■ The expected value is $70,000.
■ The most likely outcome is $70,000.
■ The range of possible outcomes is $60,000.
■ The standard deviation of the possible outcomes is $14,491.

Is Product D riskier than Product B? Product D's standard deviation is larger, but so is its expected value. Because Product B's and Product D's cash flows are of different sizes, comparing their standard deviations is meaningless without somehow adjusting for the scale of cash flows.

We can do that with the *coefficient of variation*, which translates the standard deviation of different probability distributions (because their scales differ) so that they can be compared.

The coefficient of variation for a probability distribution is the ratio of its standard deviation to its expected value:

$$\text{Coefficient of variation} = \frac{\sigma(x)}{E(x)}$$

Calculating the coefficient of variation for each of the four products' probability distributions in our examples,

Product	Expected Value	Range	Standard Deviation	Coefficient of Variation
A	$4,200	$11,000	$3,894	0.9271
B	7,000	6,000	1,449	0.2070
C	7,000	6,000	1,183	0.1690
D	70,000	6,000	14,491	0.2070

Comparing coefficients of variation among these products, we see that:

■ Product A is the riskiest.
■ Product C is least risky.
■ Products B and D have identical risk.

Risk can be expressed statistically in terms of measures such as the range, the standard deviation, and the coefficient of variation. Now that we know how to calculate and apply these statistical measures, all we need are the probability distributions of the project's future cash flows so we can apply these statistical tools to evaluate a project's risk.

Where do we get these probability distributions? From research, judgment, and experience. We can use sensitivity analysis or simulation analysis to get an idea of a project's possible future cash flows and their risk.

Sensitivity Analysis

Estimates of cash flows are based on assumptions about the economy, competitors, consumer tastes and preferences, construction costs, and taxes, among a host of other possible assumptions. One of the first things managers must consider about these estimates is how sensitive they are to these assumptions. For example, if we only sell 2 million units instead of 3 million units in the first year, is the project still profitable? Or, if Congress increases the tax rates, will the project still be attractive?

We can analyze the sensitivity of cash flows to change in the assumptions by reestimating the cash flows for different scenarios. *Sensitivity analysis*, also called *scenario analysis*, is a method of looking at the possible outcomes, given a change in one of the factors in the analysis. Sometimes we refer to this as "what if" analysis—"what if this changes," "what if that changes," and so on.

To see how sensitivity analysis works, let's look at the Williams 5 & 10 cash flows we determined in Chapter 12, where the detailed calculations were shown in Exhibit 12.4 of that chapter. The net cash flow for each year is:

Year	Net Cash Flow
Initial	−$550,000
2001	+79,809
2002	+153,409
2003	+149,569
2004	+147,265
2005	+460,946

Now let's play with the assumptions. Suppose that the tax rate is not known with certainty, but instead the tax rate may be 20%, 30%, or 40%. The tax rate that we assume affects all the following factors:

- The expected tax on the sale of the building and equipment in the last year;
- The cash outflow for taxes from the change in revenues and expenses; and
- The cash inflow from the depreciation tax shield.

Each different tax assumption changes the project's net cash flows as follows:

| Year | Net Cash Flow | | |
	Tax rate = 20%	Tax rate = 30%	Tax rate = 40%
Initial	−$550,000	−$550,000	−$550,000
2001	+86,540	+78,909	+73,079
2002	+168,940	+153,409	+137,879
2003	+166,380	+149,569	+132,759
2004	+164,844	+147,265	+129,687
2005	+467,298	+460,946	+489,987

We can see that the value of this project, hence any decision made based on this value, is sensitive to what we assume will be the tax rate.

We could take each of the "what if" tax rate assumptions and re-calculate the value of the investment.

If the tax rate is ...	... the net present value using a cost of capital of 5% is ...
20%	$331,134
30%	276,677
40%	249,954

But when we do this, we have to be careful—the net present value requires discounting the cash flows at a rate that reflects risk—but *that* is what we are trying to figure out! So we shouldn't be using the net present value method in evaluating a project's risk in our sensitivity analysis.

An alternative is to recalculate the internal rate of return under each "what if" scenario.

If the tax rate is ...	... the internal rate of return will be ...
20%	20.20%
30%	17.77%
40%	16.32%

And this illustrates one of the attractions of using the internal rate of return to evaluate projects. Despite its drawbacks in the case of mutually exclusive projects and in capital rationing, as pointed out in Chapter 13, the internal rate of return is more suitable to use in assessing a project's attractiveness under different scenarios and, hence, that project's risk. Why? Because the net present value approach requires us to use a cost of capital to arrive at a project's value, but the cost of capital is what we set out to determine! We would be caught in a vicious circle if we used the net present value approach in sensitivity analysis. But the internal rate of return method does not require a cost of capital; instead, we can look at the possible internal rates of return of a project and use this information to measure a project's risk.

If we can specify the probability distribution for tax rates, we can put sensitivity analysis together with the statistical measures of risk. Suppose that in the analysis of the Williams project it is most likely that tax rates be 30%, though there is a slight probability that tax rates will be lowered and a chance that tax rates will be increased. More specifically, suppose the probability distribution of future tax rates and, hence the project's internal rate of return, is:

Probability is ...	that the tax rate will be ...	and hence the internal rate of return will be ...
10%	20%	20.20%
50%	30%	17.77%
40%	40%	16.32%

Applying the calculations for the statistical measures of risk to this distribution,

Expected internal rate of return	= 17.433%
Standard deviation of possible internal rates of return	= 1.148%
Coefficient of variation	= 0.066

We could then judge whether the project's expected return is sufficient considering its risk (as measured by the standard deviation). We could also use these statistical measures to compare this project with other projects under consideration.

Sensitivity analysis illustrates the effects of changes in assumptions. But because sensitivity analysis focuses only on one change at a time, it is not very realistic. We know that not one, but many factors can change throughout the life of a project. In the case of the Williams project, there are a number of assumptions built into the analysis that are based on uncertainty, including the sales prices of the building and equipment in five years and the entrance of competitors no sooner than five years. And you can use your imagination and envision any new product and the attendant uncertainties including the economy, the firm's competitors, and the price and supply of raw materials and labor.

Simulation Analysis

Sensitivity analysis becomes unmanageable if we change several factors at the same time. A manageable approach to changing two or more factors at the same time is computer simulation. *Simulation analysis* allows the financial manager to develop a probability distribution of possible outcomes, given a probability distribution for each variable that may change.

Suppose you are analyzing a project having the following uncertain elements: (1) sales (number of units and price); (2) costs; and (3) tax rate. Suppose further that the initial outlay for the project is known with certainty and so is the rate of depreciation. From the firm's marketing research, you estimate a probability distribution for dollar sales. And from the firm's engineers, production management, and purchasing agents, you estimate the probability distribution for costs, which depends, in part, on the number of units sold. The firm's economists estimate the probability distribution of possible tax rates.

You have three probability distributions to work with. Now you need a computer simulation program to meet your needs—one that can:

- randomly select a possible value of unit sales for each year, given the probability distribution;
- randomly select a possible value of costs for each year, given the unit sales and the probability distribution of costs; and
- randomly select a tax rate for each year, given the probability distribution of tax rates.

While the computer cannot roll a die, spin a wheel like they do in TV game shows, or select ping-pong balls with numbers as they do with lotteries, computers can be programmed to randomly select values based on whatever probability distribution you want. For example, Lotus Development Corporation has a program, called @Risk, that allows the financial manager to assume probability distributions for different variables in an analysis and perform a simulation.

Once the computer selects the number of units sold, the cost per unit, and the tax rate, the cash flows as well as its internal rate of return are calculated. You now have one internal rate of return. Then you start all over, with the computer repeating this process, calculating an internal rate of return each time. After a large number of trials, you will have a frequency distribution of the return on investments. A *frequency distribution* is a description of the number of times you've arrived at each different return. Using the statistical measures of risk, you can evaluate the risk associated with the return on investments by applying these measures to this frequency distribution.[1]

Simulation analysis is more realistic than sensitivity analysis because it introduces uncertainty for many variables in the analysis. But if you use your imagination, this analysis may become complex since there are interdependencies among many variables in a given year and interdependencies among the variables in different time periods.

However, simulation analysis looks at a project in isolation, focusing on the project's total risk. And simulation analysis also ignores the effects of diversification for the owners' personal portfolio. If owners hold diversified portfolios, then their concern is how a project affects their portfolio's risk, not the project's total risk.

Measuring a Project's Market Risk

If we are looking at an investment in a share of stock, we could compare the stock's returns and the returns of the entire market over the same period of time as a way of measuring its market risk. While this is not a perfect measurement, it at least provides an estimate of the sensitivity of that particular stock's returns as compared to the returns of the market as a whole. But what if we are evaluating the market risk of a new product? We can't look at how that new product has affected the firm's stock return! So what do we do?

Though we can't look at a project's returns and see how they relate to the returns on the market as a whole, we can do the next best thing: Estimate the market risk of the stock of *another firm* whose only line of business is the same as the project's. If we could find such a company,

---

[1] Because the frequency distribution is a *sampling* distribution (that is, its based on a sample of observations instead of a probability distribution), its standard deviation is calculated in a slightly different manner than the standard deviation of possible outcomes. The standard deviation of a frequency distribution is:

$$\text{Standard deviation of frequency distribution} = \sqrt{\frac{\Sigma(x_i - \bar{x})^2 f_i}{N - 1}}$$

where x_i is the value of a particular outcome, $\bar{x}$ is the average of the outcomes, f_i is the number of times the particular outcome is observed (its frequency), and N is the number of trials (e.g., number of times a coin is flipped). The interpretation of this standard deviation is similar to the interpretation of the standard deviation discussed previously.

There are two differences between the standard deviation of the frequency distribution and that of the probability distribution: Instead of the probability, the weights are the frequency, and the sum of the weighted outcomes is divided by the number of trials (less one).

we could look at its stock's market risk and use that as a first step in estimating the project's market risk.

Let's use a measure of market risk, referred to as *beta* and represented by β. β is a measure of the sensitivity of an asset's returns to change in the returns of the market. β is an elasticity measure: If the return on the market increases by 1%, we expect the return on an asset with a β of 2.0 to increase by 2%; if the return on the market decreases by 1%, we expect the returns on an asset with a β of 1.5 to decrease by 1.5%, and so on. The β of an asset, therefore, is a measure of the asset's market risk. To distinguish the beta of an asset from the beta we used for a firm's stock, we refer to an asset's beta as β_{asset} and the beta of a firm's stock as β_{equity}.

Market Risk and Financial Leverage

If a firm has no debt, the market risk of its common stock is the same as the market risk of its assets. This is to say the beta of its equity, β_{equity}, is the same as the beta of its assets, β_{asset}.

Financial leverage is the use of fixed payment obligations, such as notes or bonds, to finance a firm's assets. As we will demonstrate in Chapter 18, the greater the use of debt obligations, the more financial leverage and the greater the risk associated with cash flows to owners. So the effect of using debt is to increase the risk of the firm's equity. If the firm has debt obligations, the market risk of its common stock is *greater* than its assets' risk (that is, $\beta_{equity} > \beta_{asset}$), due to financial leverage. Let's see why.

Consider the an asset's beta, β_{asset}. This beta depends on the asset's risk, *not* on how the firm chose to finance it. The firm can choose to finance it with equity only, in which case $\beta_{asset} = \beta_{equity}$. But what if, instead, the firm chooses to finance it partly with debt and partly with equity? When it does this, the creditors and the owners share the risk of the asset, so the asset's risk is split between them, but not equally because of the nature of the claims. Creditors have seniority and receive a fixed amount (interest and principal), so there is less risk associated with a dollar of debt financing than a dollar of equity financing of the same asset. So the market risk borne by the creditors is different than the market risk borne by owners.

Let's represent the market risk of creditors as β_{debt} and the market risk of owners as β_{equity}. Because the asset's risk is shared between creditors and owners, we can represent the asset's market risk as the weighted average of the firm's debt beta, β_{debt}, and equity beta, β_{equity}:[2]

---

[2] The process of breaking down the firm's beta into equity and debt components is attributed to Robert S. Hamada ["The Effect of the Firm's Capital Structure on the Systematic Risk of Common Stocks," *Journal of Finance* (May 1972) pp. 435–452].

$$\beta_{asset} = \beta_{debt}\left(\frac{debt}{debt + equity}\right) + \beta_{equity}\left(\frac{equity}{debt + equity}\right)$$

But interest on debt is deducted to arrive at taxable income, so the claim that creditors have on the firm's assets does not cost the firm the full amount, but rather the after-tax claim. Therefore, the burden of debt financing is actually less due to interest deductibility. Let τ represent the marginal tax rate. The asset beta is:

$$\beta_{asset} = \beta_{debt}\left(\frac{(1-\tau)debt}{(1-\tau)debt + equity}\right) + \beta_{equity}\left(\frac{equity}{(1-\tau)debt + equity}\right)$$

If the firm's debt does not have market risk, $\beta_{debt} = 0$. This means that the returns on debt do not vary with returns on the market. We generally assumed this to be true for most large firms. Therefore, the market risk of a firm's equity is affected by both the assets' market risk and the nondiversifiable portion of firm's financial risk. If $\beta_{debt} = 0$,

$$\beta_{asset} = \beta_{equity}\left[\frac{equity}{(1-\tau)debt + equity}\right] = \beta_{equity}\left[\frac{1}{1 + \frac{(1-\tau)debt}{equity}}\right]$$

This means that an asset's beta is related to the firm's equity beta, with adjustments for financial leverage.[3] You'll notice that if the firm does not use debt, $\beta_{asset} = \beta_{equity}$ and if the firm does use debt, $\beta_{asset} < \beta_{equity}$.

Therefore, we can translate a β_{equity} into a β_{asset} by removing the firm's financial risk from its β_{equity}. As you can see from the above, to do this we need to know:

- the firm's marginal tax rate;
- the amount of the firm's debt financing; and
- the amount of the firm's equity financing.

---

[3] This means that we can also specify the firm's equity beta in terms of its asset beta:

$$\beta_{equity} = \beta_{asset}\left(1 + \frac{(1 - \text{marginal tax rate})debt}{equity}\right)$$

The greater a firm's use of debt (relative to equity), the greater its equity's beta and hence the greater its equity's market risk.

If the firm's β_{equity}, is 1.2, its marginal tax rate is 40%, and it has $4 million of debt and $6 million of equity, and its asset risk is 0.8571:

$$\beta_{asset} = 1.2 \left[\frac{1}{1 + \frac{(1 - 0.40)\$4 \text{ million}}{\$6 \text{ million}}} \right] = 1.2(0.7143) = 0.8571$$

The process of translating an equity beta into an asset beta is referred to as "unlevering" since we are removing the effects of financial leverage from the equity beta, β_{equity}, to get a beta for the firm's assets, β_{asset}.[4]

Using a Pure-Play

A firm with a single line of business is referred to as a *pure-play*. Selecting the firm or firms that have a single line of business, where this line of business is similar to the project's, helps in estimating the market risk of a project. We estimate a project's asset beta by starting with the pure-play's equity beta. We can estimate the pure-play's equity beta by looking at the relation between the returns on the pure-play's stock and the returns on the market. Once we have the pure-play's equity beta, we can then "unlever" it by adjusting it for the financial leverage of the pure-play firm.

Examples of pure-play equity betas are shown in Exhibit 14.4. The firms listed in this table have one primary line of business. Using the information in Exhibit 14.4 for Alcan Aluminum and assuming a marginal tax rate of 35%, we see that the asset beta for aluminum products is 0.748:

$$\beta_{asset} = 1.088 \left[\frac{1}{1 + (1 - 0.35)0.700} \right] = 0.748$$

A firm with little debt relative to equity, such as Gap, Inc., will have an asset beta that is close to its equity beta.

Because many U.S. corporations whose stock's returns are readily available have more than one line of business, *finding* an appropriate pure-play firm may be difficult. Care must be taken to identify those that have lines of business similar to the project's.

---

[4] The effect of financial leverage on equity betas and the process of levering and unlevering betas is attributed to Hamada, "The Effect of the Firm's Capital Structure on the Systematic Risk of Common Stocks."

EXHIBIT 14.4   Equity and Asset Betas for Selected Firms with a Single Line of Business ("Pure-Plays"), 2002

Company	Line of Business	Equity Beta	Debt-to-Equity Ratio	Asset Beta
7-Eleven	Convenience stores	0.75	2.00	0.034
Gap	Retail apparel	1.55	0.18	1.40
Mattel	Toy manufacturer	0.75	0.13	0.69
McDonald's	Fast-food restaurants	0.85	0.30	0.70
Office Depot	Retail office supplier	1.25	0.10	1.18
Universal Corporation	Tobacco	0.60	0.47	0.46

Source: Value Line Investment Survey

INCORPORATING RISK IN THE CAPITAL BUDGETING DECISION

In using the net present value method to value future cash flows, we know that the discount rate should reflect the project's risk. In using the internal rate of return method, we know that the hurdle rate—the minimum rate of return on the project—should reflect the project's risk. Both the net present value and the internal rate of return methods, therefore, depend on using a cost of capital that reflects the project's risk.

Risk-Adjusted Rate

The cost of capital is the cost of funds (from creditors and owners). The cost of capital can be viewed as the sum of what suppliers of capital would demand for providing funds if the project were risk-free plus compensation for the risk they take on.

The compensation for the time value of money includes compensation for any anticipated inflation. We typically use a risk-free rate of interest, such as the yield on a long-term U.S. Treasury bond, to represent the time value of money.

The compensation for risk is the extra return required because the project's future cash flows are uncertain. If we assume that the relevant risk is the stand-alone risk (say, for a small, closely-held business), the greater the project's stand-alone risk, the greater the return. If we assume that the relevant risk is the project's market risk, the greater the project's market risk, the greater the return that investors require.

Return Required for the Project's Market Risk

Now let's explain how to determine the premium for bearing market risk. We do this by first specifying the premium for bearing the average amount of risk for the market as a whole. Then, using our measure of market risk, we fine tune this to reflect the market risk of the asset.

The market risk premium for the market as a whole is the difference between the average expected market return, r_m, and the risk-free rate of interest, r_f. If you bought an asset whose market risk was the same as that as the market as a whole, you would expect a return of $r_m - r_f$ to compensate you for market risk.

Next, let's adjust this market risk premium for the market risk of the particular project by multiplying it by that project's asset beta, β_{asset}:

$$\text{Compensation for market risk} = \beta_{asset} (r_m - r_f)$$

This is the extra return necessary to compensate for the project's market risk. The β_{asset} fine tunes the risk premium for the market as a whole to reflect the market risk of the particular project. If we then add the risk-free interest rate, we arrive at the cost of capital:

$$\text{Cost of capital} = r_f + \beta_{asset} (r_m - r_f)$$

Suppose the expected risk-free rate of interest is 4% and the expected return on the market as a whole is 10%. If the β_{asset} is 2.00, this means that if there is a 1% change in the market risk premium, we expect a 2% change in the return on the project. In this case, the cost of capital is 16%:

$$\text{Cost of capital} = 0.04 + 2.00 \,(0.10 - 0.04) = 0.16 \text{ or } 16\%$$

If β_{asset} is 0.75, instead, the cost of capital is 8.5%:

$$\text{Cost of capital} = 0.04 + 0.75 \,(0.06) = 0.085 \text{ or } 8.5\%$$

If we are able to gauge the market risk of a project, we estimate the risk-free rate and the premium for market risk and put them together. But often we are not able to measure the market risk or even the risk-free rate. So we need another way to approach the estimation of the project's cost of capital.

Adjusting the Firm's Cost of Capital

Another way to estimate the cost of capital for a project without estimating the risk premium directly is to use the firm's average cost of capital as a starting point. The average cost of capital is the firm's marginal cost of raising one more dollar of capital—the cost of raising one more dollar in the context of all the firm's projects considered altogether, not just the project being evaluated. We can adjust the average cost of capital of the firm to suit the perceived risk of the project using the following decision rules:

- If a new project being considered is *riskier* than the average project of the firm, the cost of capital of the new project is *greater* than the average cost of capital.
- If the new project is *less risky*, its cost of capital is *less* than the average cost of capital.
- If the project is *as risky* as the average project of the firm, the new project's cost of capital is *equal to* the average cost of capital.

As you can tell, altering the firm's cost of capital to reflect a project's cost of capital requires judgment. How much do we adjust it? If the project is riskier than the typical project do we add 2%? 4%? 10%? There is no prescription here. It depends on the judgment and experience of the decision maker.

Real Options

A significant challenge in capital budgeting is dealing with risk. The traditional methods of evaluating projects are being challenged by an alternative approach that applies option pricing methods to real assets, referred to as ***real options valuation*** (ROV). The interest in ROV arises from the fact that the traditional methods do not consider directly the options available in many investment projects. Though the importance of options in investment opportunities has long been recognized, it is only recently that a great deal of attention has been paid to incorporate options in a meaningful way.[5]

Consider the typical options inherent in an investment opportunity: (1) almost every project has an option to abandon, though there may be constraints (e.g., legally binding contracts) that affect when this option can be exercised, (2) many projects have the option to expand, and (3) many projects have an option to defer investment, putting off the major investment outlays to some future date.

So how do we consider these options within the context of the traditional methods? One approach is to use sensitivity analysis or simulation analysis. And while these analyses allow a look at the possible outcomes of

---

[5] For example, Stewart Myers recognized the importance of considering investment opportunities as growth options ["Determinants of Corporate Borrowings," *Journal of Financial Economics* (Spring 1977), pp. 147–176].

a decision, they do not provide guidance regarding which course of action—of the many—to take. Another approach is the use of a decision tree analysis, associating probabilities to each of the possible outcomes for an event and mapping out the possible outcomes and the value of the investment opportunity associated with these different outcomes. And while this approach is workable when there are few options associated with a project, option pricing provides a method of analysis that is more comprehensive.

The basic idea of ROV is to consider that the value of a project extends beyond its value as measured by the net present value; in other words, the value of project is supplemented by the value of the options. Because the options are considered strategic decisions, the revised or supplemented net present value is often referred to as the *strategic NPV*. Consider an investment opportunity that has one option associated with it. The strategic NPV is the sum of the traditional NPV (the static NPV) and the value of the option:

$$\text{Strategic NPV} = \text{Static NPV} + \text{Value of the option}$$

Options on Real Assets

The valuation of stock options is rather complex, but with the assistance of some well-accepted models such as the Black-Scholes model, we can estimate the value of an option. For example, in the Black-Scholes option pricing model discussed in Appendix A, there are five factors that are important in the valuation of an option:[6]

1. The value of the underlying asset, P
2. The exercise price or strike price of the option, E
3. The risk free rate of interest, r
4. The volatility of the value of the underlying asset, σ
5. The time remaining to the expiration of the option, T

In Chapter 9 we examine the relation between each of these factors and the value of a stock option. Our focus here is to map these factors onto a real asset option. Like other options, real options may be a call option (the option to buy an asset), a put option (the option to sell an asset), or a compound option (an option on an option). And, like other options, real options may be a European option (an option that can only be exercised on the expiration date) or an American option (an option that can be exercised at any time on or before the expiration date).

In general terms, the relation between the factors that affect the value of a stock option and those that affect a real option correspond as follows:

---

[6] Fischer Black and Myron Scholes, "The Pricing of Options and Corporate Liabilities," *Journal of Political Economy* (May/June 1973), pp. 637–659.

Parameter	Option on a Stock	Option on a Real Asset
X	The stock's price	The present value of cash flows from the investment opportunity
S	The exercise price of the option	The present value of the delayed capital expenditure or future cost savings
r	The risk-free rate of interest	The risk-free rate of interest
s	Volatility of value of the underlying asset	Uncertainty of the project's cash flows
t	The time to maturity	The project's useful life

Of course, the factors that correspond to a specific option can be better described when we examine the particular option. Consider the option to abandon. In this case, the underlying asset is continuing operations and so the value of the underlying asset is the present value of the cash flows associated with the asset. The ***strike price*** or ***exercise price*** for this option is the exit value or salvage value of the asset. A number of common real options are described in Exhibit 14.5.

EXHIBIT 14.5 Examples of Real Options

Option	Type*	Value of Underlying Asset	Exercise Price
To abandon	American put	The present value of the cash flows from the abandoned assets	The exit or salvage value
To defer an investment	American call	The present value of completed project's net operating cash flows	The deferred investment outlay
To abandon during construction	Compound option	The present value of the completed project's cash flows	The investment outlay necessary for the next stage
To contract the scale of a project	European put	The present value of potential cost savings	The costs of rescaling the project
To expand	European call	The present value of incremental net operating cash flows	The additional investment outlay
To switch inputs or outputs	American put	The present value of the incremental cash flows from the best alternative use	The cost of retooling production or distribution

*A put option is an option to sell the underlying asset; a call option is an option to buy the underlying asset. An American option is one that can be exercised at any time up to and including the expiration date; a European option is one that can only be exercised at the expiration date.

Identifying the options associated with an investment opportunity is the first step. The second step is to value these options. Consider an investment opportunity to defer an investment. This investment opportunity is similar to what a firm experiences in their investment in research and development: An expenditure or series of expenditures are made in research and development and then sometime in the future, depending on the results of the research and development, the actions of competitors, and the approval of regulators, the firm can then decide whether to go ahead with the investment opportunity.

Real Options: An Example

Let's put some numbers to the analysis of a project with a real option. Suppose that research and development is $2 million initially and $2 million more for each of the next three years. And suppose that at the end of the fourth year the firm has an option to either go ahead with the product or simply abandon it. If the firm goes ahead with the development of the product, this will require an investment of $100 million at the end of the fourth year. To make the analysis simpler, let's assume that we can sell the investment in the product to another party—that is, cash out—at the end of the fourth year for $120 million.[7] And, because we know that all of this is uncertain, let's attach probabilities of this being a marketable product and, hence, one that the firm is able to cash out. Let's assume that there is a 60% chance that the firm can cash out for $120 million and a 40% change that the firm cannot cash out at all (and will, therefore, not make the investment).

Given this scenario, it means that:

■ If the R&D is successful and the firm is able to cash out, the value at the end of the fourth period is $120 million – $100 million = $20 million.
■ If the R&D is not successful and the firm is not able to cash out, the value at the end of the fourth period is $0.

Before we can value the project with or without the option, we need to estimate the cost of capital. The cost of capital is the sum of the risk-free rate of interest and the risk premium.[8] The risk premium is determined relative to the market's risk premium. Suppose the risk-free rate

---

[7] We are simplifying this example. More realistically, we would estimate future cash flows from the successful project beyond the fourth year and discount these to the end of the fourth year—and then use this value in place of the $120 million.

[8] To be consistent with the Black-Scholes option-pricing model, we'll use continuously compounded cost of capital throughout our example.

of interest is 5%, the market risk premium is 4%, and the volatility is 5 times that of the market. If the market's volatility (i.e., the standard deviation of expected cash flows) is 15%, the cost of capital is:[9]

$$\text{Cost of capital} = \text{Risk-free rate of interest} + \text{Risk premium}$$
$$= 5\% + 5(4\%) = 25\%$$

Using a continuously compounded discount rate of 25%, the present value of the research and development costs is –$5.72 million:

	in millions			
	0	1	2	3
Research and development	–$2.00	–$2.00	–$2.00	–$2.00
Present value of research and development	–$2.00	–$1.56	–$1.21	–$0.94
Total present value of R&D	–$5.72			

Putting the R&D together with the value of the investment four years from today,

$$\text{NPV} = -\$5.720 \text{ million} + \left\{ \left[(0.60)\frac{\$20 \text{ million}}{e^{4(0.25)}} \right] + [(0.40)(\$0)] \right\}$$

$$= -\$5.720 \text{ million} + 4.415 \text{ million} = -\$1.305 \text{ million}$$

This NPV represents the cost to the firm if the firm makes the decision today to commit to both the R&D and the investment at the end of the fourth year.

Using the traditional capital budgeting NPV technique, this suggests that we should reject the project because its net present value is less than $0. But wait—we have not considered the valuable option of the deferred investment because the firm can wait until the end of the fourth year to decide on the investment.

We can see the value of the option by estimating how much value the option itself adds to the project. First, we estimate the parameters of the option pricing model. Then we see how the value of the option, when considered along with the present value of the cost of acquiring the option (that is, the present value of the research and development), can make an unattractive project into an attractive project.

---

[9] This means that the volatility of the project's cash flows are $5(15\%) = 75\%$. This is the estimate of volatility that we include in the valuation of the project's option.

The value of the underlying asset is the discounted value of the probability-weighted possible outcomes:

$$\text{Value of the underlying asset} = \left[0.6 \left(\frac{\$120 \text{ million}}{e^{4(0.25)}} \right) \right] + [(0.40)(\$0)]$$

$$= \$26.487 \text{ million}$$

Therefore, the value of the parameters in the option valuation are as follows:

Value of the underlying asset	$26.487 million
Strike price	$100.000 million
Risk-free rate of interest	5%
Volatility	75%
Number of periods to exercise	4

Using the Black-Scholes option pricing formula, the value of this option is $7.774 million. Therefore, the value of the project is:

Project NPV = Present value of the R&D + Value of the option
= – $5.72 million + 7.774 million
Project NPV = $2.054 million

Another way of looking at this is to estimate the value-added of the deferral option:

Value-added of the option = Project NPV – Static NPV
= $2.054 million – (–1.305 million)
Value-added of the option = $0.749 million

Hence, the project has a positive NPV considering the valuable option to defer investment.

Challenges

We have simplified this last example to illustrate the importance of considering options. Now let's examine a couple of the challenges in incorporating real option valuation into an actual investment opportunity analysis.

The first challenge has to do with the parameters in the model. Focusing just on the estimate of volatility, we can see that the value added of the option is sensitive to the estimate of volatility. Though we simply assumed that the volatility is 50%, it is not a simple matter to determine the volatility of a project's future cash flow. We experience the same problems that we did in trying to determine the beta of a project—it just isn't measurable directly. The volatility of an investment opportunity's cash flows affect two key elements of the strategic value: The volatility has a positive relation to the value of the option (that is, the greater the volatility, the greater the value of the option), and the volatility has a negative relation to the static NPV (that is, the greater the volatility, the greater the cost of capital and hence the lower the static NPV). If we take this last example and calculate the strategic NPV with volatility of 60% and 90%, again we see that the value of the option is affected by the choice of volatility:

	Volatility		
	60%	75%	90%
Static NPV	–$0.82	–$1.30	–$1.69
Value of the option	$0.47	$2.06	$3.14
Strategic NPV	$1.29	$3.36	$4.83

Second, most investment projects have several options, some of which interact. For example, if a firm is investing in R&D over a period of years in the development of a new product, there exists at least two options: the option to abandon during development and the option to defer investment. The valuation problem in the case of multiple options is not simply carried out by adding the separate values because the value of one option may affect the value of other options. Solving for the value of options in the case of multiple, interacting options is beyond the Black and Scholes model and is quite difficult, requiring the application of numerical methods.[10]

CERTAINTY EQUIVALENTS

An alternative to adjusting the discount rate to reflect risk is to adjust the cash flow to reflect risk. We do this by converting each cash flow and its risk into its certainty equivalent. A certainty equivalent is the certain cash flow that is considered to be equivalent to the risky cash flow. For example, if the risky cash flow two periods into the future is $1.5 million, the certainty equivalent is the dollar amount of a certain cash flow (that is, a sure thing) that the firm considers to be worth the same. This

---

[10] For a discussion of these issues and an example of option interaction, see Lenos Trigeorgis, "A Log-Transformed Binomial Numerical Analysis Method for Valuing Complex Multi-Option Investments," *Journal of Financial and Quantitative Analysis*, September 1991, pp. 309–326.

certainty equivalent could be $1 million, $0.8 million, $1.4 million, or any other amount—it depends on both the degree of riskiness of the $1.5 million risky cash flow and the judgment of the decision-maker.

The certainty equivalent approach of incorporating risk into the net present value analysis is useful for several reasons.

- *It separates the time value of money and risk.* Risk is accounted for in the adjusted cash flows while the time value of money is accounted for in the discount rate.
- *It allows each period's cash flows to be adjusted separately for risk.* This is accomplished by converting each period's cash flows into a certainty equivalent for that time period. The certainty equivalent factor may be different for each period.
- *The decision maker can incorporate preferences for risk.* This is done in determining the certainty equivalent cash flows.

However, there are some disadvantages to using the certainty equivalent approach that stymie its application in practice:

- *The net present value of the certainty equivalent is not easily interpreted.* We no longer have the clearer interpretation of the net present value as the increment in shareholder wealth.
- *There is no reliable way of determining the certainty equivalent value for each period's cash flow.*

While the certainty equivalents approach sounds great in principle, it sure is tough to apply in practice.

ASSESSMENT OF PROJECT RISK IN PRACTICE

Most U.S. firms consider risk in some manner in evaluating investment projects. But considering risk is usually a subjective analysis as opposed to the more objective results obtainable with simulation or sensitivity analysis.

Firms that use discounted cash flow techniques, such as internal rate of return and net present value methods, tend to use a single cost of capital. But using a single cost of capital for all projects can be hazardous.

Suppose you use the same cost of capital for all your projects. If all of them have the same risk and the cost of capital you are using is appropriate for this level of risk, no problem. But what if you use the same cost of capital but your projects each have *different* levels of risk?

Suppose you use a cost of capital that is the cost of capital for the firm's average risk project. What happens when you apply discounted cash flow techniques, such as the net present value or the internal rate of return, and use this one rate? You will end up:

■ rejecting profitable projects (which would have increased owners' wealth) that have risk below the risk of the average risk project because you discounted their future cash flows too much, and

■ accepting unprofitable projects whose risk is above the risk of the average project, because you did not discount their future cash flows enough.

Firms that use a risk-adjusted discount rate usually do so by classifying projects into risk classes by the type of project. For example, a firm with a cost of capital of 10% may develop from experience the following classes and discount rates:

Type of Project	Cost of Capital
New product	14%
New market	12%
Expansion	10%
Replacement	8%

Given this set of costs of capital, the financial manager need only figure out which class a project belongs to and then apply the rate assigned to that class.

Firms may also make adjustments in the cost of capital for factors other than the type of project. For example, firms investing in projects in foreign countries will sometimes make an adjustment for the additional risk of the foreign project, such as exchange rate risk, inflation risk, and political risk.

The cost of capital is generally based on an assessment of the firm's overall cost of capital. The firm first evaluates the cost of each source of capital—debt, preferred stock, and common equity. Then each cost is weighted by the proportion of each source to be raised. This average is referred to as the *weighted average cost of capital* (*WACC*).

There are tools available to assist the decision-maker in measuring and evaluating project risk. But much of what is actually done in practice is subjective. Judgment, with a large dose of experience, is used more often than scientific means of incorporating risk. Is this bad? Well, the scientific approaches to measurement and evaluation of risk depend, in part, on subjective assessments of risk, the probability distributions of future cash flows and judgments about market risk. So it is possible that bypassing the more technical analyses in favor of a completely subjective assessment of risk may result in cost of capital estimates that better reflect the project's risk. But then again it may not. The proof may be in the pudding, but it is difficult to assess the "proof" since we cannot tell how well firms could have done had they used more technical analyses.

SUMMARY

- To screen and select among investment projects, the financial manager must estimate future cash flows for each project, evaluate the riskiness of those cash flows, and evaluate each project's contribution to the firm's value and, hence, to owners' wealth.
- The financial manager has to evaluate future cash flows—cash flows that are estimates, which means they are uncertain.
- The financial manager has to incorporate risk into the analysis of projects to identify which ones maximize owners' wealth.
- Statistical measures that can be used to evaluate the risk of a project's cash flows are: the range, the standard deviation, and the coefficient of variation.
- Sensitivity analysis and simulation analysis are tools that can be used in conjunction with the statistical measures to evaluate a project's risk. Both techniques give us an idea of the relation between a project's return and its risk.
- Because the firm is itself a portfolio of projects and it is typically assumed that owners hold diversified portfolios, the relevant risk of a project is not its stand-alone risk, but rather how it affects the risk of owners' portfolios, its market risk.
- Risk is typically figured into our decision-making by using a cost of capital that reflects the project's risk.
- The relevant risk for the evaluation of a project is the project's market risk, which is also referred to as the asset beta. This risk can be estimated by looking at the market risk of firms in a single line of business similar to that of the project, a pure-play.
- An alternative to finding a pure-play is to classify projects according to the type of project (e.g., expansion) and assign costs of capital to each project type according to subjective judgment of risk.
- Most firms adjust for risk in their assessment of the attractiveness of projects. However, this adjustment is typically done by evaluating risk subjectively and making ad hoc adjustments to the firm's cost of capital to arrive at a cost of capital for a particular project.

■ Estimating the options associated with an investment opportunity may reveal value in a project that is not reflected using traditional capital budgeting techniques.

■ There are options associated with every investment opportunity, including the option to defer the investment and the option to abandon the investment.

■ The valuation of a single option is straightforward, but the valuation of multiple options that may interact is quite difficult.

■ An alternative approach to dealing with risk in a capital project is through the use of certainty equivalents, which are risk-free values that correspond to the risky cash flows.

■ In practice, the treatment of risk in capital budgeting varies, with the most basic approach being the subjective adjustment to the firm's cost of capital to arrive at a project's cost of capital.

QUESTIONS

1. Are the required rate of return and the cost of capital the same thing? Explain.
2. Suppose a discount retail chain is considering opening a new outlet in another city. What should they consider in assessing the risk associated with the future cash flows of this new outlet?
3. Suppose a cereal manufacturer is considering a new cereal based on a new, yet to be released feature film. What should the cereal manufacturer consider in assessing the risk associated with the future cash flows from this new cereal?
4. Suppose you perform calculations and determine that the expected value of first year cash flows is $1,200 and the standard deviation is $500. What does this mean?
5. What distinguishes sensitivity analysis from simulation analysis?
6. Suppose the Shell Point Shell Company evaluates most projects using the net present value method and a single discount rate that reflects its marginal cost of raising new capital. Can you see any problem with their method?
7. Suppose a firm is planning to develop a new toy product over the next two years. If the development and market testing is successful, the firm will begin production of the product in two years, with a goal of reaching the market in two and one-half years. What types of options are inherent in this investment opportunity? Are there any options whose values may interact?
8. Suppose the Destin Sand Company's management evaluates investment opportunities by grouping projects into three risk classes: low,

average, and high risk. They assign a cost of capital to each group and use this cost of capital to discount a project's future cash flows: 5% for low risk, 10% for average risk, and 15% for high risk projects. Critique their method of adjusting for risk.

9. Consider the probability distribution of the first year cash flows for the ABC Project:

Possible Cash Flow	Probability
$1,000	20%
$2,000	60%
$3,000	20%

a. Calculate the range of possible cash flows.
b. Calculate the expected cash flow.
c. Calculate the standard deviation of the possible cash flows.
d. Calculate the coefficient of variation of the possible cash flows.

10. Consider the probability distribution of the first year cash flows for the DEF Project:

Possible Cash Flow	Probability
$1,000	10%
$2,000	60%
$3,000	30%

a. Calculate the range of possible cash flows.
b. Calculate the expected cash flow.
c. Calculate the standard deviation of the possible cash flows.
d. Calculate the coefficient of variation of the possible cash flows.

11. Consider the probability distributions of the first year cash flows of two projects, GHI and JKL:

GHI Possible Cash Flow	JKL Probability
−$5,000	30%
$0	30%
+$7,000	40%

a. Calculate the range of possible cash flows for each project.
b. Calculate the expected cash flow for each project.
c. Calculate the standard deviation of the possible cash flows for each project.

  d. Calculate the coefficient of variation of the possible cash flows for each project.

  e. Which project has more risk? Why?

12. The Avalanche Snow Company is evaluating the purchase of a new snow making machine. The marketing and production managers have provided the following change in revenues and expenses associated with the new machine, and the accountant has calculated the depreciation on the machine for the next four years. Assume that there are no changes in working capital in each year.

Year	Sales	Expenses	Depreciation
2001	$100,000	$50,000	$25,000
2002	150,000	75,000	25,000
2003	125,000	75,000	25,000
2004	100,000	75,000	25,000

  a. What is the operating cash flow for each year if the tax rate is 30%?

  b. What is the operating cash flow for each year if the tax rate is 40%?

  c. What is the operating cash flow for each year if the tax rate is 50%?

  d. Suppose the probability of a 30% tax rate is 10%, the probability of a 40% tax rate is 30% and the probability of a 50% tax rate is 60%. What is the expected operating cash flow for Avalanche? What is the standard deviation of operating cash flows?

13. The Sopchoppy Motorcycle Company is considering an investment of $600,000 in a new motorcycle. They expect to increase sales in each of the next three years by $400,000, while increasing expenses by $200,000 each year. They expect that they can carve out a niche in the marketplace for this new motorcycle for three years, after which they intend to cease production on this motorcycle. Assume the equipment is depreciated at the rate of $200,000 each year. Sopchoppy's tax rate is 40%.

  a. What is the internal rate of return of this project if they sell the manufacturing equipment for $200,000 at the end of three years?

  b. What is the internal rate of return of this project if they sell the manufacturing equipment for $100,000 at the end of three years?

  c. What is the internal rate of return of this project if they sell the manufacturing equipment for $300,000 at the end of three years?

  d. Suppose the following distribution of possible sales prices on the equipment is developed:

Sales Price	Probability
$100,000	25%
$200,000	50%
$300,000	25%

What is the expected internal rate of return for Sopchoppy? What is the standard deviation of these possible internal rates of return?

14. Consider the probability distribution of possible cash flow outcomes for Project XYZ:

Possible Cash Flow	Probability
$2,000	$\frac{1}{6}$
$4,000	$\frac{2}{3}$
$6,000	$\frac{1}{6}$

Construct a simulation of the future cash flows using a six-sided die.

a. Rolling the die 30 times, what is the distribution of the possible cash flows?

b. Rolling the die a total of 60 times, what is the distribution of the possible cash flows?

c. Draw a frequency distribution of the results of rolling the die 60 times, plotting the frequency of occurrence on the vertical axis and the possible outcomes on the horizontal axis. How does this frequency distribution compare with the probability distribution?

15. Suppose the compensation for risk is based on the market risk and that market risk is estimated as the product of the asset's beta and the market risk premium for the market as a whole (that is, $r_m - r_f$). Calculate the cost of capital for each of the possible combinations of compensation for the time value of money and compensation for risk:

	Risk-Free Rate of Interest	Asset Beta	Market Risk Premium
a.	3%	1.00	4%
b.	4%	0.50	5%
c.	5%	1.50	6%
d.	4%	1.00	4%
e.	5%	1.25	4%

16. Consider the following information based on firms that are in a single line of business:

Company Name	Equity Beta	Debt in Millions	Equity in Millions
A	1.6	$320	$461
B	0.8	$365	$5,186
C	1.3	$1,447	$3,811
D	0.7	$2,332	$1,456
E	1.1	$334	$314

Calculate the asset beta for each firm, assuming a marginal tax rate of 34%.

PART

Four

Financing Decisions

CHAPTER 15

Intermediate and Long-Term Debt

In Part Four of this book, we will describe a firm's capital structure, which is the mix of debt and equity used to finance the firm. Before we deal with the decision of how much of what type of capital a firm should use, we will first take a look at the characteristics of the different types and features of debt and equity securities that are available for a firm to issue.

In this chapter, we discuss the features of debt instruments, focusing on two specific types of debt—term loans and notes/bonds. We describe these debt instruments by focusing on the different features, such as interest and maturity. From the perspective of the investor, these features affect the pattern of cash flows from the investment and the uncertainty associated with these cash flows, both of which affect the cost of debt capital to the firm. From the perspective of the issuer, the key is to package these features in a debt obligation in a way to make them attractive to investors, provide reasonable cost of debt to the issuer, and to give the firm flexibility to alter its capital structure in the future.

Short-term debt obligations (meaning repayment within one year) are the subject of Chapter 21. Other forms of borrowing are via structured finance transactions, the subject of Chapter 26, and equipment leasing, the subject of Chapter 27. In Chapter 16, we will look at common stock and in Chapter 17 we examine preferred stock as a source of capital. Once we understand the advantages and disadvantages of each type of security, we will address the capital structure decision—a firm's mix of debt and equity.

OVERVIEW OF DEBT OBLIGATIONS

In a debt obligation, the borrower receives money in exchange for a promise to repay it at some future time. The obligation to repay is referred to as *debt* or *indebtedness*; the borrower is the *debtor*; and the lender is the *creditor*. The creditor is also an investor, because he is lending money at one point in time and expecting it back in the future, along with compensation for lending his money. We refer to indebtedness between a borrower and a lender as a *loan*. If the borrower issues a security to represent the indebtedness, we usually refer to the borrower as the issuer and the lenders as noteholders or bondholders, depending on the type of security representing the indebtedness.

The amount borrowed is called the *principal* and is repaid either at the end of the period of indebtedness or at regular intervals during this period. When the entire principal is repaid only at the end of the period of the indebtedness, the debt obligation is said to have a *bullet structure*. If, instead, the principal payments are made over time based on a schedule, the debt obligation is said to have an *amortizing structure*.

The lender receives *interest* to compensate for lending funds. For some types of debt the interest is paid periodically, and for other types is paid at the end of the debt period. The interest rate can be a fixed rate or a variable rate. When the interest rate is a variable rate, more popularly referred to as a *floating rate*, there is a formula that sets forth how the interest rate on the debt obligation will be determined at the interest reset date. The formula is called the *interest rate reset formula*. The general formula for the floating rate is:

Floating rate = Reference rate + Quoted margin

The *reference rate* is the interest rate on some contractually specified market interest rate or some other benchmark. The *quoted margin* is fixed over the life of the debt obligation. The amount of the quoted margin depends on the credit quality of the borrower and other features of the debt obligation. The lower the credit quality of the borrower, the higher the quoted margin. The date on which the rate on the debt obligation is changed is called the *reset date*. The period over which the new rate applies is called the *reset period*.

For example, suppose that a debt obligation's reset period is one year and the reference rate is the 1-year London interbank offered rate (LIBOR). Suppose further that the quoted margin is 200 basis points. That is, the formula for its floating rate is

1-year LIBOR + 200 basis points

So, if 1-year LIBOR at a reset date is 3%, then the floating rate for the reset period would be 5%. If at a subsequent reset date 1-year LIBOR increases to 4.2%, then the floating rate for that reset period would be 6.2%.

A floating-rate debt obligation can have a maximum interest rate imposed. This means that if the interest rate reset formula at a reset date indicates that the interest rate is greater than the maximum interest rate specified, the formula is overridden. The maximum interest rate in a floating-rate debt obligation is referred to as a *cap*. For example, suppose that the cap is 7% and that the formula is the one used earlier, 1-year LIBOR plus 200 basis points. Then if 1-year LIBOR is 6% at the reset date, in the absence of the cap the formula would set the rate at 8%. However, this is above the cap of 7%. The rate for the period is then set at the cap, 7%. A cap is an advantage to the borrower and a disadvantage to the lender.

There are some floating-rate debt obligations that set a minimum interest rate. The minimum interest rate is called a *floor*. The floor is an advantage to the lender and a disadvantage to the borrower.

The lender cannot be absolutely sure that the borrower will repay the principal and pay the interest when promised. Realizing that, borrowers typically specify this assurance in the form of a promise to repay with property they own, if necessary. Failing to pay when promised, the creditors force the sale of this property to be repaid from the proceeds.

We refer to debt backed by property as a *secured debt* and to the property as *security* or *collateral*. If there is no security, the creditor relies entirely on the ability of the borrower to make the promised payments. We refer to this type of debt as *unsecured*.

TERM LOANS

Term loans are negotiated directly between borrower and creditor, where the creditor is typically a commercial bank, an insurance company, or a finance company. Term loans range in maturity from two to ten years, though any repayment term is possible. We refer to these debts as term loans because there is a fixed term, or fixed maturity, for the loan, as opposed to a loan that is payable on demand. Term loans can be secured or unsecured.

Interest Rate

The interest rate on term loans is usually variable, although some lenders offer a fixed rate. The reason why lenders prefer to offer a variable rate has to do with the management of risk of the lending institution. A major risk faced by a lending institution is the mismatch between the rate earned on the loans it makes and the rate it must pay to borrow funds. For example, suppose a commercial bank provides a 5-year loan with a fixed rate of 8% to a manufacturing firm. The bank must be able to fund (borrow) money in order to extend the term loan to the manufacturing firm. Typically, a lender such as a bank or a finance company borrows on a floating-rate basis. Suppose in the first year of the term loan, the bank can borrow funds at 6%. The bank has locked in a spread of 2% (8% − 6%) or 200 basis points. Suppose in the second year of the loan, interest rates in the economy increase such that the cost to the bank of borrowing is 8.5%. Then the bank will not generate enough interest from the term loan to cover the cost of its borrowing. That is, the bank will be borrowing for one year at 8.5% but will be loaning funds to the manufacturing firm at 8% (i.e., the fixed rate on the term loan).

This risk of a rise in interest rates that the lender faces is solved by loaning funds on a floating-rate basis. More specifically, the lender will tie the reference rate of the floating-rate loan to the reference rate that its cost of funds are tied to. For example, suppose that the lender borrows money tied to LIBOR. The lender will then prefer to make a loan with a floating rate that is "LIBOR based"—meaning that the interest rate on the loans it makes will vary with LIBOR. By doing so, if LIBOR increases, while the cost of borrowing for the lender increases, the loan rate it receives increases as well.

Despite this risk, some lenders are willing to provide term loans with a fixed rate. There are two reasons for this. First, a lender such as an insurance company does not borrow funds to extend a loan. Such a lender is seeking to lock in an interest rate over some period of time. Second, as we see later in this chapter, a lender can use an interest rate swap to convert cash flows from a fixed rate to a floating rate or the other way around, from a floating rate to a fixed rate. What this enables a lender to do is loan funds on a fixed-rate basis and swap the interest payments from a fixed rate to a floating rate. By doing so, a lender that borrows on a floating-rate basis can provide a matching of the loan's interest payments to its borrowing cost.

Repayment Schedule

Term loans are usually repaid in installments either monthly, quarterly, semiannually, or annually. Let's look at the typical repayment schedule for a term loan. Suppose that GemOne Corporation is a manufacturer that seeks a 4-year term loan of $100 million. Let's assume for now that the term loan carries a fixed interest rate of 8% and that level payments are made monthly. A "level payment" means that the same amount is paid each month. Thus, there will be 48 monthly payments. In a typical term loan, the payments are structured such that each month GemOne's payment will include interest and principal repayment. A loan structured in this way is what we refer to as an amortizing loan. The loan payments are determined such that after the last payment is made, there is no loan balance outstanding. Thus the loan is referred to as a *fully amortizing loan*.

For our hypothetical 4-year, $100 million term loan with an 8% rate, the monthly payment would be $2,441,292.23. This amount is determined by using the time value of money principles explained in Chapter 7. The procedure is to determine the amount of an annuity (i.e., the monthly loan payment) that will make the present value of 48 payments of the annuity equal to $100 million using a discount rate of 0.66667%. (The 0.66667% discount rate is the annual interest rate of 8% divided by 12 since the loan repays monthly.)

Exhibit 15.1 shows for each month the amount of the beginning monthly balance, the interest payment for the month, the amount of the monthly payment applied to repayment of the principal (referred to as the *scheduled principal repayment* or the *amortization), and* the ending loan balance. A schedule such as that shown in Exhibit 15.1 is referred to as an *amortization schedule*. Notice that in our illustration, the ending loan balance is zero. That is, it is a fully amortizing loan.

Suppose instead that the term loan is still fixed at 8% for the 4-year life of the loan but that instead of fully amortized, GemOne seeks to lower its monthly payment by not fully amortizing the loan. Suppose that the lender agrees that it will accept a loan balance at the end of the 4 years of $10 million. The principal outstanding at the end of 4 years that must be paid is called a *balloon payment*. The amount of the monthly loan payment for such a loan would be $2,263,829.68. At the end of year 4, GemOne must make the last monthly loan payment of $2,263,829.68 plus the balloon payment of $10 million.

In an *interest-only loan*, no scheduled principal repayment is made each month prior to the last month of the loan's term. Instead, each month interest is paid. In our GemOne 4-year term loan, the monthly interest is $666,666.67. This is simply the monthly interest rate of 0.66667% (8%/12) multiplied by the amount borrowed, $100 million. The payment at the end of the last year of the loan is the monthly interest payment of $666,666.67 plus the balloon payment of $100 million. A loan structured in this way where no principal repayments are made during the life of the loan is called a *bullet loan* and the last payment is called a *bullet payment*.

So far we have looked at a fixed-rate term loan. Suppose that the GemOne loan is a floating-rate loan and the loan resets at the beginning of each one year anniversary of the loan. Assume that for the first year the loan rate is 8% and in the second year the loan rate increases to 10%. The

EXHIBIT 15.1 Term Loan Amortization Schedule: Fixed Rate, Fully Amortized

Interest rate	8%	Loan	$100,000,000
Number of months	48	Monthly payment	$2,441,292.23

Month	Beginning Loan Balance	Interest	Scheduled Principal Repayment	Ending Loan Balance
1	$100,000,000.00	$666,666.67	$1,774,625.57	$98,225,374.43
2	98,225,374.43	654,835.83	1,786,456.40	96,438,918.03
3	96,438,918.03	642,926.12	1,798,366.11	94,640,551.91
4	94,640,551.91	630,937.01	1,810,355.22	92,830,196.69
5	92,830,196.69	618,867.98	1,822,424.26	91,007,772.44
6	91,007,772.44	606,718.48	1,834,573.75	89,173,198.69
7	89,173,198.69	594,487.99	1,846,804.24	87,326,394.44
8	87,326,394.44	582,175.96	1,859,116.27	85,467,278.17
9	85,467,278.17	569,781.85	1,871,510.38	83,595,767.79
10	83,595,767.79	557,305.12	1,883,987.12	81,711,780.68
11	81,711,780.68	544,745.20	1,896,547.03	79,815,233.65
12	79,815,233.65	532,101.56	1,909,190.68	77,906,042.97
13	77,906,042.97	519,373.62	1,921,918.61	75,984,124.36
14	75,984,124.36	506,560.83	1,934,731.41	74,049,392.95
15	74,049,392.95	493,662.62	1,947,629.61	72,101,763.34
16	72,101,763.34	480,678.42	1,960,613.81	70,141,149.52
17	70,141,149.52	467,607.66	1,973,684.57	68,167,464.95
18	68,167,464.95	454,449.77	1,986,842.47	66,180,622.49
19	66,180,622.49	441,204.15	2,000,088.08	64,180,534.40
20	64,180,534.40	427,870.23	2,013,422.00	62,167,112.40
21	62,167,112.40	414,447.42	2,026,844.82	60,140,267.58
22	60,140,267.58	400,935.12	2,040,357.12	58,099,910.46
23	58,099,910.46	387,332.74	2,053,959.50	56,045,950.96
24	56,045,950.96	373,639.67	2,067,652.56	53,978,298.40
25	53,978,298.40	359,855.32	2,081,436.91	51,896,861.49
26	51,896,861.49	345,979.08	2,095,313.16	49,801,548.33
27	49,801,548.33	332,010.32	2,109,281.91	47,692,266.42
28	47,692,266.42	317,948.44	2,123,343.79	45,568,922.63
29	45,568,922.63	303,792.82	2,137,499.42	43,431,423.21
30	43,431,423.21	289,542.82	2,151,749.41	41,279,673.80
31	41,279,673.80	275,197.83	2,166,094.41	39,113,579.39
32	39,113,579.39	260,757.20	2,180,535.04	36,933,044.35
33	36,933,044.35	246,220.30	2,195,071.94	34,737,972.42
34	34,737,972.42	231,586.48	2,209,705.75	32,528,266.66
35	32,528,266.66	216,855.11	2,224,437.12	30,303,829.54
36	30,303,829.54	202,025.53	2,239,266.70	28,064,562.84
37	28,064,562.84	187,097.09	2,254,195.15	25,810,367.69
38	25,810,367.69	172,069.12	2,269,223.12	23,541,144.57
39	23,541,144.57	156,940.96	2,284,351.27	21,256,793.30
40	21,256,793.30	141,711.96	2,299,580.28	18,957,213.02
41	18,957,213.02	126,381.42	2,314,910.81	16,642,302.21
42	16,642,302.21	110,948.68	2,330,343.55	14,311,958.66
43	14,311,958.66	95,413.06	2,345,879.18	11,966,079.48
44	11,966,079.48	79,773.86	2,361,518.37	9,604,561.11
45	9,604,561.11	64,030.41	2,377,261.83	7,227,299.28
46	7,227,299.28	48,182.00	2,393,110.24	4,834,189.04
47	4,834,189.04	32,227.93	2,409,064.31	2,425,124.74
48	2,425,124.74	16,167.50	2,425,124.74	0.00

monthly loan payment for the second year would be determined as follows. Assuming the loan is a fully amortizing loan, at the end of the first year we know what the outstanding loan balance is. This amount can be found in Exhibit 15.1. It is $77,906,042.97. Thus, GemOne is borrowing $77,906,042.97 for three years at the new rate, 10% per annum or 0.8333% per month. The monthly loan payment to fully amortize a 3-year 10% term loan is $2,513,808.87. Panel a in Exhibit 15.2 shows the amortization schedule for the 12 months in the second year on the loan.

Let's suppose in the third year of the term loan that the loan rate decreases to 9%. The loan balance at the end of the second year is $54,476,387.15 as can be seen from panel a in Exhibit 15.2. The monthly loan payment to fully amortize $54,476,387.15 for 2 years at 9% is $2,488,739.71. The amortization schedule for the third year is shown in panel b of Exhibit 15.2. At the end of the third year, the outstanding balance is $28,458,521.22. If in the fourth year the loan rate decreases to 7.8%, then the monthly loan payment necessary to fully amortize $28,458,521.22 for one year is $2,472,931.18. Panel c of Exhibit 15.2 shows the amortization schedule for the last year. Note that at the end of the fourth year the outstanding balance is zero; that is, the loan is fully amortized.

EXHIBIT 15.2 Amortization Schedule for a Term Loan with a Floating Rate: Years 2 through 4
a. Year 2

| Interest rate | 10% | Loan | $77,906,043 |
| Number of months | 36 | Monthly payment | $2,513,808.87 |

Month	Beginning Loan Balance	Interest	Scheduled Loan Repayment	Ending Loan Balance
13	$77,906,042.97	$649,217.02	$1,864,591.85	$76,041,451.12
14	76,041,451.12	633,678.76	1,880,130.11	74,161,321.01
15	74,161,321.01	618,011.01	1,895,797.86	72,265,523.15
16	72,265,523.15	602,212.69	1,911,596.18	70,353,926.97
17	70,353,926.97	586,282.72	1,927,526.15	68,426,400.82
18	68,426,400.82	570,220.01	1,943,588.87	66,482,811.95
19	66,482,811.95	554,023.43	1,959,785.44	64,523,026.52
20	64,523,026.52	537,691.89	1,976,116.98	62,546,909.53
21	62,546,909.53	521,224.25	1,992,584.63	60,554,324.91
22	60,554,324.91	504,619.37	2,009,189.50	58,545,135.41
23	58,545,135.41	487,876.13	2,025,932.74	56,519,202.66
24	56,519,202.66	470,993.36	2,042,815.52	54,476,387.15

EXHIBIT 15.2 (Continued)
b. Year 3

| Interest rate | 9% | Loan | $54,476,387 |
| Number of months | 24 | Monthly payment | $2,488,739.71 |

Month	Beginning Loan Balance	Interest	Scheduled Loan Repayment	Ending Loan Balance
25	$54,476,387.15	$408,572.90	$2,080,166.80	$52,396,220.34
26	52,396,220.34	392,971.65	2,095,768.05	50,300,452.29
27	50,300,452.29	377,253.39	2,111,486.31	48,188,965.97
28	48,188,965.97	361,417.24	2,127,322.46	46,061,643.51
29	46,061,643.51	345,462.33	2,143,277.38	43,918,366.13
30	43,918,366.13	329,387.75	2,159,351.96	41,759,014.17
31	41,759,014.17	313,192.61	2,175,547.10	39,583,467.07
32	39,583,467.07	296,876.00	2,191,863.70	37,391,603.37
33	37,391,603.37	280,437.03	2,208,302.68	35,183,300.68
34	35,183,300.68	263,874.76	2,224,864.95	32,958,435.73
35	32,958,435.73	247,188.27	2,241,551.44	30,716,884.29
36	30,716,884.29	230,376.63	2,258,363.07	28,458,521.22

c. Year 4

| Interest rate | 7.8% | Loan | $28,458,521 |
| Number of months | 12 | Monthly payment | $2,472,931.18 |

Month	Beginning Loan Balance	Interest	Scheduled Loan Repayment	Ending Loan Balance
37	$28,458,521.22	$184,980.39	$2,287,950.80	$26,170,570.42
38	26,170,570.42	170,108.71	2,302,822.48	23,867,747.95
39	23,867,747.95	155,140.36	2,317,790.82	21,549,957.13
40	21,549,957.13	140,074.72	2,332,856.46	19,217,100.67
41	19,217,100.67	124,911.15	2,348,020.03	16,869,080.64
42	16,869,080.64	109,649.02	2,363,282.16	14,505,798.48
43	14,505,798.48	94,287.69	2,378,643.49	12,127,154.98
44	12,127,154.98	78,826.51	2,394,104.68	9,733,050.31
45	9,733,050.31	63,264.83	2,409,666.36	7,323,383.95
46	7,323,383.95	47,602.00	2,425,329.19	4,898,054.76
47	4,898,054.76	31,837.36	2,441,093.83	2,456,960.94
48	2,456,960.94	15,970.25	2,456,960.94	0.00

NOTES AND BONDS

A firm may borrow money by issuing notes or bonds. Both are *certificates of indebtedness*, which are written obligations of the borrower to repay the amount borrowed under specified terms. There is a technical difference between a note and a bond. A bond has an *indenture agreement*, a note does not. An indenture agreement spells out the rights and duties of the borrower, with a trustee appointed to look out for the bondholders' interests. Though both a note and a bond are represented by legal contracts stipulating the rights and duties of the borrower, the contract representing a note is typically considered an agreement, less formal than a bond's contract, and is not referred to as an indenture. Throughout this book we will use the terms "note" and "bond" interchangeably, with a preference for the term "bond."

Bonds may be either registered or bearer. For *registered bonds*, the issuer maintains records of who owns them (the creditors) and sends any interest or principal to the registered owners. For *bearer bonds*, whoever physically possesses the certificates representing them owns them. If interest is payable, the bearer simply clips a coupon attached to the certificate and sends it in or cashes it at a specified bank. Almost all bonds issued today are in registered form.

A U.S. corporation can issue bonds anywhere in the world. Bonds issued in the United Stated must comply with U.S. securities laws as regulated by the Securities and Exchange Commission. A bond issued outside the United States need only comply with the securities laws of the countries where the securities are issued and traded. *Eurobonds* are terms for indebtedness issued and traded in markets other than the currency the debts are denominated. Eurobonds are discussed in Chapter 25.

Indenture Agreement

Because a bond is a contract between issuer and bondholders that obligates the issuer to pay the interest and principal and to abide by other terms as well, the rights of the bondholders and the obligations of the issuer must be specified. These obligations and rights are spelled out in the *indenture*. All corporate debt sold to the public (with few exceptions) is governed by the Trust Indenture Act of 1939. The act requires each bond issue to have a trustee who watches out for the interests of the bondholders. Specifically, the trustee is responsible for making sure that all provisions of the indenture are carried out.

In addition, the indenture contains:

■ A description of the bond, including the denomination of the bond payments and the interest payments and their payment dates;

■ Remedies, such as the ability to dispose of equipment or other property, in case the borrower fails to live up to provisions of the bond agreement;

■ The issuer's responsibilities to keep the bondholders informed regarding its financial condition; and

■ Covenants, which are provisions that limit or restrict the issuer's activities to insure sufficient funds are available to pay the debt's obligations. A covenant's typical provisions require the issuer to: pay interest and principal as specified; pay any real estate taxes on any secured property; and provide adequate insurance coverage on any secured property. In addition a covenant may specify a minimum amount of working capital or restrictions on the payment of dividends.

Each bond issue may have a separate indenture, or the firm may have a blanket indenture covering all its bond issues. Several debt issues covered under the same indenture are referred to as a "series," and each issue within the series is usually labeled A, B, C, and so on.[1]

Features and Provisions of a Bond Issue

In this section we describe the basic features or provisions of a bond issue. They include:

■ Denomination
■ Term to maturity
■ Interest
■ Security
■ Seniority
■ Provisions for retirement of debt
■ Convertibility

Denomination

Bonds are issued in denominations, referred to as the *par value*, representing the amount of indebtedness. The par value is also referred to as the *face value* or the *maturity value*. A face value of $1,000 means the issuer is borrowing $1,000 and will, hopefully, repay the $1,000 at the end of the debt period. Though corporate bonds are typically issued with par values of $1,000, we can find bonds with par values of $500, $5,000, or $10,000.

---

[1] Do not confuse a series of bonds with a serial debt issue. A bond series is a set of bond issues issued under one blanket indenture; serial debt is debt issued at one time that has different maturities.

Because bonds can have any denomination, when the price of a bond is quoted the convention in the bond market is to quote it as a percentage of par value. (In Chapter 9, we explained how to value or price a bond.) A price quote of "100" means that the bond's price is 100% of its par value. So, if the par value of a bond is $1,000, then a price of 100 means a price of $1,000 per bond. If the par value of a bond is $100,000 and the price is quoted as 100, the price of this bond is $100,000. If a bond is quoted at 91½, this means that the bond's price is 91% plus ½%. That is, the price is 91.5% of par value. If a bond with a par value of $1,000 is quoted at 91½ this means that its price is $915. For bond with a par value of $100,000, the price would be $915,000 if the price quote is 91½ .

Most bonds sold in the United States are denominated in U.S. dollars—the interest and principal are paid in U.S. dollars. But it is possible to denominate bonds in any currency. A firm can borrow funds today outside the United States and promise to pay a specified interest and principal in a currency other than U.S. dollars. There are some bonds whose principal and interest payments need not be in the same currency. These bonds are called *dual currency bonds*. A few bond issues even give the bondholder the choice between receiving interest and principal in U.S. dollars or some other currency.

Term to Maturity

If a firm borrows by issuing a bond, it must repay the debt obligation at some specified point in time, referred to as the *maturity date*—the date the bond "matures." The number of years until a bond matures is called the *term to maturity* or simply as the *term* or the *maturity* of the bond.

There is no limit to the maturity. Bonds and notes are often classified in terms of their maturity, though this is a very loose classification. Obligations with original maturities less than ten years are usually called notes. Bonds are generally considered to be obligations with original maturities of ten years and beyond. Corporate bonds usually have maturities ranging from 15 to 30 years, though issuers can design bonds with any maturity. In the mid-1990s, several major U.S. companies issued bonds with non-traditional maturities of 50 years (e.g., TVA, Boeing, and Ford Motor Company) and 100 years (e.g., Disney, Bell-South Corporation, and News Corporation).

Interest

In the United States, interest is typically paid twice a year at six month intervals. For example, a bond may pay interest on January 1 and July 1. Bonds issued in many other countries pay interest annually. A bond can be designed to pay interest quarterly, monthly, or even daily, any way the corporation desires. The objective is to design the interest payments to be attractive to the investors, but, at the same time minimize the costs of administering the bonds—writing and mailing interest payments.

Interest is also referred to as a *coupon*. The reference to coupons originates with bearer bonds. If you owned a bearer bond, you received the interest by clipping coupons off the side of the bond and redeeming them for cash. But over time, the interest received on both registered and bearer debt has come to be referred to as the coupon payment.

Interest is generally stated as a percentage of the par value of the bond and the rate or interest is referred to as the interest rate or the *coupon rate*. The coupon rate can be either a fixed coupon rate (fixed rate) or a floating coupon rate (floating rate). Most bonds have a fixed coupon rate and such issues are said to have a *straight coupon*.

In the past 25 years, there have been many innovations in the type of debt interest payments, so there is no longer any "typical" bond. These innovations include zero-coupon, deferred interest, floating rate, and dual coupon debt. Below we discuss the various types of coupon payments.

Zero-Coupon   Zero-coupon bonds do not have a coupon. Since there are no coupons, the only return an investor gets by holding the bond until it matures is the difference between what was paid for the bond and its maturity value. This is why zero-coupon bonds are issued and trade at a discount from their maturity value. That is, they are issued and trade at a price below 100.

Effectively, the investor in a zero-coupon bond earns interest, but the investor does not receive it until the maturity date—the interest is part of the maturity value. Consider The Walt Disney Co. Zero-coupon Subordinated Notes, due 2005. These notes were issued in June 1990 at 41.199 (41.199% of their maturity value). An investor buying a $1,000 maturity value note in June 1990 would pay $411.99. If that investor held on to the bond until the maturity date, she would not receive interest during the life of the bond, but she would receive $1,000 in June 2005.

Zero-coupon bonds were first issued by corporations in 1981 and rapidly became popular. As with interest paid on any kind of debt, the issuer may deduct the implicit interest to determine taxable income. Investors are taxed on the bond's interest income—the implicit interest—even though they receive no cash.

Consider the Disney notes. If you bought a note for $411.99 in June 1990 and hold it until maturity, you earn an annual return of 6.09%:

Present value of the investment = $411.99
Future value of the investment = $1,000.00
Number of periods   = 15

$$\text{Return} = \sqrt[15]{\frac{\$1,000.00}{\$411.99}} - 1 = 6.09\%$$

Implied interest for the first year is 6.09% multiplied by $411.99, or $25.09. Implied interest for the second year is 6.09% multiplied by $411.99 + $25.09 = $437.08, or $26.62. As time passes, the value of the note increases and the implicit interest on the note in any period is the 6.09% multiplied by the increased value. Implicit interest on the Disney note over its life is shown for each year in Exhibit 15.3.

EXHIBIT 15.3 Implied Interest on Disney Zero-Coupon Subordinated Notes, Due 2005, that were Issued June 1990 at 41.199 or $411.99 per Bond

For the year ended June ...	Beginning of the Year Value	Implied Interest = Yield × Beginning Value	End of Year Value = Beginning Value + Implied Interest
1991	$411.99	$25.09	$437.08
1992	437.08	26.62	463.70
1993	463.70	28.24	491.94
1994	491.94	29.96	521.90
1995	521.90	31.78	553.68
1996	553.68	33.72	587.40
1997	587.40	35.77	623.17
1998	623.17	37.95	661.12
1999	661.12	40.26	701.38
2000	701.38	42.71	744.10
2001	744.10	45.32	789.41
2002	789.41	48.07	837.49
2003	837.49	51.00	888.49
2004	888.49	54.11	942.60
2005	942.60	57.40	1,000.00
Total implied interest			$588.01

Note:
Yield calculation:

$$\text{Yield} = \sqrt[T]{\frac{\text{Future value}}{\text{Present value}}} - 1 = \sqrt[15]{\frac{\$1,000.00}{\$411.99}} - 1 = 6.0899\%$$

Check on the calculations:

Total implied interest + price when issued = Face value
$588.01   + $411.99   = $1,000.00

Floating Rate   In the 1970s, when bond issuers were reluctant to be locked into paying the high interest rates that prevailed in the United States, corporations began to issue bonds whose coupon rate changed as interest rates changed. Corporations thus ended up paying the "market rate" instead of a fixed rate.

Different interest rate benchmarks for floating rates include:

- The London Interbank Offered Rate (LIBOR)
- The rate on a money market instrument such a Treasury bill (T-bill) or the rate on commercial paper[2]
- A rate fixed by an auction process (specifically, a Dutch auction)

As explained earlier when we discussed the floating rate for term loans, there is an interest rate reset formula (called a *coupon reset formula*) that is used to determine the coupon rate for the reset period. The floating rate changes periodically, such as annually, semiannually, or quarterly, as specified. Many bonds with a floating rate will have a cap, the maximum coupon rate that the issuer pays. Some issues may have a floor, the minimum coupon rate.

By using derivatives and other types of derivative instruments, different types of coupon bonds can be created. Consider for example bonds that are issued in which the interest rate changes in the opposite direction from the benchmark rates. These bonds are referred to as *inverse floaters.* For example, in 1996 BMW issued 10-year bonds denominated in deutschemarks. The bonds pay interest of 9% in the first year, reverting thereafter to a semiannual interest payment that floats at 12% minus the prevailing six-month LIBOR for deutschemark. If the LIBOR falls, the coupon rate on these bonds rises. By issuing such a bond it would seem that BMW is accepting the risk that if interest rates fall, it will have to pay a higher interest rate. While not demonstrated here, this risk may be eliminated by using an interest rate swap.

Later in this chapter, we will see how swaps are used to create a bond whose coupon payment depends on the performance of a stock market index.

Deferred Interest   Somewhere between a zero-coupon bond and a straight bond lies a *deferred interest bond*—a bond whose interest payments do not start until some time after it is issued. Most deferred interest bonds have no interest for the first three to seven years and sell at a discount from their face value.

---

[2] Money market instruments are debt obligations that mature in one year or less. We describe these instruments in Chapter 19.

Deferred interest debt is usually used where cash flow problems are anticipated. For example, if a firm borrows heavily to restructure its operations, deferred interest debt offers time to turn its operations around.

Income Bonds   An *income bond* pays interest only when there are sufficient earnings to pay it. If earnings are not sufficient, the firm need not pay the interest to its income bondholders. Unlike other types of debt, failure to pay interest on an income bond is not necessarily an act of default.

Income bonds and notes are seldom issued, for two reasons. First, since they do not carry a fixed interest obligation, they are issued by companies that foresee financial difficulties—so this stigma is attached to income bonds. Second, since paying interest depends on accounting earnings, which can be manipulated, there is a potential problem—a possible conflict of interests between management, who represent shareholders, and the bondholders, who are the creditors.

Moreover, the Internal Revenue Service (IRS) is not naive. It recognizes that a firm may attempt to disguise preferred stock by packaging it as an income bond. If the IRS believes that an income bond has all of the characteristics of preferred stock, it will seek to reclassify the interest rate payments that were deducted by the firm so that they are treated as dividend payments which are not tax deductible.

Security

A bond may be unsecured or secured with the pledge of specific property called collateral. A debt that is not secured by specific property is referred to as a *debenture*. If the obligations of the loan are not satisfied, the creditor has the right to recoup the amount of principal, any accrued interest, and penalties from the proceeds from the sale of the pledged property in the case of secured debt. Unsecured bonds, as well as secured bonds, are backed by the general credit of the firm—the ability of the firm to generate cash flows that are sufficient to meet its obligations.

There are different types of secured bonds, classified by the type of property pledged. If the pledged property is real property—such as land or buildings—the debt is referred to as a *mortgage*. If the pledged property is any type of financial asset, such as stocks or bonds of other corporations, the bond is referred to as *collateral trust bond*, since the stocks and bonds are held in a trust account until the bond is satisfied. If the pledged property is equipment, the secured debt is referred to as *equipment obligation* or *equipment trust debt*. Equipment trust debt, also referred to as equipment trust certificates, are often used by railroads to purchase rolling stock and airlines to finance the purchase of aircraft.

Seniority

A firm can issue different kinds of bonds. But not all bonds are created equal. There is a pecking order of sorts with respect to each bond holder's claim on the firm's assets and income. This pecking order is referred to as *seniority*. One bond issue is *senior* to another if it has a prior claim on assets and income; one bond issue is *junior* to another if the other bond has a prior claim on assets and income. A *subordinated bond* is a bond that is junior to another.

Debt Retirement

By the maturity date of the bond, the issuer must pay off the entire par value. The issuer can do so in one of following four ways:

- Repay the entire par value in one payment at the maturity. This is the typical mechanism for bonds issued by corporations.
- Repay the par value based on an amortization schedule. This mechanism is the same as for the repayment of the amount borrowed for the term loans described earlier. That is, each periodic payment made by the firm to bond holders includes interest and scheduled principal repayment. Many asset-backed securities, discussed in Chapter 26, are paid off in this way.
- Retire a specified amount of the par value of the issue periodically. This provision is called a *sinking fund provision*.
- Pay off the entire amount of the face value prior to the maturity date by one of two mechanisms: "calling" the issue if permitted or "defeasing" the issue.

The first two mechanisms are straightforward. We describe the sinking fund, call, and defeasing mechanisms next, beginning with the call mechanism.

In addition to the above mechanisms, a bond issue may give the bondholder the right to force the issuer to retire a bond issue prior to the maturity date. This right granted is referred to as a *put prevision*. We will also describe it below.

Call Mechanism An important question in setting the terms of a new bond issue is whether the issuer shall have the right to redeem the entire amount of bonds outstanding on one or more dates before the maturity date. Issuers generally want this right because they recognize that at some time in the future the general level of interest rates may fall sufficiently below the issue's coupon rate so that redeeming the issue and replacing it with another issue with a lower coupon rate would be attractive. This right is a disadvantage to the bondholder because it forces the bondholder to reinvest the proceeds received at a lower interest rate. This is the reinvestment risk that we explained in Chapter 9.

The right of the issuer to retire an issue prior to the maturity date is referred to as the right to *call the issue*. Effectively, it is the right of the issuer to take away the bonds from the bondholder at a specified price at specified times. Consequently, this right that the issuer has is referred to as a call option. While we described a call option in Chapter 4, those options were standalone options. That is, they were not part of any debt obligation. A call option that is part of a bond issue is referred to as an *embedded option*. As we discuss other features of a bond we will see other types of embedded options.

Retiring an outstanding bond issue with proceeds from the sale of another bond issue is referred to as *refunding a bond issue*. The usual practice is a provision that denies the issuer the right to refund a bond issue during the first five to ten years following the date of issue with proceeds received from issuing lower-cost debt obligations ranking equal to or superior to the bond issue to be retired. For example, if a bond issue has a coupon rate of 10% and the issuer could issue a new bond issue with a coupon rate of 7%, then if there is a prohibition on refunding a bond issue, the issuer could not retire the 10% coupon issue with funds received from the sale of a 7% issue. While most long-term issues have these refunding restrictions, they may be immediately callable, in whole or in part, if the source of funds comes from other than lower interest cost money. Cash flow from operations, proceeds from a common stock sale, or funds from the sale of property are examples of such sources of proceeds that a firm can use to refund a bond issue.

Sometimes there is confusion between refunding protection and call protection. Call protection is much more absolute in that bonds cannot be redeemed for any reason. Refunding restrictions only provide protection against the one type of redemption mentioned above.

Typically, corporate bonds are callable at a premium above par. Generally, the amount of the premium declines as the bond approaches maturity and often reaches par after a number of years have passed since issuance.

A framework for a firm to decide whether it will refund a bond issue will be discussed later in this chapter.

Sinking Fund   Bond indentures may require the issuer to retire a specified portion of an issue each year. This is referred to as a *sinking fund requirement*. This kind of provision for repayment of a bond issue may be designed to liquidate all of a bond issue by the maturity date, or it may be arranged to pay only a part of the total by the maturity date.

The purpose of the sinking fund provision is to reduce default risk. Generally, the issuer may satisfy the sinking-fund requirement by either (1) making a cash payment of the par amount of the bonds scheduled to be retired to the trustee who then calls the bonds for redemption using a lottery, or (2) delivering to the trustee bonds with a total par value equal to the amount that must be retired from bonds the issuer purchased in the open market. Usually, the sinking-fund call price is the par value of the bonds.

Many corporate bond indentures include a provision that grants the issuer the right (i.e., option) to retire more than the required sinking fund payment. For example, suppose that the amount of the sinking fund requirement is $10 million for some year up to a specified amount. The issuer would have the right to retire more than $10 million. For some issues, the issuer may be permitted to retire twice the amount required. This is another embedded option granted to the issuer, called the *acceleration option*, because the issuer can take advantage of this provision if interest rates decline below the coupon rate. That is, suppose that an issue has a coupon rate of 10% and that current rates are well below 10%. Suppose further that there is a refunding restriction so that the issuer cannot refund the bond issue and that it does not have sufficient funds to retire the entire issue by another means that would be permitted. If there is a sinking fund requirement with an acceleration option, the issuer can use this option to get around the refunding restriction and thereby retire part of the outstanding bond issue. There is another advantage. When bonds are purchased to satisfy the sinking fund requirement, they are called by the trustee at par value. In contrast, when they are called if the issuer has the right to call an issue, for other than to satisfy the sinking fund requirement, the call price is typically above the par value.

A sinking fund adds extra comfort to the bondholder—the presence of the sinking fund reduces the default risk associated with the bond. That is, if the issuer fails to make a scheduled payment to satisfy the sinking fund provision, the trustee may declare the bond issue in default; this has the same consequences as not paying interest or principal. However, because the inclusion of the acceleration option allows the issuer to retire more of the scheduled amount prior to the maturity date, it effectively is a call option granted to the issuer and therefore increases the reinvestment risk to the bondholders.

Defeasance   Another way of effectively retiring a bond issue is to *defease* it by creating a trust to pay off the payments that must be made to the bondholders. To do this, the firm establishes an irrevocable trust (where the firm cannot get back any funds it puts in it), deposits risk-free securities into the trust (such as U.S. government bonds) such that the cash flows from these bonds (interest and principal) are sufficient to pay the obligations of the debt. The interest and principal of the defeased debt is then paid by this trust.

Defeasing debt requires that the issuer undertake the following three steps:

Step 1: Create a trust dedicated to making payments due on the bond issue.

Step 2: Place in the trust U.S. government securities having cash inflows (interest and principal) that match the cash outflows on the firm's bond (interest and principal).

Step 3: Place the securities in the trust. The bond's interest and principal payments are made by the trust.

An issuer would employ the defeasance mechanism for several reasons:

■ If the bonds cannot be bought back from the bondholders (the issue cannot be called or refunded), defeasance provides a way of retiring bonds.

■ If interest rates on the securities in the trust is high relative to the interest rate on the defeased bond, this difference ends up increasing the firm's reported earnings.

■ If certain requirements are met, as set forth in the Financial Accounting Standards Board's Statement of Financial Accounting Standards No. 76, the debt obligation is removed from the borrower's financial statements, which should lead to a an improved credit evaluation.

Owners of a bond issue that has been defeased are assured they will be paid interest and principal as promised, so their default risk is in effect eliminated.

Put Provision   A put provision grants the bondholder the right to sell the issue back to the issuer on designated dates. Bonds with such a provision are referred to as *putable bonds*. The advantage to the bondholder is that if interest rates rise after the bonds are issued, thereby reducing the value of the bond, the bondholder can put the bond to the issuer for par value. The put provision, just like the call provision, is an embedded option. Consequently, the put provision is referred as a put option. Unlike a call option which is an option granted to the issuer to retire the bond issue prior to the maturity date, a put option grants the bondholder the right to have the bond issue retired prior to the maturity date.

Put provisions have been used for reasons other than to protect the bondholder against a rise in interest rates after the bond is issued. The right to sell the debt back is permitted under special circumstances. In the late 1980s, many firms took on a great deal of debt, increasing the risk of default on all their debt obligations. Many debtholders found themselves with debt whose default risk increased dramatically. Put provisions were included in bond indentures as a way of protecting bondholders. If an event affecting the bond issue took place, such as a leveraged buyout or a downgrade in the credit rating of the issuer, bondholders have the right to sell the bonds back to the issuer.

In the late 1980s, some firms issued puts designed specifically to make takeovers more expensive. Called *poison puts*, they take affect only under some specified change in control of the firm, such as if someone acquires more than 20% of the common stock. By designing putable bonds with this feature, the management is able to make any takeover more expensive. Bondholders will want to sell the bonds back to the firm for more than its par value, draining the company of cash. A "change in control" put provision may state:

> In the event of a change-in-control of Co., each holder will have the one-time optional right to require Co. to repurchase such holder's debentures at the principal amount thereof, plus accrued interest.

If there is a change in control, as defined in more detail in the indenture, the bond holder can "put" the bond back to the issuer at par value.

Convertibility

A conversion feature gives the investor the right to exchange the bond issue for some other security of the issuer, typically shares of common stock, at a predetermined rate of exchange. A bond issue that has such a feature is called a *convertible bond*.

The conversion feature must specify the *conversion ratio*, the number of shares of stock that the bond may be exchanged for of the other security to be acquired. For example, suppose a $1,000 par value bond of ABC Company is convertible into the common stock of ABC Company and the conversion ratio is 20. This means that the bondholder can exchange one bond for 20 shares of common stock.

At the time of issuance of a convertible bond, the issuer effectively grants the bondholder the right to purchase the common stock at a price equal to the bond's par value divided by the conversion ratio. This price is called the *stated conversion price*. For the ABC Company convertible bond, the stated conversion price is $50, found by dividing the par value of $1,000 by the conversion ratio.

At the time the convertible bonds are issued, the stated conversion price is often 15 to 20% above the current market price of the common share. The bondholder must hold the bond until it becomes attractive to convert it into shares of stock. It won't be worth converting unless the price of the shares of stock increases.

After the convertible bond has been issued, the price of the convertible bond will change due to changes in interest rates (just as bonds without a conversion feature would change) and due to changes in the price of the security that the bond issue can be converted into. Subsequent buyers of the convertible bond are effectively buying the common stock when they buy the convertible bond at a price that reflects the bond's prevailing market price. This price is called the *effective conversion price* or simply *conversion price* and is found by dividing the current market price of the bond by the conversion ratio. So, for example, if the current market price of ABC Company's convertible bond is $900, the conversion price is $45 found by dividing $900 by 20.

Another measure used by buyers of convertible bonds is the bond's *conversion value*. This is the value of the convertible bonds that would be obtained by converting it. The conversion value is obtained by multiplying the current market price of the common stock by the conversion ratio. For example, suppose that the price of ABC Company's common stock is $60. Since the conversion ratio is 20, the conversion value is $1,200 ($60 × 20).

The decision to convert will be affected by the current market price of the common stock. But it is not the only factor that influences a bondholder's decision to convert the bond. By not converting, the bondholder continues to get the interest payments. If the bondholder exchanges the bond for common stock, the bondholder does not get this interest but, instead, would be entitled to receive dividends. So the bondholder must to weigh the benefits of holding the bond with the benefits of converting into common stock.

Almost all convertible issues are callable by the issuer. This is a valuable feature for issuers who deem the current market price of their stock undervalued enough so that selling stock directly would dilute the equity of current stockholders. The firm would prefer to raise common stock over incurring debt, so it issues a convertible, setting the conversion ratio on the basis of a stock price it regards as acceptable. Once the market price reaches the conversion point, the firm will want to see the conversion happen in view of the risk that the stock price may drop in the future. This gives the firm a motive to force conversion, even though this is not in the interest of the owners of the bond, whose price is likely to be adversely affected by the call.

Why does a firm needing funds issue a convertible bond? Conversion is attractive to investors because they can switch their convertible bond to common stock if the shares do well. So, investors are willing to accept a lower yield on convertible bond. This means a lower cost of financing for the issuer. Another reason a firm may issue convertible bond is weak demand for its common stock. But by issuing a convertible bond, the firm is, in effect, issuing a stock at a later time if the stock price increases.

Credit (Debt) Ratings

We say that an issuer who fails to live up to the terms of the bond agreement is "in default." Since there is always some chance the issuer will not pay interest or principal when promised, or abide by some other part of the debt agreement, there is always some chance of default. For some firms, this chance is extremely small, for others default is likely.

Organizations that analyze the likelihood of default and make the information about their opinions to the public in terms of a rating system are referred to as *rating agencies*. These organizations are private firms. Organizations that are recognized by the U.S. government as having ratings that can be used for investment purposes are referred to as "nationally recognized statistical rating organizations" (NRSROs). At the time of this writing, there are three NRSROs—Moody's Investors Service, Standard & Poor's Corporation, and Fitch. The rating systems use similar symbols, as shown in Exhibit 15.4. The ratings are referred to as *debt ratings* or *credit ratings*.

Credit ratings are important for the cost of and marketability of debt. Many banks, pension funds, and governmental bodies are restricted from investing in securities that do not have a minimum credit rating.

Because investors want to be compensated for risk, the greater the default risk associated with debt, as represented by the credit ratings, the greater the yield on debt demanded by investors. The greater the yield required means the greater the cost of raising funds via debt.

Rating Systems

In all systems the term *high grade* means low default risk, or conversely, high probability of future payments. The highest-grade bonds are designated by Moody's by the symbol Aaa, and by the other two rating agencies by the symbol AAA. The next highest grade is denoted by the symbol Aa (Moody's) or AA (the other two rating agencies); for the third grade all rating agencies use A. The next three grades are Baa or BBB, Ba or BB, and B, respectively. There are also C grades.

EXHIBIT 15.4   Summary of Corporate Bond Rating Systems and Symbols

Fitch	Moody's	S&P	Summary Description
Investment Grade—High Creditworthiness			
AAA	Aaa	AAA	Gilt edge, prime, maximum safety
AA+	Aa1	AA+	
AA	Aa2	AA	High-grade, high-credit quality
AA–	Aa3	AA–	
A+	A1	A+	
A	A2	A	Upper-medium grade
A–	A3	A–	
BBB+	Baa1	BBB+	
BBB	Baa2	BBB	Lower-medium grade
BBB–	Baa3	BBB–	
Speculative—Lower Creditworthiness			
BB+	Ba1	BB+	
BB	Ba2	BB	Low grade, speculative
BB–	Ba3	BB–	
B+	B1		
B	B2	B	Highly speculative
B–	B3		
Predominantly Speculative, Substantial Risk, or in Default			
CCC+		CCC+	
CCC	Caa	CCC	Substantial risk, in poor standing
CC	Ca	CC	May be in default, very speculative
C	C	C	Extremely speculative
		CI	Income bonds—no interest being paid
DDD			
DD			Default
D		D	

Bonds rated triple A (AAA or Aaa) are said to be *prime*; double A (AA or Aa) are of high quality; single A issues are called *upper-medium grade*; and triple B are *medium grade*. Lower-rated bonds (i.e., bonds rated below triple B) are said to have speculative elements or be distinctly speculative.

All rating agencies use rating modifiers to provide a narrower credit quality breakdown within each rating category. S&P and Fitch use a rating modifier of plus and minus. Moody's uses 1, 2, and 3 as its rating modifiers.

Bond issues that are assigned a rating in the top four categories are referred to as *investment-grade bonds*. Issues that carry a rating below the top four categories are referred to as *noninvestment-grade bonds* or *speculative bonds*, or more popularly as *high-yield bonds* or *junk bonds*. Thus, the corporate bond market can be divided into two sectors: the investment-grade and noninvestment-grade markets.

Ratings of bonds change over time. Issuers are *upgraded* when their likelihood of default (as assessed by the rating agency) decreases, and *downgraded* when their likelihood of default (as assessed by the rating agency) increases.

It is important to remember that debt ratings reflect credit quality only—no evaluation is done of other risks (e.g., interest rate risk) associated with the debt. The rating process involves the analysis of a multitude of quantitative and qualitative factors over the past, present, and future. The ratings apply to the particular issue, not the issuer. A rating is only an opinion or judgment of an issuer's ability to meet all of its obligations when due, whether during prosperity or during times of stress. The purpose of ratings is to rank issues in terms of the probability of default, taking into account the special features of the issue, the relationship to other obligations of the issuer, and current and prospective financial condition and operating performance.

Factors Considered in Assigning a Rating

In conducting its examination, the rating agencies consider the four Cs of credit—character, capacity, collateral, and covenants. The first of the Cs stands for *character* of management, the foundation of sound credit. This includes the ethical reputation as well as the business qualifications and operating record of the board of directors, management, and executives responsible for the use of the borrowed funds and repayment of those funds. Character analysis involves the analysis of the quality of management. Although difficult to quantify, management quality is one of the most important factors supporting an issuer's credit strength. When the unexpected occurs, it is management's ability to react appropriately that will sustain the company's performance. In assessing management quality, the analysts at Moody's, for example, try to understand the business strategies and policies formulated by management.

The next C is *capacity* or the ability of an issuer to repay its obligations. In assessing the ability of an issuer to pay, an analysis of the financial statements is undertaken. In addition to management quality, the factors examined by Moody's, for example, are (1) industry trends, (2) the regulatory environment, (3) basic operating and competitive position, (4) financial position and sources of liquidity, (5) company structure (including structural subordination and priority of claim), and (6) parent company support agreements. In considering industry trends, the rating agencies look at the vulnerability of the company to economic cycles, the barriers to entry, and the exposure of the company to technological changes. For firms in regulated industries, proposed changes in regulations must be analyzed to assess their impact on future cash flows. At the company level, diversification of the product line and the cost structure are examined in assessing the basic operating position of the firm.

The rating agencies must look at the *capacity* of a firm to obtain additional financing and backup credit facilities. There are various forms of backup facilities. The strongest forms of backup credit facilities are those that are contractually binding and do not include provisions that permit the lender to refuse to provide funds. An example of such a provision is one that allows the bank to refuse funding if the bank feels that the borrower's financial condition or operating position has deteriorated significantly. (Such a provision is called a "material adverse change clause.") Noncontractual facilities such as lines of credit that make it easy for a bank to refuse funding are of concern to the rating agency. The rating agency also examines the quality of the bank providing the backup facility. Other sources of liquidity for a company may be third-party guarantees, the most common being a contractual agreement with its parent company. When such a financial guarantee exists, rating agencies undertake a credit analysis of the parent company.

The third C, *collateral*, is looked at not only in the traditional sense of assets pledged to secure the debt, but also to the quality and value of those unpledged assets controlled by the issuer. In both senses the collateral is capable of supplying additional aid, comfort, and support to the bond and the bondholder. Assets form the basis for the generation of cash flow that services the debt in good times as well as bad.

The final C is for *covenants*, the terms and conditions of the lending agreement. Covenants lay down restrictions on how management operates the company and conducts its financial affairs. Covenants can restrict management's discretion. A default or violation of any covenant may provide a meaningful early warning alarm enabling investors to take positive and corrective action before the situation deteriorates further. Covenants have value because they play an important part in minimizing risk to creditors. They help prevent the unconscionable transfer of wealth from debtholders to equityholders.

Designing a Bond Issue

A corporation seeking to raise funds via a bond offering wants to issue a security with the lowest cost and the flexibility to retire the debt if interest rates fall. An investor wants a security that provides the highest yield, lowest risk, and the flexibility to sell it if other, more profitable investment opportunities arise. The best "package" of debt features will provide what investors are looking for (in terms of risk and return) and simultaneously what the firm is willing to offer (in terms of risk and cost).

There is a wide range of features available with respect to denomination, type of coupon rate, security, call features for retiring a bond issue prior to the maturity date, and conversion options that make it possible to design a bond issue to meet both the needs of the issuer and investors. Features that make an issue more attractive to investors decrease the yield investors want. As a result, the issuer's borrowing cost is reduced. For example, the inclusion of embedded options such as a conversion feature and a put option make the issue more attractive to investors, so an issuer would expect that the inclusion of such features would reduce the yield at which it would have to offer a bond. In contrast, features included in a bond issue that are an advantage to the issuer increase the yield investors want and therefore increase the cost of the bond issue. For example, the inclusion of covenants that favor the issuer or the inclusion of embedded options, such as the call option and the acceleration option, add to the cost of a bond issue.

In an efficient market, investors fairly price the value of the favorable and unfavorable features into the offering price. Opportunities for an issuer to obtain a higher offer price for a bond issue (i.e., a lower cost) arise only if for some reason the market is not pricing these features properly. For example, suppose that investors buy a particular bond issue at issuance that is callable and is undervaluing the call option. This means that the issuer is buying a cheap call option and therefore the issuer's cost for the bond issue is lower than if the call option is priced fairly. However, suppose that the same issuer did not want a call option. The issuer can take advantage of effectively buying a cheap call by issuing the callable bond and simultaneously entering into a transaction to sell a call option in the over-the-counter market. Basically, the issuer effectively bought a call option by issuing the callable bond and has sold a call option with the same terms as the embedded call option at a higher price. The net effect is that the proceeds realized from the sale of the call option in the market reduce the issuer's cost for the bond issue relative to issuing a noncallable bond.

In an efficient market, there are opportunities to reduce the cost of a bond issue if a new, innovative bond structure can be designed that is not currently available in the marketplace. What type of innovation must that be? The innovation must be such that it either enables investors to reduce a risk that previously could not have been reduced efficiently through currently available financial instruments, or takes advantage of tax or financial accounting loopholes that benefit the issuer and/or investors. The first type of innovation, risk-reducing features, eventually are introduced by other issuers so that only those issuers who are first to introduce those features will benefit. Investment bankers who see a new innovation introduced by a competitor firm promptly notify their clients about the opportunity to issue bonds with this feature. As a result, the uniqueness of the feature wanes and there is no advantage to issuing a bond with this feature—that is, the issuer gets a fair market value for the feature. For innovations that result from tax or financial accounting loopholes, those advantages disappear once the Internal Revenue Service changes tax rules or the Financial Accounting Standards Board changes the financial accounting rules that created the loophole.

A good illustration of this is the zero-coupon bond structure. In the early 1980s when interest rates were at a historical high, investors came to appreciate the concept of reinvestment risk when investing in a bond. This is the risk that when coupon payments are made by the issuer, in order to realize the yield on the bond at the time of purchase, all the coupon payments would have to be reinvested at that yield. For example, if an investor purchased a 20-year bond in 1982 with a coupon rate of 16%, at par value so that its yield is 16%, then to realize that 16% each coupon payment must be reinvested to earn at least 16%. If the coupon payments are reinvested at a rate of less than 16%, then the investor would earn less than 16%. In fact, the investor could earn less than 16% if interest rates dropped. In fact, interest rates did drop substantially since the early 1980s and investors holding a coupon bond purchased at that time would be realizing a lower return. Against this background, corporations began to issue zero-coupon bonds. This feature eliminates reinvestment risk because there are no coupons to reinvest. If an investor purchased a zero-coupon bond that was noncallable in 1982 with a yield of 16% and held the bond to maturity in 2002, the investor would have realized a 16% yield despite the fact that interest rates dropped substantially from 1982 to 2002. As a result, when zero-coupon bonds were introduced, investors were willing to pay up for newly issued zero-coupon bonds. That is not the case a few years later, as it is today, as the supply of zero-coupon bonds issued by corporations does not justify a premium price (i.e., a lower cost).

Moreover, while we previously discussed the financial accounting advantage of a zero-coupon bond from the issuer's perspective, the advantage was even greater prior to the change in the tax treatment in the mid-1980s. Specifically, the issuer prior to a change in the tax law could write off interest as an expense for tax purposes equal to the difference between the maturity value and the price received divided by the number of years to maturity. This resulted in higher interest deductions in the early years and thereby reduced the effective cost of a bond issue. This tax advantage was wiped out by a change in the tax rules for determining the annual interest expense from the issuance of a zero-coupon bond.

Fixed-Rate Versus Floating-Rate

One of the first questions a corporate treasurer seeking to borrow via a bond offering must address is whether to issue a floating-rate or fixed-rate bond. Issuers of floating-rate bonds fall into one of two categories.

The first are financial entities whose assets that they invest in pay a floating interest rate. For example, suppose that a bank makes loans where the interest payment it receives is 3-month LIBOR plus 300 basis points. If the bank issues fixed-rate bonds, the risk that it would take is that 3-month LIBOR may increase to a level where the interest payment it receives from the loans may be less than the fixed rate it pays to borrow funds. A properly designed floating-rate bond eliminates that problem. If the bank can borrow funds on a floating-rate basis where it pays, for example, 3-month LIBOR plus 30 basis points, then the bank is earning a spread of 270 basis points—the difference between 3-month LIBOR plus 300 basis points it receives from the loans and 3-month LIBOR plus 30 basis points it pays to bondholders. If 3-month LIBOR increases or decreases, the bank has locked in a spread.

The second type of issuer of floating-rate bonds is a corporation that does want to lock in a fixed-rate bond but issues a floating-rate bond. Why does a corporation take on the risk that market interest rates will rise in the future and therefore it will have to pay a higher interest rate? One possibility is that the corporation will benefit if interest rates go down and that is the expectation of the chief financial officer. Typically, that is not the reason. The reason is in fact that the corporation ultimately does not take on the risk that interest rates will rise. This is done by combining the issuance of a floating-rate bond with the use of an interest rate swap. We introduced the basic elements of an interest rate swap in Chapter 4. An interest rate swap allows an issuer to change floating-rate payments into fixed-rate payments. By doing so, the issuer of a floating-rate bond who simultaneously enters into an interest rate swap in which it receives a floating rate and pays a fixed rate has *synthetically* created a fixed-rate bond. This is because the floating rate that the issuer receives pays the bondholders of the fixed-rate bonds that it issued. We will illustrate how this is done in shortly when we discuss how swaps are used in conjunction with designing a bond offering.

Economic theory tells us that if markets are efficient then whether a corporation synthetically creates a fixed-rate bond by issuing a floating-rate bond and using a swap or by just issuing a fixed-rate bond, the cost of funds will be the same to the issuer after transaction costs. Therefore, why not just issue a fixed-rate bond? The answer lies in an understanding of how markets operate.

In the real world, institutional bond buyers impose constraints on the amount that they will invest in a particular issuer, or in fact, issuers in a particular sector of the bond market. Suppose a corporation has historically issued only fixed-rate bonds. When this corporation is contemplating a new bond offering, the chief financial officer will approach its investment banker about how much it will cost to raise the target amount of funds. The sales force of the investment banking firm will canvass its bond customers to assess what it will cost the issuer to issue a fixed-rate bond. Suppose that the banker's sales force indicates that most fixed-rate bond buyers are not willing to purchase any additional fixed-rate bonds issued by this corporation because it has realized its maximum exposure. This may mean a higher cost for issuing the bond. The sales force, however, may indicate that institutional buyers of floating-rate bonds will be more receptive to the corporation since they do not have any credit risk exposure to the corporation. The investment banker would then determine what the cost of a synthetically created fixed-rate bond issue will be if the corporation issued a floating-rate bond and used an interest rate swap. If the cost is lower, the corporation may issue the floating-rate bond. Even if the cost is close to the same, the CFO may decide to synthetically create a fixed-rate bond just to increase its presence in the floating-rate market.

It is for the same reason that corporations needing to issue bonds with a floating rate will issue a fixed-rate bond and enter into an interest rate. In this case, the corporation will agree to pay a floating rate and receive a fixed rate, thereby synthetically creating a floating-rate bond.

Use of Derivative Instruments in Designing Bonds

The flexibility in designing a bond issue today to meet the needs of investors has increased due to availability of derivative instruments. We described the basic features of these instruments in Chapter 4. We just explained that issuers can synthetically create fixed-rate or floating-rate bonds by using interest rate swaps. Next we show how this is done.

A bond issue with an unusual coupon structure (i.e., other than a traditional fixed or floating rate) that is created by using derivative instruments so that the issuer is synthetically creating the targeted fixed or floating rate is called a *structured note*. We will also show how and why an issuer can design a structured note by using a swap.

What is important to keep in mind is that any time a swap is used in a transaction, there is counterparty risk; that is, the other party to the swap agreement may default on its obligation.

Creating a Synthetic Fixed- or Floating-Rate Security   Suppose that two corporations are seeking bond financing. An independent finance company, Quick Funding Finance, and a manufacturing firm, Toys for Kids. The treasurers of both corporations want to raise $100 million for 10 years. Quick Funding Finance wants to raise floating-rate funds because the loans that it makes are floating-rate based and therefore floating-rate bonds are a better match against its assets (i.e., the loans it has made) than fixed-rate bonds. Toys for Kids wants to raise fixed-rate funds.

Suppose that the interest rates that must be paid by the two corporations in the floating-rate and fixed-rate markets for a 10-year bond offering are as follows:

For Quick Funding Finance:
    Floating rate = 6-month LIBOR + 30 bp
    Fixed rate = 10.5%

For Toys for Kids:
    Floating rate = 6-month LIBOR + 80 bp
    Fixed rate = 12%.

Suppose Quick Funding Finance issued fixed-rate bonds and Toys for Kids issued floating-rate bonds. Both issues are for $100 million par value and mature in 10 years. At the time of issuance, both corporations entered into a 10-year interest rate swap with a $100 million notional amount with Merrill Lynch, the swap dealer in our illustration. The interest rate swap is diagrammed in Exhibit 15.5. Suppose the terms of the interest rate swap are as follows:

For Quick Funding Finance:
  Pay floating rate of 6-month LIBOR
  Receive fixed rate of 10.6%

For Toys for Kids:
  Pay fixed rate = 10.85%
  Receive floating rate = 6-month LIBOR

The cost of the bond issue for Quick Funding Finance would then be as follows:

Interest paid
On fixed-rate bonds issued = 10.5%
On interest rate swap   = 6-month LIBOR
Total   = 10.5% + 6-month LIBOR

Interest received
On interest rate swap   = 10.6%

Net cost
Interest paid   = 10.5% + 6-month LIBOR
Interest received   = 10.6%
Total   = 6-month LIBOR − 10 bp

Therefore, Quick Funding Finance has achieved its financing objective of floating-rate funding.

EXHIBIT 15.5 Diagram of the Interest Payments in an Interest-Rate Swap

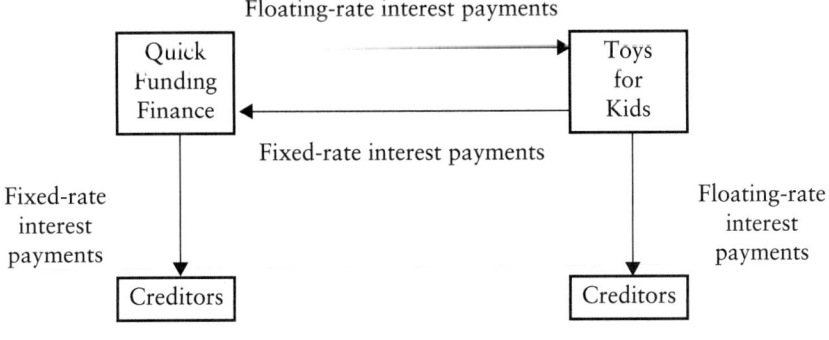

The cost of the issue for Toys for Kids would then be as follows:

Interest paid
On floating-rate bonds issued = 6-month LIBOR + 80 bp
On interest rate swap = 10.85%
Total = 11.65% + 6-month LIBOR

Interest received
On interest rate swap = 6-month LIBOR

Net cost
Interest paid = 11.65% + 6-month LIBOR
Interest received = 6-month LIBOR
Total = 11.65%

As can be seen, by using the interest rate swap Toys for Kids is able to obtain the type of coupon rate it sought, a fixed rate.

In fact, a closer examination of both transactions indicates that both firms were actually able to reduce their funding cost below what the cost would have been had they issued directly into the market for the type of coupon they sought. A comparison of the two costs for the two corporations is summarized below:

Quick Funding Finance:
    Issue floating-rate bond: 6-month LIBOR + 70 b.p.
    Issue fixed-rate bond + swap: 6-month LIBOR – 10 b.p.

Toys for Kids
    Issue fixed-rate bond: 12.5%
    Issued fixed-rate bond + swap: 11.65%

While the magnitude of the reduction in funding costs that we have just illustrated is not likely to occur in real world markets, there are opportunities to reduce funding costs for the reasons described earlier. In fact, the interest rate swaps market became the key vehicle for issuers in the United States to obtain lower funding cost in the Eurobond market in the early 1980s because of differences in the spreads demanded by fixed-rate and floating-rate investors in the U.S. bond market and in the Eurodollar bond market. In Chapter 25, we will see how a currency swap can be used to issue fixed-rate or floating-rate bonds outside of the United States where the bonds are denominated in a foreign currency.

Creating an Equity Linked Coupon Payment   There are different types of swaps that we discussed in Chapter 4—interest rate, currency, and commodity swaps. There are also swaps in which one party swaps a fixed- or floating-rate in exchange for the rate of return on a common stock index. These swaps are called *equity swaps*. Let's see how equity swaps can be used to design a bond issue with a coupon rate tied to the performance of an equity index. We then address why an issuer would want to do so.

Suppose the Universal Information Technology Company (UIT) seeks to raise $100 million for the next five years on a fixed-rate basis. UIT's investment banker, Credit Suisse First Boston (CSFB), indicates that if bonds with a maturity of five years are issued, the interest rate on the issue would have to be 8.4%. At the same time, there are institutional investors seeking to purchase bonds but are interested in making a play (i.e., betting on) on the future performance of the stock market. These investors are willing to purchase a bond whose annual interest rate is based on the actual performance of the S&P 500 stock market index.

CSFB recommends to UIT's management that it consider issuing a five-year bond whose annual interest rate is based on the actual performance of the S&P 500. The risk with issuing such a bond is that UIT's annual interest cost is uncertain since it depends on the performance of the S&P 500. However, suppose that the following two transactions are entered into:

1. On January 1, UIT agrees to issue, using CSFB as the underwriter, a $100 million five-year bond issue whose annual interest rate is the actual performance of the S&P 500 that year minus 300 basis points. The minimum interest rate, however, is set at zero. The annual interest payments are made on December 31.
2. UIT enters into a five-year, $100 million notional amount equity swap with CSFB in which each year for the next five years UIT agrees to pay 7.9% to CSFB, and CSFB agrees to pay the actual performance of the S&P 500 that year minus 300 basis points. The terms of the swap call for the payments to be made on December 31 of each year. Thus, the swap payments coincide with the payments that must be made on the bond issue. Also as part of the swap agreement, if the S&P 500 minus 300 basis points results in a negative value, CSFB pays nothing to UIT.

Consider what has been accomplished with these two transactions from the perspective of UIT. Specifically, focus on the payments that must be made by UIT on the bond issue and the swap and the payments that it will receive from the swap. These are summarized below.

Interest payments on bond issue: S&P 500 return − 300 bp
Swap payment from CSFB: S&P 500 return − 300 bp

Swap payment to CSFB:	7.9%
Net interest cost:	7.9%

Thus, the net interest cost is a fixed rate despite the bond issue paying an interest rate tied to the S&P 500. This was accomplished with the equity swap.

There are several questions that should be addressed. First, what was the advantage to UIT to entering into this transaction? Recall that if UIT issued a bond, CSFB estimated that UIT would have to pay 8.4% annually. Thus, UIT has saved 50 basis points (8.4% minus 7.9%) per year. Second, why would investors purchase this bond issue? In real world markets, there are restrictions imposed on institutional investors as to types of investment. For example, an institutional investor may be prohibited by a client from purchasing common stock, however it may be permitted to purchase a bond of an issuer such as UIT despite the fact that the interest rate is tied to the performance of common stocks. Third, is CSFB exposed to the risk of the performance of the S&P 500? While it is difficult to demonstrate at this point, there are ways that CSFB can protect itself.

Use of Warrants in a Bond Offering

Some bond issues are offered with warrants attached. A *warrant* is the right to buy the common stock of a company at a specified price, the exercise price. So a warrant is like a call option. It represents the right to buy the stock. How then is a warrant different from a convertible bond? With a convertible bond, the bond holder exchanges the bond issue for shares of stock. With a warrant, the bond holder exercises the warrant—buying the shares of stock at a specified price—but still has the bond!

Warrants may have a fixed life (i.e., use it or lose it) or may have a perpetual life—called *perpetual warrants*. The bond and its warrant together are referred to as a *unit*. Some warrants can be separated from the debt—called *detachable warrants*—and sold by the bondholder. These warrants can be traded in the market just as shares of stock are traded.

A warrant is an option and, like other types of options, its value depends on many factors. (We discussed these factors in Chapter 9.) Suppose you buy a warrant that gives you a right to buy stock for $5 per share within the next five years. The $5 is the exercise price. If the current share price is $1 per share, this right is not very valuable. But it is still worth something. However small, there is some chance that the price of the stock will get above $5 and make exercising this warrant valuable.

Factors that affect a warrant's value are:

■ *The common stock's share price.* The greater the share's price, the more valuable the warrant. If the share's price were $6 instead of $1, the warrant will be more valuable.

■ *The exercise price.* The lower the exercise price, the more valuable the warrant. The lower the warrant's exercise price—$5 in our example— the more valuable the warrant. If the exercise price were $2 instead of $5, there is a greater chance that the warrant would gives you the right to buy shares for a price below the prevailing market price.

■ *The warrant's life.* The longer the life of the warrant, the more valuable the warrant since there is more time for the share price to increase and the warrant become attractive. If the warrant expired in ten years instead of the five years, it would be more valuable since there is a greater chance of the share's price rising above $5 in ten years than in five.

■ *The opportunity cost of funds.* The greater the opportunity cost, the more valuable the warrant, because it allows us to postpone our stock purchase to a later time. Suppose the underlying stock price were $6 instead of $1. We could hold onto the warrant and buy the stock at a later time. The value of the warrant will increase along with the stock's price so we can share in the stock's appreciation without laying out the cash.

■ *The common stock's share price volatility.* The more volatile the share's price, the more valuable the warrant since a more volatile price means that there is a greater chance the share's price will change before our warrant expires. If the share's price is very stable, there is little chance that it will go above $5. But if the share's price is volatile, there is more chance that the share price will go above the exercise price, $5.

Using Financial Derivatives to Hedge Interest Rate Costs

The CFO must determine the best time to sell bonds. If the CFO expects interest rates to decline, then it may pay for an issuer to postpone a bond offering if possible. If the CFO expects interest rates to rise, then the best strategy may be for the firm to issue bonds now. Moreover, if the CFO expects that bonds will have to be issued at some future date, say six-months from now, and also expects that interest rates will be higher than they currently are, the CFO may find that the best strategy is to issue bonds now rather than wait six months. The tradeoff is that the firm will have the bond proceeds today that it will have to pay interest on. To partially offset that additional interest cost, the issuer can invest the proceeds received from the bond sale and earn interest. The CFO must evaluate the net additional cost of accelerating the bond offering versus the higher interest cost expected in the future.

While we have cast the timing of an offering in terms of interest rates, that is too general. As explained in Chapter 15, the CFO thinks in terms of two components that determine the cost of an issue: the Treasury rate (which we referred to as the base rate) and the spread. A CFO may believe that Treasury rates are declining but may want to issue a bond today because the CFO may believe that spreads in the market are widening such that the interest rate that will have to be paid will increase. For example, suppose the Treasury rate is 6% and the spread is 100 basis points for an issuer. The interest rate that the issuer pays would then be 7% if it issues bonds now. Suppose that the CFO of this firm believes that the Treasury rate six months from now will decline to 5%. The question in deciding whether or not to postpone a bond issuance is what the CFO believes will happen to the spread. If the spread is expected to widen (i.e., increase), the CFO may want to lock in the current spread.

Financial derivatives have provided CFOs with the maximum flexibility in timing their bond offerings. We will briefly discuss how interest rate futures, options, interest rate swaps, and caps can be used. Moreover, there are special products created by investment bankers as will be explained below.

There are several interest rate futures contracts. The one used by issuers to protect against a rise in interest rates in the future is a Treasury bond (or note) futures contract. This derivative instrument can be used to protect or hedge against changes in the Treasury rate. Specifically, the CFO planning a future offering of bonds and concerned with the possibility of a rise in Treasury rates uses the contract as follows. The price of a Treasury bond changes inversely with the change in Treasury rates. That is, if Treasury rates rise, the price of a Treasury bond declines. The price of a Treasury bond futures contract also falls if Treasury rates rise. So, by selling a Treasury bond futures contract, an issuer would realize a profit if Treasury rates increase. This is because the CFO sold a contract and gets to repurchase the contract at a lower price if Treasury rates rise.

Now let's combine the position in the Treasury bond futures contract with the sale of the bonds. If the CFO sells a Treasury bond futures contract and Treasury rates rise, then when the issuer issues the bonds, there will be higher interest cost that must be paid. However, there will be a gain on the Treasury bond futures position. If the CFO sells the correct number of Treasury bond futures contracts, the additional cost of the bond issue will be offset by the gain in the Treasury bond futures position. As a result, a future bond offering will be protected against a rise in Treasury rates.

Note that the issuer would not benefit from a decline in Treasury rates. This is because the lower cost of the bonds to be issued will be offset by the loss that results from the Treasury bond futures position. To overcome this problem, the CFO can buy put options on a Treasury bond rather than sell Treasury bond futures. Should Treasury rates fall, the issuer can issue bonds at a lower cost. However, this is not free. For this benefit, the issuer must pay the price for the put options and this expense increases the cost of the bond issue. If Treasury rates rise, the issuer exercises the put option to sell Treasury bonds at a higher price than in the market. This gain is used to offset the higher interest rate that must be paid on the bond issue.

With an interest rate swap, the rate that the fixed-rate payer pays is called the *swap rate*. The swap rate that the fixed-rate payer pays is equal to the Treasury rate at the inception of the swap plus a spread. The spread is called the *swap spread*. An interest rate swap can be such that it does not start until some time in the future. This type of interest rate swap is called a *forward start interest rate swap*. The CFO can use a forward start interest rate swap to lock in a spread in the future, which will be equal to the swap spread. For example, the CFO might like the spread at the time but is concerned that if 15-year bonds are issued six months from now, the spread will be higher. By entering into a forward start interest rate swap with a start date six months from now and with a 15-year maturity, the CFO can lock in a spread.

Taking the right position in a derivative instrument may not be simple for the CFO or his staff. There are several factors that may cause the strategy to fall short of its objective. To overcome this problem, investment banking firms offer their clients an alternative—the opportunity to lock in the base rate or the spread, or both. Such an agreement for locking in the spread is called a *spread lock agreement*. The investment banking firm then faces the risk of hedging the position. The benefit to the investment banking firm is that the issuer will agree to use the underwriter for the future offering of the firm.

For an issuer that seeks floating-rate financing, the concern of the CFO is that interest rates will rise. A CFO can protect itself against a rise in the reference rate used in the coupon reset formula by buying a cap agreement. This agreement results in a payment of a specified amount if the reference rate at the reset date rises above the cap rate. The issuer pays a fee for this and therefore this cost must be recognized in determining the effective cost of funds.

Bond Retirement

A bond issuer does not have to keep an issue outstanding for the bond's entire life. Bonds can be retired prior to their maturity date by:

- Calling in a bond if the issue is callable.
- A sinking fund call if there is such a provision to retire part of the issue and in the case of an acceleration provision, up the maximum amount.
- In the case of a convertible bond forcing conversion into common stock.
- Purchasing the bonds from the investor either through direct negotiation or by buying the bond in the open market.

There are a number of reasons to retire a bond issue before its maturity date:

1. The issuer may want to eliminate the fixed, legal obligations associated with the bond issue. If the interest is too burdensome, or the issuer does not have enough taxable income to use to offset the interest tax deduction, bonds may be unattractive because they increase the firm's default risk.
2. The issuer may find the indenture provisions too confining. Provisions, such as a covenant that the firm maintain a specified ratio of current assets to current liabilities, may restrict management decisions.
3. The issuer may no longer need the funds. The issuer may be generating more cash from operations than needed for other purposes, and hence will use the excess to reduce debt.
4. Market interest rates may have fallen, making the interest rate on the outstanding bonds too costly relative to the current rate.

Let's take a closer look at this last reason. Suppose a corporation currently has $100 million par value of bonds outstanding with a 10% coupon rate. The bonds were issued five years ago and they will mature in five years. Looking at current rates, the treasurer figures she can issue bonds today that have a maturity of five years with a coupon rate of 6%. Should the treasurer buy back the outstanding 10% bonds and issue new 6% bonds in their place? This is called *refunding a bond issue*.

Let's assume that it costs the firm $300,000 in fees to issue the new bonds. Does it pay to do this? It all boils down to comparing the cost of the old bonds versus the cost of the new bonds. Suppose the old bonds are trading in the market to yield 6% (that is, 3% per six-month period). The value of an old bond per $1,000 of par value is:

$$\text{Value of old bond} = \sum_{t=1}^{10} \frac{\$50}{(1+0.03)^t} + \frac{\$1,000}{(1+0.03)^{10}}$$
$$= \$426.51 + \$744.09 = \$1,170.60$$

If the old bonds are not callable and the treasurer were to buy these bonds in the financial markets, the issuer would have to pay $1,170.60 per bond, or $117,060,000 for the entire issue. The premium on these bonds $170.60 (= $1,170.60 – $1,000.00) per bond or $17,060,000 in total and the flotation expenses—the $300,000 to pay the underwriters who sell the new bonds—are deductible for tax purposes. If the firm faces a 40% tax rate, this means that the premium to buy back the old bonds only costs the firm 60% of $17,060,000, or $10,236,000, and the flotation expenses only cost 60% of $300,000, or $180,000. The government pays for the difference by allowing the firm to lower its taxable income by $17,360,000 (= $300,000 + $17,060,000):

Item	Cost	Firm's Share	Government's Share
Premium on old bonds	$17,060,000	$10,236,000	$6,824,000
Flotation costs on new bonds	300,000	180,000	120,000
Total	$17,360,000	$10,416,000	$6,944,000

Therefore, considering the flotation costs, the treasurer has to issue new 6% bonds with a par value of $110,356,000 (= $117,060,000 – $6,824,000 + $120,000) to replace the 10% bonds. If the treasurer does this, the firm will have interest payments of 3% of $110,356,000 or $3,310,680 every six months instead of 5% of $100,000,000 or $5,000,000 on the old bonds.

With the old bonds, the firm had an interest expense of $5,000,000 each period. But since interest is deductible for tax purposes, this really costs the firm only 60% of $5,000,000, or $3,000,000. For the new bonds, the after-tax cost is 60% of $3,310,680, or $1,986,408 every six months. The firm is saving $1,013,592 every six months over the next five years by retiring the old bonds and issuing new bonds.

Is the firm better off with the old bonds or refunding them and issuing new bonds? The only way to figure this out is to look at the present value of the difference in cash flows between the old and the new bonds. How do they differ? In two ways. First, every six months they have a lower interest payment, which after taxes amounts to $1,013,592. Second, we have a different maturity value to pay in five years: $110,356,000 instead of $100,000,000. Thus, there is an additional cash outlay of $10,356,000. The present value of the difference in the cash flow, discounted at the yield on the new bonds (3% per six-month period), is as follows:

$$\text{Present value of difference} = \sum_{t=1}^{10} \frac{\$1,013,592}{(1+0.03)^t} - \frac{\$10,356,000}{(1+0.03)^{10}}$$

↑   ↑

Present value   Present value

of difference in   of difference in

after-tax interest   maturity values

expense

$$= \$8,646,145 \quad - 7,705,837$$
$$= \$940,308$$

Therefore, the firm is better off by $940,308 if the treasurer buys back the old 10% bond issue and issues the new 6% bonds.

The refunding decision—whether to retire old debt and issue new debt—requires looking at whether or not it increases the value of the firm by providing increased cash flows. The way this is done is as follows:

1. Determine the cash flows with the old and with the new debt, considering the difference in interest payments, any tax effects, and any flotation costs.
2. Calculate the differences in cash flows between the old and the new bonds.
3. Calculate the present value of the differences of cash flows.

If the present value of the difference is positive, the new bond issue provides a benefit; if negative, the new bond issue represents a cost.

However, even if there is an advantage in terms of the difference in the present value of the cash flow, a firm may be reluctant to retire bonds. The reason is that the premium paid to purchase the old bond issue in the market is treated as a current expense and thereby reduces current earnings.[3]

SUMMARY

■ Intermediate and long-term debt securities include term loans and bonds (notes) that have characteristics that can be packaged in different ways.

---

[3] The difference between the debt's book value and the amount paid to retire the issue is treated as an extraordinary gain or loss [Statement of Financial Accounting Standards No. 4, *Reporting Gains and Losses from Extinguishment of Debt—An Amendment of APB Opinion No. 30*].

■ Debt may be denominated in any country's currency. They may have any maturity, though term loans tend to have shorter maturities than bonds.

■ Interest payments on debt may be variable (floating) or fixed, may start immediately or start some time in the future, and may allow debtholders to share in the good fortunes of the firm.

■ Debt may be backed by specific pledges of property or may be backed by the general credit of the firm. Some debt may have prior claims over other debt, though all debt securities have prior claim over equity.

■ Bonds may have option-like features that give the issuer or the bondholder certain rights. Call options, conversion options, put options, and warrants are valuable and affect the riskiness and attractiveness of the security they are attached to.

■ The bond indenture is the contract between the issuer and the bondholders and consists of provisions that protect the interests of the bondholders. A trustee acts in the bondholders' interest, monitoring the firm to insure that the issuer is abiding by the contract provisions.

■ Debt (credit) rating services in the United States include Moody's Investors Service, Standard & Poor's Corporation, and Fitch. These nationally recognized statistical rating organizations provide ratings that reflect their opinion regarding the possibility of default on a debt obligation. The credit rating are expressed in terms of a letter grade. Two important categories are investment grade (issues rated triple B or higher) and noninvestment grade (issues rated below triple B).

■ A bond issue can be retired by calling it, investors converting it into other securities if granted the option, and buying it back in the marketplace.

■ In designing a bond offering, corporations can use derivative instruments such an swaps to create a bond structure that offers the opportunity to reduce its funding costs. Such opportunities arise in financial markets throughout the world.

■ Financial derivatives can be used by an issuer to protect against a rise in the base interest rate and/or the spread. Caps can be used to protect against a rise in the reference rate for a floating-rate bond.

■ The decision to refund a bond issue—replace an outstanding bond issue with a new bond issue with a lower interest rate—is based on an analysis of the present value of the difference in the after-tax interest cash flows for the issuer taking into consideration the cost of retiring the old bond issue at a premium to par value and the flotation cost of the new bond issue.

QUESTIONS

1. a. What distinguishes a note from a bond?
   b. How are the terms "note" and "bond" commonly used?
2. a. What is the difference between a registered bond and a bearer bond?
   b. What is the role of the trustee designated in a bond indenture?
3. a. At whose option is a callable bond exercised?
   b. At whose option is a convertible bond exercised?
   c. At whose option is a put option exercised?
4. Explain the difference between call protection and refunding protection.
5. A sinking fund provision may appear to be a benefit to the issuer of a bond. However, if there is an acceleration provision, this is a benefit to the issuer. Explain why.
6. a. If a corporation were to issue both a convertible bond and a non-convertible bond—both identical except for the conversion feature—how would the prices of the two bonds compare?
   b. How would the yields on the two bonds compare?
7. a. How does a put option affect the cost of debt for an issuer?
   b. Why would a put feature be attractive to the investor?
8. If a corporation's bond issue is rated AAA by Standard & Poor's, does this mean that it is risk-free? Explain.
9. What factors determine whether a firm will seek floating-rate funding?
10. a. Why would an issuer that needs floating-rate financing issue a fixed-rate bond combined with an interest rate swap?
    b. Suppose an issuer seeking fixed-rate financing issues a floating-rate bond combined with an interest rate swap. In the swap, would the issuer be the fixed-rate or floating-rate payer?
11. The Buckingham Company issued a bond where the coupon rate resets every six months based on the performance of the Standard & Poor's 500 index. Is this company necessarily exposed to changes in this common stock index? Explain.
12. a. Explain why a detachable warrant to buy the common stock of a corporation may have a value, even though the exercise price of the warrant is above the current price of the common stock.
    b. Why would a corporation attach warrants to a bond?
13. Why would a corporation decide to issue debt instead of stock?
14. a. What is a "coupon reset formula"?
    b. What features may be imposed on the interest rate in a floating-rate loan or floating-rate bond?
15. When using a swap to design a bond structure, explain why an issuer must be concerned with counterparty risk.
16. The CFO of a firm plans to issue bonds with a par value of $50 million at the end of the next quarter. Economic forecasts indicate that

Treasury rates are expected to rise when the issuer plans to bring the bond issue to market.

a. Explain how the CFO can use interest rate futures to protect against a rise in Treasury rates.

b. Explain how the CFO can use an option to protect against a rise in Treasury rates.

c. Compare the strategies in (a) and (b) with respect to how they allow the CFO to take advantage of a decline in interest rates.

17. How can an issuer protect against an adverse change in the spread when it expects to issue bonds in the future?

18. Suppose that the Dante Company borrows $10 million via a term loan. The loan matures in three years and has a fixed interest rate of 10%. The loan is a fully amortizing loan and the payments are made quarterly.

a. What is the amount of the quarterly loan payment?

b. Construct an amortization schedule for this loan.

19. The Monte Company borrows $50 million via a term loan. The loan matures in two years and the payments are made monthly. The loan is a fully amortizing loan with a floating interest rate. The floating interest rate is reset at the end of the first year.

a. For the first year, the interest rate is 12%. Determine the amount of the monthly payment for the first 12 months and construct an amortization schedule for the first 12 months.

b. Suppose at the beginning of the second year, the interest rate reset formula requires an interest rate of 10%. Determine the amount of the monthly payment for the last 12 months and construct an amortization schedule for the last 12 months.

20. The Can Sell Company issued $200 million of 8% coupon bonds that mature in 15 years. These bonds pay interest semiannually. Calculate the amount of the interest to be paid each period on these bonds.

21. The Quarter Company has $300 million of 10% coupon bonds outstanding. These bonds have interest paid each quarter; that is, every three months. What is the dollar amount of interest Quarter Company pays each quarter?

22. The Drifter Corporation has $100 million in floating-rate notes outstanding, with interest paid quarterly. The coupon reset formula is 3-month LIBOR plus 300 basis points. The coupon resets at the beginning of every quarter. There is a cap of 10% but no minimum coupon rate. Given the following rates for 3-month LIBOR, what is the coupon rate for the quarter: (a) 3% (b) 4% (c) 7% (d) 9%?

23. The Cipher Corporation issued a zero-coupon that matures in eight years. Suppose you purchased one of these bonds with a maturity

value of $1,000 for $400 on January 1, Year 1. The bond was issued at $400. This bond matures on December 31, Year 8.

a. If you bought this bond when it was issued for $400 and held it to maturity, what return would you earn?

b. What is the amount of interest expense per bond that Cipher deducts each year per $1,000 maturity value?

24. A manufacturing firm, Banner Products, is seeking to raise $50 million by issuing a seven-year bond. The CFO is seeking fixed-rate financing. However, Banner Products' investment banker has informed the CFO that it could synthetically create a fixed-rate bond at a lower cost if it issued floating-rate bonds and used an interest rate swap. If the fixed-rate bonds are issued, the interest rate that Banner Products must offer is 9%. If floating-rate bonds are issued, the rate would be three-month LIBOR plus 200 basis points. The swap would be a seven-year swap that pays quarterly with a notional amount of $50 million. In the swap, Banner Products would pay 6.7% and receive three-month LIBOR.

a. Diagram the payments that must be made by Banner Products if it issues a floating-rate bond and at the same time enters into the swap.

b. What is the rate on the synthetic fixed-rate bond created and compare this rate to that of a fixed-rate bond that Banner Products could have issued?

c. What risk is Banner Products exposed to by creating a synthetic fixed-rate bond?

25. Suppose that Chuckie Munchies Company is seeking to raise $60 million for the next five years on a fixed-rate basis. The firm's investment banker indicates that if bonds with a maturity of five years are issued, the interest rate on the issue would have to be 9%. At the same time, there are institutional investors willing to purchase a bond whose annual interest rate is based on the actual performance of the S&P 500 stock market index. Specifically, the company can issue a five-year bond whose coupon rate is equal to the S&P 500 minus 250 basis points.

a. If Chuckie Munchies Company issued a bond whose coupon rate is tied to the S&P 500, what risk is it facing?

b. Suppose that the company's investment banker indicates that the firm can enter into a five-year equity swap with a notional amount of $60 million on the following terms:

- One party will pay a fixed-rate of 8.7%.
- The other party will pay a rate equal to the actual performance of the S&P 500 minus 280 basis points (with the minimum interest rate equal to zero).

How can Chuckie Munchies Company's CFO use the equity swap to create a bond structure tied to the S&P 500 so as to lower its funding cost?

26. The Basis Corporation issued $300 million of 5% coupon bonds, each with a warrant, to buy a share of Basis Corporation common stock at $20 per share.
   a. If the price of a share of stock is $15, is this warrant worthless? Explain.
   b. If the price of a share of stock is $26, what is the minimum price you would be willing to pay for the warrant?
   c. If the price of a share of stock is $22, what is the minimum price you would be willing to pay for the warrant?
   d. If the warrant had an expiration date two years into the future, how would this warrant price compare with a similar, yet perpetual warrant?

27. Doppleganger, Inc. bonds have a maturity value of $1,000 each and are convertible into common shares at $50 per share. At issuance, the bonds were sold for $1,000 each.
   a. What is the stated conversion price?
   b. What is the conversion ratio for these bonds?
   c. If the common stock is trading for $60 a share, what is the conversion value of the bonds?
   d. If the common stock is trading for $40 a share, what is the conversion value of the bonds?
   e. If the bonds are trading at 110, what is the market conversion price?

28. Changeling, Inc. bonds have a par value of $1,000 each and are convertible into common stock at $35 per share. The bonds were issued at par value.
   a. What is the stated conversion price?
   b. What is the conversion ratio of these bonds?
   c. If the common stock is trading for $30 a share, what is the conversion value of these bonds?
   d. If the common stock is trading for $40 a share, what is the conversion value of these bonds?
   e. If the bond is trading at 90, what is the market conversion price?

29. The Choice Corporation has $5 million of 6% coupon bonds outstanding, each with a maturity value of $1,000. The bonds are callable at 104 at any time, are putable at 105 in five years at par value, are convertible into 20 shares of common stock, and have a warrant attached to each that give the bondholder the right to buy a share of common stock at $50 per share.
   a. List all the embedded options in these bonds, identifying the party that has the option to exercise.

b. If each option is exercised, is there a cash inflow or outflow to Choice and, if there is some cash flow, what is the amount of the cash flow? (Treat each option independently in determining the impact on cash flow.)

30. The Pact Company is evaluating its outstanding bond issue in light of a recent drop in interest rates. Currently, it has $200 million of 8% coupon bonds (paid semiannually) outstanding that mature in five years and have a maturity value of $1,000 each. The bonds are callable at 106 at any time. Their outstanding bonds are priced to yield 6% on a bond-equivalent basis (i.e., a six-month yield of 3%) and the treasurer believes that if the bonds could retire the existing bonds, they could issue new bonds at par with a 6% coupon rate. Pact Company's marginal tax rate is 40%.
   a. What is the total market value of the outstanding bonds?
   b. Should Pact Company buy the outstanding bonds in the open market or call in the bonds at this point in time assuming no flotation costs for new bonds issued? Why?
   c. If there are no flotation costs, what is the face value of new 6% bonds that must be issued to refund the existing bonds?
   d. Should Pact refund the 8% bonds?

31. The Buffett Restaurant Company currently has $100 million of 9% coupon bonds outstanding. These bonds pay interest semiannually, mature in ten years, and are callable at 102. Buffett also has $100 million of 8½% coupon bonds outstanding. These bonds pay interest semiannually, have ten years remaining to maturity, and are callable at 101. Both issues of bonds are trading to yield 6%.
   a. What is the market value of Buffett's outstanding bonds?
   b. If Buffett is considering retiring both issues, should it buy the bonds in the open market or call the bonds? Explain.
   c. Suppose that Buffett can issue new bonds with a 6% coupon. Ignoring flotation costs, what is the face value of these new bonds that must be issued to replace each of Buffett's two outstanding issues?

32. Suppose the Fiscke Company has $100 million face value bonds outstanding with a coupon of 12% (paid semiannually) and five years remaining to maturity. And suppose that Fiscke can refund this bond issue, replacing them with 8% coupon bonds of similar remaining maturity. If flotation costs are 2% of the new bond's face value and the existing bonds are priced to yield 8%, should Fiscke refund the 12% bonds if its tax rate is:
   a. 30%?
   b. 50%?

CHAPTER 16

Common Stock

Suppose you buy a new car that costs $20,000 and you pay cash for it. You will own it completely. The value of your investment in the car— your equity—is the value of the car, $20,000. If, instead, you pay 10% in cash and finance the rest with a car loan, your equity is 10% of the value of the car, or $2,000. Your equity in the car is the value of the car, less any debt obligation. As you pay off your debt or as the car changes in value, your equity in the car changes also.

If you joined together with your roommate to buy the car, each putting up $10,000 in cash, you own 50% of the equity in the car and your roommate owns 50%. By sharing ownership, you are sharing the equity.

Like the equity in your car, the equity of a corporation is the value of its ownership. We refer to the equity of a corporation as *stock*.

A corporation's stock may be divided into two major types—common stock and preferred stock (discussed in Chapter 17). Both may be split into smaller classes of stock. And each of these classes is split into smaller pieces called *shares*. This smallest unit of ownership, one share, is represented by a stock certificate. Owners of these shares are referred to as *shareholders* or *stockholders*. As a shareholder you are not buying something that is tangible (other than the stock certificate itself), but rather you are buying rights: rights to income, rights to have a say in the corporation's activities, and so on.

Preferred stock and common stock have different rights. Preferred shareholders are given *preference* over common shareholders: They have rights to receive income *ahead* of common shareholders. You see, shareholders receive part of the return on their investment from *dividends*, which are periodic cash payments from the corporation. Dividends promised to preferred shareholders must be paid *before* common shareholders can receive any dividends.

If the firm is liquidated—that is, the business operations stopped—the assets are sold and the proceeds of the sale are distributed to creditors and owners. Preferred shareholders are given preference over common shareholders when liquidation proceeds are distributed among the owners. Preferred shareholders receive the liquidation value of their shares before common shareholders can receive anything.

Common stock is the residual ownership of a corporation, residual meaning that creditors and preferred shareholders have the right to the income and assets of a corporation before common shareholders can receive anything. Common shareholders get what is left over.

In this chapter, we take a closer look at the specific features of common stock. In particular, we examine the characteristics of these shares, a firms' dividend policy (in theory and in practice), and stock repurchases. We take a close look at preferred stock in Chapter 17. We put all the financing pieces—long-term debt, common stock, and preferred stock—together in our discussion of capital structure in Chapter 18.

COMMON STOCK

Residual ownership in a firm is common stock ownership and is represented by shares. Because the corporation has a perpetual existence granted by its charter, common stock ownership interest—also referred to as *common equity*—is also perpetual.

Common equity is created either by retaining and reinvesting earnings in the firm or by selling more shares. Whatever is left from earnings after paying what is due the creditors and preferred shareholders may be reinvested in the firm or paid as dividends to common shareholders. If these residual funds are reinvested in profitable investment opportunities, they increase the value of the firm, increasing the value of the common stock. If these residual funds are paid to shareholders, the shareholders can reinvest the dividends they receive as they wish.

There are a number of characteristics of common stock that are important in the financial manager's capital structure decision and that affect investors' decisions regarding common stock as an investment. These characteristics include:

- Limited liability
- The number of shares
- Stock ownership
- Classified stock
- Voting rights
- The right to buy more stock

Limited Liability

The corporate form of doing business is attractive to owners of a business because it limits their liability. The most owners can lose is the amount of their investment. But this is not quite true. The amount owners—the shareholders—can lose depends on whether there is a par value for their shares.

Each share of stock may have a *par value*, indicated on the stock certificate. Par value represents the maximum amount of each share shareholders can be responsible for if the firm became insolvent (that is, unable to pay its debts).

If shares are sold at or above par value, the most shareholders can lose in the case of insolvency what they paid for their shares. Suppose a share of stock has a $100 par value and is sold for $110. If the corporation is liquidated and the proceeds are not enough to pay all the creditors, the stock is worthless and shareholders have lost the $110 invested in each share.

If shares are sold for less than their par value, some states' laws require that shareholders be held liable for the difference between what they paid for the shares and the par value. Suppose a share of stock has a $100 par value and is sold for $90. If the corporation is liquidated and the proceeds are not enough to pay all the creditors, the owner of each share is liable for $10 per share—the difference between what they paid for the stock and its par value.

This potential for liability has encouraged corporations to issue stock with very low par values—say $1 or even 1 cent—or no par at all. Shares of stock issued without a par value are referred to as *no-par stock*. This creates a problem for accountants—they like to record something in the balance sheet to represent the value of the stock. Firms issuing no-par stock assign an arbitrary value per share, referred to as the *stated value*, which implies no liability.

The Numbers of Shares

The equity pie can be split into any number of pieces. There can be one share that represents 100% ownership or 100,000 shares, each share representing a 0.001% ownership share.

How many shares of stock may a corporation issue? The number—referred to as the *authorized shares*—is specified in the corporate charter. If a firm wishes to issue more shares than specified, the charter must be amended to change the number of authorized shares. But a firm does not have to issue the entire number of shares authorized. The number of *issued shares*—the number of shares sold—is equal to or fewer than the number of authorized shares.

If a firm buys back stock from investors, the number of shares left in the hands of investors—referred to as *outstanding shares*—is fewer than the number of issued shares. Shares bought back from investors may be either retired (that is, eliminated from existence), reducing the number of issued shares, or held as *treasury stock*. Shares held as treasury stock are not considered outstanding shares and can be used by the firm, for example, to provide shares to employees when they exercise their stock options.

Stock Ownership

We can classify a corporation according to whether its shares of stock can be traded in financial markets. A corporation whose shares of stock are traded in financial markets is considered a *public corporation*. A corporation whose shares cannot be traded in financial markets is considered a *private corporation*.[1]

Federal securities laws—specifically the Securities Exchange Act of 1934, as modified in 1982—requires a corporation to *register* its securities if it has more than 500 shareholders and more than $3 million of assets. To register securities, a corporation must file a detailed description of the firm and the securities, as well as:

- quarterly financial reports on Form 10-Q;
- annual reports on Form 10-K, providing financial statement information, along with other descriptive information about the firm; and
- Form 8-K detailing specific events, such as the acquisition or disposition of assets, as they occur.

We discussed these disclosures in Chapter 6.

If a corporation has either less than 500 shareholders or less than $3 million of assets, it can choose not to register, and is referred to as a private corporation or a *privately-held corporation*. If it does register with the Securities and Exchange Commission, it's considered a public corporation.

The shares of stock of a public corporation—also referred to as a *publicly-held corporation*—can be owned by and traded among the general public. Anyone can buy and sell the shares of stock in a public corporation and these shares can be traded in the financial markets—on national or regional stock exchanges or in the over-the-counter market.

---

[1] A private corporation whose stock is owned among a very few individuals is referred to as a *closely-held corporation* or a *close corporation*. In a close corporation, the stock is owned by a single shareholder or a tightly-knit group of shareholders who are active in the management of the firm.

What difference does it make whether the corporation's stock is privately held or publicly-held? There are many differences.

One difference is the stock's marketability. If the shares are publicly traded, they are marketable. Investors can easily buy or sell the shares. If shares are privately-held, there may be restrictions as to whom you can sell your shares, possibly making it difficult to get cash when you need it.

Another difference is the diversification of the owners' wealth. If the shares are closely-held, the owners are usually also the managers. Owner-managers have a great deal of their wealth tied up with the corporation. Not only does the value of their stock depend on the fortunes of the company, so does their income. In a publicly-held corporation, owner-managers can sell off parts of their ownership.

Still another difference is the firm's access to capital. A publicly-traded corporation can raise new capital by issuing more shares to the general public. A privately-held corporation may not be able to do this since ownership may be restricted to a few shareholders. In addition, a privately-held corporation may reach a point when the number of shareholders and the size of the firm increases to the point requiring the registration of securities—changing the firm's status from private to public.

A further difference is confidentiality. A publicly-held corporation is required to disclose information to shareholders and the investing public through financial statements, annual reports, and press releases. Securities laws and exchange rules require publicly-traded corporations to disclose to investors important information such as a merger, a new product or discovery, the sale of a significant asset, and labor disputes. Private corporations do not have to reveal any information to the public. Therefore, a private corporation has the advantage because it is more difficult for its publicly-traded competitors to figure out what it is doing. For example, the two candy companies, Hershey Foods Corporation (Hershey Kisses, Reeses Peanut Butter Cups) and Mars, Incorporated (M&Ms, Milky Way bars), are competitors. Hershey Foods is publicly-traded, whereas Mars is a private company. Mars has access to all of Hershey's financial statements and other disclosures, whereas Hershey has no financial information on Mars.

Another difference is the cost of communication. A publicly-traded corporation must file annual financial statements with the Securities and Exchange Commission, prepare and send annual reports to shareholders, and correspond with shareholders (Securities Exchange Act of 1934, Rule 13a). The costs of these communications can add up, in terms of both the direct expenses for accountants, lawyers, and other personnel, and the indirect expense of tying up managements' time in shareholders' affairs instead of managing the firm.

All these differences must be weighed in deciding whether to be a private or a public corporation. There are over 4 million corporations in the U.S., but only about 9,000 have publicly-traded stock. The fact that we observe some private and some public corporations tells us that the weighing these factors can go either way.

Corporations do *change* their status, going from public to private or private to public. It is possible that as a corporation changes—in terms of the ownership, the types of investments it makes, and its need for capital—a change from public to private or private to public may be appropriate. RJR Nabisco went private in 1989, only to go public once again as RJR Nabisco Holdings two years later when it needed more capital.

Classified Stock

Corporations may have more than one class of common stock, each with different rights. There is no limit on the number of different classes of common stock a corporation may issue. The different classes are usually designated class A, class B, *et cetera*. There is no rule as to how these classes must be designated.

We often find different classes of stock owned by the family that founded the corporation and stock in the same corporation owned by the public. Until 1956, Ford Motor Company was a privately-held corporation—only Ford family members owned the stock. When the company went public, the Ford family did not want to lose control of the management of the business, so the shares were divided into Class A and Class B. Class A are the publicly owned shares and Class B are owned only by Ford family members and their descendants.[2] Class B shares give their shareholders better voting rights than the Class A shares (as you will see in the next section).

Multiple classes of common stock may also arise from acquisitions. For example, General Motors (GM) acquired Hughes Aircraft Co. in 1985. As a condition of the acquisition, Hughes Aircraft shareholders were given a special class of GM stock, designated class H. When GM acquired Electronic Data Systems (EDS) in 1985 it created still another, class E.[3] General Motors common stock (which doesn't have a class designation), General Motors Class H common, and General Motors Class E common all had different rights to vote and different rights to divi-

---

[2] In addition to family members and descendants, Class B stock may be owned by trusts or corporations controlled by Ford family members or descendants.

[3] General Motors spun-off its EDS division in 1996 by exchanging each GM class E share for one new EDS share, making EDS a publicly-traded company once again.

dends. For example, Class H shares had one-half a vote per share, whereas Class E common shares had one-quarter vote per share.

Voting Rights

Common shareholders are generally granted rights to

- Elect members of the board of directors
- Vote on the merger of the corporation with another corporation
- Authorize additional shares of common stock
- Vote on amendments to the articles of incorporation

The number of votes granted per share of stock is determined by the articles of incorporation and the particular class of common stock. Different classes of stock may have different numbers of votes per share, or different classes as a whole may have specified percentages of the votes. For example, with Ford Motor Company, Class B gets 40% of the vote and Class A 60%, even though there are more than twelve times the number of Class A shares as Class B shares.

Special classes of common stock with better voting rights (that is, more votes per share than the common shares already outstanding) were created during the 1980s as a defense against takeovers. By issuing a class of common stock with superior voting rights—say, ten votes per share instead of one vote per share—to a friendly party, the management of a corporation could derail a takeover attempt.

Supervoting shares have been used since the 1990s by many companies in IPOs to insure that the controlling shareholders prior to going public remain in control following the IPO.[4] Examples of companies going public with dual classes include Estee Lauder, Intimate Brands, and Revlon.

The proliferation of multiple classes of common stock during the 1980s, along with the potential to take control of the firm from current shareholders, raised concern over whether there *should* be different classes of stock with different rights. Suppose a firm has one class of stock with 1,000 shares outstanding, where each share has one vote. If you own 100 shares, you have 10% of the stock with 10% of the votes. Now suppose the firm issues 1,000 shares of a new class of stock, with each share having 10 votes per share. What happens to your control of the firm? After it issues these shares, you have 5% of the outstanding

---

[4] In many cases, the firm was taken private by a management or investor group in the 1980s and then went public in the 1990s with dual classes, with the management or investor group retaining the supervoting shares.

shares of stock, but only $100/[1,000 + (10 \times 1,000)] = 0.91\%$ of the votes. No federal securities law prohibits multiple classes of stock with different rights, though some state laws prohibit them.

The markets where the stock is traded may prohibit the listing of multiple classes of stock. For example, the New York Stock Exchange (NYSE) and the National Association for Securities Dealers Automated Quotation (NASDAQ) system require each share to have one vote for common stocks traded in their markets. The only exceptions are for (1) classes already outstanding at the time this rule went into effect, and (2) multiple class of stock as part of an initial public offering. The American Stock Exchange (ASE), however, allows companies to list classes of stock with different voting rights.

Shareholders exercise their voting rights by either voting directly at annual meetings and special shareholder meetings or by giving their vote to another party through a proxy. A *proxy* is a written authorization for someone else to vote for the shareholder in the manner the shareholder prescribes. Corporations whose stock is publicly-traded are required by the Securities Exchange Act to send a *proxy statement*, detailing the issues subject to shareholder voting, along with the *proxy card*, the document on which the shareholder indicates her or his vote.

The use of proxies is governed by the Securities Exchange Act of 1934.[5] Though intended to encourage corporate democracy though greater disclosure of information, the regulation of the proxy system resulted in the creation of barriers among shareholders and limits on shareholder proposals. For example, the Securities and Exchange Commission instituted rules (Rules 14a-6 and 14a-7) intended to enhance the disclosure of information to shareholders, but instead slowed down the process, inhibiting shareholder-to-shareholder communication and increasing the expense of communications among shareholders.

Cumulative Voting

Because shareholders elect the board of directors, the board should be the voice of the shareholders. But if every shareholder receives one vote per share to cast for each board seat, there is no way for minority shareholders to get representation on the board of directors. The folks who own the majority of shares can elect every one of the directors!

Cumulative voting is designed to alleviate this problem, allowing a minority of shareholders to gain representation on the board. With cumulative voting, shareholders can accumulate their votes for members of the board of directors. Let's see how this works.

---

[5] Securities Exchange Act of 1934, Regulation 14A—Solicitation of Proxies.

Suppose there are 1,000 shares outstanding, seven director positions up for election, and you own 400 shares. If there is no cumulative voting, you would have 400 votes that you can cast for each director position. If there is cumulative voting, you have 7 times 400, or 2,800 votes, that you can cast any way you want:

- Cast 400 for each position (400 × 7 = 2,800);
- Cast 2,800 towards one position and none for the other six (2,800 × 1 plus 0 × 6 = 2,800);
- Cast 1,400 towards each of two positions and none for the other five (1,400 × 2 plus 0 × 5 = 2,800);
- Or any other possible allocation of your 2,800 votes.

Cumulative voting allows shareholders to pile up their votes for one or more seats, leading to more active participation in the corporation's governance, especially by shareholders with smaller holdings.

Most states permit cumulative voting rights to be included in the corporate charter. Some states' corporate laws require cumulative voting for common shareholders; a few states prohibit it.

Classified Board of Directors

In most corporations, shareholders elect the members of the board of directors annually, without cumulative voting. If a majority of shareholders desire to gain representation on the board, they simply wait until the next annual meeting or, in some cases, call a special shareholders' meeting.

Some corporations have divided their director positions into classes, where only one class of directors is voted on each year, instead of the entire board. This system is referred to as a *classified board of directors* or a *staggered board of directors*. Consider Flowers Industries which has 12 members of the board of directors: four positions voted on each year, with each member serving a three-year term.

The advantage of this system is that, by staggering terms there is continuity in the board of directors. Having multiyear terms insures that there are experienced members of the board and allows the board as a group to work on projects or issues that extend beyond one year.

However, the system has its drawbacks. As a deterrent to a changeover in the board, some corporations have classified their board positions into several classes—typically three—so only a few positions are put to a vote each year. If a shareholder wanted to elect representatives to this board and eventually get control of the board, it would take two or more years. A classified board cannot prevent a majority of shareholders from gaining control of the board, but it can slow the process down.

The Right to Buy More Stock

If a corporation issues additional shares of stock, it is available for purchase by anyone—existing shareholders and others. This opens up the possibility that a shareholder's interest in the corporation may be diluted. If you own 1,000 shares of stock in a corporation, representing 10% of the 10,000 common shares outstanding, you control 10% of that corporation. If the corporation issues 10,000 more shares and you do not buy any of these shares, your ownership drops to 5%.

Corporations can give the right to buy additional shares of new common stock through a *rights offering*—an offering of rights to existing shareholders. First, the corporation gives each shareholder *warrants*, the physical document that gives, according to the number of shares each shareholder already owns, the right to buy a *specified number of shares* at a *specified price*, within a *specified period of time*. In other words, a warrant is a call option. When a shareholder receives warrants, he or she can:

■ throw these rights away;
■ exercise these rights, buying the shares; or
■ sell these rights.

In some corporations, a current shareholder's right to buy shares of any new common stock offering is granted directly in the corporate charter. This is referred to as the *preemptive right,* and is the current shareholder's right to buy additional shares of common stock to maintain her or his proportionate share of ownership in the corporation.

Suppose you own 10% of the stock of a corporation. If the corporation has a rights offering, you have the right to buy 10% of any new stock before it is offered to the public You don't have to, but you have the right and will be given the opportunity.

A corporation makes a rights offering for two reasons. First, shareholders may view a preemptive right as attractive since they are able to maintain their proportionate ownership interest and, hence, their control of a corporation. If shareholders view this as valuable, this right has the effect of increasing the value of the stock. If the price of shares is higher, a firm need not issue as many new shares when it wants to raise new capital.

Second, it usually costs a corporation less to issue shares in a rights offering than to sell new shares to the public. And a savings for the corporation is valuable to the owners—the shareholders.

Let's look at an example of a rights offering. In 1991, Time Warner issued rights to its common shareholders.[6] For each share owned, shareholders received 6/10ths of a right to buy Time Warner stock at $80 per share. If you owned 100 shares, you were entitled to buy 60 shares of stock at $80 per share. The rights were granted July 16th and expired three weeks later, on August 5th. During that period, the higher the price of Time Warner stock, the more valuable this right.

At the time the rights were granted, Time Warner common stock was trading at $86.75 per share, making the right to buy at $80 worth *at least* $6.75 per right. But early on in this three week period the value of the right—the price of the rights traded on the stock exchange—was *greater* than the difference between the Time Warner stock price and $80. Why? Because the investors buying the rights at this price felt that before the three weeks were up, the price of the Time Warner stock would increase even more, making the right *even more* valuable. But as time passed, investors began to lose confidence that the stock would increase in price. So the value of the right wound up equal to the difference between the stock price and the $80.

We can see the relation between the value of the right and the value a share of Time Warner stock in Exhibit 16.1. The value of the right and the value of the stock move almost parallel. As the price of Time Warner stock increases, so does the value of the right to buy it at $80. Finally, just before expiration, the value of the right was equal to the difference between the Time Warner stock price and $80.

Corporate Democracy

Corporate democracy gives owners of the corporation a say in how to manage it. By law, shareholders are not allowed to interfere with the ordinary business—the day-to-day operations—of a corporation. But they elect representatives, the members of the board of directors, to oversee the management of the firm. The board of directors may be comprised of officers of the corporation or may include persons not employed by the corporation—referred to as **outside directors**.

It is not always clear just what constitutes the ordinary business of a corporation: Golden parachutes (attractive severance packages) for top management? Salary and stock options for management? Doing business with tobacco companies? Buying goods from companies employing underage workers?

---

[6] Prior to this rights offering, Time Warner did attempt another offering whose terms were not in the best interests of the shareholders. Dennis E. Logue and James K. Seward discuss the Time Warner rights offerings in detail in their article entitled "Time Warner Rights Offering: Strategy, Articulation and Destruction of Shareholder Value," *Financial Analysts Journal* (March/April 1992) pp. 37–45.

EXHIBIT 16.1   The Value of a Time Warner Common Share and the Right to Buy a
Time Warner Common Share at $80 per Share

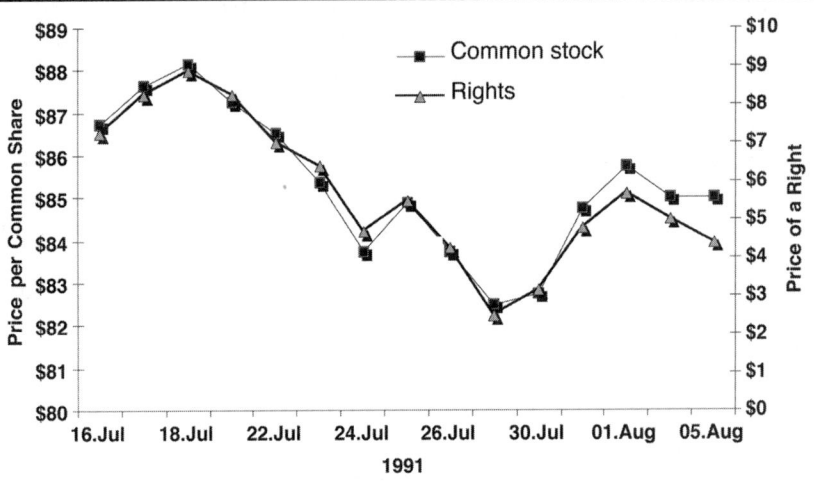

Source: Standard and Poor's Daily Stock Price Record

Any shareholder owning either $1,000 worth of the common stock
or 1% of the outstanding shares is permitted to introduce a proposal to
be voted on by shareholders.[7] To avoid having proposals that are inappropriate—in the sense that they are really about ordinary business or
simply a nuisance—the management may petition to the Securities and
Exchange Commission (SEC) to remove a proposal from the proxy. In the
past, the SEC has allowed corporate management to remove shareholder
proposals that dealt with management compensation issues, but more
recently has forced companies to include these proposals in the proxies.

A problem that became quite noticeable during the 1980s merger
mania is that most large, institutional investors tended to vote as recommended by management and individual investors were, in large part, apathetic towards corporate issues. As both institutional investors and
individual investors are forming coalitions to encourage shareholder participation in corporation issues, this situation is becoming less of a problem.

Another problem is that for most corporations, voting is not always
confidential. It may be the case that management receives your votes
and, if not pleased with how you voted, may contact you trying to persuade you to change your vote. In many cases, shareholders and managers of institutional investors have been pressured to vote in favor of the
present management.

---

[7] This requirement is set forth in the Securities Exchange Act of 1934, Rule 14a-8.

Still another problem is that if a shareholder proposal succeeds, the proposal is nonbinding. Management can simply ignore it.

Complicating shareholders' rights are provisions referred to as poison pills. *Poison pill* describes a provision that makes the target of a takeover offer unattractive. These provisions typically involve granting shareholders of the target firm special rights or privileges if the firm is the object of a takeover bid. Usually, the management of the target firm can negate the poison pill if they feel that the offer is in the shareholders' best interest.

An argument *for* these "pills" is that they allow the management of the target firm to negotiate the best price for the shareholders since the only way to avoid the costly poison is through management's approval. An argument *against* these pills is that they discourage takeover bids that would have paid shareholders more than the current stock price for their shares.

Researchers have found that poison pills have a depressing effect on share price: Investors do not like these provisions.[8] Oddly, poison pills are often referred to as *shareholder rights plans*.

Shareholder proposals represent a weak method of effecting change in a corporation. This is due to the apathetic nature of shareholders, the possibility of arm-twisting by management, and because these proposals are nonbinding. An alternative method of getting a corporation to change is to wage a *proxy fight*, gaining a voice in the corporation by getting seats on the board of directors. Usually, the board members elected each year are nominated by the current board members and run unopposed. In a proxy fight, an alternative slate of board members is nominated by someone interested in gaining representation on the board. And the battle begins.

A proxy fight pits current board members against the alternative slate, each slate vying for the votes, that is, the proxies, of the shareholders. An example of a proxy fight is the one waged (and lost) by investors Carl Icahn and Bennet LeBow for control of RJR Nabisco Holdings in the spring of 1996. Icahn and LeBow initiated the proxy fight to force RJR Nabisco to spin-off Nabsico from the tobacco company. RJR Nabisco fought back and won, defeating the Icahn and LeBow slate by a 3-to-1 margin—and costing the RJR Nabisco $11 million (or 2 cents per share).

---

[8] A detailed analysis of the different types of poison pills and how they affect share price can be found in Paul H. Malatesta and Ralph A. Walkling, "Poison Pill Securities: Stockholder Wealth, Profitability, and Ownership Structure," *Journal of Financial Economics* (January/March 1988), pp. 347–376; and Michael Ryngaert, "The Effect of Poison Pill Securities on Shareholder Wealth," *Journal of Financial Economics* (January/March 1988), pp. 377–418.

DIVIDENDS

A dividend is the cash, stock, or any type of property a corporation distributes to its shareholders. The board of directors may declare a dividend at any time, but dividends are not a legal obligation of the corporation—it is the board's choice. Unlike interest on debt securities, if a corporation does not pay a dividend, there is no violation of a contract and no legal recourse for shareholders.

Most dividends are in the form of cash. In addition to cash dividends, a corporation may provide shareholders with dividends in the form of additional shares of stock or, rarely, some types of property owned by the corporation. We will first take a look at the mechanics of paying a dividend, which applies to all types of dividends, and then we will look cash dividends, followed by stock distributions. After we have described the different types of dividends, we will look at dividend policy—both the practice and the theory of paying cash dividends.

Mechanics of Paying a Dividend

The board of directors decides whether or not to pay a dividend. The board announces a decision to pay a dividend, specifying:

- the amount of the dividend (dollars per share for a cash dividend, amount of stock for a stock dividend);
- who is to receive the dividend, specified in terms of who owns the stock on a specified date, referred to as the *record date*; and
- when the dividend is to be paid, the *payment date*.

The date the board of directors declares the dividend is referred to as the *declaration date*.

Dividend Dates are summarized as follows:

Declaration date	The day the board of directors meets and decides on the dividend.
Record date	The date specified by the board such that any shareholders who are on record as owning shares on this date are eligible to receive the dividend.
Ex-dividend date	The date, established by the financial markets as four business days prior to the record date, that determines who receives the dividend (whomever purchased and held onto the shares prior to this date) and who does not (whomever buys the shares on or after this date).
Payment date	The date the dividend checks are mailed.

Figuring out who are actually the owners of stock on the record date can be somewhat of a problem because it may take a few days for the paperwork to be completed following a sale of shares. Recognizing this situation, the stock exchanges adopted a system of figuring out who has the right to the dividend, called the ***three-day delivery plan.*** The stock exchanges identify the trading day four business days *prior* to the record date as the ***ex-dividend date.*** If you buy the shares on the day before the ex-dividend date, you are entitled to the forthcoming dividend. If you buy the shares *on* the ex-dividend date or after, you are not entitled to the forthcoming dividend.

The Board of Directors of the Wm. Wrigley Jr. Company met on May 22, 2002 and declared a $0.205 dividend on each share of Common Stock and each share of Class B Common Stock. In their declaration, the Wrigley's board declared that the dividend is payable on August 1, 2002 to stockholders of record at the close of business on July 12, 2002.

Declaration Date	Ex-Dividend Date	Record Date	Payment Date
Wednesday, May 22, 2002	Wednesday, July 10, 2002	Friday, July 12, 2002	Thursday, August 1, 2002

If you bought Wrigley common stock before July 10, 2002, and did not sell it before that same date, you were entitled to the dividend paid August 1, 2002. If you bought the stock on July 10, 2002 or after, you would not have received the dividend paid August 1, 2002.

The price of the stock on the ex-dividend date reflects the fact that you are not entitled to the next dividend. Suppose a stock is trading for $25 the day prior to the ex-dividend date. If the dividend is $1 per share, what would you being willing to pay for a share on the ex-dividend date? Remember, if you buy the share on this date, you are not entitled to this $1 dividend, *but* if you had bought it the day before, you would be getting the $1 in the near future. If nothing else happens to affect the share price, you would be willing to pay only $24 a share on the ex-dividend date. Therefore, we expect a share's price on the ex-dividend date to be less than it was the day before by approximately the amount of the dividend per share.

Cash Dividends

Cash dividends are payments made directly to shareholders in proportion to the shares they own. Cash dividends are paid on all outstanding shares of stock. That means no dividends are paid on treasury stock. Cash dividends can be paid monthly, quarterly, semiannually, or annually though most U.S. corporations that pay dividends do so on a quarterly basis. A few companies pay special or extra dividends occasionally—identifying these dividends apart from their regular dividends.

We usually describe the cash dividends that a company pays in terms of *dividends per share (DPS)*. For example, during 2001 General Electric paid $2,848 million in common dividends on the 9,925 million common shares outstanding. Therefore, General Electric paid $0.64 in dividends per share of stock. We can calculate the DPS as:

$$\text{Dividends per share} = \frac{\text{Common stock dividends}}{\text{Number of common shares outstanding}} \quad (16\text{-}1)$$

For General Electric in 2001,

$$\text{Dividends per share} = \frac{\$6,358 \text{ million}}{\$9,925 \text{ million}} = \$0.64 \text{ per share}$$

If you owned 10,000 shares of General Electric stock during 2001, you would have received cash dividends of $0.64 per share time 100 shares = $6,400.

Another way of describing cash dividends is in terms of the percentage of earnings paid out in dividends, referred to as the dividend payout (DPO). General Electric had earnings of $13,684 million of which $6,358 million or 46.5% were paid out to shareholders. General Electric's earnings per share of stock were $13,684 million/9.925 million shares = $1.38.

We can write the dividend payout in terms of dividends and shares outstanding:

$$\text{Dividend payout} = \frac{\text{Common stock dividends}}{\text{Earnings available to common shareholders}} \quad (16\text{-}2)$$

In the case of General Electric for 2001,

$$\text{Dividend payout} = \frac{\$6,358 \text{ million}}{\$13,684 \text{ million}} = 46.5\%$$

If we divide both the numerator and the denominator by the number of common shares outstanding, we can rewrite the dividend payout ratio as:

$$\text{Dividend payout} = \frac{\text{Dividends per share}}{\text{Earnings per share}}$$

In terms of General Electric's 2001 dividends and earnings per share:

$$\text{Dividend payout} = \frac{\$0.64}{\$1.38} = 46.5\%$$

Dividend Reinvestment Plans

Many U.S. corporations allow shareholders to reinvest automatically their dividends in the shares of the corporation paying them. A *dividend reinvestment plan (DRP)* is a program that allows shareholders to reinvest their dividends, buying additional shares of stock of the company instead of receiving the cash dividend.

These additional shares representing dividends reinvested may be currently outstanding (the firm buys them in the open market) or newly issued. The dividends are reinvested according to a prescribed formula. For example, you may be able to reinvest your dividend into new shares based on the average market price of a share five days prior to the dividend payment date. If you get $100 in dividends and the average price of the stock during the five preceding days is $20, you receive five more shares. The corporation keeps track of the shares you are "buying," much like a savings account. You never see the cash dividend or the shares, but you receive a periodic account of the shares you own. You can sell or keep the shares that accumulate in your account.

To encourage participation, especially in plans providing newly issued shares, some firms allow shareholders to reinvest their dividends at a discount from the current market price. These discounts range from 2% to 10%, typically 5%.

A DRP offers benefits to both shareholders and the firm. Shareholders buy shares without transactions costs—brokers' commissions—and at a discount from the current market price. The firm is able to retain cash without the cost of a new stock issue.

Alas, the dividends are taxed as income before they are reinvested, even though the shareholders never see the dividend. The result is similar to a dividend cut. Many firms are finding high rates of participation in DRPs. If so many shareholders want to reinvest their dividends—even after considering the tax consequences—why is the firm paying dividends? This suggests that there is some rationale, such as signalling (discussed later in this chapter), which compels firms to pay dividends.

Stock Distributions

When dividends aren't in cash, they are usually additional shares of stock. Additional shares of stock can be distributed to shareholders in two ways: paying a stock dividend and splitting the stock.

Stock Dividend

A *stock dividend* is the distribution of additional shares of stock to shareholders. Stock dividends are generally stated as a percentage of existing share holdings. For example, if you own 1,000 shares of stock and the firm pays a 5% stock dividend, you receive 5% more shares, or 50 shares. Before the dividend, you own 1,000 shares; after the dividend, you own 1,050 shares.

If a corporation pays a stock dividend, it is not transferring anything of value to the shareholders. The assets of the corporation remain the same and each shareholder's proportionate share of ownership remains the same. All the firm is doing is cutting its equity pie into more slices and at the same time cutting each shareholder's portion of that equity into more slices. So why pay a stock dividend?

There are a couple of reasons for stock dividends. One is to provide information to the market. A firm may want to communicate good news to the shareholders without paying cash. For example, if the firm has an attractive investment opportunity and needs funds for it, paying a cash dividend doesn't make any sense—so the firm pays a stock dividend instead. But is this an effective way of communicating good news to the shareholders? It costs very little to pay a stock dividend—just minor expenses for recordkeeping, printing, and distribution. But if it costs very little, do investors really believe in devices where management is not putting "its money where its mouth is"?

Another reason for paying a stock dividend is to reduce the price of the stock. If the price of a stock is high relative to most other stocks, there may be higher costs related to investors' transactions of the stock, as in a higher broker's commission. By paying a stock dividend—which slices the equity pie into more pieces, the price of the stock should decline.

Let's see how this works. Suppose you own 1,000 shares, each worth $50 per share, for a total investment of $50,000. If the firm pays you a 5% stock dividend, you own 1,050 shares after the dividend. Is there is any reason for your holdings to change in value? Nothing economic has gone on here—the firm has the same assets, the same liabilities, and the same equity—total equity is just cut up into smaller pieces. There is no reason for the value of the portion of the equity you own to change. But the price *per share* should decline: from $50 per share to $47.62 per share. The argument of reducing share price only works if you can bring down the price substantially, from an unattractive trading range to a more attractive trading range in terms of reducing brokerage commissions and enabling small investors to purchase even lots of 100 shares. Brokerage commissions are usually lower for shares trading in the range from $20 to $40, compared to shares trading above or below that price range, and for even lots of 100 shares.

Stock Split

A stock split is something like a stock dividend. A *stock split* splits the number of existing shares into more shares. For example, in a 2:1 split—referred to as "two for one"—each shareholder gets two shares for every one owned. If you own 1,000 shares and the stock is split 2:1, you own 2,000 shares after the split. Has the portion of your ownership in the firm changed? No, you simply own twice as many shares—and so does every other shareholder. If you owned 1% of the corporation's stock before the split, you still own 1% after the split.

So why split? Like a stock dividend, the split reduces the trading price of shares. If your 1,000 shares of stock are trading for $50 per share prior to a 2:1 split, your shares should trade for $25 per share after the split.

Aside from a minor difference in accounting, stock splits and stock dividends are essentially the same.[9] A 2:1 split has the same effect on a stock's price as a 100% stock dividend, a 1.5 to 1 split has the same effect on a stock's price as a 50% stock dividend, and so on.[10]

A *reverse stock split*, raises the price of a stock by reducing the number of shares of stock outstanding. It's the opposite of a stock split. Reducing the number of shares increases the stock's price because the equity is transformed into fewer *larger* pieces. A 1:2 reverse split—one share given in exchange for two shares—doubles the price of the stock. If you own 1,000 shares of stock and the stock is trading for $5 per share, with a 1:2 reverse split you own 500 shares after the split, each worth around $10 per share.

There are several reasons for a reverse split.

First, the firm may want to steer the price of its stock toward a more attractive trading range, reducing investors' transactions costs for trad-

---

[9] The stock dividend requires a shift within the stockholders' equity accounts, from retained earnings to paid-in capital, for the amount of the distribution, whereas the stock split requires only a memorandum entry.

[10] The basis of the accounting rules is related to the reasons behind the distribution of additional shares. If firms want to bring down their share price, they tend to declare a stock split; if firms want to communicate news, they often declare a stock dividend.

ing in the stock. The firm may also want to raise the price of the stock so that it is not a *penny stock*, a stock trading under $1 per share, since there is a negative connotation to penny stocks.

Another reason to reverse split may be to take the company private. If your firm has fewer than 500 shareholders, you can avoid the disclosure requirements of the SEC—go private. While there are other ways to go private, a reverse split is an inexpensive way.

Stock Distributions and the Market Reaction

How can we tell what the motivation is behind stock dividends, stock splits, and reverse splits? We can't. But we can get a general idea of how investors interpret these actions by looking at what happens to the firm's share price when a corporation announces its decision to pay a stock dividend, split its stock, or reverse split. If the share price tends to go up when the announcement is made, the decision is probably good news; if the price goes down, the stock dividend is probably bad news. This is supported by evidence that indicates firms' earnings tend to increase following stock splits and dividends.[11]

The share price of companies announcing stock distributions and stock splits generally increase at the time of the announcement.[12] The most likely explanation is that this distribution is interpreted as good news—that management believes that the future prospects of the firm are favorable or that the share price is more attractive to investors.

The stock price of companies announcing a reverse stock split usually decreases at the time of the announcement.[13] The most likely explanation for this decrease is that the firm is unable to increase the share price in any way *other* than through a reverse split. That is, the prospects of the firm are so bleak that this is the only way to increase the share price.

---

[11] See, for example, Maureen McNichols and Ajay Dravid, "Stock Dividends, Stock Splits, and Signaling," *Journal of Finance* (July 1990) pp. 857–879.

[12] The stock price typically increases by 1 to 2% when the split or stock dividend is announced. When the stock dividend is distributed or the split is effected (on the "ex" date), the share's price typically declines according to the amount of the distribution. Suppose a firm announces a 2:1 split. Its share price may increase by 1 to 2% when this is announced, but when the shares are split, the share price will go down to approximately half of its pre-split value. See, for example, Mark Grinblatt, Ronald Masulis, and Sheridan Titman, "The Valuation Effects of Stock Splits and Stock Dividends," *Journal of Financial Economics* (December 1984), pp. 461–490.

[13] See, for example, David Peterson and Pamela Peterson, "A Further Evidence of Stock Distributions: The Case of Reverse Stock Splits," *Journal of Financial Research* (Fall 1992), pp. 189–206.

EXHIBIT 16.2   Dividends per Share and Dividend Payout for the Cooper Tire &
Rubber Company, 1980–2001

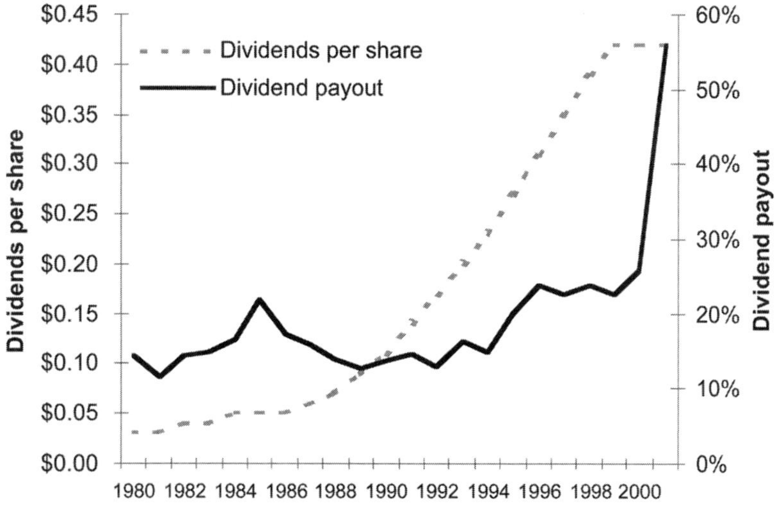

Source: Value Line Investment Survey

Dividend Policy

A dividend policy is a firm's decision about the payment of cash dividends to shareholders. Looking at the dividends per share and the dividend payout at a point in time doesn't tell us much about the firm's
dividend policy. We generally need somewhat more information than one
quarter's or one year's dividend. If we look at dividends over a longer
period, we can begin to get a better picture of the firm's dividend policy.

There are several basic ways of describing a firm's dividend policy:

- No dividends
- Constant growth in dividends per share
- Constant payout ratio
- Low regular dividends with periodic extra dividends

The firms that typically do not pay dividends are those that are generally viewed as younger, faster growing firms. For example, as of 2002,
firms such as Microsoft Corporation (computer software), Amgen (bio-
technology), and Amazon.com (internet retailer) had never paid dividends.

A common pattern of cash dividends tends to be the constant growth
of dividends per share. As we see for Cooper Tire and Rubber in Exhibit
16.2, dividends per share grew at a constant rate after 1986 and until 1999.

EXHIBIT 16.3   Dividends per Share and Dividend Payout for the Sara Lee
Corporation, 1980–2001

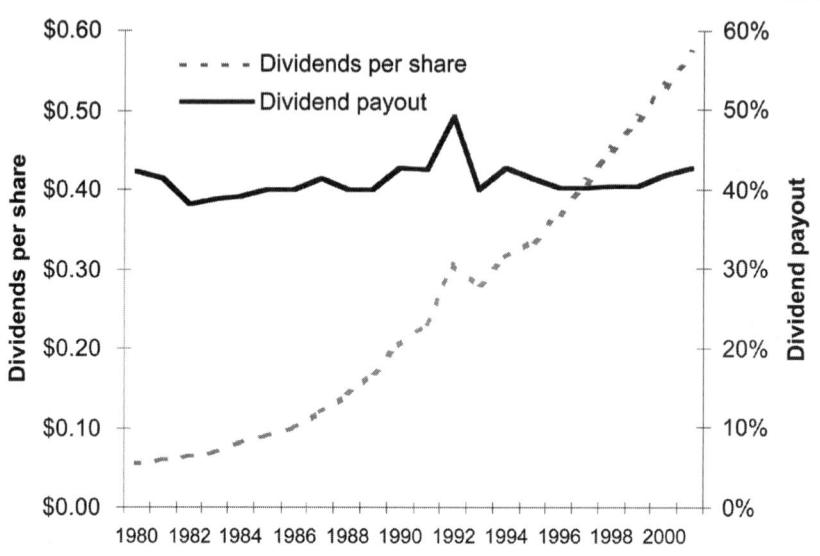

Source: Value Line Investment Survey

Another pattern is the constant payout ratio, as exhibited in Exhibit
16.3 by the Sara Lee Corporation. Sara Lee's dividend payout is around
40% each year, with the most noticeable deviation occurring when it
paid a special dividend in 1992. Many other companies in the food processing industry, such as Kellogg and Tootsie Roll Industries, pay dividends that are a relatively constant percentage of earnings.

Some companies display both a constant dividend payout and a constant growth in dividends. The dividends per share and dividend payout of
General Electric common stock over the years 1980 through 2001 are
graphed in Exhibit 16.4. Dividends per share grew steadily throughout
much of this period. Looking at the dividend payout in this same figure,
we see that it has been relatively constant throughout the period as well.
This type of dividend pattern is characteristic of large, mature companies
that have predictable earnings growth—the dividends growth tends to
mimic the earnings growth, resulting in a constant payout.

U.S. corporations that pay dividends tend to pay either constant or
increasing dividends per share. Dividends tend to be lower in industries
that have many profitable opportunities to invest their earnings. But as
a company matures and finds fewer and fewer profitable investment
opportunities, a greater portion of its earnings are paid out in dividends.

EXHIBIT 16.4 Dividends per Share and Dividend Payout for the General Electric Corporation, 1980–2001

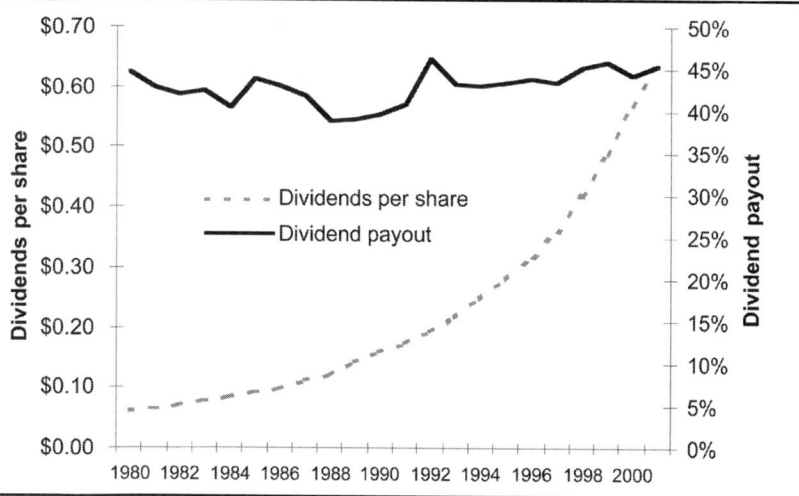

Source: Value Line Investment Survey

Many firms are reluctant to cut dividends because the firm's share price usually falls when a dividend reduction is announced.[14] For example, the U.S. auto manufacturers cut dividends during the recession in the early 1990s, as illustrated in Exhibit 16.5 by General Motors (Panel A) and Ford Motor Company (Panel B). As you can see in these graphs, as earnings per share declined the auto makers did not cut dividends until EPS were negative—and in the case of GM, not until it had experienced two consecutive loss years. But as earnings recovered in the mid-1990s, dividends were increased. Firms tend to only raise their regular quarterly dividend when they are sure they can keep it up in the future. By giving a special or extra dividend, the firm is able to provide more cash to the shareholders without committing itself to paying an increased dividend each period into the future. Let's look at an example. The fortunes of Longview Fibre, a timber growing and harvesting firm,

---

[14] A number of studies have documented the fall in share price that accompanies a cut in dividends. See, for example, Richardson Pettit, "Dividends Announcements, Security Performance, and Capital Market Efficiency," *Journal of Finance* (December 1972), pp. 86–96; and Joseph Aharony and Itzhak Swary, "Quarterly Dividend and Earnings Announcements and Stockholders' Returns: An Empirical Analysis," *Journal of Finance* (March 1980), pp. 1–12]. But just how much the share price falls depends on the reasons for the cut; see J. Randall Woolridge and Chinmoy Gosh, "Dividend Cuts: Do They Always Signal Bad News?" *Midland Journal of Corporate Finance* (Summer 1985), pp. 20–32.

vary depending on construction demand and timber cutting availability on public land, both of which are quite uncertain. Longview Fibre pays a regular quarterly dividend around $0.10 a share, but also may pay special dividends that vary according to its earnings.

EXHIBIT 16.5   Dividends and Earnings per Share for General Motors and Ford Motor Company, 1980–2001
Panel A: General Motors

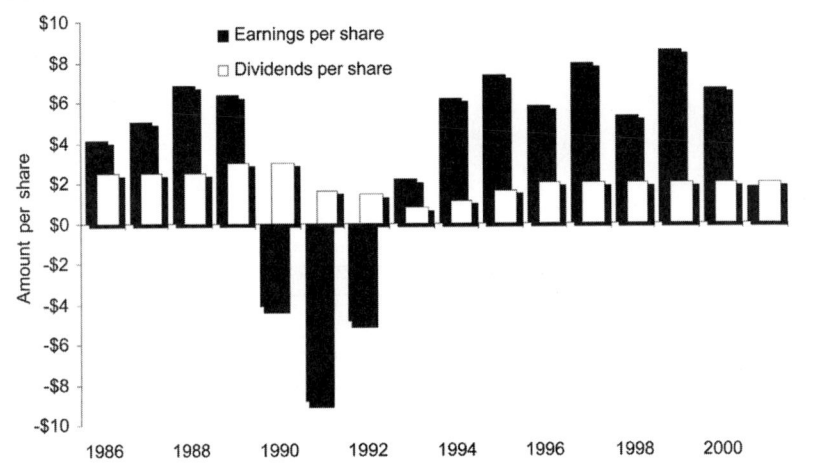

Panel B: Ford Motor Company

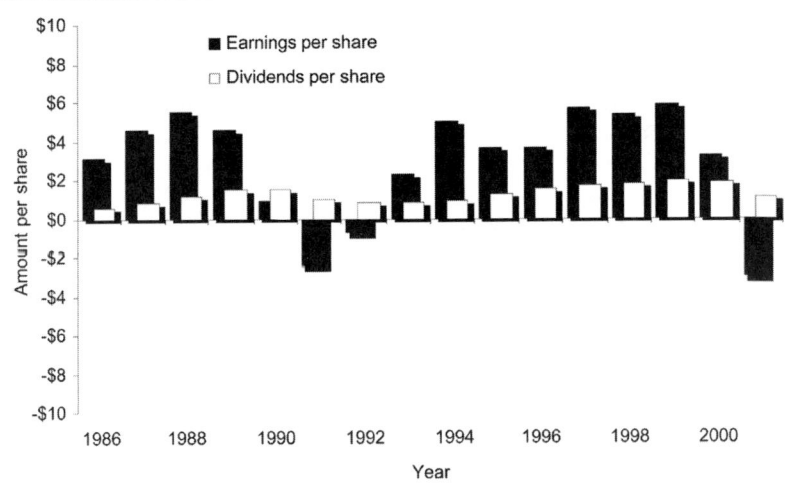

Source: Value Line Investment Survey

Dividends: To Pay or Not to Pay

There is no general agreement whether dividends should or should not be paid. Here are several views:

- **The Dividend Irrelevance Theory:** The payment of dividends does not affect the value of the firm since the investment decision is independent of the financing decision.
- **The "Bird in the Hand" Theory:** Investors prefer a certain dividend stream to an uncertain price appreciation.
- **The Tax-Preference Explanation:** Due to the way in which dividends are taxed, investors should prefer the retention of funds to the payment of dividends.
- **The Signalling Explanation:** Dividends provide a way for the management to inform investors about the firm's future prospects.
- **The Agency Explanation:** The payment of dividends forces the firm to seek more external financing, which subjects the firm to the scrutiny of investors.

Let's take a further look at each view.

The Dividend Irrelevance Theory The dividend irrelevance argument was developed by Merton Miller and Franco Modigliani.[15] Basically, the argument is that if there is a *perfect market*—no taxes, no transactions costs, no costs related to issuing new securities, and no costs of sending or receiving information—the value of the firm is unaffected by payment of dividends.

How can this be? Suppose investment decisions are fixed—that is, the firm will invest in certain projects *regardless* how they are financed. The value of the firm is the present value of all future cash flows of the firm—which depend on the investment decisions that management makes, *not* on how these investments are financed. If the investment decision is fixed, whether a firm pays a dividend or not does not affect the value of the firm.

A firm raises additional funds either through earnings or by selling securities—sufficient to meet its investment decisions and its dividend decision. The dividend decision therefore affects only the financing decision—how much capital the firm has to raise to fulfill its investment decisions.

The Miller and Modigliani argument implies that the dividend decision is a residual decision. If the firm has no profitable investments to undertake, the firm can pay out funds that would have gone to investments to shareholders. And whether or not the firm pays dividends is of no consequence to the value of the firm. In other words, dividends are irrelevant.

---

[15] Merton Miller and Franco Modigliani. "Dividend Policy, Growth and the Valuation of Shares," *Journal of Business* (October 1961), pp. 411–433.

But we don't live in a perfect world with a perfect market. Are the imperfections (taxes, transactions costs, etc.) enough to alter the conclusions of Miller and Modigliani? It isn't clear.

The "Bird in the Hand" Theory   A popular view is that dividends represent a *sure thing* relative to share price appreciation. The return to shareholders is comprised of two parts: the return from dividends—the *dividend yield*—and the return from the change in the share price—the *capital yield*. Firms generate earnings and can either pay them out in cash dividends or reinvest earnings in profitable investments, increasing the value of the stock and, hence, share price. Once a dividend is paid, it is a certain cash flow. Shareholders can cash their quarterly dividend checks and reinvest the funds. But an increase in share price is not a sure thing. It only becomes a sure thing when the share's price increases over the price the shareholder paid and he or she sells the shares.

We can see that prices of dividend-paying stocks are less volatile than nondividend-paying stocks. But are dividend-paying stocks less risky because they pay dividends? Or are less risky firms more likely to pay dividends? Most of the evidence supports the latter. Firms that have greater risk—business risk, financial risk, or both—tend to pay little or no dividends. Firms whose cash flows are more variable tend to avoid large dividend commitments that they could not satisfy during periods of poorer financial performance.

The Tax-Preference Explanation   The dividend income shareholders receive is taxed as any other income, such as wages or salaries. If shareholders sell their stock, any gain they make (called capital gains) is given preferential tax treatment—taxed effectively at a lower rate than dividend income. Capital gains are taxed at lower rates due to two aspects of the tax law.

First, capital gains are only taxed when realized—when you sell the stock. If you receive $20 of dividends in 2001, you pay taxes on that income in 2001. If you bought stock in 1990 and sell it in 2007, you do not pay tax on any gain until 2007! So, while the price of the stock may go up $20 in 2001, you don't pay any tax on that $20 until you sell the stock in 2007. And since the taxes you pay on this gain are in the future, you effectively pay lower taxes on the capital gain as compared to an equivalent amount of dividends.

Second, capital gains are taxed at relatively lower rates. Whether through a special capital gain exclusion—that means part of the gain does not get figured into your taxable income—or through a special tax rate, capital gains have been taxed at lower rates than dividend income throughout most of U.S. tax history.

But the tax impact is different for different types of shareholders. An individual taxpayer includes dividend income along with other income such as wages to determine taxable income. But a corporation receiving a dividend from another corporation may take a *dividends received deduction*—a deduction of a large portion of the dividend income.[16] Therefore, corporations pay taxes on a small portion of their dividend income. Still other shareholders may not even be taxed on dividend income. For example, a pension fund beneficiary does not pay taxes on the dividend income it gets from its investments (these earnings are eventually taxed when the pension is paid out to the employee after retirement).

Dividends are taxed at rates higher than capital gains, though there are two things that could affect this difference for some investors. First, investors that have high marginal tax rates may gravitate towards stocks that pay little or no dividends. This means the shareholders of dividend paying stocks have lower marginal tax rates. This is referred to as a *tax clientele*—investors who choose stocks on the basis of the taxes they have to pay.

Second, investors with high marginal tax rates can use legitimate investment strategies—such as borrowing to buy stock and using the deduction from the interest payments on the loan to offset the dividend income in order to reduce the tax impact of dividends.[17]

The Signalling Explanation   Firms that pay dividends seem to maintain a relatively stable dividend, either in terms of a constant or growing dividend payout or in terms of a constant or growing dividend per share. And when firms change their dividend—either increasing or reducing ("cutting") the dividend—the price of the firm's shares seems to be affected: When a dividend is increased, the price of its shares goes up; when a dividend is cut, the price goes down. This reaction is attributed to investors' perception of the meaning of the dividend change: Increases are good news, decreases are bad news.

---

[16] As we saw in Chapter 5, the dividends received deduction ranges from 70% to 100%, depending on the ownership relation between the two corporations.

[17] Several strategies that can be used to reduce the taxes on dividend income are discussed by Merton Miller and Myron Scholes in "Dividend and Taxes," *Journal of Financial Economics* (1979), pp. 333–364. However, Pamela Peterson, David Peterson, and James Ang, in their article entitled "Direct Evidence on the Marginal Rate of Taxation on Dividend Income," *Journal of Financial Economics* (1985), pp. 267–282, document that investors do not appear to take advantage of these strategies and end up paying substantial taxes on dividend income.

Managers likely have some information that investors do not have. A change in dividend may be a way for managers to signal this private information. Since we observe that when dividends are lowered, the price of a share falls, we expect managers not to increase a dividend unless they thought they could maintain it into the future. Realizing this, investors may view a dividend increase as management's increased confidence in the future operating performance of the firm.

The Agency Explanation   The relation between the owners and the managers of a firm is an *agency relationship*: The owners are the *principals* and the managers are the *agents*. The managers are charged with acting in the best interests of the owners. Nevertheless, there are possibilities for conflicts between the interests of the two. If the firm pays a dividend, managers may be forced to raise new capital outside of the firm—that is, issue new securities instead of using internally generated capital—subjecting them to the scrutiny of equity research analysts and other investors. This extra scrutiny helps reduce the possibility that managers will not work in the best interests of the shareholders. But issuing new securities is not costless. There are costs of issuing new securities—*flotation costs*. In "agency theory speak," these costs are part of *monitoring costs*—incurred to help monitor the managers' behavior and insure behavior is consistent with shareholder wealth maximization.

The payment of dividends also reduces the amount of free cash flow under control of management. *Free cash flow* is the cash in excess of the cash needed to finance profitable investment opportunities. A profitable investment opportunity is any investment that provides the firm with a return greater than what shareholders could get elsewhere on their money—that is, a return greater than the shareholders' opportunity cost.

Because free cash flow is the cash flow left over after all profitable projects are undertaken, the only projects left are the unprofitable ones. Should free cash be reinvested in the unprofitable investments or paid out to shareholders? Of course if managers make decisions consistent with shareholder wealth maximization, any free cash flow should be paid out to shareholders since—by the definition of a profitable investment opportunity—the shareholders could get a better return investing the funds they receive.

If the firm pays a dividend, funds are paid out to shareholders. If the firm needs funds, they could be raised by issuing new securities. If the shareholders wish to reinvest the funds received as dividends in the firm, they could buy these new securities. The payment of dividends therefore reduces the cash flow in the hands of management, reducing the possibility that managers will invest funds in unprofitable investment opportunities.

Summing Up: To Pay Dividends or Not   We can figure out reasons why a firm should or should not pay dividends, but not why they actually do or do not—this is the "dividend puzzle".[18] But we do know from looking at dividends and the market's reaction to them that:

- If a firm increases its dividends or pays a dividend for the first time, this is viewed as good news—its share price increases.
- If a firm decreases its dividend or omits it completely, this is viewed as bad news—its share price declines.

That's why financial managers must be aware of the relation between dividends and the value of the common stock in establishing or changing dividend policy.

Stock Repurchases

Corporations have repurchased their common stock from their shareholders. A corporation repurchasing its own shares is effectively paying a cash dividend, with one important difference: taxes. Cash dividends are ordinary taxable income to the shareholder. A firm's repurchase of shares, on the other hand, results in a capital gain or loss for the shareholder, depending on the price paid when they were originally purchased. If the shares are repurchased at a higher price, the difference may be taxed as capital gains, which may be taxed at rates lower than ordinary income.

Methods of Repurchasing Stock

A corporation may repurchase its own stock by any of three methods: (1) a tender offer, (2) open market purchases, and (3) a targeted share repurchase.

Tender Offer   A *tender offer* is an offer made to all shareholders, with a specified deadline and a specified number of shares the corporation is willing to buy back. The tender offer may be a fixed price offer, where the corporation specifies the price it is willing to pay and solicits purchases of shares of stock at that price. For example, The Limited Inc. made a repurchase tender offer in early 1996, offering to buy up to 85 million of its shares for $19 a share at a time when its shares were trading for $16.50 a share.

---

[18] The phrase "dividend puzzle" originates from Fischer Black, "The Dividend Puzzle," *Journal of Portfolio Management* (Winter 1976), pp. 5–8.

The tender offer may also be conducted as a ***Dutch auction*** in which the corporation specifies a minimum and a maximum price, soliciting bids from shareholders for any price within this range at which they are willing to sell their shares. After the corporation receives these bids, they pay all tendering shareholders the maximum price sufficient to buy back the number of shares they want. A Dutch auction reduces the chance that the firm pays a price higher than needed to acquire the shares.

To illustrate how a Dutch auction works, suppose a corporation wants to buy back 1 million shares of common stock currently trading for $25 a share. If the firm make a tender offer for the shares, it must specify the price it is willing to pay. The price must be higher than $25, or no one will be willing to sell back the shares. Because it is sometimes difficult to figure out just how much more to offer, the firm can use a Dutch auction. A Dutch auction sets the buying price for the item on the basis of bids.

For example, the firm could make a Dutch auction tender offer, specifying that it wants to buy back 1,000,000 shares, offering to buy at a minimum price of $26 and a maximum price of $29. Shareholders who want to tender their shares—sell them back to the corporation—specify how many shares they are willing to sell and at what price. Suppose the shareholders respond as follows:

Number of Shares Willing to Tender	Specified Price
200,000	$26
600,000	$27
200,000	$28
400,000	$29

The corporation will accept the first 1,000,000 shares in order of price, paying only one price and not higher than necessary to get that 1,000,000 shares. In this example, the corporation would pay $28 per share of the 1,000,000 shares. The shareholders that specified they would tender their shares at $29 per share are out of luck. The shareholders who bid $26 and $27 are paid more than the price at which they were willing to tender.

Open Market Purchases A corporation may also buy back shares directly in the open market. This involves buying the shares through a broker. A corporation that wants to buy shares may have to spread its purchases over time so as not to drive the share's price up temporarily by buying large numbers of shares.

Targeted Share Repurchase The third method of repurchasing stock is to buy it from a specific shareholder. This involves direct negotiation between the corporation and the shareholder. This method is referred to as a *targeted block repurchase*, since there is a specific shareholder (the "target") and there are a larger number of shares (a "block) to be purchased at one time. Targeted block repurchases, also referred to as greenmail, were used in the 1980s to fight takeovers.

Reasons for Repurchasing Stock

Corporations repurchase their stock for a number of reasons. First, a repurchase is a way to distribute cash to shareholders at a lower cost to both the firm and the shareholders than dividends. If capital gains are taxed at rates lower than ordinary income, which is often the case with U.S. tax law, repurchasing is a lower cost way of distributing cash. However, since shareholders have different tax rates—especially when comparing corporate shareholders with individual shareholders—the benefit is mixed. Why? Because some shareholders are tax-free (e.g., pension funds), some shareholders are only taxed on a portion of dividends (e.g., corporations receiving dividends from other corporations), and some shareholders are taxed on the full amount of dividends (e.g., individual taxpayers).

Another reason to repurchase stock is to increase earnings per share. A firm that repurchases its shares increases its earnings per share simply because there are fewer shares outstanding after the repurchase. But there are two problems with this motive:

1. Cash is paid to the shareholders, so less cash is available for the corporation to reinvest in profitable projects.
2. Because there are fewer shares, the earnings pie is sliced in fewer pieces, resulting in higher earnings per share. The individual "slices" are bigger, but the pie itself remains the same size.

Looking at how share prices respond to gimmicks that manipulate earnings, we know that you cannot fool the market by playing an earnings per share game. The market can see through the earnings per share to what is really happening and that is that the firm will has less cash to invest.

Still another reason for stock repurchase is that it could tilt the debt-equity ratio so as to increase the value of the firm. By buying back stock—thereby reducing equity—the firm's assets are financed to a greater degree by debt. Does this seems wrong? It's not. To see this, suppose a corporation has the following balance sheet:

Assets $100 Debt $50
                       Equity $50

The corporation has financed 50% of its assets with debt, and 50% with equity. If this corporation uses $20 of its assets to buy back stock worth $20, its balance sheet will be:

Assets $80 Debt $50
                  Equity $30

It now finances 62.5% of its assets with debt and 37.5% with equity.

If financing the firm with more debt is good—that is, the benefits from deducting interest on debt outweigh the cost of increasing the risk of bankruptcy—repurchasing stock may increase the value of the firm. But there is the flip-side to this argument: Financing the firm with more debt may be bad if the risk of financial distress—difficulty paying legal obligations—outweighs the benefits from tax deductibility of interest. So, repurchasing shares from this perspective would have to be judged on a case-by-case basis to determine if it's beneficial or detrimental.

One more reason for a stock repurchase is that it reduces total dividend payments—without seeming to. If you cut down on the number of shares outstanding, you can still pay the same amount of dividends *per share*, but your *total* dividend payments are reduced. Suppose you pay a regular, quarterly dividend of $2.00 per share. If there are 1,000,000 shares of stock outstanding, your quarterly dividend payment is $2,000,000. If you repurchase 10% of the outstanding shares and keep the dividends per share the same, your total quarterly dividend payment is $2.00 times 900,000 shares, or $1,800,000. You have reduced your payment by $200,000, yet have not changed the dividends per share.

If the shares are correctly valued in the market (there is no reason to believe otherwise), the payment for the repurchased shares equals the reduction in the value of the firm—and the remaining shares are worth the same as they were before. In our example, the repurchase reduces the equity pie by 10%—and the smaller pie comprises 10% fewer shares. Suppose the shares traded at $50 per share before the repurchase—total equity is $50 times 1,000,000, or $50,000,000. If the firm buys back 10% of the shares—100,000 shares at $50 each—the value of the firm should decline by $5,000,000. This leaves equity worth $45,000,000. Split among the remaining 900,000 shares, the value per share is $50—the same as before the repurchase.

Some argue that a repurchase is a signal about future prospects. That is, by buying back the shares, the management is communicating to investors that the firm is generating sufficient cash to be able to buy back shares. But does this make sense? Not really. If the firm has profitable investment opportunities, the cash could be used to finance these investments, instead of paying it out to the shareholders.

A stock repurchase may also reduce agency costs by reducing the amount of cash the management has on hand. Similar to the argument we used for dividend payments, repurchasing shares reduces the amount of free cash flow and, hence, reduces the possibility that management will invest it unprofitably.

Repurchasing shares of a firm tends to shrink the firm: Cash is paid out and the value of the firm is smaller. Can repurchasing shares be consistent with wealth maximization? Yes.

If the best use of funds is to pay them out to shareholders, repurchasing shares maximizes shareholders' wealth. If the firm has no profitable investment opportunities, it is better for a firm to shrink by paying funds to the shareholders than to shrink by investing in lousy investments.

So how does the market react to a firm's intention to repurchase shares? A number of studies have looked at how the market reacts to such announcements. In general, the share price goes up when a firm announces it is going to repurchase its own shares.

It is difficult to identify the reason the market reacts favorably to such announcements since so many other things are happening at the same time. By piecing bits of evidence together, however, we see that it is likely that investors view the announcement of a repurchase as good news—a signal of good things to come.

SUMMARY

- Stock represents ownership in a corporation in units called shares. There are two types of stock: preferred and common. Both are forms of equity, but have different priorities with respect to their claim on the firm's income and assets.
- Part of shareholders' return is in the form of cash payments called dividends. Whether a corporation should pay dividends is debatable, given the higher tax rate on dividend income relative to capital gain income. Some believe that dividends serve a purpose: either providing information about the firm's future prospects or forcing the corporation to sell more securities to raise the money to pay the dividends.
- Common stock represents ownership that is last to receive any income and any assets if the firm is liquidated. If the firm is liquidated, common shareholders have to wait until all claimants, such as creditors and preferred shareholders, are satisfied before they receive anything.

- Common shareholders are the ultimate owners of the corporation and through corporate democracy, elect members of the board of directors and have a say in major issues that affect the firm. While the current system of corporate democracy is imperfect, the current movement in shareholders' rights may put this system back on track.
- Besides cash dividends, firms may distribute additional shares of stock to shareholders through a stock dividend or a stock split. While distributing additional shares does not change the value of the stock, the announcement of the distribution may provide information about management's expectations of the firm's future prospects.
- Corporations may repurchase their own shares, resulting in lesser tax consequences than distributing cash to shareholders in the form of a dividend. Corporations can repurchase shares in the open market, use a tender offer, or buy shares in a targeted block repurchase. Corporations can repurchase shares either to change their capital structure, reduce dividend payments, signal future prospects, or to reduce free cash flow.
- Common shareholders get a return from their investment in the form of dividends and any increase (or decrease) in the market value of their share. But dividends are not a sure thing. The corporation is not obligated to pay dividends to common shareholders.

QUESTIONS

1. What are the primary differences between common and preferred stock?
2. What is the role of the par value of a stock? If a stock has no par value, does this mean that it is worthless? Explain.
3. Explain why the numbers of shares of a corporation's stock may differ among authorized, issued, and outstanding shares.
4. List the advantages of being a publicly-held corporation. List the advantages of being to privately-held corporation. Why would a large, publicly-traded corporation such as RJR Nabisco go private? Why would it go public shortly thereafter?
5. What distinguishes a stock dividend from a stock split?
6. Why may a firm use a reverse stock split? How may a reverse stock split affect the market value of a firm's equity?
7. Describe the information provided in the board of director's declaration of a dividend. Who determines the ex-dividend date?
8. Explain how cumulative voting allows a minority shareholder representation on the board of directors.
9. Describe how a classified board of directors could be used to thwart or discourage a takeover of control of a corporation's board.

10. In a rights offering, the corporation gives shareholders the right to buy shares of the stock at a discount from the current market price. Why would a corporation offer a discount?

11. What are some of the problems with the current system of corporation democracy in the U.S.?

12. List the alternative rationale for paying dividends. For each rationale, determine whether the rationale favors or does not favor the payment of dividends.

13. If a firm has more cash than it needs for its profitable investment opportunities and wishes to pay this cash out to common shareholders, would you recommend the firm do this with a special cash dividend or by repurchasing stock? Explain your choice.

14. What is a tax clientele? What role does a tax clientele play in explaining dividend policies?

15. Explain how an increase in dividends per share may be interpreted as good news from the perspective of the shareholders. Explain how an increase in dividends per share may be interpreted as bad news from the perspective of the shareholders.

16. From the perspective of a shareholder, would you rather receive a 5% stock dividend or a $2.00 per share cash dividend? Explain.

17. If a firm pays a cash dividend and sells new shares of stock, both in the same year, does this make sense? Why?

18. What is a dividend reinvestment plan? From the perspective of shareholders, what are the advantages and disadvantages of participating in such a plan? From the perspective of the corporation, what are the advantages of offering such a plan?

19. If a firm makes a Dutch auction tender offer to repurchase shares and sets a range of prices of $20 to $25, with the current share price of $19, would you tender your shares? At what price would you tender your shares? Explain your decision.

20. The Foster Corporation has paid dividends on common stock over the ten years as follows:

Year	Dividends	Earnings
1994	$3,000	$5,000
1995	3,100	5,100
1996	3,200	4,500
1997	3,300	5,400
1998	3,500	5,500
1999	3,725	5,300
2000	3,975	5,200
2001	4,200	5,600
2002	4,500	5,800

During this ten-year period, there were 1,000 common shares outstanding.

a. What are the dividends per share for each year?

b. What is the dividend payout for each year?

c. How would you describe the dividend policy of Foster Corporation?

21. The Repo Corporation currently has 1 million common shares outstanding and have been paying a $1.00 dividend per share each quarter on their common shares. The Repo Corporation has decided to repurchase 10% of their common shares.

a. If they maintain their current dividend per share, how much will they be paying in dividends each quarter after the repurchase?

b. If they decide to keep the total dividend payments the same, what would be their new dividend per share?

22. The Linen Corporation currently has a stock price of $100 per share. What would be the expected price of the Linen stock under each of the following types of distributions:

a. a 2:1 stock split

b. a 100% stock dividend

c. a 4:1 stock split

d. a 50% stock dividend

23. Oak Corporation currently has 10 million common shares outstanding, trading at $2 per share. If Oak does a reverse split of 1:4, how many shares will be outstanding after this split? What price would you expect Oak shares to be trading at after this split?

24. The Fissure Corporation currently has 2 million common shares of stock outstanding that is trading at $80 per share. The board of directors has decided that the current price per share is too high, preventing many smaller investors from buying even lots of 100 shares. They have decided that a more attractive stock price would be around $40 per share.

a. If they decide to use a stock dividend to reduce the share price, what would be the size of the stock dividend that would reduce the share price to the desirable level?

b. If they decide to use a stock split to reduce the share price, what would be the size of the stock split that would reduce the share price to the desirable level?

25. Lowly Worm Corporation's common share price is currently around $5 per share. The board of directors have decided that a more respectable share price level is around $20. The board also realizes that in the company's current circumstance, share price is not expected to increase and cannot be increased other than with a reverse stock split. What size reverse split is necessary to increase the share price to the desirable level?

26. Calculate the stock dividend rate equivalent to each of the following stock splits: a. 1.5:1 b. 2:1 c. 3:1 d. 7:5
27. The dividend payout ratio for the Albany Company is 40%. Albany has 1 million shares outstanding, sales of $15 million, and a net profit margin of 5%. What is the amount of Albany's dividends per share?
28. Determine the ex-dividend date for each of the following record dates using the three-day delivery plan:
    a. Thursday, December 27, 2001
    b. Friday, July 10, 2001
    c. Monday, December 23, 2002
29. Calculate the stock split that is equivalent to each of the following stock dividend rates: a. 50% b. 100% c. 25%
30. The Bartlett Company currently has 10 million common shares outstanding and pays a dividend of $2.50 per share on its common stock. Bartlett wants to repurchase shares such that the total dollar amount of dividends is reduced by 25%, but its dividend per share remains at $2.50. How many shares of stock must Bartlett buy back?
31. The Midnight Expresso Company is considering repurchasing shares of stock. It currently pays out $1.40 in dividends each year on its 2.2 million common shares. Midnight's goal is to buy back sufficient shares of stock so that the same dollar amount is paid out in dividends, yet the dividends per share increase by 10% over its current level. How many shares must be repurchased to satisfy this goal?
32. SunTrek Corporation is the leading U. S. producer of equipment for aerospace. SunTrek currently has over 60,000 shares of common stock outstanding. The price of a share of stock at the end of 1997 was $42, but the stock traded in the range of $35 to $42 during 1997. SunTrek's earnings and dividends are expected to grow at a rate of 10% each year over the next few years. In anticipation of the increased rate of growth, SunTrek's board of directors declared a 2 for 1 stock split, effective in March, 1998.

    Its earnings per share (EPS) and dividends per share (DPS) over the period from 1983 through 1997 (based on pre-split shares) a represented in following table.

Year	DPS	EPS	Year	DPS	EPS	Year	DPS	EPS
1983	$0.38	$1.14	1988	0.45	$1.01	1993	$0.55	1.53
1984	0.43	1.31	1989	0.45	0.61	1994	0.55	1.51
1985	0.45	0.94	1990	0.45	0.46	1995	0.59	1.49
1986	0.45	0.61	1991	0.45	−0.68	1996	0.60	1.28
1987	0.45	0.91	1992	0.45	1.40	1997	0.60	1.46

a. Describe SunTrek's dividend policy in terms of dividends per share and dividend payout. Provide graphs to illustrate Sun-Trek's policy.

b. What stock price change, if any, do you expect when the shares are split in March of 1998? Explain.

c. Discuss the reasoning behind SunTrek's splitting its shares. Do you agree with SunTrek's board's decision to split the shares? Explain.

d. Suppose that there is a difference of opinion regarding SunTrek's future growth, with estimates of future growth ranging from 5% to 14%, and a median estimate of 10%. Considering the difference of opinion on SunTrek's future growth, discuss the wisdom of splitting its shares.

CHAPTER 17

Preferred Stock

In Chapter 16 we covered the basics of common stock, which is the residual ownership of a firm. Some firms also issue preferred stock: a form of ownership that has preference over common stock ownership.[1] Like common stock, preferred stock also represents equity.

Preferred shareholders have a claim on income and assets ahead of that of common shareholders. Preferred shareholders are promised a dividend that must be paid before common shareholders receive any dividends. The consequences of not paying the preferred stock dividend are not as drastic as not paying, say, interest on a debt obligation: Unlike creditors, preferred shareholders do not have a legal claim to receive the dividend—they cannot force the firm into bankruptcy for failure to pay.

However, if the business is liquidated—all the assets sold and the proceeds used to pay off all the creditors and owners—the preferred shareholders get all that's coming to them before common shareholders get anything. While few corporations are actually liquidated, this prior claim provides preferred shareholders with an advantage in the reorganization of firms in distress or bankruptcy. The Nationally Recognized Statistical Rating Organizations that assign ratings to corporate bond issues also rate preferred stock issues.

Just as there may be different classes of common stock, there also may be different classes of preferred stock, each with different dividend rates and rights. Some classes of preferred stock are junior to others—

---

[1] Preferred stock originated in the United States as a compromise around the end of the 19th century. Creditors of financially-troubled railroads were willing to take an equity interest in exchange for the unpaid debt that was owed them, but they wanted to make sure that their claims had seniority over the existing owners of the companies. Therefore, they settled on a type of equity share that had preference over the other, or common equity.

they wait in line behind owners of more senior preferred issues in the case of dividends and liquidation. Nevertheless, all preferred shareholders have preference over the common shareholders. While common stock is never issued with a maturity date, preferred stock may be issued with or without a maturity date. Preferred stock issued without a maturity date is called *perpetual preferred stock.*

Historically, utilities have been the major issuers of preferred stock, accounting for more than half of each year's issuance. Since 1985, major issuers have become financially oriented companies—finance companies, banks, thrifts, and insurance companies.

FEATURES OF PREFERRED STOCK

The issuer of preferred stock determines, with the help of an underwriter, the features of the preferred stock. These features affect the cost of the stock, the issuer's flexibility in changing its capital structure, and the role of preferred shareholders in the governance of the firm, among other things. We'll first take a look at the different preferred stock features that are typically used. Then we'll see how these features can be packaged together to provide a source of financing that meets the issuer's needs and the investors' preferences.

Par and Liquidation Values

Preferred stock may have a par value, though it is not legally required. Nevertheless, it is convenient to have some value for accounting purposes. Some corporations specify a *stated value* for the stock—an arbitrary value, say $100.

Each preferred stock does have a *liquidation value*—the amount that preferred shareholders are paid in the event the firm is liquidated and there remain sufficient assets to pay off this value. Often, the liquidating value is equal to the stated or par value of the stock.

Dividends

Although a firm's board of directors declares a dividend on its preferred stock, it is not a legal obligation. That is, if a firm does not pay the dividend, preferred shareholders cannot legally force payment. Nevertheless, almost all firms pay their specified preferred dividend. When dividends are paid, preferred dividends must be paid first; what remains may be paid as dividends to common shareholders. Most preferred share dividends are paid in cash, though a few preferred stock issues allow the firm issuing them to pay preferred dividends in cash or shares of stock.

Most preferred dividends are paid quarterly, though monthly, semi-annual, and annual dividends are possible. And preferred dividends may be paid at either a fixed or floating rate per period.

Fixed versus Adjustable Rate Dividends

Fixed dividends are expressed as either a percentage of the par value or a fixed dollar amount per period. If you own a preferred stock with a $100 par value and an 8% annual dividend, you receive $8.00 in dividends per year. This dividend also could have been stated simply as $8.00 per share annually. Before 1982, all publicly issued preferred stock was fixed-rate preferred stock.

In May 1982, the first *adjustable-rate preferred stock* (ARPS) issue was sold in the public market. The dividend rate on an adjustable-rate preferred stock is typically fixed quarterly and based on a predetermined spread from the highest of three points on the Treasury yield curve. The predetermined spread is called the *dividend reset spread*. Most adjustable-rate preferred stock is perpetual, with a floor (i.e., a minimum rate) and a cap (i.e., a maximum or ceiling rate) imposed on the dividend rate of most issues. This maximum and minimum dividend rate feature is referred to as a *collar*. From the perspective of the issuer, a collar's maximum ensures that the costs of financing with preferred stock are limited; from the perspective of the investors, a collar's minimum ensures that the return on the preferred stock has a lower limit.

The popularity of ARPS lost favor with investors when these securities began to sell below their par value—because the dividend reset rate is determined at the time of issuance, not by market forces. In 1984, a new type of preferred stock, *auction preferred stock*, was designed to overcome this problem. The dividend rate on auction preferred stock is set periodically, as with adjustable-rate preferred stock, but it is established through an auction process. (More specifically, it is through a Dutch auction.) Participants in the auction consist of current holders and potential buyers. The dividend rate that participants are willing to accept reflects current market conditions.

Remarketed preferred stock is preferred stock where the dividend rate is determined periodically by a remarketing agent who resets the dividend rate so that any preferred stock can be tendered at par and be resold (remarketed) at the original offering price. Typically, an investor has the choice of dividend resets every seven days or every 49 days.

Since the mid-1980s, auction preferred stock and remarketed preferred stock have become the dominant type of preferred stock issued.

Cumulative versus Noncumulative Dividends

Because there is no legal requirement to pay dividends to preferred shareholders, these shareholders want some assurance that their dividend is not skipped and the funds paid instead to common shareholders. Remember: The board of directors is, for the most part, elected by the common shareholders.

But there is a way to insure that common shareholders do not take advantage of the preferred shareholders' lack of legal claim on dividends. With *cumulative preferred stock*, any dividend not paid in one period must be paid the next period before any other dividend for that class of preferred stock is paid and before any common stock dividend is paid. With *noncumulative preferred stock*, any dividend not paid in a period is not paid in any other period—it is simply forgotten and does not affect the preferred or common dividend in any future period.

If a preferred stock dividend is cumulative, any dividend passed over in one period is carried over year to year. The passed over dividend is referred to as the *arrearage* and the preferred stock dividend is said to be in *arrears*. Most preferred stock issued in the United States is cumulative preferred stock.[2]

Participating versus Nonparticipating

Preferred shareholders may also share in the earnings of the firm, along with the common shareholders. If the preferred stock is *participating*, preferred shareholders receive a share of the earnings according some prescribed formula. This share of earnings is either in addition to a stated preferred dividend or varies according to the common stock dividend.

There are very few participating preferred stock issues. There are two reasons for this. First, preferred stock originated as a substitute for debt in cases where firms were in poor financial condition. Because the prospects for a firm issuing preferred stock are viewed as dim, so is the value of participating in the firm's future earnings. Preferred shareholders prefer to receive their promised dividend, rather than to gamble on an uncertain share of earnings.

Second, participating preferred stock reduces the benefits to common shareholders. If the firm does poorly, common shareholders are protected on the downside by limited liability. If the firm does well,

---

[2] Some companies can chalk up quite a bit of dividends in arrears. For example, Gulf States Utilities began to have cash problems in 1987 and stopped paying dividends on its 23 different preferred stock issues, as well as on its common stock. Preferred dividend arrearages grew to over $282 million over 24 quarters from 1987 until mid-1991 when Gulf States began to whittle down the arrearage.

common shareholders do not have to share the good earnings with others. They simply pay the bondholders and preferred shareholders the promised interest or dividend and no more, keeping the rest. Participating preferred shares would limit this leveraging effect.

One example is the participating preferred issued by Intermark, Inc., in 1986. The dividend on this preferred stock is not fixed, but rather is one cent per share less than the common stock dividend each quarter. The preferred shareholders of Intermark therefore have the opportunity to share in the earnings along with the common shareholders, and are not limited by a specified dividend rate or amount.

Convertibility

A preferred stock may be exchangeable for common shares—called a *convertible preferred stock*. Such a conversion feature gives the shareholder the right to convert the preferred shares into common shares at a predetermined rate of exchange. Convertible preferred stock specifies the *conversion ratio*, which is the number of shares of common stock that you get when you exchange a share of preferred stock for common stock.

The investor's decision to convert preferred stock into common stock requires weighing two factors: (1) the more certain preferred dividend against the less certain common stock dividend, and (2) the limited stock price appreciation of the preferred stock against the unlimited stock price appreciation of the common stock. In this decision, the investor considers the *market conversion price*, which is the market value of the common stock the investor would have if the preferred stock is exchanged with the common stock. The market conversion price is the conversion ratio multiplied by the market value of a share of common stock. The market conversion price is also referred to as the *conversion value*. If the market value of the convertible preferred stock exceeds the conversion value, we refer to this difference as the *conversion premium*.

To see how this conversion feature works, consider the convertible preferred stock issue in November of 1991 by Ford Motor Company. Ford sold 46 million shares of its convertible preferred stock for $50 each, for a total sale of $2.3 billion. The annual dividend yield is 8.4% of the $50 par, or $4.20 per share. Each preferred share is convertible into 1.6327 shares of Ford Motor Company Class A common stock.

When is it best for a shareholder to convert Ford preferred stock into Ford common stock? You have to weigh several factors. If you keep the Ford preferred stock, you have a stream of dividends of $4.20 each year, forever. While these dividends are not certain, you at least have preference over Ford's common shareholders, whose annual dividends could be (and have been) cut. But sticking with the preferred stock, you are limited in your profit potential—if the value of Ford Motor Co. common stock increases, the only way to share in this appreciation is to convert to the common stock. At the time the preferred stock was issued, Ford common stock was trading around $25.75 a share—so exchanging the preferred stock into common stock was not attractive then since the market conversion price was around $42. The preferred stock investor must decide between keeping the preferred stock, receiving $4.20 per share per year, and converting, receiving stock equal to the market conversion value, with the prospect of receiving the less certain common stock dividend. From the perspective of Ford, the investors' decision regarding conversion affects the amount of dividends that Ford pays each year.

Recently, several firms have issued *mandatory convertible preferred stock*. This type of stock requires the investor to convert the preferred shares into common shares within a specified period of time—say, five years. From the perspective of the issuer, mandatory convertible preferred is attractive since it releases the firm from the obligation to pay preferred dividends and is, in effect, a deferred issue of common shares. From the perspective of the investor, mandatory convertible preferred provides the opportunity to convert but only within a specific period and is much like a common stock with a set dividend rate for a limited period of time.

Callability

As explained earlier, preferred stock can be issued with or without a maturity date. If an issuer wants to retire a preferred stock issue, it can do so in one of the two following ways:

1. Buy the stock in the open market; or
2. Exchange preferred shares for another security, such as common shares, with a conversion feature.

If the stock is callable, the firm has another alternative: Exercise its right to call it—buy it—from the investor. *Callable preferred stock* gives the issuer the right to buy it from the shareholder at a predetermined price. If the issuing corporation wants to buy back the stock by using the call—referred to as *exercising* the call—they pay the specified *call price*. The call price may be a set amount forever, or may change according to a preset schedule. The call price is generally greater than or equal to the stated or par value of the stock.

Conversion and Call Features Are Options

Suppose a corporation issued preferred stock at $100 par that pays a 9% dividend. If the yield on the preferred stock falls to 5%, two things happen:

1. The price of the 9% preferred stock increases to $90.05 = $180.00, a premium of $80 above par value, and
2. The corporation sees an opportunity to issue preferred stock at a lower dividend cost.

Buying the preferred stock in the open market means that the corporation pays $180 for each share. But if the preferred stock is callable at, say, $104, the corporation can buy it back at $104 a share, retire the 9% preferred stock, and issue 5% preferred stock.

The call feature provides the issuer with flexibility. But it increases the risk to the investor since the stock may be called away just when it is looking really good. Since the call feature increases the risk to the investor, investors demand a greater return—and therefore a greater cost to the issuer—on callable preferred stock relative to noncallable preferred stock.

Voting Rights

The vast majority of preferred stock issues do not include voting rights. Instead, preferred shareholders generally have *contingent voting rights*—voting rights that become active only when the firm fails to pay the promised preferred stock dividend. Contingent voting rights may be designed in any manner. But the typical voting right is triggered once the dividends are in arrears and is limited to voting on representation on the board of directors and the issuance of other securities. For example, the New York Stock Exchange requires that all preferred stock issues have contingent voting rights that allow preferred shareholders the right to vote for at least two members of the board of directors as long as dividends are in arrears.

Sinking Funds

Because there is no legal obligation to pay the preferred dividend and because bondholders and other creditors get the first crack at a firm's income and liquidation rights, preferred shareholders want some assurance they will receive preferred stock dividends. A corporation can provide this assurance in the form of a sinking fund provision. In fact, almost all preferred stock has a sinking fund provision.

As we discussed in Chapter 15 in the context of long-term debt, a *sinking fund* is like a savings account. The corporation deposits funds with a trustee, who uses these funds to periodically retire preferred stock, buying it from shareholders at a specified price, the *sinking fund call price*. The trustee acquires these shares by either buying them in the open market—calling up a broker and buying the shares—or calling in the preferred stock at a specified sinking fund call price. The amount of the periodic retirement is predetermined, which may be specified in terms of the number of shares or the percentage of total shares to be retired each year. By retiring preferred stock periodically, the firm is better able to meet the dividend payments on the remaining preferred shares.

Packaging Features

A corporation may combine any of the features we just described into its preferred stock. If they hope to sell their preferred shares, they must package them in a way that is attractive to investors and at a reasonable cost.

Features that give the issuer flexibility, such as a call feature, introduce uncertainty for investors. Investors do not know when (or if) the firm will call in the issue. Because investors do not like risk, they will demand a greater return on callable preferred shares to compensate them for the additional risk implicit in its uncertainty. Providing a greater return increases the issuer's cost.

Features that give the investor something of additional value, such as a conversion feature, lower the issuers' cost. Investors are willing to accept a lower return in exchange for convertibility. And if investors are willing to accept a lower return, the issuer's cost of capital is lower.

And like common stock, dividends received by corporations are partially excluded from taxation. And because most of the investors in preferred stock are corporations, the dividend received deduction lowers the return demanded by investors, lowering the issuing corporation's cost of financing.

Packaging a new issue of preferred stock requires considering investors' need for greater returns and lower risk and the issuer's need for greater flexibility and lower costs.

CORPORATE USE OF PREFERRED STOCK

Preferred stock is generally considered the Wall Street wallflower. Seldom issued, preferred stock is usually associated with financially troubled firms. Recently, several major U.S. companies issued preferred stock as a source of additional equity capital. Examples of preferred stock issues in the 1990s include Ford Motor Company, RJR Nabisco Holdings, Kmart, and General Motors. These issues did not do much to change preferred stock's image, since these companies issued preferred stock at times when they were cash-poor or on the brink of a debt downgrade.

Why would a company issue preferred stock? One advantage of using preferred stock as a source of capital is that, in general, the firm must pay only a fixed amount in dividends, leaving the upside potential in earnings to be reaped by common shareholders. Another advantage is that the voting control of common shareholders is not diluted, as it would be if common shares were issued. Still another advantage is the cost of preferred stock. Preferred stock is considered less risky than common stock, therefore its cost to the issuer should be less than that of common stock. Relative to issuing debt, preferred stock is more expensive since the interest paid on debt is deductible for tax purposes and the dividends paid on preferred stock is not deductible.

Mitigating this cost somewhat is the fact that a large portion (currently 70%) of the dividends received by corporate owners of preferred stock is excluded from taxable income, which therefore reduces the yields that corporate investors demand on the stock For example, if Corporation A owns the preferred stock of Corporation B, then only $30 of each $100 that A receives in dividends from B will be taxed at A's marginal tax rate. The purpose of this provision is to mitigate the effect of the double taxation of corporate earnings. There are two implications of this tax treatment of preferred stock dividends. First, the major buyers of preferred stock are the treasurers of corporations seeking tax-advantaged investments. Second, the cost of preferred stock issuance is lower than it would be in the absence of the tax provision, because the tax benefits are passed through to the issuer by the willingness of buyers to accept a lower dividend rate.

A disadvantage of preferred stock, relative to common stock, is that it has a claim on income and assets of the firm that is senior to that of common shareholders. The firm must pay the dividends owed preferred shareholders before it pays dividends to common shareholders.

Another disadvantage of using preferred stock as a source of capital is the connotation associated with these issuing firms. Historically, preferred stock issuances have been made by firms that were in financial difficulty. This is confirmed by looking at what happens to a firm's common stock price when it announces an issue of preferred stock: The price of the issuer's common shares tends to go down. For example, when RJR Nabisco Holdings announced a planned offering of $2 billion of preferred stock in 1994, its common stock price fell 8.5%. A portion of this fall in price may be attributed to the possible dilution of existing common shares since the planned preferred shares are convertible. However, the common stock price drop may also be attributed to the relatively high dividend yield needed to convince investors to buy the preferred stock and to the message conveyed by the firm that it was unable to successfully offer new common shares directly to the public.

SUMMARY

- Preferred stock has some of the features of common stock—a perpetual security with dividends. But preferred stock also shares some of the features of long-term debt, such as convertibility, callability, and sinking funds. There is some preferred stock with a maturity date.
- Preferred dividends can be specified a number of ways: fixed versus adjustable, cumulative versus noncumulative, and participating versus nonparticipating. The most common type of preferred stock with respect to dividend feature is auction preferred stock and remarketing preferred stock.
- Similar to notes and bonds, preferred stock can be convertible into common stock and callable.
- Unlike common shareholders, preferred shareholders do not have a say in the corporation. Only in extreme circumstances do preferred shareholders vote for representation on the board of directors. Therefore, features such as cumulative dividends and contingent voting rights have developed to protect the preferred shareholders' rights.
- The major issuers of preferred stock are financially oriented corporations.

QUESTIONS

1. Explain why a corporation would issue preferred stock rather than a debt security or common shares.
2. Why would a corporate treasurer prefer to buy preferred shares of another corporation rather than a bond or common shares?
3. Suppose the Multi-Facet Corporation issues a convertible callable sinking fund preferred stock.
   a. From the perspective of the issuer, which of these features contributes to financing flexibility?
   b. From the perspective of the investor, which features contribute to the uncertainty of the share's value?
4. Suppose ABC Corporation is issuing convertible, callable, fixed-rate preferred stock.
   a. What option does ABC Corporation have after it issues this stock?
   b. What option does the investor buying this stock have?
5. Some preferred stock issues give the preferred shareholders rights to vote if dividends are in arrears.
   a. Why is this provision necessary?
   b. Explain what may happen if the preferred shareholders did not have this right.

6. List the advantages and disadvantages of using preferred stock as a source of capital.

7. Why are corporate treasurers the main buyers of preferred stock?

8. What was the reason for the popularity of auction and remarketed preferred stock?

9. The Dawes Corporation has 1 million shares of 9% cumulative preferred stock outstanding with a stated value of $100 per share. If Dawes does not pay dividends for two years, what will be the amount of arrearage?

10. The Manny-Hanny Corporation issued 10.96% preferred stock in 1996 with a par value of $25. A total of 4 million shares are outstanding. Calculate the total amount of dividends that Manny-Hanny must pay each year and the annual amount of dividends per share.

11. The Insull Electric Company issued $5 million of 8.25% $50 par preferred shares in 1997. Calculate (a) the total amount of dividends paid on this issue per year and (b) the annual amount of dividends per share.

12. Suppose you own 1,000 shares of STU Corporation 10% convertible preferred stock. If each preferred share is convertible into 40 common shares, what is the conversion value of your 1,000 preferred shares if the common stock is trading at:
   a. $20 per share?
   b. $30 per share?
   c. $40 per share?

13. The Top Down Corporation has 1 million callable convertible preferred shares outstanding with a par value of $100 and a dividend rate of 5% per year, paid quarterly. The shares are callable at $105 per share and are convertible into 4 common shares.
   a. What is the dividend payment on preferred shares each quarter?
   b. Suppose Top Down determines that they can issue preferred stock that pays 3% per year. What are Top Down's possible courses of action?
   c. Suppose the common stock is currently trading at $30 per share and the preferred stock is trading at $150 per share. Is it attractive to convert to common stock? Explain.

14. The Webb Company issued $100 par preferred stock with a dividend rate of 8.5%. Each share is automatically converted into two common shares at the end of three years. The common shares of the Webb Company currently trade at $50 per share and this period's common share dividend is $1.85. If investors require a return of 12% on shares of similar risk, what is the value of a share of Webb preferred stock? Assume that dividends are paid at the end of each year.

15. The George Corporation is considering raising new funds by either issuing preferred stock or issuing additional common shares. The preferred stock alternative consists of issuing $20 million of $25 par, 5% preferred stock. The common stock alternative consists of issuing 1 million new shares at $20 per share. The George Corporation currently has 4 million shares outstanding. The expected net profits of the George Corporation for the next few years are the following:

Year	Net Profit
One year from now	$5.4 million
Two years from now	6.0 million
Three years from now	4.2 million
Four years from now	5.0 million

Calculate George's earnings available for common stock and earnings per share for each year and each alternative financing arrangement.

CHAPTER 18

Capital Structure

A business invests in new plant and equipment to generate additional revenues and income—the basis for its growth. One way to pay for investments is to generate capital from the firm's operations. Earnings generated by the firm belong to the owners and can either be paid to them—in the form of cash dividends—or plowed back into the firm. The owners' investment in the firm is referred to as *owners' equity* or, simply, *equity*. If management plows earnings back into the firm, the owners expect it to be invested in projects that will enhance the value of the firm and, hence, enhance the value of their equity.

But earnings may not be sufficient to support *all* profitable investment opportunities. In that case the firm is faced with a decision: Forgo profitable investment opportunities or raise additional capital. A firm can raise new capital either by borrowing or by selling additional ownership interests or both (see Exhibit 18.1).

DEBT VERSUS EQUITY

The combination of debt and equity used to finance a firm's projects is referred to as its *capital structure*. The capital structure of a firm is some mix of debt, internally generated equity, and new equity. But what is the right mixture?

The best capital structure depends on several factors. If a firm finances its activities with debt, the creditors expect the amount of the interest and principal—fixed, legal commitments—to be paid back as promised. Failure to pay may result in legal actions by the creditors.

EXHIBIT 18.1   Financing the Firm

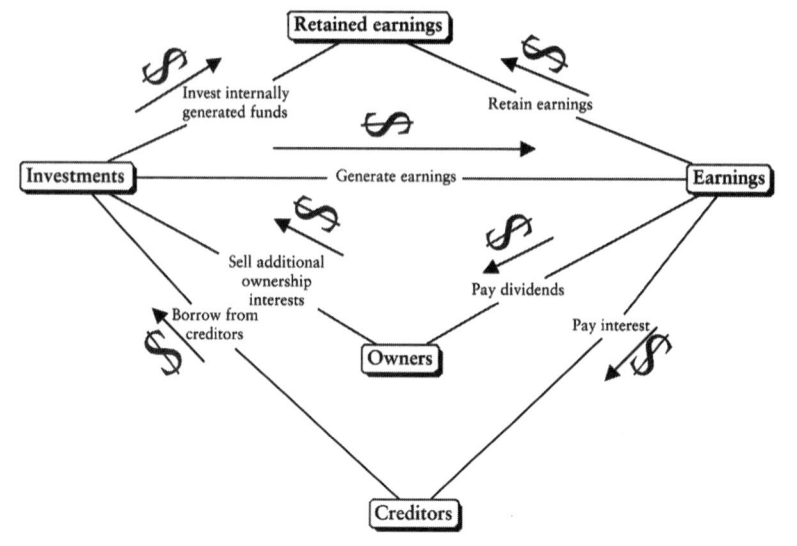

Suppose you borrow $100 and promise to repay the $100 plus $5 in one year. Consider what may happen when you invest the $100:

■ If you invest the $100 in a project that produces $120, you pay the lender the $105 you owe and keep the $15 profit.
■ If your project produces $105 back, you pay the lender $105 and keep nothing.
■ If your project produces $100, you pay the lender $105, with $5 coming out of your personal funds.

So if you reinvest the funds and get a return more than the $5 (the cost of the funds), you can keep all the profits. But if you get a return of $5 or less, the lender *still* gets her or his $5 back. This is the basic idea behind *financial leverage*—the use of financing that has a fixed, but limited payments.

If the firm has abundant earnings, the owners reap all that remains of the earnings after the creditors have been paid. If earnings are low, the creditors still *must* be paid what they are due, leaving the owners nothing out of the earnings.

Failure to pay interest or principal as promised may result in financial distress. *Financial distress* is the condition where a firm makes decisions under pressure to satisfy its legal obligations to its creditors. These decisions may not be in the best interests of the owners of the firm.

With equity financing there is no obligation. Though the firm may choose to distribute funds to the owners in the form of cash dividends, there is no legal requirement to do so. Furthermore, interest paid on debt is deductible for tax purposes, whereas dividend payments are not tax deductible.

One measure of the extent debt is used to finance a firm is the *debt ratio*, the ratio of debt to equity:

$$\text{Debt ratio} = \frac{\text{Debt}}{\text{Equity}} \tag{18-1}$$

The greater the debt ratio, the greater the use of debt for financing operations, relative to equity financing.

Another measure is the *debt-to-assets ratio*, which is the extent to which the assets of the firm are financed with debt:

$$\text{Debt-to-assets ratio} = \frac{\text{Debt}}{\text{Assets}} \tag{18-2}$$

There is a tendency for firms in some industries to use more debt than others. We see this looking at the capital structure for companies in different industries in Exhibit 18.2, where the proportion of assets financed with debt and equity are shown graphically. We can make some generalizations about differences in capital structures across industries:

- Industries that are more reliant upon research and development for new products and technology—for example, pharmaceutical companies—tend to have lower debt-to-asset ratios than firms without such research and development needs.
- Industries that require a relatively heavy investment in fixed assets, such as shoe manufacturers, tend to have lower debt-to-asset ratios.

It is also interesting to see how debt ratios compare among industries. For example, the electric utility industry has a higher use of debt than the malt beverage industry. Yet within each industry there is variation of debt ratios. For example, within the beverage industry, Cott Corporation, maker of retail-brand soft drinks, has a much higher portion of debt in its capital structure than, say, the Coca-Cola Company.

Why do some industries tend to have firms with higher debt ratios than other industries? By examining the role of financial leveraging, financial distress, and taxes, we can explain some of the variation in debt ratios among industries. And by analyzing these factors, we can explain how the firm's value may be affected by its capital structure.

EXHIBIT 18.2   Proportions of Capital from Debt and Equity, 2001

Panel A: Beverage Industry

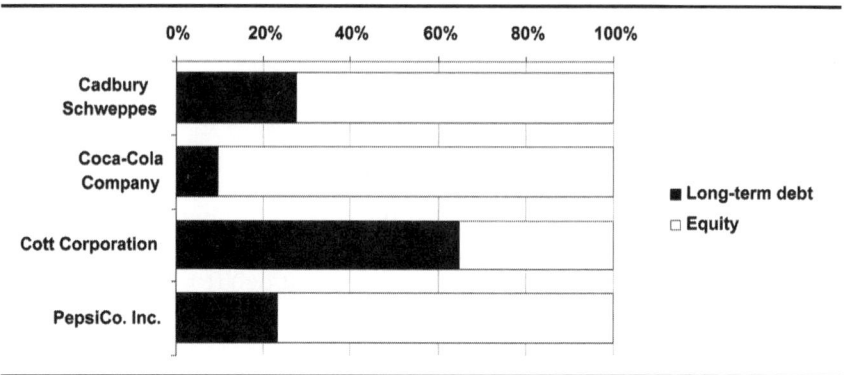

Panel B: Shoe Manufacturers

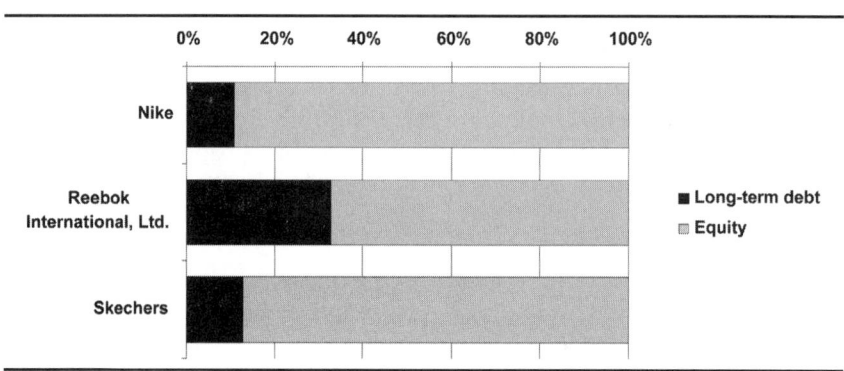

Panel C: Electric Utilities

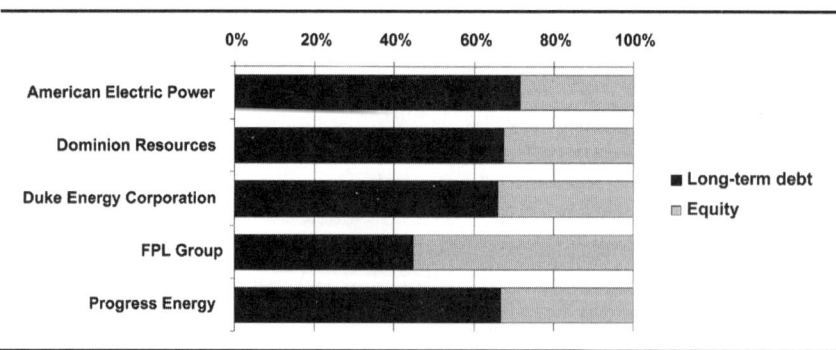

Exhibit 18.2 (Continued)

Panel D: Pharmaceutical Companies

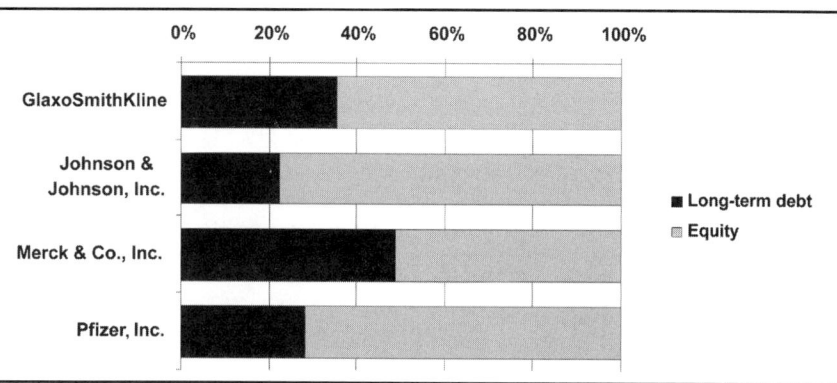

Source: Various company annual reports, 2001

CAPITAL STRUCTURE AND FINANCIAL LEVERAGE

Debt and equity financing create different types of obligations for the firm. Debt financing obligates the firm to pay creditors interest and principal—usually a fixed amount—when promised. If the firm earns more than necessary to meet its debt payments, it can either distribute the surplus to the owners or reinvest.

Equity financing does *not* obligate the firm to distribute earnings. The firm may pay dividends or repurchase stock from the owners, but there is *no* obligation to do so.

The fixed and limited nature of the debt obligation affects the risk of the earnings to the owners. Consider Capital Corporation that has $20,000 of assets, all financed with equity. There are 1,000 shares of Capital Corporation stock outstanding, valued at $20 per share. The firm's current balance sheet is simple:

		Capital Corporation	
		Balance Sheet	
Assets	$20,000	Liabilities	$0
		Equity (1,000 shares)	20,000

Suppose Capital Corporation has investment opportunities requiring $10,000 of new capital. Further suppose Capital Corporation can raise the new capital either of three ways:

EXHIBIT 18.3   Capital Corporation's Projected Balance Sheet for Alternative Financing

ALTERNATIVE 1:	$10,000 EQUITY, $0 DEBT		
Assets	$30,000	Liabilities	$0
		Equity (1,500 shares)	$30,000
ALTERNATIVE 2:	$5,000 EQUITY, $5,000 DEBT		
Assets	$30,000	Liabilities	$5,000
		Equity (1,250 shares)	$25,000
ALTERNATIVE 3:	$0 EQUITY, $10,000 DEBT		
Assets	$30,000	Liabilities	$10,000
		Equity (1,000 shares)	$20,000

Alternative 1:   Issue $10,000 equity (500 shares of stock at $20 per share)

Alternative 2:   Issue $5,000 of equity (250 shares of stock at $20 per share) and borrow $5,000 with an annual interest of 5% and

Alternative 3:   Borrow $10,000 with an annual interest of 5%

It may be unrealistic to assume that the interest rate on the debt in Alternative 3 will be the same as the interest rate for Alternative 2 since in Alternative 3 there is more credit risk. For purposes of illustrating the point of leverage, however, let's keep the interest rate the same.

The balance sheet representing each financing method is shown in Exhibit 18.3. The only difference between the three alternative means of financing is with respect to how the assets are financed:

Alternative 1:   all equity
Alternative 2:   ⅙ debt, ⅚ equity
Alternative 3:   ⅓ debt, ⅔ equity

Stated differently, the debt ratio and the debt-to-asset ratio of Capital Corporation under each alternative is:

Financing Alternative	Debt Ratio or Debt-to-Equity Ratio	Debt-to-Assets Ratio
1	$\dfrac{\$0}{\$30,000} = 0.000$ or 0%	$\dfrac{\$0}{\$30,000} = 0.000$ or 0%
2	$\dfrac{\$5,000}{\$25,000} = 0.200$ or 20%	$\dfrac{\$5,000}{\$30,000} = 0.167$ or 16.7%
3	$\dfrac{\$10,000}{\$20,000} = 0.500$ or 50%	$\dfrac{\$10,000}{\$30,000} = 0.333$ or 33.3%

How can managers interpret these ratios? Let's look at Alternative 2. The debt ratio of 20% tells us that the firm finances its assets using $1 of debt for every $5 of equity. The debt-to-assets ratio means that 16.7% of the assets are financed using debt or, in other words, almost 17 cents of every $1 of assets is financed with debt.

Suppose Capital Corporation has $4,500 of operating earnings. This means it has a $4,500/$30,000 = 15% return on assets (ROA = 15%). And suppose there are no taxes. What are the earnings per share (EPS) under the different alternatives?

	Alternative 1: $10,000 Equity	Alternative 2: $5,000 Equity and $5,000 Debt	Alternative 3: $10,000 Debt
Operating earnings	$4,500	$4,500	$4,500
Less interest expense	0	500	1,000
Net income	$4,500	$4,000	$3,500
Number of shares	÷ 1,500	÷ 1,250	÷ 1,000
Earnings per share	$3.00	$3.20	$3.50

Suppose that the return on assets is 10% instead of 15%. Then,

	Alternative 1: $10,000 Equity	Alternative 2: $5,000 Equity and $5,000 Debt	Alternative 3: $10,000 Debt
Operating earnings	$3,000	$3,000	$3,000
Less interest expense	0	500	1,000
Net income	$3,000	$2,500	$2,000
Number of shares	÷ 1,500	÷ 1,250	÷ 1,000
Earnings per share	$2.00	$2.00	$2.00

If you are earning a return that is the same as the cost of debt, 10%, the earnings per share are not affected by the choice of financing.

Now suppose that the return on assets is 5%. The net income under each alternative is:

	Alternative 1: $10,000 Equity	Alternative 2: $5,000 Equity and $5,000 Debt	Alternative 3: $10,000 Debt
Operating earnings	$1,500	$1,500	$1,500
Less interest expense	0	500	1,000
Net income	$1,500	$1,000	$500
Number of shares	÷ 1,500	÷ 1,250	÷ 1,000
Earnings per share	$1.00	$0.80	$0.50

If the return on assets is 15%, Alternative 3 has the highest earnings per share, but if the return on assets is 5%, Alternative 3 has the lowest earnings per share.

You cannot say ahead of time what next period's earnings will be. So what can you do? Well, you can make projections of earnings under different economic climates, and make judgments regarding the likelihood that these economic climates will occur.

Comparing the results of each of the alternative financing methods provides information on the effects of using debt financing. As more debt is used in the capital structure, the greater the "swing" in EPS.

Summarizing the EPS under each financing alternative and each economic climate:

	Earnings per Share under Different Economic Conditions		
Financing Alternative	Slow (ROA = 5%)	Normal (ROA = 10%)	Boom (ROA = 15%)
1. $10,000 equity	$1.00	$2.00	$3.00
2. $5,000 equity, $5,000 debt	$0.80	$2.00	$3.20
3. $10,000 debt	$0.50	$2.00	$3.50

When debt financing is used instead of equity (Alternative 3), the owners don't share the earnings—all they must do is pay their creditors the interest on debt. But when equity financing is used instead of debt (Alternative 1), the owners must share the increased earnings with the additional owners, diluting their return on equity and earnings per share.

EXHIBIT 18.4   Capital Corporation's Earnings per Share for Different Operating Earnings for Each of the Three Financing Alternatives

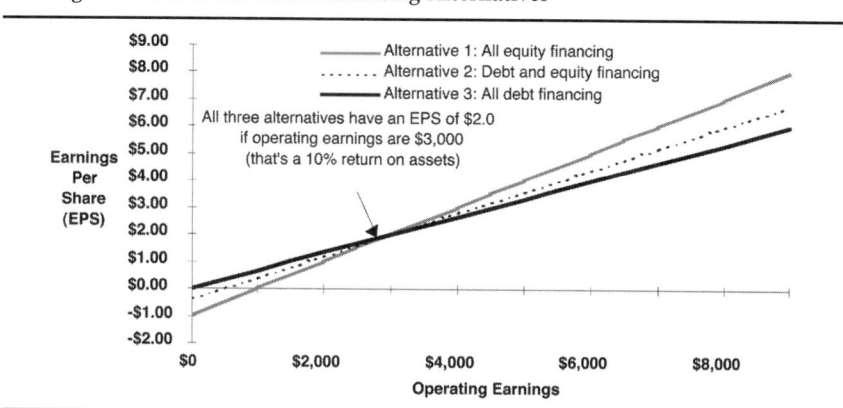

FINANCIAL LEVERAGE AND RISK

The use of financial leverage (that is, the use of debt in financing a firm), increases the range of possible outcomes for owners of the firm. As we saw previously, the use of debt financing relative to equity financing increases both the up-side and down-side potential earnings for owners. In other words, financial leverage increases the risk to owners. Now that we understand the basics of leverage, let's quantify its effect on the risk of earnings to owners.

The Leverage Effect

Equity owners can reap most of the rewards through financial leverage when their firm does well. But they may suffer a downside when the firm does poorly. What happens if earnings are down so low that they cannot cover interest payments? Interest must be paid no matter how low the earnings. How can money be obtained with which to pay interest when earnings are insufficient? It can be obtained in three ways:

- by reducing the assets in some way, such as using working capital needed for operations or selling buildings or equipment;
- by taking on more debt obligations; or
- by issuing more shares of stock.

Whichever the firm chooses, the burden ultimately falls upon the owners.
This leveraging effect is illustrated in Exhibit 18.4 for Capital Corporation. Note that we have broadened the number of possible return on asset outcomes ranging from 0% to 30%. Alternative 3 provides for

the most upside potential for the equity holders, it also provides for the most downside potential as well. Hence, Alternative 1—all equity—offers the more conservative method of financing operations.

The three alternatives have identical earnings per share when there is a 10% return on assets. Capital Corporation's 10% return on assets is referred to as the **EPS indifference point**: the return where the earnings per share (EPS) are the same under the financing alternatives. Above a 10% return on assets (that is, above operating earnings of $3,000), Alternative 3 offers the most to owners. But Alternative 3 also has the most downside potential, producing the worst earnings to owners below this 10% return on assets.

Quantifying the Leverage Effect

We can see the effects of financial leverage by putting numbers to this uncertainty of possible outcomes. Consider once again the three return on assets outcomes—5%, 10%, and 15%—but this time we are attaching probabilities; we're guessing (somehow) that each of these will happen. Suppose that the probability associated with each outcome is:

Economic Climate	Return on Assets	Probability
Slow	5%	20%
Normal	10%	60%
Boom	15%	20%

We can measure the risk associated with each alternative by calculating the standard deviation of the possible earnings per share. The larger the standard deviation, the greater the uncertainty associated with the alternative.[1]

The calculations of the expected EPS, the standard deviation of EPS, and the coefficient of variation are shown in Exhibit 18.5 for each of the three alternative financing arrangements. The expected values and corresponding standard deviations calculated in Exhibit 18.5 are summarized as follows:

Financing Alternative	Expected EPS	Standard Deviation of EPS
1. $10,000 equity	$2.00	$0.6325
2. $5,000 equity, $5,000 debt	$2.00	$0.8944
3. $10,000 debt	$2.00	$0.9487

---

[1] In the Capital Corporation example, the expected values for alternatives are the same. However, if we are trying to compare risk among different probability distributions that have different expected values, we need to scale the standard deviation to make each comparable. We do this dividing the standard deviation by the expected value, giving us a scaled down value of dispersion, referred to as the *coefficient of variation*. The larger the coefficient of variation, the greater the risk.

EXHIBIT 18.5   Capital Corporation's Expected Earnings per Share and Standard Deviation of Possible Earnings per Share Associated with Alternative Financing

ALTERNATIVE 1: $10,000 EQUITY, $0 DEBT

EPS	Probability	EPS × Probability	Deviation from Expected EPS	Deviation Squared	Squared Deviation × Probability
$1.00	20%	$0.20	−$1.00	1.0000	0.2000
2.00	60%	1.20	0.00	0.0000	0.0000
3.00	20%	0.60	1.00	1.0000	0.2000
	E(EPS) =	$2.00		σ^2(EPS) =	0.4000

σ(EPS) = $0.6325

ALTERNATIVE 2: $5,000 EQUITY, $5,000 DEBT

EPS	Probability	EPS × Probability	Deviation from Expected EPS	Deviation Squared	Squared Deviation × Probability
$0.80	20%	$0.16	−$1.60	2.5600	0.5120
2.00	60%	1.20	0.00	0.0000	0.0000
3.20	20%	0.64	1.20	1.4400	0.2880
	E(EPS) =	$2.00		σ^2(EPS) =	0.8000

σ(EPS) = $0.8944

ALTERNATIVE 3: $0 EQUITY, $10,000 DEBT

EPS	Probability	EPS × Probability	Deviation from Expected EPS	Deviation Squared	Squared Deviation × Probability
$0.50	20%	$0.10	−$1.50	2.2500	0.4500
2.00	60%	1.20	0.00	0.0000	0.0000
3.50	20%	0.70	1.50	2.2500	0.4500
	E(EPS) =	$2.00		σ^2(EPS) =	0.9000

σ(EPS) = $0.9487

Notes: E(EPS) = Expected earnings per share
$\quad\quad$ σ^2(EPS) = Variance of earnings per share
$\quad\quad$ σ(EPS) = Standard deviation of earnings per share

It happens that each alternative has the same expected EPS, but the standard deviations differ. The all-debt financing (Alternative 3) results in the highest standard deviation of EPS. This result supports the notion that financial leverage increases the returns to owners, but also increases the risk associated with the returns to owners.

CAPITAL STRUCTURE AND TAXES

We've seen how the use of debt financing increases the risk to owners; the greater the use of debt financing (vis-à-vis equity financing), the greater the risk. Another factor to consider is the role of taxes. In the U.S., income taxes play an important role in a firm's capital structure decision because the payments to creditors and owners are taxed differently. In general, interest payments on debt obligations are deductible for tax purposes, whereas dividends paid to shareholders are not deductible. This bias affects a firm's capital structure decision.

In this section, we look at the capital structure decision. At first, we look at the base-case in which individuals and corporations have the same access to capital markets. In this case there are no tax advantages to debt financing (vis-à-vis equity financing), and both debt and equity securities are perfect substitutes from the perspective of the investor. Then we'll take a look at what happens once we add a little realism into the decision.

The M&M Model

The value of a firm—meaning the value of all its assets—is equal to the sum of its liabilities and its equity (the ownership interest). Does the way we finance the firm's assets affect the value of the firm and hence the value of its owners' equity? It depends.

The basic framework for the analysis of capital structure and how taxes affect it was developed by two Nobel Prize winning economists, Franco Modigliani and Merton Miller.[2] Modigliani and Miller (M&M) reasoned that if the following conditions hold, the value of the firm is not affected by its capital structure:

Condition #1:   Individuals and corporations are able to borrow and lend at the same terms (referred to as "equal access").

Condition #2:   There is no tax advantage associated with debt financing (relative to equity financing).

---

[2] Franco Modigliani and Merton H. Miller, "The Cost of Capital, Corporation Finance, and the Theory of Investment," *American Economic Review* (June 1958).

Condition #3: Debt and equity trade in a market where assets that are substitutes for one another trade at the same price. This is referred to as a *perfect market*. If assets are traded in a perfect market, assets with the same risk and return characteristics trade for the same price.

Under the first condition, individuals can borrow and lend on the same terms as business entities. Therefore, if individuals are seeking a given level of risk, they can either (1) borrow or lend on their own or (2) invest in a business that borrows or lends. In other words, if an individual wants to increase the risk of her investment, she could invest in a company that uses debt to finance its assets. Or, the individual could invest in a firm with no financial leverage and take out a personal loan—increasing her own financial leverage.

The second condition isolates the effect of financial leverage. If deducting interest from earnings is allowed in the analysis, it would be difficult to figure out what effect financial leverage itself has on the value of the firm.

The third condition insures that assets are priced according to their risk and return characteristics.

Under these conditions, the value of Capital Corporation is the same, no matter which of the three financing alternatives it chooses.[3] The *total* income to owners and creditors is the same. For example, if the return on assets is expected to be 15%, the *total* income to owners and creditors is $4,500 under each alternative:

Financing Alternative	Income to Owners	Income to Creditors	Total Income to Owners and Creditors
1. $10,000 equity	$4,500	$ 0	$4,500
2. $5,000 equity, $5,000 debt	$4,000	$ 500	$4,500
3. $10,000 debt	$3,500	$1,000	$4,500

Assume that the expected return on assets is 15%, for each period, forever. It follows that the value of Capital Corporate can be determined using the formula for the valuation of a perpetuity, $PV = CF/r$. Expressing this in terms of the value of the firm:

$$\text{Value of the firm} = \frac{\text{Expected earnings per period}}{\text{Discount rate}}$$

---

[3] The Modigliani and Miller models are explained within in this chapter through numerical examples.

The Capitalization Rate

The discount rate is referred to as the *capitalization rate*, which is the discount rate that translates future earnings into a current value. The capitalization rate reflects the uncertainty associated with the expected earnings in the future. The more uncertain the future earnings, the less a dollar of future income is worth today and the greater the capitalization rate.

But the uncertainty regarding the earnings on the assets is not affected by how the assets are financed. How the assets are financed affects who gets what.

Assume the appropriate discount rate for Capital Corporation's future income is 15%. Then:

$$\text{Value of Capital Corporation} = \frac{\$4,500}{0.15} = \$30,000$$

Because there are no creditors to share with in the case of all-equity financing (Alternative 1), the value of equity for Capital Corporation is the present value of the earnings stream of $4,500 per period discounted at 15%, or $30,000. However, the value of Capital Corporation with debt financing (Alternatives 2 and 3), is a bit more difficult.

In the case of Alternatives 2 and 3, Capital Corporation's owners view their future earnings streams as more risky than in the case of no debt. Hence, the discount rate should be higher, reflecting the debt used.

Modigliani and Miller show that the discount rate for the earnings to equity owners is higher when there is the use of debt and the greater the debt the higher the discount rate. Specifically, they show that the discount rate of the earnings to owners is equal to the discount rate of a firm with no financial leverage plus the compensation for bearing risk appropriate to the amount of debt in the capital structure.

The Risk Premium

The compensation for bearing risk, as reasoned by Modigliani and Miller, should be the risk premium weighted by the relative use of debt in the capital structure. The *risk premium* is the difference between the discount rate for the net income to owners and the discount rate on earnings to creditors (the interest), which is assumed to be risk free. Interest is paid to creditors no matter how well or how poorly the firm is doing; hence, it is considered risk free to creditors. And the greater the use of debt, the greater the risk premium.

Let r_e be the discount rate for a risky earnings to owners and let r_d be the discount rate for risk-free debt earnings. The risk premium is equal to $r_e - r_d$ and the discount rate for the earnings to owners is:

$$\text{Discount rate} = r_e + (r_e - r_d)\left(\frac{\text{debt}}{\text{equity}}\right) \qquad (18\text{-}3)$$

In the case of the Capital Corporation, the equity discount rate for the financing alternatives is calculated by adjusting the discount rate of the earnings stream, $r_e = 15\%$, for risk associated with financial leveraging. If the interest rate on debt, r_d, is 10%, we can analyze our three alternatives as follows:

Alternative 1: $10,000 equity

$$\text{Discount rate} = 0.15 + (0.15 - 0.10)\frac{\$0}{\$30,000} = 0.15 \text{ or } 15\%$$

Alternative 2: $5,000 equity, $5,000 debt

$$\text{Discount rate} = 0.15 + (0.15 - 0.10)\frac{\$5,000}{\$25,000} = 0.16 \text{ or } 16\%$$

Alternative 3: $10,000 debt

$$\text{Discount rate} = 0.15 + (0.15 - 0.10)\frac{\$10,000}{\$20,000} = 0.175 \text{ or } 17.5\%$$

The value of Capital Corporation's equity under each alternative is calculated by valuing the earnings to the owners stream using the appropriate capitalization rate.

Alternative 1: Value of equity $= \dfrac{\$4,500}{0.15} = \$30,000$

Alternative 2: Value of equity $= \dfrac{\$4,000}{0.16} = \$25,000$

Alternative 3: Value of equity $= \dfrac{\$3,500}{0.175} = \$20,000$

Summarizing,

Financing Alternative	Equity Discount Rate (%)	Value of Debt	Value of Equity	Total Value
1	15	$0	$30,000	$30,000
2	16	$5,000	$25,000	$30,000
3	17.5	$10,000	$20,000	$30,000

Modigliani and Miller show that the value of the firm depends on the earnings of the firm, *not* on how the firm's earnings are divided between creditors and shareholders. In other words, the value of the firm—the "pie"—is not affected by how you slice it.

An implication of the Modigliani and Miller analysis is that the use of debt financing increases the expected future earnings to owners. But it also increases the risk of these earnings and, hence, increases the discount rate investors use to value these future earnings. Modigliani and Miller reason that the effect that the increased expected earnings have on the value of equity is offset by the increased discount rate applied to these riskier earnings.

Interest Deductibility and Capital Structure

The use of debt has a distinct advantage over financing with stock, thanks to Congress. The Internal Revenue Code (IRC), written by Congress, allows interest paid on debt to be deducted by the paying corporation in determining its taxable income.[4]

This deduction represents a form of a government subsidy of financing activities. By allowing interest to be deducted from taxable income, the government is sharing the firm's cost of debt. To see how this subsidy works, compare two firms: Firm U (unlevered) and Firm L (levered). Suppose both have the same $5,000 taxable income before interest and taxes. Firm U is financed entirely with equity, whereas Firm L is financed with $10,000 debt that requires an annual payment of 10% interest. If the tax rate for both firms is 30%, the tax payable and net income to owners are calculated as follows:

	Firm U (No Debt)	Firm L ($10,000 Debt)
Taxable income before taxes and interest	$5,000	$5,000
Less: interest expense	0	1,000
Taxable income before taxes	$5,000	$4,000
Less: taxes at 30% of taxable income	1,500	1,200
Net income to owners	$3,500	$2,800

By financing its activities with debt, paying interest of $1,000, Firm L reduces its tax bill by $300. Firm L's creditors receive $1,000 of income, the government receives $1,200 of income, and the owners receive $2,800. The $300 represents money Firm L does not pay because they are allowed to deduct the $1,000 interest. This reduction in the tax bill is a type of subsidy.

---

[4] Internal Revenue Code (IRC) (1986 Code) Section 163. For individuals, the interest deduction may be subject to limitations [IRC Section 163 (d)].

If Firm LL (Lots of Leverage) has the same operating earnings and tax rate as Firms U and L, but uses $20,000 of debt (at the 10% interest rate), the taxes payable and net income to owners are as follows:

	Firm U (No Debt)	Firm L ($10,000 Debt)	Firm LL ($20,000 Debt)
Taxable income before taxes and interest	$5,000	$5,000	$5,000
Less: interest expense	0	1,000	2,000
Taxable income before taxes	$5,000	$4,000	$3,000
Less: taxes at 30%	1,500	1,200	900
Net income to owners	$3,500	$2,800	$2,100

Comparing Firm LL to Firm L, we see that creditors' income (the interest expense) is $2,000 ($1,000 more than Firm L), taxes are $900 ($300 lower than Firm L's $1,200 taxes) and the net income to owners $2,100 ($700 lower than Firm L's net income). If Firm L were to increase its debt financing from $10,000 to $20,000, like Firm LL's, the total net income to the suppliers of capital—the creditors and owners— is increased $300, from $3,800 to $4,100, determined as follows:

	Firm L ($10,000 Debt)	Firm LL ($20,000 Debt)
Income to creditors	$1,000	$2,000
Income to owners	2,800	2,100
	$3,800	$4,100

The distribution of incomes for Firms U, L, and LL is shown in Exhibit 18.6. In the case of Firm U, 70% of the income goes to owners and 30% goes to the government in the form of taxes. In the case of Firm LL, 42% of the income goes to owners and 18% goes to taxes, with the remaining 40% going to creditors.

Extending this example to different levels of debt financing, a pattern emerges. A summary of the distribution of income to creditors and shareholders (as well as the government's share) for different levels of debt financing is shown in Exhibit 18.7. We are assuming, for simplicity, that the cost of debt (10%) remains the same for all levels of debt financing. And this would be the case in a perfect market. The government subsidy for debt financing grows as the level of debt financing grows. With increases in the use of debt financing, the creditors' share of earnings increases and the owners' and the government's shares decrease.

EXHIBIT 18.6   Distribution of Income Among Owners, Creditors, and the
Government for Firms U, L and LL

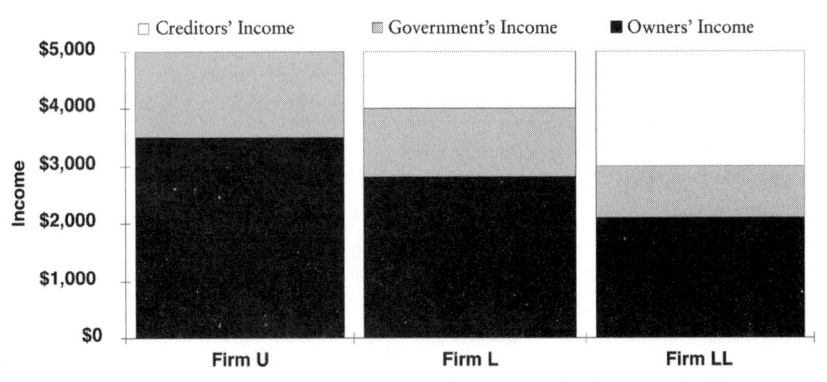

EXHIBIT 18.7   Distribution of Income between Owners, Creditors, and the
Government for Different Levels of Debt Financing, Using a 30% Tax Rate and
Assuming 10% Interest on Debt

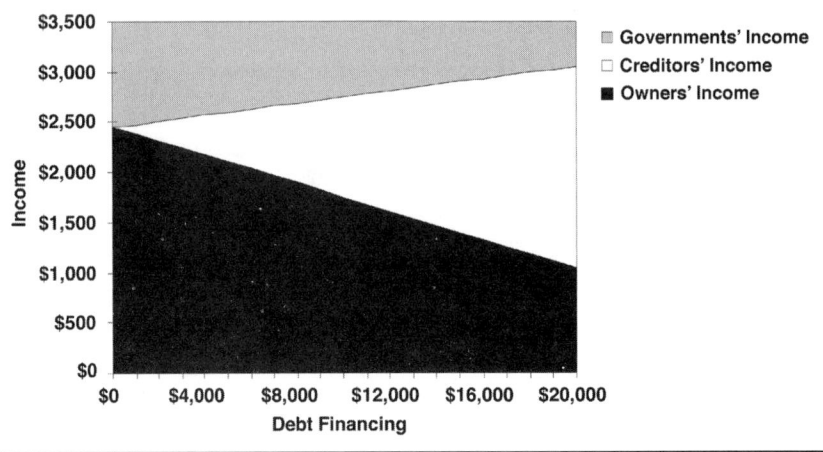

Interest Tax Shield

An interesting element introduced into the capital structure decision is
the reduction of taxes due to the payment of interest on debt. We refer
to the benefit from interest deductibility as the *interest tax shield*, since
the interest expense *shields* income from taxation. The tax shield from
interest deductibility is:

$$\text{Tax shield} = (\text{Tax rate})(\text{Interest expense})$$

If Firm L has $10,000 of 10% debt and is subject to a tax of 30% on net income, the tax shield is:

$$\text{Tax shield} = 0.30\,[\$10,000(0.10)] = 0.30(\$1,000) = \$300$$

A $1,000 interest expense means that $1,000 of income is not taxed at 30%.

Recognizing that the interest expense is the interest rate on the debt, r_d, multiplied by the face value of debt, D, the tax shield for a firm with a tax rate of τ is:

$$\begin{aligned}\text{Tax shield} &= (\text{Tax rate})(\text{Interest rate on debt})(\text{Face value of debt})\\ &= \tau r_d D\end{aligned}$$

How does this tax shield affect the value of the firm? The tax shield reduces the net income of the firm that goes to pay taxes.

We should specify that the tax rate is the **marginal tax rate**—the tax rate on the next dollar of income. Suppose you have a salary of $20,000 a year. And suppose the first $20,000 of income is taxed at 20% and any income over that is taxed at 30%. If you are considering making an investment that will generate taxable income above $20,000, what tax rate do you use in making your decision? You use 30%, because any income you earn above the $20,000 will be taxed at 30%, not 20%.

And since we are concerned with how interest protects income from taxation, we need to focus on how it shields taxable income beyond the income that is shielded by all other tax deductible expenses. Suppose you have income of $20,000 and deductible expenses *other* than interest of $20,000. If you are considering borrowing, does the interest expense shield anything? No, so the marginal tax rate is 0%.

If the level of debt financing, D, is considered permanent (that is, when the current debt matures, new debt in the same amount is issued to replace it), and *if* the interest rate on the debt, r_d, is considered fixed, and *if* the tax rate on the net income is considered to remain constant at τ, then the tax shield is expected to be generated in each period, forever. Therefore, the tax shield represents a perpetual stream whose value is:

$$\text{Present value of a perpetual stream} = \frac{\text{Periodic stream}}{\text{Discount rate}}$$

The discount rate is the interest rate on the debt and the periodic stream is the tax shield each period. The *present value of the interest tax shield (PVITS)* is:

$$PVITS = \frac{(\text{Tax rate})(\text{Interest rate on debt})(\text{Face value of debt})}{(\text{Interest rate on debt})} = \frac{\tau r_d D}{r_d}$$

Simplifying,

$$PVITS = \tau D = (\text{Tax rate})(\text{Face value of debt}) \qquad (18\text{-}4)$$

This means Firm L with $10,000 of debt at an interest rate of 10% and a tax rate on income of 30%, has a $3,000 tax shield:

$$PVITS = (0.30)(\$10,000) = \$3,000.$$

The fact that the Internal Revenue Code allows interest on debt to reduce taxable income *increases* the value of Firm L by $3,000.

Tax shields from interest deductibility are valuable: If a firm finances its assets with $50,000 of debt and has a tax rate of 30%, the tax shield from debt financing (and hence the increase in the value of the firm) is $15,000!

We can specify the value of the firm as:

Value of the firm = Value of the firm if all equity financed
　　　　　　　　　+ Present value of the interest tax shield

If the firm is expected to maintain the same amount of debt in its capital structure,

Value of the firm = Value of the firm, if all equity financed + τD

Therefore, the value of the firm is supplemented by the tax subsidy resulting from the interest deducted from income.

Personal Taxes and Capital Structure

A firm's corporate taxes and debt affects its value: The more debt it uses, the more interest is deductible, the more income is shielded from taxes.

But personal taxes also enter into the picture. Who is going to buy this debt? Investors. But investors face personal taxes and have to make decisions about what investments they want to buy. And if their income from debt securities—their interest income—is taxed differently from their income on equity securities—their dividends and capital appreciation—this may affect how much they are willing to pay for the securities.[5] This affects the return the firm must offer investors on debt and equity to entice them to buy the securities.

We won't go through the mathematics of how personal taxes affect the interest rates a firm must offer. But we can look at the major conclusions regarding personal taxes and capital structure:

1. If debt income (interest) and equity income (dividends and capital appreciation) are taxed at the same rate, the interest tax shield is still τD and increasing leverage increases the value of the firm.
2. If debt income is taxed at rates higher than equity income, some of the tax advantage to debt is offset by a tax disadvantage to debt *income*. Whether the tax advantage from the deductibility of interest expenses is more than or less than the tax disadvantage of debt income depends on: the firm's tax rate; the investor's tax rate on debt income; and the investor's tax rate on equity income. But since different investors are subject to different tax rates (for example, pension funds are not taxed), determining this is a problem.
3. If investors can use the tax laws effectively to reduce to zero their tax on equity income, firms will take on debt up to the point where the tax advantage to debt is just offset by the tax disadvantage to debt income.[6]

The bottom line from incorporating personal taxes is that there is a benefit from using debt. It may not be as large as τD because of personal taxes, but personal taxes are thought to reduce some, but not all, of the benefit from the tax deductibility of debt.[7]

Unused Tax Shields

The value of a tax shield depends on whether the firm can use an interest expense deduction. In general, if a firm has deductions that *exceed* income,

---

[5] Equity income consists of dividends and capital appreciation. Under the present U.S. tax system capital appreciation is taxed more favorably (meaning lower rates) than interest income since: (1) capital appreciation is not taxed until realized (for example, when shares of stock sold); and (2) at times, a portion of the realized capital gain has been excluded from taxable income (for individual taxpayers) or taxed at lower rates (for corporations).

[6] This reasoning was developed by Merton Miller in "Debt and Taxes," *Journal of Finance* (May 1977), pp. 261–276.

[7] Some argue that the benefit from $1 of debt is about 20 cents. See, for example, Ronald H. Masulis, "The Effect of Capital Structure Change on Security Prices: A Study of Exchange Offers," *Journal of Financial Economics* (June 1980), pp. 139–177, and Ronald H. Masulis, "The Impact of Capital Structure Change on Firm Value," *Journal of Finance* (March 1983), pp. 107–126.

the result is a *net operating loss.* The firm does not have to pay taxes in the year of the loss and may "carry" this loss to another tax year.

This loss may be applied against previous years' taxable income (with some limits). The previous years' taxes are recalculated and a refund of taxes previously paid is requested. If there is insufficient previous years' taxable income to apply the loss against, any unused loss is carried over into future years (with some limits), reducing future years' taxable income.[8]

Therefore, when interest expense is larger than income before interest, the tax shield is realized immediately—*if* there is sufficient prior years' taxable income. If prior years' taxable income is *insufficient* (that is, less than the operating loss created by the interest deduction), the tax shield is *less* valuable because the financial benefit is not received until some later tax year (if at all). In this case, we discount the tax shield to reflect both the uncertainty of benefitting from the shield and the time value of money.

To see how an interest tax shield may become less valuable, let's suppose The Unfortunate Firm has the following financial results:

	The Unfortunate Firm		
	Year 1	Year 2	Year 3
Taxable income before interest	$7,000	$8,000	$6,000
Interest expense	5,000	5,000	5,000
Taxable income	$2,000	$3,000	$1,000
Tax rate	0.40	0.40	0.40
Tax paid	$800	$1,200	$400

Suppose further that the Unfortunate Firm has the following result for Year 4:

The Unfortunate Firm	
Operating Results for Year 4	
Taxable income before interest	$1,000
Less: Interest expense	8,000
Net operating loss	−$7,000

---

[8] The tax code provisions, with respect to the number of years available for net operating loss carrybacks and carryovers, has changed frequently. For example, under the Tax Reform Act of 1986, the code permits a carryback for three previous tax years and a carryforward for fifteen future tax years [IRC Section 172 (b), 1986 Code].

Suppose the tax code permits a carryback of three years and a carry-over of 15 years. Unfortunate Firm can take the net operating loss of $7,000 and apply it against the taxable income of previous years, beginning with Year 1:

	The Unfortunate Firm		
	Calculation of Tax Refunds Based on Year 4 Net Operating Loss		
	Year 1	Year 2	Year 3
Taxable income before interest	$7,000	$8,000	$6,000
Interest expense	5,000	5,000	5,000
Taxable income—original	$2,000	$3,000	$1,000
Application of Year 4 loss	–2,000	–3,000	–1,000
Taxable income—recalculated	$0	$0	$0
Tax due—recalculated	$0	$0	$0
Refund of taxes paid	$800	$1,200	$400

By carrying back the part of the loss, the Unfortunate Firm has applied $6,000 of its Year 4 loss against the previous years' taxable income: $2,000(Year 1) + 3,000(Year 2) + 1,000(Year 3) and receives a tax refund of $2,400 (= $800 + 1,200 + 400). There remains an unused loss of $1,000 ($7,000 – $6,000). This loss can be applied toward future tax years' taxable income, reducing taxes in future years. But since we don't get the benefit from the $1,000 unused loss—the $1,000 reduction in taxes—until sometime in the future, the benefit is worth less than if we could use it today.

The Unfortunate Firm, with an interest deduction of $8,000, benefits from $7,000 of the deduction; $1,000 against current income and $6,000 against previous income. Therefore, the tax shield from the $8,000 is not $3,200 (40% of $8,000), but rather $2,800 (40% of $7,000), plus the present value of the taxes saved in future years. The present value of the taxes saved in future years depends on:

1. the uncertainty that Unfortunate Firm will generate taxable income and
2. the time value of money.

The Unfortunate Firm's tax shield from the $8,000 interest expense is less than what it could have been because the firm could not use all of it now.

The bottom line of the analysis of unused tax shields is that the benefit from the interest deductibility of debt depends on whether or not the firm can use the interest deductions.

CAPITAL STRUCTURE AND FINANCIAL DISTRESS

A firm that has difficulty making payments to its creditors is in financial distress. Not all firms in financial distress ultimately enter into the legal status of bankruptcy. However, extreme financial distress may very well lead to bankruptcy. While bankruptcy is often a result of financial difficulties arising from problems in paying creditors, some bankruptcy filings are made prior to distress, when a large claim is made on assets (for example, class action liability suit).

Costs of Financial Distress

The costs related to financial distress without legal bankruptcy can take different forms. For example, to meet creditors' demands, a firm takes on projects expected to provide a quick payback. In doing so, the financial manager may choose a project that decreases owners' wealth or may forgo a profitable project.

Another cost of financial distress is the cost associated with lost sales. If a firm is having financial difficulty, potential customers may shy away from its products because they may perceive the firm unable to provide maintenance, replacement parts, and warranties. If you are arranging your travel plans for your next vacation, do you want to buy a ticket to fly on an airline that is in financial difficulty and may not be around much longer? Lost sales due to customer concern represent a cost of financial distress—an opportunity cost, something of value (sales) that the firm would have had if it were not in financial difficulty.

Still another example of costs of financial distress are costs associated with suppliers. If there is concern over the firm's ability to meet its obligations to creditors, suppliers may be unwilling to extend trade credit or may extend trade credit only at unfavorable terms. Also, suppliers may be unwilling to enter into long-term contracts to supply goods or materials. This increases the uncertainty that the firm will be able to obtain these items in the future and raises the costs of renegotiating contracts.

The Role of Limited Liability

Limited liability limits owners' liability for obligations to the amount of their original investment in the shares of stock. Limited liability for owners of some forms of business creates a valuable right and an interesting incentive for shareholders. This valuable right is the right to default on obligations to creditors—that is, the right not to pay creditors. Because the most shareholders can lose is their investment, there is an incentive for the firm to take on very risky projects: If the projects turn out well, the firm pays creditors only what it owes and keeps the rest, and if the projects turn out poorly, it pays creditors what it owes—*if* there is anything left.

We can see the benefit to owners from limited liability by comparing the Unlimited Company, whose owners have unlimited liability, to the Limited Company, whose owners have limited liability. Suppose that the two firms have the following identical capital structures in Year 1:

	Year 1	
	Unlimited Company	Unlimited Company
Debt	$1,000	$1,000
Equity	3,000	3,000
Total value of firm's assets	$4,000	$4,000

Owners' equity—their investment—is $3,000 in both cases.

If the value of the assets of both firms in Year 2 are increased to $5,000, the value of both debt and equity is the same for both firms:

	Year 2	
	Unlimited Company	Unlimited Company
Debt	$1,000	$1,000
Equity	4,000	4,000
Total value of firm's assets	$5,000	$5,000

Now suppose the total value of both firm's assets in Year 2 is $500 instead of $5,000. If there are insufficient assets to pay creditors the $1,000 owed them, the owners with unlimited liability must pay the difference (the $500); if there are insufficient assets to pay creditors the $1,000 owed them, the owners with limited liability do not make up the difference and the most the creditors can recover is the $500.

	Year 2	
	Unlimited Company	Unlimited Company
Debt	$1,000	$500
Equity	−500	0
Total value of firm's assets	$ 500	$500

In this case, the Unlimited Firm's owners must pay $500 to their creditors because the claim of the creditors is greater than the assets available to satisfy their claims. The Limited Company's creditors do not receive their full claim and since the owners are shielded by limited liability, the creditors cannot approach the owners to make up the difference.

We can see the role of limited liability for a wider range of asset values by comparing the creditors' and owners' claims in Exhibit 18.8 for the Unlimited Company (Panel a) and the Limited Company (Panel b). The creditors make their claims at the expense of owners in the case of the Unlimited Company for asset values of less than $1,000. If the value of assets of the Unlimited Company is $500, the creditors recover the remaining $500 of their claim from the owners' personal assets (if there are any such assets). In the case of Limited Company, however, if the assets' value is less than $1,000, the creditors cannot recover the full $1,000 owed them—they cannot touch the personal assets of the owners!

The fact that owners with limited liability can lose only their initial investment—the amount they paid for their shares—creates an incentive for owners to take on riskier projects than if they had unlimited liability: They have little to lose and much to gain. Owners of the Limited Company have an incentive to take on risky projects since they can only lose their investment in the firm. But they can benefit substantially if the payoff on the investment is high.

For firms whose owners have limited liability, the more the assets are financed with debt, the greater the incentive to take on risky projects, leaving creditors "holding the bag" if the projects turn out to be unprofitable. This is a problem: There is a conflict of interest between shareholders' interests and creditors' interests. The investment decisions are made by managers (who represent the shareholders) and, because of limited liability, there is an incentive for managers to select riskier projects that may harm creditors who have entrusted their funds (by lending them) to the firm. The right to default is a call option: The owners have the option to buy back the entire firm by paying off the creditors at the face value of their debt. As with other types of options, the option is more valuable, the riskier the cash flows.

However, creditors are aware of this and demand a higher return on debt (and hence a higher cost to the firm).[9] The result is that shareholders ultimately bear a higher cost of debt.

---

[9] Michael Jensen and William H. Meckling analyze the agency problems associated with limited liability in their article "Theory of the Firm: Managerial Behavior, Agency Costs and Ownership Structure," *Journal of Financial Economics* (1976), pp. 305–360. They argue that creditors are aware of the incentives the firm has to take on riskier project. Creditors will demand a higher return and may also require protective provisions in the loan contract.

EXHIBIT 18.8 Comparison of Claims for the Unlimited Company

Panel a: Claims on Assets: Unlimited Company

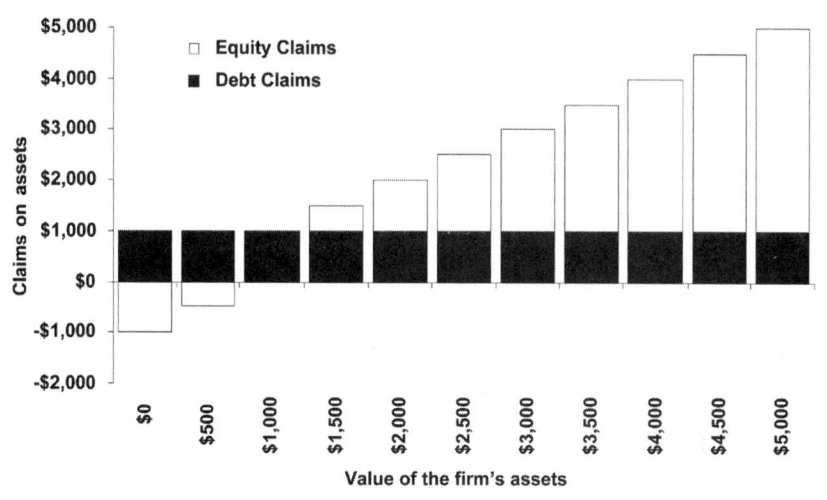

Panel b: Claims on Assets: Limited Company

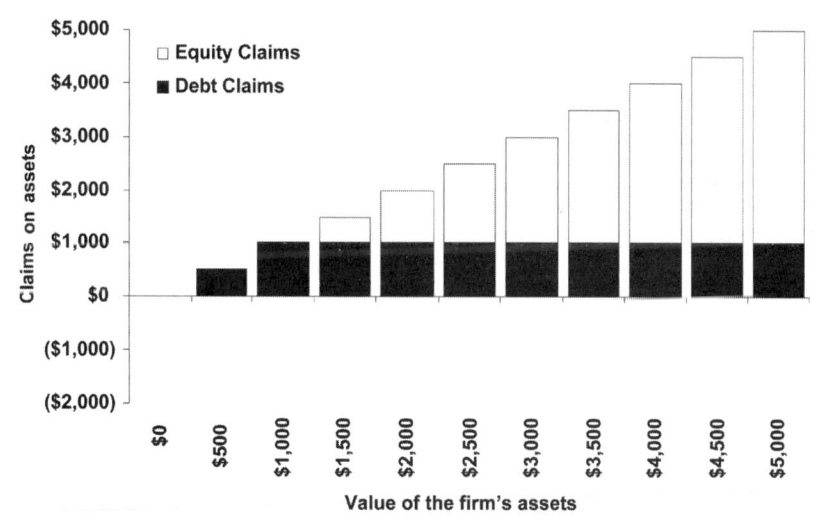

Bankruptcy and Bankruptcy Costs

When a firm is having difficulty paying its debts, there is a possibility that creditors will foreclose (that is, demand payment) on loans, causing the firm to sell assets which could impair or cease operations. But if some creditors force payment, this may disadvantage other creditors. So what has developed is an orderly way of dealing with the process of the firm paying its creditors—the process is called *bankruptcy.*

Bankruptcy in the United States is governed by the Bankruptcy Code, created by the Bankruptcy Reform Act of 1978. A firm may be reorganized under Chapter 11 of this Code, resulting in a restructuring of its claims, or liquidated under Chapter 7.[10]

Chapter 11 bankruptcy provides the troubled firm with protection from its creditors while it tries to overcome its financial difficulties. A firm that files bankruptcy under Chapter 11 continues as a going concern during the process of sorting out which of its creditors get paid and how much. On the other hand, a firm that files under bankruptcy Chapter 7, under the management of a trustee, terminates its operations, sells its assets, and distributes the proceeds to creditors and owners.

We can classify *bankruptcy costs* into direct and indirect costs. Direct costs include the legal, administrative, and accounting costs associated with the filing for bankruptcy and the administration of bankruptcy. These costs are estimated to be 6.2% of the value of the firm prior to bankruptcy.[11] For example, the fees and expenses for attorneys representing shareholders and creditors' committees in the Texaco bankruptcy were approximately $21 million.[12]

The indirect costs of bankruptcy are more difficult to evaluate. Operating a firm while in bankruptcy is difficult, since there are often delays in making decisions, creditors may not agree on the operations of the firm, and the objectives of creditors may be at variance with the objective of efficient operation of the firm. One estimate of the indirect costs of bankruptcy, calculated by comparing actual and expected profits prior to bankruptcy, is 10.5% of the value of the firm prior to bankruptcy.[13]

---

[10] Bankruptcy Reform Act of 1978, Public Law No. 95-598.92 Stat. 2549 (1978).

[11] The direct cost is taken from the study by Edward I. Altman, "A Further Empirical Investigation of the Bankruptcy Cost Question," *Journal of Finance* (September 1984), pp. 1067–1089, based on his study of industrial firms. An earlier study [Jerold B. Warner, "Bankruptcy Costs: Some Evidence," *Journal of Finance* (May 1977), pp. 337–347], estimated the direct costs of bankruptcy to be approximately 5% of the prebankruptcy market value of the firm.

[12] *Wall Street Journal* (June 2, 1988), p. 25.

[13] The indirect cost estimate is taken from Altman, "A Further Empirical Investigation," p. 1077.

Another indirect cost of bankruptcy is the loss in the value of certain assets. Because many intangible assets derive their value from the continuing operations of the firm, the disruption of operations during bankruptcy may change the value of the firm. The extent to which the value of a business enterprise depends on intangibles varies among industries and among firms; so the potential loss in value from financial distress varies as well. For example, a drug company may experience a greater disruption in its business activities, than say, a steel manufacturer, since much of the value of the drug company may be derived from the research and development that leads to new products.

Financial Distress and Capital Structure

The relationship between financial distress and capital structure is simple: As more debt financing is used, fixed legal obligations increase (interest and principal payments), and the ability of the firm to satisfy these increasing fixed payments decreases. Therefore, as more debt financing is used, the probability of financial distress and then bankruptcy increases.

For a given decrease in operating earnings, a firm that uses debt to a greater extent in its capital structure (that is, a firm that uses more financial leverage), has a greater risk of not being able to satisfy the debt obligations and increases the risk of earnings to owners.

Another factor to consider in assessing the probability of distress is the business risk of the firm. *Business risk* is the uncertainty associated with the earnings from operations. Business risk is uncertainty inherent in the type of business and can be envisioned as being comprised of sales risk and operating risk.

Sales risk is the risk associated with sales as a result of economic and market forces that affect the volume and prices of goods or services sold.

Operating risk is the risk associated with the cost structure of the business firm's assets. A cost structure is comprised of both fixed and variable costs. The greater the fixed costs relative to variable costs, the greater the operating risk. If sales were to decline, the greater the fixed costs in the operating cost structure the more exaggerated the effect on operating earnings. When an airline flies between any two cities, most of its costs are the same whether there is one passenger or one hundred passengers. Its costs are mostly fixed (fuel, pilot, gate fees, etc.), with very little in the way of variable costs (the cost of the meal). Therefore, an airline's operating earnings are very sensitive to the number of tickets sold.

The effect of the mixture of fixed and variable costs on operating earnings is akin to the effect of debt financing (financial leverage) on earnings to owners. Here it is referred to as *operating leverage*: The greater the fixed costs in the operating cost structure, the greater the leveraging effect on operating earnings for a given change in sales. The greater the business risk of the firm, the greater the probability of financial distress.

Our concern in assessing the effect of distress on the value of the firm is the present value of the expected costs of distress. And the present value depends on the probability of financial distress: The greater the probability of distress, the greater the expected costs of distress.

The present value of the costs of financial distress increase with the increasing relative use of debt financing since the probability of distress increases with increases in financial leverage. In other words, as the debt ratio increases, the present value of the costs of distress increases, lessening some of the value gained from the use of tax deductibility of interest expense.

Summarizing the factors that influence the present value of the cost of financial distress:

1. The probability of financial distress increases with increases in business risk.
2. The probability of financial distress increases with increases in financial risk.
3. Limited liability increases the incentives for owners to take on greater business risk.
4. The costs of bankruptcy increase the more the value of the firm depends on intangible assets.

We do not know the precise manner in which the probability of distress increases as we increase the debt-to-equity ratio. Yet, it is reasonable to think that the probability of distress increases as a greater proportion of the firm's assets are financed with debt.

PUTTING IT ALL TOGETHER

As a firm increases the relative use of debt in the capital structure, its value also increases as a result of the tax shield of interest deductibility. However, this benefit is eventually offset by the expected costs of financial distress. Weighing the value of the tax shield against the costs of financial distress, we can see that there is some ratio of debt to equity that maximizes the value of the firm. Because we do not know the precise relationship between the tax shield and distress costs, we cannot specify for a given firm what the optimal debt-to-equity ratio should be. And although we have not yet considered other factors that may play a role in determining the value of the firm, we can say:

■ The benefit from the tax deductibility of interest increases as the debt-to-equity ratio increases.

■ The present value of the cost of financial distress increases as the debt-to-equity ratio increases.

This "tradeoff" between the tax deductibility of interest and the cost of distress can be summarized in terms of the value of the firm in the context of the Modigliani and Miller model:

Value of the firm = Value of the firm if all-equity financed
+ Present value of the interest tax shield
− Present value of financial distress

The value of the firm is affected by taxes and the costs of financial distress. As a firm uses more debt financing relative to equity financing, its value is increased. And the costs associated with financial distress (both direct and indirect costs) reduce the value of the firm as financial leverage is increased. Hence, this is the tradeoff between the tax deductibility of interest and the costs of financial distress.

These considerations help to explain the choice between debt and equity in a firm's capital structure. As more debt is used in the capital structure, the benefit from taxes increases the firm's value, while the detriment from financial distress decreases its value. This tradeoff is illustrated in the three graphs in Exhibit 18.9, in which the value of the firm is plotted against the debt ratio.

Case 1: No interest tax deductibility, and no costs of financial distress (panel a of Exhibit 18.9).

Case 2: Tax deductibility of interest, but no costs of financial distress (panel b of Exhibit 18.9).

Case 3: Tax deductibility of interest and costs of financial distress (panel c of Exhibit 18.9).

Case 3 is the most comprehensive (and realistic) case. At moderate levels of financial leverage (low debt ratios), the value contributed by tax shields more than offsets the costs associated with financial distress. At some debt ratio, however, the detriment from financial distress may outweigh the benefit from corporate taxes, reducing the value of the firm as more debt is used. Hence, the value of the firm increases as more debt is taken on, up to some point, and then decreases.

At that point, the value of the firm begins to diminish as the probability of financial distress increases, such that the present value of the costs of distress outweigh the benefit from interest deductibility. The mix of debt and equity that maximizes the value of the firm is referred to as the *optimal capital structure*. This is the point where the benefit from taxes exactly offsets the detriment from financial distress. The optimal capital structure is that mix of debt and equity that produces the highest value of the firm.

EXHIBIT 18.9   The Value of the Firm under Different Tax and Financial Distress Scenarios

Case 1: The Value of the Firm Assuming No Interest Deductibility and No Costs of Financial Distress

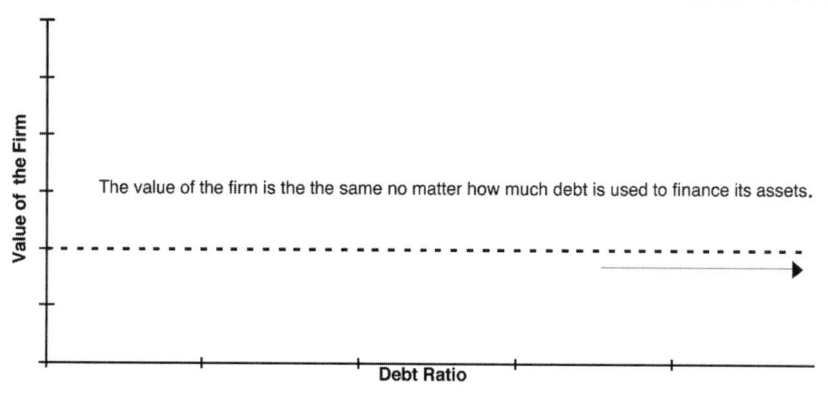

Case 2: The Value of the Firm Assuming Interest Deductibility, but No Costs of Financial Distress

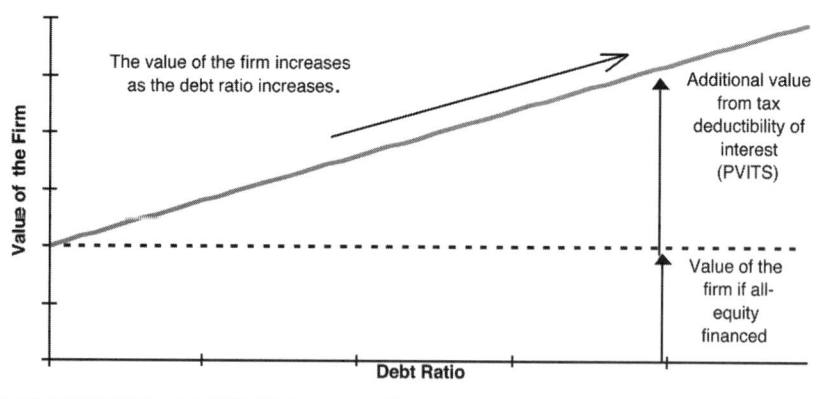

Exhibit 18.9 (Continued)

Case 3: The Value of the Firm Assuming Interest Deductibility and Costs of Financial Distress

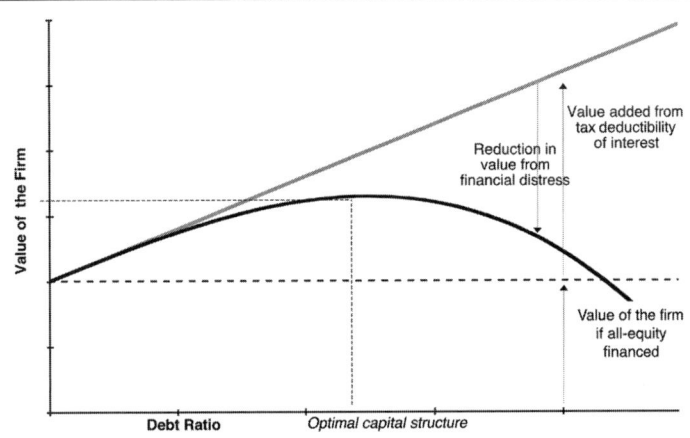

At first glance, the value enhancement from tax shields appears simple to calculate: Multiply the corporate tax rate times the face value of debt. However, it is not that simple, for many reasons. The use of the τD for valuation assumes:

1. A constant marginal corporate tax rate;
2. Refinancing debt at current interest rates; and
3. The firm will earn sufficient taxable income (before interest payments) to be able to use the interest deduction.

Marginal corporate tax rates change periodically, at the discretion of Congress. Interest rates change over time; it is therefore unlikely that refinancing in, say, 20 years will be at current interest rates. Further, you cannot always predict that a company will generate future income that will be sufficient to cover the interest expenses.

And the expected costs of financial distress are difficult to calculate. You cannot simply look at a firm and figure out the probability of distress for different levels of financial leverage. The probability of distress at different levels of debt financing may differ among firms, dependent upon their business risk. The costs of distress are also difficult to measure. These costs will differ from firm to firm, depending on the type of asset (that is, intangibles versus tangibles) and the nature of the firm's supplier and customer relationships.

RECONCILING THEORY WITH PRACTICE

So what good is this analysis of the tradeoff between the value of the interest tax shields and the costs of distress if we cannot apply it to a specific firm? While we cannot specify a firm's optimal capital structure, we *do* know the factors that affect the optimum. The analysis demonstrates that there is a benefit from taxes but, eventually, this benefit may be reduced by costs of financial distress.

Capital Structures among Different Industries

The analysis of the capital structure tradeoff leaves us with several financial characteristics of firms that affect the choice of capital structure:

- The greater the marginal tax rate, the greater the benefit from the interest deductibility and, hence, the more likely a firm is to use debt in its capital structure.
- The greater the business risk of a firm, the greater the present value of financial distress and, therefore, the less likely the firm is to use debt in its capital structure.
- The greater extent that the value of the firm depends on intangible assets, the less likely it is to use debt in its capital structure.

It is reasonable to expect these financial characteristics to differ among industries, but be similar within an industry. The marginal tax rate should be consistent within an industry since:

- The marginal tax rates are the same for all profitable firms.
- The tax law provides specific tax deductions and credits (for example, depreciation allowances and research and development credits) that creates some differences across industries, but generally apply to all firms within an industry since the asset structure and the nature of investment is consistent within an industry.
- The firms in an industry are subject to the same economic and market forces that may cause tax shields to be unusable. Therefore, it is reasonable to assume that capital structures should be similar within industry groups.

Capital Structures within Industries

The capital structures among firms within industries differ for several possible reasons.

First, within an industry there may not be a homogeneous group of firms. For example, Ben and Jerry's, Brach's Candy, and Sara Lee Corporation are all considered members of the food product industry, but they have quite different types of business risk. The problem of industry groupings is exacerbated by the recent acquisitions boom—many industries now include firms with dissimilar product lines.

Adding to the difficulty in comparing firms is the Financial Standards Accounting Board (FASB) requirement that firms consolidate the accounting data of majority-owned subsidiaries.[14] The capital structure of the automobile manufacturers (for example, General Motors and Ford Motor Company) look quite different when the financing subsidiaries are included in the calculation of their debt ratios.

Another reason an industry may appear to comprise firms having different capital structures is the way the debt ratio is calculated. We can see this in Exhibit 18.10 where the debt to market value of equity ratios are shown alongside the debt to book value of equity ratios for firms in the amusement industry.[15] With book value of equity, the debt ratio ranges from 1.405 to 34.432 times in the automotive industry, whereas the debt ratios using the market value of equity ranges from 0.106 to 15.677 times.

Tradeoff Theory and Observed Capital Structures

The tradeoff theories can explain some of the capital structure variations that we observe. Firms whose value depends to a greater extent on intangibles, such as in the semiconductor and drug industries, tend to have lower debt ratios. Firms in volatile product markets, such as the electronics and telecommunications industries, tend to have lower debt ratios.

EXHIBIT 18.10 Comparison of Debt Ratios for a Sampling of Automotive Companies

Company	Debt to Book Equity	Debt to Market Equity	Debt to Assets
DiamlerChryslerAG	4.318	4.867	77%
Ford Motor Company	34.432	15.677	97%
General Motors Corporation	1.544	14.699	94%
Toyota Motor Company	1.405	0.106	58%

Source: Yahoo! Finance

---

[14] Financial accounting Standards Board, Statement No. 94.
[15] The book value of debt is used in the calculation of both ratios in the exhibit. This is necessitated by the lack of current market value data on long-term debt.

However, the tradeoff theories cannot explain all observed capital structure behavior. We observe profitable firms in the drug manufacturing industry that have no long-term debt. Though these firms do have a large investment in intangibles, they choose not to take on *any* debt at all, even though taking on some debt could enhance the value of their firms.

We also see firms that have high business risk and high debt ratios. Firms in the air transportation industry experience a volatile product market, with a high degree of operating leverage. Firms in this industry must invest heavily in jets, airport gates, and reservations systems, and have a history of difficulty with labor. However, these firms also have high debt ratios, with upwards to 80% of their assets financed with debt. One possible explanation for airlines taking on a great deal of financial leverage on top of their already high operating leverage is that their assets, such as jets and gates, can be sold quickly, offsetting the effects of their greater volatility in operating earnings. Whereas the high business risk increases the probability of financial distress, the liquidity of their assets reduces the probability of distress. But hindsight tells us more about the airline industry. The overcapacity of the industry just prior to the recession of 1989–1991 meant that there wasn't much of a market for used jets and planes. The airlines suffered during this economic recession: Of the 14 firms in existence just prior to 1989, four firms entered bankruptcy (Continental, Pan Am, Midway, and America West), and two were liquidated (Eastern Airlines and Braniff).

OTHER POSSIBLE EXPLANATIONS

Looking at the financing behavior of firms in conjunction with their dividend and investment opportunities, we can make several observations:

- Firms prefer using internally generated capital (retained earnings) to externally raised funds (issuing equity or debt).
- Firms try to avoid sudden changes in dividends.
- When internally generated funds are greater than needed for investment opportunities, firms pay off debt or invest in marketable securities.
- When internally generated funds are less than needed for investment opportunities, firms use existing cash balances or sell off marketable securities.
- If firms need to raise capital externally, they issue the safest security first; for example, debt is issued before preferred stock, which is issued before common equity.

The tradeoff among taxes and the costs of financial distress lead to the belief that there is some optimal capital structure, such that the value of the firm is maximized. Yet, it is difficult to reconcile this with some observations in practice. Why?

One possible explanation is that the tradeoff analysis is incomplete. We didn't consider the relative costs of raising funds from debt and equity. Because there are no out-of-pocket costs to raising internally generated funds (retained earnings), it may be preferred to debt and to externally raised funds. Because the cost of issuing debt is less than the cost of raising a similar amount from issuing common stock (flotation of 2.2% versus 7.1%), debt may be preferred to issuing stock.

Another explanation for the differences between what we observe and what we believe should exist is that firms may wish to build up *financial slack*, in the form of cash, marketable securities, or unused debt capacity, to avoid the high cost of issuing new equity.

Still another explanation is that financial managers may be concerned about the signal given to investors when equity is issued. It has been observed that the announcement of a new common stock issue is viewed as a negative signal, since the announcement is accompanied by a drop in the value of the equity of the firm. It is also observed that the announcement of the issuance of debt does not affect the market value of equity. Therefore, the financial manager must consider the effect that the new security announcement may have on the value of equity, and hence, may shy away from issuing new equity.

The concern over the relative costs of debt and equity and the concern over the interpretation by investors of the announcement of equity financing leads to a preferred ordering, or *pecking order*, of sources of capital: first internal equity, then debt, then preferred stock, then external equity (new common stock). A result of this preferred ordering is that firms prefer to build up funds, in the form of cash and marketable securities, so as not to be forced to issue equity at times when internal equity (retained earnings) is inadequate to meet new profitable investment opportunities.[16]

A CAPITAL STRUCTURE PRESCRIPTION

The analysis of the tradeoff and pecking order explanations of capital structure suggests that there is no satisfactory explanation. What is

---

[16] For a more complete discussion of the pecking order explanation, especially the role of asymmetric information, see Stewart C. Myers, "The Capital Structure Puzzle," *Midland Corporate Finance Journal*, Vol. 3, No. 3 (Fall 1985).

learned from an examination of these possible explanations is that there are several factors to consider in making the capital structure decision:

- **Taxes.** The tax deductibility of interest makes debt financing attractive. However, the benefit from debt financing is reduced if the firm cannot use the tax shields.
- **Risk.** Because financial distress is costly, even without legal bankruptcy, the likelihood of financial distress depends on the business risk of the firm, in addition to any risk from financial leverage.
- **Type of asset.** The cost of financial distress is likely to be more for firms whose value depends on intangible assets and growth opportunities.
- **Financial slack.** The availability of funds to take advantage of profitable investment opportunities is valuable. Therefore, having a store of cash, marketable securities, and unused debt capacity is valuable.

The financial manager's task is to assess the business risk of the firm, predicting the usability of tax deductions in the future, evaluating how asset values are affected in the event of distress, and estimating the relative issuance costs of the alternative sources of capital. In the context of all these considerations, the financial manager can observe other firms in similar situations, using their decisions and consequences as a guide.

SUMMARY

- Financial leverage is the use of fixed cost sources of funds. The effect of using financial leverage is to increase both the expected returns and the risk to owners.
- Taxes provide an incentive to take on debt, since interest paid on debt is a deductible expense for tax purposes, shielding income from taxation. But the possibility of incurring direct and indirect costs of financial distress discourages taking on high levels of debt.
- Taxes and financial distress costs result in a tradeoff. For low debt ratios, the benefit of taxes more than overcomes the present value of the costs of financial distress, resulting in increases in the value of the firm for increasing debt ratios. But beyond some debt ratio, the benefit of taxes is overcome by the costs of financial distress; the value of the firm decreases as debt is increased beyond this point.
- An explanation for the capital structures that we observe is that firms prefer to raise capital internally, but will raise capital externally according to a pecking order from safe to riskier securities.

■ We cannot figure out *the* best capital structure for a firm. We can provide a checklist of factors to consider in the capital structure decision: taxes, business risk, asset type, issuance costs, and investor interpretations of security issuance announcements.

QUESTIONS

1. What is financial leverage and how does it affect the risk associated with future earnings to shareholders?
2. If the marginal tax rate on corporate income were to increase, what do you expect to be the effect of this on the tax shield from interest deductibility?
3. Consider three financing alternatives:
   Alternative A: Finance solely with equity
   Alternative B: Finance using 50% debt, 50% equity
   Alternative C: Finance solely with debt
   a. Which of the three alternatives involves the greatest financial leverage?
   b. Which of the three alternatives involves the least financial leverage?
4. List the potential costs associated with financial distress.
5. How does limited liability affect the incentives of shareholders to encourage investment in riskier projects?
6. List the potential direct and indirect costs associated with bankruptcy.
7. Shareholders may be viewed as having a call option on the firm. What is this call option? Identify the elements of an option in the context of the equity of a firm:
   a. exercise price
   b. expiration date
8. Explain why firms in the electric utility industry tend to have higher debt ratios than firms classified as industrials.
9. Rank the following sources of capital in order of preference, according to the pecking order explanation of capital structure:

   ■ Issue debt
   ■ Sell shares of stock
   ■ Retained earnings

10. What is financial slack? Why do firms wish to have financial slack?

11. Consider the information on the three firms A, B, and C:

Capital	Firm A	Firm B	Firm C
Debt	$1,000	$2,000	$3,000
Equity	$3,000	$2,000	$1,000

   a. Calculate the debt ratio for each firm.

   b. Calculate the debt-to-assets ratio for each firm.

12. The Chew-Z Corporation is considering three possible financing arrangements to raise $10,000 of new capital. Currently, the capital structure of Chew-Z consists of no debt and $10,000 of equity. There are 500 shares of common stock currently outstanding, selling at $20 per share. The Chew-Z is expected to generate $12,000 of earnings before interest and taxes next period. It is expected that the interest rate on any debt would be 10%. The three possible financing alternatives are:

Alternative 1: Finance completely with new equity.

Alternative 2: Finance using 50% debt and 50% new equity.

Alternative 3: Finance completely with new debt.

   a. Calculate the following items for each alternative, assuming that there are no taxes on corporate income:

■ Earnings to owners
■ Earnings per share
■ Distribution of income between creditors and shareholders

   b. Calculate the following items for each alternative, assuming that the marginal rate of tax on corporate income is 40%:

■ Earnings to owners
■ Earnings per share
■ Distribution of income among creditors, shareholders, and the government

13. The financial manager of the Variable Corporation has looked into the department's crystal ball and estimated the earnings per share for Variable under three possible outcomes. This crystal ball is a bit limited, for it can only make projections regarding the earnings per share and the probability that each will occur. Unfortunately, it cannot tell the financial manager which of the three possible outcomes will occur. The data provided by the crystal ball indicates:

Economic Environment	Probability	Earnings per Share
Good	50%	$10.00
OK	20%	$5.00
Bad	30%	$1.00

Help the financial manager assess this data by calculating the expected earnings per share and the standard deviation of earnings per share for Variable Corporation.

14. Calculate the capitalization rate (discount rate) for equity for the following three firms, D, E and F:

Capital	Firm D	Firm E	Firm F
Debt	$1,500	$1,000	$2,000
Equity	$1,500	$2,000	$1,000

Assume that there are no corporate income taxes and that the cost of equity for an unlevered firm is 10% and the cost of risk-free debt is 6%

15. The I.O. Corporation has $10,000 of debt in its capital structure. The interest rate on this debt is 10%. What is the present value of the tax shield from interest deductibility if the tax rate on corporate income is:
a. 0%?
b. 20%?
c. 40%?
d. 60%?
e. 80%?

16. The I.R.S. Corporation has $10,000 of debt in its capital structure. The interest rate on this debt is 10%. What is the present value of the tax shield from interest deductibility if the tax rate on corporate income is 45%?

17. The Lou Zer Corporation generated a net operating loss of $5,000 in 2001. Assume that the current tax law allows the loss to be carried back three years to reduce previous years' taxes and that previous tax returns reveal the following information:

Tax Year	Taxable Income	Taxes Paid
2000	$1,000	$400
1999	$2,000	$800
1998	$3,000	$1,200
1997	$2,000	$800

    a. What is the amount of tax refund that Lou Zer can apply for as a result of the 2001 loss?

    b. How would your answer differ if the tax law permitted the loss to be carried back only two years?

18. General Stuff is a food processing company that manufacturers a wide variety of food products, including pasta, cereal, juice beverages, and confectionery goods. In addition to food processing, General Stuff has acquired a small, regional restaurant chain within the past year. The management of General Stuff believes that the most profitable course would be to expand the restaurant chain to become a major player in the national market. To do this, however, requires cash—which General Stuff doesn't have quite enough of right now. General Stuff's management has determined that it needs to raise $1 million in capital next year beyond the funds generated internally.

    General Stuff had revenues of around $1.2 billion in the last fiscal year and revenues are expected to increase at a rate of 8% per year for the next five years if the restaurant chain is expanded as planned. The vast majority (80%) of the revenues are currently from the food processing business, but it is expected that the restaurant chain will provide up to 40% of General Stuff's revenues within three years. General Stuff's net profit margin last year was 5%, but the typical net profit margin for retail food businesses is 10%. General Stuff's return on assets last year was 25% and return on equity was 40%.

    The beta (an indicator of an asset's systematic risk) assigned to General Stuff's common stock by a major financial analysis service was 1.2 prior to its acquisition of the restaurant chain. The beta was revised upward slightly to 1.3 following this acquisition.

    Other firms in the food processing industry have capital structures comprising 40% debt and 60% equity, though the use of debt ranges from a low of 15% to a high of 72%. Firms in the retail food industry have capital structures of 45% debt and 55% equity, ranging from 35% to 70% debt.

    a. Compare General Stuff's capital structure with that of the industry.

    b. Provide a recommendation for the amount of debt and equity General Stuff should issue to support the expansion program. List any assumptions you have made in your analysis. Briefly discuss additional information that would be useful in making a recommendation.

Managing Working Capital

CHAPTER 19

Management of Cash and Marketable Securities

A s we saw in Part Three, managers base decisions about investing in long-term projects on judgments about future cash flows, the uncertainty of those cash flows, and the opportunity costs of the funds to be invested. As we turn in Part Five to the management of short-term assets, we will see that such decisions are made in similar ways, but over much shorter time horizons. Thus considerations of risk will take a smaller role in our discussions in the next few chapters, while the operating cycle becomes more important.

Recall from our discussion in Chapter 6 that the operating cycle refers to the time it takes to turn the investment of cash (e.g., buying raw materials) back into cash (e.g., collecting on accounts receivables). As our opening example shows, the operating cycle in part determines how long it takes for a firm to generate cash from its short-term assets and, therefore, the risk and cost of its investment in current assets, or working capital. *Working capital* is the capital that managers can immediately put to work to generate the benefits of capital investment. Working capital is also known as *current capital* or *circulating capital*.

Firms invest in current assets for the same reason they invest in long-term, capital assets: to maximize owners' wealth. But because managers evaluate current assets over a shorter time frame (less than a year), they focus more on their cash flows and less on the time value of money.

How much should a firm invest in current assets? That depends on several factors:

- The type of business and product
- The length of the operating cycle

■ Customs, traditions, and industry practices
■ The degree of uncertainty of the business

The type of business, whether retail, manufacturing, or service, affects how a firm invests. In some industries, large investments in machinery and equipment are necessary. In other industries, such as retail firms, less is invested in plant and equipment and other long-term assets, and more is invested in current assets such as inventory.

The firm's operating cycle—the time it takes the firm to turn its investment in inventory into cash—affects how much the firm ties up in current assets. The operating cycle comprises the time it takes to: manufacturer the goods, sell them and collect on their sale. The *net* operating cycle considers the benefit from purchasing goods on credit; the net operating cycle is the operating cycle less the number of days of purchases. The longer the net operating cycle, the larger the investment in current assets.

Let's look at firms' investments in current and noncurrent assets, as summarized in Exhibit 19.1. As shown in Panel (a), approximately 30 to 40% of firms' investment is in current assets. As we see in Panel (b), within current assets, inventories are the largest investment, followed by cash and cash equivalents. Firms that manufacture goods, such as steel, tend to have more invested in long-term assets than, say, retail shoe stores. Of the manufacturing firms, those with greater raw material price uncertainty, such as the sugar and confectionery processors and the beverage producers, tend to have more invested in current assets.

EXHIBIT 19.1   Asset Composition of U.S. Corporations

Panel a: Current versus Noncurrent Assets

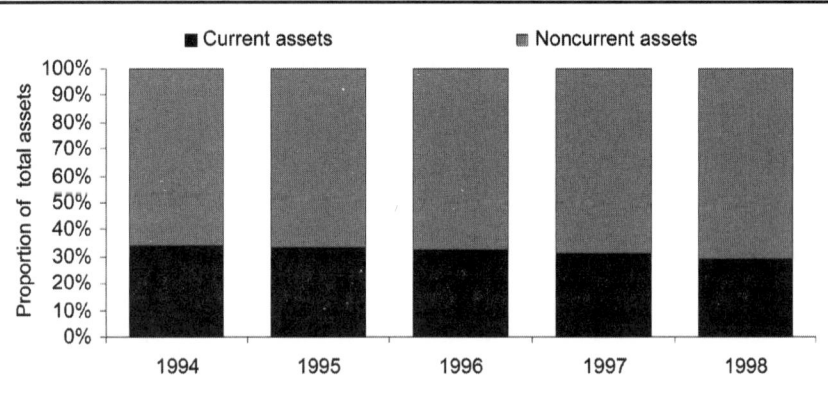

EXHIBIT 19.1   (Continued)

Panel b: Current Assets by Type

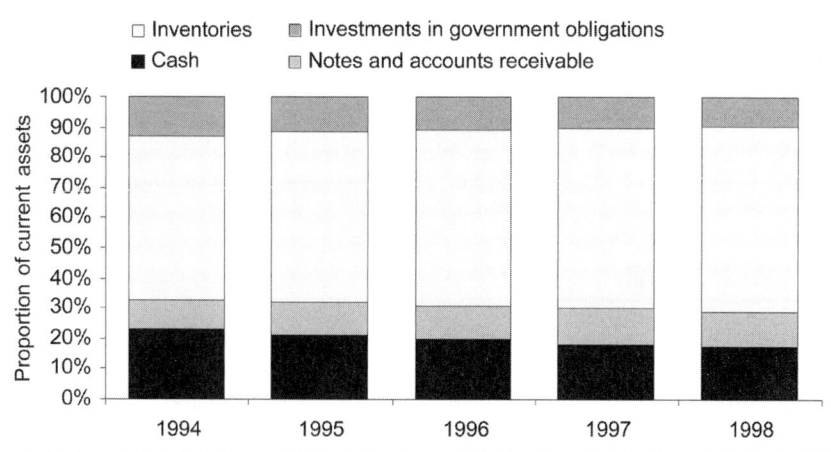

Source: Statistical Abstract of the United States, 2001, U.S. Census Bureau

EXHIBIT 19.2   Current Asset Composition for a Sample of Firms, 2001

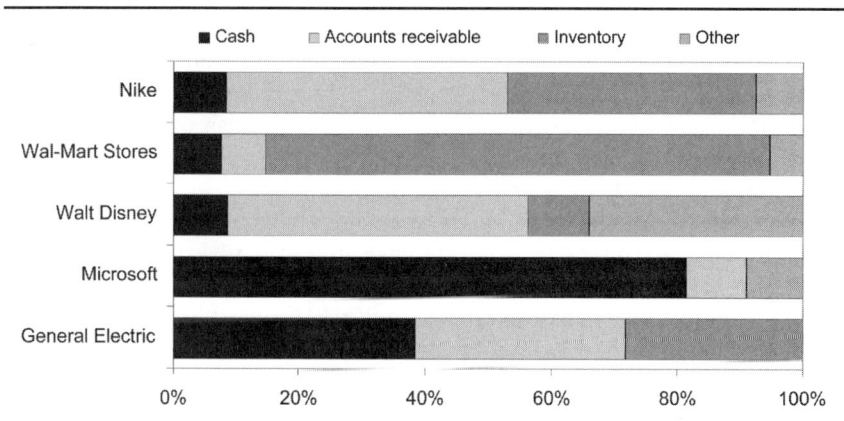

Source: Company annual reports

The differences in how these industries invest in current assets is illustrated in more detail Exhibit 19.2. Here, current assets are broken down for a sample of firms by type: cash, marketable securities, accounts receivable, inventory, and "other." "Other" includes prepaid expenses (which are short-term assets because these are expenses paid but not yet incurred) and income tax refunds (because they are refunds that are coming, but have not yet arrived). We do not discuss either in detail in this chapter.

Inventory plays a small role for Disney, but is significant for retailers, such as Wal-Mart. Accounts receivable, however, are not important to Wal-Mart, since they typically do not extend credit to customers, but they are important to shoe manufacturers, like Nike, which typically do. Manufacturers tend to have more invested in cash than, say, retailers.

The working capital decision requires an evaluation of the benefits and costs associated with each component. In this chapter, we will look at the management of cash and marketable securities and see how we can evaluate the benefits and costs associated with the investment in these assets.

CASH MANAGEMENT

Cash flows *out of* a firm as it pays for the goods and services it purchases from others. Cash flows *into* the firm as customers pay for the goods and services they purchase. When we refer to *cash*, we mean the amount of cash and cash-like assets—currency, coin, and bank balances. When we refer to *cash management*, we mean management of cash inflows and outflows, as well as the stock of cash on hand.

Monitoring Cash Needs

We can monitor our cash needs through cash forecasting. *Cash forecasting* is analyzing how much and when cash is needed, and how much and when to generate it. Cash forecasting requires pulling together and consolidating the short-term projections that relate to cash inflows and outflows. These cash flows may be a part of your capital budget, production plans, sales forecasts, or collection on accounts.

To understand the cash needs and generation, you have to understand how long it takes to generate cash, once an investment in inventory is made. We're referring to the operating cycle—the time it takes to make cash out of cash. For example, in 2001, General Electric (GE) had an operating cycle of 90 days; it took GE, on average, 62 days to convert its investment in inventory into a sold product and, on average, 28 days to collect on its customer accounts.[1]

If we consider cash disbursements, we get a better picture of the net cash—the *net operating cycle*—the time it takes to make cash from cash plus the time we delay payment on our purchases:

Net operating cycle = Operating cycle – Number of days of purchases

GE, for example, had a net operating cycle of 41 days in 2001. It took, on average, 49 days to pay for its purchases.

---

[1] This calculation assumes that all sales are on credit.

Estimating our net operating cycle gives us information on how long it takes to generate cash from our current assets. The longer the net operating cycle, the more cash we need on hand.

To understand our cash flows, we also have to have a fairly good idea of the uncertainty of our cash needs and cash generation. Cash flows are uncertain because sales are uncertain, and so is the uncertainty regarding when we will collect payment on what we do sell, as well as uncertainty about production costs and capital outlays. Forecasting cash flows requires the coordination of marketing, purchasing, production, and financial management.

Reasons for Holding Cash Balances

Firms hold some of their assets in the form of cash for several reasons. They need cash to meet the transactions in their day-to-day operations. Referred to as the *transactions balance*, the amount of cash needed for this purpose differs from firm to firm, depending on the particular flow of cash into and out of the firm. The amount depends on:

1. the size of the transactions made by the firm; and
2. the firm's operating cycle, which determines its cash outflow and inflow, depending on the firm's production process, purchasing policies, and collection policies.

There is always *some* degree of uncertainty about future cash needs. Firms typically hold an additional balance, referred to as a *precautionary balance*, just in case transactions *needs* exceed the transactions *balance*. But how much to keep as a precaution depends on the degree of the transactions uncertainty—how well we can predict our transactions needs. For example, a retail store has a good idea from experience about how much cash to have on hand to meet the typical day's transactions. In addition to what is needed for a typical day, the retail store may keep more cash on hand to meet a higher than usual level of transactions.

In addition to the precautionary balances, firms may keep cash on hand for unexpected future opportunities. Referred to as a *speculative balance*, this is the amount of cash or securities that can be easily turned into cash, above what is needed for transactions and precaution. The speculative balance enables a firm to take advantage of investment opportunities on short notice and to meet extraordinary demands for cash. For example, an automobile manufacturers may need an additional cash cushion to pay its bills in case a wildcat strike closes down a plant.

In addition to the cash balances for transactions, precautionary, and speculative needs, a firm may keep cash in a bank account in the form of a *compensating balance*—a cash balance required by banks in exchange for banking services. By keeping a balance in an account that is non-interest earning or low-interest earning, the firm is effectively compensating the bank for the loans and other services it provides. Some bank loans and bank services require a specified amount or average balance be maintained in an account.

Costs Associated with Cash

There is a cost to holding assets in the form of cash. Because cash does not generate earnings, the cost of holding assets in the form of cash, referred to as the *holding cost*, is an opportunity cost—what the cash *could* have earned if invested in another asset.

If a firm needs cash, it must either sell an asset or borrow cash. There are transactions costs associated with both. Transactions costs are the fees, commissions, or other costs associated with selling assets or borrowing to get cash; they are analogous to the ordering costs for inventory.

Determining the Investment in Cash

How much cash should a firm hold? For transactions purposes, enough to meet the demands of day-to-day operations. To determine how much is enough transactions purposes, we compare the cost of having *too* much cash to the cost getting cash—in other words, we compare the holding cost and transactions cost.

As you hold more cash, its holding cost increases. With more cash on hand, the costs of making transactions to meet your cash needs for operations declines. That's because with larger cash balances, you need fewer transactions (selling marketable securities or borrowing from a bank) to meet your cash needs.

We want to have on hand the amount of cash that minimizes the sum of the costs of making transactions to get the cash (selling securities or borrowing) and the opportunity cost of holding more cash than we need.

We will look at the Baumol Model and the Miller-Orr Model to help us decide on the level of cash we need and when we need it.

The Baumol Model

The Baumol Model is based on the ***Economic Order Quantity*** (EOQ) model developed for inventory management.[2] We will see it applied to inventory in Chapter 20. Applied to the management of cash, the EOQ model determines the amount of cash that minimizes the sum of the holding cost and transactions cost. The holding cost includes the costs

---

[2] William J. Baumol, "The Transactions Demand for Cash: An Inventory Theoretic Approach," *Quarterly Journal of Economics* (November 1952).

of administration (keeping track of the cash) and the opportunity cost of not investing the cash elsewhere. The *transaction cost* is the cost of getting more cash—either through selling marketable securities or through borrowing. The economic order quantity is the level of cash infusion (from selling marketable securities or borrowing) that minimizes the total cost associated with cash.

Suppose each time our cash balance is zero we generate $100,000 (borrowing or selling securities). Further suppose that our opportunity cost for holding cash is 5%—we could have invested the cash in something that earns 5% instead of holding it. Our holding costs are the product of the average cash balance and the opportunity cost. If we start with $0 cash and end up with $100,000 after an infusion, our average cash balance is = $50,000, so our holding cost is:

$$\text{Holding cost} = \underset{\substack{\uparrow \\ \text{Opportunity} \\ \text{cost}}}{0.05} \underset{\substack{\uparrow \\ \text{Average} \\ \text{balance}}}{\left(\frac{\$100,000}{2}\right)} = \$2,500$$

If we did not hold $50,000 of cash on average, we could have earned $2,500 by investing it.

Now suppose we need $1,000,000 cash for transactions over a given period. If we need $1,000,000 in total and we get $100,000 cash at a time, we need to make 10 transactions during the period. If it costs us $200 every time we make a cash infusion our transactions cost is $2,000:

$$\text{Transaction cost} = \underset{\substack{\uparrow \\ \text{Cost per transaction}}}{\$200 \text{ per transaction}} \underset{\substack{\uparrow \\ \text{Number of transactions}}}{\left(\frac{\$1,000,000}{\$100,000 \text{ per transaction}}\right)}$$

$$= \$200(10) = \$2,000$$

The total cost associated with cash is the sum of the holding cost and the transactions cost:

$$\text{Total cost} = \$2,500 + 2,000 = \$4,500$$

Will cash infusions of $100,000 at a time produce the lowest cost of getting cash? We can't control the cash needed for transactions purposes or the cost per transaction. But we can control how many cash infusions we make. And that number affects both the holding cost and the transactions cost.

The holding cost is a function of the amount of the cash infusion: With larger cash infusions, we hold more cash. Holding more cash, we have a greater opportunity cost to holding it. The transactions cost is also a function of the amount of cash infusion: The larger the cash infusion, the fewer the transactions, and therefore the lower our transactions costs.

Let's use these considerations and what we know about economic order quantity to determine the minimum cost of cash.

If we get cash in the amount of Q at the beginning of a period and wait until the cash balance is zero before we get more cash, the average cash balance over the period is $Q/2$. The cost of holding cash during this period is determined by the average cash balance, $Q/2$, and the opportunity cost of holding the cash, k:

$$\text{Holding cost} = k\frac{Q}{2}$$

But each time we get cash, we have to make a transaction. If we demand a total of S dollars of cash each period, we end up making S/Q transactions per period. If it costs K to make a transaction, the transactions cost for the period is:

$$\text{Transactions cost} = K\frac{S}{Q}$$

Putting the holding cost and the transaction cost together, the total cost associated with the cash balance is:

$$\text{Total cost} = \text{Holding cost} + \text{Transaction cost}$$
$$= k\frac{Q}{2} + K\frac{S}{Q}$$

The total cost associated with any given level of inventory ordering Q is:

$$\text{Total cost} = k\frac{Q}{2} + K\frac{S}{Q}$$

To calculate the minimum total cost with respect to the amount of inventory we get each time, we:

1. Calculate the first derivative of the total cost equation with respect to Q.

2. Set this first derivative equal to zero.
3. Solve for Q.

The first derivative of the total cost with respect to Q (where "d" indicates "change") is:

$$\frac{d(\text{Total cost})}{d(Q)} = \frac{k}{2} - \frac{S}{Q^2}K$$

Setting the first derivative equal to zero:

$$0 = \frac{k}{2} - \frac{S}{Q^2}K$$

Solving for the level of Q that minimizes the total cost, Q^*,

$$Q^* = \sqrt{\frac{2(\text{Cost per transaction})(\text{Total demand for cash})}{\text{Opportunity cost of holding cash}}}$$

or,

$$Q^* = \sqrt{\frac{2KS}{k}}$$

What does this mean? If we look at the relations among Q^* and K, S, and k in this equation, we see that:

■ The larger the cost per transaction, K, the greater the amount of cash, Q^*, infused in a single transaction—the larger the transaction cost, the fewer transactions we make.
■ The larger the demand for cash, S, the larger the amount of cash, Q^*, infused in a single transaction.
■ The larger the opportunity cost of holding cash, k, the smaller the amount of cash, Q^*, infused in a single transaction.

In our example, $K = \$200$ per transaction, $S = \$1,000,000$, $k = 5\%$, and

$$Q^* = \sqrt{\frac{2(\$200)(\$1,000,000)}{0.05}} = \$89,443$$

If every time we need a cash infusion, we get $89,443, the costs associated with cash will be minimized.

We can check our work by looking at the total costs of cash for levels of Q on either side of $Q^* = \$89,443$. If $Q = \$100,000$,

$$\text{Total cost} = \$2,500 + \$2,000 = \$4,500$$

as we saw before. If $Q = \$50,000$:

$$\text{Total costs} = 0.05\left(\frac{\$50,000}{2}\right) + \$200\left(\frac{\$1,000,000}{\$50,000}\right)$$

$$= \$1,250 + \$4,000 = \$5,250$$

If $Q = \$89,443$,

$$\text{Total costs} = 0.05\left(\frac{\$89,443}{2}\right) + \$200\left(\frac{\$1,000,000}{\$89,443}\right)$$

$$= \$2,236 + \$2,236 = \$4,472$$

We can see in Exhibit 19.3 that the minimum of the total cost curve is at a cash infusion level of $89,443, which corresponds to a total cost of $4,472. If the level of cash infusion is less than or more than $89,443, the cost of cash will be higher.

EXHIBIT 19.3   Costs of Cash for Different Levels of Cash Infusions

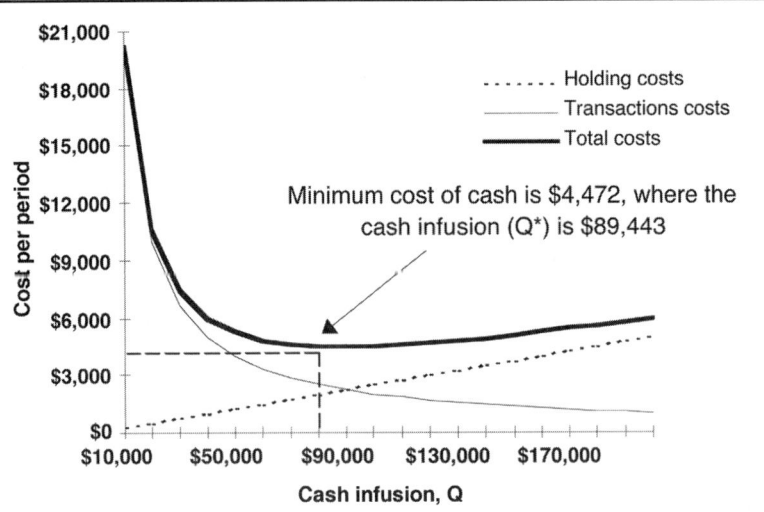

The EOQ model can be applied to any time framework—whether the period is a year, a month, a week, or any other unit of time. It is only necessary to make sure that all the elements that depend on the unit of time—the holding costs, k, and transactions demand, S—are in that same unit of time.

The economic order quantity model can be modified to suit the circumstances of different cash situations. For example, the EOQ model for cash can be modified to include a *safety stock*—a balance of cash for precautionary purposes. The safety stock is a level of cash balance that acts as a cushion in case our cash needs are suddenly greater than expected.

The Miller-Orr Model

The Baumol Model assumes that cash is used uniformly throughout the period. The Miller-Orr Model recognizes that cash flows vary throughout the period in an unpredictable manner.[3]

To see how the Miller-Orr model takes account of changes in the need for cash, consider the three key levels of inventory:

- the *lower limit*, below which inventory does not fall
- the *return point*, the level of inventory that is the target if either the lower or upper limit is reached
- the *upper limit*, above which inventory does not rise

The lower limit is really a safety stock of cash—the cash on hand must never fall below this level. We need to apply experience and judgment in determining the lower level.

Based on (a) how much needs are expected to vary each day, (b) the cost of a transaction, and (c) the opportunity cost of cash expressed on a daily basis, this model tells us:

1. *The level of cash at which a new cash infusion is needed.* This level is referred to as the *return point* (not to be confused with the level of safety stock). Levels of cash below the safety stock cannot be tolerated; levels below the return point are tolerated—until they hit the safety stock level, of course.
2. *The upper limit of cash.* The amount of cash that would exceed this limit is invested in marketable securities.

---

[3] Merton H. Miller and Daniel Orr, "A Model of the Demand for Money by Firms," *Quarterly Journal of Economics* (July 1966) pp. 413–435.

The return point and the upper limit are determined by the model as the levels necessary to minimize costs of cash, considering (a) daily swings in cash needs, (b) the transactions cost, and (c) the opportunity cost of cash. The Miller-Orr model provides us with a few decision rules:

- Our cash balance can be any level between the upper and lower limit.
- There is a cash balance (the return point) that we aim for if our cash balance exceeds the upper limit or if our cash balance is below the lower limit:

    If our cash balance *exceeds the upper limit*, any cash in excess of the return point is invested in marketable securities.

    If our cash balance is *below the lower limit*, any deficiency up to the return point is made up by selling marketable securities or borrowing.

The return point is a function of:

- the lower limit
- the cost per transactions
- the opportunity cost of holding cash (per day)
- the variability of daily cash flows, which we measure as the variance of daily cash flows

and is determined mathematically as follows:

Return point

$$= \text{Lower limit} + \sqrt[3]{\frac{0.75(\text{Cost per transcation})(\text{Variance of daily cash flows})}{\text{Opportunity cost per day}}} \quad (19\text{-}1)$$

In this equation, we see that:

- The higher the safety stock (the lower limit), the higher the return point.
- The higher the cost of making a transaction, the higher the return point.
- The greater the variability of cash flows, the higher the return point.
- The greater the holding cost of cash, the lower the return point.

The upper limit is the sum of the lower limit and three times the right-most term of the return point equation:

$$\text{Upper limit} = \text{Lower limit} + 3\left[\sqrt[3]{\frac{0.75(\text{Cost per transcation})(\text{Variance of daily cash flows})}{\text{Opportunity cost per day}}}\right] \quad (19\text{-}2)$$

To see how this model works, suppose we estimate the following items:

Opportunity cost per day   = 0.01%
Variance of daily cash flows = $20,000
Cost per transaction   = $200
Lower limit   = $10,000

Then:

$$\text{Lower limit} = \$10,000$$

$$\text{Return point} = \$10,000 + \sqrt[3]{\frac{0.75(\$200)(\$20,000)}{0.0001}} = \$13,107$$

$$\text{Upper limit} = \$10,000 + 3(\$3,107) = \$19,321$$

What we have just determined using the Miller-Orr model is that the cash balance is allowed to fluctuate between $13,107 and $19,321. If the cash balance exceeds $19,321, we invest the difference between the cash balance and the return point, restoring the cash balance to the return point. If the cash balance is below the lower limit, marketable securities are sold to bring the cash balance to the return point. Each time the cash balance is outside either the lower or the upper limit, we bounce back to the return point.

This "bouncing" is illustrated in Exhibit 19.4. In part (a) of this figure, the cash flow per day is graphed against time—sometimes cash flows in, sometimes cash flows out. In part (b) this figure, the cash balance is plotted for each day using the Miller-Orr model. Each time the balance is hits $10,000, it bounces back to $13,107 and each time the balance is hits $19,321, it bounces back to $13,107.

Other Considerations

The Baumol and Miller-Orr models both try to help us minimize the costs of cash. The Baumol model assumes a predictable, steady use of cash. The Miller-Orr model incorporates an estimate of the variability of cash flows.

But there are other factors that affect cash management. One is the seasonality of our cash needs. If our sales and collections on sales are seasonal, we must factor the pattern of cash into our cash balance—the Baumol model does not consider changing cash needs.

EXHIBIT 19.4 Illustration of the Miller-Orr Model: Cash Balance per Day with the Application of Control Limits

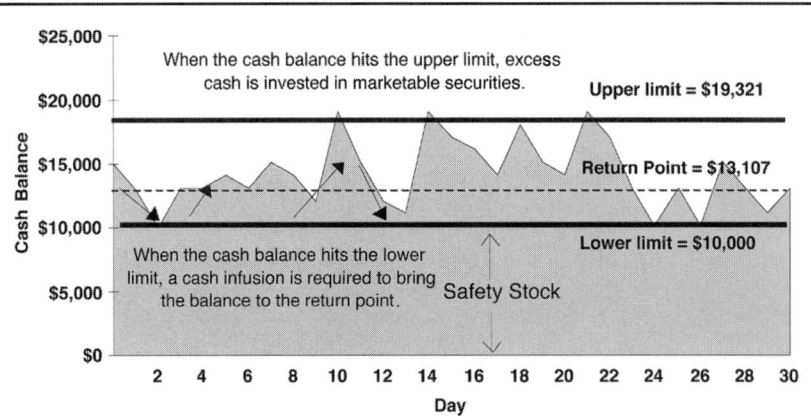

Another factor is doing business in other countries. If we do business in a foreign country, we have added complications, including:

- keeping cash in different currencies;
- restrictions on transferring currencies across borders;
- laws in many countries requiring holdings in that country's domestic currency; and
- the risk that the value of the foreign currency may change, relative to your domestic currency.

We must look very closely at our cash flows and the factors that affect our cash needs. Once we understand our cash flow needs and the predictability of these needs, we can use the basis of either model to determine cash infusions and holdings to minimize costs.

Cash Management Techniques

Cash management has very simple goals:

- Have enough cash on hand to meet immediate needs, but not too much.
- Get cash from those who owe it to you as soon as possible and pay it out to those you owe as late as possible.

The Baumol and Miller-Orr models help firms manage cash to satisfy the first goal. But the second goal requires methods that speed up incoming cash and slow down outgoing cash. To understand these methods, we need to first understand the check clearing process.

The Check Clearing Process

The process of receiving cash from customers involves several time-consuming steps:

■ The customer sends the check.
■ The check is processed within the firm—so the customer can be credited with paying.
■ The check is sent to the firm's bank.
■ The bank sends the check through the clearing system.
■ The firm is credited for the amount of the check.

Several days may elapse between the time when the firm receives the check and the time when the firm is credited with the amount of the check. During that time, the firm cannot use the funds. The amount of funds tied up in transit and in the banking system is referred to as the *float*. The float occurs because of the time tied up in the mail, in check processing within the firm, and in check processing in the banking system. (See Exhibit 19.4)

The float can be costly to those who are on the receiving end. Suppose on average your customers make $1 million in payments each day. If your float is seven days, you therefore have 7 times $1,000,000 = $7,000,000 coming to you that you cannot use. If you can speed up your collections to five days, you can reduce our float to $5 million—and use the freed-up $2 million for other things.

But the float can be beneficial to the payer. Suppose you make payments to your suppliers, on average, $1 million per day. And suppose it takes your suppliers five days after they receive your checks to complete the check processing system. You have $5 million in float per day. If you could slow down the check processing by one day, you increase the float to $6 million. That's $1 million more cash available for you to use each day.

There are several ways we can speed up incoming cash:

■ *Lockbox system* A system where customers send their checks to post office boxes and banks pick up and begin processing these checks immediately.
■ *Selection of banks* Choosing banks that are well connected in the banking system, such as clearinghouse banks or correspondent banks, can speed up the collection of checks.
■ *Check processing within the firm* Speed up processing of checks within the firm so that deposits are made quickly.

- *Electronic collection* Avoid the use of paper checks, dealing only with electronic entries.
- *Concentration banking* The selection of a bank or banks that are located near customers, reducing the mail float.

A *clearinghouse* is a location where banks meet to exchange checks drawn on each other, and a *clearinghouse bank* is a participant in a clearinghouse. Clearinghouses may involve local banks or local and other banks. Being a member of a clearinghouse can reducing check clearing time by up to one-half a day relative to clearing checks through the Federal Reserve system. A *correspondent bank* is a bank that has an agreement with a clearinghouse bank to exchange its checks in the clearinghouse. Banks can become correspondents to clearinghouses in other parts of the country, reducing their check clearing time relative to clearing checks through the Federal Reserve system.

In addition, there are several methods you can use to slow up our payment of cash:

- *Controlled disbursements* Minimizing bank balances by depositing only what is needed to make immediate demands on the account.
- *Remote disbursement* Paying what is owed with checks drawn on a bank that is not readily accessible to the payee, increasing the check processing float.

Consider the reduction in float by a local government. The city of Seattle, Washington, discovered that their float was quite large.[4] By taking a closer look at their processing of checks and banking relationships, the city was able to reduce their float substantially. They improved their float by using a number of devices: adding bar codes on envelopes, processing mail electronically through the post office, changing their mail pick-up routine, using optical scanning to record receipts, and using concentration banking. The result? They reduced the mail float by one day, reduced the office processing float by three and one-half days, and reduced the bank float by almost one day—a savings estimated to be approximately $1.3 million per year.

Whichever way you speed up the receipt of cash or slow down the payment of cash there is a cost. Firms must weigh the benefits with the cost of altering the float.

We will look closely at one speed-up device—the lockbox system—and one slow-down device—controlled disbursements—to see how the float can be altered.

---

[4] Lloyd F. Hara, "Seattle's 'No-Float Day'," *Government Finance Review*, Vol. 3 (December 1987) pp. 7–10.

EXHIBIT 19.5   An Example of the Time Line Corresponding to a Lockbox System

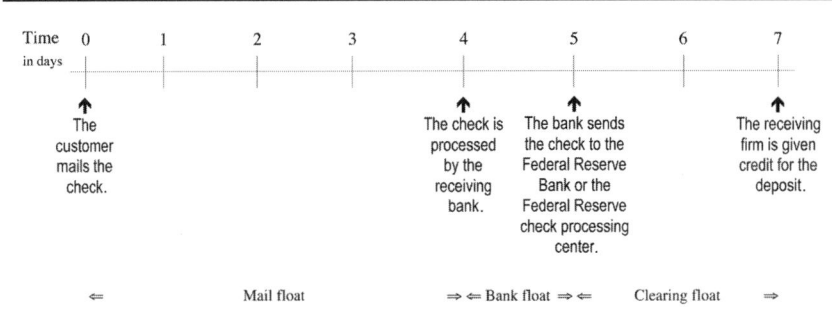

The lockbox system may reduce the mail float (due to the placement of the lockboxes near the customer) and changes what was the "firm float" to a "bank float" since the bank now processes the checks received from customers.

Lockbox System

With a *lockbox system* a firm's customers send their payments directly to a post office box controlled by the firm's bank. This skips the step where the firm receives and handles the check and paperwork (see Exhibit 19.5). The lockbox system can cut down on the time it takes to process checks in two ways. First, the firm can use post office boxes (and collecting banks) throughout the country, reducing the time a check spends in the mail—reducing the mail float. Second, because the bank processes the checks and paperwork, the lockbox avoids the time the checks spend at the receiving firm—eliminating the time it takes to process checks in the firm.

To see the savings using a lockbox, suppose it can reduce our total float from eight to five days. If we collect $1.5 million per year through the lockbox system, three days worth of collections ($1,500,000/365 × 3 days = $12,329) freed up for investment during the year. If we can earn 12% a year investing in marketable securities, this amounts to an increase in earnings of $12,329 × 0.12 = $1,479. As long as the cost of the lockbox system is less than $1,479 per year, there is a benefit to using it.

We can state the increased earnings from the lockbox system as:

Benefit from lockbox system
= (Collections per day) × (Reduction of float in days)   (19-3)
× (Opportunity cost of funds per year)

To decide whether or not to use such a system involves comparing the benefit obtained from the lockbox system with the lockbox fees charged by the bank.

There are a couple of drawbacks to a lockbox system. Because the bank receives the check and documents, it takes longer for the firm to record who has paid—the bank must forward the documents to the firm. Also, customers may become confused, since payments are sent to the lockbox's address and all other correspondence is sent to the firm's business address.

Setting up a lockbox system requires the answers to several questions:

1. How many lockboxes?
2. Where to locate the lockboxes to cut down on mail time?
3. Where to direct which customers to send their payments?

Determining the optimal lockbox set-up requires evaluating the cost of each lockbox and the opportunity cost of having checks in the mail.

CURRENT ADVANCES IN LOCKBOXES

There are a number of recent advances in lockbox systems that need to be considered in selecting a lockbox system, including:

- *Lockbox networks*—collections of banks that link lockboxes from different parts of the country to speed up the bank float.
- *Image-based processing*—computer coding, such as bar-coding of envelopes, that speeds up processing by the bank.
- *Mail interception*—banks picking up mail at the post office to reduce the mail float.
- *Nonbank lockbox systems*—firms other than banks that establish lockbox systems.

In selecting a lockbox system, we need to evaluate the speed in which we have access to funds, the recordkeeping of accounts paid, and the costs of the system.

Controlled Disbursements

If you want to have more cash available for your own use, you can slow down the payments you make—increasing the float to others. *Controlled disbursements* is an arrangement with a bank to minimize the amount that you hold in bank balances to pay what you owe. Under this system, you minimize your bank balance to only the funds you need for immediate disbursing. To make this work, you need to work closely with the bank—the bank notifies you of checks being cashed on your account and you immediately wire the necessary funds.

An extreme disbursement method is referred to as a *zero-balance account* (ZBA). In an ZBA arrangement, you keep no funds in the bank—you simply deposit funds as the checks you wrote out are presented for payment through the banking system. As this account can save you two to three days of float and cost anywhere from $20 to $200 per month in bank fees, zero-balance accounts are attractive. Some banks will even automatically invest funds in excess of the firm's payments needs into short-term securities—insuring that there are no idle funds.

As you can imagine, a controlled disbursements system requires coordination between you and your bank. If you are off just a little bit, you can lose goodwill with your suppliers or other payees. Also, this system is not costless; the bank is performing a service and charges a fee.

MARKETABLE SECURITIES

An integral part of cash management is storing excess cash in an asset that earns a return—such as marketable securities. Precautionary and speculative needs for cash can often be satisfied by funds stored in marketable securities, selling them as needs for cash arise. Models of cash management assume that managers stash cash they don't need right away into marketable securities and convert them to cash as needed. In this way, marketable securities are a substitute for cash.

If cash flows of a firm are uneven—perhaps seasonal—the firm can deal with the uneven demands for cash by either borrowing for the short-term or selling marketable securities. If short-term borrowing is not possible or is costly, marketable securities can be used: Buy marketable securities when cash inflows exceed outflows; sell marketable securities when cash inflows are less than outflows. In this way, marketable securities are a temporary investment.

Aside from the uneven cash demands from operations, marketable securities may be a convenient way of storing funds for planned expenditures. If you generate cash from operations or from the sale of securities for an investment in the near future, the funds can be kept in marketable securities until needed.

Marketable Securities and Risk

The primary role of marketable securities is to store cash that isn't needed immediately, but may be needed soon. We should therefore consider only marketable securities that provide safety and liquidity. In evaluating safety, we need to look at the risks we accept in investing in securities. The relevant risks for you to consider are:

Default risk: The risk that the issuer will not pay interest and/or principal as promised.

Purchasing power risk: The risk that inflation will erode the purchasing power of the money you receive in the form of interest and principal in the future.

Interest rate risk: The risk that interest rates will change, changing the value of your investment.

Reinvestment rate risk: The risk that interest rates will change, affecting the rate of return you can earn on reinvesting the interest and principal from your investment.

Liquidity risk: Also referred to as marketability risk, the risk that the security will not be marketable, at least at its true value, due to the lack of investor interest in the security.

Types of Marketable Securities

The marketable securities that satisfy the criteria of safety and liquidity are most likely money market securities. Money market securities are listed and described in Exhibit 19.6.

Some money market securities, such as government securities, have no default risk; the ones that do have very little default risk. Due to the short maturity of money market securities and the fact that they are generally issued by large banks or corporations (who are not likely to get into deep financial trouble in a short time), their default risk is low. Even so, you can look at the credit ratings by Moody's, Standard & Poor's, and Fitch for an evaluation of the default risk of any particular money market security.

Money market securities have relatively little purchasing power risk. The chance of inflation changing over the short horizon is slight, though a possibility. Money market securities also have relatively little interest rate risk. Since these securities are short-term, their values are not as affected by changes in interest rates as, say, a thirty-year corporate bond.

The short maturities of money market securities, however, subject the investor to reinvestment rate risk. If rates fall and the security matures, the investor must roll over—or reinvest—the funds in another security with lower rates. But since this investment's purpose is short-term, this is a risk that we must bear.

EXHIBIT 19.6   Money Market Securities

Security	Description	Yields[a] (%) 2002	2001	1999
Certificates of deposit	Debt issued by banks sold in large denominations. This debt has maturities ranging generally up to one year. Because this debt is issued by banks, but exceeds the amount for deposit guarantees by bank insurance, there is some default risk.	1.73	3.71	6.46
Commercial paper	Debt issued by large corporations that is sold in large denominations and generally matures in thirty days. While the debt is unsecured credit and is issued by corporations, there is some default risk, though this is minimized by the back-up lines of credit at commercial banks.	1.69	3.65	6.31
Eurodollars deposits	Loans and certificates of deposits of non-U.S. banks that are denominated in the U.S. dollar. These debts are generally large denominations with maturities up to six months. Like loans and certificates of U.S. banks, there is some default risk.	1.73	3.70	6.45
Treasury bills	Securities issued by the U.S. Government that have maturities of one month, three months, and six months. These securities are considered default-free and are readily marketable.	1.61	3.40	5.82

[a] *Federal Reserve Board*, www.federalreserve.gov. Yields are for three-month maturity.

RECAP

We have seen in this chapter some of the techniques managers use to decide how much cash to keep on hand and how to manage the cash that is not needed immediately. In the next chapter, we will discuss the management of the other current assets of a firm: receivables and inventory. We will see that managers must make similar kinds of balancing decisions when they decide whether to issue credit to customers or to keep large amounts of cash tied up in inventory. In Chapter 21, we will see how managers make decisions about their short-term financing needs. In Part Eight, we will see how managers make working capital decisions within the context of the firm's short-term and long-term budgeting and planning.

SUMMARY

- The management of short-term assets involves decisions related to cash, marketable securities, accounts receivable, and inventory. Because short-term assets support the long-term investments of the firm, they are linked to the firm's capital budgeting decision.
- The objective of short-term investments is the same as for long-term investment decisions: Maximize owners' wealth. But since we are basing our decision on cash flows received are over the short term, we focus less on the time value of money and more on identifying the costs and benefits associated with our decisions.
- The common purpose of our decisions related to cash and marketable securities is to minimize our investment in the short-term asset. But in all cases, we must have *some* investment in the asset because we will incur costs if we do not have enough of it. If we don't pay our bills, we may be unable to buy goods from our suppliers in the future. We may be unable to borrow in the future because we can't pay our debts on time.
- We need to strike the right balance between the cost of having and not having the asset. The "right balance" is different for each firm. Each firm must assess its costs of having and not having the asset.
- Cash management involves the tradeoff between the benefits from having enough cash to meet day-to-day operations and the costs of having cash (e.g., opportunity cost of funds and costs of getting and storing cash). The Baumol and Miller-Orr models can be used in the management of cash to determine the amount of funds to transfer in and out of cash.
- Marketable securities are a store of excess cash. A firm invests funds in marketable securities to have a ready, liquid source of cash. Marketable securities include U.S. Treasury bills, commercial paper, and certificates and deposit.

QUESTIONS

1. Why do firms hold some of their assets in the form of cash?
2. What is the benefit from using a lockbox system?
3. Suppose the post office develops new technology that speeds up mail delivery. How would such a development affect a firm's cash management decision?
4. The Peach Company has determined that it's cash EOQ is $100,000. What does this mean?
5. The Pear Company is applying the Miller-Orr model to their cash management. They determined that the return point is $12,000, the lower limit is $5,000, and the upper limit is $26,000. Explain what this information means to Pear's cash management.

6. What are the primary differences between the Baumol and Miller-Orr models of cash management?

7. Preferred stock is a long-term source of capital for a corporation. How can it be both a long-term source of capital *and* a short-term investment of funds?

8. Why do firms hold marketable securities?

9. In general, what types of risks do investors bear when investing in money market securities? What risks can be reduced or eliminated when investing in U.S. government short-term securities?

10. Why would the investment in marketable securities differ for companies domiciled in different countries?

11. Suppose you start each month with a cash balance of $100,000 and you use cash evenly throughout the month, ending each month with a zero cash balance.

    a. What is the average cash balance each month?

    b. If you could earn 1% per month investing your cash, what is the opportunity cost, per month, associated with your cash balance?

12. The Bulldog Company has cash needs of $5 million per month. If Bulldog needs more cash, it can sell marketable securities, incurring a fee of $300 for each transaction. If Bulldog leaves its funds in marketable securities, it expects to earn approximately 0.50% per month on their investment.

    a. If Bulldog gets a cash infusion of $1 million each time it needs cash, what are the holding costs associated with its cash investment?

    b. If Bulldog gets a cash infusion of $1 million each time it needs cash, what are the transactions costs per month associated its cash infusions?

    c. Using the EOQ model, what level of cash infusion minimizes Bulldog's costs associated with cash?

13. Buccaneer, Inc., has determined that it needs $10 million in cash per week. If Buccaneer needs additional cash, it can sell marketable securities, incurring a fee of $100 for each transaction. If Buccaneer leaves funds in its marketable securities, it expects to earn approximately 0.2% per week on their investment. Using the economic order quantity model, how much cash should Buccaneer raise from selling securities each week to minimize its costs of cash?

14. The Seminole Company wishes to apply the Miller-Orr model to manage its cash investment. Seminole's management has collected the following estimates:

    Cost per transaction   = $200
    Variance of daily cash flows   = $10,000
    Opportunity cost of cash, per day   = 0.05%

Seminole management has figured, based on their experience dealing with the cash flows of the company, that there should be a cushion—a safety stock—of cash of $20,000. Calculate the following:
a. the lower limit
b. the return point
c. the upper limit

15. The management of the Book Warehouse Company wishes to apply the Miller-Orr model to manage its cash investment. They have determined that the cost of either investing in or selling marketable securities is $100. By looking at Book Warehouse's past cash needs, they have determined that the variance of daily cash flows is $20,000. Book Warehouse's opportunity cost of cash, per day, is estimated to be 0.03%. Based on experience, management has determined that the cash balance should never fall below $10,000. Calculate the lower limit, the return point, and the upper limit based on the Miller-Orr model of cash management.

16. The Gator Corporation has determined that it can reduce its float by 3 days if it applies a number of different cash management techniques. If Gator typically receive $100,000 in payments from its customer per day and can earn 10% on its investments, what is the savings per year from the float reduction?

17. SNK, Inc. is considering evaluating its collection and deposit procedures. SNK typically has sales of $5 million per day. SNK's opportunity cost of investing in cash is 10%. If SNK can reduce the time it takes to clear its payments from customers from 7 to 6 days, what is the benefit to SNK? How much should SNK be willing to pay in annual fees to accomplish this float reduction?

18. Consider the following five different lockbox arrangements:

Arrangement	Float Reduction, in Days	Opportunity Cost per Year	Annual Collections	Bank Fee for Lockbox
A	3	10%	$1,000,000	$500
B	5	10%	1,000,000	600
C	5	10%	1,000,000	1,500
D	4	12%	500,000	500
E	3	5%	1,200,000	500

a. For each arrangement, calculate the benefits from using the lockbox system.
b. Considering the bank fee for each arrangement, which lockbox systems are attractive?

CHAPTER 20

Management of Receivables and Inventory

In Chapter 19, we saw how firms determine their need for current assets and manage their holdings in cash and marketable securities. The majority of a firm's investment in current assets, however, is tied up in accounts receivable and inventory. Both the accounts receivable and inventory represent investments that are necessary for day-to-day operations of the business. A firm needs inventory so that it will have goods to sell. As you see in the opening example, the type of inventory differs among firms largely because of the nature of the products they sell. A firm extends credit, and thus has accounts receivable, to encourage customers to purchase its goods or services.

Because accounts receivable and inventory are a use of funds, tying up funds in these investments has an associated cost. This cost must be considered alongside the benefits from the enhanced sales of goods and services. In this chapter, we will first look at the management decisions involving extending credit (i.e., accounts receivable) and then focus on inventory management.

RECEIVABLES MANAGEMENT

When a firm allows customers to pay for goods and services at a later date, it creates *accounts receivable*. By allowing customers to pay some time after they receive the goods or services, you are granting credit, which we refer to as *trade credit*. Trade credit, also referred to as *merchandise credit* or *dealer credit*, is an informal credit arrangement. Unlike other forms of credit, trade credit is not usually evidenced by

651

notes, but rather is generated spontaneously: Trade credit is granted when a customer buys goods or services.

Reasons for Extending Credit

Firms extend credit to customers to help stimulate sales. Suppose you offer a product for sale at $20, demanding cash at the time of the sale. And suppose your competitor offers the same product for sale, but allows customers 30 days to pay. Who's going to sell the product? If the product and its price are the same, your competitor, of course. So the benefit from extending credit is the profit from the increased sales.

Extending credit is both a financial and a marketing decision. When a firm extends credit to its customers, it does so to encourage sales of its goods and services. The most direct benefit is the profit on the increased sales. If the firm has a *variable cost margin* (that is, variable cost/sales) of 80%, then increasing sales by $100,000 increases the firm's profit before taxes by $20,000. Another way of stating this is that the *contribution margin* (funds available to cover fixed costs) is 20%: For every $1 of sales, 20 cents is available *after* variable costs.

The benefit from extending credit is:

$$\text{Benefit from extending credit} = \text{Contribution margin} \times \text{Change in sales} \qquad (20\text{-}1)$$

If a firm liberalizes its credit it grants to customers, increasing sales by $5 million and if its contribution margin is 25%, the benefit from liberalizing credit is 25% of $5 million, or $1.25 million.

Costs of Credit

But like any credit, it has a cost. The firm granting the credit is forgoing the use of the funds for a period—so there is an opportunity cost associated with giving credit. In addition, there are costs of administering the accounts receivable—keeping track of what is owed. And, there is a chance that the customer may not pay what is due when it is due.

The Cost of Discounts

Do firms grant credit at no cost to the customer? No, because as we just explained, a firm has costs in granting credit. So they generally give credit with an implicit or hidden cost:

- The customer that pays cash on delivery or within a specified time thereafter—called a discount period—gets a discount from the invoice price.

■ The customer that pays after this discount period pays the *full* invoice price.

Paying after the discount period is really borrowing. The customer pays the difference between the discounted price and the full invoice price. How much has been borrowed? A customer paying in cash within the discount period pays the discounted price. So what is effectively borrowed is the cash price.

In analyses of credit terms, the dollar cost to granting a discount is:

$$\text{Cost of discount} = \text{Discount percentage} \times \text{Credit sales using discount} \qquad (20\text{-}2)$$

If a discount is 5% and there are $20 million credit sales using the discount, the cost of the discount is 5% of $20 million, or $1 million.

But wait. Is this the only effect of granting a discount? *Only* if you assume that when the firm establishes the discount it does not adjust the full invoice price of their goods. But is this reasonable? Probably not. If the firm decides to alter its credit policy to institute a discount, most likely it will increase the full invoice sufficiently to be compensated for the time value of money and the risk borne when extending credit.

The difference between the cash price and the invoice price is a cost to the customer—and, effectively, a return to the firm for this trade credit. Consider a customer that purchases an item for $100, on terms of 2/10, net 30. This means if they pay within 10 days, they receive a 2% discount, paying only $98 (the cash price). If they pay on day 11, they pay $100. Is the seller losing $2 if the customer pays on day 10? Yes and no. We have to assume that the seller would not establish a discount as a means of cutting price. Rather, a firm establishes the full invoice price to reflect the profit from selling the item *and* a return from extending credit.[1]

Suppose the Discount Warehouse revises its credit terms, which had been payment in full in 30 days, and introduces a discount of 2% for accounts paid within 10 days. And suppose Discount's contribution margin is 20%. To analyze the effect of these changes, we have to project the increase in Discount's future sales and how soon Discount's customers will pay.

---

[1] If the customer pays within the discount period, there is a cost to the firm—the opportunity cost of not getting the cash at the exact date of the sale but rather some time later. With the terms 2/10 net 30, if the customer pays on the tenth day, the seller has just given a 10-day interest-free loan to the customer. This is part of the carrying cost of accounts receivable, which we will discuss in a moment.

Let's first assume that Discount does not change its sales prices. And let's assume that Discount's sales will increase by $100,000 to $1,100,000, with 30% paying within ten days and the rest paying within thirty days. The benefit from this discount is the increased contribution toward before tax profit of $100,000 × 20% = $20,000. The cost of the discount is the forgone profit of 2% on 30% of the $1.1 million sales, or $6,600.

Now let's assume that Discount changes its sales prices when it institutes the discount so that the profit margin (available to cover the firm's fixed costs) after the discount is still 20%:

$$\text{Contribution margin}(1 - 0.02) = 20\%$$

$$\text{Contribution margin} = \frac{0.20}{(1 - 0.02)} = 20.408\%$$

If sales increase to $1.1 million, the benefit is the difference is the profit,

Before the discount	= 20% of $1,000,000	= $200,000
After the discount	= 20.408% of $1,100,000	= $224,488

so the incremental benefit is $24,488. And the cost, in terms of the discounts taken is 2% of 30% of $1,100,000, or $6,600.

While we haven't taken into consideration the other costs involved (such as the carrying cost of the accounts and bad debts), we see that we get a different picture of the benefits and costs of discounts depending on what the firm does to the price of its goods and services when the discount is instituted. So what appears to be the "cost" from the discounts doesn't give us the whole picture, because the firm most likely changes its contribution margin at the same time to include compensation for granting credit. In that way, it increases the benefit from the change in the policy.

Other Costs

There are a number of costs of credit in addition to the cost of the discount. These costs include:

- The carrying cost of tying-up funds in accounts receivable instead of investing them elsewhere.
- The cost of administering and collecting the accounts.
- The risk of bad debts.

The carrying cost is similar to the holding cost that we looked at for cash balances: the product of the opportunity cost of investing in accounts receivable and the investment in the accounts. The opportunity cost is the return the firm could have earned on its next best opportunity. The investment is the amount the firm has invested to generate sales. For example, if a product is sold for $100, and its contribution margin is 25%, the firm has invested $75 in the sold item (in raw materials, labor, and other variable costs).

Suppose a firm liberalizes its credit policy, resulting in an increase in accounts receivable of $1 million. And suppose that this firm's contribution margin is 40% (which means its variable cost ratio is 60%). The firm's increased investment in accounts receivable is 60% of $1 million, or $600,000. If the firm's opportunity cost is 5%, the carrying cost of accounts receivable is:

Carrying cost of accounts receivable = 5% of $600,000 = $30,000

We can state the carrying cost more formally as:

$$\text{Carrying cost of accounts receivable} = (\text{Opportunity cost})(\text{Variable cost ratio}) \quad (20\text{-}3)$$
$$(\text{Change in accounts receivable})$$

In addition to the carrying cost, there are costs of administering and collecting accounts. Extending credit involves recordkeeping. Moreover, costs are incurred in personnel and paperwork to keep track of which customers owe what amount. In addition to simply recording these accounts, there are expenses in collecting accounts that are past due. Whether the firm collects its own accounts or hires a collection agency to collect these accounts, there are costs involved in making sure that customers pay.

Still another cost of trade credit is unpaid accounts—bad debts. If the firm demanded cash for each sale, there would be no unpaid accounts. By allowing customers to pay after the sale, the firm is taking on risk that the customer will not pay as promised. And by liberalizing its credit terms (for example, allowing longer to pay) or to whom it extend credit, the firm may attract customers who are less able to pay their obligations when promised.

The Implicit Cost of Trade Credit to the Customer

Trade credit is often stated in terms of a rate of discount, a discount period, and a net period when payment in full is due. The effective cost of trade credit to the customer can be calculated by determining first the effective interest cost for the period of credit and then placing this effective cost on an annual basis so that we can compare it with the cost of other forms of credit.

If the credit terms are stated as "2/10, net 30," this means that the customer can take a 2% discount from the invoice price if they pay within ten days, otherwise the full price is due within thirty days. If you purchase an item that costs $100, you would either pay $98 within the first ten days after purchase or the full $100 price if you pay after ten days.

The effective cost of credit is the discount forgone. For a $100 purchase, this is $2. Putting this in percentage terms, you pay 2% of the invoice price to borrow 98% of the invoice price:

$$\text{Cost of credit} = r = \frac{0.02}{0.98} = 0.020408 \text{ or } 2.0408\% \text{ per credit period}$$

The effective *annual* cost is calculated by determining the compounded annual cost if this form of financing is done *through the year*. Assuming that payment is made on the net day (thirty days after the sale), the credit period (the difference between the net period and the discount period) is twenty days and there are $t = 365/20 = 18.25$ such credit periods in a year. The effective annual cost is:

$$\text{Effective annual cost} = (1 + r)^t - 1$$
$$= (1 + 0.020408)^{18.25} - 1 = 44.58\% \text{ per year}$$

The flip-side of this trade credit is that the firm granting credit has an effective return on credit of 44.58% per year.

Credit and the Demand for a Firm's Goods and Services

When a firm decides to grant credit, it must consider the effect on its pricing and its sales. Let's return to the case where your competitor offers credit terms of payment in thirty days and your firm does not. While on the surface it may seem that your competitor has an advantage, this may not be. What if your competitor also charges higher prices? Perhaps these prices are just high enough to compensate it for the expected costs of bad debts and the time value of money. Does this mean that your firm will increase sale if they extend credit? Yes, if your firm does not change its prices. Maybe, if your firm increases prices when it extends credit.

To analyze the effect of extending credit, you must consider a number of factors:

- *The price elasticity of your goods and services.* How price sensitive are sales?
- *The probability of bad debts.* When you extend credit, how likely is it that some customers may pay late or never pay? How much compensation do you require to bear this risk?

■ *When customers are most likely to pay.* If you offer discount terms, will all your customers pay at the end of the discount period? What proportion of your customers will pay within the discount period?

As you can see, there are many variables to consider and these variables differ from firm to firm and industry to industry. An understanding of your market and of your customers' needs is required in analyzing the effects of a change in credit policy.

Credit and Collection Policies

A firm's credit and collection policies specify the terms of extending credit, deciding who gets credit, and procedures for collecting delinquent accounts. In deciding what its credit and collection policies will be, a firm considers the tradeoff between the costs of accounts receivable—the opportunity cost of investing in receivables, the cost of administering the receivables, and the cost of delinquent accounts—and the benefits of accounts receivable—the expected increase in profits and the return received from its trade credit.

Credit Policies

Credit terms consist of the maximum amount of credit, the length of period allowed for payment (that is, the net period), and the discount rate and discount period, if any. The purpose of discounts is to attract customers, thereby increasing sales, and to encourage the early payment of accounts, thereby reducing the amount tied up in accounts receivable.

Credit terms should somehow balance the marketing needs (increased sales) and the costs of these receivables (the cost of administration of receivables, the risk of bad debts, and the opportunity cost of funds). To design terms to meet your marketing needs, you must consider:

1. *Customers' cash flow patterns.* (Do our customers have seasonal cash flows? How long is your customers' operating cycle?) For example, if you are a toy manufacturer, your customers (toy retailers) have seasonal cash flow. You could tailor the terms using *seasonal dating*, where the discount period begins at the start of the customer's busy season.
2. *The terms competitors are offering.*
3. *The equitability of credit terms among customers.* Firms must be careful not to discriminate among customers. For example, different terms can be applied to customers with different credit risks, but there must be some basis for classifying them.

Evaluation of Creditworthiness

In Chapter 15, we described how rating agencies assess the credit quality of a corporate bond issuer. The rating agencies evaluate the four Cs of credit analysis: character, capacity, collateral, and covenants. When evaluating a customer's creditworthiness, the same four Cs are used, with one slightly modified—instead of convenants, there are "conditions." The four Cs as they apply to the analysis of a customer's creditworthiness are then:

Capacity: Ability of the customer to pay.
Character: Willingness of the customer to pay debts.
Collateral: Ability of creditors to collect on bad debts if the customer liquidates its assets.
Conditions: The sensitivity of the customer's ability to pay to underlying economic and market factors.

Firms use the following sources of information to assess the creditworthiness of customers:

- Prior experience with the customer.
- The credit rating assigned by rating agencies and reports on the customer, such as those of Dun & Bradstreet and TRW.
- Contact with the customer's bank or other creditors.
- Analysis of the customer's financial condition.

In setting credit policies, firms must consider the cost of these sources, such as fees for credit reports, as well as the costs of personnel and other resources in evaluating the information contained in the credit reports.

Often firms will extend a small amount of credit to a customer to get experience with that customer—to see whether they actually do pay on time.

Collection Policies

Collection policies specify the procedures for collecting delinquent accounts. Collection could start with polite reminders, continuing in progressively severe steps, and ending by placing the account in the hands of a collection agency, a firm that specializes in collecting accounts. The following sequence is typical:

1. When an account is a few days overdue, a letter is sent reminding the customer of the amount due and the credit terms.
2. When an account is a month overdue, a telephone call is made reminding the customer of the amount due, the credit terms, and efforts to collect the account by letter.

3. When an account is two months overdue it is handed over to a collection agency.

In designing the collection procedures, you must keep in mind that aggressive efforts to collect may result in lost future sales. We also have to consider the customers' circumstances. For example, if the customer in the midst of a labor strike, you may wish to avoid collection tactics that would be detrimental to your relationship with this particular customer.

Monitoring Accounts Receivable

You can monitor how well accounts receivable are managed using financial ratios and aging schedules. Financial ratios can be used to get an overall picture of how fast we collect on accounts receivable. Aging schedules, which are breakdowns of the accounts receivable by how long they have been around, help you get a more detailed picture of your collection efforts.

You can get an idea of how quickly we collect our accounts receivable by calculating the *Number of Days of Credit*, which is the ratio of the balance in accounts receivable at a point in time (say, at the end of a year) to the credit sales per day (on average, the dollar amount of credit sales during a day):

$$\text{Number of days of credit} = \frac{\text{Accounts receivable}}{\text{Credit sales per day}} \qquad (20\text{-}4)$$

where credit sales per day is the ratio of credit sales over a period, divided by the number of business days in that period. For example, averaging over a year:

$$\text{Credit sales per day} = \frac{\text{Credit sales}}{365 \text{ days}} \qquad (20\text{-}5)$$

The number of days credit ratio, also referred to as the *average collection period* and *days sales outstanding* (DSO), measures how long, on average, it takes us to collect on our accounts receivable.

Suppose that Whole Loaves, a wholesale bakery, has $1 million of credit sales per year and currently has a balance in accounts receivable of $80,000. Then:

$$\text{Credit sales per day} = \frac{\$1,000,000}{365 \text{ days}} = \$2,740 \text{ per day}$$

$$\text{and } \text{Number of days of credit} = \frac{\$80,000}{\$2,740 \text{ per day}} = 29 \text{ days}$$

This means the firm has, on average, 29 days worth of sales that have not been paid for as yet.

The firm can use this measure to evaluate the effectiveness of its collection policies, comparing the number of days of credit with the net period allowed in our with the credit terms. You can also use this information to help us in cash forecasting since it tells us how long before each credit sale turns into cash, on average.

But you need to consider certain factors in applying this measure. For example, if your sales are seasonal, which accounts receivable balance do you use? Over what period do you measure credit sales per day? You must be careful when you interpret this ratio since both the numerator and denominator are influenced by the pattern of sales. For example, firms tend to select the end of their accounting year to be the *low* point of their operating cycle. This is when business is slowest, which means the lowest inventory level and, possibly, the lowest receivables. If you evaluate receivables at a firm's year-end, you may not get the best measure of collections. It is preferable (though not always possible) to look at quarterly or monthly averages of receivables.

Firms also monitor receivables using an aging schedule. Preparing an aging schedule allows us to look at all our receivables and group them according to how long they were outstanding, such as 1 to 30 days, 31 to 40 days, and so on. For example,

Number of Days Outstanding	Number of Accounts	Amount Outstanding
1 to 30 days	120	$320,000
31 to 40 days	40	80,000
41 to 50 days	10	18,000
51 to 60 days	5	15,000
over 60 days	3	3,000

This schedule can represent the receivables according to how *many* there are in each age group or according to the *total dollars* the receivables represent in each age group. The higher the number of accounts or the number of dollars in the shortest term groups, the faster the collection.

Looking at a breakdown of accounts receivable in an aging schedule allows you to do the following:

1. Estimate the extent of customers' compliance with credit terms.
2. Estimate cash inflows from collections in the near future.

3. Identify accounts that are most overdue.

Keep in mind that the age of receivables may change from month to month if credit sales change. For example, your 30–60 day old accounts receivable may increase from June to July simply because credit sales increased from May to June—not because collections of receivables became slower.[2]

Establishing and Changing Credit Policies

The credit decisions involve tradeoffs, the profit from the additional sales versus the costs of extending credit, as follows:

Benefits	Costs
Increased profits from increased sales.	The opportunity cost of funds.
	Administration and collection costs.
	Bad debts.

It is difficult to measure the benefit of extending credit or changing credit terms because there are many variables to consider: If the firm liberalizes its credit policy, extending credit to more customers, do the costs associated with this increased credit change? Most likely. Do they change in a predictable manner? Most likely not, because you won't know the costs associated with these additional sales until you change the credit policy.

Ideally, a firm wants to design its credit (and collection) policy so that the marginal benefits from extending credit equals its marginal cost of extending credit. At this point, the firm maximizes owners' wealth. But the benefits and costs are uncertain. The best the firm can do in forecasting the benefits and costs from its credit and collection policies is to learn from its own experience (make changes and see what happens) or from the experience of others (look at what happens when a competitor changes its policies).

Analyzing a Change in Credit and Collection Policies: An Example

Let's look at an example of a firm changing its credit policy. All-Booked-Up Company is a wholesale distributor of books and all its sales are on credit For every book it sells, its variable costs are 70% of the sales price; in other words, its variable cost ratio is 70% (and its contribution margin is 30%). If All-Booked-Up sells $100,000 worth of books, it has $30,000 after variable costs.

---

[2] We will see in Chapter 29 how the aging schedule is useful in formulating cash budgets.

EXHIBIT 20.1   Proposed Change in Credit Policy for All-Booked-Up

From:	To:
Payment due in 30 days	Payment due in 40 days
Moderate collection efforts, costing 1 cent per dollar of accounts receivable	Intense collection efforts, costing 1 cent per dollar of accounts receivable for accounts paying within 40 days, 3 cents per dollar of accounts receivable for accounts paying beyond 40 days.

All-Booked-Up is proposing a change to its credit policy, as outlined in Exhibit 20.1.

Without the changes, All-Booked-Up expects $3 million in sales and $1 million of accounts receivable; with the changes, All-Booked-Up expects sales to be $4 million and accounts receivable to be $1.5 million. But where will these extra sales come from? We assume that the additional sales will come from slower paying customers who like the new 40 day credit period.

To analyze the benefits and costs, we need to know All-Booked-Up's opportunity cost of funds: What could they do with the funds if they didn't have them tied up in receivables? Let's assume that the firm's opportunity cost of funds (on a before-tax basis) is 20%. It is important that we are consistent in dealing with all before-tax benefits and costs or all after-tax benefits and costs. Because dealing with the before-tax benefits and costs saves us the adjustment for taxes, let's stick with these to make our analysis simpler.

The Benefits

The benefits from the change in policies are the profits from the increased sales. For each dollar of increased sales, All-Booked-Up makes 30 cents before taxes. So the added $1 million sales increase translates into $300,000 in increased profits before taxes:

$$\text{Benefit from extending credit} = (\text{Contribution margin})(\text{Change in sales})$$
$$= 30\%(\$1,000,000) = \$300,000$$

The Costs

The opportunity cost of funds is the cost of what the firm has tied up in accounts receivable. How much more will the firm invest in these accounts? The full $0.5 million? Not really, because only a portion of that represents funds the firm has actually invested. Suppose a book sells for $10. What has that book cost All-Booked-Up? As long as All-Booked-Up is not operating at full capacity (so it doesn't have to increase its investment in its fixed assets such as plant and equipment), they have invested $7 in that book. Though accounts receivable increase by $10 when it sells the book, All-Booked-Up has invested only $7.

The cost of funds is therefore the variable cost portion of the increased accounts receivable, as we saw in equation (20-3):

Carrying cost of accounts receivable
= (Opportunity cost)(Variable cost ratio)(Change in accounts receivable)
= (20%)(70%)($500,000) = $70,000

Another cost associated with change in policies is the additional collection cost. Before the change in the policies, collection costs were 1 cent per dollar of accounts, or $10,000. After the change, collections costs are still 1 cent per dollar for the accounts that tend to pay within 30 days, but increase to 3 cents per dollar for the added $0.5 million of accounts, or $15,000. So, the incremental collection costs are $15,000.

Benefits	Costs
Increased profits before taxes: $300,000	Carrying cost of accounts receivable: $70,000
	Increased collection costs: $15,000

Comparing the benefits, $300,000, with the costs, $70,000 + $15,000 = $85,000, it appears that All-Booked-Up would be better off with the change in its policies.

Some Final Considerations

We've simplified All-Booked-Up's policy change, leaving out many factors that would likely change. Consider the following:

- When the credit period is liberalized, customers that used to pay within thirty days may now pay within forty days, increasing accounts receivable (and the cost of funds tied up in these accounts), but probably not increasing collection costs since the cost of collecting should not increase as they stretch out their payments.
- When the credit period is liberalized, not only is the firm likely to increase sales from customers who like the longer credit period, but the firm may attract customers whose probability of bad debt is higher than its customers under the old policy. But it is unclear how much bad debts will increase, because collection attempts are being enhanced.

As you can see by the All-Booked-Up example and the additional considerations, there are many factors to consider when a firm adjusts its credit or collection policies. As one element is changed, there may be a "domino" effect. A lengthening in the credit period may increase expected sales, which increases the expected profit from sales but may also increase the expected level of accounts receivable. In turn, these effects may increase the expected opportunity cost of funds tied up in accounts receivable, the expected costs of administering accounts receivable, and the expected loss from the increase in bad debts.

Captive Finance Subsidiaries

Some firms choose to form a wholly-owned subsidiary—a corporation owned by the parent firm—to provide the credit granting and collection function of the parent firm. For example, if you buy a General Motors car, you can finance your purchase through General Motors Acceptance Corporation (GMAC), a wholly-owned subsidiary of General Motors.

GMAC is an example of the kind of firm referred to as *captive finance subsidiaries*. Their sole purpose is to finance the customers' purchase of the parent firm's products.

These subsidiaries can stimulate sales by providing easy access to loans. For example, Hyundai Motors of America found that customers were having difficulty getting auto loans for their low-priced cars, since loan default rates are typically high for loans on such autos. So Hyundai established their own finance company—Hyundai Motor Finance Co. (HMFC)—to finance customers' purchases and increase sales.

Another motive is to separate the credit function from the rest of the firm. By operating the credit granting and collection function as a separate profit center, it is easier to evaluate how well accounts receivable are managed.

INVENTORY MANAGEMENT

Inventory is the stock of physical goods for eventual sale. Inventory consists of raw material, work-in-process, and finished goods available for sale. There are many factors in a decision of how much inventory to have on hand. As with accounts receivable, there is a tradeoff between the costs of investing in inventory and the costs of insufficient inventory. There's a cost to too much inventory and there's a cost of too little inventory.

Reasons for Holding Inventory

There are several reasons to hold inventory. The most obvious is that if you sell a product, you can't transact business without inventory.

Another obvious reason is that goods cannot be manufactured instantaneously. If you manufacture goods, you will likely have some inventory in various stages of production. This is referred to as work-in-process.

You also may want to have some inventory of finished goods in case sales are greater than expected. Or you may want to hold some speculative inventory for dealing with events such as a change in the product or a change in the cost of the raw materials. For example, when Coca-Cola introduced "New Coke" to replace the "old" Coke, many retailers hoarded supplies of the "old" Coke product—since renamed "Classic Coke"—in anticipation of continued customer demand for the original product.

Further, some firms hold inventory to satisfy contractual agreements. For example, a retail outlet that is the sole distributor or representative of a product in a region, may be required to carry a specified inventory of goods for sale.

The decision to invest in inventory involves, ultimately, determining the level of inventory such that the marginal benefit (such as providing for transactions and precautionary needs) equal the marginal cost (such as carrying costs). The level of inventory at which the marginal benefits equal the marginal cost is the owners' wealth maximizing level.

Costs Associated with Inventory

There are two types of inventory cost—the cost of holding inventory and the cost of obtaining more inventory,

The holding cost for inventory, also referred to as the *carrying cost*, is the cost of keeping inventory—storage, depreciation, and obsolescence—and the opportunity cost of tying up funds in inventory. If we estimate holding cost on a per-unit basis:

Holding cost = (Average quantity)(Holding cost per unit)

Replenishing our inventory is costly. We must place orders—by phone, fax, or computer—and we have to pay shipping charges for each order. These costs make up the *ordering cost*. Given a cost per order, we calculate our ordering costs as:

Ordering cost = (Fixed cost per order)(Number of orders per period)

The total cost of inventory is the sum of the holding cost and ordering cost:

Total inventory cost = Holding cost + Ordering cost

Let

c = holding or carrying cost, in dollars per unit
Q = quantity ordered
K = cost per transaction
S = total number of units needed during the period

Then,

$$\text{Total inventory cost} = c \underset{\uparrow}{\frac{Q}{2}} + K \underset{\uparrow}{\frac{S}{Q}}$$

Carrying cost per unit	Average balance	Cost per order	Number of orders

The ABCD Company has a total demand for 500,000 units during a month. If you order 50,000 units at a time, that's 10 orders. If it costs us $100 each time we place an order, the ordering costs are 10 × $100 = $1,000. If you order 50,000 units each time you run out, you have, on average, 25,000 units on hand. Suppose the carrying cost per unit is 20. If you have 25,000 units, on average, on hand, you have holding costs of 20 × 25,000 or $5,000. Hence:

$$\text{Total inventory cost} = \$0.20\left(\frac{50,000}{2}\right) + \$100\left(\frac{500,000}{50,000}\right)$$
$$= \$0.20(25,000) + \$100(10) = \$6,000$$

In the next section, we examine two models of inventory management to discover ways to decrease inventory costs while still maintaining adequate inventory on hand.

Models of Inventory Management

There are alternative models for inventory management, but the basic idea for all of them is the same: Minimize inventory costs. We will look at two—the economic order quantity model and the just-in-time inventory model—to see how they minimize costs.

The Economic Order Quantity Model

The Economic Order Quantity (EOQ) model helps us determine what quantity of inventory to order each time we order so that total inventory costs throughout the period are minimized. The economic order quantity model assumes that:

- Inventory is received instantaneously.
- Inventory is used uniformly over the period.
- Inventory shortages are not desirable.

With these assumptions, firms can minimize the costs of inventory—the sum of the carrying costs and the ordering costs—by ordering a specific amount of inventory, referred to as the *economic order quantity*, each time they run out of inventory.

The economic order quantity is the value of Q in:

$$\text{Total cost} = c\frac{Q}{2} + K\frac{S}{Q}$$

that minimizes the total cost. Invoking a bit of calculus to minimize total costs with respect to Q, $d(\text{total cost})/d(Q)$, it turns out that the economic order quantity, Q^*, is:

$$\text{Economic order quantity} = \sqrt{\frac{2(\text{Cost per transaction})(\text{Total demand})}{\text{Carrying cost per unit}}}$$

or,

$$Q^* = \sqrt{\frac{2KS}{c}} \qquad (20\text{-}6)$$

If, $c = \$0.20$ per unit, $K = \$100$ per transaction, and $S = 500,000$ units, then:

$$Q^* = \sqrt{\frac{2(\$100)(500,000)}{\$0.20}} = 22,361 \text{ units}$$

Then for this order quantity:

$$\text{Total inventory cost} = \text{Holding cost} + \text{Ordering cost}$$

$$= \$0.20\left(\frac{22,361}{2}\right) + \$100\left(\frac{500,000}{22,361}\right)$$

$$= \$2,236 + \$2,236 = \$4,472$$

Are costs minimized at this point? Let's check it out by looking the costs at a couple of other order quantities. If the order quantity were 10,000 units, the total costs would be:

$$\text{Total costs at } Q \text{ of } 20,000 = \$0.20\left(\frac{20,000}{2}\right) + \$100\left(\frac{500,000}{20,000}\right)$$

$$= \$2,000 + \$2,500 = \$4,500$$

If the order quantity were 30,000 units, the total costs would be:

$$\text{Total costs at } Q \text{ of } 30,000 = \$0.20\left(\frac{30,000}{2}\right) + \$100\left(\frac{500,000}{30,000}\right)$$

$$= \$3,000 + \$1,667 = \$4,667$$

The costs are lowest at $Q = 22,361$ units.

We can modify the EOQ model to include factors such as: (1) safety stock, (2) lead time, and (3) allowance for stock-out.

Safety stock is an additional level of inventory intended to enable the firm to continue to meet demand in case sales levels turn out to be higher than predicted and in case there are unexpected delays in either receiving raw materials or in producing goods. The level of safety stock depends on the degree of uncertainty in our sales and production and the cost of lost sales (where the cost of lost sales comprises sales lost and the loss of customer goodwill).

For example, a large portion of automobile manufacturers' employees are unionized. A strike in one plant that makes parts can cause a ripple effect throughout the company, shutting down production at not only the striking plant but all others. The employees at one of General Motors' Canadian parts plants struck the firm in fall of 1996. General Motors had stocked sufficient parts at several U.S. locations and was able to maintain operations at its U.S. plants throughout the three-week strike.

Lead time is the time it takes between placing an order for more inventory and the time when it is received or produced. We can modify the EOQ model so that ordering takes place early enough so that the new inventory arrives just as the existing inventory runs out. If it takes, say, three days to receive inventory, having three days worth of inventory demand prior to reaching the reorder point is prudent.

The *allowance for stock-out* is the tolerance for a shortage of goods for sale. We can modify the EOQ model to permit shortages—though we risk the loss of sales and customer goodwill.

The EOQ model is useful in pointing out the trade off between holding and ordering costs. But there are some problems applying it to actual inventory management. One problem is that it does not consider the possibility that inventory may be held in several locations. For example, if a firm has many retail outlets and regional warehousing, the model has to be altered to consider order quantities for the firm as a whole, each warehouse, and each store. Another problem is that there may be different types of inventory—raw materials, work-in-process, and finished goods—and many different goods, requiring EOQ models for each one. Still another problem is that EOQ is not useful in cases where the demand for inventory is seasonal. Furthermore, EOQ is not readily adapted to cases when quantity discounts available.

Just-in-Time Inventory

The goal of the *just-in-time* (JIT) inventory model is to cut down on the firm's need to keep inventory on hand, coordinating the supply of raw materials with the production and marketing of the goods. In JIT, the raw materials are only acquired precisely when they are needed—just in time. The idea of JIT is to have zero inventory or as near zero as possible without adversely affecting production or sales. The goal of this strategy is to cut down on inventory costs:

1. Holding less inventory, so that there are lower storage costs, lower levels of spoilage, and less risk of obsolescence.
2. Coordinating with suppliers to minimize the cost of reordering inventory.

JIT requires coordination between a firm and its suppliers. To make JIT work, you must have timely, reliable delivery of goods and materials. Further, you must have a predictable production process so that you can determine your input needs in advance, which requires a high degree of production automation. In addition, demand must be predictable. If production is constantly modified to suit the demand for your product, JIT will not work well or may not work at all.

JIT is a strategy of coordination between suppliers, production, and marketing to minimize the amount of inventory to the point where it is always possible to supply exactly what consumers demand. Supplies and raw materials are delivered only when needed for production. The firm produces only those items that are needed for anticipated demand. This requires lots of coordination and falls apart if there is poor quality in any one part of the process—a defective bolt can gum up the works.

JIT works hand in hand with two other management techniques, total quality control (TQC) and employee involvement (EI). TQC is the principle that quality goods and services be a goal of *all* efforts of the firm—production, accounting, marketing, etc. Part of TQC is recognizing that some personnel of the firm are customers of other personnel. For example, the financial manager serves the production management by evaluating the expansion of the production facilities, whereas the accounting staff serves the financial manager, supplying financial data necessary for the financial manager's evaluation of the expansion.

EI is the philosophy that employees at all levels should be involved in the firm's decision making. By participating in decision making, employees are able to understand and perform their tasks better. Also, employees make significant contributions to the decision making process due to their unique perspective regarding the decision.

This management strategy of just-in-time inventory management is similar to the zero-balance account disbursements technique for cash management. Both are based on the idea that we can reduce costs if we carry a lower balance. And both require coordination and planning to make them work.

JIT has been used extensively in Japan, but now many U.S. firms are adopting JIT principles to inventory management. For example, Ford Motor Company allows its suppliers to tap into its inventory management system computer so they can figure out what supplies are needed and when to deliver them to Ford's production plants. This helps Ford's suppliers in their own planning, which benefits Ford through more efficient delivery of the goods it needs.

Other Considerations

The goal of both the economic order quantity and JIT is to minimize the costs of holding and ordering inventory. The EOQ model does this through the quantity of goods ordered that will minimize costs. JIT inventory management does this a bit differently, by focusing on the source of these costs and minimizing holding costs.

In addition to the holding and ordering costs, there are other considerations in determining the appropriate level of inventory. One consideration is taxes on inventory. For example, there may be a state tax based on the value of inventory held as of a specified date, say December 31st. In that case, you would hold on that date the smallest amount of inventory that would not cause a shortage of goods for your customers.

Another consideration is the possibility of expropriation. If you are doing business in another country, there may be a risk of that country's government expropriating—taking over—your goods. When doing business in other countries, you must assess the risk of expropriation and, if high, minimize your inventory holdings in that country.

Still another consideration is export-import quotas. For example, if we produce goods in the U.S. and sell them in Japan, there may be a limit on the amount Japan will import. Suppose the limit on imports into Japan is 50,000 units per month. If demand in Japan is seasonal—say, 20,000 per month every month except June when the demand shoots up to 200,000 units—the importer in Japan will have to import more than needed for several months to build up inventory for June.

Monitoring Inventory Management

We can monitor inventory by looking at financial ratios in much the same way we can monitor receivables. The *number of days of inventory* is the ratio of the dollar value of inventory at a point in time to the cost of goods sold per day:

$$\text{Number of days of inventory} = \frac{\text{Inventory}}{\text{Average day's cost of goods sold}} \quad (20\text{-}7)$$

This ratio is an estimate of the number of days' worth of sales you have on hand. Combined with an estimate of the demand for your goods, this ratio helps you in planning your production and purchasing of goods. For example, automobile manufacturers keep a close watch on the number of days of autos on car lots. If there are more than is typical, they tend to offer rebates and financing incentives. If there are fewer than is typical, they may step up production.

Another way to monitor inventory is the inventory turnover ratio—the ratio of what you sell over a period (the cost of goods sold) to what you have on hand at the end of that period (inventory):

$$\text{Inventory turnover} = \frac{\text{Cost of goods sold}}{\text{Inventory}} \quad (20\text{-}8)$$

The inventory turnover ratio tells you, on average, how many times inventory flows through the firm—from raw materials to goods sold—during the period. If the typical inventory turnover for a firm is, say, five times, that means that the firm completes the cycle of investing in inventory and selling it five times in the year. If the turnover is above the typical, this may suggest a possible stock-out. If the turnover is less than usual, this may suggest either production is slower (resulting in relatively more work-in-process) or that sales are sluggish and perhaps need a boost from providing sales incentives or discounting prices.

You must be careful, however, in interpreting these ratios. Because the production and sale of goods may be seasonal—and not always in sync—the value you put into your calculations may not represent what is actually going on. Most firms select the lowest point in their seasonal pattern of activity as their fiscal year-end. For example, Toys 'R Us ends its fiscal year on January 31 since its peak business period is the Christmas season. For the 2002 fiscal year, the Toys 'R Us inventory was:

Quarter End	Inventory (in Millions)
November 3, 2001	$3,547
February 2, 2002	2,041
May 4, 2002	2,241
August 3, 2002	2,466

The cost of goods sold for these four quarters was $7,661 million. If we calculate the inventory turnover using August 3, 2002 inventory, the Toys 'R Us inventory turnover was 3.1 times. If, on the other hand, we use average inventory (averaging the four quarter-end inventories), the inventory turnover was 2.98 times. While both are correct values for inventory turnover, 2.98 times is probably more representative of the firm's management of inventory throughout the year.

Also, interpretation of an inventory turnover ratio is not straightforward. Is a higher turnover good or bad? It could be either. A high turnover may mean that the firm is using its investment in inventory efficiently. But it might mean that the firm is risking a shortage of inventory. Not keeping enough on hand (relative to what is sold) incurs a chance of lost sales and customer goodwill. If Toys 'R Us runs out of stock on the "hottest" toys in the Christmas season, you can be sure that customers will shop elsewhere. Using inventory turnover ratios along with measures of profitability can give you a better idea of whether you are getting an adequate return on your investment in inventory.

RECAP

As we saw in Chapter 19 and again in this chapter, the management of current assets requires balancing the cost of having too much tied up in the asset against the benefits of having a sufficient amount of the asset on hand. Though business practices and customs differ among industries, the general idea in the management of receivables is to grant credit to encourage sales and stay competitive, while considering the costs of tying up funds and of possibly incurring bad debts. In the management of inventory, the investment in inventory differs among industries since the nature of the goods for sale dictates in large part the type of inventory required, as we saw in the opening example. However, even considering this, firms can manage the amount invested in inventory. The economic order quantity model and the just-in-time management technique can aid the financial manager in managing the investment in inventory.

SUMMARY

- The common purpose of decisions related to accounts receivable and inventory is to minimize investment in short-term assets. But in all cases, you must have some investment in the asset because you will incur costs if you do not have enough of the asset. If you lack sufficient inventory or you fail to offer competitive credit terms, you may lose sales to your competitors.
- Receivables management involves a tradeoff between the benefits of increased sales and the costs of credit (for example, the opportunity cost of funds and defaults by credit customers).
- Credit and collection policies must be formulated to consider the benefits arising from increasing sales and the costs associated with extending credit.
- Inventory management involves a tradeoff between the benefits of having sufficient inventory to meet demand and the costs of inventory (for example, the opportunity cost of funds, storage, and obsolescence).
- Models of inventory management, such as the economic order quantity model and the just-in-time technique, can be used to analyze and minimize the costs of inventory.

QUESTIONS

1. Granting credit to customers means that the firm will not receive the cash from their sales for some time after the sale. Why do firms extent credit to customers?
2. What do the credit terms "2/10, net 30" mean? If a firm changes their credit terms from "2/10, net 30" to "3/10, net 30," what do you expect to happen to its investment in accounts receivable?

3. List the Five C's of Credit. Suppose you own a small landscaping business and are considering granting credit to your customers. How would you apply the Five C's to your landscape customers?

4. Where inventory occupies a prominent position in business operations, it will usually play a key role in deciding the success of the venture. Comment.

5. Why do firms invest in inventory? What are the benefits from the investment in inventory? What are the costs to investing in inventory?

6. Compare and contrast the motives for holding cash and inventory. What are the similarities in these motives? What are the differences in these motives?

7. Distinguish between the economic order quantity and the just-in-time inventory models of inventory management.

8. If you are doing business in a foreign country, what factors must you consider in determining the level of your investment in inventory?

9. We observe that the amount firms invest in working capital varies from industry to industry and from firm to firm. We also observe that the amount invested in working capital varies according to the business cycle. Explain why a firm's working capital investment may vary according to the business cycle.

10. A consideration in determining the appropriateness of just-in-time inventory management that has come to light in recent years is the presence of a unionized work force. Discuss why unionized work forces may affect a firm's use of a management system such as JIT.

11. Calculate the contribution margin for each of the following discount rate and profit margin combinations:

	Discount Rate	Profit Margin
a	3%	20%
b	2%	15%
c	5%	30%

12. Calculate the carrying cost of accounts receivable for each of the following combinations of opportunity cost, variable cost ratio, and change in accounts receivable:

	Opportunity Cost	Variable Cost Ratio	Change in Accounts Receivable
a	5%	60%	$1,500,000
b	2%	55%	$2,250,000
c	1%	70%	$3,000,000

13. Calculate the cost of trade credit to your customers for each of the following credit terms, assuming they pay on the net day:
a. 2/10, net 30, b. 1/10, net 30, c. 3/20, net 30, d. 1/10, net 40, e. 3/10, net 40
14. The AR Company had sales of $5 million in 1991. It is estimated that 80% of all sales are on credit.
a. If the balance in accounts receivable at the end of 1991 was $500,000, how long did it take AR's customers to pay?
b. If the balance in accounts receivable at the end of 1991 was $750 million, how long did it take AR's customers to pay?
c. Suppose AR extends credit to customers on the basis of 2/10, net 30. How does the actual time it takes customers to pay compare with these credit terms if the accounts receivable balance is $500,000? if the accounts receivable balance is $750?
d. Critique the use of the number of days credit to evaluate AR's collections.
15. The COMP Computer Company is reevaluating its credit terms. Presently it is granting credit to customers using 1/10, net 40. COMP's competitors give their customers terms of 2/5, net 40. If COMP's customers miss the discount period, they typically pay on the net day.
a. Compare COMP's credit terms with its competitors'. Which has a higher implicit cost to the customer?
b. If COMP switched its terms to those of its competitors, what do you expect to happen to the amount of COMP's accounts receivable? Why?
16. The El Cheapo Company typically has $1 million of sales each year and a contribution margin of 20%. El Cheapo is considering offering its customers a 1% discount if they pay within five days of the sale, otherwise full payment is due within 20 days.
a. What is the effective annual cost of credit to its customers if El Cheapo changes its policy and customers pay on the net day?
b. If sales are expected to increase to $2 million per year when this discount is instituted and if 30% of its customers are predicted to take advantage of this discount, what is the cost of the discount to El Cheapo?
c. What contribution margin would El Cheapo need to insure a 20% profit margin on those accounts paid within five days (ignoring any costs of carrying accounts receivable)?
17. UO, Inc., is evaluating its present credit policy and is concerned that it may not be offering terms that are competitive. Presently, they offer terms of 1/10, net 30, with 50% of its customers paying within the discount period and the remainder paying within the net period. UO's credit department has projected that if the terms were changed

to 2/10, net 30, without changing the 25% contribution margin, annual credit sales will increase from $20 million to $30 million, with 75% of customers paying within ten days and the remainder paying within the net period. This change will decrease its days of credit from 20 to 15 days. UO's opportunity cost for its accounts receivable investment is 15% before taxes.

a. What is the cost to UO of changing its discount?

b. What is the change in the carrying cost of accounts receivable for UO?

c. Should UO change its discount? Explain.

18. Hurricane, Inc. is evaluating its management of inventory. Hurricane's management estimates that Hurricane needs 100,000 units per month. Each time it places an order to replenish inventory, it costs Hurricane $50. It costs approximately $5 per month to carry one unit.

a. If Hurricane orders 20,000 units each time it places an order, what are the ordering costs per month?

b. If Hurricane Company orders 20,000 units each time it places an order, what are the holding costs of inventory per month?

c. What is the economic order quantity for Hurricane? How do the inventory costs change if Hurricane orders 1,000 units more than the EOQ each time? How do the inventory costs change if Hurricane orders 1,000 units less than the EOQ each time?

19. Consider the following information from financial statements, with dollar amounts in millions:

Corporation	Inventory	Cost of Goods Sold	Primary Product
A	$816	$2,761	Drugs and health care
B	2,141	3,975	Tobacco products
C	1,147	17,932	Oil and gasoline
D	707	3,915	Food, soup
E	1,595	6,506	Computers
F	494	3,727	Food, cereal

Source: Standard & Poors' *Compustat PC Plus* CD-Rom

a. Calculate the inventory turnover for each firm.

b. Calculate the number of days of inventory for each firm.

c. Why might the inventory turnovers and number of days of inventory differ among these firms?

20. Paul's Pawn shop is reevaluating the credit terms for its customers in light of a new state law that limits interest rates on secured credit (which includes pawn shop credit) to an annual percentage rate of 45% (that is, rate × number of credit periods in a year = 45%).

Paul's currently has terms that require repayment of the loan plus 25% interest paid after 45 days.

a. What is the effective annual rate for Paul's customers before the change if they pay on the net day?

c. If Paul's wants to keep terms requiring payment within 45 days, what interest rate should it charge for this period to comply with the law? What is the effective annual rate on these new terms?

21. Complete the following table:

Company	Accounts Receivable	Credit Sales	Number of Days of Credit
X	$2,330,576	$28,355,341	
Y	$1,440,942		42
Z		$30,000,000	33

22. The Floppy Disk Company currently extends credit to its customers, offering a discount of 4% if the account is paid within 20 days, otherwise the full amount is due 40 days from the date of purchase. It is considering changing its credit terms to offer more incentive to its customers to pay early. It is proposing increasing its discount to 6% if accounts are paid within 20 days. Its contribution margin is 25% and its before-tax opportunity cost of funds is 15%.

a. Calculate the cost of trade credit to Floppy's customers that choose to pay on the net day under the present credit terms.

b. Calculate the cost of trade credit to Floppy's customers that choose to pay on the net day under the proposed credit terms.

c. If Floppy's sales are expected to increase by $5 million under these new credit terms and the percentage of customers paying within 10 days increases from 20% to 30%, what is the cost of the change in the discount for the Floppy Disk Company?

23. The I. Krueger Company is evaluating its credit terms. Currently, the I. Krueger Company allows its customers to pay in 30 days and gives the customers a 2% discount if they pay in within five days.

a. What is the effective interest rate on its current credit terms?

b. If I. Krueger moves the discount period from five days to three days (leaving the amount of the discount the same), what would be the effective interest rate that it charges credit customers that pay in 30 days?

c. If I. Krueger changes only the discount rate from 2% to 3% (leaving the discount period the same), what would be the effective interest rate that it charges its credit customers that pay in 30 days?

d. If I. Krueger changes the discount rate from 2% to 3% and changes the discount period from five to three days, what would

be the effective interest rate that it charges its credit customers
that pay in 30 days?

24. The Teeny Tiny Toy Company (often referred to as the 3T Company) manufactures toys with themes tied to recent movie releases.
3T's sales in the last fiscal year were $3 billion and sales have been
growing at a rate of 5% per year. Sales are seasonal, with the peak
sales in August of each year. 3T's fiscal year ends in January. The
forecasted sales for 3T for the next fiscal year, in millions, are:

Month	Estimated Sales	Month	Estimated Sales
February	$150	August	$450
March	160	September	370
April	170	October	320
May	230	November	300
June	250	December	230
July	380	January	140

Sales for December and January of the most recent fiscal year
are $215 million and $130 million, respectively. 3T's gross and contribution margins were 30% and 40%, respectively, in the last fiscal
year. No change in margins is expected in the next fiscal year.

3T sells its goods to retail stores on credit, with terms of 4/30,
net 90. Under the present credit terms, 30% of its customers pay
within 30 days, 60% pay within 60 days, and the rest pay within 90
days. 3T is considering changing its credit policy to stimulate sales.
Based an examination of competitors' terms, if they alter the policy
to 4/60, net 90, 3T management anticipates increasing sales by
10%, but collections are expected to slow down: Only 10% of its
sales on credit will be paid within 30 days, 80% paid within 60
days, and the rest paid within 90 days.

The costs of administering and collecting accounts receivables is
expected to increase by $200,000 since the customer base will be
increased and credit will be extended to slower-paying customers.
The cost of carrying accounts receivable (that is, the opportunity
cost) is 10%.

a. Estimate the effect that the change in the credit policy would have
on monthly sales and accounts receivable. Graph monthly sales
and accounts receivable for each month in the next fiscal year.

b. Prepare a recommendation regarding the change in the credit policy.
Be sure to list any assumptions that are necessary and discuss the
benefits and costs associated with a change in 3T's credit policy.

CHAPTER 21

Management of Short-Term Financing

As we have seen in previous chapters, a corporation invests in long-term assets, such as plant and equipment, and short-term assets, such as cash, accounts receivable, inventory, and marketable securities. Short-term assets are also referred to as *working capital*, since they are put to work to generate sales which eventually result in cash flow which ultimately generates profit. Working capital comprises *permanent* working capital and *temporary* working capital.

Permanent working capital is that investment necessary to satisfy the continual demands of operations. As we saw in Chapter 20, a firm invests cash in inventory, which is then sold for credit (creating accounts receivable), which are then collected in cash. This process continues throughout the year, with some funds circulating as current assets over time. Permanent working capital is most likely financed with long-term capital, since it represents ongoing investment of the firm.

Temporary working capital is the difference between actual working capital and permanent working capital. It arises from seasonal fluctuations in a firm's business. Because firms do not have to maintain this form of working capital throughout the year, nor year after year, it may be better to use short-term rather than long-term sources of capital to satisfy temporary needs.

As an example, let's look at how Mattel, Inc.'s investment in current assets changes during the year. Since Mattel's primary business is toy manufacturing, most of its sales are during the summer and fall months. Accounts receivable build-up in the summer and fall—the second and third quarters of the year—as toy retailers stock up for the holiday season. These increased purchases mean increased accounts receivable for

679

the toy manufacturers. As the toy retailers pay their bills—usually their sales increase around the December holidays—the toy manufacturer's accounts receivable shrink. We can see this effect in the graph in Exhibit 21.1. Mattel's total current assets increase during the third quarter of the year due to the increase in accounts receivable. During the fourth quarter, toy retailers pay their bills and Mattel's accounts receivable decrease.

The focus of this chapter is on short-term financing. We will look at alternative sources of short-term financing and their costs. We'll start with the different ways the costs of financing can be stated. This allows us to look at the benefits and the costs of alternative financing arrangements as we discuss each one.

COSTS OF SHORT-TERM FINANCING

The interest paid on any financing arrangement may be either simple interest or compound interest. Recall from Chapter 7 that *simple interest* is interest paid on only the loaned amount, and *compound interest* is interest paid on both the loaned amount and any interest due.

EXHIBIT 21.1   Mattel, Inc.'s Current Assets by Quarter, June 2000 through September 2002

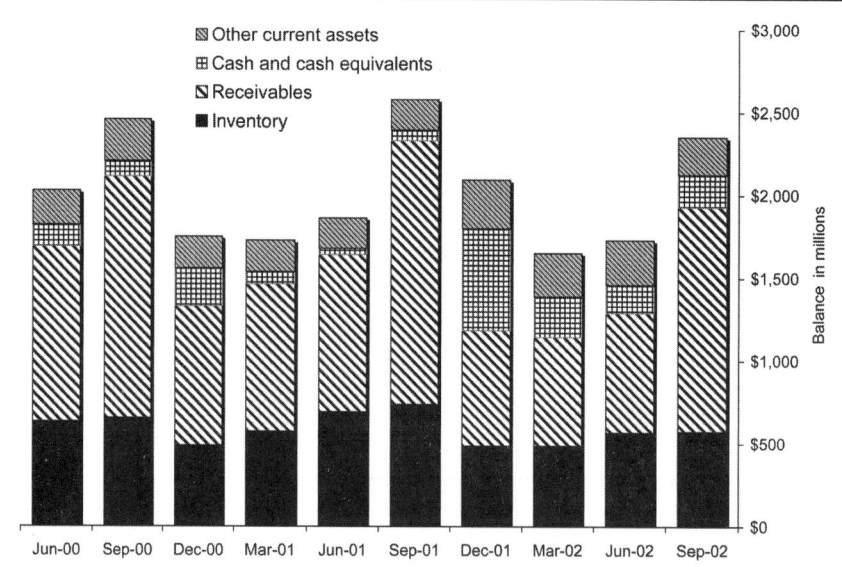

Source: Mattel Inc., financial statements, various quarters

Effective Cost of Borrowing

The *effective cost* of borrowing is the cost of financing, considering both direct and indirect costs. This effective cost is the cost of funds for a given period, the duration of time over which interest is paid and the end of which compounding (if there is compounding) is calculated. For example, if we borrow $1,000 today and must repay it plus $50 after three months, the period is three months and the cost of funds expressed in percent is $50/$1,000 = 5% for the period of the loan. Suppose we borrow $1,000 today and must repay it at the end of the year, plus 5% each quarter, with interest compounded at the end of each quarter. The "period" is three months and the amount repaid after one year is $1,000 compounded four periods at 5% per period or $1,000 \times (1 + 0.05)^4 = $1,215.51.

To compare alternative forms of financing that may have different terms, including different periods, we convert the effective cost of financing into a common unit of time—by convention, one year. Returning to our last example, suppose we use this same financing arrangement throughout a year. At the end of the first three months we borrow the amount we owe—the $1,050—for three more months. At the end of the second three months, we owe $1,050 plus the interest on $1,050:

$$\text{Amount owed} = \$1,050 + (0.05)\$1,050 = \$1,102.50$$

Borrowing once again for three more months, at the end of the second three-month period we owe $1,102.50(1.05) = $1,157.63. Borrowing again for the last three months, at the end of the year we owe $1,157.63 (1.05) = $1,215.51.

If we borrow $1,000 for one year and pay 5% interest every three months, we pay $1,215.51 − $1,000.00 = $215.51 interest. Comparing the $215.51 interest with the amount we borrowed, the effective cost over the year is:

$$\text{Effective cost of borrowing} = \frac{\$215.51}{\$1,000.00} = 0.2155 \text{ or } 21.55\% \text{ per year}$$

By stepping through this example with interest compounded every three months, we see the effect of compounding: 5% for three months compounded over one year translates into 21.55% for one year. We can look at this another way by combining our compounding into one step:

$$\text{Interest} = \underbrace{\$1,000(1.05)(1.05)(1.05)(1.05)}_{\text{Balance due after one year}} - \underbrace{\$1,000}_{\text{Principal}}$$

$$= \$1,000(1 + 0.05)^4 \qquad\qquad -\$1,000$$

The *effective annual rate (EAR)* on the borrowing is the ratio of the interest paid in one year to the principal, the amount borrowed:

$$\text{EAR} = \frac{\text{interest}}{\text{principal}}$$

Substituting the interest on the borrowing for a year,

$$\text{EAR} = \frac{\$1,000(1 + 0.05)^4 - \$1,000}{\$1,000}$$

which we can break into two fractions,

$$\text{EAR} = \frac{\$1,000(1 + 0.05)^4}{\$1,000} - \frac{\$1,000}{\$1,000}$$

Simplifying the fractions, we arrive at the formula for the effective annual rate:

$$\text{EAR} = (1 + 0.05)^4 - 1 = 0.2155 \text{ or } 21.55\% \text{ per year}$$

Designating the rate per compounding period r and the number of compounding periods within a year t, we have in general terms:

$$\text{EAR} = (1 + r)^t - 1 \tag{21-1}$$

Now let's see why the effective cost, as expressed by EAR, is the true cost of borrowing.

Annual Percentage Rate

The costs of borrowing are often stated on an *annualized basis* by multiplying the rate per compounding period by the number of compounding periods in a year. This is done partly because of custom and partly to simplify matters. The *annual percentage rate (APR)* is the annualized cost of financing (or lending, if you are on the other side of the transaction) *without considering the compounding of interest.* The APR is the product of the rate per period, r, and the number of periods in a year, t:

$$\text{APR} = r \times t \tag{21-2}$$

This APR is also referred to as the *nominal rate* or the *stated rate.* If $50 interest is paid every three months on a loan of $1,000, the APR is 5% times 4 = 20%.

The APR is simple to compute, but it is not very useful for comparing costs of alternative financing arrangements since it ignores compounding. For example, if 1% interest is paid each month, the APR is:

$$APR = 0.01(12) = 0.1200 \text{ or } 12\% \text{ per year}$$

But each month this loan's effective annual cost with compounding is:

$$EAR = (1 + 0.01)^{12} - 1 = 0.1268 \text{ or } 12.68\% \text{ per year}$$

The APR understates the effective cost of financing if interest is compounded each period during the year.

The costs of short-term financing, however, are not always straightforward. The costs of short-term financing may be direct, such as interest or commitment fees, or indirect, such as discount interest and compensating balances (we explain these terms later in the chapter). Managers must understand how to calculate the cost of financing for the alternative ways in which these costs may be stated so that we can compare them. In the remainder of this section, we demonstrate how to calculate EAR for a variety of loans.

Single Payment Interest

A *single payment loan* is a specified amount borrowed at the beginning of the loan period; it is repaid plus interest at the end of the period. The interest on this type of loan is referred to as *single payment interest* and is paid at the same time the loan is repaid.

Suppose you borrow $100,000 for six months, with an interest rate of 6% for this six-month period. After six months you repay the $100,000 plus $6,000 interest. The cost of the financing is $6,000 for the six months. To put this cost on an annual basis we need to consider the compounding effect for the second six months in the year. In our example, $r = 6\%$ and $t = 2$, and the effective annual rate is:

$$EAR = (1 + 0.06)^2 - 1 = 0.1236 \text{ or } 12.36\% \text{ per year}$$

Borrowing under these terms for one year means that you pay interest of 12.36% on the $100,000, or $12,360.

Discount Interest

A *discount loan* is a loan in which the proceeds—the funds you have available to use—are a *portion* of the stated loan amount. The interest is paid up front, deducted from the funds at the beginning of the loan.

Discount interest is the difference between the amount that must be paid back and the amount that you have available to use.

Suppose you borrow $200,000 from a bank for four months. If this is a discount loan with a rate of 5%, you have available for your use 95% of the loan amount, or $190,000. You use the $190,000 for the period of the loan and then pay the full $200,000 at the end of the loan period. The $10,000 difference is the interest on the loan—the discount interest. You effectively pay $10,000/$190,000 = 0.0526 or 5.26% for the use of the $190,000 for four months.

The effective annual rate of a discount loan is calculated in the same way as the EAR of a single payment loan once you have figured out r, the effective cost for the period. In this example, $r = 0.0526$ and there are three four-month periods in a year. The EAR is:

$$\text{EAR} = (1 + 0.0526)^3 - 1 = 1.1662 - 1 = 0.1662 \text{ or } 16.62\% \text{ per year}$$

The only difference in calculation between the single payment and the discount loan cost is how we determine r: For the single payment we determine r using the end-of-period interest, whereas for the discount loan we use the amount of the discount relative to the funds available for use.

Suppose you are given only the discount rate and the time to maturity for the loan. You can still determine the effective annual rate without knowing the amount of the loan. The rate per period is:

$$r = \frac{\text{costs}}{\text{funds available}}$$

If there is a 1% discount (the cost) we have use of 99% of the funds (funds available). If there is a 5% discount, we have use of 95% of the funds. And so on. If we let d represent the discount rate, the rate per period is:

$$r = \frac{d}{1 - d} \tag{21-3}$$

For example, if there is a 1% discount, the funds available are 99% of the face value of the loan and the rate per period is:

$$r = \frac{0.01}{0.99} = 0.0101 \text{ or } 1.01\% \text{ per period}$$

EXHIBIT 21.2   Effective Cost per Period of Loans for Alternative Discount
Percentages

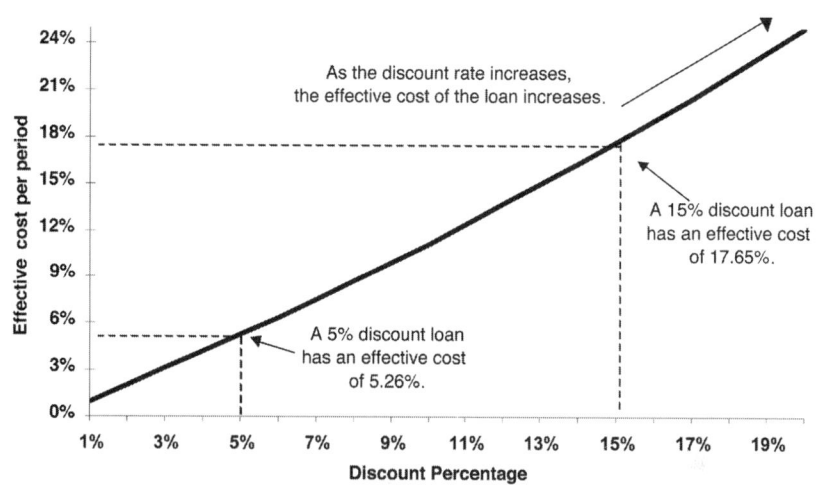

If the discount rate is 5%,

$$r = \frac{0.05}{0.95} = 0.0526 \text{ or } 5.26\% \text{per period}$$

which is what we figured out earlier by using the comparison of the discount and the funds available.

The greater the discount rate, the higher the effective cost per period. We can see this in Exhibit 21.2, where the effective cost is plotted against the discount percentage. For larger discounts, the effective cost is larger than the discount percentage. As another example, a 15% discount results in an effective cost of $r = 0.15/0.85 = 17.65\%$ per period.

Add-on-interest

Another way of stating interest is with **add-on interest**, where the total interest is *added* to the principal amount of the loan and interest is paid on both the amount borrowed and the interest to be paid on the loan. Used primarily in consumer installment loans, add-on effectively increases the effective cost of the loan.

Consider a loan of $1,000 for five years with 10% add-on interest and the loan is to be paid off in five year-end payments. The funds that are borrowed (available to the borrower) are $1,000 and the "interest" is $100 × 5 = $500. The installments are calculated based on a loan principal amount of $1,000 + 500 = $1,500: $1,500/5 = $300 each.

How much is the borrower really paying to borrow $1,000? Let's restate this loan in more familiar terms:

Present value = $1,000
Number of payments = 5
Amount of each payment = $300

and

$1,000 = $300(present value of an annuity for $T = 5$ and $r = ?$)

The effective annual cost of this loan is $r = 15.23\%$, which is more than one and one-half times the stated rate of 10%!

Compensating Balance

Some financing arrangements require that a balance be maintained in an non-interest-bearing account with the lender. This balance is referred to as a *compensating balance* because it compensates the lender for making the loan. Like in the case of a discount loan, this may have the effect of raising the cost of borrowing since you do not have the use of the funds you deposited in this balance for the period of the loan.

The amount of the compensating balance depends on the amount of the loan, ranging from 5% to 20% of the amount of the loan. Once used with nearly all bank loans, the use of compensating balances has declined in the U.S. over the years, replaced with service fees and other direct fees. However, more than two-thirds of U.S. banks still require compensating balances in their lending arrangements.

Let's see the effective cost of a compensating balance loan. First, suppose you borrow $300,000 for one year from a bank with a single payment loan that requires interest of 10% payable at the end of the year. The cost of this financing is $30,000 or 10%. We don't have to worry about compounding of interest here since interest is paid at the end of the year.

Now suppose the bank will lend to you on these same terms, with an additional stipulation: you leave 5% of the loan amount (hence, it's a discount loan) in a non-interest-bearing account for the entire year. What is the cost of the loan now? The cost is more than the 10% since we now are paying 10% of $300,000, but have the use of only 95% of the funds, or $285,000. The effective cost is:

$$\text{Effective cost} = \frac{\$30,000}{\$285,000} = 0.1053 \text{ or } 10.53\% \text{ per year}$$

The compensating balance increases the cost of the financing from 10% to 10.53%.

We can generalize the cost of financing with the compensating balance. Let r once again represent the effective cost per period, i represent the stated interest rate per compounding period on the face value of the loan, and b represent the compensating balance as a percentage of the loan face value. Then,

$$r = \frac{\text{costs}}{\text{funds available}} = \frac{i(\text{loan amount})}{(1 - b)(\text{loan amount})}$$

$$r = \frac{i}{1 - b} \tag{21-4}$$

Suppose you borrow $500,000 from the bank for three months, with a nominal annual rate of 12% (compounded every three months), and the bank requires you to maintain a compensating balance for 10% of the loan. Then, the stated quarterly rate is:

$$i = \frac{0.12}{4} = 0.03 \text{ or } 3\% \text{ for a three-month period}$$

and the compensating balance is $b = 10\%$. The *effective* cost for a three-month period is:

$$r = \frac{0.03}{1 - 0.10} = 0.0333 \text{ or } 3.33\% \text{ per period}$$

Since there are four three-month periods in a year, the effective annual cost of this financing is:

$$\text{EAR} = (1 + 0.0333)^4 - 1 = 0.1400 \text{ or } 14\% \text{ per year}$$

If there were no compensating balance requirement, the effective annual cost is:

$$\text{EAR} = (1 + 0.03)^4 - 1 = 0.1255 \text{ or } 12.55\% \text{ per year}$$

The compensating balance requirement raises the effective annual cost from 12.55% to 14%. We can see the effect of the compensating balance requirement on the effective cost of the loan in Exhibit 21.3, where the cost of the 12% loan is plotted against the compensating balance as a percentage of the loan face value. The larger the compensating balance percentage, the higher the effective cost of the loan.

Other Costs

Besides interest, discount interest, add-on interest, and compensating balances, there may be other costs associated with financing. The lender may charge a *loan origination fee*, which covers the lender's costs of credit checks and legal fees to make the loan available to you. A lender may also charge a *commitment fee*, which is compensation for the promise to make a loan since the bank stands ready to lend the funds whether used or not. All these fees increase the cost of financing.

Suppose you arrange to borrow $50,000 from the bank for three months with a single payment loan at a rate of 2.5% for three months. The effective annual cost of this credit is:

$$EAR = (1 + 0.025)^4 - 1 = 0.1038 \text{ or } 10.38\% \text{ per year}$$

If the bank charges a loan origination fee of $500, taken as a discount from the amount loaned, the effective cost for the three-month period is:

EXHIBIT 21.3   Effective Annual Cost of a Bank Loan with an Annual Percentage Rate of 12% (Interest Compounded Quarterly) for Alternative Compensating Balances

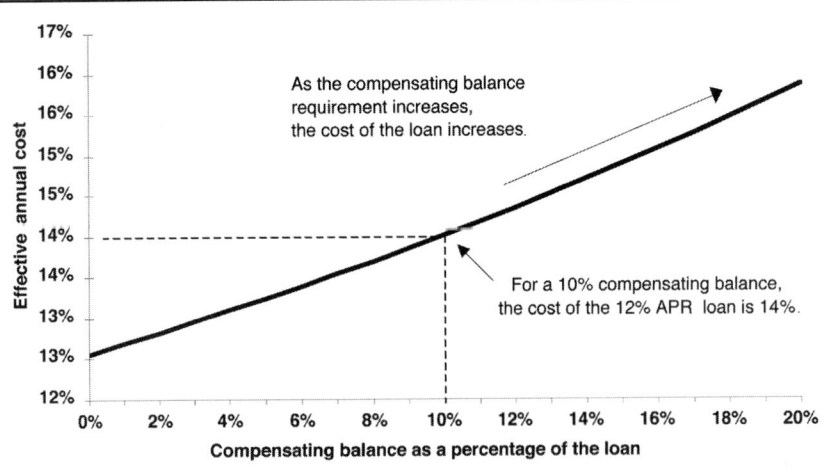

$$r = \frac{\text{costs}}{\text{funds available}} = \frac{0.025(\$50,000) + \$500}{\$50,000 - \$500}$$
$$= 0.0354 \text{ or } 3.54\% \text{ per period}$$

Taking into consideration the origination fee as a discount from the face value of the loan, the effective annual cost is:

$$\text{EAR} = (1 + 0.0354)^4 - 1$$
$$= 1.1493 - 1$$
$$= 0.1493 \text{ or } 14.93\% \text{ per year}$$

The fee raises the effective annual cost from 10.38% to 14.93%. The higher the fees, the less funds available and the higher the effective cost of the loan.

It makes a difference whether the fees are paid at the beginning of the period or the end of the period. Consider a one-year loan of $10,000 with single payment interest of 5%. If there were no fees, the effective cost of credit is 5% per year.

Suppose there is a fee of $300 associated with this loan. If the fees are paid at the beginning, you are effectively borrowing $10,000 less the fee, or $9,700. The effective cost is:

$$r = \frac{\$500 + \$300}{\$9,700} = 0.0825 \text{ or } 8.25\%$$

Suppose instead that the $300 fee is paid at the end of the loan period. You then have $10,000 to use during the entire year, so the effective cost is:

$$r = \frac{\$500 + \$300}{\$10,000} = 0.0800 \text{ or } 8.00\%$$

Paying the fee up-front effectively increases the cost of financing compared to paying the same fee at the end of the loan period.

UNSECURED FINANCING

In some types of financing, the creditor is counting on being paid the promised interest and principal, relying on the general creditworthiness of the borrower. But other creditors want more assurance of being paid back. This assurance is provided in the form of the borrower's property specified to be transferred to the lender if the borrower fails to pay as promised.

A loan that is "backed" by specific property is a *secured loan*. A loan that is backed only by the general credit of the borrower is an *unsecured loan*. There are several different types of unsecured loans. We take a look at the more widely used types of unsecured credit: trade credit, bank loans, and money market securities.

Trade Credit

Trade credit is granted by a supplier to a customer purchasing goods or services. Trade credit arises spontaneously as the customer acquires goods or services and promises to pay some time in the future. From the seller's point of view, trade credit is a way of making more sales. From the customer's point of view, trade credit is an easy way to finance the purchase of goods. Once a satisfactory relationship is established between the seller and the customer, trade credit is granted automatically. For the seller, trade credit creates accounts receivables; for the customer, trade credit creates accounts payable.

Cost of Trade Credit

There is no explicitly stated interest rate for trade credit. But there is an *implicit* cost. Suppliers allow customers to pay at a later date but offer a discount if payment is made within a specified time period. The implicit cost is the difference between the cash price (the cost after the discount) and the full invoice price. Trade credit terms customarily state the discount terms: the discount percentage, period in which the payment must be received to take advantage of the discount, and the final due date.

For example, the terms "1/15, net 30" means that if payment is made during the first 15 days, there is a 1% discount from the invoice amount, otherwise full payment of invoice amount must be paid by day 30. Exhibit 21.4 shows a time line that represents the amounts due on a $100 purchase. The figure shows that if you pay *on* or *before* the fifteenth day, your cost of the goods is $99. If you pay *after* the fifteenth day, your cost of the goods is $100. The credit period begins after day 15. You start incurring a higher cost on day 16, and the cost of the credit is $1 (the difference between $100 and $99). The credit period covers the number of days payment is delayed *beyond* the fifteenth day.

EXHIBIT 21.4   Time Line of Payments Required Under Terms 1/15, Net 30

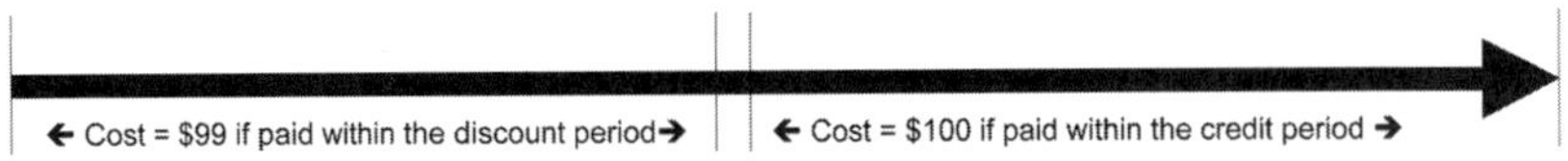

← Cost = $99 if paid within the discount period→   ← Cost = $100 if paid within the credit period →

The effective cost of credit depends on the number of days payment is delayed beyond the fifteenth day. Because terms of credit from different suppliers may be stated using different credit periods and because we may wish to compare the cost of alternative forms of credit, it is convenient to calculate the effective cost of trade credit for some common period, say a year.

What is the effective annual rate of using trade credit if terms are 1/15, net 30, and payment is made on the tenth day? Because the cash price is paid on day 10, there is no cost of credit—EAR = 0%.

What if payment is made on the twentieth day under these terms? The rate of interest is 1% of invoice price. But how much are you really borrowing? If you paid within fifteen days from the date of purchase, the cost is $99. If you pay *after* fifteen days, the cost is $100. Therefore, by paying on day 20, you are paying $1 to borrow $99 for five days:

$$r = \frac{\$1}{\$99} = 0.0101 \text{ or } 1.01\% \text{ per period (5 days in this case)}$$

If you pay on day 20, you have effectively borrowed funds for five days (from day 16 through day 20). How many five-day periods (compounding periods) are there in a year? There are 73 ($t = 365/5$). The effective annual cost of trade credit if you pay 20 days after your purchase is:

$$\text{EAR} = (1 + 0.0101)^{73} - 1 = 1.0826 \text{ or } 108.26\% \text{ per year.}$$

What this means is that you effectively borrowed $1 from the sixteenth day to the twentieth day and paid an annual rate of 109% for these five days.

What if you pay on the "net" day—thirty days after purchase? The interest rate for the credit period remains the same, since you are still paying 1% of the invoice price to borrow 99% of the invoice:

$$r = \frac{0.01}{0.99} = 0.0101 \text{ or } 1.01\% \text{ per period (15 days in this case)}$$

But the credit period is now fifteen days, so there are fewer compounding periods in a year, 24.33 ($t = 365/15$). The effective annual rate when you pay 30 days after the purchase is:

$$\text{EAR} = (1 + 0.0101)^{24.33} - 1 = 0.2770 \text{ or } 27.70\% \text{ per year.}$$

EXHIBIT 21.5   Effective Annual Cost of Trade Credit Financing with Terms of 1/15, Net 30, with Payment 18 to 50 Days After the Sale

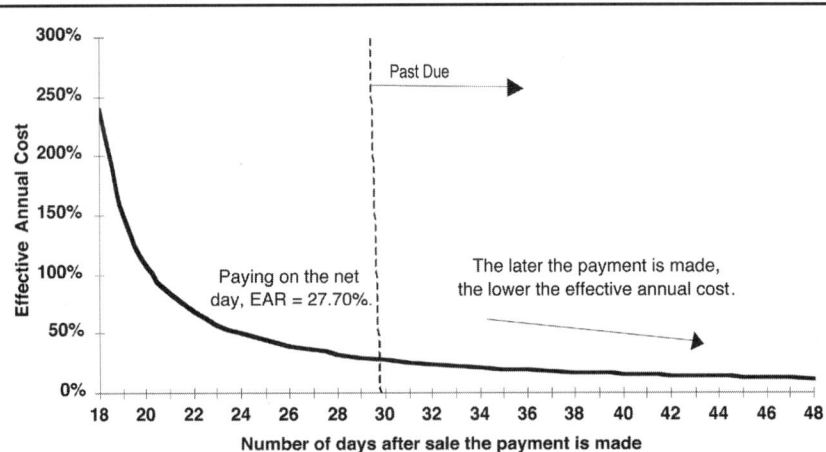

As the credit period is lengthened, the cost of trade credit declines. Why? The later within the credit period that you pay your bill, the longer you have the creditor's $1 and the lower the effective annual cost. The cost of credit for the credit period remains the same once you pay after the fifteenth day and through the thirtieth day, 1.01%, but the credit period *lengthens*. You can see this in Exhibit 21.5, where the effective annual rate of trade credit under these terms is plotted against the number of days payment is made after the purchase date, starting with the eighteenth day.[1] The effective rate drops swiftly as we stretch out our payments beyond the discount period.

Managing Accounts Payable

Managing accounts payable involves negotiating the terms of purchases, as well as deciding when to pay amounts due. Remember that accounts payable are the "flip side" of accounts receivable—your accounts payable are someone else's accounts receivable. Your suppliers are trying to minimize their costs, in terms of funds tied up in accounts receivable and bad debts. Yet, at the same time they are extending credit to generate more sales.

---

[1] We did not start graphing the effective cost in Exhibit 21.5 until 18 days from the sale because the effective interest cost is extraordinarily high for days 16 and 17.

$$\text{EAR paying 16 days after the sale} = (1.0101)^{365} - 1 = 3,817\%$$

$$\text{EAR paying 17 days after the sale} = (1.0101)^{182.5} - 1 = 526\%$$

Firms try to set these policies with an eye on the policies of their competitors, so terms of credit are uniform within industries. However, if your firm is an important customer of a particular supplier, you may be able to negotiate better terms of credit.

In calculating the cost of trade credit, managers know:

- If you pay within the discount period you are using free credit—you can delay payment by, say, ten days and pay the same as if you paid in cash on the date of purchase.
- If you pay beyond the discount period, the later you pay, the lower the cost of credit.

While paying beyond the due date does reduce the cost of trade credit even further, some other issues arise. First, paying taxes, insurance, or license fees late may cost you dearly in legal costs and sanctions. Second, your creditors may impose penalties for payments beyond the due date. Third, if you consistently pay late, you may damage your relationship with a creditor. Also, paying beyond the due date may hurt your credit rating, making it more difficult or more expensive to borrow funds from banks or to purchase goods on credit in the future.

Aside from the legal costs and the indirect and direct costs of paying late, there is an important ethical issue: You agree to specific terms when you purchase the goods on credit. Intentionally (or even unintentionally) violating these terms is unethical business behavior.

It is important to monitor accounts payable to ensure that discounts are taken when possible and payments are made within the specified period. You can evaluate your accounts payable management by examining the accounts payable turnover, a measure of how many times within a specific period the accounts payable are created and paid:

$$\text{Accounts payable turnover} = \frac{\text{credit purchases}}{\text{accounts payable}} \qquad (21\text{-}5)$$

The numerator is the total credit purchases made in the period. The denominator is a typical accounts payable balance over this period. The larger the turnover, the faster you are paying your accounts. For example, if you have \$2,000,000 of credit purchases in a year and your ending balance in accounts payable (using the ending balance as typical accounts payable) is \$200,000, the turnover is 10 times:

$$\text{Accounts payable turnover} = \frac{\$2,000,000}{\$200,000} = 10 \text{ times}$$

A high turnover may be good news or bad news: good news since you are probably establishing goodwill with your suppliers by paying quickly; bad news if you are not taking discounts but paying your bills before they are due. A low turnover may be good news, since you are stretching your payments out, lowering the effective cost of trade credit; bad news if you are paying beyond the due date, which may harm your credit standing.

Deciding whether a specific accounts payable turnover ratio is good news or bad news requires a bit more information. You can learn more about our payable management by calculating how long, on average, it takes us to pay. If you know the accounts payable you generate on a typical day and your typical balance of accounts payable, you can calculate the number of days' worth of payables you have in accounts payable. The number of days in accounts payable is calculated as:

$$\text{No. of days in accounts payable} = \frac{\text{accounts payable}}{\text{average daily credit purchases}} \quad (21\text{-}6)$$

If total credit purchases for the year are \$2,000,000, your average daily credit sales are \$2,000,000/365 = \$5,479. This implies that the number of days in your accounts payable balance is \$200,000/\$5,479 per day 36.5 days. This tells us that it takes, on average, 36.5 days to pay your accounts. Is this good or bad? It depends on your credit terms. If your credit terms all have net days of 30, then having 36.5 days in your ending balance tells you that you are, on average, paying late. If your credit terms all have net days of 60, then having 36.5 days tells you that you are, on average, paying too early.

If the credit terms you face are varied, it is difficult to evaluate the number of days in accounts payable. A more detailed breakdown of accounts payable is necessary. One breakdown is to classify it into three groups:

■ Payables that are still within the discount period
■ Payables that are beyond the discount period, yet are not overdue
■ Payables that are overdue

Once you have this classification, you can focus on why each of the accounts payable is not paid when due and why discounts were not taken. This also allows you to plan for discounts that can be taken in the near future.

Another classification scheme is to "age" the accounts payable; that is, classify the accounts by the number of days since the purchase. This breakdown allows you to identify the older accounts payable, as well as to plan ahead for the ones that must soon be paid.

Accounts payable management is a balancing act: The cost of trade credit must be balanced against the cost of alternative sources of financing. For example, if bank loans cost effectively 10% per year, should the firm borrow from the bank or use trade credit with terms of 1/15, net 30? Answer: the bank, since it costs less (10% versus 27.706%). But many times, especially for small businesses, bank loans may not be available and trade credit is the only source of financing the purchases.

Bank Financing

Banks lend money to firms under different financing arrangements. The financing arrangement may be straightforward, such as a single payment loan. Or a firm may obtain from a bank its promise to lend, such as a line of credit or revolving credit.

Single Payment Loan

A single payment loan is the simplest short-term financing arrangement. In a single payment loan, the borrower negotiates a loan of a specific sum from the lender, usually a bank, and agrees to repay the loaned amount at the end of a specified period.

Short-term bank loans are generally self-liquidating. That is, they are used to acquire assets and the cash flows from these assets are sufficient to pay off the loan. Bank loans are represented in the form of a promissory note, which specifies the amount of the loan, the maturity date, and any interest.

The interest on a single payment loan may be either discount interest or single payment interest. With discount interest, the borrower receives less than the amount of the loan, paying back the full amount of the loan at maturity. The interest is the difference between the amount of the loan—the face value—and the funds actually available to the borrower. With single payment interest, the borrower receives the amount of the loan, paying back the full amount of the loan plus interest at maturity.

The interest rate in a single payment loan may be either fixed or floating. That is, the amount of interest may be fixed at the beginning of the loan period at a specified amount, or may vary, according to some specified formula.

Rates are often quoted relative to the London Interbank Offered Rate (LIBOR) or the *prime rate*. The prime rate is the rate banks charge their most creditworthy customers.

Line of Credit

A *line of credit* is an agreement wherein a bank will make available to a firm, a loan up to a specific limit—the "line"—if the firm requests these funds. The bank extends this line of credit for a specified period, typically one year.

A line of credit is a flexible source of credit. When a firm borrows under a line of credit, it takes out notes payable to the bank, which range in maturity from one to 90 days. A bank may require that the borrower "clean-up" the line—pay off the borrowings completely—for a specified period of time.

A line of credit may be uncommitted or committed. In an *uncommitted line of credit*, the bank makes a verbal agreement to lend funds up to the line within the specified period, but is not legally bound to do so. In a *committed line of credit*, the bank makes a written agreement to lend funds and is legally bound to do so under the terms of the line of credit.

The cost of the line of credit comprises two costs. First, the borrower pays interest at a specified rate only on the funds borrowed and for the time borrowed. Second, if the agreement is a committed line of credit, the borrower pays either a commitment fee—from ¼ to ½% of the unused portion of the line of credit—or must maintain a specified compensating balance for the period of the line of credit. Either way, the firm incurs some cost, though likely quite small, for the line of credit even if it does not borrow anything against the line.

In addition to the fee or compensating balance, there may be some *covenants*—conditions that limit the actions of the borrower. Covenants may require that the borrower provide financial statements periodically or that the certain financial ratios, such as a minimum interest coverage or current ratio, be satisfied. These covenants do not usually restrict the decision-making of the borrower, but serve to protect the lender in extreme cases.

Revolving Credit

A *revolving credit agreement* is similar to a line of credit agreement, but is usually for a longer period—two to three years. The borrower can borrow and repay the credit many times *within* this period in a series of short-term notes.

The cost of the revolving credit comprises two parts: (1) the commitment fee or compensating balance, and (2) the interest on any borrowings under the agreement. Unlike the line of credit, revolving credit agreements usually specify a floating interest rate.

Typically, the borrower and lender renegotiate the revolving line of credit prior to maturity, insuring a continuous source of funds for the borrower.

Letter of Credit

Suppose you just started an import-export business and you are importing calculators made in Taiwan. Your supplier in Taiwan may not want to grant you trade credit for your purchase of the calculators—it may be too expensive or time-consuming for the supplier to evaluate your creditworthiness. But since your business is just getting started and you have very little funds, you may not want to pay outright for the calculators. You can solve this dilemma by getting a letter of credit from your local bank.

A *letter of credit* is a written promise by a bank to make a loan if specific conditions are met. In the case of your importing calculators, the condition may be that you receive the goods. The Taiwanese supplier may be willing to ship the goods to you if you have the promise from the bank: They have the assurance of your bank that payment will be made as soon as the goods are received. You will receive a loan in the amount of this payment, hence you can pay for the goods.

A letter of credit may be either revocable or irrevocable. If revocable, the bank can cancel the letter of credit; if irrevocable, the bank is committed to making the loan.

The cost of a letter of credit comprises two parts: a commitment fee for writing the letter of credit and the interest on the loan once it is made. The loan typically has a fixed interest rate.

Comparing Forms of Bank Financing

Let's see what the alternative ways of stating the costs for bank credit do to the borrower's cash flows and the effective cost of financing. Suppose there are four alternative loan arrangements, as follows:

Alternative #1 A loan with 10% single payment interest.

Alternative #2 A loan with a 10% discount.

Alternative #3 A loan with 10% single payment interest and a 20% compensating balance.

Alternative #4 A $150,000 line of credit, where any borrowings have a single payment interest of 10% and there is a 1% fee for any unused line of credit.

If you need to borrow $100,000 for one year, which of these alternatives has the lowest effective cost of financing? Let's look at each one.

Alternative #1: Single Interest Payment Since there is only a single interest payment of 10%, the effective cost of credit is 10%.

Alternative #2: Discount Loan If $100,000 of funds are needed, we have to first determine the principal amount of the loan:

$$\text{Loan amount} - 0.10(\text{loan amount}) = \$100,000$$

$$\text{Loan amount} = \frac{\$100,000}{0.90} = \$111,111$$

The principal amount of the loan is $111,111 and the discount is 10% of $111,111, or $11,111. Therefore, the effective cost of the loan is:

$$r = \frac{\$11,111}{\$100,000} = 0.1111 \text{ or } 11.11\%$$

You receive $100,000 at the beginning of the year and pay $111,111 at the end of the year.

Alternative #3: Compensating Balance If you want to borrow $100,000 and there is a 20% compensating balance, you need to borrow more than $100,000:

$$\text{Loan amount} - 0.20(\text{Loan amount}) = \$100,000$$

$$\text{Loan amount} = \frac{\$100,000}{0.80} = \$125,000$$

You therefore need to borrow $125,000 so that you can have $100,000 to use during the year, leaving $25,000 on deposit at the bank. At the end of the year you pay the interest of 10% on $125,000, or $12,500, so the effective cost of the loan is:

$$r = \frac{\$12,500}{\$100,000} = 0.1250 \text{ or } 12.50\%$$

At the end of the year, you repay the loan amount, $125,000, plus the $12,500 interest. And since you get back the use of the compensating balance, your payment to the bank (after considering getting the compensating balance back) is $125,000 + 12,500 − 25,000 = $112,500.

Alternative #4: Line of Credit If you borrow only $100,000 of the $150,000 line, your cost is comprised of two parts: (1) the 10% interest on the $100,000 you borrowed, or $10,000, and (2) the 1% fee for the $50,000 unused line of credit, or $500. The effective cost of financing is:

$$r = \frac{\$10,000 + 500}{\$100,000} = 0.1050 \text{ or } 10.50\%$$

At the end of the year, you repay the $100,000 borrowed, pay the $10,000 interest, and pay the $500 fee.

Exhibit 21.6 compares the four alternatives. As can be seen, the compensating balance, discount, and fees increase the effective cost of the loan over the 10% cost of a single payment loan.

Money Market Securities

In addition to trade credit and bank loans, there are loans that become marketable—loans that can be bought and sold on the open market. Two short-term financing arrangements that create a *money market security*—short-term securities that can be bought or sold in financial markets by investors—are commercial paper and bankers' acceptances.

Commercial Paper

Commercial paper is an unsecured promissory note with a fixed maturity issued by the borrower. Commercial paper notes have denominations (face values) starting at $25,000 each, although most have denominations of $100,000 or larger.

Commercial paper is unsecured, so the lender (the party buying the commercial paper) is counting on the borrowers ability to pay the face amount of the note at maturity. Nevertheless, almost all commercial paper is backed up by a line of credit from a bank. If commercial paper is backed and the borrower is unable to pay the lender at maturity, the bank stands ready (for a fee) to lend the borrower funds to pay off the maturing paper.

Most commercial paper notes issued in the U.S. have maturities from 3 to 270 days. Why? Because if a security has a maturity over 270 days, the issuer must register the security with the Securities and Exchange Commission. Doing so would delay the issuance and increase the cost of issuing the paper. Though these maturities are relatively short, some firms tend to use commercial paper for financing over longer periods of time. They do this by rolling over the paper—as the paper matures, they issue new commercial paper to pay off the maturing commercial paper.

EXHIBIT 21.6 Comparison of the Cost of Alternative Financing Arrangements

Financing Alternative	Arrangement	Beginning of the Year Cash Flow		End of the Year Cash Flow	Effective Cost of Financing
1	A loan with a single interest rate of 10%	$100,000 cash available	→	$110,000 paid to the bank	10.00%
2	A loan with a 10% discount	$100,000 cash available	→	$111,111 paid to the bank	11.11%
3	A loan with a single interest payment of 10% and a 20% compensating balance	$100,000 cash available	→	$125,000 + 12,500 − 25,000 = $112,500 paid to the bank	12.50%
4	A $150,000 line of credit from which any borrowings incur a single interest payment of 10 percent; in addition, there is a 1% fee on any unused credit	$100,000 cash available	→	$100,000 + 10,000 + 500 = $110,500 paid to the bank	10.50%

Finance companies and nonfinancial companies issue commercial paper. Finance companies, such as General Motors Acceptance Corporation (GMAC) and C.I.T. Financial Corporation, are in the business of lending funds to consumers, usually for consumer durables such as automobiles. Finance companies tend to continually roll over their commercial paper since it is the major source of funds to use for their lending business. Nonfinancial companies are not finance companies, but instead are manufacturing firms and public utilities. They tend to issue commercial paper to meet their seasonal financing needs.

Commercial paper is classified as either direct paper or dealer paper. *Direct paper* is sold by an issuing firm directly to investors without using a securities dealer as an intermediary. The vast majority of the issuers of direct paper are financial firms. Because financial firms require a continuous source of funds in order to provide loans to customers, they find it cost effective to establish a sales force to sell their commercial paper directly to investors. Direct issuers post rates at which they are willing to sell commercial paper with financial information vendors such as Bloomberg, Reuters, and Telerate. In the case of dealer-placed commercial paper, the issuer uses the services of a securities firm to sell its paper.

Although commercial paper is a short-term security, it is issued within a longer term program: U.S. commercial paper programs are often open-ended. For example, a company might establish a five-year commercial paper program with a limit of $300 million. Once the program is established, the company can issue commercial paper up to this amount. The program is continuous and new commercial paper can be issued at any time, daily if required.

The interest on commercial paper is generally stated as discount interest, though in recent years some commercial paper with single payment interest—interest bearing—has been issued. The interest is quoted on the basis of a 360-day year and is fixed for the maturity of the paper.

All investors in commercial paper are exposed to credit risk. Credit risk is the possibility the investor will not receive the timely payment of interest and principal at maturity. While some institutional investors do their own credit analysis, most investors assess a commercial paper's credit risk using ratings by a Nationally Recognized Statistical Rating Organizations (NRSROs). The SEC currently designates only Moody's, Standard & Poor's, and Fitch as NRSROs for rating U.S. corporate debt obligations. Exhibit 21.7 presents the commercial paper ratings from the NRSROs.

EXHIBIT 21.7   Ratings of Commercial Paper

	Fitch	Moody's	S&P
Superior	F1+/F1	P1	A1+/A1
Satisfactory	F2	P2	A2
Adequate	F3	P3	A3
Speculative	F4	NP	B, C
Defaulted	F5	NP	D

The risk that the investor faces is that the borrower will be unable to issue new paper at maturity. As a safeguard against "rollover risk," commercial paper issuers secure backup lines of credit sometimes called "liquidity enhancement." Most commercial issuers maintain 100% backing because the NRSROs that rate commercial paper usually require a bank line of credit as a precondition for a rating. However, some large issues carry less than 100% backing. Backup lines of credit typically contain a "material adverse change" provision that allows the bank to cancel the credit line if the financial condition of the issuing firm deteriorates substantially.[2]

Historically, defaults on commercial paper are relatively rare. As of the end of 2001, the last default of any consequence occurred on January 31, 1997 when Mercury Finance Co.—a sizeable player in the automobile lending business—defaulted on $17 million in commercial paper. The amount of paper in default mushroomed to $315 million by the end of the next month. Fortunately, the Mercury default inflicted minimal damage on commercial paper market.

The commercial paper market is divided into tiers according to credit risk ratings. The "top top tier" consists of paper rated A1+/P1/F1+. "Top tier" is paper rated A1/P1, F1. Next, "split tier" issues are rated either A1/P2 or A2/P1. The "second tier" issues are rated A2/P2/F2. Finally, "third tier" issues are rated A3/P3/F3.

The cost of commercial paper varies along with other market interest rates, such as the rate on a 3-month Treasury bill. In addition to general market rates, the credit rating of the issuer of commercial paper affects the cost of this form of financing. Specifically, the higher the credit rating, the lower the cost.

---

[2] Dusan Stojanovic and Mark D. Vaughan, "Who's Minding the Shop?" *The Regional Economist*, The Federal Reserve Bank of St. Louis (April 1998), pp. 1–8.

Bankers' Acceptance

A *bankers' acceptance* is a bank's commitment to pay someone else's promise to pay a specified amount at a specified date. With a bankers' acceptance, the bank is committing itself to making the specified payment at the maturity of the draft *if* the issuer of the draft does not pay. A *draft* is a written order by one party that orders a second party to make payments to a third party. A check is a draft: written by a depositor, ordering the second party (the financial institution) to pay a third party (an institution or individual). A *sight draft* orders the payment immediately (on "sight") upon presentation. A *time draft* orders payment after a specified period of time. Bankers' acceptances are typically used in international trade, though they may be used domestically as well. They generally have maturities less than 270 days, hence, they are time drafts.

Although there are a variety of ways a bankers' acceptance can be arranged, the basic idea behind all of them is that a letter of credit is transformed into a security that can be bought and sold in the open market.

Suppose a bank issues a letter of credit to assist an importer in the payment of goods. The exporter wants cash now, not the letter of credit. So the exporter takes the letter of credit to her bank and receives her funds now. But she receives *less* than the face value of the letter of credit. By cashing it in, rather than waiting for maturity, she receives less money. The exporter's bank may not want to hold onto the letter of credit until maturity, so the exporter's bank exchanges it for funds with the importer's bank. First the letter of credit is exchanged for a time draft—a promise of the importer's bank to pay. Then the draft is exchanged into funds with the importer's bank. The importer's bank is now holding a time draft that it issued. The bank can either hold it as an investment, or sell it to an investor. This process is diagrammed in Exhibit 21.8.

EXHIBIT 21.8   How Bankers' Acceptances Provide Financing for Export-Import Transactions

Round 1: Exporter Sells Goods to Importer

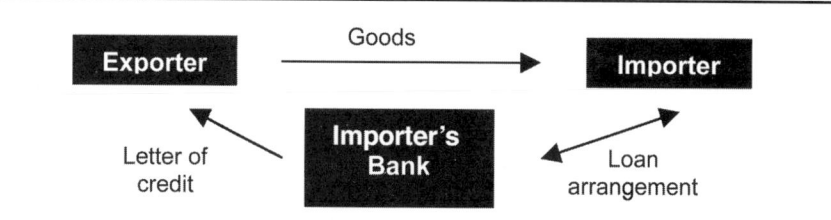

EXHIBIT 21.8   (Continued)

Round 2: Exporter Presents Letter of Credit to its Bank

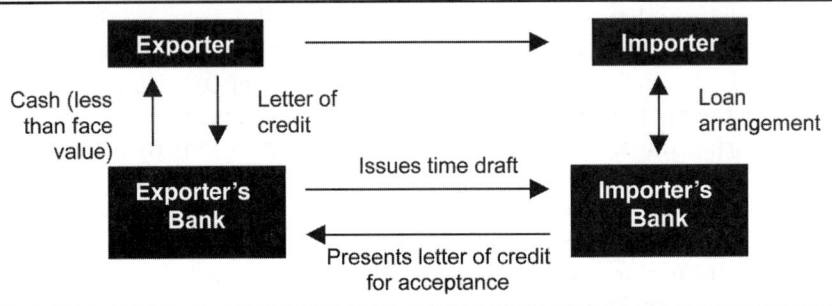

Round 3: Exporter's Bank Sells Time Draft to Importer's Bank

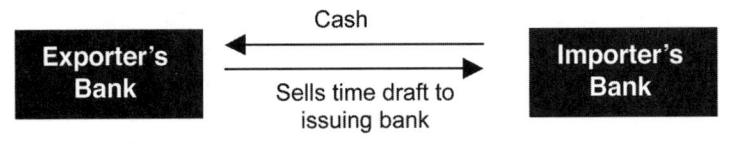

Round 4: Importer's Bank Sells Acceptance to an Investor

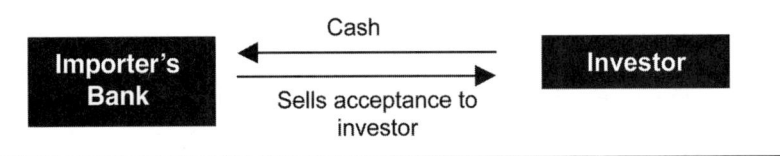

Round 5: The Banker's Acceptance Matures and the Importer's Bank Pays Cash to the Investor

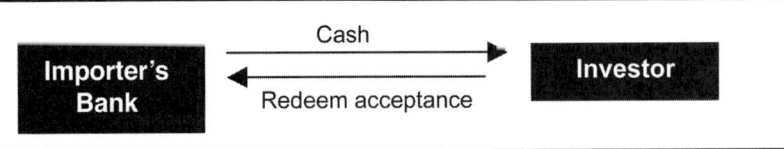

The cost of a bankers' acceptance comprises: a commitment fee or commission for the commitment, and the interest rate on the loan if the bank makes the payment for the issuer. The interest is usually stated as discount interest—the difference between the price paid and face value. The amount specified in the letter of credit is for the price of the goods plus interest; the face value of the acceptance is some amount larger than the price of the goods, with the difference being the interest on the loan. This is similar to trade credit: The exporter, by cashing in the letter of credit gets the cash price of the goods, but if he waited, he would get this cash price plus interest.

When the bankers' acceptance is sold to investors, it is sold at a discount from the face value, so when it matures, the purchaser of the goods (the importer in our example) pays face value. If the purchaser cannot pay the face value, the bank will because it has accepted the responsibility for payment.

A bankers' acceptance is similar to commercial paper. They both can be traded among investors, both have maturities less than 270 days, and both generally have discount interest. But they differ in two ways:

1. The way that they are created.
2. Their risk. Commercial paper is backed by the issuer, which *may* have a back-up line of credit; bankers acceptance is backed by the issuer, yet the bank stands ready to pay the face value. The lower risk on the bankers' acceptances results in slightly lower yields than the yields on the commercial paper.

SECURED FINANCING

Secured financing is "backed" by some specific asset or assets of the borrower. A borrower's assets used in this way are referred to as *collateral*. The collateral acts as a back-up source of funds for the lender if the borrower fails to abide by the terms of the loan.

The collateral for short-term financing arrangements are usually current assets—marketable securities, accounts receivable, or inventory. In this section we will describe two types of secured financing arrangements: accounts receivable financing and inventory financing. Another form of financing uses securities as collateral and is called a *repurchase agreement*. This form of financing is predominately used by financial institutions.

Accounts Receivable

Accounts receivable can be used as collateral for a secured loan. There are three types of financing arrangements that use accounts receivable as security assignment, factoring, and securitizing. Securitizing assets, also referred to as *asset securitization*, is an important financing arrangement for raising short- to intermediate-term funds. We devote all of Chapter 26 to the process of asset securitization.

Assignment of Receivables

The simplest form of accounts receivable financing is the assignment of receivables. In an *assignment of receivables*, the lender makes a loan accepting the borrower's accounts receivable as the collateral. The borrower receives immediate cash, in exchange for a promissory note to the lender. The borrower's customers are generally instructed to send their payments to the lender, who uses these payments to reduce the amount of the loan. This type of financing is flexible since the lender increases the loan as more receivables are generated (as acceptable collateral by the borrower) and reduces the loan as these receivable are paid off. Therefore the loan fluctuates with the needs of the borrower.

If payments on the accounts receivable are sent directly to the lender, there are potential problems. First, part of the motivation that customers have to repay their trade credit is to maintain the customer-supplier relationship. If payments are made to a party (the lender) *other* than the supplier, the customer may not be as motivated to pay.

Second, if there are disputes over goods or services, it is difficult to resolve them if payments are made to a third party. Suppose the customer refuses to pay because the goods were defective. The third party (the lender) is not in a position to resolve this dispute and part of the loan collateral may not have value.

In general, lenders loan up to 70 to 85% of the value of the accounts receivable, though the amount varies. Lenders do not accept accounts receivable that are grossly past due.

The cost of a loan that is secured with accounts receivable depends on the amount of the loan, the turnover (the rate of collection) and the creditworthiness of the accounts receivable. The interest rates charged on loans backed by accounts receivable are usually variable, tied to the interest rate on some other security. For example, a loan backed by accounts receivable may by specified as 50 basis points (0.5%) above the prime rate. If the lender performs any credit functions (such as approving credit or collecting accounts), service fees will increase the cost of the loan.

Factoring

A borrower can go a step further in financing with accounts receivable. Instead of simply using accounts receivable as collateral, the borrower can sell them outright to another party—called a *factor*—typically a bank or a commercial finance company. Selling the receivables—called *factoring*—may be done with or without recourse. In a factoring arrangement *without recourse*, the factor performs all the accounts receivable functions: evaluating customers' credit, approving credit, and collecting on accounts receivable. If any of the accounts turn out to be uncollectible, the factor bears the bad debt. If a borrower has an arrangement with a factor *with recourse* and the borrower grants credit without permission from the factor, the borrower assumes responsibilities for collection of the account.

There are basically two types of factoring, maturity factoring and conventional factoring. They differ with respect to when cash is received for the receivables. In *maturity factoring*, the customer sends cash to the factor, who then sends the cash (less a commission) to the seller. In *conventional factoring*, the factor advances cash to the seller when the accounts are factored, and then keeps the customers' payments as they come in.

Factors charge a commission of 0.75% to 1.5% of the face value of the accounts receivable. In addition, if funds are advanced, as in the case of conventional factoring, the factor charges interest on those funds, usually at a rate of 2½ to 3% above the prime rate. Because factoring is a substitute for having accounts receivable personnel, whether a firm should use factoring requires comparing what it costs to operate the receivables function with the factor's commission.

Suppose a firm borrows using conventional factoring for its $10 million accounts receivable. And suppose the factor charges a fee of 1% of the face value of the receivables, payable up front, and interest at 3% over prime. If the prime rate is 12% APR, what does it effectively cost the firm to borrow under these terms for one month?

If the factor lends the firm $10 million but then charges a fee of 1% at the beginning of the loan, the borrower has the use of only 99% of the $10 million, of $9.9 million. Interest is 3% over prime, or 15% a year. As the prime rate is an annual percentage rate, the monthly rate is 15%/12 = 1.25%. The interest is therefore 1.25% of $10 million, or $125,000. The effective cost over a month is:

$$r = \frac{\$125,000 + \$100,000}{\$9,900,000} = 0.0227 \text{ or } 2.27\%$$

and the effective annual rate is:

$$EAR = (1 + 0.227)^{12} - 1 = 30.91\%$$

Inventory

Inventory can also be used as collateral for financing since it is a fairly liquid asset. Not all inventory is of equal importance as security: The amount of funds loaned depends on how easy it is for the lender to turn the inventory into cash. In general,

- standardized inventory is much better than specialized inventory.
- nonperishable inventory is better than perishable inventory.
- raw materials and finished goods are better than work-in-process.

Types of Inventory Financing

There are several different types of loan arrangements that involve inventory as collateral. These arrangements differ in terms of the control that the lender has over the location and disposition of the inventory.

A *floating lien* is the most flexible type of inventory loan. A floating lien gives the lender a lien on all inventory of the borrower—that is, all inventory is security for the loan. Therefore the security of the loan changes as the borrower buys and sells inventory.

A *chattel mortgage* is a loan secured by specified inventory. In other words, inventory items are uniquely identified, such as by serial number, as collateral for the loan. The borrower retains title of the inventory. And although the borrower still owns the inventory, she or he cannot sell it unless the lender gives permission. This type of loan is best suited for inventory that consists of large, slow moving items.

In a *trust receipts loan*, the borrower holds the inventory in trust for the lender. As the inventory is sold, the borrower keeps the proceeds in trust for the lender. This type of arrangement is also referred to as *floor planning* and is used often with auto dealerships. First, the borrower arranges a loan with the finance company. The borrower then orders and receives the inventory, with the finance company paying the supplier. As the borrower sells the inventory items, the borrower remits the payments to the finance company, reducing the amount of the loan. Because the finance company is counting on the borrower to maintain the inventory (keep it in good condition) and send the payments when sales are made, the lender must devise a way to monitor the borrower.

In a *field warehouse loan* the lender has tighter control over the inventory. The collateral (the inventory) is kept in a separate, secured area within the borrower's premises and is monitored by a field warehouse agent. This agent keeps control over the inventory in this area and issues receipts to the lender, indicating the existence of the inventory. As the lender receives these receipts, she makes a loan based on the collateral value of the inventory. This arrangement is more expensive than the floating lien, chattel mortgage, and trust receipts arrangements because a third party—the field warehouser—must be compensated for his services. This arrangement offers the lender more peace of mind over the inventory.

Even tighter control over collateral inventory is maintained in a public warehouse loan arrangement. In a *public warehouse loan*, collateral inventory is kept in a secured area away from the borrower's premises, such as in a public warehouse, and is only released to the borrower if the lender gives permission. The warehouser issues to the lender receipts (similar to the field warehouse arrangement) from which the lender acknowledges in the form of money loaned to the borrower. In this arrangement, the *lender* has title to the goods instead of the borrower.

Cost of Inventory Financing

Suppose a firm borrows $1,000,000 for one month under a field warehousing arrangement. And suppose the interest rate on the loan is 12% APR. The interest on the loan is therefore 1% of $1,000,000, or $10,000. If the field warehouse charges a $5,000 fee, payable at the end of the month, the cost of this financing is:

$$r = \frac{\$10,000 + \$5,000}{\$1,000,000} = 0.0150 \text{ or } 1.50\%$$

and:

$$EAR = (1 + 0.0150)^{12} - 1 = 0.1956 \text{ or } 19.56\%$$

If the field warehouse charges the $5,000 fee at the *beginning* of the month, the cost for the month is more since effectively the firm has only borrowed $995,000:

$$r = \frac{\$10,000 + \$5,000}{\$995,000} = 0.0151 \text{ or } 1.51\%$$

and:

$$EAR = (1 + 0.0151)^{12} - 1 = 0.1970 \text{ or } 19.70\%$$

EXHIBIT 21.9   Annual Cost of Short-Term Financing Alternatives, 1997–2002

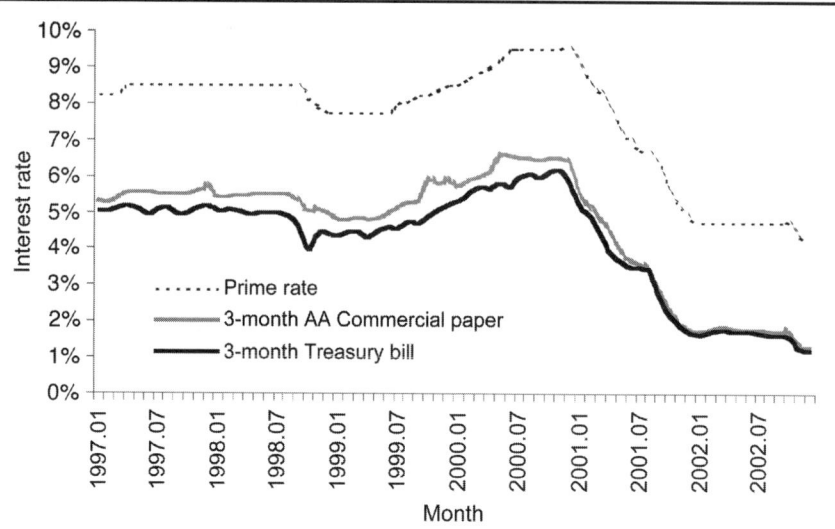

Source: Federal Reserve Bank of St. Louis

ACTUAL COSTS OF SHORT-TERM FINANCING

The cost of short-term financing is a function of many factors, including

- prevailing interest rates
- creditworthiness of borrower (credit rating)
- length of maturity of borrowing
- level of seniority
- collateral
- backup line of credit

The costs of different forms of financing vary, due to these factors. We can see the difference in the costs of several different forms of short-term financing in Exhibit 21.9, where the costs of several types of financing are shown, along with the rate on the 6-month T-Bill—the government's cost of short-term financing. We use the T-Bill rate for comparison purposes since this is the rate on a short-term security with no risk of default—the U.S. government can always print more money to cover its debts.

We see that bankers' acceptance rates are higher than the T-Bill rates. This is because there is some default risk with acceptances. Commercial paper rates are slightly higher than those for acceptances, since they are also considered to have little default risk yet may or may not be backed by a line of credit. The prime rate, which is what banks use as a base rate for their loans, is above the commercial paper rate, reflecting a generally greater risk associated with the bank loans relative to the commercial paper, which are issued by large, creditworthy corporations.

SPECIALIZED COLLATERALIZED BORROWING ARRANGEMENT FOR FINANCIAL INSTITUTIONS

There are special borrowing arrangements for financial institutions such as commercial banks and securities firms in which the securities (particularly, bonds) that they own or want to acquire are used as collateral. The arrangement is called a *repurchase agreement*.

A repurchase agreement, commonly referred to as a *repo*, is the sale of a security with a commitment by the seller to buy the same security back from the purchaser at a specified price at a designated future date. The price at which the seller must subsequently repurchase the security is called the *repurchase price* and the date that the security must be repurchased is called the *repurchase date*. Basically, a repurchase agreement is a collateralized loan, where the collateral is the security that is sold and subsequently repurchased. The term of the loan and the interest rate that the securities firm agrees to pay are specified. The interest rate is called the *repo rate*. When the term of the loan is one day, it is called an *overnight repo;* a loan for more than one day is called a *term repo.*

The transaction is referred to as a repurchase agreement because it calls for the sale of the security and its repurchase at a future date. Both the sale price and the purchase price are specified in the agreement. The difference between the purchase (repurchase) price and the sale price is the dollar interest cost of the loan.

The following illustration describes the mechanics of a repo. Suppose a securities firm wants to purchase for 10 days $10 million of a particular Treasury security using a repo to finance the purchase. Suppose further that a customer of the securities firm has excess funds of $10 million to invest for 10 days. (The customer might be a municipality with tax receipts that it has just collected, and no immediate need to disburse the funds, or a mutual fund with cash it wants to invest for 10 days.) The securities firm would agree to deliver ("sell") $10 million of the Treasury security to the customer for an amount determined by the repo rate and buy in 10 days ("repurchase") the same Treasury security from the customer for $10 million the next day. Suppose that the overnight repo rate is 3%. Then, as will be explained below, the securities firm would agree to deliver the Treasury securities for $9,991,667 and repurchase the same securities in 10 days for $10 million. The $8,333 difference between the "sale" price of $9,991,667 and the repurchase price of $10 million is the dollar interest on the financing.

The following formula is used to calculate the dollar interest on a repo transaction:

Dollar interest = (Dollar principal) × (Repo rate) × (Repo term/360)

Notice that the interest is computed on a 360-day basis. In our example, at a repo rate of 3% and a repo term of 10 days, the dollar interest is $8,333 as shown below:

$$\$10,000,000 \times 0.03 \times 10/360 = \$8,333$$

The advantage to financial institutions of using the repo market for borrowing on a short-term basis is that the rate is lower than the cost of bank financing. The reason for this is that the borrowing is secured by the collateral and if the market value of the security declines, the securities firm would be required to put up more collateral or return cash.

Four final points about repos. First, there is not one repo rate. The rate varies from transaction to transaction. One factor that affects the repo rate is the term of the borrowing. As explained in Chapter 3, there is a term structure of interest rates. The same is true in the repo market.

Second, in practice the amount loaned will not be equal to the market value of the securities. Instead, less will be loaned. By doing so, the lender reduces credit risk because the loan is overcollateralized (i.e., the amount lent is less than the market value). The difference between the market value of the security and the amount loaned is called the haircut.

Third, one can be confused by whether a repurchase agreement is a financing arrangement or an investment vehicle if one does not understand which side of the transaction a party is on. For example, in our illustration we demonstrated how a financial institution can use a repo to finance the purchase of a security. From the perspective of the customer that loaned the funds, the transaction is a short-term investment. Consequently, repos are referred to as money market instruments because they have a maturity of less than one year.

Finally, some financial institutions earn income by borrowing and lending the same security in a repo transaction with the same maturity. This is referred to as running a "matched book." For example, suppose that a securities firm enters into a term repo of 10 days with a mutual fund and lends funds to a commercial bank for 10 days using a term repo. The securities involved in both transactions are the same. If the repo rate on the repo transaction with the mutual fund is 3.30% and the repo rate on the repo transaction with the commercial bank is 3.25%, then the financial institution is earning a spread of 0.05% (5 basis points).

SUMMARY

- Short-term financing includes trade credit, bank financing, money market securities, and secured financing.
- You must calculate the effective cost of short-term financing arrangements in order to compare them. Putting the cost of financing on an effective annual basis facilitates this comparison. To calculate an effective cost, you must consider any discount interest, compensating balance requirements, and fees.
- Trade credit arises out of ordinary business transactions, where suppliers permit firms to pay at some later date. The cost of trade credit is from any discount not taken.
- Accounts payable management requires us to compare the cost of trade credit with the cost of other forms of credit. We also must weigh the benefits of paying our accounts later with the costs late payments will have in the form of our relationship with suppliers.
- Bank financing comes in many forms, including single payment loans, which may arise from simple lending arrangements or from promises to lend in the form of lines of credit, revolving credit agreements, or letters of credit.
- Short-term financing can also be obtained using loans that create marketable securities, such as commercial paper and bankers' acceptances. Because these securities have lower risk, due to the creditworthiness of the parties that issue the security and backup credit by banks, they are also lower cost ways of financing.
- There are a variety of secured financing arrangements, including accounts receivable (assignment and factoring), inventory (floating liens, chattel mortgages, trust receipts, and warehousing), and marketable securities (repurchase agreements).
- Accounts receivable may be used as collateral in a loan. In the assignment of receivables, the lender loans funds with the accounts receivable as collateral. As payments are made on the accounts (generally directly to the lender), the lender accepts these as repayment of the loan. In factoring, the borrower sells the accounts receivable to the lender, the factor.
- There are several types of loans that involve inventory as collateral. These loans differ in terms of the control that the lender has over the

inventory, ranging from little control (i.e., a floating lien) to tight control (field warehouse loan).
- The costs of short-term financing depend on many features of the loan, including the creditworthiness of the borrower, the amount borrowed, any backup line of credit, and the maturity of the loan. Generally, commercial paper and bankers' acceptances have lower costs than bank loans and loans secured with accounts receivable or inventory.
- A repurchase agreement is a specialized financing arrangement used by financial institutions to finance their purchase of securities.

QUESTIONS

1. Consider a single payment loan with interest of 10% and a discount loan with a discount of 10%. If the loan amounts and the loan periods are the same for both loans, which loan has a higher effective cost of financing? Why?
2. If a bank states 5% interest on a 360-day basis, is this stated rate less then, equal to, or more than 5% interest on a 365-day basis? Why?
3. Consider two loans with equal maturity and identical face values: a discount loan that has a discount of 10% and a single payment loan with a 10% compensating balance requirement. Which loan has the higher interest rate? Explain.
4. Consider two loans with equal maturity and identical loaned amounts: a discount loan that has a discount of 10% and a single payment loan with no interest but an origination fee of 10%. Which loan has the higher interest rate? Explain.
5. Explain the advantages and disadvantages of stretching payments on trade credit.
6. There are different ways a firm may use its inventory as collateral in financing arrangements. How do these alternative arrangements differ?
7. OEA, Inc., a manufacturer of aerospace and automobile products, at the end of their 1992 fiscal year-end had a $2.5 million line of credit, with the interest rate equal to the lending institution's prime interest rate minus 0.5%. OEA is required to keep a compensating balance on deposit with the lending institution equal to 5% of the line of credit, plus add 5% of any usage. [Source: *OEA 35th Annual Report—1992*, page 14].
   a. What do you need to consider in determining OEA's cost of the line of credit?
   b. How does the compensating balance affect OEA's cost of borrowing?
8. If there is no stated interest on trade credit, how can there be a cost to trade credit as a source of short-term financing?

9. In using trade credit, if there is a lower effective cost of paying later, what incentive is there to pay early? What incentive is there to pay within the net period?
10. Explain how the assignment of receivables differs from factoring.
11. Distinguish between maturity factoring and conventional factoring of accounts receivable.
12. Calculate the effective annual rate that corresponds to each of the following alternative financings' annual percentage rates:

Alternative	APR	Frequency of Compounding
A	12%	annually
B	12	semiannually
C	18	monthly
D	10	weekly
E	5	quarterly

13. Calculate that effective annual cost of each of the following trade credit terms and payment dates:
   a. 1/10, net 30, paying on day 20.
   b. 2/10, net 40, paying on day 30.
   c. 3/15, net 60, paying on day 60.
   d. 5/15, net 50, paying on day 50.
14. Calculate the effective annual cost of trade credit for the terms of 1/10, net 40, if payment is made:
   a. 9 days after the sale.
   b. 11 days after the sale.
   c. 20 days after the sale.
   d. 30 days after the sale.
   e. 40 days after the sale.
15. What is the effective annual cost of a single payment loan that requires interest of 6% after three months?
16. What is the effective annual cost of a discount loan that has a discount of 5% and a loan period of four months?
17. Calculate the effective annual cost of a six-month loan of $100,000 that has a 7% interest rate, and:
   a. no compensating balance nor loan origination fee.
   b. a 20% compensating balance and no loan origination fee.
   c. a 20% compensating balance and a loan origination fee of $1,000, taken as a discount.
18. Calculate the effective annual cost of a three-month loan of $1 million that has a 16% APR, and:
   a. no compensating balance nor loan origination fee.

    b. a 10% compensating balance and no loan origination fee.

    c. a 10% compensating balance and a loan origination fee of $1,000, paid at the beginning of the loan.

19. The Dieu Company had sales of $1 million in 1996, with 60% of its sales made on credit. If the average accounts payable are $100,000, what is Dieu's accounts payable turnover?

20. At the end of 1996, Golden Motors Corporation had $10 billion of accounts payable. If this balance is representative of GM's payables, and if it takes GM 30 days to pay on its accounts, how much did GM have in credit purchases during 1996?

21. Suppose that a factor is willing to lend you $6 million for one month, using your firm's accounts receivable as collateral. If the annual percentage rate on this loan is 12%, what is the effective interest rate? If the factor charges an up-front fee of 2%, what is the effective annual cost of this loan?

22. The Cash Poor Company is considering using its $1 million of accounts receivable to secure financing for the next month. Cash Poor has approached two financing firms, each offering different arrangements. Firm A is willing to lend Cash Poor 75% of the face value of the receivables at 60 basis points above the prime rate. Firm B is willing to factor Cash Poor's receivables, advancing 75% of the receivables, collecting a fee up front of 1% of all receivables, and charging interest at 30 basis points above the prime rate. In the case of Firm A's arrangement, Cash Poor continues with its evaluation and collection of credit, but in the case of Firm B's arrangement, Firm B performs all the credit functions, saving Cash Poor an estimated $10,000 over the next month. If the prime rate is 12% APR, which arrangement is less costly for Cash Poor?

23. What is the effective cost of financing for a six-month inventory field warehouse loan of $100,000 that requires interest of $6,000 to be paid at the end of six months and a warehouse fee of $5,000 to be paid at the beginning of the loan period?

24. A firm is considering using a field warehousing arrangement as part of its short-term financing. The field warehouse requires a once-a-year payment of $10,000, paid at the beginning of the year, no matter how much the firm borrows. Interest on the loan is a single payment of 10% per year, paid at the end of the year. What is the effective annual cost of borrowing using field warehousing if the amount borrowed is:

    a. $150,000?

    b. $200,000?

    c. $300,000?

    d. $500,000?

25. Evaluate the effective annual cost of each of the following credit terms:
    a. Trade credit, with terms of 2/10, net 30, paying on the net day.
    b. Bank loan with single payment interest at 5% for six months.
    c. Bank loan with discount interest of 4% for six months.
    d. Bank loan with single payment interest of 2% for three months, with a compensating balance of 10%.
    e. Bank loan with single payment interest of 3% for three months, with a compensating balance of 5%.
    f. A one-year loan secured with accounts receivable, with a service fee of 5% (payable at the end of the loan) and a 5% rate of interest.
26. Which of the following financing arrangements provides the lowest effective annual cost to the borrower?

    Arrangement #1: Commercial paper with a maturity of 91 days sold at a 14% discount from its face value.
    Arrangement #2: A bank loan with no compensating balance, but with discount interest of 14%.
    Arrangement #3: A one-year bank loan with a 10% compensating balance and 5% single payment interest.

27. If the A Company loans the B Company $100,000 for six months, with discount interest of 5%, what is the effective cost of this credit to B company?
28. Bank C requires all borrowers to maintain a 20% compensating balance during the loan periods. Company D borrows from Bank C for six months at an APR of 10%. What is Company D's effective annual cost of borrowing from Bank C?
29. What is the effective annual rate of interest for trade credit with the terms 3/10, net 40, with payment made:
    a. 20 days after the sale?
    b. 30 days after the sale?
    c. 40 days after the sale?
30. Frich Corporation is considering the use a field warehousing loan, which has a fee of $25,000 up front (that is, at the beginning of the three months of financing) and interest of 8% on all outstanding loans. If Armour borrows $2 million for one month with this field warehousing loan, what is the cost of financing for one month? What is the effective annual cost of using this financing?
31. Evaluate the effective annual cost of each of the following credit terms:
    a. Trade credit, with terms of 2/10, net 30, paying on the net day.
    b. Bank loan with single payment interest of 5% for six months.
    c. Bank loan with discount interest of 4% for six months.

    d. Bank loan with single payment interest of 2% for three months, with a compensating balance of 10%.

    e. Bank loan with single payment interest of 3% for three months, with a compensating balance of 5%.

    f. A one-year loan secured with accounts receivable, with a service fee of 5% (payable at the end of the loan) and a 5% rate of interest.

32. Financial institutions typically use a repurchase agreement to finance the purchase of a security.

    a. What a repurchase agreement?

    b. What is the advantage of using a repurchase agreement rather than borrowing from a bank?

    c. Is a repurchase agreement a lending arrangement or an investment vehicle?

33. Suppose that a commercial bank wants to purchase $1 million of a bond for five days using a repurchase agreement to finance the purchase. Suppose further that the repo rate is 2.7%.

    a. What is the dollar interest cost of borrowing?

    b. What is the repurchase price?

    c. What is the price that the commercial bank will sell the bond for to the lender in the repurchase agreement?

Financial Statement Analysis

CHAPTER 22

Financial Ratio Analysis

In this chapter, we introduce you to financial ratios—one of the tools of financial analysis. In financial ratio analysis we select the relevant information—primarily the financial statement data—and evaluate it. We show how to incorporate market data and economic data in the analysis and interpretation of financial ratios. Finally, we show you how to interpret financial ratio analysis, warning you of the pitfalls that occur when it's not done properly.

Financial analysis is one of the many tools useful in valuation because it helps the financial analyst gauge returns and risks. We begin the analysis with a fictitious firm as our example, allowing us to use simplified financial statements and allowing you to become more comfortable with the tools of financial analysis. After we cover the basics, we use these same tools with data from an actual firm in an integrative example.

RATIOS AND THEIR CLASSIFICATION

A *ratio* is a mathematical relation between two quantities. Suppose you have 200 apples and 100 oranges. The ratio of apples to oranges is 200/100, which we can conveniently express as 2:1 or 2. A financial ratio is a comparison between one bit of financial information and another. Consider the ratio of current assets to current liabilities, which we refer to as the current ratio. This ratio is a comparison between assets that can be readily turned into cash—current assets—and the obligations that are due in the near future—current liabilities. A current ratio of 2 or 2:1 means that we have twice as much in current assets as we need to satisfy obligations due in the near future.

Ratios can be classified according to the way they are constructed and the financial characteristic they are describing. For example, we will see that the current ratio is constructed as a coverage ratio (the ratio of current assets—available funds—to current liabilities—the obligation) that we use to describe a firm's liquidity (its ability to meet its immediate needs).

There are as many different financial ratios as there are possible combinations of items appearing on the income statement, balance sheet, and statement of cash flows. We can classify ratios according to how they are constructed or according to the financial characteristic that they capture.

Ratios can be constructed in the following four ways:

1. As a *coverage ratio*. A coverage ratio is a measure of a firm's ability to "cover," or meet, a particular financial obligation. The denominator may be any obligation, such as interest or rent, and the numerator is the amount of the funds available to satisfy that obligation.
2. As a *return ratio*. A return ratio indicates a net benefit received from a particular investment of resources. The net benefit is what is left over after expenses, such as operating earnings or net income, and the resources may be total assets, fixed assets, inventory, or any other investment.
3. As a *turnover ratio*. A turnover ratio is a measure of how much a firm gets out of its assets. This ratio compares the gross benefit from an activity or investment with the resources employed in it.
4. As a *component percentage*. A component percentage is the ratio of one amount in a financial statement, such as sales, to the total of amounts in that financial statement, such as net profit.

In addition, we can also express financial data in terms of time—say, how many days' worth of inventory we have on hand—or on a per share basis—say, how much a firm has earned for each share of common stock. Both are measures we can use to evaluate operating performance or financial condition.

When we assess a firm's operating performance, we want to know if it is applying its assets in an efficient and profitable manner. When we assess a firm's financial condition, we want to know if it is able to meet its financial obligations. We can use financial ratios to evaluate five aspects of operating performance and financial condition:

1. Return on investment
2. Liquidity
3. Profitability

4. Activity
5. Financial leverage

There are several ratios reflecting each of the five aspects of a firm's operating performance and financial condition. We apply these ratios to the Fictitious Corporation, whose balance sheets, income statements, and statement of cash flows were discussed in Chapter 6 and were presented in Exhibits 6.1, 6.4, and 6.6 of that chapter. The ratios we introduce now are by no means the only ones that can be formed using financial data, though they are some of the more commonly used. After becoming comfortable with the tools of financial analysis, you will be able to create ratios that serve your particular evaluation objective.

RETURN-ON-INVESTMENT RATIOS

Return-on-investment ratios compare measures of benefits, such as earnings or net income, with measures of investment. For example, if you want to evaluate how well the firm uses its assets in its operations, you could calculate the *return on assets*—sometimes called the *basic earning power ratio*—as the ratio of earnings before interest and taxes (EBIT) (also known as *operating earnings*) to total assets:

$$\text{Basic earning power} = \frac{\text{Earnings before interest and taxes}}{\text{Total assets}}$$

For Fictitious Corporation, for 1999:

$$\text{Basic earning power} = \frac{\$2,000,000}{\$11,000,000} = 0.1818 \text{ or } 18.18\%$$

For every dollar invested in assets, Fictitious earned about 18 cents in 1999. This measure deals with earnings from operations; it does not consider how these operations are financed.

Another return-on-assets ratio uses net income—operating earnings less interest and taxes—instead of earnings before interest and taxes:[1]

---

[1] In actual application the same term, return on assets, is often used to describe both ratios. It is only in the actual context or through an examination of the numbers themselves that we know which return ratio is presented. We use two different terms to describe these two return-on-asset ratios in this chapter simply to avoid any confusion.

$$\text{Return on assets} = \frac{\text{Net income}}{\text{Total assets}}$$

For Fictitious in 1999:

$$\text{Return on assets} = \frac{\$1,200,000}{\$11,000,000} = 0.1091 \text{ or } 10.91\%$$

Thus, without taking into consideration how assets are financed, the return on assets for Fictitious is 18%. Taking into consideration how assets are financed, the return on assets is 11%. The difference is due to Fictitious financing part of its total assets with debt, incurring interest of $400,000 in 1999; hence, the return-on-assets ratio excludes 1999 taxes of $400,000 from earnings in the numerator.

If we look at Fictitious' liabilities and equities, we see that the assets are financed in part by liabilities ($1 million short term, $4 million long term) and in part by equity ($800,000 preferred stock, $5.2 million common stock). If we look at the information as investors, we may not be interested in the return the firm gets from its *total* investment (debt plus equity), but rather shareholders are interested in the return the firm can generate on their investment. The **return on equity** is the ratio of the net income shareholders receive to their equity in the stock:

$$\text{Return on equity} = \frac{\text{Net income}}{\text{Book value of shareholders' equity}}$$

For Fictitious Corporation, there is only one type of shareholder: common. For 1999:

$$\text{Return on equity} = \frac{\$1,200,000}{\$6,000,000} = 0.2000 \text{ or } 20.00\%$$

Recap: Return-on-Investment Ratios

The return-on-investment ratios for Fictitious Corporation for 1999 are:

Basic earning power = 18.18%
Return on assets = 10.91%
Return on equity = 20.00%

These return-on-investment ratios tell us:

- Fictitious earns over 18% from operations, or about 11% overall, from its assets.
- Shareholders earn 20% from their investment (measured in book value terms).

These ratios do not tell us:

- Whether this return is due to the profit margins (that is, due to costs and revenues) or to how effectively Fictitious uses its assets.
- The return shareholders earn on their actual investment in the firm, that is, what shareholders earn relative to their actual investment, not the book value of their investment. For example, you may invest $100 in the stock, but its value according to the balance sheet may be greater than or, more likely, less than $100.

The Du Pont System

The returns on investment ratios give us a "bottom line" on the performance of a company, but don't tell us anything about the "why" behind this performance. For an understanding of the "why," the analyst must dig a bit deeper into the financial statements. A method that is useful in examining the source of performance is the Du Pont system. The *Du Pont system* is a method of breaking down return ratios into their components to determine which areas are responsible for a firm's performance. To see how it's used, let's take a closer look at the first definition of the return on assets:

$$\text{Basic earning power} = \frac{\text{Earnings before interest and taxes}}{\text{Total assets}}$$

Suppose the return on assets changes from 20% in one period to 10% the next period. We do not know whether this decreased return is due to a less efficient use of the firm's assets—that is, lower activity—or to less effective management of expenses (i.e., lower profit margins). A lower return on assets could be due to lower activity, lower margins, or both. Because we are interested in evaluating past operating performance to evaluate different aspects of the management of the firm and to predict future performance, knowing the source of these returns is valuable.

Let's take a closer look at the return on assets and break it down into its components: measures of activity and profit margin. We do this by relating both the numerator and the denominator to sales activity. Divide both the numerator and the denominator of the basic earning power by sales:

$$\text{Basic earning power} = \frac{\text{Earnings before interest and taxes/Sales}}{\text{Total assets/Sales}}$$

which is equivalent to:

$$\text{Basic earning power} = \left(\frac{\text{Earnings before interest and taxes}}{\text{Sales}}\right)\left(\frac{\text{Sales}}{\text{Total assets}}\right)$$

This says that the earning power of the company is related to profitability (in this case, operating profit) and a measure of activity (total asset turnover).

Basic earning power = (Operating profit margin) (Total asset turnover)

If we are analyzing a change in basic earning power, we therefore know that we could look at this breakdown to see the change in its components: operating profit margin and total asset turnover.

This method of analyzing return ratios in terms of profit margin and turnover ratios, referred to as the Du Pont System, is credited to the E.I. Du Pont Corporation, whose management developed a system of breaking down return ratios into their components.[2]

Let's look at the return on assets of Fictitious for 1998 and 1999. Its returns on assets were 20% in 1998 and 18.18% in 1999. We can decompose the firm's returns on assets for the two years, 1998 and 1999, to obtain:

Year	Basic Earning Power	Operating Profit Margin	Total Asset Turnover
1998	20.00%	22.22%	0.9000 times
1999	18.18	20.00	0.9091 times

We see that operating profit margin declined from 1998 to 1999, yet asset turnover improved slightly, from 0.9000 to 0.9091. Therefore, the return-on-assets decline from 1998 to 1999 is attributable to lower profit margins.

The return on assets can be broken down into its components in a similar manner:

---

[2] American Management Association, *Executive Committee Control Charts*, AMA Management Bulletin No. 6, 1960, p. 22.

$$\text{Return on assets } = \left(\frac{\text{Net income}}{\text{Sales}}\right)\left(\frac{\text{Sales}}{\text{Total assets}}\right)$$

or

$$\text{Return on assets} = (\text{Net profit margin})\,(\text{Total asset turnover})$$

We can relate the basic earning power ratio to the return on assets, recognizing that:

$$\text{Net income} = \text{Earnings before tax }(1 - \text{Tax rate})$$

$$\text{Net income} = \text{Earnings before interest and taxes}$$
$$\times \left(\frac{\text{Earnings before taxes}}{\text{Earnings before interest and taxes}}\right)(1 - \text{Tax rate})$$

$$\underset{\text{equity's share of earnings}}{\uparrow} \qquad \underset{\text{tax retention \%}}{\uparrow}$$

The ratio of earnings before taxes to earnings before interest and taxes reflects the interest burden of the company, where as the term $(1 - \text{tax rate})$ reflects the company's tax burden. Therefore,

$$\text{Return on assets } = \left(\frac{\text{Earnings before interest and taxes}}{\text{Sales}}\right)\left(\frac{\text{Sales}}{\text{Total assets}}\right)$$
$$\times \left(\frac{\text{Earnings before taxes}}{\text{Earnings before interest and taxes}}\right)(1 - \text{Tax rate})$$

or

$$\text{Return on assets } = (\text{Operating profit margin})(\text{Total asset turnover})$$
$$\times (\text{Equity's share of earnings})(\text{Tax retention \%})$$

The breakdown of a return-on-equity ratio requires a bit more decomposition because instead of total assets as the denominator, we want to use shareholders' equity. Because activity ratios reflect the use of all of the assets, not just the proportion financed by equity, we need to adjust the activity ratio by the proportion that assets are financed by equity (i.e., the ratio of the book value of shareholders' equity to total assets):

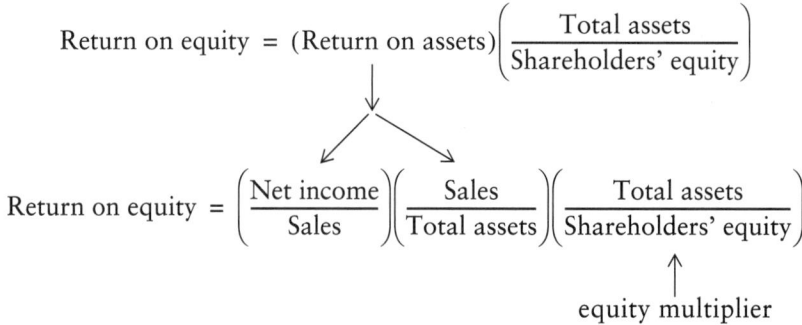

$$\text{Return on equity} = (\text{Return on assets})\left(\frac{\text{Total assets}}{\text{Shareholders' equity}}\right)$$

$$\text{Return on equity} = \left(\frac{\text{Net income}}{\text{Sales}}\right)\left(\frac{\text{Sales}}{\text{Total assets}}\right)\left(\frac{\text{Total assets}}{\text{Shareholders' equity}}\right)$$

equity multiplier

The ratio of total assets to shareholders' equity is referred to as the *equity multiplier*. The equity multiplier, therefore, captures the effects of how a company finances its assets, referred to as its financial leverage. Multiplying the total asset turnover ratio by the equity multiplier allows us to break down the return-on-equity ratios into three components: profit margin, asset turnover, and financial leverage. For example, the return on equity can be broken down into three parts:

$$\text{Return on equity} = (\text{Net profit margin})(\text{Total asset turnover})$$
$$(\text{Equity multiplier})$$

Applying this breakdown to Fictitious for 1998 and 1999:

Year	Return on Equity	Net Profit Margin	Total Asset Turnover	Total Debt to Assets	Equity Multiplier
1998	22.73%	11.11%	0.9000 times	56.00%	2.2727
1999	20.00	12.00	0.9091	45.45%	1.8332

We see that the return on equity decreased from 1998 to 1999 because of a lower operating profit margin *and* less use of financial leverage.

We can decompose the return on equity further by breaking out the equity's share of before-tax earnings (represented by the ratio of earnings before and after interest) and tax retention percent:

$$\text{Return on equity} = \left(\frac{\text{Earnings before interest and taxes}}{\text{Sales}}\right)\left(\frac{\text{Sales}}{\text{Total assets}}\right)$$
$$\times \left(\frac{\text{Earnings before taxes}}{\text{Earnings before interest and taxes}}\right)(1 - \text{Tax rate})$$
$$\times \frac{\text{Total assets}}{\text{Shareholders' equity}}$$

This decomposition allows the financial analyst to take a closer look at the factors that are controllable by a company's management (e.g., asset turnover) and those that are not controllable (e.g., tax retention). As you can see, the breakdowns lead the analyst to information on both the balance sheet and the income statement. And this is not the only breakdown of the return ratios—further decomposition is possible.

LIQUIDITY

Liquidity reflects the ability of a firm to meet its short-term obligations using those assets that are most readily converted into cash. Assets that may be converted into cash in a short period of time are referred to as *liquid assets*; they are listed in financial statements as current assets. Current assets are often referred to as *working capital*, since they represent the resources needed for the day-to-day operations of the firm's long-term capital investments. Current assets are used to satisfy short-term obligations, or current liabilities. The amount by which current assets exceed current liabilities is referred to as the *net working capital*.

The Operating Cycle

How much liquidity a firm needs depends on its operating cycle. The *operating cycle* is the duration from the time cash is invested in goods and services to the time that investment produces cash. For example, a firm that produces and sells goods has an operating cycle comprising four phases:

1. Purchase raw materials and produce goods, investing in inventory.
2. Sell goods, generating sales, which may or may not be for cash.
3. Extend credit, creating accounts receivable.
4. Collect accounts receivable, generating cash.

The four phases make up the cycle of cash use and generation. The operating cycle would be somewhat different for companies that produce services rather than goods, but the idea is the same—the operating cycle is the length of time it takes to *generate* cash through the *investment* of cash.

What does the operating cycle have to do with liquidity? The longer the operating cycle, the more current assets are needed (relative to current liabilities) since it takes longer to convert inventories and receivables into cash. In other words, the longer the operating cycle, the greater the amount of net working capital required.

To measure the length of an operating cycle we need to know:

1. The time it takes to convert the investment in inventory into sales (that is, cash → inventory → sales → accounts receivable).
2. The time it takes to collect sales on credit (that is, accounts receivable → cash).

We can estimate the operating cycle for Fictitious Corporation for 1999, using the balance sheet and income statement data. The number of days Fictitious ties up funds in inventory is determined by the total amount of money represented in inventory and the average day's cost of goods sold. The current investment in inventory—that is, the money "tied up" in inventory—is the ending balance of inventory on the balance sheet. The *average day's cost of goods sold* is the cost of goods sold on an average day in the year, which can be estimated by dividing the cost of goods sold (which is found on the income statement) by the number of days in the year. The average day's cost of goods sold for 1999 is:

$$\text{Average day's cost of good sold} = \frac{\text{Cost of goods sold}}{365 \text{ days}}$$
$$= \frac{\$6,500,000}{365 \text{ days}} = \$17,808 \text{ per day}$$

In other words, Fictitious incurs, on average, a cost of producing goods sold of $17,808 per day.

Fictitious has $1.8 million of inventory on hand at the end of the year. How many days' worth of goods sold is this? One way to look at this is to imagine that Fictitious stopped buying more raw materials and just finished producing whatever was on hand in inventory, using available raw materials and work-in-process. How long would it take Fictitious to run out of inventory?

We compute the *number of days of inventory* by calculating the ratio of the amount of inventory on hand (in dollars) to the average day's cost of goods sold (in dollars per day):

$$\text{Number of days of inventory} = \frac{\text{Amount of inventory on hand}}{\text{Average day's cost of goods sold}}$$
$$= \frac{\$1,800,000}{\$17,808 \text{ per day}} = 101 \text{ days}$$

In other words, Fictitious has approximately 101 days of goods on hand at the end of 1999. If sales continued at the same price, it would take Fictitious 101 days to run out of inventory.

If the ending inventory is representative of the inventory throughout the year, then it takes about 101 days to convert the investment in inventory into sold goods. Why worry about whether the year-end inventory is representative of inventory at any day throughout the year? Well, if inventory at the end of the fiscal year-end is lower than on any other day of the year, we have understated the number of days of inventory. Indeed, in practice most companies try to choose fiscal year-ends that coincide with the slow period of their business. That means the ending balance of inventory would be *lower* than the typical daily inventory of the year. To get a better picture of the firm, we could, for example, look at quarterly financial statements and take averages of quarterly inventory balances. However, here for simplicity we make a note of the problem of representatives and deal with it later in the discussion of financial ratios.[3]

We can extend the same logic for calculating the number of days between a sale—when an account receivable is created—to the time it is collected in cash. If we assume that Fictitious sells all goods on credit, we can first calculate the *average credit sales per day* and then figure out how many days' worth of credit sales are represented by the ending balance of receivables.

The average credit sales per day are:

$$\text{Credit sales per day} = \frac{\text{Credit sales}}{365 \text{ days}} = \frac{\$10,000,000}{365 \text{ days}} = \$27,397 \text{ per day}$$

Therefore, Fictitious generates $27,397 of credit sales per day. With an ending balance of accounts receivable of $600,000, the **number of days of credit** in this ending balance is calculated by taking the ratio of the balance in the accounts receivable account to the credit sales per day:

$$\text{Number of days of credit} = \frac{\text{Accounts receivable}}{\text{Credit sales per day}}$$
$$= \frac{\$600,000}{\$27,397 \text{ per day}} = 22 \text{ days}$$

---

[3] As an attempt to make the inventory figure more representative, some suggest taking the average of the beginning and ending inventory amounts. This does nothing to remedy the representativeness problem because the beginning inventory is simply the ending inventory from the previous year and, like the ending value from the current year, is measured at the low point of the operating cycle. A preferred method, if data are available, is to calculate the average inventory for the four quarters of the fiscal year.

If the ending balance of receivables at the end of the year is representative of the receivables on any day throughout the year, then it takes, on average, approximately 22 days to collect the accounts receivable. In other words, it takes 22 days for a sale to become cash.

Using what we have determined for the inventory cycle and cash cycle, we see that for Fictitious:

$$\text{Operating cycle} = \text{Number of days of inventory} + \text{Number of days of credit}$$
$$= 101 \text{ days} + 22 \text{ days} = 123 \text{ days}$$

We also need to look at the liabilities on the balance sheet to see how long it takes a firm to pay its short-term obligations. We can apply the same logic to accounts payable as we did to accounts receivable and inventories. How long does it take a firm, on average, to go from creating a payable (buying on credit) to paying for it in cash?

First, we need to determine the amount of an *average day's purchases on credit*. If we assume all the Fictitious purchases are made on credit, then the total purchases for the year would be the cost of goods sold less any amounts included in cost of goods sold that are not purchases. For example, depreciation is included in the cost of goods sold yet is not a purchase. Since we do not have a breakdown on the company's cost of goods sold showing how much was paid for in cash and how much was on credit, let's assume for simplicity that purchases are equal to cost of goods sold less depreciation. The average day's purchases then become:

$$\text{Average day's purchases} = \frac{\text{Cost of goods sold} - \text{Depreciation}}{365 \text{ days}}$$
$$= \frac{\$6,500,000 - \$1,000,000}{365 \text{ days}} = \$15,068 \text{ per day}$$

The number of days of purchases represented in the ending balance in accounts payable is calculated as the ratio of the balance in the accounts payable account to the average day's purchases:

$$\text{Number of days of payables} = \frac{\text{Accounts payable}}{\text{Average day's purchases}}$$

For Fictitious in 1999:

$$\text{Number of days of payables} = \frac{\$500,000}{\$15,068 \text{ per day}} = 33 \text{ days}$$

This means that on average Fictitious takes 33 days to pay out cash for a purchase.

The operating cycle tells us how long it takes to convert an investment in cash *back into* cash (by way of inventory and accounts receivable). The number of days of payables tells us how long it takes to pay on purchases made to create the inventory. If we put these two pieces of information together, we can see how long, on net, we tie up cash. The difference between the operating cycle and the number of days of purchases is the *net operating cycle*:

Net operating cycle = Operating cycle – Number of days of payables

Or, substituting for the operating cycle,

Net operating cycle = Number of days of inventory
+ Number of days of credit – Number of payables

The net operating cycle for Fictitious in 1999 is:

Net operating cycle = 101 + 22 – 33 = 90 days

The net operating cycle is how long it takes for the firm to get cash back from its investments in inventory and accounts receivable, considering that purchases may be made on credit. By not paying for purchases immediately (that is, using trade credit), the firm reduces its liquidity needs. Therefore, the longer the net operating cycle, the greater the required liquidity.

Measures of Liquidity

We can describe a firm's ability to meet its current obligations in several ways. The *current ratio* indicates the firm's ability to meet or cover its current liabilities using its current assets:

$$\text{Current ratio} = \frac{\text{Current assets}}{\text{Current liabilities}}$$

For the Fictitious Corporation, the current ratio for 1999 is the ratio of current assets, $3 million, to current liabilities, the sum of accounts payable and other current liabilities, or $1 million.

$$\text{Current ratio} = \frac{\$3,000,000}{\$1,000,000} = 3.0 \text{ times}$$

The current ratio of 3.0 indicates that Fictitious has three times as much as it needs to cover its current obligations during the year. However, the current ratio groups all current asset accounts together, assuming they are all as easily converted to cash. Even though, by definition, current assets can be transformed into cash within a year, not all current assets can be transformed into cash in a short period of time.

An alternative to the current ratio is the *quick ratio*, also called the *acid-test ratio*, which uses a slightly different set of current accounts to cover the same current liabilities as in the current ratio. In the quick ratio, the least liquid of the current asset accounts, inventory, is excluded. Hence:

$$\text{Quick ratio} = \frac{\text{Current assets} - \text{Inventory}}{\text{Current liabilities}}$$

We typically leave out inventories in the quick ratio because inventories are generally perceived as the least liquid of the current assets. By leaving out the least liquid asset, the quick ratio provides a more conservative view of liquidity.

For Fictitious, in 1999:

$$\text{Quick ratio} = \frac{\$3,000,000 - 1,800,000}{\$1,000,000} = \frac{\$1,200,000}{\$1,000,000} = 1.2 \text{ times}$$

Still another way to measure the firm's ability to satisfy short-term obligations is the *net working capital-to-sales ratio*, which compares net working capital (current assets less current liabilities) with sales:

$$\text{Net working capital-to-sales ratio} = \frac{\text{Net working capital}}{\text{Sales}}$$

This ratio tells us the "cushion" available to meet short-term obligations relative to sales. Consider two firms with identical working capital of $100,000, but one has sales of $500,000 and the other sales of $1,000,000. If they have identical operating cycles, this means that the firm with the greater sales has more funds flowing in and out of its current asset investments (inventories and receivables). The firm with more funds flowing in and out needs a larger cushion to protect itself in case of a disruption in the cycle, such as a labor strike or unexpected delays in customer payments. The longer the operating cycle, the more of a cushion (net working capital) a firm needs for a given level of sales.

For Fictitious Corporation:

$$\text{Net working capital-to-sales ratio} = \frac{\$3,000,000 - 1,000,000}{\$10,000,000}$$

$$= 0.2000 \text{ or } 20\%$$

The ratio of 0.20 tells us that for every dollar of sales, Fictitious has 20 cents of net working capital to support it.

Recap: Liquidity Ratios

Operating cycle and liquidity ratio information for Fictitious, using data from 1999, in summary, is:

Number of days of inventory	=	101 days
Number of days of credit	=	22 days
Operating cycle	=	123 days
Number of days of payables	=	33 days
Net operating cycle	=	90 days
Current ratio	=	3.0
Quick ratio	=	1.2
Net working capital-to-sales ratio	=	20%

Given the measures of time related to the current accounts—the operating cycle and the net operating cycle—and the three measures of liquidity—current ratio, quick ratio, and net working capital-to-sales ratio—we know the following about Fictitious Corporation's ability to meet its short-term obligations:

- Inventory is less liquid than accounts receivable (comparing days of inventory with days of credit).
- Current assets are greater than needed to satisfy current liabilities in a year (from the current ratio).
- The quick ratio tells us that Fictitious can meet its short-term obligations even without resorting to selling inventory.
- The net working capital "cushion" is 20 cents for every dollar of sales (from the net working capital-to-sales ratio.)

What don't ratios tells us about liquidity? They don't provide us with answers to the following questions:

■ How liquid are the accounts receivable? How much of the accounts receivable will be collectible? Whereas we know it takes, on average, 22 days to collect, we do not know how much will never be collected.

■ What is the nature of the current liabilities? How much of current liabilities consists of items that recur (such as accounts payable and wages payable) each period and how much consists of occasional items (such as income taxes payable)?

■ Are there any unrecorded liabilities (such as operating leases) that are not included in current liabilities?

PROFITABILITY RATIOS

We have seen that liquidity ratios tell us about a firm's ability to meet its immediate obligations. Now we extend our analysis skills by adding profitability ratios, which help us gauge how well a firm is managing its expenses. *Profit margin ratios* compare components of income with sales. They give us an idea of which factors make up a firm's income and are usually expressed as a portion of each dollar of sales. For example, the profit margin ratios we discuss here differ only in the numerator. It's in the numerator that we can evaluate performance for different aspects of the business.

For example, suppose the analyst wants to evaluate how well production facilities are managed. The analyst would focus on gross profit (sales less cost of goods sold), a measure of income that is the direct result of production management. Comparing gross profit with sales produces the *gross profit margin*:

$$\text{Gross profit margin} = \frac{\text{Sales} - \text{Cost of goods sold}}{\text{Sales}}$$

This ratio tells us the portion of each dollar of sales that remains after deducting production expenses. For Fictitious Corporation for 1999:

$$\text{Gross profit margin} = \frac{\$10,000,000 - \$6,500,000}{\$10,000,000} = \frac{\$3,500,000}{\$10,000,000}$$
$$= 0.3500 \text{ or } 35\%$$

For each dollar of sales, the firm's gross profit is 35 cents. Looking at sales and cost of goods sold, we can see that the gross profit margin is affected by:

■ Changes in sales volume, which affect cost of goods sold *and* sales.
■ Changes in sales price, which affect sales.
■ Changes in the cost of production, which affect cost of goods sold.

Any change in gross profit margin from one period to the next is caused by one or more of those three factors. Similarly, differences in gross margin ratios among firms are the result of differences in those factors.

To evaluate operating performance, we need to consider operating expenses in addition to the cost of goods sold. To do this, we remove operating expenses (e.g., selling and general administrative expenses) from gross profit, leaving us with operating profit, also referred to as earnings before interest and taxes (EBIT). The *operating profit margin* is therefore:

$$\text{Operating profit margin} = \frac{\text{Sales} - \text{Cost of goods sold} - \text{Operating expenses}}{\text{Sales}}$$
$$= \frac{\text{Earnings before interest and taxes}}{\text{Sales}}$$

For Fictitious in 1999:

$$\text{Operating profit margin} = \frac{\$2,000,000}{\$10,000,000} = 0.20 \text{ or } 20\%$$

Therefore, for each dollar of sales, Fictitious has 20 cents of operating income. The operating profit margin is affected by the same factors as gross profit margin, plus operating expenses such as:

■ Office rent and lease expenses
■ Miscellaneous income (for example, income from investments)
■ Advertising expenditures
■ Bad debt expense

Most of these expenses are related in some way to sales, though they are not included directly in the cost of goods sold. Therefore, the difference between the gross profit margin and the operating profit margin is due to these indirect items that are included in computing the operating profit margin.

Both the gross profit margin and the operating profit margin reflect a company's operating performance. But they do not consider how these operations have been financed. To evaluate both operating *and* financing decisions, we need to compare net income (that is, earnings after deducting interest and taxes) with sales. Doing so, we obtain the *net profit margin*:

$$\text{Net profit margin} = \frac{\text{Net income}}{\text{Sales}}$$

The net profit margin tells us the net income generated from each dollar of sales; it considers financing costs that the operating profit margin doesn't consider. For Fictitious, for 1999:

$$\text{Net profit margin} = \frac{\$1,200,000}{\$10,000,000} = 0.12 \text{ or } 12\%$$

For every dollar of sales, Fictitious generates 12 cents in profits.

Recap: Profitability Ratios

The profitability ratios for Fictitious in 1999 are:

Gross profit margin	= 35%
Operating profit margin	= 20%
Net profit margin	= 12%

They tell us the following about the operating performance of Fictitious:

- Each dollar of sales contributes 35 cents to gross profit and 20 cents to operating profit.
- Every dollar of sales contributes 12 cents to owners' earnings.
- By comparing the 20-cent operating profit margin with the 12-cent net profit margin, we see that Fictitious has 8 cents of financing costs for every dollar of sales.

What these ratios do not tell us about profitability is the sensitivity of gross, operating, and net profit margins to:

- Changes in the sales price
- Changes in the volume of sales

Looking at the profitability ratios for one firm for one period gives us very little information that can be used to make judgments regarding future profitability. Nor do these ratios give us any information about why current profitability is what it is. We need more information to make these kinds of judgments, particularly regarding the future profitability of the firm. For that, we turn to activity ratios, which are measures of how well assets are being used.

ACTIVITY RATIOS

Activity ratios—for the most part, turnover ratios—can be used to evaluate the benefits produced by specific assets, such as inventory or accounts receivable or to evaluate the benefits produced by the totality of the firm's assets.

Inventory Management

The *inventory turnover ratio* indicates how quickly a firm has used inventory to generate the goods and services that are sold. The inventory turnover is the ratio of the cost of goods sold to inventory:[4]

$$\text{Inventory turnover ratio} = \frac{\text{Cost of goods sold}}{\text{Inventory}}$$

For Fictitious, for 1999:

$$\text{Inventory turnover ratio} = \frac{\$6,500,000}{\$1,800,000} = 3.61 \text{ times}$$

This ratio tells us that Fictitious turns over its inventory 3.61 times per year. On average, cash is invested in inventory, goods and services are produced, and these goods and services are sold 3.6 times a year. Looking back to the number of days of inventory, we see that this turnover measure is consistent with the results of that calculation: We have 101 calendar days of inventory on hand at the end of the year; dividing 365 days by 101 days, or 365/101 days, we find that inventory cycles through (from cash to sales) 3.61 times a year.

Accounts Receivable Management

In much the same way we evaluated inventory turnover, we can evaluate a firm's management of its accounts receivable and its credit policy. The

---

[4] A common alternative to this is the ratio of sales to inventory. But there is a problem with this alternative: The numerator is in terms of sales (based on selling prices), whereas the denominator is in terms of costs. By including the sales price in the numerator, the result is not easily interpreted.

accounts receivable turnover ratio is a measure of how effectively a firm is using credit extended to customers. The reason for extending credit is to increase sales. The downside to extending credit is the possibility of default—customers not paying when promised. The benefit obtained from extending credit is referred to as *net credit sales*—sales on credit less returns and refunds.

$$\text{Accounts receivable turnover} = \frac{\text{Net credit sales}}{\text{Accounts receivable}}$$

Looking at the Fictitious Corporation income statement, we see an entry for sales, but we do not know how much of the amount stated is on credit. This is often the case when we analyze companies from the outside looking in. Let's assume that the entire sales amount represents net credit sales. For Fictitious, for 1999:

$$\text{Accounts receivable turnover} = \frac{\$10,000,000}{\$600,000} = 16.67 \text{ times}$$

Therefore, almost 17 times in the year there is, on average, a cycle that begins with a sale on credit and finishes with the receipt of cash for that sale. In other words, there are 17 cycles of sales to credit to cash during the year.

The number of times accounts receivable cycle through the year is consistent with the number of days of credit (22) that we calculated earlier—accounts receivable turn over 17 times during the year, and the average number of days of sales in the accounts receivable balance is 365 days/16.67 times = 22 days.

Overall Asset Management

The inventory and accounts receivable turnover ratios reflect the benefits obtained from the use of specific assets (inventory and accounts receivable). For a more general picture of the productivity of the firm, we can compare the sales during a period with the total assets that generated these sales.

One way is with the *total asset turnover ratio* which tells us how many times during the year the value of a firm's total assets is generated in sales:

$$\text{Total assets turnover} = \frac{\text{Sales}}{\text{Total assets}}$$

For Fictitious Corporation in 1999:

$$\text{Total assets turnover} = \frac{\$10,000,000}{\$11,000,000} = 0.91 \text{ times}$$

The turnover ratio of 0.91 indicated that during 1999, every dollar invested in total assets generates 91 cents of sales. Or, stated differently, the total assets of Fictitious "turn over" almost once during the year. Because total assets include both tangible and intangible assets, this turnover tells us how efficiently all assets were used.

An alternative is to focus only on fixed assets, the long-term, tangible assets of the firm. The *fixed asset turnover* is the ratio of sales to fixed assets:

$$\text{Fixed asset turnover ratio} = \frac{\text{Sales}}{\text{Fixed assets}}$$

For Fictitious Corporation for 1999:

$$\text{Fixed asset turnover ratio} = \frac{\$10,000,000}{\$7,000,000} = 1.43 \text{ times}$$

Therefore, for every dollar of fixed assets, Fictitious is able to generate $1.43 of sales.

Recap: Activity Ratios

The activity ratios for Fictitious Corporation are:

Inventory turnover ratio	=	3.61 times
Accounts receivable turnover ratio	=	16.67 times
Total asset turnover ratio	=	0.91 times
Fixed asset turnover ratio	=	1.43 times

From these ratios we can determine that:

- Inventory flows in and out almost four times a year (from the inventory turnover ratio).
- Accounts receivable are collected in cash, on average, 22 days after a sale (from the number of days of credit). In other words, accounts receivable flow in and out almost 17 times during the year (from the accounts receivable turnover ratio).

What these ratios do not tell us about the firm's use of its assets:

■ The number of sales not made because credit policies are too stringent.
■ How much of credit sales is not collectible.
■ Which assets contribute most to the turnover.

FINANCIAL LEVERAGE RATIOS

A firm can finance its assets with equity or with debt. Financing with debt legally obligates the firm to pay interest and to repay the principal as promised. Equity financing does not obligate the firm to pay anything because dividends are paid at the discretion of the board of directors. There is always some risk, which we refer to as business risk, inherent in any business enterprise. But how a firm chooses to finance its operations—the particular mix of debt and equity—may add financial risk on top of business risk. *Financial risk* is risk associated with a firm's ability to satisfy its debt obligations, and is often measured using the extent to which debt financing is used relative to equity.

Financial leverage ratios are used to assess how much financial risk the firm has taken on. There are two types of financial leverage ratios: component percentages and coverage ratios. Component percentages compare a firm's debt with either its total capital (debt plus equity) or its equity capital. Coverage ratios reflect a firm's ability to satisfy fixed financing obligations, such as interest, principal repayment, or lease payments.

Component Percentage Ratios

A ratio that indicates the proportion of assets financed with debt is the *debt-to-assets ratio*, which compares total liabilities (short-term + long-term debt) with total assets:

$$\text{Total debt-to-assets ratio} = \frac{\text{Debt}}{\text{Total assets}}$$

For Fictitious in 1999:

$$\text{Total debt-to-assets ratio} = \frac{\$5,000,000}{\$11,000,000} = 0.4546 \text{ or } 45.46\%$$

This ratio tells us that 45% of the firm's assets are financed with debt (both short-term and long-term).

We may also look at the financial risk in terms of the use of debt relative to the use of equity. The *debt-to-equity ratio* tells us how the firm finances its operations with debt relative to the book value of its shareholders' equity:

$$\text{Debt-to-equity ratio} = \frac{\text{Debt}}{\text{Book value of shareholders' equity}}$$

For Fictitious, for 1999, using the book-value definition:

$$\text{Debt-to-equity ratio} = \frac{\$5,000,000}{\$6,000,000} = 0.8333 \text{ or } 83.33\%$$

For every one dollar of book value of shareholders' equity, Fictitious uses 83 cents of debt.

Both of these ratios can be stated in terms of total debt, as above, or in terms of long-term debt. And it is not always clear which form—total or long term debt—the ratio is calculated. Additionally, it is often the case that the current portion of long-term debt is excluded in the calculation of the long-term versions of these debt ratios.

Book Value versus Market Value

One problem with using a financial ratio based on the book value of equity to analyze financial risk is that there is seldom a strong relationship between the book value and market value of a stock. We can see the distortion in values on the balance sheet by looking at the book value of equity and comparing it with the market value of equity. The book value of equity consists of:

1. The proceeds to the firm of all the stock issues since it was first incorporated, less any stock repurchased by the firm.
2. The accumulative earnings of the firm, less any dividends, since it was first incorporated.

Let's look at an example of the book value versus the market value of equity. IBM was incorporated in 1911, so the book value of its equity represents the sum of all its stock issued and all its earnings, less any dividends paid since 1911. As of the end of 2002, IBM's book value was approximately $21 billion, yet its market value was $137 billion.

Book value generally does not give a true picture of the investment of shareholders in the firm because:

1. Earnings are recorded according to accounting principles, which may not reflect the true economics of transactions.
2. Due to inflation, the earnings and proceeds from stock issued in the past do not reflect today's values.

Market value, on the other hand, is the value of equity as perceived by investors. It is what investors are willing to pay. So why bother with book value? For two reasons: First, it is easier to obtain the book value than the market value of a firm's securities, and second, many financial services report ratios using book value rather than market value.

However, any of the ratios presented in this chapter that use the book value of equity can be restated using the market value of equity. For example, instead of using the book value of equity in the debt-to-equity ratio, you can use the market value of equity to measure the firm's financial leverage.

Coverage Ratios

The ratios that compare debt to equity or debt to assets tell us about the amount of financial leverage, which enables us to assess the financial condition of a firm. Another way of looking at the financial condition and the amount of financial leverage used by the firm is to see how well it can handle the financial burdens associated with its debt or other fixed commitments.

One measure of a firm's ability to handle financial burdens is the *interest coverage ratio*, also referred to as the *times interest-covered ratio*. This ratio tells us how well the firm can cover or meet the interest payments associated with debt. The ratio compares the funds available to pay interest (that is, earnings before interest and taxes) with the interest expense:

$$\text{Interest coverage ratio} = \frac{\text{EBIT}}{\text{Interest expense}}$$

The greater the interest coverage ratio, the better able the firm is to pay its interest expense. For Fictitious, for 1999:

$$\text{Interest coverage ratio} = \frac{\$2,000,000}{\$400,000} = 5 \text{ times}$$

An interest coverage ratio of 5 means that the firm's earnings before interest and taxes are five times greater than its interest payments.

The interest coverage ratio tells us about a firm's ability to cover the interest related to its debt financing. However, there are other costs that do not arise from debt but which nevertheless must be considered in the same way we consider the cost of debt in a firm's financial obligations. For example, lease payments are fixed costs incurred in financing operations. Like interest payments, they represent legal obligations.

What funds are available to pay debt and debt-like expenses? We can start with EBIT and *add back* expenses that were deducted to arrive at EBIT. The ability of a firm to satisfy its fixed financial costs—its fixed charges—is referred to as the *fixed charge coverage ratio*. One definition of the fixed charge coverage considers only the lease payments:

$$
\begin{aligned}
&\text{Fixed charge coverage ratio} \\
&= \frac{\text{Earnings before interest and taxes} + \text{Lease expense}}{\text{Interest} + \text{Lease expense}}
\end{aligned}
$$

For Fictitious Corporation, for 1999:

$$
\text{Fixed charge coverage ratio} = \frac{\$2,000,000 + \$1,000,000}{\$400,000 + \$1,000,000} = 2.14 \text{ times}
$$

This ratio tells us that Fictitious' earnings can cover its fixed charges (interest and lease payments) more than two times over.

What fixed charges to consider is not entirely clear-cut. For example, if the firm is required to set aside funds to eventually or periodically retire debt—referred to as *sinking funds*—is the amount set aside a fixed charge? As another example, since preferred dividends represent a fixed financing charge, should they be included as a fixed charge? From the perspective of the common shareholder, the preferred dividends must be covered to enable either the payment of common dividends or to retain earnings for future growth. Because debt principal repayment and preferred stock dividends are paid on an after-tax basis—paid out of dollars remaining after taxes are paid—we must translate this fixed charge into equivalent before-tax dollars. The fixed charge coverage ratio can be expanded to accommodate the sinking funds and preferred stock dividends as fixed charges.

Up to now we considered earnings before interest and taxes as funds available to meet fixed financial charges. The EBIT we have used thus far included noncash items such as depreciation and amortization. Because we are trying to compare funds available to meet obligations, a better measure of available funds is cash flow from operations, which we can find in the statement of cash flows. A ratio that considers cash flows from operations as funds available to cover interest payments is referred to as the *cash flow interest coverage ratio*.

$$\text{Cash flow interest coverage ratio} = \frac{\text{Cash flow from operations} + \text{Interest} + \text{Taxes}}{\text{Interest}}$$

The amount of cash flow from operations that is in the statement of cash flows is net of interest and taxes. So we have to add back interest and taxes to cash flow from operations to arrive at the cash flow amount *before* interest and taxes in order to determine the cash flow available to cover interest payments.

For Fictitious Corporation in 1999:

$$\text{Cash flow interest coverage ratio} = \frac{\$1,800,000 + \$400,000 + \$400,000}{\$400,000}$$

$$= \frac{\$2,600,000}{\$400,000} = 6.5 \text{ times}$$

This coverage ratio tells us that, in terms of cash flows, Fictitious has 6.5 times more cash than is needed to pay its interest. This is a better picture of interest coverage than the five times reflected by EBIT. Why the difference? Because cash flow considers not just the accounting income, but noncash items as well. In the case of Fictitious, depreciation is a noncash charge that reduced EBIT but not cash flow from operations—it is added back to net income to arrive at cash flow from operations.

Recap: Financial Leverage Ratios

Summarizing, the financial leverage ratios for Fictitious Corporation for 1999 are:

Debt-to-assets ratio	=	45.45%
Debt-to-equity ratio	=	83.33%
Interest coverage ratio	=	5.00 times
Fixed charge coverage ratio	=	2.14 times
Cash flow interest coverage ratio	=	6.50 times

These ratios tells us Fictitious uses its financial leverage as follows:

■ Assets are 45% financed with debt, measured using book values.
■ Long-term debt is approximately two-thirds of equity. When equity is measured in market value terms, long-term debt is approximately one-sixth of equity.

These ratios do not tell us:

■ What other fixed, legal commitments the firm has that are not included on the balance sheet (for example, operating leases).
■ What the intentions of management are regarding taking on more debt as the existing debt matures.

COMMON SIZE ANALYSIS

We have looked at a firm's operating performance and financial condition through ratios that relate various items of information contained in the financial statements. Another way to analyze a firm is to look at its financial data more comprehensively.

Common-size analysis is a method of analysis in which the components of a financial statement are compared with each other. The first step in common-size analysis is to break down a financial statement—either the balance sheet or the income statement—into its parts. The next step is to calculate the proportion that each item represents relative to some benchmark. In common-size analysis of the balance sheet, the benchmark is total assets. For the income statement, the benchmark is sales.

Let's see how it works by doing some common-size financial analysis for the Fictitious Corporation. The company's balance sheet is restated in Exhibit 22.1. This statement does not look precisely like the balance sheet we have seen before. Nevertheless, the data are the same but reorganized. Each item in the original balance sheet has been restated as a proportion of total assets for the purpose of common size analysis. Hence, we refer to this as the *common-size balance sheet*.

In this balance sheet, we see, for example, that in 1999 cash is 3.6% of total assets, or $400,000/$11,000,000 = 0.036. We can also see that the largest investment is in plant and equipment, which comprises 63.6% of total assets. On the liabilities side, we can see that current liabilities are a small portion (9.1%) of liabilities and equity.

The common-size balance sheet tells us in very general terms how Fictitious has raised capital and where this capital has been invested. As with financial ratios, however, the picture is not complete until we look at trends and compare these proportions with those of other firms in the same industry.

EXHIBIT 22.1   Fictitious Corporation Common Size Balance Sheets for Years Ending December 31

	1999		1998	
Asset Components				
Cash	3.6%		2.0%	
Marketable securities	1.8%		0.0%	
Accounts receivable	5.5%		8.0%	
Inventory	16.4%		10.0%	
Current assets		27.3%		20.0%
Net plant and equipment		63.5%		70.0%
Intangible assets		9.2%		10.0%
Total assets		100.0%		100.0%
Liability and shareholders' equity components				
Accounts payable	4.6%		4.0%	
Other current liabilities	4.6%		1.0%	
Long-term debt	36.4%		50.0%	
Total liabilities		45.4%		56.0%
Shareholders' equity		54.6%		44.0%
Total liabilities and shareholders' equity		100.0%		100.0%

In the income statement, as we did in the balance sheet, we can restate items as a proportion of sales; this statement is referred to as the *common-size income statement*. The common-size income statements for Fictitious for 1999 and 1998 are shown in Exhibit 22.2. For 1999, we see that the major costs are associated with goods sold (65%); lease expense, other expenses, interest, taxes, and dividends make up smaller portions of sales. Looking at gross profit, EBIT, and net income, we see that these proportions are the profit margins we calculated earlier. The common-size income statement provides information on the profitability of different aspects of the firm's business. Again, the picture is not complete until we look at trends over time and comparisons with other companies in the same industry.

USING FINANCIAL RATIO ANALYSIS

Financial analysis provides information concerning a firm's operating performance and financial condition. This information is useful to an analyst in evaluating a firm's operations and to an investor in evaluating the risk and potential returns to investing in a firm's securities.

But financial ratio analysis cannot tell the whole story and must be interpreted and used with care. When we discussed each ratio, we noted what we need to assume or what it might not tell us. For example, in calculating inventory turnover, we need to assume that the inventory shown on the balance sheet is representative of inventory throughout the year. Another example is in the calculation of accounts receivable turnover. We assumed that all sales were on credit. If we are on the outside looking in—that is, evaluating a firm based on its financial statements only—and therefore do not have data on credit sales, we have to start making assumptions, which may or may not be correct.

In addition, there are other areas of concern you should be aware of in using financial ratios:

- Limitations in the accounting data used to construct the ratios, as discussed in a previous chapter.
- Selection of an appropriate benchmark firm or firms for comparison purposes.
- Interpretation of the ratios.
- Pitfalls in forecasting future operating performance and financial condition based on past trends.

Let's take a closer look at some of these concerns.

EXHIBIT 22.2 Fictitious Corporation Common Size Income Statement for Years Ending December 31

	1999	1998
Sales	100.0%	100.0%
Cost of goods sold	65.0%	66.7%
Gross profit	35.0%	33.3%
Lease and administrative expenses	15.0%	16.7%
Earnings before interest and taxes	20.0%	16.7%
Interest expense	4.0%	5.6%
Earnings before taxes	16.0%	16.7%
Taxes	4.0%	5.7%
Net income	12.0%	11.1%
Common dividends	6.0%	5.6%
Retained earnings	6.0%	5.5%

Example: Wal-Mart, 1996–2001

Applied to a fictitious company, the ratio calculations are rather straight-forward: We form a ratio of two items derived from the balance sheet or the income statement. However, it is usually not as straightforward when applying these tools to an actual company. Let's look at the case of Wal-Mart and its ratios for a two-year period. Wal-Mart's balance sheets for the 2001 and 2000 fiscal years (years ending January 31, 2002 and 2001, respectively) are shown in Exhibit 22.3 and Wal-Mart's income state-ments for these same fiscal years are shown in Exhibit 22.4.

Selected financial ratios for Wal-Mart Stores for the two years are shown in Exhibit 22.5. As you can see by comparing the financial ratios and the financial statement data, not all figures are taken directly from these statements. For example, gross profit is not given, so the analyst must calculate that as the difference between total revenues and cost of sales. As another example, total debt is not given as a subtotal on the bal-ance sheet, so the analyst must combine the different debt items to arrive at the total debt amount that is used in the financial leverage ratios.

Using a Benchmark

To interpret a firm's financial ratios we need to compare them with the ratios of other firms in the industry since these other firms are in a similar line of business and face some of the same market pressures—for example, competition in the input and output markets—as the firm we are evaluating.

But finding the appropriate comparable firms is difficult for many large firms that have operations spanning many different lines of business. For example, in 2001, the Walt Disney Company reported the following:[5]

Segment	Dollar Amounts, in Millions, with the Percentage of the Total in [ ]		
	Revenues	Operating Income	Assets
Media networks	$9,569	$1,758	$20,357
	[37.87%]	[43.90%]	[46.58%]
Theme parks and resorts	$7,004	$1,586	$11,369
	[27.72%]	[39.60%]	[26.02%]
Studio entertainment	$6,106	$260	$6,614
	[24.16%]	[6.49%]	[15.14%]
Consumer product	$2,590	$401	$1,041
	[10.25%]	[10.01%]	[2.38%]
Corporate			$4,318
			[9.88%]

---

[5] *The Walt Disney Company 2001 Annual Report.*

EXHIBIT 22.3   Wal-Mart Stores Balance Sheet for Fiscal Years 2001 and 2000

Period Ending	Jan 31, 2002	Jan 31, 2001
Assets		
Current Assets		
Cash and cash equivalents	$2,161	$2,054
Net receivables	2,000	1,768
Inventory	22,614	21,442
Other current assets	1,471	1,291
Total current assets	$28,246	$26,555
Long-Term Assets		
Property plant and equipment	$45,750	$40,934
Goodwill	8,595	9,059
Other assets	860	1,582
Total assets	$83,451	$78,130
Current Liabilities		
Payables and accrued expenses	$24,134	$22,288
Short-term and current long term debt	3,148	6,661
Total current liabilities	$27,282	$28,949
Long-Term Liabilities		
Long-term debt	$18,732	$15,655
Deferred long-term liability charges	1,128	1,043
Minority interest	1,207	1,140
Total liabilities	$48,349	$46,787
Stockholders Equity		
Common atock	$445	$447
Retained carnings	34,441	30,169
Capital surplus	1,484	1,411
Other stockholdcr equity	(1,268)	(684)
Total stockholder equity	$35,102	$31,343
Total liabilities and equity	$83,451	$78,130

EXHIBIT 22.4   Wal-Mart Stores Income Statement for 2001 and 2000 Fiscal Years

Period Ending:	Jan 31, 2002	Jan 31, 2001
Total Revenue	$219,812	$193,295
Cost of Revenue	171,562	150,255
Gross Profit	$48,250	$43,040
Selling General and Administrative Expenses	36,173	31,550
Earnings Before Interest and Taxes	$12,077	$11,490
Interest Expense	1,326	1,374
Income Before Tax	$10,751	$10,116
Income Tax Expense	3,897	3,692
Minority Interest	(183)	(129)
Net Income	$6,671	$6,295

EXHIBIT 22.5   Selected Financial Ratios for Wal-Mart Stores for 2001 and 2000

Ratio	2001	2000
Return		
Basic earning power	$12,077/$83,451 = 14.47%	$16,490/$78,130 = 21.11%
Return on assets	$6,671/$83,451 = 7.9%	$6,295/$78,130 = 8.06%
Return on equity	$6,671/$35,102 = 19.00%	$6,295/$31,343 = 20.03%
Liquidity		
Current ratio	$28,246/$27,282 = 1.04 times	$26.555/$28,949 = 0.92 times
Quick ratio	$5,628 /$27,282 = 0.21 times	$5,113/$28,949 =0.18 times
Profitability		
Gross profit margin	$48,250/$219,812 = 21.95%	$43,040/$193,295 = 22.27%
Operating profit margin	$12,877/$219,812 = 5.86%	$11,490/$193,295 = 5.94%
Net profit margin	$6,671/$219,812 = 3.03%	$6,295/$193,295 = 3.26%
Activity		
Inventory turnover	$171,562/$22,618 = 7.59 times	$150,255/$21,442 = 7.01 times
Total asset turnover	$219,812/$83,451 = 2.63 times	$193,295/$78,130 = 2.47 times
Financial leverage		
Total debt-to-assets	$48,319/$83,451 = 58.90%	$46,787/$78,130 = 59.88%
Total debt-to-equity	$48,319/35,102 = 1.38 times	$46,787/$31,343 = 1.49 times
Interest coverage	$12,077/$1,326 = 9.11 times	$11,490/$1,374 = 8.36 times

In what industry do we classify the Walt Disney Company? Media networks, where it has invested almost 50% of its assets but derives only 38% of its revenues? Studio entertainment, where it derives 24% of its revenues and invests only 15% of its assets? What are the comparable companies? It is not always clear. In the case of Disney, there are no companies with the same *mix* of lines of business, so we end up comparing it with similar companies, such as AOL Time Warner, that are in the same lines of business—amusements and film entertainment (i.e., creative contents)—but with different revenue, income, and asset mixes.

Suppose we find a comparable firm or set of firms. The average ratios of these comparable firms do not necessarily constitute a good benchmark. Finding that a firm is about average is not necessarily the same as saying that it is doing well. A better comparison may be with those firms that are in similar lines of business and are also the industry's leaders.

Selecting and Interpreting Ratios

It is difficult to say whether a comparison is good or bad. Suppose we find a firm has a current ratio greater than the industry leaders. This could mean the firm is more liquid than the others and there is less risk that it cannot meet its near-term obligations. But it may also mean that the company is tying up its assets in low- or no-earning assets, which reduces its profitability.

Because ratios cannot be viewed in isolation, we need to look at several different characteristics of a firm *at the same time* in order to make judgments regarding its operating performance and financial condition. Statistical models have been developed that incorporate several aspects of a firm's operating performance and financial conditions at the same time in order to make assessments of a firm's creditworthiness. With the help of computers, these models enable us to translate financial ratios into meaningful measures.

Another issue of interpretation is the appropriateness of particular ratios to the firm. Consider an electric utility whose sole line of business is generating electricity. The only inventory that such a utility has on hand will be nuts, bolts, and a few spare parts—which do not amount to much. Calculating an inventory turnover doesn't make sense for this type of firm—and any attempts to do so will result in an absurd inventory turnover, perhaps over 2,000 times! The selection of ratios must make sense for the firm being analyzed.

Still another issue is trying to make sense out of ratios that are out of reasonable bounds. Suppose a firm has a negative book value of equity—it can happen. If we calculate its total debt-to-assets ratio, we get a value greater than 1.0, meaning that more than 100% of the firm's assets are financed with debt. In this case, some other ratio—say, total debt-to-market-value of equity—should be used instead.

INTEGRATIVE EXAMPLE: FINANCIAL ANALYSIS OF WAL-MART STORES[6]

Now that you are familiar with the concepts behind the financial ratios, we will demonstrate how to look at ratios over time and across an industry, using data for an actual firm that has a past (and a future). Let's look at and analyze the financial ratios of Wal-Mart Stores. But first, we'll take a brief look at the business of Wal-Mart, the industry, and the economy, which we must always do to properly analyze any financial ratio.

The Business

Sam Walton founded Wal-Mart Stores in 1945. Its main business is operating discount department stores (Wal-Mart stores and Wal-Mart Supercenters) and wholesale clubs (Sam's Clubs). By the end of 2001, Wal-Mart had 1,647 department stores, 1,066 supercenters, and 500 wholesale clubs and was the largest retailer in the United States in terms of dollar sales. It operates over 1,100 foreign stores, mostly in Canada, Mexico, and the United Kingdom. Wal-Mart leases the vast majority of its stores from developers and local governments.

Most of Wal-Mart's new stores in the United States are supercenters, which sell grocery products in addition to general consumer goods. The grocery line of business traditionally has smaller profit margins than the general consumer goods.

The Industry

Wal-Mart is a discount retailer. Other discount retailers include Kmart, Target Stores, and Costco Wholesale. Kmart was once the industry leader, but in recent years it has retrenched, closing stores and restructuring; in 1992, Kmart had over 4,000 stores, but in 2002 Kmart had less than 2,100. Kmart filed for bankruptcy in January 2002.

Traditionally, retailers such as Sears Roebuck and Company and J.C. Penney did not compete with the discount retailers, but in the past decade they have entered the fray, making for a very competitive retail industry. The leaders in the industry and the breakdown of the industry's sales for 2001 are shown in Exhibit 22.6.

---

[6] The sources of information used in this analysis are the companies' annual reports for various years and Yahoo! Finance.

EXHIBIT 22.6   Retail Industry Sales, 2001

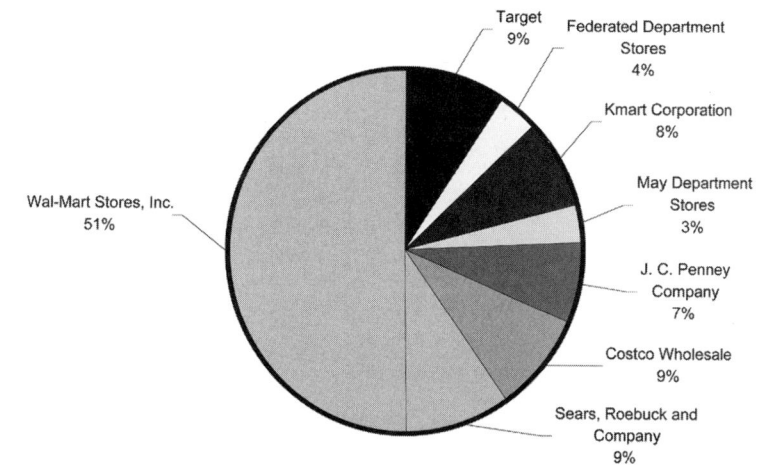

Source: Based on data obtained from *Value Line Investment Survey*

Much of Wal-Mart's growth in the 1970s and 1980s was at the expense of small, local retailers. In the 1990s and beyond, Wal-Mart's competition consists of the other behemoth retail companies; growth can no longer come from mom-and-pop stores because many of these smaller stores have gone out of existence.

Because most of these retailers have expanded as far as they can in the United States, future growth requires expansion outside of the United States or expansion into different lines of business. Wal-Mart has recently opened stores in China and Germany, though the initial success is limited.

Several retailers are shifting more of their stocked goods to private-label brands, which can provide much lower, competitive prices. Further, several retailers are focusing on operating efficiencies in warehousing, distribution, and store layout, which may pay off in lowering operating costs.

A big uncertainty is whether Kmart will be able to emerge from bankruptcy and regain its position in the industry. It will be some time before we know whether Kmart will continue to play a role in the industry.

The Economy

To evaluate Wal-Mart's financial condition and operating performance with an eye on the future, we need to look at how it has done under different economic conditions: Has the firm fared well during recessions? Has it fared well during periods of high inflation? How has it done during periods of economic prosperity?

EXHIBIT 22.7   Annual Percentage Change in Sales and Net Income for
Wal-Mart Stores, 1993–2001

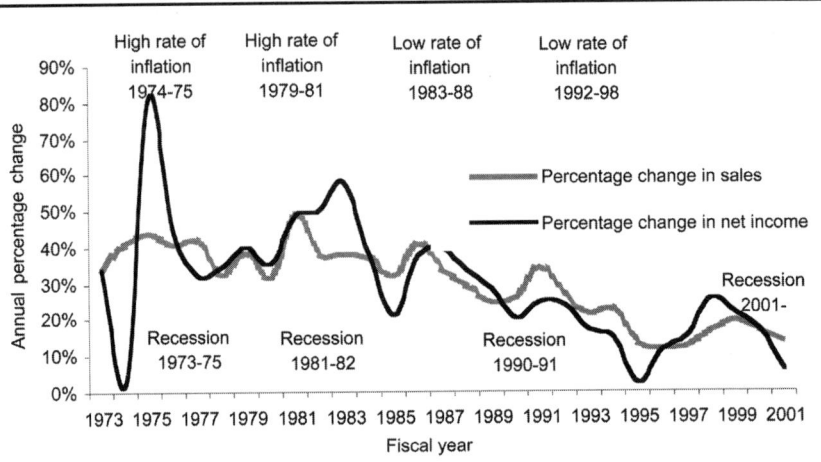

To gain a perspective on the firm's management under different economic conditions, we have to evaluate the financial ratios within the
economic climate over which they are measured. To do this, we could
look back at economic history, mapping out the indicators, such as
gross domestic production (GDP), which is a measure of the goods and
services produced in a nation, and the consumer price index (CPI),
which measures the general level of prices, to get an idea of economic
conditions and how Wal-Mart fared under different conditions.

The changes in annual sales and net income for Wal-Mart over the 29-
year period 1973–2001 are shown in Exhibit 22.7, with economic climates
indicated. We see that Wal-Mart does well in most poor economic climates: The growth in sales and net income is strongest during recessionary
and inflationary periods. This makes sense, because consumers are likely
to seek out discounts when their personal financial condition worsens.

At the end of 2001 (the point of reference for this analysis), inflation is forecast to remain low and the economy is showing signs of
recovering from the most recent recession.

Financial Ratios of the Firm and the Industry

To analyze Wal-Mart Stores, we have graphed selected ratios for Wal-
Mart over the 13-year period, 1988–2001, along with the corresponding
average ratio for the industry. We have included four companies as defining the "industry" by which we make comparisons with Wal-Mart:
Sears, Roebuck and Company, J.C. Penney, Kmart, and Target.

EXHIBIT 22.8   Return on Equity for Wal-Mart Stores and the Industry, 1988–2001

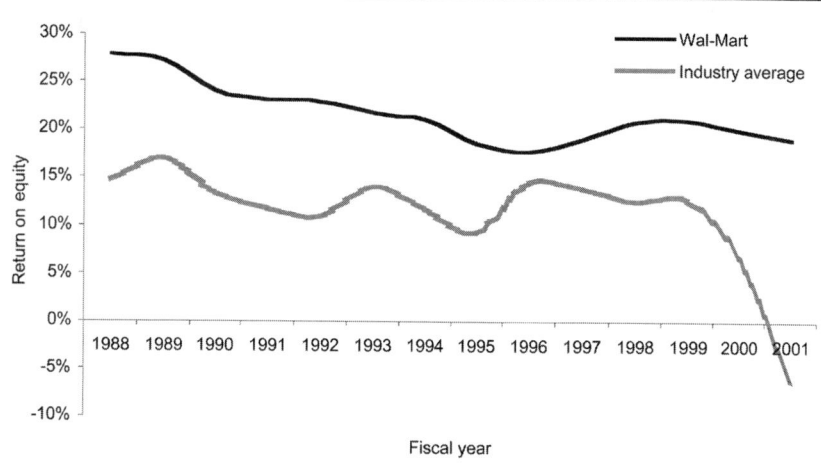

Return

Exhibit 22.8 shows that Wal-Mart's return on equity is better than the industry's. We attribute a company's return on equity to: (1) its efficiency in using assets (turnover), (2) its ability to manage expenses (profit margin), (3) its use of financial leverage (debt ratios), (4) the tax burden, and (5) the interest burden.

We can use the Du Pont system to analyze Wal-Mart's returns on equity. For example, we see that Wal-Mart's return on equity in 1988 differs from that for 2001 (28% versus 19%). Using the Du Pont breakdown of the return on equity,

$$\text{Return on equity} = \left(\frac{\text{Earnings before interest and taxes}}{\text{Sales}}\right)\left(\frac{\text{Sales}}{\text{Total assets}}\right)$$

$$\times \left(\frac{\text{Earnings before taxes}}{\text{Earnings before interest and taxes}}\right)(1 - \text{Tax rate})$$

$$\times \frac{\text{Total assets}}{\text{Shareholders' equity}}$$

we can break down Wal-Mart's 2001 return on equity into its components:

Return on equity = (Operating profit margin)(Total asset turnover)

(Equity share of before-tax earnings)(Tax retention)(Equity multiplier)

$$19.01\% = \left(\frac{\$12,077}{\$219,812}\right)\left(\frac{\$219,812}{\$83,451}\right)\left(\frac{\$10,751}{\$12,077}\right)\left(1 - \frac{\$3,897}{\$10,751}\right)\left(\frac{\$83,451}{\$35,102}\right)$$

Getting to the root of the difference using the Du Pont system results in the following:

Characteristic	1988	2001
Return on equity	27.83%	19.00%
Operating profit margin	6.41%	5.49%
Total asset turnover	3.59 times	2.63 times
Equity share of before-tax earnings	90.89%	89.02%
Tax retention	63.06%	63.75%
Equity multiplier	2.11 times	2.38 times

This information tells the analyst that the difference is attributed to many factors, including a lower profit margin and a lower asset utilization in 2001. But as you can see, the increased use of debt also contributes to the decline in the return on equity. However, the comparison of these two years does not give a complete picture of Wal-Mart and its return. A more thorough analysis would compare these components for Wal-Mart for each year and compare Wal-Mart's component ratios with those of the industry.

Understanding the industry's trends may also help explain the changes in performance and financial condition over time. The increased competitiveness in the industry is apparent in the declining return on equity for both Wal-Mart and its competitors. If the industry remains very competitive, we should expect to see further convergence in the return on equity for Wal-Mart and its competitors.

Liquidity

The current ratios for Wal-Mart and the retail store industry are graphed in Exhibit 22.9. We can easily see that Wal-Mart is less liquid than the other companies, as indicated by its lower current ratios. Both the industry and Wal-Mart have experienced declining liquidity over time.

We can't tell whether this is good or bad because we are looking at only one piece in the puzzle. On the one hand, relatively lower liquidity could mean that Wal-Mart is having difficulty meeting its short-term obligations, perhaps forcing it to seek additional short-term financing. On the other hand, relatively lower liquidity could mean that Wal-Mart is managing its current assets efficiently. Because current assets provide a low return—a firm earns less from its current assets than from its investment in plant and equipment—a smaller investment in current assets may mean that Wal-Mart is investing in noncurrent assets that provide a higher return. So let's withhold judgment on a declining current ratio until we examine Wal-Mart's profitability.

Profitability

The gross profit margins for both Wal-Mart and the industry are graphed in Exhibit 22.10. We see that Wal-Mart has lower gross margins than the rest of the industry. This may be attributed to the inclusion in the industry average of traditionally non-discounters such as J.C. Penney, which typically has a gross margin around 33%. This may also be due to Wal-Mart's expansion into the lower-margin grocery business. The lower gross profit margins combined with about the same operating profit margins as the industry tells us that Wal-Mart is better at managing its operating costs (e.g., the day-to-day operating costs of running its stores) than its competitors.

Wal-Mart's gross margins declined from around 25% to 22%. The declining gross margins for Wal-Mart and the rest of the industry from 1988–1994 may be the result of the increased competition as traditional non-discounters (e.g., J.C. Penney) began to compete with the discount retailers. Further, Wal-Mart's entry into grocery items (through its supercenters) may account for the slightly lower margins, since grocery retailers typically have gross margins in the 21% to 25% range. The increased gross and operating profit margins in the industry from 1995 to 1997 may reflect some retailers' shift to higher-margin goods.

EXHIBIT 22.9   Current Ratio for Wal-Mart and the Industry, 1988–2001

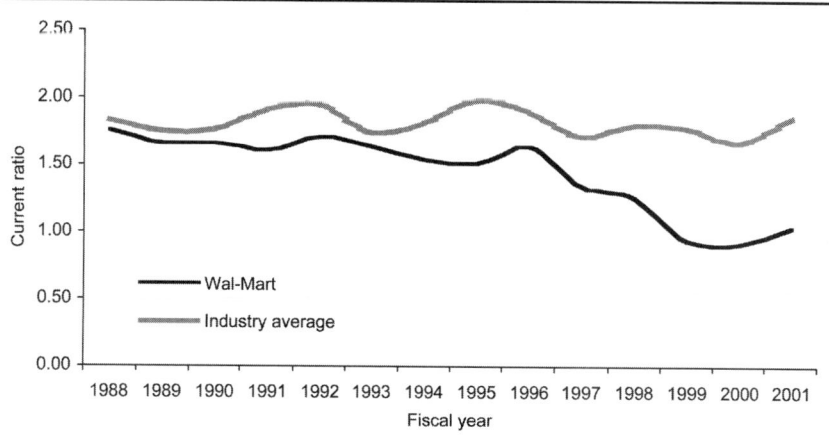

EXHIBIT 22.10 Gross Profit Margin and Operating Profit Margin for Wal-Mart Stores and the Industry, 1988–2001

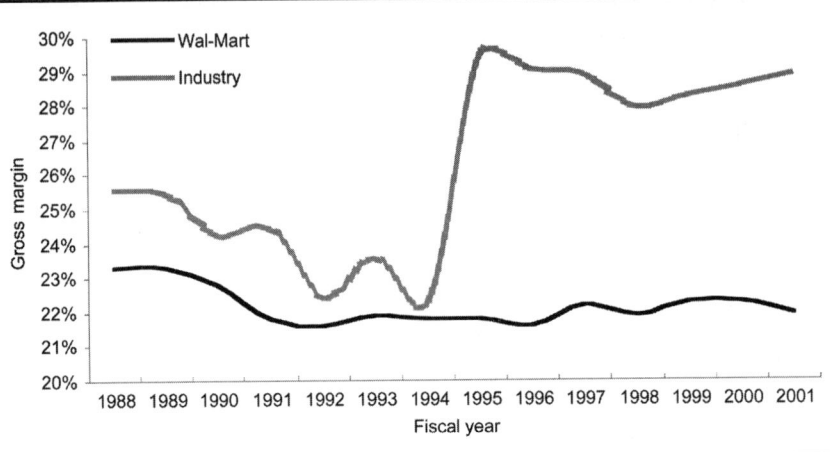

EXHIBIT 22.11 Inventory Turnover for Wal-Mart Stores and the Industry, 1988–2001

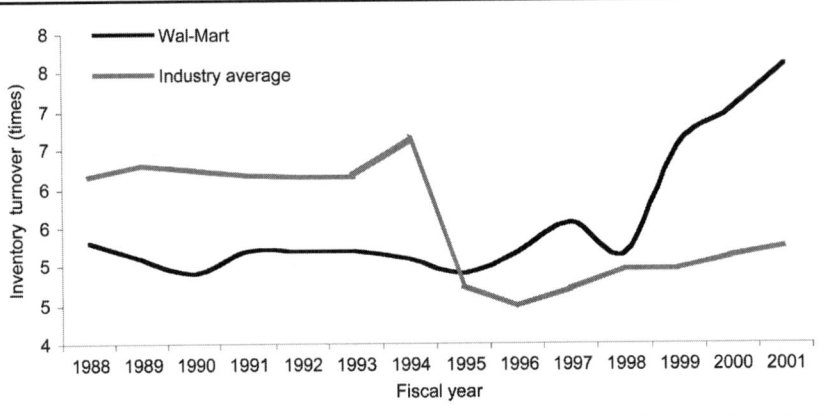

Activity

The inventory turnover for Wal-Mart and the industry is shown in Exhibit 22.11. Inventory turnover is slower for Wal-Mart than the rest of the industry for the 1988–1994 period, but faster in the 1995–2001 period. This indicates that there may be a difference between either the type of inventory or the inventory management systems of Wal-Mart and its competitors.

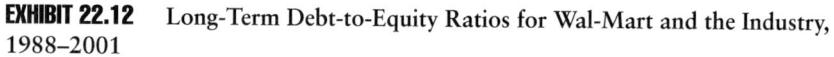

EXHIBIT 22.12 Long-Term Debt-to-Equity Ratios for Wal-Mart and the Industry, 1988–2001

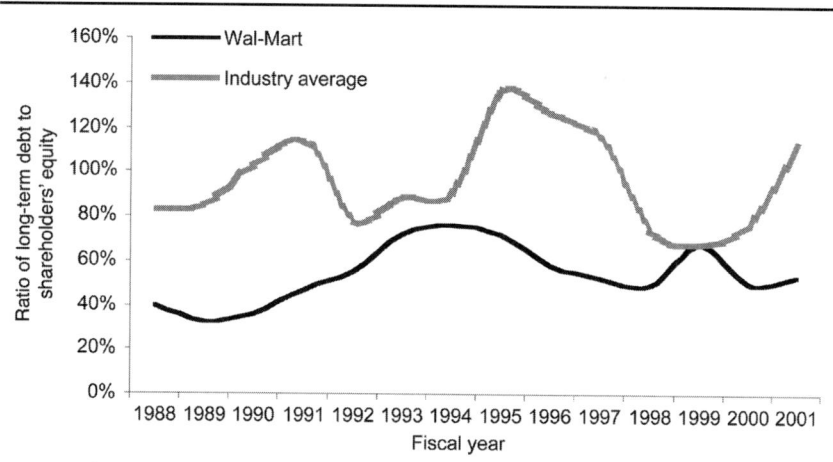

One of the aspects that helped Wal-Mart grow and become profitable has been its warehousing system. By using distribution warehousing and its own fleet of trucks, Wal-Mart is able to maintain a relatively low level of inventory. Wal-Mart's inventory turnover is, in fact, higher than most firms in the industry, but the inclusion of Sears in the industry average obscures the industry statistics. Before 1994, Sears had a catalog system which allowed it to keep less inventory on hand in its stores and in its warehouses, resulting in a high inventory turnover (around 13 times). The drop in the industry average turnover in 1995 illustrates the sensitivity of the industry average to Sears' dropping its catalog business. Another factor is that Wal-Mart has increased its grocery business, a business that has a higher turnover rate than its general retail line.

Is the slower turnover bad? Not necessarily. A slower turnover may be good news (lower risk of stock-outs) or bad news (less efficient use of existing assets). Whether good news or bad news is determined by looking at the whole picture.

Financial Leverage

Exhibit 22.12 shows the long-term debt-to-equity ratio for Wal-Mart and the industry. We see that for most of the time, Wal-Mart had a lower debt-to-equity ratio than the industry, but Wal-Mart's use of debt increased after 1991 only to decline once again after 1994 and again in 1999. The industry debt-to-equity ratio increased after 1994 because of changes in two companies: Kmart restructured, which required it to take on additional debt and

close many stores, and Sears discontinued its catalog and sold 80% of All-
state Insurance, reducing its assets but not its level of debt.

Common Size Analysis

A thorough common size analysis requires looking at financial statement
components over time. Exhibit 22.13 uses a bar graph to represent each of
the three major components of Wal-Mart's assets as a proportion of total
assets (panel A) and to represent the three major components of liabilities
and equity as proportions of total liabilities and equity (panel B).

EXHIBIT 22.13   Common Size Balance Sheets for Wal-Mart Stores, 1988–2001

Panel a: Assets

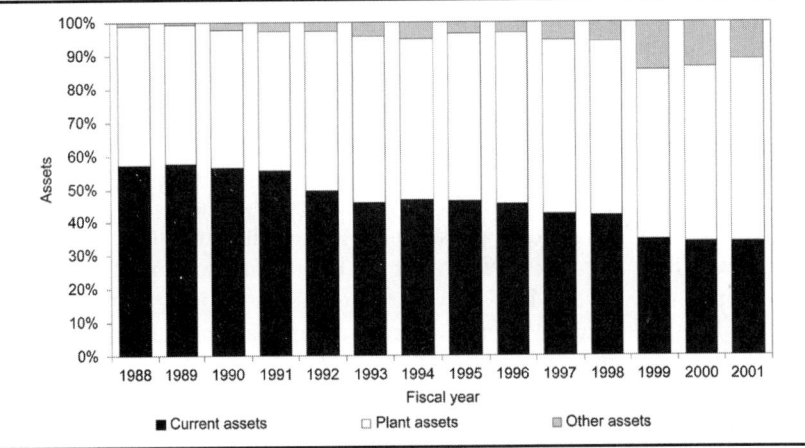

Panel b: Liabilities and Equity

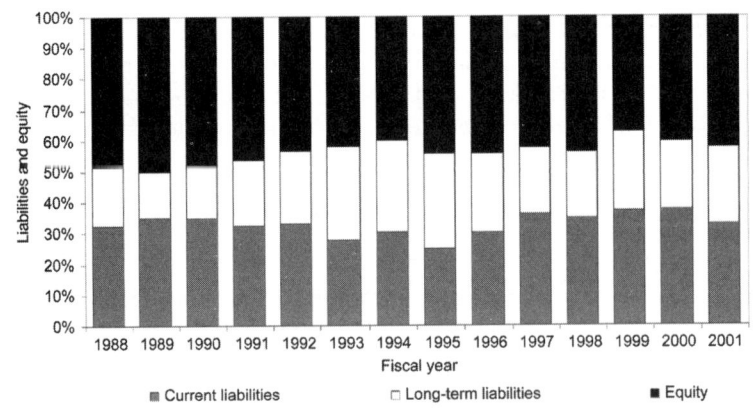

As we see in Exhibit 22.13, current assets (which consist primarily of inventory) have diminished in importance over the years, especially after 1991, as Wal-Mart shifted more of its investment towards plant assets (buildings). As we also see in this exhibit, Wal-Mart has increased its reliance on long-term debt to finance its expansion, substituting longer-term sources (in particular, notes payable) for shorter-term sources (trade credit, as represented by accounts payable), but reducing its reliance on long-term debt after 1995.

Other Factors

In addition to the financial statement data and economic forecasts, there are factors that should be considered by the financial analyst in addressing the performance and condition of the companies in this industry. Factors that should be included in the analysis of companies in the retail industry include the following:

- Same store's sales, where upward movement in his indicator is perceived as favorable.
- Changes in the number of stores, relative to competitors.
- Progress or success in strategies to alter sales mix (e.g., Sears' "softer side" campaign).
- Market share nationally, internationally, and in specific geographic or demographic markets.
- Mergers or acquisitions within the industry (e.g., Proffitt's acquisitions of Carson Pirie Scott and Saks Holdings) that may alter the market share of both minor and major firms in the industry.
- Effects of "category killers," specialty stores that may take away sales in specific product lines (e.g., electronics).

Financial Analysis of Wal-Mart: Summary

Using the information about Wal-Mart and its competitors and looking at not only the ratios of the most recent fiscal years but a time-series of these financial ratios, we can draw a number of conclusions regarding Wal-Mart and its operating performance and financial condition:

- Wal-Mart appears to do best in periods of high inflation and recession.
- The industry is currently comprised of large national chains: Wal-Mart's major competitors are Target, Kmart, J.C. Penney, and Sears Roebuck & Co. Both Kmart and Sears were troubled companies in 1993–1995, but Sears has been recovering and is becoming a stronger competitor for Wal-Mart.

- Wal-Mart provides superior return on equity (relative to its competitors), most likely because of its operating efficiency; compared to its competitors, Wal-Mart has lower gross margins yet similar operating profit margins.
- The industry has become more competitive in recent years, which is reflected in lower operating margins, return on equity, and price-to-earnings ratios.
- Wal-Mart has shifted its use of assets toward plant assets and away from current assets, which is reflective of its growth through opening more stores.
- Wal-Mart has shifted its mix of liabilities over time.
- The analysis suggests that the prospects for Wal-Mart continue to be good, but the growth in sales and profits has slowed considerably. The increased degree of competitiveness will affect all firms in the industry, resulting in lower profit margins and returns in the future.

SUMMARY

- Financial analysis is the basis for investment and financing decisions. The basic data for financial analysis is the financial statement data. We use this data to analyze relationships between different elements of a firm's financial statements. Through this analysis, we develop a picture of the operating performance and financial condition of a firm.
- Looking at the calculated financial ratios, in conjunction with industry and economic data, we can make judgments about past and future financial performance and condition.
- We can classify ratios by type—coverage, return, turnover, or component percentage—or by the financial characteristic that we wish to measure—liquidity, profitability, activity, financial leverage, or return.
- Liquidity ratios tell us about a firm's ability to satisfy short-term obligations. These ratios are related closely to a firm's operating cycle, which tells us how long it takes a firm to turn its investment in current assets back into cash.
- Profitability ratios tell us how well a firm manages its assets, typically in terms of the proportion of revenues that are left over after expenses.
- Activity ratios tell us how efficiently a firm manages its assets; that is, how effectively a firm uses its assets to generate sales.
- Financial leverage ratios tell us (1) to what extent a firm uses debt to finance its operations and (2) its ability to satisfy debt and debt-like obligations.

- Return on investments ratios tell us how much of each dollar of an investment is generated in a period. The Du Pont system breaks down return ratios into their profit margin and activity ratios, allowing us to analyze changes in return on investments.
- Common size analysis expresses financial statement data relative to some benchmark item—usually total assets for the balance sheet and sales for the income statement. Representing financial data in this way allows an analyst to spot trends in investments and profitability.

QUESTIONS

1. What is the relation between a firm's operating cycle and its need for liquidity?
2. Why is inventory removed from assets available to cover current liabilities in the calculation of the quick ratio?
3. Suppose you calculate the following ratios for two firms, A and B.

	Firm A	Firm B
Current ratio	2.0	2.0
Quick ratio	1.0	1.5

   What can you say about the relative investment in inventory?
4. Suppose you are comparing two firms that are in the same line of business. Firm C has an operating cycle of 40 days, and D has an operating cycle of 60 days. Firm C has a current ratio of 3, and D has a current ratio of 2.5. Comment on the liquidity of the two firms. Which firm has more risk of not satisfying its near-term obligations? Why?
5. A rule of thumb in financial analysis is that a current ratio of 2 is adequate.
   a. If this is so, how much could a firm's current assets shrink and still be sufficient to satisfy current obligations?
   b. Explain how a current ratio of 2 may be inadequate to meet current obligations.
   c. Explain how a current ratio of 2 may be more than sufficient to meet current obligations.
6. Suppose you calculate an inventory turnover for the Rapid Corporation of three times.
   a. Explain why a high turnover may be seen as favorable information about the management of the firm.
   b. Explain why a low turnover may be seen as unfavorable information about the management of the firm.

   c. Explain how you would determine whether Rapid's inventory turn-
      over indicates good operating performance.
 7. Suppose you calculate a return on fixed assets of 20% for 1998 and
    15% for 1999 for a company. Explain how you would use the Du
    Pont System to further investigate this change in the return on fixed
    assets.
 8. Suppose you must select ratios to evaluate the returns on assets of a
    manufacturing firm. Which ratios would you select? Why?
 9. Suppose you must select ratios to evaluate the returns on assets of
    an airline. Which ratios would you select? Why?
10. In examining the trend of returns on assets over a 20-year period for
    a firm, you find that the returns have been declining gradually over
    this period. What information would you look at to further explain
    this trend?
11. In preparing your financial ratio analysis of a firm, your supervisor
    has suggested you add another ratio:

$$\text{Working capital-to-assets ratio} = \frac{\text{Net working capital}}{\text{Total assets}}$$

    where net working capital is the difference between current assets
    and current liabilities.
    a. What type of ratio is this: coverage, return, turnover, or compo-
       nent percentage?
    b. What financial characteristic of a firm does this ratio capture?
    c. Suppose you calculated a value of 10% for this ratio. What does
       that mean?
12. Data for the Ray Shio Corporation is provided below:

Ray Shio Corporation
Balance Sheet
As of December 31, 1999 (in millions)

Cash	$100	Accounts payable	$300
Marketable securities	300	Other current liabilities	200
Accounts receivable	600	Long-term debt	500
Inventory	1,000	Common stock	2,000
Net plant and equipment	4,000	Retained earnings	3,000
Total assets	$6,000	Total liabilities and equity	$6,000

Ray Shio Corporation
Income Statement
For Year Ending December 31, 1999 (in millions)

Sales	$12,000
Cost of goods sold*	10,800
Gross profit	$1,200
Administration expenses	150
Earnings before interest and taxes	$1,050
Interest expense	50
Earnings before taxes	$1,000
Taxes	400
Net income	$600

* Includes depreciation of $800

Calculate the following ratios for the Ray Shio Corporation:
a. Current ratio
b. Quick ratio
c. Inventory turnover ratio
d. Total asset turnover ratio
e. Gross profit margin
f. Operating profit margin
g. Net profit margin
h. Debt-to-assets ratio
i. Debt-to-equity ratio
j. Return on assets (basic earning power)
k. Return on equity
13. Using the data for the Ray Shio Corporation in the previous question, calculate the following assuming a 365-day year and all sales and purchases on credit:
a. Number of days of inventory
b. Number of days of credit
c. Number of days of purchases
d. Operating cycle
e. Net operating cycle
14. Consider two firms, each with a return on assets of 10%. Firm X has a return on equity of 15%, and Y has a return on equity of 20%. Which firm uses more financial leverage? Explain.
15. Consider the following financial data (in millions of dollars) for Costello Laboratories over the period of 1992–1996:

Year	Sales	Net Income	Total Assets	Common Equity
1995	$3,800	$500	$3,900	$1,800
1996	4,400	650	4,400	2,100
1997	5,000	750	4,800	2,500
1998	5,400	860	4,900	2,700
1999	6,200	1,000	5,600	2,800

a. Calculate Costello's return on assets for each year.
b. Calculate Costello's return on equity for each year.
c. Using the Du Pont System, describe the changes in the return on assets from year to year.
d. Using the Du Pont System, describe the changes in the return on equity from year to year.

16. Look at the balance sheets and income statements for Toys R Us for the five years from 1993 to 1997 taken from its 10-K reports:

Toys R Us Balance Sheet (in millions)

	1997	1996	1995	1994	1993
Assets					
Cash and marketable securities	$214	$761	$203	$370	$792
Receivables	175	142	129	116	99
Inventory	2,464	2,215	2,000	1,999	1,778
Other current assets	51	42	87	46	39
Net property and equipment	4,212	4,047	3,858	3,669	3,185
Intangibles	356	365	0	0	0
Other assets	491	451	460	371	257
Total assets	$7,963	$8,023	$6,737	$6,571	$6,150

Toys R Us Balance Sheet (in millions)

	1997	1996	1995	1994	1993
Liabilities					
Notes payable	$134	$303	$333	$123	$240
Accounts payable	1,280	1,347	1,182	1,339	1,156
Accrued expenses	680	720	438	473	472
Income taxes payable	231	171	140	202	207
Deferred taxes	219	223	229	220	203
Long-term debt	851	908	827	785	710
Other long-term liabilities	140	161	156	0	13
Total liabilities	$3,535	$3,833	$3,305	$3,142	$3,001

Toys R Us Balance Sheet (in millions) (Cont.)

	1997	1996	1995	1994	1993
Common stock	$30	$30	$30	$30	$30
Capital surplus	467	489	543	521	454
Retained earnings	4,610	4,120	3,693	3,545	3,013
Equity adjustments	(122)	(60)	13	(25)	(56)
Treasury stock	557	388	846	642	293
Shareholders' equity	$4,428	$4,190	$3,433	$3,429	$3,149
Total liabilities and shareholders equity	$7,963	$8,023	$6,738	$6,571	$6,150

Toys R Us Income Statements (in millions)

	1997	1996	1995	1994	1993
Net sales	$11,038	$9,932	$9,427	$8,746	$7,946
Cost of goods sold	7,710	6,892	6,592	6,008	5,495
Gross profit	$3,328	$3,040	$2,835	$2,738	$2,451
Selling, general, and administrative expenses	2,484	2,226	2,087	1,826	1,630
Operating profit	$844	$814	$748	$912	$821
Nonoperating income (expense)	13	(42)	(379)	16	24
Interest expense	85	99	103	84	72
Income before taxes	$772	$673	$266	$844	$773
Provision for income taxes	282	246	118	312	290
Net income	$490	$427	$148	$532	$483

Note: The amounts shown in these statements may differ slightly from the reported amounts due to rounding.

a. Using financial ratios, describe the company's operating performance and financial condition over this five-year period.
b. What other information do you need to complete your financial analysis of Toys R Us?

17. The Walt Disney Company had sales over the period 1981 through 1990 as follows:

Year	Sales (in millions)	Year	Sales (in millions)
1981	$1,005	1986	$2,471
1982	1,030	1987	2,877
1983	1,307	1988	3,438
1984	1,656	1989	4,594
1985	2,015	1990	5,844

Source: Value Line Investment Survey, various issues

a. Looking at the trend of Disney's sales over this period, what sales do you predict for 1991? 1992?

b. What factors do you consider important in predicting Disney's future sales?

c. Disney had the following results for the years 1991 through 1997:

Year	Sales (in millions)
1991	$6,182
1992	7,504
1993	8,529
1994	10,055
1995	12,112
1996	21,238
1997	22,473

How do these amounts differ from those you predicted based on the 1981–1990 data? Is this rate of growth in the later period different from the rate of growth in the earlier (1981–1990) period? What company-specific events explain the changes in the growth in sales?

18. Suppose a company has a return on equity of 20%. If this company has an asset turnover of 4 times and a profit margin of 5%, what is its debt-to-assets ratio?

19. The Astor Company had the following results for the most recent fiscal year:

Sales	$10 million
Net profit margin	5%
Interest	$1 million
Tax rate	40%

Calculate the interest coverage ratios for Astor.

20. The Cooke Corporation had the following results for the most recent fiscal year:

Sales $5 million
Operating profit margin   25%
Interest coverage ratio   6 times
Tax rate   45%

Calculate Cooke's net profit margin.

21. The following information concerning the financial results for the Imhoff Corporation for 1997 is available:

Current ratio   = 3.0 times
Current liabilities   = $500,000
Net working capital to sales ratio   = 10%
Total asset turnover   = 2.0 times

a. What is the dollar amount of Imhoff's sales?
b. What is the amount of Imhoff's 1997 total assets?
c. What is the amount of Imhoff's 1997 net working capital?

22. In 1997, Drexel Corporation had a current ratio of 3.0 and a quick ratio of 1.5. If net working capital is $2 million, what is the amount of Drexel's 1997 inventory?

23. In 1998, Bagehot Corporation's debt-to-assets ratio was 30%, its net profit margin was 15%, and its total asset turnover was 1.25 times. What is Bagehot's return on equity for 1998?

24. Complete the following balance sheet for the Fisk Company for 1998:

Cash	$50,000	Current liabilities	$
Accounts receivable	50,000	Long-term debt	
Inventory		Shareholders' equity	
Plant and equipment			
Total assets	$_____	Liabilities and equity	$_____

The following information is also available:

Quick ratio   = 1.0 time
Net working capital to sales ratio   = 10%
Total asset turnover   = 2 times
Sales   = $2 million
Debt to assets   = 50%

25. Construct the common size balance sheet for Grisham Company for 1997:
Balance Sheet (in millions)

Cash	$50	Current liabilities	$30
Accounts receivable	30	Long-term debt	90
Inventory	80	Equity	240
Plant and equipment	200	Total liabilities and equity	$360
Total assets	$360		

26. The Barron Company had the following results for the period 1998–2003:

Year	Net Profit Margin	Return on Assets
1998	5%	10%
1999	6%	9%
2000	4%	3.2%
2001	4%	2.8%
2002	4%	3%
2003	5%	3%

Barron's management was concerned about the declining return on assets.

a. Calculate the total asset turnover for Barron Company for each year.

b. Explain the trend in return on assets using the trends in net profit margin and asset turnover.

27. The Toyota Motor Company had the following financial results for the year ended June 30, 1994:

Net sales	=	9,362,732 million yen
Cost of goods sold	=	7,725,931 million yen
Operating income	=	136,226 million yen
Net income	=	125,807 million yen

Calculate the gross profit margin, operating profit margin, and net profit margin for Toyota Motor Corporation.

28. Bayer AG, a German corporation, reported the following for the year ended December 31, 1994:

Current assets	=	25,069 million deutsche marks
Inventories	=	8,333 million deutsche marks
Current liabilities	=	8,167 million deutsche marks

a. Calculate net working capital for Bayer AG.

b. Calculate the current ratio and the quick ratio for Bayer AG.

29. Suppose you are asked to provide an opinion regarding the financial condition and operating performance of a computer manufacturing firm, Wang Laboratories. Wang Laboratories filed for Chapter 11 bankruptcy in 1992 and reemerged a little more than a year later, having shed some of its debt and restructured some of its operations.

Before its bankruptcy, Wang's lines of business consisted of minicomputers and software services. Following bankruptcy, Wang is more focused on the software services, de-emphasizing the minicomputer lines. Financial data are available for Wang Laboratories just before and after bankruptcy.

Balance Sheet	Year ended June 30, 1995	9-mos. ended June 30, 1994	Year ended June 30, 1992	Year ended June 30, 1991	Year ended June 30, 1990
Assets					
Cash and equivalents	$181	$189	$184	$233	$169
Accounts receivable	182	129	344	316	481
Inventories	24	28	118	163	246
Other current assets	37	37	57	110	187
Total current assets	$425	$383	$702	$822	$1,082
Depreciable assets, net	$134	$80	$316	$495	$732
Intangible assets, net	274	198	0	0	4
Other assets	26	26	47	101	129
Total assets	$859	$686	$1,065	$1,418	$1,946
Liabilities					
Current liabilities	$381	$288	$716	$727	$872
Long-term liabilities	32	2	453	500	556
Other liabilities	81	79	184	139	103
Total liabilities	$494	$369	$1,352	$1,365	$1,531
Shareholders' equity	366	317	−286	53	415
Total liabilities and equity	$859	$686	$1,066	$1,418	$1,946

Income Statement	Year ended June 30, 1995	9-mos. ended June 30, 1994	Year ended June 30, 1992	Year ended June 30, 1991	Year ended June 30, 1990
Revenues	$946	$644	$1,896	$2,092	$2,498
Cost of goods sold	656	408	1,003	1,016	1,212
Gross profit	$290	$237	$893	$1,075	$1,286
Other operating expenses	353	225	938	1,186	1,410
Operating income	−$63	$12	−$45	−$111	−$124
Interest expense	4	5	45	44	76
Other income or expense	13	−22	−305	−208	−378
Income tax expense	4	10	12	9	46
Net income	−$58	−$24	−$407	−$372	−$624

Financial ratios for the computer software industry for the corresponding period are as follows:

Ratio	1995	1994	1993	1992	1991
Operating profit margin	25.0%	25.7%	24.5%	23.0%	20.4%
Net profit margin	12.6%	12.6%	11.9%	11.0%	9.1%
Return on equity	21.5%	22.3%	21.8%	21.6%	18.9%
Net working capital to sales	29.0%	24.7%	22.4%	21.3%	16.1%
Debt to equity	11.0%	13.6%	13.9%	16.9%	11.7%

Requirements: Analyze the financial and operating condition of Wang Laboratories as of the end of the 1995 fiscal year. Use only the financial data from 1990–1995 to develop your analysis. In addition, list and briefly describe any additional information that would be useful in the analysis of Wang Laboratories. In your analysis, be sure to include the following:

- The types of financial problems experienced by Wang prior to the bankruptcy.
- A comparison of the financial condition and operating performance from before to after bankruptcy.
- A comparison of Wang Laboratories' condition and performance with that of the industry.

CHAPTER 23

Earnings Analysis

What determines the market price of a share of common stock? Like anything, price depends on what people are willing to pay. The price of a share of stock today depends on what investors believe is today's value of all the cash flows that will accrue in the entire future from that share of stock. In other words, no one is going to pay any more today for a share of stock than they think it is worth—based on what they get out of it in terms of future cash flows. What people are willing to pay for a share of stock today determines its market value.

The theory of stock prices makes sense. If we could accurately forecast a company's cash flows in the future, we could determine the value of the company's stock today and determine whether the stock is over- or undervalued by the market. But forecasting future cash flows is difficult. As an alternative, what is typically done is to examine the historical and current relation between stock prices and some fundamental value, such as earnings or dividends, using this relation to estimate the value of a share of stock.

In this chapter and the one to follow, we take a closer look at the fundamental factors of earnings and dividends and their relations with share price as expressed in such commonly used ratios as the price-earnings ratio and the dividend yield. Our focus in this chapter is on earnings.

VARIOUS EARNINGS MEASURES

A commonly used measure of a company's performance over a period of time is its earnings, which is often stated in terms of a return—earnings scaled by the amount of the investment. But earnings can really mean many different things depending on the context. If a financial analyst is evaluating the performance of a company's operations, the focus is on the operating earnings of the company—its *earnings before interest and taxes*, EBIT. If the analyst is evaluating the performance of a company overall, the focus is upon net income, which is essentially EBIT less interest and taxes. If the analyst is evaluating the performance of the company from a common shareholder's perspective, the earnings are the *earnings available to common shareholders*—EBIT less interest, taxes, and preferred stock dividends. Muddying the financial waters further is the issue of nonrecurring earnings or losses. Should the analyst focus on earnings before nonrecurring items or after? Therefore, it is useful to be very specific in the meaning of "earnings."

CAN EARNINGS BE MANAGED?

As we discussed in Chapter 3, there is a possibility that reported financial information may be managed or manipulated by the judicious choice of accounting methods and timing. In particular, earnings can be manipulated using a number of devices, including the selection of inventory method (e.g., FIFO versus LIFO) and the selection of depreciation method and lives. The possibility of manipulation exists, so the burden is on the financial analyst to understand a company's financial reporting, accounting methods, and the likelihood of manipulation.

There are many pressures that a company may face that affect the likelihood of manipulation. These pressures include:

- Executive compensation based on earnings targets.
- Reporting ever-increasing earnings, especially when the business is subject to variations in the business cycle.
- Meeting or beating analyst forecasts.

Earnings targets comes in various forms, but typically schemes on earnings targets provide for a bonus if earnings meet or exceed a specified target such as a return on equity. Disney, for example, provides cash bonuses based on adjusted net income.[1]

One-sided incentives such as this—rewards for beating the target return, but no penalty for not making the target—create problematic situations. If, for example, management knows that the earnings target

---

[1] For many years, Disney paid Michael Eisner a bonus equal to 2% of the difference between the actual net income and that net income that produces an 11% return on equity. Currently, however, the target returns are not disclosed [2002 Proxy Statement, p. 24].

cannot be met in a period, there may be an incentive to take large write-offs in that period to increase chances of making earnings targets in future periods—referred to as taking a "big bath."

The pressure to report constant or constantly increasing earnings may also result in earnings management, manipulation, or, in extreme cases, even fraud. For example, Leslie Fay reported relatively constant earnings in 1990 and 1991, even though its business was subject to the whims of fashion fads and trends. The perceived pressure by some employees to show constant increasing earnings were significant to encourage not only earnings management (through items such as prepaid expenses and accrued expenses) but also through fraudulent accounting entries.[2] The manipulation of financial results has been a recurring problem and in recent years has shaken investor confidence in accounting data as the scandals involving Enron, Worldcom, and others have unfolded. Therefore, the financial analyst must not only look for unusual patterns in earnings, but also earnings that are perhaps *too* predictable.[3]

Meeting analysts' forecasts presents still another pressure for the management of earnings. We know from the wealth of empirical evidence that stock prices react to *earnings surprises*, where surprises are defined as a difference between expected and actual earnings.[4] In general, the price of a company's stock will jump upward at the announcement of better-than-expected earnings and the price of a company's stock will fall quickly at the announcement of worse-than-expected earnings. The typical reaction to a positive earnings surprise is shown in Exhibit 23.1 for the case of Qualcomm, which reported third quarter 1998 earnings per share of $0.33, compared to the forecasted $0.26 per share. As you can see in this graph, both the volume of shares traded and the share prices jumped upward in response to the earnings sur-

---

[2] Martin I. Gosman, Janice L. Ammons, Mary G. Murphy, and Stephanie A. Watts, "Fraudulent Reporting at Leslie Fay: Lessons for Lenders," *Commercial Lending Review* (Fall 1996), p. 23.

[3] The pressure to meet targets is so well known that customers and suppliers of companies under pressure can take advantage of the pressure to extract discounts or otherwise favorable terms (Greg Ip, "Growth Companies Feel Pressure to Book Sales," *Wall Street Journal* (September 16, 1997), pp. C1, C13.)

[4] Richard J. Rendleman, Charles P. Jones, and Henry A. Latané document that abnormal returns (i.e., returns in excess of that expected in absence of an earnings announcement) persist beyond the initial "surprise" ("Empirical Anomalies Based on Unexpected Earnings and the Importance of Risk Adjustment," *Journal of Financial Economics* [1982], pp. 269–287). The existence of these post-announcement abnormal returns may be the result of a market inefficiency or an empirical measurement problem, as argued by Ray Ball ("The Earnings-Price Anomaly," *Journal of Accounting and Economics* [1992], pp. 319–345).

prise. Negative earnings surprises are similar in nature, with increased volume yet lower share prices associated with the earnings announcement. However, there is usually a lot else going on in the market, so earnings surprises may not always be accompanied by large price adjustments. For example, many 1998 quarterly earnings announcements were tempered with gloomy forecasts about the effects of the Asian crisis on future earnings, dampening any price reaction to a positive earnings surprise for many companies.

Because there is a market reaction to surprises—negative for earnings less than expected and positive for earnings better than expected—companies have an incentive to manage earnings to meet or exceed forecasted earnings. Frustrating the efforts to beat analysts' forecasts is the tendency of analysts to be overly optimistic about earnings.[5] In fact, the overestimation of earnings is more pronounced in cases in which companies report negative earnings.

EXHIBIT 23.1   Volume and High-Low-Closing Stock Prices for Qualcomm for Trading Days Surrounding the July 22, 1998 Positive Earnings Surprise

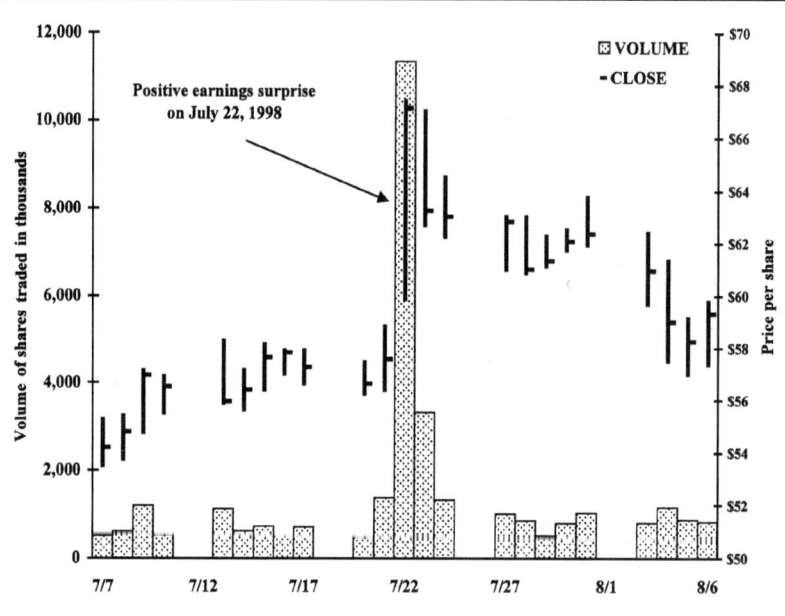

Source: Microsoft Investor, investor.msn.com

---

[5] This over-optimism is documented in the study by Richard J. Dowen entitled "Analyst Reaction to Negative Earnings for Large Well-Known Firms," *Journal of Portfolio Management* (Fall 1996).

EXHIBIT 23.2   General Electric's Earnings and Market Value of Equity, 1987–2001

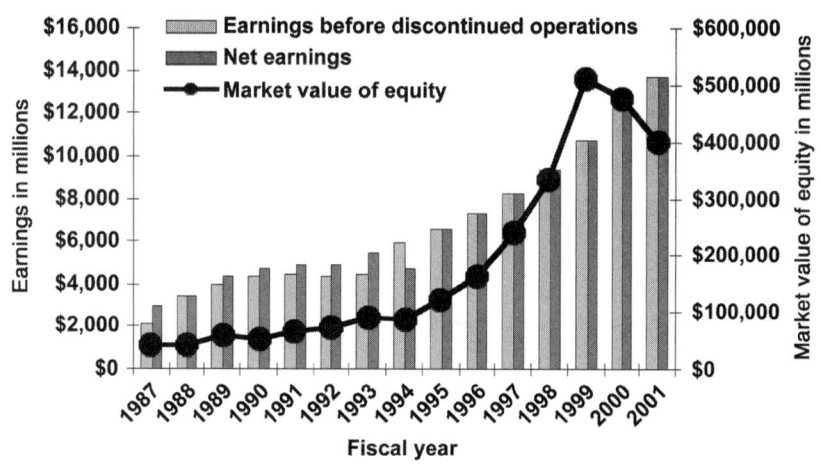

Source: General Electric's 10-K statements and annual reports, various years.

Even with the potential for managed earnings, is there a relation between earnings and stock value? Consider General Electric's earnings and prices over the period 1987–2001, as illustrated in Exhibit 23.2. As you can see, the market value of GE's common stock moves along in tandem with GE's net earnings, yet the relation between market value and earnings before discontinued items is not as strong. In the case of the period 1999–2001, market value does not move in tandem with either earnings.

Though the example using General Electric illustrates the relation for one company over a specific range of years, the issue is whether earnings and market value are related for most companies. The research into the relation between earnings and value concludes the following:

- Stock prices change in response to an announcement of unexpected earnings, and
- Accounting earnings are correlated with stock returns, especially returns measured over a long horizon following the release of earnings.[6]

The strong relation between earnings and stock prices may be due to reported earnings being strongly correlated with true earnings (that is,

---

[6] See, for example, the following study: Peter D. Easton, Trevor S. Harris, and James A. Ohlson, "Aggregate Accounting Earnings Can Explain Most of Security Returns," *Journal of Accounting and Economics* (1992), pp. 119–142.

earnings in absence of management). Or the earnings-stock price relation may be due to stocks' valuation being dependent on *reported* earnings.

EARNINGS PER SHARE

We often refer to earnings in terms of the amount per share of stock, rather than as a total dollar amount generated in a period. Expressing a company's net income in terms of income per share allows us to compare it with the company's market price per share. *Earnings per share* (EPS) is earnings available for common shareholders, divided by the number of common shares outstanding:

$$\text{Earnings per share} = \frac{\text{Earnings available to common stockholders}}{\text{Number of common shares outstanding}}$$

This ratio indicates each share's portion of how much is earned by the firm in a given accounting period:

Suppose a company has $5 million of earnings and 4 million shares outstanding. Its earnings per share is:

$$\text{Earnings per share} = \frac{\$5,000,000}{5,000,000 \text{ shares}} = \$1.25 \text{ per share}$$

This company earned $1.25 for each common share outstanding.

The EPS doesn't tell us anything about the preferred shareholders. And that's acceptable because preferred shareholders, in most cases, receive a fixed dividend amount. Because the common shareholders are the residual owners of the firm—they are the last ones in line after creditors and preferred shareholders—we are interested in seeing just what is left over for them.

When we see an amount given for EPS, we have to be sure we know what it really means. But what is there to interpret? Net income available to common shares is pretty clear-cut (with some exceptions). What about the number of common shares outstanding? Can that change during the period of time under consideration? It can, affecting the calculated value of earnings per share. The number of common shares outstanding can change for two reasons:

1. *Timing:* Net income is earned over a specific period of time, yet the number of shares outstanding may change over this period.
2. *Dilutive securities:* The company may have securities outstanding that can be converted into common stock or employee stock options and

warrants that may be exercisable (i.e., potentially dilutive securities), so the number of shares of common that potentially may share in this net income is greater than the number reported as outstanding.

Timing

Timing requires us to consider the net income relative to some meaningful measure of common shares outstanding during the same period. We can do this by first calculating the *weighted average number of shares outstanding* during the period.

Suppose the ABC company has income available for common shareholders of $2 million over 1999 and there are no potentially dilutive securities. ABC provides you with the following information:

Number of shares outstanding January 1, 1999　　= 200,000 shares
Number of shares issued July 1, 1999　　　　　　= 　50,000 shares
Number of shares outstanding December 31, 1999 = 250,000 shares

The weighted average number of shares outstanding is then:

Weighted average number of shares outstanding
= 0.50(200,000 shares) + 0.50(250,000 shares)
= 100,000 shares + 125,000 shares = 225,000 shares

What are the earnings per share for 1999?

$$\text{Earnings per share} = \frac{\$2,000,000}{225,000} = \$8.89 \text{ per share}$$

We can represent the earnings per share adjusted for the change in the shares outstanding as:

$$\text{Earnings per share} = \frac{\text{Net income available for common stockholders}}{\text{Weighted average number of shares outstanding}}$$

Dilutive Securities

For a company having securities that are dilutive—meaning they could share in net income—there are two earnings per share amounts that are reported in financial statements. Beginning with fiscal years ending after December 15, 1997, companies must report both basic and diluted earnings per share.[7] This replaces the previous requirement of simple, primary, and fully diluted EPS.[8]

Basic earnings per share are earnings (minus preferred dividends), divided by the average number of shares outstanding, which is the previous standard's simple earnings per share. *Diluted earnings per share* is earnings (minus preferred dividends), divided by the number of shares outstanding considering all dilutive securities (e.g., convertible debt, options), which is the previous standard's fully diluted earnings per share. Companies that report earnings per share for any prior period must restate these amounts in terms of the new basic and diluted calculations. The objective of the new reporting standard is to bring U.S. accounting in line with international accounting for earnings per share.

To see how the new earnings per share figures are calculated, consider American Express's 2001 earnings per share. Net income for 2001 was $1,991 million. The average number of shares for the basic earnings per share figure was 464.2 million. Therefore,

$$\text{Basic earnings per share} = \frac{\$1,311 \text{ million}}{1,324 \text{ million}} = \$0.99 \text{ per share}$$

As of 2001, American Express had the potential to issue 12 million additional shares that dilute earnings per share.[9] Adding the potential shares to the weighted average outstanding shares in the denominator,

$$\text{Diluted earnings per share} = \frac{\$1,311 \text{ million}}{1,336 \text{ million}} = \$0.98 \text{ per share}$$

What difference does the new earnings per share reporting make? Prior to 1998, companies reported simple, primary, and fully diluted earnings per share. What is missing under the new standards is the primary earnings per share amount that reflects *some* (but not all) dilution. Does it matter to the financial analyst which earnings per share data are presented? In one sense, it should not matter if we assume that analysts consider potential dilution in assessing a company's earnings per share,

---

[7] Statement of Financial Accounting Standards No. 128, "Earnings Per Share" (Stamford: Financial Accounting Standards Board, 1997).

[8] Primary earnings per share is the earnings per share calculation that reflects the dilutive effects of securities considered likely to be transformed into common stock, such as convertible securities, options, and warrants. Fully diluted earnings per share are earnings per share that reflect the dilutive effects of all potentially dilutive securities (for example, including options that are "out-of-the-money").

[9] Source: American Express 2001 annual report.

focusing on the diluted earning per share. If analysts focus on primary earnings per share (that is, factoring in some, but not all dilution), that value would not be presented directly on financial statements and would have to be calculated using data on options and securities found in the notes to financial statement. Because many financial services have used primary earnings per share in their financial analyses, such as in the case of the price-earnings ratio (P/E) used by Bloomberg and Standard & Poor's, among others, the new standard to report only basic and fully diluted earnings per share requires some adjustment of these analyses.

Does it make a difference in the reported figures? Consider the information provided by American Express that provides earnings stated according to the old standard and the new standard:[10]

	1997	1996
Basic earnings per share	$4.29	$4.02
Primary earnings per share	4.16	3.90
Diluted earnings per share	4.15	3.89

As you can see in the case of American Express, the primary earnings per share falls between the basic and diluted earning per share amounts.

The difference between the basic and diluted earnings per share over time can be seen for Microsoft Corporation in Exhibit 23.3. The difference between the basic and diluted earnings per share varies over time, due to differences in the denominator of diluted earning per share—the number of dilutive securities outstanding.

ANALYSTS' FORECASTS

There are many financial services firms offering projections on different aspects of a firm's performance. The most common financial ratio forecast is future earnings per share of a firm, though projections of cash flows and stock prices are available. For most companies whose stock is publicly traded, there are a number of analysts who analyze the stock and make forecasts regarding earnings in the future.

In addition to the forecasts made by individual analysts, several service providers collect and report statistics of analysts' forecasts. Several of these service providers are identified in Exhibit 23.4. One of the most common statistics is the consensus earnings forecast. The *consensus earnings forecast* is the average of the earnings per share forecasts for a

---

[10] *American Express 1997 Annual Report*, "Consolidated Highlights."

given loose stock.[11] Services that provide analyst forecast information also provide earnings surprise analysis—the difference between actual earnings per share and the forecasted earnings per share, where the consensus forecast is used as the forecasted earnings per share.

EXHIBIT 23.3 Microsoft's Basic and Diluted Earnings Per Share, 1985–2002

Source: Earnings per share data from Microsoft's Investor Relations web site, www.microsoft.com/msft/ar98/fins.htm

EXHIBIT 23.4 Analyst Forecast Service Provider

Service Provider	Address
First Call	www.firstcall.com
Institutional Brokers Estimate System (I/B/E/S)	www.ibes.com
Multex	www.multexnet.com
Zacks Investment Research*	www.zacks.com

* Zacks' analysts' forecast information is available through other sites, including Yahoo! Finance [biz.yahoo.com/zacks/]

---

[11] Though the average of forecasts is typically used to represent the consensus forecast, the distribution of analysts' forecasts may not be normal (that is, symmetric and centered on the average). Further, the range in forecasts may be large. For example, the distribution of Zacks' reported 1999 forecasts for Disney has an average of $1.06, ranging from $0.95 to $1.25.

There are three issues related to using analysts forecasts in investment analysis. First, different providers define actual and forecasted earnings differently. There are different earnings per share amounts historically (simple, primary, and fully-diluted) and currently (basic and diluted) and different analysts will forecast for different earnings per share.

Second, analysts' forecasts are made at different points in time. Not all analysts sit down at the same time to make forecasts, so consensus forecasts are an average of forecasts made at different point in time. Because we know that analysts' forecasts are more accurate as the time approaches to release actual earnings, this means that a set of forecasts at a point in time is a collection of forecasts that have different degrees of accuracy.

Finally, there are differing degrees of analyst following. There are some companies for which few analysts make forecasts, whereas other companies have many analysts following. An earnings surprise in a company for which there are few analysts following it may have a different stock market reaction as compared to a surprise of similar magnitude for a well-followed company. For example, there are 26 analysts reporting forecasts to Zacks Investment Research for the 1998 fiscal year for Walt Disney Company, compared to four analysts for OEA Inc.

Consensus earnings forecasts and the forecasts of individual analysts are used to compute several measures that researchers have found to be important factors in explaining stock returns. The first measure is *earnings momentum*. This is a measure of consensus earnings growth found by computing the growth in earnings based on actual earnings for the current period and the consensus earnings forecasts for the next period. Some analysts and services refer to this as *earnings torpedo*. A second measure is the number of analysts that have increased their estimate of earnings less the number that have decreased their estimate of earnings, divided by the total number of analysts who have provided estimates. A variant of this measure is the percentage of analysts who have revised upwards their earnings estimate for the next period.

Analyst Forecasting Ability

A study by Elton, Gruber, and Gultekin demonstrated the value of accurate forecasts.[12] They found that if an investor was armed with perfect information about the growth of earnings that would occur, an investor could have generated significant abnormal positive returns.

---

[12] Edwin Elton, Martin Gruber, and M. Gultekin, "Expectations and Share Prices," *Management Science* (September 1981).

Given the value of good forecasts, let's look at how well analysts do in forecasting EPS.

There has been extensive research dating back to the late 1960s that has investigated how well analysts do in forecasting earnings. We'll look at some recent evidence on the subject. Before we discuss the recent evidence, we must first define how to measure the forecast error.

A simple procedure is to look at the difference between the actual EPS and the forecasted EPS. The latter is measured by the consensus EPS. The result is a measure of the earnings surprise. The problem with using this measure of earnings surprise is that it does not take into account the severity of the error based on the level of EPS. For example, a $0.02 difference between the actual and consensus EPS is more significant for a company with actual EPS of $0.20 than it is for a company with actual EPS of $10. Thus, the dollar difference in the error must be deflated or standardized by the level of EPS. Two measures have been used by researchers. Earnings surprise can be standardized by dividing by either actual EPS or consensus EPS. In fact, because researchers want to know the bias of the forecast error (overestimate or underestimate), the practice is to divide by the absolute value of the actual EPS or consensus EPS. That is, the forecast error can be measured in either of the following ways:

$$\text{Forecast error} = \frac{\text{Actual EPS} - \text{Consensus EPS}}{\text{Absolute value of the Actual EPS}}$$

or,

$$\text{Forecast error} = \frac{\text{Actual EPS} - \text{Consensus EPS}}{\text{Absolute value of the Consensus EPS}}$$

The forecast errors as measured above are also referred to as a measure of "standardized earnings surprise." Using the Qualcomm example, the two measures of forecast error are:

$$\text{Forecast error} = \frac{\text{Actual EPS} - \text{Consensus EPS}}{\text{Absolute value of the Actual EPS}}$$
$$= \frac{\$0.33 - \$0.26}{\$0.33} = 21.21\%$$

and

$$\text{Forecast error} = \frac{\text{Actual EPS} - \text{Consensus EPS}}{\text{Absolute value of the Consensus EPS}}$$
$$= \frac{\$0.33 - \$0.26}{\$0.26} = 26.92\%$$

To assess the forecasting ability of analysts, researchers then analyze these forecasting errors by looking at the mean absolute forecasting error and the proportion of the sample of forecasts outside of practical error bands (e.g., the percentage of forecasts that fall outside a plus or minus a 10% interval around the actual earnings).

Recent studies by David Dreman and Michael Berry[13] and by Lawrence Brown[14] have examined the ability of analysts to forecast quarterly EPS and whether or not there is a bias in analyst forecasts. Dreman and Berry found that the average forecast errors are too high— more than 20% when not standardized and double that amount when standardized. They also found that when a 10% forecast band is used, more than half of the forecasts were outside the band. Dreman and Berry used other bands but the 10% figure is what they state is "a level that many Wall Street professionals consider minimally acceptable."[15] Moreover, they find that forecasts overestimate actual earnings. That is, analysts tend to be optimistic about a firm's future earnings. In concluding their study, they write:

> The observed frequency, size, and increasing trend of all of the error metrics for quarterly estimates bring into question many important methods of stock valuation, which rely on precise earnings estimates sometimes years into the future. The growth, earnings momentum, discounted cash flow, and earnings yield techniques, for example, require fine-tuned estimates often a decade or more into the future. Thus, a significant portion of current security analysis requires a precision in earnings forecasts that is increasingly difficult for analysts to meet.[16]

---

[13] David N. Dreman and Michael A. Berry, "Forecasting Errors and Their Implications for Security Analysis," *Financial Analysts Journal* (May/June 1996), pp. 30–41.

[14] Lawrence D. Brown, "Analyst Forecasting Errors: Additional Evidence," *Financial Analysts Journal* (November/December 1997), pp. 81–88.

[15] Dreman and Berry, "Forecasting Errors and Their Implications for Security Analysis," p. 39

[16] Dreman and Berry, "Forecasting Errors and Their Implications for Security Analysis," p. 39.

The database used in the Dreman-Berry study was the Abel-Noser database. This database uses information from Value Line, I/B/E/S, Zacks Investment Research, and First Call. The potential problem with such a database is that providers define actual earnings and forecasted earnings differently and as a result this could make the forecast errors larger than they actually are.[17] In a study published a year after the Dreman-Berry study, Brown reexamined the ability of analysts to forecast earnings relying only on the I/B/E/S database. He also reported results using the Abel-Noser database used in the Dreman-Berry study. Brown found that for the two databases, the results supported the position that analyst forecasting errors are large. In addition, he finds that there is an optimistic bias in the forecasts.

Brown extended his investigation to determine whether the types of firms that analysts follow have an effect on their forecasting ability. Brown examined this question by looking at analyst forecasts based on the following firm-specific factors: whether a firm is included in the S&P 500, market capitalization, the absolute value of earnings forecast, and analyst following. He found that for firms in the S&P 500, the forecasting errors are smaller compared to firms not in the S&P 500. For firms with comparatively large capitalization, absolute value of earnings forecast, and analyst following, the forecasting error was relatively small. He continued to observe an optimistic bias. When Brown investigated analyst forecast errors for 14 industries, he found that the forecasting errors for some are substantially greater than for others.

There are other findings reported in the Brown study that warrant noting because they shed some light on other questions we raised earlier in this chapter regarding earnings management. Brown, as well as Dreman and Berry, found that the median and modial value of earnings surprise was zero, suggesting that analysts forecasts tended to be on target (although the average forecast was too large relative to actual earnings). Brown found that the number of small positive errors was greater than the number of small negative errors. Based on this finding, Brown suggested that corporate managers may manage earnings so as to not fall below the consensus estimate. Moreover, Brown also found that the number of large negative errors was greater than the number of large positive errors. This finding sheds some light on the "big bath" observation that we discussed earlier, whereby managers create large negative earnings surprises relative to the number of large positive earnings surprises.

---

[17] D.R. Philbrick and W.E. Ricks, "Using Value Line and I/B/E/S Analysts Forecasts in Accounting Research," *Journal of Accounting Research* (Autumn 1991), pp. 397–417.

Forecasts Based on Extrapolative Statistical Models

Our discussion focused only on analyst forecast errors, not on how analysts develop their forecasts. Some analysts use the techniques of fundamental analysis. Cragg and Malkiel in their assessment of analysts forecasts in late 1968 found that most analysts projected future earnings based on a linear extrapolation of recent trends in earnings.[18]

Today, some analysts use statistical models to extrapolate future earnings. The models range from very simple regression models in which time is the explanatory variable and earnings per share is the dependent variable to much more sophisticated time series statistical models. For example, in the simple model, the equation that is estimated to forecast EPS for time period t is:

$$\text{EPS for time period } t = a + b \text{ Time}$$

where a and b are the parameters estimated using regression analysis. The above model assumes a linear relationship between EPS and time. Nonlinear relationships can also be estimated.

An example of a time-series of EPS for a company is shown in Exhibit 23.5, with EPS for the Crane Co. shown in Panel A for the 1983–1997 period. A time-series linear trend is estimated and shown in Panel B. This linear time-trend captures the general trend of Crane's EPS, but appears to be ill-fitting starting in 1990. A better fitting time-trend is found using a nonlinear relationship (specifically a polynomial time trend), as shown in Panel C.

Other statistical models use previous period's EPS as the explanatory variable in the model. For example, the forecasting model can be formulated as:

$$\text{EPS for time period } t = a + b \times (\text{EPS for time period } t\text{-}1)$$

Relationships in which EPS in a future period is assumed to depend on EPS in one or more previous periods are called *autoregressive models*.

Often the data used in forecasting EPS are time and historical EPS of the company, but it is critical that EPS be adjusted to reflect changes in accounting requirements. For example, an analyst who used a statistical model would want to adjust previously reported EPS based on primary, diluted, or fully diluted EPS for the new reporting requirements.

---

[18] J. G. Cragg and Burton Malkiel, "The Consensus and Accuracy of Some Predictions of the Growth of Corporate Earnings," *Journal of Finance* (March 1969), pp. 67–84.

EXHIBIT 23.5   Earnings per Share for Crane Co., 1983–1997

Panel A: Actual Earnings per Share

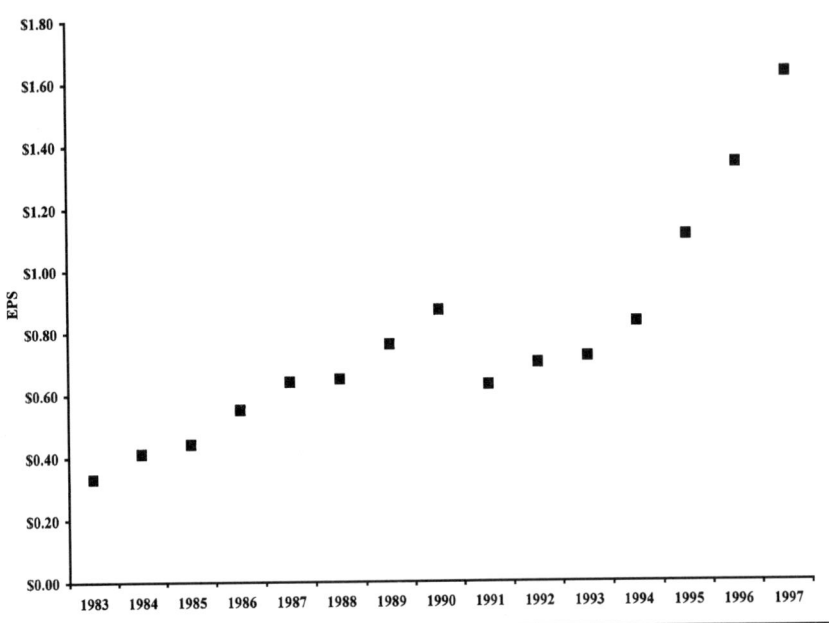

Panel B: Linear Trend Fit to the Earnings per Share

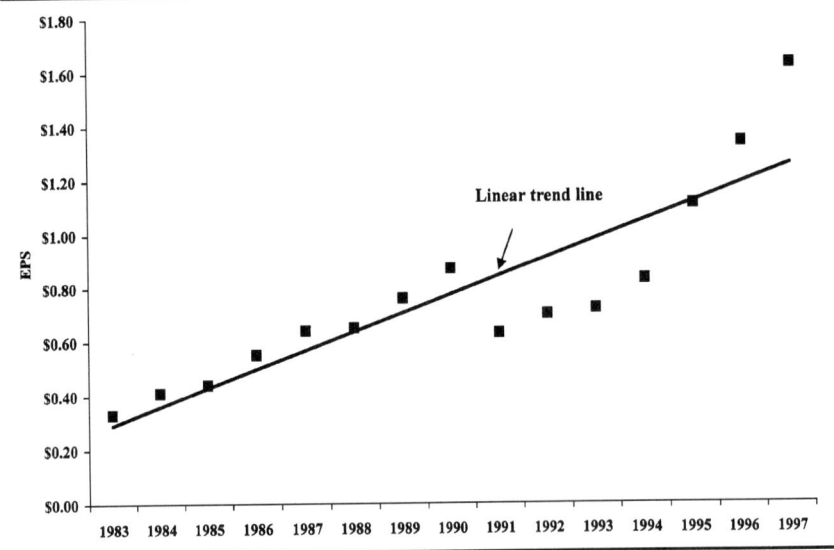

EXHIBIT 23.5 (Continued)

Panel C: A Nonlinear Trend Fit to the Earnings per Share

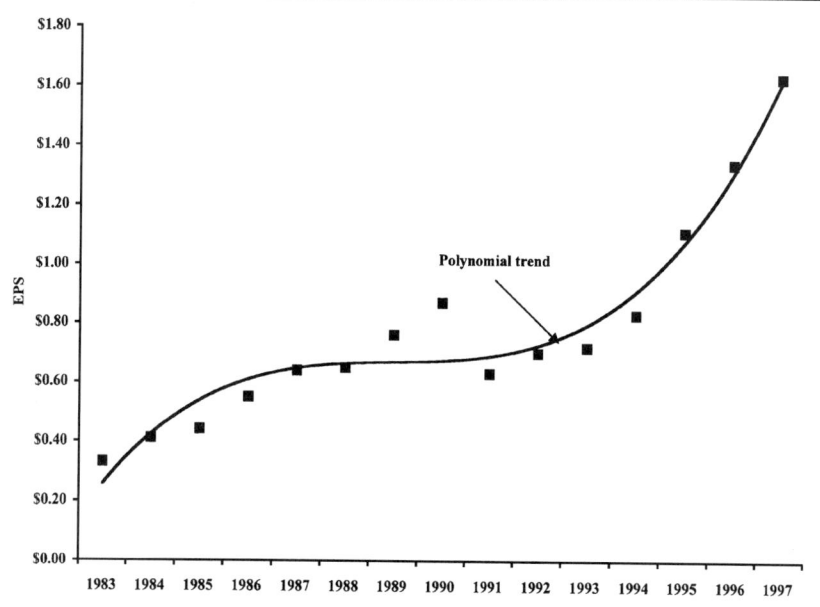

Source: Earnings per share figures are from the *Value Line Investment Survey,* various issues

Forecasting based on trends of EPS can be hazardous and does depend on the particular model used to capture the trend in EPS. Consider the Crane Co. example in Exhibit 23.5. If a forecast for 1998 EPS is made from the linear trend, EPS are forecasted to be around $1.20. If, on the other hand, the nonlinear trend is selected, the EPS forecast would be much higher, over $1.60 per share.

The question is, how good are EPS forecasts based on extrapolative statistical models compared to analysts' forecasts based on fundamental analysis? There is an extensive literature that supports the view that analyst forecasts do *not* outperform forecasts based on naive extrapolative statistical models. But there are some studies that do suggest superiority because of the advantages that analysts have in utilizing more current information.[19] The preponderance of the evidence, however, certainly supports what two researchers found back in 1972 which still

---

[19] For an overview of this literature, see T. Daniel Coggin, "The Analysts and the Investment Process: An Overview," in Frank J. Fabozzi (ed.), *Managing Institutional Assets* (New York, NY: Harper & Row, 1990).

holds, "... mechanical techniques have been shown to do about as good a job of forecasting earnings as do security analysts."[20]

Why might extrapolative statistical models do better in forecasting earnings than fundamental analysis? Daniel Coggin suggests based on studies in the area of clinical psychology why forecasts from statistical models might be superior to that of trained experts.[21] Specifically, he cites studies that show that for classifying subjects, statistical models outperformed psychologists. The reason preferred is that statistical models are not biased by human judgment and other imperfections in processing information. Another reason is that researchers find that in forecasting earnings, analysts do not employ time series properties of earnings correctly.[22]

Most of the studies have used simple or naive extrapolative statistical models. Statisticians have developed more complex models for forecasting time series data. Do such complex models do a better job of forecasting earnings than simple or naive models? The evidence does not suggest that complex statistical models lead to significantly better forecasts.[23]

PRICE-EARNINGS RATIO

Many investors are interested in how the earnings are valued by the market. A measure of how these earnings are valued is the *price-earnings ratio* (P/E). This ratio compares the price per common share with earnings per common share:

$$\text{Price-earnings ratio} = \frac{\text{Market price per share}}{\text{Earnings per share}}$$

The result is a multiple—the value of a share of stock expressed as a multiple of earnings per share. The inverse of this measure is referred to as the *earnings yield*, or E/P:[24]

---

[20] Edwin Elton and Martin Gruber, "Earnings Estimates and the Accuracy of Expectational Data," *Management Science* (April 1972), p. B-423.

[21] Coggin, "The Analysts and the Investment Process: An Overview."

[22] Jeffrey S. Abarbanell and Victor Bernard, "Tests of Analysts' Overreaction/Underreaction to Earnings Information as an Explanation for Anomalous Stock Price Behavior," *Journal of Finance* (July 1992), pp. 1181–1208.

[23] Robert Conroy and Robert Harris, "Consensus Forecasts of Corporate Earnings: Analysts Forecasts and Time Series Methods," *Management Science* (June 1987), pp. 724–738.

[24] Though the earnings yield provides the same information as the price-earnings ratio, it is often used to avoid the problem of dividing by zero in the cases in which earnings are zero.

$$\text{Earnings yield} = \frac{\text{Earnings per share}}{\text{Market price per share}}$$

Because investors are forward-looking in their valuation, earnings per share in this ratio represents the *expected normal earnings per share* for the stock. If a company has a share price of $17 and earnings per share of 80 cents, the price-earnings ratio is:

$$\text{Price-earnings ratio} = \frac{\$17.00}{\$0.80} = 21.25 \text{ times}$$

and the earnings yield is:

$$\text{Earnings yield} = \frac{\$0.80}{\$17.00} = 4.71\%$$

If the market value of the stock represents today's forecast of future earnings to common shareholders and if current earnings are an indication of future earnings, this ratio tells us that each dollar of earnings represents $21.25 of value today.

P/E ratios vary over time for the S&P 500, typically ranging from 8 to 20 times, averaging around 14.2 times as illustrated in Exhibit 23.6. In recent years the P/E ratio has gone out of these bounds, reaching record-breaking highs toward 30 times.[25]

An interesting issue arises in deciding the appropriate inputs to the P/E ratio. The numerator is rather straightforward: Use a recent market price per share. The denominator presents a number of issues. Aside from the issue of whether the denominator is the basic or diluted earnings per share, an important issue is over what period to measure earnings per share. At any point in time, the most recently ending annual period or quarter's earnings may not be available. Further muddying the waters is whether the P/E ratio should be measured over a historical period (backward-looking) or measured using forecasted earnings (forward-looking). So what is the analyst to do? There are several approaches that are used:

■ The sum of the latest available four reported quarters.

---

[25] See John Y. Campbell and Robert J. Shiller, "Valuation Ratios and the Long-Run Stock Market Outlook," *Journal of Portfolio Management* (Winter 1998), p. 11, and E. S. Browning, "Bulls Use Convoluted Measures to Justify View," *Wall Street Journal* (April 20, 1998), p. C1.

EXHIBIT 23.6   Average Annual P/E for the S&P 500, 1958–2001

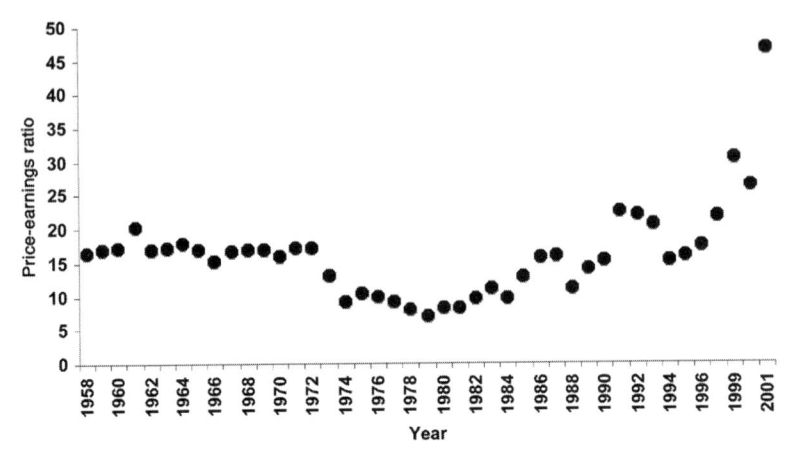

Source: Standard & Poor's Stock Market Encyclopedia and www.standardandpoors.com.

- ■ Estimated earnings for the next fiscal year.
- ■ Earnings per share averaged over several historical, annual periods.

The last approach is suggested by Graham and Dodd and uses an EPS that is the average of EPS for "not less than five years, preferably seven or ten years."[26]

Taking a closer look at the determinant of P/E ratios, we see that this ratio is related to a number of fundamental factors:

Factor	Relationship with P/E
EPS growth	+
Stability of earnings growth	+
Earnings quality	+
Dividend payout	−
Financial leverage	−
Market capitalization	−
P/E ratio of similar stocks	+
P/E ratio of the market	+
Level of interest rates	−
Inflation	−

[26] Benjamin Graham and David L. Dodd. *Security Analysis* (New York: McGraw-Hill, 1934), p. 452.

As pointed out by Eugene Fama and Kenneth French in their study of the relation between stock returns and fundamental factors, E/P (or its inverse P/E) includes the stock price in its construction and hence should be correlated with stock returns.[27] This has been supported in research that finds that E/P explains stock returns.[28] Additional evidence of this is found in Chapter 9 where we discuss fundamental factor models.

SUMMARY

- Earnings are used in the valuation of stock because of the close relation that has been observed between earnings and stock prices.
- There are many definitions of earnings, with the appropriate definition being dependent on the particular use of earnings in the analysis.
- A measure of earnings is earnings per share (EPS).
- Complications arise in the calculation of EPS not only because of the definition of earnings, but in the determination of the number of shares of stock outstanding.
- Recent accounting principle changes require the use of basic earnings per share and diluted earnings per share in financial reporting.
- Basic and diluted earnings per share replace the simple, primary, and fully diluted earnings per share.
- The consensus earnings forecast is the average of the earnings per share forecasts for a given stock and these forecasts are provided by several services. These forecasts are used to measure earnings surprises and they are standardized (deflated) to account for the level of earnings.
- Studies of the ability of analysts to forecast earnings suggests that the forecast errors are too large to make the forecasts useful in models that rely on earnings estimates and that the forecasts have an optimistic bias.
- Studies of earnings forecasts based on simple or naive extrapolative statistical models find that these forecasts are just as good as forecasts based on fundamental analysis. Moreover, forecasts based on complex statistical models do not improve the forecasting ability significantly.
- The relation between earnings and stock prices is often summarized using the price-to-earnings ratio (P/E), or its inverse, the earnings yield (E/P).

---

[27] Eugene F. Fama and Kenneth R. French. "The Cross-Section of Expected Stock Returns," *Journal of Finance* (June 1992), pp. 427–465.
[28] See, as an example, the following study: Sanjoy Basu, "The Relationship Between Earnings Yield, Market Value, and Return for NYSE Common Stocks: Further Evidence," *Journal of Financial Economics* (1983), pp. 129–156.

■ Calculation of the P/E or E/P is complicated by the issue of what earnings per share amount to use—historical, current, or expected.

QUESTIONS

1. What is the difference between earnings before interest and taxes and earnings available to common stockholders?
2. What pressures are there on management that may cause it to manage earnings?
3. Suppose a company had 2 million shares of stock outstanding at the beginning of the year and 2.25 million shares at the end of the year after issuing 0.25 million shares at the beginning of the fourth quarter. And suppose the company had earnings available to common shareholders of $4 million. What is this company's earnings per share?
4. a. What is meant by an earnings surprise?
   b. Describe the typical stock price response to an earnings surprise.
5. Why in measuring earnings surprise is the difference between actual and consensus earnings deflated?
6. a. Distinguish between basic earnings per share and diluted earnings per share.
   b. What is the difference between how earnings per share numbers are reported before and after 1998?
7. For the 1997 fiscal year, Intel Corporation had a net income of $6,945 million. At the beginning of the year, there were 1,642 million shares outstanding and at the end of the year there were 1,628 million shares. There are 160 million potentially dilutive shares during 1997 from employee stock option plans and warrants. Calculate Intel's 1997 basic and diluted earnings per share.
8. a. What is a consensus earnings forecast?
   b. What are the issues related to using analysts' forecasted earnings per share?
9. The Close-Call Co. announced earnings of $2.15 per share for the 1998 fiscal year. The consensus analyst forecast for 1998 earnings was $2.10.
   a. Calculate the forecast error for Close-Call.
   b. Explain the expected stock price reaction in response to the better-than-expected earnings.
10. What has been the evidence on the ability of analysts to forecast earnings?
11. In calculating a stock's price-earnings ratio, what earnings per share number is used?

CHAPTER 24

Cash Flow Analysis

An objective of financial analysis is to assess a company's operating performance and financial condition. The information that an analyst has available includes economic, market, and financial information. But some of the most important financial data are provided by the company in its annual and quarterly financial statements. However, the choices available in the accrual accounting system make it difficult to compare companies' performance. These choices also provide the opportunity for the management of financial numbers through judicious choice of accounting methods. For example, $1 of net income for one company may not be equivalent to $1 of net income of another company. Cash flows provide the financial analyst with a way of transforming net income based on an accrual system to a more comparable medium. Additionally, cash flows are essential ingredients in valuation: The value of a company today is the present value of its expected future cash flows. Therefore, understanding past and current cash flows may help the analyst in forecasting future cash flows and, hence, determine the value of the company. Moreover, understanding cash flow allows an analyst to assess the ability of a firm to maintain current dividends and its current capital expenditure policy without relying on external financing.

DIFFICULTIES WITH MEASURING CASH FLOW

The primary difficulty with measuring a cash flow is that it is a flow: Cash flows into the company (cash inflows) and cash flows out of the company (cash outflows). At any point in time there is a stock of cash on hand, but the stock of cash on hand varies among companies because of the size of the company, the cash demands of the business, and a company's management of working capital. So what is cash flow? Is it the total amount of cash flowing into the company during a period? Is it the total amount of cash flowing out of the company during a period? Is it the net of the cash inflows and outflows for a period? Well, there is no specific definition of cash flow—and that's probably why there is so much confusion regarding the measurement of cash flow. Ideally, the analyst needs a measure of the company's operating performance that is comparable among companies—something other than net income.

A simple, yet crude method of calculating cash flow requires simply adding noncash expenses (e.g., depreciation and amortization) to the reported net income amount to arrive at cash flow. For example, the estimated cash flow for Procter & Gamble (P&G) for 2002, is:

$$
\begin{aligned}
\text{Estimated cash flow} &= \text{Net income} \quad + \text{depreciation and amortization} \\
\text{Estimated cash flow} &= \$4{,}352 \text{ million} \quad + 1{,}693 \text{ million} \\
&= \$6{,}045 \text{ million}
\end{aligned}
$$

This amount is not really a cash flow, but simply earnings before depreciation and amortization. Is this a cash flow that analysts should use in valuing a company? Though not a cash flow, this estimated cash flow does allow a quick comparison of income across firms that may use different depreciation methods and depreciable lives.[1]

The problem with this measure is that it ignores the many other sources and uses of cash during the period. Consider the sale of goods for credit. This transaction generates sales for the period. Sales and the accompanying cost of goods sold are reflected in the period's net income and the estimated cash flow amount. However, until the account receivable is collected, there is no cash from this transaction. If collection does not occur until the next period, there is a misalignment of the income and cash flow arising from this transaction. Therefore, the simple estimated cash flow ignores some cash flows that, for many companies, are significant.

Another estimate of cash flow that is simple to calculate is *EBITDA*—earnings before interest, taxes, depreciation, and amortization. However, this measure suffers from the same accrual-accounting bias as the previous measure, which may result in the omission of significant cash flows.

---

[1] An example of the use of this estimate of cash flow, *The Value Line Investment Survey*, published by Value Line, Inc., reports a cash flow per share amount, calculated as reported earnings plus depreciation, minus any preferred dividends, stated per share of common stock [*Guide to Using the Value Line Investment Survey*, New York: Value Line, Inc., p. 19, available at http://www.valueline.com].

Additionally, EBITDA does not consider interest and taxes, which may also be substantial cash outflows for some companies.[2]

These two rough estimates of cash flows are used in practice not only for their simplicity, but because they experienced widespread use prior to the disclosure of more detailed information in the statement of cash flows. Currently, the measures of cash flow are wide-ranging, including the simplistic cash flows measures, measures developed from the statement of cash flows, and measures that seek to capture the theoretical concept of "free cash flow."

CASH FLOWS AND THE STATEMENT OF CASH FLOWS

Prior to the adoption of the statement of cash flows, the information regarding cash flows was quite limited. The first statement that addressed the issue of cash flows was the statement of financial position, which was required starting in 1971.[3] This statement was quite limited, requiring an analysis of the sources and uses of funds in a variety of formats. In its earlier years of adoption, most companies provided this information using what is referred to as the working capital concept—a presentation of working capital provided and applied during the period. Over time, many companies began presenting this information using the cash concept, which is a most detailed presentation of the cash flows provided by operations, investing, and financing activities.[4]

Consistent with the cash concept format of the funds flow statement, the statement of cash flows is now a required financial statement. The requirement that companies provide a statement of cash flows applies to fiscal years after 1987.[5] As discussed in Chapter 2, this state-

---

[2] For a more detailed discussion of the EBITDA measure, see Kent Fastman, "EBIT-DA: An Overrated Tool for Cash Flow Analysis," *Commercial Lending Review* (Spring 1997) p. 64.

[3] *APB Opinion No. 19*, "Reporting Changes in Financial Position," AICPA (New York: 1971). Prior to this APB, *APB Opinion No. 3*, "The Statement of Source and Application of Funds," AICPA (New York: 1963) encouraged, but did not require, companies to report a information regarding the changes in cash over a period (referred to as the *flow of funds*).

[4] This change in format generally followed the recommendations of the Financial Executives Institute and the Financial Accounting Standards Board recommendations [*FASB Discussion Memorandum*, "Conceptual Framework for Accounting and Reporting" (Stamford: Financial Accounting Standards Board, 1974)].

[5] *Statement of Financial Accounting Standards No. 95*, "Statement of Cash Flows" (Stamford: Financial Accounting Standards Board, 1987).

ment requires the company to classify cash flows into three categories, based on the activity: operating, investing, and financing. Cash flows are summarized by activity and within activity by type (e.g., asset dispositions are reported separately from asset acquisitions).

The reporting company may report the cash flows from operating activities on the statement of cash flows using either the *direct method*— reporting all cash inflows and outflows—or the *indirect method*—starting with net income and making adjustments for depreciation and other noncash expenses and for changes in working capital accounts. Though the direct method is recommended, it is also the most burdensome for the reporting company to prepare. Most companies report cash flows from operations using the indirect method. The indirect method has the advantage of providing the financial statement user with a reconciliation of the company's net income with the change in cash. The indirect method produces a cash flow from operations that is similar to the estimated cash flow measure discussed previously, yet it encompasses the changes in working capital accounts that the simple measure does not. For example, Procter & Gamble's cash flow from operating activities (taken from their 2002 statement of cash flows) is $7,742 million, which is over $1 billion more than the cash flow that we estimated earlier.[6]

The classification of cash flows into the three types of activities provides useful information that can be used by the analyst to see, for example, whether the company is generating sufficient cash flows from operations to sustain its current rate of growth. However, the classification of particular items is not necessarily as useful as it could be. Consider some of the classifications:

- Cash flows related to interest expense are classified in operations, though they are clearly financing cash flows.
- Income taxes are classified as operating cash flows, though taxes are affected by financing (e.g., deduction for interest expense paid on debt) and investment activities (e.g., the reduction of taxes from tax credits on investment activities).
- Interest income and dividends received are classified as operating cash flows, though these flows are a result of investment activities.

Whether these items have a significant affect on the analysis depends on the particular company's situation. Procter & Gamble, for example, has very little interest and dividend income, and its interest expense of $603 million is not large relative to its earnings before interest and taxes ($6,986 million). Adjusting P&G's cash flows for the interest expense

---

[6] Procter & Gamble's fiscal year ends June 30, 2002.

only (and related taxes) changes the complexion of its cash flows slightly to reflect greater cash flow generation from operations and less cash flow reliance on financing activities:[7]

(In millions)	As Reported	As Adjusted
Cash flow from operations	$7,741	$8,134
Cash flow for investing activities	(6,835)	(6,835)
Cash flow from (for) financing activities	197	(195)

Source: Source: Procter & Gamble 2002 Annual Report

For other companies, however, this adjustment may provide a less flattering view of cash flows. Consider Amazon.com's fiscal year results. Interest expense to financing, along with their respective estimated tax effects, results in more reliance on cash flow from financing:[8]

(In millions)	As Reported	As Adjusted
Cash flow from operations	$(120)	$(30)
Cash flow for investing activities	(253)	(253)
Cash flow from financing activities	(107)	17

Source: Amazon.com 2001 10-K

Looking at the relation among the three cash flows in the statement gives the analyst a sense of the activities of the company. A young, fast growing company may have negative cash flows from operations, yet positive cash flows from financing activities (i.e., operations may be financed to a large part with external financing). As a company grows, it may rely to a lesser extent on external financing. The typical, mature company generates cash from operations and reinvests part or all of it back into the company. Therefore, cash flow related to operations is positive (i.e., a source of cash) and cash flow related to investing activities is negative (i.e., a use of cash). As a company matures, it may seek less financing externally and may even use cash to reduce its reliance on external financing (e.g., repay debts). We can classify companies on the basis of the pattern of their sources of cash flows, as shown in Exhibit 24.1. Though additional information is required to assess a company's

---

[7] The adjustment is for $603 million of interest and other financing costs, less its tax shield (the amount that the tax bill is reduced by the interest deduction) of $211 (estimated from the average tax rate of 35% of $603): adjustment = $603 (1 − 0.35) = $392.

[8] The adjustment is based on interest expense of $139 million, and a tax rate of 35%.

financial performance and condition, examination of the sources of cash flows, especially over time, gives us a general idea of the company's operations. P&G's cash flow pattern is consistent with that of a mature company, whereas Amazon.com's cash flows are consistent with those of a fast growing company that is reliant on outside funds for growth.

Martin Fridson suggests reformatting the statement of cash flows as shown in Exhibit 24.2.[9] From the basic cash flow, the nondiscretionary cash needs are subtracted resulting in a cash flow referred to as *discretionary cash flow*. By restructuring the statement of cash flows in this way, the analyst can see how much flexibility the company has when it must make business decisions that may adversely impact the long-run financial health of the enterprise.

For example, consider a company with a basic cash flow of $800 million and operating cash flow of $500 million. Suppose that this company pays dividends of $130 million and that its capital expenditure is $300 million. Then the discretionary cash flow for this company is $200 million found by subtracting the $300 million capital expenditure from the operating cash flow of $500 million. This means that even after maintaining a dividend payment of $130 million, its cash flow is positive. Notice that asset sales and other investing activity are not needed to generate cash to meet the dividend payments because in Exhibit 24.2 these items are subtracted after accounting for the dividend payments. In fact, if this company planned to increase its capital expenditures, an analyst can use the format in Exhibit 24.2 to assess how much that expansion can be before affecting dividends and/or increasing financing needs.

EXHIBIT 24.1   Patterns of Sources of Cash Flows

Cash Flow	Financing Growth Externally and Internally	Financing Growth Internally	Mature	Temporary Financial Downturn	Financial Distress	Downsizing
Operations	+	+	+	−	−	+
Investing activities	−	−	−	+	−	+
Financing activities	+	−	+ or −	+	−	−

[9] Martin S. Fridson, *Financial Statement Analysis: A Practitioner's Guide* (New York: John Wiley & Sons, 1995).

EXHIBIT 24.2 Suggested Reformatting of Cash Flow Statement to Analyze a Company's Flexibility

	Basic cash flow
Less:	Increase in adjusted working capital
	Operating cash flow
Less:	Capital expenditures
	Discretionary cash flow
Less:	Dividends
Less:	Asset sales and other investing activities
	Cash flow before financing
Less:	Net (increase) in long-term debt
Less:	Net (increase) in notes payable
Less:	Net purchase of company's common stock
Less:	Miscellaneous
	Cash flow

Notes:
1. The basic cash flow includes net earnings, depreciation, and deferred income taxes, less items in net income not providing cash.
2. The increase in adjusted working capital excludes cash and payables.
Source: This format was suggested by Martin S. Fridson, *Financial Statement Analysis: A Practitioner's Guide* (New York: John Wiley & Sons, 1995).

Though we can classify a company based on the sources and uses of cash flows, more data are needed to put this information in perspective. What is the trend in the sources and uses of cash flows? What market, industry, or company-specific events affect the company's cash flows? How does the company being analyzed compare with other companies in the same industry in terms of the sources and uses of funds?

Let's take a closer look at the incremental information provided by cash flows. Consider Wal-Mart Stores, Inc., which had growing sales and net income from 1988 to 2001, as summarized in Exhibit 24.3. We see that net income grew each year, with the exception of 1995, and that sales grew each year.

We get additional information by looking at the cash flows and their sources, as graphed in Exhibit 24.4. We see that the growth in Wal-Mart was supported by both internally generated funds and, to a lesser extent, through external financing. Wal-Mart's pattern of cash flows suggests that Wal-Mart is a mature company that has become less reliant on external financing, funding most of its growth in recent years (with the exception of 1999) with internally generated funds.

EXHIBIT 24.3   Wal-Mart Stores, Inc., Net Income and Sales, 1988–2001

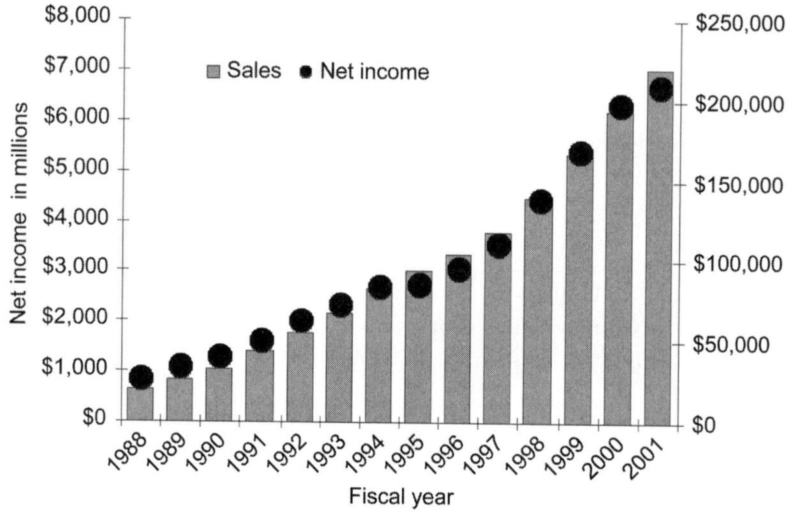

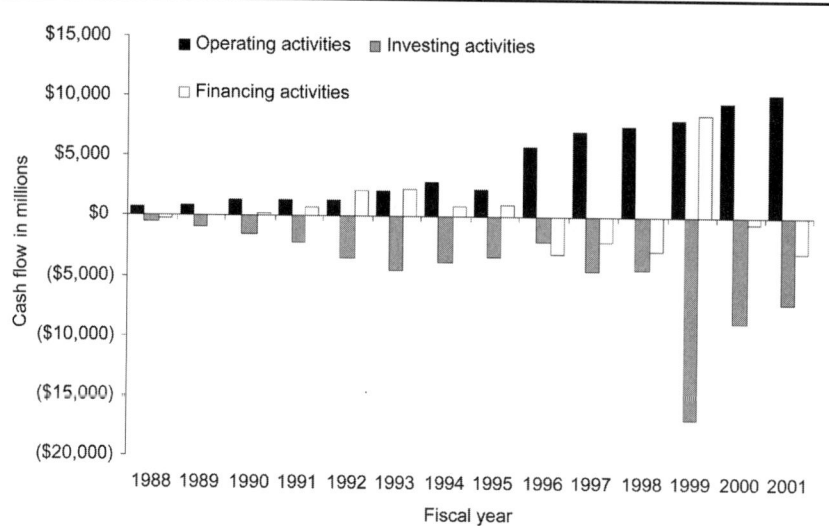

Source: Wal-Mart Stores, Inc., Annual Report, various years

EXHIBIT 24.4   Wal-Mart Stores, Inc., Sources of Cash Flow, 1988–2001

Source: Wal-Mart Stores, Inc., Annual Report, various years

FREE CASH FLOW

Cash flows without any adjustment may be misleading because they do not reflect the cash outflows that are necessary for the future existence of a firm. An alternative measure, free cash flow, was developed by Michael Jensen in his theoretical analysis of agency costs and corporate takeovers.[10] In theory, *free cash flow* is the cash flow left over after the company funds all positive net present value projects. *Positive net present value projects* are those projects (i.e., capital investments) for which the present value of expected future cash flows exceeds the present value of project outlays, all discounted at the cost of capital.[11] In other words, free cash flow is the cash flow of the firm, less capital expenditures necessary to stay in business (i.e., replacing facilities as necessary) and grow at the expected rate (which requires increases in working capital).

The theory of free cash flow was developed by Jensen to explain behaviors of companies that could not be explained by existing economic theories. Jensen observed that companies that generate free cash flow should disgorge that cash rather than invest the funds in less profitable investments. There are many ways in which companies can disgorge this excess cash flow, including the payment of cash dividends, the repurchase stock, and debt issuance in exchange for stock. The debt-for-stock exchange, for example, increases the company's leverage and future debt obligations, obligating the future use of excess cash flow. If a company does not disgorge of this free cash flow, there is the possibility that another company—a company whose cash flows are less than its profitable investment opportunities or a company that is willing to purchase and lever-up the company—will attempt to acquire the free-cash-flow-laden company.

As a case in point, Jensen observed that the oil industry illustrates the case of wasting resources: The free cash flows generated in the 1980s were spent on low return exploration and development and on poor diversification attempts through acquisitions. He argues that these companies would have been better off paying these excess cash flows to shareholders through share repurchases or exchanges with debt.

By itself, the fact that a company generates free cash flow is neither good nor bad. What the company *does* with this free cash flow is what

---

[10] Michael Jensen, "Agency Costs of Free Cash Flow, Corporate Finance, and Takeovers," *American Economic Review* (May 1986), pp. 323–329.

[11] The cost of capital is the cost to the company of funds from creditors and shareholders. The cost of capital is basically a hurdle: If a project returns more than its cost of capital, it is a profitable project.

is important. And this is where it is important to measure the free cash flow as that cash flow in excess of profitable investment opportunities. Consider the simple numerical exercise with the Winner Company and the Loser Company:

	Winner Company	Loser Company
Cash flow before capital expenditures	$1,000	$1,000
Capital expenditures, positive net present value projects	(750)	(250)
Capital expenditures, negative net present value projects	0	(500)
Cash flow	$250	$250
Free cash flow	$250	$750

These two companies have identical cash flows and the same total capital expenditures. However, the Winner Company spends only on profitable projects (in terms of positive net present value projects), whereas the Loser Company spends on both profitable projects and wasteful projects. The Winner Company has a lower free cash flow than the Loser Company, indicating that they are using the generated cash flows in a more profitable manner. The lesson is that the existence of a high level of free cash flow is not necessarily good—it may simply suggest that the company is either a very good takeover target or the company has the potential for investing in unprofitable investments.

Positive free cash flow may be good or bad news; likewise, negative free cash flow may be good or bad news:

	Good News	Bad News
Positive free cash flow	The company is generating substantial operating cash flows, beyond those necessary for profitable projects.	The company is generating more cash flows than it needs for profitable projects and may waste these cash flows on unprofitable projects.
Negative free cash flow	The company has more profitable projects than it has operating cash flows and must rely on external financing to fund these projects.	The company is unable to generate sufficient operating cash flows to satisfy its investment needs for future growth.

Therefore, once the analyst calculates free cash flow, other information (e.g., trends in profitability) must be considered to evaluate the operating performance and financial condition of the firm.

CALCULATING FREE CASH FLOW

There is some confusion when this theoretical concept is applied to actual companies. The primary difficulty is that the amount of capital expenditures necessary to maintain the business at its current rate of growth is generally not known; companies do not report this item and may not even be able to determine how much of a period's capital expenditures are attributed to maintenance and how much is attributed to expansion.

Consider Procter & Gamble's property plant and equipment for 2002, which comprise some, but not all, of P&G's capital investment:[12]

Additions to property, plant, and equipment	$1,679 million
Dispositions of property, plant and equipment	(227)
Net change before depreciation	$1,452 million

How much of the $1,679 million is for maintaining P&G's current rate of growth and how much is for expansion? Though there is a positive net change of $1,452 million, does it mean that P&G is expanding? Not necessarily: The additions are at current costs, whereas the dispositions are at historical costs. The additions of $1,679 are less than P&G's depreciation and amortization expense for 2001 of $1,693 million, yet it is not disclosed in the financial reports how much of this latter amount reflects amortization.[13] The amount of necessary capital expenditures is therefore elusive.

Some estimate free cash flow by assuming that all capital expenditures are necessary for the maintenance of the current growth of the company. Though there is little justification in using all expenditures, this is a practical solution to an impractical calculation. This assumption allows us to estimate free cash flows using published financial statements.

Another issue in the calculation is defining what is truly "free" cash flow. Generally we think of "free" cash flow as that being leftover after all necessary financing expenditures are paid; this means that free cash flow is after interest on debt is paid. Some calculate free cash flow before such financing expenditures, others calculate free cash flow after interest, and still others calculate free cash flow after both interest and dividends (assuming that dividends are a commitment, though not a *legal* commitment).

There is no one correct method of calculating free cash flow and different analysts may arrive at different estimates of free cash flow for a

---

[12] In addition to the traditional capital expenditures (i.e., changes in property, plant, and equipment), P&G also has cash flows related to investment securities and acquisitions. These investments are long-term and are hence part of P&G's investment activities cash outflow of $6,835 million.

[13] P&G's depreciation and amortization are reported together as $1,693 million on the statement of cash flows.

company. The problem is that it is impossible to measure free cash flow as dictated by the theory, so many methods have arisen to calculate this cash flow. A simple method is to start with the cash flow from operations and then deduct capital expenditures. For P&G in 2002,

Cash flow from operations	$7,742
Deduct capital expenditures	(1,692)
Free cash flow	$6,050

Though this approach is rather simple, the cash flow from the operations amount includes a deduction for interest and other financing expenses. Making an adjustment for the after-tax interest and financing expenses, as we did earlier for Procter & Gamble,

Cash flow from operations (as reported)	$7,742
Adjustment	392
Cash flow from operations (as adjusted)	$8,134
Deduct capital expenditures	(1,692)
Free cash flow	$6,442

We can relate free cash flow directly to a company's income. Starting with net income, we can estimate free cash flow using four steps:

Step 1: Determine earnings before interest and taxes (EBIT).
Step 2: Calculate earnings before interest but after taxes.
Step 3: Adjust for noncash expenses (e.g., depreciation).
Step 4: Adjust for capital expenditures and changes in working capital.

Using these four steps, we can calculate the free cash flow for Procter & Gamble for 2002, as shown in Exhibit 24.5.

NET FREE CASH FLOW

There are many variations in the calculation of cash flows that are used in analyses of companies financial condition and operating performance. As an example of these variations, consider the alternative to free cash flow developed by Fitch IBCA, a company that rates corporate debt instruments.[14] This cash flow measure, referred to as *net free cash*

---

[14] See the research reports at http://www.fitchibca.com for descriptions of this method.

flow (NFCF), is free cash flow less interest and other financing costs and taxes. In this approach, free cash flow is defined as earnings before depreciation, interest, and taxes, less capital expenditures. Capital expenditures encompass all capital spending, whether for maintenance or expansion, and no changes in working capital are considered.

EXHIBIT 24.5   Calculation of Procter & Gamble's Free Cash Flow for 2002, in Millions*

Step 1:		
Net income	$4,352	
Add taxes	2,031	
Add interest	603	
Earnings before interest and taxes	$6,986	
Step 2:		
Earnings before interest and taxes	$6,986	
Deduct taxes (@35%)	(2,445)	
Earnings before interest	$4,541	
Step 3:		
Earnings before interest	$4,541	
Add depreciation and amortization	1,693	
Add increase in deferred taxes	389	
Earnings before noncash expenses	$6,623	
Step 4:		
Earnings before noncash expenses		$6,623
Deduct capital expenditures		(1,679)
Add decrease in receivables	$ 96	
Add decrease in inventories	159	
Add cash flows from changes in accounts payable, accrued expenses, and other liabilities	684	
Deduct cash flow from changes in other operating assets and liabilities	(98)	
Cash flow from change in working capital accounts		841
Free cash flow		$5,785

*Procter & Gamble's fiscal year ended June 30, 2002. Charges in operating accounts are taken from Procter & Gamble's Statement of Cash Flows.

The basic difference between NFCF and free cash flow is that the financing expenses—interest and, in some cases dividends—are deducted. If preferred dividends are perceived as nondiscretionary—that is, investors come to expect the dividends—dividends may be included with the interest commitment to arrive at net free cash flow. Otherwise, dividends are deducted from net free cash flow to produce cash flow. Another difference is that NFCF does not consider changes in working capital in the analysis.

Further, cash taxes are deducted to arrive at net free cash flow. Cash taxes is the income tax expense restated to reflect the actual cash flow related to this obligation, rather than the accrued expense for the period. Cash taxes are the income tax expense (from the income statement) adjusted for the change in deferred income taxes (from the balance sheets).[15] For Procter & Gamble in 2002,

Income tax expense	$2,031
Deduct increase in deferred income tax	(389)
Cash taxes	$1,642

In the case of Procter & Gamble for 2002,

EBIT	$6,986
Add depreciation and amortization	1,693
Earnings before interest, taxes, depreciation, and amortization	$8,679
Deduct capital expenditures	(1,679)
Free cash flow	$7,000
Deduct interest	(603)
Deduct cash taxes	(1,642)
Net free cash flow	$4,755
Deduct cash common dividends	(2,095)
Net cash flow	$2,660

The free cash flow amount per this calculation differs from the $5,785 that we calculated earlier for two reasons: Changes in working capital and the deduction of taxes on operating earnings were not considered.

Net cash flow gives the analyst an idea of the unconstrained cash flow of the company. This cash flow measure may be useful from a creditor's perspective in terms of evaluating the company's ability to fund additional debt. From a shareholder's perspective, net cash flow (i.e., net

---

[15] Cash taxes require taking the tax expense and either increasing this to reflect any decrease in deferred taxes (that is, the payment this period of tax expense recorded in a prior period) or decreasing this amount to reflect any increase in deferred taxes (that is, the deferment of some of the tax expense).

free cash flow net of dividends) may be an appropriate measure because this represents the cash flow that is reinvested in the company.

THE USEFULNESS OF CASH FLOWS IN FINANCIAL ANALYSIS

The usefulness of cash flows for financial analysis depends on whether cash flows provide unique information or provide information in a manner that is more accessible or convenient for the analyst. The cash flow information provided in the statement of cash flows, for example, is not necessarily unique because most, if not all, of the information is available through analysis of the balance sheet and income statement. What the statement does provide is a classification scheme that presents information in a manner that is easier to use and, perhaps, more illustrative of the company's financial position.

An analysis of cash flows and the sources of cash flows can reveal information to the analyst, including:

- *The sources of financing the company's capital spending.* Does the company generate internally (i.e., from operations) a portion or all of the funds needed for its investment activities? If a company cannot generate cash flow from operations, this may indicate problems up ahead. Reliance on external financing (e.g., equity or debt issuance) may indicate a company's inability of to sustain itself over time.
- *The company's dependence on borrowing.* Does the company rely heavily on borrowing that may result in difficulty in satisfying future debt service?
- *The quality of earnings.* Large and growing differences between income and cash flows suggests a low quality of earnings.

Consider financial results of OEA, Inc., a manufacturer of propellants and pyrotechnic devices (such as those used in air bags), as presented in Exhibit 24.6.[16] As we can see in this exhibit, both operating income and net income are growing over time, with a slight interruption of this growth in 1992. We can take off the "rose-colored glasses" of income and look at cash flows to get a much different picture of the company, as shown in Exhibit 24.7. As we can see in this exhibit, the growth in investment expenditures has continued over time, yet the company is less able to generate funds from operations; in fact, in 1997 OEA relied entirely on external financing. This difficulty is associated with the recent concerns over air bags, the reengineering of air bags, and

---

[16] OEA, Inc. was acquired in 2000 by Autoliv Inc.

OEA's heavy reliance on the airbags for its revenues (80%). OEA's recent financial challenges are not reflected in the income figures, but are detected with an analysis of the sources of cash flows.

Ratio Analysis

One use of cash flow information is in ratio analysis, much like we did in Chapter 4 primarily with the balance sheet and income statement information. In that chapter we used a cash flow-based ratio, the cash flow interest coverage ratio, as a measure of financial risk. There are a number of other cash flow-based ratios that the analyst may find useful in evaluating the operating performance and financial condition of a company.

A useful ratio to help further assess a company's cash flow is the *cash flow to capital expenditures ratio*, or *capital expenditures coverage ratio*:[17]

$$\text{Cash flow to capital expenditures} = \frac{\text{Cash flow}}{\text{Capital expenditures}}$$

EXHIBIT 24.6   OEA Inc., Operating and Net Income 1988–1997

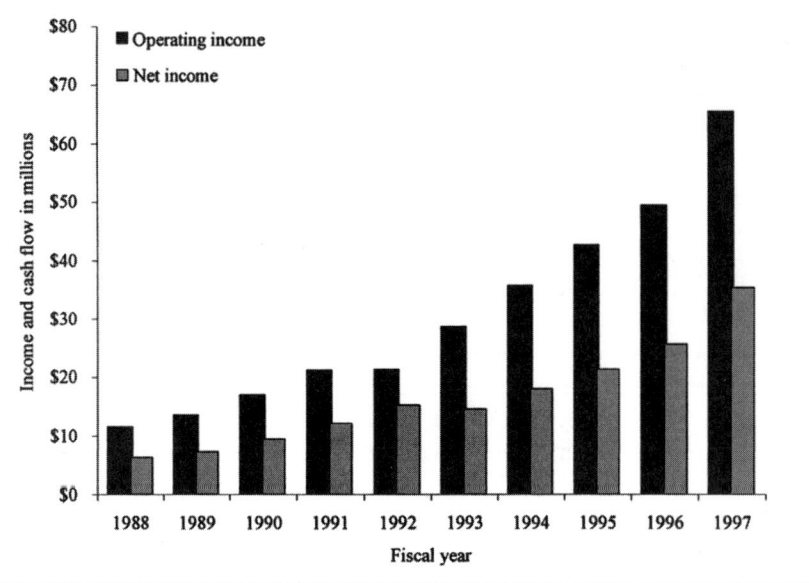

Source: OEA, Inc., Annual Reports, various years

---

[17] The cash flow measure in the numerator should be one that has not already removed capital expenditures; for example, including free cash flow in the numerator would be inappropriate.

EXHIBIT 24.7   OEA, Inc., Sources of Cash Flows, 1988-1997

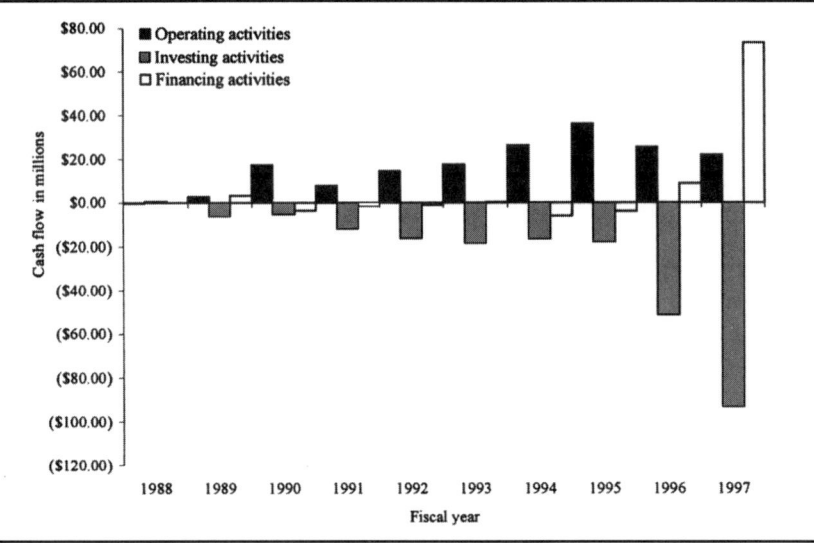

Source: OEA, Inc., Annual Reports, various years

This ratio gives the analyst information about the financial flexibility of the company and is particularly useful for capital-intensive firms and utilities.[18] The larger the ratio, the greater the financial flexibility. The analyst, however, must carefully examine the reasons why this ratio may be changing over time and why it might be out of line with comparable firms in the industry. For example, a declining ratio can be interpreted in two ways. First, the firm may eventually have difficulty adding to capacity via capital expenditures without the need to borrow funds. The second interpretation is that the firm may have gone through a period of major capital expansion and therefore it will take time for revenues to be generated that will increase the cash flow from operations to bring the ratio to some normal long-run level.

Another useful cash flow ratio is the *cash flow to debt ratio*:

$$\text{Cash flow to debt} = \frac{\text{Cash flow}}{\text{Debt}}$$

where debt can be represented as total debt, long-term debt, or a debt measure that captures a specific range of maturity (e.g., debt maturing in 5 years). This ratio gives a measure of a company's ability to meet maturing debt obligations. A more specific formulation of this ratio is Fitch's CFAR

[18] Fridson, *Financial Statement Analysis*, p. 173.

ratio, which compares a company's 3-year average net free cash flow to its maturing debt over the next five years.[19] By comparing the company's average net free cash flow to the expected obligations in the near term (i.e., five years), this ratio provides information on the company's credit quality.

Using Cash Flow Information

The analysis of cash flows provides information that can be used along with other financial data to help the analyst assess the financial condition of a company. Consider the cash flow to debt ratio calculated using three different measures of cash flow—EBITDA, free cash flow, and cash flow from operations (from the statement of cash flows)—each compared with long-term debt, as shown in Exhibit 24.8 for Weirton Steel.

This example illustrates the need to understand the differences among the cash flow measures. The effect of capital expenditures in the 1988–1991 period can be seen by the difference between the free cash flow measure and the other two measures of cash flow; both EBITDA and cash flow from operations ignore capital expenditures, which were substantial outflows for this company in the earlier period.

EXHIBIT 24.8   Cash Flow to Debt Using Alternative Estimates of Cash Flow for Weirton Steel, 1988–1996

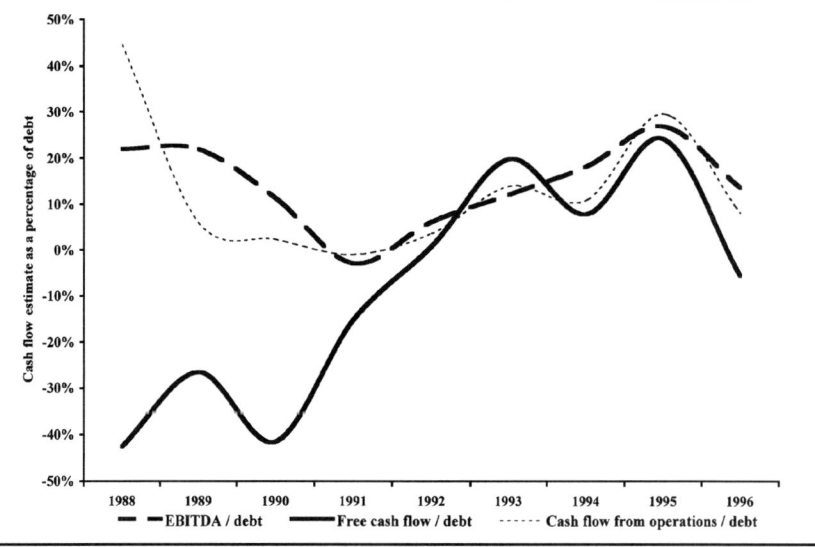

Source: Weirton Steel's 10-K reports, various years

---

[19] Daniel J. McConville, "Cash Flow Ratios Gains Respect as Useful Tool for Credit Rating," *Corporate Cashflow Magazine* (January 1996), p. 18.

Cash flow information may help the analyst identify companies that may encounter financial difficulties. Consider the study by Largay and Stickney that analyzed the financial statements of W.T. Grant during the 1966–1974 period preceding its bankruptcy in 1975 and ultimate liquidation.[20] They noted that financial indicators such as profitability ratios, turnover ratios, and liquidity ratios showed some down trends, but provided no definite clues to the company's impending bankruptcy. A study of cash flows from operations, however, revealed that company operations were causing an increasing drain on cash, rather than providing cash.[21] This necessitated an increased use of external financing, the required interest payments on which exacerbated the cash flow drain. Cash flow analysis clearly was a valuable tool in this case since W.T. Grant had been running a negative cash flow from operations for years. Yet none of the traditional ratios discussed above take into account the cash flow from operations. Use of the cash flow to capital expenditures ratio and the cash flow to debt ratio would have highlighted the company's difficulties.

More recently, Dugan and Samson examined the use of operating cash flow as an early warning signal of a company's potential financial problems.[22] The subject of the study was Allied Products Corporation because for a decade this company exhibited a significant divergence between cash flow from operations and net income. For parts of the period, net income was positive while cash flow from operations was a large negative value. In contrast to W.T. Grant that went into bankruptcy, the auditor's report in the 1991 Annual Report of Allied Products Corporation did issue a going concern warning. Moreover, the stock traded in the range of $2 to $3 per share. There was then a turnaround of the company by 1995. In its 1995 annual report, net income increased dramatically from prior periods (to $34 million) and there was a positive cash flow from operations ($29 million). The stock traded in the $25 range by the Spring of 1996.[23] As with the W.T. Grant study, Dugan and Samson found that the economic realities of a firm are better reflected in its cash flow from operations.

---

[20] J.A. Largay III and C.P. Stickney, "Cash Flows, Ratio Analysis and the W.T. Grant Company Bankruptcy," *Financial Analysts Journal* (July/August 1980), pp. 51–54.
[21] For the period investigated, a statement of changes of financial position (on a working capital basis) was required to be reported prior to 1988.
[22] Michael T. Dugan and William D. Samson, "Operating Cash Flow: Early Indicators of Financial Difficulty and Recovery," *Journal of Financial Statement Analysis* (Summer 1996), pp. 41–50.
[23] As noted for the W.T. Grant study by Largay and Stickney, cash flow from operations had to be constructed from the statement of changes in financial positions that companies were required to report prior to 1988.

The importance of cash flow analysis in bankruptcy prediction is supported by the study by Benjamin Foster and Terry Ward, who compared trends in the statement of cash flows components—cash flow from operations, cash flow for investment, and cash flow for financing—between healthy companies and companies that subsequently sought bankruptcy.[24] They observe that healthy companies tend to have relatively stable relations among the cash flows for the three sources, correcting any given year's deviation from their norm within one year. They also observe that unhealthy companies exhibit declining cash flows from operations and financing and declining cash flows for investment one and two years prior to the bankruptcy. Further, unhealthy companies tend to expend more cash flows to financing sources than they bring in during the year prior to bankruptcy. These studies illustrate the importance of examining cash flow information in assessing the financial condition of a company.

SUMMARY

- The term "cash flow" has many meanings and the analyst's challenge is to determine the cash flow definition and calculation that is appropriate.
- The simplest calculation of cash flow is the sum of net income and noncash expenses. This measure, however, does not consider other sources and uses of cash during the period.
- The statement of cash flows provides a useful breakdown of the sources of cash flows: operating activities, investing activities, and financing activities. Though attention is generally focused on the cash flows from operations, the analyst must also examine what the company does with the cash flows (i.e., investing or paying off financing obligations) and what are the sources of invested funds (i.e., operations versus externally financing).
- Minor adjustments can be made to the items classified in the statement of cash flows to improve the classification.
- The analyst can examine different patterns of cash flows to get a general idea of the activities of the company. For example, a company whose only source of cash flow is from investing activities, suggesting the sale of property or equipment, may be experiencing financial distress.

---

[24] Benjamin P. Foster and Terry J. Ward, "Using Cash Flow Trends to Identify Risks of Bankruptcy," *The CPA Journal* (September 1997), p. 60.

■ Free cash flow is a company's cash flow that remains after making capital investments that maintain the company's current rate of growth. It is not possible to calculate free cash flow precisely, resulting in many different variations in calculations of this measure.

■ A company that generates free cash flow is not necessarily performing well or poorly; the existence of free cash flow must be taken in context with other financial data and information on the company.

■ One of the variations in the calculation of a cash flow measure is net free cash flow, which is, essentially, free cash flow less any financing obligations. This is a measure of the funds available to service additional obligations to suppliers of capital.

QUESTIONS

1. A temporary downturn in a company's fortunes may be suggested by the presence of a negative operating cash flow and positive cash flows from investing and financing activities. Explain how these cash flows may suggest a temporary financial problem.

2. Classify each of the following according to the statement of cash flow activity (i.e., operating, investing, or financing):
   a. Cash received from the issuance of bonds
   b. Cash dividends paid
   c. Cash from the sale of equipment
   d. Cash paid for treasury stock
   e. Cash received from the sale of inventory

3. Classify each of the following companies as mature, growing, or downsizing based on these cash flows:

Company	Cash Flow from Operations	Cash Flow from (for) Investing Activities	Cash Flow from (for) Financing Activities
A	$550,345,890	$(300,532,400)	$(232,221,891)
B	$33,114,893	$(145,231,879)	$120,133,155
C	$2,900,311	$3,000,200	$(5,444,656)
D	$1,918,777	$(5,506,990)	$3,899,231

4. Consider the following statement: "Companies that consistently generate free cash flows are good performing companies that will do quite well in the future." Is this statement true? Explain.

5. Explain briefly what is meant by cash flow, discretionary cash flow, free cash flow, and net free cash flow. What are the distinguishing characteristics of each of these measures?

6. The following are adjustments to net income to arrive at cash flow from operations from Kmart's 1997 Consolidated Statement of Cash Flows:

- Asset impairment charges
- Cash used for store restructuring and other charges
- Decrease in other long-term liabilities
- Cash used for discontinued operations
- Loss on disposal of discontinued operations

Support the classification of these items as adjustments to arrive at cash flows from operations or suggest and support a reclassification to either the cash flows for investing or cash flows from financing.
7. Calculate the amount of free cash flow for Gap Inc., for the year ended January 31, 1998. State any assumptions that you make in your calculations.

Gap Inc., Statement of Cash Flows, in thousands

CASH FLOWS FROM OPERATING ACTIVITIES	
Net earnings	$53,901
Adjustments to reconcile net earnings to net cash provided by operating activities	
Depreciation and amortization	269,706
Tax benefit from exercise of stock options by employees and from vesting of restricted stock	23,682
Deferred income taxes	(13,706)
Change in operating assets and liabilities	
Merchandise inventory	(156,091)
Prepaid expenses and other	(44,736)
Accounts payable	63,532
Accrued expenses	107,365
Income taxes payable	(8,214)
Deferred lease credits and other long-term liabilities	69,212
Net cash provided by operating activities	$844,651
CASH FLOWS FROM INVESTING ACTIVITIES	
Net maturity (purchase) of short-term investments	174,709
Net purchase of long-term investments	(2,939)
Net purchase of property and equipment	(465,843)
Acquisition of lease rights and other assets	19,779
Net cash used for investing activities	(313,852)

CASH FLOWS FROM FINANCING ACTIVITIES	
Net increase in notes payable	44,462
Net issuance of long-term debt	495,890
Issuance of common stock	30,653
Net purchase of treasury stock	(593,142)
Cash dividends paid	(79,503)
Net cash used for financing activities	(101,640)

Gap Inc., Income Statement, in thousands

Net sales	$6,507825
Costs and expenses	
Cost of goods sold and occupancy expenses	4,021,541
Operating expenses	1,635,017
Net interest income	(2,975)
Earnings before income taxes	$842,242
Income taxes	320,341
Net earnings	$533,901

Selected Topics in Financial Management

CHAPTER 25

International Financial Management

Financial management decisions of most firms are not confined to domestic borders. Many financing and investment decisions involve economies and firms outside a firm's own domestic borders either directly, through international transactions, or indirectly, through the effects of international issues on the domestic economy. *International financial management* is the management of a firm's assets and liabilities considering the global economy in which the firm operates.

Many U.S. firms derive a large part of their income from international operations. Exhibit 25.1 shows the proportion of 2001 sales derived from domestic and foreign sales for a sample of U.S. companies. Walt Disney derives a small portion of its sales from outside the United States, whereas Coca-Cola, the second-largest U.S. corporation, derives most of its sales from outside the United States.

EXHIBIT 25.1 Sales Derived from Domestic and Foreign Sales for a Sample of U.S. Companies: 2001

Company	Domestic Sales	Foreign Sales
Coca-Cola	38	62
Dow Chemical	42	58
General Electric	50	50
International Business Machines	41	59
Philip Morris	57	43
Timberland Co.	70	30
Walt Disney	83	17

Source: Company annual reports

In this chapter, we discuss special factors that must be considered in international corporate financial management. We begin with a review of the global economy, looking at recent international agreements that affect financial decisions. We will also examine the reasons why firms expand operations beyond their domestic borders and the issues related to taxes and with foreign currencies. Finally we discuss issues related to financing, capital structure, investing, and working capital management.

THE GLOBAL ECONOMY

Many countries export a substantial portion of the goods and services they produce. Looking at just the United States, we see in Exhibit 25.2 that the role of exports and imports in the economy is ever increasing. In panel (a), we see the imports and exports growing through time. In panel (b), we see the net trade balance (that is, exports less imports), which illustrates that the United States has maintained a negative trade balance (referred to as a "deficit") for an extended period. The major exports of the United States are chemicals, computers, and consumer durable goods. The major imports of the United States are petroleum, automobiles, clothing, and computers. The top three trading partners of the United States in 2001, in terms of exports and imports, were Canada, Mexico, and Japan.

Countries trade with each other, exporting and importing, because it allows them to specialize. This ability to specialize makes for more efficient production and, ultimately, greater output. Countries will produce and export goods and services for which they have a comparative or competitive advantage and countries will import goods and services for which other countries have a comparative or competitive advantage. A comparative or competitive advantage may originate from a country's natural resources (such as petroleum), its human resources (such as education), its capital investment (which may or may not be aided by the government), or its laws or regulations that may promote certain activities. For example, the chief exports of the United States are machinery, transportation equipment (e.g., trucks and aircraft), chemicals, and grain products, which relate to the vast capital investment in the heavy industries (e.g., steel production) and the acreage devoted to farm products. The chief import of the United States is petroleum because of the diminished U.S. oil reserves combined with the strong demand for fuel and petroleum-based products (e.g., plastics).

EXHIBIT 25.2 United States' Exports and Imports, 1919–2001 in Real Dollars

Panel a: Exports and Imports

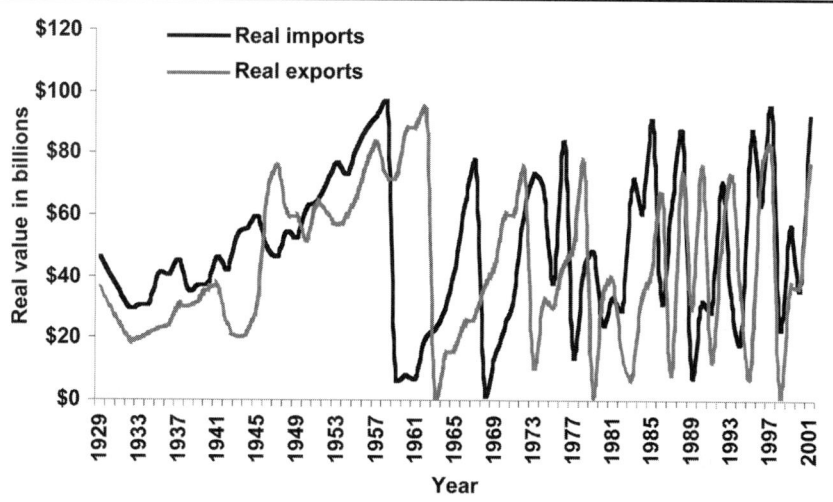

Panel b: Net Trade Balance

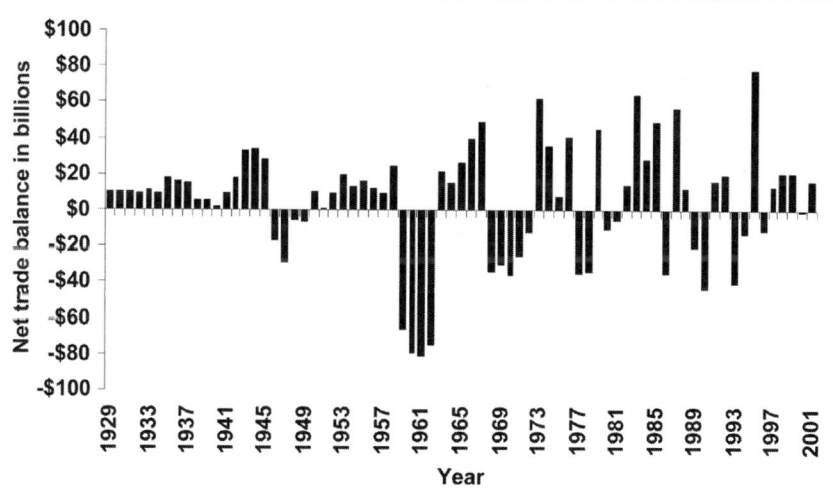

Source: Federal Reserve Bank of St. Louis

Many advocate *free trade*, which is trading among countries without barriers such as export or import quotas and tariffs (taxes on imported goods). The benefits of free trade include enhanced competition, which ultimately benefits the consumer. However, for countries for which there are few or no comparative or competitive advantages, free trade may not be beneficial, and such countries may impose barriers to protect their own companies. These barriers may affect foreign companies' investment and financing decisions in that country.

Throughout history, most countries have exercised some protectionism. However, trends throughout the twentieth century reduced protectionism. One such agreement is the *General Agreement on Tariffs and Trade* (GATT), which was first signed by 23 countries in 1947. GATT is basically a forum for negotiating the reduction in trade barriers on a multilateral basis—that is, many countries agreeing to such reductions at one time. Through time, other nations joined in GATT.

Monetary cooperation is facilitated through the *International Monetary Fund* (IMF), an agency of the United Nations, which began operations in 1947. The objective of the IMF is to promote monetary cooperation and encourage international trade. An important function of the IMF is to facilitate trade through a system of payments for current transactions. Further, the IMF strives to reduce and eliminate restrictions on foreign exchange. In 2001, there were 184 member nations of the IMF.

Two recent major agreements affect trade among major industrialized nations: the European Union and the North American Free Trade Agreement. The *European Union* (EU) is an organization, consisting in 1996 of 15 European countries, whose goal is to increase economic cooperation and integration among its member countries. The European Union was established with the *Maastricht Treaty* in November 1993, which was then ratified by the member nations, forming the European Economic Community (EEC). Under this treaty, citizens of the member countries gain mobility because immigration and customs requirements are reduced. An objective of this union was the development of a common currency for all member nations. The European countries that did not join the European Union remained in its predecessor, the *European Free Trade Association* (EFTA), which was formed to reduce trade barriers and to enhance economic cooperation. A January 1994 agreement eliminated trade barriers between the EU and the EFTA by creating the *European Economic Area*, and creating the largest free trading area in the world.

The *North American Free Trade Agreement* (NAFTA) is a pact among Canada, Mexico, and the United States for the gradual removal of trade barriers for most goods produced and sold in North America. This pact became effective January 1, 1994, and makes North America the world's second largest free trade zone. It is expected that this pact will expand to encompass Latin American countries, but the economic requirements imposed upon included countries may be difficult for some countries to satisfy, as least in the near term.

Most of the significant trade pacts involve major industrial nations. However, because many of the future growth opportunities are in lesser-developed nations, barriers to free trade exist and are important considerations in many aspects of financial decision making.

MULTINATIONAL FIRMS

A *multinational company* is a firm that does business in two or more countries. Most large U.S. corporations are multinational firms, deriving a large part of their income from operations beyond the U.S. borders.

The largest multinational firms at the end of 2001 are listed in Exhibit 25.3, along with their home countries and their revenues in U.S. dollars. Many U.S. firms derive a large portion of their sales and income from their foreign operations as we saw in Exhibit 25.1.

Companies expand beyond their domestic borders for many reasons, including:

■ **To gain access to new markets.** Growth in the domestic market may slow, but there may be opportunities to grow in other countries. For example, as the domestic discount retail market became saturated in the mid-1990s, Wal-Mart opened stores in Mexico.

EXHIBIT 25.3 The Largest Multinational Companies, 2001

Rank	Company	Country	Revenues (Millions of $ U.S.)
1	Wal-Mart Stores	United States	$219,812
2	Exxon Mobil	United States	191,581
3	General Motors	United States	177,260
4	BP PLC	United Kingdom	174,218
5	Ford Motor	United States	162,412
6	Enron	United States	138,718
7	DaimlerChrysler AG	Germany	136,897
8	Royal Dutch/Shell Group	Netherlands & United Kingdom	135,211
9	General Electric	United States	125,913
10	Toyota Motor	Japan	120,814

Source: www.fortune.com, 2002 Global 500

■ **To achieve production efficiency.** By shifting operations to other, lower-cost nations, a company can reduce its operating costs.

■ **To gain access to resources.** Companies that rely on natural resources, such as oil companies, establish access to these resources by establishing subsidiaries in other countries. This assures these companies of their basic materials to maintain uninterrupted operations.

■ **To reduce political and regulatory hurdles.** Shifting operations to other countries may be necessary to overcome the many hurdles established by nations to protect their domestic businesses. For example, in the 1970s Japanese auto firms established manufacturing and assembly plants in the United States to avoid import quotas imposed by the United States.

■ **To diversify.** Over any given period of time, the level of business activity may be different in different countries. This results in opportunities to reduce the overall fluctuations in a firm's business revenues and/or costs by doing business abroad. For example, in the 1980s, the Japanese economy was flourishing, while the U.S. economy was in a recession; in contrast, during the early 1990s, the Japanese economy did poorly, while the U.S. economy was prospering.

■ **To gain access to technology.** As technology is developed in other countries, a firm may expand operations in other countries, say, through joint ventures, to assure access to patents and other developments that ensure its competitiveness both domestically and internationally.

The many changes in the world political economy have enhanced opportunities. These changes include changes in domestic laws and regulations, such as increased import quotas and the reduction in regulations on banking activities, and changes outside the United States, such as NAFTA and the European Free Trade Association (EFTA).

FOREIGN CURRENCY

Doing business outside of one's own country requires dealing with the currencies of other countries. Financial managers must be aware of the issues relating to dealing with multiple currencies. In particular, the financial manager must be aware of exchange rate and the related currency risk.

Exchange Rates

The *exchange rate* is the number of units of a given currency that can be purchased for one unit of another country's currency; the exchange rate tells us about the relative value of any two currencies. The exchange rate can be quoted in term of the number of units of the domestic currency relative to a unit of the foreign currency (referred to as a *direct quotation*), or in terms of the number of units of the foreign currency relative to a unit of the domestic currency (referred to as an *indirect quotation*).

Consider the exchange rate of U.S. dollars and Swiss francs. From the perspective of the U.S. firm, the exchange rate would be the number of U.S. dollars needed to buy a Swiss franc. If the rate is 0.70, this means that it takes $0.70 to buy one Swiss franc, 1CHF. From the perspective of the Swiss firm, the rate is US$0.70/1CHF = 1.4286; that is, it takes 1.4286 Swiss francs to buy one U.S. dollar.

Countries have different policies concerning their currency exchange rate. In the *floating exchange rate system*, the currency's foreign exchange rate is allowed to fluctuate freely by supply and demand for the currency. Another type of policy is the *fixed exchange rate system*, where the government intervenes to offset changes in exchange rates caused by changes in the currency's supply and demand. The third type of policy is a *managed floating exchange rate system*, which falls somewhere between the fixed and floating systems. In the managed floating rate system, the currency's exchange rates are allowed to fluctuate in response to changes in supply and demand, but the government may intervene to stabilize the exchange rate in the short-run, avoiding short-term wild fluctuations in the exchange rate.

The international foreign currency market has undergone vast changes since the gold standard was abolished in 1971. Prior to August 1971, the value of the U.S. dollar was tied to the value of gold (fixed at $35 per ounce) and the value of other countries' currency was tied to the value of the U.S. dollar. In other words, the world's currencies were on a type of fixed exchange rate system. Since August 1971, the values of the U.S. dollar and other currencies have been allowed to change according to supply and demand. However, the United States, like other countries, does occasionally intervene. Therefore, the U.S. currency policy is best described as a managed floating rate system.

The value of a country's currency depends on many factors, including the imports and exports of goods and services. As the demand and supply of countries' currencies rises and falls, the exchange rates, which reflect the currencies' relative values, change if rates are allowed to "float." For example, if a Swiss company purchases U.S. goods, the Swiss company must buy U.S. dollars to purchase the goods, thus creating demand for U.S. dollars. If a U.S. company purchases Swiss goods, the U.S. company must buy Swiss francs, thus creating demand for Swiss francs. If there is increased demand for U.S. dollars, the price of the dollar relative to the Swiss franc increases—the U.S. dollar appreciates and the Swiss franc depreciates. But this system does not go unchecked—countries' central banks may buy or sell currencies to affect the exchange rates, thus managing the rate changes. Usually, the role of the central banks is to smooth out any sudden fluctuations in exchange rates.

Another factor that affects the relative value of currencies is the movement of investment capital from one country to another. If interest rates are higher in one country, investors may buy the currency of that country in order to buy the interest-bearing securities in that country. This shifting of investment capital increases the demand for the currency of the country with the higher interest rate.

When a currency loses value relative to other currencies, we say that the currency has "depreciated" if the change is due to changes in supply and demand, or has been "devalued" if the change is due to government intervention. If the currency gains value relative other currencies, we say that the currency has "appreciated" or been "revalued."

Currency Risk

The uncertainty of exchange rates affects a financial manager's decisions. Consider a U.S. firm making an investment that produces cash flows in British pounds, £. Suppose you invest £10,000 today and expect to get £12,000 one year from today. Further suppose that £1 = $1.48 today, so you are investing $1.48 times 10,000 = $14,800. If the British pound does not change in value relative to the U.S. dollar, you would have a return of 20%:

$$\text{Return} = \frac{£12,000 - £10,000}{£10,000} \text{ or } \frac{\$17,760 - \$14,800}{\$14,800} = 20\%$$

But what if one year from now £1 = $1.30 instead? Your return would be less than 20% because the value of the pound has dropped in relation to the U.S. dollar. You are making an investment of £10,000, or $14,800, and getting not $17,760, but rather $1.30 times £12,000 = $15,600 in one year. If the pound loses value from $1.48 to $1.30, your return on your investment is:

$$\text{Return} = \frac{\$15,600 - \$14,800}{\$14,800} = \frac{\$800}{\$14,800} = 5.41\%$$

Currency risk, also called *exchange-rate risk*, is the risk that the relative values of the domestic and foreign currencies will adversely change in the future, changing the value of the future cash flows. Financial managers must consider currency risk in investment decisions that involve other currencies and make sure that the returns on these investments are sufficient compensation for the risk of changing values of currencies.

The buying and selling of foreign currency takes place in the foreign exchange market, which is an over-the-counter market consisting of banks and brokers in major world financial centers. Trading in foreign currencies may be done in the spot market, which is the buying and selling of currencies for immediate delivery, or in the *forward market*, which is the buying and selling of contracts for future delivery of currencies. If a U.S. firm needs euros in 90 days, it can buy today a contact for delivery of euros in 90 days.

Forward contracts can be used to reduce uncertainty regarding foreign exchange rates. By buying a contract for euros for 90 days from now, the firm is locking in the exchange rate of U.S. dollars for euros. This use of forward contracts in this manner is referred to as *hedging*. By hedging, the financial manager can reduce a firm's exposure to currency risk.

Purchasing Power Parity

If there are no barriers or costs to trade across borders (including costs to move the good or service), the price of a given product will be the same regardless of where it is sold. This is referred to as the *law of one price*. Applied to a situation in which there are different currencies on either side of the borders, this means that after adjusting for the difference in currencies, the price of a good or service is the same across borders. In the case of different currencies, the law of one price is known as *purchasing power parity* (PPP).

If purchasing power parity holds, we can evaluate the exchange rate of two currencies by looking at the price of a good or service in the two different countries. In a light-hearted look at purchasing power parity, the financial magazine, the *Economist*, periodically publishes the price of the McDonald's Big Mac in different countries. The *Economist* uses the price of the Big Mac in different countries, along with information on current exchange rates, to predict future exchange rates. For example, in April 2002, the Big Mac price in China was Yuan 10.50, which was equivalent to $1.27 using the exchange rate in existence then of 8.28 Yuan/USD [*Economist*, April 25, 2002]. Comparing this Big Mac price with that of the Big Mac in the U.S. at the time, $2.49, this suggests—if you believe that this is a good indicator of relative valuation—that the Yuan in undervalued by 49% relative to the U.S. dollar.

Any mispricing in terms of current exchange rates is interpreted as a sign of future changes in currency valuations. In most situations, there are barriers (e.g., import or export quotas) and costs (e.g., tariffs) associated with moving goods across borders. Therefore, purchasing power parity does not likely hold precisely.[1]

The Euro

The *European Union* consists of 15 European member countries that engage in European economic and political activities. In February 1992, the *Treaty on European Union of 1992* established that monetary union would take place by January 1999. The treaty, also called the Maastricht Treaty because its terms were agreed to at the European Council meeting in Maastricht (Netherlands) in December 1991, called for a single currency and monetary policy for member countries in Europe. Monetary policy was to be administered by the *European Central Bank*. The *Economic and Monetary Union* (EMU) represents the member countries that are part of the European Union that have adopted the single currency and monetary policy.

At the time of the treaty, the single currency was to be the *economic currency unit* (ECU). This was the most widely used composite currency unit for capital market transactions. It was created in 1979 by the European Economic Community (EEC). The currencies included in the ECU were those that were members of the European Monetary System (EMS). The weight of each country's currency is figured according to the relative importance of a country's economic trade and financial sector within the EEC. Exchange rates between the ECU and those countries not part of the EEC float freely. The exchange rate between countries in the EEC, however, may fluctuate only within a narrow range.

However, at a meeting of the heads of government in Madrid in December 1995, it was agreed that the name of the single currency would be called the *euro*. The reason that the ECU was not selected as the single currency was due to the opinion of Germans that the ECU was perceived to be a weak currency. For the countries of the European Union electing to be members of the EMU, there is a fixed conversion rate against their national currencies and relative to the euro. However, the value of the euro against all other currencies, including member states of the European Union that did not elect to join the EMU, fluctuate according to market conditions.

Members of the EMU are said to be part of "euroland" or the "euro zone" because the euro became the only legal currency. Initially, the member countries maintained their own physical currencies, although

---

[1] There is a variation of purchasing power parity that states that changes in the relative inflation rates between two countries is reflected in the change in the exchange rate between the two currencies.

they were fixed in value relative to the euro, and the euro had no physical existence. The actual euro currency physically replaced the individual currencies of the participating countries on January 1, 2002. The relevant authorities of each member country began to withdraw their old national currency from circulation and when this process is completed, their old national currency will no longer be legal tender.

For corporations, the primary issuance of corporate debt denominated in the euro has become large and liquid. Both European and U.S. investment banks play significant roles in these fundings.

TAX CONSIDERATIONS

Taxes paid by corporate entities can be classified into two types: income taxes and indirect taxes. The former includes taxes paid to the central government based on corporate income and possibly any local income taxes. Indirect taxes include real estate value-added and sales taxes, as well as miscellaneous taxes on business transactions. In this section, we provide an overview of the key corporate income tax issues that affect investing decisions and financing decisions in foreign countries.

Establishing a Business Entity

As explained in Chapter 5, the United States has several forms of taxable entities: individuals, partnerships, and corporations. The choice of the structure is determined by a myriad of factors, including the minimization of taxes (income taxes and other business taxes), the desire for limited liability, and the ease with which ownership can be transferred. The same factors also influence the structure a firm elects when establishing a subsidiary in a foreign country. The form of business entity chosen by major commercial entities in the United States is the corporation.

As examples of the business entities that are available outside the United States, let's look at Germany and France. Germany has six forms of commercial enterprises: (1) the corporation (*Aktiengellschaft*— abbreviated AG), (2) limited liability company (*Gesellschaft mit beschrankter Haftung*—GmbH), (3) general commercial partnership (*offene Handelgellschaft*—oHG), (4) limited partnership (*Kommanditgesellschaft*—KG), (5) limited partnership with share capital (*Kommanditgellschaft auf Aktien*—KGaA), and (6) branch of a domestic or foreign company (*Zweignierderlassung*). Corporate income taxes are assessed on AGs, GmbHs, and nonresident companies that establish German branches. The other forms are not taxed at the entity level but at the individual level; that is, the income is allocated to the individual partners who are then taxed at their appropriate tax rate. The preferred form used by foreigners is either the GmbH or a branch.

The principal forms of French commercial enterprises are (1) the corporation (*societe annonyme*—abbreviated SA), (2) limited liability company (*societe a responsabilite limitee*—SARL), (3) general partnership (*societe en nom collectif*—SCS), (4) partnership limited by shares (*societe en commandite par actions*—SCPA), (5) joint ventures, and (6) branch (*succursale*). The commercial entities liable for corporate income taxes are SAs, SARLs, SCPAs, and nonresident companies with branches. The other entities may elect to be taxed as corporate entities or as individuals. Foreign entities predominately use SAs and SARLs.

Corporate Income Tax Rates

The basic corporate income tax imposed by central governments is a fixed percentage or an increasing percentage of the statutorily determined corporate income. The rate varies significantly from country to country. Countries typically tax resident corporations on worldwide income regardless of whether the income is repatriated. Nonresident corporations, that is, corporations whose corporate seat and place of management are outside the country, are typically subject only to corporate taxes derived from within the country.

To list the basic tax rates by country would be misleading for several reasons. First, the calculation of corporate income varies based on the types of revenues that may or may not be included as taxable and permissible deductions. Second, there may be a refund for corporate income distributed to shareholders that lowers the effective tax rate or an additional corporate tax paid on distributed income that raises the effective tax rate. Third, there may be a different tax rate based on the characteristics of the commercial entity, such as its size. Fourth, the effective tax rate may be different for undistributed income and income distributed to shareholders. Finally, the tax rate can vary for resident and nonresident business entities.

Several countries impose no tax or minimal tax rates. These countries are referred to as **tax havens**. The Cayman Islands and Bermuda are examples. Tax havens are used by some entities to avoid or reduce taxes. The use of tax havens by U.S. entities was significantly reduced by the Tax Reform Act of 1986.

A country's tax authorities withhold taxes on income derived in their country by nonresident corporations. The withholding tax rate may vary, depending on the type of income: dividends, interest, or royalties. Major trading countries often negotiate tax treaties to reduce the double taxation of corporate income.

A corporation's effective tax rate on its worldwide income therefore depends on tax treaties between its home country and all the foreign countries where it has established a nonresident corporation. Moreover, the rate also depends on whether a corporation is permitted a credit by the tax authorities in its home country against taxes paid in foreign countries. Many countries permit this credit, called a *foreign tax credit*. The limitation is usually that the tax credit paid to a foreign country may not exceed the amount that would have been paid in the home country.

Determining Taxable Income

Varying definitions of taxable revenue and deductible expenses cause the determination of corporate profits to vary from country to country. By far, the largest variance can be attributed to the differences in the treatment of items that are deductible for tax purposes. Different methods of treating of noncash expenses such as depreciation and inventory valuation can affect the calculation of taxable income.

Two other considerations affect the determination of taxable income. Both of these matters relate to the deductibility of items that foreign tax authorities view as legitimate expenses but are incurred to minimize taxes in the foreign country. The first is the deductibility of interest expense when that expense may be viewed as excessive. The second is the inflation of expenses associated with the sale or purchase of goods and services by a nonresident company with an associated company (that is, a parent company or another subsidiary of the parent) outside the foreign country. These two factors are interest expense and transfer prices used in intercompany transactions.

Interest Expense

In most countries, the interest expense associated with borrowed funds is tax deductible. Dividends, in contrast, are treated as distributed profits and are not tax deductible.[2] This difference is particularly important when a parent company provides financing to a foreign subsidiary. Interest paid by a subsidiary to its parent is deductible for the subsidiary but taxable for the parent. Dividends, in contrast, are taxable for both the subsidiary and the parent.

An increasing number of firms have employed financing arrangements to take advantage of the tax advantage associated with debt. It can be done in two ways. First, a financing agreement can be called "debt" even though it is effectively a form of equity. For example, an instrument may be called a debt obligation but, unlike legitimate debt, it

---

[2] However, some countries allow the dividend-paying company to receive a tax credit for distributed profits.

allows the "borrower" to miss periodic payments if sufficient cash flow is unavailable. Or the priority of the "creditors" can be subordinated to all other creditors and to preferred stockholders. Both of these provisions indicate that the instrument may be more appropriately classified as a form of equity rather than debt. Second, several companies have employed capital structures that predominately consist of debt. Such companies are commonly referred to as *thin capitalization.*

In some countries, tax authorities have challenged whether, in fact, some of the debt should be appropriately recharacterized as equity for tax purposes, thereby eliminating the deductibility of interest for the reclassified portion. The recharacterization of debt to equity may be due to the terms of the individual agreement or security regardless of the ratio of debt to equity. When a company's debt-to-equity ratio is high, tax authorities may seek to recharacterize a portion of the debt to equity for tax purposes. The Committee on Fiscal Affairs of the Organization on Economic Cooperation and Development (OCED) addressed the issue of thin capitalization in a 1987 publication, *The OECD Report on Thin Capitalization.* The report identifies the general issues but does not provide any guideline as to what constitutes an excessive debt-to-equity ratio.

Tax authorities or finance ministries use other methods to attempt to curtail what they perceive to be an abuse of borrowing to benefit from interest deductibility. One way is to place an explicit restriction on the amount of interest that may be deductible. To restrict resident companies controlled by foreign entities from being thinly capitalized, some countries, requiring approval of the investments by foreign entities, do not grant that approval unless they deem the capitalization adequate. When approval is necessary, minimum equity or maximum debt levels may be imposed. Or countries can use restrictions on the transfer of funds abroad to mitigate the problem of thin capitalization.

Intercompany Transactions and Transfer Prices

As just explained, to minimize taxes in foreign countries with high tax rates, a firm may use excessive debt in controlled entities. To further reduce taxes, the interest rate on the "loan" may be above market rates. An excessive interest rate charged to subsidiaries in high tax countries is but one expense that a company with foreign operations can consider to reduce worldwide taxes.

It is common for a company's subsidiaries in different countries to buy and sell goods from each other. The price for the goods in such intercompany transactions is called a *transfer price.* Establishing transfer prices to promote goal congruence within a multinational company is a complicated topic. In practice, goal congruence seems to be of secondary importance to the minimization of worldwide taxes—income taxes and import duty taxes—in the establishment of transfer prices.[3]

The following illustration demonstrates how the establishment of a transfer price affects income taxes. Suppose that a parent company resides in the United States where it faces a marginal tax rate of 35% and has only one subsidiary located in a foreign country where the marginal tax rate is 42%. The parent company manufactures a product for US$20 a unit and sells 100,000 units to the subsidiary each year. The subsidiary, in turn, further processes each unit at a cost of $10 per unit and sells the finished product for $80 per unit. The parent company's sale represents its revenue, and the subsidiary's purchase represents part of its production cost. It is assumed that fixed costs for the parent and the subsidiary are $1,000,000 and $500,000, respectively.

Panel a of Exhibit 25.4 shows the taxes and the net income of the parent, the subsidiary, and the company as a whole if the transfer price is set at $40 per unit. Panel b of the exhibit shows the same analysis if the parent company sets a transfer price of $60 per unit. Notice that by increasing the transfer price from $40 to $60, worldwide income increases by $140,000, the same amount by which worldwide taxes decline.

FINANCING OUTSIDE THE DOMESTIC MARKET

Because of the globalization of capital markets throughout the world, a corporation is not limited to raising funds in the capital market where it is domiciled. *Globalization* means the integration of capital markets throughout the world into a global capital market.

From the perspective of a given country, capital markets can be classified into two markets: an *internal market* and an *external market*. The internal market is also called the *national market*. It can be decomposed into two parts: the domestic market and the foreign market. The domestic market is where issuers domiciled in the country issue securities and where those securities are subsequently traded.

The *foreign market* of a country is where issuers not domiciled in the country issue securities and where the securities are then traded. The rules governing the issuance of foreign securities are those imposed by regulatory authorities where the security is issued. For example, securities issued by non-U.S. corporations in the United States must comply with the regulations set forth in U.S. securities law and other requirements imposed by the Securities and Exchange Commission. A non-Japanese

---

[3] R.L. Benke, Jr. and J.D. Edwards, *Transfer Pricing: Techniques and Uses* (New York: National Association of Accountants, 1980).

corporation that seeks to offer securities in Japan, for example, must comply with Japanese securities law and regulations imposed by the Japanese Ministry of Finance.

EXHIBIT 25.4   Illustration of Effect of Transfer Price on Worldwide Net Income

Assumptions: Units sold by parent = 100,000
U.S. parent tax rate = 35%
Subsidiary tax rate = 42%

	Price and Costs in U.S. dollars	
	Parent	Subsidiary
Selling price	Transfer price	$80
Unit variable manufacturing cost	$20	Transfer price + $10
Fixed manufacturing costs	$1,000,000	$500,000

a. Transfer price = $40

	U.S. Parent Company Alone	Subsidiary
Revenue	$4,000,000	$8,000,000
Variable manufacturing costs	2,000,000	5,000,000
Fixed manufacturing costs	1,000,000	500,000
Taxable income	$1,000,000	$2,500,000
Income taxes	350,000	1,050,000
Net income after taxes	$650,000	$1,450,000

Worldwide income taxes = $1,400,000
Worldwide net income after taxes = $2,100,000

b. Transfer price = $60

	U.S. Parent Company Alone	Subsidiary
Revenue	$6,000,000	$8,000,000
Variable manufacturing costs	2,000,000	7,000,000
Fixed manufacturing costs	1,000,000	500,000
Taxable income	$3,000,000	$500,000
Income taxes	1,050,000	210,000
Net income after taxes	$1,950,000	$290,000

Worldwide income taxes = $1,260,000
Worldwide net income after taxes = $2,240,000

The *external market*, also called the *international market*, includes securities with the following distinguishing features: (1) they are underwritten by an international syndicate, (2) they are offered at issuance simultaneously to investors in a number of countries, and (3) they are issued outside the jurisdiction of any single country. The external market is commonly referred to as the *offshore market* or, more popularly, the *Euromarket*.[4]

We refer to the collection of all these markets—the domestic market, the foreign market, and the Euromarket—as the *global capital market*. The global capital market can be further divided based on the type of financial claim: equity or debt.

Several factors have lead to the better integration of capital markets throughout the world. We can classify these factors as follows: (1) deregulation or liberalization of capital markets and activities of market participants in key financial centers of the world; (2) technological advances for monitoring world markets, executing orders, and analyzing financial opportunities; and, (3) increased institutionalization of capital markets. These factors are not mutually exclusive. We discuss each factor below.

Motivation for Raising Funds Outside of the Domestic Market

There are four reasons why a corporation may seek to raise funds outside of its domestic market. First, in some countries, large corporations seeking to raise a substantial amount of funds may have no other choice but to obtain financing in either the foreign-market sector of another country or the Euromarket. This is because the fund-raising corporation's domestic market is not fully developed to be able to satisfy its demand for funds on globally competitive terms. Governments of developing countries have used these markets in seeking funds for government-owned corporations that they are privatizing.

The second reason is that there may be opportunities for obtaining a reduced cost of funding (taking into consideration issuing costs) compared to that available in the domestic market. With the integration of capital markets throughout the world, such opportunities have diminished. Nevertheless, there are imperfections in capital markets throughout the world that prevent complete integration and thereby may permit a reduced cost of funds. These imperfections, or market frictions, occur because of differences in: security regulations in various countries, tax

---

[4] This classification is by no means universally accepted. Some market observers and compilers of statistical data on market activity refer to the external market as consisting of the foreign market and the Euromarket.

structures, restrictions imposed on regulated institutional investors, and the credit risk perception of the issuer. In the case of common stock, a corporation is seeking to gain a higher value for its stock and to reduce the market impact cost of floating a large offering.

The third reason to seek funds in foreign markets is a desire by corporate treasurers to diversify their source of funding in order to reduce reliance on domestic investors. In the case of common stock, diversifying funding sources may encourage investment by foreign investors who have different perspectives of the future performance of the corporation. There are two additional advantages of raising foreign equity funds from the perspective of U.S. corporations: (1) some market observers believe that certain foreign investors are more loyal to corporations and look at long-term performance rather than short-term performance as do investors in the United States; and (2) diversifying the investor base reduces the dominance of U.S. institutional holdings and its impact on corporate governance.

Finally, a corporation may issue a security denominated in a foreign currency as part of its overall foreign-currency management. For example, consider a U.S. corporation that plans to build a factory in a foreign country where the construction costs will be denominated in that foreign currency. Also assume that the corporation plans to sell the output of the factory in the same foreign country. Therefore, the revenue will be denominated in the foreign currency. The corporation then faces exchange-rate risk: The construction costs are uncertain in U.S. dollars because during the construction period the U.S. dollar may depreciate relative to the foreign currency. Also, the projected revenue is uncertain in U.S. dollars because the foreign currency may depreciate relative to the U.S. dollar. Suppose that the corporation arranges debt financing for the plant in which it receives the proceeds in the foreign currency and the liabilities are denominated in the foreign currency. This financing arrangement can reduce risk because the proceeds received will be in the foreign currency and will be used to pay the construction costs, and the projected revenue can be applied to service the debt obligation.

Corporate Financing Week asked the corporate treasurers of several multinational corporations why they used nondomestic markets to raise funds.[5] Their responses reflected one or more of the reasons cited above. For example, the director of corporate finance of General Motors said that the company uses the Eurobond market with the objective of "diversifying funding sources, attracting new investors and achieving comparable, if not, cheaper financing." A managing director of Sears

---

[5] Victoria Keefe, "Companies Issue Overseas for Diverse Reasons," Corporate Financing Week (November 25, 1991, Special Supplement), pp.1 and 9.

Roebuck stated that the company "has a long-standing policy of diversifying geographical [funding] sources and instruments to avoid reliance on any specific market, even if the cost is higher."

Implications of Global Market Integration for Funding Costs

As explained above, a firm may seek funds outside its local capital market with the expectation of doing so at a lower cost than if its funds are raised in its own capital market. Whether this is possible depends on the degree of integration of capital markets. At the two extremes, the world capital markets can be classified as either *completely segmented* or *completely integrated.*

In the case of a completely segmented capital market, investors in one country are not permitted to invest in the securities issued by an entity in another country. As a result, in a completely segmented market, the required return of securities of comparable risk that are traded in different capital markets throughout the world will be different even after adjusting for taxes and foreign-exchange rates. This implies that a firm may be able to raise funds in the capital market of another country at a cost that is lower than doing so in its local capital market.

At the other extreme, in a completely integrated capital market, there are no restrictions to prevent investors from investing in securities issued in any capital market throughout the world. In such an ideal world capital market, the required return on securities of comparable risk will be the same in all capital markets after adjusting for taxes and foreign-exchange rates. This implies that the cost of funds will be the same regardless of where in the capital markets throughout the world a fund-seeking entity elects to raise funds.

Real-world capital markets are neither completely segmented nor completely integrated, but fall somewhere in between. Such markets can be referred to as *mildly segmented* or *mildly integrated.* This implies that in a world capital market characterized in this way, there are opportunities for firms to raise funds at a lower cost in some capital markets outside their own capital market.

Global Equity Market

In 1985, *Euromoney* surveyed several firms that either listed stock on a foreign stock exchange or had a stock offering in a foreign market to find out why they did so.[6] While the study is now quite old, the results of the survey are still informative.

---

[6] "Why Corporations Gain from Foreign Equity Listings," *Euromoney Corporate Finance* (March 1985), pp. 39–40.

One corporation surveyed was Scott Paper, a U.S. corporation, which listed its stock on the London Stock Exchange in November 1984. The stock had already been listed on the NYSE and a regional stock exchange. The following reason for listing was given by an official in the company's public relations department:

> We had no immediate need for extra equity, but may well do so at some time in the future. We would like a broader stockholder base, and felt there would be some interest in the company overseas. The London Stock Exchange has high visibility, so it best served the purpose of getting the company's name known.[7]

A second firm surveyed was Saatchi & Saatchi, a U.K. corporation that raised equity in the United States in the over-the-counter market. Several reasons were given for Saatchi & Saatchi's raising of equity in the United States. The firm had considerable U.S. activities and therefore felt it necessary to establish a presence in the U.S. equity market and a higher profile in the United States in general. Also, the firm wanted to offer stock options to its U.S. employees and apparently felt that having stocks traded in the U.S. equity market would make the options more attractive to employees.

Yet another set of reasons discussed earlier was given by a third firm in the *Euromoney* survey, Norsk Data, a Norwegian firm. It is in the high technology industry and before it sought foreign listing had a history of earning per share growth of 60%. In 1981, the firm listed its stock on the London Stock Exchange and followed this several months later with an offering of new shares in London. In 1983 the firm raised funds in the U.S. equity market with the stock traded in the U.S. over-the-counter market. The chief executive officer of the firm gave the following reasons for listing:

> For major computer companies, the U.S. market is a very important source of funds, since it is alive to the possibility of high technology. However, we went to London first, since we felt a leap straight from Oslo to New York would be too great. Our major customers are in Germany, the UK and to a lesser extent, the U.S.[8]

In 1984, Norsk Data raised equity funds in a simultaneous United States and European offering. With respect to its various equity offerings, the chief executive officer stated:

---

[7] "Why Corporations Gain from Foreign Equity Listings," p. 39.
[8] "Why Corporations Gain from Foreign Equity Listings," p. 40.

We have now brought equity up to the level of our competitors, and we have a natural balance sheet for a high growth, high technology company. *That would have been very difficult if we had been limited to the Oslo stock market.*[9] [Emphasis added.]

In addition, after these equity offerings on foreign markets, the firm was 60% owned by foreign investors, most of which was nonvoting common stock. Thus, corporate control was not sacrificed.

A 1992 survey of corporate managers investigating why U.S. corporations list on the London, Frankfurt, and Tokyo stock exchanges found the following four major motives:[10]

1. Increased visibility (awareness, name recognition, or exposure).
2. Broadened shareholder base (diversify ownership).
3. Increased access to financial markets.
4. Possible future market for products.

The most popular motive was the first.

International Depositary Receipts

When a corporation issues equity outside of its domestic market and the equity issue is subsequently traded in the foreign market, it is typically in the form of an *international depositary receipt* (IDR). Banks issue IDRs as evidence of ownership of the underlying stock of a foreign corporation that the bank holds in trust. Each IDR may represent ownership of one or more shares of common stock of a corporation. The advantage of the IDR structure is that the corporation does not have to comply with all the regulatory issuing requirements of the foreign country where the stock is to be traded. IDRs are typically sponsored by the issuing corporation. That is, the issuing corporation works with a bank to offer its common stock in a foreign country via the sale of IDRs.

As an example, consider the United States version of the IDR, the *American depositary receipt* (ADR). The success of the ADR structure resulted in the rise of IDRs throughout the world. ADRs are denominated in U.S. dollars and pay dividends in them. The holder of an ADR does not have voting or preemptive rights.

---

[9] "Why Corporations Gain from Foreign Equity Listings," p. 40.

[10] H. Kent Baker, "Why U.S. Companies List on the London, Frankfurt and Tokyo Stock Exchanges," *The Journal of International Securities Markets* (Autumn 1992), pp. 219-227.

ADRs can arise in one of two ways. First, one or more banks or security firms can assemble a large block of the shares of a foreign corporation and issue ADRs without the participation of that foreign corporation. More typically, the foreign corporation that seeks to have its stock traded in the United States sponsors the ADRs. In these instances, only one depository bank issues them. A sponsored ADR is commonly referred to as an *American depositary share* (ADS). Periodic financial reports are provided in English to the holder of an ADS. ADSs can either be traded on one of the two major organized exchanges (the New York Stock Exchange and the American Stock Exchange), traded in the over-the-counter market, or privately placed with institutional investors. The nonsponsored ADR is typically traded in the over-the-counter market.

Euroequity Issues

Euroequity issues are those issued simultaneously in several national markets by an international syndicate. The first modern Euroequity offering was in 1983. Since that time an increasing number of U.S. firms had equity offerings that included a Euroequity "tranche." (In the financial vocabulary, the word "tranche," which is French for slice or segment or cut, means a distinctive portion of the issue of a financial security. In this context, the word means that some of the newly issued equity shares were reserved for sale in Euromarkets.) Similarly, more European firms began offering equity securities with a U.S. tranche.

Corporations have not limited their equity offerings to just their domestic equity market and a foreign market of another country. Instead, the offerings have been more global in nature. For example, the initial public offering (IPO) of British Telecommunications (the United Kingdom's government-owned telephone company) in 1984 was offered simultaneously in the United Kingdom, the United States, Japan, and Canada.

The innovation in the Euroequities markets is not in terms of new equity structures. Rather, it is in the development of an efficient international channel for distributing equities.

Eurobond Market

A corporate treasurer seeking to raise funds via a bond offering can issue in the foreign sector of another country's bond market or the Euromarket. Let us focus on the Euromarket. The distinguishing features of the securities in this market are that (1) they are underwritten by an international syndicate, (2) at issuance they are offered simultaneously to investors in a number of countries, (3) they are issued outside the jurisdiction of any single country, and (4) they are in unregistered form. The sector of the Euromarket in which bonds are traded is called the *Eurobond market.*

Eurobonds can be denominated in any major currency. Eurobonds are referred to by the currency in which the issuer agrees to denominate the payments. For example, U.S. dollar-denominated bonds are called *Eurodollar bonds* and Japanese yen-denominated bonds are called *Euroyen bonds.*

Although Eurobonds are typically registered on a national stock exchange, the most common being the Luxembourg, London, or Zurich exchanges, the bulk of all trading is in the over-the-counter market. Listing is purely to circumvent restrictions imposed on some institutional investors who are prohibited from purchasing securities that are not listed on an exchange. Some of the stronger issuers have their issues privately placed with international institutional investors.

Calculating the Cost of a Eurobond Issue

To compare the cost of issuing bonds in the domestic and Eurobond market, the first step is to calculate the all-in-cost of funds of an issue. The all-in-cost of funds considers the interest cost and the costs associated with issuing a bond issue. The all-in-cost of funds of a bond issue is the interest rate that will make the present value of the cash flow that the issuer must make to bondholders equal to the net proceeds received by the issuer. Once the all-cost-of-funds is calculated, adjustments must be made to consider differences in the frequency at which interest payments are made.

For example, consider a U.S. corporation that plans to issue $50 million of 10-year bonds in the United States. Suppose further that its investment banker indicates that 9% coupon bonds can be issued and that the issuance costs will be: (1) $300,000 in underwriter spread and (2) $184,683 in registration and legal fees. Thus, the net proceeds to the issuer would be $49,515,317.

The coupon payments are semiannual payments since this is the practice in the U.S. bond market. The all-in-cost of funds is the interest rate that will make the present value of the semiannual payments equal to the proceeds of $49,515,317. It can be shown that 4.575% is the *semiannual* all-in-cost of funds. The cost is annualized by doubling the semiannual cost and is called the bond-equivalent yield. In our illustration, the all-in-cost of funds calculated on a bond equivalent basis is 9.150% ($2 \times 4.575\%$).

Consider now the same corporation that can issue a 10-year $50 million Eurodollar bond. Its investment banker indicates that a 9.125% coupon is required and that the issuance costs would be: (1) $290,000 in underwriter spread and (2) $43,543 in registration and legal fees.

Thus, the net proceeds to the issuer would be $49,666,457. The payments are annual, not semiannual as with the U.S. bond issue. It can be shown that an annual interest rate of 9.23% makes the present value of the annual payments equal to the proceeds, $49,666,457.

It would seem that for our two hypothetical bond issues, the all-in-cost of funds is lower for the U.S. bond issue (9.15%) than for the Eurodollar bond issue (9.23%) by eight basis points. This is an incorrect conclusion because of the convention used in the United States to annualize a semiannual rate. An adjustment is required to make a direct comparison between the all-in-cost on a U.S. bond issue and that on a Eurodollar bond issue. It should be clear that the ability to pay annually rather than semiannually effectively reduces the cost of funding for an issuer. Given the all-in-cost on a Eurodollar bond issue, its all-in-cost (AIC) on a bond-equivalent basis is computed as follows:

$$2[(1 + \text{AIC on Eurodollar bond})^{1/2} - 1]$$

Using our hypothetical Eurodollar bond issue that has a 9.23% all-in-cost, the all-in-cost on a bond equivalent basis is:

$$2[(1.0923)^{1/2} - 1] = 0.0903 = 9.03\%$$

Notice that the bond-equivalent yield will always be less than the Eurodollar bond's yield to maturity. Now comparing the all-in-cost of the two bond issues on a bond equivalent basis, it can be seen that the Eurobond issue is cheaper by 12 basis points (9.03% versus 9.15%).

Alternatively, to convert the all-in-cost on a bond-equivalent basis of a U.S. bond issue to an annual pay basis so that it can be compared to the all-in-cost of a Eurodollar bond, the following formula can be used:

$$\text{AIC on an annual-pay basis} = \left[\left(1 + \frac{\text{AIC on a bond-equivalent basis}}{2}\right)^2 - 1\right]$$

For example, the all-in-cost on a bond equivalent basis for the U.S. bond issue is 9.15%, so the all-in-cost on an annual pay basis would be:

$$[(1 + 0.0915/2)^2 - 1] = 0.0936 = 9.36\%$$

The all-in-cost on an annual basis is always greater than the all-in-cost on a bond-equivalent basis. Our conclusion once again is that the all-in-cost is higher for the U.S. bond issue relative to the Eurodollar bond issue.

FINANCIAL ANALYSIS ISSUES

The financial statements of U.S. firms are prepared according to generally accepted accounting standards (GAAP). Information about the U.S. firms' foreign subsidiaries is incorporated with the results of the firms' domestic operations. There are two methods that may be used to translate financial data stated in foreign currency into U.S. dollars.[11] The first method uses end-of-period exchange rates to translate the amounts into U.S. dollars. The second method uses end-of-period exchange rates to translate monetary assets and liabilities, but uses historical exchange rates for all other accounts. If there are substantial changes in exchange rates over the accounting period, substantial differences may arise from these two methods.

The financial statements of non-U.S. firms may be prepared according to different accounting standards. Many non-U.S., exchange-listed companies are adopting accounting practices that conform to the ***International Accounting Standards*** (IAS), which are issued by the International Accounting Standards Committee. These standards are similar to U.S. GAAP, providing financial data in a uniform manner. An advantage of a company reporting its financial data according to IAS is that investors do not have to understand each country's accounting practices. Like GAAP, IAS allows companies a choice in how they present some information, which means that familiarity with the standards is necessary in financial analysis. The primary differences between GAAP and IAS methods relate to reporting goodwill, depreciation, discretionary reserves, and cash flows. Understanding these differences is important in analyzing non-U.S. companies.

In fact, financial statements are not always prepared according to GAAP nor IAS. For example, the financial information of Russian banks is reported using the Soviet system, which is quite different from other accounting standards. The bottom line is that the financial analyst must be aware of the financial standards and methods used to report information for international firms.

CAPITAL BUDGETING

Capital budgeting involves (1) estimating future cash flows from investments, (2) assessing the investment's risk and estimating its cost of capital, and (3) determining whether the investment will add value. The

---

[11] Statement of Financial Accounting Standards No. 52.

important elements of cash flows, cost of capital, and analysis are present in the international capital budgeting decision whether or not the investment is domestic or international. However, the decision becomes more complex in the international setting. There are several sources of the added complexity:

- *Foreign currency risk.* Investing in assets in other countries adds value only if the benefits from these assets can eventually by reflected in greater cash flows for the company's owners, where these cash flows are ultimately converted into the domestic currency. Consider McDonalds, which owns and operates restaurants in many European cities, including Switzerland. The cash flows that are generated from its restaurants in, say, Zurich, are in Swiss francs. Evaluating cash flows requires estimating not only the future cash flow in Swiss francs, but also the future exchange rate of Swiss francs for dollars.
- *Restrictions on repatriation.* Some countries may limit the amount of the cash flows that a subsidiary may send to the parent company in another country; the transfer of funds across borders to the parent is referred to as *repatriation.*
- *Political risk.* In some countries, there exists the risk that the government will reduce the value of the investment through increased taxes, currency controls, change in repatriation laws, price controls, and, in the extreme, expropriation of assets. Though this risk is minimal in many developed nations, this risk is substantial in some of the very same countries for which there is the most growth potential—developing nations.

These risks and restrictions affect not only an investment's cost of capital but also make the estimation of cash flows all the more difficult.

CAPITAL STRUCTURE

The capital structures of companies differ substantially among companies in different countries. There are several explanations for these differences:

- *Accounting standards.* Different accounting standards result in different methods of reporting debt and equity.
- *Taxes.* The different treatment of dividend and interest income results in different costs of capital, which influences a company's choice between debt and equity.

■ *Role of creditors.* In some countries, such as Japan, companies typically borrow from banks that closely monitor the management of the company. This close monitoring may reduce the likelihood of the companies defaulting on their debt obligations.

WORKING CAPITAL MANAGEMENT

Political risk, foreign currency risk, and restrictions on repatriation affect the working capital management of firms with international operations. In addition, there is a host of unique issues that arise concerning working capital.

Cash management requires working with one or more global center banks that can assist in the transfer of funds across borders. These global center banks specialize in seeking out the best rates of foreign exchange. To avoid having numerous cash balances, each denominated in a different currency, companies can pool these cash balances in cooperation with a global bank. Cross-currency pooling systems essentially offset credits in one currency with debits in another, allowing the company to earn interest on the net credit balance without having to physically convert currencies. For example, if a company has a credit balance (that is, a deposit) in British pounds and a debt balance in Singapore dollars (that is, a deficiency), without cross-currency pooling, the company would have to borrow Singapore dollars on a short-term basis and would earn interest (most likely at a lower rate) on its British pounds. With cross-currency pooling, the two balances are netted and the company earns interest or pays interest on the net amount only, resulting in a savings. The two currencies are translated at the going exchange rate, but no actual exchange takes place—avoiding transactions costs.

Accounts receivable management is especially important in the international setting because extending credit is an important part of doing business in developing countries. Many growth opportunities exist in the developing countries and granting credit is sometimes the only way to do business. The evaluation of credit is more difficult in developing countries because in most cases reliable, historical financial information is not available. This means that the evaluation of credit must rely on other information.

Inventory management is more complex because the geographical range is expanded, often requiring inventory to be maintained at one or more locations in foreign countries. This geographical span also requires more lead time in ordering and, perhaps, more time in getting the goods to customers. Another consideration is the possible restrictions or costs of moving inventory from one country to another because of import or export taxes. Still another consideration is that some countries impose taxes on property, which includes inventory, as of some specific date. For example, a country may impose a tax on all property owned on March 1st; this may inspire companies to move inventory out of that country prior to this date and to move inventory into that country after that date.

HEDGING CURRENCY RISK

Given the existence of currency risk, the natural question is how a firm can hedge this risk. There are four derivative instruments that firms can use to protect against adverse foreign exchange rate movements: (1) currency forward contracts, (2) currency futures contracts, (3) currency swaps, and (4) currency options. We discuss each below.

Currency Forward Contracts

Recall from our introduction to financial derivatives in Chapter 4 that a forward contract is one in which one party agrees to buy the underlying asset, and another party agrees to sell that same underlying asset at a designated price and date in the future. Forward contracts in which the underlying asset is foreign exchange is called a *currency forward contract*.

Most currency forward contracts have a maturity of less than two years. For longer-dated forward contracts, the bid-ask spread for a forward contract increases; that is, the size of the spread for a given currency increases with the maturity. Consequently, forward contracts become less attractive for hedging long-dated foreign currency exposure.

Forward contracts, as well as futures contracts, can be used to lock in a foreign exchange rate. In exchange for locking in a rate, the hedger forgoes the opportunity to benefit from any advantageous foreign exchange rate movement. Futures contracts that are creations of an exchange have certain advantages over forward contracts for types of underlying assets. For foreign exchange, however, the forward market is the market of choice rather than futures contracts, which we describe next.

Currency Futures Contracts

There are U.S.-traded currency futures contracts for the major currencies traded on the International Monetary Market (IMM), a division of the Chicago Mercantile Exchange, as well as other exchanges. The maturity cycle for currency futures is March, June, September, and December. The longest maturity is one year. Consequently, as in the case of a currency forward contract, currency futures are limited with respect to hedging long-dated foreign-exchange risk exposure.

Currency Swaps

When issuing bonds in another country where the bonds are not denominated in the base currency, the issuer is exposed to currency risk. One way to hedge this risk is to use currency futures contracts or currency forward contracts. While these derivative instruments allow an issuer to lock in an exchange rate, they are difficult to use in protecting against the currency risk faced when issuing a bond or when facing other long-term liabilities. The reason is that a currency futures or forward contract is needed to protect against each payment that must be made by the issuer. So, if a bond is issued with a maturity of 20 years and interest payments are made annually, 20 currency futures or forward contracts must be used for each year when payment is to be made. The major problem is that currency futures contracts have settlement dates that go out only one year and therefore cannot be used. Currency forward contracts can be obtained from a commercial bank for longer terms. However, they become expensive because dealers in this market charge a larger spread for long-dated forward contracts.

Today, when an issuer wants to protect itself against bonds denominated in a foreign currency, the treasurer will use a currency swap. Recall from our discussion in Chapter 4, a swap is an agreement whereby two counterparties agree to exchange payments. In an interest rate swap, only interest payments are exchanged. In a currency swap, there is an exchange of both interest and principal. The best way to explain a currency swap is with an illustration.

Consider two companies, a U.S. company and a Swiss company. Each company seeks to borrow for 10 years in its domestic currency; that is, the U.S. company seeks $100 million U.S.-dollar-denominated debt, and the Swiss company seeks CHF 127 million Swiss-franc-denominated debt. Suppose that both companies want to issue 10-year bonds in the bond market of the other country, denominated in the other country's currency. That is, the U.S. company wants to issue the Swiss-franc equivalent of $100 million in Switzerland, and the Swiss company wants to issue the U.S.-dollar equivalent of CHF 127 million in the United States.

For this illustration we will assume the following:

1. At the time that both companies want to issue their 10-year bonds, the spot exchange rate between U.S. dollars and Swiss francs is one U.S. dollar for 1.27 Swiss francs.
2. The coupon rate that the U.S. company would have to pay on the 10-year Swiss-franc-denominated bonds issued in Switzerland is 6%.
3. The coupon rate that the Swiss company would have to pay on the 10-year U.S.-dollar-denominated bonds issued in the U.S. is 11%.

By the first assumption, if the U.S. company issues the bonds in Switzerland, it can exchange the CHF 127 million for $100 million. By issuing $100 million of bonds in the U.S., the Swiss company can exchange the proceeds for CHF 127 million. Therefore, both get the amount of financing they seek. Assuming the coupon rates given by the last two assumptions, and assuming for purposes of this illustration that coupon payments will be made annually,[12] the cash outlays that the companies must make for the next 10 years are summarized below:

Year	U.S. Company	Swiss Company
1–10	CHF 7,620,000	$11,000,000
10	127,000,000	100,000,000

Each issuer faces the risk that at the time the liability payment must be made its domestic currency will have depreciated relative to the other currency, requiring more of the domestic currency to satisfy the liability. That is, both are exposed to foreign-exchange risk.

In a currency swap, the two companies will issue bonds in the other's bond market. The currency swap agreement will require that:

1. The two parties exchange the proceeds received from the sale of the bonds.
2. The two parties make the coupon payments to service the debt of the other party.
3. At the termination date of the currency swap (which coincides with the maturity of the bonds), both parties agree to exchange the par value of the bonds.

In our illustration, these requirements mean the following.

a. The U.S. company issues 10-year, 6% coupon bonds with a par value of CHF 127 million in Switzerland and gives the proceeds to the Swiss company. At the same time, the Swiss company issues 10-year, 11% bonds with a par value of $100 million in the U.S. and gives the proceeds to the U.S. company.
b. The U.S. company agrees to service the coupon payments of the Swiss company by paying $11,000,000 per year for the next 10 years to the Swiss company; the Swiss company agrees to service the coupon payments of the U.S. company by paying CHF 7,620,000 for the next 10 years to the U.S. company.

---

[12] In reality U.S. coupon payments are made semiannually. The typical practice for bonds issued in Europe is to pay coupon interest once per year.

c. At the end of 10 years (this would be the termination date of this currency swap because it coincides with the maturity of the two bond issues), the U.S. company agrees to pay $100 million to the Swiss company, and the Swiss company agrees to pay CHF 127 million to the U.S. company.

This currency swap is illustrated in Exhibit 25.5.

EXHIBIT 25.5 Illustration of a Currency Swap between a U.S. Company and a Swiss Company

Panel a: Initial Cash Flow for the Currency Swap

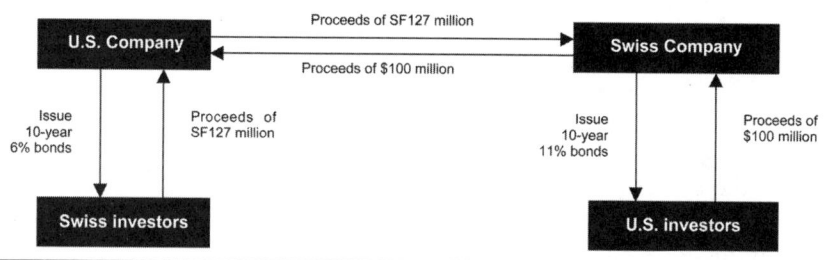

Panel b: Interest Servicing for the Currency Swap

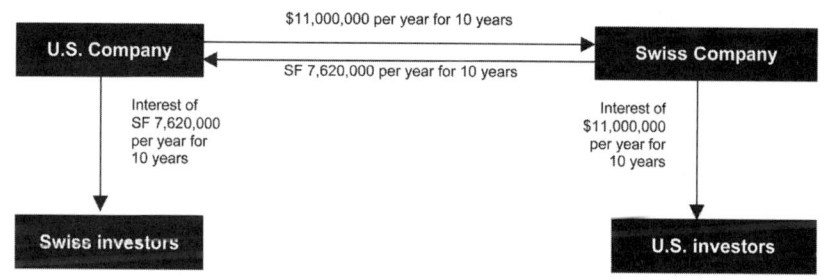

Panel c: Termination of the Currency Swap

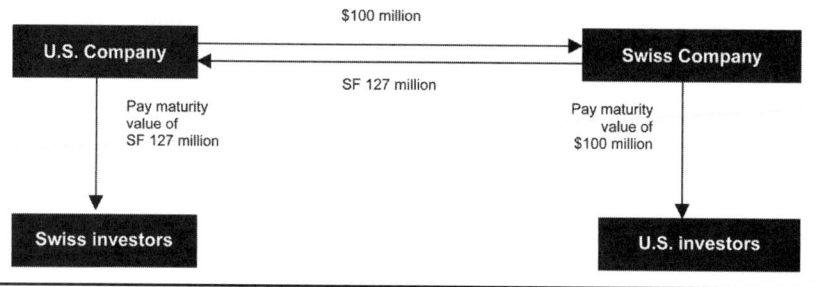

Now let's assess what this transaction has done. Both parties received the amount of financing they sought. The U.S. company's coupon payments are in dollars, not Swiss francs; the Swiss company's coupon payments are in Swiss francs, not U.S. dollars. At the termination date, both parties will receive an amount sufficient in their local currency to pay off the holders of their bonds. With the coupon payments and the principal repayment in their local currency, neither party faces foreign-exchange risk.

In practice, the two companies would not deal directly with each other. Instead, either a commercial bank or investment banking firm would be involved as an intermediary in the transaction either as a broker or a dealer. As a broker, the intermediary simply brings the two parties together, receiving a fee for the service. If instead the intermediary serves as a dealer, it not only brings the two parties together, but also guarantees payment to both parties. Thus, if one party defaults, the counterparty will continue to receive its payments from the dealer. Of course, in this arrangement, both parties are concerned with the credit risk of the dealer. When the currency swap market started, transactions were typically brokered. The more prevalent arrangement today is that the intermediary acts as a dealer.

In our illustration, we assumed that both parties made fixed cash-flow payments. Suppose instead that one of the parties sought floating-rate rather than fixed-rate financing. Assume in our illustration that instead of fixed-rate financing, the Swiss company wanted LIBOR-based financing. In this case, the U.S. company would issue floating-rate bonds in Switzerland. Suppose that it could do so at a rate of LIBOR plus 50 basis points. Because the currency swap calls for the Swiss company to service the coupon payments of the U.S. company, the Swiss company will make annual payments of LIBOR plus 50 basis points. The U.S. company will still make fixed-rate payments in U.S. dollars to service the debt obligation of the Swiss company in the United States. Now, however, the Swiss company will make floating-rate payments (LIBOR plus 50 basis points) in Swiss francs to service the debt obligation of the U.S. company in Switzerland.

Currency swaps in which one of the parties pays a fixed rate and the counterparty a floating rate are called *currency coupon swaps*.

Currency Option Contracts

In contrast to a forward or futures contract, an option gives the option buyer the opportunity to benefit from favorable exchange rate movements but establishes a maximum loss. The option price is the cost of establishing such a risk/return profile.

There are two types of foreign currency options traded on exchanges: options on the foreign currency and futures options. The latter is an option to enter into a foreign exchange futures contract which has the same effect in hedging exposure to currency risk.

There is also an over-the-counter (OTC) market for options on currencies. The markets for these products are made by commercial banks and investment banking firms. OTC options are tailor-made products to accommodate the specific needs of corporate clients. While options on the major currencies are traded on the exchange, an option on any other currency may be purchased in the OTC market.

There are variations on the standard call and put options in the OTC market. These options are called **exotic options**. Two common types of exotic options on currencies used by firms are the lookback currency option and the average rate currency option.

A **lookback currency option** is an option where the option buyer has the right to obtain the most favorable exchange rate that prevailed over the life of the option. For example, consider a two-month lookback call option to buy yen when the exchange rate between the U.S. dollar and Japanese yen is $1 for 105 yen on Day 0. Suppose that the next day, Day 1, the exchange rate changes to $1 for 110 yen—the option buyer has the right to exchange $1 for 110 yen. Suppose that on Day 2 the exchange rate changes to $1 for 108 yen. The option buyer still has the right to exchange $1 for 110 yen. Regardless of what happens to the exchange rate over the 60 days, the option buyer gets to exercise the option at the exchange rate that prevailed that gave the largest number of yen for $1 (or, equivalently, at the lowest price per yen).

An **average rate currency option**, also called an **Asian currency option**, has a payoff that is the difference between the strike exchange rate for the underlying currency and the *average* exchange rate over the life of the option for the underlying currency. In the case of a call option, if the average exchange rate for the underlying currency is greater than the strike exchange rate, then the option seller must make a payment to the option buyer. The amount of the payment is:

Payoff for average rate currency call option
= (Average exchange rate − Strike exchange rate) × Underlying units

In the case of a put option, if the strike exchange rate for the underlying currency is greater than the average exchange rate, then the option seller must make a payment to the option buyer that is equal to:

Payoff for average rate currency put option
= (Strike exchange rate − Average exchange rate) × Underlying units

SUMMARY

- International financial management is the management of a firm's assets and liabilities in the global economy. Issues such as foreign currency exchange, taxes, and unique risks, such as political and currency risk, make the financial management of a firm more challenging.

- Countries trade with each other, exporting goods and services for which they have a comparative advantage and importing goods and services for which they do not have a comparative advantage. In the past twenty years, the United States has operated at a trade deficit; that is, imports exceed exports.

- Trade agreements, such as NAFTA and the Maastricht Treaty, seek to reduce trade barriers. As these trade barriers fall, the opportunities for international trade expand.

- Companies do business outside of their own country's borders to gain access to new markets, to enhance production efficiency, to gain access to resources, to reduce hurdles to expand in other nations, to diversify, and to gain access to certain technology.

- Financial managers of companies doing business abroad must be aware of foreign currency exchange and its associated risk. Changes in foreign currency exchange rates can affect a company's profitability.

- Making decisions in foreign countries, however, requires an understanding of domestic tax regulations as well as foreign tax regulations. Taxes paid by corporate enterprises are income taxes (taxes paid to the central government based on corporate income and possibly any local income taxes) and indirect taxes (real estate value-added and sales taxes, as well as miscellaneous taxes on business transactions).

- The reasons why a corporation may seek to raise funds outside of its domestic market are (1) in some countries a firm may not have a choice but to obtain financing because of the funding needed relative to the size of the domestic market, (2) opportunities for obtaining a reduced cost of funding, (3) to diversify the source of funding in order to reduce reliance on domestic investors, and (4) issuance of a security denominated in a foreign currency as part of its overall foreign-currency management. The ability of an issuer to obtain lower cost funding depends on the degree of capital market integration.

- Currency forward contracts, currency futures contracts, currency swaps, and currency options are four derivative instruments that firms and investors can use to protect against adverse foreign exchange rate movements.

QUESTIONS

1. List reasons why firms may want to do business outside of their own country's borders.
2. Identify major trade agreements that have served to substantially reduce barriers to trade.
3. a. How does a fixed-rate exchange rate system differ from a floating-rate exchange system?
   b. Which system is currently used for the U. S. dollar?
4. a. What is a spot exchange rate?
   b. How does a spot rate differ from a forward rate?
5. If the Japanese yen were to depreciate against the U. S. dollar, can you buy more or fewer Japanese yen with a U.S. dollar after this depreciation?
6. You are the assistant treasurer of a corporation. The treasurer has asked you make a list of basic corporate tax rates by country. Why would a simple listing of the basic tax rates by country be misleading?
7. What is the controversy regarding the classification of corporate funds as debt or equity?
8. a. What is meant by a "thin capitalization company"?
   b. What might the tax authorities of a country do if a corporation is viewed as a thin capitalization company?
9. a. What is meant by the *classical system* of taxing distributed earnings?
   b. What is meant by the *imputation system* of taxing distributed earnings?
10. a. What is a *tax credit*?
    b. What is meant by a *tax holiday*?
11. a. What are the differences between a country's internal market and external market?
    b. Distinguish between a country's domestic market and a foreign market.
12. a. What is meant by a completely segmented world capital market and what are the implications of such a market for raising funds?
    b. What is meant by a completely integrated world capital market and what are the implications of such a market for raising funds?
13. Why might a corporation seek to raise funds outside of its local capital market even if it results in a higher cost of funds?
14. Some stocks are listed on several exchanges around the world. What are three reasons that a firm might want its stock to be listed on an exchange in the firm's home country as well as on exchanges in other countries?
15. a. What does it mean that a U.S. firm's new stock offering might contain a Euroequity tranche?

  b. How does an IDR avoid the often cumbersome and usually costly regulations about the issuance of a domestic firm's securities in a foreign country?

  c. What is the major difference between an American depositary receipt and an American depositary share?

16. List and briefly describe the additional risks that must be evaluated in assessing non-U.S. investments.

17. Many firms use a higher cost of capital for investments abroad. Explain why this may be appropriate.

18. List and explain at least three recent trends in international financial management.

19. The number of units of foreign currency equivalent to $1 U.S. is shown below for each of six countries' currencies. For each currency, restate the exchange rate in terms of U.S. dollars per foreign currency unit.

Currency	Units of Foreign Currency to US$1
British pound	0.6552
Canadian dollar	1.3688
Mexican new peso	7.565
Japanese yen	105.73
Swiss franc	1.1888

20. Consider the following two exchange rates:
  1.41 Singapore dollars to US$1
  5.19 French francs to US$1
  a. Calculate the exchange rate of Singapore dollars to a French franc.
  b. Calculate the exchange rate of French francs to a Singapore dollar.

21. Consider the foreign exchange rates for the following, stated in terms of foreign currency per U.S. dollar:

Currency	Foreign Currency per US$1, Year1	Foreign Currency per US$1, Year 2
Belgian franc	36.785	39.409
Netherlands guilder	1.9778	2.1219
Swiss franc	1.4643	1.6369

  a. Calculate the number of U.S. dollars per foreign currency unit for each year and each currency.
  b. For each currency, describe whether the currency has appreciated or depreciated relative to the U.S. dollar.

22. Suppose that the exchange rate for one U.S. dollar for another currency, say the euroyen (EY), is $1 US = 2EY. And suppose that if the

exchange rate remains the same, you will get a 20% return on your investment in the EY's currency over a one-year period.
a. If the exchange rate were to change such that $1 = 3 EY, what return do you expect on your investment?
b. If the exchange rate were to change such that $1 = 1.5 EY, what return do you expect on your investment?

23. Suppose you invest $100,000 in a project that provides 150,000 British pounds at the end of one year. And suppose that the exchange rate when you make this investment is $1 US = £1.5.
a. If the exchange rate does not change during the year, what is your return on the investment?
b. If the exchange rate at the end of one year is $1 US = £1.6, what is your return on the investment?
c. If the exchange rate at the end of one year is $1 US = £1.4, what is the return on your investment?

24. The XYZ Corporation is a United States corporation with subsidiaries in several countries. Suppose that the United States corporate marginal tax rate is 35% and that one of its subsidiaries is operating in a foreign country where the marginal tax rate is 47%. XYZ Corporation manufactures a product for US$60 a unit and sells 50,000 units to the subsidiary each year. The subsidiary, in turn, further processes each unit at a cost of $40 per unit and sells the finished product for $240 per unit. The fixed costs for XYZ Corporation and the subsidiary are $2,000,000 and $1,000,000, respectively.
a. What are the taxes and the net income of the parent, the subsidiary, and the company as a whole if the transfer price is set at $90 per unit?
b. What are the taxes and the net income of the parent, the subsidiary, and the company as a whole if the transfer price is set at $120 per unit?
c. Given your answers to (a) and (b), how does the choice of a transfer price affect the company as a whole?

25. Why is the all-in-cost of funds for an 8.125% coupon, 10-year Eurobond issue with a par value of $100 million and in which the proceeds to the issuer are $98,187,562 equal to 8.4%?

26. A financial manager is considering issuing a bond in the United States or in the Eurobond market. The manager has calculated that the all-in-cost of funds for a bond issued in the United States is 8.25% and 8.35% in the Eurobond market. In which market would the manager realize a lower all-in-cost of funds?

27. Consider this excerpt from *Euromoney* of September 1989:

Enterprise Oil itself recently purchased what it claims to be the biggest currency option obtained by a corporate client. In March it spent over $15 million as the premium on a 90-day currency option.

The Chemical [Bank]-arranged option was used to lock in exchange rate protection on $1.03 billion of a $1.45 billion liability incurred in the acquisition of US-based gas transmission company, Texas Eastern.

The need for the option arose since Enterprise Oil was paying for a dollar liability by raising sterling-denominated equity. The option is a dollar-call option which gives the company the right to buy dollars at a dollar/sterling exchange rate of $1.70 for a 90-day period.

Discuss Enterprise Oil's financing strategy and rationale for the purchase of the currency options.

28. Explain whether you agree or disagree with the following statement: "As with an interest rate swap, there is no exchange of principal with a currency swap."

29. Explain whether you agree or disagree with the following statement: "A currency swap is a redundant financial instrument since a bond issuer can accomplish the same hedging objective with a series of foreign currency forward contracts that settle on the date that a bond payment must be made."

30. A financial manager seeks to hedge the currency risk of a transaction to take place three years from now. Explain whether the financial manager can use a currency futures contract to protect against the currency risk.

31. Explain how the payoff of an average rate currency option is determined.

CHAPTER 26

Borrowing Via Structured Finance Transactions

As an alternative to the issuance of a corporate bond, a corporation can issue a security backed by loans or receivables. Securities that have as their collateral loans or receivables are referred to as *asset-backed securities*. The transaction in which asset-backed securities are created is referred to as a *structured finance transaction* or *structured financing*. In this chapter, we will explain what is meant by a structured finance transaction, the reasons why a corporation would use a structured finance transaction rather than issue a corporate bond, and how rating agencies assess the credit risk of a structured finance transaction. While our focus in this chapter is on structured financing used by corporations, it should be noted that some municipal governments use this form of financing rather than issuing municipal bonds and several European central governments use this form for financing.

WHAT IS A STRUCTURED FINANCE TRANSACTION?

The term "structured finance" refers to a wide variety of debt and related securities. The key element of structured financing is that the obligation of the issuer to repay lenders is backed by the value of a financial asset or credit support provided by a third party to the transaction.[1] When we say the value of a "financial asset" we mean a loan, an account receivable, or a note receivable. Keep in mind that a loan or a

---

[1] Andrew A. Silver, "Rating Structured Securities," Chapter 5 in *Issuer Perspectives on Securitization* (New Hope, PA: Frank J. Fabozzi Associates, 1998), p. 5

receivable is a financial asset to the lender but a liability to the borrower. So, in a structured financing, the lender is using a pool of loans or receivables as collateral for debt instruments that it issues. To obtain a desired credit rating sought by a corporation for the asset-backed securities created by using a structured financing, both the value of the financial assets and a third-party credit support may be needed.

In Chapter 15 where we discuss intermediate- and long-term debt instruments, we described secured debt instruments whose credit standing is supported by a lien on specific assets (i.e., a mortgage bond or collateral trust bond) or by a third-party guarantee. However, with traditional secured bonds, it is the ability of the issuer to generate sufficient earnings to repay the debt obligation that is necessary for the issuer to repay the debt. So, for example, if a manufacturer of farm equipment issues a mortgage bond in which the bondholders have a first mortgage lien on one of its plants, the ability of the manufacturer to generate cash flow from all of its operations is required to pay off the bondholders.

In contrast, in a structured financing, the burden of the source of repayment shifts from the cash flow of the issuer to the cash flow of the pool of financial assets and/or a third-party that guarantees the payments if the pool of financial assets does not generate sufficient cash flow. For example, if the manufacturer of farm equipment has receivables from installment sales contracts to customers (i.e., a financial asset for the farm equipment company) and uses these receivables in a structured financing as described in this chapter, payment to the buyers of the bonds backed by these receivables depends only on the ability to collect the receivables. That is, it does not depend on the ability of the issuer to generate cash flow from operations.

The process of creating securities backed by a pool of financial assets is referred to as *asset securitization*. The financial assets included in the collateral for an asset securitization are referred to as *securitized assets*.

The issuers of asset-backed securities include:

- Captive finance companies of manufacturing firms that provide financing only for their parent company's products.
- Financing subsidiaries of major industrial corporations.
- Independent finance companies.
- Domestic and foreign commercial banks.

An example of the first type of issuer is the captive finance companies of automobile manufacturers. For example, Ford Credit is a captive finance company of Ford Motor Company. It provides financing for individuals who want to purchase a motor vehicle or commercial financing for companies that want to purchase a fleet of motor vehicles manufactured by Ford Motor Company.

Financing subsidiaries of major industrial corporations provide financing for not only their parent company's products but products of other vendors. Three examples are GE Capital Commercial Finance, IBM Global Financing, and Caterpillar Financial. GE Capital Commercial Finance, a wholly-owned subsidiary of General Electric, is a diversified financial servicing company. IBM Global Financing is a wholly-owned subsidiary of IBM that provides financing for both IBM and non-IBM equipment. Caterpillar Financial, the financial arm of Caterpillar Inc. (the world's largest manufacturer of construction and mining equipment, natural gas and diesel engines, and industrial gas turbines) offers a wide range of financing alternatives for Caterpillar equipment, Solar gas turbines, products equipped with Caterpillar components, fork lift trucks manufactured by Mitsubishi Caterpillar Forklift of America, Inc., and related products sold through Caterpillar dealers.

ILLUSTRATION OF A STRUCTURED FINANCE TRANSACTION

Let's use an illustration to describe a structured finance transaction. (We'll review an actual structured financing transaction at the end of this chapter after we have explained all of the key features in these transactions.) In our illustrations throughout this chapter, we will use a hypothetical firm, Farm Equip Corporation. This company is assumed to manufacturer farm equipment. Some of its sales are for cash, but the bulk of its sales are from installment sales contracts. Effectively, an installment sale contract is a loan to the buyer of the farm equipment who agrees to repay Farm Equip Corporation over a specified period of time. For simplicity we will assume that the loans are typically for four years. The collateral for the loan is the farm equipment purchased by the borrower. The loan specifics an interest rate that the buyer pays.

The credit department of Farm Equip Corporation makes the decision as to whether or not to extend credit to a customer. That is, the credit department will receive a credit application from a customer and, based on criteria established by the firm, will decide on whether to extend a loan and the amount. The criteria for extending credit or a loan are referred to as *underwriting standards*. Because Farm Equip Corporation is extending the loan, it is referred to as the *originator* of the loan.

Moreover, Farm Equip Corporation may have a department that is responsible for servicing the loan. *Servicing* involves collecting payments from borrowers, notifying borrowers who may be delinquent, and, when necessary, recovering and disposing of the collateral (i.e., farm equipment in our illustration) if the borrower does not make loan repayments by a specified time. While the servicer of the loans need not be the originator of the loans, in our illustration we are assuming that Farm Equip Corporation is the servicer.

Now let's get to how these loans can be used in a structured finance transaction. We will assume that Farm Equip Corporation has more than $200 million of installment sales contracts. This amount is shown on the corporation's balance sheet as an asset. We will further assume that Farm Equip Corporation wants to raise $200 million. Rather than issuing corporate bonds for $200 million (for the reasons explained in the next section), the treasurer of the corporation decides to raise the funds via a structured financing.

To do so, the Farm Equip Corporation will set up a legal entity referred to as a special purpose vehicle (SPV). At this point, we will not explain the purpose of this legal entity, but it will be made clearer later that the SPV is critical in a structured finance transaction. In our illustration, the SPV that is set up is called FE Asset Trust (FEAT). Farm Equip Corporation will then sell to FEAT Company $200 million of the loans. Farm Equip Corporation will receive from FEAT $200 million in cash, the amount it wanted to raise. But where does FEAT get $200 million? It obtains those funds by selling securities that are backed by the $200 million of loans. The securities are the asset-backed securities we referred to earlier. These asset-backed securities issued in a structured finance transaction are also referred to as bond classes or *tranches*.

The structure is diagrammed in Exhibit 26.1.

EXHIBIT 26.1   Structured Financing

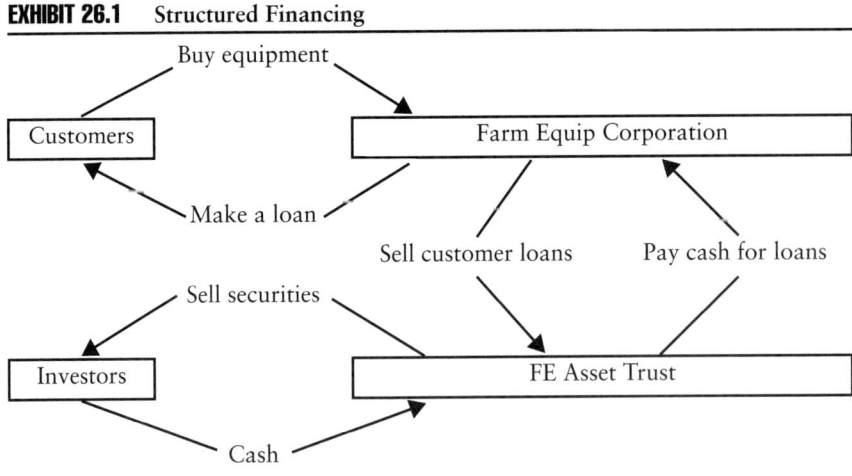

A simple transaction can involve the sale of just one bond class with a par value of $200 million. We will call this Bond Class A. Suppose that 200,000 certificates are issued for Bond Class A with a par value of $1,000 per certificate. Then, each certificate holder would be entitled to 1/200,000 of the payment from the collateral. Each payment made by the borrowers (i.e., the buyers of the farm equipment) consists of principal repayment and interest.

A structure can be more complicated. For example, there can be rules for distribution of principal and interest other than on a pro rata basis to different bond classes. It may be difficult to understand why such a structure should be created. What is important to understand is that there are institutional investors who have needs for bonds with different maturities and price volatility characteristics. A structured finance transaction can be designed to create bond classes with investment characteristics that are more attractive to institutional investors to satisfy those needs.

An example of a more complicated transaction is one in which two bond classes are created, Bond Class A1 and Bond Class A2. The par value for Bond Class A1 is $90 million and for Bond Class A2 is $110 million. The priority rule can simply specify that Bond Class A1 receives all the principal that is paid by the borrowers (i.e., the buyers of the farm equipment) until all of Bond Class A1 has paid off its $90 million and then Bond Class A2 begins to receive principal. Bond Class A1 is then a shorter term bond than Bond Class A2.

As will be explained later, there are structures where there is more than one bond class but the two bond classes differ as to how they will share any losses resulting from defaults of the borrowers. In such a structure, the bond classes are classified as *senior bond classes* and *subordinate bond classes*. This structure is called a *senor-subordinate structure*. Losses are realized by the subordinate bond classes before there are any losses realized by the senior bond classes. For example, suppose that FEAT issued $180 million par value of Bond Class A, the senior bond class, and $20 million par value of Bond Class B, the subordinate bond class. As long as there are no defaults by the borrower greater than $20 million, then Bond Class A will be repaid fully its $180 million.

REASONS FOR USING A STRUCTURED FINANCE TRANSACTION

There are four principal reasons why a corporation may elect to issue an asset-backed security rather than a corporate bond. They are:

1. The potential for reducing funding costs
2. To diversify funding sources
3. To accelerate earnings for financial reporting purposes
4. For regulated entities, potential relief from capital requirements

We will focus on the first three reasons here.

The Potential for Reducing Funding Costs

To understand the potential for reducing funding costs by issuing an asset-backed security rather than a corporate bond, suppose that Farm Equip Corporation has a triple B credit rating. If it wants to raise funds equal to $200 million and it issues a corporate bond, its funding cost would be whatever the benchmark Treasury yield is plus a yield spread for triple B issuers. Suppose, instead, that Farm Equip Corporation uses $200 million of its installment sales contracts (i.e., the loans it has made to customers) as collateral for a bond issue. What will be its funding cost? It probably will be the same as if it issued a corporate bond. The reason is that if Farm Equip Corporation defaults on any of its outstanding debt, the creditors will go after all of its assets, including the loans to its customers.

However, suppose that Farm Equip Corporation can create another legal entity and sell the loans to that entity. That entity is the special purpose vehicle that we described earlier in our hypothetical structured finance transaction. In our illustration, it is Farm Equipment Asset Trust (FEAT). If the sale of the loans by Farm Equip Corporation to FEAT is done properly—that is, the sale is at the fair market value of the loans—FEAT then *legally* owns the receivables, not Farm Equip Corporation. This means that if Farm Equip Corporation is forced into bankruptcy, its creditors *cannot* try to recover the loans (sold to FEAT) because they are legally owned by FEAT. What is the implication of structuring a transaction in this way?

When FEAT sells bonds backed by the loans, those interested in buying the bonds will evaluate the credit risk associated with collecting the payments due on the loans independent of the credit rating of Farm Equip Corporation. What credit rating will be received for the bonds issued by FEAT? Whatever FEAT wants the credit rating to be! It may seem strange that the issuer (the SPV, FEAT) can get any credit rating it wants, but that is the case. The reason is that FEAT will show the characteristics of the collateral for the asset-backed securities (i.e., the loans to Farm Equip's customers) to a rating agency. In turn, the rating agency will evaluate the credit quality of the collateral and inform the issuer what must be done to obtain a desired credit rating.

More specifically, the issuer will be asked to "credit enhance" the structure. There are various forms of credit enhancement that we will review later. Basically, the rating agencies will look at the potential losses from the collateral and make a determination of how much credit enhancement is needed for the bond classes issued to achieve a rating targeted by the issuer. The higher the credit rating sought by the issuer, the more credit enhancement a rating agency will require. Thus, Farm Equip Corporation which is triple B rated can obtain funding using its loans to its customers as collateral to obtain a better credit rating for the bonds issued than its own credit rating. In fact, with enough credit enhancement, it can issue a bond of the highest credit rating, triple A.

The key to a corporation issuing bonds with a higher credit rating than the corporation's own credit rating is the SPV. Its role is critical because it is the SPV (FEAT in our illustration) that separates the assets used as collateral from the corporation that is seeking financing (Farm Equip Corporation in our illustration).

Why doesn't a corporation always seek the highest credit rating (triple A) for the bonds backed by the collateral in a structured financing? The answer is that credit enhancement does not come without a cost. As described later, there are various credit enhancement mechanisms and they increase the costs associated with securitized borrowing via an asset-backed security. So, the corporation must assess the tradeoff when it is seeking a higher rating between the additional cost of credit enhancing the bonds versus the reduction in funding cost by issuing a bond with a higher credit rating.

It is important to realize that if a bankruptcy of the corporation seeking funds occurs (Farm Equip Corporation in our example), a bankruptcy judge may decide that the assets of the SPV are assets that the creditors of the corporation seeking financing may go after. This is an unresolved legal issue in the United States. Legal experts have argued that this is unlikely. In the prospectus of an asset-backed security, there will be a legal opinion addressing this issue. This is the reason why special purpose vehicles in the United States are referred to as "bankruptcy remote" entities.

Diversifying Funding Sources

An issuer seeking to raise funds via a structured financing must establish itself as an issuer in the asset-backed securities market. Once an issuer establishes itself in the market, it can look at both the corporate bond market and the asset-backed securities market to determine the better funding source. That is, it will compare the all-in-cost of funds in the corporate bond market and the asset-backed securities market and select the one with the lower cost.

Accelerating Earnings for Financial Reporting Purposes

Generally accepted accounting principles permit a corporation to use a portfolio of its receivables or assets to accelerate earnings for shareholder reporting. This reason is best described by means of an illustration.

Consider again Farm Equip Corporation, the manufacturer of farm equipment. Suppose that this firm has $200 million in installment sales contracts. For financial reporting purposes, the installment sales contracts are not realized as revenue until the installment payments are received. Suppose that the agreement with the buyer of the farm equipment requires that the buyer pay 8% interest per annum. Suppose further that the treasurer of Farm Equip Corporation approaches the firm's investment banker and is told that it can sell an asset-backed security backed by the installment sales contracts at a cost of 5%. This means that Farm Equip Corporation is receiving from the installment sales contracts 8% and would pay investors in the asset-backed securities 5%. The difference between what Farm Equip Corporation is receiving and paying is 3% or 300 basis points. Part of that difference represents a cost to Farm Equip Corporation for "servicing" the installment sales contracts. For now, assume that the servicing fee is 1%.

Reducing the 300 basis points by the 100 basis point servicing fee, means that there are 200 basis points remaining. This is referred to as the **net interest spread**. This is a profit to Farm Equip Corporation that will be realized by the sale of the asset-backed securities and it can be booked as income immediately. The income is effectively in the form of an asset referred to as **interest-only strip**. How much is the income that will be realized by Farm Equip Corporation for financial reporting purposes? Or equivalently, what is the value of the interest-only strip? We can apply the basic principle of valuation to determine it. This is done as follows. First, Farm Equip Corporation's treasurer must determine the dollar amount of the 200 basis points for each year over the expected life of the asset-backed security. Then the present value of this dollar amount for each period is computed.

For example, suppose that the $200 million in installment sales contracts call for a repayment of principal of $50 million per year for the next four years. Then assuming that none of the borrowers default on their contractual obligation or pay off their loans earlier than the scheduled principal repayment date (referred to as a "prepayment"), this means that each year the dollar net interest based on the net interest spread of 200 basis points is as follows:

Beg. of Year	Balance Outstanding	Dollar Net Interest
1	$200,000,000	$4,000,000
2	150,000,000	3,000,000
3	100,000,000	2,000,000
4	50,000,000	1,000,000

The next step is to compute the present value of the dollar net interest. The question is: What is the appropriate discount rate? The discount rate should reflect the uncertainty of realizing the projected dollar net interest over the next four years. Let's suppose that a fair market rate is 12%. Then the present value of the dollar net interest 12% is $8,022,088.78 as shown below:[2]

Beg. of Year	Balance Outstanding	Dollar Net Interest	PV Factor at 12%	Present Value ($)
1	$200,000,000	$4,000,000	0.89286	$3,571,428.57
2	150,000,000	3,000,000	0.79719	2,391,581.63
3	100,000,000	2,000,000	0.71178	1,423,560.50
4	50,000,000	1,000,000	0.63552	635,518.08
		Value of interest-only strip		$8,022,088.78

The $8,022,088.78 would be reported as income in the year that the asset-backed securities are issued and is the value of the interest-only strip.

The key in the valuation of the interest-only strip is determining the dollar net interest spread each year and the appropriate interest rate at which to discount the dollar amount for each year. Consider first the dollar net interest each year. In the analysis above, it is assumed that the $200 million in installment sales contracts will be paid—that is, no defaults are assumed. Suppose instead that, due to defaults, the treasurer projects that the balance outstanding after defaults is as follows:

Beg. of Year	Balance Outstanding	Dollar Net Interest
1	$199,000,000	$3,980,000
2	147,000,000	2,940,000
3	95,000,000	1,900,000
4	42,000,000	840,000

---

[2] Notice that calculations have been simplified by assuming that all of the dollar net interest spread is received at the end of the year.

Then the dollar net interest and the present value at 12% each year are shown below, along with the value of the interest-only strip:

Beg. of Year	Balance Outstanding	Dollar Net Interest	PV Factor at 12%	Present Value ($)
1	$199,000,000	$3,980,000	0.89286	$3,553,571.43
2	147,000,000	2,940,000	0.79719	2,343,750.00
3	95,000,000	1,900,000	0.71178	1,352,382.47
4	42,000,000	840,000	0.63552	533,835.19
		Value of interest-only strip		$7,783,539.09

Thus, based on this, the reported income due to the securitization would be $7,783,539.09 (the value of the interest-only strip) versus $8,022,088.78, in the case where no defaults are assumed. If a more appropriate discount rate is higher than 12%, then the value of the interest-only strip is reduced. For example, at a 15% rate, the value of the interest-only strip is $7,633,477.58, assuming no defaults and $7,413,485.51, assuming the defaults in the table above.

If there are prepayments, this reduces the value of the interest-only strip. This is because when a borrower repays a loan, this reduces the loan balance. The issuer receives the dollar net interest only on the outstanding loan balance. For example, suppose that there are no defaults but that the borrowers prepay their loans such that the balance outstanding each year is as follows:

Beg. of Year	Balance Outstanding	Dollar Net Interest
1	$200,000,000	$4,000,000
2	70,000,000	1,400,000
3	20,000,000	400,000
4	10,000,000	200,000

It can be shown that the present value of the interest-only strip in this case is $5,099,315.71. When discounted at a 12% rate, the value is less than even the case above, where there are defaults.

It is not a simple task to determine the defaults and therefore the dollar net interest and the appropriate interest rate for discounting. Consequently, the firm's external auditors must assess the assumptions made by management in determining income resulting from a securitization. There are shareholder suits against management and its external auditors in cases where shareholders have challenged income generated from a securitization for a firm that has faced financial difficulties. The issue is whether reasonable assumptions were made regarding defaults and whether the appropriate discount rate was used.

It is important to understand that a corporation can use a structured financing to achieve a target income. Stock analysts project a consensus earnings for a corporation. Suppose that management in the absence of securitization needs $0.10 per share to achieve the target earnings. Management can use all or part of its receivables or loans to achieve the targeted amount via securitization.

One more advantage should be noted. Our discussion here deals with realization of income for financial reporting purposes. How about the tax treatment? Under the tax code, the sale of the assets to the SPV and the resulting income need not be recognized for this purpose. That is, income realized for financial reporting purposes need not be realized for tax purposes. So, income can be accelerated for financial reporting purposes by selling financial assets but taxes on that income can be postponed for tax purposes.

WHAT RATING AGENCIES LOOK AT IN RATING ASSET-BACKED SECURITIES

In Chapter 15, we described the factors that the rating agencies—Moody's Investors Service, Standard & Poor's, and Fitch—consider in assigning a credit rating to a corporate bond. Here we discuss the factors considered by rating agencies in assigning a credit rating to an asset-backed security.

In analyzing credit risk, the rating agencies focus on (1) credit quality of the collateral, (2) the quality of the seller/servicer, and (3) cash flow stress and payment structure. We discuss each below.

Credit Quality of the Collateral

Analysis of the credit quality of the collateral depends on the asset type. The rating agencies will look at the underlying borrower's ability to pay and the borrower's equity in the asset. By the "borrower" we mean the individual or business entity that took out the loan. In our Farm Equipment Corporation illustration, the borrowers are the entities that purchased the farm equipment via an installment sales contract. The borrower's equity will be a key determinant as to whether a borrower has an economic incentive to default or to sell the asset and pay off a loan.

For example, suppose three years ago a farmer purchased equipment that currently has a market value of $200,000 and the outstanding balance of the installment sales contract is $30,000. The farmer's equity in the equipment is $170,000 ($200,000 minus $30,000). It is highly unlikely that the farmer will default on the installment sales contract. It would be expected that the farmer would sell the equipment to realize the equity of $170,000 rather than default and have the equipment repossessed. In contrast, if the equipment has a market value of $200,000 but the outstanding balance of the installment sales contract is $320,000, it is likely that the farmer will default if the farmer does not have the ability to pay.

The rating agencies will also look at the experience of the originators of the underlying loans and will assess whether the loans underlying a specific transaction have the same characteristics as the experience reported by the issuer. That is, the originator of the loan or installment sales contract—Farm Equip Corporation in our illustration—will have a credit department that will assess whether to extend credit to a customer. If the underwriting standards are lax, then this will be reflected in high default rates; tough underwriting standards will be reflected in low default rates. Rating agencies will assess the underwriting standards by looking at historical default rates of an originator and will monitor the default rates over time to determine if there has been a deterioration or an improvement in underwriting standards.

In addition to default rates, rating agencies will look at historical recovery rates. It is the default rates combined with recovery rates that determine what the potential loss will be. For example, suppose that the historical recovery rate is 40% and that the historical default rate for the collateral is 2%. This means that for every $100 of collateral, there will be defaults of about $2. Of the $2 of defaults, $0.80 will be recovered and therefore $1.20 will be lost. This is a rate of 1.2% and is referred to as the *loss rate*.

The concentration of loans is examined by rating agencies. The underlying principle of asset securitization is that the large number of borrowers in the collateral pool will reduce the credit risk via diversification. If there are a few borrowers included in the collateral pool that are significant in size relative to the entire pool balance, this diversification benefit can be lost, resulting in a higher level of default risk. This risk is called *concentration risk*. Rating agencies will set concentration limits on the amount or percentage of loans or receivables from any one borrower. If the concentration limit at issuance is exceeded, the issue will receive a lower credit rating than if the concentration limit was not exceeded. If after issuance the concentration limit is exceeded, the bonds may be downgraded.

Quality of the Seller/Servicer

All loans and receivables must be serviced. These responsibilities are fulfilled by a third party to an asset-backed securities transaction called a *servicer*. While viewed as a "third-party," in many asset-backed securities transactions, the servicer is effectively the originator of the loans used as the collateral for the corporation seeking funding.

The servicer may also be responsible for advancing payments when there are delinquencies in payments (that are likely to be collected in the future) resulting in a temporary shortfall in the payments that must be made to the investors in the securities issued in a structured finance transaction.

The role of the servicer is critical in a structured finance transaction. Therefore, rating agencies look at the ability of a servicer to perform all the activities that a servicer will be responsible for before they assign a credit rating to the bonds issued. For example, the following factors are reviewed when evaluating servicers: servicing history, experience, servicing capabilities, human resources, financial condition, and growth/competition/business environment.

Based on its analysis, a rating agency determines whether the servicer is acceptable or unacceptable. If a servicer is unacceptable, a structured finance transaction will not be rated. The rating agency may require a "backup" servicer if there is a concern about the ability of a servicer to perform.

Remember that the issuer of an asset-backed security, the special purpose vehicle, is not a corporation with employees. It simply has loans and receivables. The servicer therefore plays an important role in assuring that the payments are collected from the borrowers.

Cash Flow Stress and Payment Structure

The rating agencies will analyze the extent to which the cash flow from the collateral can satisfy all of the obligations of the asset-backed securities transaction. The cash flow of the collateral consists of interest and principal repayment. The cash flow payments that must be made are interest and principal to investors, servicing fees, and any other expenses for which the issuer is liable. The rating companies analyze the structure to test whether the collateral's cash flows match the payments that must be made to satisfy the issuer's obligations. This requires that the rating company make assumptions about losses and delinquencies under various interest rate scenarios.

Based on its analysis of the collateral and the stress testing of the structure to assess the risk that the bondholders will not be repaid in full, a rating agency will determine the amount of credit enhancement necessary for an issue to receive a particular credit rating.

CREDIT ENHANCEMENT

The way credit enhancement works is some third party is either paid a fee (or an insurance premium) or earns extra yield on a security in the structure to assume credit risk. There are two forms of credit enhancement—external and internal. *External credit enhancement* involves third-party guarantees such as insurance or a letter of credit. *Internal credit enhancement* includes overcollateralization, senior-subordinated structure, and reserves. Deals will often have more than one form of credit enhancement. The rating agencies specify the amount of credit enhancement to obtain a specific credit rating. The issuer decides on what mechanisms to use.

It is critical for the issuer to examine each form of credit enhancement prior to issuance to determine the enhancement mechanism or combination of credit enhancement mechanisms that is most cost effective. Over time, due to changing market conditions, the least expensive form of credit enhancement today may not be the least expensive in a subsequent securitization transaction.

As explained earlier, the reason why an issuer does not simply seek a triple A rating for all the securities in the structure is that there is a cost to doing so. The issuer must examine the cost of credit enhancing a structure to obtain a triple A rating versus the reduction in the yield (i.e., the increase in price) at which it can offer the securities due to a triple A rating. In general the issuer, in deciding to improve the credit rating on some securities in a structure, will evaluate the tradeoff associated with the cost of enhancement versus the reduction in yield required to sell the security.

Below we describe the various forms of credit enhancement mechanisms.

Third-Party Guarantees

Perhaps the easiest form of credit enhancement to understand is insurance or a letter of credit. In this form of credit enhancement, an insurance provider agrees, for a fee, to guarantee the performance of a certain amount of the collateral against defaults. If, for example, a loan in the collateral pool goes into default and the underlying collateral is repossessed and then sold at a loss resulting in a partial payoff of the outstanding loan balance, the bondholders would be in a position not to recover the principal outstanding for that loan. To provide protection to the bondholders, an insurance provider will pay the difference between the loan payoff amount and the amount due to the bondholders, thereby absorbing the loss.

The rating agencies decide on the creditworthiness of the insurance provider to determine the credit rating of the bonds. Perhaps the biggest perceived disadvantage to this form of credit enhancement is so called *event risk*. Triple A rated bondholders, for example, can enjoy triple A status only as long as the enhancement provider retains its triple A credit rating status. If the credit enhancement provider is downgraded (i.e., its credit rating is lowered by a rating agency), the bonds guaranteed by the enhancement provider are typically downgraded as well.

Overcollateralization

One form of internal credit enhancement is *overcollateralization*. In this form of credit protection, credit enhancement is provided by issuing bonds with a par value that is less than the par value of the loans or receivables in the collateral pool. For example, if there are $200 million of loans in a collateral pool and the issuer wanted to use overcollateralization for credit enhancement to achieve, say, a triple A credit rating for the bonds to be issued, the issuer would obtain from the rating agencies an indication as to how many bonds it could issue versus the $200 million par value of loans in the collateral pool to obtain the target credit rating. Depending on the characteristics of the loans and their perceived creditworthiness, the rating agencies might allow $190 million of par value of bonds to be issued.

This means that cash flows for $200 million par value of loans is available to bondholders but only $190 million par value of bonds need to be paid interest and principal. The cash flows from the extra $10 million of loans can either flow into a "reserve account" where the flows are reserved until such a time as they are needed to cover losses or the funds are used to retire bonds early. If a $3 million loss is realized by the collateral pool, there will still be enough cash flow from the other loans to insure that the triple A rated bonds receive their payments. After all the bonds have been retired, the remaining funds in the reserve account and any remaining collateral are distributed to the originator (assuming the originator has not sold its interest in the collateral).

The cost of such an arrangement is implicit in the price paid for $200 million par value of collateral versus the proceeds of issuing only $190 million par value of bonds.

Senior-Subordinate Structure

Another form of internal credit enhancement is the senior-subordinate structure mentioned earlier. This involves the subordination of some bond classes for the benefit of attaining a high investment-grade rating for other bond classes in the structure. Based on an analysis of the collateral, a rating agency will decide how many triple A bonds can be issued, how many double A bonds, and so forth down to non-rated bonds. A structure can have simply two bond classes, a senior bond class and a subordinate bond class. Or it can have several subordinate bond classes in addition to the senior bond class.

For example, suppose that a senior-subordinate structure for $200 million of collateral for the Farm Equip Corporation is as follows:

Bond Class	Rating	Percent of Structure	Par value
A	AAA	65%	$130 million
B	AA	20%	$40 million
C	BBB	10%	$20 million
D	Not rated	5%	$10 million

Bond class A is the senior bond class. The subordinate bond classes are B, C, and D.

The rule for recognizing losses is as follows. As a $1 of loss on the collateral is realized, that loss is first applied to bond class D. When bond class D has no balance, the next dollar of loss is applied to bond class C, and then bond class B. After all the subordinate bond classes are wiped out due to losses, the losses are realized by the senior bond class.

The cost of this form of credit enhancement is based on the proceeds for selling the bonds which is, in turn, determined by the demand for the bonds. The yields that must be offered on the bond classes are affected by the yields demanded by investors. The lower the credit rating of the bond class (i.e., the more likely the bond class is to realize a loss), the more yield is demanded and the lower will be the proceeds received from the sale of the bonds for that bond class. The proceeds for the sale of all the bonds have to be compared to the cost of the collateral pool.

One of the perceived advantages of internal credit enhancements such as the overcollateralization and the senior-subordinate structure is the lack of event risk that accompanies external credit enhancement (i.e., a third-party guarantee). The assets in the collateral pool provide all credit support and investors are at risk only with regard to the performance of those assets.

Reserve Funds

Reserve funds come in two forms, cash reserve funds and excess spread. Cash reserve funds are straight deposits of cash generated from issuance proceeds. In this case, part of the underwriting profits from the deal are deposited into a fund and used to offset any losses. Excess spread accounts involve the allocation of excess spread into a separate reserve account after paying out the coupon to bondholders, the servicing fee, and all other expenses on a monthly basis.

EXAMPLE OF AN ACTUAL STRUCTURED FINANCE TRANSACTION

We conclude this chapter with an actual structured finance transaction—Caterpillar Financial Asset Trust 1997-A. Caterpillar Financial Asset Trust 1997-A is the special purpose vehicle and is referred to in the prospectus as the "Issuer" and the "Trust."

The collateral (i.e., financial assets) for the transaction is a pool of fixed-rate retail installment sales contracts that are secured by new and used machinery manufactured primarily by Caterpillar Inc. The retail installment sales contracts were originated by the Caterpillar Financial Funding Corporation, a wholly-owned subsidiary of Caterpillar Financial Services Corporation. Caterpillar Financial Services Corporation is a wholly-owned subsidiary of Caterpillar Inc. Because Caterpillar Financial Funding Corporation sold the retail installment sales contracts to Caterpillar Financial Asset Trust 1997-A, Caterpillar Financial Funding Corporation is referred to in the prospectus as the "Seller."

The prospectus states that:

> "THE NOTES REPRESENT OBLIGATIONS OF THE ISSUER ONLY AND DO NOT REPRESENT OBLIGATIONS OF OR INTERESTS IN CATERPILLAR FINANCIAL FUNDING CORPORATION, CATERPILLAR FINANCIAL SERVICES CORPORATION, CATERPILLAR INC. OR ANY OF THEIR RESPECTIVE AFFILIATES."

This is the key feature of a structured financing—the separation of the collateral from the creditors of Caterpillar Inc.

The servicer of the retail installment sales contracts is Caterpillar Financial Services Corporation, a wholly-owned finance subsidiary of Caterpillar Inc. and is referred to as the "Servicer" in the prospectus. For servicing the collateral, Caterpillar Financial Services Corporation receives a servicing fee of 100 basis points of the outstanding loan balance.

The securities were issued on May 19, 1997 and had a par value of $337,970,000. In the prospectus the securities were referred to as "asset-backed notes." The structure was as follows. There were four rated bond classes:

	Par Value
Class A-1	$88,000,000
Class A-2	$128,000,000
Class A-3	$108,100,000
Class B	$13,870,000

This is a senior-subordinate structure. The senior classes in this transaction are Class A-1, Class A-2, and Class A-3. The subordinate class is Class B. The senior classes are paid off in sequence—first Class A-1 is paid principal until it is paid off its entire balance, then Class A-2 starts receiving principal payments until it is paid off entirely, and then finally Class A-3 is paid off. Class B begins receiving principal payments after Class A-3 is paid off. Any losses on the collateral are realized by Class B. If the losses exceed $13,870,000 (the par value of Class B) plus the losses that can be absorbed by the reserve account (discussed later), the senior classes absorb the loss on a pro rata basis.

Consequently, credit enhancement for the senior classes is provided by the subordinate class, Class B. Additional credit enhancement was provided by a reserve fund of $7,799,325. This initial reserve account is provided by the Seller via a deposit of that amount. The Seller receives a note for this amount.

Over time, as losses on the collateral are realized, the amount of the reserve fund would decline if there is no mechanism to prevent this from occurring. To prevent this, the structure provides for a "specified reserve account balance" to be maintained. In the Caterpillar Financial Asset Trust 1997-A, the specified reserve account balance must be equal to the (1) lesser of the principal balance of the outstanding asset-backed notes in the structure and (2) $7,799,325 (the amount of the initial reserve account balance). If there is a shortfall in the specified reserve account balance in a month, any payments from the collateral that exceed the interest payments to all the classes, the servicing fee, and administrative fees are deposited into the reserve fund until the shortfall is eliminated.

In the Caterpillar Inc. 2001 10-K filing with the SEC, the following is noted regarding securitized receivables:

> "When finance receivables are securitized, we retain interest in the form of interest-only strips, servicing rights, cash reserve accounts, and subordinate certificates."

It should be clear what all of forms of the retained interest are. The interest-only strips are what we described earlier in this chapter. The servicing rights are the value of the servicing fee of 1% of the outstanding pool balance not only for the Caterpillar Financial Asset Trust 1997-A discussed above, but all of its structured finance transactions to date. The cash reserve account is the amount remaining in the reserve fund ($7,799,325 in the structure discussed less any reserves used). Subordinate certificates are any certificates retained by Caterpillar in a structured financing because they are not sold to investors.

As explained earlier in this chapter, the value for the interest-only strips must be calculated. In the 10-K report, it is explained that this is done as follows for the securitized receivables:

> "Gains or losses on the securitization are dependent upon the purchase price being allocated between the carrying value of the securitized receivables and the retained interests based upon their relative fair value. We estimate fair value based on the present value of future expected cash flows using key assumptions for credit losses, prepayment speeds, . . . and discount rates. . ."

In our discussion of the value of the interest-only strips, we explained why these assumptions are important.

SUMMARY

- Structured finance transactions (or structured financings) provide an alternative to the issuance of a corporate bond.
- The securities issued in a structured finance transaction are backed by loans, accounts receivable, or notes receivable and are referred to as asset-backed securities. The process of creating securities backed by a pool of financial assets is referred to as asset securitization.
- It is the collateral combined with any third-party guarantees that will determine the ability of an issuer to pay the obligation to the holders of the asset-backed securities. To obtain a desired credit rating sought by a corporation by using a structured financing, both the value of a financial asset and a third-party credit support may be needed.
- The four principal reasons why a corporation may elect to issue an asset-backed security rather than a corporate bond are (1) potential for lower funding cost, (2) diversification of funding sources, (3) acceleration of earnings for financial reporting purposes, and (4) potential for reducing capital requirements for regulated entities.

■ The key to a corporation issuing asset-backed securities with a higher credit rating than the corporation's own credit rating via a structured financing is the special purpose vehicle. Its role is critical because it is the special purpose vehicle that legally separates the assets used as collateral from the corporation that is seeking financing.

■ When assigning a credit rating to an asset-backed security issued via a structured finance transaction, the rating agencies analyze (1) the credit quality of the collateral, (2) the quality of the seller/servicer, and (3) the cash flow stress and payment structure.

■ There are two forms of credit enhancement that can be used in a structured finance transaction. External credit enhancement involves third-party guarantees such as insurance or a letter of credit. Internal credit enhancement includes overcollateralization, senior-subordinated structures, and reserves.

QUESTIONS

1. Explain how, using a structured finance transaction, a corporation seeking to reduce its funding costs may be able to do so issuing an asset-backed security rather than a corporate bond.

2. Why is it not likely that corporations with a triple A rating will issue asset-backed securities for the sole purpose of reducing their funding costs?

3. Explain how a corporation can use a structured finance transaction to manage the earnings it reports to stockholders.

4. In a meeting with its investment banker, the treasurer of E-Z Loans Corporation was told that it would be unlikely that there would be a reduction in its funding costs by issuing an asset-backed security rather than a corporate bond. The investment banker, however, felt that there could be other advantages of issuing an asset-backed security. What are those advantages?

5. A finance company issued an asset-backed security backed by home equity loans to individuals. The average interest rate on the loans is 9.7%. The fee for servicing the loans is 70 basis points. The finance company can issue an asset-backed security in which it pays 5.7%. What is the net interest spread?

6. What is an interest-only strip and why is it created in a structured finance transaction?

7. In valuing an interest-only strip, what factors affect the cash flow?

8. Why should the investor in an asset-backed security be concerned with the underwriting standards of the loan originator?

9. Why should the investor in an asset-backed security be concerned with the capability of the servicer?
10. What are the obligations that must be paid by the issuer of an asset-backed security?
11. What determines the amount of credit enhancement a rating agency will require an issuer to obtain in order to achieve a target credit rating?
12. Why doesn't an issuer of an asset-backed security seek the highest credit rating of triple A?
13. Explain each of the following types of credit enhancement:
    a. overcollateralization
    b. senior-subordinate structure
    c. excess spread account
    d. external credit enhancement

CHAPTER 27

Equipment Leasing*

A lease is a contract wherein, over the term of the lease, the owner of the equipment permits another entity to use it in exchange for a promise by the latter to make a series of payments. The owner of the equipment is referred to as the *lessor.* The entity that is being granted permission to use the equipment is referred to as the *lessee.*

Most corporate financial executives recognize that earnings are derived from the use of an asset, not its ownership, and that leasing is simply an alternative financing method. More equipment is financed today by equipment leases than by bank loans, private placements, or any other method of equipment financing. Nearly any asset that can be purchased can also be leased, from aircraft, ships, satellites, computers, refineries, and steam-generating plants, on the one hand, to typewriters, duplicating equipment, automobiles, and dairy cattle, on the other hand.

In order to compare leasing with other methods of financing, it is necessary to understand the basics of how leasing works and the differences among the general categories of equipment leases. This will be explained in the present chapter, along with the reasons often cited for leasing, the types of lessors, and tax and financial reporting requirements. At the end of the chapter we provide an analytical framework for deciding between leasing or borrowing to buy.

HOW LEASING WORKS

A typical leasing transaction works as follows. The lessee first decides on the equipment needed. The lessee then decides on the manufacturer,

---

*This chapter draws from Peter K. Nevitt and Frank J. Fabozzi, *Equipment Leasing: Fourth Edition* (New Hope, PA: Frank J. Fabozzi Associates, 2000).

the make, and the model. The lessee specifies any special features desired, the terms of warranties, guaranties, delivery, installation, and services. The lessee also negotiates the price. After the equipment and terms have been specified and the sales contract negotiated, the lessee enters into a lease agreement with the lessor. The lessee negotiates with the lessor on the length of the lease; the rental; whether sales tax, delivery, and installation charges should be included in the lease; and other optional considerations.

After the lease has been signed, the lessee assigns its purchase rights to the lessor, which then buys the equipment exactly as specified by the lessee. When the equipment is delivered, the lessee formally accepts the equipment to make sure it gets exactly what was ordered. The lessor then pays for the equipment, and the lease goes into effect.

When all costs associated with the use of the equipment are to be paid by the lessee and not included in the lease payments, the lease is called a *net lease* or *triple net lease.* Examples of such costs are property taxes, insurance, and maintenance. These costs are paid directly by the lessee and may not be deducted from the lease payments.

At the end of the lease term, the lessee usually has the option to renew the lease, to buy the equipment, or to terminate the agreement and return the equipment. As we shall see later in this chapter, the options available to the lessee at the end of the lease are very significant in that the dimensions of such options determine the nature of the lease for tax purposes and the classification of the lease for financial accounting purposes.

TYPES OF EQUIPMENT LEASES

Equipment leases fall into the following two general categories: (1) non-tax-oriented leases and (2) tax-oriented true leases. We discuss each type of lease in the following sections.[1]

Non-Tax-Oriented Leases

Non-tax-oriented leases, most commonly referred to as a *conditional sale leases*, transfer all incidents of ownership of the leased property to the lessee and usually give the lessee a fixed price bargain purchase option or renewal option not based on fair market value at the time of exercise.

---

[1] There is a third type of specialized lease called a *tax-oriented TRAC lease for over-the-road vehicles.* We will not discuss this type of lease in this chapter.

We will discuss the guidelines under the Internal Revenue Code for a lease to be classified as a conditional sale leases for tax purposes later in this chapter. If a lease is classified as a conditional sale lease, the lessee treats the property as owned thereby entitling the lessee to depreciate the property for tax purposes, claim any tax credit which may be available, and deduct as an expense the imputed interest portion of the lease payments. The lessor under a conditional sale lease treats the transaction as a loan and cannot offer the low lease rates associated with a true lease since the lessor does not retain the tax benefits available to the owner of the equipment.

Tax-Oriented True Leases

The *true lease* offers all of the primary benefits commonly attributed to leasing. Substantial cost savings can often be achieved through the use of tax-oriented true leases in which the lessor claims and retains the tax benefits of ownership and passes through to the lessee a portion of such tax benefits in the form of reduced lease payments. The lessor claims tax benefits resulting from equipment ownership such as tax depreciation deductions, and the lessee deducts the full lease payment as an expense. The lessor in a true lease owns the leased equipment at the end of the lease term. A tax-oriented true lease (also sometimes called a *guideline lease*) either contains no purchase option or has a purchase option based on fair market value.

The principal advantage to a lessee of using a true lease to finance an equipment acquisition is the economic benefit that comes from the indirect realization of tax benefits that might otherwise be lost because the lessee cannot use the tax benefits. This occurs when the lessee does not have a sufficient tax liability, nor expects to be able to fully use the tax benefits in the future if those benefits are carried forward.

If the lessee is unable to generate a sufficient tax liability to currently use all tax benefits, the cost of owning new equipment will effectively be higher than leasing the equipment under a true lease. Under these conditions, leasing is usually a less costly alternative because the lessor uses the tax benefits from the acquisition and passes on a portion of these benefits to the lessee through a lower lease payment.

The lower cost of leasing realized by a lessee throughout the lease term in a true lease must be weighted against the loss of the leased equipment's market value at the end of the lease term, referred to as the *residual value.* A framework for evaluating the tax and timing effects is presented later in this chapter.

The Internal Revenue Service is well aware that parties to a lending transaction may find it more advantageous from a tax point of view to characterize an agreement as a "lease" rather than as a conditional sale agreement. Therefore, guidelines have been established by the IRS to distinguish between a true lease and a conditional sales agreement. These guidelines are discussed later.

Single-Investor Leases versus Leveraged Leases

There are two categories of true leases: single-investor leases (or direct leases) and leveraged leases. *Single-investor leases* are essentially two-party transactions, with the lessor purchasing the leased equipment with its own funds and being at risk for 100% of the funds used to purchase the equipment.

The leveraged form of a true lease of equipment is the ultimate form of lease financing. The most attractive feature of a *leveraged lease,* from the standpoint of a lessee unable to use tax benefits of depreciation, is its low cost as compared to that of alternative methods of financing. Leveraged leasing also satisfies a need for lease financing of especially large capital equipment projects with economic lives of up to 25 or more years, although leveraged leases are also used where the life of the equipment is considerably shorter. The leveraged lease can be a most advantageous financing device when used for the right kinds of projects and structured correctly.

A leveraged lease of equipment is conceptually similar to a single-investor lease. The lessee selects the equipment and negotiates the lease in much the same manner. Also, the terms for rentals, options, and responsibility for taxes, insurance, and maintenance are similar. However, a leveraged lease is appreciably more complex in size, documentation, legal involvement, and, most importantly, the number of parties involved and the unique advantages that each party gains.

Leveraged leases of equipment are generally offered only by corporations acting as lessors. This is because in a leveraged lease the tax benefits available to individual lessors are much more limited than those available to a corporation.

The lessor in a leveraged lease of equipment becomes the owner of the leased equipment by providing only a percentage (20%–30%) of the capital necessary to purchase the equipment. The remainder of the capital (70%–80%) is borrowed from institutional investors on a nonrecourse basis to the lessor. This loan is secured by a first lien on the equipment, an assignment of the lease, and an assignment of the lease payments. The cost of the nonrecourse borrowing is a function of the credit standing of the lessee. The lease rate varies with the prevailing interest rates and with the risk of the transaction.

A "leveraged lease" is always a true lease. The lessor in a leveraged lease can claim all of the tax benefits incidental to ownership of the equipment even though the lessor provides only 20% to 30% of the capital needed to purchase the equipment. This ability to claim the tax benefits attributable to the entire cost of the leased equipment and the right to 100% of the residual value provided by the lease, while providing and being at risk for only a portion of the cost of the equipment, is the "leverage" in a leveraged lease. This leverage enables the lessor in a leveraged lease to offer the lessee much lower lease rates than the lessor could provide under a single-investor nonleveraged lease.

Single-investor nonleveraged leases are basically two-party transactions with a lessee and a lessor. However, leveraged leases by their nature involve a minimum of three parties with diverse interests: a lessee, a lessor, and a nonrecourse lender. Indeed, leveraged leases are sometimes called *three-party transactions.*

FULL PAYOUT LEASES VERSUS OPERATING LEASES

Thus far, the leases we have discussed are comparable to equipment financing transactions in that the lease term is for a substantial portion of the economic life of the leased equipment. In these leases the lessor expects to recover its entire investment plus (1) a targeted return on its investment from the lease payments received, (2) any tax benefits the lessor is entitled to receive, and (3) the residual value the lessor anticipates receiving when the lease terminates. These types of leases are called *full payout leases.* Such leases are essentially financing transactions.

Other types of leases called *operating leases*, in contrast to full payout lease, are not financing transactions. Operating leases may be for only a fraction of the life of the asset. An operating lease is always a true lease for tax purposes. That is, the lessor is entitled to all the tax benefits associated with ownership, and the lessee is entitled to deduct the lease payments.

We shall explain later in this chapter the special meaning of the term "operating lease" for financial accounting purposes. Transactions classified as operating leases are not disclosed in the body of the balance sheet as financial obligations. Instead, they are shown in the footnotes to the financial statement as fixed obligations. This classification may arise despite the fact that the transaction, for all intents and purposes, is a financing transaction.

REASONS FOR LEASING

Leasing is an alternative to purchasing. Because the lessee is obligated to make a series of payments, a lease arrangement resembles a debt contract. Thus, the advantages cited for leasing are often based on a comparison between leasing and purchasing using borrowed funds.

Cost

Many lessees find true leasing attractive because of its apparent low cost. This is particularly evident where a lessee cannot currently use tax benefits associated with equipment ownership due to such factors as lack of currently taxable income or net operating loss carryforwards.

If it were not for the different tax treatment for owning and leasing equipment, the costs would be identical in an efficient capital market. However, due to the different tax treatment as well as the diverse abilities of tax entities to currently utilize the tax benefits associated with ownership, no set rule can be offered as to whether borrowing to buy or a true lease is the cheaper form of financing. Various factors must be analyzed to assess the least costly financing method. A framework for such an analysis is provided later in this chapter.

The cost of a true lease depends on the size of the transaction and whether the lease is tax-oriented or non-tax-oriented. The equipment leasing market can be classified into the following three market sectors: (1) small-ticket retail market with transactions in the $5,000 to $100,000 range, (2) middle market with large-ticket items covering transactions between $100,000 and $5 million, and (3) special products market involving equipment cost in excess of $5 million.

Tax-oriented leases generally fall into the second and third markets. Most of the leveraged lease transactions are found in the third market and the upper range of the second market. The effective interest cost implied by these lease arrangements is considerably below prevailing interest rates that the same lessee would pay on borrowed funds. Even so, the potential lessee must weigh the lost economic benefits from owning the equipment against the economic benefits to be obtained from leasing.

Non-tax-oriented leases fall primarily into the small-ticket retail market and the lower range of the second market. There is no real cost savings associated with these leases compared to traditional borrowing arrangements. In most cases, however, cost is not the dominant motive of the firm that employs this method of financing.

From a tax perspective, leasing has advantages that lead to a reduction in cost for a company that is in a tax loss carryforward position and is consequently unable to claim tax benefits associated with equipment ownership currently or for several years in the future.

Conservation of Working Capital

The most frequent advantage cited by leasing company representatives and lessees is that leasing conserves working capital. The reasoning is as follows: When a firm borrows money to purchase equipment, the lending institution rarely provides an amount equal to the entire price of the equipment to be financed. Instead, the lender requires the borrowing firm to take an equity position in the equipment by making a down payment. The amount of the down payment will depend on such factors as the type of equipment, the creditworthiness of the borrower, and prevailing economic conditions. Leasing, in contrast, typically provides 100% financing since it does not require the firm to make a down payment. Moreover, costs incurred to acquire the equipment, such as delivery and installation charges, are not usually covered by a loan agreement. They may, however, be structured into a lease agreement.

The validity of this argument for financially sound firms during normal economic conditions is questionable. Such firms can simply obtain a loan for 100% of the equipment or borrow the down payment from another source that provides unsecured credit. On the other hand, there is doubt that the funds needed by a small firm for a down payment can be borrowed, particularly during tight money periods. Also, some leases do, in fact, require a down payment in the form of advance lease payments or security deposits at the beginning of the lease term.

Preservation of Credit Capacity by Avoiding Capitalization

Current financial reporting standards for leases require that lease obligations classified as capital leases (discussed later) be capitalized as a liability on the balance sheet. According to FASB Statement No. 13, the principle for classifying a lease as a capital lease for financial reporting purposes is as follows:

> A lease that transfers substantially all of the benefits and risks incident to ownership of property should be accounted for as the acquisition of an asset and the incurrence of an obligation by the lessee.

FASB Statement No. 13 specifies four criteria for classifying a lease as a capital lease. We will discuss these four criteria later in this chapter. Leases not classified as capital leases are considered operating leases. Unlike a capital lease, an operating lease is not capitalized. Instead, certain information regarding such leases must be disclosed in a footnote to the financial statement.

Many chief financial officers are of the opinion that avoiding capitalization of a lease will enhance the financial image of their corporations. Because there is generally ample room for designing lease arrangements so as to avoid having a lease classified as a capital lease, chief financial officers generally prefer that lease agreements be structured as operating leases.

As a practical matter, most long-term true leases (payout type leases for the lessors) are structured to qualify as operating leases for financial accounting purposes for the lessees at the request of the lessees.

Risk of Obsolescence and Disposal of Equipment

When a firm owns equipment, it faces the possibility that at some future time the equipment may not be as efficient as more recently manufactured equipment. The owner may then elect to sell the original equipment and purchase the newer, more technologically efficient version. The sale of the equipment, however, may produce only a small fraction of its book value. By leasing, it is argued, the firm may avoid the risk of obsolescence and the problems of disposal of the equipment. The validity of this argument depends on the type of lease and the provisions therein.

With a *cancelable* operating lease, the lessee can avoid the risk of obsolescence by terminating the contract. However, the avoidance of risk is not without a cost since the lease payments under such lease arrangements reflect the risk of obsolescence perceived by the lessor. At the end of the lease term, the disposal of the obsolete equipment becomes the problem of the lessor. The risk of loss in residual value that the lessee passes on to the lessor is embodied in the cost of the lease.

The risk of disposal faced by some lessors, however, may not be as great as the risk that would be encountered by the lessee. Some lessors, for example, specialize in short-term operating leases of particular types of equipment, such as computers or construction equipment, and have the expertise to release or sell equipment coming off lease with substantial remaining useful life. A manufacturer-lessor has less investment exposure since its manufacturing costs will be significantly less than the retail price. Also, it is often equipped to handle reconditioning and redesigning due to technological improvements. Moreover, the manufacturer-lessor will be more active in the resale market for the equipment and thus be in a better position to find users for equipment that may be obsolete to one firm but still satisfactory to another. IBM is the best example of a manufacturer-lessor that has combined its financing, manufacturing, and marketing talents to reduce the risk of disposal. This reduced risk of disposal, compared with that faced by the lessee, is presumably passed along to the lessee in the form of a reduced lease cost.

Restrictions on Management

When a lender provides funds to a firm for an extended period of time, provisions to protect the lender are included in the debt contract. The provisions are called covenants and were discussed in Chapter 15. The purpose of protective provisions, or protective covenants, is to ensure that the borrower remains creditworthy during the period over which the funds are borrowed. Protective provisions impose restrictions on the borrower. Failure to satisfy such a protective covenant usually creates an event of default that, if not cured upon notice, gives the lenders certain additional rights and remedies under the loan agreement, including the right to perfect a security agreement or to demand the immediate repayment of the principal. In practice, the remedy and ability to cure vary with the seriousness of the event of default.

An advantage of leasing is that lease agreements typically do not impose financial covenants and restrictions on management as does a loan agreement used to finance the purchase of equipment. The historical reason for this in true leases is that the Internal Revenue Service discouraged true leases from having attributes of loan agreements. Leases may contain restrictions as to location of the property and additional investments by the lessee in the leased equipment in order to ensure compliance with tax laws.

Flexibility and Convenience

In addition to the flexibility and convenience that may result from leasing due to fewer restrictions being imposed on management, four other reasons are often cited for leasing. These reasons are characterized by flexibility and convenience.

Tailor-Made Lease Payments

Lease payment schedules can sometimes be designed to meet the specific needs of the lessee. For example, lease payments can be reduced or not scheduled during the period when the firm has its greatest needs for working capital. Payments can be set higher during the later years of the lease and lower in the earlier years, subject to Internal Revenue requirements. Although it may be possible to structure a term loan in the same way, it is generally difficult to do so. Moreover, the term for a true lease can usually be structured for a longer period than is customary for conventional loan agreements. Lessors can offer longer terms than bank term loans because of longer-term borrowing to fund activities and faster return of capital as a result of cash flow generated by tax benefits.

Speed in Obtaining Financing

E-commerce leases make a routine lease closing almost instantaneous with the decision to acquire certain types of equipment. A more complex single investor lease can generally be arranged more quickly than financing with other sources of intermediate-term debt. Documentation is usually simpler for closing leasing deals than for other financing arrangements. However, where large-ticket items are financed using a leveraged lease, it may take just as much time, or possibly longer, to put together an acceptable package for all parties as it would take to structure a term loan or arrange a private placement of bonds.

Some lessors write *master leases* to facilitate quick handling of a series of deliveries of various equipment. A master lease agreement works like a line of credit. Such an arrangement permits the lessee to acquire equipment when needed without having to negotiate a new lease agreement each time equipment is acquired. A restriction is placed on both the dollar amount of equipment to be leased and the time period over which the master lease is to apply. Generally, the time period is less than one year. The interest rate is either agreed to at the outset or is indexed to a reference interest rate at the time of acceptance. As equipment is delivered and accepted by the lessee, the lessee and lessor sign a schedule describing the equipment and lease term which is then incorporated into the master lease agreement by reference. One major advantage to the lessee is that financing costs and conditions of the lease are known in advance. Another advantage is the simple documentation requirements after the master lease agreement is in place.

Regulatory Ease

Public disclosure of financial information and confidential trade information is not required in connection with a lease transaction, as is the case with a prospectus for a public offering of debt or equity and as is sometimes the case with a private offering prospectus or memorandum. Moreover, compliance by the lessee with SEC regulations governing the issuance of securities is not required under a lease.

Eliminates Maintenance Problems

Of course, for a lease structured as a net lease, maintenance problems are not eliminated but are the responsibility of the lessee. Although an operating lease, in which the lessor agrees to maintain the equipment, eliminates maintenance problems for the lessee, the cost of maintenance is reflected in the lessor's pricing of the lease. If the lessor, under an operating lease, is the manufacturer and provides a service contract if the equipment is purchased, the relative unbundled maintenance cost implied in the lease must be compared with the same cost if the equipment is purchased in conjunction with a service contract in order to determine the least expensive operating lease arrangement.

Impact on Cash Flow and Book Earnings

In a properly structured true lease arrangement, the lower lease payment from leasing rather than borrowing can provide a lessee with a superior cash flow. Whether the cash flow on an after-tax basis after taking the residual value of the equipment into account is superior on a present value basis must be ascertained. The analysis of cash flows from leasing versus borrowing to purchase is explained later in this chapter.

Lease payments under a true lease will usually have less impact on book earnings during the early years of the lease than will depreciation and interest payments associated with the purchase of the same equipment.

TYPES OF LESSORS

Corporate lessors may be generally categorized as commercial banks or their subsidiaries, independent leasing companies, captive leasing subsidiary companies of nonfinance companies, finance companies or their subsidiaries, investment banking firms, and subsidiaries of life or casualty insurance companies.

Many banks and bank holding companies or their subsidiaries participate indirectly in leasing through working relationships with independent and captive leasing companies. Independent leasing companies engage in equipment leasing in the same way as banks. After purchasing and taking title to the equipment requested by the lessee, most such companies lease the equipment to lessees as full payout type leases. However, some independent leasing companies may specialize in short-term operating leases. Specialized leasing companies provide leasing and servicing of specific equipment in a particular industry. For example, many independent leasing companies concentrate on data processing equipment.

Captive leasing or finance companies are generally subsidiaries of equipment manufacturers, and their primary purpose is to secure financing for the customers of the parent company. Captives may also be involved in the lease financing of equipment other than that manufactured by their parent company.

In recent years, many nonfinance industrial and service companies without a need to finance their own products have established captive leasing companies to engage in tax-oriented leasing of equipment. These companies have become important participants in the market.

LEASE BROKERS AND FINANCIAL ADVISERS

The growth of the leasing industry has produced a demand for intermediaries to assist lessors in servicing lessees. Lease brokers and financial advisers serve as architects or packagers of lease transactions by bringing together lessors, lessees, and, in the case of a leveraged lease, third-party lenders. Leasing subsidiaries of banks and bank holding companies, investment bankers, commercial banks, and small independent leasing companies have all played an important role as lease brokers and financial advisers.

Lease brokers and financial advisers can perform a useful service for both lessees and lessors in arranging equipment leases. They can be especially helpful to a lessee by obtaining attractive pricing from a legitimate investor and advising the lessee in structuring and negotiating the transaction. While lease brokers and financial advisers typically represent lessees, they can be helpful to a lessor in finding solutions to negotiating issues.

For its services as an intermediary, the lease broker or financial adviser receives a brokerage commission. The amount of the remuneration can vary widely, depending on the complexity of the deal and the attractiveness of the deal to the lessor in the prevailing economic environment. The standard fee usually ranges from ½% to 4% of the cost of the equipment, depending on the services performed or provided by the broker and the size and difficulty of the transaction. In some brokered transactions, the lease broker or financial adviser also may receive at least a portion of its compensation in the form of a share participation in the residual value of the leased equipment. And in still other situations the broker or financial adviser will work for a flat fee.

LEASE PROGRAMS

Lessors can structure lease transactions to suit the needs of most companies. Examples of various lease programs available are described below.

A *standard lease* provides 100% long-term financing with level payments over the term of the lease. Standard documentation facilitates quick handling and closing of the lease transaction. Installation costs, delivery charges, transportation expense, and taxes applicable to the purchase of the equipment may be included as part of the lease financing package.

A *custom lease* contains special provisions designed to meet particular needs of a lessee. It may, for example, schedule lease payments to fit cash flow. Such a lease can be particularly helpful to a seasonal business.

A master lease, as discussed earlier, works like a line of credit. It is an agreement that allows the lessee to acquire, during a fixed period of time, equipment as needed without having to renegotiate a new lease contract for each item. With this arrangement, the lessee and lessor agree to the fixed terms and conditions that will apply for various classifications of equipment for a specified period, usually six months to one year. At any time within that period, the lessee can add equipment to the lease up to an agreed maximum, knowing in advance the rate to be paid and the leasing conditions.

Designed as a sales tool for equipment manufacturers or distributors, a *vendor lease* program permits suppliers to offer financing in the form of true or conditional sale leases. Vendor leases may be structured as tax-oriented or non-tax-oriented leases. They may be either short-term operating leases or full payout leases. Vendor lease programs can be offered directly by manufacturers and distributors or in conjunction with a third-party leasing company.

An *offshore lease* is an agreement to lease equipment to be used outside the United States. Offshore lease programs offer leases calling for payments to U.S. lessors in U.S. dollars or local currencies for equipment used abroad. Both true leases and conditional sale leases can be arranged for firms requiring equipment in overseas operations. However, the tax benefits to U.S. lessors are insignificant since little depreciation is available on equipment located outside of the United States.

Sale-and-leaseback transactions can be used by a company to convert owned property and equipment into cash. The equipment is purchased by the lessor and then leased back to the seller.

Under a *facility lease*, an entire facility—a plant and its equipment—can be leased. Under this arrangement, a lessor may provide or arrange construction financing for a facility. Interest costs during construction can often be capitalized into the lease. The lease commences when the completed facility has been accepted by the lessee.

FINANCIAL REPORTING OF LEASE TRANSACTIONS BY LESSEES

Financial reporting considerations are important for most lessees and potential lessees. At one time, lessees needed only to disclose information regarding lease commitments in footnotes to their financial statements. Hence, leasing was often referred to as "off balance sheet financing."

With the issuance by the Financial Accounting Standards Board (FASB) of Statement of Financial Accounting Standards No. 13 (FAS 13), the accounting treatment of lease commitments changed. FAS 13 required that certain leases be recorded on the lessee's balance sheet as a liability and the leased property reported as an asset. This procedure is called "capitalizing a lease" or "lease capitalization." For leases that fail to meet the test specified by FAS 13, the lessee need only disclose certain information regarding lease commitments in a footnote.

Classification of Leases

According to FAS 13 (paragraph 60), a lease is classified as either an operating lease or a capital lease. The principle for classifying a lease as either operating or capital for reporting purposes is as follows:

> [A] lease that transfers substantially all of the benefits and risks incident to the ownership of property should be accounted for as the acquisition of an asset and the incurrence of an obligation by the lessee....All other leases should be accounted for as operating leases.

But how should the accountant interpret when substantially all of the benefits and risks of ownership are transferred? FAS 13 specifies that if one or more of the following four criteria are met for a noncancelable lease at the date of the lease agreement, the lease is to be accounted for as a capital lease:

1. The lease transfers ownership of the property to the lessee by the end of the lease term.
2. The lease contains a bargain purchase option.
3. The lease term is equal to 75% or more of the estimated economic life of the leased property.
4. The present value of the minimum lease payments (excluding executory costs)[2] equals or exceeds 90% of the fair value of the leased property.

A lease that does not satisfy at least one of the above four criteria is classified as an operating lease.

For reasons to be discussed below, lessees prefer a lease to be classified as an operating lease. While it may appear that FAS 13 limits management's ability to structure how a lease will be treated for financial reporting purposes, this is not true in practice. There are several ways in which a lessee can structure a lease to meet its objectives, as will be discussed later.

---

[2] Executory costs include insurance, maintenance, and property taxes.

Accounting for Operating Leases

Because an operating lease does not represent the transfer of substantially all of the benefits and risks of ownership, the leased property is not capitalized, nor is the lease obligation shown as a liability on the balance sheet. Instead, the lease payments are charged to expenses over the lease term as they become payable.

Although neither the leased asset nor the obligation appears in the balance sheet, the lessee must disclose the following information in footnotes to its financial statements: (1) a general description of the leasing arrangement, which would include restrictions imposed by the lease arrangement, the existence of renewal or purchase options, and escalation clauses; (2) the lease expense for each year in which an income statement is presented; and, (3) future minimum lease payments required in the aggregate and separately for each of the next five years.

Exhibit 27.1 is an illustration of a footnote disclosure of lease commitments taken from the fiscal 1999 annual report of Circuit City Stores, Inc. The disclosure of commitments for both operating and capital leases is shown. The latter disclosure requirements are explained in the next section.

Accounting for Capital Leases

A capital lease is treated for accounting purposes as if the leased asset were purchased and financed over time. The question then arises as to how the value of the leased asset and the corresponding liability should be recorded on the lessee's balance sheet at the inception of the lease. FAS 13 requires that these amounts be recorded at the inception of the lease as the lower of (1) the present value of the minimum lease payments during the lease term or (2) the fair market value of the leased asset.[3]

Once the asset and liability at the inception of the lease have been determined, the depreciation charge and the interest expense associated with the liability must be determined. Although the amounts of the asset and liability are the same at the inception of the lease, the subsequent depreciation and interest expense are computed independently.

---

[3] The minimum lease payments are defined as the sum of (i) the minimum lease payments required during the lease term and (ii) the amount of any bargain purchase option. In the absence of a bargain purchase option, the amount of any guarantee of the residual value and the amount specified for failure to extend or renew the lease are used in lieu of (ii). Excluded from the minimum lease payments are executory costs where these are required to be paid by the lessee to the lessor.

EXHIBIT 27.1   Lease Commitments Footnote Disclosure in Fiscal 1999 Annual
Report of Circuit City Stores, Inc.

```
10. LEASE COMMITMENTS
The Company conducts a substantial portion of its business in leased premises.
The Company's lease obligations are based upon contractual minimum rates. For

certain locations, amounts in excess of these minimum rates are payable based
upon specified percentages of sales. Rental expense and sublease income for all
operating leases are summarized as follows:
```

| (Amounts in thousands) | Years Ended February 28 | | |
	1999	1998	1997
Minimum rentals..............	$302,724	$248,383	$184,618
Rentals based on sales volume.	1,247	730	2,322
Sublease income..............	(20,875)	(12,879)	(11,121)
Net.......................	$283,096	$236,234	$175,819

```
      The Company computes rent based on a percentage of sales volumes in excess
of defined amounts in certain store locations. Most of the Company's other
leases are fixed-dollar rental commitments, with many containing rent
escalations based on the Consumer Price Index. Most provide that the Company pay
taxes, maintenance, insurance and certain other operating expenses applicable to
the premises.
      The initial term of most real property leases will expire within the next
25 years; however, most of the leases have options providing for additional
lease terms of five years to 25 years at terms similar to the initial terms.
      Future minimum fixed lease obligations, excluding taxes, insurance and
other costs payable directly by the Company, as of February 28, 1999, were:
```

(Amounts in thousands) Fiscal	Capital Leases	Operating Lease Commitments	Operating Sublease Income
2000........................	$1,662	$296,674	$(14,684)
2001........................	1,681	293,961	(12,817)
2002........................	1,725	289,553	(11,605)
2003........................	1,726	285,710	(10,624)
2004........................	1,768	283,422	(9,123)
After 2004..................	16,464	3,289,107	(55,144)
Total minimum lease payments.................	25,026	$4,738,427	$(113,997)
Less amounts representing interest.................	12,298		
Present value of net minimum capital lease payments (NOTE 5)........	$12,728		

In addition, the following footnote disclosures for capital leases are
required in the lessee's financial statement:

1. The gross amount of assets recorded under capital leases presented by
   major classes according to nature or function. The lessee can combine
   this information for owned assets, which the company must also disclose.
2. Future minimum lease payments in the aggregate and for each of the
   five succeeding years (deducting executory costs) and the amount of
   imputed interest in reducing the minimum lease payments to present
   value.

3. Total contingent lease payments actually incurred for each period for which an income statement is presented.
4. A general description of the leasing arrangement, which would include restrictions imposed by the lease arrangement, the existence of renewal or purchase options, and escalation clauses.

Exhibit 27.1 illustrates the footnote disclosure for capital lease commitments.

The impact of the accounting treatment of leases on reported income is usually minimal. The primary concern of management is, therefore, not with the impact on reported income but with the effect on the firm's debt-to-equity ratio. As explained in Chapter 22, this ratio is commonly employed by creditors and investors to determine whether a company is overburdened with debt. With a capital lease, the debt-to-equity ratio will be greater than if the lease is treated as an operating lease because of the lease obligation reported in the balance sheet. However, it is naive to assume that market participants are untutored about the impact of noncapitalized leases on the debt-equity ratio. Certainly rating agencies take into account leasing arrangements in assigning a credit rating.

The Role of Interpretation in the Implementation of FAS 13

The test set forth in FAS 13 may suggest that the lessee cannot influence the classification of a lease. Every accountant knows how to classify a lease given the required information about the lease. But there's the rub! All but the first criterion, transfer of ownership by the end of the lease term, require sufficient judgment by the individual gathering the data that can influence the classification.[4] Let's look at Criterion 2 and 3 to see how this is possible.

Criterion 2 involves the existence of a bargain purchase price. To say that an option to purchase some asset at a future date is a bargain purchase requires judgment as to the expected projected fair market value at the exercise date. What you may perceive as a bargain purchase given your projected fair market value may not be a bargain to another individual who has determined a different projected fair market value for the same product. We constantly observe differences of opinion of projected future values in the marketplace for equipment. The person responsible for gathering the data must resolve whether a bargain purchase option exists.

---

[4] Dan Palmon and Michael Kwatinetz, "The Significant Role Interpretation Plays in the Implementation of SFAS No. 13." *Journal of Accounting, Auditing & Finance* (Spring 1980).

Even if the projected fair market value could be estimated with some degree of certainty, internally or externally from expert appraisers, judgment is still required to determine whether it is a bargain. Is the option to buy a leased asset for $15 million five years from now when the projected fair market value has been estimated to be $15.2 million a bargain? To resolve this question, management must specify criteria for the presence of a bargain purchase. An extreme case would categorize a bargain purchase when the option price is less than the projected fair market value. More than likely, management will arbitrarily set a minimum percentage for the purchase option price to the projected fair market value. What seems to be a very simple criterion can now be seen to require considerable judgment by management and the individual designated to gather the information.

Criteria 3 classifies a lease as a capital lease if the lease term is 75% or more of the estimated economic life of the leased asset. At first, it may appear that the lease term is readily available from the lease agreement but that judgment is required to estimate the economic life. In fact, both permit managerial discretion in implementation in the absence of a bargain purchase option. When a bargain purchase option exists, the lease term is defined as the period between the inception of the lease and the date on which the bargain purchase option becomes exercisable. The lease agreement may permit additional lease periods so the lease term may not be clear.

The problems associated with estimating the economic life of the leased asset are the same as those experienced by management when estimating the economic life of owned assets it must depreciate. For certain types of assets, this task may not be difficult because of company or industry experience. For other assets, different estimates may exist for the same asset. Lengthening the estimated economic life will influence the outcome of Criterion 3 for classification.

FEDERAL INCOME TAX REQUIREMENTS FOR TRUE LEASE TRANSACTIONS

Remember that the Internal Revenue Service is concerned with the classification of a lease because tax benefits are affected. The Internal Revenue Code (IRC) has requirements for a lease to be treated as a true lease. These rules are independent of the rules for classifying a lease as set forth in FAS 13. The IRC distinguishes between non-tax-oriented leases (i.e., conditional sale leases) and tax-oriented true leases. The major characteristic differentiating non-tax-oriented and tax-oriented true leases is the type of purchase options available to the lessee. True leases have fair-market-value types of purchase options. Conditional sale leases have nominal fixed-price purchase options or automatically pass the title to the lessee at the end of the lease.

Revenue Ruling 55-540 (1955-2 Cum. Bull. 39) states:

> Whether an agreement, which in form is a lease, is in substance a conditional sales contract depends upon the intent of the parties as evidenced by the provisions of the agreement, read in light of the facts and circumstances existing at the time the agreement was executed. In ascertaining such intent no single test, nor special combination of tests, is absolutely determinative. No general rule, applicable in all cases, can be laid down. Each case must be decided in the light of its particular facts.

A purchase option based on fair market value rather than a nominal purchase option is a strong indication of intent to create a lease rather than a conditional sale or lease. The test is whether the interest of the lessor in the leased property is a proprietary interest with attributes of ownership rather than a mere creditor's security interest in the leased property.

A lease *generally* qualifies as a true lease for tax purposes if all of the following criteria are met:

1. At the start of the lease, the fair market value of the leased property projected for the end of the lease term equals or exceeds 20% of the original cost of the leased property (excluding front-end fees and any cost to the lessor for removal).
2. At the start of the lease, the leased property is projected to retain at the end of the initial term a useful life that (a) exceeds 20% of the original estimated useful life of the equipment and (b) is at least one year.
3. The lessee does not have a right to purchase or release the leased property at a price that is less than its then fair market value.
4. The lessor does not have a right to cause the lessee to purchase the leased property at a fixed price.
5. At all times during the lease term, the lessor has a minimum unconditional "at-risk" investment equal to at least 20% of the cost of the leased property.
6. The lessor can show that the transaction was entered into for profit, apart from tax benefits resulting from the transaction.
7. The lessee does not furnish any part of the purchase price of the leased property and has not loaned or guaranteed any indebtedness created in connection with the acquisition of the leased property by the lessor.

Additional criteria and guidelines for true leases are described in various IRS Revenue Rulings and Revenue Procedures.

In structuring a tax-oriented lease transaction, corporations requiring the use of equipment will seek to have the lease treated as a capital lease for financial reporting purposes to avoid showing a debt obligation on the balance sheet but as a true lease for tax purposes so that the tax benefits of ownership can be transferred to the lender.

While the requirements and guidelines set forth for a lease transaction to be treated as a true lease for tax purposes, there are transactions that the IRS might view as a conditional sales lease. If this were to occur for a tax-oriented transaction, the economics of such a transaction would be changed by an adverse IRS ruling. Consequently, for complex transactions in which the parties fear they might be viewed by the IRS as not meeting the requirements and guidelines, the parties would seek an advanced ruling from the IRS as to how it would treat the transaction.

Lease agreements generally provide for an indemnity against the possible loss by the lessor of the income tax benefits the lessor expects to receive.

SYNTHETIC LEASES

One of the attractions of a true lease of equipment for lessees is the off-balance sheet treatment of the lease obligation. One of the drawbacks of a true lease of equipment for many lessees (and particularly those able to utilize tax benefits associated with equipment ownership) is the possible loss to be experienced when the true lease terminates and the equipment may have to be acquired from the lessor.

The *synthetic lease* was developed to meet this need by providing the lessee with off-balance sheet treatment of the lease obligation while at the same time protecting the lessee's cost of acquiring the residual value of the leased equipment at the termination of the lease. Tax benefits of equipment ownership are claimed by the lessee in a synthetic lease. The rental in a synthetic lease is approximately equivalent to the lessee's debt rate for comparable maturities.

Synthetic leases are off-balance sheet leases in which the lessee retains tax benefits associated with ownership. Such synthetic leases are structured using a lease agreement between the user or owner of equipment as the "lessee" and an investor as the "lessor" in a manner which satisfies the requirements for an operating lease defined in FAS 13 and related accounting rules.

VALUING A LEASE: THE LEASE OR BORROW-TO-BUY DECISION

Now that we know what a lease is and the key role of the treatment of tax benefits and residual value in a lease transaction, we will show how to value a lease. Several economic models for valuing a lease have been proposed in the literature. The model used here requires the determination of the net present value of the direct cash flow resulting from leasing rather than borrowing to purchase an asset, where the direct cash flow from leasing is discounted using an "adjusted discount rate."[5] The model is derived from "the objective of maximizing the equilibrium market value of the firm, with careful consideration of interactions between the decision to lease and the use of other financing instruments by the lessee."[6]

Direct Cash Flow from Leasing

When a firm elects to lease an asset rather than borrow money to purchase the same asset, this decision will have an impact on the firm's cash flow. The cash flow consequences, which are stated relative to the purchase of the asset, can be summarized as follows:

1. There will be a cash inflow equivalent to the cost of the asset.
2. The lessee may or may not forgo some tax credit. For example, prior to the elimination of the investment tax credit, the lessor could pass this credit through to the lessee.
3. The lessee must make periodic lease payments over the life of the lease. These payments need not be the same in each period. The lease payments are fully deductible for tax purposes if the lease is a true

---

[5] The adjusted discount rate technique presented in this chapter is fundamentally equivalent to and results in the same answer as is obtained by comparing financing provided by a loan that gives the same cash flow as the lease in every future period. This will be illustrated below.

 Although the adjusted discount rate technique is fundamentally equivalent to calculating the adjusted present value of a lease, it is less accurate. The adjusted present value technique takes into consideration the present value of the side effects of accepting a project financed with a lease. (The adjusted present value technique was first developed by Stewart C. Myers, "Interactions of Corporate Financing and Investment Decisions: Implications for Capital Budgeting," *Journal of Finance* (March 1974), pp. 1–26.) The reason for a possible discrepancy between the solutions to the lease versus borrow-to-buy decision using the adjusted discount rate technique and adjusted present value technique is that different discount rates are applied where necessary in discounting the cash flow when the latter technique is used.

[6] Stewart C. Myers, David A. Dill, and Alberto J. Bautista, "Valuation of Financial Lease Contracts," *Journal of Finance* (June 1976), p. 799.

lease. The tax shield is equal to the lease payment times the lessee's marginal tax rate.

4. The lessee forgoes the tax shield provided by the depreciation allowance since it does not own the asset. The tax shield resulting from depreciation is the product of the lessee's marginal tax rate times the depreciation allowance.

5. There will be a cash outlay representing the lost after-tax proceeds from the residual value of the asset.

For example, consider the capital budgeting problem faced by the Hieber Machine Shop Company. The company is considering the acquisition of a machine that requires an initial net cash outlay of $59,400 and will generate a future cash flow for the next five years of $16,962, $19,774, $20,663, $21,895, and $26,825. Assuming a discount rate of 14%, the net present value (NPV) for this machine was found to be $11,540.

Let's assume that the following information was used to determine the initial net cash outlay and the cash flow for the machine:

Cost of the machine = $66,000
Tax credit[7] = $6,600
Estimated pre-tax residual = $6,000 value after disposal costs
Estimated after-tax proceeds from residual value = $3,600
Economic life of the machine = 5 years

Depreciation is assumed to be as follows:[8]

Year	Depreciation Deductions
1	$9,405
2	13,794
3	13,167
4	13,167
5	13,167

---

[7] We use a tax credit in this illustration to show how the model can be applied should Congress decide to introduce some form of tax credit for capital investments in future tax legislation.

[8] The depreciation schedule used in this illustration is not consistent with the tax law at the time of this writing and is used for illustrative purposes only. The depreciation in this example is based on a depreciable basis comprised of the cost of the asset, less one-half of the tax credit, or $66,000 − 3,300 = $62,700. The rates of depreciation for the five years, in order, are 15%, 22%, 21%, 21%, and 21%.

The same machine may be leased by the Hieber Machine Shop Company. The lease would require five annual payments of $13,500, with the first payment due immediately. The lessor would retain the assumed tax credit. The tax shield resulting from the lease payments would be realized at the time that Hieber Machine Shop Company made the payment. No additional annual expenses will be incurred by Hieber Machine Shop Company by owning rather than leasing (that is, the lease is a net lease). The lessor will not require Hieber Machine Shop Company to guarantee a minimum residual value.

Exhibit 27.2 presents the worksheet for the computation of the direct cash flow from leasing rather than borrowing to purchase. The marginal tax rate of Hieber Machine Shop Company is assumed to be 40%. The direct cash flow is summarized below:

			Year		
0	1	2	3	4	5
$51,300	($11,862)	($13,618)	($13,367)	($13,367)	($8,867)

The direct cash flow from leasing was constructed assuming that (1) the lease is a net lease and (2) the tax benefit associated with an expense is realized in the tax year the expense is incurred. These two assumptions require further discussion.

First, if the lease is a gross lease instead of a net lease, the lease payments must be reduced by the cost of maintenance, insurance, and property taxes. These costs are assumed to be the same regardless of whether the asset is leased or purchased with borrowed funds. Where have these costs been incorporated into the analysis? The cash flow from owning an asset is constructed by subtracting the additional operating expenses from the additional revenue. Maintenance, insurance, and property taxes are included in the additional operating expenses. There may be instances when the cost of maintenance differs depending on the financing alternative selected. In such cases, an adjustment to the value of the lease must be made.

Second, many firms considering leasing may be currently in a nontaxpaying position but anticipate being in a taxpaying position in the future. The derivation of the lease valuation model presented in the next section does not consider this situation. It assumes that the tax shield associated with an expense can be fully absorbed by the firm in the tax year in which the expense arises. There is a lease valuation model that, under certain conditions, will handle the situation of a firm currently in a nontaxpaying position.[9]

---

[9] The generalized model is explained and illustrated in Julian R. Franks and Stewart D. Hodges, "Valuation of Finance Contracts: A Note," *Journal of Finance* (May 1978), pp. 657–669.

EXHIBIT 27.2 Worksheet for Direct Cash Flow from Leasing: Hieber Machine Shop Company*

	End of Year				
	0	1	2	3	4	5
Cost of machine	$66,000					
Lost tax credit	(6,600)					
Lease payment	(13,500)	($13,500)	($13,500)	($13,500)	($13,500)	
Tax shield from lease payment**	5,400	5,400	5,400	5,400	5,400	
Lost depreciation tax shields***		(3,762)	(5,518)	(5,267)	(5,267)	($5,267)
Lost residual value						(3,600)
Total	$51,300	($11,862)	($13,618)	($13,367)	($13,367)	($8,867)

* Parentheses denote cash outflow.

** Lease payment multiplied by the marginal tax rate (40%).

*** Depreciation for year multiplied by the marginal tax rate (40%).

906

Valuing the Direct Cash Flow from Leasing

Because the lease displaces debt, the direct cash flow from leasing should be further modified by devising a loan that in each period except the initial period engenders a net cash flow that is identical to the net cash flow for the lease obligation; that is, financial risk is neutralized. Such a loan, called an *equivalent loan*, is illustrated later. Fortunately, it has been mathematically demonstrated that rather than going through the time-consuming effort to construct an equivalent loan, all the decision-maker need do is discount the direct cash flow from leasing by an adjusted discount rate. The adjusted discount rate can be approximated using the following formula:[10]

> Adjusted discount rate
> = (1 − Marginal tax rate) × (Cost of borrowing money)

The formula assumes that leasing will displace debt on a dollar-for-dollar basis.[11]

Given the direct cash flow from leasing and the adjusted discount rate, the NPV of the lease can be computed. We shall refer to the NPV of the lease as simply the *value of the lease*. A negative value for a lease indicates that leasing will not be more economically beneficial than borrowing to purchase. A positive value means that leasing will be more economically beneficial. However, leasing will be attractive only if the NPV of the asset assuming normal financing is positive *and* the value of the lease is positive, or if the sum of the NPV of the asset assuming normal financing and the value of the lease is positive.

In order to evaluate the direct cash flow from leasing for the machine considered by the Hieber Machine Shop Company in our illustration, we must know the firm's cost of borrowing money. Suppose that the cost of borrowing money has been determined to be 10%. The adjusted discount rate is then found by applying the formula:

> Adjusted discount rate = (1 − 0.40) × (0.10) = 0.06, or 6%

---

[10] As noted by Brealey and Myers, "The direct cash flows are typically assumed to be *safe* flows that investors would discount at approximately the same rate as the interest and principal on a secured loan issued by the lessee" (Richard Brealey and Stewart Meyers, *Principles of Corporate Finance* [New York: McGraw Hill, 1981], p. 629). There is justification for applying a different discount rate to the various components of the direct cash flow from leasing.

[11] Brealey and Myers, *Principles of Corporate Finance*, p. 634. The formula must be modified, as explained later, if the lessee believes that leasing does not displace debt on a dollar-for-dollar basis.

EXHIBIT 27.3   Worksheet for Determining the Value of a Lease

End of Year	Direct Cash Flow from Leasing	Present Value of $1 at 6%	Present Value
0	$51,300	1.0000	$51,300
1	(11,862)	0.9434	(11,191)
2	(13,618)	0.8900	(12,120)
3	(13,367)	0.8396	(11,223)
4	(13,367)	0.7921	(10,588)
5	(8,867)	0.7473	(6,626)
Value (or NPV) of lease			$(448)

The adjusted discount rate of 6% is then used to determine the value of the lease. The worksheet is shown as Exhibit 27.3. The value of the lease is –$448. Hence, from a purely economic point of view, the machine should be purchased by the Hieber Machine Shop Company rather than leased. Recall that the NPV of the machine assuming normal financing is $11,540.

Concept of an Equivalent Loan

The value of the lease considered by the Hieber Machine Shop Company was shown to be –$448. Suppose the firm had the opportunity to obtain a $51,748 five-year loan at 10% interest with the following principal repayment schedule:[12]

End of year	0	1	2	3	4	5
Repayment	0	$8,757	$11,039	$11,450	$12,137	$8,365

(Recall that the firm's marginal borrowing rate was assumed to be 10%.)

Exhibit 27.4 shows the net cash flow for each year if the loan is used to purchase the machine. In addition to the loan, the firm must make an initial outlay of $7,652.

The net cash flow for each year if the machine is leased is also presented in Exhibit 27.4. Notice that the net cash flows of the two financing alternatives are equivalent, with the exception of year 0. Therefore, the loan presented above is called the *equivalent loan for the lease.*

---

[12] The loan payments are determined by solving for the set of repayments and interest each period that would result in the value of purchase (accompanied by a loan) being equivalent to leasing.

EXHIBIT 27.4 Equivalent Loan for Lease versus Borrow-to-Buy Decision Faced by Hieber Machine Shop Company

Period	0	1	2	3	4	5
Leasing: Cash flows:						
− Lease payments	−$13,500	−$13,500	−$13,500	−$13,500	−$13,500	$0
+ Tax shield	5,400	5,400	5,400	5,400	5,400	0
Net cash flow	−$8,100	−$8,100	−$8,100	−$8,100	−$8,100	$0
Purchasing: Cash flows:						
− Purchase cost	−$66,000					
+ Tax credit	6,600					
+ Residual value						$3,600
+ Depreciation tax shield	0	$3,762	$5,518	$5,267	$5,267	5,267
+ Loan	51,748					
− Principal repayment	0	−8,757	−11,039	−11,450	−12,137	−8,365
− Interest on loan	0	−5,175	−4,299	−3,195	−2,050	−836
+ Interest tax shield	0	2,070	1,720	1,278	820	334
Net cash flow	−$7,652	−$8,100	−$8,100	−$8,100	−$8,100	$0
Loan account:						
Previous balance	$0	$51,748	$42,991	$31,953	$20,503	$8,365
Principal repayment (+ loan)	+51,748	−8,757	−11,039	−11,450	−12,137	−8,365
New balance	$51,748	$42,991	$31,953	$20,503	$8,365	$0
Value (NPV) of lease*	−$448					

* Difference between the net cash flows in year 0 [−8,100 − (−7,652)].

We can now understand why borrowing to purchase is more economically attractive for Hieber Machine Shop Company. The equivalent loan produces the same net cash flow as the lease in all years after year 0. Hence, the equivalent loan has equalized the financial risk of the two financing alternatives. However, the net cash outlay in year 0 is $7,652 compared to $8,100 if the machine is leased. The difference, –$448, is the value of the lease. Notice that the lease valuation model produced the same value for the lease without constructing an equivalent loan.

Comparison of Alternative Leases

The potential lessee may have the opportunity to select from several leasing arrangements offered by the same lessor or different lessors. From a purely economic perspective, the potential lessee should select the leasing arrangement with the greatest positive value. This requires an analysis of the direct cash flow from leasing for each of the leasing arrangements available.

For example, suppose that a firm has two leasing arrangements available to lease a given asset. The direct cash flow from leasing is shown below for each alternative:

End of Year	Direct Cash Flow from Leasing	
	Lease 1	Lease 2
0	$42,000	$45,800
1	(15,000)	(13,000)
2	(15,000)	(16,000)
3	(15,000)	(18,000)
4	(1,000)	(4,000)

The value of the lease using an adjusted discount rate of 6% and 8% is summarized below:

Adjusted Discount Rate	Value of	
	Lease 1	Lease 2
6%	$1,109	$1,015
8	2,663	2,818

When the adjusted discount rate is 6%, both leases are economically beneficial. However, Lease 1 is marginally superior to Lease 2. The value of both leases increases when the adjusted discount rate is 8%. In this case, Lease 1 is slightly less attractive than Lease 2. The NPVs of both leases for discount rates ranging from 4% to 10% are shown in Exhibit 27.5.

EXHIBIT 27.5   The NPV of Lease 1 and Lease 2 for Different Adjusted Discount Rates

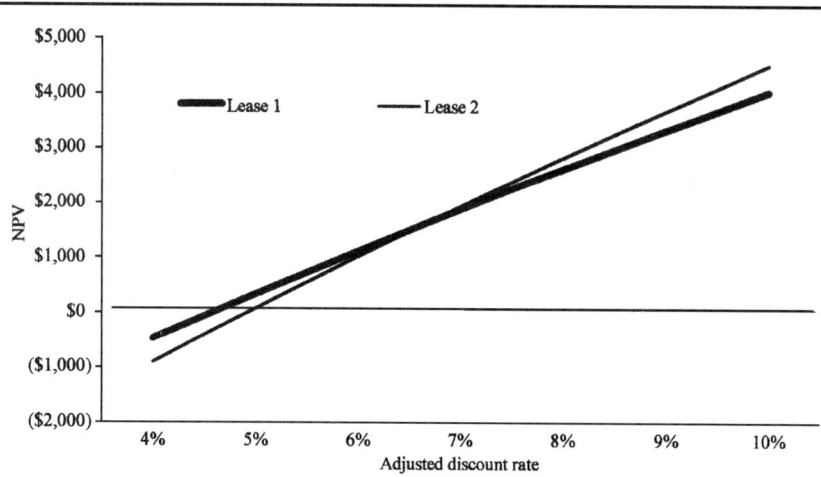

Another Approach to Lease Valuation

Rather than determining the NPV of a lease, many lessors use a different approach when attempting to demonstrate to potential lessees the economic attractiveness of a particular leasing arrangement. The approach is a comparison of the after-tax interest rate on the lease with the after-tax cost of borrowing money. The reason this approach appears to be popular is that management finds it easy to comprehend a rate concept but difficult to appreciate the NPV of a lease concept.

The after-tax interest rate on the lease is found by determining the discount rate that equates the direct cash flow from leasing to zero; that is, it is the discount rate that makes the value of the lease equal to zero. This discount rate is also referred to as the *internal rate of return*. The after-tax interest rate on the lease is then compared to the after-tax cost of borrowing money. When the after-tax interest rate on the lease exceeds the after-tax cost of borrowing money, borrowing to purchase is more economical than leasing. Leasing is more economical when the after-tax cost of borrowing money is greater than the after-tax interest rate on the lease.

Exhibit 27.2 shows the direct cash flow from leasing for the lease arrangement available to the Hieber Machine Shop Company. The discount rate that produces a present value close to zero for the direct cash flow from leasing is 6.3%. Hence, the after-tax interest rate on the lease is about 6.3%.[13]

---

[13] The precise answer may be obtained using a financial calculator that has the IRR program or by using a spreadsheet program function, such as the IRR function in Microsoft's Excel.

When the after-tax cost of borrowing is 6%, the lease arrangement is not attractive. However, when the after-tax cost of borrowing money is 8%, the lease arrangement is attractive.

In the previous illustration, the determination that was made as to whether the lease was economically attractive was precisely the same determination that was made when the NPV lease valuation model was used. The identity of the result is not peculiar to this illustration. The two approaches will always produce the same result.

The advantage of the NPV lease valuation model presented is that it permits interaction of the investment and financing decisions. As a result, it is simple to determine whether an investment proposal that has a negative NPV assuming normal financing can be made economically attractive by a favorable lease arrangement. With the after-tax interest on the lease approach, this is not done as easily. That approach requires management to revise its estimate of the cost of capital when the after-tax interest rate on the lease is less than the after-tax cost of borrowing money and then to reevaluate the investment proposal with the revised cost of capital. This is an extremely complicated and awkward approach since it requires a continuous revision of the cost of capital as attractive lease arrangements become available. No simple solution to this problem has been proffered in the literature.

The rate approach will not always provide the same solution as the NPV approach when lease arrangements are compared. Differences in the selection of the best lease arrangement may result when the number of advance payments is different, when the lease payments are not uniform, or when the tax credit is handled any differently.[14] The best lease arrangement is the one with the greatest NPV. Therefore, if conflicts arise when comparing lease arrangements by the two methods, the decision should be based on the NPV of the lease.

SUMMARY

■ A lease is a contract wherein, over the term of the lease, the owner of equipment (the lessor) permits another entity (the lessee) to use that equipment in exchange for a promise by the lessee to make a series of lease payments.

---

[14] The situation is analogous to conditions in which the yield technique in capital budgeting may produce rankings conflicting with those produced by the net present value technique.

- The options available to the lessee at the end of the lease term are critical in determining the nature of the lease for tax purposes and the classification of the lease for financial accounting purposes.
- Non-tax-oriented leases or conditional sale leases transfer all incidents of ownership of the leased property to the lessee and usually give the lessee a fixed price bargain purchase option or renewal option not based on fair market value at the time of exercise. For tax purposes, the transaction is treated as a loan.
- In a tax-oriented true leases, the lessor claims and retains the tax benefits of ownership and passes through to the lessee most of such tax benefits in the form of reduced lease payments. The principal advantage to a lessee of using a true lease to finance an equipment acquisition is the economic benefit that comes from the indirect realization of tax benefits that might otherwise be lost because the lessee cannot use the tax benefits.
- True leases are categorized as single-investor leases (or direct leases) and leveraged leases. Single-investor leases are essentially two-party transactions, with the lessor purchasing the leased equipment with its own funds and being at risk for 100% of the funds used to purchase the equipment. Conceptually, a leveraged lease of equipment is similar to a single-investor lease. However, it is more complex in size, documentation, legal involvement, and, most importantly, the number of parties (particularly lenders who provide the major portion of funds to purchase the equipment) involved and the unique advantages that each party gains.
- Full payout leases are basically financing transactions. In contrast, an operating lease is one for which the lease term is much shorter than the expected life of the equipment.
- The reasons cited for leasing rather than borrowing to purchase equipment are cost savings, conservation of working capital, preservation of credit capacity by avoiding capitalization, elimination of risk of obsolescence and disposal of equipment, less restrictions on management, and flexibility and convenience. Not all of these claims are valid, particularly cost savings since cost reduction depends on whether the lease is tax-oriented.
- For financial reporting purposes, a lease is classified as either an operating lease or a capital lease. FAS 13 sets forth the conditions for classifying a lease. For a capital lease, the transaction is shown on the lessee's balance sheet as a liability and the leased property reported as an asset. For an operating lease, the lessee need only disclose certain information regarding lease commitments in a footnote.
- The value of the lease is found by discounting the direct cash flow from leasing by the adjusted discount rate. A negative value for a lease indi-

cates that leasing will not be more economically beneficial than borrowing to purchase. A positive value means that leasing will be more economically beneficial. However, leasing will be attractive only if the NPV of the asset assuming normal financing is positive and the value of the lease is positive, or if the sum of the NPV of the asset assuming normal financing and the value of the lease is positive.

QUESTIONS

1. Why in a tax-oriented true lease can the lessee benefit from a lower leasing cost?
2. How does a single-investor lease differ from a leveraged lease?
3. Explain how a lessor expects to recover its investment in a full payout lease.
4. How does an operating lease differ from a full payout lease?
5. How is an operating lease treated for tax purposes?
6. How can a corporation that cannot currently use tax benefits associated with equipment ownership because it lacks currently taxable income or net operating loss carryforward benefits from leasing?
7. Why, if it were not for the different tax treatment for owning and leasing equipment, would the costs be identical in an efficient capital market?
8. Explain why the cost of a true lease depends on the size of the transaction and whether the lease is tax-oriented or non-tax-oriented.
9. A frequently cited advantage for leasing is that it conserves working capital. The validity of this advantage for financially sound firms during normal economic conditions is questionable. Explain why.
10. Why do chief financial officers generally prefer that lease agreements be structured as an operating lease for financial accounting purposes?
11. Critically evaluate the claim that by leasing, a corporation can avoid the risk of obsolescence of equipment and the risk of disposal of the equipment.
12. Who are corporate lessors?
13. Explain the role of lease brokers and financial advisers in a lease transaction.
14. a. What is a master lease?
    b. What is a sale-and-leaseback transaction?
15. a. For financial reporting purposes, what determines if a lease is treated as an operating lease or capital lease?
    b. If a lease for equipment that has a 15-year expected economic life has a lease term of two years, how will the lease be treated for financial reporting purposes?

c. If a lease for equipment allows the lessee to buy the equipment at the end of the lease term for $1, how will the lease be treated for financial reporting purposes?

16. For tax reporting purposes, explain why a purchase option based on fair market value rather than a nominal purchase option is a strong indication of intent to create a lease rather than a conditional sale lease.

17. Explain why when structuring a tax-oriented lease transaction, corporations requiring the use of equipment will seek to have the lease treated as an operating lease for financial reporting purposes but as a true lease for tax purposes.

18. What is a synthetic lease?

19. The Mishthosi Company is considering the acquisition of a machine that costs $50,000 if bought today. The company can buy or lease the machine. If it buys the machine, the machine would be depreciated as a 3-year MACRS asset and is expected to have a salvage value of $1,000 at the end of the 5-year useful life. If leased, the lease payments are $12,000 each year for four years, payable at the beginning of each year. The marginal tax rate of Mishthosi is 30% and its cost of capital is 10%. Assume that the lease is a net lease, that any tax benefits are realized in the year of the expense, and that there is no investment tax credit.

MACRS rates of depreciation on a 3-year asset are:

Year	Rate
1	33.33%
2	44.45%
3	14.81%
4	7.41%

a. Calculate the depreciation for each year in the case of the purchase of this machine.

b. Calculate the direct cash flows from leasing initially and for each of the five years.

c. Calculate the adjusted discount rate.

d. Calculate the value of the lease.

20. The Mietet Company is considering the acquisition of a machine that costs $1 million if bought today. The company can buy or lease the machine. If it buys the machine, the machine would be depreciated as a 3-year MACRS asset and is expected to have a salvage value of $10,000 at the end of the 5-year useful life. If leased, the lease payments are $250,000 each year for four years, payable at the beginning of each year. Mietet's marginal tax rate is 35% and the cost of capital is 12%. Use the MACRS rates as provided in Problem 1.

Assume that the lease is a net lease, that any tax benefits are realized in the year of the expense, and that there is no investment tax credit.

a. Calculate the depreciation for each year in the case of the purchase of this machine.

b. Calculate the direct cash flows from leasing initially and for each of the five years.

c. Calculate the adjusted discount rate.

d. Calculate the value of the lease.

21. The Rendilegping Company is considering the acquisition of a machine that costs $100,000 if bought today. The company can buy or lease the machine. If it buys the machine, the machine would be depreciated as a 3-year MACRS asset and is expected to have a salvage value of $5,000 at the end of the 5-year useful life. If leased, the lease payments are $24,000 each year for four years, payable at the beginning of each year. The marginal tax rate of the Rendilegping Company is 30% and the cost of capital is 15%. Use the MACRS rates as provided in Question 19 and assume that the lease is a net lease, that any tax benefits are realized in the year of the expense, and that there is no investment tax credit.

a. Calculate the depreciation for each year in the case of the purchase of this machine.

b. Calculate the direct cash flows from leasing initially and for each of the five years.

c. Calculate the adjusted discount rate.

d. Calculate the value of the lease.

e. Calculate the amortization of the equivalent loan.

22. The Arrende Corporation is considering the acquisition of a machine that costs $73,000 if bought today. The company can buy or lease the machine. If it buys the machine, the machine would be depreciated using the straight-line method, depreciating the full asset cost over five years, and is expected to have a salvage value of $2,000 at the end of the 5-year useful life. If leased, the lease payments are $17,500 each year for four years, payable at the beginning of each year. Arrende's marginal tax rate is 38% and the appropriate cost of capital is 10%. Assume that the lease is a net lease, that any tax benefits are realized in the year of the expense, and that there is no investment tax credit.

a. Calculate the depreciation for each year in the case of the purchase of this machine.

b. Calculate the direct cash flows from leasing initially and for each of the five years.

c. Calculate the adjusted discount rate.

d. Calculate the value of the lease.

e. Calculate the amortization of the equivalent loan.

CHAPTER 28

Project Financing

Structured financing is a debt obligation that is backed by the value of an asset or credit support provided by a third party. In Chapter 26 we described one form of structured finance transaction—asset securitization. The key in an asset securitization is to remove the assets (i.e., loans and receivables) from the balance sheet of an entity. Recall that the special purpose vehicle (SPV) is the entity that acquires the asset and sells the securities to purchase the assets.[1] Structured finance is also used by corporations to fund major projects so that the lenders look to the cash flow from the project being financed rather than corporation or corporations seeking funding. This financing technique is called *project financing* (or *project finance*) and uses the SPV to accomplish its financing objectives. Both project financing and asset securitization use SPVs, yet project financing involves cash flows from operating assets, whereas asset securitization involves cash flows from financial assets, such loans or as receivables.

Industries engaged in the production, processing, transportation or use of energy have been particularly attracted to project financing techniques because of the needs of such companies for new capital sources. Enterprises located in countries privatizing state-owned companies have made extensive use of project financing.

In this chapter we look at the basic features of project financing. Discussions associated with project financing tend to focus on large complex projects. This might lead one to the conclusion that the project financing principles discussed in this chapter have little application to smaller, more ordinary financings. This is not the case. The same principles used to finance a major pipeline, copper mine, or a power plant can be used to finance a cannery, a hotel, a ship, or a processing plant.

---

[1] Another name for the SPV is the special purpose entity, or SPE.

The use of project financing, and the use of an SPV to accomplish it, have been under attack by the press and some legislative leaders. This attack is the result of the bankruptcy of Enron in 2002. Enron used project financing in a manner that made little economic sense and purely as a means for avoiding disclosing information to shareholders and creditors. At the end of this chapter, we discuss the impact of Enron's bankruptcy on the use of project financing by corporations.

WHAT IS PROJECT FINANCING?

Although the term "project financing" has been used to describe all types of financing of projects, both with and without recourse, the term has evolved in recent years to have a more precise definition:

> A financing of a particular economic unit in which a lender is satisfied to look initially to the cash flows and earnings of that economic unit as the source of funds from which a loan will be repaid and to the assets of the economic unit as collateral for the loan.[2]

A key word in the definition is "initially." While a lender may be willing to look initially to the cash flows of a project as the source of funds for repayment of the loan, the lender must also feel comfortable that the loan will in fact be paid on a worst case basis. This may involve undertakings or direct or indirect guarantees by third parties who are motivated in some way to provide such guarantees.

Project financing has great appeal when it does not have a substantial impact on the balance sheet or the creditworthiness of the sponsoring entity. Boards of directors are receptive to proceeding with projects which can be very highly leveraged or financed entirely or substantially on their own merits.

The moving party in a project is its *promoter* or *sponsor*. A project may have one or several sponsors. The motivation of construction companies acting as sponsors is to profit in some way from the construction or operation of the project. The motivation of operating companies for sponsoring a project may be simply to make a profit from selling the product produced by the project. In many instances the motivation for the project is to provide processing or distribution of a basic product of the sponsor or to ensure a source of supply vital to the sponsor's business.

---

[2] Peter K. Nevitt and Frank J. Fabozzi, *Project Financing: Seventh Edition* (London: Euromoney, 2001), p. 1.

The ultimate goal in project financing is to arrange a borrowing for a project which will benefit the sponsor and at the same time be completely non-recourse to the sponsor, in no way affecting its credit standing or balance sheet. One way this can be accomplished is by using the credit of a third party to support the transaction. Such a third party then becomes a sponsor. However, projects are rarely financed independently on their own merits without credit support from sponsors who are interested as third parties and who will benefit in some way from the project.

There is considerable room for disagreement between lenders and borrowers as to what constitutes a feasible project financing. Borrowers prefer their projects to be financed independently off-balance sheet with appropriate disclosures in financial reports indicating the exposure of the borrower to a project financing. Lenders, on the other hand, are not in the venture capital business. They are not equity risk takers. Lenders want to feel secure that they are going to be repaid either by the project, the sponsor, or an interested third party. Therein lies the challenge of most project financings.

The key to a successful project financing is structuring the financing of a project with as little recourse as possible to the sponsor while at the same time providing sufficient credit support through guarantees or undertakings of a sponsor or third party, so that lenders will be satisfied with the credit risk.

There is a popular misconception that project financing means off-balance sheet financing to the point that the project is completely self-supporting without guarantees or undertakings by financially responsible parties. This leads to misunderstandings by prospective borrowers who are under the impression that certain kinds of projects may be financed as stand-alone, self-supporting project financings and, therefore, proceed on the assumption that similar projects in which they are interested can be financed without recourse to the sponsor, be off-balance sheet to the sponsor, and be without any additional credit support from a financially responsible third party.

It would be a happy circumstance if it were possible simply to arrange a 100% loan for a project (non-recourse to sponsors) which looked as though it would surely be successful on the basis of optimistic financial projections. Unfortunately, this is not the case. There is no magic about project financing. Such a financing can be accomplished by financial engineering which combines the undertakings and various kinds of guarantees by parties interested in a project being built in such a way that none of the parties alone has to assume the full credit responsibility for the project, yet when all the undertakings are combined and reviewed together, the equivalent of a satisfactory credit risk for lenders has resulted.

REASONS FOR JOINTLY OWNED OR SPONSORED PROJECTS

There has been an increasing trend towards jointly owned or controlled projects. Although most corporations prefer sole ownership and control of a major project, particularly projects involving vital supplies and distribution channels, there are factors that encourage the formation of jointly owned or controlled projects that consist of partners with mutual goals, talents, and resources. These factors include:[3]

- The undertaking is beyond a single corporation's financial and/or managerial resources.
- The partners have complementary skills.
- Economics of a large project lower the cost of the product or service substantially over the possible cost of a smaller project if the partners proceeded individually.
- The risks of the projects are shared.
- One or more of the partners can use the tax benefits (i.e., depreciation and any tax credit).
- Greater debt leverage can be obtained.

The joint sponsors will select the legal form of the SPV (corporation, partner, limited partnership, limited liability company, contractual joint venture, or trust) that will be satisfy their tax and legal objectives.

CREDIT EXPOSURES IN A PROJECT FINANCING

To place a project financing into perspective, it is helpful to review the different credit exposures that occur at different times in the course of a typical project financing.

Risk Phases

Project financing risks can be divided into three time frames in which the elements of credit exposure assume different characteristics:

- engineering and construction phase
- start-up phase
- operations according to planned specifications

---

[3] Nevitt and Fabozzi, *Project Financing, Seventh Edition*, p. 265.

Different guarantees and undertakings of different partners may be used in each time frame to provide the credit support necessary for structuring a project financing.

Engineering and Construction Phase

Projects generally begin with a long period of planning and engineering. Equipment is ordered, construction contracts are negotiated, and actual construction begins. After commencement of construction, the amount at risk begins to increase sharply as funds are advanced to purchase material, labor, and equipment. Interest charges on loans to finance construction also begin to accumulate.

Start-Up Phase

Project lenders do not regard a project as completed on conclusion of the construction of the facility. They are concerned that the plant or facility will work at the costs and to the specifications which were planned when arranging the financing. Failure to produce the product or service in the amounts and at the costs originally planned means that the projections and the feasibility study are incorrect and that there may be insufficient cash to service debt and pay expenses.

Project lenders regard a project as acceptable only after the plant or facility has been in operation for a sufficient period of time to ensure that the plant will in fact produce the product or service at the price, in the amounts, and to the standards assumed in the financial plan which formed the basis for the financing. This start-up risk period may run from a few months to several years.

Operations According to Specification

Once the parties are satisfied that the plant is running to specification, the final operating phase begins. During this phase, the project begins to function as a regular operating company. If correct financial planning was done, revenues from the sale of the product produced or service performed should be sufficient to service debt—interest and principal—pay operating costs, and provide a return to sponsors and investors.

Different Lenders for Different Risk Periods

Some projects are financed from beginning to end with a single lender or single group of lenders. However, most large projects employ different lenders or groups of lenders during different risk phases. This is because of the different risks involved as the project facility progresses through construction to operation, and the different ability of lenders to cope with and accept such risks.

Some lenders like to lend for longer terms and some prefer short-term lending. Some lenders specialize in construction lending and are equipped to monitor engineering and construction of a project, some are not. Some lenders will accept and rely on guarantees of different sponsors during the construction, start-up or operation phases, and some will not. Some lenders will accept the credit risk of a turn-key operating project, but are not interested in the high-risk lending during construction and start-up.

Interest rates will also vary during the different risk phases of project financing and with different credit support from sponsors during those time periods.

Short-term construction lenders are very concerned about the availability of long-term "take out" financing by other lenders upon completion of the construction or start-up phase. Construction lenders live in fear of providing their own unplanned take out financing. Consequently, from the standpoint of the construction lender, take out financing should be in place at the outset of construction financing.

KEY ELEMENTS OF A SUCCESSFUL PROJECT FINANCING

There are several elements that both sponsors and lenders to a project financing should review in order to increase the likelihood that a project financing will be successful. The key ones are listed below:[4]

- A satisfactory feasibility study and financial plan should be prepared with realistic assumptions regarding future inflation rates and interest rates.
- The cost of product or raw materials to be used by the project is assured.
- A supply of energy at reasonable cost has been assured.
- A market exists for the product, commodity, or service to be produced.
- Transportation is available at a reasonable cost to move the product to the market.
- Adequate communications are available.
- Building materials are available at the costs contemplated.
- The contractor is experienced and reliable.
- The operator is experienced and reliable.
- Management personnel are experienced and reliable.
- Untested technology is not involved.

---

[4] Nevitt and Fabozzi, *Project Financing, Seventh Edition*, p. 7.

- The contractual agreement among joint venture partners, if any, is satisfactory.
- The key sponsors have made an adequate equity contribution.
- Satisfactory appraisals of resources and assets have been obtained.
- Adequate insurance coverage is contemplated.
- The risk of cost overruns have been addressed.
- The risk of delay has been considered.
- The project will have an adequate return for the equity investor.
- Environmental risks are manageable.

When the project involves a sovereign entity, the following critical elements are important to consider to ensure the success of a project:

- A stable and friendly political environment exists; licences and permits are available; contracts can be enforced; legal remedies exist.
- There is no risk of expropriation.
- Country risk is satisfactory.
- Sovereign risk is satisfactory.
- Currency and foreign exchange risks have been addressed.
- Protection from criminal activities such as kidnaping and extortion.
- Existence of a commercial legal system protecting property and contractual rights.

CAUSES FOR PROJECT FAILURES

The best way to appreciate the concerns of lenders to a project is to review and consider some of the common causes for project failures, which include the following:[5]

- Delay in completion, with consequential increase in the interest expense on construction financing and delay in the contemplated revenue flow
- Capital cost overrun
- Technical failure
- Financial failure of the contractor
- Uninsured casualty losses
- Increased price or shortages of raw material
- Technical obsolescence of the plant or equipment
- Loss of competitive position in the marketplace

---

[5] Nevitt and Fabozzi, *Project Financing, Seventh Edition*, p. 2.

■ Poor management
■ Overly optimistic appraisals of the value of pledged security, such as oil and gas reserves

In addition, for projects in a foreign country, the following are causes for project failures:

■ Government interference
■ Expropriation
■ Financial insolvency of the host government

For a project financing to be successfully achieved, these risks must be properly considered, monitored, and avoided throughout the life of the project.

CREDIT IMPACT OBJECTIVE

While the sponsor or sponsors of a project financing ideally would prefer that the project financing be a non-recourse borrowing which does not in any way affect its credit standing or balance sheet, many project financings are aimed at achieving some other particular credit impact objective, such as any one or several of the following:[6]

■ To avoid being shown on the face of the balance sheet
■ To avoid being shown as debt on the face of the balance sheet so as not to impact financial ratios
■ To avoid being shown in a particular footnote to the balance sheet
■ To avoid being within the scope of restrictive covenants in an indenture or loan agreement which precludes direct debt financing or leases for the project
■ To avoid being considered as a cash obligation which would dilute interest coverage ratios, and affect the sponsor's credit standing with the rating services
■ To limit direct liability to a certain period of time such as during construction and/or the start-up period, so as to avoid a liability for the remaining life of the project
■ To keep the project off-balance sheet during construction and/or until the project generates revenues

---

[6] Nevitt and Fabozzi, *Project Financing, Seventh Edition*, p. 4.

Any one or a combination of these objectives maybe sufficient reason for a borrower to seek the structure of a project financing.

Liability for project debt for a limited time period may be acceptable in situations in which liability for such debt is unacceptable for the life of the project. Where a sponsor cannot initially arrange long-term non-recourse debt for its project that will not impact its balance sheet, the project may still be feasible if the sponsor is willing to assume the credit risk during the construction and start-up phase, and provided lenders are willing to shift the credit risk to the project after the project facility is completed and operating. Under such an arrangement, most of the objectives of an off-balance sheet project financing and limited credit impact can be achieved after the initial risk period of construction and start-up. In some instances, the lenders may be satisfied to rely on revenue produced by unconditional take-or-pay contracts from users of the product or services to be provided by the project to repay debt.[7] In other instances, the condition of the market for the product or service may be such that sufficient revenues are assured after completion of construction and start-up so as to convince lenders to rely on such revenues for repayment of their debts.

ACCOUNTING CONSIDERATIONS

Project financing is sometimes called off-balance sheet financing. However, while the project debt may not be on the sponsor's balance sheet, the project debt will appear on the face of the project balance sheet. In any event, the purpose of a project financing is to segregate the credit risk of the project in order that the credit risk of lending to either the sponsor or the project can be clearly and fairly appraised on their respective merits. The purpose is *not* to hide or conceal a liability of the sponsor from creditors, rating agencies, or stockholders.

Significant undertakings of sponsors and investors in projects subject to the Financial Accounting Standards Board must usually be shown in footnotes to their financial statements if not in the statements themselves.

---

[7] A *take-or-pay contract* is a long-term contract to make periodic payments over the life of the contract in certain minimum amounts as payments for a service or a product. The payments are in an amount sufficient to service the debt needed to finance the project which provides the services or the product and to pay operating expenses of the project. The obligation to make minimum payments is unconditional and must be paid whether or not the service or product is actually furnished or delivered. In contrast, a *take-and-pay contract* is a contact in which payment is contingent upon delivery and the obligation to pay is not unconditional.

Because project financings are concerned with balance sheet accounting treatment, familiarity with accounting terms used to describe or rationalize balance sheet reporting is important. Terms such as contingent liability, indirect liability, deferred liability, deferred expense, fixed charges, equity accounting, and materiality are used to rationalize the appropriate positioning of entries in a sponsor's financial statements and footnotes. Accounting rules for reporting these types of liabilities are under continual review, as the accounting profession grapples with the problem of proper and fair disclosure and presentation of objective information to stockholders, lenders, rating agencies, guarantors, government agencies, and other concerned parties.[8]

MEETING INTERNAL RETURN OBJECTIVES

As explained in Chapter 13, corporations set target rates of return for new capital investments. If a proposed capital expenditure will not generate a return greater than a company's target rate, it is not regarded as a satisfactory use of capital resources. This is particularly true when a company can make alternative capital expenditures which will produce a return on capital in excess of the target rate.

Project financing can sometimes be used to improve the return on the capital invested in a project by leveraging the investment to a greater extent than would be possible in a straight commercial financing of the project. This can be accomplished by locating other parties interested in getting the project built, and shifting some of the debt coverage to such parties through direct or indirect guarantees. An example would be an oil company with a promising coal property which it did not wish to develop because of better alternative uses of its capital. By bringing in a company which required the coal, such as a public utility, an indirect guarantee might be available in the form of a long-term take-or-pay contract which would support long-term debt to finance the construction of the coal mine. This, in turn, would permit the oil company's investment to be highly leveraged and consequently to produce a much higher rate of return.

---

[8] On June 28, 2002, the Financial Accounting Standards Board (FASB) issued an exposure draft of a proposed interpretation of Accounting Research Bulletin No. 51, "Consolidation of Certain Special-Purpose Entities." This exposure draft, which is subject to public comment, is an attempt to clarify the issue of whether to consolidate special purpose entities within the sponsor company's financial statements.

OTHER BENEFITS OF A PROJECT FINANCING

There are often other side benefits resulting from segregating a financing as a project financing which may have a bearing on the motives of the company seeking such a structure. These benefits include:[9]

- Credit sources may be available to the project that would not be available to the sponsor.
- Guarantees may be available to the project that would not be available to the sponsor.
- A project financing may enjoy better credit terms and interest costs in situations in which a sponsor's credit is weak.
- Higher leverage of debt to equity may be achieved.
- Legal requirements applicable to certain investing institutions may be met by the project but not by the sponsor.
- Regulatory problems affecting the sponsor may be avoided.
- For regulatory purposes, costs may be clearly segregated as a result of a project financing.
- Construction financing costs may not be reflected in the sponsor's financial statements until such time as the project begins producing revenue.

In some instances, any one of the reasons stated above may be the primary motivation for structuring a new operation as a project financing.

TAX CONSIDERATIONS

Tax benefits from any applicable tax credits, depreciation deductions, interest deductions, depletion deductions, research and development tax deductions, dividends-received credits, foreign tax credits, capital gains, and non-capital start-up expenses are very significant considerations in the investment, debt service, and cash flow of most project financings. Care must be used in structuring a project financing to make sure that these tax benefits are used. Where a project financing is housed in a new entity that does not have taxes to shelter, it is important to structure the project financing so that any tax benefits can be transferred to parties in a position currently able to use such tax benefits.

For U.S. federal income tax purposes, 80% control is required for tax consolidation, except in the case of certain foreign subsidiaries, in which 50% control may require consolidation.

---

[9] Nevitt and Fabozzi, *Project Financing, Seventh Edition,* p. 6.

DISINCENTIVES TO PROJECT FINANCING

Project financings are complex. The documentation tends to be complicated, and the cost of borrowing funds may be higher than conventional financing. If the undertakings of a number of parties are necessary to structure the project financing, or if a joint venture is involved, the negotiation of the original financing agreements and operating agreements will require patience, forbearing, and understanding. Decision making in partnerships and joint ventures is never easy, since the friendliest of partners may have diverse interests, problems, and objectives. However, the rewards and advantages of a project financing will often justify the special problems that may arise in structuring and operating the project.

ENRON'S EFFECT ON PROJECT FINANCING

Because of Enron's use of project financing, concerns have been expressed over the use of this method of financing. Unfortunately, attacks on project financing that were reported in the press and concerns expressed by members of Congress simply failed to recognize that what Enron did had very little to do with traditional project financing. Enron used partnerships as its legal entity in project financing and these partnerships had little of the characteristics of a project financing described in this chapter. Instead, according to Barry Gold, a managing director at Salomon Smith Barney, the project financings used by Enron were an "attempt to unduly benefit from accounting, tax, and disclosure requirements and definitions."[10]

In a project financing, there is transparency about the economics of the project. The project lenders are well informed of the risks and are furnished the financial projections and economic analysis along with the assumptions. In general, there is more information provided in a project financing than there is in a typical corporate bond prospectus. All parties to a project financing can perform due diligence and raise questions with the sponsor. In contrast, in the project financings of Enron, the firm's shareholders and creditor did not have enough information to undertake due diligence.

While project financing as discussed in this chapter had nothing to do with the use of off-balance sheet SPVs utilized by Enron, there have been some changes in the market. As a result of the Enron bankruptcy, major corporate users of project financing are providing even more disclosure

---

[10] Henry A. Davis, "How Enron Has Affected Project Finance," *The Journal of Structured and Project Finance* (Spring 2002), p. 19.

about projects.[11] What management will want to be sure of is that any project financings that are treated as off-balance sheet are truly non-recourse to the sponsor. If there is potential recourse to the sponsor that may be significant in nature, management should report the project financing on the balance sheet. That is, the debt of the project should be treated as a liability and the value of the project should be treated as an asset.

In concluding his analysis of the use of project finance after Enron, Henry Davis, managing editor of *The Journal of Structured and Project Finance*, writes:

> ... project finance is alive and well. We just need to remind a few people of its basic fundamentals. Neither project finance nor sensible innovations in structured finance with sound, well-explained business reasons have been shaken by Enron. The principal lessons learned from the Enron debacle have to do with transparency and disclosure. When some of your businesses or your financing structures become hard to explain, you may begin to question whether they make sense in the first place.[12]

SUMMARY

- In a project financing or project finance, lenders initially look to the cash flow from the project being financed rather than the corporation or corporations seeking funding. The moving party in a project is its *promoter* or *sponsor*.
- The ultimate goal in project financing is to arrange a borrowing for a project which will benefit the sponsor and, at the same time, be completely non-recourse to the sponsor, in no way affecting its credit standing or balance sheet. This can be accomplished by using the credit of a third party to support the transaction. However, projects are typically not financed independently on their own merits without credit support from sponsors who are interested third parties who will benefit in some way from the project.
- Although most corporations prefer sole ownership and control of a major project, there are several factors that encourage the formation of jointly owned or controlled projects. Joint sponsors will select the legal form of the SPV that will satisfy their tax and legal objectives.

---

[11] Davis, "How Enron Has Affected Project Finance."
[12] Davis, "How Enron Has Affected Project Finance," p. 25.

■ There are three time frames that are associated with the risk of a project financing: (1) engineering and construction phase, (2) start-up phase, and (3) operations according to planned specifications. Different guarantees and undertakings of different partners may be used in each time frame to provide the credit support necessary for structuring a project financing. Most large projects employ different lenders or groups of lenders because of the different risks involved as the project facility progresses through construction to operation, and the different ability of lenders to cope with and accept such risks.

■ For a project financing to be successfully achieved, the risks associated with a project must be understood and monitored throughout the life of the project.

QUESTIONS

1. What types of industries have been engaged in project financing?
2. Why do lenders in a project financing look very closely at the project's expected cash flows?
3. Comment on the following statement: "The sole purpose of a project financing is to provide the sponsors with off-balance sheet financing."
4. What are the advantages of a jointly sponsored project financing?
5. The key to a project financing is to finance a project with as little recourse to the sponsor as possible. Explain why.
6. Comment on the following statement: "Project financing means off-balance sheet financing to the point that the project is completely self-supporting without guarantees or undertakings by financially responsible parties."
7. What types of risk are associated with the following phases of a project financing:
   a. engineering and construction phase?
   b. start-up phase?
   c. operations according to planned specifications?
8. For most large projects there are different lenders or groups of lenders during different risk phases. Explain why.
9. What is the concern of short-term construction lenders to a project financing?
10. Identify some important factors that a company considering a project financing in another country should consider.
11. Identify some of the common causes for project failures.
12. What are some of the ways that a project financing can be used to improve the return on the capital invested in a project?

13. Identify some of the motives for a project financing.
14. Comment on the following statement: "Enron Corporation used project financing and got itself into a lot of trouble. Enron is a perfect example of why project financing and special purpose vehicles should not be used by reputable firms."

CHAPTER 29

Strategy and Financial Planning

A business that maximizes its owners' wealth allocates its resources efficiently, resulting in an efficient allocation of resources for society as a whole. Owners, employees, customers, and anyone else who has a stake in the business enterprise are all better off when its managers make decisions that maximize the value of the firm.

Just as there may be alternative routes to a destination, there may be alternative ways to maximize owners' wealth. A *strategy* is a sense of how to reach an objective such as maximizing wealth. And just as some routes may get you where you are going faster, some strategies may be better than others.

Suppose a firm has decided it has an advantage over its competitors in marketing and distributing its products in the global market. The firm's strategy may be to expand into European market, followed by an expansion into the Asian market. Once the firm has its strategy, it needs a plan, in particular the *strategic plan,* which is the set of actions the firm intends to use to follow its strategy.

The investment opportunities that enable the firm to follow its strategy comprise the firm's *investment strategy.* The firm may pursue its strategy of expanding into European and Asian markets by either establishing itself or acquiring businesses already in these markets. This is where capital budgeting analysis comes in: We evaluate the possible investment opportunities to see which ones, if any, provide a return greater than necessary for the investment's risk. And let's not forget the investment in working capital, the resources the firm needs to support its day-to-day operations.

Suppose as a result of evaluating whether to establish or acquire businesses, our firm decides it is better—in terms of maximizing the value of the firm—to acquire selected European businesses. The next step is to figure out how it is going to *pay* for these acquisitions. The financial managers must make sure that the firm has sufficient funds to meet its operating needs, as well as its investment needs. This is where the firm's *financing strategy* enters the picture. Where should the funds needed come from? What is the precise timing of the needs for funds? To answer these questions, working capital management (in particular, short-term financing) and the capital structure decision (the mix of long-term sources of financing) enters the picture.

When managers look at the firm's investment decisions and consider how to finance them, they are budgeting. *Budgeting* is mapping out the sources and uses of funds for future periods. Budgeting requires both economic analysis (including forecasting) and accounting. Economic analysis includes both marketing and production analysis to develop forecasts of future sales and costs. Accounting techniques are used as a measurement device: but instead of using accounting to summarize what has happened (its common use), in budgeting firms use accounting to represent what we expect to happen in the future. The process is summarized in Exhibit 29.1

EXHIBIT 29.1   The Firm's Planning Process

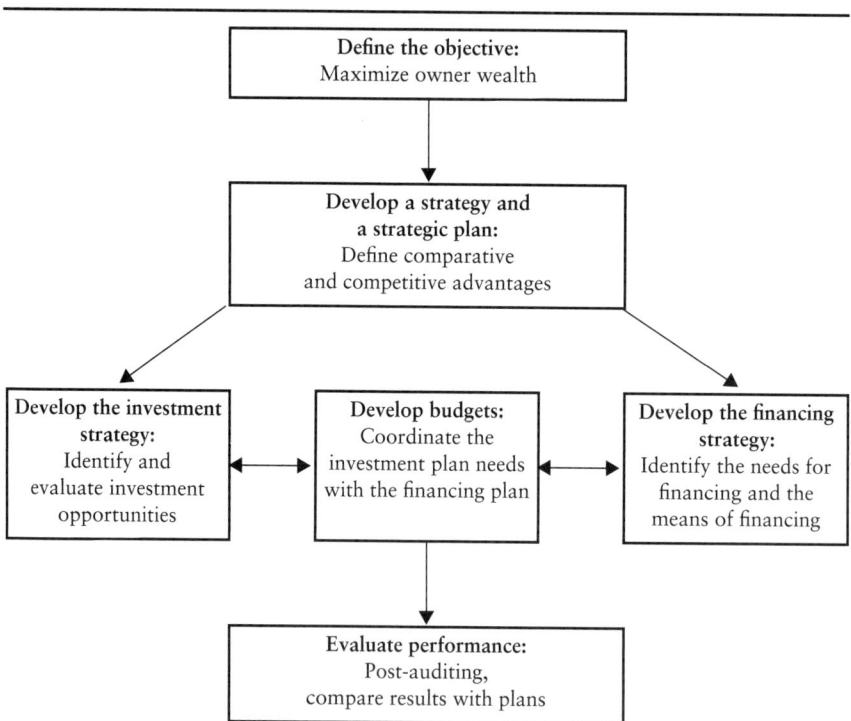

Once these plans are put into effect, they must compare what happens with what was planned. This is referred to as *post-auditing*, which firms use to:

- evaluate the performance of management,
- analyze any deviations of actual results from planned results, and
- evaluate the planning process to determine just how good it is.

STRATEGY

"Whilst every man is free to employ his capital where he pleases, he will naturally seek for it that employment which is most advantageous; he will naturally be dissatisfied with a profit of 10 per cent, if by removing his capital he can obtain a profit of 15 per cent."
David Ricardo, *The Principles of Political Economy and Taxation* (London, 1817).

The way to create wealth from investments is to invest in projects that have positive net present values. But where do these positive net present values come from? From the firm's comparative advantage or its competitive advantages.

Comparative and Competitive Advantages

A *comparative advantage* is the advantage one firm has over others in terms of the cost of producing or distributing goods or services. For example, Wal-Mart Stores, Inc. had for years a comparative advantage over its competitors (such as K Mart) through its vast network of warehouses and its distribution system. Wal-Mart invested in a system of regional warehouses and its own trucking system. Combined with bulk purchases and a unique customer approach (such as its "greeters"), Wal-Mart's comparative advantages in its warehousing and distribution systems helped it grow to be a major (and very profitable) retailer in a very short span of time. However, as with most comparative advantages, it took competitors a few years to catch up and for Wal-Mart's advantage to disappear.

A *competitive advantage* is the advantage one firm has over another because of the structure of the markets, input and output markets, they both operate in. For example, one firm may have a competitive advantage due to barriers to other firms entering the same market. This happens in the case of governmental regulations that limit the number of firms in a market, as with banks, or in the case of governmental granted monopolies. A firm itself may create barriers to entry (although with the help of the government) that include patents and trademarks. NutraSweet Company, a unit of Monsanto Company, had the exclusive patent on the artificial sweetener, aspartame, which it marketed under the brand name, NutraSweet. However, this patent expired December 14, 1992. The loss of the monopoly on the artificial sweetener reduced the price of aspartame from $70 per pound to $20–35 per pound, since other firms could produce and sell aspartame products starting December 15, 1992.[1,2]

NutraSweet had a competitive advantage as long as it had the patent. But as soon this patent expired, this competitive advantage was lost and competitors were lining up to enter the market.

Only by having some type of advantage can a firm invest in something and get more back in return. So first you have to figure out where your firm has a comparative or competitive advantage before you can determine your firm's strategy.

Strategy and Owners' Wealth Maximization

Often firms conceptualize a strategy in terms of the consumers of the firm's goods and services. For example, you may have a strategy to become the world's leading producer of microcomputer chips by producing the best quality chip or by producing chips at the lowest cost, developing a cost (and price) advantage over your competitors. So your focus is on product quality and cost. Is this strategy in conflict with maximizing owners' wealth? No.

To maximize owners' wealth, we focus on the returns and risks of future cash flows to the firm's owners. And we look at a project's net present value when we make decisions regarding whether or not to invest in it. A strategy of gaining a competitive or comparative advantage is consistent with maximizing shareholder wealth. This is because projects with positive net present value arise when the firm has a competitive or comparative advantage over other firms.

Suppose a new piece of equipment is expected to generate a return greater than what is expected for the project's risk (its cost of capital). But how can a firm create value simply by investing in a piece of equipment? How can it maintain a competitive advantage? If investing in this equipment can create value, wouldn't the firm's competitors also want this equipment? Of course—if they could use it to create value, they would surely be interested in it.

---

[1] Lois Therrien, Patrick Oster, and Chuck Hawkins, "How Sweet It Isn't At Nutra-Sweet," *Business Week* (December 14, 1992), p. 42.
[2] Monsanto sold its sweetener division in 2000.

Now suppose that the firm's competitors face no barriers to buying the equipment and exploiting its benefits. What will happen? The firm and its competitors will compete for the equipment, bidding up its price. When does it all end? When the net present value of the equipment is zero.

Now suppose instead that the firm has a patent on the new piece of equipment and can thus keep its competitors from exploiting the equipment's benefits. Then there would be no competition for the equipment and the firm would be able to exploit it to increase its owners' wealth.

Consider an example where trying to gain a comparative advantage went wrong. Schlitz Brewing Company attempted to reduce its costs to gain an advantage over its competitors: It reduced its labor costs and shortened the brewing cycle. Reducing costs allow it to reduce its prices below competitors' prices. But product quality suffered—so much that Schlitz lost market share, instead of gaining it.

Schlitz attempted to gain a comparative advantage, but was not true to a larger strategy to satisfy its customers—who apparently wanted quality beer more than they wanted cheap beer. And the loss of market share was reflected in Schlitz's declining stock price.[3]

Value can only be created when the firm has a competitive or comparative advantage. If a firm analyzes a project and determines that it has a positive net present value, the first question should be: Where did it come from?

FINANCIAL PLANNING AND BUDGETING

"As certainly as financial planning centers about commitments and utilization of capital, the protective function of management is also germane to the process. This function comprehends the integrity of capital, the profitable survival of the business entity, and the safe-guarding of the rights of the capital contributors," Paul M. Van Arsdell, *Corporation Finance* (New York: The Ronald Press Company, 1968), p. 550.

A strategy is the direction a firm takes to meet its objective. A strategic plan is how a firm intends to go in that direction. In financial management, a strategic investment plan includes policies to seek out possible investment opportunities: Do we spend more on research and development? Do we look globally? Do we attempt to increase market share?

A strategic plan also includes resource allocation. If a firm intends to expand, where does it get the capital to do so? If a firm requires more

---

[3] The case of Schlitz Brewing is detailed in George S. Day and Liam Fahey in "Putting Strategy into Shareholder Value Analysis," *Harvard Business Review* (March–April 1990), pp. 156–162.

capital, the timing, amount, and type of capital (whether equity or debt) comprise elements of a firm's financial strategic plan. These things must be planned to implement the strategy.

Financial planning allocates a firm's resources to achieve its investment objectives. Financial planning is important for several reasons.

First, financial planning helps managers assess the impact of a particular strategy on their firm's financial position, its cash flows, its reported earnings, and its need for external financing.

Second, by formulating financial plans, the firm's management is in a better position to react to any changes in market conditions, such as slower than expected sales, or unexpected problems, such as a reduction in the supply of raw materials. By constructing a financial plan, managers become more familiar with the sensitivity of the firm's cash flows and its financing needs to changes in sales or some other factor.

Third, creating a financial plan helps managers understand the tradeoffs inherent in its investment and financing plans. For example, by developing a financial plan, the financial manager is better able to understand the tradeoff that exists between having sufficient inventory to satisfy customer demands and the need to finance the investment in inventory.

Financial planning consists of the firm's investment and financing plans. Once we know the firm's investment plan, we need to figure out when funds are needed and where they will come from. We do this by developing a *budget*,[4] which is basically the firm's investment and financing plans expressed in dollar terms. A budget can represent details such as what to do with cash in excess of needs on a daily basis, or it can reflect broad statements of a firm's business strategy over the next decade. Exhibit 29.2 illustrates the budgeting process.

Budgeting for a short-term (less than a year) is usually referred to as *operational budgeting*; budgeting for the long-term (typically three to five years ahead) is referred to as *long-run planning* or *long-term planning*. But since long-term planning depends on what is done in the short-term, the operational budgeting and long-term planning are closely related.

The budgeting process involves putting together the financing and investment strategy into terms that allow the financial manager to determine what investments can be made and how these investments should be financed. In other words, budgeting pulls together decisions regarding capital budgeting, capital structure, and working capital. Managers prepare budgets by preparing financial statements that represent these decisions.

---

[4] The term "budget" originates from the French *bouge*, meaning a bag and its contents. We use the term budget to refer to the allocation of a firm's resources (in dollars) over future periods. The bag is therefore the firm; its contents are the firm's resources, its funds.

EXHIBIT 29.2   The Budgeting Process of a Firm

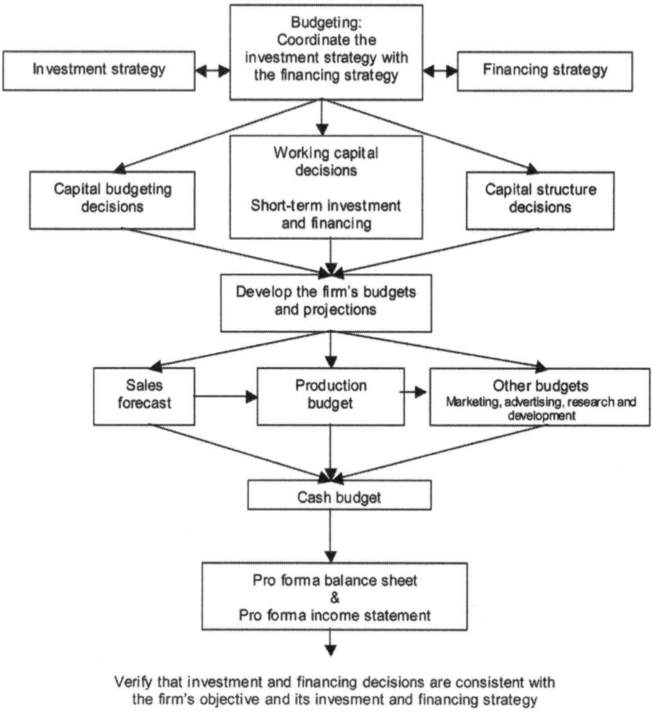

Verify that investment and financing decisions are consistent with
the firm's objective and its invesment and financing strategy

Consider Sears. Its store renovation plan is part of its overall strategy of regaining its share of the retail market by offering customers better quality and service. Fixing up its stores is seen as an investment strategy. Sears evaluates its renovation plan using capital budgeting techniques (e.g., net present value). But the renovation program requires financing—this is where the capital structure decision comes in. If it needs more funds, where do they come from? Debt? Equity? Both? And let's not forget the working capital decisions. As Sears' renovates its stores, will this change its need for cash on hand? Will the renovation affect inventory needs? If Sears expects to increase sales through this program, how will this affect its investment in accounts receivable? And what about short-term financing? Will Sears need more or less short-term financing when it renovates?

While Sears is undergoing a renovation program, it needs to estimate what funds it needs, in both the short-run and the long-run. This is where a cash budget and pro forma financial statements are useful. The starting point is generally a sales forecast, which is related closely to the purchasing, production, and other forecasts of the firm. What are Sears' expected sales in the short term? In the long term? Also, the amount that Sears expects to sell affects its purchases, sales personnel, and advertising forecasts. Putting together forecasts requires cooperation among Sears' marketing, purchasing, and financial management.

Once Sears has its sales and related forecasts, the next step is a cash budget, detailing the cash inflows and outflows each period. Once the cash budget is established, pro forma balance sheet and income statements can be constructed. Following this, Sears must verify that its budget is consistent with its objective and its strategies.

Budgeting generally begins four to six months prior to the end of the current fiscal period. Most firms have a set of procedures that must be followed in compiling the budget. The budget process is usually managed by either a Vice-President to Planning, the Director of the Budget, the Vice-President of Finance, the Chief Financial Officer, or the Corporate Controller. Each division or department provides its own budgets that are then merged into a firm's centralized budget by the manager of the budget.

A budget looks forward and backward. It identifies resources the firm will generate or need in the near- and long-term, and it serves as a measure of the current and past performance of departments, divisions, or individual managers. But we have to be careful when we measure deviations between budgeted and actual results. We must separately identify deviations that were controllable from deviations that were uncontrollable. For example, suppose we develop a budget expecting $10 million sales from a new product. If actual sales turn out to be $6 million, do we interpret this result as poor performance on the part of management? Maybe, maybe not. If the lower-than-expected sales are due to an unexpected downturn in the economy, probably not. But yes, if they are due to what turns out to be obviously poor management forecasts of consumer demand.

Sales Forecasting

Sales forecasts are an important part of financial planning. Inaccurate forecasts can result in shortages of inventory, inadequate short-term financing arrangements, and so on.

If a firm's sales forecast misses its mark, either understating or overstating sales, there are many potential problems. Consider Coleco Industries, which missed its mark. This company introduced a toy product in 1983, its Cabbage Patch doll, which enjoyed runaway popularity. In fact, this doll was so popular, that Coleco could not keep up with demand. It was in such demand and inventory so depleted that fights broke out in toy stores, some parents bribed store personnel to get scarce dolls just before Christmas, and fake dolls were being smuggled into the country.

Coleco missed its mark, significantly underestimating the demand for these dolls. While having a popular toy may seem like a dream for a toy manufacturer, this doll turned into a nightmare. With no Cabbage Patch dolls on the toy shelves, other toy manufacturers introduced dolls with similar (but not identical) features, capturing some of Coleco's market. Also, many consumers—the parents—became irate at Coleco's creating the demand for the toy through advertising, but not having sufficient dolls to satisfy the demand.

Coleco Industries tried but failed to introduce a toy as successful as the Cabbage Patch doll. It filed for bankruptcy in 1988, with most of its assets (including its Cabbage Patch doll line) sold to Hasbro Inc., a rival toy company. Hasbro was then acquired by Mattel, Inc. Cabbage Patch Dolls are experiencing a resurgence of interest, thanks to the increased marketing power of Mattel and a tie-in with the 1996 summer Olympics.

To predict cash flows we forecast sales which are uncertain because they are affected by future economic, industry, and market conditions. Nevertheless, we can usually assign meaningful degrees of uncertainty to our forecasts. We forecast sales in one of the following ways:

- regression analysis;
- market surveys; and
- opinions of management.

Forecasting with Regression

Regression is a statistical method that enables us to "fit" a straight line that on average represents the best possible graphical relationship between sales and time. This best "fit" is called the *regression line*. One way regression can be used is to simply extrapolate future sales based on the trend in past sales. In Exhibit 29.3, let's look at the sales of International Business Machines' sales over the period 1976 through 1999. During much of this period, sales increased each year, hence the sales trend is positive. If we were to connect each point representing sales and time, the result would look almost like a straight line that slopes upward. But we can't do much with an "almost" straight line. We need a straight line.

Let's simplify the regression against time by noting the years 1976, 1977, ..., 1999 as 1, 2, ..., 24. Regressing IBM's sales against time we estimate a regression line described as:

IBM annual sales, in billions = $14.67 + $3.00 × time

$\qquad\qquad\qquad\qquad\qquad\qquad\quad\uparrow\qquad\qquad\quad\uparrow$

$\qquad\qquad\qquad\qquad\qquad\quad$ Intercept of $\qquad$ Slope of
$\qquad\qquad\qquad\qquad\qquad\quad$ line with $\qquad\quad$ the line, in
$\qquad\qquad\qquad\qquad\qquad\quad$ vertical axis, $\qquad$ billions of
$\qquad\qquad\qquad\qquad\qquad\quad$ in billions $\qquad$ dollars per year

EXHIBIT 29.3   Sales of IBM

Panel a: Sales, 1976 through 1999

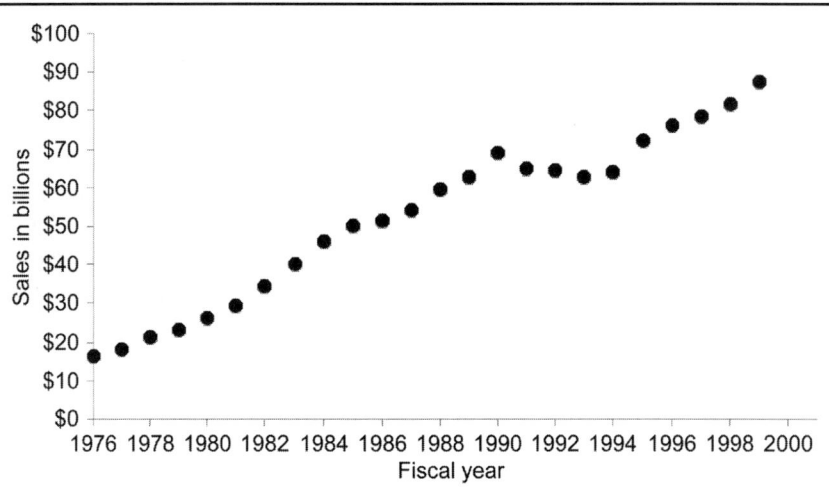

Panel b: Sales and Fitted Regression Line, 1976 through 1999

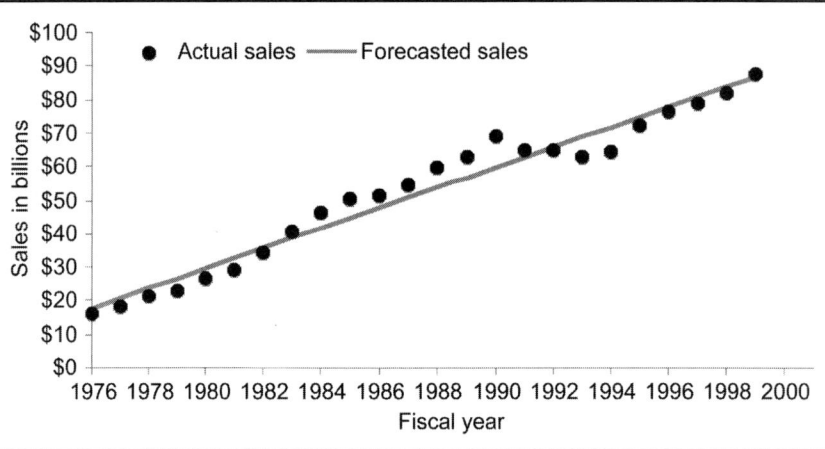

This line tells us that on average, from 1976 through 1999, IBM's sales increased $3.19 billion each year. This regression line is also plotted in Exhibit 29.3. You'll notice that the line intersects the vertical axis at $14.67 billion sales and has a slope (a rate of change in sales each year) of $3.00 billion.

EXHIBIT 29.3 (Continued)

Panel c: Actual Sales and Forecasted Sales for 2000 and 2001

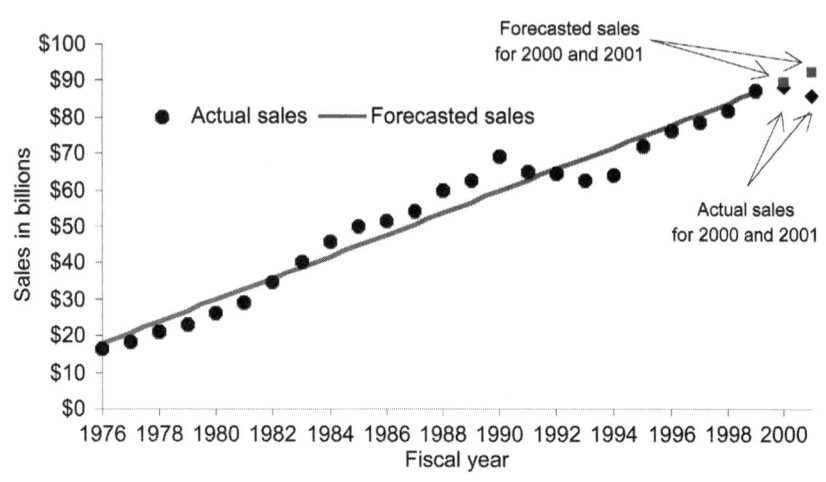

Source: IBM Annual Reports, various years

If we assume the current trend continues, we would predict sales to increase in 2000. Let 2000 be represented as time = 25, then

$$\text{IBM 2000 sales, in billions} = \$14.67 + \$3(25) = \$89.72$$

And for 2001 (time = 20):

$$\text{IBM 2001 sales, in billions} = \$14.67 + \$3(26) = \$92.76$$

The difference between what was forecasted and what actually occurred is the *forecast error.* Were actual 2000 and 2001 sales close to what we predicted? Not really: We have predicted higher sales than actually occurred.

	Actual Sales in Billions	Sales Predicted by Regression Line in Billions	Forecast Error in Billions
2000	$88.40	$89.72	−$1.32
2001	$85.87	$92.76	−$6.79

EXHIBIT 29.4   Sales and Capital Expenditures for IBM
Predicted Sales for 2000 and 2001, Based on Regression of Sales and Capital
Expenditures for 1976–1999

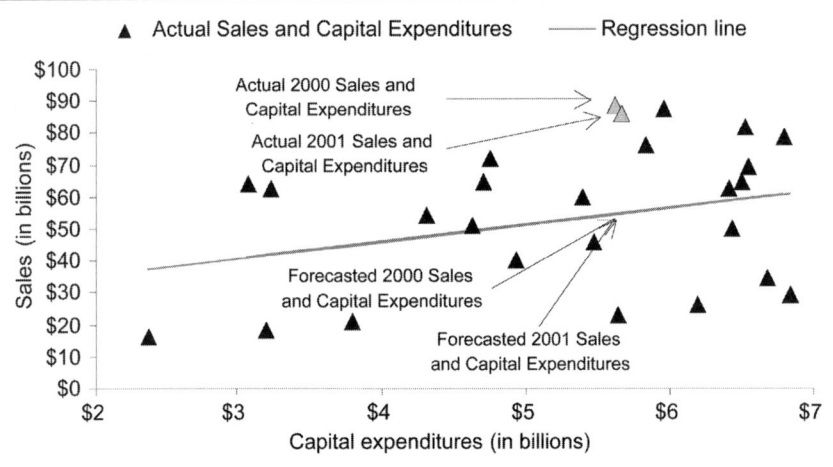

Source: IBM Annual Reports, various years

Predicted and actual 2000 and 2001 sales are shown in Exhibit 29.3, panel c. You'll notice that we overestimated sales. This illustrates a problem with regression analysis: Past trends do not always continue. Sales growth slowed in 2000 and 2001.

Another way of using regression is to look at the relation between two measures, say, sales and capital expenditures. Exhibit 29.4, which shows the relation between sales and capital expenditures for the period 1976 through 1999, indicates that the greater the capital expenditures, the greater IBM's sales. The straight line shown in this figure is the regression line, which represents the best summary of the relation between IBM's sales and capital expenditures from 1976 through 1999. Based on the relation between sales and capital expenditures during the 1976–1999 period and using actual capital expenditures for 2000 and 2001, we would have underestimated IBM's sales in these years using the regression:

Year	Actual Capital Expenditures	Predicted Sales	Actual Sales	Forecast Error
2000	$5.62 billion	$54.10 billion	$88.40 billion	$34.30 billion
2001	5.66 billion	54.33 billion	85.97 billion	31.64 billion

As you can see, we have forecast errors that are quite large relative to actual sales.

We also could look at the relation between IBM's sales and a number of factors, such as IBM's capital expenditures, a measure of economic activity such as Gross Domestic Product (GDP), and IBM's competitor's capital expenditures. Estimating the relation among these factors over a number of years, combined with forecasts of GDP and competitors' expenditures, we could predict IBM's sales for 1994. The more factors we include, the more accurate should be our predictions.

While regression analysis gives us what may seem to be a precise measure of the relationship among variables, there are a number of warnings that the financial manager must heed in using it:

- Using historical data to predict the future assumes that the past relationships will continue into the future, which is not always true.
- The period over which the regression is estimated may not be representative of the future. For example, data from a recessionary period of time will not tell much about a period that is predicted to be an economic boom.
- The reliability of the estimate is important: If there is a high degree of error in the estimate, the regression estimates may not be useful.
- The time period over which the regression is estimated may be too short to provide a basis for projecting long-term trends.
- The forecast of one variable may require forecasts of other variables. For example, you may be convinced that sales are affected by GDP and use regression to analyze this relationship. But to use regression to forecast sales, you must first forecast GDP. In this case, your forecast of sales is only as good as your forecast of GDP.

Market Surveys

Market surveys of customers can provide estimates of future revenues. In the case of IBM, we would need to focus on the computer industry and, specifically, on the personal computer, mini-computer, and mainframe computer markets. For each of these markets, we would have to assess IBM's market share and also the expected sales for each market. We should expect to learn from these market surveys:

- product development and introductions by IBM and its competitors; and
- the general economic climate and the projected expenditures on computers.

A firm can use its own market survey department to survey its customers. Or it can employ outside market survey specialists.

Management Forecasts

In addition to market surveys, the firm's managers may be able to provide forecasts of future sales. The experience of a firm's management and their familiarity with the firm's products, customers, and competitors make them reliable forecasters of future sales.

The firm's own managers should have the expertise to predict the market for the goods and services and to evaluate the costs of producing and marketing them. But there are potential problems in using management forecasts. Consider the case of a manager who forecasts rosy outcomes for a new product. These forecasts may persuade the firm to allocate more resources—such as a larger capital budget and additional personnel—to that manager. If these forecasts come true, the firm will be glad these additional resources were allocated. But if these forecasts turned out to be too rosy, the firm has unnecessarily allocated these resources.

Forecasting is an important element in planning for both the short-term and the long-term. But forecasts are made by people. Forecasters tend to be optimistic, which usually results in rosier than deserved forecasts of future sales. In addition, people tend to focus on what worked in the past, so past successes carry more weight in the developing forecasts than an analysis of the future.

One way to avoid this is to make managers responsible for their forecasts, rewarding accurate forecasts and penalizing the ones for being way off the mark.

Seasonal Considerations

The operating activities of a firm typically vary throughout the year, depending on seasonal demand and supply factors. Seasonality influences a firm's short-term investment and financing activities.

Let's look at a few U.S. corporations' quarterly revenues to get an idea of different seasonal patterns of activity:

- Coca Cola, a beverage producer
- Amazon.com, an online retailer
- Walt Disney, a film and amusement firm
- Nike, a shoe manufacturer
- Delta Airlines, a national airline

The quarterly revenues for each of these firms is plotted in Exhibit 29.5 from the first quarter 1999 through the fourth quarter 2002. The seasonal patterns are quite different:

EXHIBIT 29.5   Sales of Selected U.S. Companies, Quarterly
First Quarter 1999 through First Quarter 2002

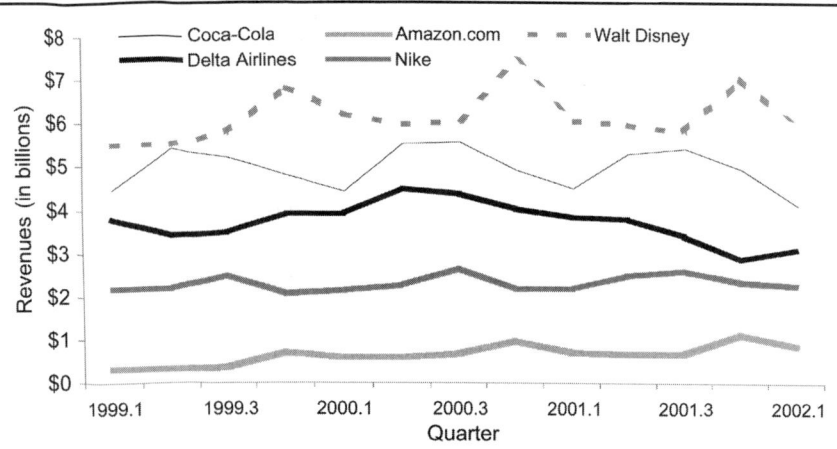

Source: Company annual reports, various years.

- Coca Cola tends to have increased sales in the summer months, driven, most likely, by their larger segment, soft drinks.
- Disney has a high degree of seasonality, with sales dependent on the December holiday season, with sales highest in the fourth quarter.
- Walt Disney Company has sales that tend to increase around the fourth quarter of each year, influenced by their two major product lines, movie production and amusement parks.
- Nike has seasonal sales, with sales increasing around the "back-to-school" time of year
- Delta sales increase somewhat during the summer months, due to summer vacation travel, but this seasonality is not as pronounced as that of, say, Nike or Disney.

Looking closer at what seasonality has to do with cash flows, let's focus on the likely cash flow pattern for Amazon.com. Sales are greatest in the fourth quarter of the year due to holiday shopping. As a retail operation that does not extend credit, its cash inflows will be highest in the fourth quarter also.

But what about cash *out*flows? To have the merchandise to sell in the fourth quarter, Amazon.com must increase its inventory prior to or during the fourth quarter. Depending on its credit arrangements with its suppliers, cash will be flowing out of the firm before or during the fourth quarter. This means that for some period of time Amazon.com will have more cash going out than in, and then more cash coming in than out.

Budgeting

In budgeting, we bring together analyses of cash flows, projected income statements, projected balance sheets. The cash flow analyses are most important, though you also need to generate the income statement and balance sheet as well.

Most firms extend or receive credit, so cash flows and net income do not coincide. Typically, you must determine cash flows from accounting information on revenues and expenses. Combining sales projections with our estimates of collections of accounts receivable results in an estimate of cash receipts.

Suppose you have the following sales projections for the next six months:

Month	Sales	Month	Sales	Month	Sales
July	$300,000	September	$900,000	November	$300,000
August	600,000	October	600,000	December	300,000

How do you translate these sales estimates into cash receipts? First, you need an estimate of how long it takes to collect on your accounts.

You can estimate the typical time it takes to collect on your accounts using the financial ratio,

$$\text{Number of days of credit} = \frac{\text{Accounts receivable}}{\text{Credit sales per day}}$$

This tells you how long it takes, on average, to collect on accounts receivable. Suppose the number of days credit is thirty. This means that a sale made in January is collected in February, a sale made in February is collected in March, and so on. If you had sales of $300,000 in the previous June, your estimate of cash receipts for July through December is:

Month	Sales	Collections on Receivables
July	$300,000 ———————	$300,000 ← From June sales
August	600,000 ———————	300,000
September	900,000 ———————	600,000
October	600,000 ———————	900,000
November	300,000 ———————	600,000
December	300,000 ———————	300,000

An alternative, and more precise method, is to look at the aging of receivables—how long each account has been outstanding—and use this information to track collections. However, this requires a detailed estimate of the age of all accounts and their typical collection period.

Whether you use an overall average or an aging approach, you need to consider several factors in our cash collections estimate:

- An estimate of bad debts—accounts that will not be collected at all;
- An analysis of the trend in the number of days it takes customers to pay on account; and
- An estimate of the seasonal nature of collections of accounts; often customers' ability to pay is influenced by the operating cycle of their own firm.

As with revenues and cash receipts, there is a relation between expenses and cash disbursements. Firms typically do not pay cash for all goods and services; purchases are generally bought on account (creating accounts payable) and wages and salaries are paid periodically (weekly, bi-monthly, or monthly). Therefore, there's a lagged relationship between expenses and cash payments.

You can get an idea of the time it takes to pay for your purchases on account with the number of days of purchases:

$$\text{Number of days of purchases} = \frac{\text{Accounts payable}}{\text{Average day's purchases}}$$

And you can determine the time it takes to pay for wages and salaries by looking at the firm's personnel policies. Putting these two pieces together, you can estimate how long it takes to pay for the goods and services you acquire.

The Cash Budget

A *cash budget* is a detailed statement of the cash inflows and outflows expected in future periods. This budget helps you identify our financing and investment needs. You can also use a cash budget to compare your actual cash flows against planned cash flows so that you can evaluate both your performance and your forecasting ability.

Cash flows in to the firm from:

1. Operations, such as receipts from sales and collections on accounts receivable;
2. The results of financing decisions, such as borrowings, sales of shares of common stock, and sales of preferred stock; and

3. The results of investment decisions, such as sales of assets and income from marketable securities.

Cash flows *out* of the firm for:

1. Operations, such as payments on accounts payable, purchases of goods, and the payment of taxes;
2. Financing obligations, such as the payment of dividends and interest, and the repurchase of shares of stock or the redemption of bonds; and
3. Investments, such as the purchase of plant and equipment.

As we noted before, the cash budget is driven by the sales forecast. Consider the following sales forecasts for the Imagined Company for January through June:

Month	Forecasted Sales	Month	Forecasted Sales
January	$1,000	April	$2,000
February	2,000	May	1,000
March	3,000	June	1,000

Using the forecasted sales, along with a host of assumptions about credit sales, collections on accounts receivable, payments for purchases, and financing, we can construct a cash budget, which tells us about the cash inflows and the cash outflows.

Let's look at Imagined's cash budget for January 2005. Sales are expected to be $1,000. Now let's translate sales into cash flows, focusing first on the cash flows from operations.

Let's assume that an analysis of accounts receivable over the past year reveals that:

■ 10% of a month's sales are paid in the month of the sale.
■ 60% of a month's sales are paid in the month following the sale.
■ 30% of a month's sales are paid in the second month following the sale.

This means that only 10% of the $1,000 sales, or $100 is collected in January. But this also means that in January Imagined collects 60% of 2004's December sales and 30% of 2004's November sales. If December 2004 sales were $1,000 and November 2004 sales were $2,000, this means that January collections are:

Collections on January 2005 sales	$100	← 10% of $1,000
Collections on December 2004 sales	600	← 60% of $1,000
Collections on November 2004 sales	600	← 30% of $2,000
Total cash inflow from collections	$1,300	

Now let's look at the cash flows related to Imagined's payment for its goods. We first have to make an assumption about how much Imagined buys and when it pays for its goods and services. First, assume that Imagined has a cost of goods (other than labor) of 50%. This means that for every $1 it sells, it has a cost of 50%. Next, assume that Imagined purchases goods two months in advance of when the firm sells them (this means the number of days of inventory is around 60 days). Finally, let's assume that Imagined pays 20% of its accounts payable in the month it purchases the goods and 80% of its accounts payable in the month after it purchases the goods.

Putting this all together, we forecast that in January, Imagined will purchase 50% of March's forecasted sales, or 50% of $3,000 = $1,500. Imagined will pay 20% of these purchases in January, or 20% of $1,500 = $300. In addition, Imagined will be paying 80% of the purchases made in December 2004. And December's purchases are 50% of *February's* projected sales. So in January, Imagined will pay 50% of 80% of $2,000, which is 50% of $1,600 or $800.

We assume that Imagined has additional cash outflows for wages (5% of current month's sales) and selling and administrative expenses (also 10% of current month's sales). Imagined's cash outflows related to operations in January consist of:

Payments of current month's purchases	$300	← 20% of $1,500
Payments for previous month's purchases	800	← 80% of $1,600
Wages	50	← 5% of $1,000
Selling and administrative expenses	100	← 10% of $1,000
Operating cash outflows	$1,250	

The cash flows pertaining to Imagined Company's operations are shown in the top portion of Exhibit 29.6. In January, there is a net cash *in*flow from operations of $50. Extending what we did for January's cash flows to the next five months as well, we get a projection of cash inflows and outflows from operations. As you can see, there are net outflows from operations in February and March, and net inflows in other months.

But cash flows from operations do not tell us the complete picture. We also need to know about Imagined's nonoperating cash flows. Does it intend to buy or retire any plant and equipment? Does it intend to retire any debt? Does it need to pay interest on any debt? And so on. These projections are inserted in the lower portion of Exhibit 29.6.

But there is one catch here: Cash inflows must equal cash outflows (unless Imagined has found a way to create cash!). So we have to decide where Imagined is going to get its cash if its *in*flows are less than its *out*flows. And we have to decide where it is going to invest its cash if its *out*flows are less than its *in*flows.

EXHIBIT 29.6 Imagined Company Monthly Cash Budget, January–June 2005

	January	February	March	April	May	June
Sales	$1,000	$2,000	$3,000	$2,000	$1,000	$1,000
Operating Cash Flows						
Cash Inflows						
Collections on accounts receivables:						
Collections on current month's sales	$100	$200	$300	$200	$100	$100
Collections from previous month's sales	600	600	1,200	1,800	1,200	600
Collections from two months' previous sales	600	300	300	600	900	600
Operating cash inflows	$1,300	$1,100	$1,800	$2,600	$2,200	$1,300
Cash Outflows						
Payments of purchases on account:						
Payments for current month's purchases	$300	$200	$100	$100	$100	$100
Payments for previous month's purchases	800	1,200	800	400	400	400
Wages	50	100	150	100	50	50
Selling and administrative expenses	100	200	300	200	100	100
Operating cash outflows	$1,250	$1,700	$1,350	$800	$650	$650
Operating net cash flow	$50	($600)	$450	$1,800	$1,550	$650
Nonoperating Cash Flows						
Cash Inflows						
Retirements of plant and equipment	$0	$0	$0	$500	$0	$0
Issuance of long-term debt	0	3,000	0	0	0	0
Issuance of common stock	0	0	0	0	0	0
Nonoperating cash inflows	$0	$3,000	$0	$500	$0	$0

EXHIBIT 29.6 (Continued)

	January	February	March	April	May	June
Cash Outflows						
Acquisitions of plant and equipment	$1,000	$3,000	$0	$0	$3,500	$0
Payment of cash dividends	0	0	100	0	0	100
Retirement of long-term debt	0	0	0	0	0	1,000
Retirement of common stock	0	0	0	0	0	0
Interest on long-term debt	10	10	10	10	10	10
Taxes	69	165	271	168	53	53
Nonoperating cash outflows	$1,079	$3,175	$381	$178	$3,563	$1,163
Nonoperating cash flows	–$1,079	–$175	–$381	$322	–$3,563	–$1,163
Analysis of cash and marketable securities						
Balance, beginning of month	$1,500.00	$1,000.00	$1,000.00	$1,069.25	$2,000.00	$1,000.00
Net cash flows for the month	(1,029.00)	(775.33)	69.25	2,122.34	(2,012.55)	(513.05)
Balance without any change in bank loans	$471.00	$224.67	$1,069.25	$3,191.59	($12.55)	$486.95
Bank loans to maintain minimum balance	529.00	775.33	0.00	0.00	1,012.55	513.05
Available to pay off bank loans	0.00	0.00	0.00	1,191.59	0.00	0.00
Balance, end of month	$1,000.00	$1,000.00	$1,069.25	$2,000.00	$1,000.00	$1,000.00

Assumptions:
(1) Cash sales are 10% of current month's sales
(2) Collections on accounts receivables are 60% of previous month's sales and 30% of the two months previous' sales
(3) Purchases are 50% of two months ahead sales
(4) Payments on accounts are 20% of current month's purchases, plus 80% of previous month's purchases
(5) Wages are 5% of current month's sales
(6) Selling and administrative expenses are 5% of current month's sales
(7) July and August sales are forecasted to be $1,000 each month

953

Let's assume that Imagined will borrow from the bank when it needs short-term financing and it will pay off its bank loans or invest in marketable securities (if it has no outstanding bank loans) if it has more cash than needed. In our example, let's group cash and marketable securities and cash into one item, referred to as "cash."

The bank loan-marketable securities decision is a residual decision: We make decisions about such things as when we pay out accounts, but we use the bank loan or marketable securities investment as a "plug" figure to help balance our cash inflows and outflows. But this "plug" is very important—it tells us what financing arrangement we need to have in place (such as a line of credit) or that we need to make decisions regarding short-term investments (such as U.S. Treasury bills).

Comparing inflows with outflows from operations, we see that if Imagined requires a minimum cash balance of $1,000, it needs to use bank financing in January, February, May, and June. We also see that if Imagined does not need to maintain a cash balance above $2,000, it can pay off some of its bank loans in April.

We've forecasted cash inflows and outflows for several months into the future. But these are forecasts and lots of things can happen between now and then. The actual cash flows can easily differ from the forecasted cash flows. Furthermore, we've made a host of assumptions and decisions along the way, some that we have control over, such as dividend payments, and some that we have no control over, such as how long customers take to pay. Economic conditions, market conditions, and other factors will affect actual cash flows.

Two methods to help us look as the uncertainty of cash flows are sensitivity analysis and simulation analysis. *Sensitivity analysis* involves changing one of the variables in our analysis, such as the number of units sold, and looking at its affect on the cash flows. This gives us an idea of what cash flows may be under certain circumstances. We can pose different scenarios: What if customers take 60 days to pay instead of 30? What if we sales are actually $1,000 in February instead of $2,000?

But sensitivity analysis can become unmanageable if we start changing two or more things at a time. A manageable approach to doing this is with computer simulation. *Simulation analysis* allows you to develop a probability distribution of possible outcomes, given a probability distribution for each variable that may change.

Suppose you can develop a probability distribution—that is, a list of possible outcomes and their related likelihood of occurring—for sales. (A *probability distribution* is the set of possible outcomes and their likelihood of occurrence.) And suppose you can develop a probability distribution for costs of the raw materials that are needed in producing the product. Using simulation, a probability distribution of cash flows can be produced, providing information on the uncertainty of the firm's future cash flows, as shown in Exhibit 29.7.

Once we produce the probability distribution of future cash flows, we have an idea of the possible cash flows and can plan accordingly. The cash budget produced using the possible cash flows is a *flexible budget.* With this information, we can then determine the more appropriate short-term financing and short-term investments to consider.

Pro Forma Financial Statements

A *pro forma balance sheet* is a projected balance sheet for a future period— a month, quarter, or year—that summarizes assets, liabilities, and equity. A *pro forma income statement* is the projected income statement for a future period—a month, quarter, or year—that summarizes revenues and expenses. Together both projections help you identify your firm's investment and financing needs.

The analysis of accounts and the percent-of-sales method are two ways of projecting financial statements.

Analysis of Accounts

The *analysis of accounts method* starts with the cash budget. Before putting together the pro forma income statement and balance sheet, we need to see how the various asset, liability, and equity accounts change from month to month, based on the information provided in the cash budget. The analysis of accounts is shown in Exhibit 29.8, where each account is analyzed starting with the beginning balance and making any necessary adjustments to arrive at the ending balance.

EXHIBIT 29.7   Simulation and Cash Flow Uncertainty

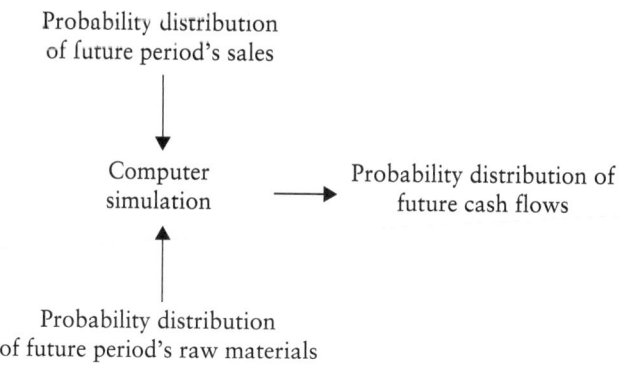

EXHIBIT 29.8 Imagined Company Analysis of Monthly Changes in Accounts, January through June 2005

	January	February	March	April	May	June
Accounts receivable						
Month's beginning balance	$2,000	$1,700	$2,600	$3,800	$3,200	$2,000
plus, credit sales during the month	900	1,800	2,700	1,800	900	900
less, collections on accounts	1,200	900	1,500	2,400	2,100	1,200
Month's ending balance	$1,700	$2,600	$3,800	$3,200	$2,000	$1,700
Inventory						
Month's beginning balance	$2,500	$3,500	$3,500	$2,500	$2,000	$2,000
plus, purchases	1,500	1,000	500	500	500	500
plus, wages and other production expenses	50	100	150	100	50	50
less, goods sold	550	1,100	1,650	1,100	550	550
Month's ending balance	$3,500	$3,500	$2,500	$2,000	$2,000	$2,000
Accounts payable						
Month's beginning balance	$2,000	$2,400	$2,000	$1,600	$1,600	$1,600
plus, purchases on account	1,200	800	400	400	400	400
less, payments on account	800	1,200	800	400	400	400
Month's ending balance	$2,400	$2,000	$1,600	$1,600	$1,600	$1,600
Bank loans						
Month's beginning balance	$1,000	$1,529	$2,304	$2,304	$1,113	$2,125
plus, borrowings	529	775	0	0	1,013	513
less, repayment of loans	0	0	0	1,192	0	0
Month's ending balance	$1,529	$2,304	$2,304	$1,113	$2,125	$2,638
Plant and equipment						
Month's beginning balance	$10,000	$10,890	$13,751	$13,614	$12,982	$16,318
plus, acquisitions	1,000	3,000	$0	0	3,500	0
less, retirements	0	0	0	500	0	0
less, depreciation*	110	139	137	131	165	163
Month's ending balance	$10,890	$13,751	$13,614	$12,982	$16,318	$16,154
Long-term debt						
Month's beginning balance	$5,000	$5,000	$8,000	$8,000	$8,000	$8,000
plus, issuances of long-term debt	0	3,000	0	0	0	0
less, retirements of long-term debt	0	0	0	0	0	1,000
Month's ending balance	$5,000	$8,000	$8,000	$8,000	$8,000	$7,000
Common equity						
Month's beginning balance	$8,000	$8,161	$8,547	$9,079	$9,470	$9,592
plus, earnings retained during the month	161	386	532	391	123	24
plus, issuances of common stock	0	0	0	0	0	0
less, retirements of common stock	0	0	0	0	0	0
Month's ending balance	$8,161	$8,547	$9,079	$9,470	$9,592	$9,616

*1% of gross plant and equipment

We can see how the cash budget interacts with the pro forma income statement and balance sheet by looking at the change in accounts receivable. Consider what happens in January:

The analysis of accounts receivable . . .		. . . affects financial planning through the . . .)
Balance at the beginning of the month	$2,000 →	pro forma balance sheet (accounts receivable)
Plus credit sales during January	+900 →	pro forma income statement (sales) and pro forma balance sheet (accounts receivable)
Less collections on accounts during January	−1,200 →	cash budget (cash flow from operations)
Balance at the end of the month	$1,700 →	pro forma balance sheet (accounts receivable)

As you can see, the balances in these accounts are all interrelated with the cash budget.

In doing our cash budget, we have begun to make projections based on the following information:

- Changes in the cash account are determined by the difference between our cash inflows and outflows.
- Changes in accounts receivables are determined by our sales and collections projections.
- Changes in inventory are determined by our purchase and sales projections.
- Changes in plant and equipment are determined by our capital budgeting.
- Changes in long-term debt are determined by our financing projections.
- Changes in common equity are determined by both the financing projections and the projected retained earnings.
- Changes in retained earnings are determined by the projected income.

If we put together all these pieces, we have a pro forma balance sheet for Imagined Company, as shown in Exhibit 29.9. Looking at the cash budget in Exhibit 29.7, the analysis of accounts in Exhibit 29.8, and the balance sheet in Exhibit 29.9, we can follow through to see the interactions among the various assets, liabilities, equity accounts, and cash flows as we did for accounts receivable.

The pro forma income statement for Imagined Company is shown in the lower part of Exhibit 29.9. Though our interest is ultimately on cash flows, the income statement provides useful summary information on the expected performance of the firm in months to come. As you can see in Exhibit 29.9, net income tends to increase in March, which accompanies the increased revenues in that month.

EXHIBIT 29.9   Imagined Company Monthly Pro Forma Balance Sheet and Income Statement, January through June 2005
Pro Forma Balance Sheet

	January	February	March	April	May	June
Assets						
Cash and marketable securities	$1,000	$1,000	$1,069	$2,000	$1,000	$1,000
Accounts receivable	1,700	2,600	3,800	3,200	2,000	1,700
Inventories	3,500	3,500	2,500	2,000	2,000	2,000
Plant and Equipment	10,890	13,751	13,614	12,982	16,318	16,154
Total Assets	$17,090	$20,851	$20,983	$20,182	$21,318	$20,854
Liabilities and Equity						
Accounts payable	$2,400	$2,000	$1,600	$1,600	$1,600	$1,600
Bank loans	1,529	2,304	2,304	1,113	2,125	2,638
Long-term debt	5,000	8,000	8,000	8,000	8,000	7,000
Common equity	8,161	8,547	9,079	9,470	9,592	9,616
Total Liabilities and Equity	$17,090	$20,851	$20,983	$20,182	$21,318	$20,854

Pro Forma Income Statement

	January	February	March	April	May	June
Sales	$1,000	$2,000	$3,000	$2,000	$1,000	$1,000
less, Cost of goods sold	550	1,100	1,650	1,100	550	550
less, Depreciation	110	139	138	131	165	163
Gross profit	$340	$761	$1,212	$769	$285	$287
less, Selling and administrative expenses	100	200	300	200	100	100
Earnings before interest and taxes	$240	$561	$912	$569	$185	$187
less, Interest	10	10	10	10	10	10
Earnings before taxes	$230	$551	$902	$559	$175	$177
less, Taxes	69	165	271	168	53	53
Net income	$161	$386	$632	$391	$123	$124
less, Cash dividends	0	0	100	0	0	100
Retained earnings	$161	$386	$532	$391	$123	$24

We are interested in the pro forma balance sheet and income statement not just as a product of our cash flow analysis. Suppose the bank financing is secured financing, limited to 80% of accounts receivable. If this is the case, we may be limited in how much we can borrow from the bank in any particular month. We are also interested in the balance sheet since some of our short-term or long-term debt may have covenants that prescribe the firm to maintain specific relations among its accounts; for example, a current ratio of 2:1. In addition, we may be concerned about the firm's perceived riskiness. If we must borrow heavily at certain times within a year, does this affect the riskiness of our debt securities, increasing the cost of financing?

These considerations point out the importance of reviewing the projected balance sheet. In fact, these considerations may point out the need for the financial manager to explicitly build constraints into the budget to ensure that, say, a current ratio of 2 is maintained each month. These constraints add complexity to an already complex system of relationships, the detail of which is beyond the scope of this text.

Percent-of-Sales Method

The *percent-of-sales method* uses historical relationships between sales and each of the other income statement accounts and between sales and each of the balance sheet accounts. There are two steps to this method.

First, previous periods' income statement and balance sheet accounts are restated in terms of a percentage of sales for the year. Let's look at the Imagined Corporation balance sheet and income statement for 2004 shown in the left-most column of Exhibit 29.10. Because we are projecting monthly sales, each item in both statements is restated as a percent of December 2004 sales, as shown in the second column of this table.

Second, based on the forecasted sales for the future years and the percentages each account represents, projections for January through June are calculated. For example, cost of goods sold are 55% of sales. Because January sales are predicted to be $1,000, cost of goods sold are predicted to be 55% of $1,000, or $550. And as sales for February are predicted to be $2,000, cost of goods sold for February are predicted to be $1,100. Likewise for balance sheet accounts. Cash and marketable securities are 75% of monthly sales, so we expect $750 in this account in January. Each of the balance sheet and income statement accounts is forecasted January through June, as shown in Exhibit 29.10.

This method of creating pro forma statements is simple. But it may make inappropriate assumptions, such as that: (1) all costs vary with sales, even though most firms have fixed costs; or (2) assets and liabilities change along with sales, even though firms tend to make capital investments that generate cash flows far into the future, not necessarily in the year they are put in place.

And there is another drawback: The percent-of-sales method focuses on accounts in the financial statements, not cash flows. Because it doesn't, it cannot help us identify when a firm needs cash and when it has excess cash to invest.

But the percent-of-sales method is used frequently because of its simplicity. And since we are dealing with forecasts, which are themselves estimates (and not actual fact), the simpler approach is sometimes more attractive.

EXHIBIT 29.10   Pro Forma Financial Statements for January through June 2005, Using the Percent-of-Sales Method

Pro Forma Balance Sheet

	As of the End of 2004	Percentage of December 2004 Sales	Forecasted Accounts for 2005					
			January	February	March	April	May	June
Cash and marketable securities	$1,500	75%	$750	$1,500	$2,250	$1,500	$750	$750
Accounts receivable	2,000	100%	1,000	2,000	3,000	2,000	1,000	$1,000
Inventories	2,500	125%	1,250	2,500	3,750	2,500	1,250	$1,250
Plant and equipment	10,000	500%	5,000	10,000	15,000	10,000	5,000	$5,000
Total Assets	$16,000	800%	$8,000	$16,000	$24,000	$16,000	$8,000	$8,000
			$0	$0	$0	$0	$0	$0
Accounts payable	$2,000	100%	$1,000	$2,000	$3,000	$2,000	$1,000	$1,000
Bank loans	1,000	50%	500	1,000	1,500	1,000	$500	$500
Long-term debt	5,000	250%	2,500	5,000	7,500	5,000	2,500	2,500
Common stock and paid-in capital	2,000	100%	1,000	2,000	3,000	2,000	1,000	1,000
Retained earnings	6,000	300%	3,000	6,000	9,000	6,000	3,000	3,000
Total Liabilities and Equity	$16,000	800%	$8,000	$16,000	$24,000	$16,000	$8,000	$8,000

Pro Forma Income Statement

	December 2004	Percentage of December 2004 Sales	Forecasted Accounts for 2005					
			January	February	March	April	May	June
Sales	$2,000	100%	$1,000	$2,000	$3,000	$2,000	$1,000	$1,000
less, Cost of goods sold	1,100	55%	550	1,100	1,650	1,100	550	550
less, Depreciation	200	10%	100	200	300	200	100	100
Gross profit	$700	35%	350	700	1,050	700	350	350
less, Selling and administrative expenses	10	1%	5	10	15	10	5	5
Earnings before interest and taxes	$690	35%	$345	$690	$1,035	$690	$345	$345
less, Interest	20	1%	10	20	30	20	10	10
Earnings before taxes	$670	34%	$335	$670	$1,005	$670	$335	$335
less, Taxes	12	1%	6	12	18	12	6	6
Net income	$658	33%	$329	$658	$987	$658	$329	$329

Previous December's sales	$1,000
Previous November's sales	$2,000

LONG-TERM FINANCIAL PLANNING

Long-term planning is similar to what we have just completed for the operational budget for January through June 2005, but for a longer span of time into the future and with less detail.

Projections for 2005 through 2010 are shown in Exhibit 29.11, where the cash budget is shown in panel (a) and the pro forma financial statements are shown in panel (b). You'll notice that we are not as concerned about the details, say, concerning the source of cash flows from operations, but rather the bottom line. However, these statements must be compiled as we have done with the operational budget: Based on projections and assumptions that are built into our cash budget, we integrate the investment decisions with the financing decisions.

By looking at the long-term plan, we get an idea of how the firm intends to meet its objective of maximizing shareholder wealth. For example, in the operational budget we are concerned about meeting monthly cash demands and we assume Imagined Company borrows from banks to meet any cash shortages. But with the long-term plan, we can address the issue of what capital structure (the mix of debt and equity) the firm wants in the long-run. In the case of Imagined Company, we assume:

- Any bank loans are reduced to $1,000 at the end of each year.
- When long-term capital is needed, we raise one-half using debt, one-half issuing new equity.
- When the firm is able to reduce its reliance on external funds, it will reduce its long-term debt.

Long-term plans should be evaluated periodically as are operational budgets. And since the two are closely tied (what we do in the short-term influences what happens in the long-term), it is convenient to update both types of budgets simultaneously.

FINANCIAL MODELING

A *financial model* is the set of relationships that are behind the calculations we perform in putting together the cash budget and the pro forma statements. In financial modeling, we generally focus on the essential features of the budget and statements, and try not to get bogged down in the details. In our Imagined Company example, we looked at the relation between cash and marketable securities, but we avoided getting into detail of where the cash is held or which securities we buy or sell.

EXHIBIT 29.11   Imagined Company Long-Term Planning, 2005 through 2010

Panel a: Cash Budget

Projected Sales	$20,000	$22,000	$25,000	$26,000	$27,000	$28,000
Operating Cash Flows						
	2005	2006	2007	2008	2009	2010
Cash Inflows						
Cash sales	$2,000	$2,200	$2,500	$2,600	$2,700	$2,800
Collections on account:	19,000	19,820	21,250	22,040	24,100	26,270
Operating cash inflows	$21,000	$22,020	$23,750	$24,640	$26,800	$29,070
Cash Outflows						
Payments of purchases on account:	$10,067	$10,917	$12,375	$12,958	$13,458	$13,958
Wages	1,000	1,100	1,250	1,300	1,350	1,400
Selling and administrative expenses	2,000	2,200	2,500	2,600	2,700	2,800
Operating cash outflows	$13,067	$14,217	$16,125	$16,858	$17,508	$18,158
Operating net cash flows	$7,933	$7,803	$7,625	$7,782	$9,292	$10,912
Nonoperating Cash Flows						
Cash inflows						
Retirement of plant and equipment	$500	$0	$0	$0	$1,000	$2,000
Nonoperating cash inflows	$500	$0	$0	$0	$1,000	$2,000
Cash outflows						
Maturing long-term debt	$1,000	$1,000	$1,000	$1,000	$1,000	$1,000
Acquisitions of plant and equipment	10,000	7,500	7,500	5,000	1,000	5,000
Payment of cash dividends	400	400	400	400	400	400
Interest on long-term debt	0,300	0,350	0,400	0,350	0,300	0,250
Taxes	1,308	1,317	1,454	1,520	1,773	1,901
Nonoperating cash outflows	$13,008	$10,567	$10,754	$8,270	$4,473	$8,551
Nonoperating net cash flows	−$12,508	−$10,567	−$10,754	−$8,270	−$3,473	−$6,551
Analysis of cash						
Cash balance, beginning of year	$1,500	$1,500	$1,500	$1,500	$1,500	$4,000
Net cash flows during year	−4,575	−2,764	−3,129	−488	5,819	4,360
Cash balance without any financing	−$3,075	−$1,264	−$1,629	$1,012	$7,319	$8,360
Long-term debt issuance	2,287	1,382	1,564	244	0	0
Common stock issuance	2,287	1,382	1,564	244	0	0
Available to pay off long-term debt	0	0	0	0	3,319	4,360
Cash balance, end of year	$1,500	$1,500	$1,500	$1,500	$4,000	$4,000

EXHIBIT 29.11 (Continued)
Imagined Company Long-Term Planning, Analysis of Accounts

	2005	2006	2007	2008	2009	2010
Accounts receivable						
Year's beginning balance	$2,000	$1,000	$980	$2,230	$3,590	$3,790
plus, credit sales during the year	$18,000	19,800	22,500	23,400	24,300	25,200
less, collections on accounts	$19,000	19,820	21,250	22,040	24,100	26,270
Year's ending balance	$1,000	$980	$2,230	$3,590	$3,790	$2,720
Inventory						
Year's beginning balance	$2,500	$2,500	$2,500	$2,500	$2,500	$2,500
plus, purchases	10,000	11,000	12,500	13,000	13,500	14,000
plus, wages and other production expenses	1,000	1,100	1,250	1,300	1,350	1,400
less, goods sold	11,000	12,100	13,750	14,300	14,850	15,400
Year's ending balance	$2,500	$2,500	$2,500	$2,500	$2,500	$2,500
Accounts payable						
Year's beginning balance	$2,000	$1,933	$2,017	$2,142	$2,183	$2,225
plus, purchases on account	10,000	11,000	12,500	13,000	13,500	14,000
less, payments on account	10,067	10,917	12,375	12,958	13,458	13,958
Year's ending balance	$1,933	$2,017	$2,142	$2,183	$2,225	$2,267
Bank loans						
Year's beginning and ending balance	$1,000	$1,000	$1,000	$1,000	$1,000	$1,000
Plant and equipment						
Year's beginning balance	$10,000	$17,160	$21,701	$25,697	$27,013	$23,772
plus, acquisitions	9,500	7,500	7,500	5,000		3,000
less, depreciation	2,340	2,959	3,504	3,684	3,242	3,213
Year's ending balance	$17,160	$21,701	$25,697	$27,013	$23,772	$23,559
Long-term debt						
Year's beginning balance	$5,000	$6,287	$6,669	$7,234	$6,478	$2,159
plus, long-term debt issued	2,287	1,382	1,564	244		
less, long-term debt retired or matured	1,000	1,000	1,000	1,000	4,319	5,360
Year's ending balance	$6,287	$6,669	$7,234	$6,478	$2,159	-$3,202
Common equity						
Year's beginning balance	$8,000	$12,939	$16,995	$21,551	$24,942	$28,678
plus, issuance of new shares of stock	2,287	1,382	1,564	244	0	0
plus, earnings retained during the year	2,652	2,674	2,992	3,146	3,736	4,036
Year's ending balance	$12,939	$16,995	$21,551	$24,942	$28,678	$32,714

EXHIBIT 29.11   (Continued)

Panel b: Imagined Company Pro Forma Financial Statements, 2005 through 2010

Pro Forma Balance Sheet

	2005	2006	2007	2008	2009	2010
Assets						
Cash and marketable securities	$1,500	$1,500	$1,500	$1,500	$4,000	$4,000
Accounts receivable	1,000	980	2,230	3,590	3,790	2,720
Inventories	2,500	2,500	2,500	2,500	2,500	2,500
Plant and Equipment	17,160	21,701	25,697	27,013	23,772	23,559
Total Assets	$22,160	$26,681	$31,927	$34,603	$34,062	$32,779
Liabilities and Equity						
Accounts payable	$1,933	$2,017	$2,142	$2,183	$2,225	$2,269
Bank loans	1,000	1,000	1,000	1,000	1,000	1,000
Long-term debt	6,287	6,669	7,234	6,478	2,159	(3,202)
Stockholders' equity	12,939	16,995	21,551	24,942	28,678	32,714
Total Liabilities and Equity	$22,160	$26,681	$31,927	$34,603	$34,062	$32,779

Pro Forma Income Statement

	2005	2006	2007	2008	2009	2010
Sales	$20,000	$22,000	$25,000	$26,000	$27,000	$28,000
less, Cost of goods sold	11,000	12,100	13,750	14,300	14,850	15,400
less, Depreciation	2,340	2,959	3,504	3,684	3,242	3,213
Gross profit	$6,660	$6,941	$7,746	$8,016	$8,908	$9,387
less, Selling and administrative expenses	2,000	2,200	2,500	2,600	2,700	2,800
Earnings before interest and taxes	$4,660	$4,741	$5,246	$5,416	$6,208	$6,587
less, Interest	300	350	400	350	300	250
Earnings before taxes	$4,360	$4,391	$4,846	$5,066	$5,908	$6,337
less, Taxes	1,308	1,317	1,454	1,520	1,773	1,901
Net income	$3,052	$3,074	$3,392	$3,546	$4,136	$4,436
less, Cash dividends	400	400	400	400	400	400
Retained earnings	$2,652	$2,674	$2,992	$3,146	$3,736	$4,036

In the case of Imagined Company, the following relations between cash inflows and sales are "modeled":

$$\text{Cash inflows} = 10\% \begin{pmatrix} \text{This} \\ \text{month's} \\ \text{sales} \end{pmatrix} + 60\% \begin{pmatrix} \text{Preceding} \\ \text{month's} \\ \text{sales} \end{pmatrix} + 30\% \begin{pmatrix} \text{Second} \\ \text{preceding} \\ \text{month's sales} \end{pmatrix}$$

Cash outflows are similar, but instead of collecting on sales and receivables, we are paying expenses and paying on our accounts payable:

Cash outflows

$$= 20\% \begin{pmatrix} \text{This} \\ \text{month's} \\ \text{purchases} \end{pmatrix} + 80\% \begin{pmatrix} \text{Last} \\ \text{month's} \\ \text{purchases} \end{pmatrix} + 5\% \begin{pmatrix} \text{This} \\ \text{month's} \\ \text{sales} \end{pmatrix} + 10\% \begin{pmatrix} \text{This} \\ \text{month's} \\ \text{sales} \end{pmatrix}$$

$$\underbrace{\phantom{= 20\% \text{This month's purchases} + 80\% \text{Last month's purchases}}}_{\text{Payments on purchases}} \quad \underbrace{\phantom{5\% \text{This month's sales}}}_{\text{Wages}} \quad \underbrace{\phantom{10\% \text{This month's sales}}}_{\text{Other expenses}}$$

Purchases are determined by projected sales, so we can rewrite this as:

$$\text{Cash outflows} = 20\% \begin{pmatrix} \text{Sales} \\ \text{forecasted} \\ \text{two months} \\ \text{out} \end{pmatrix} + 80\% \begin{pmatrix} \text{Next} \\ \text{month's} \\ \text{sales} \end{pmatrix} + 15\% \begin{pmatrix} \text{This} \\ \text{month's} \\ \text{sales} \end{pmatrix}$$

The cash inflows and outflows from operations are therefore dependent on the forecast of sales in future periods. By changing forecasted sales, the cash inflows and outflows change as well.

We could continue modeling the relations expressed in the cash budget and pro forma financial statements until we have represented all the relationships. Once we have done this, we have our financial model. By playing "what if" with the model—changing one item and observing what happens to the rest—managers can see the consequences of their decisions.

Building the financial model forces the manager to think through the relationships and consequences of investment and financing decisions. Much of the computation in financial modeling can be accomplished using computers and spreadsheet programs.

The task of modeling financial relationships is made easier by computer programs. Many software packages are available, including:

Excel (Microsoft Corporation)
Lotus 1-2-3 (Lotus Development Corporation)
VisiCalc (Lotus Development Corporation)
Multiplan (Microsoft Corporation)

These programs reduce the modeling effort because they enable the user to program a financial model using understandable phrases instead of programming code.

BUDGETING AND FINANCIAL PLANNING PRACTICES

Based on numerous surveys of budgeting practices in U.S. companies, we can make some general statements regarding budgeting and financial planning practices:[5]

- Most firms start with sales forecasts.
- Most use historical data analysis to forecast sales and expenses, though some use opinions of management and economic models.
- Most firms have budget manuals, detailing budget procedures and forms to be completed.

The survey indicates the following recent changes in firms' financial planning:

- An increasing number of firms have established formal budget programs.
- There is a decreasing role of Board of Directors in approving budgets.
- Strategy is becoming more centralized within the companies.
- There is more frequent updating of long-run plans.
- There is an increasing use of flexible budgets that separate controllable and uncontrollable revenues and expenses.

Over time, the level of sophistication of capital budgeting in the United States has increased. This is due to two factors. First, there is an increased awareness of the need to plan a firm's finances to meet its objective of maximizing owners' wealth. Second, technological advances in computer software and hardware make financial planning less time consuming and less costly.

SUMMARY

- The goal of financial management is to maximize shareholder wealth. Like any goal, it requires a strategy.
- As part of its strategy, the firm needs to plan the sources and uses of funds. The investment strategy is the plan of what investment opportunities are needed to meet the firm's goals. The financing strategy is the plan of where the firm is going to get the funds to make these investments.

---

[5] See Srinivasan Umapathy's book entitled *Current Budgeting Practices in U.S. Industry* (New York: Quorum Books, 1987) for a detailed survey of budgeting and planning practices.

■ Financial planning is where decisions, actions, and goals are brought together with forecasts about the firm's sales.

■ In financial planning we need to know what sales will be to determine what are cash flows will be. We can forecast sales using regression analysis, market surveys, or management forecasts.

■ The cash budget is used to coordinate the investment decisions—which often require cash outlays—with the financing decisions—where the cash is coming from.

■ Pro forma financial statements can be generated using the percent of sales method or analyzing accounts based on the cash budget. Whereas the percent of sales method is simpler, the analysis of accounts gives the financial manager a better idea of the cash flows of the firm and their relation to the financial statements.

■ Long-term financial planning is less detailed than the operational budgets, but not less important. Long-term planning helps keep financial managers focused on the objective of the firm and the strategy to achieve it.

■ Financial modeling is a useful tool in looking at the array of relationships that exist in financial planning. It enables managers to examine the consequences of their decisions.

■ Budgeting practices of U.S. companies have become more sophisticated, with more formalized procedures and more attention to long-term financial planning.

QUESTIONS

1. Suppose the financial manager of the Sooner Company had projected sales in 2001 of $4 million and actual sales for that year were $3 million. What should you consider in evaluating this difference? Why?

2. How does the process of selecting projects on the basis of net present values, as done in capital budgeting, relate to a firm's strategy? Explain.

3. How does a firm's capital structure decision relate to its strategy? Explain.

4. Consider a discount retail store chain. List the factors that influence future sales for the chain. Identify the factors over which the firm's management exercises some control.

5. What are the advantages and disadvantages of using the percent-of-sales method in constructing pro forma financial statements?

6. Describe the methods a financial manager could use to assess the uncertainty of a firm's future cash flows.

7. Explain how long-term financial planning is related to operational budgeting.

8. What is financial modeling and how does it assist the financial manager in planning?
9. What distinguishes simulation analysis from sensitivity analysis?
10. Why is it important for a firm to analyze its comparative and competitive advantages in assessing its strategy?
11. The quarterly sales for Powder Corporation for the period from the first quarter of 2002 through the second quarter in 2005 are as follows:

Quarter	Sales in Millions	Quarter	Sales in Millions
1Q02	$671	4Q03	$640
2Q02	658	1Q04	561
3Q02	580	2Q04	568
4Q02	600	3Q04	551
1Q03	636	4Q04	595
2Q03	660	1Q05	614
3Q03	656	2Q05	633

Powder Corporation's products include chemicals, metal products, and ammunition.
a. Plot these sales over time.
b. Do you detect any seasonality in Powder's sales? What do you envision to be Powder's pattern of cash flows from operations?
c. Looking at your graph, what sales do you predict for Powder for the third quarter of 2005?

12. The quarterly sales of Banana Brands International, Inc., from the first quarter of 2003 through the second quarter of 2005 are as follows:

Quarter	Sales in Millions	Quarter	Sales in Millions
1Q03	$895	4Q04	$1,050
2Q03	1,023	1Q05	1,179
3Q03	903	2Q05	1,256
4Q03	1,004	3Q05	1,036
1Q04	1,025	4Q05	1,156
2Q04	1,137	1Q06	1,158
3Q04	1,060	2Q06	1,230

Banana Brands' products include bananas, other fruits, and packaged meats.
a. Plot these sales over time.
b. Do you detect any seasonality in Banana Brands' sales? What do you envision to be the pattern of Banana Brands' cash flows?

    c. Looking at your graph, what sales do you predict for Banana Brands for the third quarter of 2006?

13. Consider the financial statements for the Pretend Corporation for 2003:

Balance Sheet		Income Statement	
Current assets	$1,000	Sales	$15,000
Plant and equipment	8,500	Cost of goods sold	10,000
Other assets	500	Gross profit	$5,000
Total assets	$10,000	Other operating expenses	500
		Operating profit	$4,500
Current liabilities	$500	Interest expense	200
Long-term liabilities	5,000	Taxes	1,720
Stockholders' equity	4,500	Net profit	$2,580
Total liabilities and equity	$10,000	Dividends	1,032
		Retained earnings	$1,548

Forecasted sales for the years 2004 through 2006 are as follows:

Year	Forecasted Sales
2004	$17,000
2005	18,000
2006	19,000

    a. Using the percent-of-sales method, create a pro forma balance sheet for each of the years 2004 through 2006 for the Pretend Corporation.

    b. Using the percent-of-sales method, create a pro forma income statement for each of the years 2004 through 2006 for the Pretend Corporation.

14. The financial manager of the AppleCart Company has prepared the following pro forma balance sheet for the next month:

Assets		Liabilities and Equity	
Cash	$150	Accounts payable	$200
Accounts receivable	50	Long-term debt	200
Inventory	200	Common equity	600
Plant and equipment	600	Total liabilities and equity	$1,000
Total assets	$1,000		

a. After preparing this budget, the financial manager learned that Apple Cart needs to maintain a current ratio of 3 (current assets are three times the current liabilities) at all times. If the only way this can be accomplished is to reduce the amount of cash on hand, propose an alternative pro forma balance sheet that satisfies this constraint.

b. How does the reduction in cash on hand alter AppleCart's risk?

c. Propose two other approaches AppleCart can use to satisfy the current ratio constraint. What risks are involved in each?

15. Consider the Plum Computer Company's sales for three months:

January	$10,000
February	$8,000
March	$7,000

90% of Plum's sales are for credit. 80% of all credit sales are paid the following month and the remainder are paid two months after the sale. Estimate Plum's cash flow from these sales.

16. Suppose a firm had the following assets at the end of a year:

Current assets	$10,000
Plant assets	20,000
Total assets	$30,000

And suppose the firm had sales of $100,000. Using the percentage of sales methods and using this year as the base year, what are the predicted current assets and plant assets of the firm in the following year if sales are predicted to be $125,000?

17. Evaluate Sears' change in strategy from a financial supermarket to a greater concentration on its retail stores.

a. How has Sears fared since 1995 in terms of revenues and profits?

b. Calculate the return on Sears' common stock each year since 1995. How has Sears fared since 1995 in terms of returns to shareholders? How do the returns to shareholders compare with the returns on the market as a whole?

18. Nano Seconds is a chain of retail stores specializing in purchasing, refurbishing, and reselling personal computer systems. Nano Seconds extends no credit to its customers and uses trade credit, paying all trade obligations within one month of purchase. The company has expanded at a rate of one store every six months, leasing all its retail space and making little investment in plant and equipment.

The management of Nano Seconds is concerned about the cash needs of the company in the next year. Forecasted sales for the next four quarters are as follows:

Quarter	Forecasted Sales
June 2005	$600 million
September 2005	$550 million
December 2005	$610 million
March 2006	$650 million

Nano Seconds has a line of credit of $250 million from banks, any loans from which must be fully paid back by the end of the September quarter; any financing needs beyond short-term bank loans will be met with long-term debt.

a. Prepare a cash budget for Nano Seconds and a pro forma balance sheet and income statement using the analysis-of-accounts method. List any assumptions.

b. Discuss the role of the bank financing constraint on the pro forma statements. If Nano Seconds is able to renegotiate its line of credit, what maximum amount would you recommend? Explain you recommendation.

Nano Seconds, Inc.
Quarterly Income Statement
($ millions, except per share)

	Mar-05	Dec-04	Sep-04	Jun-04	Mar-04
Sales	$593.000	$524.000	$539.000	$494.000	$529.000
Cost of Goods Sold	424.000	359.000	358.000	340.000	375.000
Gross Profit	$169.000	$165.000	$181.000	$154.000	$154.000
Selling, General, and Administrative Expense	58.000	56.000	76.000	40.000	49.000
Operating Profit	$111.000	$109.000	$105.000	$114.000	$105.000
Interest Expense	70.000	68.000	65.000	64.000	65.000
Special Items	0.000	0.000	−70.000	−10.000	0.000
Pretax Income	$41.000	$41.000	−$30.000	$40.000	$40.000
Total Income Taxes	15.000	16.000	−12.000	16.000	16.000
Net Income	$26.000	$25.000	−$18.000	$24.000	$24.000
Preferred Dividends	2.000	2.000	3.000	2.000	2.000
Available for Common	$24.000	$23.000	−$21.000	$22.000	$22.000
Dividends Per Share	$0.090	$0.090	$0.090	$0.090	$0.090

Nano Seconds, Inc.
Quarterly Balance Sheet

	Mar-05	Dec-04	Sep-04	Jun-04	Mar-04
Assets					
Cash and Equivalents	$106	$100	$88	$93	$122
Net Receivables	2,310	2,350	2,313	2,310	2,239
Inventories	154	171	145	148	158
Total Current Assets	$2,570	$2,621	$2,546	$2,551	$2,519
Net Plant, Property, and Equip	2,069	1,963	1,864	1,870	1,889
Other Assets	391	411	397	410	426
Total Assets	$5,030	$4,995	$4,807	$4,831	$4,834
Liabilities					
Accounts Payable	$104	$132	$84	$69	$62
Notes Payable	235	239	0	218	211
Total Current Liabilities	$339	$371	$84	$287	$273
Long-Term Debt	$3,631	$3,580	$1,759	$3,508	$3,546
Deferred Taxes and Inv. Tax Credits	0	0	229	0	0
Other Liabilities	311	299	248	264	256
Total Liabilities	$4,281	$4,250	$4,066	$4,059	$4,075
Equity					
Preferred Stock	$95	$95	$100	$100	$100
Common Stock	$5	$5	$5	$5	$5
Capital Surplus	138	125	129	129	128
Retained Earnings	734	701	681	700	674
Less: Treasury Stock	223	181	174	162	148
Common Equity	$654	$650	$641	$672	$659
Total Equity	$749	$745	$741	$772	$759
Total Liabilities and Equity	$5,030	$4,995	$4,807	$4,831	$4,834
Common Shares Outstanding	35.25	36.35	36.70	37.34	38.03

19. Consider the financial statements for the Carpenter Corporation for 20X1, stated in millions:

Balance Sheet		Income Statement	
Current Assets	$3,513	Sales	$8,995
Net Plant, Property, and Equipment	3,492	Cost of Goods Sold	4,901
		Gross Profit	$4,094
Other Assets	2,231	Selling, General, and Admin-	
Total Assets	$9,236	istrative Expenses	2,485
		Depreciation	700
Current Liabilities	$2,190	Operating Profit	$1,785
Long-Term Liabilities	2,957	Interest Expense	208
Stockholders' Equity	4,089	Other Nonoperating Items	120
Total Liabilities and Equity	$9,236	Taxes	263
		Net Profit	$1,194
		Dividends	1,050
		Retained Earnings	$144

Forecasted sales for the years 20X2 through 20X4 are as follows:

Year	Forecasted Sales
20X2	$9,000
20X3	9,500
20X4	10,000

a. Using the percent-of-sales method, create a pro forma balance sheet for each of the years 20X2 through 20X4 for the Carpenter Corporation.

b. Using the percent of-sales method, create a pro forma income statement for each of the years 20X2 through 20X4 for the Carpenter Corporation.

20. Forecasted sales for Outlook, Inc. for each of the next four months are as follows:

Month	Forecast
March	$100,000
April	250,000
May	125,000
June	150,000

Actual sales in April were $150,000. Outlook generally collects 20% of its sales in cash and collects 80% the following month. Outlook purchases amount to 70% of the current month's sales, and it pays 50% of its purchases during the current month and 50% during the following month. Determine the net cash flows from operations forecasted for each of the four months.

Appendix

Black-Scholes Option Pricing Model

An option is an asset that derives its value from some other asset; hence, as we saw in Chapter 4, an option is a derivative instrument. An option may be a stand-alone security, or be embedded in financial instruments such as a callable bond and a convertible bond, as well as options embedded in financial decisions such as real options in capital budgeting decisions, discussed in Chapter 14.

In Chapter 8 we explained the basic factors that affect the "value of an option," also referred to as the "option price." The option price is a reflection of the option's intrinsic value and any additional amount over its intrinsic value, called the time premium. In this appendix we will explain how the theoretical price of an option can be determined using a well-known financial model, the *Black-Scholes option pricing model*.[1] This model is viewed by many in the financial community as one of the path-breaking innovations in financial management and analysis. We will not provide the details with respect to how the model was derived by its developers, Myron Scholes and Fischer Black. Rather, we will set forth the basics of the model.[2]

---

[1] Fischer Black and Myron Scholes, "The Pricing of Options and Corporate Liabilities," *Journal of Political Economy* (May-June 1973), pp. 637–654.

[2] Since the introduction of the Black-Scholes option pricing, there have been numerous modifications and extensions of the model. We will not review these in this appendix.

THEORETICAL UPPER AND LOWER VALUES OF AN OPTION

By examining the features of an option and the value of its underlying asset, we can determine the highest and lowest values that an option may take on. These values are referred to as theoretical boundary conditions. The theoretical boundary conditions for the price of an option can be derived using simple economic arguments. For example, it can be shown that the minimum price for an American call option (i.e., an option that can be exercised at any time up to and including the expiration date) is its intrinsic value. That is,

Call option price $\geq$ maximum[0, Price of underlying – Strike price]

This expression says that the price of a call option will be greater than or equal to either the difference between the current price of the underlying asset and the strike price (intrinsic value) or zero, whichever is higher. Why zero? Because the option holder can simply choose not to exercise the option.

The boundary conditions can be "tightened" by using arbitrage arguments coupled with certain assumptions about the cash distribution of the underlying asset. For example, when the underlying is common stock, the cash distribution is the dividend payment.

The extreme case is an option pricing model that uses a set of assumptions to derive a single theoretical price for an option, rather than a range. As we shall see below, deriving a theoretical option price is complicated because the option price depends on the expected price volatility of the value of the underlying asset over the life of the option.

BLACK-SCHOLES OPTION PRICING MODEL

Several models have been developed to determine the theoretical value of an option. The most popular one was developed by Fischer Black and Myron Scholes in 1973 for valuing European call options on common stock. Recall that a European option is one that cannot be exercised prior to the expiration date.

Basically, the idea behind the arbitrage argument in deriving the option pricing model is that if the payoff from owning a call option can be replicated by (1) purchasing the stock underlying the call option and (2) borrowing funds, then the price of the option will be (at most) the cost of creating the payoff replicating strategy.

By imposing certain assumptions (to be discussed later) and using arbitrage arguments, the Black-Scholes option pricing model computes the fair (or theoretical) price of a European call option on a non-dividend-paying stock with the following formula:

$$C = SN(d_1) - Xe^{-rt} N(d_2)$$

where

$$d_1 = \frac{\ln(S/K) + (r + 0.5s^2)t}{s\sqrt{t}}$$

d_2 = $d_1 - s\sqrt{t}$
ln = natural logarithm
C = call option price
S = price of the underlying asset
K = strike price
r = short-term risk-free rate
e = 2.718 (natural antilog of 1)
t = time remaining to the expiration date (measured as a fraction of a year)
s = standard deviation of the value of the underlying asset

$N(.)$ = the cumulative probability density[3]

Notice that five of the factors that we indicated in Chapter 8 that influence the price of an option are included in the formula. Anticipated cash dividends are not included because the model is for a non-dividend-paying stock. In the Black-Scholes option pricing model, the direction of the influence of each of these factors is the same as stated in Chapter 8. Four of the factors—strike price, price of underlying asset, time to expiration, and risk-free rate—are easily observed. The standard deviation of the price of the underlying asset must be estimated.

The option price derived from the Black-Scholes option pricing model is "fair" in the sense that if any other price existed, it would be possible to earn riskless arbitrage profits by taking an offsetting position in the underlying asset. That is, if the price of the call option in the market is higher than that derived from the Black-Scholes option pricing model, an investor could sell the call option and buy a certain quantity of

---

[3] The value for $N(.)$ is obtained from a normal distribution function that is tabulated in most statistics textbooks or from spreadsheets that have this built-in function.

the underlying asset. If the reverse is true, that is, the market price of the call option is less than the "fair" price derived from the model, the investor could buy the call option and sell short a certain amount of the underlying asset. This process of hedging by taking a position in the underlying asset allows the investor to lock in the riskless arbitrage profit.

To illustrate the Black-Scholes option pricing formula, assume the following values:

Strike price = $45
Time remaining to expiration = 183 days
Stock price = $47
Expected price volatility = standard deviation = 25%
Risk-free rate = 10%

In terms of the values in the formula:

S = $47
K = $45
t = 0.5 (183 days/365, rounded)
s = 0.25
r = 0.10

Substituting these values into the Black-Scholes option pricing model, we get:

$$d_1 = \frac{\ln(\$47/\$45) + [0.10 + 0.5(0.25)^2]0.5}{0.25\sqrt{0.5}} = 0.6172$$

$$d_2 = 0.6172 - 0.25\sqrt{0.5} = 0.4404$$

From a normal distribution table:

$$N(0.6172) = 0.7315 \text{ and } N(0.4404) = 0.6702$$

Then:

$$C = \$47(0.7315) - \$45(e^{-(0.10)(0.5)})(0.6702) = \$5.69$$

Let's look at what happens to the theoretical option price if the expected price volatility is 40% rather than 25%. Then:

$$d_1 = \frac{\ln(\$47/\$45) + [0.10 + 0.5(0.40)^2]0.5}{0.40\sqrt{0.5}} = 0.4719$$

$$d_2 = 0.4719 - 0.40\sqrt{0.5} = 0.1891$$

From a normal distribution table:

$$N(0.4719) = 0.6815 \text{ and } N(0.1891) = 0.5750$$

Then:

$$C = \$47(0.6815) - \$45(e^{-(0.10)(0.5)})(0.5750) = \$7.42$$

Notice that the higher the assumed expected price volatility of the underlying asset, the higher the price of a call option.

Exhibit App.1 shows the option value as calculated from the Black-Scholes option pricing model for different assumptions concerning (1) the standard deviation, (2) the risk-free rate, and (3) the time remaining to expiration. Notice that the option price varies directly with all three variables. That is, (1) the lower (higher) the volatility, the lower (higher) the option price; (2) the lower (higher) the risk-free rate, the lower (higher) the option price; and, (3) the shorter (longer) the time remaining to expiration, the lower (higher) the option price. All of this agrees with what we stated in Chapter 8 about the effect of a change in one of the factors on the price of a call option.

Value of a Put Option

How do we determine the value of a put option? There is a relationship among the price of the underlying asset, the call option price, and the put option price. This relationship, called the *put-call parity relationship*, is given below for European options:

> Put option price = Call option price + Present value of strike price
> − Price of the underlying asset

or, using the notation we used previously,

$$P = C + Xe^{-rt} - S$$

If there are cash distributions on the underlying asset (e.g., dividends), these would be added to the right-hand side of this equation. The relationship is approximately true for American options.

If this relationship does not hold, arbitrage opportunities exist. That is, portfolios consisting of long and short positions in the underlying asset and related options that provide an extra return with (practical) certainty will exist.

EXHIBIT APP.1 Comparison of Black-Scholes Call Option Prices Varying One Factor at a Time

Base case:
Strike price = $45
Current stock price = $47
Time remaining to expiration = 183 days
Risk-free rate = 10%
Expected price volatility = standard deviation = 25%

Panel A: Holding All Factors Constant Except Expected Price Volatility

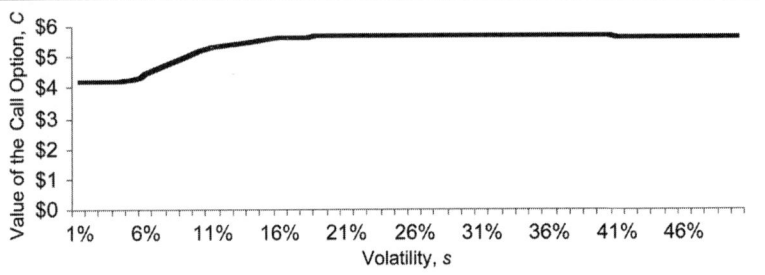

Panel B: Holding All Factors Constant Except for the Risk-Free Rate

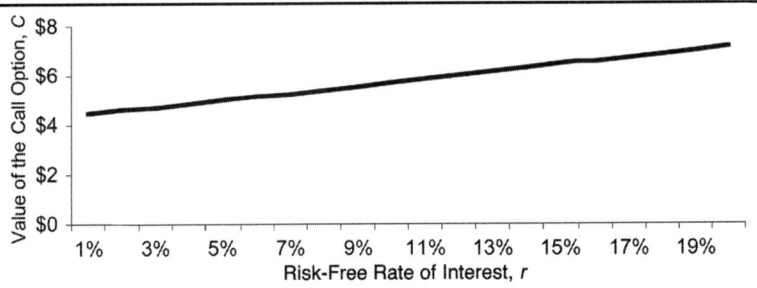

Panel C: Holding All Factors Constant Except for the Time Remaining to Expiration

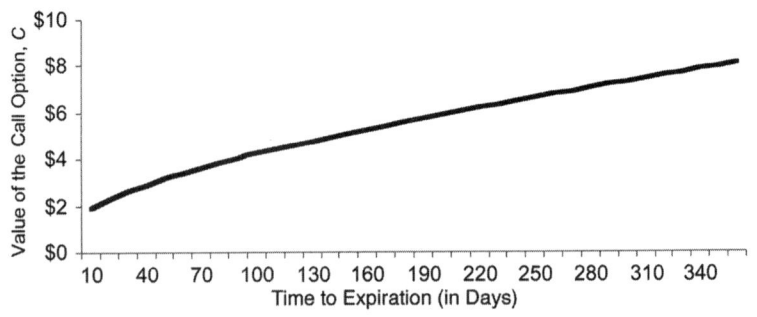

EXHIBIT APP.2   Relation Between Call and Put Option Features and the Value of an Option

Factor	Description	Relation to Call Option Value	Relation to Put Option Value
S	Value of the underlying asset, S	Direct relation	Inverse relation
X	Exercise price, X	Inverse relation	Direct relation
r	Time value of money, r	Direct relation	Inverse relation
s	Volatility of the value of the underlying asset, s	Direct relation	Direct relation
t	Time to maturity, t	Direct relation	Direct relation

If we can calculate the fair value of a call option, the fair value of a put with the same strike price and expiration on the same stock can be calculated from the put-call parity relationship.

Black-Scholes Option Pricing Model Assumptions

The relation between the value of an option and the five factors in the Black-Scholes model are summarized in Exhibit App.2. The Black-Scholes option pricing model is based on several restrictive assumptions. These assumptions were necessary to develop the hedge to realize riskless arbitrage profits if the market price of the call option deviates from the value obtained from the model.

The Option is European

The Black-Scholes option pricing model assumes that the call option is a European call option. Because the model is for a non-dividend-paying stock, early exercise of an option will not be economical because by selling rather than exercising the call option, the option holder can recoup the option's time premium.[4]

Variance of the Price of the Underlying

The Black-Scholes model assumes that the variance of the price of the underlying asset is (1) constant over the life of the option and (2) known with certainty.

---

[4] An option pricing model called the "lattice model" can easily handle American call options. For a description of this model, see John C. Cox, Stephen A. Ross, and Mark Rubinstein, "Option Pricing: A Simplified Approach," *Journal of Financial Economics*, (1979), pp. 229–263.

Stochastic Process Generating Stock Prices

To derive an option pricing model, an assumption is needed about the way the price of the underlying asset may change over time. The Black-Scholes model is based on the assumption that the price of the underlying asset is generated by one kind of stochastic (random) process called a "diffusion process." In a diffusion process, the underlying asset's price can take on any positive value, but when it moves from one price to another, it must take on all values in between. That is, the stock price does not jump from one stock price to another, skipping over interim prices.

Risk-Free Rate

In deriving the Black-Scholes option pricing model, two assumptions are made about the risk-free rate. First, it is assumed that the interest rates for borrowing and lending are the same. Second, it is assumed that the interest rate was constant and known over the life of the option.

Dividends

The original Black-Scholes option pricing model is for a non-dividend-paying stock. In the case of a dividend-paying stock, it may be advantageous for the holder of the call option to exercise the option early. To understand why, suppose that a stock pays a dividend such that if the call option is exercised, dividends would be received prior to the option's expiration date. If the dividends plus the accrued interest earned from investing the dividends from the time they are received until the expiration date are greater than the option's time premium, then it would be optimal to exercise the option. In the case where dividends are not known with certainty, it will not be possible to develop a model using arbitrage arguments.[5]

Taxes and Transaction Costs

The Black-Scholes option pricing model ignores taxes and transaction costs. The model can be modified to account for taxes, but the problem is that there is not just one tax rate. Transaction costs include both commissions and the bid-ask spreads for the underlying asset and the option, as well as other costs associated with trading options.

---

[5] In the case of known dividends, a shortcut to adjust the Black-Scholes model is to reduce the stock price by the present value of the dividends. Fischer Black suggested an approximation technique to value a call option for a dividend-paying stock. A more accurate model for pricing call options in the case of known dividends has been developed by several researchers.

Index